Security Analysis and
Investment Strategy

Security Analysis
and Investment Strategy

Geoffrey Poitras

Blackwell
Publishing

BLACKWELL PUBLISHING
350 Main Street, Malden, MA 02148–5020, USA
108 Cowley Road, Oxford OX4 1JF, UK
550 Swanston Street, Carlton, Victoria 3053, Australia

First published 2005 by Blackwell Publishing Ltd

Library of Congress Cataloging-in-Publication Data

Poitras, Geoffrey, 1954–
  Security analysis and investment strategy / Geoffrey Poitras.
    p. cm.
  Includes bibliographical references and index.
  ISBN 1-4051-1248-4 (hardcover : alk. paper)
  1. Investment analysis. 2. Portfolio management. I. Title
HG4529.P65 2005
332.6–dc22

                                        2004007688

A catalogue record for this title is available from the British Library.

Set in 10/12^1/$_2$ Rotis Serif
by Graphicraft Limited Hong Kong
Printed and bound in the United Kingdom
by TJ International, Padstow, Cornwall

The publisher's policy is to use permanent paper from mills that operate a sustainable forestry policy, and which has been manufactured from pulp processed using acid-free and elementary chlorine-free practices. Furthermore, the publisher ensures that the text paper and cover board used have met acceptable environmental accreditation standards.

For further information on
Blackwell Publishing, visit our website:
www.blackwellpublishing.com/poitras/

Contents

Detailed Contents   vi
List of Figures   viii
List of Tables   x
Notes for Instructors   xiii
Preface   xix
Acknowledgments   xxi

Part 1   Philosophy, History and Core Theory   1

1   The Philosophy of Investment   4
2   The History of Security Analysis   71
3   Theoretical Developments in Modern Finance   136

Part 2   Fixed Income Valuation   181

4   Basics of Fixed Income Valuation   184
5   Convexity, Time Value and Immunization   247
6   Bonds with Embedded Options   302

Part 3   Equity Valuation and Investment Strategy   353

7   Fundamental Analysis and Value Investing   356
8   Valuation Techniques for Equity Securities   421
9   Technical Analysis Demystified   489
10 Investment Strategy   558

References   614
Index   637

Detailed Contents

# Indicates some sub-sections contain advanced material.
* Indicates complete section is advanced material

Part 1 Philosophy, History and Core Theory	1
Chapter 1 *The Philosophy of Investment*	4
1.1 The Investor's Landscape	4
1.2 The Efficient Markets Hypothesis	34
1.3 The Philosophy of Investment*	50
Chapter 2 *The History of Security Analysis*	71
2.1 Life Annuity Valuation#	71
2.2 Writers on Stock Markets up to the Early Twentieth Century	86
2.3 Graham and Dodd (1934) and After	110
2.4 The Emergence of Modern Finance	119
Chapter 3 *Theoretical Developments in Modern Finance*	136
3.1 Basics of Mean-Variance Portfolio Analysis	136
3.2 Separation, the CAPM and the Market Model#	148
3.3 Decision Making under Uncertainty*	157
3.4 Financial Engineering with Derivative Securities	165
Part 2 Fixed Income Valuation	181
Chapter 4 *Basics of Fixed Income Valuation*	184
4.1 Basics of Fixed Income Securities	184
4.2 The Concept of Duration	210
4.3 The Term Structure of Interest Rates	220
4.4 Basics of Credit Risk and Default Risk	230

Chapter 5   *Convexity, Time Value and Immunization*   247
5.3   Fixed Income Portfolio Management   247
5.2   Mathematics for Advanced Fixed Income Analysis*   257
5.3   The Time Value–Convexity Tradeoff*   275
5.4   Immunization with Non-Parallel Yield Curve Shifts*   285

Chapter 6   *Bonds with Embedded Options*   302
6.1   Types of Bonds with Embedded Options   302
6.2   Greeks for Bonds with Embedded Options*   318
6.3   Option Adjusted Spread Analysis*   331
6.4   Modeling and Analyzing Default Risk[#]   341

Part 3   Equity Valuation and Investment Strategy   353

Chapter 7   *Fundamental Analysis and Value Investing*   356
7.1   Characteristics of Equity Securities   356
7.2   The Basics of Fundamental Analysis   365
7.3   What is Value Investing?   381
7.4   Observations from the Classics   395

Chapter 8   *Valuation Techniques for Equity Securities*   421
8.1   Discounted Cash Flow Modeling   421
8.2   Interpreting Financial Statements   437
8.3   Forecasting the Inputs   465

Chapter 9   *Technical Analysis Demystified*   489
9.1   What is Technical Analysis?   489
9.2   The Technician's Toolkit   498
9.3   Behavioral Foundations?   529
9.4   Relative Strength, Momentum and the Oscillator   538

Chapter 10   *Investment Strategy*   558
10.1   Investment Strategy: Basic Concepts   558
10.2   Tactical and Strategic Asset Allocation   571
10.3   Investment Strategy for Value Investors   581
10.4   Advanced Topics in Investment Strategy*   593

References   614
Index   637

Figures

1.1	Money rates	20
1.2	An example of a binomial process for stock prices	29
2.1	Price-earnings ratio	103
3.1	Capital allocation line (CAL) with efficient frontier	143
3.2	Expected utility map for the mean-variance expected utility function	145
3.3	Security market line (SML)	151
4.1	Interest spreads for investment grade bonds, 1980–2002	242
5.1	Linear approximation to a convex function	258
5.2	Quadratic approximation to a convex function	258
5.3	Binomial process of the one-period zero and associated bond prices	273
5.4	Higher convexity provides superior return	276
6.1	Price-yield relationship for a callable bond and a straight bond	326
6.2	Price-yield function for a putable and a straight bond	329
7.1	Dividend yields and AAA nominal bond yields	386
8.1	Relationship among the four financial statements	447
8.2	Financial highlights statement for RCCC	476
8.3	Internet site information for Ford Motor Company	480
9.1	Example of a Dow theory confirmation signal	502
9.2	Dow Jones Transportation Index, 5 year, 09/98–09/03	503
9.3	Five year DJIA chart, November 1998–November 2003	504
9.4	Bar chart, S&P 500 futures	510
9.5	Candlestick chart, S&P 500 futures	511
9.6	S&P 500 (SPY), 1 year sample, 05/02–05/03	514
9.7	S&P 500 (SPY), 3 year sample, 05/00–05/03	515
9.8	Trading range for Procter & Gamble	517
9.9	200 day vs. 10 day MA chart for SPY, July 1998–July 2003	520
9.10	50 day vs. 10 day MA chart for SPY, November 2002–May 2003	521
9.11	Procter & Gamble 50 day vs. 10 day MA, 1 year sample	522
9.12	Procter & Gamble 50 day vs. 10 day MA, 5 year sample	523
9.13	Advance-decline for DJIA, 11/02–11/03	524
9.14	Investors' intelligence NYSE bullish	528

9.15   GM, Ford and S&P, September 2002–September 2003   540
9.16   Momentum: 3, 9, 20 day   543
9.17   The 12-day momentum ratio $\{ROC\ (t,\ 12)\}$ 544
9.18   MACD diagram   549
9.19   MACD and other technical indicators, DJIA, November 2003–July 2004   550

Tables

1.1	Relative size of world bond markets, January 2000	7
1.2	Boeing Corporation, balance sheet, annual report, 2002	8
1.3	Boeing Corporation note to financial statements, annual report, 2002	9
1.4	Preferred stock quotes	12
1.5	Common stock quotes	14
1.6	The top ten stock exchanges in the world	17
1.7	Capitalization of world stock markets, January 2000	18
1.8	List of the primary government securities dealers reporting to the Market Reports Division of the Federal Reserve Bank of New York	19
1.9	Treasury bonds, notes and bills	21
1.10	Corporate bonds	23
1.11	Tax-exempt bonds, mortgage-backed securities and high-yield bonds	24
1.12	Foreign government and international bonds	25
1.13	Annual returns for US stocks, bonds, bills and inflation over the 1974–98 market cycle	26
1.14	Decomposition of the variance of the US $ currency return for six foreign equity and bond indices, 1978–89	30
2.1	Timeline for intellectual and historical events, 1602–1776	87
2.2	Components of the Dow Jones Industrial Average: 1896, 1916, 1928 and 1997	99
2.3	Stocks in the Dow Jones Industrial Average, September 5, 2003, 4.30 pm, EST	100
3.1	Stock index futures prices	170
3.2	NYSE program trading	171
3.3	Examples of portfolio insurance: static insurance and continuous rebalancing	174
3.4	Examples of portfolio insurance: no rebalancing and discrete rebalancing	176
4.1	Outstanding level of public and private debt, 1985–2002	187
4.2	Summary of Treasury securities outstanding, November 30, 2002	188
4.3	Maturity distribution and average length of marketable US Treasury debt held by private investors	188

4.4	Closed-end bond funds	193
4.5	Canadian bonds	198
4.6	Summary of corporate bond rating systems and symbols	233
4.7	Default rates and losses, 1978–2002	235
4.8	Weighted average recovery rates on defaulted debt by seniority per $100 face amount, 1978–2002	236
4.9	Selected transition matrices based on S&P rated issues	238
4.10	Defaults by original rating (investment grade vs. non-investment grade, by year)	240
4.11	Distribution of years to default from original issuance date (by year of default, 1990–2002)	241
4.12	Reuters corporate spreads for banks for February 10, 2003	242
5.1	Correlation coefficients for monthly changes in 10-year government bond interest rates, February 1984–October 1990	253
5.2	Government bond interest rate risk measures, February 1984–October 1990	254
5.3	Components of the risk of the domestic currency return for foreign government bonds divided by total foreign bond risk, February 1984–October 1990	256
5.4	Example of the % price change using modified duration and convexity for a 20-year 10% coupon selling at par to yield 10%	277
5.5	Decomposition of the Taylor series expansion: default free par bonds from 1 year to 30 years to maturity	281
5.6	Decomposition of the Taylor series expansion: default free par bonds from 1 year to 30 years to maturity	281
5.7	Decomposition of the Taylor series expansion default free par bonds from 1 year to 30 years to maturity	282
5.8	Partial durations, $\{n_t\}$ and extreme bounds for the high and low surplus examples	294
5.9	Partial durations $\{n_t\}$ and extreme bounds for the maturity bond and split maturity examples	295
6.1	Issuance of agency mortgage-backed securities, 1980–2002	316
6.2	Mortgage pass-through cash flow, at 100% PSA	317
6.3	Mortgage pass-through cash flow, at 150% PSA	318
6.4	Cumulative normal distribution values	322
6.5	Eurodollar futures and options prices	323
6.6	Monte Carlo simulation of ten binomial paths	334
6.7	Calculated Treasury spot rates for the ten paths in table 6.6	335
6.8a	Refinancing rate paths and callable bond cash flow for each refinancing path	337
6.8b	Refinancing rate paths and callable bond cash flow for each refinancing path	337
6.9	Present value of each path and average present value using various spreads	338
6.10	Option adjusted spreads for various types of bonds with embedded options	339

7.1	Cost of preferred stock of financial, utility and other companies, 1980–99	359
7.2	Post-World War II recessions, expansions and stock returns	375
7.3	Philip Fisher's eighteen common stocks	377
7.4	Berkshire's corporate performance vs. the S&P 500	409
7.5	Berkshire Hathaway Inc.: major operating companies	410
7.6	Berkshire Hathaway Inc.: acquisition criteria	412
8.1	Ford Motor Company and subsidiaries, sector statement of income	439
8.2	United States Steel corporation, statement of operations	441
8.3	Ford Motor Company and subsidiaries, sector balance sheet	444
8.4	United States Steel Corporation, balance sheet data	446
8.5	Ford Motor Company and subsidiaries, condensed sector statement of cash flows	448
8.6	United States Steel Corporation, cash flow statement	450
8.7	Operating cash flows before securities trading, Ford Motor Company, 2000–2002	453
8.8	Example of different methods for calculating invested capital, Hershey Foods Corporation, 1990–92	457
8.9	The top 30 firms in the Stern Stewart Performance 1000	459
8.10	ROE and levers of performance for ten diverse companies, 1995	467
8.11	The Coca-Cola Company and subsidiaries, selected financial data	469
8.12	Financial highlights statement for RCCC	475
9.1	Current components for Dow Jones transportation average, Friday, April 25, 2003	501
10.1	Annualized excess returns and risk measures, 1970–99	580
10.2	Common stock positions of Berkshire Hathaway, larger than $500 million	585
10.3	Berkshire Hathaway Inc. and subsidiaries, selected financial data	587
10.4	Berkshire Hathaway, sources of profit	588
10.5	Asset allocations recommended by selected financial advisors	595

Notes for Instructors

USING THE BOOK FOR SENIOR UNDERGRADUATE AND MBA COURSES

This book is intended to be an advanced treatment of security analysis and investment strategy for students that have already completed, at least, a university level introductory investments class using a course text at the level of, say, Bodie, Kane and Marcus (1999). Though there is some basic background material in this book, the treatment is too brief to support the use of the book at the introductory level. The basic background that is included is intended only to be a brief review of the requisite introductory foundation. As such, this book is designed to be used in courses aimed at the next and subsequent higher levels of instruction, including senior undergraduate and generalist MBA courses as well as specialist or second year MBA courses, M.Sc. courses and those at the Ph.D. level.

As a consequence of being suitable for use at more than one subsequent level of instruction, there is a considerable amount of material in the book that is also not suitable for the next level of instruction beyond introductory investments – effectively senior undergraduate and generalist MBA courses. This advanced material has been identified in the text using an asterisk (*) to mark the appropriate subsections. It is strongly recommended that subsections marked with an asterisk be skipped by senior undergraduate and generalist MBA level courses. This book is *not* intended to be used by sequentially following the chapters, starting with chapter one and proceeding through week-by-week to chapter 10. The asterisk is intended to be used as a guide to make a distinction between the difficulty level of the material and provide users of the book with some direction as to whether specific material is to be covered. This use of the asterisk extends to the end of chapter questions.

Instructors are advised to examine the various sections and subsections to determine which particular parts are suitable for inclusion in a particular course. A number of factors such as the variation in teaching styles and the number of lecture hours in the teaching term make it difficult to provide a precise model course outline with appropriate readings. Example outlines of general coverage for Security Analysis course which includes both equity and fixed income securities and is being taught at the senior undergraduate level would be:

With student cases	Without student cases
Unstarred sections in part I	Unstarred sections in part I
Part II, chapter 4, sections 5.1 and 6.1	Part II, chapter 4, sections 5.1 and 6.1

Part III, all chapters, excluding
    section 10.4
	Part III, all chapters, excluding
	    section 10.4

While there are certain pedagogical disadvantages to having a non-sequential coverage of the text in a particular course, the advantage is that the book can be used in more than one course, including courses at increasingly higher levels of technical sophistication.

Another possible use of the text is for courses specializing in Fixed Income Analysis. An advanced undergraduate class or generalist MBA class could cover chapter 4 and sections 5.1 and 6.1 in detail, supplemented by portions of sections 5.2, 5.3, 6.2 and 6.3. In situations where students have already had exposure to the foundational material found in the excellent texts by Fabozzi (2002) or Sundaresan (2002) and have sufficient mathematical preparation, part II could be covered completely doing approximately one section per week. There is considerable advanced material in chapters 5 and 6 and instructors are advised to exercise individual judgment about which material is appropriate.

Another use of this book is in advanced undergraduate and generalist MBA classes on Equity Analysis. Such courses could cover part III in detail. This part contains few sections marked with an asterisk and could also form a core part for a more general Security Analysis course aimed at students with only the preparation of an introductory investments class. Dropping coverage of the bulk of the material on bonds in part II as well as the historical and philosophical material in part I would permit the instructor to spend more time on the material in chapter 8 dealing with discounted cash flow models. Instructors that have students with exposure to modern portfolio theory will benefit from detailed examination of sections 10.1 and 10.2.

It is strongly suggested that, whenever class size permits, a course in equity analysis involve student group presentations. Model examples of such presentations are available on the Blackwell website, www.blackwellpublishing.com/poitras/ for the following industries: US biotechnology; global airlines; global breweries; US semiconductor; US computers; Canadian oil and gas. These presentations are available for download through the website for this book. The group presentation module involves valuing the common stock of a number of companies in a selected industry. In classes of 20–25 students doing a three lecture hour course, this may involve the loss of two or more lectures to allow time for students to make class presentations, but the instructional gains are considerable. For example, a group of four or five students would be required to do a valuation of three companies in the global airline industry. One or two students would each be responsible for discussing the macroeconomic and industry analysis, while the other three students would examine one of the three companies. The objective of the exercise is to make an assessment of the company's common stock value using the methods presented in part III.

Recognizing that a substantial portion of business school instruction uses, in some form or other, the case method, this book has made a specific commitment to the case approach. Those who use *the case approach* will appreciate the difficulty of containing the amount of material needed in a case analysis within the confines of the conventional textbook format. This book identifies the value of the internet to case instruction, by distributing the case material in a web-based format. The specific cases available for download from the book website involve: (1) the US brewery industry, with a company analysis of Anheuser-Busch; (2) resource companies; with a company analysis of the Canadian Oil Sands unit trust; and, (3) the US airline industry, with a company analysis of Delta Airlines. These cases can be used to motivate the types of material to examine in the student presentations. The website also contains additional material such as writeups on the recent changes in the industry classification scheme used by the Economic Census.

One feature of this book that some instructors may find undesirable is the lack of a sizeable number of end of chapter questions. The questions that are included are typically targeted at going beyond specific points in the text. The set of questions provided in a given chapter does not provide full coverage of topics examined in the chapter. This absence of a sizeable number of end of chapter questions is primarily aimed at restraining the length of the book. Instructors who desire such questions will be pleased to find that there are additional question sets available for download at www.blackwellpublishing.com/poitras. These question sets are designed to provide questions compatible with full coverage of the main topics examined in the book. Those desiring model solutions to the end of chapter questions that are contained within the text will also find those at the Blackwell site. A number of other instructional aids are also available.

USING THE BOOK FOR ADVANCED MBA, MSC. (FIN.) AND PH.D. LEVEL COURSES

Instruction of advanced students poses a more complicated problem than for senior undergraduates and MBA students. The diversity of possible topics makes it difficult to provide a sufficiently indepth discussion that will satisfy students that have already taken a number of courses in the subject and have acquired sufficient mathematical training. For this reason, courses at the Ph.D. or M.Sc. level in Finance often appear as thinly disguised topics courses that focus on the instructor's specialization within Finance. Those with quantitative background teach a course on financial econometrics, perhaps using Campbell et al. (1997). Those with an asset pricing background teach a theoretical course, perhaps using Duffie (2001). The primary difficulty with such courses is that students capable of handling the advanced mathematical and statistical material often have a less than sound grounding in the more institutional aspects of the subject. It is not unusual to find Ph.D. graduates from the most prestigious Finance faculties that are capable of accurately conceptualizing the equivalent martingale measure but are unable to provide even a rough estimate for the value of, say, Microsoft common stock.

At one level, this book is designed to rectify some of the foundational shortcomings that are often observed in Ph.D. (Finance) graduates. A model for such a Ph.D. level course would cover:

Model for general Ph.D. level course
Starred sections in part I
Part II, chapters 5 and 6
Part III, chapters 8, 9 and 10.

Students without sufficient foundational background could expand this core material by doing supplementary reading covering the basic material contained in the sections not covered in the model syllabus. For example, a student that has had little exposure to the bond market could include chapter 4 as well as chapters 5 and 6. Within this general instructional model, the philosophical and historical material plays a key role in rectifying an element of graduate Finance education that has been decidedly lacking in recent years. Understanding the philosophical perspective of modern Finance is a key to making a reasoned assessment of the modern portfolio theory that forms such an essential component of the instructional approach currently used in many Finance programs.

For a number of reasons, some instructors may find that the philosophical and historical material in part I and the discussion of technical analysis in part III is irrelevant. Such instructors could follow a model that omits such material. An example of such a model is:

Model for a technical Ph.D. level course
Part I, sections 2.1, 2.4, and 3.3
Part II, chapters 5 and 6
Part III, chapter 8, section 9.3 and chapter 10.

Though historical, the material on life annuity valuation in section 2.1 provides an excellent base for motivating the contingent claims analysis of bonds in chapter 6. The solutions to variations of this valuation problem provided by de Moivre, Halley and others all warrant close inspection. It is possible to further reduce the coverage by omitting additional sections. For example, section 10.3 could easily be omitted in a Ph.D. level course. Some instructors may opt to omit chapter 9 altogether, feeling that there is little value added in this material. An alternative possibility is to cover only section 9.4 on momentum and oscillators. Some attention could also be given to the Dow theory in section 9.2.

   Ultimately, it is not possible to do sufficient justice to the complexity of the numerous topics that have received intensive and not so intensive study in Finance. Students
have to take the initiative and pursue topics through additional study. To facilitate this
process, ample references are provided throughout the text to help students pursue
further discussion of a specific notion. In many cases, the intellectual history is traced
back decades, if not centuries. The objective in providing the more dated references
is that past interpretations may take a different perspective than more recent and
often quantitatively oriented studies. This is a feature of this text that is different from
conventional Ph.D. level texts. There is a constant effort to expand the field of view
beyond the narrow confines of the intellectual approach used in modern Finance, that
emphasizes results of the Markowitz-Sharpe-Fama line of thought, often to the exclusion of alternative approaches. In addition, students will find that the end of chapter
questions marked with an asterisk to be challenging, with solutions that provide insight
into the in-text discussion.

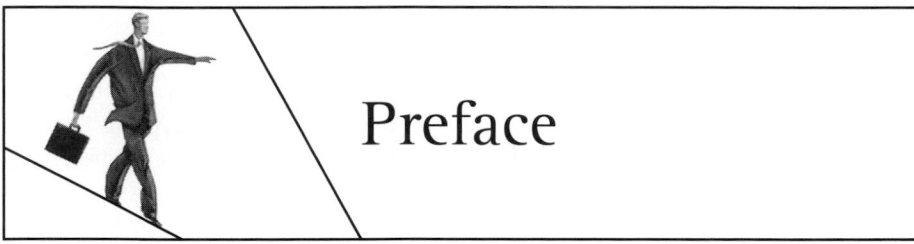

Preface

To some, this book may appear to be a well timed attempt to cash in on the financial market debacles that started with the collapse of Enron and have spread like a contagion to engulf Arthur Anderson, Worldcom, Adelphia, Global Crossing, and Tyco, to name only a few. Even major investment banking institutions, such as Citigroup and JP Morgan Chase have been exposed for participating in the accounting shenanigans that hid the activities of Enron and others from the glare of public disclosure. Yet, even though the timing of this book seems like an exercise in current affairs, this is more of a fortuitous coincidence than a primary motivation. Recent events do provide a useful backdrop for the arguments advanced in this book but the substance would be largely unchanged even if the roaring bull market of the second half of the 1990s had continued unabated. Though current events are closely examined at various points, the substance of this book has been a long time in preparation. Lecture notes from classes taught as long ago as the early 1980s form the backbone of this book, though the bulk of the material has been developed since the mid-1990s. The book is designed to be an advanced textbook treatment of security analysis and investment strategy that integrates the best of academic and practitioner insights on the subject.

Casual inspection of the text will reveal an approach to the subject that is somewhat different than the usual fare. In particular, this book takes direct aim at the limitations of the prevailing positivist epistemology that dominates both the instructional and research agenda of modern Finance. It argues that Finance is a use oriented subject and, as such, needs to keep one eye squarely fixed on the needs of practitioners in the securities industry. The theoretical ideas of Finance are explored in considerable detail with the objective of demonstrating that the positivist approach is insufficient for dealing with the pervasive uncertainty in securities markets. Though there is much of value in the received theories of modern Finance, the analysis has to be expanded along historical and philosophical lines in order to deal with the practical valuation problems encountered in securities markets, especially the market for common stocks. Mantras such as "stock returns outperform bond returns in the long run" and investment strategies derived from two fund separation are examined in detail, with a view to extracting the insights for making security valuation and investment strategy decisions.

Those aiming to use this book as the backbone of an advanced course on security analysis may be concerned that the philosophical explorations and some other topics lie too far outside the knowledge base of the typical advanced Finance student. Most such students have never taken a course on, say, the history of science or epistemology. Similarly, some of the mathematical content, such as the discussion of stochastic differential equations in section 5.2, will be too technical for the typical Finance student. To alleviate such concerns, an asterisk is used to mark chapter subsections that likely fall into the "too advanced" or "too unfamiliar" category. As a casual inspection of the book will reveal, such subsections form only a fraction of the book's content. Though this material is essential to developing key themes in the book, such as demonstrating the biases in modern Finance that arise from philosophical concerns, the informational and practical content contained in the book can be readily digested without giving much consideration to these issues.

The layering of material by level of sophistication and analytical complexity makes the book suitable for a range of course levels and course content. Though there is some foundational material similar to what is contained in an introductory investments text such as Bodie et al. (1999), it is not pedagogically sensible to use this book as the core text in an introductory investments course. Depending on instructor preferences, various chapters or subsections could be of value in an introductory investments course, making the book suitable as a supplementary text. The bulk of material in the book is targeted at courses in security analysis and investment strategy at the senior undergraduate and second year MBA level. If the more advanced material is included, the book is also suitable for a Ph.D. level course in, say, fixed income analysis or equity valuation. The cases and *case oriented material downloadable from the book website* also makes the book useful as a supplementary text in trade courses or as a self-study guide for real-time security market combatants.

Those familiar with my other books on finance, *The Early History of Financial Economics, 1478–1776* (2000) and *Risk Management, Speculation and Derivative Securities* (2002) may be concerned that this effort is, yet again, an example of the creeping incursion of typographical and editing errors into modern academic texts. Though there are no guarantees in life, rest assured that a herculean effort has been made to keep the bugs out of this effort. As with my previous books, my website at www.sfu.ca/~poitras will have posted an up to date listing of the typos and other errors that have been uncovered in this book. (The website also contains errata lists for my previous books.) This book has benefitted considerably from the comments of anonymous and not-so-anonymous reviewers on preliminary drafts of the text. Feedback and discussion from numerous students over the years has had a significant impact on the topic coverage. At Blackwell Publishing, I would like to give special thanks to the efforts of Seth Ditchik, Laura Stearns and Elizabeth Wald without whom this book would not have been produced.

Acknowledgments

The preparation of this book required permission to reproduce copyright material from journal articles, websites, newspapers, books, and magazines. The author and publishers gratefully acknowledge permission from the following:

The Princeton University Press (tables 1.1 and 1.7)
The Wall Street Journal (tables 1.4, 1.5, 1.9, 1.10, 1.11, 1.12, 3.1, 4.4, 6.5 and figure 1.1)
The International Federation of Stock Exchanges (table 1.6)
The New York Stock Exchange (table 3.2)
Southwestern Publishing Company (tables 3.3 and 3.4)
The Bond Market Association (tables 4.1, 4.12 and 6.1)
Globe and Mail (table 4.5)
Professor Edward Altman, New York University (tables 4.7, 4.8, 4.10 and 4.11)
Standard and Poor's Corporation (table 4.9)
The New Yorker Collection 1997 Warren Miller from cartoonbank.com. All Rights Reserved (cartoon on p. 195)
National Bureau of Economic Research (table 7.2)
Berkshire Hathaway, Inc. and Warren Buffett (tables 7.4, 7.5, 7.6, 10.2, 10.3 and 10.4)
Prentice-Hall, Inc. (figure 8.1)
John Wiley & Sons, Inc. (table 8.8)
Stern Stewart, www.sternstewart.com (table 8.9)
www.bloomberg.com (figures 8.3 and 9.15)
www.globeinvestor.com (figures 9.2, 9.9, 9.10, 9.11 and 9.12)
www.bigchart.com (figures 9.3, 9.6, 9.7 and 9.8)
www.futuresource.com (figures 9.4, 9.5 and 9.16)
Barrons' (figure 9.13)
www.investorsintelligence.com (figure 9.14)
www.clearstation.com (clearstation.etrade.com) (figures 9.18 and 9.19)
Journal of Economics and Finance (table 10.1)
American Economic Review (table 10.5)

The publishers apologize for any errors or omissions in the above list and would be grateful to be notified of any corrections that should be incorporated in the next edition or reprint of this book.

part 1   Philosophy, History and Core Theory

One thing badly needed by investors – and a quality they rarely seem to have – is a sense of financial history.

Benjamin Graham, The Intelligent Investor (1949)

Ye wise Philosophers explain
What Magick makes our Money rise

Jonathan Swift, first two lines of the poem, The Bubble (1721)

One who aspires to explain or understand human behavior must be, not finally but first of all, an epistemologist.

Frank Knight, Economic Psychology and the Value Problem (1925)

Chapter
Summary

Chapter 1 *The Philosophy of Investment*

1.1　The Investor's Landscape
　　　What is a security?
　　　The securities universe, institutions and regulations
　　　Basics of the risk and return tradeoff
　　　Risk and uncertainty: Frank Knight and J.M. Keynes

1.2　The Efficient Markets Hypothesis
　　　Basic insights
　　　Testing the efficient markets hypothesis
　　　Evidence of anomalies
　　　The tradeoff between risk and return revisited

1.3　The Philosophy of Investment*
　　　The epistemology of modern Finance*
　　　Truth and method in the human sciences*
　　　The ergodic hypothesis*

Questions
Notes

* Indicates section contains advanced material

<table>
<tr><td>chapter 1</td><td># The Philosophy
of Investment</td></tr>
</table>

 ## 1.1 THE INVESTOR'S LANDSCAPE

What is a security?

A useful starting point for a book on security analysis is the question: what is a security? The answer to this question is seemingly so obvious that most introductory investment texts do not deal with it.[1] Instead, securities are implicitly defined to be publicly traded stocks and bonds, together with derivative securities – futures, forward and option contracts. Yet, "investments" such as whole life insurance, real estate, securities issued by privately held companies and various other types of real assets and financial instruments are either ignored or given only passing mention. An even narrower definition of a security is provided in the so-called "Bible of Security Analysis," Graham and Dodd (1934), where the securities to be analyzed are "publicly held corporate stock or bond issue(s)." This approach to defining a security permits the intensive scrutiny of financial statements, for which Graham and Dodd (1934) and later versions of this text – Graham, Dodd and Tatham (1951) and Graham, Dodd and Cottle (1962) – are justly recognized. However, the omission of securities such as government debt is difficult to rationalize.

What about using a *legal approach* to defining a security? The Securities Act (1933), as currently amended (2000), defines a "security" to mean:

> any note, stock, treasury stock, security future, bond, debenture, evidence of indebtedness, certificate of interest or participation in any profit-sharing agreement, collateral-trust certificate, preorganization certificate or subscription, transferable share, investment contract, voting-trust certificate, certificate of deposit for a security, fractional undivided interest in oil, gas, or other mineral rights, any put, call, straddle, option, or privilege on any security, certificate of deposit, or group or index of securities (including any interest therein or based on the value thereof), or any put, call, straddle, option, or privilege entered into on a national securities exchange relating to foreign currency, or, in general, any interest or instrument commonly known as a "security," or any certificate of interest or participation in, temporary or interim certificate for, receipt for, guarantee of, or warrant or right to subscribe to or purchase, any of the foregoing.

Legally, most futures contracts, together with options on those contracts, fall outside the scope of the Securities Act, coming instead under the scope of the Commodity Exchange Act (1936). However, futures contracts on a security, including security indexes, do fall within the scope of the Securities Act, as do options on a security. In this context, it would seem that a "derivative security" is only a security if the underlying commodity is a security.[2]

In addition to confusions over whether to classify derivative securities as securities, the Securities Act (section 3) makes provision for a range of securities which are exempted from the Act. Most important of these exempted securities are:

> Any security issued or guaranteed by the United States or any territory thereof, or by the District of Columbia, or by any State of the United States, or by any political subdivision of a State or territory, or by any public instrumentality of one or more States or territories, or by any person controlled or supervised by and acting as an instrumentality of the Government of the United States pursuant to authority granted by the Congress of the United States.

Also included on the exempted list are "any security issued or guaranteed by any bank," "a collective trust fund maintained by a bank," "any note, draft, bill of exchange, or banker's acceptance which arises out of a current transaction or the proceeds of which have been or are to be used for current transactions, and which has a maturity at the time of issuance of not exceeding nine months, exclusive of days of grace, or any renewal thereof the maturity of which is likewise limited," "any security issued by a person organized and operated exclusively for religious, educational, benevolent, fraternal, charitable, or reformatory purposes and not for pecuniary profit," "any insurance or endowment policy or annuity contract or optional annuity contract, issued by a corporation subject to the supervision of the insurance commissioner, bank commissioner, or any agency or officer performing like functions," and "any security which is a part of an issue offered and sold only to persons resident within a single State or Territory, where the issuer of such security is a person resident and doing business within or, if a corporation, incorporated by and doing business within, such State or Territory."

This sizeable list of exemptions would seem to nix the possibility of using contracts falling within the scope of the Securities Act to define securities. At the least, would not government bonds have to be included in the definition? What about using a definition involving both exempted and included securities? Ignoring the difficulties of handling derivative securities, this approach would admit too wide a class to be practical for purposes of defining the scope of securities analysis. Giving coverage to insurance policies, not-for-profit liabilities, even some types of bank deposits would involve taking the discussion quite far afield. Some insight on this point can be gleaned from Graham, Dodd and Cottle (1962), where substantive analytical advantages were obtained from limiting the securities to be analyzed to publicly held corporate stock or bond issues. By ignoring the valuation of government bonds, this approach is going most of the way back to defining securities as contracts falling within the scope of the Securities Act.

Historically, the notion of what constitutes a security has undergone considerable evolution. For example, the original text of the Securities Act, as amended in 1934, did not make reference to "put, call, straddle, option or privilege" or to "security future" in the definition of a security. Much farther in the past, the English 1697 Act "To Restrain the number and ill Practice of Brokers and Stockjobbers" makes reference to "Talleys, Bank Stock, Bank Bills, Shares and Interests in Joint Stocks" when referring to securities that were being actively traded. At this time, the English financial markets were in the early stages of the financial revolution (Dickson 1967) in government debt and trading in longer term debt issues was relatively limited. As reflected in the trade publications at this time, such as John Houghton's *A Collection for the Improvement of Husbandry and Trade* (1692–1703), trading in stocks was lumped in with trading in other "Actions" such as copper, lead and lottery tickets. It seems that the definition of a security does change significantly over time.

One possible approach to defining a security is "*functionality.*" For example, introductory investments texts presume that a security is some type of "investment." However, this approach can lead to confusion as to the classification of, say, futures and forward contracts for securities. Being only agreements to buy or sell a security at a future date, these contracts do not formally qualify as investments as there is no cash flows involved when the contract is created. The issue is even more confusing when option contracts are considered. Unlike futures and forwards, options on a security do involve a cash flow (payment) when the contract is purchased, much the same as with a purchase of the underlying security. Yet, lottery tickets also involve a cash flow when purchased and, like options, feature a contingent payoff that could be made on a future date. Of course, the distinction between lottery tickets and options is that the contingency in one case is based on a randomizer and in the other case the payoff depends on the future value of a security.

Another problem with making a direct connection between a security and an investment is that securities may be exchanged for reasons other than making investments. In other words, the transaction may be more speculative than investment driven. As it turns out, the speculative motive is an essential component in determining the valuation of a significant number of securities. At a deeper level, this distinction between speculation and investment is intimately connected to the rhetoric of finance. For example, despite certain legal restrictions, considerable rhetorical effort is expended by some market participants to convince retail investors that a particular common stock which is highly speculative is a "good investment." To counteract this, a key element of traditional security analysis for common stocks revolves around specifying methods for distinguishing between speculative securities and investments.

Perhaps a more appropriate method of arriving at an acceptable definition for a security is to use observation. More precisely, securities can be defined by identifying what the informed public at large recognize as being securities. To do this, it is possible to look at the securities that are of interest in popular financial media, such as the *Wall Street Journal* or the business section of the *New York Times*, as well as the financial news shows such as CNBC or CNN.fn. This approach reveals a decided emphasis on publicly traded securities, especially common stocks and, to a lesser extent, government and corporate bonds. There is also considerable interest in exchange rates, money market securities, exchange traded derivative securities and mutual funds. For lack of a better alternative, this is the approach to defining securities used in this book. Given the disproportionate amount of attention given to common stocks, these securities will receive the greatest attention. In keeping with the modern analysis of fixed income securities, and in contrast to the approach of Graham, Dodd and Cottle (1962), it is recognized that a sufficient discussion of government bond issues is also necessary.

The securities universe, institutions and regulations

Though the securities that receive a substantial amount of attention in the financial press share some general features, such as a relatively high level of liquidity, it is also possible to describe some general distinguishing features. For example, securities can be classified according to type of issuer, e.g., *government* versus *corporate*. The only securities of interest issued by government entities are debt instruments. These debt securities are classified according to the type of issuer and term to maturity. The types of issuers include: the different levels of government, federal, state/provincial, municipal; government agencies, such as the Federal Home Loan Bank; government sanctioned agencies, such as the Government National Mortgage Association; and the international agencies, such as the World Bank. Also included in this group are the fully owned government corporations, such as the provincial Hydro companies in Canada. Summary data on the size and composition of the bond market across a range of countries is given in table 1.1.

Securities issued by corporations are typically classified with reference to the right hand side of the balance sheet, i.e., as **debt** or **equity** securities. To better see the relationship between the balance sheet and securities issued, tables 1.2 and 1.3 provide an example: the balance sheet and selected notes to the financial statements for Boeing

Table 1.1 Relative size of world bond markets, January 2000

Country/region	Total outstanding (billion)	% of world	Rank in world	Bond value as % GDP	% bonds which are government	% of equity market size
United States	14,595	47.0	1	159	53	88
Japan	5,669	18.3	2	130	72	125
Germany	3,131	10.1	3	148	25	219
Italy	1,374	4.4	4	117	68	189
France	1,227	4.0	5	86	58	83
United Kingdom	939	3.0	6	65	50	32
Canada	539	1.7	7	85	73	67
The Netherlands	458	1.5	8	116	38	66
Belgium	324	1.0	9	131	60	175
Spain	304	1.0	10	51	73	70
World total (40 countries)	31,054	100	1–40	109	55	

Source: World Bank and Merrill Lynch (2000); Dimson et al. (2002)

Table 1.2 Boeing Corporation, balance sheet, annual report, 2002

Consolidated statements of financial position

(in $ millions except per share data) December 31,	2002	2001
Assets		
Cash and cash equivalents	2,333	633
Accounts receivable	5,007	5,156
Current portion of customer and commercial financing	1,289	1,053
Deferred income taxes	2,042	2,444
Inventories, net of advances, progress billings and reserves	6,184	7,559
Total current assets	16,855	16,845
Customer and commercial financing, net	10,922	9,345
Property, plant and equipment, net	8,765	8,459
Goodwill	2,760	5,127
Other acquired intangibles, net	1,128	1,320
Prepaid pension expense	6,671	5,838
Deferred income taxes	2,272	
Other assets	2,969	2,044
	52,342	48,978
Liabilities and shareholders' equity		
Accounts payable and other liabilities	13,739	14,237
Advances in excess of related costs	3,123	4,021
Income taxes payable	1,134	909
Short-term debt and current portion of long-term debt	1,814	1,399
Total current liabilities	19,810	20,566
Deferred income taxes		177
Accrued retiree health care	5,434	5,367
Accrued pension plan liability	6,271	555
Deferred lease income	542	622
Long-term debt	12,589	10,866
Shareholders' equity:		
Common shares, par value $5.00 – 1,200,000,000 shares authorized;		
Shares issued – 1,011,870,159 and 1,011,870,159	5,059	5,059
Additional paid-in capital	2,141	1,975
Treasury shares, at cost – 171,834,950 and 174,289,720	(8,397)	(8,509)
Retained earnings	14,262	14,340
Accumulated other comprehensive income	(4,045)	(485)
Unearned compensation		(3)
ShareValue Trust shares – 40,373,809 and 39,691,015	(1,324)	(1,552)
Total shareholders' equity	7,696	10,825
	52,342	48,978

Table 1.3 Boeing Corporation note to financial statements, annual report, 2002

Debt at December 31 consisted of the following ($ millions):	2002	2001
Boeing Capital Corporation debt		
Non-recourse debt and notes		
2.540% – 14.280% notes due through 2012	50	60
Senior debt securities		
1.400% – 7.375% notes due through 2013	5,006	4,737
Senior medium-term notes		
1.440% – 7.530% notes due through 2017	3,113	2,039
Euro medium-term notes		
3.410% due through 2004	51	
Subordinated notes		
3.900% – 8.310% due through 2012	24	24
Capital lease obligations due through 2008	362	392
Retail notes	487	
Commercial paper securitized due 2012	299	
Commercial paper	73	43
Subtotal Boeing Capital Corporation	9,465	7,295
Other Boeing debt:		
Non-recourse debt and notes		
Enhanced equipment trust	566	593
Unsecured debentures and notes		
49, 7.565% due Mar. 30, 2002		46
120, 9.250% due Apr. 1, 2002		120
300, 6.750% due Sep. 15, 2002		300
300, 6.350% due Jun. 15, 2003	300	300
200, 7.875% due Feb. 15, 2005	203	204
199, 0.000% due May 31, 2005	174	
300, 6.625% due Jun. 1, 2005	297	295
250, 6.875% due Nov. 1, 2006	249	249
175, 8.100% due Nov. 15, 2006	175	175
350, 9.750% due Apr. 1, 2012	348	348
400, 8.750% due Aug. 15, 2021	398	398
300, 7.950% due Aug. 15, 2024	300	300
250, 7.250% due Jun. 15, 2025	247	247
250, 8.750% due Sep. 15, 2031	248	248
175, 8.625% due Nov. 15, 2031	173	173
300, 6.625% due Feb. 15, 2038	300	300
100, 7.500% due Aug. 15, 2042	100	100
175, 7.875% due Apr. 15, 2043	173	173
125, 6.875% due Oct. 15, 2043	125	125
Senior medium-term notes		
6.840% – 7.460% due through 2006	60	70
Capital lease obligations due through 2005	337	67
Other notes	165	139
Subtotal other Boeing debt	4,938	4,970
Total debt	14,403	12,265

Corporation are taken from the 2002 Annual Report. While publicly traded companies are required to follow Generally Accepted Accounting Principles (GAAP) when preparing accounts, there is considerable latitude in the detail provided for the various items of interest. Boeing is only used as an example, not as a model, for how the accounts are to be prepared. GAAP is applicable to corporations having securities listed and traded on US markets. The securities of corporations traded outside the US are subject to the laws of the relevant jurisdiction. In general, the detail and clarity of accounts for firms subject to US rules set a standard that is a model for reporting requirements in other jurisdictions.

In the Boeing balance sheet, the traded securities are associated with the line items, "Short term debt and the current portion of long term debt" (STD), "Long term debt" (LTD) and "Shares issued." The debt items are further clarified in the notes to the financial statements. In tables 1.2 and 1.3 observe that the total debt number given in table 1.3 ($14,403) equals STD ($1,814) plus LTD ($12,589). The annual report provides some additional discussion of these debt securities, e.g., the $300 million debenture (unsecured debt issue) due in 2024 is redeemable at the holder's option in 2012. However, sources beyond the financial statements and notes contained in the annual report are needed to get precise information about each debt issue. As for equity, the balance sheet indicates that 1,011,870,159 shares have been issued with 171,834,950 held in Treasury stock and 40,373,809 held in ShareValue Trust, a trust which holds Boeing stock for the purpose of making distributions to employees. Boeing has no outstanding preferred stock. Further discussion on the equity account is provided in in the statement of shareholders' equity and in the notes to the financial statements, e.g., Boeing has issued performance shares.

Corporate securities differ with respect to *priority of claim* against both income and assets. Debt securities have a priority claim over equity securities, with default on the promise to make an income payment on a debt security being grounds for initiating a bankruptcy proceeding against the corporation. The specific contract governing a corporate bond issue is the *bond indenture* for that issue. The bond indenture is a legal document, monitored and enforced by a trustee, that contains the terms and conditions governing that issue. Where applicable, the indenture contains information about coupon payment schedules, protective provisions and covenants, priority of claim relative to other bond issues, conversion conditions, sinking fund payment schedules, and the like. Due to the difficulty of obtaining and digesting bond indenture contracts, there are a number of information sources, such as Moody's Investor Services, that provide summary information about the contents of the bond indenture for specific bond issues.

The bond indenture typically provides a number of conditions under which the bond holder can initiate a *bankruptcy proceeding* against the issuing corporation. Where applicable, these conditions include failure to make a scheduled coupon payment or violation of a bond covenant governing, say, the net asset value of the company. In the event that a bankruptcy proceeding is initiated, debt claims are paid according to the seniority of the issue, as laid out in the indentures of the different bond issues made by the corporation. Debt issues which are secured by specific property, such as mortgage bonds, are repaid either by repossessing the asset or from the proceeds of the disposition of the asset. Debentures are unsecured issues that do not have a lien against a specific asset identified in the indenture. When a number of debentures are issued by a corporation, the issues are usually further classified as senior, senior subordinated and subordinated debentures to reflect the associated priority of claim. In a bankruptcy proceeding, debenture holders have the status of general creditors.

Because an equity security is an ownership claim, failure by the corporation to make an income (dividend) payment to holders of equity securities is permissible. In turn, equity securities feature *limited liability*, meaning that in the event of bankruptcy shareholders are only liable to the extent of the amount that was paid for the shares. Equity securities are composed of common stock, preferred stock and claims against equity such as warrants. Preferred stock differs from common stock in a number of ways. Though there are a number of possible variations for preferred stock, e.g., it may be redeemable, convertible or floating rate, all preferred stock is non-voting. In most cases, there is a regularly (usually quarterly) scheduled dividend payment of a fixed dollar amount. Because the size of the dividend payment is fixed, as the price of the preferred changes, the dividend yield will change. As indicated in table 1.4, even though preferred stock is traded on the same exchange as the common stock, the price quotes are listed separately in the *Wall Street Journal*.

Most *preferred share issues* have cumulative dividend provisions, meaning that if scheduled preferred dividend payments are not made, all unpaid preferred share dividends have to be made good before any dividend payments can be made to common shareholders. Because preferred stock is an equity claim, the dividend payments are not a tax-deductible expense for the corporation (in contrast to interest payments on corporate debt). The associated negative tax implications are offset by the favorable tax treatment given to inter-corporate dividend payments. Traditionally, the corporate tax advantages for preferred stock meant that preferred shares were priced to be attractive mainly to corporate investors. However, due to changes in the tax code that have eroded the corporate tax advantages of preferred stock dividends, combined with a number of other considerations, table 1.4 demonstrates that yields for preferred stock on 1/14/2004 were attractive relative to comparable yields for both Treasury securities and corporate debt.

Common stock stands last in the priority ranking, making common stock the *residual claim* to income payments. The priority of preferred over common also applies in the event of firm liquidation, recognizing that equity is the residual claim against assets.[3] Typically, each share of common stock is entitled to one vote that can be used in the election of the board of directors held at the annual meeting of the shareholders. In turn, the board of directors is responsible for selecting the senior management, e.g., chief executive officer and president, that actually runs the company. Votes may also be held at the annual meeting or at special meetings when substantive initiatives are being undertaken by management, e.g., a merger or takeover. Shareholders not attending a meeting may vote by *proxy* that allows a named person, usually a member of management, to vote the shares. A *proxy fight* occurs when a dissident shareholder group solicits proxies to vote against current management. A good example of a proxy fight occurred in 2002 when a dissident group led by the son of a company founder sought to prevent the merger of Hewlett-Packard with Compaq.

Table 1.4 Preferred stock quotes

NYSE: Wednesday, January 14, 2004				
Stock	Div.	Yield	Close	Net price chg.
ABN Am pfF	0.39p	–	26.03	0.13
ABN Am pfB	1.78	7.0	25.28	−0.01
ABN Am pfE	1.48	6.0	24.60	0.02
ACE CapTr	2.22	8.4	26.40	−0.01
ACE pfC	1.95	7.1	27.63	−0.07
AES Tr	3.38	7.8	43.40	−0.55
AGL Cap Trups	2.00	7.3	27.38	0.14
AMB Prop pfL	1.63	6.6	24.80	−0.04
AMB Prop pfM	0.23p	–	25.10	0.05
AMR Pines	1.97	9.7	20.35	0.37
AT&T 8.25Pines	2.06	8.2	25	0.02
AbbeyNtl	1.75	6.9	25.32	0.04
AbeyNtl ADS	1.84	6.6	27.90	0.01
AbeyNtl 7 1/4%	1.81	7.1	25.54	−0.05
AbeyNtl nts	1.81	6.7	26.90	0.01
AbbeyNt pfC	1.84	6.7	27.37	0.07
Aetna nts	2.13	7.7	27.68	−0.05
AffMagrlnm	1.50	5.8	26.08	0.70
Agrium Coprs	2.00	7.9	25.35	–
AL Pwr pfO	1.46	5.5	26.61	−0.09
AL Pwr pfN	1.30	4.9	26.60	−0.05
AL Pwr ntsJ	1.69	6.7	25.38	−0.02
AlexREEq pfB	2.28	8.2	27.80	0.14
AlexREEq pfA	2.38	9.3	25.63	−0.08
AlldWaste pfC	3.13	4.1	76.94	−0.21
AmbacFnl 5.875	1.47	5.8	25.31	0.01
Ambac 7%	1.75	6.5	26.87	−0.12
AmbacFnl 5.95	1.49	5.9	25.39	−0.05
AmBev ADS	1.04e	3.9	26.90	−0.29
AmerHess pf		–	58.17	−0.13
Amerco pfA		–	25.35	−0.15
Ameren Aces	2.44	8.3	29.30	0.15
AmAnnty Toprs	2.31	9.0	25.64	0.19
AmFnlCap Toprs	2.28	8.9	25.65	0.06

See notes to table 1.5

In a sense, the common stockholders are the owners of the firm, though in practice there are considerable impediments to achieving this objective. For example, many companies use a *statutory* voting procedure where each individual member of the board of directors is voted on separately. In this model, the group holding the majority of the shares is able to elect the full board. In an attempt to address the problem of under-representation, in some states corporation law requires common stock to have cumulative voting rights where each share is entitled to a number of votes equal to the number of board members being elected, with all board members being elected according to the number of votes cast for each. In this type of voting, a minority group voting as a block is able to get a voice on the board by electing a member or members to the board.

In addition to voting rights, common stockholders have a number of other rights and protections. The extent of these rights depends on the corporation law of the state of incorporation. *Preemptive rights* allow stockholders to subscribe pro rata to any new issues of stock. This right prevents undesired dilution of ownership. Other rights include protections against stock repurchases or recapitalizations. Though these rights may extend to certain types of non-cash dividends, the size of dividend payments made to the common shares is typically at the discretion of management. As indicated in table 1.5, there are many firms that do not make cash dividend payments. There are also numerous firms that have a long unbroken record of regular, quarterly dividend payments that have grown gradually over time. Earnings that are not paid to shareholders as dividends are retained within the firm and, presumably, go to the purchase of assets, thereby enhancing the claim of common stock against assets and, hopefully, producing an increased common stock price and a capital gain for stockholders.

In the US, except in a few special cases, e.g., nationally chartered banks, corporations come into being when chartered under a particular state code. Each state has a corporation law outlining rules for incorporation and general rules for operation. As such, the state of incorporation defines rules governing corporate status. While conducting business in states other than the state of incorporation, the corporation is subject to the commercial laws and taxes of that state. At the time of incorporation, a *corporate charter* has to be filed which contains the articles of incorporation. The corporate charter provides information about: the methods by which the articles of incorporation can be amended; the classes of stock and the par values; features protecting the preferred stock; voting rights for the stock; powers of the board of directors; rules for retiring common stock; dividend payment provisions; rights of prior security holders in the event of new issues; merger and reorganization procedures. Due to differences in corporation laws across states, many of the largest corporations have opted to incorporate in Delaware. (Why?) A useful reference on relevant corporation law issues is the Commerce Clearing House, *Corporation Law Guide*.

In some jurisdictions, the corporation law permits different *classes of common stock* to be issued, usually differentiated by voting rights. Such types of common stock are referred to as dual-class shares, restricted shares or classified common stock. While such common stock issues are not uncommon in Canada or China, for example, they are unusual in the US, e.g., Partch (1987), Chen et al. (2002). Due to perceived and actual abuses, the New York Stock Exchange has not listed non-voting common stock since 1924. Where companies do issue common stock with different voting rights, the different classes trade as separate issues, permitting different prices to be quoted. For example, Canadian Tire Corporation traded on the Toronto Stock Exchange (TSX) has class A common stock with no voting rights and regular common stock that does have voting rights. Other than voting rights, both classes of common stock have equal claims, e.g., to common stock dividends. The 1/10/2002 closing price for the class A shares was C$29.12 and C$36.00 for the regular shares.

Table 1.5 Common stock quotes

NEW YORK STOCK EXCHANGE COMPOSITE TRANSACTIONS

How to Read the Stock Tables

The following explanations apply to the New York and American exchange listed issues and the Nasdaq Stock Market. NYSE and Amex prices are composite quotations that include trades on the Chicago, Pacific, Philadelphia. Boston and National (NSX) exchanges and reported by the National Association of Securities Deafers.

Boldfaced quotations highlight those issues whose price changed by 5% or more if their previous closing price was $2 or higher.

Underlined quotations are those stocks with large changes in volume, per exchange, compared with the issue's average trading volume. The catcutation includes common stocks of $5 a share or more with an average volume over 65 trading days of at least 5,000 shares. The underlined quotations are for the 40 largest volume percentage leaders on the NYSE and the Nasdaq National Market. It includes the 20 largest volume percentage gainers on the Amex.

YTD percentage change reflects the stock price percentage change for the calendar year to date, adjusted for stock splits and dividends over 10%.

The 52-week high and low columns show the highest and lowest price of the issue during the preceding 52 weeks plus the current week, but not the latest trading day. These ranges are adjusted to reflect stock payouts of 1% or more, and cash dividends or other distributions of 10% or more.

Dividend/Distribution rates, unless noted, are annual disbursements based on the last monthly, quarterly, semiannual, or annual declaration. Special or extra dividends or distributions, including return of capital, special situations or payments not designated as regular are identified by footnotes.

Yield is defined as the dividends or other distributions paid by a company on its securities, expressed as a percentage of price.

The P/E ratio is determined by dividing the closing market price by the company's diluted per-share earnings, as available, for the most recent four quarters. Charges and other adjustments usually are excluded when they qualify as extraordinary items under generally accepted accounting rules.

Sales figures are the unofficial daily total of shares traded, quoted in hundreds (two zeros omitted; f-four zeros omitted.)

Exchange ticker symbols are shown for all New York and American exchange common stocks, and Dow Jones News/Retrieval symbols are listed for Class A and Class B shares listed on both markets. Nasdaq symbols are listed for all Nasdaq NMS issues. A more detailed explanation of Nasdaq ticker symbols appears with the NMS listings.

Footnotes:

a-Extra dividend or extras in addition to the regular dividend.

b-indicates annual rate of the cash dividend and that a stock dividend was paid.

c-Liquidating dividend.

cc-P/E ratio is 100 or more.

dd-Loss in the most recent four quarters.

e-Indicates a dividend was declared in the preceding 12 months, but that there isn't a regular dividend rate. Amount shown may have been adjusted to reflect stock split, spinoff or other distribution.

FD-First day of trading.

f-Annual rate, increased on latest declaration.

g-indicates the dividend and earnings are expressed in Canadian money. The stock trades in U.S. dollars. No yield or P/E ratio is shown.

n-Newly issued in the past 52 weeks. The high-low range begins with 'the start of trading and doesn't cover the entire period.

p-Initial dividend; no yield calculated.

pf-Preferred.

pp-Holder owes installment(s) of purchase price.

pr-Preference.

r-Indicates a cash dividend declared in the preceding 12 months, plus a stock dividend.

rt-Rights.

s-Stock split or stock dividend, or cash or cash equivalent distribution, amounting to 10% or more in the past 52 weeks. The high-low price is adjusted from the old stock. Dividend calculations begin with the date the split was paid or the stock divident occurred.

stk-Paid in stock in the last 12 months. Company doesn't pay cash dividend.

A

YTD % CHG	52-WEEK HI	52-WEEK LO	STOCK (SYM)	DIV	YLD %	PE	VOL 100s	CLOSE	NET CHG
4.3	16.87	3.55	AAR AIR		–	dd	4178	15.60	−0.05
6.5	18.33	12.50	ABM Ind ABM	0.40f	2.2	10	1129	18.55	0.22
0.9	24.19	12.98	ABN Am ADS ABN	1.01e	4.3	–	1441	23.70	0.15
4.8	43.25	23.59♣	ACE Ltd ACE	0.76	1.8	16	9726	43.40	0.34
5.9	10.20	2.63♣	AES Cp AES		–	dd	16159	10	0.04
−2.0	36.91	28	AFLAC AFL	0.32	0.9	20	7483	35.44	0.27
5.9	22.80	14.30	AGCO Cp AG		–	dd	10584	21.32	0.22
0.0	29.35	21.90	AGL Res ATG	1.12	3.8	13	1268	29.11	0.14
−10.7	47.28	34.15	AIPC PLB	0.19p		16	6331	37.43	0.28
−11.8	8.23	1.74♣	AK Steel AKS		–	dd	11142	4.50	−0.02
2.8	33.60	25.90♣	AMB Prop AMB	1.66	4.9	22	2895	33.79	0.79
18.8	24.75	5.40	Amcol ACO	0.20f	0.8	38	5530	24.11	−0.25
−2.8	27.28	19.82	AMLI Rsdntl AML	1.92	7.4	34	552	26.05	0.25
4.2	15.46	1.25	AMR AMR		–	dd	36160	13.50	0.33
18.1	4.60	1.10	APT Satelt ATS		–	–	1489	2.81	0.11
25.0	9.18	5.17	AT&T Wrls AWE		–	71	732365	9.99	1.44
5.3	27.55	13.45	AT&T T	0.95	4.4	8	46745	21.38	0.33
9.1	18.30	8.27	AVX Cp AVX	0.15	0.8	dd	3073	18.13	0.17
8.7	23.43	9.93♣	AXA ADS AXA	0.44e	1.9	–	3030	23.33	0.65
20.3	14.95	8.30	AZZ AZZ		–	19	347	16.06	1.46
1.0	25.98	24.60	AAG Hldg GFW n	0.29p	–	–	228	25.65	−0.05
11.3	23.63	11.37	AaronRent RNT s	0.04f	0.2	22	1047	22.41	0.31
8.2	21.67	12.53	AaronRent A RNTA s	0.04f	0.2	19	8	20	0.25
21.5	5.95	1.53	ABB ADS ABB s	1.23e	19.9	dd	4851	6.17	0.31
−4.5	47.25	33.75	Abboltlab ABT	0.98	2.2	29	46183	44.50	0.07
3.8	33.65	23.07	Abercrombie A ANF		–	13	18457	25.64	0.05
−0.6	8.54	6.10	Abitibi ABY	0.10g	–	–	2639	8.06	0.06
0.1	12.73	7.40♣	AcadiaRlty AKR	0.64f	5.1	21	182	12.51	−0.09
−10.0	26.95	13.45	Accenture ΛCN		–	21	81475	23.69	1.03
−8.2	27.71	14.65	ActionPerf ATN	0.20	1.1	13	6899	18	0.12
4.8	38.38	16.25	Actuant A ATU s		–	34	2045	37.93	0.47
−2.8	26.44	12.24	Acuity Br AYI	0.60	2.4	21	1446	25.09	−0.12
−25.9	17.10	6.35	Adecco ADO	0.11e	0.9	–	15874	11.94	0.18
5.0	18.23	4.42	Administaff ASF		–	83	1062	18.25	0.20
0.5	28.67	21.55	AFP Prov ADS PVD	1.70e	6.0	–	22	28.36	−0.03
3.4	42.75	18.50	AdvanceAuto AAP s		–	30	3752	42.10	0.20
−11.0	14.24	9.35	AdvMktg MKT	0.04	0.4	18	11741	10.15	−1.82
5.3	22.25	11.30	AdvMedOp AVO		–	–	1537	20.70	−0.11
2.0	18.50	4.78	AdvMicro AMD		–	dd	129465	15.20	0.01
11.9	5.75	2.23	AdSemEg ADS ASX s	stk	–	–	4912	5.65	0.35
8.2	21.36	7.86	Advntst ADS ATE	0.05e	0.2	–	153	21.49	0.56
1.4	33.57	19.67	ADVO AD s	0.11	0.4	20	2380	32.20	−0.12
6.6	15.58	6.44♣	Aegon AEG	0.23e	1.5	13	3900	15.77	0.50
3.2	34.70	9.66	Aeropostale ARO		–	25	6914	28.29	−0.48
1.0	70.25	39.90	Aetna AET	0.04	0.1	14	11336	68.24	2.24
−0.6	25.65	16.50	AFCCapTrl Corts KRH	1.94	7.7	–	8	25.25	−0.01
4.5	57.85	40.01	AffilCmptr A ACS		–	25	6791	56.92	0.50
12.0	75.87	36.52	AffilMangr AMG		–	30	5728	77.95	2.70
11.5	3.93	1.29	AgereSys A AGRA		–	dd	232790	3.40	−0.06
9.7	3.75	1.19	AgereSys B AGRB		–	dd	34123	3.18	−0.11
9.9	32.60	11.30	AgilentTch A		–	dd	32402	32.14	−0.10
5.7	16.47	9.72♣	AgnicoEgl AEM	0.03g	0.2	dd	10873	12.76	−0.23
0.1	28.58	16.83	AgreeRlty ADC	1.94	6.9	14	161	28.32	0.13
−3.7	16.96	9.40	Agrium AGU	0.11g	0.7	25	2904	15.85	−0.41

Wall Street Journal stock tables reflect composite regular trading as of 4 p.m. and changes in the closing prices from 4 p.m. the previous day. Wednesday, January 14, 2004

Besides restrictions imposed by the corporation law governing the corporate charter, there are a number of other laws that govern the issuance of corporate securities. Most prominent are the federal regulations that are administered by the *Securities and Exchange Commission* (SEC) (www.sec.gov), especially the Securities Act (1933, most recently amended 2000), the Securities and Exchange Act (1934), the Investment Company Act (1940), the Public Utility Holding Company Act (1935) and the Sarbanes-Oxley Act (2002). These regulations cover filing requirements for all firms with publicly traded securities. The most prominent filing requirement is the 10-K form, required under the Securities and Exchange Act (1934), that provides annual financial statements of the corporation, certified by a chartered public accountant. Under the Securities Act (1933), companies issuing publicly traded securities for the first time also must meet SEC filing requirements in the form of a prospectus providing full disclosure of pertinent facts about the issue. The SEC is also responsible for monitoring regulations governing insider trading. The regular and irregular filings with the SEC are essential sources of information for security analysis of publicly traded companies.

The rules and regulations administered by the SEC are not the only ones relevant to corporate securities. There are also state "*blue-sky laws*" that can cover the licensing of securities firms, filing information requirements, oversight responsibilities and penalties relating to violating the statutes. A useful reference on these laws is the Commerce Clearing House *Blue-Sky Law Reporter*. State securities laws can have national significance. For example, blue-sky laws of New York, Massachusetts and other states played an important role in the prosecution of major securities firms such as Merrill-Lynch when analysts and investment advisors were found to be unfairly touting stocks such as Worldcom to retail accounts. In addition to state–blue-sky laws, there are also federal and state laws governing corporate mergers, such as the federal Sherman Anti-Trust Act, and corporate bankruptcies, such as the federal Bankruptcy Reform Act of 1978.

Securities are traded in a range of different venues. The method of issue and exchange for securities differs according to whether the security is a *primary issue* or a *secondary issue*. A primary issue is a new security that is just coming to market, generating a cash inflow to the issuing entity. Some primary issues are *seasoned*, i.e., are increases in the outstanding issues for companies which are already publicly traded. For example, if Ford Motor makes a new issue of common stock this would be a seasoned primary issue. Other primary issues are *unseasoned*, being made by companies which are making a first issue of publicly traded securities.[4] The primary market for equity securities, such as common stock, is the initial public offering (IPO) market. Though some companies do sell primary security issues directly to investors, it is conventional to employ an investment banking firm to market the securities. For historical reasons, this investment banking activity is called underwriting. Investment banks also do underwriting of debt issues for both corporations and governments.

There are a number of variations on *underwriting* that are used by investment bankers in the distribution of primary issues. The mainstay of the investment banking business involves purchasing-distributing where a lead investment bank (or banks) will set up a purchase group or *syndicate* with a number of other investment banks. All the investment banks in the group agree to purchase a specified portion of the new issue for sale and distribution to customer accounts. As such, the ability to evaluate the price and

Table 1.6 The top ten stock exchanges in the world

	Market capitalization ($ millions)		Value of trading ($ millions)	
	2002	2001	2002	2001
1 NYSE	9,015,270.5	11,026,586.5	10,311,155.7	10,489,030.6
2 Tokyo	2,069,299.1	2,264,527.9	1,564,243.9	1,659,908.7
3 Nasdaq	1,994,494.0	2,739,674.7	7,254,594.3	10,934,572.5
4 London	1,800,658.0	2,164,716.2	4,001,339.9	4,520,183.2
5 Euronext Paris	1,538,654.2	1,889,455.1	1,988,358.6	2,092,540.4
6 Deutsch Borse	686,013.5	1,071,748.7	1,212,301.6	1,423,370.8
7 Toronto	570,223.5	611,492.8	408,164.9	461,556.5
8 Switzerland	547,020.4	625,908.7	599,749.1	591,064.9
9 Italy	477,075.4	527,467.3	634,634.6	633,936.5
10 Hong Kong	463,054.9	506,072.9	194,003.6	241,012.6

Source: International Federation of Stock Exchanges (FIBV)

marketability of a new issue is crucial to investment banking as are a substantial sales force and connections to the purchasers of new issues. Because the process of under-writing is risky, e.g., the firm could be left holding a sizeable amount of unmarketable issue due to changes in market conditions in the period between the pricing agreement with the issuer and distribution of the issue, sometimes agency marketing or **best efforts** marketing is used to distribute the issue. In this case, the issuing corporation seeks to reduce investment banking fees by taking on some or all of the risk that the issue will not be sold. Some types of primary issues, e.g., rights issues that are sold directly to shareholders, permit the use of standby underwriting where the firm markets the issue and the investment bank agrees to take up any unsold securities at a given price.

In order to attract attention from the financial media, securities usually have to be **publicly traded** and **transferable**. The main exception is certain mutual funds (open end funds) which are issued directly by the fund company and are **redeemable** instead of transferable.[5] The secondary market for publicly traded securities is composed of ex-changes, such as the New York Stock Exchange, and the over-the-counter (OTC) market, such as the NASDAQ. The various stock exchanges also trade other securities than individual stocks, such as corporate debt and closed end funds. Some exchanges, such as the AMEX and PHLX also trade options and indexes. The relative sizes of the major stock markets is given in table 1.6 which illustrates the importance of the NYSE, a stock exchange, and the NASDAQ, the primary OTC stock market.[6] The relative size of the US market compared to stock markets around the world is given in table 1.7.

Though government bonds in some jurisdictions are traded on exchanges, as in the case of British government gilts, in the US and Canada the secondary market for government bonds is OTC. In contrast, a significant proportion of corporate debt is traded on exchanges, though there is also considerable OTC trading. (In the corporate market there is also a significant number of "bought deals" which are issues purchased by a single investor or group of investors. Such issues are not continuously priced.) In

Table 1.7 Capitalization of world stock markets, January 2000

Country/region	Market capitalization ($ billion)	% of world	World rank	% of market capitalization in largest three stocks
United States	16,635	46.1	1	7
Japan	4,547	12.6	2	14
United Kingdom	2,933	8.1	3	22
France	1,475	4.1	4	19
Germany	1,432	4.0	5	21
Canada	801	2.2	6	21
Italy	728	2.0	7	23
The Netherlands	695	1.9	8	43
Switzerland	693	1.9	9	38
Hong Kong	609	1.7	10	
Australia	478	1.3	11	24
Spain	432	1.2	12	39
World total	36,099	100	1–111	

Source: Global Financial Data (market capitalizations); Dimson et al. (2002)

the US, agency issues, mortgage backed securities and municipal debt are all traded OTC. Some of this debt is traded indirectly on exchanges via closed end funds that hold these types of debt. Due to the widespread use of specialized brokers, e.g., Prebon Yamane (www.prebon.com), the OTC market has different segments that specialize in different securities. Important market participants, e.g., Salomon Smith Barney, will operate as dealers in most active parts of the securities markets.[7]

Though some primary issues of government debt are made through investment bankers, major issuers of government debt such as the US Treasury make primary issues of debt directly to the public through a regular sealed-tender auction process. Only short-dated maturities of debt – currently 4 week, 13 week and 26 week "Treasury bills" – are offered each week. Primary issues of 2–10 year "Treasury notes" and 10–30 year "Treasury bonds" are issued according to a regularized schedule that varies according to funding requirements. Currently, the 2 year note is issued monthly, with the 5 and 10 year notes being issued quarterly in February, May, August and November and a 10 year inflation indexed note in January, July and October (see www.treasury.gov). Around April 2004, there were no 30 year Treasury bond issues, though this may change depending on government financing requirements.

In the US, the public is permitted to participate in the Treasury auction but only to purchase securities for their individual account. The prices charged to individuals are based on the prices charged to the accepted competitive tenders, where registered government securities dealers (primary dealers) submit sealed bids for the issues available at that auction. Only registered government securities dealers are permitted to

Table 1.8 List of the primary government securities dealers reporting to the Market Reports Division of the Federal Reserve Bank of New York

ABN AMRO Incorporated
BNP Paribas Securities Corp.
Bank of America Securities LLC
Barclays Capital Inc.
Bear, Stearns & Co., Inc.
Chase Securities Inc.
CIBC World Markets Corp.
Credit Suisse First Boston Corporation/Donaldson, Lufkin & Jenrette Securities Corporation[a]
Daiwa Securities America Inc.
Deutsche Bank Securities Inc.
Dresdner Kleinwort Benson North America LLC.
Fuji Securities Inc.
Goldman, Sachs & Co.
Greenwich Capital Markets, Inc.
HSBC Securities (USA) Inc.
J.P. Morgan Securities, Inc.
Lehman Brothers Inc.
Merrill Lynch Government Securities Inc.
Morgan Stanley & Co. Incorporated
Nesbitt Burns Securities Inc.
Nomura Securities International, Inc.
SG Cowen Securities Corporation
Salomon Smith Barney Inc.
UBS Warburg LLC
Zions First National Bank

[a] Donaldson, Lufkin & Jenrette Securities Corporation (DLJ) has been acquired by Credit Suisse First Boston Corporation, effective November 3, 2000. DLJ will cease to be a primary dealer by December 31, 2000.
Source: Securities Reports Division Federal Reserve Bank of New York, December 4, 2000

purchase securities at the auction for distribution in the OTC market.[8] However, there are many more dealers that are active in trading Treasury securities once the securities have been distributed to the OTC market by the primary dealers. As of December 5, 2000 there were 27 primary dealers (see table 1.8). In order to qualify as a primary dealer, a securities firm is required to satisfy a range of stringent requirements associated with auction participation, firm capitalization and the like. The current primary dealer list and requirements that have to be satisfied to obtain primary dealer status are available at the Federal Reserve Bank of New York website (www.ny.frb.org).

One possible convention for organizing the various issues in the fixed income market is to decompose the issues by *maturity*.[9] Issues with a year or less to maturity are listed as money market securities while issues with more than a year to maturity are listed in the bond market. In the money market, securities are quoted by maturity and the type of issuer. The main categories of US money market securities are: Treasury bills, issued by the US government; commercial paper, unsecured liabilities of corporations

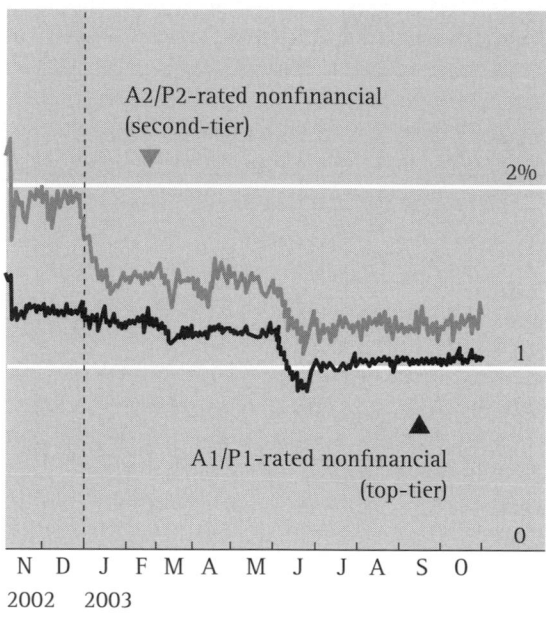

Figure 1.1 Money rates
Source: Federal Reserve

(see figure 1.1); certificates of deposit (CDs), issued by commercial banks; and Eurodollars, effectively CDs issued by banks operating offshore. Also included in the money market are federal funds, which are traded by banks seeking to balance reserve positions, and repurchase agreements, which are of interest to dealers seeking to fund the securities inventories used to support trading in government securities. Single direct transactions in the money market are in the millions of dollars and are executed OTC, often through specialized brokers or directly with dealers specializing in the specific security.

Unlike the money market, the US bond market is segmented by *type of issuer.* The convention is to list available issues according to term to maturity, providing a tabular presentation of the yield curve for that issuer. (The yield curve is the functional relationship between yield to maturity and term to maturity.) This is indicated in table 1.9, Treasury securities. Other categories that are identified, as indicated in tables 1.10 and 1.11 are: municipal bonds, which have different types of tax-exempt status; exchange traded corporate bonds, where the exchange trades debt of companies with listed common stock; high yield bonds, typically traded OTC through specialized dealers; and mortgage backed securities, bonds issues used to fund pools of mortgages. The final category in the bond market of immediate interest, foreign government bonds, is given in table 1.12. These bonds are different from the other categories of bonds in having the price being denominated in a foreign currency, resulting in two types of return calculations: local currency returns, which accounts for coupon yield and price changes due to movements in interest rates; and, US dollar returns, which augments the local currency return to include the impact changes in the local currency relative to the US dollar.

Table 1.9 Treasury bonds, notes and bills

Explanatory Notes

Representative Over-the-Counter quotation based on transactions of $1 million or more. Treasury bond, note and bill quotes are as of mid-afternoon. Colons in bid-and-asked quotes represent 32nds: 101:01 means 101 1/32. Net changes in 32nds, n-Treasury note, i-Inflation-Indexed issue. Treasury bill quotes in hundredths, quoted on terms of a rate of discount. Days to maturity calculated from settlement date. All yields are to maturity and based on the asked quote. For bonds callable prior to maturity, yields are computed to the earliest call date for issues quoted above par and to the maturity date for issues below par. *When issued.

Source: eSpeed/Cantor Fitzgerald

U.S. Treasury strips as of 2 p.m. Eastern time, also based on transactions of $1 million or more. Colons in bid and asked quotes represent 32nds: 99:01 means 99 1/32. Net changes in 32nds. Yields calculated on the asked quotation, ci-stripped coupon interest, bp-Treasury bond, stripped principal, np-Treasury note, stripped principal. For bonds callable prior to maturity, yields are computed to the earliest call date for issues quoted above par and to the maturity date for issues below par.

Source: Bear, Stearns & Co. via Street Software Technology Inc

RATE	MATURITY MO/YR	BID	ASKED	CHG	ASK YLD	RATE	MATURITY MO/YR	BID	ASKED	CHG	ASK YLD
Government Bonds & Notes						3.625	Jan 08i	110:26	110:27	3	0.89
3.250	Dec 03n	100:00	100:01	—	0.12	3.000	Feb 08n	100:24	100:25	6	2.80
3.000	Jan 04n	100:05	100:06	—	0.83	5.500	Feb 08n	110:18	110:19	5	2.76
4.750	Feb 04n	100:15	100:16	−1	0.82	2.625	May 08n	98:25	98:26	4	2.91
5.875	Feb 04n	100:20	100:21	−1	0.72	3.375	Jan 12i	112:12	112:13	8	1.72
3.000	Feb 04n	100:10	100:11	−1	0.84	4.875	Feb 12n	106:22	106:23	10	3.90
3.625	Mar 04n	100:21	101:22	−1	0.88	3.000	Jul 12i	109:15	109:16	7	1.80
3.375	Apr 04n	100:25	100:26	−1	0.89	4.375	Aug 12n	102:25	102:26	9	3.98
5.250	May 04n	101:19	101:20	−1	0.91	4.000	Nov 12n	99:29	99:30	10	4.01
7.250	May 04n	102:11	102:12	−1	0.91	10.375	Nov 12	128:00	128:00	4	2.71
12.375	May 04	104:09	104:10	−4	0.87	3.875	Feb 13n	98:22	98:23	10	4.04
3.250	May 04n	100:29	100:30	−1	0.96	3.625	May 13n	97:00	97:00	9	4.01
2.875	Jun 04n	100:29	100:30	−1	0.97	1.875	Jul 13i	99:25	99:26	8	1.90
2.250	Jul 04n	100:22	100:23	−1	1.02	4.250	Aug 13n	101:00	101:01	10	4.12
2.125	Aug 04n	100:22	100:23	—	1.04	12.000	Aug 13	138:13	138:14	5	3.03
6.000	Aug 04n	103:02	103:03	−2	1.04	4.250	Nov 13n	100:24	100:25	9	4.15
7.250	Aug 04n	103:27	103:28	−2	1.04	13.250	May 14	149:07	149:08	6	3.20
13.750	Aug 04	107:28	107:29	−3	1.05	12.500	Aug 14	146:23	146:24	6	3.32
1.875	Sep 04n	100:18	100:19	—	1.08	11.750	Nov 14	144:04	144:05	5	3.39
2.125	Oct 04n	100:25	100:26	−1	1.14	11.250	Feb 15	161:12	161:13	12	4.26
5.875	Nov 04n	104:02	104:03	−1	1.16	10.625	Aug 15	157:00	157:01	12	4.33
7.875	Nov 04n	105:26	105:27	−2	1.15	9.875	Nov 15	150:13	150:14	11	4.38
11.625	Nov 04	109:02	109:03	−2	1.16	9.250	Feb 16	144:27	144:28	13	4.43
2.000	Nov 04n	100:22	100:23	−1	1.19	7.250	May 16	126:00	126:00	12	4.49
1.750	Dec 04n	100:16	100:17	−1	1.20	7.500	Nov 16	128:17	128:18	10	4.54
1.625	Jan 05n	100:13	100.14	—	1.22	8.750	May 17	141:17	141:18	13	4.56
7.500	Feb 05n	107:00	107:00	−2	1.23	8.875	Aug 17	143:01	143:02	14	4.59
1.500	Feb 05n	100:08	100:09	1	1.26	9.125	May 18	146:18	146:19	13	4.65
1.625	Mar 05n	100:11	100:12	—	1.31	9.000	Nov 18	145:26	145:27	14	4.69
1.625	Apr 05n	100:10	100:11	1	1.36	8.875	Feb 19	144:20	144:21	12	4.71
6.500	May 05n	107:00	107:00	—	1.35	8.125	Aug 19	136:24	136:25	13	4.76
6.750	May 05n	107:10	107:11	—	1.33	8.500	Feb 20	141:12	141:13	11	4.78
12.000	May 05	114:18	114:19	−2	1.27	8.750	May 20	144:19	144:20	14	4.79
1.250	May 05n	99.24	99.25	1	1.41	8.750	Aug 20	144:25	144:26	11	4.80
1.125	Jun 05n	99:15	99:16	—	1.45	7.875	Feb 21	134:25	134:26	11	4.86
1.500	Jul 05n	99:30	99:31	1	1.51	8.125	May 21	138:02	138:03	11	4.85
6.500	Aug 05n	108:00	108:00	—	1.50	8.125	Aug 21	138:07	138:08	13	4.87
10.750	Aug 05	114:24	114:25	−1	1.51	8.000	Nov 21	136:29	136:30	12	4.88
2.000	Aug 05n	100:21	100:22	—	1.57	7.250	Aug 22	128:00	128:00	11	4.93
1.625	Sep 05n	100:00	100:00	1	1.62	7.625	Nov 22	132:27	132:28	12	4.93
1.625	Oct 05n	99:28	99:29	1	1.67	7.125	Feb 23	126:19	126:20	10	4.95
5.750	Nov 05n	107:15	107:16	—	1.67	6.250	Aug 23	115:22	115:23	10	4.98
5.875	Nov 05n	107:23	107:24	1	1.66	7.500	Nov 24	132:10	132:11	11	4.99
1.875	Nov 05n	100:08	100:09	2	1.73	7.625	Feb 25	134:00	134:01	10	5.00
1.875	Dec 05n	100:03	100:04	2	1.81	6.875	Aug 25	124:05	124:06	8	5.03
5.625	Feb 06n	107:28	107:29	1	1.82	6.000	Feb 26	112:18	112:19	4	5.05
9.375	Feb 06	115:21	115:22	−1	1.82	6.750	Aug 26	122:28	122:29	9	5.04
2.000	May 06n	100:03	100:04	3	1.95	6.500	Nov 26	119:13	119:14	4	5.06
4.625	May 06n	106:03	106:04	3	1.97	6.625	Feb 27	121:07	121:08	7	5.05
6.875	May 06n	111:09	111:10	2	1.97	6.375	Aug 27	117:29	117:30	8	5.06
7.000	Jul 06n	112:05	112:06	3	2.06	6.125	Nov 27	114:15	114:16	7	5.07
2.375	Aug 06n	100:20	100:21	3	2.12	3.625	Apr 28i	124:27	124:28	6	2.28
6.500	Oct 06n	111:17	111:18	2	2.20	5.500	Aug 28	105:25	105:26	6	5.08
2.625	Nov 06n	101:00	101:00	4	2.26	5.250	Nov 28	102:10	102:11	5	5.08
3.500	Nov 06n	103:15	103:16	4	2.23	5.250	Feb 29	102:15	102:16	5	5.07
3.375	Jan 07i	108:16	108:17	3	0.54	3.875	Apr 29i	130:16	130:17	6	2.28
6.250	Feb 07n	111:22	111:23	4	2.34	6.125	Aug 29	115:04	115:05	7	5.06
6.625	May 07n	113:14	113:15	6	2.44	6.250	May 30	117:07	117:08	6	5.06
4.375	May 07n	106:02	106:03	4	2.48	5.375	Feb 31	106:00	106:00	4	4.97
3.250	Aug 07n	102:06	102:07	5	2.60	3.375	Apr 32i	124:19	124:20	16	2.20
6.125	Aug 07n	112:06	112:07	5	2.57						
3.000	Nov 07n	101:01	101:02	4	2.70						

Table 1.9 (*Cont'd*)

U.S. Treasury Strips

MATURITY	TYPE	BID	ASKED	CHG	ASK YLD	MATURITY	TYPE	BID	ASKED	CHG	ASK YLD
Jan 04	ci	99:31	99:31	—	0.89	Nov 09	bp	80:22	80:25	4	3.66
Feb 04	ci	99:28	99:28	—	0.88	Feb 10	ci	80:02	80:05	7	3.64
Feb 04	np	99:28	99:28	—	0.90	Feb 10	np	80:13	80:16	10	3.57
May 04	ci	99:20	99:20	—	0.97	May 10	ci	79:01	79:04	7	3.70
May 04	np	99:20	99:21	—	0.96	Aug 10	ci	78:02	78:05	7	3.75
Jul 04	ci	99:16	99:17	1	0.89	Aug 10	np	78:11	78:14	10	3.70
Aug 04	ci	99:14	99:14	1	0.89	Nov 10	ci	77:13	77:16	8	3.74
Aug 04	np	99:13	99:13	1	0.95	Feb 11	ci	75:22	75:25	8	3.93
Nov 04	ci	99:01	99:01	1	1.10	Feb 11	np	76:07	76:11	10	3.82
Nov 04	bp	99:01	99:01	1	1.10	May 11	ci	74:21	74:24	8	3.98
Nov 04	np	99:01	99:01	1	1.10	Aug 11	ci	73:25	73:28	8	4.01
Jan 05	ci	99:04	99:05	1	0.82	Aug 11	np	74:03	74:07	8	3.95
Feb 05	ci	98:21	98:22	2	1.19	Nov 11	ci	72:29	73:00	8	4.03
Feb 05	np	98:20	98:20	2	1.22	Feb 12	ci	71:16	71:20	8	4.15
May 05	ci	98:06	98:07	2	1.31	Feb 12	np	72:04	72:08	9	4.04
May 05	bp	98:09	98:10	2	1.24	May 12	ci	70:12	70:15	9	4.22
May 05	np	98:04	98:05	2	1.36	Aug 12	ci	69:13	69:17	9	4.26
May 05	np	98:03	98:04	2	1.38	Aug 12	np	70:08	70:12	9	4.12
Jul 05	ci	98:10	98:11	2	1.09	Nov 12	ci	68:14	68:17	9	4.30
Aug 05	ci	97:20	97:21	2	1.46	Nov 12	np	69:15	69:19	2	4.13
Aug 05	bp	97:16	97:17	2	1.53	Feb 13	ci	67:17	67:21	9	4.33
Aug 05	np	97:17	97:18	2	1.52	May 13	ci	66:17	66:21	9	4.37
Nov 05	ci	96:30	96:31	2	1.64	Aug 13	ci	65:18	65:22	9	4.41
Nov 05	np	96:28	96:29	2	1.68	Nov 13	ci	64:17	64:21	9	4.47
Nov 05	np	96:28	96:29	2	1.69	Feb 14	ci	63:18	63:22	9	4.51
Jan 06	ci	96:28	96:30	3	1.53	May 14	ci	62:17	62:21	9	4.56
Feb 06	ci	96:02	96:04	3	1.87	Aug 14	ci	61:19	61:23	9	4.59
Feb 06	bp	96:04	96:06	3	1.84	Nov 14	ci	60:20	60:24	10	4.64
Feb 06	np	96:06	96:07	3	1.82						
May 06	ci	95:12	95:13	3	1.99						
May 06	np	95:09	95:11	3	2.02						
Jul 06	ci	95:18	95:19	4	1.78						
Jul 06	np	94:24	94:25	4	2.12						
Aug 06	ci	94:18	94:20	4	2.12						
Oct 06	np	93:30	94:00	4	2.23						
Nov 06	ci	93:19	93:21	4	2.29						
Nov 06	np	93:22	93:24	4	2.26						
Feb 07	ci	92:20	92:22	5	2.44						
Feb 07	np	92:24	92:26	5	2.40						
May 07	ci	91:26	91:28	5	2.52						
May 07	np	91:26	91:27	5	2.53						
Aug 07	np	90:28	90:30	5	2.64						
Aug 07	ci	90:24	90:26	5	2.67						
Aug 07	np	90:27	90:29	5	2.64						
Nov 07	ci	90:01	90:03	6	2.71						
Nov 07	np	89:30	90:00	6	2.73						
Feb 08	ci	88:25	88:27	6	2.89						
Feb 08	np	88:31	89:01	6	2.83						
May 08	ci	87:21	87:23	6	3.01						
May 08	np	87:25	87:28	6	2.98						
Aug 08	ci	86:28	86:31	6	3.04						
Nov 08	ci	85:20	85:23	7	3.19						
Nov 08	np	85:25	85:28	7	3.15						
Feb 09	ci	84:11	84:14	7	3.33						
May 09	ci	83:10	83:13	7	3.41						
May 09	np	84:06	84:09	7	3.21						
Aug 09	ci	82:12	82:15	7	3.46						
Aug 09	np	82:20	82:23	7	3.40						
Nov 09	ci	81:21	81:24	7	3.46						

Treasury Bills

MATURITY	DAYS TO MAT	BID	ASKED	ASK CHG	YLD
Jan 02 04	4	0.81	0.80	−0.05	0.80
Jan 08 04	10	0.81	0.80	−0.02	0.80
Jan 15 04	17	0.80	0.79	−0.06	0.80
Jan 22 04	24	0.80	0.79	−0.06	0.80
Jan 29 04	31	0.80	0.79	−0.02	0.80
Feb 05 04	38	0.80	0.79	−0.03	0.80
Feb 12 04	45	0.80	0.79	−0.03	0.80
Feb 19 04	52	0.80	0.79	−0.03	0.80
Feb 26 04	59	0.82	0.81	−0.03	0.82
Mar 04 04	66	0.83	0.82	−0.03	0.83
Mar 11 04	73	0.85	0.84	−0.02	0.85
Mar 18 04	80	0.85	0.84	−0.02	0.85
Mar 25 04	87	0.85	0.84	−0.03	0.85
Apr 01 04	94	0.86	0.85	−0.02	0.86
Apr 08 04	101	0.86	0.85	−0.02	0.86
Apr 15 04	108	0.88	0.87	−0.02	0.88
Apr 22 04	115	0.89	0.88	−0.01	0.89
Apr 29 04	122	0.89	0.88	—	0.89
May 06 04	129	0.90	0.89	−0.01	0.91
May 13 04	136	0.90	0.89	−0.02	0.91
May 20 04	143	0.91	0.90	−0.01	0.92
May 27 04	150	0.90	0.89	−0.01	0.91
Jun 03 04	157	0.93	0.92	—	0.94
Jun 10 04	164	0.94	0.93	—	0.95
Jun 17 04	171	0.94	0.93	−0.01	0.95
Jun 24 04	178	0.97	0.96	−0.01	0.98

Table 1.10 Corporate bonds

Tuesday, November 4, 2003: forty most active fixed-coupon corporate bonds

Company (ticker)	Coupon	Maturity	Last price	Last yield	Est. spread[a]	UST[b]	Est. $ Vol (000s)
Ford Motor Credit (F)	7.000	Oct. 01, 2013	97.780	7.317	302	10	189,538
DaimlerChrysler North America Holding (DCX)	6.500	Nov. 15, 2013	100.794	6.391	209	10	180,670
Sprint Capital (FON)	8.375	Mar. 15, 2012	113.650	6.251	195	10	118,969
Altria Group (MO)	7.000	Nov. 04, 2013	101.381	6.807	251	10	96,499
BP Capital Markets PLC (BZ)	2.750	Dec. 29, 2006	99.734	2.840	57	3	93,570
Abbey National First Capital BV (ABBEY)	8.200	Oct. 15, 2004	106.254	1.467	n.a.	n.a.	83,645
FirstEnergy (FE)	6.450	Nov. 15, 2011	105.253	5.627	133	10	80,159
Sprint Capital (FON)	8.750	Mar. 15, 2032	113.675	7.570	244	30	74,163
Time Warner (TWX)	6.875	May 01, 2012	110.646	5.300	100	10	72,520
Cendant (CD)	7.375	Jan. 15, 2013	114.891	5.305	101	10	67,743
Ford Motor Credit (F)	5.625	Oct. 01, 2008	97.941	6.116	286	5	63,581
Goldman Sachs Group (GS)	5.250	Oct. 15, 2013	100.297	5.211	92	10	62,189
SLM (SLM)	5.625	Apr. 10, 2007	107.764	3.212	n.a.	n.a.	62,000
Weyerhaeuser (WY)	6.750	Mar. 15, 2012	108.310	5.495	120	10	61,625
Metlife (MET)	6.125	Dec. 01, 2011	108.043	4.905	59	10	60,616
Ford Motor (F)	7.450	Jul. 16, 2031	89.067	8.479	335	30	59,743

Volume represents total volume for each issue; price/yield data are for trades of $1 million and greater.
[a] Estimated spreads, in basis points (100 basis points is 1 percentage point), over the 2, 3, 5, 10 or 30-year on the run Treasury note/bond. 2-year: 1.625 10/05; 3-year: 2.375 08/06; 5-year: 3.125 10/08; 10-year: 4.250 08/13; 30-year: 5.375 02/31. [b] Comparable US Treasury issue. c-Convertible bond.
Source: MarketAxess Corporate BondTicker

Basics of the risk and return tradeoff

The tradeoff between risk and expected return is, perhaps, the most fundamental notion in Finance.[10] This result has been approached at a number of levels. At one level, the result is empirical. There are legions of studies, e.g., Ibbotson and Sinquefield (1976), Siegel (1998, ch. 2), Dimson et al. (2002), which provide empirical estimates for various types of unconditional mean return and volatility of return measures. These empirical results cover a wide range of countries, securities and time periods. At another level, the tradeoff between risk and expected return is theoretical. Starting with Markowitz (1952) and Roy (1952), the tradeoff has been examined in the context of the optimal selection problem for a portfolio of securities. Over time, this approach developed into so-called "modern portfolio theory." At yet another level, the tradeoff between risk and expected return is rhetorical. In the spirit of McCloskey (1994), the tradeoff is an essential component of the arguments that academics and practitioners in Finance use to persuade others.

Table 1.11 Tax-exempt bonds, mortgage-backed securities and high-yield bonds

Tax-Exempt Bonds

Representative prices for several active tax-exempt revenue and refunding bonds, based on institutional trades, but may not reflect actual transactions. Yield is to maturity. n-new.

Source: The Bond Buyer/Standard & Poor's Securities Evaluations.

ISSUE	COUPON	MAT	PRICE	CHG	BID YLD	ISSUE	COUPON	MAT	PRICE	CHG	BID YLD
CA Infr&EcoDevBayAr toll	5.000	07-01-33	100.603	+0.306	4.92	NYC Muni Wtr Fin Auth	5.000	06-15-35	99.695	+0.314	5.02
CA Infr&EcoDevBayAr toll	5.000	07-01-36	100.526	+0.229	4.93	NYC Transitional Fin	5.000	08-01-32	99.992	+0.302	5.00
CA Infr&EcoDevBayAr toll	5.000	07-01-29	100.832	+0.229	4.89	NYS Envir Facs Corp	5.000	06-15-33	101.060	+0.153	4.86
ChicagoIL genarpt 3rdref	5.250	01-01-34	100.934	+0.237	5.13	Orlando Orange Co Exprwy	5.000	07-01-35	100.986	+0.230	4.87
ChicagoIL genarpt 3rdref	5.250	01-01-30	101.567	+0.238	5.05	Penn St Pub Sch Bldg	5.000	06-01-33	100.677	+0.228	4.91
Cincinnati Sch Dist OH	5.000	12-01-31	100.942	+0.237	4.88	Port Auth NY&NJ consol	5.000	09-01-38	99.340	+0.325	5.04
DallasFtWorthTX JointRvO	5.000	11-01-32	98.822	+0.447	5.08	Port of Seattle WA	5.200	07-01-29	101.067	+0.228	5.06
Denver ConvHotelAthCoSnr	5.000	12-01-33	100.232	+0.236	4.97	Puerto Rico ElecPwrAuth	5.125	07-01-29	100.865	+0.304	5.01
Detroit MI SewageDispSys	5.000	07-01-32	100.641	+0.229	4.92	Puerto Rico ElecPwrAuth	5.000	07-01-33	101.951	+0.232	4.75
Forsyth Mont Poll Cntrl	5.000	03-01-31	100.554	+0.241	4.93	Puerto Rico pub Imprv	5.000	07-01-33	99.381	+0.607	5.04
Highlands Co Hlth FL	5.375	11-15-35	99.242	+0.449	5.42	Puerto Rico pub Imprv	5.000	07-01-27	99.966	+0.549	5.00
Illinois Educ Facs Auth	5.000	07-01-33	99.840	+0.459	5.01	PuertoRicoHwyTransAthSnr	5.000	07-01-42	98.612	+0.499	5.08
IndianaTrans FinAuthhwy	5.000	06-01-28	100.571	+0.228	4.93	Rev Sr 03 NrWstrn Univ	5.000	12-01-38	99.341	+0.487	5.04
MA consolidated loan	5.000	10-01-27	100.174	+0.275	4.98	S.CarolinaPubSvcAuthRev	4.750	01-01-32	97.865	+0.447	4.89
MD Hlth & Hghr Ed	5.125	11-15-34	101.132	+0.236	4.98	SaltRiver Prj Agri Imprv	4.750	01-01-32	97.865	+0.447	4.89
MetropolitanTransAthNY	5.000	11-15-31	100.721	+0.145	4.90	SaltRiver Prj Agri Impry	5.000	01-01-31	100.798	+0.220	4.89
MetroTran AthNY trans	5.250	11-15-32	101.400	+0.235	5.07	SanDiego Unif SchDistCal	5.000	07-01-28	100.909	+0.230	4.89
Miami-DadeCoFLAviationRv	5.000	10-01-33	99.228	+0.456	5.05	TexasTpkeAuthRvBds	5.000	08-15-42	100.204	+0.212	4.97
NYC bds Fiscal 2004	5.000	10-15-27	98.978	+0.409	5.07	Triborough Bdg & Tunl NY	5.000	11-15-32	100.721	+0.145	4.90
NYC bds Fiscal 2004	5.000	10-15-29	98.851	+0.425	5.08	Univ of CA Regents	5.000	05-15-33	100.601	+0.302	4.92

Mortgage-Backed Securities

Indicative, not guaranteed; from Bear Stearns Cos./Street Pricing Service

RATE	PRICE (DEC) (PTS-32DS)	PRICE CHANGE (32DS)	AVG LIFE (YEARS)	SPRD TO AVG LIFE (YEARS)	SPREAD CHANGE (BPS)	PSA (PREPAY SPEED)	YIELD TO MAT*
30-year							
FMAC GOLD 5.5%	100–29	+10	6.6	172	+2	229	5.34
FMAC GOLD 6.0%	102–23	+07	3.6	246	+11	436	5.10
FMAC GOLD 6.5%	104–01	+03	2.0	235	−12	708	4.17
FNMA 5.5%	100–29	+09	6.6	169	+2	232	5.31
FNMA 6.0%	102–22	+06	3.4	246	+9	470	5.01
FNMA 6.5%	103–29	+03	2.0	234	−11	705	4.18
GNMA** 5.5%	101–13	+11	6.2	169	—	238	5.22
GNMA** 6.0%	103–13	+09	3.9	218	+5	388	4.94
GNMA** 6.5%	104–22	+04	2.4	222	−6	584	4.29
15-year							
FMAC GOLD 5.0%	101–13	+07	4.0	175	+8	292	4.58
FNMA 5.0%	101–15	+07	4.3	160	+8	264	4.55
GNMA** 5.0%	101–30	+07	4.6	139	+4	254	4.51
FMAC GOLD 5.0%	(PTS-32DS)	CHANGE	(YEARS)	AVG LIFE	CHANGE	(PREPAY	YIELD

Collateralized Mortgage Obligations

Spread of CMO yields above U.S. Treasury securities of comparable maturity, in basis points (100 basis points = 1 percentage point of interest)

MAT	SPREAD	CHG FROM PREV DAY
Sequentials		
2-year	190	—
5-year	190	—
7-year	170	—
10-year	140	—
20-year	84	—
PACS		
2-year	110	—
5-year	130	—
7-year	129	—
10-year	115	—
20-year	64	—

* Extrapolated from benchmarks based on projections from Bear Stearns prepayment model, assuming interest rates remain unchanged. ** Government guaranteed.

High-Yield Bonds

Tuesday, November 4, 2003
Ten most active fixed-coupon high-yield, or "junk," corporate bonds

COMPANY (TICKER)	COUPON	MATURITY	LAST PRICE	LAST YIELD	*EST SPREAD	UST†	EST VOL (000's)
Tyco International Group SA (TYC)-c	2.750	Jan 15, 2018	114.838	1.579	n.a.	n.a.	66,196
Tenet Healthcare (THC)	7.375	Feb 01, 2013	96.750	7.871	356	10	36,105
J.C. Penney (JCP)-c	5.000	Oct 15, 2008	104.625	2.659	n.a.	n.a.	27,531
Georgia-Pacific (GP)	8.125	May 15, 2011	109.000	6.588	229	10	18,329
Qwest Capital Funding (QUS)	7.750	Aug 15, 2006	99.625	7.896	562	3	16,318
Freeport-McMoran Copper & Gold (FCX)-c	7.000	Feb 11, 2011	161.761	1.131	n.a.	n.a.	15,000
DEX Media East LLC (DEXME)	12.125	Nov 15, 2012	120.625	7.420	312	10	13,100
Ahold Finance U.S.A. (AHOLD)	8.250	Jul 15, 2010	110.000	6.387	207	10	11,500
Playtex Products (PYX)	9.375	Jun 01, 2011	98.500	9.657	534	10	9,827
Chesapeake Energy (CHK)	8.125	Apr 01, 2011	109.750	5.347	103	10	7,270

Volume represents total volume for the market; price/yield data are for trades of $250,000 and greater. * Estimated spreads, in basis points (100 basis points is one percentage point), over the 2, 3, 5, 10 or 30-year on the run Treasury note/bond. 2-year: 1.625 10/05; 3-year: 2.375 08/06; 5-year: 3.125 10/08; 10-year: 4.250 08/13; 30-year: 5.375 02/31. †Comparable U.S. Treasury issue. c-Convertible bond.
Source: MarketAxess Corporate BondTicker; *Wall Street Journal*, November 4, 2003

Table 1.12 Foreign government and international bonds

Total rates of return on international bonds in %, based on J.P. Morgan Government Bond Index, Dec. 31, 1987 = 100

	Local currency terms					$ TERMS				
	Index value	1 Day	1 Mo	3 Mos	Since 12/31	Index value	1 Day	1 Mo	3 Mos	Since 12/31
Japan	216.26	−0.19	−0.46	−1.98	−1.70	239.08	+1.38	+0.63	+7.71	+6.54
Britain	413.83	+0.42	−1.23	−1.94	−0.47	368.26	+0.25	−0.58	+2.20	+3.76
Germany	280.45	+0.27	−0.90	+0.15	+2.63	258.71	+0.52	−1.98	+1.59	+12.48
France	374.47	+0.27	−0.29	+0.12	+2.62	349.12	+0.52	−1.38	+1.56	+12.47
Canada	410.00	+0.28	−0.32	+1.20	+3.91	399.51	+0.01	+0.35	+6.46	+23.08
Netherlands	301.43	+0.25	−0.28	+0.16	+2.86	277.64	+0.50	−1.37	+1.60	+12.73
EMU-[c]	198.53	+0.27	−0.43	+0.15	+2.80	186.18	+0.53	−1.51	+1.59	+12.66
Global-[a]	329.86	+0.16	−0.44	−0.10	+1.28	313.51	+0.67	−0.58	+3.37	+8.24
EMBI+-[b]	284.31	+0.52	+1.75	+9.82	+24.23	284.31	+0.52	+1.75	+9.82	+24.23

International government bonds

Coupon	Maturity Mo/Yr	Price	Change	Yield[d]	Coupon	Maturity Mo/Yr	Price	Change	Yield[d]
Japan (3 p.m. Tokyo)					**Germany (5 p.m. London)**				
2.90%	12/05	105.76	−0.04	0.17%	2.50%	09/05	99.64	+0.08	2.702%
1.10	12/08	101.98	−0.18	0.70	3.50	10/08	99.41	+0.23	3.633
1.40	09/13	99.14	−0.34	1.50	4.25	01/14	99.17	+0.44	4.351
1.70	06/33	87.81	−1.08	2.41	4.75	07/34	96.27	+1.06	4.984
United Kingdom (5 p.m. London)					**Canada (3 p.m. Eastern Time)**				
8.50%	12/05	107.60	+0.08	4.635%	3.00%	12/05	99.58	+0.01	3.210%
5.00	03/08	100.20	+0.29	4.948	4.25	09/08	100.64	+0.21	4.102
8.00	09/13	122.87	+0.73	5.036	5.25	06/13	102.93	+0.40	4.863
4.25	06/32	90.76	+1.25	4.851	5.75	06/29	105.03	+0.53	5.385

[a] 18 int'l govt. markets. [b] external-currency emerging mkt. debt, Dec. 31, 1993 = 100.
[c] Jan. 2, 1995 = 100. [d] Equivalent to semi-annual compounded yields to maturity
Source: Wall Street Journal, November 4, 2003

At an introductory level, some basic empirical evidence about risk and return estimates is presented in table 1.13 for US data. As will be demonstrated, this basic data can be extended into various forms dealing with extensions and limitations arising from this baseline. Before doing this, the basics need description. The main item of interest is the values for the mean and standard deviation over the full sample. Casual inspection reveals that, for the categories selected, stocks exhibit the highest estimated (arithmetic average) return and highest estimated standard deviation of return, followed by long term bonds and Treasury bills.[11] Also included for comparison is the inflation rate,

Table 1.13 Annual returns for US stocks, bonds, bills and inflation over the 1974–98 market cycle

Year	Small stocks	Large stocks	Long-term T-bonds	Intermediate term T-bonds	T-bills	Inflation
1974	−29.74	−26.40	5.53	6.03	7.93	12.34
1975	69.54	37.26	8.50	6.79	5.80	6.94
1976	54.81	23.98	11.07	14.20	5.06	4.86
1977	22.02	−7.26	0.90	1.12	5.10	6.70
1978	22.29	6.50	−4.16	0.32	7.15	9.02
1979	43.99	18.77	9.02	4.29	10.45	13.29
1980	35.34	32.48	13.17	0.83	11.57	12.52
1981	7.79	−4.98	3.61	6.09	14.95	8.92
1982	27.44	22.09	6.52	33.39	10.71	3.83
1983	34.49	22.37	−0.53	5.44	8.85	3.79
1984	−14.02	6.46	15.29	14.46	10.02	3.95
1985	28.21	32.00	32.68	23.65	7.83	3.80
1986	3.40	18.40	23.96	17.22	6.18	1.10
1987	−13.95	5.34	−2.65	1.68	5.50	4.43
1988	21.72	16.86	8.40	6.63	6.44	4.42
1989	8.37	31.34	19.49	14.82	8.32	4.65
1990	27.08	−3.20	7.13	9.05	7.86	6.11
1991	50.24	30.66	18.39	16.67	5.65	3.06
1992	27.84	7.71	7.79	7.25	3.54	2.90
1993	20.30	9.87	15.48	12.02	2.97	2.75
1994	−3.34	1.29	−7.18	−4.42	3.91	2.67
1995	33.21	37.71	31.67	18.07	5.58	2.54
1996	16.50	23.07	−0.81	3.99	5.50	3.32
1997	22.40	33.17	15.08	7.69	5.32	1.70
1998	2.50	28.53	13.02	8.62	5.11	1.61
Average	20.737	16.161	10.055	9.436	7.092	5.2488
Standard dev.	4.51	3.247	2.042	1.655	0.56	0.693
Minimum	−29.74	−26.4	−7.18	−4.42	2.97	1.1
Maximum	69.54	37.71	32.68	33.39	14.95	13.29

which has an average rate of increase below that of bills. Only the standard deviation of inflation for the US, which is above that for bills, is anomalous. Unfortunately, upon closer inspection, the number of questions raised by these empirical results is substantial. The implications for portfolio management and security selection are not as apparent as initial appearances indicate.

The first type of question that comes to mind concerns the form of the estimators used to compare the performance of the securities selected. At the basic level, parameters of the *unconditional distribution* are evaluated, i.e., the expected return for security

i is estimated using the arithmetic average of the time series of the observed returns for security i, $R_i(t)$, risk is estimated using the standard deviation of returns, i.e., the square root of the variance:[12]

$$\bar{R}_i = \frac{\sum_{t=1}^{T} R_i(t)}{T} \qquad \hat{\sigma}_i = \sqrt{\frac{\sum_{t=1}^{T} (R_i(t) - \bar{R}_i)^2}{T-1}}$$

Expected return is estimated using the arithmetic mean of the time series of the security return and risk is estimated using the standard deviation of the time series. The use of the arithmetic mean to estimate the expected return is justified under the assumption that the returns are independently, identically distributed (iid) random variables, i.e., the process is strictly stationary (see section 1.3). In this case, the arithmetic mean has the desirable property that it is a best linear unbiased estimate of the return to be obtained in the next period.[13] A similar conclusion applies to the use of the standard deviation to estimate the risk.

For statistical purposes, being the best estimator in the class of linear unbiased estimators is a desirable property. Yet, when used in the context of calculating the returns from holding a security, the use of this estimate embeds assumptions about the underlying investment strategy. In particular, it assumes that the security selection process and associated portfolio rebalancing occurs each sampling period ($t = 1, 2, 3 \ldots$). Alternatively, it is also possible to assume that the trader is entering the market for the first time that period and will hold the security for one period. If the objective is to determine the return on a security that was purchased and then held over multiple periods, the *arithmetic average return* will give a biased result when compared to the *geometric average return*. The arithmetic average only gives an unbiased estimate of the return over the next period. It can give misleading results when used to describe the return over more than one period.

Similarly, the "best" property of the arithmetic average is achieved by weighting each observation equally by $1/T$. Best means the mean squared error for the estimator is the smallest. In the class of unbiased estimators this translates into the smallest variance around the true population parameter. Weighted average estimators which, say, give more weight to observations that are more recent and less weight to observations in the more distant past would not be statistically "best," but do have the intuitively appealing property of giving more weight to recent changes in market conditions. However, this requires some method of determining the relationship between the various observations. If sufficient information is available to formulate prior distributions, the weights could even be determined in a Bayesian fashion.

To better understand the investment strategy implications of basing decisions on arithmetic averages, consider the method used for calculating the one-period return on a domestic security, $R(1)$. It is assumed that at $t = 0$ the security is purchased at price $P(0)$, held for one period and then sold at price $P(1)$. For simplicity, it is assumed that any dividend payment (*Div.*) paid during the holding period is received at the time the security is sold. The return can now be calculated as:

$$R(1) = (P(1) - P(0) + Div.)/P(0) = [P(1)/P(0)] + [Div./P(0)] - 1$$

$$= [(P(1) - P(0))/P(0)] + [Div./P(0)]$$

$$= Capital\ Gain\ (Loss) + Dividend\ (or\ Coupon)\ Yield$$

The funds received from the sale of the security can now be reinvested at $t = 1$. This same security can now be purchased at price $P(1)$, held for one period and then sold at price $P(2)$, with any dividend payment again assumed to be paid at the time the security is sold. This second, one period return is $R(2)$. And so it goes for $R(3)$, $R(4)$, $R(5)$ . . .

For purposes of illustration, assume that the security does not pay dividends and that $P(0) = \$100$, $P(1) = \$50$ and $P(2) = \$100$. It follows that $R(1) = (\$50 - \$100)/\$100 = -50\%$ and $R(2) = (\$100 - \$50)/\$50 = 100\%$. The arithmetic average for this process is $(-50\% + 100\%)/2 = 25\%$. But the security which was purchased at \$100 at $t = 0$ is only worth \$100 at $t = 2$. The security value is unchanged from $t = 0$ to $t = 2$ yet the arithmetic average rate of return is 25%. These same numbers can be used to illustrate the properties of the geometric mean:

$$(1 + \bar{R}_i^G) = \left[\prod_{t=1}^{T} (1 + R_i(t)) \right]^{1/T}$$

The geometric mean can now be calculated as $\sqrt{(1 + -.5)(1 + 1)} = 1$, implying a geometric mean equal to zero. Hence, if the investor is concerned with the terminal value of the investment, then the geometric average would seem to be more appropriate.

The advantages of using the geometric mean to guide investment decisions has been recognized at least since Latane (1959) and Brieman (1960). Often being referenced as the "growth optimal" model, early explorations in Finance on the implications of using the geometric mean were developed by Young and Roberts (1969), Hakansson (1971), Roll (1973) and Elton and Gruber (1974). Relevant issues raised along this line will be explored in chapter 10. Proponents of the arithmetic average would observe that the illustration used in the example is not fair as the probabilities of future movements in rates are not given accurate accounting. Say the probability of the 100% increase is 50% and for the −50% reduction is also 50%. Then there are four possible paths as shown in figure 1.2. Given the probabilities the expected terminal value at time $t = 2$ would be: $E[V] = .25(400) + .5(100) + .25(25) = \$156.25 = \$100(1.25)^2$. Assuming that −50% and +100% are both equally likely then the expected return is 25%, not 0%.

As noted, differences between the geometric and arithmetic mean can translate into potential differences in investment strategies. Conventionally, use of the geometric mean has been associated with an investment strategy that maximizes the expected terminal value of a portfolio while the arithmetic average has been associated with maximizing the expected utility of the terminal value, where expected utility is identified with a mean-variance objective function. Considerable effort has been given to identifying cases where these two objectives will produce the same portfolio. Not surprisingly, one case that has been identified occurs when returns are identically normally distributed. Introductory statistics texts observe that a limitation of the arithmetic mean is that it can give misleading results when there are extreme observations. In practice, differences

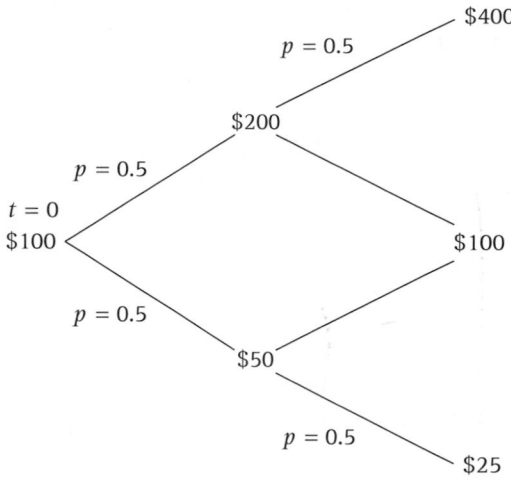

Figure 1.2 An example of a binomial process for stock prices

between the geometric and arithmetic means are only significant when returns are decidedly non-normal, as in the case of small stocks, and are almost identical when returns are approximately normal, as in the case of bills and inflation.

The return calculation becomes more complicated when the security selection process is permitted to include foreign assets, where the price is denominated in foreign currency terms. Showing the distinction requires some notation. Let: the domestic currency denominated return on a foreign security position be $R_\$$; the foreign currency denominated return on a foreign asset be $R_£$; let e be the growth rate of the currency, $(S(1) - S(0))/S(0) = (\Delta S/S(0))$, where S is the spot exchange rate measured as units of domestic currency for one unit of foreign currency. In order to distinguish from the domestic values, let Div^* be the single dividend which is known to be paid in units foreign currency at $t = 1$ and P^* be the security price in foreign currency terms. Given this notation:

$$1 + R_\$ = 1 + \frac{[P^*(1) + Div^*(1)]S(1) - P^*(0)S(0)}{P^*(0)S(0)} = \frac{P^*(1) + Div^*(1)}{P^*(0)} \frac{S(1)}{S(0)}$$

$$= [1 + R_£][1 + e]$$

In effect, the security return can be decomposed into the returns associated with local factors, $R_£$, and currency changes, e.

The presence of foreign securities in the portfolio selection problem raises substantive difficulties, if only because the relevant return, $R_\$$, is a function of two random variables, $R_£$ and e. This complicates the calculation of the variance:

$$var[R_\$] = var[1 + R_£ + e + R_£e]$$

$$= var[R_£] + var[e] + cov[R_£, e] + var[R_£e] + cov[R_£e, R_£] + cov[R_£e, e]$$

Table 1.14 Decomposition of the variance of the US $ currency return for six foreign equity and bond indices, 1978–89[a]

	$var[R_{is}]$	$var[R_i]$	Components of $var(R_{is})$		
			$var[e_i]$	$2 \, cov[R_i, \, e_i]$	Δvar
Bonds					
Canada	15.29	10.82	1.72	2.67	0.08
France	16.48	2.82	12.74	0.60	0.32
Germany	21.53	2.59	13.84	4.91	0.19
Japan	24.70	3.03	15.13	6.09	0.45
Switzerland	21.16	1.14	17.64	2.34	0.04
United Kingdom	27.67	8.88	12.39	6.08	0.32
United States	10.24	10.24	0.00	0.00	0.00
Stocks					
Canada	37.70	30.58	1.72	5.37	0.03
France	59.75	43.03	12.74	3.75	0.23
Germany	43.82	29.27	13.84	0.00	0.71
Japan	41.47	19.45	15.13	5.83	1.06
Switzerland	34.81	20.07	17.64	−3.76	0.86
United Kingdom	40.96	29.27	12.39	−1.52	0.82
United States	21.16	21.16	0.00	0.00	0.00

[a] The variances are computed using monthly percentage returns.
Source: (Poitras 2002), Eun and Resnick (1994)

It is conventional to simplify this calculation by using the approximation, $\ln[1 + R_\$] \simeq R_\$ \simeq \ln[1 + R_£] + \ln[1 + e] \simeq R_£ + e$ (where $\simeq$ means "approximately equal to"). This permits all the terms in $var[R_\$]$ involving $(R_£e)$ to be ignored. However, this approximation is only valid if $R_£$ and e are sufficiently small (see end of chapter questions).

A number of sources provide information on the relative contributions to $var[R_\$]$ of the local return ($R_£$) and the exchange rate (e). For example, table 1.14 reports empirical results for the decomposition of $var[R_\$]$ into these components (see also table 1.12). Evidence is presented for the US$ denominated monthly returns of securities from seven different countries. Returns for both intermediate term bonds and the major stock index for each country are provided. Returns are measured monthly. The fifth and last column gives the contribution due to ($R_£e$) and indicates that this component is not significant. Hence, for these returns measured at a monthly frequency, the log approximation is valid. The results also indicate that, with the exception of Canada, the component of the variance of bond returns due to local price changes is significantly less than that due to exchange rate changes. This result is changed for the variance of stock returns where the component associated with changes in the local stock prices is significantly larger than that due to exchange rate changes.

Risk and uncertainty: Frank Knight and J.M. Keynes[14]

The distinction between risk and uncertainty was at one time a hotly debated subject which fell well within the confines of active academic discussion. However, under the currently prevailing orthodoxy in Finance, this distinction has come to be either discarded or ignored. Parametric inferences drawn from conditional or unconditional distributions are now the fashion. The cudgel of dispensing notions derived from the implications of uncertainty have been relegated to non-mainstream proponents, such as the post-Keynesian economists, e.g., Davidson (1991) and Bernstein (1997, 1998). This is unfortunate. Though difficult to handle within the positivist theoretical and empirical framework of modern Finance, inclusion of uncertainty into the analysis of securities and investment strategies does have profound implications for both the modeling process and the conclusions reached. As argued by J.M. Keynes in *The General Theory* the implications of uncertainty extend well into the realm of public policy about the role of securities markets in determining aggregate investment behavior.

Modern financial theory is careful to develop logical relationships based on parameters from the conditional (or unconditional) distribution. Typically, attention focuses on the expected value (mean) and variance of the distribution, though attention is sometimes given to higher moments such as skewness and kurtosis. Precisely how to model predictions for random variable outcomes, e.g., using the conditional distribution, raises deep philosophical questions, variants of which have been debated for centuries. For example, Thomas Bayes (1701–1761) suggested that the conditional (posterior) distribution is determined by combining prior beliefs with available empirical evidence. In the twentieth century, both J.M. Keynes (1883–1946) and Frank Knight (1885–1972) advanced the notion that the variation in future outcomes is a combination of a measurable component, risk, and an unmeasurable component, uncertainty. At the time, this was an intellectual step forward, a reaction to the nineteenth-century beliefs of Stanley Jevons, Francis Galton and others that future outcomes were ultimately measurable.

Knight and Keynes were both struggling with different facets of the impact of randomness on economic activity. When put within the context of the problems at hand, their seemingly arcane ideas still have considerable relevance, though proponents of modern Finance argue otherwise (see section 1.3). Knight worked within the tradition of classical economics, seeking to explain how economic profits can arise from uncertainty in the process of production and distribution. Classical economic theory depends on the assumption that outcomes are certain, if there is randomness then the probabilities of the possible outcomes are known with certainty. In the absence of market imperfections, such as monopoly, classical economic theory argues that economic profits will dissipate to zero and each of the factors of production will earn their value of marginal product. Knight questioned this view, arguing that economic profits could still arise from the ability of entrepreneurs to resolve the uncertainty facing factors of production.

Frank Knight still has relevance, not because of his theoretical musings, but because of his interpretation of the randomness arising from commercial risks. Part three of *Risk, Uncertainty and Profit* (1921), especially the chapters on "The meaning of risk and uncertainty" and "Structures and methods for meeting uncertainty," contain many insights. For example, Knight discusses the application of "the principle of insurance" to "business hazards." After recognizing the wide divergence of insurable risks, from life to fire to marine to theft and burglary, Knight concludes (p. 252): "The possibility of . . . reducing uncertainty by transforming it into a measurable risk . . . constitutes a strong incentive to extend the scale of operations of a business establishment. This fact must constitute one of the important causes of the phenomenal growth in the average size of industrial establishments which is a familiar characteristic of modern life." Knight also clearly recognizes "specialization" in activities which isolate the "true uncertainty" in business risk including "organized speculation as carried on in connection with produce and security exchanges" (p. 257).

Perhaps the most important point involves Knight's interpretation of commercial risks, for example (p. 226):

> A manufacturer is considering the advisability of making a large commitment in increasing the capacity of his works. He "figures" more or less on the proposition, taking account as well as possible of the various factors more or less susceptible of measurement, but the final result is an "estimate" of the probable outcome of any proposed course of action. What is the "probability" or error (strictly, of any assigned degree of error) in the judgment? It is manifestly meaningless to speak of either calculating such a probability *a priori* or of determining it empirically by studying a large number of instances. The essential and outstanding fact is that the "instance" in question is so entirely unique that there are no others or not a sufficient number to make it possible to tabulate enough like it to form a basis for any inference of value about any real probability in the case we are interested in.

It is not a stretch to replace this "manufacturer" with an investor seeking to make a substantial investment in a particular security. Risk is associated with objectively measured probabilities, while uncertainty requires subjective probability assessments. The economic rents to business ownership or, for that matter, security selection arises from correctly anticipating uncertain outcomes.

As for methods of dealing with uncertainty, Knight (p. 239) recognizes four general approaches:

> We may call the two fundamental methods of dealing with uncertainty, based respectively upon reduction by grouping and upon selection of men to "bear" it, "consolidation" and "specialization," respectively. To these two methods we must add two others . . . (3) control of the future, (4) increased power of prediction.

Knight recognizes the complementarity among the different approaches for dealing with uncertainty. For example, increased specialization permits more firm resources to be devoted to data collection and analysis which increases power of prediction. Writing in 1921, Knight has little to say about the use of derivative securities to "control the future." Other than occasional references, Knight also does not deal with specific aspects of financial risk and uncertainty. What Knight does say very clearly is that the randomness associated with economic risks, such as business risk, is composed of "risk," which is measurable in an objective sense, and "uncertainty," which is only measurable subjectively. It is in dealing correctly with uncertainty that "entrepreneurs" earn value.

In contrast to Knight, Keynes provides little guidance on general methods of managing risks. Whereas Knight's *Risk, Uncertainty and Profit* wanders toward an endpoint, in *The General Theory of Employment, Interest and Money* (1936) Keynes proposes "not one, or two, but three or four 'models' of the workings of a modern economy" (Blaug 1978, p. 682). Chapter 12 of *The General Theory* is a largely self-contained essay on "The State of Long Term Expectation." In this chapter, Keynes is concerned with the social consequences of instability in stock markets, arguing for government intervention to offset inherent deficiencies. The core of the argument revolves around an examination of the process by which expectations are formed in financial markets. Due to an excess bias towards maintaining liquidity, expectations in financial markets are focused on near-term prospects (p. 157): "Investment based on genuine long-term expectation is so difficult today as to be scarcely practicable."

The General Theory is a difficult book to read, quite untidy and poorly written. The importance of the book lies in the substance of certain arguments, who was making those arguments and when the book was presented, i.e., during the stagnation following the economic collapse of the early 1930s. Many ideas are presented, some seemingly off the cuff, such is the case with chapter 12. Some of the observations are insightful, for example (pp. 154–5):

> It might be supposed that competition between expert professionals, possessing judgment and knowledge beyond that of the average private investor, would correct the vagaries of the ignorant individual left to himself. It happens, however, that the energies and skill of the professional investor and speculator are mainly occupied otherwise. For most of those persons are, in fact, largely concerned, not with making superior long-term forecasts of the probable yield of an investment over its whole life, but with forecasting changes in the conventional basis of valuation a short time ahead of the general public. They are concerned, not with what an investment is really worth to a man who buys it "for keeps," but with what the market will value it at, under the influence of mass psychology, three months or a year hence. Moreover, this behaviour is not the outcome of a wrong-headed propensity. It is an inevitable result of an investment market organized (to concentrate resources upon the holding of "liquid" securities). For it is not sensible to pay 25 for an investment of which you believe the prospective yield to justify a value of 30, if you also believe that the market will value it at 20 three months hence.

In true Keynesian fashion, this is shortly followed with the rhetorical statement (p. 155): "The social objective of skilled investment should be to defeat the dark forces of time and ignorance which envelop our future." The modern reader is left glancing about for a Wall Street investment banker dressed as Batman or Spiderman.

What Keynes develops in chapter 12 is a model where the heterogeneous, subjective expectations of market participants leads to a financial market equilibrium in which prices are "subject to waves of optimistic and pessimistic sentiment, which are unreasoning and yet in a sense legitimate where no solid basis exists for a reasonable calculation" (p. 154). The implication is that prices can change "violently as the result of a sudden fluctuation of opinion due to factors which do not really make much difference to the prospective yield" (p. 154). Not only will prices be considerably more volatile than is justified by the long term expectation, prices will typically depend more on "what average opinion expects average opinion to be" rather than on valuations which capture "the prospective yield of an investment over a long term of years" (p. 155). Prices are determined more by "*speculation* . . . the activity of forecasting the psychology of the market" than by "*enterprise* . . . the activity of forecasting the prospective yield of assets over their whole life" (p. 158).

Keynes was concerned about the potentially negative impact that price formation in capital markets can have on the macroeconomy: "When the capital development of a country becomes a by-product of the activities of a casino, the job is likely to be ill-done" (p. 159). As evidenced by the technology-led stock price bubble of 1997–2000, such observations still have relevance. However, this is not a book on macroeconomics. While Keynes has only general or cursory insights about security analysis and investment strategy, there is considerable insight about the stochastic properties of financial prices and the role of speculation in determining financial prices. Modern investment strategy is largely concerned with managing financial risks to achieve the objective of investor wealth maximization. Keynes warns about the possibility that financial prices may not reflect long term expectations of prospective yields and will likely be subject to inexplicable volatility. If so, this substantially complicates the problem of formulating optimal portfolio management strategies.

Though both Keynes and Knight have been duly recognized for examining the role of uncertainty on random economic outcomes, the predictions that they made about the impact of uncertainty on the evolution of financial markets seem to be at odds. Knight argues that increasing the scale of activities will permit firms to increasingly specialize, permitting a reduction in the scope of uncertainty. Keynes (1936, p. 158) seems to have the opposite view: "As the organization of investment markets improves, the risk of the predominance of speculation does, however, increase." In one case, the impact of uncertainty seems to be dissipating over time, in the other case it is increasing. It seems that agreement over the implications of uncertainty are difficult to obtain. The implications of uncertainty for security analysis and investment strategy will be developed in considerably greater detail at various points in the following chapters. The key point to take away at this stage is that the handling of uncertainty is an essential element in security analysis and investment strategy.

1.2   THE EFFICIENT MARKETS HYPOTHESIS

Basic insights

The roots of the efficient markets hypothesis (EMH) are as murky as the hypothesis itself. There are hints of the EMH as far back as de la Vega (1688) with both J.M. Keynes (1936, ch. 12) and Irving Fisher (1930, ch. 13) having well developed notions that could qualify as precursors of the EMH. The reference to "efficiency" is misleading, as this term is also used to refer to a number of related concepts. For example, there is the "efficient frontier" associated with the Markowitz optimization model and there is "Pareto efficiency" associated with the properties of a perfectly competitive equilibrium in theoretical microeconomics. As presented by Fama (1970, 1976) and by numerous others, the efficient markets hypothesis is related to information processing. "An efficient capital market is a market that is efficient in processing information. The prices of securities observed at any time are based on the 'correct' evaluation of all information available at that time. In an efficient market, prices 'fully reflect' available information" (Fama 1976, p. 133). While accurate processing of information is a noble goal for a security market, there are real difficulties in specifying tests of the EMH. Testing of efficiency also requires the "correct" evaluation method to be specified. Hence, the EMH is inherently a joint hypothesis of efficiency and a return generating model.

Perhaps the defining moment for the EMH came with Samuelson (1965). By proving that "properly anticipated prices fluctuate randomly," Samuelson brought the theory of security pricing into congruence with a myriad of statistical results about security prices that had been developing since the early 1950s. An early example of this work, Kendall (1953) found that stock prices had no identifiable pattern. Prices evolved in a random fashion, with no predictable component. More precisely, successive changes in security prices were independent of each other. More recent research, e.g., Lo and MacKinlay (1988), has found some evidence of positive serial correlation in common stock returns over short intervals. In some cases, the evidence is only weak and does not extend much beyond weekly sampling intervals.[15] However, using Center for Research in Security Prices (CRSP) value weighted and equally weighted indexes, Campbell et al. (1997) provide somewhat stronger evidence of generally positive serial correlation for daily, weekly and monthly stock returns (1962–94). Lo and MacKinlay (1999) extend these results even further. This line of research on the randomness properties of stock prices speaks to one form of the EMH, whether current prices fully reflect the information in past prices. In this form, the EMH is often reformulated as the "random walk hypothesis," e.g., Malkiel (1995).

It is conventional to present different versions of the EMH associated with different possible types of information sets which are "fully reflected" in security prices. Three versions are usually identified: *weak* form, where the information set is the past history of the security price (sometimes this form includes all market generated data such as up/down volume, number of 52 week highs and lows, etc.); the *semi-strong* form, where the information set is publicly available information, such as firm accounting data, newspaper articles, analysts' recommendations and so on; and, *strong* form, where the information set is all publicly and privately available information, including insider information. If the EMH is correct, then it is not possible to achieve abnormal returns from trading on the available information set. When the weak form information set is defined to be a subset of the semi-strong form which is also a subset of the strong form, it follows that a strong form efficient market is also semi-strong form and weak form efficient. Similarly, it does not follow that a weak form efficient market will be semi-strong or strong form efficient. As will be discussed shortly, because the EMH is a joint hypothesis, rejection of any version of the EMH could be due to a rejection of the return generating model rather than the EMH.

The focus on information processing provides a direct connection between security pricing and the evaluation of a conditional expectation. Specifying the security price, or some appropriate transformation of the security price, as the conditional expectation evaluated with respect to a particular conditioning information set makes a direct connection to the theory of stochastic processes, including results on *martingale* processes. Under the assumption of ergodicity, the connection to stochastic processes provides a structure for the statistical testing of hypotheses about security prices. The connection to martingale theory can be used to motivate the correspondence between trading of securities and gambling. More precisely, a martingale process can be identified with the *fair game* model that Feller (1957, pp. 233–5) and many others use to motivate the law of large numbers. In turn, closer examination of the fair game model is useful in establishing a precise connection between gambling theory and the security pricing models used in Finance.

Martingale theory has been something of a revolution in a number of areas of mathematics and mathematical statistics, including the solving of partial differential equations.[16] The most basic definition of a martingale is (Karlin and Taylor 1975, p. 238):

Definition

The elementary martingale process

A stochastic process $\{X(t): t = 0, 1, 2, \ldots\}$ is a martingale if, for $t = 1, 2, \ldots$:

(i) $E[\,|X(t)|\,] < \infty$
(ii) $E[X(t + 1) \mid X(0), X(1), X(2) \ldots X(t)] = X(t)$

Condition (i) is a restriction on the probability distribution from which the $\{X(t)\}$ can be drawn, the unconditional expected value of $X(t)$ has to be finite. This rules out processes with infinite mean values, such as the Cauchy process, but does admit processes with infinite variance, such as the stable processes with characteristic exponent less than two. Condition (ii) is the martingale property which says that, given the information on the $\{X(t)\}$ up to time t, the best prediction of the next $(t + 1)$ observation is the current (t) observation.

The conditioning information set can be expanded considerably to be, say, $\{Y(0), Y(1), Y(2) \ldots Y(t)\}$ where $\{Y(t)\}$ is some stochastic process or set of stochastic processes which could include $\{X(t)\}$. In this case (ii) can be expressed as $E[X(t + 1) \mid Y(0), Y(1), Y(2) \ldots Y(t)] = X(t)$, i.e., $\{X(t)\}$ is a martingale with respect to conditioning information set $\{Y(t)\}$, where $X(t)$ is a function of $\{Y(0), Y(1), Y(2) \ldots Y(t)\}$.[17] Within this framework, the strong, semi-strong and weak form versions of the efficient markets hypothesis can be represented by expanding the appropriate conditioning information set associated with the conditional expectation. For the weak form, the past history of prices is the conditioning information set; for the semi-strong form, the information set is potentially all publicly available information; and, for the strong form, the information set is all available information, public and private. However, while this interpretation of the EMH is appealing, a substantial amount of development is required. A useful starting point for this development is the fair game model.

The connection of a martingale with a fair game arises when $\{X(n)\}$ is the amount of money that a player has after $n \in \{1, 2, \ldots, N\}$ trials when playing a fair game. The game involved here is a repeated trial of some game of chance, e.g., throwing dice or flipping a coin. Following Feller, the fair game model requires two key assumptions: that the gambler has unlimited capital, i.e., no amount of loss can force termination of the game; and, that the total number of trials (N) is fixed at the start of the game and independent of the way the game develops, i.e., the gambler cannot terminate the game at a favorable point. The first assumption prevents the game being reduced to the gambler's ruin problem. The second assumption prevents the game from being an optional sampling problem where the gambler has the ability to terminate the game after a run of good luck.

Given these two assumptions, the definition of a fair game follows by letting μ be the expected payoff from a winning gamble where $\mu = E[X(k)] < \infty$. Letting $\gamma =$ the cost (entrance fee, ante) required to undertake a single trial of the game, then it is often said that a "fair" game occurs when $\gamma = \mu$, though Feller wrangles at the use of this name because it is still possible for $\gamma = \mu$ and for the accumulated winnings to be positive or negative. For a game played to the fixed termination time, the expected winnings would be $S(N) = X(1) + X(2) + \ldots + X(N)$. Observing that the cost of achieving these winnings is $N\gamma$, then the net gain from playing the game would be $S(N) - N\gamma$. Recognizing that the law of large numbers says $S(N) - N\mu$ will become small as the number of trials gets large, it follows that when $\gamma = \mu$ the net gain or loss from playing the game will be small relative to N as N gets large. As Feller observes, it is possible for the net gain or loss of a fair game to be non-zero as long as the gain or loss is small when N gets large.

To see the connection between the fair game model and a martingale, consider the expectation of $S(n + 1)$ given the information on accumulated winnings up to time n:

$$E[S(n + 1) \mid S(n), \, S(n - 1) \ldots S(0)] = E[S(n + 1) \mid X(n), \, X(n - 1), \ldots X(0)] = S(n)$$

This result captures the essence of Feller's (1966, p. 211) observation about the fair game model: "The idea of a fair game is that the knowledge of the past should not enable the gambler to improve on his fortunes. Intuitively, this means that an absolutely fair game should remain absolutely fair under any system of gambling, that is, under rules of skipping individual trials." (For example, betting rules in a fair game such as "bet on tails after k heads in a row occur" will not be successful.) The fair game model, the martingale process, and the expected value conditional on the past history of the random variable all come together to provide a foundation for the weak form of the efficient markets hypothesis. In the weak form version, the securities market is being modeled as a fair game.

While it may be intuitively appealing to model the weak form of the EMH by taking the current price for a security to be a martingale with respect to the past history of security prices, the actual formulation of the hypothesis is more complicated. For example, consider the price of a non-dividend paying stock where: $P(t + 1) = (1 + R(t + 1))P(t)$. It follows that this price process will not follow a martingale unless expected returns are zero. More precisely, the price process will follow a submartingale:

Definition

The submartingale process

A stochastic process $\{X(t): t = 0, 1, 2, \ldots\}$ is a submartingale with respect to $\{Y(t): t = 0, 1, 2, \ldots\}$ if, for $t = 1, 2, \ldots$:

(i) $E[X(t)^+] < \infty$ where $X(t)^+ = max[0, X(t)]$
(ii) $E[X(t + 1) \mid Y(0), Y(1), Y(2) \ldots Y(t)] \geq X(t)$
(iii) $X(t) = f[Y(0), Y(1), \ldots Y(t)]$

Basically, a submartingale is a martingale with the $\geq$ replacing $=$ that applies to the martingale definition, condition (ii). It follows that $E[P(t + 1) \mid Y(0), Y(1) \ldots Y(t)] \geq P(t)$ whenever $E[R(t + 1) \mid Y(0), Y(1) \ldots Y(t)] \geq 0$, i.e., prices for non-dividend paying securities follow a submartingale. This result explains the reliance on returns, as opposed to prices, in testing asset pricing models.

To see the statistical advantages of using returns instead of prices observe that if $R(t + 1) = (P(t + 1) - P(t))/P(t)$ then, evaluating the expectation conditional on information available at $t = 0$, $E[R(t + 1)] = (E[P(t + 1)] - P(t))/P(t)$. Observing that $R(t) = (P(t) - P(t - 1))/P(t - 1)$, then the requirement that security returns follow a martingale becomes $E[R(t + 1)] = (E[P(t + 1)] - P(t))/P(t) = R(t) = (P(t) - P(t - 1))/P(t - 1)$. This reduces to the condition that $E[P(t + 1)]/P(t) = P(t)/P(t - 1)$. (By taking logs, this condition can be formulated in terms of the log differences in prices.) It follows that, if the return generating process is ergodic, then it is returns, not prices, that follow a martingale. Various generalizations of this basic result have been explored. Recognizing that the return to holding a security is associated with compensation for invested capital, the relevance of using returns instead of prices may not extend to futures and forward contracts that, ignoring the opportunity cost of margin funds, do not require a cash outflow when created.

Because of the key role that empirical testing plays in the positivist philosophy of modern Finance, it becomes imperative to identify a procedure or rationale for converting the stochastic price process to a martingale. This is because of the importance that martingale difference sequences can have in testing theory, e.g., Hendry (1995, pp. 733–8). As discussed in section 1.3, the theory of classical hypothesis testing involves the laws of large numbers and the central limit theorem, results that rely on iid or, with appropriate adjustments, independent random variables. These results can be generalized using martingale limit theory that, in turn, depends on the properties of martingale difference sequences. These generalizations permit the assumption of independence to be relaxed to where the random variables are uncorrelated. Recognizing that sums of independent (and iid) random variables, expressed as deviations from the mean value, are martingales, it follows that the classical results can also be formulated and derived using the properties of martingale difference sequences.

A *martingale difference sequence* is constructed by differencing a martingale process. (In time series econometrics, martingale differences are referred to as "innovations.") More precisely, if $\{X(t)\}$ is a martingale with respect to $\{Y(t)\}$, then the martingale difference process $\{Z(t)\}$ can be constructed by defining $Z(t) = X(t) - X(t-1)$. It follows that $\{Z(t)\}$ has the property that $E[Z(t+1) \mid Y(0), Y(1) \ldots Y(t)] = 0$. The analytical advantages of the using the martingale difference process is that standard results such as versions of Chebychev's inequality and the laws of large numbers can be derived for $\{X(t)\}$ with finite second moments, permitting asymptotic distributions to be derived for cases where the independence assumption is relaxed to require only uncorrelated random variables. The asymptotic distribution theory follows from the associated central limit theorem for the martingale difference sequence. (A fair game can be expressed as a martingale difference sequence where $Z(t) = E[S(N+1) \mid X(0)$. $X(1) \ldots X(N)] - S(N)$.)

Testing the efficient markets hypothesis

From a testing perspective, it is essential to recognize that the EMH necessarily involves a *joint hypothesis*. Any empirical test of the EMH, a hypothesis that is concerned with the efficient processing of information into market prices, is also a test of the model being used to generate returns (prices). Empirical rejection of the EMH could be due to a rejection of the model for the return generating process, to a rejection of the EMH, or both. To see this, observe that, if the EMH is true, then it is not possible to generate (positive) abnormal returns from trading on the strategies exploiting the relevant information set. At any time t, this requires some hypothesis about the return generating process for $E[R(t+1) \mid Y(0), Y(1) \ldots Y(t)]$ in order to determine when a return is abnormal, i.e., where the actual return minus the predicted return is positive, $R(t+1) - E[R(t+1) \mid Y(0), Y(1) \ldots Y(t)] > 0$. Where applicable, the trading strategy is associated with the model used to specify $R(t+1)$ while $E[R(t+1) \mid Y(0), Y(1) \ldots Y(t)]$ is the expected return that the return generating model indicates is appropriate.

Following Fama (1976), the range of possible return generating models include: simple models, where the only restriction is that expected returns are positive; models of expected return resulting in the restriction that expected returns are constant over time, i.e., the conditional and unconditional means are equal; more sophisticated models that require expected returns to conform to the "market model" (see section 3.2); and, models that require expected returns to "conform to a risk return relationship." In this classification, there is a progressive nesting of the model types. For example, the models that imply expected returns are constant over time also impose the restriction that expected returns are positive. Similarly, requiring expected returns to follow the market model is imposed when a time series of observations on $\{R(t+1) - E[R(t+1) \mid Y(0),$ $Y(1) \ldots Y(t)]\}$ is used to test market efficiency. Because expected returns are associated with the conditional distribution, the market model is used to update the conditional expectation to account for the market risk inherent in the strategy. Tests of market efficiency based on constancy of the expected return are typically based on an information set that only considers the history of past returns.

Some empirical tests examine the time series of the abnormal returns, other tests examine the properties of the sum of abnormal returns over some time period (cumulative abnormal returns). For example, consider empirical tests of the weak form EMH based on the significance of serial correlation coefficients of returns, e.g., Lo and Mackinlay (1988, 1999). If there are identifiable trends in returns, then time series models, such as the ARMA (p,d,q) models popularized by Box and Jenkins (1970), could be used to predict next period's return from the history of current and past returns, including previous errors in forecasting past returns. The ARMA model would provide an atheoretical return generating model. However, if it was possible to use ARMA models to predict security returns, then under the EMH rational traders would seek out the profit opportunities by fitting the time series model and initiating a price adjustment process that would eliminate the predictable trends. If returns are not predictable using ARMA models, then returns are serially uncorrelated "white noise." Hence, a test of weak form efficiency is that returns be serially uncorrelated.

In general, the return generating model is used to determine if the return from the trading strategy is actually abnormal, e.g., accounts for systematic risk and provides an adequate return on invested capital. Given that the return generating model predicts that returns follow a martingale, empirical tests can be conducted by examining the statistical properties of $R(t + 1) - E[R(t + 1) | Y(0), Y(1) \ldots Y(t)] = R(t + 1) - R(t) = Z(t + 1)$. Recognizing that the null hypothesis of no abnormal returns requires that $E[Z(t)] = 0$, the EMH can be tested by determining whether $E[Z(t + 1) | Y(0), Y(1) \ldots Y(t)] = 0$, i.e., the tests can be conducted on the martingale difference sequence $\{Z(t)\}$. Which specific version of the EMH is tested depends on the information set that is used in the return generating model to determine $E[R(t + 1) | Y(0), Y(1) \ldots Y(t)]$. In practice, the econometric approach selected does not directly employ the martingale approach but, rather, will use an approach that possesses the martingale property in addition to imposing additional conditions. For example, tests of the weak form EMH usually use a random walk model instead of a martingale.

The random walk is a useful econometric model for testing the EMH, if only because of the substantial statistical theory that has been developed for this model. Different variations of the random walk are available. The basic random walk model is specified: $X(t + 1) = \mu + X(t) + u(t + 1)$, where μ is the constant "drift" in the process and the $u(t)$ is a random variable with a conditional mean of zero. Different versions of the random walk model can be formulated depending on the process being "driftless" ($\mu = 0$), whether $\{u(t)\}$ is assumed to be iid (σ_u is constant over time) or independent (σ_u is not constant over time) or uncorrelated (requires only that $E[u(t)u(t + 1)] = 0$ and allows for higher moments of the distribution to be dependent). A specific distributional assumption such as normality may also be imposed on $\{u(t)\}$ for testing purposes. Because of the failure to distinguish the specific form of the model being used, the random walk hypothesis has been the subject of considerable misinterpretation.

Early tests of the statistical properties of security prices, such as the studies in Cootner (1965), often employed the random walk model. By taking an expectation conditional on the information available at $t = 0$ it is possible to show that the driftless random walk obeys the martingale property, i.e., $E[X(t + 1) | Y(0), Y(1) \ldots Y(t)] = X(t)$. But if returns are positive, modeling the statistical behavior of security prices with a driftless random walk is incorrect. If returns are assumed to be positive and constant then a random walk with drift is required to model prices. If returns are only constant then it is possible that the estimate of the drift may be biased because the return is time varying. In most cases, a more appropriate formulation is to specify the log of prices as following a driftless random walk: $\ln[P(t + 1)] = \ln[P(t)] + u(t)$. Allowing $u(t)$ to be only independent instead of iid allows for the time varying volatility that is a commonly observed characteristic of security returns.

In general, there are a myriad of possible methods of testing the EMH. Because of the pervasive use of market efficiency in specifying asset pricing models, tests of such models are also indirectly tests of market efficiency. More immediate tests of the semi-strong form can be examined using event-study methodology, e.g., Campbell et al. (1997, ch. 4). Other tests use grouping methods and test for significant differences between groups using techniques such as regression analysis or variance ratio tests, e.g., comparing the returns from the month of January with other months or from the returns from low capitalization firms with the returns not in that group. It is even possible to use anecdotal studies, e.g., to examine the investment performance of successful investors such as Warren Buffett or Li Ka Shing or Ben Graham to identify heuristic characteristics not associated with lucky guessing or high initial wealth levels.

Whatever the methodology selected, the acid test of market efficiency is the requirement that investors cannot make abnormal profits from exploiting the relevant information set after deducting all the costs of trading and making the appropriate adjustments for risk. This means that tests of market efficiency have to be, either directly or indirectly, related to trading rules. In most situations, it is possible to account for the risk in a trading rule by discounting the expected profit at an interest rate that is sufficient to account for the risk. The appropriately discounted expected profit can then be compared to the initial capital required to implement the strategy. Costs of trading are incorporated in the trading rule. There are various sources of trading costs such as commissions, bid/offer spreads, asynchronous prices and "shoe leather." It is not enough to show that the relevant information is not fully incorporated in prices, e.g., by estimating a statistically significant serial correlation coefficient for returns. It is also necessary to demonstrate that it is possible to generate risk adjusted net profits from the market's slow interpretation of the relevant information.

Following Leitch and Tanner (1991), conventional statistical criteria may be inappropriate for identifying trading rules that are profitable. For example, a statistically significant positive serial correlation coefficient may not be sufficient to generate statistically significant profits. For example, consider the following string of numbers that can be assumed to be price changes for a stock price that is quoted in dollars: $\{x(t) = P(t) - P(t - 1)\} = \{5, 4, 1, -10, 0, 3, 2, 0, 1, -4\}$. This sequence of ten numbers has a serial correlation coefficient of .12 and a covariance of 2.25. These statistics are calculated using the nine available observations on $x(t)$ and $x(t - 1)$. The positive serial correlation coefficient implies that positive (negative) price changes tend to be followed by positive (negative) price changes. A possible trading rule to exploit the positive serial correlation would be to establish a long position following an up move, switching to a short position after a down move. Starting with $x(1) = 5$, the sequence of trading profits would be $\{\pi(t)\} = \{4, 1, -10, 0, -3, 2, 0, 1, -4\}$. Total profit would be -9.

There is nothing tricky about this particular string of numbers. Even without making reference to transactions costs, it is not difficult to specify sequences that have positive or negative serial correlation coefficients and produce negative trading rule profits. Statistical significance is achieved by taking the string to a sufficient number of terms. In general, statistical significance does not necessarily translate into trading rule profitability. Making the statistical analysis more complicated ("sophisticated") tends to make the specification of the trading rule less apparent. Though there may be more value associated with making the trading rule more sophisticated, with few exceptions this approach is not used. In this vein, Leitch and Tanner (1991) suggest the use of trading rule profitability as a measure of parameter significance instead of, say, minimum mean square error. To date, this suggestion has not been widely adopted.

Evidence of anomalies

Elton and Gruber (1984, p. 379) provide a pedagogically useful description of the initial development of the EMH:

> The efficient market hypothesis had a strange beginning. Generally, a theory is suggested and then extensive tests are undertaken to try to see if it better describes reality than previously accepted theories. The efficient market theory was developed in the opposite way. First, extensive tests were undertaken that demonstrated that, contrary to popular belief, certain types and ways of using information (usually past prices) did not lead to superior profits. When evidence along these lines accumulated, academics went in search of a theory to explain these findings and the efficient market theory was born.

This description captures many essential features of the process by which knowledge is "created" in modern Finance. The epistemology that is prescribed in modern Finance requires that a theory or model is "suggested" using logical deduction from stated assumptions. "Extensive tests" of the model are then conducted to establish empirical validity. If the model is supported by the data it becomes part of received theory until a "better," more empirically descriptive, model is developed. If the model is rejected, the process of logical deduction is iterated until a model is identified that explains the "stylized facts."

In contrast to the prescribed epistemology, the EMH developed inductively. Initial results, such as those presented in Fama (1965) and Cootner (1965), provided "strong empirical evidence" that changes in security prices, particularly common stock prices, were random or, at least, random enough. The empirical tests usually involved an examination of the serial correlation coefficients for the difference in the log of prices though, in some cases, the serial correlation for the difference in prices was examined. Recognizing that serial correlation tests can be affected by a small number of large observations (outliers), some studies also provided results for runs tests, e.g., Fama (1965). Though such tests typically have low power to reject the null hypothesis of random behavior, runs tests assess whether there are an inordinate number of positive or negative changes that occur in sequence. Results from the runs tests were much as with the serial correlation tests, daily time intervals indicated a slight positive relationship with longer intervals appearing random.

Serial correlation and runs tests only examine statistical properties without making a direct connection to the evaluation of trading rules designed to exploit the potential profitability of non-random behavior. This issue was addressed in other early tests, such as those of Fama and Blume (1966), that compared the profitability of filter rules to buy-and-hold strategies. The filter trading rules examined in the early studies were relatively simple. For example, a *k* percent filter rule would be: if the price of a security rises *k* percent, buy the security and hold it until it drops *k* percent from a subsequent high. At that time the security is sold and a short position is established and held until the price rises *k* percent at which time the short position is covered and a long position is again established. This process is continued until the end of the trading horizon is reached at which time the profits from the filter rule are compared with the return from buying the security at the beginning of the horizon and holding it until the end.

Early tests of filter rules generally found that buy-and-hold was at least as profitable as pursuing a *filter rule trading strategy.* However, when *k* was small and the trading intervals were for daily or intra-daily moves then there was sometimes a small advantage in favor of the filter rule. Because small *k* percent filter rules generate a large number of trades, these small profits would aggregate into sizeable total profits. Fama (1976, p. 142) discusses this evidence: "When one takes account of even the minimum trading costs that would be generated by small filters ... their advantage over a buy-and-hold strategy disappears." At the time, this was taken to be conclusive evidence against the profitability of technical analysis – the use of security market generated data to forecast future security price movements. Over time, the conclusion that technical analysis is a profitless exercise has become less certain as the trading rules being studied have become more closely aligned to the rules currently proposed by practicing technical analysts, e.g., relative strength, momentum and oscillator models. These studies are examined in chapter 9.

The early evidence on the serial correlation of security returns (price changes), runs tests and filter rules facilitated an inductive process that led to the formulation of the hypothesis that the observed randomness was the outcome of efficient processing of information by the securities market. Though the use of induction in hypothesis development is an essential element of the scientific approach, the positivist epistemology expounded in modern Finance required the development of a theory using logical processes, confronting the theory with empirical evidence and iterating as appropriate. Though this did not happen with the EMH, by the time of Fama (1976, p. 142) the inconsistency was largely ignored:

> no null hypothesis, such as the hypothesis that the market is efficient, is a literally accurate view of the world. It is not meaningful to interpret the tests of each hypothesis on a strict true-false basis. Rather, one is concerned with testing whether the model at hand is a reasonable approximation to the world, which can be taken as true, at least until a better approximation comes along. What is a reasonable approximation depends on the use to which the model is to be put. For example, since traders cannot use filters to beat buy and hold, it is reasonable for them to assume that they should behave as if the market were efficient, at least for the purposes of trading on information in past prices.

It seems that, through the empirical analysis of selected data, an agreeable method for determining when "a better approximation comes along" is available. The possibility that ideas can become entrenched and that complicated issues cannot be resolved empirically is not part of the philosophy.

Over time, numerous empirical studies have presented various types of evidence rejecting, or purporting to reject, the null hypothesis of the EMH. These results can be classified according to whether it is the weak form or semi-strong form versions of EMH that have been rejected. Such rejections of the EMH are classified as "anomalies" associated with the particular type of information considered. In contrast, rejections of the strong form version of EMH are not considered as anomalous where trading on insider information is the relevant information variable. As the weak form tests relate to "technical analysis" and the semi-strong form tests relate to "fundamental analysis" (see end of chapter questions), the empirical results for the two versions are typically considered separately, though there are good reasons to try to reconcile the results of the two versions. Given this, rejections of the weak form include the January effect, as well as other calendar and seasonality effects such as the day-of-the-week effects, the weekend effect and the daylight-savings-time effect. Rejections of the semi-strong form include the small firm effect, the book-to-market effect, the neglected firm effect and the P/E ratio effect.

Because the EMH is a joint hypothesis, it follows that rejection of the EMH could be due to inadequate specification of the return generating process, rather than a violation of the accurate processing of information. An example of this is provided by the P/E ratio effect proposed by Basu (1977, 1983). The P/E ratio plays an important role in a number of the rules-of-thumb suggested by fundamental analysts, e.g., Graham (1949) suggests a criterion for buying a security is that the price does not exceed 20 times the average earnings over the previous 6 years (Oppenheimer 1981, p. 9). Using a sample of NYSE stocks, Basu presented empirical evidence that portfolios of low P/E stocks have higher average returns than portfolios of high P/E stocks, after appropriate adjustment is made for systematic risk of the portfolios using the capital asset pricing model (CAPM). Is this result due to a violation of EMH or to the inadequacy of the CAPM to adjust for risk or both? Perhaps the result could be proxying for some other type of anomaly such as the small firm effect?

Of all the various effects, the *small firm effect* (small firms have systematically higher risk-adjusted returns), and the *January or turn-of-the-year effect* (risk-adjusted returns are systematically higher in January than in other months) have the strongest level of empirical support. Yet, Dimson et al. (2002, p. 8) make the following observation about the size or small firm effect: "A frustrating feature of the size effect is that soon after its discovery the size premium went into reverse with smaller companies subsequently underperforming their larger counterparts. We show that this reversal was a worldwide phenomenon." Similarly, the possibility of exploiting the January effect only comes around once a year. Because it is a statistical result, there is no guarantee that the January effect will appear in any given year. A trading rule designed to exploit the effect would likely require leveraging up at the end of December and leveraging back down at the end of January as indicated. Also the effect appears to be related to the small firm effect (Dimson et al., p. 136): "For US large-caps, there is no turn-of-the-year effect. Returns are not low in December, and January does not have the highest return, but ranks fifth." Similar results are reported for the UK (if one "outlier" is removed).

Where does all this to and fro on the EMH lead? The epistemology of modern Finance suggests that, if the evidence of anomalies is correct, new hypotheses will be formed that are "a better approximation" to the world. However, such hypotheses would represent an assault on received knowledge. Academics who have invested large amounts of human capital in the "old theory" would be faced with personal obsolescence and the battle lines would be drawn. Such is the case with the now emerging theory of behavioral finance (see chapter 9). As a leader of the old guard, Fama (1998) is not persuaded either by the bulk of the evidence on market anomalies or by the evidence being provided by behavioral finance. Fama claims that behavioral finance does not impose adequately defined alternative hypotheses to market efficiency. A similar comment is also advanced to explain much of the evidence on market efficiency anomalies: there is inadequate specification of alternative hypotheses.

As discussed in Haugen (1999a, b), the subject of Finance has undergone an evolution from Old Finance to Modern Finance to New Finance (see section 2.4). The Old Finance harkens back to the teachings of Graham and Dodd, when Finance was deeply concerned with the tools of security analysis. Modern Finance supplemented the Old Finance during the 1960s and was in ascendancy until the 1990s when the accumulation of empirical and theoretical results produced a vulnerability that the behavioral theories of the New Finance are seeking to exploit. Oddly enough, proponents of modern Finance are finding refuge in some of the insights that were the stock and trade of the Old Finance. More precisely, during the 1990s there has been an increasing accumulation of results associated with importance of "value" and "growth" in determining stock returns.

Much as with the early results on the EMH, modern Finance has used inductive methods to arrive at results for value and growth stocks. Dimson et al. (2002, p. 148) summarize the evidence:

> Value and growth investing have given rise to dramatically different methods of long-term performance. Value strategies typically emphasize stocks with a high dividend yield, or with a high ratio of book value to market value of equity. A large body of US based evidence shows that there has been a higher long-run return, at least over the period 1926– 2000, from investing in value stocks . . . we also find a strong value premium in the United Kingdom. The value premium exists within the small cap as well as the large cap universe.

At least since Fama and French (1992), leading figures of modern Finance have been exploring the empirical implications of value stocks, e.g., Fama and French (1995), and value vs. growth stocks, e.g., Lakonishok et al. (1994) and Fama and French (1998). Decades of empirical studies in the trade literature have grudgingly become relevant, even though the chauvinism of the academics in modern Finance still remains, e.g., Dimson et al. (2002, p. 141): "The pre-eminent measure of value is at present the book-to-market ratio. Some two decades ago, work by Stattman (1980) . . . encouraged the view that there may be above-average returns to high book-to-market stocks." Stattman (1980) is an MBA honors paper at the University of Chicago.

That the adherents of modern Finance have slowly uncovered the insights of the Old Finance is both puzzling and discomforting. It is discomforting because the approach of modern Finance is based on averaging methods. Large numbers of firms across a large number of years are examined to determine if, say, a low price-to-book ratio generates abnormal returns. The process by which price-to-book is used to determine whether a particular common stock will generate value is not substantively considered because that would require an analysis of the specifics of each firm, typically requiring a detailed understanding of financial statement analysis (see chapter 8). A low price-to-book has different implications depending on, say, whether there are a considerable amount of intangible assets on the balance sheet. It is difficult to reduce the procedure to an empirically implementable hypothesis that can be tested across a sample of firms. Information derived from averaging procedures gives the appearance of having more content than it actually does.

The puzzling part regarding the recognition of notions from the Old Finance relates to the no-more-than-passing recognition given to the well-developed state these ideas achieved in the Old Finance. For example, Graham, Dodd and Cottle (1962, pp. 488–9) explicitly examined the use of price-to-book value to determine firm value. Examining data for the S&P 425, IBM and GE from 1929 to 1959, there is explicit recognition of the relationship between book value, market value and earnings:

> let us define a successful company as one which has earned and is expected to earn a large enough return on shareholders' equity to produce (or justify) an average market price for the shares in excess of their book value. Let us assume further that these "excess" or "premium" earnings can be maintained on a large amount of reinvested profits. The logical deduction from these assumptions is that *all* profits should be reinvested by such companies – at least up to the point, if any, where diminishing returns vitiate the premise of superior profitability.

The data for the S&P indicates that the value to shareholders from high reinvestment rates was not supported while it was supported for IBM and GE. This discussion is followed by numerous other insights on this issue.

The tradeoff between risk and return revisited

To those concerned about security analysis and investment strategy, the philosophical problems associated with "what constitutes knowledge" are likely to seem sterile and irrelevant (see section 1.3). How to value a common stock or whether to add a convertible bond to a given portfolio or what fraction of a portfolio to hold in foreign stocks seem to be problems far removed from questions about what constitutes objective truth. Yet, it is relatively easy to show that such views are mistaken. Consider the positivist approach of estimating parameters from past (*ex post*) empirical data and using these estimates as a basis for predicting future (*ex ante*) values. This is the procedure underlying the mantra of modern Finance: the return on common stocks will outperform the return on bonds in the long run. The parameters of interest in this case are the average returns estimated from past values of the security returns. "Facts" derived from past data are used to make "conjectures" about the future performance of security returns. The mantra provides a useful illustration of the rhetoric used in security analysis and investment strategy.

Following Siegel (1998, p. 45), the empirical proposition that stocks returns will be superior to bond returns in the long run can be traced to Edgar Lawrence Smith (1925). Prior to Smith, the prevailing wisdom, as reflected in Fisher (1912), was that stocks would outperform bonds during periods of inflation while bonds would outperform stocks during periods of deflation. Smith was the start of a long train of empirical research that fleshed out the details of the relative performance of common stocks and bonds. It was not long before Irving Fisher was drawn in by the rhetoric, becoming a leading bull by the late 1920s. Yet, Fisher was to be embarrassed by the collapse in stock values that started around September 1929 and continued until February 1933. The collapse precipitated a long period of generally negative perceptions about common stock investment, relative to bonds. The general view was still decidedly negative when Eiteman and F. Smith (1953) demonstrated that an equally weighted buy-and-hold strategy for 92 common stocks of widely held industrial companies averaged a 12.2% return over a 14 year holding period from 1936 to 1950.

Eiteman and Smith marks a resurrection of the mantra that common stock returns will outperform bond returns in the long run. The significant run-up in common stock values during the 1950s permitted Fisher and Lorie (1964) and others to demonstrate that common stock returns were significantly higher over the 1926–60 period. Even the collapse of common stock values associated with the Great Depression could be overcome, if the long run was long enough. The appearance of Ibbotson and Sinquefield (1976) not only exhaustively confirmed the results of Fisher and Lorie over an even longer and more detailed sample (1926–74), it is also the start of a time series on stock returns that is updated in an annual yearbook. The view that common stock returns are superior to bond returns in the long run has continued unabated until the present, though the accumulation of significant common stock losses that started in early 2000 and continued to March 2003 did shake the confidence of some investors.

In the academic realm of studies on common stock returns, Dimson et al. (2002) is an impressive recent effort. In addition to providing much useful empirical information on the tradeoff between risk and return over a long time period – 100 years – across a large number of countries (16), it is also an excellent example of the rhetoric and assumptions that modern Finance researchers employ in seeking to develop empirical results. In particular, the restrictions associated with ergodicity are accurately identified (Dimson et al. 2002, p. 3):

> We . . . need to look at the long run. Brief snippets of stock market history are not very helpful . . . if we wish to say something about the expected return over the next five years, we cannot extract much information from the last five years . . . To estimate the expected return we need a long run of data. We cannot improve estimates of the expected return by subdividing an interval into many short subperiods. While there are also benefits to looking at risk over the long haul, the need for long-term data is especially great when we are interested in expected returns.

As evidenced in numerous sources, e.g., Siegel (1998), the importance to modern Finance of considering the long run is not confined to Dimson et al. (2002).

Yet, confronted with evidence such as the efficient market "anomalies," the run-up in stock prices in the last decade of the twentieth century and the inability of core theories such as the CAPM to withstand close empirical scrutiny from insiders of modern Finance such as Fama and French (1992), adherents of modern Finance such as Dimson et al. (2002) and Constantinides (2002) have been looking for wriggle room from the positivist strait-jacket. For example, Dimson et al. (2002, p. 9) observe:

> Many people argue that the historical risk premium, if measured over a long enough time span, gives an unbiased estimate of the prospective (equity risk) premium. We review evidence that suggests that academic experts typically subscribe to this view, and that their own forecasts are heavily influenced by the historical record. The research conducted for (Dimson et al. 2002), however, leads us to question whether the historical risk premium really does provide a reasonable estimate of the prospective premium. Our belief is that historical equity returns have almost certainly exceeded investors' *ex ante* risk premium requirements, and also that the required risk premium has itself fallen over time. We use evidence from historical dividend growth to back up these assertions, and to suggest an alternative, rather lower, estimate of the future risk premium.

The rationale for undertaking this reconsideration sounds somewhat out of step with the positivist approach of modern Finance (Dimson et al. 2002, p. 5):

> Measuring what has happened in the past is only the starting point for assessing the future. Interpretation of the data and being able to apply it to a modern-day canvas are as important. Throughout (Dimson et al. 2002), therefore, our emphasis is not simply on describing the past but also on interpreting what has happened, with an eye to what it tells us about the future.

Such an approach, in a book concerned with detailing 101 years of security returns across 16 countries seems somewhat incongruent, if not misplaced.

Another form of expression about the uneasiness of modern Finance adherents is captured by Constantinides (2002, p. 1567):

> A central theme in finance and economics is the pursuit of a *unified* theory of the rate of return across different classes of financial assets . . . The neoclassical rational economic model is a *unified* model that views [the difference between the riskfree rate and the rate of return on specific financial assets] as the reward to risk-averse investors that process *information rationally* and *have unambiguously defined preferences over consumption* . . . The cause of much anxiety over the last quarter of a century is evidence interpreted as failure of the rational economic paradigm to explain the price level and rate of return of financial assets both at the macro and micro levels. A celebrated example of such evidence, although by no means the only one, is the failure of the *representative agent* rational economic paradigm to account for the large average premium of the aggregate return of stocks over short-term bonds and the small average return of short-term bonds from the last quarter of the 19th century to the present. Dubbed the "Equity Premium Puzzle" . . . it has generated a cottage industry of rational and behavioral explanations of the level of asset prices and their rate of return.

This is followed by a string of statements such as "even though one may introduce one's own strong prior beliefs and adjust downwards the sample-average estimate of the premium, the unconditional mean premium is at least 6 percent per year and the annual Sharpe ratio is at least 32 percent. These numbers are large and call for an economic explanation."

Not surprisingly, after relaxing "assumptions," making a distinction between conditional and unconditional asset pricing distributions and providing a discussion that "is eclectic and mirrors in part my own research interests," Constantinides (2002, p. 1589) reports: "I conclude that the observed asset returns do not support the case for abandoning the rational economic theory as our null hypothesis. Much more remains to be done to fully exploit the ramifications of the rational asset-pricing paradigm." This conclusion is reached without identification of what "their" alternative null hypothesis would be. Presumably the alternative null hypothesis is an irrational, uneconomic, atheoretical blurb produced by the cottage industry of believers in behavioral explanations of asset prices. Yet, after some fifty years of developing and testing theories based on the "rational asset-pricing paradigm," there is still "much more that remains to be done." It is difficult for those not indoctrinated by the paradigm to read such statements without a healthy dose of anti-cynicism.

If there are substantive difficulties with the rational economic asset-pricing paradigm, then what are some feasible alternatives? Perhaps the problem is not with the paradigm, per se, but rather with the types of questions the paradigm is trying to answer. For example, Constantinides argues that "the construct of per capita consumption" is irrelevant for explaining the equity risk premium. This is important because rational asset-pricing models are usually formulated in terms of consumption. Considerable time and effort is expended on demonstrating that the form of a model is empirically inapplicable. This type of discussion is far removed from practical questions such as whether an investor seeking to purchase common stocks in 1995 or 1999 or 2002 can expect to do better at retirement than an investor purchasing bonds. Despite the pervasiveness of the equity risk premium over 130 years, the long run common stock investor in, say, 1927–1929 would have had to wait until the 1950s to have outperformed the Treasury bond investor.

Considerable effort in modern Finance is expended rediscovering results that were developed by writers of the past. For example, Constantinides (2002, pp. 1588–9) observes: "Labor income is by far the single most important source of household saving and consumption. The shocks to labor income are uninsurable and persistent and arrive with greater frequency during economic contractions. Idiosyncratic income shocks go a long way toward explaining the unconditional moments of assets returns and the predictability of returns." In the *General Theory*, J.M. Keynes argued forcefully that stock market valuation is intimately connected to macroeconomic activity. A severe collapse of stock prices, such as that from 1929 to 1933 or from 2000 to 2003, has a psychological impact on aggregate investment activity that can produce a significant and persistent affect on aggregate income. In the language of the rational economic model, there is a feedback loop from asset pricing behavior to the generation of labor income.

Modern Finance operates within a positivist framework which assumes that the techniques of the natural sciences are the appropriate model for generating knowledge about financial activities such as security pricing. One implication of treating Finance as a human science is that knowledge is not viewed in a linear fashion where increasing the amount of data and the techniques of statistical analysis will result in a better understanding of the subject. As such, knowledge takes on a timeless quality. Writers from the past may have a better understanding of certain aspects of current events than contemporary observers. The implication is that there is considerable value in examining what insightful writers in the past had to say. Because these writers were often motivated by events of the time, this requires adequate treatment of the historical context to interpret their musings. This is the subject matter of chapter 2.

1.3   THE PHILOSOPHY OF INVESTMENT*

*The epistemology of modern Finance**

Academics in modern Finance have to face an enigma surrounding common stock valuation. For example, in a widely used and admired investments text, Elton and Gruber (1995, p. 449) observe:

> The search for the "correct" way to value common stocks, or even one that works, has occupied a huge amount of effort over a long period of time. Attempts have ranged from simple mechanical techniques for picking winners to hypotheses about the broad influences affecting stock prices. At one extreme, the attempt to find a simple rule for selecting stocks that will have above-average performance can be likened to the search for a perpetual motion machine . . . At the other extreme the determinants of common stock prices are quite easy to specify in general terms. The price of common stock is a function of the level of a company's earnings, dividends, risk, the cost of money and future growth rate. While it is easy to specify these broad influences, the implementation of a system that uses these concepts to successfully value or select common stocks is a difficult task.

Confronted with the difficulties of common stock valuation, academics have found comfort in an analytical perspective based on investor rationality and market efficiency. Recognizing that market efficiency dictates against systematic abnormal gains to individual security selection, the upshot is an approach to security analysis and investment strategy which emphasizes optimal diversification.

All this is not meant to imply that the subject of modern Finance has not made substantive contributions to understanding various aspects of security analysis and investment strategy; quite the contrary. Rather, the perspective and approach to what constitutes knowledge in modern Finance differs from that of industry practitioners, such as security analysts and portfolio managers, and most of the investing public. Stickney (1997) provides some insight on these differences:

> There is a fundamental difference between the research conducted by academics and by professional security analysts. For the most part, academic research focuses on the *average* relation between selected accounting information and stock prices across a large number of firms. Equity analyst research, in contrast, uses accounting information of *individual* firms,

along with other information, to make buy, sell and hold recommendations ... inherent differences will always exist between research conducted across large sets of firms and that conducted on individual firms.

As it turns out, Stickney's observations only scratch the surface of a complicated matter. Despite a general lack of attention to philosophical matters, Finance is not immune to the issues which have been at the core of the debates that have raged in modern epistemology.

In Finance, various philosophical approaches compete to explain what constitutes knowledge and objective truth in security analysis and investment strategy.[18] Finance is, at root, a human science, concerned with explaining and predicting that aspect of human behavior associated with financial activities. Much of interest has appeared in the epistemological debates about knowledge and objectivity in the human sciences since, say, Hayek's *The Counter-Revolution of Science* (1955) or Gadamer's *Truth and Method* (1960). Unlike the natural sciences, what is required in the human sciences is recognition that there are differing approaches to what constitutes knowledge. It is naive to believe the route to knowledge and truth in valuing securities or specifying investment strategies is unproblematic, provided that one adheres to the prevailing positivist approach of modern Finance: it is inappropriate to conclude that deviations from the narrow parameters of the prescribed positivist epistemology are unscientific rubbish not worthy of academic pursuit.

Knowledge appears in various guises: empirical observations, logical deductions and informed conjectures can all be part of the final picture. Making sense of the different facets requires that careful attention be given to the language being used. For example, a logical relationship derived from a theoretical model may have only limited empirical applicability. Yet, the logical relationship may be presented as though it has a strong "factual" basis. This may confuse an uninitiated audience into concluding that the factual basis, which is logical, extends into the empirical realm. Academics in modern Finance are inherently attracted to logical facts, such as the capital asset pricing model or the Markowitz mean-variance optimization model. Whether logical facts have any *ex ante* empirical validity requires careful analysis that extends beyond the theoretical structure used to develop the model. Though this point may seem obvious, the resulting confusions are apparent in introductory investments textbooks that tend to present logical relationships as though there were an empirical validity which corresponds to the logical validity.

Many of the arguments being advanced in this book revolve around concepts such as "epistemology," "methodology," "positivism" and the like. Yet, no precise explanation of these concepts has been provided. In a book concerned with practical problems of security analysis and investment strategy, this is somewhat presumptuous. As evidenced by the more obvious philosophical biases of those expounding modern Finance, the core subject matter will not necessarily appeal to those who also have a detailed knowledge of philosophy. Without a sufficient exposure to philosophical conversations, it is unlikely that the relevance of how knowledge is created will be adequately appreciated. This lack of appreciation is compounded by the apparent lack of agreement among philosophers on these issues. The centuries of seemingly endless debate without resolution have taken a toll on those outside philosophy seeking clear-cut answers to questions such as how knowledge is properly identified. However, lack of agreement need not be confused with lack of importance or understanding.

The term *epistemology* comes from the Greek word for knowledge. Simply put, epistemology is the philosophy of knowledge. The central question of epistemology is how individuals come to know or, in slightly different terms, how knowledge is created. Methodology is concerned with the methods that are used in creating knowledge and, as such, is more practical in nature. Positivism is a philosophical movement, concerned with epistemology, characterized by an emphasis upon science and scientific method as the only sources of knowledge. Though the roots of positivism can be traced back to Francis Bacon (1561–1626), the beginnings of the movement are usually credited to Auguste Comte (1798–1857). Over time, positivism evolved substantively to the point where, in the 1920s, a new version, known as *logical positivism* (also known as logical empiricism, logical neopositivism, neopositivism) emerged. Reflecting the German and Austrian roots of the so-called Vienna school, the leading founding figure is usually identified as Rudolf Carnap (1891–1970). However, the English philosopher A.J. Ayer (1910–1989) is usually credited with the most influential contribution *Language, Truth and Logic* (1936). The branch of positivism reflected in modern Finance can be traced to Friedman (1953).

Comte argued the search for knowledge had gone through three historical phases: the theological, that was concerned with obtaining knowledge about God and spirituality; the metaphysical, where the search was for philosophical truths; and, the positive or scientific phase, that involved the search for objective facts or "positive truths." It was this last phase that Comte associated with positivism. As initially conceived by Comte, the positivist approach to knowledge made a sharp distinction between the realms of fact and value. There was also a strong hostility toward religion and traditional philosophy, in general, and metaphysics, in particular. The positivist philosophy maintained that all sciences rely upon the same methodology for determining facts about the physical and material world. As such, there are no important differences between, say, biology, physics or economics. This was referred to as the so-called "unity of science project." Facts are to be collected and summarized through a process of induction.

Echoes of positivism constantly resonate through modern Finance. Elton and Gruber (1984, p. 273) provide an excellent example: *"As the physicist builds models of the movement of matter in a frictionless environment, the economist builds models where there are no institutional frictions to the movement of stock prices"* (emphasis added). The epistemology of modern Finance can be traced to Friedman (1953) where the distinction between fact and value appears as a distinction between "positive economics" and "normative economics" (p. 4):

> Positive economics is in principle independent of any particular ethical position or normative judgments . . . it deals with "what is" not with "what ought to be." Its task is to provide a system of generalizations that can be used to make correct predictions about the consequences of any change in circumstances. Its performance is to be judged by the precision, scope, and conformity with experience of the predictions it yields. In short, positive economics is, or can be, an "objective" science, in precisely the same sense as any of the physical sciences.

Much of Friedman (1953) is concerned with the issue whether a theory with unrealistic assumptions, even "wildly inaccurate descriptive representations of reality" can be "important and significant." For Friedman, the ultimate test of a theory was "whether it yields sufficiently accurate predictions," not whether the assumptions are realistic.

The concern of Friedman (1953) with the form of the theory being examined is consistent with the evolution of positivist epistemology. Initially, positivism placed heavy reliance on the inductive process of collecting facts. Spurred by the remarkable successes of the natural sciences during the late nineteenth and early twentieth centuries, this view evolved into logical positivism, an epistemology that placed emphasis on theories and the logical deduction of hypotheses to test those theories as well as the collection of facts. The epistemology of logical positivism allows only two grounds for truth: there are deductive truths such as those in mathematics and formal logic, e.g., $12 - 3 = 9$; and inductive statements that match reality precisely. As a consequence, truthful statements have to be verifiable to be meaningful. In logical positivism, statements have meaning relative to the conditions under which the statement can be verified. Friedman adapts this approach to where the test of verification for a hypothesis is the ability to predict. That is consistent with the tenet of logical positivism that a statement that does not describe an "experiential proposition" carries no significance, i.e., it is not knowledge.

Friedman (1953, p. 7) clearly reflects these tenets of logical positivism:

> Viewed as a language, theory has no substantive content; it is a set of tautologies . . . The canons of formal logic alone can show whether a particular language is complete and consistent, that is, whether propositions in the language are "right" or "wrong." Factual evidence alone can show whether the categories of the "analytical filing system" have a meaningful empirical counterpart, that is, whether they are useful in analyzing a particular class of concrete problems.

Statements that are verifiable provide a basis for building a science. Under positivism, science is the source of knowledge. As such, both positivism and logical positivism share a fundamental commitment to empiricism, an epistemology where claims that have no empirical consequences are without meaning. Logical positivism extends empiricism by arguing that science can also seek to build theories to describe the regularities of cause and effect in order to explain the world. This requires theories to be expressed as a set of axioms or, less formally, basic assumptions. These theories have rules to systematically link the predictions with objective measurements of the real world. The connection to Friedman (1953), von Neumann and Morgenstern (1947) and innumerable other projects in positivist economics and modern Finance is apparent.

At this point, the proponent of modern Finance is compelled to ask: so what is wrong with logical positivism? There are a number of answers to this question, some of which are given in the latter parts of this section. At this point, it is relevant to observe that positivism maintains that science is the only way to create knowledge, to allow individuals to understand the world well enough to predict and control outcomes. In the positivist framework, the objective world is viewed as deterministic, operated by laws of cause and effect that can be identified if the unique approach of the scientific method is correctly applied. Science is conceived as a mechanistic operation. It is possible to use deductive reasoning to postulate theories that can be empirically tested. Based on the results of these empirical tests, it is determined whether a theory "fits the facts" or whether the theory needs to be revised in order to provide better predictions of reality. Ultimately, there is an objective reality that can be discovered if there is sufficient empirical information available to verify the "true" deductive hypotheses.

Criticisms of logical positivism are numerous. One type of criticism focuses on the misunderstanding of the process by which science is conducted. Is there really a unity of science? Are the procedures used in physics and chemistry directly applicable to economics or psychology? Do scientists really develop deductive hypotheses that are then "verified" on empirical data? Another related criticism observes that logical positivism says little or nothing about how axioms (or Friedman's assumptions) are translated into possible testable hypotheses. In other words, positivism has no substantive insight into the process by which knowledge is created. Positivism is only interested in specifying the scientific process, without recommending criteria for selecting among permitted ideas. This leads to Friedman (1953) and the criteria of predictive ability. But, this leads to the problem of measuring predictive ability. The distinction between *ex ante* and *ex post* predictability is one key example of this type of problem in modern Finance.

Positivism proposes that there is a unity of science. The development of epistemology after positivism denies this proposition. As such, schools of thought have emerged that are concerned specifically with the epistemological problems arising in the human sciences. One such epistemology is critical realism, a school that observes all measurement is fallible is some way. For example, critical realists maintain that all observations are theory-laden and that individuals, in general, and scientists, in particular, are inherently biased by their cultural experiences, world views, and so on. Friedman (1953, pp. 4–5) recognizes this issue but does not view it as a basis for "a fundamental distinction" between economics and the natural sciences. For critical realists the challenge is how to move from a notion of objectivity that is inherently a social phenomenon to the identification of knowledge. If objectivity is not perfect, then how are these separate and imperfect individual interpretations of reality to be combined?

Truth and method in the human sciences*

Compared to the easy, irreverent style of McCloskey (1985, 1994) or Shefrin (2000), Gadamer (1960) is almost mentally unhealthy. The style is ponderous and the ideas often buried in a hodgepodge of obscure words. Perhaps this is due to the English translation of a German text, but not likely. Words like "hermeneutics" and "ontology" are essential to the discussion, though references to notions such as "the questionableness of romantic hermeneutics" could almost certainly be tidier. Despite this, the thrust of the message is worth the effort. Gadamer is part of a long line of thought that questions the ability to apply techniques of the natural sciences to the human sciences, e.g., (p. 6): "the real problem that the human sciences present to thought is that one has not properly grasped the nature of the human sciences if one measures them by the yardstick of an increasing knowledge of regularity. The experience of the socio-historical world cannot be raised to a science by inductive procedure of the natural sciences." Though Gadamer's notion of the human sciences may seem to have more applicability to, say, political science or sociology, it is difficult to evade the observation that the prices of securities are set in markets and are the outcome of a social interaction. Security analysis lies within the domain of the human sciences.

How is Gadamer's distinction between human and natural sciences of relevance to the analysis of securities? There are a number of ways to answer this question. One way deals with the issue of method. It is one thing to observe that application of the method and techniques from the natural sciences to the human sciences is inadequate, it is quite another to advance an alternative approach or method that can yield some superior results. This creates a quandary. The natural sciences seek to uncover universal rules governing natural phenomena. Insofar as such universal rules are discoverable, progress in the natural sciences is cumulative. Increasingly greater knowledge obtained from inductive analysis of better data enables more accurate prediction about the natural subject of interest. This leads to a prominent place for "reason" and no place for "prejudice" towards particular ideas. Discrimination between different predictions of an event can be made based on the use of reason to interpret the "facts" available about that event. The possibility of different forms of "certainty" cannot be admitted.

Absent the concept of certain knowledge associated with the natural sciences, the quandary for the human sciences is to determine how knowledge about subjects can be generated when different interpretations are possible. This problem has concerned philosophers, especially German philosophers, going back at least to Kant. Unlike the natural sciences, human sciences have to contend with the implications of free will. Recognizing that the human sciences are fundamentally concerned with explaining historical events, the problem can be stated as: "Historical study is different because there are no natural laws but, rather, the voluntary acceptance of practical laws . . . The world of human freedom does not manifest the same absence of exceptions as natural laws" (Gadamer, p. 10). In an attempt to address the differences between the human and natural sciences, some important nineteenth-century philosophers, such as Hermann Helmholtz, proposed using two different methods of induction applicable to the different sciences. While reason would guide the inductive process of the natural sciences, key factors such as memory, authority and psychological tact would guide the inductive process in the human sciences.

Yet, despite recognizing the possibility of different methods, little progress was made toward developing such methods. "For Helmholtz, the methodological ideal of the natural sciences needed neither historical derivation nor epistemological restriction, and that is why he could not logically comprehend the method of the human sciences any differently." Gadamer explicitly recognizes the futility of the approach proposed by Helmholtz and accepts that the general method of induction is as essential to the human sciences as in the natural sciences (pp. 5–6):

> it is not a question of recognizing that the human sciences have their own logic but, on the contrary, that it is the inductive method, basic to all experimental science, which alone is valid in this field too . . . Human science also is concerned with establishing similarities, regularities and conformities to a law which would make it possible to predict the individual

phenomena and processes . . . it is quite unimportant whether one believes, say, in the freedom of will or not – one can still make predictions in the sphere of social life . . . The involvement of free decisions – if they exist – does not interfere with the regular process, but itself belongs to the general and regular quality which is discovered through the method of induction.

In other words, following Gadamer: "The human sciences have no special method." Gadamer's essential insight is to recognize that the "science" in the human sciences lies in the method by which inferences are drawn from the inductive method.

The next step in Gadamer's approach to the human sciences is to develop the notion of "interpretation through understanding." For this purpose, Gadamer draws on the work of the twentieth-century philosopher Martin Heidegger (1889–1976). In *Being and Time* (1927), Heidegger says: "we genuinely take hold of the possibility [of knowing] only when, in our interpretation, we have understood that our first, last and constant task is never to allow our fore-having, fore-sight, and fore-conception to be presented to us by fancies and popular conceptions, but rather to make the scientific theme secure by working out these fore-structures in terms of the things themselves." In Gadamer's words: "All correct interpretation must be on guard against arbitrary fancies and the limitations imposed by imperceptible habits of thought and direct its gaze 'on the things themselves'." The process of interpretation "begins with fore-conceptions that are replaced with more suitable ones. This constant process of new projection is the movement of understanding and interpretation" (p. 236).

The subtle point being made here involves a shift from the absolute objectivity of the natural sciences to the objectivity of the human sciences (pp. 236–7):

> A person who is trying to understand is exposed to distraction from fore-meanings that are not borne out by the things themselves. The working-out of appropriate projects, anticipatory in nature, to be confirmed "by the things" themselves, is the constant task of understanding. The only "objectivity" here is the confirmation of the fore-meaning in its being worked out. The only thing that characterizes the arbitrariness of inappropriate fore-meanings is that they come to nothing in the working-out. But understanding achieves its full potentiality only when the fore-meanings that it uses are not arbitrary.

How then are arbitrary fore-meanings to be identified? On this point Gadamer observes: "Methodologically conscious understanding will be concerned not merely to form anticipatory ideas, but to make them conscious, so as to check them and thus acquire right understanding from the things themselves" (p. 239).

To the modern student of Finance, all this might seem quite hazy. How is it that fore-structures are worked out by things in themselves? How are fore-meanings which correctly anticipate the working out of the things in themselves to be determined? Heuristically, these questions can be illustrated with the general security valuation problem. Given that inductive observation reveals "stock returns out perform bond returns in the long run," a plausible fore-structure or fore-meaning would be that the stocks would be a preferable long run investment to bonds. Yet, the working out of the things themselves may not be supportive of this fore-meaning. Stock and bond returns are the outcome of the human interactions in security markets. An investor purchasing cyclical stocks in, say, early 1929, or technology stocks at the beginning of 2000, would find that the working-out of the arbitrary fore-meaning comes to nothing if the investor's holding period is shorter than the time needed to realize the higher anticipated returns to holding stocks. Purchasers at other times or with different holding periods may come to a different conclusion. This raises the problem of identifying, at a given point in historical time, the fore-meaning that correctly anticipates the working-out.

Gadamer observes that "it is the tyranny of hidden prejudices that makes us deaf" to hearing the correct fore-meanings. The "fundamental question" follows appropriately (p. 246): "where is the ground of the legitimacy of prejudices? What distinguishes legitimate prejudices from all the countless ones that it is the undeniable task of critical reason to overcome?" In all of this, Gadamer uses "prejudice" in a precise and non-negative way. For Gadamer, prejudice does not mean a false or unfounded judgment. Rather, prejudice "means a judgment that is given before all elements that determine a situation have been finally examined . . . it can have a positive and a negative value" (p. 240). In the rationalist approach of the natural sciences, hypotheses are evaluated using reason to analyze the available facts. Reason provides the yardstick for determining whether a judgment is unfounded, "methodologically disciplined use of reason can safeguard us from all error" (p. 246). In the human sciences, the standard of certainty this imposes leaves no room for prejudice. As Gadamer observes, this involves "prejudice against prejudice itself."

Unlike the natural sciences, the human sciences have to allow for prejudice derived from authority. In contrast, methodologically disciplined use of reason cannot accept arguments based on authority for that involves not using one's reason to reach conclusions. "If the prestige of authority takes the place of one's own judgment, then authority is in fact a source of prejudices." But the approach toward the human sciences proposed by Gadamer does not view prejudice either negatively or positively. As such, authority as a positive prejudice provides a basis for knowledge (p. 249):

> the recognition of authority is always connected with the idea that what authority states is not irrational or arbitrary, but can be seen, in principle, to be true. This is the essence of the authority claimed by the teacher, the superior, the expert. The prejudices that they implant are legitimized by the person who presents them. But this makes them then, in a sense objective prejudices, for they bring about the same bias in favor of something that can come about through other means, e.g., through solid ground offered by reason.

The process of interpretation and understanding is fundamental to the human sciences. While knowledge about an object in the natural sciences gets progressively deeper over time, the same is not true about the human sciences where great achievements of the past "hardly ever grow old."

For Gadamer, the interpreter is an essential component of knowledge in the human sciences: "the object appears truly significant only in the light of him who is able to describe it to us properly. Thus it is certainly the subject that we are interested in, but the subject acquires its life only from the light in which it is presented to us." Subjects appear historically "under different aspects at different times or from a different standpoints" (p. 252). Insightful interpretations require the past to be echoed in the present.

As such, the human sciences are involved not only in the accumulation of empirical results but in the transmission of an important source of authority: tradition. "That which has been sanctioned by tradition and custom has an authority that is nameless, and our finite historical being is marked by the fact that always the authority of what has been transmitted – and not only what is clearly grounded – has power over our attitudes and behavior" (p. 249).

Gadamer sees an essential role for tradition in the human sciences (pp. 251–2):

> That there is an element of tradition active in the human sciences, despite the methodological nature of its procedures, an element that constitutes its real nature, and is its distinguishing mark, is immediately clear if we examine the history of research and note the difference between the human and natural sciences with regard to their history . . . the natural scientist writes the history of his subject in terms of the present stage of knowledge. For him errors and wrong turnings are of historical interest only, because the progress of research is the self-evident criterion of his study . . . the human sciences cannot be described adequately in terms of this idea of research and progress.

Knowledge in the human sciences does not proceed by distancing and freeing ourselves from what has been transmitted through tradition. Rather, the problem is to find the relationship of the present with the traditions of the past.

The positivist superstructure of modern Finance is predicated on the premise that knowledge in the subject is obtained solely from the methodology of the natural sciences. Somehow, increasingly greater knowledge is obtainable about the natural phenomena of security markets, such as prices or returns, as increasingly larger amounts of data are examined. The historical evolution of markets is unimportant. The views of writers in the past, such as Graham and Dodd or J.M. Keynes or Irving Fisher, are only of historical interest, useful illustrations of how far knowledge has progressed since that time. Gadamer, and other philosophers of his ilk, would argue that this approach is predicated on Finance being a natural science. However, the objects of interest in Finance are the result of human interactions and, as such, belong in the realm of the human sciences. If correct, knowledge of the subject could be substantively increased by proceeding beyond the inductive process to incorporate the notion of tradition and appreciate the contributions of authorities from the past.

The ergodic hypothesis

In aiming to achieve a scientific approach, positivism is fundamentally concerned with the quantification, measurement and empirical verification of hypotheses. As a key assumption in the application of statistical methodology to time series data, ergodicity lies at the philosophical core of the positivism of modern Finance. This statement captures the thrust of the strong criticisms that Davidson (1991, pp. 132–3) and others make about the economic foundations of modern Finance: "Acceptance of the presumption of an ergodic economic environment is often rationalized by the necessity of developing economics as an empirically based science. Indeed, Samuelson has made the acceptance of the 'ergodic hypothesis' the sine qua non of the scientific method in economics." In Finance, ergodicity plays a fundamental role in converting *ex post* logical relationships, such as the CAPM or Markowitz mean-variance diversification models, into *ex ante* prescriptions for investment strategy. It is an essential component of the efficient markets hypothesis and is the driving force behind the fascination with the risk-return tradeoff and the equity risk premia, e.g., Mehra and Prescott (1986), Kocherlakota (1996), Constantinides (2002).

Ergodicity is a property of stochastic processes. Formally, a stochastic process can be defined:

Definition

Let $\{X(t)\}$ be a family of random variables indexed by the linear (index) set $\mathfrak{F}$, where $t \in \mathfrak{F}$. Then $\{X(t)\}$ is said to be a *stochastic process*.

In Finance, the terms stochastic (random) process and time series are often used interchangeably, though it is possible for the index set to refer to some linear variable other than time. Following Karlin and Taylor (1975, p. 32), "a stochastic process may be considered as well defined once its state space, index parameter and family of joint distributions are prescribed." Similar approaches can be found in other sources, e.g., Dhrymes (1974, p. 383): "The probability characteristics of a stochastic process $\{X(t)\}$ are completely specified if we determine the joint density function of a finite number of members of the family of random variables comprising the process."

Heuristically, the theory of stochastic processes describes the behavior of random variables, the X's, over time, $t \in \mathfrak{F}$. Conventionally, a random variable is a function that maps from a prespecified domain, or sample space, to some portion of the real line, $\mathfrak{R}^1$. In the theory of stochastic processes, a single realization of X defines a sample path starting at, say, $X(0)$ and ending at $X(T)$. When the distribution of X is continuous, there are an infinite number of such possible sample paths. In order to make reference to individual sample paths, it is necessary to further introduce another indexing variable for X, $\xi \in \Xi$. This index allows individual sample paths or "states" of X to be identified. It follows that $X(\xi, T)$ would refer to the time $t = T$ observation from a single sample path in $\{X(t)\}$ that starts at $X(0)$ and ends at $X(T)$ and $\{X(\xi, T)\}$ would be the set of all $X(\xi, T)$ at $t = T$. The $\xi \in \Xi$ index makes it possible to define the operation of summing over the ξ at any time $t = T$. Such operations are relevant to identifying the properties of one of the joint distributions of the $\{X(t)\}$ at a single point in time.

In certain financial applications, e.g., where X refers to a security price, X takes values only on the positive, half line. In this case as well as when the X values are allowed to assume any value along the real line, it is conventional to assume that there is a zero probability of X being equal to plus or minus infinity. When t is fixed at a given point, $X(t)$ has the conventional interpretation of a random variable, with associated (one-dimensional) probability density function. In contrast, the ergodicity assumption is concerned with using the $X(\xi, t)$, $X(\xi, t+1)$, $X(\xi, t+2) \ldots X(\xi, T)$ observations from a single sample path to estimate the parameters of the joint distributions defining the $\{X(t)\}$. Specification of the stochastic process for X requires specification of the joint density functions that relate X's at different points in time: the joint densities provide a probabilistic specification of how X evolves over time. This potentially complicated mapping can involve various combinations of discrete or continuous observations on X and t.

In many empirical applications of stochastic process theory, the objective is to rationalize how to use past and present observations on $X(t)$ $(t \le 0)$ to predict future values $(t > 0)$. A classical example of this type of reasoning in Finance is: "Stock returns will outperform bond returns in the long run." Based on past realizations of the time series of returns on stocks and bonds, a prediction is made about the future path for returns. The task of prediction is difficult because the past and present $X(t)$ represent only one realization of the process, i.e., there is only one observed sample path. Yet, for any given $t \in \mathfrak{F}$ the joint probability densities can be used to specify an infinite number of future possible paths for $X(t)$. Theoretically, an *assumption* is required to permit the statistics for the joint probability densities, i.e., the means, variances and other parameters, to be calculated from a single realization of the process. The requisite assumption invokes some form of ergodicity for the stochastic process.

To visualize how an ergodicity assumption works, choose a given starting value for a stochastic process, $X(0)$. From this starting point, the (continuous) joint probability distributions of the stochastic process define an infinite number of possible future paths for $X(t)$. Between $t = 0$ and $t = T$ each of these paths will start at $X(0)$ and reach some point $X(\xi, T)$ at time T. It is now possible to take a "large number" of the points for these paths at T and calculate an *arithmetic mean* of the $\{X(\xi, T)\}$. Setting N to be a large number this gives:

$$\bar{X}[N, T] = \frac{1}{N} \sum_{\xi=1}^{N} X(\xi, T)$$

The set of X defined by the ξ is referred to as the *ensemble* of time paths. Ergodic theorems are concerned with the conditions under which $M(T)$, the arithmetic average calculated from an individual time path from $t = 1$ to $t = T$, converges to the same limit (mean value) as the ensemble average taken at T. More precisely, for t measured discretely:

$$M(T) = \frac{1}{T} \sum_{t=1}^{T} X(t) = \frac{1}{T} \sum_{t=1}^{T} X(t \mid \xi = a) \Leftrightarrow \bar{X}[N, T]$$

Being concerned with the convergence properties of the arithmetic mean, ergodic theorems are closely related to the strong and weak laws of large numbers, e.g., Feller (1957, ch. X).

An important convergence property of the arithmetic mean of the ensemble of time paths is given by the strong law of large numbers. Under certain conditions, such as stationarity of the stochastic process, the process is ergodic and the strong law also applies to time averages. More precisely, if the $\{X(\xi, T)\}$ are independently and identically distributed (iid) with mean $|\mu| < \infty$, the *strong law of large numbers* for the ensemble average states:

$$Pr\{\lim_{N \to \infty} \bar{X}[N, T] = \mu\} = 1$$

where μ is the population mean of $\{X(\xi, T)\}$, i.e., $\mu = E[X(\xi, T)]$. In words, the strong law states that, for a random sample of iid $\{X(\xi, T)\}$ observations, the sample mean will converge to the population mean with probability 1. This is purely a convergence property of the mean, no restriction is imposed on the variance or higher moments. Because $\{X(\xi, T)\}$ is iid, it follows that $\mu = E[X(\xi, t)]$.

The weak law of large numbers is so called because it deals with convergence in probability. A process which converges with probability one will also converge in probability, but not conversely. Applied to the ensemble averages, the *weak law of large numbers* requires:

$$\lim_{N \to \infty} Pr\{| \bar{X}(N, T) - \mu | > \varepsilon\} = 0$$

where, for large enough N, ε can be chosen to be an arbitrarily small positive number. A key result, due to Khinchine (Khintchine), is that if $\{X(\xi, T)\}$ or, more generally, $\{X(\xi, t)\}$ is a sequence of independently, identically distributed random variables with a finite mean μ, then this sequence will obey the weak law. The difference between the strong and weak law relates to the type of convergence which is imposed. By imposing convergence with probability one, the strong law applies to the properties of the arithmetic average as N increases to the limit. In using convergence in probability, the weak law only applies to the arithmetic average at the limit.

In modern presentations, the strong and weak laws apply to the properties of the arithmetic mean. Where additional conditions are imposed on the variance and, possibly, higher moments, then attention shifts to the central limit theorems which provide information not only about the mean but also the distribution of the sequence. In particular, by imposing additional restrictions to those required for the strong law, the central limit theorem can be used to estimate the size of the discrepancy between the arithmetic average and the population mean.[19] This is accomplished by demonstrating that the distribution of the arithmetic average is asymptotically normal. The central limit theorem is a development on *Chebyshev's inequality* which states:

$$Pr\{| X(\xi, T) - \mu | \geq \theta\} \leq \frac{\sigma^2}{\theta^2}$$

where $\sigma^2 = E[(X(\xi, t) - \mu)^2]$ and θ is a given constant. In this form, Chebyshev's inequality provides a relationship between the variance of a distribution and the probability for the size of observed deviations from the mean.

Feller (1966, p. 219) observes: "Chebyshev's inequality must be regarded as a theoretical tool rather than a practical method of estimation. Its importance is due to its universality, but no statement of great generality can be expected to yield sharp results in individual cases." The use of the variance to specify Chebyshev's inequality is an essential component of the result. However, if it assumed that the random variable $X(\xi, T)$ is strictly positive, as is the case where X refers to a security price, then it is possible to derive a form of the inequality that does not involve the variance, i.e.:

$$Pr\{X(\xi, T) \geq \alpha\} \leq \frac{E[X(T)]}{\alpha}$$

where $\alpha > 0$ is a given constant. This form of Chebyshev's inequality illustrates the extensions that are possible where X can be restricted to be positive.

The central limit theorem goes well beyond Chebyshev's inequality to make a precise statement about the form of the probability distribution which, in turn, can be used to provide a practical estimate of the size of the deviation of the arithmetic average from the mean ($|\mu| < \infty$) of the distribution, in terms of the distribution's standard deviation ($0 < \sigma < \infty$). More precisely, at any arbitrary time $t = T$:

Central limit theorem

Let $\{X(\xi, T)\}$ be a sequence of independently, identically distributed random variables with $\mu = E[X(\xi, T)]$ and $\sigma^2 = E[(X(\xi, T) - \mu)^2]$. Then for every fixed β:

$$\lim_{N \to \infty} Pr\left\{\sqrt{N} \frac{\bar{X}[N, T] - \mu}{\sigma} < \beta\right\} = \frac{1}{\sqrt{2\pi}} \int_{-\infty}^{\beta} e^{\frac{-u^2}{2}} du = \Phi[\beta]$$

where $\Phi[\cdot]$ is the standard normal distribution.

This basic result has been generalized in a number of different ways, e.g., to stable processes that do not have a finite variance. The central limit theorem forms the basis of classical parametric tests of empirical hypotheses. As such, the central limit theorem is a key element in the arsenal of positivist methodology.

With this background, it is now possible to proceed to the key logical step that has been identified as the sine qua non of the scientific method in modern Finance: the ergodicity theorem. Much as with the laws of large numbers and the central limit theorem, there are a number of possible variations of the ergodic hypothesis that depend on different assumptions. In comparison to the results which have already been presented, the ergodic theorems are something of a hybrid. As used in Finance, the theorems require assumptions about the stationarity of the stochastic process which, at the least, impose conditions on the covariance function relating $X(t)$ with $X(t + i)$ for all t and $t + i$ defined by the time index set $\mathfrak{F}$. However, as the ultimate objective is to identify conditions under which time averages equal ensemble averages, a correspondence is usually drawn between the ergodic theorems and the strong and weak laws, e.g., Karlin and Taylor (1975, pp. 474–89). As such, results about ergodicity rely on assumptions about the stationarity of the stochastic process.

Two definitions for stationarity are usually presented: *strict stationarity* and *covariance stationarity*. Strict stationarity applies to the joint distributions of the stochastic process:

Definition

A stochastic process $\{X(t)\}$ is a *strictly stationary* process if, for any positive integer k, for all t to $t + k$ and $t + i$ to $t + i + k$ in the time index set $\mathfrak{F}$, the joint distribution of $\{X(t), X(t + 1), X(t + 2) \ldots X(t + k)\}$ has the same joint distribution as $\{X(t + i), X(t + i + 1), X(t + i + 2) \ldots X(t + i + k)\}$.

It is possible for a strictly stationary process to have no finite moments, e.g., a strictly stationary Cauchy process. Strict stationarity could be considered to be a strong assumption because it imposes requirements on the joint distributions when, for many results, all that is required are restrictions on the first two moments of the distribution. With this in mind, the definition for a covariance stationary (*weakly* stationary) process follows:

Definition

A stochastic process $\{X(t)\}$ is a *covariance stationary* process if the second moment $E[X(t)^2]$ (or variance) is finite, the mean $E[X(t)] = \mu$ is constant and the temporal covariance $E[(X(t) - \mu)(X(s) - \mu)] = E[(X(t + i) - \mu)(X(s + i) - \mu)]$ depends only on the time difference $t - s$.

In the same fashion that a strictly stationary process may not satisfy covariance stationarity because the variance (and possibly the mean) are not finite as $T \to \infty$, it is also possible for a covariance stationary process to not be strictly stationary. In the special case where the joint distribution of the stochastic process is Gaussian, then covariance stationarity and strict stationarity have the same meaning. The covariance stationary process leads naturally to the definition of the covariance function, $C[k]$, that defines the temporal covariance $E[(X(t) - \mu)(X(t - k) - \mu)]$ for lag k.

This considerable background is now sufficient to state the conditions under which a single realization of a stochastic process $\{X(0), X(\xi, 1), \ldots, X(\xi, T)\}$ can be used to estimate the constant mean value of the joint distributions. Two types of ergodic theorems are available, one type which applies to covariance stationary processes and "corresponds" to the weak law and one type which applies to strictly stationary processes and "corresponds" to the strong law. The weak law variation takes the form:

Mean-square ergodicity theorem[20]

Suppose $\{X(t)\}$ is a covariance stationary process with covariance function $C[k]$. Then:

$$\lim_{M \to \infty} \frac{1}{M} \sum_{k=0}^{M-1} C[k] = 0$$

if and only if:

$$\lim_{T \to \infty} E[(M(T) - \mu)^2] = 0$$

Because the process is assumed to be covariance stationary with $\mu = E[X(t)]$, the convergence in quadratic mean part of the theorem relates to the limit of the variance of $M(T)$. The first condition relates to the convergence of covariance between $M(T)$ and $X(0)$. It follows that the mean square ergodic theorem says that the variance of $M(T)$ will go to zero in the limit if, and only if, the covariance between $M(T)$ and any arbitrary starting point $X(0)$ also goes to zero in the limit.

The connection of this theorem to the weak law is facilitated by observing that convergence in quadratic mean implies convergence in probability (but not the converse). In terms of quadratic mean convergence, the weak law applies when the elements of the sequence $\{X(t)\}$ are asymptotically uncorrelated.[21] In this vein, the mean-square ergodic theorem requires that as the lag (k) increases in the covariance function between $X(t)$ and $X(t - k)$, the covariance function goes to zero. If this condition is satisfied, then a single realization (time path) of a covariance stationary process can be used to estimate the mean of the ensemble of time paths, provided that the observed time path has a large enough number of observations. Though not easy to prove, this result is intuitive. The action, so to speak, is in the assumption of stationarity.

Casual inspection of the weak and strong laws, as well as the condition for mean square ergodicity reveals the dependence of these results on taking the limit as N or T goes to infinity. Hence, even accepting that the stochastic process satisfies the conditions needed for stationarity, a time path of "a sufficiently long duration" (Karlin and Taylor 1975, p. 475) is still needed. In Finance applications this requirement can create complications, e.g., the longer is the time path the greater the possibility that the fundamentals driving the stochastic process will change due, say, to substantive regulatory changes or evolution of investor sentiments. If the time path is not sufficiently long enough, then the distribution governing the outcomes will be subject to short run influences, such as the picking of an $X(0)$ which is too high or low relative to μ or to the possible impact of boundary conditions. More formally, for "short" time paths the observed distribution will be a combination of the ergodic distribution and a sequence of transient terms, e.g., Heaney and Poitras (1992). Only if the process is allowed to run for a sufficiently long duration will the stochastic process dampen out the possible transients and permit the ergodic distribution to determine the properties of the arithmetic average.

Key elements in the specification of the strong and weak laws of large numbers and the related central limit theorem are the properties of independence and identical distribution. The statement of the strong law given above is only applicable if the $\{X(t)\}$ are independently and identically distributed. It is possible to generalize this result to the case where the random sample uses $\{X(t)\}$ that are only independently distributed, i.e., values of X observed at times up to and including T will not necessarily have constant mean, e.g., Dhrymes (1974, p. 102). This generalization requires a $\mu(t)$, the mean at time t, to be introduced. Invoking ergodicity, the strong law can now be stated:

$$Pr\left\{\lim_{T\to\infty} \frac{\sum\limits_{t=1}^{T} |X(\xi, t) - \mu(t)|}{T} = 0\right\} = 1$$

It is in this form that the strong and weak laws, the central limit theorem and related results are typically applied in applications using regression analysis. The operative random variable is the error term in a regression equation: $y = W\beta + u$, where y is a $Tx1$ vector containing a time series of observations on the dependent variable of interest, W is a $Tx(k + 1)$ matrix of the time series for k independent variables and a constant, β is a $(k + 1)x1$ parameter vector to be estimated and u is a $Tx1$ vector of unobserved error terms that is assumed to be strictly stationary with $E[u] = 0$. To see the connection to the independence form of the strong law, let $y(t) = X(\xi, t)$ and $W(t)\beta = \mu(t)$. It follows that the law of large numbers applies to $u(t)$.

Based on this discussion, a number of observations can be made about the validity of using time averages to estimate the mean value of the joint distributions generating a stochastic process. Heuristically, the modeling process can be summarized as: "The more things change, the more they remain the same." This old adage appears to be an apt description of the ergodicity assumption. In practice, ergodicity permits relationships which are estimated over long time periods to be used to make predictions about those relationships over long time periods in the future. Because security prices are the outcome of human interactions, assuming that such processes are ergodic requires a philosophy that admits the constancy of factors driving human behavior. This could be rationalized along the lines of: "You can't teach an old dog new tricks." Alternatively, it could be assumed that the factors influencing security pricing do change. The upshot is a world where uncertainty is pervasive and real gains are possible from not putting too much faith in old adages.

? Questions

MARKET EFFICIENCY

1 "Even if the market is efficient, there's no need to lose money unnecessarily. I can still reduce my losses by making sure that I always buy after a fall in price rather than after a price rise." Discuss.

2 Respond to the following comment: "The random walk theory, with its implication that investing in stocks is like playing roulette, is a powerful indictment of our capital markets."

3 Some authors argue that professional investment managers are incapable of outperforming the market. Others come to an opposite conclusion. Compare and contrast the assumptions about the stock market that support (a) passive portfolio management, and (b) active portfolio management.

4 Dollar-cost averaging means that you buy equal dollar amounts of a stock every period, e.g., $X per month. The strategy is based on the idea that when the stock price is low, your fixed monthly purchase will buy more shares, and when the price is high, fewer shares will be purchased. Averaging over time, you will end up buying more shares when the stock is cheaper and fewer when it is relatively expensive. Therefore, by design, you will exhibit good market timing. Evaluate this strategy.

5 For what purpose are (a) runs tests, (b) serial correlations, and (c) filter rules used in testing the efficient markets theory? What investment information was obtained from these tests?

6 Technical analysis refers to the use of market generated data to predict future price changes. As such, technical analysis includes the use of price chart patterns, moving average systems, momentum indicators, up/down volume and the like. After reviewing the relevant material in chapter 3, answer the following questions: Does the Markowitz mean-variance optimization model fall within the scope of technical analysis? What about the use of beta to form portfolios? In other words, does modern portfolio theory fall under the weak form or the semi-strong form version of the EMH?

7 Fundamental analysis refers to the use of publicly available information to predict future price changes. As such, fundamental analysis includes the use of corporate financial statements, news stories, government reports, and the like. Does the Dow theory fall within the scope of technical analysis or fundamental analysis? More generally, would a newspaper article that

discussed predictions about future market movements based on resistance and support levels in a chart pattern qualify as fundamental analysis or technical analysis?

BASIC INVESTMENTS

1 Explain each of the following: (a) blue chips; (b) growth stocks; (c) defensive stocks; (d) preferred stocks; (e) income stocks; (f) cyclical stocks; (g) speculative stocks; (h) short selling; (i) brokers and dealers; (j) underwriters

2 In the event of bankruptcy and liquidations in what order (from first to last) will the contributors of capital be repaid? What types of claims will be settled prior to payments made to the contributors of capital?

3 Could Singapore business executives incorporate a corporation in Delaware and cause it to do all its business in Colorado? If this is possible, which state laws would govern the corporation with respect to its power to pay dividends, repurchase its stock or merge with another corporation? Which state laws would apply to the meaning of its contracts for the sale of merchandise?

4 What are the advantages and disadvantages of trading on margin?

5 Suppose a UK zero coupon bond was purchased by a US investor and held for one year. The bond was purchased for £500 when the $/£ exchange rate was $2. (The bond cost $1000.) Due to increases in UK interest rates, the bond was sold for £475 when the exchange rate was $2.20.
(a) What was the rate of return on the bond in £ ($R_£$)?
(b) What was the rate of return on the bond in $ ($R_\$$)?
(c) What portion of the $ return was due to exchange rate changes (e)?
(d) Determine the error of approximation that is introduced by using:
$R_\$ \cong R_£ + e.$

STATISTICS AND ERGODICITY*

1* Outline the proof of the mean square ergodic theorem. How would the theorem have to be changed if it was assumed that the mean of each of the joint distributions was a function of time?

2* Show that if the random variables are iid that the arithmetic mean is the best linear unbiased estimator. Does this result apply if it is only assumed that the process is covariance stationary?

3* Identify hypothetical investment situations where the median, the mode and the harmonic mean of returns would be useful measures of central tendency for guiding security selection. Identify at least three alternatives to the standard deviation as a measure of dispersion, e.g., the square root of the sum of squared deviations from the median. Under what conditions would each of the alternatives be preferred to the standard deviation?

4* Develop the theoretical relationship between the arithmetic, geometric and harmonic means (see Kendall and Stuart 1963, pp. 37–8). Under what conditions will the geometric and arithmetic means be equal?

5* Under what conditions will an efficient security market also be Pareto efficient (Hint: see Mossin 1973)? What happens to the Pareto efficiency of a securities market if it assumed that there is separation of ownership from management?

NOTES

1 An exception is Francis (1983, p. 12): "A security is a document that gives the investor who owns it specific claims on particular assets; it provides evidence of creditorship or ownership. There are two main types of securities – stocks and bonds."

2 The text of the Act can be obtained at the URL www.law.uc.edu/CCL/sldtoc.html. If this link is inactive, the SEC site, www.sec.gov will likely have an active link to a site with the text of the Act. The text of the Commodity Exchange Act, which provides explicit discussion of the jurisdiction of the SEC in the regulation of futures contracts on securities, can be found by following the links at the CFTC site, www.cftc.gov/cftc, which points to the URL www4.law.cornell.edu/uscode/7/ch1.html.

3 Liquidation refers only to the winding up of the firm. It is possible for a firm to be liquidated that has a healthy surplus of marketable assets over liabilities. In the event of bankruptcy, i.e., a surplus liabilities over marketable assets, a liquidation means no payments will be available to equity holders, though in some jurisdictions exceptions may be made for small payments made to speed up legal proceedings.

4 The distinction between seasoned and unseasoned issues is blurred in certain cases. For example, consider a company with publicly traded common stock and no debt on the balance sheet. Would a new issue of bonds by this company be a seasoned or unseasoned issue? Because there is no market price available for the bonds, the issue would typically be considered as unseasoned. Now consider a company with outstanding issues of both straight debt and common stock that is seeking to make a new convertible bond issue. Is this a seasoned or unseasoned issue?

5 Open-ended funds are distinguished from the two other types of fund groups specified in the Investment Company Act (1940) which are closed end funds and unit investment trusts (unit trusts). These types of funds are publicly traded on the stock exchanges or OTC.

6 The emergence of third and fourth markets for trading securities is a recent development. The third market is an OTC market which trades dual listed stocks. The Chicago Stock Exchange is an example of the third market. The fourth market involves direct sales between traders acting outside the conventional trading process making, mostly, large block trades of securities. An important development in this area is the emergence of after-hours trading markets.

7 There are numerous sources which provide discussions of the institutional details of securities markets, e.g., Livingston (1996).

8 Since November 2, 1998 all competitive bids are allocated at the stop-out price, the highest discount rate of the bids accepted at the tender.

9 Another convention is to classify according to credit quality. Combining these two conventions results in the usual two dimensional classification scheme that is often employed in the securities market. For example, this two dimensional classification scheme is used in Lehman Brothers bond pricing matrix. Sorting first by credit quality and then by maturity is also consistent with the typical organization of the trading desks of securities firms. Another possible classification scheme uses the special features of issues, such as convertibility and callability.

10 Various interesting internet searches could be done to show the pervasiveness of risk and return in the teaching of Finance, in general, and investment analysis, in particular. For example, in Yahoo, try the search "Bodie, Kane and Marcus & Risk and Return." This will generate well over 1,000 hits for course outlines and descriptions which use this popular textbook and emphasize risk and return in the course content. The universities involved extend globally and include some of the most prestigious, e.g., Princeton, MIT and Chicago.

11 It is possible to pick specific sample periods where these results do not apply. For example, taking a 1974–2001 sample for Canadian data, the ranking is reversed to have government of Canada Treasury bills with the highest return, followed by long-term bonds and then common stocks.

12 These estimators for the expected return and standard deviation are a function of the time series sample that is selected. Different samples will likely produce somewhat different results. Because the calculation of returns involves taking a difference of prices at different points in time. The sampling frequency will also be relevant. For example, for annual data, the introduction of ERISA in 1974 will impact the results when estimating the expected return over a 1972–2002 sample of annual returns.

13 See the end of chapter problem that queries whether this is also the case if the process is covariance stationary.

14 This section follows Poitras (2002a, pp. 116–20).

15 There is disagreement about whether the Lo and Mackinlay (1988) results are evidence against the EMH. For example, Conrad and Kaul (1993) argue the results can be explained by other factors such as bid/ask spreads. The evidence about the random properties of successive price changes typically involves the use of closing prices. When intra-day transaction to transaction prices are used, there is stronger evidence in favor of short-term trending in prices.

16 The name "martingale" is derived from a French acronym for a gambling strategy which involves doubling up bets until a win is achieved.

17 In more advanced mathematical treatments, the approach is to define $\{Y(t)\}$ as a σ-field of an appropriately defined probability space, e.g., Karlin and Taylor (1975, pp. 297–325).

18 Much of modern Finance lies within the realm of positivism (see section 1.3), also referred to as logical positivism or modernism, e.g., Friedman (1953), Blaug (1992). Positivism strives to achieve a scientific approach, divorced from normative values, emphasizing quantification, measurement and empirical verification of hypotheses. Competing approaches include structural realism, critical realism, post-modernism and pragmatism, e.g., Bhaskar (1978), Lawson (1997).

19 Reference to "the" central limit theorem is somewhat misplaced as there are numerous varieties of central limit theorems which vary according to the initial assumptions imposed, e.g., Feller (1966, ch. 8). Reference to the central limit theorem is to the general result which establishes the conditions under which sums of independent random variables are asymptotically normally distributed.

20 See Karlin and Taylor (1975, p. 476) for a proof of this theorem. Because a covariance stationary process has a constant mean, the theorem says that the time variance of the stochastic process will converge to zero if and only if the covariance between elements of the process goes to zero as the time distance between the elements increases.

21 If the elements are correlated, it is possible to specify the correlation between elements, form correlation adjusted differences and then apply the weak law to these differences. For example, assume that the elements have a first order correlation ρ where $X(t) = \rho X(t-1) + u(t)$. The weak law can be applied to $(X(t) - \rho X(t-1))$.

Chapter
Summary

Chapter 2 *The History of Security Analysis*

2.1 Life Annuity Valuation#
Development of life contingent contracts
De Witt and Halley
De Moivre's approximations and Bernoulli's problem*

2.2 Writers on Stock Markets up to the Early Twentieth Century
Early European writers: J. de la Vega and T. Mortimer
Reminiscences of the US stock operators
Irving Fisher, stock valuation and the 1929 crash
Keynes, uncertainty and the stock market

2.3 Graham and Dodd (1934) and After
The historical context
Defining security analysis
Lasting insights: Graham, Dodd and Cottle (1962)

2.4 The Emergence of Modern Finance
History of portfolio diversification theory before Markowitz
Old Finance, modern Finance and New Finance
Conquering the Old Finance: from Markowitz to Fama

Questions
Notes

# Indicates some sub-sections contain advanced material
* Indicates section contains advanced material

The History of Security Analysis

chapter 2

2.1 LIFE ANNUITY VALUATION[1]

Development of life contingent contracts

An aleatory contract has a payoff that depends on a random outcome. Examples of such contracts arise in the early history of insurance where, say, a contract would be made to protect against the loss of a cargo at sea. In a sense, any security that is not riskless is aleatory but this stretches the notion in a direction that is not too helpful. In the early history of security analysis, it is aleatory contracts with outcomes dependent on life contingencies which are, by far, the most significant. Not only were such contracts socially important prior to the development of modern pension plans and life insurance schemes, life contingent contracts also provide the first instance of significant analytical solutions to security pricing problems. In providing contingent claims pricing formulas for the range of life annuity contracts that were traded in the late seventeenth and early eighteenth centuries, intellectual giants of that era, such as Edmond Halley and Abraham de Moivre, laid the foundations for modern security analysis.

The origins of life annuities can be traced to ancient times. Socially determined rules of inheritance usually meant a sizeable portion of the family estate would be left to a predetermined individual, often the first born son. Bequests such as usufructs, maintenances and life incomes were common methods of providing security to family members and others not directly entitled to inheritances.[2] One element of the Falcidian law of ancient Rome, effective from 40 BC, was that the rightful heir(s) to an estate was entitled to not less than one-quarter of the property left by a testator, the so-called "Falcidian fourth" (Bernoulli 1709/1975, ch. 5). This created a judicial quandary requiring any other legacies to be valued and, if the total legacy value exceeded three-quarters of the value of the total estate, these bequests had to be reduced proportionately.

The Falcidian fourth created a legitimate valuation problem for jurists because many types of bequests did not have observable market values. Because there was not a developed market for life annuities, this was the case for bequests of life incomes. Some method was required to convert bequests of life incomes to a form that could be valued. In Roman law, a legal solution was introduced by the jurist Ulpian (Domitianus Ulpianus,

?–228) who devised a table for the conversion of life annuities to annuities certain, a security for which there was a known method of valuation. Ulpian's conversion table is given by Greenwood (1940) and Hald (1990, p. 117):

Age of annuitant in years								
0–19	20–24	25–29	30–34	35–39	40 . . . 49	50–54	55–59	60–
30	28	25	22	20	19 . . . 10	9	7	5
Comparable Term to maturity of an annuity certain in years								

The connection between age and the pricing of life annuities is a fundamental insight of Ulpian's table. However, it seems that, in practice, the use of Ulpian's table did not produce accurate valuations. For example, Nicholas Bernoulli in the *De Usu Artis Conjectandi in Jure* (1709) indicates that values were often determined by taking the annual value of the legacy, and multiplying this value by the term to maturity of the annuity certain to get the associated legacy value (Hald 1990, p. 117). For example, if the individual was 37 years old and was receiving a life income of £100 per year, then the legacy value according to Ulpian's table would be £2000. Bernoulli correctly identifies the method of multiplying the table value by the size of the payment as faulty due to the omission of the value of interest. Bernoulli observes that at, say, 5% interest the value of the legacy would be only £1246.22.

Ulpian's table was concerned with life incomes, maintenances and the like, which are not quite the same as life annuities which are traded securities with defined cash flow patterns dependent on life contingencies. The life annuity evolved from the *census* which was a form of investment dating at least to feudal times. The English word annuity is an approximate translation, but annuity does not make the appropriate connection to the source of the *census* return being derived from a "fruitful good" (Noonan 1957, p. 155). In Roman law, the *census* was not used, though various types of annuities were available. The various forms of *census* contracts formed the basis for the emergence of government debt issues of annuities certain (fixed term annuities), perpetual annuities and life annuities to fund, first, municipal and, eventually, national borrowing.

Census contracts were initially designed, in feudal times, as a type of barter arrangement, present goods for future goods. The contract appears to have originated in continental Europe, eventually facilitating the evolution of a market for long-term debt (Tracy 1985, pp. 7–8):

> Continental landholders had, since the twelfth century or earlier, been possessed of a technique for converting their property to credit. In France, at least, the practice of borrowing by "constituting" a *rente* on one's land, or of extending credit on this basis, was pioneered by monastic institutions. As the agrarian economy improved, twelfth-century lords found they could obtain credit from the local monastery by pledging the usage fees (*cens*) paid by their peasants instead of having to mortgage the land itself. From this

practice, there derived the idea of creating an artificial income on one's property by constituting a rente (= annual income) on it. In default of annual interest payments at the stipulated rate, creditors had the right to seize the property against whose "income" the contract had been secured. Such rents could either be for the life of the creditor or his assignee, or, at an appreciably lower rate, perpetual. By the late Middle Ages, however, all perpetual or "heritable" rentes in France were generally considered redeemable in principle, in deference to canon law prohibitions against usury. It was this form of private credit, widely diffused in Spain, Germany, northern France, and the Low Countries, which subsequently became the basis for long-term public credit in the same regions.

The conventional *census* contract gradually took the form of a modern annuity where cash was received by the seller of the annuity in exchange for an agreement to make a stream of annual payments over time. By the end of the fifteenth century, the nobility, the church, the state and the landed gentry were all involved as sellers of *census*. Many different variations of *census* were offered: a life *census* in which payments were made over the life of a buyer, or their designee; a perpetual *census*, that had no fixed maturity date; and, a temporary or term *census* that ran for a fixed number of years, similar to a mortgage. A *census* could have conditions that permitted it to be redeemable at the option of either the buyer or seller. Noonan (1957) estimates that credit raised using *census* arrangements may have exceeded that raised through *societas* (business partnerships).

The growth of markets, the Reformation, and a host of other factors contributed to the further evolution of securities derived from the *census*. In turn, this led to the evolution of security pricing techniques. By the sixteenth century, financial markets had developed to the point where an array of investment securities were available. There were short-term commercial loans, often implicitly constructed in the form of bills obligatory or bills of exchange that disguised the direct payment of interest. Other short-term financial securities included bank deposits and triple contracts. The conventional *census* contract had also evolved. There was a range of mortgage contracts, secured by land and there was a range of life annuities often, though not always, issued by states and municipalities. Other instruments of government finance included long-term and perpetual annuities.

A major impetus to the development of securities markets was provided by the various "financial revolutions" in government finance. These revolutions started at different times, in different countries, beginning with the Italian city states and, somewhat later, extending to the cities in northern France and Flanders. The key feature of these revolutions was the transition of government debt from the status of a short-term loan to an individual, debt as an obligation of the sovereign, to a long-term loan to a political entity independent of the ruler (Hamilton 1947, p. 118):

> The nascent states of Western Europe began to borrow by the middle of the thirteenth century, and modern methods of issuing and transferring public obligations arose even earlier in the Italian city states. But owing to the scarcity of liquid capital, the canonical and civil opposition to interest upon loans, and the instability of central governments, the sums borrowed were never large. The debts were usually guaranteed by pledges of jewelry, specific revenues, or real property; and almost invariably they were regarded as personal obligations of the reigning sovereign. The prevalent tendency for monarchs to default upon the debts of their predecessors prevented continuity and accumulation.

The revolutions in government finance transformed government debt operations from the realm of individual borrowing, which was typically short-term and secured by assets, to long-term borrowings which were secured by specific funding sources and were, to varying degrees, independent of the creditworthiness of the monarch.

The earliest forms of "public debt," issued by Italian city states and the northern European cities and municipalities, were either forced loans on wealthy citizens, for example, the *prestiti* in Venice, or were *rentes* backed by specific revenue sources of the sovereign or town government. Northern European towns favoured annuities or *rentes* secured by urban taxes. As early as 1260, such early issues of *rentes heritables* and *rentes vagieres* (life annuities) appeared in the French cities of Calais and Douai, spreading to the Low Countries and German towns such as Cologne (Tracy 1985, p. 13). Between 1275 and 1290 the city of Ghent in Flanders issued *lijfrenten* or life annuities followed by issues of *erfrenten* or redeemable *rentes*. There was a form of guarantee by the sovereign associated with some of these municipal issues, for example, the Court of Flanders "undertook to see that the city lived up to its promises." Municipalities, particularly in Holland, Flanders and Brabant, continued to issue life and redeemable annuities leading to increasingly larger stocks of public debt and, ultimately, to repayment difficulties for some towns by the sixteenth century.

The transition from municipal to national public debt issues was gradual. Though claims could be made for certain German territories, Dutch provinces or the Spanish monarchies, Hamilton (1947) traces the beginnings of national public debt to sixteenth century France. For some centuries before, the French had a tradition of the monarch selling long-term *rentes*, supported by the income from royal properties. These sales were often sold at deep discounts to royal officials and could not be considered "public debt" but, rather, were obligations of the sovereign. Hamilton (1947, p. 119) marks 1522 as a turning point:

> For practical purposes, the national debt began in the reign of Francis I. Following the loss of Milan, the key to northern Italy, on September 15, 1522, Francis I borrowed 200,000 francs, then called *livres tournois*, at $12\frac{1}{2}$ per cent from the merchants of Paris, to intensify the war against Charles V. Administered by the city government, this loan inaugurated the famous series of bonds based on revenues from the capital and known as *rentes sur l'Hotel de Ville* . . . the public debt rose to 100 million francs by 1576 and to 300 million, of which 157 million were funded, by 1595.

Though sovereigns had recognized the importance of the debt market in financing state military ventures for some time, the emergence of the public debt gave the debt market a new status as an instrument of state power.

Despite this claim to first-mover status by the French, there were numerous difficulties with the administration of the French public debt. Large increases in outstanding principal to sustain various military adventures led to periods of suspended interest payments and forced reduction through partial bankruptcy. By the beginning of the eighteenth century, French national finances were in a sorry condition. The Dutch were decidedly more successful in developing their public debt. The Dutch provincial governments pioneered various innovations in public debt issues during the sixteenth century, including the development of a "free market" for provincial *renten* issued in Holland (Tracy 1985, ch. IV). The English were relative late comers in developing public debt issues, with the beginnings of English public debt starting only with the reign of William and Mary in 1688.[3] However, by the mid-eighteenth century the English had assumed front-runner status and the system of English public debt had become a model for European governments.[4]

In the medieval and Renaissance periods, difficulties associated with valuing a life annuity were advantageous from the perspective of avoiding usury laws, e.g., Noonan (1957), Poitras (2000, ch. 3). However, by the later seventeenth century financial markets required more precise methods of handling the pricing risks associated with issuing life annuities. In addition to improvements in pricing techniques, different variations on the life annuity were proposed to deal with the difficulty of valuing the life contingency risk. The most important of these proposals was the tontine, a funding scheme recommended to Cardinal Mazarin of France in 1652 by Lorenzo Tonti, an expatriate Neapolitan banker living in Paris.

While a number of variations were used, for example, compound tontines, the generic tontine classified the subscribers' nominees into groups, by age class, creating a fund for each group. Each of the surviving persons in a group would share the interest from the fund associated with that group. When the last member of a group was dead, payments would cease. After two aborted 1653 attempts at issuing state tontines in France and Denmark, the first tontine was issued in 1670 by the Dutch town of Kampen. Following an initial issue in 1689, the tontine became an important source of state finance in France during the eighteenth century (Weir 1989; Alter and Riley 1986). Starting in 1693, the tontine was also used, though less extensively, for state finance in England.[5]

De Witt and Halley[6]

In the late seventeenth and early eighteenth centuries, analytical solutions were proposed to the problem of valuing life annuities. Arguably, these analytical solutions represent the most important theoretical contributions to the early history of security analysis. The intellectual preliminaries required to sustain these contributions start around the latter part of the sixteenth century in Holland where important university mathematicians, such as Simon Stevin, were drawn to solving practical fixed income valuation problems, complementing the work of the commercial algorists. Even though the development of discounting and compounding techniques were important for determining the return from partnerships and valuing commonly traded term annuities such as mortgages and lease-purchase transactions, these techniques were not sufficient to value life annuities and other types of securities involving life contingent claims. Such problems were important because, in the absence of pension funds and life insurance, life annuities performed an essential social function.

The life annuity usually was a contract between three parties, the subscriber who provided the initial capital, the shareholder who was entitled to receive the annuity payments and the nominee on whose life the payout was contingent, e.g., Weir (1989). Different variations were possible. For example, one person could be subscriber, shareholder and nominee; a parent could be a subscriber and designate a child as the nominee with the shareholder status passing from parent to child as an inheritance; or, joint life annuities could be specified where more than one nominee was designated and payments continued until both nominees died. The life annuity was further complicated by the need to establish proof of survival for the nominee prior to each annuity payment date. While it was technically possible to resell most life annuity contracts to third parties, the difficulties associated with verifying the survival and probability of survival for the nominee made resale difficult. Oddly enough, until the nineteenth century, market practice usually involved selling life annuities without taking accurate consideration of the age of the nominee.

Life annuities have a long history with the earliest transactions involving individuals. Issues of *rentes vagieres* by municipalities in northern France, such as Calais, appeared around 1260 (Tracy 1985, p. 13). The practice of raising municipal funds using life annuities soon spread to the Low Countries and the German towns. By the fifteenth century, it was common for cities and religious orders to use life annuities to raise funds in Germany and the Low Countries, though Italian public finance appears to have adopted the practice somewhat later with "the Venetian mint (*zecca*) offering life annuities at 14% between 1536 and 1540." Issues of life annuities for national financing appear somewhat later in France and England; the French government first using *rentes vagieres* during the Nine Years' War (1688–1697) and the English government making a first issue of life annuities in 1693 (Velde and Weir 1992).

Though there were larger and less frequent issues of life annuities by the emerging nation states starting in the seventeenth century, the typical government issuers of life annuities were municipalities, with prices varying widely from town to town depending on prevailing local interest rates and pricing conventions. Amsterdam, for example, sold municipal annuities at regular intervals starting in 1402, typically "charging flat rates of $9\frac{1}{11}$ percent for annuities on two heads and $11\frac{13}{17}$ percent for one, regardless of age" (Daston 1988, p. 121). Annuity prices were quoted in "*years' purchase*," which is the price of the annuity divided by the annual annuity payment. For a perpetual annuity, years' purchase is the inverse of the annual yield to maturity.

Nicholas Bernoulli (1709) provides historical examples of life annuities selling for 6 to 12 years' purchase, without allowance being made for the age of nominee.[7] De Witt quotes a 1671 price for a single life annuity in Amsterdam of 14 years' purchase with a 4% interest rate and no allowance for age of nominee; this is compared with a price of 25 years' purchase for a redeemable annuity, effectively a perpetual annuity with an embedded option for the borrower to redeem at the purchase price. Houtzager (1950) quotes a sixteenth and early seventeenth century Dutch pricing convention of 1.5 to 2 times the years' purchase for a redeemable annuity to determine the price for life annuities, i.e., the years' purchase of a life annuity equaled the years' purchase for a redeemable annuity divided by 1.5 to 2. The inefficiency of the practice of selling life annuities without reference to the age of the nominee did not escape the notice of those responsible for government finance. However, solving the problem of determining a correct price was not easy. The first sound solution to this difficult analytical problem was proposed by Jan de Witt.[8]

Jan de Witt was not a professional mathematician. He was born into a burgher-regent family. While attending university at Leiden as a student of jurisprudence, de Witt lived in the house of Frans van Schooten who, while a professor of jurisprudence, was also deeply involved in mathematical studies. Van Schooten encouraged Christian Huygens, Jan Hudde and de Witt in their mathematical studies and published their efforts as appendices to two of his mathematical books. De Witt's contribution on the dynamics of conic sections was written around 1650 and published as an appendix to van Schooten's 1659 exposition of Cartesian mathematics, *Geometria a Renato Des Cartes*. From the perspective of the history of mathematics, de Witt's contribution is an interesting and insightful exposition on the subject but "marks no great advance" (Coolidge 1990, p. 127).

Around 1650, de Witt began his career in Dutch politics as the pensionary of Dordrecht. In 1653, at the age of 28, de Witt became the grand pensionary or prime minister of Holland. During his term as grand pensionary, de Witt was confronted with the need to raise funds to support Dutch military activities, first in the Anglo-Dutch war of 1665–67 and later in anticipation of an invasion by France which, ultimately, came in 1672. Life annuities had for many years been a common method of municipal and state finance in Holland and de Witt also proposed that life annuity financing be used to support the war effort. However, de Witt was not satisfied that the convention of selling of life annuities at a fixed price, without reference to the age of the annuitant, was a sound practice. Instead de Witt proposed a method of calculating the price of life annuities which would vary with age. This remarkable contribution can be considered the start of modern contingent claims analysis.

More precisely, aided by contributions from Huygens in probability and Hudde in mortality statistics, in *Value of Life Annuities in Proportion to Redeemable Annuities* (1671, in Dutch) de Witt provided the first substantive analytical solution to the difficult problem of valuing a life annuity.[9] Unlike the numerous variations of fixed term annuity problems which had been solved in various commercial arithmetics, the life annuity valuation required the weighting of the relevant future cash flows by the probability of survival for the designated nominee. De Witt's approach, which is somewhat computationally cumbersome but analytically insightful, was to compute the value of a life annuity by applying the concept of mathematical expectation advanced by Huygens in 1657.[10]

De Witt's approach involved making theoretical assumptions about the distribution of the number of deaths. To provide empirical support for his calculations, he gave supplementary empirical evidence derived from the register at The Hague for life annuitants of Holland and West Friesland for which he calculated the average present values of life annuities for different age classes, based on the actual payments made on the annuities. This crude empirical analysis was buttressed by the considerably more detailed empirical work of Hudde on the mortality statistics of life annuitants from the Amsterdam register for 1586–90. For the next century, the development of pricing formulas for life annuities is intimately related to progress in the study of life contingency tables, a subject which is central to the development of modern statistical theory and actuarial science.

Not long after submitting his *Value of Life Annuities* to the States General, de Witt's life came to a tragic end. The invasion of the Dutch Republic by France in 1672 led to a public panic which precipitated de Witt's forced resignation and his replacement by the Stadholder William III. However, the demand for public retribution for the grand pensionary's perceived failings did not end with his resignation. Later in 1672, de Witt was set upon by a mob and shot, publicly hanged and his body then violated. However, despite the tragic demise of de Witt, Jan (Johan) Hudde had been consulted by de Witt on various aspects of the results contained in the *Value of Life Annuities*, particularly the validity of the calculations, the empirical evidence on mortality of annuitants and the theoretical procedures required to calculate annuities on two or more lives. Hudde continued and expanded de Witt's work on life annuity valuation.[11]

The solution to the problem of pricing life annuities given by de Witt uses an age interval between 3 and 80.[12] Hence, de Witt is considering the value of a life annuity written on the life of a 3-year-old nominee. As the practice up to his time was to sell life annuities at the same price, regardless of the age of the nominee, it was conventional to select younger nominees from healthy families. Based on Hudde's data for 1586–90 Amsterdam life annuity nominees, approximately 50% were under 10 years of age, and 80% under 20 (Alter and Riley, p. 33). *Throughout the following annuities will be assumed to make a payment of 1 unit of currency (florin, dollars, etc.) each period.*

Instead of assuming a uniform distribution where death at each age would be equally likely, De Witt divided the interval between 3 and 80 into four subperiods: (3, 53), (53, 63), (63, 73) and (73, 80). Within each subperiod, an equal chance of mortality is assigned. The number of chances assigned to each subgroup is 1, 2/3, 1/2, 1/3. The chance of living beyond 80 is assumed to be zero. While de Witt corresponded with Hudde about mortality data he was collecting and tabulating for the 1586–9 Amsterdam annuitants, these probabilities were assumed and not directly derived from a life table.

From these assumptions, de Witt constructs a distribution for the number of deaths and calculates the life annuity price as the expectation of the relevant annuity present values. In doing this, de Witt explicitly recognizes that life annuities were paid in semi-annual instalments, requiring time to be measured in half years and for survivors to be living at the end of the half year in order to receive the payment. The 77-year period translates into 154 half years. Using a discount rate of 4% per annum, De Witt uses his assumed chances of mortality in any half year to calculate a weighted average of the present values for the certain annuities associated with each half year. The resulting value is the expected present value of the life annuity which is the recommended price at which the annuity should be sold.

Algebraically, de Witt's technique can be illustrated by defining A_n to be the present value of an annuity with a 4% annual rate to be paid at the end of the half year n (Hald, pp. 124–5):

$$A_n = \sum_{t=1}^{n} \frac{1}{(1 + r)^t} = \frac{1}{r} - \frac{1}{r(1 + r)^n} \quad \text{where} \quad (1 + r) = \sqrt{1.04}$$

To evaluate the expected present value of the life annuity, de Witt performs the calculation:

$$E[A_n] = \frac{\sum\limits_{n=1}^{99} A_n + \dfrac{2}{3}\sum\limits_{n=100}^{119} A_n + \dfrac{1}{2}\sum\limits_{n=120}^{139} A_n + \dfrac{1}{3}\sum\limits_{n=140}^{153} A_n}{128}$$

Interpretation of the sums is aided by observing that individuals must be alive at the end of the half year to qualify for annuity payments. For example, dying in the first half year means that no payments will be received. The divisor of 128 is calculated by determining the total number of chances as:

$$(100)1 + (20)\frac{2}{3} + (20)\frac{1}{2} + (14)\frac{1}{3} = 128$$

where the number in brackets is the number of half years in each subgroup. De Witt's solution can be compared to the less realistic case where the distribution of deaths is assumed to be uniform:

$$E[A_n] = \frac{\sum\limits_{n=1}^{153} A_n}{154} = \frac{1}{154}(0) + \frac{1}{154}\frac{1}{1+r} + \frac{1}{154}\sum\limits_{t=1}^{2}\frac{1}{(1+r)^t}$$

$$+ \ldots + \frac{1}{154}\sum\limits_{t=1}^{153}\frac{1}{(1+r)^n} + 0$$

By assigning less weight to the largest cash flows, de Witt's calculated expected value of 16.0016 florins for *annual* payments of 1 florin differs from the expected value of 17.22 florins calculated using a uniform distribution.

It is difficult to assess the impact of de Witt's contribution to the practice of pricing life annuities. Based on his recommendation, in 1672 the city of Amsterdam began offering life annuities with prices dependent on the age of the nominee. However, this practice did not become widespread and by 1694, when Edmond Halley (1656–1742) published his influential paper "An Estimate of the Degrees of Mortality of Mankind, drawn from the curious Tables of the Births and Funerals at the City of Breslaw; with an Attempt to ascertain the Price of Annuities upon Lives," the English government was still selling life annuities at seven years' purchase, independent of age.[13] Halley's paper is remarkable in providing substantive contributions to both demography and to security analysis. The importance of this paper reinforces the intellectual stature of an individual who is recognized in modern times primarily for his contributions to astronomy.

The Breslau data used in the preparation of Halley's "Estimate . . ." was much better suited to construction of a life table than the bills of mortality data used by John Graunt. Thanks to Leibnitz, the data set came to attention of the Royal Society and Halley, the editor of the Society's journal, was selected to analyze the data. From the end of the sixteenth century, Breslau, a city in Silesia, had maintained a register of births and deaths, classified according to sex and age. For the purpose of constructing a precise life table, only the population size is missing. The paper is primarily concerned with constructing Halley's life table and touches on the valuation of life annuities only as an illustration of applying the information in the life table. In the process, Halley presents a somewhat more general approach than de Witt to the valuation of a life annuity. While this paper was Halley's primary effort in demographics, he did make other contributions to security analysis, such as detailing the use of logarithms in solving present value problems, e.g., Poitras (2000, p. 155).

General details of Halley's life are available in numerous sources, e.g., Ronan (1978): Halley was born in Haggerston, England on October 29, 1656; the eldest son of a well-to-do landowner, soapmaker and salter from the City of London, also known as Edmond Halley. The father had sufficient means to ensure an impressive education for his son, who showed an interest in astronomy from an early age. Together with an extensive and valuable collection of astronomical instruments that had been purchased by his father and in part made for himself, the younger Edmond Halley set off to study at Oxford at the age of 17. After three productive years of study, which included three papers published in the *Philosophical Transactions* of the Royal Society, at the age of 20 Halley moved from the overachieving to the remarkable (Pearson 1978, p. 82):

> at the age of 20 an idea occurred to this young undergraduate. Why should he not go to the Southern Hemisphere and catalogue the stars which never rose above the horizon of either Dantzig or Greenwich? No sooner thought of than carried out. Halley packed up his telescope, left Oxford without a degree ... and sailed under the auspices of the East India Company to St. Helena, where he arrived after three months' (!) voyage and set up his telescope, sticking to the work for eighteen months, until he had completed his star catalogue, reaching England again, exactly two years after he had left it, to be hailed as the Tycho Brahe of the Southern Hemisphere.

The star map by itself was considered sufficient for the King, Charles II, to issue a *mandamus* to Oxford for granting Halley a Master of Arts. In 1678, at the age of 22, Halley was made a Fellow of the Royal Society.

Unfortunately, there is so much in the life of Edmond Halley that a conventional historiography quickly covers many pages, the writer is overwhelmed and the process of sifting out important details becomes unmanageable. For example, Halley had an important relationship with Sir Isaac Newton. Some of the connections between Halley and Newton were immediate, such as Halley being instrumental in getting the *Principia* published: "There is little doubt that we owe its publication to the good offices of Halley" (Pearson 1978, p. 86). This aid came both in financial support for publication from both the Royal Society and Halley, as well as "important editorial aid" (Ronan 1978, p. 68) in preparing the manuscript. Newton was a reluctant author, if only because he was not fully satisfied with the results that were being published.

The connections between Halley and Newton were not all so apparent. For example, in addition to the star map, Halley also returned with some puzzling observations about the behaviour of an English clock pendulum in St Helena. "Halley found that his clock pendulum, which kept good time in England, had to be shortened to do so in St. Helena." When this information was passed on to Newton, he was able to interpret Halley's observations as being due to gravity. From this Newton drew the conclusion that the earth was not a sphere, but rather is an oblate spheroid. In another instance, Halley designed a diving bell and a diver's helmet. In experiments on this equipment, Halley reports "on the colour of sunlight that he observed at various depths were sent to Newton, who incorporated them in his *Opticks*." In an interesting development, Halley formed a public company for the purposes of developing commercial applications of the bell and helmet, in particular wreck salvaging. Shares in Halley's company were quoted from 1692–6.

Halley is best known for his work on the periodicity of comet orbits. The naming of Halley's comet was a posthumous recognition for his theoretical and empirical work on a particular bright comet which exhibited a periodicity of 75 years. Though Halley's observations were well known to astronomers, "it was not until the 1682 comet re-appeared as predicted in 1758 that the whole intellectual world of western Europe took notice. By then Halley had been dead fifteen years; but his hope that posterity would acknowledge that this return "was first predicted by an Englishman" was not misplaced, and the object was named "Halley's comet'" (Ronan 1978, p. 69). This recognition was a fitting tribute for someone who had contributed to so many fields, from astronomy and mathematics to history and philology.

As was the fashion at the time, Halley's presentation of the life annuity pricing problem was done by presenting mathematical concepts in a verbal format. With this in mind, it is possible to reexpress Halley's formula in more mathematical form by observing that the total number of annuities sold on a life starting at year x, ℓ_x, equals the sum of $d_x + d_{x+1} + \ldots + d_{w-1}$ where d_i is the number of annuities which terminate in period i due to the death of annuitant nominees in that half year and that $d_i = 0$ for $x \geq w$. Taking ℓ_{x+t} to be the number of nominees, starting in year x surviving in period $x + t$, it follows that: $d_{x+t} = \ell_{x+t} - \ell_{x+t+1}$ and that the probability of death in any given half year j is (d_{x+j}/ℓ_x). The general pricing formula for a life annuity follows:

$$E[A_n] = \frac{1}{\ell_x} \sum_{n=1}^{w-x-1} A_n d_{x+n} = \frac{1}{\ell_x} \sum_{n=1}^{w-x-1} d_{x+n} \sum_{t=1}^{n} \frac{1}{(1+r)^t}$$

$$= \frac{1}{\ell_x} \sum_{t=1}^{n} \sum_{n=1}^{w-x-1} d_{x+n} \frac{1}{(1+r)^t} = \frac{1}{\ell_x} \sum_{n=1}^{w-x-1} \ell_{x+n} \frac{1}{(1+r)^n}$$

The last step in the derivation comes from progressively collecting terms associated with $(1 + r)^{-t}$. For example, the $(1 + r)^{-1}$ term will appear in each annuity and will, as a result, have coefficients which are the sum of $d_{x+1}, d_{x+2}, \ldots d_{w-1}$. Recalling the definition of d in terms of ℓ, this sum returns ℓ_{x+1}. In symbolic form, this is the life annuity pricing formula presented by Halley (1694).

De Moivre's approximations and Bernoulli's problem*

In assessing Halley's contribution to the history of financial economics, it is natural to immediately mention Abraham de Moivre (1667–1754), an expatriate Frenchman transplanted to London following the Repeal of the Edict of Nantes. Halley and de Moivre were first acquainted in 1692 and in 1695 de Moivre's first paper contributed to the Royal Society was presented by Halley. Unlike Halley who touched only briefly on the pricing of securities, de Moivre spent much of his productive life studying the practical problem of pricing life annuities. By the time de Moivre undertook his work on life annuities, the basic groundwork had been laid. However, Halley and others recognized that the brute force approach to calculating tables for valuing life annuities would require "a not ordinary number of Arithmetical operations." Halley attempted to develop simplifying mathematical procedures, "to find a Theorem that might be more concise than the Rules there laid down, but in vain."

In the early history of security analysis de Moivre can be recognized for fundamental contributions involving the application of applied probability theory to the valuation of life annuities. This work laid the theoretical foundation for Richard Price, James Dodson and others to develop the actuarially sound principles required to implement modern life insurance. The immediate incentive for de Moivre was to value the various aleatory contracts which became increasingly popular as the eighteenth century progressed. Being (together with Laplace) one of two giants of probability theory in the eighteenth century (Pearson 1978, p. 146), de Moivre was singularly well suited to the task of developing the foundations of insurance mathematics. It is one of the quirks of intellectual history that de Moivre's most significant contributions, which lay primarily in the areas of probability theory and applied mathematics, contributed little to his personal comfort while his contributions to security analysis and valuation managed to help de Moivre maintain body and soul.

To the modern reader, it is strange that a person of de Moivre's stature had to endure most of his life in "the hardest poverty." Never able to secure an academic position, de Moivre earned a living as an eighteenth-century reckoning master and algorist, tutoring mathematics, calculating odds for gamblers and reckoning values for underwriters and annuity brokers. Pearson (1978, p. 143) observes that "this seamy side of life had a golden lining. Every evening (Sir Isaac) Newton would come and fetch de Moivre from (Slaughter's) Coffee House, and take him for philosophical discussion to his own house in Golden Square. I picture De Moivre working at a dirty table in the coffee house with a broken-down gambler beside him and Isaac Newton walking through the crowd to his corner to fetch out his friend. It would make a great picture for an inspired artist."

De Moivre began his close friendships with Newton and Halley around the same time in the early 1690s. The timing of the 1694 publication of Halley's "Estimate..." and Halley's subsequent presentation of de Moivre's first paper to the Royal Society in 1695 make it possible that de Moivre played some role in the inclusion of the life annuity valuation problem in the "Estimate..." It is not difficult to conceive enlightened interaction between the two on the subject of applying Halley's life table and de Moivre suggesting and explaining the important problem of life annuities. However, de Moivre's primary contribution to pricing life annuities did not appear until much later in the *Annuities Upon Lives* (1725) with a second edition (1743). Also important is the 1756 edition of his *The Doctrine of Chances* which contains a section titled "A Treatise of Annuities on Lives" together with discussion of the life tables of Halley, Kersseboom, Simpson and Deparcieux.

In *Annuities*, de Moivre examined a wide variety of the life annuities available in the early eighteenth century: single life annuities, joint annuities (annuities written on several lives), reversionary annuities, and annuities on successive lives. His general approach to these valuation problems involves two steps: first, to develop a general valuation formula for each type of annuity based on Halley's approach; and, second, to produce an approximation to the general formula suitable for calculating prices without the considerable efforts involved in evaluating the more exact formula. In order to implement some of the approximations, de Moivre developed a mathematical formulation, a piecemeal linear approximation, of the information contained in the life table.

The computational advantages of de Moivre's approximations were considerable and the methods became widely used in day-to-day commercial practice. The ensuing development of actuarial science and insurance mathematics progressed by working with the more tedious exact formulae, estimating more accurate life tables and calculating tables with exact prices for different situations and levels of interest rates. The next important person in the intellectual linkage developing life insurance mathematics was James Dodson, a pupil and friend of de Moivre. While admitting that Dodson's interest in life contingencies almost surely originated with de Moivre, Ogborn (1962, p. 23) speculates that it "is an interesting question whether (Dodson and de Moivre) ever discussed the mathematics of life assurance but there is no published evidence that they did so and it seems that the work is wholly Dodson's."

De Moivre provided an important simplification for the value of a single life annuity under the assumption that the "Probabilities of Life . . . decrease in Arithmetic Progression" or, in other words, are uniformly distributed starting at year x up to some terminal year w, $n = w - x$. Generalizing the uniformly distributed case, de Moivre's result is derived by observing that for the uniform case:

$$E[A_n] = \frac{n-1}{n}\frac{1}{1+r} + \frac{n-2}{n}\frac{1}{(1+r)^2} + \ldots + \frac{n-(n-1)}{n}\frac{1}{(1+r)^{n-1}} + \frac{n-n}{n}\frac{1}{(1+r)}$$

$$= \sum_{t=1}^{n}\frac{1}{(1+r)^t}\left(1 - \frac{t}{n}\right) = \sum_{t=1}^{n}\frac{1}{(1+r)^t} - \sum_{t=1}^{n}\frac{t}{n(1+r)^t}$$

From this point, de Moivre provides an obscure derivation in the first edition of *Annuities upon Lives* and a more tedious demonstration in later editions. A more modern derivation is provided in Pearson (1978, pp. 147–8) where it is observed that:

$$\sum_{t=1}^{n}\frac{t}{n(1+r)^t} = \frac{1+r}{n}\sum_{t=1}^{n}\frac{t}{(1+r)^{t+1}} = -\frac{1+r}{n}\frac{dA_n}{d(1+r)}$$

It follows that:

$$E[A_n] = \left[A_n + \frac{1+r}{n}\frac{dA_n}{d(1+r)}\right] = \frac{A_n}{n}\left[n + \frac{1+r}{A_n}\frac{dA_n}{d(1+r)}\right]$$

The last term, not provided by Pearson, contains the familiar Macaulay duration for the annuity applicable to the longest life.

Substituting the relevant expressions back into $E[A_n]$ and evaluating the derivative gives:

$$E[A_n] = \left[A_n + \frac{1+r}{n} \frac{dA_n}{d(1+r)} \right]$$

$$= \left(\frac{1}{r} - \frac{1}{r(1+r)^n} \right) + \frac{1+r}{n} \left[\frac{n}{r(1+r)^{n+1}} + \frac{1}{r^2(1+r)^n} - \frac{1}{r^2} \right]$$

$$= \frac{1}{r} - \frac{1+r}{n} \left[\frac{1}{r} \left\{ \frac{1}{r} - \frac{1}{r(1+r)^n} \right\} \right] = \frac{1}{r} \left\{ 1 - \frac{1+r}{n} A_n \right\}$$

The final right-hand-side expression is de Moivre's approximation to the value of a single life annuity. If only for the computational savings provided, this formula is a considerable advance. From the tedious calculation of a long weighted sum, with weights extracted from the not completely accurate life tables available at his time, de Moivre provides a calculation which could be done in a matter of seconds with or without the aid of an appropriate table for annuities certain. While the derivation provided is not precisely de Moivre's (see Hald, pp. 521–2), the connection to the familiar notion of Macaulay duration is instructive for modern readers. Similar to the improvement of the duration measure provided by the introduction of convexity, the accuracy of de Moivre's formula can be improved by considering higher order derivative terms (Pearson, pp. 150–2). In this case, the higher order terms improve on the accuracy of the solution associated with the assumption of uniformly distributed death rates.

De Moivre provided numerous approximations relevant for other cases, such as joint life annuities, where two lives are nominated and the annuity payments continue until both are dead. Some of de Moivre's approximations were more successful than others and Simpson expended considerable effort showing that direct calculation making use of life tables was substantially better for pricing the joint life annuity (Hald, p. 532). De Witt also considered the problem of joint life annuities and, implementing an early version of Pascal's triangle, provided an insightful solution, considered to be his "most important contribution to mathematics" (Coolidge 1990, p. 131). De Moivre, Simpson and later writers used a more direct approach to the price of a joint life annuity, $E[A_{mn}]$ for two joint lives, involving the price of the single life annuities $E[A_n]$ and $E[A_m]$ and an annuity for joint life continuance which makes payments only when both nominees are alive $E[_mA_n]$. Because the pricing problem for single life annuities was solved, the joint life annuity problem involved solving for $E[_mA_n]$.

The de Moivre approach to solving a joint life annuity written on two lives involved the relationship:

$$E[A_{mn}] = E[A_n] + E[A_m] - E[_mA_n]$$

This result follows from observing that the probability of having survival of at least one of the two lives at time t is $1 - (1 - Prob[x, t])(1 - Prob[y, t]) = Prob[x, t] + Prob[y, t] - Prob[x, t]Prob[y, t]$ where $Prob[x, t]$ is the probability of $x(y)$ surviving at time t which can be related to ℓ_{x+t}/ℓ_x in the $E[A_n]$ formula given previously. Multiplying by $(1 + r)^{-t}$ and summing gives the required result. From this point de Moivre used two approaches to solve for approximations to $E[_mA_n]$, one involved taking $Prob[\cdot]$ to be arithmetically declining and the other geometrically declining. While the former leads to a more exact result for $E[A_{mn}]$, the latter has a less complicated formula (Hald, pp. 528–30). An example of market prices for joint annuities are the 14%, 12% and 10% (7, 8.5 and 10 years' purchase) rates offered on annuities for one, two and three lives, irrespective of age, in a 1694 issue by the government of England.

A final point to be considered is the relationship between $E[A_n]$ and the value of a term annuity for the expected duration of life from a given starting age x. The difference between these two valuations was recognized by de Witt but the point was still a revelation to Nicholas Bernoulli (1709) who stated: "I notice that the value of (life annuity) incomes is not correctly calculated by supposing that the return will last as many years as someone is supposed probably to live." To illustrate this problem, for simplicity assume all deaths occur at the beginning or end of period. This assumption permits the exclusion of the problem of evaluating where the average time of death will be in the year for persons that die after s but before $s + 1$, e.g., averaging would give $s + 1/2$ years. Given this, the expectation of life at birth, D, can be compared with $E[A_n]$ starting at birth and the associated value of the term annuity with length D:

$$D = \sum_{t=1}^{w-x-1} t \frac{d_{x+t}}{\ell_x} \qquad E[A_n] = \sum_{n=1}^{w-x-1} A_n \frac{d_{x+n}}{\ell_x} \qquad A_d = \sum_{t=1}^{D} \frac{1}{(1+r)^t}$$

Comparing D with $E[A_n]$ and A_d it is apparent that $D > E[A_n]$ and $D > A_d$, due to the impact of discounting on the terms in $E[A_n]$ and A_d. Even if interest rates are zero and $D = A_d$, $E[A_n]$ and D are still not equal due to the $E[A_n]$ only crediting the cash flow if the end of period is reached. (This is the point that was suppressed for simplicity).

The difference between D and $E[A_n]$ is well known, e.g., Alter and Riley (p. 9), Hald (p. 128). However, the comparison between A_d, a certain annuity with term equal to expected life, and $E[A_n]$, the expected value of an annuity lasting for the duration of a life, is not as obvious. Under the simplifying assumption, these values will be equal if interest rates are zero. However, for $r > 0$, $A_d \geq E[A_n]$ with $=$ only when all deaths occur at n. To see this, consider the uniformly distributed case where:

$$E[A_n] = \frac{1}{r}\left\{1 - \frac{1+r}{n}A_n\right\} \qquad A_d = \frac{1}{r} - \frac{1}{r(1+r)^D}$$

It follows:

$$A_d - E[A_n] = \frac{1}{r(1+r)^D} - \left[\frac{1+r}{n} \cdot \frac{1}{r}\right]\left\{\frac{1}{r} - \frac{1}{r(1+r)^n}\right\}$$

$$= \frac{1}{r^2}\left\{\frac{r}{(1+r)^D} - \left[\frac{1+r}{n}\left\{1 - \frac{1}{(1+r)^n}\right\}\right]\right\}$$

$$= \frac{1}{r^2}\left\{\frac{nr(1+r)^{n-D} + (1+r) - (1+r)^{n+1}}{n(1+r)^n}\right\} > 0$$

In more general form, this was the relationship observed by Nicholas Bernoulli.

2.2   WRITERS ON STOCK MARKETS UP TO THE EARLY TWENTIETH CENTURY

Early European writers: J. de la Vega and T. Mortimer[14]

Shares in joint stock companies are the precursors of modern common shares. The joint stock form of ownership evolved somewhat slowly from earlier forms of business organization. Most of the early joint stock companies retained some of the essential features of partnerships. Hecksher (1955) makes an important distinction between partnerships and joint stock companies by referring to the latter as "capital associations of a corporative character." As such, the early joint stock companies were an alternative form of business organization to the regulated companies which had a business structure evolved along the lines of the medieval guilds. Unlike joint stock companies where capital contributions were combined and subject to the control of a single management, the regulated companies were associations of independent traders and merchants, each with their own independent capital, operating under a grant of monopoly in a specific type of trade. The Fellowship of Merchant Adventurers was an important example of an English regulated company.

Joint stock companies differed in a number of significant ways from modern publicly traded corporations. As late as the eighteenth century, transferability of joint stock shares was restricted in various ways. For example, there was a process requiring approval and registration of new shareholders. In addition, many of the earlier joint stock companies were involved in long-distance trade, with paid-in capital being dispersed together with any profits after the completion of a voyage. Sometimes profits were distributed in the form of goods such as spice. Increases in capital were usually achieved by making calls on existing shareholders, rather than issuing new shares. It was during the seventeenth century that joint stock companies with modern features started to emerge (Parker 1974). Starting with the creation of the Dutch East India Company (VOC) in 1602, these more modern joint stock companies included ready transferability of shares, a permanent capital stock, profits-only distributed as dividends and new capital requirements being raised by new stock issues (see table 2.1).

Table 2.1 Timeline for intellectual and historical events, 1602–1776

1602	Formation of Dutch East Indies Company (VOC); shares start trading in Amsterdam
1618–48	Thirty Years War, last of the major religious wars in Europe, decimates Germany
1637	Rene Descartes publishes the *Discourses*
1660	The British Restoration of Charles II
1662	John Graunt publishes *Natural and Political Observations*
1671	J. de Witt submits the *Value of Life Annuities* to the Dutch States General
1687	Isaac Newton publishes first edition of the *Principia*
1688	Glorious Revolution in Britain; J. de la Vega publishes *Confusion des Confusiones*
1693	Edmond Halley publishes "An Estimate of the Degrees of Mortality"
1694	Bank of England founded
1719–20	John Law's Mississippi Scheme in France
1720	South Sea Bubble in England
1725	A. de Moivre publishes first edition of *Annuties Upon Lives*
1761	Thomas Mortimer publishes first edition of *Everyman His Own Broker*
1771	Richard Price publishes first edition of *Observations on Reversionary Payments*
1776	Adam Smith publishes *Wealth of Nations*; American Declaration of Independence

Starting with the trading of VOC shares on the Amsterdam bourse at the beginning of the seventeenth century, joint stocks proved to be an excellent trading vehicle for the merchants populating the bourses. Shares were allocated a designated area within the bourse and were traded alongside a range of other commodities such as spice goods and copper. Even though there was sporadic trading in Dutch West Indies Company shares and selected Dutch government debt issues, VOC shares were the primary security being traded. During the seventeenth century, the Amsterdam share market achieved an extremely sophisticated level of development featuring both forward and option transactions. In addition, possibly as early as 1640, the *rescontre* system of clearing and settling accounts was perfected. This system used quarterly settlement intervals that permitted payment of differences and allowed for "continuations," similar to the operations of a clearing house at a modern futures exchange.

The emergence and growth of joint stocks was accompanied by considerable public discussion and debate which is captured in the pamphlet literature and parliamentary records of the time. However, unlike the pricing theories for fixed income securities that were relatively well developed by the end of the seventeenth century, much of the analysis of joint stock companies was concerned with describing manipulative trading practices by stockjobbers and proposing remedies for the "infamous practice," rather than with developing methods of security valuation. For example, di Marchi and Harrison (1994) describe the seventeenth-century Dutch pamphlet literature which attacked the practice of short selling securities that were not owned by the individual making the short sale. Against the polemical backdrop of the pamphlet literature can be found a number of interesting anomalies that stand out as early classics of security analysis: Joseph de la Vega's *Confusion de Confusiones* (1688) and Thomas Mortimer's *Everyman His Own Broker* (1761).

To say that *Confusion de Confusiones* is an isolated gem in the history of financial economics is an understatement. The book itself is an oddity, initially written in Spanish, published in Amsterdam by a Jewish writer of Portuguese descent. Joseph de la Vega was the second son in a family of four sons and six daughters. His parents were Isaac Penso and Esther de la Vega. Though his formal name was Joseph Penso de la Vega Passarinho, according to custom he typically used the shortened name derived from his mother. Isaac Penso was born in Spain though the family's ancestral roots appear to have been in Portugal. As was the case with many Jews in seventeenth-century Spain, the Inquisition produced a forced emigration and his parents moved first to Antwerp, then Hamburg and finally Amsterdam. Joseph was likely born sometime around 1650, soon after the family had relocated to northern Europe.

Isaac Penso achieved success as a banker in Amsterdam and became a prominent member of the local community. Though Jews in Amsterdam were relatively unrestricted in comparison to almost all other cities, there were still considerable barriers to Jewish participation in various trades. However, Jews were permitted to engage in activities such as wholesale trading in goods, shipping and banking functions such as money lending and money changing. Some Jews were also permitted to engage in brokering. Not surprisingly, Jews were central players in the business of trading stocks. Anecdotal evidence indicates that as much as 85% of Amsterdam stock trading circa 1700 was in the hands of Jews, many of whom were of Iberian descent.[15] Based on this, de la Vega was in an excellent situation to gather the type of information needed to write a detailed account of stock trading on the seventeenth-century Amsterdam bourse.

Confusion de Confusiones is written as four dialogues between a shareholder, a philosopher and a merchant. Each dialogue describes different features of the activities of the Amsterdam bourse in the later seventeenth century. In *Confusion*, de la Vega (1688, p. 156) demonstrates a modern understanding of the use of fundamental information to value stocks:

> The price of shares [in the Dutch East India Company] is now 580 . . . it seems to me that they will climb to a much higher price due to extensive cargoes that are expected from India, because of the good business of the Company, of the reputation of its goods, of the prospective dividends and of the peace in Europe.

Recognizing the uncertainties in seaborne trade and the difficulty in obtaining information about incoming cargoes, de la Vega goes on to describe how some traders could profitably trade on information about incoming cargoes from the East. He correctly recognizes that such information alone is insufficient but would depend also on European conditions and the safe arrival and unloading of cargo.

Modern Finance typically models the security valuation problem as determining the discounted value of expected future cash flows. This reliance of the valuation problem on expectations is explicitly recognized by de la Vega (1688, p. 165), who gives this story an additional twist:

> The expectation of an event creates a much deeper impression upon the exchange than the event itself. When large dividends or rich imports are expected, shares will rise in price; but

if the expectation becomes a reality, the shares often fall; for the joy over the favourable development and the jubilation over a lucky chance have abated in the meantime.

Recognizing that there are "natural reasons for this phenomenon," de la Vega attributes this share pricing behavior to a struggle between bulls and bears over market sentiment: "the leaves tremble in the softest breeze, and the smallest shadow causes fear."[16]

In the second dialogue, de la Vega (pp. 158–9) provides four useful rules to guide investment activities in shares: "The first principle: . . . Never give anyone the advice to buy or sell shares . . . The second principle: Take every gain without showing remorse about missed profits . . . The third principle: Profits on the exchange are the treasure of goblins . . . The fourth principle: Whoever wishes to win in this game must have patience and money." Variations of the second and third of these principles could easily pass as commonsense advice given to modern security traders. The fourth principle is evidence that de la Vega, an astute seventeenth-century observer of stock trading, was an adherent to "long-run investment strategies." Combining this fourth principle with de la Vega's recognition of the importance of fundamental information anticipates the approach to security investment pioneered by Benjamin Graham more than two hundred and fifty years later.

Even though de la Vega identifies how the price of joint stocks can be determined by fundamental information, much of his dialogue is taken up in a description of how prices will deviate from the fundamental values based on the expectations of bulls and bears. In particular, the last of the four dialogues is concerned with detailing methods of market manipulation: "the acme of Exchange operations, the craftiest and most complicated machinations which exist in the maze of the Exchange and which require the greatest possible cunning" (*Confusion*, p. 191). The manipulation of securities markets in the seventeenth and eighteenth centuries was facilitated by the social practice of using securities for purposes of gambling. This practice was in keeping with the widespread public acceptance of gambling reflected, for example, in the use of lotteries to increase the attractiveness of government debt operations (Daston 1988; Cohen 1953).

In contrast to the almost voluminous discussion of the nefarious practice of stockjobbing, eighteenth-century English publications dealing with the use of security analysis to value joint stocks are relatively scarce. The success of *Every Man His Own Broker* by Thomas Mortimer speaks to the lack of such a guide prior to this time. Originally published in 1761 with a further 14 editions to follow, the last being in 1807, the book was intended as a practical guide to investors seeking to make investment in the English security market without the aid of a broker. Cope (1978) describes *Every Man His Own Broker* as the first detailed account of the English stock market. Mortimer was compelled to write the book based on his experiences from dealing on his own at Jonathan's without a broker in order to save the cost of brokerage. As a result of these activities, Mortimer managed to lose a "genteel fortune" and, in the process, acquired a genuine hostility to stockjobbers and other such speculators. The book goes far beyond the basic objective of being a how-to-book for trading in the British funds to provide numerous insights on the workings of the English stock market.

A constant theme in *Every Man* is the need to be wary of "this medley of Barbers, Bakers, Butchers, Shoe-makers, Plasterers, and Taylors, whom the mammon of unrighteousness has transformed into Stock-Brokers" (p. xiii). This wariness is not to be restricted to tradesman turned stock brokers, for even stock brokers from the higher ranks of society can be corrupted as "both ancient and modern history, furnishes us with many remarkable instances of the basest actions being committed by men of high rank, and the most exalted stations in government, for smaller pecuniary advantages than those which might arise in cases here supposed" (p. 45). As for the types of advice to be suspected Mortimer observes: "Always suspect the man who wants to engage you to be continually changing the situation of your money, to be influenced by some private motive, unless you are a JOBBER yourself" (pp. 22–3). Similarly, Mortimer also advises: "it is almost impossible for a broker, to give any gentleman, candid disinterested advice, when to buy into, or sell out of, the funds" (p. xvi).

As for the specific topic of joint stock valuation, Mortimer (1761, p. 9) states:

> Every original share of a trading company's STOCK must greatly increase in value, in proportion to the advantages arising from the commerce they are engaged in; and such is the nature of trade in general, that it either considerably increases, or falls into decline; and nothing can be a greater proof of a company's trade being in a flourishing condition, than when their credit is remarkably good, and the original shares in their stock will sell at a considerable premium.

This reference to stock selling at a premium harkens back to a time when stock was issued with a par value. Writing at a time when accounting information for publicly traded securities was cursory, at best, Mortimer suggests that the ability of a firm to borrow was an important signal of fundamental value. In modern times, this could be translated into a statement about factors that would provide a basis for a firm to access credit markets such as the credit rating as well as the state of a firm's balance sheet and debt service capacity. Mortimer also makes reference to the type of "advantages" of the particular business of the firm. This hints at the sector specific approach to common stock investing which is pervasive in the modern security industry.

Mortimer proceeds to explain this general valuation approach using one of the important British public companies, the British East India Company, as an example:

> This, for instance, has always been, and still is the case of EAST INDIA STOCK in particular, not to instance any other. The present price of a share of £100 in the company's stock is £134. The reason of this advance on what cost the original proprietor only £100 is, that the company, by the profits they have made in trade, are enabled to pay £6 *per annum* interest or dividend for £100 share. But then it is uncertain how long they may continue to make so large an annual dividend, especially in time of war; for several circumstances may occur (though it is not likely they should) that may molest their trade in their settlements, and diminish their profits.

It follows that Mortimer subscribed to the view that share price was driven by the sustainable level of dividend payout that, in turn, was affected by the various factors driving firm profitability. The dividend level is implicitly being compared to the prevailing level of interest rates. Dividends, firm profitability and interest rates drive stock valuation. This view is an early precursor of what, in modern times, is referred to as fundamental analysis.[17]

Perhaps the most interesting view presented in *Every Man* concerns Mortimer's views on the superiority of fixed income investments over joint stocks. For example (pp. 20–1):

> That shares in annuities, bought at a great discount, that is to say, greatly under par, are the cheapest and most advantageous to the purchaser; and considerably more profitable than any STOCKS bought at a high premium. Because the probability of the premium (given on any STOCK) totally subsiding, is infinitely greater, than that the low price at present given for a *3 per cent Annuities*, should fall much lower; and there is a greater probability of their rising, and a greater likelyhood of its continuance, than there is, the premium now given on any STOCK should rise much higher, or continue so high as it is, for any number of years; therefore shares in STOCKS that bear a premium, are the dearest; and shares in funds or annuities under par, the cheapest to purchase.

Though difficult to translate into modern terms due to the differing characteristics of today's security markets and those of eighteenth-century England, Mortimer is clearly arguing in favor of the superiority of fixed income investment over stocks when interest rates are high relative to long term level of interest rates. This echoes the modern views of individuals in the trade such as Bill Gross of PIMCO Funds questioning the prevailing view that stock returns will outperform bond returns in the long run.

Reminiscences of the US stock operators

Much as in more modern times, the literature on security analysis of the late nineteenth and early twentieth centuries is populated by two general types of contributions. On the one hand, are the works written by academics, designed primarily to appeal to other academics. Included in this grouping are contributions by Irving Fisher, Edgar Smith, John Maynard Keynes and John Burr Williams.[18] On the other hand, are the contributions from those in the trade and the financial press, such as Henry Clews (1908), Alexander Noyes (Klein 2001), Edwin Lefèvre (1923) and Hartley Withers (1911). Though these contributions were aimed at a broad audience, the best of the contributions contain fundamental insights about views on security analysis and investment strategy prevailing at that time. Even though some members of the academic grouping, such as Irving Fisher and J.M. Keynes, did make some contributions that could easily be included in the second grouping, there is generally a different flavor to the contributions of the two groupings.

This dichotomy between academic and trade publications serves to reinforce the importance and relevance of Graham and Dodd (1934): a book written by individuals with academic standing that is fundamentally concerned with the types of problems that are at the core of what practitioners do. Graham and Dodd (1934) redefined the role of academics in relation to the practice of security analysis. Benjamin Graham (1894–1976), the senior author of the book, was well suited to this task. Born in London in 1894 as Benjamin Grossbaum, he immigrated to the US in 1895. Following an undergraduate education at Columbia, Graham graduated in 1914 and went to work at the Wall Street firm of Newburger, Henderson, and Loeb, performing mostly lower level tasks. By 1920, Graham had worked his way up to partner. During the 1920s, Graham went on to form a number of investment firms in which he was a principal. It was a keen mind and a wealth of market experience that Graham brought to his classes at Columbia. Starting in 1928, Graham was a part-time instructor of investment classes at Columbia University. It was in one of these classes that David Dodd was a student.

To appreciate the importance of Graham and Dodd (1934) for the development of security analysis as a subject, it is useful to recognize what had been written up to that time and to recount some historical background. With this in mind, it is not easy to pick a starting point for a discussion of the relevant contributions from those in the trade and financial press. In general, the published contributions chronologically increase in depth and understanding of security valuation issues. This development is roughly consistent with the growth of New York as the world's financial capital. As late as the 1820s, Philadelphia had as strong a claim as New York to be the nation's financial capital. In the period before the Civil War, London was still, by far, the world's dominant securities market. Even with the sizeable influx of funding issues associated with the war, around 1866 London still had a market cap of some $10 billion compared to $3 billion for New York (Gordon 1999, p. 123).

From the beginning of trading in joint stocks, a range of trade publications covering a number of different facets of security analysis and the securities industry have appeared. One type of publication is articles in the business press. In the US, the *Commercial and Financial Chronicle* was a key source until it was superseded by the *Wall Street Journal* (first published in 1884).[19] The business section of the major newspapers, such as the *New York Times* in the US and the *London Times* in England, also are important sources. As daily or weekly publications, these sources did not usually proceed much beyond a focus on current events. Though this often involved discussion about the valuation of specific stock issues, there was no scope to present a reasoned development for the methods of security valuation. Much like a business reporter today, the financial reporter would gather information from those involved in the trade knowledgeable about security analysis as it pertained to the topic of the interest.

Almost from the beginning of securities trading in the US, it is evident from some of the articles in the financial press that the practice of security analysis was more than rudimentary. This is not that surprising when it is recognized that market practices in the US were transplanted from European centers, such as London and Amsterdam, where there was more than a century of prior development in securities trading. Despite the availability of expertise in the industry, before Graham and Dodd there is no source which systematically develops the techniques of security analysis. This does not mean that the methods of security analysis being used at the time are completely unknown today; rather, much of the information is contained in studies that are biographical or autobiographical accounts of those involved in the industry, such as Henry Clews *Fifty Years on Wall Street* (1908) or Edwin Lefèvre *Reminiscences of a Stock Operator* (1923). There are also insightful accounts of the securities being traded such as Hartley Withers *Stocks and Shares* (1911).

In examining the various stories and accounts of the activities of market participants, it is possible to go back as far as, say, 1792 when the 21 individual brokers and 3 firms signed the Buttonwood Agreement "not to buy or sell from this day for any person whatsoever any kind of Public Stock, at a rate less than one quarter per cent Commission on the specie value, and that we will give preference to each other in our negotiations." This arrangement was eventually to evolve into the New York Stock Exchange (NYSE), a title that was introduced in 1863 as a name change for the Regular Board of the New York Stock and Exchange Board. The New York Stock Exchange emerged as the dominant exchange for trading stocks in New York with its merger with the Open Board of Brokers in 1869 (Gordon 1999, pp. 95, 124–5). The New York Stock and Exchange Board, formed in 1817 (Eames 1894, p. 18), could trace its pedigree to the Buttonwood Agreement. The Open Board was a relative newcomer that flourished in the face of the flood of issues arising from the Civil War.

Until the emergence of a dominant exchange, stock trading in New York was scattered across a range of venues. For example, in 1856 Gordon (1999, p. 87) reports there were 360 railroad stocks, 985 bank stocks, 75 insurance stocks, in addition to hundreds of corporate, municipal, state and federal bonds and other types of stocks being traded in New York. Of these most were not traded on the New York Stock and Exchange Board, the lineal precursor of the NYSE, as the Board did not trade new and untested issues. These issues were curb traded. The primary venue for curb trading was various lamp posts in the Wall Street area where brokers who were not Board members, as well as some Board members, would meet to trade securities. Though the volume of curb trading was usually higher than trading on the Board, the market cap of curb issues was lower. In contrast, to curb trading, activities of the Board were conducted at daily auctions which were held in fixed quarters.

The tales of American stock operators predate the Buttonwood Agreement. Notoriety was, and still is, the result of doing something on a grand scale, often in conjunction with a massive bull market speculation, or the creation of a colossal conglomerate or the execution of an immense market manipulation. An early example is William Duer who was at the center of a 1791–92 speculative scheme to inflate the value of bank stocks, particularly the Bank of New York (Gordon 1999, pp. 40–5). The scheme was based on leveraged speculation and trading on insider information. At the height of the speculative frenzy, a number of banks were incorporated that, ultimately, did not open. As such, these stocks represent an early US instance of bull market "paper hanging." The collapse of the scheme resulted in the bankruptcy of many of the players, including Duer. The scheme prompted Alexander Hamilton to write: "'Tis time there should be a line of separation between honest Men and knaves, between respectable Stockholders and dealers in the funds, and mere unprincipled Gamblers." This seeking of the line of separation is a task that has occupied regulators up to the present day.

The formation of the New York Stock and Exchange Board in 1817 also marks the beginning of the Wall Street career of Jacob Little, the first of a long line of big-time Wall Street speculative operators (Gordon 1999, pp. 59–62, 89–90). Unlike Duer who only used Wall Street as a trading venue, Little made a career on Wall Street. Though Little was also a broker, gaining membership to the Board in 1825, it is his activities as a speculator that made his reputation. Little's trading strategies were typically short-term, aimed at anticipating market movements. During his career, Little made and lost four fortunes in speculative trading activities. In the end, he was unable to recover from his last insolvency brought on by the market panic of 1857. From that time, until his death a few years later, Little ended his Wall Street career as a trader of penny stocks and odd lots.

Though Little was primarily a short seller, he made his first fortune in a 1834 short squeeze involving the Morris Canal and Banking Company. The objective of a short squeeze in a stock issue is to gain control of the quantity of that stock available for trading (the "float" or "floating supply") at a time when a sizeable amount of stock has been sold short by traders who do not have a sufficient amount of stock to deliver. As was the case in the squeeze on Morris Canal and Banking, the capital requirements for gaining control of the stock for delivery usually involved a group or pool of speculators operating in concert. When the time comes for the short to make delivery of the stock, the short has to enter the market to buy – but there is no supply available because the short squeezers have already gained control. The result is a rapid rise in stock prices as short sellers bid up prices to tempt new supply onto the market (either from accounts of long-term investors or from the short squeezers). At Little's time, most short sellers were brokers that had sold stock they did not own to investors, speculators or other brokers. The short position was sometimes the outcome of longer settlement periods than in modern times. In other cases, the objective of both parties was to engage in speculative forward trading, resulting in delivery dates on the short that could be many months in the future.

Prior to the wide reaching regulatory reforms of 1933–34, stock market self-regulation was an important theme of government policy toward the securities market. Yet, self-regulation suffered from the conflicting interests of the legitimate brokers, who recognized the negative impact associated with widespread unscrupulous trading activities, and the big-time speculators, who saw the market as a conduit for achieving big profits from a range of trading schemes. Many practices that are illegal in modern markets were considered fair game, such as trading on insider information or the formation of pools to engage in trading activities aimed at creating price movements favorable to speculation on stock price changes. The process of reform using self-regulation was slow and problematic. It was not until November 1868, just prior to the merger of the Open Board and the New York Stock and Exchange Board, that registration of securities and 30 days notice of new issues was required of companies listed on the two Boards.

The imposition of the listing requirement had an immediate impact on the activities of the big-time speculators, Daniel Drew, Jay Gould and James Fisk, involving the Erie Railway. The 1864–9 manipulations associated with the securities of the Erie are almost epic, reflecting the state of securities markets of that time. On one side of the struggle was "Commodore" Cornelius Vanderbilt, a giant in the transportation industry, who wanted to control the Erie in order to be able to control the pricing of railway freight rates into and out of New York City. On the other side was a group including Drew, Gould, Fisk and other big-time speculators who were seeking to control the Erie as a vehicle for making speculative gains through manipulation of the company's security issues. The machinations of the two camps has been captured in some of the early classics of business finance, e.g., Adams and Adams, *Chapters of Erie* (1871) and Henry Clews, *Fifty Years on Wall Street* (1908). The struggle between these two groups is the epitome of the problems that prevailed in securities markets of that time, e.g., Medbery (1870, ch. 9), Gordon (1999, ch. 6).

Vanderbilt was concerned with securities markets only as a vehicle for creating and managing a business empire, primarily involving railways. As part of the ongoing process of expanding this empire, Vanderbilt moved to acquire a controlling position on the Erie board of directors during the late summer and early fall of 1867. Vanderbilt had been involved with the Erie as recently as 1865, when he resigned from the board over concerns about the evident manipulations in the stock that took place during 1864–5. A major player in these manipulations was Daniel Drew, also a board member who, conveniently, served as treasurer. In his position as treasurer, Drew was able to issue securities, and in 1866 had done so by loaning the company $3.5 million in exchange for 28,000 unissued shares and $3 million in convertible bonds that had the provision that the 30,000 shares obtained from conversion could be reconverted back into convertible bonds. This provided Drew with the ability to expand and then contract about 10% of the outstanding stock – providing effective control of the floating supply.

When Vanderbilt was unsuccessful in using his influence to control the Erie board of directors, starting in January 1868 he moved to gain control of the company by making purchases of as much of the outstanding stock as could be obtained. The speculators saw this as an opportunity to issue more convertible bonds that became a conduit to print stock certificates that were then sold to Vanderbilt. From late February to mid-March, Drew and his group were able to sell 100,000 newly issued shares. The absence of registration and listing requirements prevented the New York Stock and Exchange Board from knowing what was happening. All this was set against a backdrop of corrupt judges issuing injunctions and arrest warrants and legislators being bribed to pass laws favorable to one or the other of these groups. On April 19, Vanderbilt was able to strike a deal with Drew, Gould and Fisk and recoup his potential losses from his stock dealing. Following this, Gould and Fisk continued to manipulate Erie stock issues, until the listing and registration requirements were introduced by the two Boards. Gould attempted to resist the requirements, even trying to establish a new exchange for the purposes of trading Erie stock. In September 1869, Gould capitulated and agreed to the new regulations. At that time, it was revealed that the number of Erie shares outstanding was around 700,000, about double the 351,000 shares outstanding at the time of the Vanderbilt agreement of April 1868.

To modern observers, events surrounding the Erie have the appearance of a classical farce. A business titan attempting to rest control of a railway company in order to implement a pricing cartel enters battle with a group of big time speculators seeking to use the company as a vehicle for generating profits from stock price manipulation. Drew, Gould and Fisk are usually lumped in with Andrew Carnegie, J.D. Rockefeller and Commodore Vanderbilt and recognized as the "robber barons" who dominated American industry through their financial dealings in the 1870–90 period, e.g., Geisst (1997, ch. 3). The activities of the robber barons took place against a backdrop of increasing concentration of economic power in the hands of the trusts such as American Telephone and Telegraph, General Electric, Standard Oil and the American Tobacco Company. The trusts were formed largely as a way of dealing with the legal restriction that corporations had up to around 1900 that prevented the holding of stock of other corporations. During the 1890s there were about fifty trusts operating throughout the US, involving most of the major industries. This number includes some agricultural trusts that were concentrated primarily in the south.

Trusts were formed as a legal device largely to circumvent state corporation laws that restricted the ability of a corporation to expand using mergers and takeovers. Prior to the changes in state corporation law that started with New Jersey during the 1890s, the ability of a corporation to act as a holding company was quite limited. Trusts provided a legal avenue around these restrictions. In a trust, the companies being merged or taken over would exchange the common shares in the original corporations for trust certificates that possessed a claim to earnings of the trust as well as voting rights to elect the trustees that ran the trust. Standard Oil, for example, had nine trustees. Trust certificates traded like common stocks on the stock exchanges. The trust was a useful legal mechanism for the takeover ambitions of the emerging industrialists. Instead of having to issue new shares to raise new capital for a takeover, trusts could pay for the takeover using trust certificates or internal sources of funds.

Due to changes in various state corporation laws, the trusts had a relatively short lifespan. The legal status of trusts did not prevent various states from initiating legal actions under other grounds, such as the common law restrictions on monopoly, aimed at preventing the increasing monopolization of specific industries. In addition, the public perception of economic and social problems posed by the trusts were addressed in 1890 with the passage of the Sherman Anti-Trust Act. Though this Act did not result in many successful prosecutions, it did provide a federal definition and jurisdiction for what constituted a monopoly. The trusts gradually reorganized as holding companies and trust certificates were replaced by common shares. Standard Oil, for example, completed the shift in 1899. Whether it was trading in trust certificates or the common shares, the changes in American industrial structure were good for Wall Street. The importance of trading in shares of these industrial companies gradually came to surpass the railroads. The volume and value of trade on the NYSE doubled between 1875 and 1885 with more growth on the horizon.

Yet, despite the growth, the securities markets of that era justly deserved the public perception as a speculator's haven. Henry Clews (1908, p. 19), a veteran broker and investment advisor with fifty years experience on Wall Street from 1857 to 1907, provides an informed view of "How to Make Money on Wall Street":

> To the question often put, especially by men outside of Wall Street, "How can I make money in Wall Street?" there is probably no better answer than the one given by old Meyer Rothschild to a person who asked him a similar question. He said, "I buys 'sheep' and sells 'dear'."
>
> Those who follow this method always succeed. There has hardly been a year within my recollection, going back nearly thirty years, when there has not been two or three squalls in "the Street," during the year, when it was possible to purchase stocks below their intrinsic value. The squall usually passes over in a few days, and then the lucky buyers of stocks at panic prices come in for their profits ranging from five to ten per cent on the entire venture.
>
> The question of making money, then becomes a mere matter of calculation, depending on the number of squalls that may occur during any particular year.
>
> If the venture is made at the right time – at the lucky moment so to speak – and each successive venture is fortunate, as happens often to those who use their judgment in the best way, it is possible to realize a net gain of fifty per cent. per annum on the aggregate of the year's investments.

Coming from an individual so intimately connected to the dealings of "the Street," it is difficult to deny the essential role played by speculation in US securities markets of the time. Given the numerous abuses associated with common stocks, the disposition of the small investor to favor bonds over stocks during this period is understandable.

Many of the systemic problems raised by the predominance of speculators in securities markets persisted until the regulatory reforms following the Great Depression. The introduction of legislation such as the Securities Act (1933) involved a radical realignment of the federal government's role in securities markets. The collapse of securities markets from late 1929 to early 1933 was sufficient to end the period of self-regulation that had largely governed securities trading up to that time. Yet, the period of self-regulation was not without contributions. Many of the tools needed to lay the foundation that Graham and Dodd used to launch security analysis had evolved without government intervention. The growth of securities markets witnessed the emergence of professionals who made their living in the market and had a vested interest in making sure the game was played, if not always fairly, at least according to accepted rules. For example, the listing and registration requirements imposed by the newly formed NYSE were a direct assault on Jay Gould's manipulations of Erie Railroad Company securities.

A key element in self-regulation involved the availability of accurate information. It was during the 1890s that the New York Stock Exchange required listed companies to produce annual reports. Though, even with this change, many of the annual reports that were produced did not have much substance by modern standards, the rise of the professional investment advisor necessitated that some useful information be made available. Though much of the literature of the time is largely concerned with pontificating on the good or evil of speculation, or glorifying the deeds of the big-time speculators or documenting use of the securities market to propel the rise of a business titan, the financial press did spearhead a number of important innovations. Of particular importance is the introduction of the indexes to measure the performance of the stock market. The introduction and subsequent use of indexes represents a major advance in the sophistication of market participants. Though there were some other indexes around previously, it is Charles Dow (1851–1902) who is often credited with being the father of the modern stock market index. Dow is also important in having, together with Edward Jones and Charles Bergstresser, founded Dow Jones & Co., the company that created the *Wall Street Journal.*

Charles Dow is a caricature of the changes that were taking place in the US securities markets of the later nineteenth century. Dow was a lifelong newspaper journalist who converted to financial news after covering a mining story for the *Providence Journal* in 1879. Dow was able to achieve success in financial reporting by feeding the growing need for information to do security analysis. In 1880, Dow moved to New York where he started with a stint reporting on mining stocks. In 1882, he joined together with Edward Jones, a fellow reporter from his days in Providence who also had relocated to New York, to form Dow Jones & Company. With offices behind a soda shop located next door to the entrance of the New York Stock Exchange, the main activity of the company was to collect and distribute "flimsies" or "slips" containing market news of the day. It was in this "Customers Afternoon Newsletter" that on July 3, 1884 the first version of the index appeared. The price-weighted average was calculated by summing the prices of the stocks in the index and dividing by the number of stocks.

According to Siegel (1998, p. 55), Dow began publishing a daily index of actively traded, high capitalization stocks starting in February of 1885. The original index contained 10 railways and 2 industrials. This collection was roughly consistent with the importance that railway stocks played in the stock market of that era. Dow expanded the index four years later to cover 18 railways and 2 industrials. The same year, Dow Jones & Co. started the *Wall Street Journal*. At this time the *Commercial and Financial Chronicle* was the most important financial newspaper. (Judging from accounts of Richard Wyckoff (1930, p. 44), the *Chronicle* continued to be the leading source of financial news until after Dow's death.) Recognizing the importance of the emerging industrial sector, in May 1896 Dow changed the index to a 12-stock index of industrial stocks. The first version of the Dow Jones Industrial Average appeared in the *Wall Street Journal* in October 1896. The index of 20 railway stocks, the precursor of the modern Dow Transportation Index, was renamed the Rail Average.

The original 12 stocks of the Dow Jones Industrial Average (DJIA) reflect the nature of the stock market at that time (see table 2.2). The stocks were: American Cotton Oil, American Sugar, American Tobacco, Chicago Gas, Distilling and Cattle Feeding, General Electric, Laclede Gas, National Lead, North American, Tennessee Coal and Iron, US Leather and US Rubber. All but US Leather survives today in some form, though only General Electric remains in the DJIA. In 1916, the DJIA was expanded to 20 stocks and to 30 stocks in 1928. The use of 30 stocks has continued up to the present day. Only three stocks (American Sugar, General Electric and US Rubber) of the original 12 appear in 1916, with 7 of the 20 from 1916 appearing in 1928. Oddly enough, American Tobacco and North American reappear in 1928 after being left off the 1916 list. This reflects the ongoing practice, still used today, to update the average to reflect the changing composition of trading, market capitalization and industrial composition of the leading common stocks.[20] The current 30 DJIA stock listings, together with some trading information, are given in table 2.3.

Irving Fisher, stock valuation and the 1929 crash

The roots of modern Finance can arguably be traced back to Irving Fisher. As time has advanced, a tendency has emerged to start the chronology of modern Finance in 1952 with the Markowitz portfolio diversification model, e.g., Markowitz (1999). Given the substantive institutional changes in securities markets that have taken place since World War II, this tendency is understandable. However, Fisher's seminal contributions spanned so many related areas, from index numbers to the theory of interest to the use of mathematical analysis in valuation problems, that Fisher can reasonably be identified as having laid the foundations for the theoretical superstructure that dominates the landscape of Finance. Siegel (1998, p. 44), for example, refers to Fisher as "the founder of modern capital theory." Yet, Fisher's importance to security analysis extends beyond his academic contributions. Fisher harks back to an era when leading academics, such as J.M. Keynes, also played important roles outside the academic realm. In addition to

Table 2.2 Components of the Dow Jones Industrial Average: 1896, 1916, 1928 and 1997

1896	1916	1928	1997
American Cotton Oil	American Beet Sugar	Allied Chemical	Allied-Signal
American Sugar	American Can	American Can	Aluminum Co. of
American Tobacco	American Car & Foundry	American Smelting	America
Chicago Gas	American Locomotive	American Sugar	American Express
Distilling & Cattle	American Smelting	American Tobacco	American Tel & Tel
Feeding	American Sugar	Atlantic Refining	Boeing
General Electric	American Tel & Tel	Bethlehem Steel	Caterpillar
Laclede Gas	Anaconda Copper	Chrysler	Chevron
National Lead	Baldwin Locomotive	General Electric	Coca-Cola
North American	Central Leather	General Motors	Du Pont
Tennessee Coal	General Electric	General Railway Sig.	Eastman Kodak
and Iron	Goodrich	Goodrich	Exxon
US Leather pfd.	Republic Iron & Steel	International Harvester	General Electric
US Rubber	Studebaker	International Nickel	General Motors
	Texas Co.	Mack Trucks	Goodyear
	US Rubber	Nash Motors	Hewlett-Packard
	US Steel	North American	IBM
	Utah Copper	Paramount Publix	International Paper
	Westinghouse	Postum, Inc.	J.P. Morgan
	Western Union	Radio Corp.	Johnson & Johnson
		Sears, Roebuck	McDonald's
		Standard Oil (NJ)	Merck
		Texas Corp.	Minn. Mining
		Texas Gulf Sulphur	Philip Morris
		Union Carbide	Procter & Gamble
		US Steel	Sears Roebuck
		Victor Talking Machine	Travelers Group
		Westinghouse Electric	Union Carbide
		Woolworth	United Technologies
		Wright Aeronautical	WalMart
			Walt Disney

writing investment newsletters and giving speeches to business leaders on financial topics, Fisher also started a profitable card indexing firm based on an invention that he had patented. Prior to the stock market collapse of 1929, his personal net worth was around $10 million.[21]

Based on this background, it is somewhat unfortunate that, in the annals of securities analysis, Fisher is most remembered for comments and prognostications made just prior to the stock market collapse of 1929 and in the following year, e.g., Fisher (1930). Siegel (1998, pp. 43–44) provides a lively description of a most telling incident:

> It was a seasonably cool Monday evening on October 14, 1929 when Irving Fisher arrived at the Builders' Exchange Club at 2 Park Avenue in New York City. Fisher, a professor of

Table 2.3 Stocks in the Dow Jones Industrial Average, September 5, 2003, 4.30 pm, EST

Company Name	Ticker	Price	Change	% change	Volume
3M Co	MMM	138.68	−1.32	−0.94	2,633,500
Alcoa	AA	27.99	−0.10	−0.36	2,748,100
Altria Group	MO	41.50	−0.28	−0.67	4,395,300
American Express	AXP	45.20	−0.29	−0.64	2,747,400
AT&T Corp	T	22.69	0.17	0.75	4,350,200
Boeing Co	BA	37.16	−0.73	−1.93	3,939,900
Caterpillar Inc	CAT	70.13	−0.96	−1.35	3,828,500
Citigroup Inc.	C	44.34	−0.07	−0.16	10,245,700
Coca-Cola Co.	KO	44.15	−0.35	−0.79	3,837,700
Disney (Walt) Co.	DIS	21.19	−0.27	−1.26	7,479,100
Du Pont (EI)	DD	44.37	−0.08	−0.18	2,628,800
Eastman Kodak	EK	28.80	−0.50	−1.71	3,025,600
Exxon Mobil Corp	XOM	37.97	−0.19	−0.50	8,708,600
General Electric	GE	31.04	−0.28	−0.89	18,545,900
General Motors	GM	41.71	−0.76	−1.79	6,090,700
Hewlett-Packard	HPQ	20.23	−0.55	−2.65	13,569,000
Home Depot inc	HD	33.76	−0.48	−1.40	11,734,700
Honeywell Intl	HON	29.68	0.23	0.78	4,476,900
IBM	IBM	86.95	−0.96	−1.09	7,896,800
Intel Corp	INTC	28.71	0.11	0.38	68,483,289
Intl Paper Co.	IP	39.65	−0.29	−0.73	1,879,400
Johnson & Johnson	JNJ	50.50	−0.62	−1.21	6,486,000
JP Morgan Chase	JPM	34.19	−0.49	−1.41	6,752,900
McDonalds Corp.	MCD	23.30	−0.09	−0.38	5,618,500
Merck & Co.	MRK	51.00	0.40	0.79	5,987,900
Microsoft Corp.	MSFT	28.38	−0.05	−0.18	64,049,179
Procter & Gamble	PG	90.98	−0.45	−0.49	3,960,000
SBC Communications	SBC	23.00	−0.12	−0.52	7,321,800
United Tech Corp.	UTX	78.05	−1.43	−1.80	2,943,900
Wal-Mart Stores	WMT	58.89	−1.19	−1.98	10,593,500

economics at Yale University and the most renowned economist of his time, was scheduled to address the monthly meeting of the Purchasing Agents Association . . . Members of the association and the press crowded into the meeting room. Fisher's speech was mainly designed to defend investment trusts, the forerunner of today's mutual funds. But the audience was most eager to hear his views on the stock market.

Investors had been nervous since early September when Roger Babson, businessman and market seer, predicted a "terrific" crash in stock prices. Fisher had dismissed this pessimism, noting that Babson had been bearish for some time. But the public sought to be reassured by the great man who had championed stocks for so long.

The audience was not disappointed. After a few introductory remarks, Fisher uttered a sentence that, much to his regret, became one of the most quoted phrases in stock market history: "Stock prices have reached what looks like a permanently high plateau."

On October 29, two weeks to the day after Fisher's speech, stocks crashed. Fisher's "high plateau" transformed into a bottomless abyss.

Keen to promote the notion of "Stocks for the Long Run," Siegel is something of an apologist for Fisher. The depth of Fisher's misconceptions are not adequately explored or recognized. For example, the actual quote by Fisher could be more accurately given as: "Stocks have reached what looks like a permanently high plateau . . . I expect to see the stock market a good deal higher than it is today within a few months" (Klein 2001, p. 201). Fisher was not the only prominent academic bulling the stock market. For example, just prior to the crash, Charles Amos Dice, a professor at Ohio State, published *New Levels for the Stock Market* (1929) which provided a range of arguments as to why stock prices had to continue climbing.

Though Fisher was only a leading voice in a chorus of academics cheering the virtues of stock investment, it is disturbing to see the soundness of his arguments being undercut by the brutal reality of the collapse in stock prices. Fisher's outstanding academic and public reputation was justly deserved. He was a careful and methodical researcher employing valuation models that are similar to those employed today. For example, Fisher (1930, p. xxii) explicitly uses discounted cash flow valuation to arrive at estimates for common stock prices:

> Since every stock price represents a discounted value of the future dividends and earnings of that stock, there are four reasons that may justify a rise in the price level of stocks: (1) Because the earnings are continually plowed back into the business instead of being declared in dividends, this plowing-back resulting in an accumulation at compound interest, so to speak; (2) Because the expected earnings will increase on account of technical progress within the industry; (3) Because less risk is believed to attach to those earnings than formerly; (4) Because the "basis" by which the discounting is made has been lowered.

Writing at the end of 1929, following the 40+% decline in stock prices of September to mid-November, Fisher (1930) explores all of these four points in detail and concludes (pp. 267–9): "the general plateau of the stock market is still the plateau of 1926–1929, still 55% higher than it was in 1926, and still higher than any previous plateau . . . For the immediate future, at least, the outlook is bright."

Fisher went far beyond a simple recognition that earnings were the key factor driving stock prices (p. 67): "The percentage increase in prices of stocks should be equal to the percentage increase in earnings per share if the ratio of price to earnings were to remain constant." Yet, the available data indicated that from 1922–27 industrial stock prices increased at 14.1% per year while "total profits" (earnings?) increased only 9%. This difference Fisher attributed to the gains to common stock from the low "rate of return on preferred stock" that permitted a greater share of the earnings growth to be captured by the common stock. In addition, the plowing-back of earnings permitted industrial corporations to purchase new plant and equipment that enhanced earnings capacity. Fisher recognized that the plow-back rate for industrial corporations had increased since 1927 and viewed this as a reinforcing influence (p. 80): "During the long bull market there was the record of increased real income, while plowed-back earnings gave promise of future values resident in the productive and consuming plant of the nation that were properly reflected in a heightened level of stock prices."

Fisher (1930, p. 67) credits Edgar Smith with the argument that the plowing-back of earnings was the main factor driving the increase in common stock prices. Fisher (p. 66) puts the argument this way:

> The increase both in dividend payments and in plowed-back earnings during 1929 over 1928, was not only a primal cause of the new plateau of stock prices, but gave promise of continuing prosperity to business for 1930. This increase should minimize the effects of the panic, which was largely restricted to the stock market.
>
> When earnings are turned back into a business it is in order to increase the rate of profits according to the same method by which interest is compounded on savings. There has always been a plowing-back of earnings, but it has been especially done in the last few years.

Having proposed the importance of plowing-back of earnings, Fisher (p. 81) asks the question: "Are the conclusions ... with respect to the increased rate of plowed-back earnings, stated with too great optimism?" Fisher addresses this question with a reasoned analysis of the behavior of the aggregate price-earnings (P/E) ratio.

Modern security analysts are well versed in the difficulties of interpreting P/E ratios. Earnings can be an elusive number that, to be adequately interpreted, requires careful inspection of additional information from the financial statements and other sources. Unlike modern stock market prognosticators, Fisher was hampered by lack of data on earnings and many other variables that are considered essential today for doing security analysis. For example, data on both a price index of industrial stocks and the associated earnings of those companies, calculated by the Standard Statistics Company (later to merge with the publisher of *Poor's Manual* to form Standard and Poors), are only available from May 1927. Fisher was able to obtain his estimate of the increase in earnings of industrial companies over 1922–27 of 9% from a government report (Committee of Recent Economic Changes). From the bulletin of the National City Bank of New York he was able to obtain evidence that the increase in earnings from 3Q 1928 to 3Q 1929 was 14%. Excluding railways and utilities, the remaining manufacturing and trading companies had a gain of 15%.

Given the state of financial reporting requirements prior to the Securities Act (1933), the crude earnings numbers that Fisher had to work with are somewhat suspect. Fisher (1930, p. 88) observes: "There are also difficulties to be faced in the choice of stocks that publish annual earnings figures, and in those stocks where there is concealment of earnings for tax evasion purposes." Fisher is also somewhat unclear about what P/E multiple to apply to individual stocks:

> The price-earnings ratios of the old-fashioned type should be perhaps ten times annual earnings, which is the traditional ratio for a fair selling price for stocks during the period prior to 1922. But for the new type of rapidly expanding corporation the price-earnings ratio might be 100 to 1, or even literally to infinity in the initial stages of investment when earnings are not being realized.

With this background, Fisher proceeds to examine aggregate stock price index and earnings data from the Standard Statistics Company (see figure 2.1). Examining the aggregate data (industrials including railways) Fisher concludes that the 9.8 P/E for

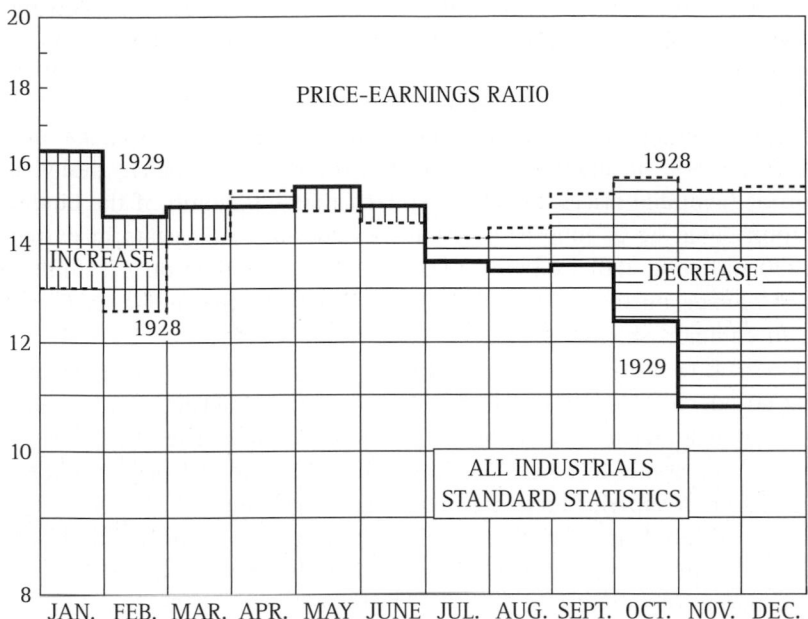

For all Industrial common shares earnings increased far more rapidly than the increase of stock prices during 1929. But this group is open to the objection that it is a variable group of stocks from Fisher (1930, chart 10).

Figure 2.1 Price-earnings ratio

November 1925 was justified. It was 40% below the peak of 16.2 in January 1929 and lower than the previous low of 11.2 for May 1927 "the earliest month for which such statistics are available."

In addition to examining the aggregate P/E data, Fisher made a number of astute observations about the behavior of aggregate and individual stock prices in the months surrounding the crash. In particular, Fisher observes that the run-up in prices was selective (p. 93): "As the market marched to its peak about half of the groups listed (on the NYSE) receded in price, while half went up." It was the high flyers that came crashing down. Using his own index for aggregate stock prices that took in all NYSE groups, Fisher estimates that stocks fell 38% overall during the crash, with railways down only 28%, the most speculative stocks fell over 50%. He attributes the downturn in "the best stocks" to the impact of "overextension of loans" to buy stocks. After reviewing the data surrounding the crash, Fisher remained a bull (p. 98): "the precipitous fall in the market went too far, in the light of sound reasons justifying the long bull market, namely, justifiable expectation of great and increasing earnings, the fact they were so generously plowed-back, the warranted expectation of safety through diversification of investments and, finally, a consequent lowered basis of discounting the future as apparently reflected in price earnings ratios."

As were many others at the time, Fisher was deeply impressed with the work of Edgar L. Smith on the long run performance of common stocks versus bonds. Prior to the appearance of Smith's *Common Stocks as Long-Term Investments* (1925), Fisher (1912) held to the prevailing view that stocks would outperform bonds in periods of rising prices, while bonds would outperform stocks during periods of falling prices. Smith carefully demonstrated that this view was mistaken. Smith took care in recognizing that the stock holdings had to be well-diversified across companies that represented the major industries. In addition, stocks had to be held a sufficient period to permit liquidation at favorable prices. Smith recognized that the length of the holding period to liquidation could be as long as 6 years – extending to 15 years in extreme cases. Fisher (1930, pp. 198–200) explicitly recognized the contribution of Smith (1925) to "a material change during (1923–30) in the estimate of the public as to the risk of investing in common stocks."

Fisher (1930) is well off the mark in terms of predicting future stock price movements. Yet, Fisher (1930, ch. 13) is an excellent illustration of why Fisher can be considered as laying the methodological foundation for modern Finance. The chapter is concerned with "Flight from Bonds to Stocks" – developing a theoretical basis for the rationale of why stocks are a superior long run investment than bonds. Fisher first explores the notion that bonds are "far safer" than stocks. Working with Smith's data, Fisher adjusts for the impact of price level changes and estimates the yield on a bond investment for 1866–85, a period of falling prices, as 11.7% in real terms (6.8% nominal), the same calculation for 1901–22 was 1.1% real (4% nominal). "This analysis indicates clearly enough that during periods of marked fluctuations in the general price level, bonds have a speculative character . . . bonds are not, as compared with a well-selected and diversified stocks, what they have been cracked up to be . . . even when prices are falling they are not usually superior to stocks" (p. 202).

In a precursor of modern portfolio theory, Fisher (p. 203) identifies "five reasons for the now proved fact that stocks are a better investment than bonds":

> first, because the stockholder stands to win as well as to lose; second, because modern dividend policy is toward steadiness; third, because a portion of stockholders' earnings is reinvested for him and ultimately yields further dividends; fourth, because the unstable dollar tricks the bondholder, but any effect on the shareholder is largely neutralized; and fifth, because diversification can correct the irregularities of the stockholder's income but not that of the bondholder.

Fisher recognizes that Smith, K. van Strum and other writers emphasize the importance of diversification – he does not claim originality on this point. Yet, Fisher was a vocal and active proponent of "investment trusts" run by "expert counsel" – precursors of modern mutual funds. For Fisher, diversification had to have another element added: "It is the principle of constant inspection or check-up as to the status of companies issuing stocks, and constant turnover accordingly . . . For the sound investor in common stocks must turn them over constantly, selling those that are losing in value and investing in those that are gaining" (p. 207). The skilled investment counsel situated in investment trusts were an essential element to achieving the gains associated with diversification that allowed stocks to be a superior investment than bonds.

Based on the limited data available, Fisher was able to observe the phenomenon, common to periods of intense speculation in stocks, of substantially increased equity issues at the end of the 1920s. A comparison is made between corporate financing during the first eight months of 1925 ($2.353 billion in long and short term corporate bonds with $804 million in stock issues) with the first eight months of 1929 ($2.360 billion in long and short corporate bonds with $4.794 billion in stock issues). Fisher also observes that the bond issues in 1929 had relatively more equity related provisions such as conversion features. Oddly enough, Fisher interpreted this data as a positive development for stock valuation.

Fisher failed to foresee the precipitous fall in stock prices in the two plus years from 1930 to 1932. More importantly from the standpoint of individual investors at that time, he also failed to foresee that the general level of stock prices would not recover to 1929 levels until after WWII. It is convenient to look back on what Fisher said and conclude that he was just another prognosticator that got it wrong. Yet, Fisher was so much more than being just another prognosticator. With all the skills and information at his disposal, Fisher fails to be able to answer the American question: if you're so smart, why ain't you rich? Though adherents to modern Finance may want to ignore Fisher's foibles, perhaps this is a reflection on the positivist approach to security valuation. Based on as careful an implementation of the scientific approach as he could muster, Fisher was a strong proponent of stocks for the long run – a view that, in his time, proved to be profoundly incorrect. Perhaps more personally disturbing to Fisher was that his long time academic rival, J.M. Keynes, was so much closer to the mark.

Keynes, uncertainty and the Stock Market[22]

Chapter 12 (and to a lesser extent chapters 13 and 15) of the *General Theory* is an essential source for the views of Keynes on the role of uncertainty in pricing of securities, though the story provided in chapter 12 is far from complete. "For convenience of exposition" (p. 149) chapter 12 abstracts from interest rate changes. While this abstraction does have pedagogical benefits, permitting Keynes to examine the process of changes in long term expectations of "prospective yield" on "the values of investments," it does suppress the portfolio management problem of determining the division of investments between fixed income and equity securities. Though these issues are incrementally developed in chapters 13 and 15, integration of the concepts is not presented, say, in the form of a security investment strategy. Given the key role attributed to the "speculative motive" in liquidity preference, e.g., p. 196, this is a significant limitation. In addition, there is limited discussion regarding both the maturity composition of the fixed income component of the investment portfolio and the riskiness of the bonds to be selected, e.g., corporate bonds vs. government bonds.

Given this, early in chapter 12 (p. 149) Keynes hints at a fundamental pricing model which can be used to value securities: "The outstanding fact is the extreme precariousness of the basis of knowledge on which our estimates of prospective yield have to be made. Our knowledge of factors which will govern the yield of an investment some years hence is usually very slight and often negligible . . . those who seriously attempt to make any such estimate are often so much in the minority that their behaviour does not govern the market." In this context, the market is "the Stock Exchange" which "revalues many investments every day" (p. 151). After observing that, due to the separation of ownership from management, the price of shares on the Stock Exchange will be determined by stock traders rather than by the "professional entrepreneur" who has direct knowledge of the underlying business, Keynes asks a key question (p. 151): "How then are these highly significant daily, even hourly, revaluations of existing investments carried out in practice?" The answer provided to this question encompasses the philosophical foundations of the impact that uncertainty has on the human condition.

McKenna and Zannoni (1993, pp. 400–1) capture the basic issue where investment decisions are concerned: "situations may arise in which individuals may not have any knowledge at all concerning the probability distribution function of future outcomes." Yet, decisions have to be made and "economic agents must create alternative mechanisms that enable decisions to be made in the face of uncertainty." Confronted with uncertainty, the crux of the decision making process relies on *convention.* In a remarkable precursor to the modern EMH, Keynes observes that in the face of uncertainty the investor accepts the prevailing evaluation of market prices (p. 152): "the existing market valuation, however arrived at is uniquely *correct* in relation to our existing knowledge of the facts which will influence the yield of the investment, and that it will change in proportion to changes in this knowledge." In following this convention, "the only risk (an investor) runs is that of a genuine change in the news *over the near future*, as to the likelihood of which he can attempt to form his own judgment" (p. 153).

For Keynes, the EMH is a convention. This is an important observation because in the Keynesian model, "conventions are essentially shared rules of behavior that enable individuals to take actions in situations where the future results of these actions are unknowable . . . though the future may be unknowable the existence of conventions and the belief that they will be maintained provide a basis for decision making under uncertainty" (McKenna and Zannoni 1993, pp. 402–3).[23] The weakness of the EMH as a convention is that the actual security prices are not being determined with reference to the long-term prospective yield. Rather, prices are being determined "as the outcome of a large number of ignorant individuals" and misguided professional investors and speculators. This produces a stock market that, when confidence in the convention is "less plausible than usual," is "subject to waves of optimistic and pessimistic sentiment, which are unreasoning and yet in a sense legitimate, where no solid basis exists for a reasonable calculation" (p. 154). Such fluctuations are so pervasive that "the energies and skill of the professional investor and speculator are mainly occupied . . . not with making superior long-term forecasts of the probable yield of an investment over its whole life, but with foreseeing changes in the conventional basis of valuation a short time ahead of the general public" (p. 154).

This reference to convention has deep philosophical implications that cannot be ignored. Conventions are the result of social interaction, what McKenna and Zannoni (1993) pedantically refer to as the social matrix (the cultural context within which individuals exercise their freedom). As a consequence of the EMH being a convention, the extent of the violent fluctuations in the market depend on the temporal state of the social matrix. In other words, the institutional, social and historical context will impact the security pricing process. The same event occurring at different times may produce a violent fluctuation in pricing in one period and have no impact at another time. Uncertainty is created by the infinite number of future outcomes which are possible at a given point in time. The specific outcome which occurs "is the result of individual choice in the context of social interaction . . . It is not the case that the far distant future is sometimes more knowable than at other times. It is always simply unknowable. What does change . . . is the meaning people choose to attach to this fact, and hence the manner in which people's behavior responds to this uncertainty" McKenna and Zannoni (1993, p. 403).

It is evident that Keynes was not a fully fledged dis-believer in the EMH and, as a result, cannot be considered in the same camp as the technical analysts. Yet, there are substantive misgivings about the success of fundamental analysis: "Investment based on genuine long-term expectation is so difficult to-day as to be scarcely practicable. [An investor] who attempts it must surely lead much more laborious days and run greater risks than [an investor] who tries to guess better than the crowd how the crowd will behave; and given equal intelligence, he may make more disastrous mistakes . . . It needs *more* intelligence to defeat the forces of time and our ignorance of the future than to beat the gun" (p. 157). Besides, there is more excitement in the chase after speculative profit: "life is not long enough; – human nature desires quick results, there is a peculiar zest in making money quickly, and remoter gains are discounted by the average man at a very high rate" (p. 157).

The reliance on the social matrix is one element of the Keynesian approach that is worrisome to neo-classical economists and, in the present context, presumably also to modern portfolio theorists. Yet, to be relevant to present day security markets, this material has to be reworked to fit the contemporary social matrix. Conventions, which are so important for decision making under uncertainty, depend fundamentally on the social matrix. In this vein, Keynes was writing at a time that was different in many ways from the world of today. There has certainly been substantive changes in financial markets since the time of the *General Theory*. Perhaps the world has changed enough that the investor motivated by long-term expectations has come to predominate, inducing an EMH convention which is more stable and less susceptible to violent fluctuation? Putting aside for the moment the empirical evidence to the contrary provided by the high tech/dot com/NASDAQ 5000 stock bubble of the recent past, what suggestions would Keynes have for those seeking to employ a security investment strategy based on fundamental analysis?

It is difficult to deny that the "zest" for quick profit is any less vigorous today than in times gone by. It is also still the case that (p. 157): "The game of professional investment is intolerably boring and overexacting to anyone who is entirely exempt from the gambling instinct." The investor who would seek to engage in fundamental analysis, i.e., "an investor who proposes to ignore near-term market fluctuations" and purchase a security on the basis of long-term prospective yield, is advised of the need for "greater resources for safety" and not to "operate on so large a scale, if at all, with borrowed money." All these potential difficulties are compounded by the following prediction (p. 158): "If I may be allowed to appropriate the term *speculation* for the activity of forecasting the psychology of the market, and the term *enterprise* for the activity of forecasting the prospective yield on assets over their whole life, it is by no means always the case that speculation predominates over enterprise." Unfortunately, this hopeful statement is followed by: "As the organization of investment markets improves, the risk of predominance of speculation does, however, increase." If this prediction is correct, fundamental analysis is likely to be even more difficult today than at the time of the *General Theory*.

Based on these observations, it seems that the conclusions about fundamental analysis will extend into the modern world. For Keynes, uncertainty plays a fundamental role in the investment process. It is in the process of dealing with uncertainty that security markets produce violent and not so violent fluctuations in prices, causing unpredictable and potentially persistent deviations of prices from the values indicated by pricing models which accurately reflect the fundamentals of the security ("the long-term prospective yield"). This makes fundamental analysis a decidedly difficult, if not "risky," activity. For example, casual inspection of the current (post-tech-bubble) prices for stocks in sectors such as bio-technology and internet retailing are still confounding to explain using the techniques of fundamental analysis. The observation that stock prices move substantially more than is indicated by changes in underlying fundamentals has much the same truth today as at the time of the *General Theory*. This, again, creates real complications for fundamental analysts.

Recognizing the difficulties associated with fundamental analysis, the security investment strategy that Keynes apparently felt would produce the highest profit was to exploit predictions aimed at market instability. To leverage up (increase invested capital with borrowing) and ride the waves of exuberance and "spontaneous optimism" in the stock market until "animal spirits are dimmed" and pessimism besets the market: "if the animal spirits are dimmed and the spontaneous optimism falters, leaving us to depend on nothing but a mathematical expectation, enterprise will fade and die; – though fears of loss may have a basis no more reasonable than hopes of profit had been before" (p. 162). As outlined in chapters 13 and 15 of the *General Theory*, when the dark clouds are gathering, the investor liquidates stock and moves funds to short-term liquid assets, soldiering resources until the next wave of spontaneous optimism grips the market and the cycle is repeated.

Keynes concludes chapter 12 with a number of qualifications that, while relatively innocuous in terms of the macroeconomic theory being presented, are confounding from a security investment strategy viewpoint. For example, there is the statement: "We should not conclude from this that everything depends on waves of irrational psychology. On the contrary, the state of long-term expectation is often steady, and, even when it is not, the other factors exert their compensating effects" (p. 162). Is this arguing for a less than complete liquidation of the stock position? Perhaps a reduction in leveraged purchasing of stocks is indicated? Even more confounding is the following statement (p. 163): "There are, moreover, certain important factors which somewhat mitigate in practice the effects of our ignorance of the future. Owing to the operation of compound interest combined with the likelihood of obsolescence with the passage of time, there are many individual investments of which the prospective yield is legitimately dominated by the returns of the comparatively near future." Investments in buildings and utilities are identified as belonging to this class. These types of assets have predictable and relatively stable cash flow patterns extending out long enough that "compound interest" would produce cash flows in distant periods which have a present value approaching zero.[24]

Having developed an elaborate theory of the impact of uncertainty on stock prices, Keynes explicitly recognizes that there may be types of investments which are not subjected to these forces. Keynes (p. 149) identifies a long list of investments which are subject to uncertainty: railways, mines, textiles, drug companies, shipping transport, and certain types of real estate ("a building in the City of London"). Yet, there are other types of companies which do have stable and relatively predictable cash flows. Hence, there appears to be a distinction being made between issues which are "speculative" and subject to the waves of optimism and pessimism and those which are "non-speculative" and relatively immune to the mis-pricing arising from uncertainty. If this is correct, then Keynes is moving some way towards the fundamental analysts where a similar distinction is made.[25] However, unlike the fundamental analysts, the set of securities which Keynes would classify as non-speculative is significantly smaller than that claimed by the fundamental analysts. Upon closer examination, the number potentially qualifying securities appears to be a set that is so small as to not be a practical basis for a widely acceptable security investment strategy.

In selecting an appropriate security investment strategy, there is also an ethical dilemma. Keynes (p. 157) captures the essence of the problem: "There is no clear evidence from experience that the investment policy which is socially advantageous coincides with that which is most profitable." An investment strategy which follows the socially responsible road is fraught with difficulty (pp. 157–8): "it is the long-term investor, he who most promotes the public interest, who will in practice come in for most criticism . . . if he is unsuccessful, which is very likely, he will not receive much mercy." Yet, Keynes still exhorts that "the social objective of skilled investment should be to defeat the dark forces of time and ignorance which envelop our future" (p. 155).

In the end, the investment strategy selected speaks to the philosophical inclinations of the individual investor. Some investors may be compelled to lead by example, attempting to conquer the dark forces of time and ignorance by selecting investments on the basis of the long term prospective yields. If a sufficient number of investors adopt this approach then, if Keynes is correct, there will be less instability in financial markets, the "game of Snap, of Old Maid, of Musical Chairs" (p. 156) will be replaced by more "socially advantageous" investment activities which contribute to stabilizing security prices at levels that reflect "long-term prospective yields." Others may take a more fatalistic view of the social matrix. The "zest" for the game may be viewed as too compelling to resist, both for themselves and for others. Uncertainty is too daunting an adversary. They will be drawn into "estimating the prospects of investment . . . (by considering) . . . the nerves and hysteria and even the digestions and reactions to the weather of those upon whose spontaneous activity it largely depends" (p. 162).

The realm of possible investment strategies extends well beyond these two general alternatives. Some may take solace in the possibility of investing in securities which are not as subject to the waves of pessimism and optimism, taking refuge in securities such as utility stocks and long-term high grade corporate securities leaving the game of Old Maid to be played by more intrepid investors with the zest for these activities. Still others may avoid financial assets altogether, preferring investments in real property which generates a predictable return, e.g., residential buildings as opposed to commercial properties. Finally, some may seek innovative investment solutions, believing that socially responsible investments, such as ethical funds, have potential long-term prospective yields which, though they cannot be measured *ex ante*, provide something intangibly more than an investment in a tobacco or chemical company. For these investors, uncertainty is a refuge that prevents an investor from accurately identifying the most profitable securities, *ex ante*. In such a climate, investment selection can be made without giving undue consideration to profitability, leaving room for other characteristics of the investment to be determining factors for inclusion in the portfolio.

2.3 GRAHAM AND DODD (1934) AND AFTER

The historical context

Graham and Dodd (1934) is a product of the severe collapse in the corporate securities markets that started in October 1929 and continued until February 1933. This is evident from page one: "Any present examination into financial principles or methods must start with recognition of the distinctive character of our recent experiences, and it must face and answer the numerous questions which these experiences inspire." For Graham and Dodd, "recent experiences" stretch back to 1927, where the advance to the October 1929 peak is identified as beginning. Words like "unprecedented," "tidal wave," "special causes" and "unparalleled effects" are used to describe this period relative to the usual "repetition of business and stock market cycles" that typically characterize stock market price behavior. In contrast, a number of recent studies, e.g., Santoni (1987), Bierman (1991, 1998), have concluded that "overall (the) stock market was not obviously excessively high in September 1929 and the business outlook was favorable. Thus the October crash did not occur because the market was too high" (Bierman 1998, p. 17).

Were Graham and Dodd incorrect in their observations about security markets events that were, perhaps, too close to be judged accurately? This seems unlikely. If Graham and Dodd were correct, then Bierman and the other observers have misinterpreted the significance of "the crash of 1929" by focusing on the mechanics of common stock valuations surrounding the crash instead of dealing with the role of the crash in contributing to the ongoing collapse of stock market values that continued until February of 1933. Based on analyses starting from Fisher (1930) and continuing to the present, it is evident that theoretically sound rationales for the level that stock prices attained in 1929 can be provided. Yet, consistent with the argument of J.M. Keynes in *The General Theory*, e.g., chapter 11, the crash acted by changing investor perceptions; it was the severity of the negative shock to the perception of the prospective return to investments that was the key driving factor behind the aggregate economic problems that plagued the industrial world in the 1930s.

Security valuation requires more than an mechanical application of predefined rules. The uncertainty inherent in common stock returns can be resolved in different ways, depending on the impact of the historical context on investor psychology. Graham and Dodd (1934, p. 6) clearly recognized this point:

we do not accept the premise that 1927–1933 experience affords a proper norm by which to judge the future of investment. The swing of the speculative pendulum during this period was of such unprecedented amplitude as to warrant the belief that it will not recur in similar intensity for a long time to come. In other words, we should regard it more as an economic phenomenon akin to the South Sea Bubble and other isolated instances of abnormal gambling frenzy than as an indication of what the typical speculative cycle will be. As a *speculative* experience, the recent cycle differed from previous ones in kind rather than degree; but in its effects upon the *investment fabric* it had unique characteristics, seemingly of a nonrecurrent type.

This is by no means an isolated quote, e.g., "One of the striking features of the past five years has been the domination of the financial scene by purely psychological elements" (p. 11). The impact of the historically abnormal previous five years of common stock pricing on the analysis and principles advanced by Graham and Dodd (1934) is systemic, it affects the whole text.

Graham and Dodd were concerned about the inadequacies of an approach to security analysis that appeared in the latter part of the 1920s. Graham and Dodd (1934, p. 307) referred to this approach as "*The New Era Theory*":

During the postwar period, and particularly during the latter stage of the bull market culminating in 1929, the public acquired a completely different attitude towards the investment merits of common stocks . . . The new theory or principle may be summed up in the sentence: "The value of a common stock depends entirely upon what it will earn in the future."

From this dictum the following corollaries are drawn:

1. That the dividend rate should have slight bearing upon the value.

2. That since no relationship apparently existed between assets and earning power, the asset value was entirely devoid of importance.

3. The past earnings were significant only to the extent that they indicated what changes in earnings were likely to take place in the future.

This complete revolution in the philosophy of common stock investment took place virtually without realization by the stock buying public and with only the most superficial recognition by financial observers.

For those with the valuations of the NASDAQ-5000 tech stock bubble still fresh in memory, these statements by Graham and Dodd (1934) almost certainly have a timeless quality (see section 1.3).

By referring to "a completely different attitude towards the investment merits of common stocks," Graham and Dodd's observations about the New Era Theory implicitly make reference to the previous approaches to security analysis that, presumably, took a more informed view of "investment merits." As such, Graham and Dodd (1934) represents a revival of the "advance of security analysis (that) proceeded uninterruptedly until about 1927, covering a long period in which increasing attention was paid on all sides to financial reports and statistical data." The "new era" was a diversion where facts and figures were "manipulated by a sort of pseudo-analysis to support the delusions of the period" (p. 14). The reliance on the analysis of financial reports permits a rough correspondence between the development of security analysis and the emergence

of the professional accountants required to prepare the corporate accounts. "The importance and prestige of security analysis have tended to increase over the years, paralleling
roughly the steady improvement in corporation reports and other statistical data which
supply its raw material" (Graham, Dodd and Cottle (GDC) 1962, p. 24). In the pre-1933
world of security market self-regulation, a professional accounting profession was
needed to ensure that financial reports issued by companies would be a reliable source
of information.

Compared to the English security markets, professional accounting was relatively slow
to develop in the US. A useful reference date is 1882 when the Institute of Accountants
and Bookkeepers was formed in New York state. The Institute issued certificates upon
successful completion of a comprehensive examination. This development was significant because it reflected the growing need for independent accountants to prepare and
audit accounts. While, in 1884, there were only 81 independent accountants "listed in
the city directories of New York, Chicago and Philadelphia. Just five years later there
were 322" (Gordon 1999, p. 173). In 1887 the precursor of the modern day American
Institute of Certified Public Accountants was established as the American Association of
Public Accountants. Recognizing the important role of states in regulating the accounting profession, in 1896 New York state established the legislation that designated
criteria for individuals to be qualified to prepare and audit company accounts. This New
York legislation, which was soon adopted by other states, is responsible for introducing
the term certified public accountant.

While the 1890s is a potential reference date for exploring the precursors, Graham
and Dodd (p. 14) make specific reference to "the last three decades" of security analysis.
This suggests the first decade of the twentieth century as a starting point. Though written
by a financial journalist from "the City" in London, Hartley Withers (1911) provides an
excellent benchmark for examining the techniques of security analysis that predate
Graham and Dodd. Withers' objective was "to glean among the best brains of the world
of finance" and "to pass on the gleanings to readers." There is ample attention given to
both English and US securities markets. Withers (1911) contains twelve chapters. After
an initial chapter on the historical evolution of securities, starting from the sixteenth
century, Withers proceeds with a chapter on the form of securities, dealing with the
topics such as the definitions of stocks, shares and bonds and the difference between
registered and bearer securities. While this material is somewhat pedestrian, the next
four chapters are recognizable precursors of Graham and Dodd (1934).

The first of the four chapters details how the capital structure of companies relate to
the various classes of securities. In this chapter there are the expected topics such as the
role of the shareholders in choosing the board of directors, the difference between
preferred and ordinary shares and stock splits. The presentation is structured around the
fictionalized creation of the "Hygienic Tooth-powder Company" by "Mr. Cleanbite" who
lives in Brixton and has a small dental practice in Finsbury Circus. The dentist has
developed an effective toothpowder but does not have the capital for making it on a
large scale. As chance would have it, one of his business neighbors in Finsbury Circus,
"a certain Mr. Mortimer . . . who carries on the mysterious profession of company,
promoter, underwriter, financier, and organizer of syndicates" happens to visit Cleanbites
dental office for treatment of a painful molar. The machinations and complications of

the ensuing formation of a public company, complete with issuing of stock, selection of the board of directors, watering of stock and so on reflects a solid understanding of the initial public offering. Having laid this foundation, Withers proceeds to a chapter with detailed examination of prospectuses.

Chapters 5 and 6 can fairly be considered as early gems of security analysis, in the sense of the Graham and Dodd mantra: "All security analysis involves the use of financial statements." Chapter 5 is a detailed dissection of the balance sheet and income statement of Babcock and Wilcox Ltd, a well known engineering firm at that time. After going over items on the liabilities side of the balance sheet, Withers (p. 127) observes:

> It is when we come to the assets side of the balance-sheet that its difficulty really begins. On the liabilities side we have been faced with sums about which there is no doubt. Every penny that the company has to account for to its shareholders or pay to its creditors is a definite penny, no more and no less. But when we look into the assets that it holds against these liabilities there is room for infinite variety in the meaning of the figures attached to them.

Withers goes on to demonstrate that the simple process of accounting for asset values according to the values paid for purchase is "quite useless as a guide to its actual position at the moment." This lays the basis for chapter 6 which is concerned with the notions of depreciation and profitability. The connection of these concerns with Graham and Dodd (1934) are apparent in part IV which is composed of four chapters concerned with the implications of asset values for balance sheet analysis. In addition, part V is concerned with analysis of the income account and has a chapter on "the relation of depreciation and similar charges to earnings power."

Accounting standards were considerably less well defined at the time Withers was writing. Rules and practices that are taken for granted today were either non-existent or subject to dispute. Legal decisions associated with bankruptcies, securities frauds and the like often acted as a barrier to implementing sound accounting practices. This leads Withers (p. 151) to make the following statement about the position of the auditor:

> The position of an auditor of a joint stock company is doubly difficult, from the indefinite and hazy nature of his duties, and from his relation to the shareholders and the Board. As we have seen, his duties are reduced by legal pronouncements to those of a checking-clerk, and the fees that he receives are very inadequate to the real importance of his task; while in practice, if a company gets into difficulties, the auditors are always likely to be blamed for not having pointed out that its published figures, though correct, were not veracious. Though originally, as a rule, appointed to be watch-dogs in the interests of the shareholders, to see that the Board and the officials are publishing true and correct statements. Their duty is to the shareholders, but their direct relations are with the Board and officials. When they take a high view of their duties, and call attention in their reports to matters which ought to be amended, it sometimes happens that their action is very foolishly resented by the shareholders, whose best interests they are trying to serve, and they sometimes get removed from office for having done their duty well.

In light of the recent events surrounding Enron and the collapse of one of the big five accounting firms, Arthur Anderson, this statement seems almost prophetic.

After three chapters, one on government and municipal securities, one on the stock exchange, and one on stock exchange transactions, Withers concludes with three remarkable chapters that explicitly deal with the implications of the distinction between speculation and investment, a distinction that also plays a key role in Graham and Dodd. Yet, Withers in these chapters goes beyond Graham and Dodd in some ways. The last three chapters of Withers have many elements that later appear in J.M. Keynes (1936, ch. 12). It is difficult to do justice in a short discussion. Chapter 10 is concerned with the price movements of securities. In this chapter, Withers starts by recognizing the role of psychological factors in determining stock prices, "price movements are chiefly a psychological question" (p. 283). After an insightful observation about the impact of dealers on pricing ("it often happens that an unexpectedly favourable traffic return or dividend announcement makes the dealers in a market raise the price of stock because they infer a quick rush of buying that will follow it"), Withers recognizes that share pricing ultimately has to be supported "by the action of the public."

Withers follows this introduction with a discussion that is clearly reminiscent of Keynes:

> One curious result of this dependence of securities on public opinion in the matter of their price movements, is that it is often dangerous to be too clever and far-seeing concerning the influences that may be expected to improve or depress prices. It has happened before now that long-sighted operators have foreseen trade developments or other happenings that could not fail ultimately to have an important effect on prices, have backed their opinion by buying the securities likely to be affected, and have lost money by being too keen of vision. All that they foresaw may have happened, but if its effects did not dawn on the intelligence of a large enough number of buyers, the stocks that ought to be affected would not move . . . It is not enough for a stock to be worth buying. It must be recognized to be worth buying by the multitude before it will go up in price. Further, the fact that a stock may be absurdly over-valued will not for a moment prevent its rising still further if there are folk enough who believe that it is still cheap and are prepared to back their opinions by buying it.

This is not the only connection to Keynes (1936, ch. 12). After examining the bull and bear operations of speculators, Withers observes that the impact of such operations on security prices are "more or less temporary" and "what finally determines the price of a security is what the real investor thinks about it. Bulls and bears produce the waves on the surface, real buying and selling are the flow and ebb of the tide which determine the depth of the water" (pp. 293–4). This is followed by the remarkable statement: "The real investor . . . is likely to be guided by convention." Though the connection to the elaborate process of decision making under "true uncertainty" is unrecognized, Withers does devote substantial discussion to the social status of the real investor, "in most cases a member of the upper or middle classes of society" and the various social and psychological factors that would influence the conventions that guide their investment decisions, e.g., "old-time convention had been very much in favour of investments at home." It is difficult to tell whether Keynes was aware of Withers (1911) as Keynes did little referencing of the ideas gleaned from others and no reference is given to Withers in Keynes (1936).

The last two chapters of Withers (1911) are devoted to detailed examination of "the real investor" and "the speculative investor." After recognizing that making such a distinction is artificial because "every investor is a speculator, and the difference between the two classes is finally, like most other differences, one of degree," Withers observes that real investors "look most of all to security of income and least to the hope of capital appreciation, while the pure speculator sets no store by income, and looks entirely to the chance of being able to make a big profit by a resale" (p. 317). Between these polar extremes are a range of speculative investors and investing speculators. The motivations of these speculative investors and investing speculators are of interest. In particular, much like the "value investor" of modern times, the investing speculator can follow the course "of buying good securities which the investing public is at present neglecting, knowing that some day or other it will come back to them, and in the meantime earning a good round yield on his money by buying stocks which are discredited."

A final point of interest in Withers (1911) are two "well known saws on the subject of investment" that are explored: "the higher the yield, the lower the security" and "never put all your eggs in one basket." On the latter saw Withers makes the remarkable (why?) statement: "expert advisers of the public are fertile in schemes for scientific distribution of risks by climate, or by geography, or by industries, etc., etc." Withers finds that neither of the old saws is "quite sound." The text ends with an exhortation (pp. 344–5): "the preceding pages have been written in vain if they have not shown that stocks and shares and market movements are a weltering chaos of uncertainty and haphazard guesswork, based on figures that often mean nothing – or worse than nothing, because they seem to mean so much – and on gusts of opinion blown hither and thither by causes which have no logical connections with the merits of the stocks affected. Whosoever is wise will ponder these things and try to be a real investor, exposing himself as little as possible to speculative anxieties and pitfalls." Sounds like a strong vote for bonds over stocks, circa 1911.

Defining security analysis[26]

In contrast to Withers (1911), Graham and Dodd (1934) is a significant advancement in terms of depth and breadth. Seeing that Withers was a journalist recounting ideas that he had gleaned from discussions with market practitioners, this is not surprising. By 1934, Graham was a market practitioner, par excellence, with a wealth of personal experience about the practice of security analysis to draw on. In addition, in the quarter of a century separating these two texts there was also a substantive increase in the breadth and depth of available accounting and other statistical information that is an essential ingredient in security analysis. The two texts were also separated by a major security market event, the collapse of security markets from 1929 to 1933. Yet there are enough significant similarities that Graham and Dodd (1934) can be seen to be part of a progression of ideas about security analysis. The seminal status often attributed to Graham and Dodd (1934) is due more to the impact and influence that the text had, rather than to the seminal nature of the ideas being presented.

Graham and Dodd (1934) possesses the constant themes that precursors in the realm of security analysis, such as Withers (1911), also possess. These themes include the relevance of the distinction between investment and speculation, the emphasis on the use of financial statements to form opinions, and the problems raised by the vagaries of market pricing. For example, chapter 4 of Graham and Dodd (1934) is dedicated to "distinctions between investment and speculation." On the vagaries of market pricing, Graham and Dodd (p. 23) explicitly recognize that the "intrinsic value" of a security may well differ from the market price:

> the influence of what we call analytical factors over the market price is both *partial* and *indirect* – partial because it frequently competes with purely speculative factors which influence the price in the opposite direction; and indirect, because it acts through the intermediary of people's sentiments and decisions. In other words, the market is not a *weighing machine*, on which the value of each issue is recorded by an exact and impersonal mechanism, in accordance with its specific qualities. Rather we should say that the market is a *voting machine*, whereon countless individuals register choices which are the product of and partly of emotion.

Together with "inadequate or incorrect data" and "uncertainties of the future," the "irrational behavior of the market" is a principal obstacle to the success of the security analyst.

In a way, Graham and Dodd deal with the philosophical implications of the process of generating knowledge in the field of security analysis. In discussing Gadamer (1960) in section 1.3, it was argued that knowledge in the human sciences does not progress in the same fashion as in the natural sciences. Whereas knowledge in the natural sciences progresses linearly as more theoretical and empirical information is obtained about a given phenomenon, in the human sciences authoritative contributions can be timeless. Graham and Dodd (1934) is an excellent example of this point. To be sure, the historical context has changed since the text was written, but many of the insights still retain contemporary value. Consider the following comment about the objectives of security analysis (p. 14):

> Analysis connotes the careful study of available facts with the attempt to draw conclusions therefrom based on established principles and sound logic. It is part of the scientific method. But in applying analysis to the field of securities we encounter the serious obstacle that investment is by nature not an exact science. The same is true, however, of law and medicine, here also both individual skill (art) and chance are important factors in determining success or failure. Nevertheless, in these professions analysis is not only useful but indispensable, so that the same should probably be true in the field of investment and possibly in that of speculation.

It seems that Graham and Dodd were grappling with many of the epistemological issues raised in section 1.3.

In surveying the scope of security analysis, three functions are identified: descriptive, selective and critical. Of these, it is the selective function that deals with "whether a given issue should be bought, sold, retained, or exchanged for some other" – the other two functions deal with the preparing of company reports or evaluating the terms and conditions of a particular security issue. As such, it is the selective function that is of general interest, with the other two functions being primarily of interest to practitioners. The key element in the selective function is the "intrinsic value" of the security: "the intrinsic value is an elusive concept. In general terms, it is understood to be that value which is justified by the facts, e.g., the assets, earnings, dividends, definite prospects, as distinct, let us say, from market quotations established by artificial manipulation or distorted by psychological excesses" (p. 17). Much of Graham and Dodd (1934) is concerned with the appropriate methods for determining the intrinsic value of a security.

Graham and Dodd (1934) is often credited for defining security analysis to mean "the use of fundamental analysis to value securities issued by publicly traded corporations." This has led to the mantra: "All security analysis involves the use of financial statements" (e.g., GDC 1962, p. 105). As such, security analysis is intimately connected to accounting practices. Yet, this interpretation of Graham and Dodd is too narrow. Determination of the intrinsic value requires analysis of both quantitative and qualitative factors. Quantitative factors are associated with statistical information from the income statement, balance sheet and additional data on factors such as capacity utilization, unit prices, costs and the like. Qualitative factors include: the nature of the business; the relative position of the company in the industry; physical, geographical and operating characteristics; the character of management; the longer term outlook for the unit, industry and business in general. Precisely how all these elements fit together to form an assessment of intrinsic value is the essence of security analysis.

Lasting insights: Graham, Dodd and Cottle (1962)

Even though a portion of Graham, Dodd and Cottle (1962) is material carried forward, unchanged from Graham and Dodd (1934), there is so much more in the 1962 edition that it can safely be considered as a separate text. To be sure, the themes of the two editions are consistent, but so were the themes that connected Withers (1911) with the 1934 edition. One of the features separating Graham, Dodd and Cottle (1962) is the substantive change in the approach to security analysis from the views advanced in the previous editions of 1951, 1940 and 1934. The change is attributed to a change in historical context (p. vi):

> Beginning sometime in 1955, our value standards and the actual market level parted company, and the gap has tended to widen through the ensuing years. Thus we are not able to proceed in 1960–1961 with the same comforting assurance as formerly that our standards are in accordance with both long-term and recent-term experience. In this respect we face a three-pronged dilemma, which we share with all serious-minded security analysts. If we persist in clinging to our old, highly conservative standards of common-stock appraisal, we risk not only the certain charge of old-fogeyism, but a real possibility of failing to recognize important changes in the underlying structure of common-stock values.

Gone is the overwhelming concern with the collapse of investor confidence associated with the pre-WWII period. In its place is a "confident appraisal of the market's future on the general expectation of continued prosperity and growth" (p. 417).

Even in the material carried forward, the changes between the 1934 and 1962 editions are more than cosmetic. In particular, where the 1934 edition presented a uniform notion of security analysis, the 1962 edition maintained: "we should acknowledge that there are some serious differences among practicing security analysts as to the basic approach to the selective function of security analysis" (p. 25). Speaking of the use of quantitative and qualitative information, the 1934 edition maintained (p. 34):

> Broadly speaking, the quantitative factors lend themselves far better to thoroughgoing analysis than do the qualitative factors. The former are fewer in number, more easily obtainable, and much better suited to the forming of definite and dependable conclusions. Furthermore, the financial results will themselves epitomize many of the qualitative elements, so that a detailed study of the latter may not add much of importance to the picture. The typical analysis of a security . . . will treat the qualitative factors in a superficial or summary fashion and devote most of its space to the figures.

The 1962 edition takes a decidedly different tone about the qualitative factors. Leaving the first two sentences unchanged, the 1962 edition says: "Furthermore, the financial results in themselves epitomize such qualitative elements as the ability of a reasonably long-entrenched management. This point of view does not minimize the importance of qualitative factors in appraising the performance of a company, but it does indicate that a detailed study of them – to be justified – should provide sufficient additional insight to assist significantly in appraising the company" (p. 86). Similarly, the 1962 edition advocates: "the weight given to financial material may vary enormously, depending upon the kind of security studied and basic motivation of the prospective purchaser" (p. 105).

This emphasis on differences is not meant to imply that the texts are diametrically opposed. For example, on the distinction between speculation and investment the texts are still in agreement. Both editions italicize the statement: "*An investment operation is one which upon thorough analysis, promises safety of principal and a satisfactory return. Operations not meeting these requirements are speculative*" (1934, p. 54). Both texts explicitly recognize that security analysis has considerable limitations in speculative situations, e.g., "It is only where chance plays a subordinate role that the analyst can properly speak in an authoritative voice and accept responsibility for the results of his judgments" (1934, p. 26; 1962, p. 52). In other words, "the value of analysis diminishes as the element of chance increases." Both the 1934 edition and the 1962 edition continues with a discussion about the benefits of holding a diversified portfolio of securities: "the element of diversification is counted upon to offset the recognized risk existing in individual securities" (p. 54). Insofar as fundamental analysis seeks to benefit from firm specific risks, it would seem that relatively undiversified portfolios would be more attractive. However, the diversification envisaged is much less than the market portfolio suggested by modern portfolio theory, more along the lines of a specialized investment trust.

In contrast to the earlier editions, the 1962 edition was profoundly influenced by the emerging subject of modern Finance, the rudiments of which were appearing at that time. There are discussions related to optimal capital structure (pp. 548–9) and impact of dividend payments on firm value. The discussion about dividends moves from the "greater benefits to stockholders from dividends" in the 1934 edition to a more ambiguous view in the 1962 edition. There are also chapters dedicated to "newer methods for valuing growth stocks" and "market analysis and security analysis." The 1962 edition is also filled with copious footnotes that contain references to recent journal articles and trade publications. Where the 1934 edition examined fixed income investments and proceeded to common stocks, with a view of applying valuation principles for bonds to common stocks, the 1962 edition has a substantial examination of the principles of financial statement analysis before proceeding to fixed income securities and common stocks. On balance, there is much new material presented in the 1962 edition.

Modern students of Finance would probably not bother to read the original texts, relying instead on what a long list of journal articles propose as the "Ben Graham approach." This approach is typically characterized by mechanical rules for security selection using selected financial ratios. Sometimes these rules are taken from the various editions of Graham and Dodd, in other cases from one of the editions of Graham *The Intelligent Investor* (1949, 1st edn.). For example, Oppenheimer (1981, p. 9) identifies four selection criteria for a defensive investor from the five editions of *The Intelligent Investor*. The rules differ only slightly from edition to edition. The rules from the 1973 edition are: (1) Some dividend paid each year since 1950; (2) the firm has at least $50 million in assets or annual sales and is in the upper $\frac{1}{4}$ or $\frac{1}{3}$ of its industry in size; (3) the security price does not exceed 25 times average earnings of the past 7 years and does not exceed 20 times earnings over the last 12-month period; and, (4) the equity at book value is at least 50% of the total market capitalization (for utilities this value is 30%). Oppenheimer also suggests criteria for the enterprising investor, e.g., market capitalization of common stock is two-thirds or less of current assets less total liabilities (including preferred stock).

There are a number of other mechanical security selection criteria that have been attributed to the Graham and Dodd approach. A partial list would include: an earnings-to-price yield at least twice the AAA bond yield; a P/E ratio less than 40% of the highest P/E ratio the stock had over the past five years; a dividend yield of at least two-thirds the AAA bond yield; and, a stock price below two-thirds of tangible book value per share. In addition, Lowe (1994) provides a list of "Ben Graham's investment principles" that includes the following: be an investor, not a speculator; know the asking price; rake the market for bargains; regard corporate figures with suspicion; don't stress out; don't sweat the math; diversify, rule #1, minimum of 25% bonds, 25% stocks; diversify, rule #2, hold a large number of securities; when in doubt, stick to quality; dividends are a clue to value; defend your shareholder rights; be patient; and, think for yourself. Finally, armed with all this background, those seeking to undertake a security analysis need to consider the basic elements of fundamental analysis: profitability; stability; growth in earnings; financial position; dividends; and price history.

2.4 THE EMERGENCE OF MODERN FINANCE

History of portfolio diversification theory before Markowitz

While recognizing that the benefits of diversification had been identified long before, Markowitz (1999) emphasizes the contributions of Markowitz (1952, 1959): "What was lacking prior to 1952 was an adequate *theory* of investment that covered the effects of diversification where risks are correlated, distinguished between efficient and inefficient portfolios, and analyzed risk-return trade-offs on the portfolio as a whole." Markowitz

(1999) recounts that his motivation to develop a formal optimization model of the risk–return tradeoff for a portfolio of securities was inspired by a rejection of Williams (1938) where the rule guiding investment decisions was to "maximize the discounted . . . (expected) value of future returns." For Williams, the value of a stock was the discounted expected value of future dividend payments. The resulting investment strategy called for selection of securities with the highest expected return. For Markowitz, the Williams approach to investment decisions ignored benefits of diversification. Though Williams (1938) did deal with the impact of uncertainty, the approach suggested was to assign probabilities to possible future states and evaluate the expected value of the investment. Williams felt that diversification would result in an elimination of security risk premia, a view that does not deal adequately with security covariances.

Markowitz (1999) reviews many contributions dealing with aspects of diversification, the risk-return tradeoff and the like appearing in the two decades before Markowitz (1952, 1959). The general assessment of prior contributions is that the discussion did not provide much beyond general terms and "did not clearly indicate why it is desirable." Yet, contributions such as Fisher (1930) receive no mention. In a discussion of "Taking Risk from Speculation" (pp. 204–7) Fisher clearly deals with the issue of diversification:

> A little reasoning permits of a startling corollary. It is this: If we can, by sufficient diversification in investments, get a greater certainty and thus run less risks from our speculation, then the more unsafe the investments are, taken individually, the safer they are taken collectively, to say nothing of profitableness, provided that the diversification is sufficiently increased.
>
>   This paradox is derived directly from exploiting the old-fashioned fear of common stocks and the consequent refusal to deal in them, except well below their "mathematical value."

What follows is a delightful discussion of the fair game model that is used to motivate the notion of the "caution coefficient" – Fisher's term for the cost of risk, a concept developed in Fisher (1906).

Fisher measures the cost of risk as the difference between the expected value ("mathematical value") and the price that will be paid for the gamble: "a sound minded investor will pay less than the mathematical value for a chance to gain money on a risk. That is, he will trim the price by means of a 'caution coefficient'" (p. 205). It is clear that Fisher was advocating the use of mean-variance expected utility functions to model investor choice:

> The "caution coefficient" becomes, in practice, greater and greater as the risk grows. If my chance of getting a dollar is a certainty, there would be no reduction on account of the caution factor. If it is like the chance of betting on "heads" or "tails," the caution factor may trim the price of the chance down from fifty cents, in mathematical value, to say, forty cents for the chance to win the dollar. That is a reduction on account of caution to 20 per cent. But if one bets on two heads in succession, the reduction on account of caution would be correspondingly greater, so that instead of paying twenty-five cents, the mathematical value, the investor might insist on a reduction of more than 20 per cent to say, fifteen cents. It is both normal and proper that the higher the risk the cheaper the chance of winning can be obtained, compared to its mathematical value.

What remains is for Fisher to translate this risk-return tradeoff into a portfolio context.

A key result of modern portfolio theory is that the market does not reward the total variability of a security's return, only that part which cannot be eliminated in an efficiently diversified portfolio. Whether Fisher grasped this point is unclear from the key part of the discussion:

> Hence, the more risky the investment would be to a lone individual playing the game, the safer it is, if, by pooling in an investment trust with wide diversification in investment, the individual risk is thereby absorbed. For as the (individual) risk grows it can be constantly absorbed by corresponding increases in diversification. Thus the individual investor of the trust may gain more on the riskier investments, bought by the trusts at much less than their mathematical value, than if he played the market alone with less risky investments, but bought at much nearer their mathematical value.

Fisher goes on to observe that the aggregate risk reducing benefits associated with increasing use of "investment trusts, investment counsels and other skilled means of diversifying" contributed to the overall rise in stock prices during the 1920s.

Fisher (1930, ch. 13) contains a number of other intellectual gems. For example, Fisher (p. 206) seems to anticipate what Markowitz was to do over two decades later: "This principle (of higher expected return for the same level of risk through diversification), so far as I know, never has been definitively formulated in the investment market." Fisher directly ties the benefits of diversification to the "principle of constant inspection." Portfolios have to be actively monitored – "rebalanced" in modern terminology – in order to achieve the anticipated portfolio expected return. Bond portfolios require less monitoring than stock portfolios. Fisher explicitly identifies the value of "scientific appraisals of the stock market" to increasing the value of stocks in general and spoke favorably about the benefits of what has come to be called "fundamental analysis." Fisher recognizes the differences between the various entities using the moniker "investment trusts" – some of which were "avowedly of the most speculative type ... because they may heavily concentrate their holdings." Finally, Fisher explicitly recognized the diversification benefits of holding foreign securities.

As for the identification of an historical starting point for diversification models, Markowitz proposes Shakespeare's *Merchant of Venice* (1600). As discussed in Poitras (2000, p. 110), this choice is somewhat misguided. A more appropriate starting point would be the 1770s in Geneva. By this time, security markets had achieved a remarkable level of sophistication about the notions that Markowitz and others were to explore almost two centuries later under the guise of "modern portfolio theory." In particular, an investment scheme appeared in the early 1770s that reflected intimate understanding of the gains accruing to portfolio diversification (Alter and Riley 1986; Velde and Weir 1992). The scheme, colloquially referred to as "*trente demoiselles de Geneve*" involved a number of Genevan banks creating "investment trusts" that were formed by pooling life annuities issued by the French government. At this time the French government was still using flat-rate pricing of life annuities, that took little account of the age of the nominee in setting the price. Using actuarially sound pricing methods, the flat-rate prices were fairly priced for an adult about age 50 (Velde and Weir 1992).

Even though there was an expected gain to purchasing life annuities written on young nominees, there was still the risk of unforeseen events. According to Velde and Weir (1992), the Genevan banks:

> developed lists of young girls from Genevan families to name as the contingent lives. The families were selected for their record of health and longevity. The girls were mostly between the ages of five and ten, and were selected only after surviving smallpox . . . The Genevan banks purchased large amounts on each life to reduce transactions costs, but pooled together annuities on enough different lives to reduce the risk. The most common number of lives in a pool was 30, hence the name of the scheme.

The banks then "resold small fractions of their pools of annuities to individual investors." Sometimes the cash flows from the life annuities were passed-through directly to investors, in other cases the cash flows were repackaged in other forms, such as tontines.

All this reflects a relatively modern state of financial sophistication. In addition to capturing the gains from risk pooling, claims against the pools were "an easily negotiated asset . . . because the bank's dispassionate selection of lives eliminated problems of asymmetric information and moral hazard" associated with life annuities written on single lives (Velde and Weir 1992). This process was facilitated by the substitution of "the paper of the investment trust for the paper of the annuities themselves." In addition to capturing the French government's sizeable mispricing of life annuities written on young, healthy lives, the pools were able to capture the risk premium available from portfolio diversification. The result was that the claims against the pools could be sold at yields well below those directly paid on individual life annuities issued by the French government (see end of chapter questions).

Over time, the investment technology developed by the Genevan banks spread to other countries, most notably the Dutch republic. The Dutch schemes, often organized by important brokers instead of banks, introduced an additional wrinkle. This involved using the surplus of interest received from the French government over interest paid to claim holders to buy back shares in the pool. In some cases, the allocation of surplus was not complete, with the residual cash flow going to the brokers who originated the scheme (Alter and Riley 1986, p. 28). In any event, the "share buyback" feature would act to reduce the number of claims on the fund, thereby increasing potential future returns of pool claimholders. In summary, the pooling scheme involved many modern notions including: the gains to diversification; investment trust/mutual fund origination; security pass-through; and share buybacks. This combination of these features provides strong support for the selection of the "*trente demoiselles de Geneve*" as the most appropriate historical starting point for the theory of portfolio diversification.

Old Finance, modern Finance and New Finance[27]

While the "*trente demoiselles de Geneve*" investment scheme is of historical interest, it is not possible to date the beginnings of modern Finance from this date. Not only is this date far removed from the institutional context of modern financial markets, the subject of modern Finance is much more than a collection of notions such as "the gains to portfolio diversification." The various notions are connected by a philosophical approach – logical positivism – that unifies these notions to create a coherent and persuasive school of thought. The relevance of this school is clarified by considering the process by which modern Finance was able to supplant during the 1950s and 1960s the "Old Finance" school epitomized by the "Graham and Dodd approach" that emphasized the security selection aspect of investment. By shifting focus onto the portfolio diversification problem, modern Finance argued for the elimination of the firm specific risk that was the stock in trade of the Old Finance adherents. In this process, a new philosophy of investment analysis emerged.

As discussed in section 1.3, a range of philosophical issues need to be addressed in order to develop insight into the prevailing approaches to security analysis and investment strategy. It was argued that modern Finance has an inherent positivist bias that is reflected in both the rhetoric and the prescriptions of academics and, to a lesser extent, practitioners. This bias has resulted in a methodological approach to the subject that seeks to emulate the natural sciences. Yet, being concerned with variables that are the outcome of human interaction, Finance is a human science. While the inductive methods of the natural sciences are necessary to the progress of knowledge in Finance, these techniques are insufficient in the human sciences. Knowledge about phenomena in the human sciences is not rigidly cumulative. Events are historical and, as such, require interpretation in the context of the times. The process of interpretation and prediction is complicated by having to deal with the "uncertainty" of future events. Unlike in the natural sciences, it is possible for writers of the past, working with less data and knowledge, to have insightful understandings of a specific phenomenon that compares favorably with the views of contemporary writers.

This chapter has been concerned with developing the intellectual history of security analysis. This also required some selected discussion of financial history. The time line incorporates Graham and Dodd (1934), a text that is heavily influenced by the historical events which preceded its publication. Yet, the text stands as an example of how writers from a previous era, working with less data and "knowledge," produce results that have a timeless quality. To be sure, Graham and Dodd (1934) has to be read in the context of the time the book was written as do other such books from that period, e.g., J.M. Keynes (1936). However, given this, Graham and Dodd (1934) acts like a beacon that can be used to determine where modern Finance is now situated on the intellectual landscape – how far positivism has come to dominate the approach to the subject. As a consequence of recognizing the biases in modern Finance, even basic results such as "stock returns will outperform bond returns in the long run" can be given a more useful interpretation in terms of predicting what type of investment strategy to employ or which particular securities to purchase.

Haugen (1999a,b) provides a refreshing description of the academic evolution from the "Old Finance" of Graham and Dodd to the world of "Modern Finance" (modern Finance) associated with modern portfolio theory, the CAPM and the EMH. Haugen proposes that the evidence against modern Finance, in terms of anomalies and the poor predictive ability of the models, is so strong that a "New Finance" is emerging to replace modern Finance. For Haugen (1999b, p. 8), the New Finance represents the complete supremacy of the inductive method:

> And now Modern Finance begins to teeter.
> And a New Finance appears.
> Discard those theories that obviously have *no* predictive power. Discard the requirement that all explanations must be based on rational economic behavior. Look carefully at the data and measure accurately without preconception. Discard the tradition that you must model *first* without looking and *then* verify. Carefully measure behavior first, and then find *reasonable* and *plausible* explanations for what you see. Ascension of the *ad hoc*, expected return, factor model. The measure of any model's relative merit: the *unmined, out-of-sample, relative accuracy of its predictions.*

For those unable to see whether this is sincerity or sarcasm, the next sentence is telling: "Go back to teaching students a *craft* rather than a *religion*." For Haugen, the New Finance achieves complete supremacy for the inductive methods of the natural sciences.

Putting aside Haugen's enthusiastic views concerning the emergence of the New Finance, Haugen (1999b, pp. 3–8) does give a useful analysis concerning the progression of Finance from the time of Graham and Dodd (1934) to the present. Haugen obtained his education in Finance in the early 1960s, "when Modern Finance was relatively young and when the Old Finance was dying." Accounting and law were the basic foundations of the Old Finance and the professors of the time were experts in those fields. The theme of the Old Finance was the analysis of financial statements and the nature of financial claims. Classic texts were Graham, Dodd and Tatham (1951) and Dewing (1953). "Graham and Dodd spent most of their book showing us the painful process of adjusting accounting statements so that earnings and assets of different companies could be directly compared... In (Dewing), we learned the legal rights of financial claims – *in great detail*. We learned the laws relating to merger and acquisition as well as those governing bankruptcy and reorganization."

Haugen describes Graham and Dodd as "very *dry* stuff and not too interesting." Dewing, on the other hand, made Graham and Dodd "look like a Stephen King thriller." Haugen views the professors of the Old Finance as teachers of a craft. "As possible future financial executives, we needed to know the rules of the game if we had to merge or go bust, as well as the legal impediments on our firm's behavior created by the financial claims that were there today or might be there tomorrow." The time of Haugen's graduate finance education, the early 1960s, was "an interesting time indeed" as modern Finance was breaking onto the academic scene, doing battle with and, eventually vanquishing the Old Finance. Though the birth of modern Finance can be traced to the portfolio optimization model of Markowitz (1952, 1959), the model was largely unnoticed until the emergence during the late 1950s and early 1960s of the other pillars of modern Finance: the Modigliani-Miller irrelevance theorems; the capital asset pricing model; and the efficient markets hypothesis. In contrast to the accounting and law foundations of the Old Finance, modern Finance was a product of financial economics. The central theme was that securities could be valued using models assuming rational economic behavior.

The emergence of modern Finance represented a direct attack on the teachings of the Old Finance. Haugen (1999b, p. 6) observes: "The craft of finance and the teachings of my old professors had been rendered *obsolete. It's not nice to be obsolete.* The professors of the Old Finance fought very hard to retain their relevance. The battles of this intellectual war are still recorded in the pages of the old issues of the *Journal of Finance* and the *American Economic Review.* But the professors of the Old (Finance) lost most of these battles, and eventually they lost the war itself." The winning of the rhetorical intellectual battle brought a wave of new professors into Finance programs, trained in graduate programs that emphasized theorizing using the assumption of rational economic behavior. The position of the proponents of modern Finance was buttressed by the emergence of option pricing theory: "Modern Finance took off. It became the dominant discipline in business schools, and it carried great influence in the real world." Having gained a position of intellectual superiority, proponents of modern Finance actively promoted the paradigm.

The intellectual history of modern Finance from the mid-1960s until the present makes for an interesting case study in the process by which knowledge is created in an academic environment. The developments are similar to those in economics where the assumption that economic agents are rational also became the central theme of economic theory, e.g., Kindleberger (1989, p. 29). Even though rationality is only an assumption that may or may not be an accurate description of the world, Haugen, Kindleberger and others observe that the validity of the assumption was "intellectually enforced" by the younger network of academics. This enforcement process took place in the journals and in the classrooms. Given the substantial investment of human capital that had been made by the younger network in the techniques and knowledge associated with the rational maximizing models, such enforcement activities are not surprising. However, as Haugen puts it (1999b, p. 7), "even when the mud is thick, truth always makes its way to the surface."

Haugen provides an interesting description of the enforcement process:

> Those who would dare to question the validity of the (Modern Finance) paradigm – especially that of efficient markets – were summarily dismissed as *gauche.*
>
> Those who dared to publish papers contradicting the paradigms were ridiculed. Their studies were supposedly replete with bias. And their methods, of course, were naive.
>
> Their studies included only firms that survived the study period – survival bias. They used earnings numbers that may not have been publicly available at the time they bought the stocks – look-ahead bias. They spun the computer countless times until they got an interesting result – data mining. They didn't take transactions costs into account. They didn't risk adjust their returns. They didn't test for statistical significance. Their results weren't robust in different time periods.
>
> On and on . . .

Haugen is quick to point out that the early studies that were critical of the paradigms of modern Finance did turn out to be on the mark: "But (were) summarily *dismissed,* in any case." Haugen traces the emergence of the New Finance to the accumulation of empirical results that invalidated the main propositions of modern Finance. New Finance is based on the theme of inefficient markets. The main paradigm, for what it is worth, is inductive ad hoc factor models. The operative techniques are inductive methods from statistics and econometrics. There is a substantial overlap, if not a formal equivalence between Haugen's New Finance and behavioral Finance, e.g., Shefrin (2000).

While Haugen's description of the progress of modern Finance is helpful, the notion that there is a "New Finance" emerging is suspect. It seems to be predicated on a misunderstanding of the positivist philosophy that underpins modern Finance albeit with less emphasis on the formal logic of model development. The New Finance is just an evolutionary branch of modern Finance. Even an individual as jaded as Haugen about modern Finance still clings to the belief that the inductive process will lead to an accumulation of knowledge that progressively uncovers the true nature of the subject. There are physical laws of nature governing financial activities. Given enough data, these laws can be identified and used to make valid predictions about optimal portfolios or security prices. Whatever the philosophical basis, chapter 3 is concerned with developing the elements of modern Finance that are applicable to security analysis and investment strategy.

Modern Finance approaches security analysis and investment strategy within the context of models that assume rational economic behavior. A strong belief in market efficiency provides a basis for arguing that traditional security analysis, along the lines of Graham and Dodd, will not be able to consistently earn abnormal returns. Given this belief about the analysis of individual securities, rationality dictates that investment strategy focus on the identification of optimally diversified portfolios. Assuming that the capital asset pricing model is an accurate description of security market equilibrium, it follows that the rational investor will hold portfolios that are composed of the riskless asset and the market portfolio. The weights in which these two assets are held depends on the risk attitudes of the investor. For example, investors with a high level of risk tolerance would borrow at the riskless rate (negative weight on the riskless asset) and leverage up in the market portfolio (positive weight greater than one). Those with low levels of risk tolerance would hold both the riskless asset and the market portfolio (both weights positive and less than one).

In section 1.3, it was argued that: "It is naive to believe that the route to knowledge and truth about the subject at hand is unproblematic, providing that one adheres to the prevailing positivist ideology." Chapter 3 takes a different slant. In much the same way that it is inappropriate for adherents of the prevailing positivist ideology to suppress contrary notions, it is equally inappropriate to dismiss the insights that the positivism of modern Finance has provided. Once the philosophical biases and rhetorical approach of the subject have been accurately assessed, there is much of value in modern Finance that is relevant to security analysis and investment strategy. For example, there is the notion that rational investors are well advised to avoid the hazards of selecting individual securities and, instead, invest in risky assets by purchasing the market portfolio. This prescription is intuitively persuasive and insightful. Another useful insight is the notion that investment strategy needs to focus on the weights for the riskless asset and the market portfolio. This idea is readily extended to the practice of fund managers periodically rebalancing the fixed income and equity proportions in the model portfolio.

Positivism strives to achieve a scientific approach, divorced from normative values, emphasizing quantification, measurement and empirical verification of hypotheses. As such, modern Finance is a combination of theoretical hypotheses and the accumulation of empirical results aimed at testing those hypotheses. Initially, considerable effort was expended in developing models, based on rational maximizing behavior of economic agents. Included among the most important models are the Markowitz portfolio optimization model and the capital asset pricing model. The theoretical framework employed to model the rational decision making process usually involved agents, subject to a budget constraint, choosing among available securities or capital assets in order to maximize the expected utility of terminal wealth. Because the value of terminal wealth depends on the prices of securities or assets that are not known at the time the optimization decision is being made, the models of modern Finance are examples of the more general decision making under uncertainty problem.

Conquering the Old Finance: from Markowitz to Fama

A number of candidates are available for selection as the intellectual beginning of modern Finance. Numerous sources identify Markowitz (1952, 1959) as the starting point, e.g., Brealey (1991), Rubinstein (2002), Markowitz (1999). In contrast, Rubinstein (2003) suggests an earlier beginning, tracing the roots back to Fisher (1906, 1907, 1930a) and Williams (1938). Accepting that the Markowitz approach was not widely recognized until after the contributions by W. Sharpe (Sharpe 1963, 1964), the contributions of Modigliani and Miller (Modigliani and Miller 1958; Miller and Modigliani 1961) (MM1; MM2) are arguably an appropriate starting point. This position is supported by a close reading of the literature at the time. For example, in launching a "hostile review" of MM1 (Bernstein 1992, p. 175), Durand (1959) represented a broad consensus of academic opinion at the time that MM1 appeared. Durand (1960) demonstrates that, at the time, the Markowitz model had not received the close scrutiny that was given to MM1. Initial criticisms of the evolving modern Finance approach included individuals that, at first glance, would seem to be disposed to MM1, MM2 and the Markowitz approach, e.g., Durand (1957).

As Rubinstein (2003) recognizes, the attribution of ideas to specific individuals is a difficult task, particularly where the individuals involved are no longer living. As such, the task of identifying the origins of modern Finance has been simplified significantly by Bernstein (1992) who provides a wonderful collection of first hand insights into the individuals involved at the beginnings of modern Finance in the 1950s and early 1960s. While it is tempting to push back the time line to individuals writing prior to this period, such as L. Bachelier, J.B. Williams and I. Fisher, there is too much of a temporal gap separating these contributors from the widespread recognition of the "bombshell assertions" (Bernstein 1992, ch. 9) that modern Finance adherents used to supplant the Old Finance from the core curriculum of business schools. In this interpretation, the modern Finance revolution begins with Modigliani and Miller (1958), gathers steam during the 1960s and reaches fruition by the middle of the 1970s. Though Markowitz (1952) appears at an earlier date, it is Markowitz (1959) that more appropriately fits into the time line suggested here.

The selection of MM1 for the beginning date of the modern Finance revolution is not intended to imply that MM1 was the most theoretically significant of the early contributions. Bernstein (1992, p. 41) reflects the generally accepted view among modern Finance adherents about the relative significance of Markowitz's contribution:

> The most famous insight in the history of modern finance and investment appeared in a short paper titled: "Portfolio Selection." It was published in the March 1952 issue of the *Journal of Finance*, the only journal then in existence for scholars in the field. Its author was an unknown 25-year old graduate student from the University of Chicago named Harry Markowitz.

Having said this, Bernstein proceeds to recognize a time line that supports the primacy of MM1:

> No one, including Markowitz, was aware that his paper would turn out to be a landmark in the history of ideas. Although his achievements would earn him a Nobel Prize in economic sciences 38 years later, the paper languished for nearly ten years after publication attracting fewer than twenty citations in the academic literature until after 1960. By that time, Markowitz had written his dissertation on the subject and had converted it into a full-length book.

In contrast to the slow acceptance of the Markowitz theory of portfolio optimization, MM1 gained almost instant notoriety.

Markowitz (1952, 1959), ultimately, became the theoretical foundation for the "modern portfolio theory" that is at the center of the modern Finance approach. In contrast, MM1 and MM2 did not make such a wide reaching contribution. This is, at least partly, due to the nature of the results being presented. MM1 demonstrated that, in perfect capital markets, the capital structure of the firm will be irrelevant to the market value of the firm, i.e., there is no optimal capital structure. Similarly, MM2 demonstrated, again in perfect capital markets, that the dividend policy of the firm was also irrelevant to the market value of the firm. In the case of the firm's capital structure, MM1 proposes that the market value of the firm (= market value of debt + market value of equity) is determined by the assets side of the balance sheet. The liabilities plus equity side of the balance sheet only determines the division of the asset cash flows between security claimholders. It is not possible to change the market value of the cash flows from the assets by reorganizing the division of those cash flows between claimholders.

In addition to the basic demonstration that the value of the firm is determined by the assets side of the balance sheet, the MM1 argument also had to deal with investor preferences for a specific type of capital structure. Given the random behavior of asset cash flows, firms with more debt on the balance sheet will have a higher variability in the payments made to equity claims. While this would seem to indicate that the common stock in firms with higher debt levels is riskier and, as a consequence, will have a different market value than the common stock of an otherwise identical firm with a lower debt level, MM1 demonstrates that by engaging in borrowing or lending activities in conjunction with purchases of the common stock, individual investors are able to create a "synthetic capital structure" for the firm that is consistent with the desired portfolio cash flow variability associated with holdings of the firm's securities. Because the individual investor is able to synthetically achieve a desired capital structure through portfolio allocation, the market value of the firm's debt and equity claims will not be priced to reflect differences in firm capital structure.

MM2 follows lines similar to MM1. The dividend policy of the firm is irrelevant because individuals are able to create a synthetic dividend that is consistent with the individual's desired dividend payout. From the firm's perspective, dividend payments made to shareholders represent forgone retained earnings. In cases where retained earnings are insufficient to sustain the capital requirements needed to fund the firm's growth, the dividend payments are recouped through new share issues. Where the dividend policy is lower than dictated by the firm's capital requirements, then the excess retained earnings will be used to repurchase the firm's common stock. Within this context, if the individual finds the firm's dividend policy is lower than desired, then a fraction of the share holdings can be sold each period to obtain the desired level of "synthetic dividend" cash flow. Similarly, if the dividend payout is higher than desired, the surplus can be used to purchase shares. While, over time, the number of shares outstanding will differ between otherwise identical firms with different dividend policies, the market value of the equity claims will be the same. As in MM1, this occurs because the value of the firm is determined by the assets side of the balance sheet.

Though MM1 and MM2 did not go on to play a central role in the theoretical development of modern portfolio theory – the core of modern Finance – MM1 and MM2 did play a central role in the attack on the Old Finance. Dividend policy and the capital structure of the firm are key concerns in traditional security analysis. The theoretical claim that such concerns are irrelevant is potentially devastating. More importantly, the irrelevance results were made by exploiting the analytical properties of perfect capital markets. The rational, maximizing individual operating in a "frictionless" market environment – a central feature of the theories that characterize modern Finance – represented a metaphor that was to prove irresistible compared to the institutionally and legally driven model of the Old Finance. However, the topics that concerned MM1 and MM2 were focused largely on the central issues of Old Finance and did not play a crucial role in the evolution of the core theory of modern Finance.

What early contributions did play a key role in the evolution of the core theory of modern Finance? The general consensus among adherents of modern Finance, e.g., Rubinstein (2002), is that at the head of the list are the seminal contributions that led to the capital asset pricing model (CAPM) and the market model (see section 3.2): Markowitz (1952, 1959) and Sharpe (1963, 1964). In addition, as recognized in Markowitz (1999), Tobin (1958) can also be given some credit for containing the essence of the two fund separation result, albeit within the context of modeling the demand for money in a portfolio optimization framework. Markowitz (1999, p. 10) observes: "At a meeting with Tobin in attendance, I once referred to his 1958 article as the first capital asset pricing model." Apparently Tobin did not accept this interpretation. In any event, while making an important contribution to monetary economics, Tobin (1958) did not have a similar impact on Finance. It was Sharpe (1963, 1964) that recognized the key revolutionary result: "the expected return on each security is linearly related to its beta and only its beta."

The core theory of modern Finance is not limited to the Markowitz mean-variance optimization framework and the CAPM. Running roughly in parallel with the development of these concepts was the work on the random character of stock market prices that culminated in Cootner (1965) and Fama (1965). While interesting in itself, this work also laid the foundation for the efficient markets hypothesis (EMH), and the modeling of stock prices (returns) as conditional expectations with information sets characterized as weak form, semi-strong form and strong form (see section 1.2).[28] This progression was aided considerably by Fama et al. (1969) which introduced a novel statistical methodology, based on cumulative abnormal residuals, that could be used to empirically test the semi-strong (and strong) form of the EMH. In turn, development of the EMH strengthened the argument for using the CAPM and Markowitz model. More precisely, under the EMH, it was not possible to use available information to earn systematic, risk-adjusted abnormal returns. This substantively undermined the basis for doing Old Finance security analysis, strengthening the rationale for the elimination of diversifiable risk through portfolio optimization methods.

While circa 1965 modern Finance was still in the process of evolving into a coherent package, Fama (1970) illustrates that by the end of the decade modern Finance had developed into something resembling a coherent whole. With the appearance of Fama (1976) (*Foundations of Finance*), the revolution against the Old Finance was largely completed, the corpus of modern Finance was solidified and the program of future research was well defined. In addition, by the mid-1970s, attention of the modern Finance school was shifting to extending and exploring the seminal contribution of Black and Scholes (1973). Though a connection can be made between the CAPM and the Black-Scholes formula, it is difficult to meld the notion of pricing by arbitrage with that of pricing by expectation. Though there were substantive efforts to exploit the continuous time pricing technology used in Black and Scholes (1973) to the CAPM framework, e.g., Merton (1969, 1973a), a disconnect between these two streams of modern Finance survives to the present day.

Consistent with the positivist approach, modern Finance has adopted the rational, maximizing individual as the central abstraction upon which theoretical knowledge about security pricing can be obtained. Inductive methods – especially variants of regression analysis – are used to determine whether a particular version of a theoretical model is consistent with observed data. If the null hypothesis is not empirically supported, the model is restructured, typically by altering an assumption, and retested. While sharing this general epistemological approach, there have been three distinct tracks in modern Finance: the *CAPM* and Markowitz mean-variance portfolio optimization model; the *EMH*; and, the *contingent claims pricing models* that emerged following Black and Scholes (1973). Though there has been some complementarity between each of these tracks, each evolved somewhat differently and, as a consequence, modern Finance cannot be viewed as a coherent doctrine of interlocking parts. Questioning of one part – such as the EMH being questioned by the "New Finance" – does not necessarily involve questioning of another part – such as contingent claims pricing models.

The lack of initial coherence between the inductive EMH and the theoretical CAPM created a number of confusions that, at the time, puzzled those seeking to understand the emerging school of thought. Some of these confusions still survive to puzzle those being introduced to the dictates of modern Finance. This is illustrated by the use of the term "efficient frontier" to define a central concept in the Markowitz approach. The "efficiency" in this case is only loosely connected to the informational "efficiency" that concerns the EMH or the Pareto "efficiency" that arises in microeconomic theory. Similarly, the different tracks in modern Finance each lead to somewhat different implications for security analysis and investment strategy. For example, while the CAPM leads to two fund separation as the appropriate investment strategy, contingent claims pricing technology suggests that dynamic portfolio insurance is an appropriate strategy. In the end, what binds the strands of modern Finance together is the underpinnings provided by the positivist approach.

Questions ?

1 In discussing the investment mantra, "never put all your eggs in one basket," Withers (1911) observes that "expert advisers of the public are fertile in schemes for scientific distribution of risks by climate, or by geography, or by industries, etc., etc." Explain the connection of this statement to the development of modern portfolio theory.

2 Ben Graham made the following observation in the *Intelligent Investor*: "The distinction between investment and speculation in common stocks has always been a useful one and its disappearance is a cause for concern. We have often said that Wall Street as an institution would be well advised to reinstate this distinction and to emphasize it in all dealings with the public. Otherwise the stock exchanges may some day be blamed for heavy speculative losses, which those who suffered them had not been properly warned against."

Comment on the implications of this statement for the valuation of securities. In your answer be sure to provide an assessment of the validity of the statement as well as a discussion of how security valuation would have to be conducted if the statement were correct.

3 In chapter 12 of *The General Theory* J.M. Keynes described the process of valuing common stocks as: "a game of Snap, of Old Maid, of Musical Chairs – a pastime in which he is victor who says *Snap* neither too soon nor too late, who passes the Old Maid to his neighbor before the game is over, who secures a chair for himself when the music stops." Comment on the implications of this statement for the valuation of securities. In your answer be sure to provide an assessment of the validity of the statement as well as a discussion of how security valuation would have to be conducted if the statement were correct.

NOTES

1   This section is based on Poitras (2000), chapter 6.

2   An usufruct is the right of temporary possession, use or enjoyment of the advantages of property belonging to another, so far as may be had without causing damage or prejudice to the property.

3   Prior to this time, English government debt was almost exclusively short term. Tracy (1985) examines the implications of this for the relatively slower development of English financial markets, relative to those in northern Europe.

4   A major part of the success of the English public debt system is due to the allocation of control over taxation to the Parliament, arising from the Glorious Revolution. With this reform, Parliament was able to ensure that the funding of interest payments with specific taxes was removed from the meddling of sovereigns.

5   The tontine has an interesting connection to the early history of the NYSE. The signatories to the Buttonwood Agreement of 1792 required a meeting place suitable to their needs. Banding together with other merchants and commercial interests, the brokers formed the "New York Tontine Coffee House Company" in which 203 subscribers contributed $200 each for the construction of the Tontine Coffee House at the corner of Wall and Water Streets. The construction was finished in 1793 and the Tontine Coffee House acted as a meeting place for "merchants, brokers and various commercial bodies, till 1827" (Eames 1894, p. 17) when the first Merchants Exchange was constructed at Wall and Hanover Streets. The name of the coffee house came from the tontine associated with the original articles of the corporation that called for the property to be held by the corporation until only seven members remained alive at which time the property would be sold and the proceeds distributed to the survivors.

6   Material in this section requires fixed income concepts that are developed in chapter 4, especially section 4.1.

7   Daston (1987, n. 5) quotes James (1853) for a 14% rate on English life annuities, for any age, issued by the state under William III. This translates into approximately 7 years' purchase.

8   It was common at this time for a number of spelling variants to be used, all of which can be considered correct spelling. The spelling Jan de Witt is found in Hald (1990), Coolidge (1990) and Pearson (1978). Hald also gives the variant Johan de Witt while Pearson reports John de Witt. Heywood (1985) uses Johannes de Wit while Hendricks (1852–3) uses John de Wit. In the *Valuation*, the author is listed as "J. de Wit."

9   Karl Pearson, who had strong views on a number of individuals involved in the history of statistics, depreciates de Witt's work by claiming: "the data are uncertain and the method of computation is fallacious" (Pearson 1978, p. 100). This is at variance with Hald (1990), Alter and Riley (1986) and others. Pearson (1978, p. 702) also appears to have been unaware of Hudde's contribution, "I was unaware that [Hudde] had contributed to the theory of probability." Hecksher (1955, v. 1, p. 214) also raises the possibility that de Witt might not have written all the works which are credited to him by referring to "the Dutchman, Pieter de la Court, whose main work often went under the name of the well-known statesman Jan de Witt." The practice of contracting-out of intellectual contributions was not uncommon around this time, e.g., Joshua Child and the work of Philopatris (Letwin 1963). However, it is highly unlikely that there were more than a handful of individuals both informed and capable enough to appreciate the relevance of Huygens's contribution on mathematical expectation to pricing life annuities. De Witt must be included in this handful of individuals.

10 There are various sources on the valuation of life contingencies, e.g., Alter and Riley (1986), Hald (1990) and Pearson (1978).

11 De Witt's submission to the States General was "a prime minister's attempt to convince the States General that the price of annuities should be raised from 14 to 16 years' purchase. Typical of other prime ministers in critical situations, de Witt was short of time, and he had presumably

no hope of getting the price raised to more than 16 years' purchase. This may explain the inconsistencies in the paper" (Hald 1990, p. 130). This situation speaks to the importance of Hudde's contribution in checking and expanding the original work of de Witt. In a modern setting, it is possible that de Witt and Hudde would have combined to produce a finished publication in which both were co-authors.

12 See Alter and Riley (1986), Hald (1990) and Pearson (1978) for more indepth and contrasting views on the history of pricing for life annuities. The use of age 3 as a starting point is due to the high infant mortality of the time making it too risky to designate an infant as the nominee. Though the pricing is done for a nominee age 3, calculating the value of a life annuity for older nominees is straight forward.

13 Halley's paper also did not have any impact on English government borrowing practices as life annuities continued to be sold at seven years' purchase without reference to the age of the annuitant (Hald 1990, p. 139).

14 This section is based on Poitras (2000) chapter 8. The discussion in section 2.2 focuses on early trading of equity securities with little attention being given to the development of debt securities that have a much longer history than common and joint stocks. The history of debt securities is discussed in more detail in section 2.1.

15 This evidence, quoted in Kellenbenz (1957, p. 128) is not claiming that Jews owned 85% of the stock. Rather, Jews, as the brokers, market markers and gamblers, did 85% of the trading.

16 De Marchi and Harrison (1994, p. 62) appear to claim that de la Vega proposed a model where stock prices were a random process, quoting de la Vega as saying: "shares are enveloped in a veil of almost religious mystery such that the more one reasons the less one grasps, and the more cunning one tries to be the more mistakes one makes." The solution, according to de la Vega, is to trade randomly. Is it possible to claim de la Vega was a precursor of the random walk model of stock prices?

17 Modern security analysis has a much more refined treatment of firm profitability, based on exploiting the much more elaborate accounting information now available. Graham and Dodd's dictum that security analysis involves the use of financial statements would have been lost on Mortimer because, at his time, accounting information was quite rudimentary and was often proprietary.

18 Though Edgar Smith was also a financial analyst and investment manager during the 1920s, he is included in the academic group as many of his contributions were targeted at the academic audience, e.g., Smith (1927, 1931). In McCloskey's terminology, Smith was actively involved in conversations with academics.

19 Wendt (1982) discusses the history of the *Wall Street Journal*.

20 The complete history of changes in the Dow Jones Averages can be downloaded from the Dow-Jones website: www.dowjones.com.

21 The life of Irving Fisher extended well beyond the world of academics, e.g., Klein (2001, pp. 86–8). Born in 1867, the son of a Congregationalist minister, Fisher studied mathematics and political economy at Yale University. The claim that Fisher was a self-made business success has to be tempered by the fact that in 1893 Fisher married Margaret Hazard, daughter of Rowland Hazard, a wealthy woolen manufacturer. As a wedding gift, the happy couple was presented with a palatial abode in New Haven. It was not until 1912 that Fisher developed his card index system that he marketed through his Index Visible Company. In 1926, this company was merged with its major competitor to form what was eventually to become the Remington Rand Company. During the 1920s he was able to turn part of the house into a home for his Index Number Institute, staffed by more than a dozen people. The institute prepared a weekly newsletter that was distributed to various newspapers around the world. Having suffered and survived tuberculosis in 1898, Fisher was for the rest of his life devoted to pursuing and promoting clean living. This part of his life found him to be a confirmed prohibitionist and one of the founders and organizers of the American Eugenics Society. This Society was an active promoter of the cause of "race betterment."

22 This section is based on Poitras (2002a).

23 While it is tempting to extend the discussion to notions of individual liberty and freedom, this would take the discussion too far afield. However, it is worth observing at this point that this concept of uncertainty "requires a social matrix for its existence" (McKenna and Zannoni 1993, p. 405). This is almost diametrically opposed to the neo-classical approach, of which the modern portfolio theory is an extension. In this approach, decisions are absolute and social conventions and institutions are not required to situate the optimal solution, which is conceived to be immutable.

24 If this interpretation is correct, then long-term high grade corporate bonds would also belong to this category. In any event, this discussion does not deal in a substantive fashion with a key element of Keynesian analysis set out in Keynes (1936): the empirical relationship between the cost of capital (marginal efficiency of investment) and the development of economic activity.

25 For example, Graham, Dodd and Cottle (1962) explicitly state that fundamental analysis is only applicable to securities which are non-speculative. The determination of whether a security is speculative depends on the assets owned by the firm, the presence of tangible cash flows from those assets and the like. Railways, textile companies, shipping companies and the like would typically fall within the scope of fundamental analysis.

26 To the uninitiated, security analysis brings to mind visions of the Cold War or the war on terrorism. Graham and Dodd are to be credited for this seeming misnomer that has been chiseled into the syllabus of Finance. A potentially more attractive title would be "securities analysis," though this could be misconstrued to mean the analysis of combinations involving more than one security.

27 Haugen uses upper case letters for New Finance, Old Finance and Modern Finance. In this text, the classifications roughly correspond to behavioral Finance, traditional Finance and modern Finance. Even though there is more than substantial overlap between the two classification schemes, when reference is being made to Haugen's notions, then upper case will be used, e.g., New Finance. Otherwise, when notions being developed in this book are being referenced, lower case letters will be used, e.g., behavioral Finance.

28 Though Fama (1970) can be credited with popularizing the weak, semi-strong and strong form terminology, Fama credits the origination of these terms to a colleague at the University of Chicago, Harry Roberts.

Chapter Summary

Chapter 3   *Theoretical Developments in Modern Finance*

3.1   Basics of Mean-variance Portfolio Analysis
      The analytical preliminaries
      The optimization model
      Capital allocation lines: introducing a riskfree asset
      The capital market line and market equilibrium
      Criticism of mean-variance portfolio analysis

3.2   Separation, the CAPM and the market model#
      Two fund separation
      The capital asset pricing model*
      The market model*

3.3   Decision making under uncertainty*
      Expected utility theory*
      Cost of risk and risk aversion properties*
      Expected utility and moment preference*

3.4   Financial Engineering with Derivative Securities
      The derivative security renaissance
      The history of portfolio insurance
      Dynamic portfolio insurance

Questions
Notes

# Indicates some sub-sections contain advanced material
* Indicates complete section is advanced material

Theoretical Developments in Modern Finance

chapter **3**

3.1   BASICS OF MEAN-VARIANCE PORTFOLIO ANALYSIS

The analytical preliminaries

Many of the essential analytical tools used in mean-variance portfolio analysis can be found in the results for linear combinations of random variables from mathematical statistics. One basic result is the following, e.g., Freund (1971, p. 195):

> ### Theorem: Moments of linear combinations of random variables
>
> If $X(1)$, $X(2)$, ..., $X(N)$ are random variables and a_1, a_2, ..., a_N are constants and $Y = a_1X(1) + a_2X(2) + \ldots + a_NX(N)$ then:
>
> $$E[Y] = \sum_{i=1}^{N} a_i E[X(i)]$$
>
> $$var[Y] = \sum_{i=1}^{N} a_i^2 \, var[X(i)] + 2 \sum\sum_{i>j} a_i a_j \, cov[X(i), X(j)]$$
>
> where the double sum over $i > j$ extends over all values of i and j, from 1 to N, for which $i > j$.

Derivation of $var[Y]$ requires the observation that $cov[X(i), X(j)] = cov[X(j), X(i)]$. One immediate corollary is that if $cov[X(i), X(j)] = 0$ for all i and j where $i \neq j$, i.e., the random variables are all independent, and $a_1 = a_2 = \ldots = a_N = 1/N$ then $var[Y]$ has the property:

$$\lim_{N \to \infty} var[Y] = \lim_{N \to \infty} \left\{ \sum_{i=1}^{N} a_i^2 \, var[X(i)] \right\} = 0$$

This result has applications in insurance where the random variables are policy payouts and each a_i is the fraction of the portfolio of policies attributable to policy i.

Extending these results to portfolios follows immediately from identifying the random variables as the returns on individual securities held in a given portfolio, i.e., let $X(i) = R_i$ for all i. The definition of the portfolio expected return follows:

Definition

The expected return on the portfolio $E[R_p]$ is the value weighted sum of the expected returns on the individual securities, the $E[R_i]$:

$$E[R_p] = \sum_{i=1}^{k} w_i E[R_i]$$

where k is the number of securities in the portfolio. To calculate the value weights, w_i:

$$w_i = \frac{\$A_i}{\sum_{i=1}^{k} A_i} \quad where \quad \sum_{i=1}^{k} w_i = 1$$

with $\$A_i$ being the dollar value invested in security i and the sum over all $\$A_i$ being the total amount of money invested in the portfolio.

As a simple example, consider having $1 million invested in a portfolio of 2 securities, and there is $500,000 in each security, then each $w_i = .5$. As a slightly more complicated example consider the following problem: At the beginning of the year, Joe Investor owned four securities in the following amounts: A, 100 shares; B, 400 shares; C, 200 shares; D, 200 shares. The current prices of the securities are: A = $12.50; B = $17.50; C = $25; and, D = $50. In one year's time, Joe expects the prices to be: A = $25; B = $20; C = $30; and D = $55. What is the expected return on Joe's portfolio for the year? The solution to this problem is determined by calculating the total value invested as: $100(12.50) + 400(\$17.50) + 200(\$25) + 200(\$50) = \$23,250$. This permits the calculation of the value weights: $w_A = 1,250/23,250 = .054$; $w_B = .301$; $w_C = .215$; $w_D = .430$. The expected return on the portfolio can now be calculated as: $E[R_p] = .054(E[R_A]) + .301(E[R_B]) + .215(E[R_C]) + .430(E[R_D]) = .054(1.00) + .301(.143) + .215(.2) + .430(.1) = .183$ (18.3%).

The other key element in the mean-variance portfolio model is the standard deviation of portfolio returns. As with calculating the risk for individual securities, calculations are done for the variance and the standard deviation is determined by taking a square root. The standard deviation, as opposed to the variance, is of the appropriate measure of risk because it is in the same units as the expected returns. However, calculations are done using the variance.

Definition

The standard deviation of portfolio returns, σ_p is the square root of the variance of portfolio returns $var[R_p] \equiv \sigma_p^2$. Various *equivalent* forms for the portfolio variance formula are available:

$$var[R_p] = \sigma_p^2 = \sum_{i=1}^{k} \sum_{j=1}^{k} w_i w_j \sigma_{ij} = \sum_{i=1}^{k} w_i^2 \sigma_i^2 + 2\sum_{i>j}^{k} w_i w_j \sigma_{ij}$$

$$= \sum_{i=1}^{k} w_i^2 \sigma_i^2 + 2\sum_{j=1}^{k} \sum_{i=1,i>j}^{k} w_i w_j \sigma_{ij} = \sum_{i=1}^{k} w_i^2 \sigma_i^2 + 2\sum_{i>j}\sum w_i w_j \sigma_{ij}$$

where $cov[R_i, R_j] = \sigma_{ij}$. In the double sum expression, when $i = j$ the covariance is a variance. These expressions can be further manipulated by making further substitutions using the definition for ρ_{ij}, the correlation between R_i and R_j, i.e., $cov[R_i, R_j] = \sigma_{ij} \equiv \rho_{ij}\sigma_i\sigma_j$.

It is easiest to understand these results for the case where $k = 2$, when there are only two securities in the portfolio. In this case:

$$\sigma_p^2 = w_1^2\sigma_1^2 + w_2^2\sigma_2^2 + 2w_1 w_2 \sigma_{12} = w_1^2\sigma_1^2 + (1 - w_1)^2\sigma_2^2 + 2w_1(1 - w_1)\rho_{12}\sigma_1\sigma_2$$

An end of chapter exercise is provided to illustrate the manual application of this result. Similarly for 3 assets in the portfolio:

$$\sigma_p^2 = w_1^2\sigma_1^2 + w_2^2\sigma_2^2 + w_3^2\sigma_3^2 + 2\{w_1 w_2 \sigma_{12} + w_1 w_3 \sigma_{13} + w_2 w_3 \sigma_{23}\}$$

When there are k securities in the portfolio, the resulting portfolio variance will contain k variance terms and $\{k(k-1)\}/2$ covariance terms. The substitutions using the definition for the correlation coefficient and the restriction that the sum of the value weights equals one is left as an exercise.

Having the formula for the variance of portfolio return permits the ready identification of an important special case of an optimum portfolio: the minimum variance portfolio, the portfolio that has the smallest risk in the set of all possible portfolios. The formula for this portfolio can be derived by minimizing $var[R_p]$ with respect to the choice variables, the value weights for each of the individual securities, subject to the restriction that the sum of the value weights be equal to one. In the simple case of the minimum variance portfolio for two securities, using the result that $w_1 + w_2 = 1$:

$$\sigma_p^2 = w_1^2\sigma_1^2 + (1 - w_1)^2\sigma_2^2 + 2w_1(1 - w_1)\sigma_{12}$$

$$\frac{d\sigma_p^2}{dw_1} = 2w_1\sigma_1^2 - 2(1 - w_1)\sigma_2^2 + 2(1 - 2w_1)\sigma_{12} = 0$$

$$w_1^* = \frac{\sigma_2^2 - \sigma_{12}}{\sigma_1^2 + \sigma_2^2 - 2\sigma_{12}}$$

This result demonstrates that the minimum variance portfolio will be a combination of the two securities and not just be fully invested in the security with the lowest risk.

The intuition behind the portfolio diversification problem can be illustrated with the following artificial situation: assume that all the securities in the market have the same expected return of 10% and the same standard deviation of security return of 15% with the covariance between all security returns being .02. Construct an equally weighted portfolio containing N securities. While the expected return on this portfolio will be 10%, the variance of the equally weighted portfolio containing N securities will be:

$$\sigma_p^2 = \sum_{i=1}^{N} \frac{\sigma_i^2}{N^2} + 2\sum_{i>j}^{N} \frac{\sigma_{ij}}{N^2} < .15$$

While the expected return is a linear combination of the individual security expected returns, the same result does not apply to the variance. This property of the variance for a linear combination of random variables is an essential ingredient in the portfolio optimization models.

Recall the result stated previously where, if the random variables are uncorrelated, then the variance of an equally weighted linear combination will go to zero as N goes to infinity. What happens to the portfolio expected return and standard deviation of this portfolio as N gets large? Because it is assumed that all standard deviations are the same, there are N equal terms in the first sum and, because the covariances have been assumed to be equal, there are $N(N - 1)$ terms in the second sum and the portfolio variance reduces to:

$$\sigma_p^2 = \frac{\sigma_i^2}{N} + N(N - 1)\frac{\sigma_{ij}}{N^2} = \frac{\sigma_i^2}{N} + \left(1 - \frac{1}{N}\right)\sigma_{ij}$$

As $N \to \infty$, the first term goes to zero and the portfolio variance is reduced to the covariance. To get this result, N must be very large. Even for portfolios containing, say, 100 securities, there is still some contribution to variance from the σ_i. As noted, when the covariance between all available securities is zero (independent returns), the standard deviation of the portfolio will go to zero as N gets large.

This simple example provides a pedagogical basis for illustrating the gains to diversification. Examining the variance of the equally weighted portfolio described above, the (σ_i^2/N) term applies to the specific risk associated with the individual securities, where the σ_i^2 for each individual security are associated with individual firm specific risks. Because this component of portfolio variance goes to zero as the number of securities gets large, it is appropriately described as *diversifiable risk*. The $(1 - (1/N))\sigma_{ij}$ term is associated with the covariance between security returns. Because this source of portfolio risk does not go to zero as N goes to infinity, it is appropriately described as *nondiversifiable risk*. It follows that the portfolio standard deviation can be decomposed into the sum of diversifiable risk and nondiversifiable risk. Hence, the risk associated with any portfolio of securities equals the sum of the diversifiable risk and nondiversifiable risk for that specific portfolio. "Efficiently diversified" portfolios have eliminated diversifiable risk.

As securities are added to the equally weighted portfolio, the risk of the portfolio is reduced until the lower bound provided by non-diversifiable risk is reached. However, the amount of risk reduction decreases as the number of the securities in the portfolio increases to the point where there is no more firm specific risk that can be eliminated. The lower bound on portfolio risk, associated with the non-diversifiable risk, is due to the covariance between security returns. Modern portfolio theory expends considerable theoretical effort in developing the capital asset pricing model (CAPM) where individual security returns depend on a combination of the riskless interest rate and the covariance of the individual security return with the return on the market portfolio. In this model, it is the nondiversifiable risk, referred to as systematic risk, that is compensated with higher expected return. Hence, *there is a tradeoff between systematic risk and expected return.* Because firm specific risk (unsystematic risk) can be eliminated in an efficiently diversified portfolio, the security market will not reward this source of risk with higher expected return.

The optimization model

The mean-variance portfolio optimization model is a central paradigm of modern Finance. The essence of the model is captured in the following quadratic optimization problem, e.g., Elton and Gruber (1995), Luenberger (1998):[1]

$$\min_{\{w_i\}} var[R_p] = \sum_{i=1}^{k} \sum_{j=1}^{k} w_i w_j \sigma_{ij}$$

$$subject\ to:\quad E[R_p] = \sum_{i=1}^{k} w_i E[R_i] = \bar{c}_n$$

$$for\quad \bar{c}_n \in \{c_0, c_1, c_2, \dots\}\quad where:\quad c_0 = c_{mv}\quad and:\quad \sum_{i=1}^{k} w_i = 1$$

where: k is the number of risky securities or assets available for investment; $E[R_i]$ is the (conditional) expected return on security or asset i; $E[R_p]$ is the expected return on the portfolio; c_{mv} is the return on the minimum variance portfolio; and, $var[R_p]$ is the variance of portfolio return. In this model, the $\{w_i\}$ are the value weights, the fraction of the total value of the portfolio invested in each asset. Though it is conventional to develop the model under the assumptions of perfect capital markets, it is possible, even desirable, to impose additional restrictions on the optimization problem. One such additional restriction is $w_i \geq 0$ for all i. This restriction prevents short selling of securities. Without this restriction, all or almost all securities will be held in some form, either long or short. With the short selling restriction, the resulting optimal portfolios will have many securities that have value weights equal to zero.

The quadratic optimization problem is to determine the value weights for each security which minimize the variance of the return on the portfolio, subject to a target level of expected return. Because there is range of possible expected returns that can be chosen, *the solution to the optimization problem will be a set of portfolios*, each with its own set of optimal weights. This set of optimal portfolios is typically referred to as the *efficient frontier*. Other terms such as efficient set (Fama 1976), portfolio possibilities curve (Elton and Gruber 1995) and mean-variance efficient locus (Ingersoll 1987) are also used. There are a number of solution methodologies that can be used to solve quadratic optimization problems. A simple iterative method involves initially solving the minimum variance problem. The resulting optimal minimum variance weights are used to identify c_{mv}. This value is used to specify $c_1 = c_{mv} + \varepsilon$, where ε (> 0) is specified according to the desired precision required in the solutions. Using c_1 it is now possible to solve the Lagrangian problem for the next portfolio along the frontier. This process continues for $c_2 = c_{mv} + 2\varepsilon$, $c_3 = c_{mv} + 3\varepsilon$ and so on until the desired efficient frontier is determined. With the short sales constraint $\{w_i \geq 0\}$, the maximum c_i is given by having all funds invested in the highest returning security. Without the short sales constraint, the efficient frontier can be extended indefinitely. Because the underlying problem is quadratic, there will be two "optimal" solutions, one of which is ignored because it will have higher risk for the same expected return. Hence, the efficient frontier only contains the portfolios with high return/lowest risk.

The number of variations that have emerged from this basic model is staggering.[2] Initially, implementation of the model was impeded by the large number of parameters required to make the model operational. In addition to the k individual asset returns, $E[R_i]$, there are k variances, σ_i^2, and $\{k(k-1)\}/2$ covariances which have to be estimated from past data. Even if these parameters are available, the model is only capable of generating a set of mean-variance optimal portfolios, the efficient frontier. Additional structure is needed to select a specific portfolio from the set of optimal portfolios. Tobin (1958), Sharpe (1963, 1964) and others handled this problem by introducing a riskless asset. This permits the investor to form portfolios which combine the riskless asset with an efficient frontier portfolio. In this fashion, the investor is able to achieve the same level of expected return as that generated by an efficient frontier portfolio, again with a lower level of risk. Effectively, the addition of a riskless asset transforms the investment opportunity set from a convex function, the efficient frontier, to a set of linear functions, the capital allocation lines.

In general, where there are many possible securities available for inclusion in the portfolio, solution of the efficient set from the optimization problem is complicated. For purposes of illustration, it is convenient to assume that there are only two risky securities. In this case it is possible to derive the efficient frontier directly, permitting basic concepts to be illustrated. So, assume you are considering creating a portfolio combining a stock fund composed of large stocks (S) and a bond fund (B). The statistics for these funds are: $E[R]$, large stock fund = 12%, bond fund = 5%; σ for the large stock fund = 15%, and for the bond fund = 8%. For ease of calculation, assume the correlation coefficient between the funds is zero. It is now possible to calculate $E[R_p]$ and σ_p for all possible portfolios, starting from 0% invested in the stock fund ($w_s = 0$) and going to 100% ($w_s = 1$), in increments of 20%. This produces:

w_s	$E[R_p]$	σ_p
0	5.0%	8.0%
0.2	6.4%	7.07%
0.4	7.8%	7.68%
0.6	9.2%	9.55%
0.8	10.6%	12.11%
1.0	12%	15%

From these values, it is apparent that an investment of 100% in the bond fund ($w_s = 0$) does not make sense because portfolios with value weights such as $w_s = .2$ and $w_s = .4$ both provide a higher portfolio expected return with a lower level of portfolio risk. Recalling that the returns were assumed to be independent, the portfolio weights, $E[R_{mv}]$ and σ_{mv} for the minimum-variance portfolio are:

$$w_s = \frac{\sigma_b^2}{\sigma_s^2 + \sigma_b^2} = \frac{.08^2}{.15^2 + .08^2} = .2215 \quad \rightarrow \quad w_b = .7785$$

It follows that $E[R_{mv}] = .0655$ and $\sigma_{mv} = .0706$. The plot in $\{E[R], \sigma\}$ space of the values from the minimum variance values to the maximum return portfolios is the efficient frontier (with no short sales).

    Suppose the number of securities available for selection in the portfolio included a third fund composed of small stocks which has $E[R] = 15\%$ and $\sigma = .20$. How would you derive the efficient frontier for portfolios combining the three funds? Attempting to use the method of direct calculation that worked for the two security case is no longer possible. The two security cases reduced to solving for one weight because it was possible to substitute out the other weight using the constraint that the sum of the weights equals one. Hence, there was no optimization problem to solve as there was only one effective weight. Barring trivial cases, when there are three or more securities the optimal weights have to be determined by solving the first order conditions of the optimization problem in order to identify how much of a given frontier portfolio is invested in each security. Ingersoll (1987) discusses the relevant solution procedure.

Capital allocation lines: introducing a riskfree asset

The efficient frontier specifies a set of portfolios that achieve optimal combinations of the available *risky* assets. In order to provide a practical guide to portfolio selection, some method is required to identify a specific portfolio from the efficient frontier. Observing that the efficient frontier is a convex relationship between $E[R]$ and σ for portfolios of risky assets, by introducing a *riskfree* asset it is possible to produce a linear set of available portfolios. In particular, when a riskfree asset is introduced a range of portfolios can be identified which are not available with risky assets alone. What is the riskfree asset? This depends on the investment horizon or the portfolio rebalancing period. The riskfree asset must be free of default risk, have no coupons to reinvest (this would create coupon reinvestment risk), have maturity equal to the investment horizon or rebalancing period and be denominated in domestic currency. For US investors, it is typical to use the 3 month Tbill rate as the riskfree interest rate. Though it is conventional to proxy the riskfree asset with a 3 month US Treasury bill, some presentations, e.g., Damodaran (1994), argue that the US Treasury long term bond yield is appropriate. The problem of specifying the riskfree asset will be explored in more detail shortly.

The riskfree asset permits the creation of portfolios which combine the riskfree asset with a risky portfolio located on the efficient frontier (see figure 3.1). In $(E[R], \sigma)$ space, the line connecting the riskfree rate with a point on the efficient frontier is referred to

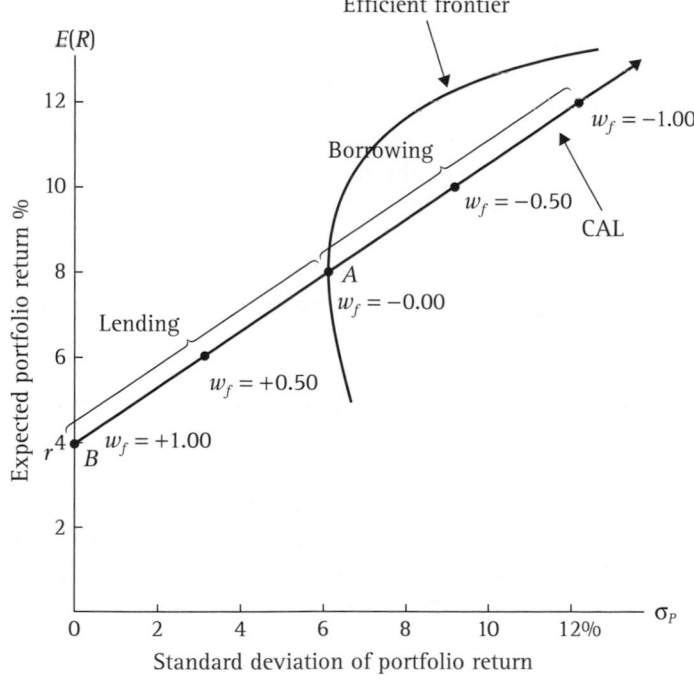

Figure 3.1 Capital allocation line (CAL) with efficient frontier

as a *capital allocation line* (CAL). (This terminology is used in Bodie, Kane and Marcus 1999.) There are as many capital allocation lines as there are portfolios on the efficient frontier. Each point on a given capital allocation line defines a range of possible portfolios which combine the riskfree asset and an efficient portfolio composed of risky assets. Along a given capital allocation line connecting the riskfree rate, r, with an efficient portfolio X, the expected return ($E[R_R]$) and standard deviation (σ_R) of a portfolio combining the efficient frontier portfolio and the riskfree asset can be specified:

$$E[R_R] = w_r r + (1 - w_r)E[R_x]$$

$$\sigma_R^2 = w_r^2 \sigma_r^2 + (1 - w_r)^2 \sigma_x^2 + 2w_r(1 - w_r)\sigma_{rx} = (1 - w_r)^2 \sigma_x^2 \quad \rightarrow \quad \sigma_R = (1 - w_r)\sigma_x$$

The result for the variance of the portfolio follows because the riskfree asset has no risk or covariance because it is risk free.

Some care has to be taken in interpreting the weight w_r. Though the notation w is used, this weight is not associated with the w_i weights for the various efficient frontier portfolios. The w_r weight is the fraction of the portfolio in the riskfree asset and $(1 - w_r)$ is the fraction held in the efficient portfolio. When $1 \geq w_r \geq 0$, this implies that the portfolio involves a positive investment in both the riskfree asset and the efficient portfolio. In figure 3.1 this condition is applicable to all the portfolios lying on the portion of the CAL between r and A. At r, $w_r = 1$ and at A on the efficient frontier $w_r = 0$. When $w_r \leq 0$, this implies that the riskfree asset is held short, i.e., the investor is borrowing at the riskless rate. This is equivalent to saying that, in addition to invest-ment of the original capital, the investor has also borrowed money at the riskfree rate and has purchased additional units of the risky portfolio A. For example, if the investor has $1 million of original capital to invest and $w_r = -.5$ ($w_X = 1.5$), then the investor has borrowed an additional $500,000 and has used this money to purchase an additional $500,000 of A. Portfolios where $w_r \leq 0$ lie to the right of A on the CAL. The key point to recognize is that the presence of the riskfree asset permits the investor to attain portfolios which are not available using risky assets alone.

The capital market line and market equilibrium

To this point, the problem of picking an individual portfolio from the set of efficient frontier portfolios has not been solved. A convex set has been replaced by a set of CAL's, each of which has a theoretically infinite number of possible portfolios. What has been demonstrated is that, with a riskfree asset, it is possible to specify ($E[R]$, σ) tradeoffs that are unattainable with risky assets alone. In order to identify the best CAL and the appropriate portfolio to select on that CAL, it is conventional to introduce the mean-variance expected utility function: $EU[R] = E[R] - b \, var[R]$. As depicted in figure 3.2, the mean-variance EU function defines a preference ordering over the ($E[R]$, σ) space. Movements in a northwest direction indicate increasingly higher levels of expected utility. It follows that the CAL which is just tangent to efficient frontier will attain

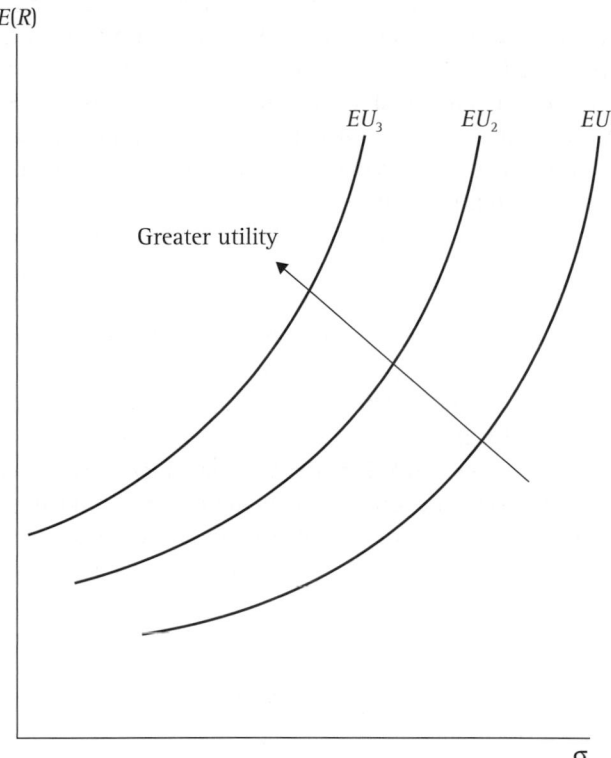

Figure 3.2 Expected utility map for the mean–variance expected utility function

the highest level of expected utility and the tangency of that CAL with the highest *EU* curve will be the specific portfolio that maximizes *EU*. The importance of this particular CAL is recognized specifically by referring to it as the ***capital market line*** (CML).

As it turns out, the slope of the capital allocation line for any efficient portfolio X will be of interest in identifying the properties of the capital market line. Observing that the rise of the CAL is $E[R_x] - r$ and the run from the origin is σ_x it follows that the slope of any CAL is $(E[R_x] - r)/\sigma_x$. Using this result, the equation of the capital allocation line for X becomes:

$$E[R_R] = r + \frac{E[R_x] - r}{\sigma_x}\sigma_R$$

Refer to figure 3.2 describing the indifference curves in $(E[R], \sigma)$ space for a risk averse investor. Because utility increases as the slope of the capital allocation line increases, the rational investor will achieve the maximum level of utility by selecting the capital allocation line with maximum slope, i.e., the CAL that is just tangent to the efficient set.

Under perfect market assumptions, the CAL that is just tangent to the efficient set represents the highest level of utility. This *tangency portfolio* is the portfolio which represents the *market equilibrium*. With the additional theoretical apparatus provided by the capital asset pricing model (CAPM) it can be demonstrated that the tangency portfolio associated with the capital market line is the *market portfolio.*

To illustrate the process of identifying a specific portfolio, refer back to the stock/bond fund portfolio discussed previously. Assume that a riskfree asset is available with $r = 3\%$. By maximizing the slope of the CAL, the weights for the tangency portfolio are given to be $w_s = .561$ and $w_B = .439$. For these weights, $E[R_M] = .0893$ and $\sigma_M = .0912$ where M indicates the tangency portfolio. Observing that the slope of CML is $(.0893 - .03)/.0912 = .65$, the equation of the capital market line can be specified as: $E[R_R] = .03 + .65\sigma_R$. Now, suppose the investor's indifference map is given by the expected utility function: $EU[R] = E[R] - \{3.25\ var[R]\}$. Recognizing that $var[R] = ((1 - w_r)\sigma_M)^2$ and $E[R_R] = w_r r + (1 - w_r)E[R_x]$, the process of maximizing $EU[R]$ gives $w_r = -.096$ as the optimal holding for the riskless asset. This implies that, for the specified mean-variance expected utility function, the optimal solution involves a point on the CML to the right of the tangency with the efficient frontier. It can be verified that alternative values of the risk aversion parameter b give: $b = 5$, $w_r = .2875$; $b = 3$, $w_r = -.01786$; and, $b = 2$, $w_r = -.78125$.

Criticism of mean-variance portfolio analysis

While the mean-variance portfolio model has considerable theoretical appeal, there are a number of substantive problems that arise in implementing the model. One obvious problem concerns the large number of parameters that have to be estimated. Even if this problem can be overcome, attempting to capture the gains, *out-of-sample*, has proved to be illusive, particularly when international assets are permitted to be part of the set of available securities. In practice, the use of *ex post* (in-sample) data to estimate the relevant *ex ante* (out-of-sample) parameters creates numerous problems, not the least of which is instability in both the mean and variance–covariance parameter estimates. This is especially the case where expected returns are of interest. As pointed out by Eaker, et al. (1991): "The problem with including returns in the portfolio selection decision is that such portfolios generally perform poorly in out-of-sample tests."

The mean-variance portfolio model is a central tenet of modern Finance. Much like another central tenet, the efficient markets hypothesis, enthusiasm for the mean-variance portfolio model within Finance has evolved considerably. In recent years the model has been subjected to substantial critical scrutiny. The first wave in the assault on the mean-variance approach can be attributed to Jorion (1985, p. 265), which describes the problems emphatically in the context of internationally diversified portfolios:

> Mean-variance analysis has serious shortcomings which are too often ignored . . . Perhaps the most serious defect in the classical [portfolio] approach is the poor out-of-sample performance of the optimal portfolios. Performance measures always deteriorate substan-

tially outside the sample period, and the supposedly optimal choice is sometimes dominated by a naive method ... Another problem is the instability in the optimal portfolio: the proportions allocated to each asset are extremely sensitive to variations in expected returns, and adding a few observations may change the portfolio distribution completely. Also, optimal portfolios are not necessarily well diversified. Often a corner solution appears, where most of the investments are zero and large proportions are assigned to countries with relatively small capital markets and high average returns.

As it turns out, this attack is decidedly overstated. However, the basic point remains: *ex post* estimates of expected returns, based on arithmetic or weighted average estimators, are not reliable estimates of future returns. Relative to estimates of variances and covariances, Jorion (1985), Eun and Resnick (1988) and others demonstrate that estimates of expected returns are considerably more unstable over time.

Empirically, the parameter instability problem has a number of implications. For example, *ex ante* results concerning the return on a given portfolio may vary significantly from sample to sample. Jorion (1985) examines the out-of-sample performance of the two *ex post* optimal internationally diversified portfolios identified by Grubel (1968) and Levy and Sarnat (1974), together with two "naive" portfolios, the equally weighted and market value weighted portfolios. As measured by the Sharpe ratio, Jorion found that over the next investment horizon, the *ex ante* performance of the two mean-variance efficient portfolios was inferior to the performance of the naive equally weighted portfolio. Jorion (1985) also provides evidence that, in estimating *ex post* returns, longer sampling windows, e.g., five years for monthly data, provides superior *ex ante* forecasting when compared with shorter sampling windows, e.g., 1 year of monthly data. The difficulty with longer sampling windows is that it takes a longer time interval for the estimates to react to changing market conditions.[3]

In addition to the estimation method used to determine the relevant parameter inputs, the presence or absence of short selling has been found to be fundamental in assessing the performance of mean-variance efficient portfolios. Even though the early studies implicitly assumed short selling was not permitted, at least since Jorion (1985) it has been recognized that odd results can be obtained when short selling is permitted. For example, Jorion reports results for the time series properties of the optimal weight on domestic assets in the *ex post* tangency portfolio (see below). A considerable amount of short-selling is indicated at various times, as much as −2.4 times the total principal value of the portfolio at one point in 1978. For many types of investment situations, e.g., pension funds, life insurance companies, this amount of short selling would be unacceptable and unobtainable. Evidence on portfolio composition with short selling restrictions, e.g., Glen and Jorion (1993), indicates a dramatic narrowing of the number of assets held in the portfolio is likely, amplifying the concentration of a given portfolio in a small number of assets.

Somehow, proponents of the model believe that the out-of-sample prediction problems can be resolved by improving the estimation methods that are used. This still leaves the problem of identifying the appropriate portfolio from the set of mean-variance efficient portfolios. Following Sharpe and others, the efficient frontier portfolio to be selected is that portfolio associated with the capital allocation line which is just tangent to the efficient frontier, i.e., the portfolio associated with the *capital market line.* This tangency portfolio can be determined by solving the following optimization problem, e.g., Eun and Resnick (1994):

$$\max_{\{w_i\}} \frac{E[R_p] - r}{\sigma_p} \quad \textit{subject to:} \quad \sum_{i=1}^{k} w_i = 1$$

On theoretical grounds, the tangency portfolio is the *ex ante* mean-variance-expected-utility optimizing risky portfolio. Even though the precise combination of riskless asset and risky tangency portfolio for any given investor requires specification of the relevant parameters for the investor's mean-variance expected utility function, the optimal risky portfolio has been determined.

Given the *ex post* estimates of the relevant means, variances and covariances, the optimality problem is solved and the resulting tangency portfolio will represent the optimal *in-sample* portfolio. Whether this in-sample optimality translates into superior *out-of-sample* performance is an open question. The answer to this question becomes even more complex when foreign assets are admitted into the asset universe. In particular, the domestic currency return on a foreign asset depends on a combination of two random variables: the return denominated in foreign currency terms; and, the change in the exchange rate. The correlation between foreign and domestic asset returns will tend to be lower than the correlations between domestic assets, making foreign assets excellent candidates for diversification. In addition, foreign assets can also provide the possibility of significantly higher returns than domestic assets. As demonstrated by Eun and Resnick (1994), the difficulties associated with estimating expected returns results in the minimum variance portfolio having generally superior *ex ante* performance compared to the tangency portfolio.

3.2 SEPARATION, THE CAPM AND THE MARKET MODEL

Two fund separation

The combination of mean-variance expected utility, perfect markets and the capital market line (CML) provides the basis for a version of the *two fund separation property*: in market equilibrium, rational risk averse investors will hold portfolios which combine the riskfree asset with the tangency portfolio. The precise combination of the riskfree asset and the tangency portfolio will depend on the risk preferences of the individual investor. The CML result does not provide any information about how to determine the return on individual assets, or any portfolio of assets which is not efficient. The CML also does not provide specific information about the asset composition of the tangency portfolio. This information is provided by the capital asset pricing model (CAPM). If the

CAPM is incorporated, then it can be shown that the tangency portfolio will be the market portfolio. In this case, the two fund separation property says that, in market equilibrium, *rational risk averse investors will hold portfolios which combine the riskfree asset and the market portfolio.*

Two fund separation provides the theoretical basis for a persuasive and implementable investment strategy. This strategy requires a strong belief in efficient markets. If markets are efficient then the gains to individual security selection strategies, using either fundamental or technical analysis, will be illusory. The decision problem facing the rational investor is to determine what fraction of invested capital to hold in the risky market portfolio and what fraction to hold in the riskfree assets. Investors with high levels of risk tolerance will leverage up, by borrowing at the riskfree rate, and purchase more of the market portfolio. Investors with moderate to low levels of risk tolerance will have positive investment weights for both the riskfree asset and the market portfolio. Though this perfect markets result requires some adjustment to account for market imperfections, e.g., differences between lending and borrowing rates, the basic intuition survives intact. As pointed out by Roll (1978), the main practical ambiguities lie with the specification of the riskfree asset and the market portfolio.

The CAPM provides a method for determining the expected return, $E[R_i]$, for any asset i, not just for portfolios on the efficient frontier. The CAPM is an *ex ante* model that can be expressed as:

$$E[R_i] = r + \{E[R_m] - r\}\beta_i$$

where $E[R_m]$ is the expected return on the market portfolio and β_i is a measure of the *systematic risk* of asset i. In words, the CAPM can be expressed as: the expected return on asset i = risk free rate + systematic risk premium for asset i. A key variable in the CAPM is β which is specified as:

$$\beta_i = \frac{cov[R_i, R_m]}{\sigma_m^2} \equiv \frac{\sigma_{im}}{\sigma_m^2}$$

where σ_m^2 is the variance of the return on the market portfolio.

Some examples of mechanical calculations that can be done with CAPM are: assume that the rate of return on the market $E[R_m] = .15$ and $r = .05$ and $\beta_i = 1.5$ then the expected return on asset i is $E[R_i] = .05 + (.15 - .05)(1.5) = .20$; assume that $E[R_i] = .1$, $E[R_m] = .105$ and $\beta_i = .9$ then the riskfree rate r is 5.5%; assume that $E[R_i] = .2$, $E[R_m] = .15$ and $r = .10$, then $\beta_i = 2$. Beta is applicable not only for individual securities but also for portfolio of securities. The following useful result can readily be derived: the beta of a portfolio, β_p is the value weighted sum of the individual betas (the β_i's). This follows because the CAPM holds for any asset, including individual assets as well as portfolios of assets. Recognizing that the CAPM will hold for the efficient portfolios on the efficient frontier, the CAPM can be used to show that the tangency portfolio in the CML is the market portfolio.

To demonstrate this result, assume that the CAPM is true. If the tangency portfolio is the market portfolio, the CML provides the result:

$$E[R_R] = r + \frac{E[R_m] - r}{\sigma_m} \sigma_R$$

where m refers to the market portfolio. Using the result that $\sigma_R = (1 - w_f)\sigma_m$ this can be rewritten:

$$E[R_R] = r + \frac{E[R_m] - r}{\sigma_m}(1 - w_r)\sigma_m = r + \{E[R_m] - r\}(1 - w_r)$$

If the CAPM is true then it will hold for any portfolio along the CML. If the market portfolio is the tangency portfolio for the CML then $E[R] = w_r r + (1 - w_r)E[R_m]$ and evaluating β gives:

$$\beta = \frac{cov[E[R], E[R_m]]}{\sigma_m^2} = \frac{cov[\{w_r r + (1 - w_r)E[R_m]\}, E[R_m]]}{\sigma_m^2}$$

$$= \frac{(1 - w_r)\sigma_m^2}{\sigma_m^2} = (1 - w_r)$$

Substituting this result back into the CML shows that the CAPM and CML are equivalent when the tangency portfolio is the market portfolio.

The relationship between the CAPM and the CML can be expressed in a linear form in $(E[R], \beta)$ space. This linear relationship is the *security market line* (SML) (see figure 3.3). While the CAL and CML provide a linear relationship in $(E[R], \sigma)$ space between total risk, as measured by standard deviation, and expected return, the SML provides a linear relationship between systematic risk, as measured by β, and expected return. The equation for the SML can be derived by identifying two points on the line: the riskfree rate where $\beta_f = 0$ and $E[R_i] = r$ and the market portfolio where $\beta_m = 1$, $E[R_i] = E[R_m]$. It follows that the slope is $(E[R_m] - r)$. From this the equation for the SML can be stated: $E[R_i] = r + (E[R_m] - r)\beta_i$. Hence, the SML is the graphical representation of the CAPM. A useful pedagogical application of the SML is to describe whether a particular security is over or underpriced relative to its measure of systematic risk.

The capital asset pricing model*

The Markowitz model of mean-variance portfolio optimization is concerned with the behavior of an individual investor selecting securities for inclusion in an optimal portfolio. Practical application of this model is complicated by the large number of parameters that have to be estimated and the associated complexity of the solutions as the number of securities is increased. The CAPM provided a theoretical mechanism for handling this problem. Using the CAPM, the problem of estimating the optimal weights

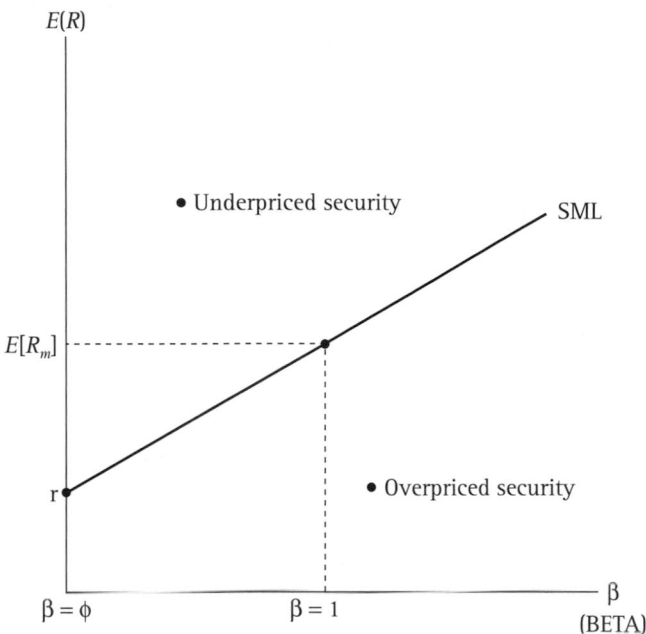

Figure 3.3 Security market line (SML)

for the individual assets in the tangency portfolio is replaced with a method of identifying the predetermined set of weights associated with the market portfolio. Though the notion of a "market portfolio" is somewhat nebulous, in practice it has been interpreted to be a widely diversified value-weighted portfolio of common stocks such as the S&P 500, e.g., Damodaran (1994). This all raises the need to examine the derivation of the CAPM in more detail.

In the years since the CAPM was introduced by Sharpe (1964), Lintner (1965) and Mossin (1966), considerable effort has been given to extending and expanding the basic model (see chapter 10). The basic CAPM, also referred to as the one factor or single index model, is derived under perfect markets assumptions. The process of extending and expanding has been largely concerned with relaxing these assumptions. Unlike the partial equilibrium approach of the mean-variance portfolio model, the CAPM is a general equilibrium model. It is this feature that permits the CAPM to go beyond the basic portfolio structure to make statements about the expected returns for individual assets. General equilibrium requires market clearing conditions for all assets to be satisfied. To accomplish this, the CAPM relies on the assumption that investors are homogeneous, possessing the same expectations about the means and variances of returns and the same investment horizon. All investors are assumed to have the same form of mean-variance expected utility function.

Much of the derivation of the CAPM follows the mean-variance optimization procedure. The homogeneity assumption is invoked after the riskfree rate is introduced and the optimality of the tangency portfolio is established. Because investors are homogeneous and market clearing is required, it must be that the tangency portfolio is the market portfolio. Fama (1976, pp. 274–5) describes the logical argument:

> a market equilibrium requires a market-clearing set of prices; a market equilibrium requires that, in aggregate, investors demand them in the proportions in which they are outstanding. Given the nature of the efficient set when there is risk-free borrowing and lending, this market-clearing condition means that a market equilibrium is not attained until the one tangency portfolio that all investors try to combine with risk-free borrowing or lending is a portfolio of all the positive variance securities in the market, where each security is weighted by the ratio of the total market value . . . of all its outstanding units to the total market value of all outstanding units of securities. In short, a market equilibrium is not reached until the tangency portfolio . . . is the value-weighted version of the market portfolio . . . A market equilibrium – a set of security prices that clears the securities market and a value of (the risk-free rate) that clears the borrowing-lending market – requires that the tangency portfolio be the market-weighted version of the market portfolio.

This last step, the identification of the tangency portfolio with the market portfolio, follows immediately from the investor homogeneity assumption. In the derivation of the CAPM, this step is something of an afterthought.

The key parts of the CAPM relate to developing the relationship between the expected return on a given asset and the expected return on an efficient portfolio. This derivation requires one useful result associated with linear combinations of random variables:[4]

$$var[R_p] = \sum_{i=1}^{k}\sum_{j=1}^{k} w_i w_j \sigma_{ij} = \sum_{i=1}^{k} w_i \left(\sum_{j=1}^{k} w_j \sigma_{ij} \right) = \sum_{i=1}^{k} w_i \, cov[R_i, \, R_p]$$

Given this, the derivation of the CAPM proceeds by solving the Lagrangian arising from the mean-variance portfolio model:

$$\max_{\{w_i\}} L = var[R_p] - 2\lambda_1 \left(\sum_{i=1}^{k} w_i E[R_i] - \bar{c}_n \right) - 2\lambda_2 \left(\sum_{i=1}^{k} w_i - 1 \right)$$

This optimization problem will produce k first order conditions associated with the $\{w_i\}$ together with two additional first order conditions for the constraints to produce a system of $k + 2$ equations.

For jth security, the first order condition provides:

$$\sum_{i=1}^{k} w_i \, cov[R_i, \, R_j] - \lambda_1 E[R_j] - \lambda_2 = 0$$

As the ordering of the securities is arbitrary, this result can be equated with the first order condition for the first security to obtain:

$$\sum_{i=1}^{k} w_i \, cov[R_i, \, R_j] - \lambda_1 E[R_j] = \sum_{i=1}^{k} w_i \, cov[R_i, \, R_1] - \lambda_1 E[R_1]$$

The next step involves multiplying both sides by w_j and summing over j. This affects the right and left hand sides differently. The left hand side produces:

$$\sum_{j=1}^{k} w_j \sum_{i=1}^{k} w_i \, cov[R_i, \, R_j] - \lambda_1 \sum_{j=1}^{k} w_j E[R_j] = var[R_p] - \lambda_1 E[R_p]$$

The right hand side produces:

$$\sum_{j=1}^{k} w_j \left(\sum_{i=1}^{k} w_i \, cov[R_i, \, R_1] - \lambda_1 E[R_1] \right) = \sum_{i=1}^{k} w_i \, cov[R_i, \, R_1] - \lambda_1 E[R_1]$$

This result follows because there is no j on the right hand side and, as a result, the sum of the weights equals one and has no impact.

Observing that the weights apply to a mean-variance efficient portfolio, i.e., R_p is on the efficient frontier, manipulating the right and left hand sides produces the result:

$$E[R_1] - E[R_p] = \frac{1}{\lambda_1} \left(\sum_{i=1}^{k} w_i \, cov[R_i, \, R_1] - var[R_p] \right) = \frac{1}{\lambda_1} (cov[R_1, \, R_p] - var[R_p])$$

What remains is to determine λ, which is the Lagrange multiplier associated with the impact of changes in the target level of portfolio expected return on the variance of the portfolio. When there is a riskfree rate, the λ for the tangency portfolio can be determined as:

$$2\lambda_1 = \frac{d \, var[R_p]}{dE[R_p]} = \frac{d \, var[R_p]}{d\sigma_p} \frac{d\sigma_p}{dE[R_p]} = 2\sigma_p \left(\frac{\sigma_p}{E[R_p] - r} \right)$$

Substituting this λ result back into the prior equation and manipulating gives the CAPM.

Nothing in this derivation demonstrates that the tangency portfolio is the market portfolio. This result is obtained from the logical argument about market clearing with homogeneity of consumers. In a sense, two fund separation, where the rational investor holds combinations of the market portfolio and the riskless asset, is too strong a condition. A more appropriate result would be a partial equilibrium result where the rational investor holds combinations of a mean-variance efficient portfolio and the riskless asset. But this would require the mean-variance efficient portfolio to be determined, falling back to the problems associated with complexity, number of parameters to estimate, estimator forecasting error and the like. That the CAPM assumptions make proponents of modern Finance queezy is apparent in the following quote from Elton and Gruber (1984, p. 273):

> It is worthwhile pointing out . . . that the final test of a model is not how reasonable the assumptions behind it appear but how well the model describes reality. As the reader proceeds with this chapter, he will, no doubt, find many of its assumptions objectionable. Furthermore, the final model is so simple the reader may well wonder about its validity. As we shall see, despite the stringent assumptions and the simplicity of the model, it does an amazingly good job of describing prices in capital markets.
>
> The real world is sufficiently complex that to understand it and construct models of how it works, one must assume away those complexities that, hopefully have only a small (or no) affect on its behavior. As the physicist builds models of the movement of matter in a frictionless environment, the economist builds models where there are no institutional frictions to the movement of stock prices.

These words reflect the place of the CAPM at the foundation of the positivist super-structure that is modern Finance.

The market model*

Because the CAPM is an *ex ante* model it depends on expected returns and other unknown values, that are not directly observable or testable. The statistical representation of the CAPM which is testable is known as the **market model**. The market model is a bivariate regression model of the form:

$$R_{it} = \alpha_i + \beta_i R_{mt} + e_{it}$$

where R_{it} is the observed return on asset i at time t, R_{mt} is the observed return on the market portfolio at time t, α_i and β_i are statistical parameters to be estimated and e_{it} is the asset specific error which is assumed to obey the statistical properties for ordinary least squares regression. For the market model the ordinary least squares (OLS) assumptions (in vector notation) are: $E[e_i] = 0$, the firm specific error has mean zero; $E[e_i R_m] = 0$, the firm specific risks are uncorrelated with the market return; $E[e_i e_j] = 0$ for i not equal to j, the firm specific risks for different securities are uncorrelated; in addition, it is assumed that the e_i are iid random variables. The additional assumption of normality of e_i facilitates hypothesis testing. With these assumptions, ordinary least squares can be used to estimate the coefficients α_i and β_i. The market model is sometimes referred to as the single index model, e.g., Elton and Gruber (1995).

Taking expected values for the market model gives for any t:

$$E[R_i] = \alpha_i + \beta_i E[R_m] \quad \text{because } E[e_i] = 0$$

If the CAPM is true, it follows that $\alpha_i = (1 - \beta_i)r$, ($\beta_i$ has the same interpretation as $cov[R_i, R_m]/var[R_m]$). This interpretation for α depends on the riskless rate being a constant. While this assumption is correct in one-step-ahead decision making, it is problematic when estimating parameters in a time series. To account for changes in *r* over time, the market model is often expressed in **risk premium form**, by subtracting the observed riskless rate, in any given period, from the observed returns:

$$R_{it} - r_t = \alpha_i + \beta_i[R_{mt} - r_t] + u_{it}$$

where u_i is also a firm specific risk with ordinary least squares properties. In this form, taking expectations and assuming that the CAPM holds gives $\alpha_i = 0$ and β_i with the same interpretation.

Beta is a measure of systematic or **market risk**. It provides information on how the stock return reacted historically when the return on the market portfolio changed. Beta estimates are reported at a number of websites, such as www.bloomberg.com. For $\beta_i > 1$ (high beta), when the return on the market portfolio changes, the return on the stock will tend to change by **more** than the return on the market portfolio. Stocks with higher than market betas are considered to be **aggressive**. When the market is expected to move up, shifting into stocks with high beta is indicated. In the US market, examples of high beta stock groups occur in industries such as trucking, consumer durables, construction and air transport. For $\beta_i < 1$ (low beta) when the return on the market portfolio changes, the return on the stock will tend to change by **less** than the return on the market portfolio. Stocks with lower than market betas are considered to be **defensive**. When the market is expected to move down, shifting into stocks with high beta is indicated. In the US market, examples of low beta stock groups occur in telephone stocks, utilities, breweries and food producers/distributors.

Alpha is an **asset specific** measure which indicates the **excess return** that the security earned beyond that warranted by the risk premium captured by the security's beta. For the market model expressed in risk premium form, positive alpha indicates that the stock outperformed the market, after adjusting for systematic risk. Negative alpha indicates that the stock underperformed the market, after adjusting for systematic risk. The market model provides a useful simplification for determining the betas and alphas for a portfolio from the alphas and betas of the individual securities:

$$E[R_p] = \sum_{i=1}^{k} w_i E[R_i] = \sum_{i=1}^{k} w_i\{\alpha_i + \beta_i E[R_m]\}$$

$$\sum_{i=1}^{k} w_i \alpha_i + \sum_{i=1}^{k} \beta_i E[R_m] = \alpha_p + \beta_p E[R_m]$$

In other words, the alpha and beta for the portfolio are the value weighted sums of the individual portfolio alphas and betas.

The market model can also be used to demonstrate that portfolio diversification leads to the elimination of unsystematic or **firm specific** risk leaving only systematic risk as the determinant of portfolio variance. If the market model is true then the variance for individual security returns reduces to:

$$\sigma_i^2 = \beta_i^2 \sigma_m^2 + \sigma_{e_i}^2$$

Similarly, the covariance between the security returns becomes:

$$\sigma_{ij} = \beta_i \beta_j \sigma_m^2$$

These results follow from the assumptions made in the market model. Substituting these results into the formula for the portfolio variance, σ_p^2, gives:

$$\sigma_p^2 = \sum_{i=1}^{k} w_i^2 \beta_i^2 \sigma_m^2 + \sum_{i=1}^{k} w_i^2 \sigma_{e_i}^2 + \sum_{i>j} w_i w_j \beta_i \beta_j \sigma_m^2$$

$$= \sum_{i=1}^{k} \sum_{j=1}^{k} w_i w_j \beta_i \beta_j \sigma_m^2 + \sum_{i=1}^{k} w_i^2 \sigma_{e_i}^2$$

Observing that the variance of the market portfolio is a common term in the double sum, it is possible to do some factoring:

$$\sigma_p^2 = \left\{ \sum_{i=1}^{k} w_i \beta_i \right\} \left\{ \sum_{i=1}^{k} w_i \beta_i \right\} \sigma_m^2 + \sum_{i=1}^{k} w_i^2 \sigma_{e_i}^2$$

Using the result that the beta of the portfolio is the value weighted sum of the individual security betas, the following simplification is available for the portfolio variance:

$$\sigma_p^2 = \beta_p^2 \sigma_m^2 + \sum_{i=1}^{k} w_i^2 \sigma_{e_i}^2$$

$$\sigma_p \to \beta_p \sigma_m \quad as \quad k \to \infty \quad and \quad w_i \Downarrow$$

The term involving β_p is the *systematic* or market related risk. It depends only on the composition of the portfolio and the variance of the return on the market. The second term involves only firm specific or *unsystematic* risks.

To show the impact of diversification on both systematic (market) risk and unsystematic (firm specific) risk, observe that the first term involving the beta of the portfolio is not much affected by increases in the number of securities in the portfolio. The second term involving the firm specific risks is directly affected by the number of securities in the portfolio. Take the case of an equally weighted portfolio where $w_i = 1/N$. In this case, as the number of the securities in the portfolio increases the firm specific risks are reduced at the rate of $(1/N^2)$, which is converging to zero quite rapidly. This follows from observing that when the firm specific risk has been eliminated then the last term on the rhs of the last equation is zero. Taking square roots and observing that the portfolio beta is the weighted sum of the individual security betas provides the required result. However, because there are a large number of securities in a portfolio, this does *not* mean that the firm specific risks are eliminated. Rather, the elimination of firm specific risk depends on reducing the value weights attached to each security as N increases. For example, if $w_1 = .5$ for a particular security, and this value does not change as the number of securities in the portfolio increases, then the firm specific risk associated with that security is not eliminated as the number of securities in the portfolio increases.

3.3   DECISION MAKING UNDER UNCERTAINTY

Expected utility theory*

The study of decision making under uncertainty is a vast subject. Theoretical applications in Finance almost invariably proceed under the guise of the expected utility hypothesis: people rank random prospects according to the expected utility of those prospects. Analytically, financial decisions typically involve solving optimization problems by selecting choice variables to maximize an expected utility function subject to a budget constraint. The choice variables are typically the proportion of the initial budget to allocate to a given asset or security. In some cases, such as the basic optimal hedging problem, e.g., Poitras (2002, ch. 2), the budget constraint is embedded in the argument of the utility function. In other cases, such as in optimal portfolio diversification models, the budget constraint appears as the restriction that the sum of the value weights equals one. In either event, the central concern is expected utility. As such, a key step in the optimization problem is to specify an expected utility function which captures the preference mapping of the decision maker over random outcomes.

Expected utility calculations involve taking expectations, which are conventionally modeled using statistical properties of random variables. This may entail the explicit introduction of probability densities. There is a profound connection between the choice of a specific probability distribution and the risk aversion properties required of the expected utility function, e.g., Heaney and Poitras (1994). As for the utility component of the expected utility function, even before von Neumann and Morgenstern (1947), it had been recognized that choosing over risky prospects is decidedly different than the textbook model of consumer choice under certainty. As is well known, von Neumann and Morgenstern made a seminal contribution by proposing a set of axioms governing choice under uncertainty. Accepting that the axioms are difficult to reject lends strong support to the von Neumann and Morgenstern approach.[5]

The key construct of the axiomatic approach to decision making under uncertainty is the "linear choice function over risky prospects," better known as the *expected utility function*:

$$EU[x] = \sum_{j=1}^{S} \theta_j U_j[x]$$

where: $EU[x]$ is the expected utility of x; S is the number of possible futures states of the world; θ_j is the probability that state j will occur, where the sum of the θ's across all

$j = 1$ to S states is equal to one; and, $U[x_j]$ is the utility associated with the amount of x received in state j. While there are a number of possible selections for x, in what follows variables such as terminal wealth, portfolio return or terminal profit will typically be used. (The implications of this selection will be examined shortly.) The *EU* function ranks risky prospects with an ordering that is unique up to a positive linear transformation. This is different than the case where just $U[x_j]$ is being maximized, as in the theory of consumer choice in microeconomics where the amounts are known with certainty. In this case, the U ranking is unique up to a positive monotonic transformation.

While the *difference between a monotonic and linear transformation* may not seem too significant, demonstrating the difference does provide some insight into the mechanics of the expected utility calculation. Consider the case where there is a single good, x. Two prospects A and B have to be ranked with $EU[x]$, prospect A is a lottery with two possible outcomes of either 0 units of x or 16 units of x, with each event equally likely, $\theta_1 = \theta_2 = .5$. This lottery is being compared with prospect B which is a certain outcome of 7 units of x. Let the utility function be $U[x] = x$, the expected utility is then $EU[A] = .5(16) + .5(0) = 8 > 7 = EU[B]$. Now consider what happens when a square root transformation is applied to the x: $EU[A] = .5(4) + .5(0) = 2 < \sqrt{7} = EU[B]$. Though the utility ranking is unchanged under the monotonic transformation of taking a square root, $U[16; 4] > U[7; \sqrt{7}] > U[0]$, the *EU* ranking did change. However, when $U[x] = a + bx$, then the expected utility calculation gives: $EU[A] = .5(a + b(16)) + .5(a + b(0)) = a + .5b(16) > a + b(7) = EU[B]$ for all positive linear transformations, $b > 0$.

Given the basic specification of the *EU* function, developing the empirical implications of models based on *EU* can be tricky because *EU* is a construct that cannot be directly observed. In addition to the difficulties of specifying $U[x_j]$ encountered in microeconomics (e.g., satiation points and externalities) it is also not apparent how to determine the θ_j. The axiomatic foundation cannot say much more than that the probabilities are available. Davidson (1991) and others emphasize the importance of the approach taken to identifying the probabilities in the expected utility calculation. In modern Finance, it is conventional to proceed, either explicitly or implicitly, along the lines of Ingersoll (1987, p. 30): "We assume throughout the discussion that the economic agents making the decisions know the true objective probabilities of the relevant events. This is not in the tradition of using subjective probabilities but will suffice for our purposes." In assuming that the probabilities are objective, Ingersoll follows the approach used in rational expectations modeling in economics.

Davidson (1991, p. 132) develops the philosophical *implications of assuming that the probabilities are objective*:

> The objective probability environment associated with the rational expectations hypothesis presumes not only that probability distributions regarding historical phenomena have existed, but also that the same probabilities which determined past outcomes will continue to govern future events. In the context of forming expectations which do not exhibit persistent errors, it holds that time averages calculated from past data will converge with the statistical averages computed from any future time series. Knowledge of the future merely involves projecting averages based on past or current realizations to forthcoming events. The future is merely the statistical reflection of the past and economic actions are

in some sense timeless. There can be no ignorance of upcoming events for those who believe the past provides reliable, unbiased, statistical information (price signals) regarding the future, and this knowledge can be obtained if only one is willing to spend the resources to examine the past.

Ergodicity provides the basis for empirically extracting objective probabilities from past data (see section 1.3). As such: "In the ergodic circumstances of objective probability distributions, probability is knowledge, not uncertainty." This is strong stuff. If correct, it means that the core theories of modern Finance deal with the uncertainty of future outcomes in a fashion that could be called into question. As such, predictions derived from the core models require, at the least, careful interpretation.

Taking probabilities as objectively determined proceeds beyond the intentions of the developers of the axiomatic approach to decision making under uncertainty where probabilities are subjectively determined. In the case of von Neumann-Morgenstern (1947), the subjective probabilities are given by assumption while in Savage (1954) the subjective probability assessments can be deduced. Yet, objective probabilities are implied by the general equilibrium formulation needed to derive models of security prices or returns, such as the CAPM. General equilibrium models often proceed by assuming that expectations are homogeneous or that individual agents are homogeneous, both of which are facilitated by objective probabilities. If probabilities are subjective then it is necessary to assume investor heterogeneity. However, if heterogeneity is the case, then key results, such as those concerning the properties of the market portfolio, are undermined. As a consequence, essential prescriptions, such as two fund separation, require reinterpretation.

In the absence of objectively known probabilities or, less stringently, probabilities estimated from past data under the assumption of ergodicity, it is still possible to use the techniques of decision making under uncertainty to develop useful prescriptions and predictions. In the world of Old Finance, for example, the theoretical requirements needed to satisfy general equilibrium concerns were of little use. The decision problems typically encountered were partial equilibrium. The ad hoc theoretical results applied to investors and traders confronted with a parametric world of atomistic competition where their activities did not impact prices. In this process, the expected utility function can still be an invaluable analytical tool. A number of useful results can be readily derived by applying an essential tool from functional analysis: the Taylor series expansion (see section 5.2). In addition, much of the intuition of the mean-variance portfolio optimization model can still be exploited, albeit in the framework of subjective estimates of risk and expected return.

Given the probabilities, analytical solutions derived using $EU[x]$ will depend on the selection of the argument x. In the *theory of consumer choice* under certainty covered in basic microeconomics, e.g., Henderson and Quandt (1980), x refers to two or more goods, e.g., $U[q_1, q_2]$. Analysis of the consumer choice problem for a two good world proceeds by maximizing $U[q_1, q_2]$ subject to a budget constraint, $y = p_1q_1 + p_2q_2$, where y is the initial endowment level and p and q refer to the price and quantity of the commodity. Solving the first order conditions for *the Lagrangian problem* (L) gives the results:

$$L = U[q_1, q_2] + \lambda(y - p_1 q_1 - p_2 q_2)$$

Solving the foc $\rightarrow \quad \dfrac{\dfrac{\partial U[q_1, q_2]}{\partial q_1}}{\dfrac{\partial U[q_1, q_2]}{\partial q_2}} \equiv \dfrac{U_1'}{U_2'} = \dfrac{p_1}{p_2} \qquad \dfrac{\partial L[q_1, q_2; y]}{\partial y} = \lambda$

By specifying a functional form for U together with specific prices and an endowment level, it is possible to solve the optimal quantities of q_1 and q_2. Varying prices will permit demand functions to be determined and so on. Using appropriate mathematical complications, the results generalize in a natural way to n commodities. Useful results are obtained when q_1 and q_2 refer to income and leisure or consumption in two different time periods.

Despite the use of U there is a significant change in orientation when attention shifts from the certainty model of consumer choice to decision problems involving $EU[x]$. Instead of being concerned with allocating a fixed income endowment among a number of goods, concern shifts to a one good (plus numeraire) world of allocating the endowment between current consumption $C(0)$ and the purchase of capital assets that generate the endowment in the next period. As discussed in chapter 10, there is an assumed separation between the generation of future income from the asset investment decision and from future labor income, with the implications of the latter usually being suppressed. The initial endowment, $W(0)$, is conventionally referred to as initial wealth. For the simple two period case where there is only one capital asset that has a random return, then terminal wealth, $W(1)$, is specified:

$$W(1) = \{W(0) - C(0) - A(0)\}(1 + r) + A(0)(1 + R(1))$$

$$= \{W(0) - C(0) - A(0)\}(1 + r) + \{A(0) + \pi(1)\}$$

where $A(0) = P(0)Q(0)$ is the value of the capital asset purchased at $t = 0$, r is the riskless return on holding the numeraire (cash), $C(0)$ is the consumption at $t = 0$. Unless the consumption decision is of immediate interest, it is conventional to omit consideration of $C(0)$.

Given this, because the choice variable is $A(0)$, the amount of the capital asset to purchase at $t = 0$, it follows that the decision problem can be specified with terminal wealth, $EU[W(1)]$, asset returns, $EU[R(1)]$, or profit, $EU[\pi(1)]$. Though there is no substantive difference between the selection of x in the simple case, the level of $W(0)$ can be important in some cases making the selection of $EU[W(1)]$ appropriate in those cases. In other cases, such as the important mean-variance optimization model, attention focuses on the portfolio returns and how to allocate the initial wealth among k assets. This leads to the use of $EU[R(1)]$, where $R(1)$ refers to the return on the asset portfolio which is, in turn, dependent on the individual asset returns. The use of $EU[\pi(1)]$ is common in problems involving derivative securities, such as the selection of the optimal amount of a forward contract to establish in order to hedge a spot position. In this case the profit on the forward contract is of interest.

Many of the basic properties of *EU* in the portfolio selection problem can be illustrated by *a simple two state example* (Mossin 1973, pp. 16–9). Setting $r = 0$ and $C(0) = 0$ for convenience, assume that the value of the asset in state 1 is zero with probability θ_1 and in state 2 is $2A(0)$ with probability $\theta_2 = (1 - \theta_1)$. Taking the initial endowment to be $W(0) = 100$, these payoffs define a range of outcomes. For example: if $A(0) = 0$, then $W(1) = 100$; if $A(0) = 20$, then $W(1) = \theta_1(80) + (1 - \theta_1)(140)$; and if $A(0) = 60$, then $W(1) = \theta_1(40) + (1 - \theta_1)(220)$. In general:

$$EU[W(1)] = \theta_1 U[W(0) - A(0)] + (1 - \theta_1)U[W(0) + 2A(0)].$$

The optimization problem is to choose the amount of the risky asset to purchase in order to maximize the expected value of terminal wealth. Assuming that the initial price, $P(0)$, is not affected by the quantity of the asset purchased, $A(0)$, it is sufficient to solve this problem using the first order condition (foc) (dEU/dA) and evaluating the second derivative to ensure the solution is a maximum.

Evaluating the foc for the simple problem gives:

$$\frac{dEU}{dA} = \theta_1 \left\{ \frac{dU[W(0) - A]}{dW} \frac{dW}{dA} \right\} + (1 - \theta_1)\left\{ \frac{dU[W(0) + 2A]}{dW} \frac{dW}{dA} \right\}$$

$$= -\theta_1 U'[W(0) - A] + 2(1 - \theta_1)U'[W(0) + 2A]$$

Solving for an optimal value of A requires a specific functional form for U to be assumed. For example, let $U[W(1)] = \ln[W(1)]$. It follows that:

$$\frac{dEU}{dA} = \frac{-\theta_1}{W(0) - A} + \frac{2(1 - \theta_1)}{W(0) + 2A} = 0$$

$$\rightarrow \quad A^* = \frac{2 - 3\theta_1}{2} W(0) = \frac{E[R_A]}{2} W(0)$$

where $E[R_A] = \{E[W(1)] - W(0)\}/A(0)$. This illustrates an important property of the log utility function: that the proportion of initial wealth invested in the risky asset, $(A(0)/W(0))$, is constant and independent of the amount of initial wealth.

Cost of risk and risk aversion properties*

The expected utility function is a useful tool for analyzing the problem of determining the cost of risk. The solution to this problem would be useful in assessing whether to buy insurance or to invest in a risky capital project. While there are a number of possible methods to extract the cost of risk, consider the following solution. Let the expected value of terminal wealth be: $E[W(t + 1)] = \Omega$. Observe that Ω is a parameter which permits the *certainty equivalent* income of a risky prospect to be defined as $\Omega - C$, where C is the cost of risk. It follows from the expected utility axioms that the cost of risk, C, can be calculated as the difference between the expected value of the risky prospect and the associated certainty equivalent income:

$$U[\Omega - C] = \sum_{i=1}^{S} \theta_i U[W_i] = EU[W(t + 1)]$$

It is now possible to expand $U[\Omega - C]$ in a Taylor series and estimate the cost of risk by manipulating the first and second order approximations.

More precisely, expanding the function $U[\Omega - C]$ around Ω the first order approximation is:

$$U[\Omega - C] = U[\Omega] + U'[\Omega] (\Omega - C - \Omega) = U[\Omega] - U'[\Omega]C$$

Similarly, a second order approximation for the function $U[W(t + 1)]$ can provide:

$$U[W(t + 1)] = U[\Omega] - U'[\Omega] (W(t + 1) - \Omega) + \tfrac{1}{2} U''[\Omega] (W(t + 1) - \Omega)^2$$

$$\rightarrow \quad EU[W(t + 1)] = U[\Omega] + \tfrac{1}{2} U''[\Omega] var[W(t + 1)]$$

Using $U[\Omega - C] = EU[W(t + 1)]$ and manipulating gives:

$$C = -\frac{U''[\Omega]}{2U'[\Omega]} var[W(t + 1)] \quad \rightarrow \quad \frac{C}{W(t)} = -\frac{U''[\Omega] \, W(t)}{2U'[\Omega]} var[1 + R]$$

where $W(t + 1) = W(t)(1 + R)$. This demonstrates theoretically that the cost of risk will vary across utility functions. This result also provides theoretical measures of the cost of risk. The measures of absolute risk aversion, $A[W] = -\{U''/U'\}$, and relative risk aversion, $R[W] = -\{U''W(t)\}/U' = W(t)A[W]$ are now textbook concepts, e.g., Elton and Gruber (1995). The risk tolerance function is defined to be $T[W] = (1/A[W])$.

The notions of *relative and absolute risk aversion*, $R[W]$ and $A[W]$, provide tools for evaluating the properties of various possible functional forms that could be used to model the $EU[W]$ function. Following Ingersoll (1987, pp. 39–40), the most widely used functions belong to the hyperbolic absolute risk aversion (HARA) or linear risk tolerance class. These functions can be represented, in general form, as *the HARA utility function*:

$$U[W] = \frac{1 - \gamma}{\gamma} \left(\frac{\alpha W}{1 - \gamma} + b \right)^{\gamma} \quad b > 0$$

where α, γ and b are parameters and the function is defined for $(b + \{\alpha W/(1 - \gamma)\}) > 0$. It can be verified by evaluating the first and second derivatives of the HARA function and solving for the risk tolerance function that $T[W] = (W/(1 - \gamma)) + (b/\alpha)$. It follows that the level of risk tolerance is linear with $T[W]$ increasing for $\gamma > 1$ and decreasing for $\gamma < 1$. Recalling that $T[W] = 1/A[W]$, the measure of absolute risk aversion will be increasing for $\gamma < 1$ and decreasing for $\gamma > 1$.

Specific functional forms for the HARA class can be derived by assuming values for the parameters of the HARA utility function. For example, the theoretically important quadratic utility function is specified using $\gamma = 2$. Setting $b = 1/\alpha$ for convenience, evaluating the HARA function for this case gives:

$$U[W] = W - \frac{\alpha^2}{2} W^2 - \frac{1}{\alpha^2} \quad \rightarrow \quad U[W] = W - cW^2$$

It follows that the quadratic utility function possesses increasing absolute risk aversion ($A[W] = \{2c/(1 - 2cW)\} \rightarrow A'[W] = \{4c^2/(1 - 2cW)^2\} > 0$) and increasing relative risk aversion ($R[W] = \{2cW/(1 - 2cW)\} \rightarrow R'[W] = \{2c/(1 - 2cW)^2\} > 0$). These properties of quadratic utility imply that investors will reduce both the dollar amount and the percentage amount invested in risky assets as wealth increases. This result is, seemingly, contrary to generally observed behavior: don't the richest people hold the bulk of risky assets?

The properties of the quadratic utility function create a potential quandary for modern portfolio theory. This is because quadratic utility functions provide a possible and expedient theoretical rationale for the use of *mean-variance expected utility* functions, a fundamental building block used to develop the Markowitz mean-variance portfolio optimization model and the capital asset pricing model. The other possible and expedient rationale is to assume that the relevant random variables, the security returns, are normally distributed. To see how quadratic utility leads to mean-variance expected utility, take expectations of the quadratic $U[W]$ and manipulate to get $EU[W] = E[W] + c\{var[W] + E[W]^2\}$. It follows that assuming quadratic utility leads to mean-variance expected utility. Given the theoretical importance of mean-variance models, at least since Mossin (1973) there have been efforts to rescue quadratic utility. For example, by allowing the parameter c to vary as wealth changes it is possible to specify a quadratic utility function that has, say, constant absolute or relative risk aversion.

Though quadratic utility has a direct correspondence to mean-variance expected utility functions, it is a natural progression to consider the implications for asset pricing and portfolio selection models of assuming other possible specifications of the utility function. Three popular models are the log utility function, $U[W] = \ln[W]$, the power utility or isoelastic utility function, $U[W] = \{W^\gamma/\gamma\}$ and the negative exponential utility function, $U[W] = -exp[-\alpha W]$. In the general HARA function: negative exponential utility is specified with $\gamma = -\infty$ and $b = 1$; power utility is specified with $\gamma < 1$ and $b = 0$; and log utility is specified with $\gamma = b = 0$ (with L'Hospital's rule being needed to make the requisite derivations in this case). It follows that the negative exponential utility function possesses constant absolute risk aversion and decreasing relative risk aversion; while both the power utility and log utility functions have decreasing absolute risk aversion and constant relative risk aversion. The presence of different utility functions with different risk aversion properties begs the question: which theoretical specification is most descriptive of investor behavior?

It is difficult to obtain empirical evidence that directly addresses the absolute and relative risk aversion properties of a "representative investor." The risk aversion measures are applicable to the behavior of a given investor at different wealth levels. Evidence on the holdings of risky assets for different investors at different wealth levels are only suggestive. For example, Blume and Friend (1975) examined Federal Reserve data on the financial holdings of consumers and found evidence in favor of constant relative risk aversion (decreasing absolute risk aversion). Recent research has found that risk aversion varies across individuals due to a range of factors such as age, income, even gender, e.g., Donkers et al. (2001), Jianakoplos and Bernasek (1998). Estimates of aggregate risk aversion also vary over time, with the state of the market and where the investor is situated in their life cycle. Many studies employ complicated joint hypotheses to arrive at specific estimates of an aggregate risk aversion coefficient. For example, Hahm (1998) estimates the coefficient of relative risk aversion to be 1.25.

Expected utility and moment preference*

Given the theoretical importance of the mean-variance expected utility function, the relationship between moment preference and expected utility has received considerable academic attention. Important topics have included: the conditions under which mean-variance analysis is consistent with maximizing expected utility, e.g., Kroll, Levy and Markowitz (1984); and, the implications of introducing skewness preference into the mean-variance framework, e.g., Poitras and Heaney (1999). Brockett and Kahane (1992) among others, have shown that there is not a direct correspondence between the derivatives of the expected utility function and moments of the return distribution. The implication is that maximization of a function defined over moments, such as mean-variance or mean-variance-skewness, may not give the same solution as directly maximizing expected utility. Yet, Ormiston and Quiggin (1994) and others demonstrate that the conditions on the random variables sufficient for mean-variance rankings to provide solutions consistent with expected utility rankings are relatively weak.

As discussed in numerous sources, e.g., Loistl (1976), Poitras and Heaney (1999), the relationship between expected utility and moment preference objective functions can be motivated using a Taylor series expansion (see section 5.2) of $U[W]$, the decision maker's utility function for wealth $U[W]$, evaluated at the expected value for terminal wealth $[\Omega]$ $(E[W(t + 1)] = \Omega)$:

$$U[W(t + 1)] = U[\Omega] + U'[\Omega](W(t + 1) - \Omega) + \frac{U''[\Omega]}{2!}(W(t + 1) - \Omega)^2$$

$$+ \frac{U'''[\Omega]}{3!}(W(t + 1) - \Omega)^3 + \ldots$$

Exploiting this type of expansion requires certain technical conditions be satisfied. For example, convergence of the series within the interval of interest is needed.[6] In addition, desirable properties for utility functions require: $U'[W] > 0$, non-satiation; $U''[W] < 0$, risk aversion; and, $U'''[W] > 0$, preference for positive skewness.

With relatively weak distributional restrictions, e.g., Hassett et al. (1985), the Taylor series representation of $U[W]$ can be transformed into an approximation for a general expected utility function based on the moments of the conditional distribution for $W(t + 1)$. The relevant approximation is derived by taking conditional expectations at time t and ignoring terms associated with moments higher than the second, for a mean-variance approximation, and moments higher than the third, for a mean-variance-skewness approximation. Taking expectations for the mean-variance and mean-variance-skewness case gives:

$$EU_{MV}[W(t + 1)] \equiv EU_{MV} = U[\Omega] + 0 + \frac{U''[\Omega]}{2!} var[W(t + 1)]$$

$$= U[\Omega] - b\, var[W(t + 1)]$$

$$EU_{MVS}[W(t + 1)] \equiv EU_{MVS}$$

$$= U[\Omega] + 0 + \frac{U''[\Omega]}{2!} var[W(t + 1)] + \frac{U'''[\Omega]}{3!} skew[W(t + 1)]$$

$$= U[\Omega] - b\, var[W(t + 1)] + c\, skew[W(t + 1)]$$

where $var[W(t + 1)]$ is the variance of terminal wealth, $skew[W(t + 1)]$ is the skewness or centralized third moment for terminal wealth. Restrictions imposed by assuming risk aversion and positive skewness preference permit the coefficients in EU_{MVS} to be immediately signed as $b, c > 0$. Further restrictions on b and c, as well as the admissible range of W, can be derived by taking further derivatives of the Taylor series expansion and invoking Jensen's inequality. Setting $c = 0$ permits the mean-variance-skewness moment preference function to be reduced to the mean-variance function, EU_{MV}.

What are the implications of introducing this additional skewness term into the moment preference objective function? Currently, limited information is available comparing solutions from mean-variance and mean-variance-skewness approximations. Information about such comparisons would be relevant for a range of decision making situations, especially those involving skewness altering securities such as options and insurance. The few studies that do compare the mean-variance and mean-variance-skewness objective functions illustrate some confusion as to the implications of introducing skewness, e.g., Poitras and Heaney (1999). Studies examining the impact of skewness on the asset pricing and portfolio theory problems include Sears and Trennepohl (1983), and Simaan (1993). Combining securities into portfolios almost certainly reduces the skewness of the portfolio relative to the value weighted sum of the individual asset skewness values.

3.4   FINANCIAL ENGINEERING WITH DERIVATIVE SECURITIES

The derivative security renaissance

The Securities Act (1933, as amended 2000) makes specific reference to both options and futures contracts written on securities. Extending the scope of the Securities Act to include derivative securities captured the growth and importance of these contracts. The substantive increase in the practical importance of derivative securities has been paralleled by a corresponding increase in the theoretical and empirical analysis of these contracts within modern Finance. To this point, modern Finance has been associated primarily with the elements of modern portfolio theory, i.e., the EMH, the CAPM, the Markowitz portfolio optimization model and related concepts. Yet, in addition to these developments, modern Finance has also been intensely concerned with the development of financial engineering. This aspect of modern Finance is sufficiently distinct from the security pricing and portfolio optimization aspect that there has been little loss in content from treating it separately for pedagogical purposes. However, the practical implications of derivative securities for security analysis and portfolio strategy cannot be overlooked and the subject has to be addressed at some point.

Derivative securities are contingent claim contracts that have payoffs that depend on the future value of some commodity, where the "commodity" is broadly interpreted to include securities. Conventionally, the set of derivative securities is defined to be options, futures, forward and swap contracts, though there are also numerous hybrids that embed a contingent claim, e.g., convertible preferred stock, callable bonds. When added to a portfolio of securities, derivative securities can permit the investor to significantly alter the distribution of terminal wealth. For example, forming a portfolio that contains a common stock together with a put option on the stock produces a truncated payoff distribution for the portfolio that is bounded below. The payoff on this portfolio replicates the payoff of another portfolio that combines a call option on that stock with an investment in bonds. In other words, the availability of derivative securities opens up the practical possibility of strategy replication providing the basis for a range of new securities products that can be financially engineered. The practical implementation of these notions has created the hugely successful financial engineering industry.

The practical developments of the financial engineering industry have been accompanied by a corresponding revolution in modern Finance. This revolution has resulted in the development of a corpus of theory and empirical evidence that lies outside the stream of the developments associated with modern portfolio theory. This is possible because modern portfolio theory is concerned with the valuation of the underlying commodity while derivative security analysis is concerned with the valuation and application of contracts written on the commodity. Attempts to integrate the two streams are difficult because the notions of derivative security analysis are derived from a distinct approach to valuation. In particular, derivative securities are largely priced using absence-of-arbitrage, an approach that is concerned with the relationship between current prices. Modern portfolio theory, on the other hand, is concerned with the expected values and variances of prices that are not currently known.

To observe that derivative securities have revolutionized modern Finance is, at the same time, both an understatement and a misleading statement. The statement is misleading because revolutions in academia usually involve the removal of one body of theory and its replacement with another. In this case, modern Finance has been expanded to encompass a new body of theories and empirical results that are treated separately from the other body of theory and empirical results. In addition, in terms of intellectual history there has been a rough correspondence in the development of modern portfolio theory and derivative security pricing theory. Important contributors in the derivative pricing stream, such as Robert Merton and Fischer Black, were also major contributors to the modern portfolio stream. The practical successes that were facilitated by the derivative pricing theories of academics implicitly gave credence to the security pricing and portfolio management theories that were being advanced by the same group of academics.

Poitras (2002) refers to the renaissance in derivative securities that can, roughly, be dated from the creation of the Chicago Board Options Exchange in 1973 and the introduction of a range of exchange and OTC traded derivative securities over the following decade. Historically, derivative securities trading, especially options trading, has been the subject of considerable criticism and legislative sanction due to the potential for speculative abuses. The last quarter of the twentieth century is remarkable in the breadth and depth of derivative security trading. Securities markets both in the US and globally have embraced these new products. The financial engineering industry has become an important profit center for many of the largest firms in the securities industry. Within academic Finance, the virtues of derivative securities are expounded in introductory investment texts and advanced courses. The importance of financial engineering has permitted a proliferation of advanced graduate programs with titles such as Masters in Financial Engineering.

Yet, the renaissance in derivative securities has had its blemishes. Due to a significant number of high profile and expensive losses, trading of derivative securities attracted considerable attention during the 1990s (e.g., Poitras 2002, ch. 1). The list of companies involved is striking, as is the size of the losses. From Barings Bank to Gibson's Greetings to Sumitomo Corporation, from Long Term Capital Management to Procter & Gamble to Orange County, individual firm losses ranging from hundreds of millions to billions of dollars have been reported. Such events induce a state of uneasiness among policy makers, corporate managers, investment professionals, even academics. While it is tempting to draw glib generalizations about the apparent misunderstanding of risk management practices, closer inspection reveals a decidedly more complicated situation. In some cases, the relevant lessons that could be learned cannot be convincingly determined, due to the veil of corporate secrecy surrounding specific events. In cases where the activities and motivations of the participants can be precisely determined, it seems that different debacles raise different types of quandaries. Upon closer inspection, it seems that some so-called debacles were not debacles at all.

Large losses associated with derivative security trading are not unique to the 1990s. Even though the largest losses in absolute terms have happened more recently, this is consistent with the increasing use, availability and complexity of derivative products. This has produced an evolution in the types of problems which are arising. Since the early 1970s, there has been a progressive relaxation in the US of restrictions on derivative security trading, many of which had originated in the anti-speculation atmosphere of the post-Depression era. In conjunction with this relaxation, there has been an almost bewildering expansion in the variety of derivative securities being traded, both on the OTC markets and on the futures and options exchanges. From financial commodities to energy to equities to currencies, it is difficult to keep track of the rapid progress which has been and is being made in the development and application of derivative securities.

The history of portfolio insurance

Despite the role that derivative securities have played in the evolution of modern Finance, this book is not about the pricing of derivative securities. This subject is covered to great depth in other sources, e.g., Poitras (2002). Rather, practical applications of derivative securities to security analysis and investment strategy are of interest. In particular, derivative securities facilitate the implementation of risk management strategies that fall under the general title of portfolio insurance. The different forms of portfolio insurance illustrate the replication properties of derivative securities and how concepts from financial engineering can be used to guide portfolio allocation decisions. In other words, it is the "investment strategy" implications of derivative securities that will be examined. The "security analysis" of derivative securities would require consideration of pricing with arbitrage methods, a subject that would take the discussion too far afield.

Though portfolio insurance techniques were popularized during the 1980s, heuristic forms of portfolio insurance have been used for decades. For example, a form of portfolio insurance can be achieved with the systematic use of order placement strategies, such as stop-loss and limit orders which have been acceptable market practice at least since the nineteenth century. These types of trading dependent strategies suffer from the defect of being path dependent, an undesirable property of insurance schemes. In addition to trading related techniques, option replication strategies using stock/bond combinations were also probably in use, though in the realm of proprietary management practices. These techniques also suffer from the defect of path dependence and, in the absence of "Greek" information, would probably have been imprecise (Poitras 2002, ch. 9). The application of option replication to specifying dynamically traded stock/bond portfolios was not of academic interest until much later, after the development of the Black-Scholes formula.

As for the history of insurance related financial products, some of the insurance schemes of the late seventeenth and eighteenth century did offer payouts based on specific outcomes associated with joint stock performance. Being introduced prior to the development of actuarial science, these insurance schemes were more like gambling than insurance. In more recent history, Benninga and Blume (1985) report the selling of insurance against investment losses in the UK as early as 1956. In the US, Gatto et al. (1980) report on portfolio insurance plans offered to individuals by both the Harleysville Mutual Insurance Company and Prudential Insurance Company of America. Brennan and Schwartz (1987) observe that the Harleysville plan was the first without any element of mortality insurance. Academically, Brennan and Schwartz (1976) were the first to make the connection between the potential for integrating insurance and equity returns. Leland, O'Brien, Rubinstein and Associates were important proponents in the marketing of dynamically traded option replication strategies to institutional clients.

The explosion in the use of the various types of portfolio insurance techniques can be traced to the introduction of exchange trading in stock options. Liquid options markets made possible the implementation of numerous portfolio insurance strategies. Even more strategies were permitted with the development of futures and options markets for stock indices. Analytical contributions based on Black-Scholes resulted in further portfolio insurance strategies being introduced. Many "alternative paths to portfolio insurance" (Rubinstein 1985) were proposed and implemented. The widespread use of dynamically traded portfolio insurance techniques has been identified as an important contributing factor in the October 1987 stock market "crash," e.g., Tosini (1988). Academic understanding of notions associated with portfolio insurance have expanded considerably since the early work by Leland (1980) and Rubinstein and Leland (1981). The 1987 "crash" provided a textbook illustration of the inadequacies of the academically inspired option replication strategies; sizeable unexpected losses were experienced by investors holding what were expected to be "insured" portfolios.

One of the fundamentals driving institutions to use dynamic trading strategies was the absence of risk management products with maturities and other characteristics that captured the time profile of their particular risk exposures. Since the crash, an array of OTC and exchange traded risk management products have been introduced which greatly enhance the ability to implement path independent strategies. Included in the list of such new products would be: long dated exchange traded option products, such as LEAPS for individual stocks and longer dated index options and equity swaps. Despite these improvements, the bulk of contract liquidity on both the exchanges and OTC is still concentrated in short dated contracts (see tables 3.1 and 3.2). The relative absence of strict mark-to-market rules in OTC contracts provides a strong incentive to use short dated contracts.

An important element in the modern renaissance in derivative securities was the emergence of trading in stock index futures (see table 3.1). Sufficient liquidity in these futures contracts has facilitated the trading of futures options on these indexes. The first stock index futures contract, based on the Value Line Index, was introduced in February 1982 on the KCBT. The most important stock index futures contract, the S&P 500 traded on the CME/IMM, was introduced shortly thereafter in April 1982. A raft of stock index futures contracts has appeared since that time, starting with the introduction of the NYSE Composite on the NYFE in May 1982 and the Major Market Index on the CBT in 1984. More recently, there has been the introduction of foreign indexes traded on US exchanges, such as the Nikkei 225 on the CME. This has been accompanied by the trading of domestic equity indexes on futures markets around the world, including markets in Japan, Hong Kong, Holland, Australia, England, France, Germany, Switzerland, and Canada. Another development has been the start of trading in the DJIA index futures in October 1997. The slow pace associated with the introduction of the DJIA was not due to a lack of interest in such a contract. On the contrary, perceiving considerable demand, the CBT had attempted to introduce a DJIA contract as early as July 1984. However, these plans were thwarted by Dow Jones and Company which initiated legal action to prevent trading of the contract. What ensued was a process lasting over a dozen years, ending with the CBT eventually introducing DJIA futures and options contracts.

Dynamic portfolio insurance

The basic mechanics of "path independent" portfolio insurance can be isolated from the put-call parity arbitrage condition for a non-dividend paying stock: $S + P = C + Xe^{-rt^*}$.

Table 3.1 Stock index futures prices

Index Futures

	Open	High	Low	Settle	Change	Lifetime High	Low	Open Interest

DJ Industrial Average (CBT)-$10 × index
Mar   10,292   10,310   10,272   10,281   −27   10,354   8,580   31,900
Est vol 1,814; vol Tue 6,958; open int 32,197, −121.
Idx prl: Hi 10,341.48; Lo 10,305.12; Close 10,305.19; −36.07.

S&P 500 Index (CME)-$250 × index
Mar   109,360   109,500   108,990   109,290   −60   123,950   77,700   589,587
June   −   −   −   109,180   −70   109,500   78,000   10,554
Est vol 9,980; vol Tue 25,659; open int 602,593, −939.
Idx prl: Hi 1,096.40; Lo 1,092.73; Close 1,094.04. −1.98.

S&P Midcap 400 (CME)-$500 × index
Mar   −   −   −   571.00   −2.25   573.00   559.75   16,032
Est vol 250; vol Tue 705; open int 16,033, +306.
Idx prl: Hi 572.98; Lo 570.82; Close 571.96, −0.81.

Nasdaq 100 (CME)-$100 × index
Mar   −   −   −   144,650   200   145,100   121,500   68,591
Est vol 2,330; vol Tue 9,663; open int 68,640, +548.
Idx prl: Hi 1,447.57; Lo 1,439.71; Close 1,443.19 −4.98.

TRAKRS Long-Short Tech (CME)-$1 × index
JI05   39.46   40.02   39.46   39.92   0.13   41.41   19.76   429,029
Est vol 2,750; vol Tue 0; open int 429,029, unch.
Idx prl: Hi 38.85; Lo 38.47; Close 38.73, −0.06.

Russell 2000 (CME)-$500 × index
Mar   −   −   −   552.50   −1.00   554.00   519.75   22,097
Est vol 876; vol Tue 826; open int 22,097, −127.
Idx prl: Hi 555.03; Lo 552.23; Close 552.35, −2.68.

Russell 1000 (NYFE)-$500 × index
Mar   −   −   −   584.50   −0.25   582.50   566.25   56,403
Est vol 361; vol Tue 79; open int 56,403, −35.
Idx prl: Hi 586.43; Lo 584.48; Close 585.26, −0.93.

NYSE Composite Index (NYFE)-$50 × index
Mar   −   −   −   6,332.50   10.00   6,217.00   6,115.00   710
Est vol 0; vol Tue 1; open int 710, unch.
Idx prl: Hi 6,356.40; Lo 6,330.82; Close 6,350.34, +12.86.

Nikkei 225 Stock Average (CME)-$5 × index
Mar   10,360   10,380   10,315   10,380   −75   11,155   7,670   22,883
Est vol 456; vol Tue 1,093; open int 22,927, +315.
Index: Hi 10,400.25; Lo 10,326.17; Close 10,371.27, −1.24.

Share Price Index (SFE)-AUD 25 × index
Mar   3,284.0   3,288.0   3,278.0   3,281.0   −5.0   3,325.0   2,700.0   154,059
June   −   −   −   3,291.0   −6.0   3,312.0   2,700.0   2,999
Est vol 4,104; vol Tue 10,254; open int 160,128, +1,208.
Index: Hi 3,267.0; Lo 3,257.4; Close 3,265.6, +10.8.

CAC-40 Stock Index (MATIF)-€10 × index
Dec   3,499.5   3,516.0   3,498.0   3,513.5   12.5   3,555.0   2,850.0   605,449
Ja04 3,508.5   3,519.5   3,505.0   3,518.0   12.0   3,545.0   3,406.0   89,162
Mar   3,519.5   3,531.0   3,513.5   3,529.5   12.5   3,542.5   2,885.0   93,849
Est vol 40,828; vol Tue 93,339; open int 800,061, +37,002.
Index: Hi 3,512.32; Lo 3,495.07; Close 3,510.30, +10.21.

FTSE 100 Index (LIFFE)-€10 × index
Mar   4,428.0   4,452.5   4,427.0   4,434.0   13.0   4,508.0   3,895.5   376,719
June   −   −   −   4,441.5   13.0   4,422.0   4,019.5   10,248
Vol Wed 8,506; open int 391,592, −111.
Index: Hi 4,457.40; Lo 4,432.90; Close 4,444.70, +3.80.

Index Options

Calls				Puts		

DJ Industrial Avg (CBOT)
$100 times premium

Price	Jan	Feb	Mar	Jan	Feb	Mar
101	25.50	33.35	39.40	7.50	15.80	21.50
102	18.00	27.10	33.00	10.00	−	25.00
103	12.00	21.30	27.10	14.00	−	−
104	7.50	16.20	21.90	19.50	−	−
105	4.50	11.90	17.30	−	−	−
106	2.50	8.60	13.60	−	−	−

Est vol 1,134 Tu 1,512 calls 433 puts
Op int Tues 12,552 calls 3,693 puts

S&P 500 Stock Index (CME)
$250 times premium

Price	Jan	Feb	Mar	Jan	Feb	Mar
1,085	20.40	30.00	35.90	12.50	22.10	28.00
1,090	17.20	27.00	32.90	14.30	24.10	30.00
1,095	14.40	24.10	−	16.50	26.20	−
1,100	11.90	21.50	27.40	19.00	28.60	34.50
1,105	9.80	19.10	−	−	31.20	−
1,110	8.00	16.90	22.60	−	34.00	−

Est vol 3,600 Tu 2,762 calls 6,483 puts
Op int Tues 67,029 calls 133,000 puts

Other Index Options

Nasdaq 100 (CME)
$100 times NASDAQ 100 index

Price	Jan	Feb	Mar	Jan	Feb	Mar
1,450	26.00	−	64.00	−	−	67.50

Est vol 0 Tu 25 calls 4 puts
Op int Tues 1,695 calls 111 puts

NYSE Composite (NYFE)
$50 times premium

Price	Jan	Feb	Mar	Jan	Feb	Mar
6,340	7,050	12,400	15,150	7,800	13,150	15,900

Est vol 50 Tu 0 calls 110 puts
Op int Tues 0 calls 6,981 puts

Table 3.2 NYSE program trading

NYSE PROGRAM TRADING

Program trading is the purchase or sale of at least 15 different stocks with a total value of $1 million or more. Stock-index arbitrage is defined as the sale or purchase of derivatives such as stock-index futures, to profit from the price difference between the basket and the derivatives. Under Rule 80A, when the DJIA moves 50 points or more from the previous day's close, index arbitrage orders in stocks of the Standard & Poor's 500 are subject to a special tick test.

November 14, 2003

(Volume Mil. Shares)	11/14 Week	11/7 Week	10/31 Week
NYSE avg daily	1,304.9	1,421.3	1,569.3
NYSE prog trad	515.0	587.2	643.3
Buy programs	255.2	296.4	335.3
Sell programs	259.8	290.8	308.0
Program % NYSE	39.5	41.3	41.0
Index Arbitrage, %	4.42	4.79	4.55
Other 80A trades, %	0.00	0.04	0.00
Other trading, %	35.08	36.51	36.45

The Top Program Traders

(Mil. Shrs)	Index Arbitrage	Derivative-Related–z	Other Strategies	Total
Morgan Stanley	7.9	0.7	426.8	435.4
Deutsche Banc	60.3	—	295.7	356.0
UBS Warburg	—	—	264.3	264.3
Goldman Sachs Group	1.7	—	235.3	237.0
Credit Suisse 1st Boston	4.1	—	173.2	177.3
Lehman Brothers	2.2	—	156.2	158.4
RBC Dominion	114.3	0.3	21.9	136.5
Bear Sterns	4.1	—	113.8	117.9
Merill Lynch	—	—	90.2	90.2
Major League Securities	—	—	72.1	72.1
Overall Total	250.6	1.0	2,086.6	2,338.2

z-Other derivative-related strategies besides index arbitrage.

Source: New York Stock Exchange

Because the concern is portfolio insurance, S refers to the price of a portfolio of stocks (instead of an individual stock), X is the exercise price (strike price), t^* is the time to expiration measured as the fraction of a year remaining to expiration, P is the price of a put written on the portfolio with exercise price X and time to expiration t^*, C is the call price written on the portfolio with the same X and t^* as the put, and r is the riskless interest rate. Dividends have been ignored for simplicity of exposition. As stated, put-call parity provides two path independent insurance strategies. One strategy is $S + P$, buy puts against the portfolio. If S is an index portfolio, relevant exchange traded puts may be available. Another strategy is $C + Xe^{-rt^*}$, buy calls and invest the remainder in appropriately dated bonds. Again, if the portfolio is an index portfolio, exchange traded calls may be available. One important practical advantage of this strategy is that transactions costs in bond markets are typically lower than transactions costs for stocks and the bond portfolio can be actively managed, e.g., by riding the yield curve, to earn potentially higher returns than the $S + P$ approach.

While the path independent strategies have certain desirable features, there are some drawbacks. One disadvantage is the inability to accurately replicate insurance for portfolios that do not track an index for which there are traded options, i.e., the relevant portfolio options are not available. Constructing a portfolio of options using options on the individual stocks will be more expensive and there is the possibility that not all stocks will have traded options. Using index options as surrogates for the portfolio options eliminates the potential for gains from individual security selection. Combining index options with options on individual stocks raises the problem of finding the appropriate combination of these options to replicate the payout on the desired portfolio. Another disadvantage is that the maturity dates for options may not be long enough to match the portfolio's investment horizon, i.e., there is insufficient time invariance. This requires options positions to be rolled forward which is more expensive and has pricing risk.

To handle these types of problems, dynamic trading strategies have been developed that involve actively trading portfolios composed of stocks and bonds in order to replicate the payoff on an insured stock portfolio. Such strategies are intuitively appealing to large institutional investors such as pension funds and insurance companies that already hold stock/bond portfolios that are actively managed. These strategies can be illustrated by substituting the Black-Scholes formula into the put-call parity condition:

$$S + P = SN[d_1] - Xe^{-rt^*}N[d_2] + Xe^{-rt^*} = SN[d_1] + Xe^{-rt^*}(1 - N[d_2])$$

$$= w_1 S + w_2 Xe^{-rt^*}$$

where $N[d]$ is the cumulative normal distribution evaluated at d with d_1 and d_2 as specified in the Black-Scholes formula, e.g., Poitras (2002, p. 441). The weights w_1 and w_2 indicate the proportions of the portfolio held in stock and bonds in order to achieve insurance with an exercise price of X and time to maturity of t^*. Unlike the portfolio optimization models, the weights here will not sum to one, as the relationship is derived to equate values on the rhs and lhs. The sum of the weights will be close to one but not equal to one unless the put value is zero.

From a practical perspective, it is important for the potential portfolio insurer to identify why dynamic replication strategies, i.e., strategies dynamically replicating a call option payoff using stock/bond positions, should be used. Related to this are subsidiary issues concerning how to replicate and when to replicate. In this vein, large fund managers would consider the liquidity needed to establish large enough positions using derivatives and whether there are suitable X and expiration dates available. For example, while a well-diversified fund (e.g., a portfolio composed of an index fund) could make use of options or futures written on the appropriate index, funds targeted at non-systematic risk are more likely to be obligated to use dynamic replication strategies. However, even a well-diversified fund may find that available expiration dates on traded derivatives are not long enough, i.e., sufficient "time convexity" cannot be achieved. Because the dynamic replication strategies can be designed to theoretically achieve almost any desired expiration date and exercise price, this provides another reason for the use of these strategies.

To illustrate the use of dynamic replication where dividends are paid on the portfolio, consider the creation of a synthetic put option for an index portfolio. Given that the dividend yield on the index is q, Hull (1987, p. 204) shows that the delta of a European put on the index is:

$$\Delta_P = \exp\{-qt^*\}[N[d_1] - 1] = \exp\{-qt^*\}(\Delta_c - 1)$$

where:

$$d_1 = \frac{\ln\left\{\dfrac{S}{X}\right\} + \left(r - q + \dfrac{\sigma^2}{2}\right)t^*}{\sigma\sqrt{t^*}}$$

Assuming that $S = 300$, $X = 290$, $r = .09$, $q = .03$, $\sigma = .25$ and $t^* = .5$, evaluation of the delta of the put gives $\Delta_P = -0.322$. It follows that if dynamic replication of a put is being used that 32.2% of the index fund should be sold and invested in (riskfree) fixed income securities. From the properties of the put delta (Poitras 2002, p. 486), as the value of the index fund drops, the delta of the put will become more negative, indicating that a larger proportion of the index fund has to be sold, i.e., a larger fraction of the portfolio will be invested in fixed income securities. A similar result would hold where the value of the index was increasing. In this case the delta of the put would be less negative, indicating that fixed income securities should be sold to purchase more units of the index fund. In this case, the proportion of the portfolio invested in the index fund would increase.

There are a number of different methods of approaching the portfolio insurance problem. In addition to strategies already examined such as combining stocks with purchased puts or dynamically replicating such positions, the remaining strategies attempt to achieve the same objectives by using derivative positions as surrogates for stock ownership, on the presumption that there are execution advantages (e.g., greater liquidity and lower transactions costs) to using derivatives. For example, instead of owning stock, it is possible to form portfolios composed of purchased call options and fixed income securities. Another strategy would alter the dynamic replication strategies by substituting short futures positions for the stock sales required when the value of the stock position declines. However, if this approach is used, for example, to insure an index fund, it is

Table 3.3 Examples of portfolio insurance: static insurance and continuous rebalancing

Insured stock portfolio value at alternative stock index levels, using static portfolio insurance[a]			Insured stock portfolio value at alternative index levels, using dynamic portfolio insurance with continuous rebalancing[a]				
Index level S	Put option P	Portfolio value $S + P$	Index level S	T-bill price Xe^{-rT}	Stock portfolio weight w_1	T-bill weight w_2	Portfolio value
59.87	36.21	96.08	59.87	96.08	0.001	1.000	96.08
63.02	33.06	96.08	63.02	96.08	0.002	0.999	96.08
66.34	29.75	96.09	66.34	96.08	0.005	0.996	96.09
69.83	26.29	96.13	69.83	96.08	0.014	0.990	96.13
73.51	22.70	96.21	73.51	96.08	0.034	0.975	96.21
77.38	19.03	96.41	77.38	96.08	0.072	0.945	96.41
81.45	15.38	96.83	81.45	96.08	0.136	0.892	96.83
85.74	11.87	97.61	85.74	96.08	0.231	0.809	97.61
90.25	8.67	98.92	90.25	96.08	0.355	0.696	98.92
95.00	5.94	100.94	95.00	96.08	0.496	0.560	100.94
100.00	3.79	103.79	100.00	96.08	0.638	0.416	103.79
105.00	2.29	107.29	105.00	96.08	0.758	0.289	107.29
110.25	1.27	111.52	110.25	96.08	0.852	0.183	111.52
115.76	0.65	116.42	115.76	96.08	0.918	0.106	116.42
121.55	0.31	121.86	121.55	96.08	0.959	0.056	121.86
127.63	0.13	127.76	127.63	96.08	0.981	0.026	127.76
134.01	0.05	134.06	134.01	96.08	0.992	0.011	134.06
140.71	0.02	140.73	140.71	96.08	0.997	0.004	140.73
147.75	0.01	147.75	147.75	96.08	0.999	0.001	147.75
155.13	0.00	155.13	155.13	96.08	1.000	0.000	155.13
162.89	0.00	162.89	162.89	96.08	1.000	0.000	162.89

[a] To value the European put, it is assumed: the index pays no dividends; $r = .08$; $\sigma = .2$; $X = 100$; and $t^* = .5$.

important to recognize that the number of stock index futures to be shorted for a given long index fund will be different than in the case where the stock position is being sold directly (and invested in bonds). In addition, there is the mechanical problem of calculating the dollar equivalency hedge ratio for the futures and cash positions.

Table 3.3 (adapted from Stoll and Whalley, 1993) has a helpful tabular presentation of how various methods of portfolio insurance would perform to insure a stock index across a range of index levels. The first table gives payoff for the path independent strategy, $S + P$. Comparing the distribution of S with $S + P$ reveals, in a simple tabular form, what Bookstaber and Clarke (1983) have examined in much more detail using distributional plots. The addition of a put transforms the symmetric S distribution to a positively skewed $S + P$ distribution. In terms of the return distribution, the additional cost of the put will result in a lower mean value for the $S + P$ distribution. The second table gives the results from applying the dynamic replication portfolio insurance strategy derived from $S + P = SN[d_1] + Xe^{-rt^*}(1 - N[d_2])$.

In practice, dynamic replication faces substantive implementation issues. Trading cannot be conducted under the perfect markets, continuous trading assumptions required for the Black-Scholes formula to capture the price of the option. Nevertheless, assuming that the Black-Scholes assumptions apply permits the decomposition of $S + P$ into the exact holdings of stocks and bonds to hold in order to precisely replicate the $S + P$ payoff. As the stock index level falls away from $S = 100$, the stock index position will be continuously reduced to the point where the stock position is nearly zero at $S = 59.87$. Similarly, as the stock index rises, the bond is sold to the point where at $S = 162.89$, there are no funds left in bonds. From this, it is apparent that dynamic portfolio insurance strategies, if applied by a large enough fraction of market traders, would amplify market movements.

In practice, dynamic trading strategies have to deal with the realities of discrete trading. Rules have to be determined about how large a movement in S is required before the rebalancing decision is executed. There are a number of possible methods of specifying a rebalancing trigger value. The example in table 3.4 assumes that the trigger value is 5%. From this point, the tabular presentation method can only provide an approximate picture of the distribution of weights, and the associated impact on portfolio value. For example, upside movements of S will produce increasing weights for S which lag the continuously rebalanced weights, resulting in a slight reduction in portfolio value. A similar result happens for downside movements of S where the reduction in S weights lags the continuously rebalanced weights, again resulting in a slight reduction in portfolio value. Hence, the simple introduction of discrete rebalancing results in a deterioration of the performance of the dynamic replication strategy.

As it turns out, the discretely rebalanced case has considerably more complications than can be captured in one table. Being *path dependent*, the terminal portfolio value can take a range of values, depending on the particular time path realized by S. For the *path independent* cases, $S + P$ and continuous rebalancing, the distribution of portfolio value can be determined precisely because the terminal portfolio value does not depend on the particular time path realized by S. This does not happen with discrete rebalancing. For example, a price path which starts at 100 and goes to 95 generates a rebalancing involving a sale of S to produce a weight change of .638 to .495. If the next step is back to 100, the rebalancing involves the weight returning from .495 to .638. The resulting portfolio value will now be less than a portfolio value along a price path where S was unchanged and no rebalancing happened.

Table 3.4 also provides results for the case where a stock/bond portfolio is created using the initial dynamic portfolio weights but no rebalancing is done along the time path. This is another type of path independent strategy. Though not immediately apparent from the tabular presentation, the distribution of the portfolio value for the no rebalancing case is not unlike the S distribution. Unlike the dynamically traded portfolio, the no rebalancing distribution retains the symmetric shape of the S distribution, though there is less dispersion due to the presence of a long investment in the riskless

Table 3.4 Examples of portfolio insurance: no rebalancing and discrete rebalancing

Insured stock portfolio value at alternative stock index levels, using dynamic portfolio insurance with no rebalancing[a]					Insured stock portfolio value at alternative stock index levels using dynamic portfolio insurance with discrete rebalancing[a]				
Index level S	T-bill price Xe^{-rT}	Stock portfolio weight w_1	T-bill weight w_2	Portfolio value	Index level S	T-bill price Xe^{-rT}	Stock portfolio weight w_1	T-bill weight w_2	Portfolio value
59.87	96.08	0.638	0.416	78.18	59.87	96.08	0.001	0.985	94.65
63.02	96.08	0.638	0.416	80.19	63.02	96.08	0.002	0.984	94.66
66.34	96.08	0.638	0.416	82.31	66.34	96.08	0.005	0.982	94.67
69.83	96.08	0.638	0.416	84.53	69.83	96.08	0.014	0.976	94.72
73.51	96.08	0.638	0.416	86.88	73.51	96.08	0.034	0.961	94.85
77.38	96.08	0.638	0.416	89.35	77.38	96.08	0.071	0.933	95.12
81.45	96.08	0.638	0.416	91.95	81.45	96.08	0.135	0.882	95.67
85.74	96.08	0.638	0.416	94.68	85.74	96.08	0.229	0.802	96.65
90.25	96.08	0.638	0.416	97.56	90.25	96.08	0.353	0.691	98.24
95.00	96.08	0.638	0.416	100.59	95.00	96.08	0.495	0.558	100.59
100.00	96.08	0.638	0.416	103.79	100.00	96.08	0.638	0.416	103.79
105.00	96.08	0.638	0.416	106.98	105.00	96.08	0.755	0.288	106.98
110.25	96.08	0.638	0.416	110.33	110.25	96.08	0.847	0.183	110.94
115.76	96.08	0.638	0.416	113.84	115.76	96.08	0.911	0.105	115.61
121.55	96.08	0.638	0.416	117.54	121.55	96.08	0.951	0.055	120.89
127.63	96.08	0.638	0.416	121.42	127.63	96.08	0.973	0.026	126.67
134.01	96.08	0.638	0.416	125.49	134.01	96.08	0.984	0.011	132.87
140.71	96.08	0.638	0.416	129.76	140.71	96.08	0.988	0.004	139.46
147.75	96.08	0.638	0.416	134.25	147.75	96.08	0.990	0.001	146.42
155.13	96.08	0.638	0.416	138.97	155.13	96.08	0.991	0.000	153.73
162.89	96.08	0.638	0.416	143.92	162.89	96.08	0.991	0.000	161.41

[a] To value the European put, it is assumed: the index pays no dividends; $r = .08$; $\sigma = .2$; $X = 100$; and $t^* = .5$. The discrete rebalancing case assumes a trigger value of 5%.

asset.[7] In all of this, the no rebalancing and static portfolio insurance cases are being unfavorably compared with the discrete rebalancing case because there are no transactions costs factored into the various calculations. In the limit, i.e., continuous rebalancing with transactions costs, the dynamic strategies may produce infinite losses. In practice, there will be a tradeoff between rebalancing frequency, the various transactions and execution costs and the terminal value of the insured portfolio. Wider rebalancing frequencies will permit greater deviation from the path independent static portfolio insurance case, but this loss of precision will be balanced out with a savings in transactions costs due to reduced trading frequency.

As discussed in Poitras (2002, pp. 523–4), there is nothing unique about a portfolio of domestic stocks. The notions of portfolio insurance can be applied to any commodity. One useful extension involves insuring the domestic currency value of a foreign bond position. Much as with dynamic portfolio insurance for stocks, dynamic portfolio insurance for foreign bonds can be derived using put-call parity for currency options. The objective is to dynamically trade a portfolio composed of domestic bonds and foreign bonds in order to achieve the same payout as a path independent portfolio composed of a foreign bond plus a currency put option. If the exchange rate increases, the value of the domestic currency rises relative to foreign currency, then the dynamic strategy involves selling foreign bonds and buying domestic bonds. If the exchange rate deteriorates, the domestic bond is sold in favor of buying the foreign bond. As before, the Black-Scholes formula for a call can be substituted into the put-call parity condition to derive the appropriate portfolio weights.

To see this consider the path independent value of a portfolio which contains a foreign currency bond which has the domestic currency value protected with a currency put option. The associated dynamic replication portfolio can now be derived:

$$V = S \exp\{-r_f t^*\} + P = C + X \exp\{-rt^*\}$$

$$= S \exp\{-r_f t^*\} N[d_1] - X \exp\{-rt^*\} N[d_2] + X \exp\{-rt^*\}$$

$$= S \exp\{-r_f t^*\} N[d_1] + X \exp\{-rt^*\}(1 - N[d_2])$$

In this formulation, $S \exp\{-r_f t^*\}$ is the domestic currency value of the foreign bond position and $X \exp\{-rt^*\}$ is the domestic currency value of the domestic bond. More precisely, $\exp\{-r_f t^*\}$ is the foreign currency value of a continuously compounded zero coupon bond which matures to one unit of domestic currency; multiplying this foreign bond price by S, the time t spot exchange rate expressed in domestic direct terms, converts the foreign bond price to units of domestic currency. Similarly, $X \exp\{-rt^*\}$ is the domestic currency value of a continuously compounded zero coupon bond which matures to the number of units of domestic currency reflected in the exercise price for the currency option.

As with portfolio insurance for stocks, portfolio insurance for foreign bonds involves dynamic trading of the position. When the value of domestic currency rises relative to foreign currency, S will fall and the dynamic strategy requires selling a portion of the foreign bond and using the funds to purchase domestic bonds. The dynamic replication formulation identifies the precise amount of foreign bonds which have to be sold in order to maintain the same payout as the path independent portfolio $[S \exp\{-r_f t^*\} + P]$. While much the same theoretically, dynamic replication for foreign bonds can differ in practice. Unlike the dynamic strategies for stock portfolios, which can suffer from inaccurate replication due to illiquidity in the underlying stocks, the cash markets involved in the dynamic insurance for foreign bonds are typically liquid. The foreign exchange market, as well as the domestic and foreign bond markets, are unlikely to be subject to the types of pricing discontinuities which precipitated the October 1987 market break.

Questions

1*(a) For the simple expected utility example in section 3.3, solve for the optimal investment in the risky asset $(A(0)^*)$ when the utility function has the quadratic form: $U[W(1)] = W(1) - bW(1)^2$. Demonstrate that $A(0)$ decreases with the amount of initial wealth $W(0)$, i.e., the greater the initial wealth level, the smaller is the investment in the risky asset.

  (b) Evaluate the second derivative of the general *EU* function and derive the conditions required for solution to be a maximum.

2* By evaluating the first derivatives for $A[W]$ and $R[W]$, solve for the relative and absolute risk aversion properties of the log utility, negative exponential and power utility functions.

3 To see how to use this formula to evaluate the variance of portfolio return, consider the following information given about three securities, A, B and C:

Stock	Expected return (%)	Standard deviation (%)	Correlation coefficients		
			A	B	C
A	14	12	1.00	0	0.20
B	16	15	0	1.00	0.60
C	12	10	0.2	0.60	1.00

(a) If the market value of a portfolio is composed of 30% of A and 70% of C, what is the expected return and standard deviation of the portfolio?
(b) If the portfolio is 21% in A, 30% in B and 49% in C what is the expected return and standard deviation of the portfolio?
(c) If a portfolio contains only A and C, what combination of A and C has the lowest possible standard deviation? What is the expected return and standard deviation on this portfolio?

4 Create a numerical example applicable to the *trente demoiselles* to illustrate how the basic notions of portfolio diversification apply to this case. To construct this example define the risk associated with one individual and carry this through to the case of a portfolio of life annuities written on the lives of thirty individuals. This will involve decomposing the basic risk into parts and assessing the impact of increasing the number of lives affecting the portfolio. (Hint: see the discussion of diversification in section 3.1).

5 Given the following information about four risky securities:

$$\sigma_1 = .2 \quad \sigma_2 = .2 \quad \sigma_{1,2} = 0 \quad E[R_1] = .05 \quad E[R_2] = .15$$

$$\sigma_3^2 = .04 = \sigma_4^2 \quad \sigma_{1,3} = \sigma_{1,4} = \sigma_{2,3} = \sigma_{2,4} = \sigma_{3,4} = 0 \quad E[R_3] = .20 = E[R_4]$$

(a) Derive the value weights (w_1, w_2, w_3, w_4), mean and variance of the minimum variance portfolio which combines these four securities.

(b) How do the value weights (w_1, w_2, w_3, w_4), mean and variance of the minimum variance portfolio change if $\rho_{1,2} = \rho_{1,3} = \rho_{2,3} = \ldots = \rho_{3,4} = .5$?

6 Assume the standard capital asset pricing model is true, e.g., there is unrestricted lending or borrowing at the same riskfree rate of interest. From your stock broker you are able to obtain the following information about two stocks:

	Expected return	Standard deviation	Correlation with the market portfolio
Stock (A)	0.18	0.30	0.4
Stock (B)	0.30	0.60	0.75

The *variance* of the return on the market is 0.16.

(a) Compute the β's for each security?

(b) What is the expected return on the market portfolio?

(c) What are the equations for the Capital Market Line and the Security Market Line?

7 Assuming the market model holds, explain why unsystematic risk is diversifiable while systematic risk is not diversifiable. Be sure to identify the relevant assumptions which are being made about the error terms and where these assumptions are used in your derivation. What is the standard deviation of a fully diversified portfolio?

8(a) A long stock position can be "protected" by buying a put. How can the payoff on this portfolio of a stock and option be replicated using "dynamic hedging" strategies involving portfolios which combine only stock and bond positions?

(b) Describe the various forms of portfolio insurance. How would these various forms of portfolio insurance perform in the face of discontinuous movements in equity prices such as the July 2002 market break?

NOTES

1 The σ_{ij} term is interpreted as being a covariance when $i \neq j$ and as a variance when $i = j$. Because the basic optimization problem is quadratic, it follows that the complete set of optimal solutions will take the form of an ellipse or a parabola. Consider the case where the $\{w_i\}$ are restricted to be non-negative, then the solution will be an ellipse. At any given target level of expected return, there will be two values of σ which solve the optimization problem. In evaluating the solutions, it is conventional to ignore the optimal solution which has the higher level of σ and consider only the portfolios which have the lowest σ.

2 Markowitz (1999) reviews the historical development of the model.

3 Such is the reason for using moving sampling windows instead of using all the data available. For example, 100 years of monthly data produces estimates of the arithmetic average which would not be affected by an additional observation. Hence, the optimal weights would not change over time.

4 The general approach in the following discussion is adapted from Fama (1976).

5 The axiomatic approach to choice under uncertainty has produced a considerable number of studies. Accessible and brief overviews are available in various sources, e.g., Henderson and Quandt (1980, section 3.8), Ingersoll (1987, ch. 1) Duffie (1988, ch. 1, section 5). A more advanced and complete treatment is available in Fishburn (1982). The following discussion presumes that the student has already had an introductory exposure to expected utility theory.

6 Further discussion of issues related to the general properties of a Taylor series expansion for approximating a general expected utility function can be found in Loistl (1976). Hassett et al. (1985) examine specific types of problems with the Taylor series which arise where skewness is involved. Brockett and Kahane (1992) discuss the connection between preference for moments and expected utility rankings of risky prospects, arguing that $U'' < 0$ and $U''' > 0$ are not related to variance avoidance or skewness preference. Poitras and Heaney (1999) illustrate a theoretical difficulty that can arise when optimizing a mean-variance-skewness objective function.

7 This observation provides a window into the various complications that non-linear payoffs, such as options, can have for mean-variance optimization analysis.

part 2   Fixed Income Valuation

Since the chief emphasis must be placed on the avoidance of loss, bond selection is primarily a negative art. It is a process of exclusion and rejection, rather than of search and acceptance. In this respect the contrast with common-stock selection is fundamental in character. The prospective buyer of a given common stock is influenced more or less equally by the desire to avoid loss and the desire to make profit. The penalty for mistakenly rejecting the issue may conceivably be as great as that for mistakenly accepting it. But an investor may reject any number of good bonds with virtually no penalty at all, provided he does not eventually accept an unsound issue.

Graham and Dodd (1934) on the selection of corporate bonds

The difficulties connected with the problem of arriving at a concept of duration are, indeed, extremely great.

Macaulay (1938, p. 52) on the concept of duration

It should always be kept in mind that corporate managements generally do not have bondholders' interests at heart; they are elected by, and beholden to, the owners of the business, namely the common shareholders. Their duty is to increase shareholder wealth, not that of bondholders. They do not owe any fiduciary duty to bondholders, their only responsibility is contractual.

Wilson and Fabozzi (1996, p. 114)

Chapter
Summary

Chapter 4 *Basics of Fixed Income Valuation*

4.1   Basics of Fixed Income Securities
      The philosophy of fixed income analysis
      Types of securities and markets
      Types of interest rates
      Some examples of valuation problems

4.2   The Concept of Duration
      The concept of duration
      Historical background: Macaulay, Hicks, Samuelson and Redington
      The uses and calculation of duration

4.3   The Term Structure of Interest Rates
      Calculation of implied zero coupon interest rates
      Traditional theories of the term structure
      Estimating term structure models

4.4   Basics of Credit Risk and Default Risk
      The legal aspects of default
      Assessment of credit risk and default risk
      The empirical evidence on credit risk and default risk

Questions
Notes

Basics of Fixed Income Valuation

4.1 BASICS OF FIXED INCOME SECURITIES[1]

The philosophy of fixed income analysis

Section 1.3 dedicated considerable attention to expanding the notion that Finance is a human science. For this purpose, the uncertainty associated with common stock valuation provided a useful basis for illustrating why the approach and techniques of the natural sciences are not fully adequate to develop understanding of problems being examined in Finance. Other than the historical discussion of life annuity valuation, only passing attention was given to fixed income securities. This omission was intentional, as fixed income security valuation poses a different shade of the epistemological problems than were raised for common stock valuation. Fixed income security analysis is based on valuation methods, derived from discounted cash flow models, that are "accurate" when applied appropriately. These valuation methods also are the basic tools for, say, actuarial science, which is a branch of applied mathematics. Is it possible that the epistemology of the natural sciences is appropriate for the fixed income element of Finance?

Sorting out the philosophy of fixed income analysis poses something of a quandary. The methods and procedures used to value these securities differ in form, if not in substance, from those used to value common stocks. Though still present, uncertainty plays a different and seemingly less pervasive role in fixed income analysis. To value the return to common stocks in excess of the riskless rate of return, modern Finance uses the concept of systematic risk that is measured relative to an "asset market" proxied by a broadly based domestic stock market index such as the S&P 500. In contrast, the return on fixed income securities is decomposed into a combination of the riskless return and components associated with term to maturity, coupon, default risk, option features, tax status and the like. The notion of an "asset market return" similar to that for common stocks is difficult to identify in the case of fixed income securities. Instead, the comparable concept for fixed income securities focuses on the level and term structure of a set of default free securities, usually proxied by available maturities for US Treasury debt.

Examined in isolation, with no reference to other securities, the valuation of default free fixed income securities could be approached as a purely mathematical problem. However, this would require unrealistic assumptions to be made. For example, if the default free security were a fixed coupon bond, then some assumption would have to be made about the interest rate at which the future coupon payments were reinvested. Alternatively, it could be assumed that the default free securities were zero coupon bonds, but this still raises the problem of comparing the certain return on a k period bond with the uncertain return from investing in k successive one period zero coupon bonds. It does not take much consideration to see that the semantics of "fixed income" securities is misleading. All that is fixed is the size of the coupon payment, and for some "fixed income" securities even this may not be fixed, e.g., tontines, mortgage pass throughs, floating rate notes. In other cases, the term over which the fixed payments are made may be unknown, e.g., life annuities, callable bonds.

Though the cash flow patterns of fixed income securities differ from common stocks in being more well defined, the problem of dealing with uncertainty is still present. In addition, situations where a decision has to be made about, say, whether to purchase a common stock or a bond or how to allocate capital invested in a portfolio between bonds and stocks, there is still the problem of assessing the uncertainty associated with common stock valuation. In other words, investment strategy requires assessments of relative valuation. Even in the extreme case where one type of security has a purely deterministic return, the decision about whether to purchase such a security and, if so, how much, still has to deal with the other securities that are available for purchase. As such, it is not possible to develop a philosophy of fixed income analysis that would conform to the epistemological approach of the natural sciences.

The contrast between actuarial science and fixed income analysis is revealing. There are some close correspondences. However, actuarial science, the mathematical science of insurance, is not concerned with the range of risks that are conventionally encountered in securities markets. Actuaries are concerned with the probability of loss versus no loss. Many of the risks encountered in securities markets are *speculative risks*, where there is a possibility of loss, as well as a possibility of gain. Such risks can be distinguished from *pure risks* that involve situations with only the chance of loss or no loss (Vaughan 1982, p. 8): "The distinction between pure and speculative risks is an important one, because normally only pure risks are insurable. Insurance is not concerned with the protection of individuals against those losses arising out of speculative risks. Speculative risk is voluntarily accepted because of its two-dimensional nature, which includes the possibility of gain." It is apparent that the valuation problems being modeled differ between actuarial science and fixed income analysis. The problem of determining the actuarially sound premium for a life insurance policy is substantively different than determining whether, say, a corporate bond is a desirable investment at a given price.

Given this, actuarial science and fixed income analysis still have some close correspondences. As Graham and Dodd (1934) observe: "Since the chief emphasis must be placed on the avoidance of loss, bond selection is primarily a negative art." The methods of valuation for fixed income securities are more mathematical and empirically precise than for common stocks. If an investor has a well defined investment horizon, it is even possible to buy a fixed income security that provides a return that is known with relative certainty. For fixed income securities issued by corporations, the uncertainty associated with both the cash flow and the asset base sustaining the security is less than for common stocks because of the higher priority of claim. As such, the inductive method of the natural sciences explains substantially more of security analysis for fixed income securities than for common stocks. Yet, there is still the human element in fixed income security valuation and the linear progression of knowledge is still unavailable. In the end, fixed income valuation still lies within the realm of the human sciences.

Given that analysis of fixed income securities has to account for the human aspect, this analysis does proceed much farther towards an understanding of the valuation problem than is the case with common stocks. The essential characteristics of fixed income securities are more readily adaptable to the techniques of discounted cash flow analysis. While there are problems with determining the cash flows and discount rates, there is relatively little debate about the applicability of the discounted cash flow model. The same cannot be said about common stock valuation where it is not clear whether discounted cash flow analysis can be effectively applied. This leads to a fundamental question confronting security analysis: to what extent can the discounted cash methods used to value fixed income securities be applied in the valuation of common stocks? Is security analysis a subject with a homogeneity of technique or is there two or more distinct subjects involved, each requiring a distinct approach to the valuation problem?

Types of securities and markets

Section 1.1 gave a cursory overview of the types of fixed income securities that are available. Various classification schemes are available: by type of issuer, e.g., corporate vs. government; by country of issue, e.g., national vs. international; by credit rating, e.g., investment grade vs. speculative; classification by features, e.g., callable, putable, convertible, and tax status; and, by term to maturity, e.g., bond market vs. money market. In the US, a breakdown by type of issuer reveals the relative importance of mortgage related issues, effectively collaterized mortgage obligations and mortgage pass throughs. This category and the corporate debt category are the two largest and are the two categories most characterized by issues with embedded options. The municipal government debt category, which includes both state and local issuers, is characterized by issues with favorable tax status. Including other issues with special features, e.g., callable US Treasury bonds, it is apparent that a large part of the US publicly traded debt market is characterized by special features.

Table 4.1 is only given as a crude reference point. There are substantial difficulties in assembling numbers on the relative size of the outstanding issues. For example, as illustrated in table 4.2, the outstanding amount reported for the US Treasury ignores non-marketable debt, such as US Savings bonds, and other types of US federal government debt obligations such as those for intra-government holdings of Government Account Series issues that are held by entities such as the Social Security trust fund, the Civil Service Retirement and Disability Fund, the Federal Hospital Insurance Trust Fund, and the Federal Retirement Thrift Savings Fund (G Fund).[2] There are also implied and

Table 4.1 Outstanding level of public and private debt 1985–2002:Q3[a] ($ billions)

Year	Municipal	US Treasury[1]	Mortgage-related[2]	Corporate[a]	Federal agencies	Money market[3]	Asset-backed[a4]	Total
1985	859.5	1,437.7	372.1	776.5	293.9	847.0	0.9	4,587.6
1986	920.4	1,619.0	534.4	959.6	307.4	877.0	7.2	5,225.0
1987	1,010.4	1,724.7	672.1	1,074.9	341.4	979.8	12.9	5,816.2
1988	1,082.3	1,821.3	772.4	1,195.7	381.5	1,108.5	29.3	6,391.0
1989	1,135.2	1,945.4	971.5	1,292.5	411.8	1,192.3	51.3	7,000.0
1990	1,184.4	2,195.8	1,333.4[b]	1,350.4	434.7	1,156.8	89.9	7,745.4
1991	1,272.2	2,471.6	1,636.9	1,454.7	442.8	1,054.3	129.9	8,462.4
1992	1,302.8	2,754.1	1,937.0	1,557.0	484.0	994.2	163.7	9,192.8
1993	1,377.5	2,989.5	2,144.7	1,674.7	570.7	971.8	199.9	9,928.8
1994	1,341.7	3,126.0	2,251.6	1,755.6	738.9	1,034.7	257.3	10,505.8
1995	1,293.5	3,307.2	2,352.1	1,937.5	844.6	1,177.3	316.3	11,228.5
1996	1,296.0	3,459.7	2,486.1	2,122.2	925.8	1,393.9	404.4	12,088.1
1997	1,367.5	3,456.8	2,680.2	2,346.3	1,022.6	1,692.8	535.8	13,102.0
1998	1,464.3	3,355.5	2,955.2	2,666.2	1,296.5	1,978.0	731.5	14,447.2
1999	1,532.5	3,281.0	3,334.2	3,022.9	1,616.5	2,338.2	900.8	16,026.4
2000	1,567.8	2,966.9	3,564.7	3,372.0	1,851.9	2,661.0	1,071.8	17,056.1
2001	1,688.4	2,967.5	4,125.5	3,818.2	2,143.0	2,542.4	1,281.1	18,566.1
2002:Q3[a]	1,782.4	3,121.4	4,589.8	3,987.6	2,282.8	2,516.2	1,489.9	19,770.1

[a] The Bond Market Association estimates
[b] Denotes break in series due to the inclusion of additional source data on private-label MBS/CMOs;
(1) interest bearing marketable public debt; (2) includes GNMA, FNMA, and FHLMC mortgage-backed securities and CMOs and private-label MBS/CMOs; (3) includes commercial paper, bankers' acceptances, and large time deposits; (4) includes public and private placements.
Sources: US Department of Treasury; Federal Reserve System; Federal National Mortgage Association; Government National Mortgage Association; Federal Home Loan Mortgage Corporation; Bond Market Association

explicit federal obligations in the form of guarantees on other debt issues. Another example of the vagaries of the aggregate debt numbers in Table 4.1 are the reported outstanding amounts for mortgage-backed securities that are only for the agencies solely issuing that type of security, i.e., the Government National Mortgage Association (GNMA), the Federal National Mortgage Association (FNMA) and the Federal Home Loan Mortgage Corporation (FHLMC). Such issues by other agencies are included under Federal Agencies.

The composition of marketable US federal government debt by maturity and type of security is given in tables 4.2 and 4.3. Information on pricing of specific issues was given in chapter 1, table 1.9. In addition to offering debt such as the Tbills, Tnotes and Tbonds discussed in chapter 1, the US Treasury also offers debt with a number of different features. Savings bonds, inflation-indexed notes and bonds, STRIPS (Separate Trading of Registered Interest and Principal Securities), in addition to the outstanding

Table **4.2** Summary of Treasury securities outstanding, November 30, 2002 (US $ millions)

Type of debt	Amount Outstanding		
	Debt held by public	Intragovernmental holdings	Total
Marketable			
Bills	901,417	26	901,444
Notes	1,568,838	26	1,568,864
Bonds	588,465	310	588,775
Inflation-indexed notes	101,250	0	101,250
Inflation-indexed bonds	45,357	0	45,357
Total marketable	3,205,328	362	3,205,690
Non-marketable			
Domestic series	29,995	0	29,995
Foreign series	12,519	0	12,519
State and local govt series	154,090	0	154,090
US savings securities	194,443	0	194,443
Government account series	48,883	2,693,746	2,742,628
Other	4,095	0	4,095
Total nonmarketable	444,025	2,693,746	3,137,771
Total public debt outstanding	3,649,353	2,694,108	6,343,460

Source: US Bureau of Public Debt

Table **4.3** Maturity distribution and average length of marketable US Treasury debt held by private investors (US $ millions)

End of fiscal year	Amount outstanding privately held	Maturity classes					Average length	
		Within 1 year	1–5 years	5–10 years	10–20 years	20 years or more		
1998	2,856,637	940,572	1,105,175	319,331	157,347	334,212	5 yrs	10 months
1999	2,728,011	915,145	962,644	378,163	149,703	322,356	6 yrs	0 months
2000	2,469,152	858,903	791,540	355,382	167,082	296,246	6 yrs	2 months
2001	2,328,302	900,178	650,522	329,247	174,653	273,702	6 yrs	1 month
2002	2,492,821	939,986	802,032	311,176	203,816	235,811	5 yrs	6 months

Source: US Treasury Bulletin obtained from Office of Market Finance, Office of the Under Secretary for Domestic Finance

long term bonds with call features, all qualify as being debt with special features.[3] STRIPS are not actually a different security but, rather, STRIPS is a US Treasury program that lets investors hold and trade the individual interest and principal components of eligible Treasury notes and bonds as separate securities. When a Treasury fixed-principal or inflation-indexed note or bond is stripped, each coupon payment and the principal payment becomes a separate zero-coupon security. For example, consider a Treasury note with 10 years remaining to maturity that consists of a single principal payment at maturity and the 20 semi-annual coupon payments that are made every 6 months for 10 years. When this note is converted to STRIPS form, each of the 20 coupon payments and the principal payment becomes a separate security.

All marketable Treasury notes and bonds are eligible for STRIPS though, as yet, there is no trading in STRIPS for inflation indexed bonds and notes. Only the conventional fixed coupon notes and bonds are currently traded in STRIPS format. It is important to recognize that the US Treasury does not issue or sell STRIPS directly to investors. STRIPS are traded only through eligible financial institutions and government securities brokers and dealers. As indicated in table 1.9, the traded zero coupon securities that originate from STRIPS are identified by the payment date and whether the zero coupon security originated from a coupon or a principal payment. All STRIPS from coupon payments that occur on the same day are considered the same security but principal payments occurring on the same day are distinguished as different securities. This distinction is important because STRIPS components can be reassembled or "reconstituted" into a fully constituted security through the commercial book-entry system.

Reconstituting a security requires the financial institution or government securities broker or dealer to obtain the principal component and all unmatured interest components for the security being reconstituted where the principal and interest components satisfy the appropriate minimum or multiple amounts for a security to be reconstituted. It is usually the case that market prices of STRIPS fluctuate more than the prices of fully constituted securities of the same maturity. This is a consequence both of the longer duration of the STRIPS for the same term to maturity and the liquidity of the STRIPS market relative to the fully constituted market. As the STRIPS market has grown in size and volume, the flexibility to strip and reconstitute securities can allow investors to take advantage of trading strategies that exploit discrepancies between the pricing of STRIPS and fully constituted Treasury securities.

The STRIPS program is only one of a number of interesting initiatives that the US Treasury has pursued in an effort to minimize US federal government interest costs and to increase the accessibility of Treasury securities to individual investors. One such initiative has been the introduction and expansion of the Treasury-online program that will allow individual investors to purchase Treasury securities on-line. Other initiatives include the introduction of inflation-indexed Treasury securities (I-bonds, I-notes), a type of security that has been used in a number of other countries, e.g., England, Canada, Israel. An I-security has a floating rate coupon that is equal to the fixed "real" rate of interest that is set at the time the security is issued plus the value of a reference inflation index, such as the CPI. The US Treasury has also introduced 4 week Tbills and has made a number of adjustments to the US Savings bond.

Determining the value of outstanding debt for government entities is relatively easy compared to the difficulties of determining a number for the outstanding amount of corporate debt issues. Unlike government entities that report outstanding debt issues in a systematic fashion through well defined public channels, there is no formal public entity responsible for collecting data on corporate debt. In addition, there are also classification problems such as whether to include issues by foreign corporations in the US market or US dollar issues by US corporations in offshore markets, such as the Eurobond market. There is also the problem of whether to include foreign government owned corporations, e.g., Ontario Hydro, or the corporate divisions of the supranational government entities, e.g., the International Financing Corporation of the World Bank. As such, any value for outstanding corporate debt is a best-guess estimate. The number reported was obtained from the Bond Market Association (www.bondmarkets.com) and is on the high side of the range of reported estimates.

Unlike government and agency debt that is relatively homogeneous in terms of the types of features, corporate debt offers a wide array of special features. In general, the use of specific features will be associated with the economic category of the issuer. These general categories are: utilities; industrial companies; transportation companies; and finance and banking companies. Using "bond" to refer to all debt issues including notes and debentures as well as bonds, a taxonomy of some important features together with brief definitions includes:

- *Call feature*: a callable bond has a provision that permits the issuer to buy back the issue at a predetermined price (the call price) at a prespecified future date (the call date). The predetermined price is usually either par value, par value plus coupon or primary issue offering price. If there is more than one call date, then it is typical for the call price to be higher for closer call dates, say, starting at par plus coupon for the first call date and scaling down to par on the last call date. If the issue has no protection against an immediate call, the issue is referred to as *currently callable*. In some cases, the call provision may be combined with *refunding protection* that restricts the firm from paying for the redemption of the issue by issuing a new series of bonds with a lower coupon, i.e., by doing a refunding.
- *Sinking fund provision*: in order to reduce the credit risk of a bond issue, the bond indenture may require the issuer to retire a prespecified portion of the bond issue at regular intervals up to the term to maturity. If the sinking fund provision does not require the issue to be fully retired by the maturity date, the unpaid balance is referred to as the *balloon maturity*. Depending on the form of the sinking fund provision, the bonds to be retired may be selected by lottery or by purchases in the open market. If selected by lottery, the repurchase price is usually the primary issue price. This feature is commonly used for bond issues by industrial companies. It is seldom used for issues by banking and finance companies. A sinking fund provision done by lottery has an expected term to maturity that is less than the stated term to maturity.
- *Put feature*: a putable (retractable) bond has a provision that permits the bond-holder to sell back the issue at a predetermined price (the put price) at a prespecified future date (the put date). The *encashability* feature of some government savings bonds is a form of put option. Between 1986 and 1996, 203 putable bond issues were made in the investment grade corporate bond market raising $39 billion (Crabbe and Nikoulis 1997). Most issues set the put price at par and have one put date. Two reasons for exercising the put are higher market rates and a deterioration in credit quality.

- *Extendible feature*: this feature is not found on many issues. Extendible bonds permit the bondholder to redeem the bonds at a later date than the stated maturity date. One example of this provision was the extendible bond issues made by the government of Canada during the high interest rate period of the late 1970s. These issues permitted bondholders to extend bonds that were, say, 15 years to maturity at original issue for another 5 years at the same coupon. Extendible bonds with above market coupons would be extended.

- *Conversion feature*: a convertible bond permits the bondholder to convert the bond issue to another security, usually the common stock for corporate bonds, at a predetermined price (the conversion price) at a prespecified future date (the conversion date). A typical convertible bond issue would have 10 to 15 years to maturity with the conversion price set 15–25% above the common stock price on the primary issue date. It is possible for a convertible bond to have a number of conversion dates and conversion prices. As with common stock warrants, the indenture for a convertible bond has to contain information about the treatment of the conversion feature in the event of recapitalization, a stock split, a stock dividend, an issuance of warrants or additional amounts of common stock.

- *Warrant bond feature*: unlike a convertible bond where the conversion feature is embedded in the bond, a warrant bond feature permits the convertibility feature to be detached and sold as a warrant, e.g., Vaidya et al. (1995). Unlike convertible bonds where the conversion price at primary issue is set so that the "call option" to convert is deep out of the money, a warrant bond sets the exercise price to be either at the money or in the money. A typical warrant bond would have approximately 30–40% of the value of the purchase price associated with the value of the warrant. Such issues are popular in East Asian markets such as Singapore, Hong Kong and Japan.

- *Floating rate feature*: a bond with a floating rate has a provision to reset the coupon at regular intervals to track a well-defined reference rate, such as LIBOR. As most debt issues with the floating rate feature are 2 to 7 years to maturity, the reference to FRN (floating rate notes) is commonly used to refer to issues with this feature. At primary issue, coupon rates are set at a spread to the reference rate that reflects the credit status of the borrower and liquidity of the issue. Typical reset rates are equal to the maturity of the reference rate, e.g., reset every 3 months when 3 month LIBOR is the reference rate. Due to changes in credit status and liquidity, the value of a floating rate note for corporate borrowers can deviate substantially from par. Default free issues will have prices close to par (equal to par on reset/coupon payment dates).

- *Cap, floor and collar features*: a bond with a floating rate may have an additional feature that sets either a ceiling (cap) on the upward adjustment of the coupon, or a lower limit (floor) on the downward adjustment of the coupon, or both a cap and a floor (collar).

This is only a partial listing of possible features, albeit those that are most commonly observed. It is possible for more than one feature to appear, e.g., a floating rate note with a collar that is both putable and callable.

In practice, retail investors may find it more attractive to purchase bond funds rather than purchase the underlying bonds directly. For example, this would be the case where the objective is to purchase high yield, below investment grade debt issues. Due to limitations on capital, a retail investor will often be unable to purchase enough issues to achieve sufficient diversification to manage firm specific default risk, an important element in high yield debt securities. In addition, liquidity and availability concerns may make it difficult for the retail investor to purchase such securities. In addition to liquidity and capital considerations, the element of professional money management is also an important incentive for purchasing bond funds. This rationale has been recognized going back at least to Irving Fisher. While the benefits of professional management are generally less for bond funds than equity funds, this is usually reflected in the lower management expense ratios for bond funds. In addition, there are still the vagaries of specialized types of bonds, e.g., international bond funds, where specialized knowledge may be valuable.

Investors purchasing bond funds can choose between a range of **open-end** and *closed-end funds.* An open-end bond fund is much the same as an open-end equity fund. Transactions in open-end funds are done directly with the fund company, e.g., Vanguard or Fidelity, or through an intermediary that deals with the fund company. Various types of fees are associated with the purchase, sale and management of these funds, e.g., front-load fees that are paid at the time of purchase and back-load fees that are paid at the time of sale. The fee structure is an important consideration in the purchase of an open-end fund. The Investment Company Institute reports that the number of open-end funds at year end 2001 was 2,091 bond funds, 4,717 equity funds, 484 hybrid (bond/equity combination) funds and 1,015 taxable/non-taxable money market funds. Total net assets in these funds were (in US$ billions): $925.1 bond, $3,418 equity, $346.3 hybrid, and $2,285.3 in money markets. The growth in open-ended funds has been staggering. For comparison, in 1991 the number of funds and net assets (in $US billions) were: 1,180 funds with $393.8 for bonds; 1,191 funds with $404.7 for equity; 212 funds with $52.2 for hybrids; and, 820 funds with $543.5 money market funds.

Within the general class of bond funds, there is considerable variation in the fund objectives. Though the Investment Company Institute does not provide a breakdown by fund objectives for open-end bond funds, a general picture can be taken from the closed-end bond funds for which data is provided. Unlike open-end funds that increase (decrease) security holdings as investors invest (withdraw) money from the fund, closed-end funds involve an initial public offering (IPO) of securities that represent claims against the fund. The capital raised by the IPO is then invested and managed according to the stated fund objectives. As such, closed-end fund shares are similar to common stock. Closed-end funds are also traded in much the same fashion as common stocks, with most issues being traded on the NYSE or AMEX. Closed-end bond funds can be classified into three groups, according to the tax treatment of the income distribution.[4] Some of these funds, which hold bonds from issuers such as corporations or the US Treasury, have income distributions that are fully taxable (taxable bond funds). Other funds, which hold issues of municipal bonds from a number of states, are exempt from federal tax, but subject to state taxes (national municipal funds). Finally, there are funds that hold municipal bonds from a single state (state municipal funds). For qualifying investors, state municipal funds are exempt from both federal and state taxes.

As indicated in Table 4.4, the financial press provides a further decomposition of closed-end bond fund types by identifying the specific types of securities held, e.g., fully taxable bond funds can be classified as: US Treasury; mortgage-backed securities; investment grade (mainly corporate); high yield; and hybrid. Within the taxable bond fund group, the Investment Company Institute also identifies convertible bond funds.

Table 4.4 Closed-end bond funds

STOCK (SYM)	EXCH	NAV	CLOSE	NET CHG	VOL 100s	PREM /DISC	DIV	12 MO YIELD
U.S. Gov't. Bond Funds								
ACM OppFd AOF	N	8.78	9.10	0.06	58	3.4	0.72	8.0
ACM IncFd ACG	N	8.40	8.51	0.05	2745	1.3	0.81	10.5
MFS GvMkTr MGF	N	7.50	6.75	−0.02	1403	−10.1	0.36	5.4
MS GvtIn GVT	N	9.87	9	0.00	178	−8.7	0.41	4.7
♣ScudderGvt KGT	N	7.43	6.72	0.00	245	−9.6	0.30m	5.3
U.S. Mortgage Bond Funds								
AmIncmFd MRF c	N			−0.03	174	NA	0.66	7.7
AmSelPort SLA c	N			−0.00	25	NA	1.05	7.9
AmStrat ASP c	N			−0.02	9	NA	0.87	6.8
AmStratII BSP c	N			−0.02	31	NA	1.14	8.3
AmStratIII CSP c	N			0.03	272	NA	1.05	8.0
BlkRkAdvTr BAT a	N	11.41	11.22	−0.06	33	−1.6	0.70	6.2
BlkRkBIG Tr BCT a	A	16.01	15.91	−0.01	4	−0.7	0.90	7.6
BlkRkInco Tr BKT a	N	7.10	7.57	0.02	444	6.3	0.61	13.5
BlkRkInv Tr BQT a	N	9.64	9.60	0.01	160	−0.4	0.03	1.3
Hyperion05 HTO c	N	9.75	9.66	0.06	8	−0.8	0.30	4.2
Hyperion HSM	N	14.47	14.60	0.09	203	0.9	1.30	8.8
HyperionFd HTR c	N	9.34	10.38	0.09	269	10.9	0.90	8.9
NationsGov04 NGF	N	10.04	10	0.00	4	−0.4	0.33	3.4
♣PIMCO Comrd PCM c	N	12.63	14.41	−0.14	90	14.1	1.13	9.8
TCW/DW 03 TMT	N				NA	NA		4.0
Investment Grade Bond Funds								
BlkRkCB Tr BHK a	N	14.89	13.79	0.08	592	−7.5	1.05	8.6
BlkRkIncoOpp Tr BNA ac	N	12.03	11.07	0.01	73	−8.2	0.84	7.4
CignaInv IIS a	N	18.96	17.04	−0.12	29	−10.2	0.92	5.5
EtnVncLtdFd EVV a	A	19.15	18.44	0.03	2342	−3.8	1.61	NS
♣1838BondFd BDF	N			0.23	308	NA	1.25m	7.1
♣FtDeaborn FTD	N	16.47	14.85		NA	−9.9	0.80	5.6
♣HnckJ IncSec JHS	N	16.56	15.41	0.13	66	−6.9	0.92	4.5
HrtfrdIncoFd HSF a	N	8.25	7.63	−0.07	27	−7.6	0.55	7.6
HatterasSec HAT	N	14.84	13.22	−0.02	3	−10.9	0.78	5.4

Table 4.4 (*Cont'd*)

STOCK (SYM)	EXCH	NAV	CLOSE	NET CHG	VOL 100s	PREM /DISC	DIV	12 MO YIELD
♣MotgmrySt MTS	N	19.67	18.41	−0.01	47	−6.4	1.63	6.9
MS InSec ICB	N	17.62	16.16	0.00	52	−8.2	0.96	5.9
PacAmShis PAI	N	16.60	15.16	0.03	3	−8.7	0.96m	6.5
♣PIMCO OppFd PTY a	N	17.19	17.22	0.02	1452	0.2	1.65	NS
PionrIntrst MUO a	N	12.61	11.47	0.01	20	−9.0	0.68	6.2
TransamInco TAI	N	24.21	23.69	0.04	53	−2.1	1.80	7.2
♣VnKmBond VBF	N	19.77	17.97	0.10	51	−9.1	1.04	6.5
VestaurSec VES c	A	14.26	13.22	0.00	11	−7.3	1.14	7.0
WesternAssetPremBd WEA a	N	15.02	15.66	NA	NA	4.2	NA	8.4
High Yield Bond Funds								
40/86StrInco CFD	N	11.09	11.13	0.10	91	0.4	1.02	8.7
BlkRkHiYld Tr BHY a	N			−0.01	98	NA	1.01	10.7
BlkRkDurInco Tr BLW a	N	19.93	18.82	0.12	464	−5.6	1.50	NS
CignaHiInco HIS a	N	2.85	2.91	0.02	385	2.1	0.28	9.7
CIM HiYld CIM a	A	4.56	4.85	0.06	41	6.1	0.45	9.2
♣ColonialIntr CIF	N	3.69	3.69	−0.02	336	−0.3	0.32	9.3
CpHiYld COY	N	8.82	9.76	0.05	462	10.5	1.07	10.5
CpHiYld III CYE	N	8.69	8.79	−0.01	424	1.2	1.00	11.1
CpHiYld V HYV	N	16.25	16	−0.05	789	−1.5	1.82	11.0
CpHiYld VI HYT	N	15.72	14.85	0.06	1018	−5.5	0.68	NS
CrSuisHighYld DHY	N	4.44	5.29	0.05	495	18.9	0.69	12.3
DDJ Cndn Hi Yld HYB.U y	T			NA	NA	NA	NA	12.7
DebtStratFd DSU	N	6.65	7.04	0.03	1036	5.7	0.88	11.7
DryfsHiYldFd DHF a	N	4.77		−0.03	1097	NA	0.59	12.2
EvrgrnIncoFd EAD	A	15.73	15.66	−0.02	889	−0.5	1.65	NS
FrnkInUnvlTr FT	N	6.35	5.75	−0.02	196	−9.3	0.36	7.5
HiIncoFd HIO	N	7.31	7.13	0.00	1490	−2.3	0.60	9.4
HiYldFd HYI	N	5.60	6	0.04	139	7.0	0.51	9.4
HiYldPlsFd HYP	N	4.04	4.72	0.09	255	16.8	0.42	9.0
LBFirstTrIncOpp LBC a	N	15.46	15.51	NA	NA	0.2	NA	NS
MgdHiInc MHY	N	7.12	6.97	0.03	1003	−2.3	0.60	9.4
MgdHiYldPI HYF a	N	5.17	5.75	0.01	758	11.0	0.63	11.1
MS HiYld MSY a	N	6.94	6.54	−0.01	185	−5.8	1.56	7.5
NewAmFd HYB	N	2.20	2.16	0.01	2689	−1.4	0.21	10.6
♣PachldrHi PHF c	A	8.52	9.22	0.07	162	8.3	0.90	10.2
♣PIMCO HiInco PHK	N	15.65	14.94	0.03	1684	−4.5	1.46	NS
PionrHl Tr PHH	N	15.97	16.35	−0.04	471	2.3	1.65	10.2
♣ProspctSt PHY	N	2.68	3.22	0.02	283	20.2	0.33	9.9
PutnmMgdYld PTM a	N	9.04	8.66	−0.05	121	−4.3	0.65	8.6
RMK HiIncoFd RMH a	N	14.83	16.13	−0.11	808	8.8	1.56	NS
SIBrHIF FIF	N	10.43	11.47	0.00	10	10.0	0.96	8.4
SIBrHIF II HIX	N	11.36	12.97	−0.02	1019	14.3	1.38	10.9

Table 4.4 (*Cont'd*)

STOCK (SYM)	EXCH	NAV	CLOSE	NET CHG	VOL 100s	PREM /DISC	DIV	12 MO YIELD
♣ScudderHigh KHI	N	5.96	7.47	0.03	193	25.3	0.64	8.9
SrHighInc ARK	N	6.02	6.35	−0.03	396	5.2	0.71	10.4
♣VnKmHiInc VIT	N	3.64	4.29	0.00	183	17.6	0.36	9.4
♣VnKmTrII VLT	N	4.56	5.19	0.12	135	13.8	0.44	8.7
ZenixFd ZIF	N	3.13	3.94	−0.05	242	25.6	0.39	11.3

Source: Wall Street Journal, January 2004

"And please let Alan Greenspan accept the things he cannot change, give him the courage to change the things he can and the wisdom to know the difference."

There are also funds that hold international bonds. These funds can be further classified as single country or multi-country. The Investment Company Institute reports that at year-end 2001 there was in the US (millions US$) $1,510.8 in outstanding closed-end multi-country bonds funds and $1,296,6 in single country funds. Finally, it is also possible to classify bond funds according to the frequency of the distributions with most funds making monthly payouts, though some funds (< 20%) make quarterly payouts. Much as with open-end funds, the aggregate US market for closed-end funds experienced considerable growth during the 1990s, with much of this growth concentrated in domestic bond funds.[5] The Investment Company Institute reports that, at year-end 1990, the four general classes of closed-end funds had market values (in billions) of $9.6 for domestic equity funds, $28 for domestic bond funds, $5.5 for international and global equity funds and $9.3 for international and global bond funds. By year-end 2000, these values were domestic equity $23.6, domestic bond $89.3, global equity $12.9 and global bond $8.7, respectively.

Types of interest rates

Due to the large number of possible definitions, reference to "the interest rate" can be confusing. The number of possible definitions that appear in fixed income analysis include: *yield to maturity; spot interest rate (implied zero coupon interest rate); implied forward (interest) rate; simple interest rate; continuously compounded interest rate; coupon interest rate; discount rate; annual percentage rate (APR); effective interest rate; zero coupon interest rate*; and, *current yield*. This list is not exhaustive. Of these variations, each has particular relevance, depending on the valuation problem at hand. Perhaps the most widely used definition for "the interest rate" is the yield to maturity. This concept of the interest rate is a direct application of the internal rate of return to the valuation for the cash flow from a fixed income security. The internal rate of return (*IRR*) is an important interest rate concept that appears, for example, in capital budgeting theory, e.g., Brealey and Myers (1991). The *IRR* is the rate of interest that equates the discounted future net cash flows produced by a capital asset with the value of the initial investment in the capital asset.

Yield to maturity

Although the *yield to maturity* can be used as the interest rate for a range of fixed income securities, the most important practical application is, arguably, to describe the interest rate for a bond. For a simple bond valuation problem, where the bond pays annual coupons and is being valued on the issue date or a coupon payment date, the annualized yield to maturity (*y*) is obtained by solving:

$$P_B = \left\{ \sum_{t=1}^{T} \frac{C}{(1 + y)^t} \right\} + \frac{M}{(1 + y)^T}$$

In this formulation, T is the number of annual coupon payments remaining to be paid on the bond, (T = term to maturity in years), C is the annual coupon payment, M is the par value of the bond which is repaid at maturity and P_B is the price of the bond. Because the calculation assumes that future coupon cash flows can be reinvested at the stated y, it follows that y is only a *promised* yield to maturity. In other words, reinvestment of coupons at the promised yield is required in order for the bond to actually earn the stated yield if the bond is held to maturity. As such, the yield to maturity is an *ex ante* forecast of the *ex post realized yield*. When $C = 0$, the bond is referred to as a pure discount or zero coupon bond. If held to maturity, a default and option free zero coupon bond will have the promised yield to maturity equal to the realized yield.

In practice, the formula given for the price of an annual coupon bond is useful for pedagogical purposes. Only a relatively small number of bonds, e.g., Eurobonds, pay annual coupons. Most government issued bonds, such as those issued by the US Treasury, pay coupons semi-annually. As reflected in tables such as 1.10 and 4.5, the convention in the bond market is to express the coupon as the sum of the coupon payments made in one year. For example, the 11.75% coupon US Treasury bond maturing in November 2014 pays a $5.875 coupon every six months for a bond with a par value of $100. Valuing the semi-annual coupon bond on an issue date or coupon payment date, the valuation formula is:

$$P_B = \left\{ \sum_{t=1}^{2T} \frac{C/2}{\left(1 + \dfrac{y}{2}\right)^t} \right\} + \frac{M}{\left(1 + \dfrac{y}{2}\right)^{2T}}$$

The sum is now over $2T$ because there are now two payments per year (T is term to maturity measured in years). The convention of dividing the (annualized) yield to maturity creates a situation where the yield on annual coupon bonds is not directly comparable to the (annualized) yield to maturity calculated from this formula. The *effective rate of interest* is used to reconcile this difference.

The importance of the yield to maturity in practical applications is illustrated in table 4.5. The yield to maturity provides a measure that can be used to compare relative value across different types of bonds. For example, convention in the bond market is to execute trades using prices. Due to the variation in term to maturity and coupon, it is difficult to assess bond value by comparing prices. The yield to maturity provides a method to compare value across bonds. The simple rule of thumb for using yield to identify value is: "All other things equal, choose the bond with the highest yield to maturity." However, if all things are equal, then efficient pricing requires that the yields will be the same. Hence, the yield to maturity can be used as a measure to assess bonds that have one or more features that are different. This leads to the notion of what Fabozzi (1989) refers to as "*traditional yield spread analysis*" where the difference in yield for bonds with different features, e.g., different levels of default risk but the same term to maturity, is used as a measure of relative value.

In the situations involving coupon bonds, the relationship between term to maturity and the yield to maturity for the set of available bonds is referred to as the *yield curve*.

Table 4.5 Canadian bonds

Federal	Coupon	Mat. date	Bid $	Yld%
Canada	12.000	Mar. 01/05	110.38	2.44
Canada	3.500	Jun. 01/05	101.39	2.45
Canada	6.000	Sep. 01/05	105.33	2.59
Canada	12.250	Sep. 01/05	115.11	2.59
Canada	8.750	Dec. 01/05	110.89	2.70
Canada	12.500	Mar. 01/06	119.28	2.99
Canada	5.750	Sep. 01/06	106.81	3.01
Canada	14.000	Oct. 01/06	128.06	3.05
Canada	7.000	Dec. 01/06	110.56	3.11
Canada	7.250	Jun. 01/07	112.43	3.30
Canada	4.500	Sep. 01/07	103.71	3.40
Canada	13.000	Oct. 01/07	133.03	3.39
Canada	10.000	Jun. 01/08	125.53	3.61
Canada	6.000	Jun. 01/08	109.42	3.64
Canada	4.250	Sep. 01/08	102.30	3.70
Canada	11.000	Jun. 01/09	134.23	3.86
Canada	5.500	Jun. 01/09	107.64	3.90
Canada	4.250	Sep. 01/09	101.41	3.97
Canada	10.750	Oct. 01/09	134.43	3.93
Canada	9.750	Mar. 01/10	130.40	4.07
Canada	9.500	Jun. 01/10	130.04	4.08
Canada	5.500	Jun. 01/10	107.62	4.12
Canada	9.000	Mar. 01/11	128.91	4.24
Canada	6.000	Jun. 01/11	110.50	4.32
Canada	8.500	Jun. 01/11	126.30	4.29
Canada	5.250	Jun. 01/12	105.55	4.45
Canada	5.250	Jun. 01/13	105.38	4.54
Canada	10.250	Mar. 15/14	145.82	4.56
Canada	5.000	Jun. 01/14	103.15	4.61
Canada	11.250	Jun. 01/15	158.81	4.56
Canada	9.750	Jun. 01/21	155.36	4.96
Canada	9.250	Jun. 01/22	150.97	4.98
Canada	8.000	Jun. 01/23	135.78	5.07
Canada	9.000	Jun. 01/25	149.65	5.14
Canada	8.000	Jun. 01/27	138.32	5.16
Canada	5.750	Jun. 01/29	108.30	5.16
Canada	5.750	Jun. 01/33	109.35	5.13

Source: Globe and Mail, Jan. 2004; supplied by RBC Dominion Securities Inc.

Different yield curves can be identified for different types of bonds, e.g., the corporate bond yield curve or Treasury bond yield curve. As will be discussed below, analysis of "the yield curve" poses a range of problems. For example, bonds with the same term to maturity may have different coupons and, as a consequence, different yields. This leads to the introduction of the abstract relationship between term to maturity and the spot interest rate (implied zero coupon interest rate) referred to as the **term structure of interest rates**. These definitions are not always adhered to in various texts and financial newspapers where the terminology "term structure of interest rates" can be used synonymously with "the yield curve." (The end of chapter questions deal with the plotting of the yield curve from actual data, as well as an analysis of the relationship between the yield curve and the spot rate curve.)

EFFECTIVE INTEREST RATE

In presenting the yield to maturity, it was observed that the convention used to calculate yields for semi-annual coupon bonds resulted in stated yields that were not directly comparable to yields calculated from annual coupon bonds. The **effective interest rate** or **effective yield** provides the annualized equivalent for a stated interest rate involving compounding at a greater than annual frequency. This problem of having the calculated yield changing with the compounding frequency is not specific to bonds but occurs with all fixed income transactions where compounding occurs. In particular, changing the compounding frequency is one of a number of possible methods of confusing consumers about the actual interest rate that is being charged on loans. In the US, truth in lending laws have codified the use of the effective yield where the concept is referred to as the **annual percentage rate** or **APR**. In others words, loan transactions are required to quote an effective yield when stating the lending rates for consumer loans. (In Canada, the APR has a different legal meaning.)

　To illustrate the methodology for calculating the effective interest rate, consider the following problem: a 10% coupon government bond (paid semi-annually) currently sells at par. At current market prices, what coupon rate would be required if the coupons were paid annually? To solve this problem, step one requires equating future values for single payments: the future value of one payment received in T years, compounded m times per year at interest rate r produces:

$$FV^m = (1 + (r/m))^{Tm}$$

For annual compounding $m = 1$ at interest rate y this reduces to $FV^A = (1 + y)^T$. Equating the future values $FV^m = FV^A$ produces:

$$(1 + y)^T = (1 + (r/m))^{Tm} \quad \rightarrow \quad y = (1 + (r/m))^m - 1 \quad \rightarrow \quad r = [(1 + y)^{1/m} - 1]m$$

For a single cash flow occurring T years ahead, this result provides the method for transforming an interest rate for compounding m times a year to an interest rate compounded annually.

The next step involves converting the future value (FV) to a present value (PV). Present and future value represent the valuation of cash flows at different points in time. To translate a future value at time T to a present value involves discounting the value at the appropriate interest rate:

$$PV^A = FV/(1 + y)^T \quad PV^{SA} = FV/(1 + (r/m))^{mT}$$

When the effective yield is used, equating the future values is the same as equating the present values.

It is now possible to extend these results for single cash flows to coupon bonds. Working by example, consider a 1 year par bond with an 10% coupon. *In all cases, it is assumed that the cash flows from the bond are reinvested at the stated yield to maturity.* A semi-annual bond has cash flows of $C/2 = \$5 = (r/2)M$ which produces a time line of:

$\$5$		$\$105$
$t = 0$	$t = 6$ months	$t = 1$ year

The future value of this stream of cash flows is:

$$FV^S = \left(\frac{r}{2}M\right)\left(1 + \frac{r}{2}\right) + M\left(1 + \frac{r}{2}\right) = M\left(1 + 2\frac{r}{2} + \frac{r}{2}\right) = M\left(1 + \frac{r}{2}\right)^2$$

This can be compared with the future value for annual payments of $FV^A = M(1 + y)$. It follows that for 1 year bonds, the effective yield formula holds: $y = (1 + (r/2))^2 - 1$. For the annual coupon bond to be sold at par, the coupon on the bond would have to be 10.25%.

For a 2 year bond, the analysis is much the same. The time line for the semi-annual coupon bond is:

$\$5$	$\$5$	$\$5$	$\$105$
$t = 0$	$t = 6$ months	$t = 1$ year	$t = 1.5$ years	$t = 2$ years

To calculate the future value of the semi-annual cash flows:

$$FV^S = \frac{r}{2}M\left(1 + \frac{r}{2}\right)^3 + \frac{r}{2}M\left(1 + \frac{r}{2}\right)^2 + \frac{r}{2}M\left(1 + \frac{r}{2}\right) + M\left(1 + \frac{r}{2}\right) = M\left(1 + \frac{r}{2}\right)^4$$

This can be compared with the future value of the annual coupons: $FV^A = M(1 + y)^2$. It follows that for 2 year bonds to have equal prices (from step two):

$$(1 + y)^2 = (1 + (r/2))^4 \quad \rightarrow \quad y = (1 + (r/2))^2 - 1$$

The effective yield result also holds in this case, and the annual coupon bond would have a coupon of 10.25% when the semi-annual coupon bond has a coupon of 10%, for both bonds to sell at par. By induction, this method for transforming the semi-annually compounded yield to an annually compounded yield extends to bonds with T years to maturity.

SPOT INTEREST RATE (IMPLIED ZERO COUPON INTEREST RATE)

As with any internal rate of return calculation, the yield to maturity has a number of limitations. One limitation involves applying the same interest rate to discount cash flows occurring at different points in time. This approach would only be valid if yield curves were flat, i.e., yields were the same for all terms to maturity. Casual inspection of real world bond markets reveals that near term cash flows are usually discounted at lower interest rates than longer term cash flows. This limitation leads directly to the concept of the **spot interest rate** or, more descriptively, the **implied zero coupon interest rate** (implied zero rate). Whereas there is a yield to maturity that can be calculated for every bond, the implied zero coupon interest rate applies to the term to maturity. There is an implied zero coupon interest rate for every fixed income payment date. For example, when the US Treasury issued 30 year bonds, there were 60 implied zero coupon interest rates that could be calculated, one for each of the 60 coupon payment dates.

To see the connection between the implied zero rate and the yield to maturity, consider the following valuation formulas for bonds with annual coupons:

$$P_B = \left\{ \sum_{t=1}^{T} \frac{C}{(1 + y)^t} \right\} + \frac{M}{(1 + y)^T} = \left\{ \sum_{t=1}^{T} \frac{C}{(1 + z_t)^t} \right\} + \frac{M}{(1 + z_T)^T}$$

Recognizing that the implied zero rate or spot interest rate (z_t) is the interest rate applicable to cash flows occurring at time t, it follows that valuation with implied zero rates values the bond by treating each of the cash flows (coupon payments and return of principal) as zero coupon bonds. The price of the bond is then calculated as the sum of the prices of the zero coupon bonds, valued using the implied zero rate applicable to single cash flows for that term to maturity, i.e., the price of the bond is the sum of the appropriately discounted zero coupon bond prices. For default free (riskless) zero coupon bond prices, the spot interest rate (implied zero rate) is equal to the yield to maturity.

While each bond has an associated yield to maturity, each coupon payment date will have an implied zero rate. To make sense of such an interest rate, it is necessary to abstract from default risk and other features. Hence, the implied zero rates are extracted from the relevant default free bond prices, i.e., the US Treasury debt issues are used to extract the implied zero rates for the US debt market. Though it would be conceptually possible to use the observed interest rates for zero coupon bonds, such as the rates for US Treasury strip securities (STRIPS), for the implied zero rates, this raises a number of difficulties. Sundaresan (2002, p. 231) specifically addresses this point: "It should be stressed that strips are not implied zeroes. Strips are traded securities directly subject to demand and supply. Implied zeroes are estimated pure discount functions derived from the prices of coupon-paying Treasury securities. Yet, as expected, implied zeroes provide a benchmark for assessing the relative richness or cheapness of Treasury securities."

Fabozzi (1989, pp. 192–3) identifies three reasons why stripped Treasury securities are not an adequate substitute for implied zeros: problems of liquidity in the Treasury strips market; maturity preferences in specific segments of the Treasury strip market may cause mispricing of certain maturities; and, differences in the tax treatment of stripped Treasuries and coupon Treasury bonds. Sundaresan (2002, pp. 237–41), Mason et al. (1995, pp. 48–55) and others demonstrate that, while not dramatically different, US Treasury strip rates do differ empirically from implied zero rates calculated from US Treasury coupon bonds.[6]

While each bond has an associated yield to maturity, each coupon payment date will have an associated implied zero coupon interest rate. As such, the method for calculating the implied zero rate differs from the method for calculating the yield to maturity. Mathematically, the yield to maturity calculation for a bond with T coupon payments involves one equation with one unknown. A bond with T coupon payments would have T unknown spot rates. This requires T equations to determine the T unknowns. Because the market used to calculate implied zero coupon rates is the US Treasury coupon bond market, a ***bootstrap*** technique is needed to extract the spot interest rates from the observed coupon yields (see section 4.3). A bootstrap is the name given to a generic algorithm that uses an stepwise solution procedure to arrive at the solution for a number of unknowns. In particular, the first step solves for the first unknown using one equation with one unknown. This solution is then used to solve a second equation that is specified with the first unknown (now solved) and the second unknown. These two solutions are then used to solve the third equation that is specified with the first two unknowns (now solved) and the third unknown. This procedure continues until all the unknowns are solved.

IMPLIED FORWARD INTEREST RATES

The ***implied forward interest rate*** (implied forward rate) has a number of possible uses in theoretical modeling. This interest rate concept is an extension of the ***breakeven interest rate*** associated with comparing a rollover investment strategy with a buy and hold strategy. To see this, consider the following comparison involving a two period, two portfolio model where z_i is the zero coupon yield on a bond maturing i periods from now, $z_{i,j}$ is the $(i$–$j)$ period interest rate starting at $t = i$ and maturing at $t = j$, e.g., $z_{1,2}$ is the one period interest rate that starts at $t = 1$ and ends at $t = 2$:

- ***Portfolio A***: buy and hold a 2 year zero coupon bond. If the initial investment is \$1 the return at the end of 2 years is $(1 + z_2)^2$.
- ***Portfolio B***: buy and mature a 1 year zero coupon and use the proceeds to purchase another 1 year zero coupon bond, 1 year in the future. If the initial investment in this portfolio is \$1 then the expected return at end of year two is: $(1 + z_1)(1 + E[z_{1,2}])$.

Portfolio A is referred to as the ***buy and hold*** portfolio and Portfolio B as the ***rollover*** portfolio.

To derive the **breakeven interest rate**, assume that the expected returns on the two portfolios are equal, then:

$$(1 + z_2)^2 = (1 + z_1)(1 + E[z_{1,2}])$$

It follows that the breakeven expected interest rate can be calculated as:

$$(1 + E[z_{1,2}]) = \frac{(1 + z_2)^2}{(1 + z_1)}$$

Using this result, the correspondence between the breakeven interest rate and the definition of the implied forward rate $f_{1,2}$ follows appropriately: $f_{1,2} = E[z_{1,2}]$. (The notation for the implied forward rate differs across the various textbooks on the subject, i.e., there is no generally accepted notational convention.)

The use of $\{z_i\}$ to define $\{f_{i,j}\}$ is intentional. In the absence of representative zero coupon interest rates, implied forward rates are calculated using spot interest rates. The extension of the definition of an implied forward rate from the two period case to the n period case follows appropriately. For example, consider the one year implied forward interest rate that will apply from period t to $t + 1$. This is given by:

$$(1 + f_{t,t+1}) = \frac{(1 + z_{t+1})^{t+1}}{(1 + z_t)^t}$$

It is also possible to define implied forward rates applying to the interest rates longer than one year. For example, the five year implied forward interest rate between $t = 5$ and $t = 10$ can be calculated using the 10 and 5 year spot rates:

$$(1 + f_{5,10}) = \sqrt[5]{\frac{(1 + z_{10})^{10}}{(1 + z_5)^5}}$$

Similarly the implied forward rate for a three year zero coupon bond that starts at $t = 2$ and matures at $t = 5$, using the two and five year spot rates, is specified:

$$(1 + f_{2,5}) = \sqrt[3]{\frac{(1 + z_5)^5}{(1 + z_2)^2}}$$

Given this, the general formula for the implied forward interest rate is specified:

$$(1 + f_{t,t+k}) = \sqrt[k]{\frac{(1 + z_{t+k})^{t+k}}{(1 + z_t)^t}}$$

It follows that an observed yield curve for, say, n maturities will produce $(n - 1) + (n - 2) + \ldots + 1$ implied forward rates (see end of chapter questions).

CURRENT YIELD

There are so many different approaches to calculating interest rates that it is not practical to give a detailed account of each method. Though not used much in recent years, prior to the advent of computerized calculations, the current yield was a commonly quoted approximation to the yield to maturity. The "current yield" is defined as: Current Yield = CY = (Annual Coupon Paid)/(Bond Price) = C/P_B. The relationship between the current yield and the yield to maturity is useful for pedagogical purposes. When $P_B = M$, the bond sells at par, then $CY = y$. When $P_B > M$, for premium bonds $CY > y$ with the difference increasing as the bond has a greater premium. When $P_B < M$, for discount bonds $CY < y$ with the difference increasing as the bond has a greater discount. For a zero coupon bond, $CY = 0$.

In general:

$$CY = \frac{C}{\displaystyle\sum_{t=1}^{T} \frac{C}{(1+y)^t} + \frac{M}{(1+y)^T}} \quad \rightarrow \quad CY\left\{\sum_{t=0}^{T-1} (1+y)^t\right\} + \frac{M}{P_B} = (1+y)^T$$

Some special cases follow, e.g., for $T = 1$:

$$CY + \frac{M}{P_B} = (1+y) \quad \rightarrow \quad y = CY + \left\{\frac{M}{P_B} - 1\right\}$$

For $T = 2$:

$$CY(1+y) + \frac{M}{P_B} = (1+y)^2 \quad \rightarrow \quad y = CY + \left\{\frac{M}{P_B(1+y)} - 1\right\}$$

As T increases, the size of the deviation shrinks to the point where, for a perpetuity:

$$CY = \frac{C}{\dfrac{C}{y}} = y$$

i.e., when T goes to infinity, the current yield equals the yield to maturity.

MONEY MARKET CALCULATIONS: THE DISCOUNT RATE

Some basic background is required to interpret the interest rate quotes for money market securities provided in the financial press. Unlike bonds, money market securities are quoted and traded using interest rates. When comparing interest rates derived from US money market securities with other fixed income securities, it has to be recognized that most US money market securities, Tbills, BA's, commercial paper and term repos, are quoted on a *discount rate* and *not* a true yield basis, e.g., Stigum (1990). In addition to using a different pricing formula, the discount rate calculation also involves calculating the year as though it has 360 days. To see this, consider the US method for determining the purchase price of a 1 year, $1 million par value Tbill sold at a discount rate of 8%:

Discount = ($1,000,000)(.08)(364/360) = $80,888.89

As a result, the price paid for this Tbill maturing in one year is the maturity (par) value minus the discount or $919,111.11. The general formula for arriving at the discount is:

$$D = dF(tsm/360)$$

where D is the discount, F is the maturity value, d is the discount rate and *tsm* is the time from settlement to maturity.[7] Similarly, for a Tbill with 3 days to maturity, par value of $1 million and discount rate of 9%:

$$D = (.09)($1,000,000)(3/360) = $750$$

The bill is purchased for $999,250 and matures in 3 days for $1 million, returning $750 in interest.

The method for valuing an 01 or one basis point (.0001 expressed as a decimal) for the 3 month $1 million par value Tbill position is:

$$D = (.0001)($1,000,000)(90/360) = $25$$

The value of an 01 (one basis point) for a $1 million, 6 month Tbill:

$$D = (.0001)($1,000,000)(180/360) = $50$$

Observing that the Eurodollar (and Tbill) futures contracts are written on 1 million dollar par value 3 month deliverable securities, it is necessary to use two Eurodollar futures contracts to provide a dollar value equivalent movement for a 6 month, $1 million dollar par value Eurodollar cash position.

It should be recognized that the discount rate understates the simple interest, true yield or bond equivalent yield formula which is used in Canada and other countries for money market securities. The formula for calculating the annualized true yield (y) is the familiar:

$$r = \frac{F - P}{P}\frac{365}{tsm} \quad or \quad P = \frac{F}{1 + \left(r\dfrac{tsm}{365}\right)}$$

where P is the price paid or $D = F - P$. Substituting this result gives:

$$y = (D/(F - D)) \, (365/tsm)$$

This can be solved in terms of the discount rate by substituting the method for calculating D for discount securities to give:

$$y = \frac{(365)d}{360 - d(tsm)}$$

This is the formula for converting a discount rate into a true or simple interest yield.

To see how this works, consider the discount rate for the US BA quoted at .0477 or 4.77%. Using the conversion formula:

$$y = [365(.0477)]/[360 - \{(.0477)90\}] = .0489462$$

Similarly for the CP rate of .0480:

$$y = [365(.0480)]/[360 - \{(.0480)90\}] = .0492577$$

The general formula can also be used to show that the quoted discount rate will always be below the true yield, $y > d$, as well as showing that the discrepancy between y and d will be greater the higher is the rate of discount and the longer is the term to maturity. Some manipulation gives the discount rate associated with a given true yield:

$$d = \frac{360y}{365 + y(tsm)}$$

In recent years, the relationship between d and y is reported in the financial press, as reflected in the US Treasury bill rates reported in table 1.9.

To verify the formula for deriving the discount rate associated with an observed yield, consider the November 3, 1994 bill observed on August 4, 1994. This three month Tbill would typically be indicated in bold in the quotes in the financial press because on August 4 it is the most recently issued 3 month bill and, due to the focus of market trading on the most recently issued maturities, this bill will tend to be the most liquid. The *tsm* for this bill is 12 weeks plus 3 days or 87 days with a reported yield of 4.56. Evaluating for d gives:

$$d = [360(.0456)]/[365 + \{(.0456)(87)\}] = .0445$$

As an exercise, calculate and verify the values for the current three month Tbill reported in table 1.9.

Some examples of valuation problems

The history of interest rate calculations stretches back centuries, e.g., Poitras (2000, chs 4–5). In this history, the use of worked examples has played an important role in illustrating concepts. An early example of the sophistication of such problems can be found in Witt (1613): "A oweth to B £1,200 to be paid in 6 yeares, in 12 equall payments, viz. at the end of each halfe yeare £100. They agree to cleare this debt in 3 yeares, in 6 equall payments, viz. at the end of each halfe yeare, one payment. The Question is, what each payment ought to be, reckoning interest after the rate of 10 per cent per Ann. and int. upon int." A conventional solution to this problem can be determined by equating the discounted value of the annuity stream of £100 for 12 half-year periods with the discounted value of £ C for 6 half-year periods and solving for C. The exact solution requires recognizing Witt's practice of using $(1 + r)^{T/2}$ instead of the modern convention of $(1 + r/2)^T$ to discount the T period cash flow.

More precisely, the solution can be determined by solving:

$$\frac{100}{(1+r)^{1/2}} + \frac{100}{(1+r)} + \ldots + \frac{100}{(1+r)^6}$$

$$= \frac{C}{(1+r)^{1/2}} + \frac{C}{(1+r)} \ldots + \frac{C}{(1+r)^3} = 100\{1 + (1+r)^{1/2}\}\left\{\frac{1}{r} - \frac{1}{r(1+r)^6}\right\}$$

$$= C\{1 + (1+r)^{1/2}\}\left\{\frac{1}{r} - \frac{1}{r(1+r)^3}\right\}$$

Solving this for $r = .10$ gives the solution stated by Witt of £175.13145 or £175. 2s. 7d. Yet, Witt is able to show that this solution can be obtained as:

$$100 + \frac{100}{(1+r)^3} = £175.\ 2s.\ 7d.$$

Lewin (1970, p. 126) describes the method Witt uses to arrive at this solution as "extremely elegant."

Though no longer used for government financing activities, during the early years of government finance perpetuity issues were commonly used. The perpetuity is still of theoretical interest today. What is a perpetuity? A perpetuity is a security that offers to pay a fixed or variable coupon, at regular intervals, forever (in perpetuity). If the coupon is variable, then it is referred to as a floating rate perpetuity. Almost all perpetuities issued in recent years have been floating rate perpetuities, e.g., the floating rate perpetuities issued by financial institutions in the Euromarkets during the 1980s. The most well known perpetuity is a *consol*, originally issued by the British government in the eighteenth and early nineteenth century, which pays a fixed coupon. This perpetuity was so named because it originated from the consolidation of a number of different types of government debt issues, i.e., consol is a short form for consolidated debt issue. Consol issues traceable back to these early debt operations are still traded on the English exchanges.

The perpetuity is more than a historical curiosity. The pricing formula for this security is of theoretical value, if only to illustrate a geometric series. Consider deriving the pricing formula for such a security when coupons are fixed and paid annually:

$$P^{perp} = \sum_{t=1}^{\infty} \frac{C}{(1+y)^t} = \frac{C}{(1+y)} \left\{ 1 + \frac{1}{1+y} + \frac{1}{(1+y)^2} + \frac{1}{(1+y)^3} \cdots \right\}$$

Recall: $\quad \dfrac{1}{1-x} = 1 + x + x^2 + x^3 + x^4 + \ldots$

$$\therefore \quad P^{perp} = \frac{C}{(1+y)} \left[\cfrac{1}{1 - \cfrac{1}{(1+y)}} \right] = \frac{C}{y}$$

It can be immediately verified that, when coupons are fixed and paid quarterly, the perpetuity has the same pricing formula. Because quarterly coupons are paid sooner than annual coupons, this result may seem odd. However, this result can be explained when it is observed that the annual and quarterly coupon perpetuities will sell for different prices. Hence, even though the pricing formula is the same, the yields will not be the same.

Another interesting result occurs for the default free floating rate perpetuity where the coupon is variable (floating) and equal to the current interest rate times the par value of the perpetuity, i.e., $C = yM$. It follows that this perpetuity will always sell at par because the coupon will adjust to keep the price of the perpetuity equal to par. This was the idea behind the floating rate perpetuities issued in the Euromarkets during the 1980s. Because financial institutions are regularly coming to the market to reissue short maturity debt, issuers could save on financing costs by offering a security that has a floating coupon. Similarly purchasers could save on commissions and other costs associated with rolling over short term debt issues. However, this analysis depends on the level of default risk staying relatively constant. In the face of actual default risk shocks, market makers were forced to absorb large amounts of these securities at falling prices. The losses incurred led to a collapse of the market for this type of security (Parente and Weintraub 1987).

One interesting extension of the fixed coupon perpetuity pricing formula occurs with the pricing of fixed coupon, fixed term annuities. The basic formula for pricing such an annual pay annuity can be stated as:

$$PV_A = \sum_{t=1}^{T} \frac{\$A}{(1+y)^t}$$

where $\$A$ is the annual coupon payment, y is the applicable interest rate and T is the term over which the annuity payment is received. This general pricing formula appears in numerous guises, such as in consumer loans for automobiles, house mortgages and the like. In these applications, the payment frequency is monthly. By observing that the cash flow stream from a fixed term annuity can be conceived as a perpetual annuity minus a perpetuity that starts at $T + 1$ (valued at T) the perpetuity formula can be used to reexpress this sum as a single closed form expression, i.e.:

$$PV_A = \frac{\$A}{y} - \left[\frac{\$A}{y}\frac{1}{(1+y)^T}\right] = \frac{\$A}{y}\left[1 - \frac{1}{(1+y)^T}\right] = \sum_{t=1}^{T}\frac{\$A}{(1+y)^t}$$

In effect, the price of a fixed coupon annuity is equal to the price of a perpetuity minus the present value of a perpetuity that starts at $T + 1$ (with price taken at T).

In contrast to perpetuities that are something of an oddity in modern fixed income markets, much of the modern focus and discussion of fixed income securities is concerned with bond valuation. Various quirks can arise in bond pricing problems. One useful example arises with using the same yield to maturity to value bonds with different coupon payment frequencies. For example, consider the following problem: a bond offers eight annual coupon payments of $8 and will repay its face value of $100 at the end of eight years. You observe that other similar bonds have yields to maturity of 10%. How much is this bond worth? If the coupons are paid semi-annually, how much is the bond worth? To solve this basic problem, let $C = \$8$, $M = \$100$, and the term to maturity (T) be $T = 8$:

$$P_B^A = \$8\sum_{t=1}^{8}\frac{1}{(1.1)^t} + \frac{\$100}{(1.1)^8} = \$8(5.335) + \$100(.467) = \$89.38$$

$$P_B^{SA} = \$4\sum_{t=1}^{16}\frac{1}{(1.05)^t} + \frac{100}{(1.05)^{16}} = \$4(10.84) + \$45.80 = \$89.16$$

where P_B^A is the price of the annual coupon bond and P_B^{SA} is the price of the semi-annual bond.

The impact of increasing the coupon payments can be established with the following two problems: if these bonds have coupon payments of $12 annually, how much is the bond worth? If the coupons are paid semi-annually how much is the bond worth? These questions can be solved as: $P_B^A = \$12(5.335) + \$46.70 = \$110.72$ and $P_B^{SA} = \$6(10.84) + \$45.80 = \$110.84$. To assess the impact of increasing the term to maturity, compare these bond prices with the 8% coupon prices calculated with 10 years to maturity. Do the same for the bonds with the 12% coupon. What do you observe about the relationships between the prices? Solving for the bond prices gives for $C = \$8$, $T = 10$, $y = .10$, $P_B^A = \$8(6.145) + \$38.60 = \$87.76$ and $P_B^{SA} = \$4(12.46) + \$37.70 = \$87.54$. Similarly, for $C = \$12$, $T = 10$, $y = .10$, $P_B^A = \$12(6.145) + \$38.60 = \$112.34$ and $P_B^{SA} = \$6(12.46) + \$37.70 = \$112.46$.

This series of bond valuations illustrates the pricing differences that arise for discount and premium bonds. This illustration requires some definitions to be introduced. A "*straight bond*" requires a stream of fixed coupon payments paid at regular intervals plus a "return of principal" at maturity that involves a payment on the maturity date equal to the stated *par value* (M) of the bond. If no coupons are offered the bond is said to be a *zero coupon* or *pure discount* bond. If the price of the bond $P_B > M$, then the bond is referred to as a *premium* bond. This occurs when the annual coupon payment C satisfies: $(C/M) > y$, i.e., the coupon rate exceeds the yield to maturity on the bond.

If the price of the bond $P_B < M$, then the bond is referred to as a *discount* bond and $(C/M) < y$. If $P_B = M$, the bond sells at its par value, then $(C/M) = y$ and the bond is referred to as a *par bond*.

In the bond valuation solutions, it can be observed that, for discount bonds with the same yield but different term to maturity, $P_B^{10} < P_B^8$. For premium bonds, with the same yield but different term to maturity, $P_B^{10} > P_B^8$. Shorter term bonds have higher prices when the bonds sell at a discount and longer term bonds sell at higher prices when the bonds sell at a premium. For discount bonds, with the same term to maturity and yield to maturity: $P_B^{SA} < P_B^A$. This result seems counter-intuitive because the semi-annual bond pays the coupon sooner than for the annual bond. For premium bonds, with the same term to maturity and yield to maturity: $P_B^{SA} > P_B^A$. All these results are somewhat misleading because with the same C and T a semi-annual coupon bond will always be preferred to an annual coupon bond, because a portion of the cash flows are received sooner. Hence, the semi-annual bond will sell for a higher price, and lower stated yield to maturity.

In a era of calculators, workstations and computerized calculation, the problem of directly calculating the yield to maturity has lost its sharp edge. The days of starting with an observed coupon, bond price and term to maturity, looking up present value factors and present value of annuity factors in tables and painstakingly interpolating to arrive at a yield to maturity are rapidly receding into the past. Instead of interest tables, introductory investment texts now include a CD with the appropriate yield calculation programs. Consider a question designed to provide a glimpse into times past. The objective is to arrive at a solution problem by hand: a bond offers semi-annual coupon payment of $5 (i.e., it is a 10% coupon bond) and will repay its face value of $100 at the end of twenty years. The bond is currently selling for $84.95. What is the offered yield to maturity on the bond?

How to solve for the yield to maturity given the P_B? As bonds are traded in terms of price, this is the typical calculation that has to be done in practice. Absent some type of financial calculator with the appropriate present value functions, it is necessary to solve by hand using the trial and error method, i.e., guess a yield and solve for the bond price. If the calculated price is above the observed price, then try a higher yield and recalculate the price. If the calculated price is below the observed price, then try a lower yield and recalculate the price. Continue this process until a yield is determined that has a desirable level of precision. In doing these calculations without present value and present value of annuity tables it is necessary to make use of the expression for the present value of an annuity given previously.

4.2   THE CONCEPT OF DURATION

The concept of duration

Duration is a fundamental concept in the analysis of fixed income securities, both for individual securities and for portfolios. Though duration has a number of different applications, the basic concept can be motivated by considering the question: what is an appropriate measure for the sensitivity of the price of a fixed income security to a change in the interest rate? For purposes of illustration, this question can be evaluated by taking the derivative of the bond price with respect to the interest rate. More precisely, observing that $d(1 + y) = dy$:

$$\frac{dP_B}{d(1 + y)} = -\left\{\sum_{t=1}^{T} \frac{tC}{(1 + y)^{t+1}} + \frac{TM}{(1 + y)^{T+1}}\right\}$$

$$\rightarrow \quad -\frac{1 + y}{P_B} \frac{dP_B}{d(1 + y)} = \frac{\sum_{t=1}^{T} \frac{tC}{(1 + y)^{t}} + \frac{TM}{(1 + y)^{T}}}{P_B} = D^* = \text{Macaulay duration}$$

Elementary economics teaches that using the unadjusted derivative to measure the sensitivity of a variable X, say quantity demanded, with respect to the change in another variable Y, say the price of the commodity or income of the consumer, is ineffective because the starting level of X and Y will impact the result. Instead, the elasticity measure is used where the derivative is scaled by the level of X and Y. This is the case with **Macaulay duration**, which is the elasticity of the bond's price with respect to a change in interest rates. Though an elasticity number is usually dimensionless (dollars divided by dollars), due to the presence of compound interest it is acceptable to express duration in years, e.g., Hicks (1939, p. 187, n. 1). An important property of D^* occurs for a zero coupon bond ($C = 0$) where $D^* = T$, i.e., the duration of a zero coupon bond equals the term to maturity.

In practice, two closely related forms of duration are encountered, Macaulay duration and **modified duration**. The difference can be illustrated with the following question: given D^*, calculate the change in the price of a bond for a given change in interest rates. This leads to:

$$D^* = -\frac{1 + y}{P_B} \frac{dP_B}{d(1 + y)} \quad \rightarrow \quad -dP_B = \frac{D^*}{1 + y} P_B dy = DP_B dy$$

$$\text{where:} \quad D = -\frac{1}{P_B} \frac{dP_B}{dy} = \frac{D^*}{1 + y}$$

The measure D is the modified duration. As discussed below, Macaulay duration is typically used in situations where the duration concept is being used as an adjusted term to maturity while the modified duration occurs in theoretical analysis of bond portfolio management applications.

Making use of the ratio expression for the present value of an annuity, some tedious algebra permits the duration for an annual coupon bond to be reexpressed as a number of different possible ratio expressions. Two such expressions are:

$$D^* = \frac{\sum_{t=1}^{T} \frac{tC}{(1+y)^t} + \frac{TM}{(1+y)^T}}{P_B} = \frac{1+y}{y} - \frac{1+y+T\left(\frac{C}{M}-y\right)}{\frac{C}{M}\{(1+y)^T - 1\} + y}$$

$$= \frac{1+y}{P_B}\left\{\frac{C}{y}\left[\frac{1}{y} - \frac{1}{(1+y)^T y} - \frac{T}{(1+y)^{T+1}}\right] + \frac{TM}{(1+y)^{T+1}}\right\}$$

The final expression follows from direct evaluation of the derivative. Such formulas are useful when programming duration into a spread sheet or hard coding into a statistical or mathematical programming package (see end of chapter questions for the par bond simplification).

The duration formula has to be adjusted when the coupon payment frequency is not annual. For example, the Macaulay duration of a semi-annual coupon bond is determined as:

$$\frac{dP_B}{d\left(1+\frac{y}{2}\right)} = -\left\{\sum_{t=1}^{2T} \frac{t(C/2)}{\left(1+\frac{y}{2}\right)^{t+1}} + \frac{2TM}{\left(1+\frac{y}{2}\right)^{2T+1}}\right\}$$

$$\rightarrow \quad -\frac{1+\frac{y}{2}}{P_B}\frac{dP_B}{d\left(1+\frac{y}{2}\right)} = \frac{\sum_{t=1}^{2T} \frac{t(C/2)}{\left(1+\frac{y}{2}\right)^t} + \frac{2TM}{\left(1+\frac{y}{2}\right)^{2T}}}{P_B} = D^{*SA} = \text{Macaulay duration (in half years)}$$

It follows that modified duration has to be adjusted appropriately, i.e., for semi-annual bonds $D^{SA} = (D^{*SA})/(1 + (y/2))$. Given that the conventional unit of measurement for duration is years, to be comparable to duration for annual coupon bonds both D^{SA} and D^{*SA} have to be divided by two to get a value that is measured in years and is comparable to duration for annual coupon bonds.

Some examples (taken from CFA Level I examinations) serve to illustrate the basic points: "An 8%, semi-annual coupon, 20 year corporate bond is priced to yield 9%. The Macaulay duration for this bond is 8.85 years. Given this information, the bond's modified duration is . . ." (1992 exam). Recognizing that the Macaulay duration in half years has been divided by two to get a value measured in years, the solution follows appropriately: (Macaulay duration)/(1 + (y/2)) = D^*/(1 + (y/2)) = 8.85/1.045 = 8.47. In words, modified duration gives the percentage change in the bond price for a given change in yield (not percentage change in yield as required for Macaulay duration). Similarly: "An 8%, 15 year bond has a yield-to-maturity of 10% and a modified duration of 8.05 years. If the market yield changes by 25 basis points, how much change will there be in the bond's price?" (1991 exam). The solution is determined as: $\%\Delta P_B$ = modified duration $\times dy$ = 8.05 $\times$ .25 = 2.01%.[8]

A final example question is: "A 6% coupon bond paying interest semi-annually has a modified duration of 10 years and sells for $800, and is priced at a yield to maturity (YTM) of 8%. If the YTM increases to 9%, the predicted change in price, using the duration concept, decreases by ..." (1994 exam). The solution to this question follows from observing that modified duration for semi-annual coupon bonds is:

$$D = \text{Modified duration} = \left(1 + \frac{y}{2}\right)^{-1} \text{Macaulay duration (in years)}$$

$$-dP = (D^*)(dy)(P) \quad \rightarrow \quad PVBP = \frac{D^* \times P}{10{,}000}$$

where *PVBP* is the present (price) value of a basis point. It follows: (10 × 800 × 100 basis points)/10,000 = $80. This formula for calculating price volatility is referred to a *dollar duration* (Fabozzi 1989, p. 74). Why divide by 10,000? This converts to one basis point (*bp*) = .0001 from 1 which is the unit of measurement for *bp* in the calculation.

The duration concept applies not only to bonds but to any sequence of future cash flows. As long as a single interest rate is used to discount the cash flows, the calculation of a duration measure is not complicated. For example, consider the duration of a perpetuity:

$$\frac{dP^{perp}}{d(1+y)} = \frac{dP^{perp}}{dy} = -\frac{C}{y^2} \quad \rightarrow \quad D^* = \frac{C}{y^2}\frac{1+y}{\frac{C}{y}} = \frac{1+y}{y}$$

As an example, if $y = 10\%$, then the duration of the perpetuity is 11 years. Changing to $y = 5\%$ the duration increases to 21 years. Similarly, the duration of a fixed annual coupon annuity can be calculated as:

$$\frac{dPV^A}{d(1+y)} = \frac{d}{dy}\left[\frac{1}{y} - \frac{1}{y(1+y)^T}\right]$$

$$\rightarrow \quad D^* = -\frac{1+y}{PV^A}\frac{dPV^A}{d(1+y)} = \frac{1+y}{y} - \frac{T}{(1+y)^T - 1}$$

As an example, if $T = 10$ years and $y = 8\%$ then an annual fixed coupon annuity will have a duration of 4.87 years.

Assuming the constant growth in dividends required for the Gordon stock pricing model to hold (see section 8.1), it is also possible to calculate the duration of the common stock price (P_S) with respect to changes in the expected return on the stock (k):

$$P_S(0) = \frac{Div(1)}{k-g} \quad \rightarrow \quad \frac{dP}{dk} = -\frac{Div(1)}{(k-g)^2} \quad \rightarrow \quad D^* = \frac{1+k}{k-g}$$

where $Div(1)$ is the dividend paid at $t = 1$. For example, if the expected return on the stock is $k = 12\%$ and the growth rate of dividends is $g = 8\%$ then the duration of the stock taken with respect to a change in expected returns is 28 years. To be comparable to the duration for, say, a bond some assumptions need to be made about dk/dy. A simpler formula would apply for the case where the preferred stock is being valued with the perpetuity pricing formula.

Historical background: Macaulay, Hicks, Samuelson and Redington

Following Bierwag et al. (1983) and others, it is conventional to date the starting point for the intellectual history of the duration concept as Macaulay (1938). This starting point has validity in a number of ways. One obvious way is in terms of the introduction of a specific formula; Macaulay stated the analytical solution for duration both in terms of the sum of discounted cash flows and as a closed form ratio expression. Macaulay can also be considered as a starting point for indepth analysis of the types of questions that the duration concept is designed to address. Though some such questions were identified previously, the empirical implications of interest rate changes and yield curve behavior were of secondary importance to theoretical questions about the origins of interest or the impact of changing price levels on the rate of interest, e.g., Fisher (1896). Solutions to the types of questions being addressed by Macaulay had not been systematically proposed. As such, the seminal contributions of Macaulay (1938) extend well beyond the introduction of the analytical formula for duration.

Section 1.3 advanced the position that Finance is a human science. As such, there is an element of timelessness in the intellectual contributions of the past. Unlike the natural sciences where knowledge about the external world is cumulative, progressing inductively toward an increasingly greater knowledge of natural phenomenon, understanding in the human sciences is more elusive. When accurate accounting has been made of differences in the historical context, classics of the past still can provide insights that may be of value to contemporary observers. In the same fashion that, say, Keynes (1936) or Graham and Dodd (1934) still contain insights, Macaulay (1938) also has contemporary relevance. Like Keynes and Graham and Dodd, Macaulay was profoundly influenced by the economic and social events associated with the Great Depression. The limitations of theoretical models based on rational decision makers are explicitly recognized in many places, e.g., "the 'laws' of a *completely* 'rational' economy cannot be formulated." Yet, like Keynes and Graham and Dodd, Macaulay (1938, p. 10) does see value in such analysis, if the limitations are correctly interpreted: "the relations that would exist under specific instances of accurate forecasting of *particular aspects* of human nature are ... often easily uncovered."

Macaulay (1938) clearly understood the need to provide a better measure of the "length" of a bond than the term to maturity. Bonds provide a sequence of coupon cash flows together with the return of principal at maturity. By considering only the term to maturity, bonds with different coupons but the same maturity date appear to have the same length even though the lower coupon bond has a larger portion of the cash flow being paid farther in the future. To address this shortcoming of the term to maturity, Macaulay proposed the weighted average term to maturity concept now justly referred to as Macaulay duration. The use of "duration" to refer to the weighted average term to maturity can be traced to the verbal description that accompanies the mathematical derivation:

> Now, if present value weighting be used, the "duration" of a bond is an average of the durations of the separate single payment loans into which the bond may be broken up. To calculate this average the durations of each individual single payment loan must be weighted in proportion to the size of the individual loan; in other words, by the ratio of the present value of the individual future payment to the sum of all the present values, which is, of course, the price paid for the bond.

The notion of the price of a bond as the sum of the prices of the zero coupon component payments is clearly recognized. The mathematical statement of the formula is unambiguous.

The contrast between Macaulay (1938) and Hicks (1939) can be used as a pedagogical illustration of the difference between Finance and Economics, even though at the time both Macaulay and Hicks identified themselves as "economists." Where Macaulay is concerned with evaluating properties of traded securities, i.e., long-term and short-term bonds, Hicks (1939, p. 3) aims to "reconsider the value theory of Pareto and then to apply this improved value theory to those dynamic problems of capital that Wicksell could not reach with the tools at his command."[9] In effect, Hicks (1939, p. 5) aims to develop a theoretical apparatus: "This is a work on Theoretical Economics, considered as the logical analysis of an economic system of private enterprise, without any inclusion of reference to institutional controls." This exercise is confounded by Hicks' claim to be deeply influenced by Keynes (1936), stating that Hicks (1939) is a "pedestrian" effort by comparison. The concern with abstract notions such as "value" and "capital" seems far removed from Macaulay's concerns with the yields on bonds.

Despite the concern with abstract notions, the duration concept is clearly presented in Hicks (1939, p. 186), not in the specific context of bond valuation but, rather, in the more general context of valuing a capital asset:

> The capital value of a stream of payments $(x_0, x_1, x_2, \ldots x_v)$ is $x_0 + \beta x_1 + \beta^2 x_1 + \ldots + \beta^v x_v$. The elasticity of this capital value with respect to the discount ratio β is
>
> $$\frac{\beta x_1 + 2\beta^2 x_2 + 3\beta^3 x_3 + \ldots + v\beta^v x_v}{x_0 + \beta x_1 + \beta^2 x_2 + \beta^3 x_3 + \ldots + \beta^v x_v}$$
>
> (for the elasticity of a sum is the *average* of the elasticities of its parts). Now when we look at the form of this elasticity we see that it may be very properly described as the *Average Period* of the stream: for it is the *average length of time for which the various payments are deferred from the present, when the times of deferment are weighted by the discounted values of the payments.*

where $\beta = 1/(1 + r)$. Because Hicks is examining a capital asset, the future payments $\{x_i\}$ can take a wide range of values. For example, if the capital asset is a "wasting asset liable to give out at some future date" then the payments from the asset will be declining over time. Hicks is concerned with evaluating the impact of interest rate changes on these variable payments relative to the impact on a "standard stream" where the payments are "constant in money terms from week to week." In order to account for the depreciation of a wasting asset, to be equal in present value to a standard stream the receipts from the wasting asset would have to be higher that the standard stream in the near term and be "re-lent" in order to have sufficient payments in the future: "the lower the rate of interest is, the greater the sum he will have to re-lend in order for the interest on it to make up for the expected failure of receipts from his wasting asset in the future" (p. 187).

Hicks (1939, p. 187) clearly evaluates the impact of an interest rate change on capital assets of unequal durations:

> It follows from all this that if the average period of the stream of receipts is greater than the average stream with which we are comparing it, a fall in the rate of interest will raise the capital value of the receipts stream more than that of the standard stream, and will therefore increase income. But if the average period of the stream of receipts is less than that of the standard stream, it is a rise in the rate of interest which will increase income.

In interpreting Hicks, it is important to recognize that, instead of a bond as the basic cash flow pattern, Hicks is concerned with a fixed annuity, i.e., the standard stream. Hicks (1939, p. 188) evaluates the duration of a perpetuity:

> What is in fact the average period of a stream of constant size and indefinite length, discounted throughout at the same rate of interest? It can easily be shown that it is equal to the reciprocal of the rate of interest, i.e., to the number of "years purchase." If the rate of interest is 5 per cent. per annum, the average period of a standard stream is 20 years.

In a footnote, Hicks solves for the duration of the perpetuity as $1/r$. Hence, despite defining the average period as an elasticity, i.e., Macaulay duration, Hicks actually has the modified duration in mind.

By comparison to the tomes of Macaulay (1938) and Hicks (1939), the short journal article of Samuelson (1945) is a pale effort. Upon closer inspection it is difficult to see why Bierwag et al. (1983) and Bierwag (1987) give it recognition similar to Hicks (1939) and Redington (1952). The primary contribution is that Samuelson (1945) takes a step towards the use of duration in fixed income portfolio management, moving away from the use of duration as an adjusted term to maturity measure of Macaulay and as a analytical tool in the theoretical abstractions of Hicks. The basic insight is to consider the impact of interest rate changes on the banking system by evaluating the relative change in value of asset and liabilities. This evaluation is accomplished by taking a derivative of the aggregated fixed income prices with respect to a change in interest rates. The implications of interest rate changes for insurance companies and universities with endowment funds are also considered. Recognizing what was later called the "duration gap," Samuelson (1945) recognizes that an increase in interest rates will impact the value of assets differently from that of liabilities when the "durations" are not equal.

Bierwag (1987, p. 58) claims that "Samuelson (1945)... independently invented the duration measure." This statement is difficult to sustain. Observing that there are no references given in the article, Samuelson uses the term "weighted average time period" to refer to the duration concept. The derivation of the weighted average time period is given as (p. 19):

Let N_t = inpayment t years after the present, C_t = corresponding outpayments, V = present value, i = interest rate per annum averaged over time. Then:

$$V = \sum \frac{N_t}{(1 + i)^t} - \sum \frac{C_t}{(1 + i)^t}$$

$$and \quad \frac{dV}{dt} = -\frac{\ln(1 + i)}{(1 + i)^2} \left\{ \sum \frac{tN_t}{(1 + i)^{t-1}} - \sum \frac{tC_t}{(1 + i)^{t-1}} \right\}$$

By rearranging terms we find that $(dV/dt) > 0, = 0, < 0$ depending upon whether $\bar{N} > \bar{C}$, $\bar{N} = \bar{C}$, $\bar{N} < \bar{C}$, where $\bar{N}$, $\bar{C}$ are respectively weighted average time periods of inpayments and outpayments, whose weights are proportional to discounted dollar amounts.

Though there are some interesting elements, this formulation cannot fairly be called an independent invention of the duration measure. The formula is not expressed as an elasticity and not identified as relating to adjusted term to maturity.

Bierwag et al. (1983, p. 16) correctly observe that Samuelson (1945, p. 19) reaches the conclusion: "increased interest rates will help any organization whose [weighted] average time period of disbursements is greater than the average time period of receipts." In modern terms, if the duration of liabilities is greater than the duration of assets, increasing interest rates will increase net worth. Yet, Samuelson (p. 25) goes on to conclude: "the banking system as a whole is immeasurably helped rather than hindered by an increase in interest rates. Indeed, it receives much greater benefit than either universities or insurance companies, and commercial banks would profit more than savings banks." The basis for this conclusion is that "the average time period of its inpayments is less than that of its outpayments." This is contrary to the received view that financial institutions such as banks face a duration gap where the duration of assets, e.g., mortgages, exceeds the duration of liabilities, e.g., checking deposits.

In contrast to Samuelson (1945), by explicitly introducing and developing the concept of "immunization" Redington (1952) does represent a significant advancement in the development of the duration concept, though Redington works only with the derivatives and does not recognize the connection to an elasticity measure. Redington (1952, pp. 288–9) introduces immunization as a fundamental improvement on the concept of "matching" where: "The word 'matching' implies the distribution of assets to make them, as far as possible, equally as vulnerable as the liabilities to those influences which affect both. In its widest sense this principle includes such important aspects as the matching of assets and liabilities in currencies." Given this, Redington makes the following observation:

The word "matching" has such a wide and general connotation that it is necessary to adopt a new label with a more precise significance. For this purpose, I use the word "immunization" to signify the investment of the assets in such a way that the existing business is immune to general change in the rate of interest. The definition is not exact, but it should not mislead. On the basis of this definition immunization is to be regarded as a particular form of matching.

From this point Redington explicitly assumes a "uniform rate of interest whatever the term," i.e., a flat yield curve, and then proceeds to apply a Taylor series expansion to derive the conditions on assets and liabilities required to achieve immunization.

As discussed in section 5.1, Redington is able to theoretically derive the two rules for classical immunization: match the duration of assets and liabilities; ensure that the convexity of assets is greater than liabilities. For this contribution, Redington has been justly recognized. However, development of the classical immunization rules occupies only a small part of Redington (1952). The bulk of the article is concerned with practical application of the rules. In this discussion, Redington recognizes numerous limitations that represent a contribution over and above the theoretical analysis. For example, Redington recognizes the following complications: difficulties in determining the yields on assets and liabilities; the presence of options in both the assets and liabilities; indeterminancy in cash flow estimation where the assets contain equities, properties and certain types of mortgages; the need to actively manage asset portfolios; and the presence of surplus funds.

The uses and calculation of duration

Duration is one of those fascinating concepts that have applications that extend well beyond the basic mechanics of the calculation. The discussion of the historical background reveals at least three different uses that can be identified: a measure of the adjusted or weighted average term to maturity (Macaulay); an elasticity measure of the sensitivity of a sequence of fixed income cash flows to changes in the interest rate (Hicks); and, as reflected in Redington's rules for classical immunization, as a tool for the management of fixed income portfolios. As an adjusted term to maturity, inspection of the duration formula reveals that, for a zero coupon bond, $D^* = T$. Hence, any calculated duration value reexpresses the "term to maturity" of a cash flow pattern in terms of the term to maturity of a zero coupon bond. This raises the practical question of how much the stated term to maturity will differ from the duration. Numerous examples will be given in section 5.1. At this point, all that is being illustrated is some basic calculations.

Observing that $D^* = T$ for a zero coupon bond, it is apparent that as C increases the duration will fall. This raises the question about how much the duration falls as the coupon rises. To see an example of this effect, calculate the durations of a 3 year, 4% annual coupon bond, a 3 year 8% annual coupon bond and a 3 year 10% annual coupon bond – all priced to yield 8% to maturity. These durations are:

$y = 8\%$	$C = \$4$	$C = \$8$	$C = \$10$
Duration (D^*)	2.879	2.783	2.742
P_B	89.6916	100	105.154

The duration values are not much different than the zero coupon duration (= 3) because the total value of the bonds has relatively little coupon income compared to the principal plus coupon value that is paid at $t = 3$. For example, when $C = \$4$ only $8 (not adjusted for discounting) is paid prior to maturity while $104 is paid at maturity. The impact of increasing the number of coupon payments is evident from setting $T = 30$ and $C = \$8$, then the duration is 12.16 years.

As will be apparent in section 5.2, duration is a point elasticity measure. It is well known that point elasticities can be quite inaccurate for large changes in the exogenous variables. To see this, consider how much the value of a 3 year, 4% coupon bond changes if interest rates increase 400 basis points from 8% to 12%. What would the duration formula predict? The relevant calculations reveal:

$$y = 12\% \qquad \text{Duration } (D^*) = 2.87211 \qquad \Delta P = (D^*)(\Delta y/(1 + y_0)^* P_0$$
$$P_B[y = .08] = 80.7853 \qquad = 9.56438$$

The duration estimate can be compared with the actual $\Delta P = 89.6916 - 80.78653 = 8.90507$. Even for the case of short term bonds, where the impact on price of a change in interest rates is not large, duration gives a relatively inaccurate estimate. Recognizing that the bond price function can be expanded in a Taylor series, to correct for this inaccuracy higher order terms in the Taylor series, i.e., the convexity term, can be included. The conclusion required at this point is that, for large changes in yield, the duration estimate deviates significantly from actual price change.

Duration measures the impact of a change in the interest rate on the price of the bond. When interest rates change there are two inversely related impacts on the bond value. Consider the case of an increase (decrease) in interest rates. In this case, the principal value plus last coupon will fall (rise) in price due to the impact of compounding. This is the *principal risk*. However, a higher (lower) interest rate means that coupons paid prior to the maturity can be reinvested at a higher (lower) interest rate. This is *reinvestment risk*. When used as a tool in balance sheet immunization, duration provides a method of determining when the positive (negative) reinvestment risk just balances against the negative (positive) principal risk. Such duration matching considerations arise in other contexts, such as a bond trader making a yield curve play by, say, shorting an intermediate-term bond and buying a short term and long term bond. Duration provides a guide to the relative amounts of the short term and long term bonds that have to be purchased to just offset the interest rate risk of the intermediate-term bond.

Though most of the discussion to this point has been concerned with the duration of individual bonds, duration also plays an important role in bond portfolio management. The extension from portfolios with single bond positions to portfolios with many bonds is straightforward. Consider a portfolio containing three bonds with prices P_1, P_2, P_3. These prices are actual prices making the total value of the portfolio (V): $V = P_1 + P_2 + P_3$. It follows:

$$\frac{dV}{dt} = \frac{dP_1}{dt} + \frac{dP_2}{dt} + \frac{dP_3}{dt} \rightarrow \frac{1}{V}\frac{dV}{dt} = \frac{P_1}{V}\frac{1}{P_1}\frac{dP_1}{dt} + \frac{P_2}{V}\frac{1}{P_2}\frac{dP_2}{dt} + \frac{P_3}{V}\frac{1}{P_3}\frac{dP_3}{dt}$$

$$D_V = w_1 D_1 + w_2 D_2 + w_3 D_3$$

where the value weights w_i are the same as those defined in the mean-variance portfolio model in section 3.1. For example, if the portfolio is composed of equal amounts of the three 3 year bonds described above:

$$D_p = \sum_{i=1}^{3} w_i D_i \quad where \quad w_i = \frac{\$P_i}{\sum_{i=1}^{3} P_i}$$

The duration of portfolio = (1/3)2.87918 + (1/3)2.78326 + (1/3)2.74236 = 2.8016.

4.3 THE TERM STRUCTURE OF INTEREST RATES

Calculation of implied zero coupon interest rates

The **term structure of interest rates** is concerned with the empirical relationship between term to maturity and the implied zero coupon rates calculated from the default free coupon bond market.[10] Because implied zero rates are not directly observed, it is necessary to estimate these variables from observed coupon bond prices. This involves bootstrapping spot interest rates from semi-annual coupon bond prices. The bootstrapping technique, e.g., Fabozzi (2000), Sundaresan (2002), is an iterative process for calculating implied zero coupon interest rates (spot interest rates) from observed coupon bond rates. The process requires the observed yields for coupon bonds of each relevant term to maturity along the yield curve. In practice, spot rates would typically be extracted from the yield curve for federal government bonds, Treasury bonds in the US or government of Canada bonds in Canada. Because these types of bonds pay semi-annual coupons, precision requires that the bootstrap be executed at semi-annual intervals.

For purposes of illustrating the bootstrap technique, assume that the relevant bonds are sold at par and pay coupons semi-annually. Further assume that the observed 6 month yield is 8.87%. For the US implied zero curve, this rate would be obtained by taking the observed 6 month Treasury bill discount rate and converting to a true yield basis. Because Tbills do not pay coupons this means that the quoted yield is for a 6 month zero coupon bond. If the observed yield on a 1 year semi-annual coupon bond is assumed to be 9.04, for a $100 par value bond this implies a semi-annual coupon payment of 4.52. Given this, the iteration for solving a sequence of implied zero coupon rates begins by discounting the first semi-annual coupon payment at the 6 month, zero coupon rate and solving for the implied 1 year zero coupon rate. For a bond sold at par this requires that:

$$100 = \frac{4.52}{1 + \frac{.0887}{2}} + \frac{104.52}{\left(1 + \frac{z_1}{2}\right)^2}$$

where z_1 is the implied 1 year zero coupon rate, which can be calculated as 0.090438.

Having solved for z_1, the next step in the iteration involves using z_1 to solve the implied zero coupon rate, $z_{1.5}$, using a 1.5 year par coupon bond. If the observed rate on 1.5 year coupon bonds is 9.155, then this implies a semi-annual coupon payment on a $100 par bond of 4.5775. This leads to:

$$100 = \frac{4.5775}{1 + \dfrac{0.0887}{2}} + \frac{4.5775}{\left(1 + \dfrac{z_1}{2}\right)^2} + \frac{104.5775}{\left(1 + \dfrac{z_{1.5}}{2}\right)^3}$$

Substituting the value for z_1 determined previously and solving gives $z_{1.5} = 0.091629$. The next step in the iteration involves solving for z_2. Taking the observed 2 year yield to be 9.2% produces:

$$100 = \frac{4.6}{1 + \dfrac{z_{.5}}{2}} + \frac{4.6}{\left(1 + \dfrac{z_1}{2}\right)^2} + \frac{4.6}{\left(1 + \dfrac{z_{1.5}}{2}\right)^3} + \frac{104.6}{\left(1 + \dfrac{z_2}{2}\right)^4}$$

This formula can be used to solve for z_2, using the previously computed values for z_1 and $z_{1.5}$. This iterative process continues until the zero coupon rate for the desired term to maturity is calculated. The relevant zero coupon rate can be used to do calculations involving implied zero rates, e.g., solving for implied forward interest rates.

In certain cases, exactly precise implied zeros are not required. If this is the case, then it is possible to achieve computational simplifications by proceeding under a number of assumptions. In particular it is possible to reduce the number of computations by a factor of two by assuming that the observed government bond prices are for annual coupon bonds. Another simplification can be achieved by taking the nearest available bond instead of estimating a par bond yield curve. To see how this simplified calculation process works, consider the example in Poitras (2002, p. 250) that involves solving for the Canadian spot interest rates from quotes obtained from the *Globe and Mail* for August 28, 1994. This involves picking the following bills/bonds from the available maturities:

1 year Tbill $z_1 = .0720$

6.5% 1 Aug. 1996 $P_2 = 97.505$ ($y_2 = .07887$)

7.5% 1 Jul. 1997 $P_3 = 98.225$ ($y_3 = .08197$)

6.5% 1 Sep. 1998 $P_4 = 93.350$ ($y_4 = .08474$)

7.75% 1 Sep. 1999 $P_5 = 96.800$ ($y_5 = .08542$)

These bonds were selected because they were closest to the required maturity dates.

Two possible bootstrap solution techniques are available: the direct approach and the par bond approach. The direct approach involves using the observed price and coupon to solve for the spot interest rate. Solving for z_2:

$$97.505 = 6.5/(1 + z_1) + 106.5/(1 + z_2)^2$$

Using this method, $z_2 = .0792$. As given above, the par bond approach uses the result that when the stated yield to maturity equals the C/M then the bond sells at par:

$$100 = 7.887/(1 + z_1) + 107.887/(1 + z_2)^2$$

Using this method $z_2 = .0791428$. The difference of .6 of a basis point is due to a combination of the assumption that the bond pays annual coupons, i.e., a semi-annual yield is used as an annual yield, and to the difference between the actual maturity date (August 1) and the required maturity date (August 28). Calculating the spot rates out to 5 years, it is evident that the differences involved are generally small:

Par bond: $z_3 = .082423$ $z_4 = .0854697$ $z_5 = .0861374$

Price/coupon: $z_3 = .08232$ $z_4 = .08595$ $z_5 = .08630$

Even for the 5 year implied zero, the difference is only 1.7 basis points. Observe that when the yield curve slopes up, as in this case, the implied zero curve will be above the yield curve. Similarly, when the yield curve slopes down, the implied zero curve will be below the yield curve. When the yield curve is flat, then both curves will be equal. This relationship follows mathematically from observing that the yield to maturity acts as a form of geometric average of the spot rates.

Traditional theories of the term structure

As noted, the term structure of interest rates refers to the functional relationship between the term to maturity and the associated implied zero coupon interest rates. This is a theoretical development on the yield curve that refers to the functional relationship between term to maturity and yield to maturity. Though the yield curve can be readily determined from inspection of bond price/yield quotes available every day in the financial press, the yield curve suffers from the defect that the term to maturity is an inaccurate measure of the true "length" of the cash flow from a bond. As observed in the discussion of duration, differences in coupons for bonds with the same term to maturity means that the time pattern of the cash flows for these bonds will differ. Because a greater proportion of the cash flow will occur later in the future, a bond with a lower coupon will behave like a longer term bond compared to a bond with a higher coupon. This problem is corrected by considering the term structure of interest rates. Changes in the shape, slope and level of the term structure are a fundamental source of risk in the valuation of individual bonds and in the management of bond portfolios, e.g., Crack and Nawalkha (2000).

Explaining the empirical behavior of the term structure of interest rates at a given point in time and over time is a fundamental problem in fixed income security analysis. Analysis of this problem has a long history. Traditional explanations use the interpretation of implied forward rates as the defining elements to distinguish different explanations. These explanations can be roughly divided into three separate categories: the unbiased expectations hypothesis; the liquidity premia or risk premia hypothesis; and the market segmentation or preferred habitat hypothesis. Under the unbiased expectations hypothesis of the term structure, implied forward rates are the market's prediction about what interest rates will be in future periods. Under the liquidity premia hypothesis, implied forward rates are upwardly biased predictors of future interest rates. Under the market segmentation hypothesis, it is not possible to formulate predictions about future interest rates from the shape of the observed term structure of interest rates.

Given the importance of the implied forward rate to the theoretical analysis of term structure behaviour, it is somewhat surprising that a standard notation for forward rates is not available. Complete notation requires three variables: the time the forward interest rate starts, the time the forward interest rate ends and the date the yield curve which is used to derive the forward interest rate is observed. As bonds are typically used to derive the implied forward rates, time is measured in years. Different sources use notation that only takes account of some of these three variables while others, e.g., van Horne (2001) use a complete notation such as $_{t+n}r_{jt}$ where $t + n$ is the start date, j is the term to maturity of the implied security and t is the date the term structure is observed. In contrast, Bodie, et al. (p. 589) use an incomplete notation: f_t where t refers to the start date, and it is assumed that all the terms to maturity for the implied securities are 1 year and that the date for observing the term structure is t. This is very limited notation.

It is assumed in developing the notation used here that the term structure is always observed at $t = 0$, i.e., in the notation $f_{i,j}$, this is the implied forward interest rate observed at $t = 0$, starting at time i and ending at time j. It is assumed in developing the notion used here that the term structure is always observed at time $t = 0$, so the time date is dropped from the notation. In this case, j minus i gives the term to maturity of the implied security. For example: $f_{1,2}$ is the implied forward interest rate starting at year 1 and ending at year 2; $f_{5,10}$ is the implied forward interest rate starting at year 5 and ending at year 10. This method of subscripting is also applied to future spot interest rates, i.e., the notation applied to future spot interest rates is $z_{i,j}$, the spot interest rate for a zero coupon bond which starts at time i and ends at time j. It is important to recognize that, in the following discussion, all expectations are assumed to be conditional and taken on information available at $t = 0$.

The three general groups of theories about term structure behaviour are concerned with different explanations of the relationship between the current term structure and future term structure level, slope and shape. These theories of the term structure of interest rates are motivated using the relationship between implied forward rates and expected spot interest rates. Because implied forward rates depend on the shape of the term structure, the various theories of the term structure seek to make predictions about the behaviour of future interest rates based on the level, slope and shape of the observed term structure of interest rates. The different theories each have a different interpretation about the relationship between the implied forward interest rate and predictions about future spot interest rates.

UNBIASED EXPECTATIONS HYPOTHESIS

The sharpest group of theories fall into the general category of the **unbiased expectations hypothesis** (UEH). Under the UEH, implied forward rates are unbiased predictors of future spot rates: $f_{i,j} = E[z_{i,j}]$. To identify the relationship between the current term structure and predictions of future interest rates under the UEH, assume that interest rates are expected to be unchanged, then: $E[z_{1,2}] = z_1$. From the two portfolio (rollover vs. buy and hold) example given above, it follows that in this case:

$$(1 + z_1)(1 + E[z_{1,2}]) = (1 + z_1)^2 = (1 + z_2)^2$$

Hence, under the UEH assuming interest rates will not change implies $z_1 = z_2$ and the observed yield curve will be flat. In other words, under the UEH a flat yield curve at $t = 0$ implies that future spot interest rates are expected to be unchanged. If this is not true, then under the UEH investors will sell the portfolio with the lower expected return and purchase the higher expected return portfolio. This will produced an adjustment in the prices for the 1 year and 2 year securities to the point where the yield curve shape reflects the underlying market expectations.

Assuming that interest rates are expected to rise, then: $E[z_{1,2}] > z_1$. From the two portfolio example, it follows that because:

$$(1 + z_1)(1 + E[z_{1,2}]) = (1 + z_2)^2$$

It must be that $z_1 < z_2$ and the observed ($t = 0$) yield curve will be upward sloping, i.e., under the UEH an upward sloping yield curve implies that future spot interest rates are expected to be higher than current rates. Similarly, when interest rates are expected to fall, $E[z_{1,2}] < z_1$ and the $t = 0$ yield curve will be downward sloping. UEH is attractive because it gives sharp predictions but it is not clear that these predictions are always accurate.

The UEH argument becomes more complicated if a three period investment horizon is considered. In this case, the two portfolio problem is expanded to compare a three period buy and hold strategy with a strategy of buying a 1 year and rolling forward either into another one year (followed by another one year) or into a 2 year. Consider the equality of the buy and hold with rolling three 1 years:

$$(1 + z_3)^3 = E[(1 + z_1)(1 + z_{1,2})(1 + z_{2,3})]$$

$$= E[1 + z_1 + z_{1,2} + z_{2,3} + z_1 z_{1,2} + z_1 z_{2,3} + z_{1,2} z_{2,3} + z_1 z_{1,2} z_{2,3}]$$

In this case, if rates are expected to be unchanged, $E[z_{1,2}] = z_1$, $E[z_{2,3}] = z_1$, it does **not** follow that the UEH implies the current yield curve is flat.

To see this, refer back to the two period case:

$$(1 + z_2)^2 = 1 + 2z_2 + z_2^2 = E[(1 + z_1)(1 + z_{1,2})]$$

$$= E[1 + z_1 + z_{1,2} + z_1 z_{1,2}] = 1 + z_1 + E[z_{1,2}] + z_1 E[z_{1,2}]$$

It follows that if rates are expected to be unchanged, $E[z_{1,2}] = z_1$, then the current yield curve will be flat ($E[z_{1,2}] = z_1 = z_2$) and the implied forward rate will equal the market expectation of the future spot rate. This result does not follow for the three period (and greater) case because:

$$E[z_{1,2}z_{2,3}] \neq E[z_{1,2}]E[z_{2,3}] \quad \rightarrow \quad E[z_{1,2}z_{2,3}] = cov[z_{1,2}, z_{2,3}] + E[z_{1,2}]E[z_{2,3}]$$

Hence, unless implied zeros are serially uncorrelated ($cov[z_{1,2}, z_{2,3}] = 0$) then there will be an advantage to the rollover strategy compared to the buy and hold strategy.

Faced with a flat yield curve, the presence of serial correlation in future implied zero rates permits the rollover strategy to achieve, on average, higher returns compared to the buy and hold strategy. In the three period case, this follows because after one period the rollover strategy can observe the direction of rates and, if rates move adversely, then the rollover can be made into a 2 year security, avoiding the potential loss associated with the future rollover into a 1 year security. Similarly, if rates move favorably, then it is possible to rollover into another 1 year seeking to gain from a further favorable movement in rates that is captured by the final rollover into a 1 year security. Though the analysis is more complicated, this argument generalizes to longer holding periods and yield curves that slope upward or downward. In effect, there is a form of "liquidity premium" associated with serial correlation in spot rate changes. Hence, even if rates are expected to be unchanged, the UEH could imply that this is consistent with an upward sloping yield curve because short rates would have to be lower than long rates to compensate for the higher potential expected return associated with the rollover strategy compared to buy and hold.

The complication in specifying the precise specification and associated implications of the UEH have been explored by Ingersoll (1987, ch. 18) where three distinct forms of the UEH are identified: the local expectations hypothesis; the yield to maturity expectations hypothesis; and the return to maturity expectations hypothesis. The return to maturity version applies to the UEH where accurate accounting is given to the possibility of positive covariance between future spot rates. The yield to maturity version converts the spot rates to yields and still accounts for the positive covariance. The local expectations hypothesis retains the condition that the t to $t + 1$ implied forward rate $f_{t,t+1} = E[z_{t,t+1}]$. Ingersoll expends considerable effort to demonstrate that the local expectations hypothesis is the only version of the UEH that is consistent with absence of arbitrage. As demonstrated in chapters 5 and 6 and other sources, e.g., Sundaresan (2002, p. 230) this result is employed in binomial and other models of term structure behavior that, in turn, are used to value fixed income contingent claims and other securities.

LIQUIDITY PREMIUM HYPOTHESIS

The potential for serial correlation in implied zero rates is not the only possible theoretical argument for a liquidity premium in implied zero rates. For example, the need to hold precautionary cash balances could produce a higher demand for short term securities relative to long term securities that would appear as a liquidity premium in short rates. An important motivation for liquidity premia is risk aversion. As a consequence of this motivation, the next group of explanations for term structure behavior, the liquidity premia hypothesis (LPH), is sometimes referred to as the risk premia hypothesis (RPH). The LPH maintains that, because the buy and hold portfolio is less liquid (or, under RPH, has greater price risk) than the rollover portfolio, then the return on the buy and hold portfolio has to be higher in order to compensate, i.e., if rates are expected to be unchanged:

$$(1 + z_1)(1 + E[z_{1,2}]) < (1 + z_2)^2$$

It follows that, under LPH, the implied forward rate will no longer be an unbiased predictor of future interest rates:

$$1 + f_{i,j} > 1 + E[z_{i,j}]$$

In other words, the $f_{i,j}$ are **upward biased predictors** of future interest rates.

This upward bias associated with implied forward rates can be used to define the **liquidity premia** (LP):

$$1 + f_{i,j} = 1 + E[z_{i,j}] + LP_{i,j} \quad or \quad f_{i,j} - LP_{i,j} = E[z_{i,j}]$$

Under the LPH, an important feature of the liquidity premia is the **monotonicity property**:

$$0 < LP_{1,2} < LP_{1,3} < LP_{1,4} < \ldots$$

In other words, the longer the term to maturity of the implied security, the higher will be the liquidity premia.

One drawback of the LPH is the lack of sharpness for making interest rate predictions from the shape of term structure. Assume that interest rates are expected to be unchanged, then: $E[z_{1,2}] = z_1$. From the two portfolio example, it follows that in this case: $(1 + z_1)^2 < (1 + z_2)^2$. This result is due to the presence of the liquidity premia. Hence, $z_1 < z_2$ and the observed yield curve will be upward sloping when rates are expected to be unchanged. This result makes it more difficult to make predictions about future interest rates if LPH is correct. Under the LPH a flat or downward sloping yield curve implies that future spot interest rates are expected to fall. However, when the yield curve is **upward sloping** the LPH is unable to make precise predictions. On balance, under LPH there is a wide range of yield curve shapes for which no prediction is possible, the prediction depends on the size of the liquidity premia. Empirical attempts to estimate the liquidity premia are mixed. At best, the premia appear to be **time varying**.

MARKET SEGMENTATION AND PREFERRED HABITAT HYPOTHESES

The UEH made sharp predictions about the relationship between implied forward rates and expected implied zero rates. The LPH made less sharp predictions but still imposed monotonicity restrictions on the liquidity premia. The last group of theories is characterized by making either a weak or no connection between implied forward rates and future implied zero rates. There are subtle differences between the two main theories in the last group. One theory is the *preferred habitat hypothesis*. The basic idea of this hypothesis is that investors prefer to invest in certain maturity segments of the yield curve but will switch to other maturities if the premia are high enough. This hypothesis has two implications: there are still liquidity premia; and, the liquidity premia no longer obey the monotonicity property, i.e., liquidity premia do not necessarily increase in size with term to maturity. In order to make inferences about the connection between yield curve shape and market expectations about future interest rate changes, some versions of the preferred habitat hypothesis incorporate other variables to explain liquidity premia behavior.

In contrast to the preferred habitat hypothesis, the *market segmentation hypothesis* maintains that investors are rigidly restricted in the maturities in which to invest. Maturity switching costs are very high, significantly higher than in the preferred habitat hypothesis, leaving yield curve shape to be fully determined by the supply and demand within the various maturity segments along the yield curve. This approach is commonly found in the financial press where considerable attention is given to, say, the impact on the yield curve of the specific tranche sizes at the US Treasury auction. Both of the preferred habitat and market segmentation hypotheses are unable to formulate predictions about future interest rates from the shape of the observed term structure of interest rates. Both of these theories explain, either in whole or in part, specific yield curve shapes by referencing the relative supply and demand for securities along the yield curve.

Estimating term structure models

Term structure estimation appears in a number of distinct forms. One form deals with the problem of getting the best fit equation, at a given point in time, to the observed set of bond yields. This estimation problem is aimed at providing a complete estimated set of par bond yields that can be used to determine implied zeros for each cash flow payment date. Given a best fit equation, the relevant estimated bond yields (or prices) can be determined from the fitted equation and used to solve for the implied zeros using the method described above. Alternatively, following McCulloch (1971), Linton et al. (2001) and others, it is possible to estimate the *discount function* directly and use this estimated function to directly derive the implied zero coupon interest rates. These implied zeros can then be used to calculate implied forward rates and to provide an estimated yield curve.

The general procedure suggested by McCulloch (1971) and adapted and extended by others can be motivated by observing that the discount function at time t, $DF(t)$, can be approximated by a smoothly declining polynomial function. The discount function is defined by the bond pricing function:

$$P_B = \sum_{t=1}^{T} \frac{C}{(1 + z_t)^t} + \frac{M}{(1 + z_T)^T} = \sum_{t=1}^{T} C\,DF(t) + M\,DF(T)$$

While this specification is for a discrete $DF(t)$, in general the function is continuous and the discrete form is only used for pedagogical and practical purposes. For simplicity of exposition, assume that $DF(t)$ is a quadratic function:

$$DF(t) = d_0 + d_1 t + d_2 t^2$$

Substituting in the bond price function gives:

$$P_B = \left(\sum_{t=1}^{T} C(d_0 + d_1 t + d_2 t^2) \right) + M(d_0 + d_1 T + d_2 T^2)$$

Reexpressing this in terms of the cash flows occurring at each period of time ($CF(t)$) produces:

$$P_B = \sum_{t=1}^{T} CF(t) \, (d_0 + d_1 t + d_2 t^2)$$

$$= d_0 \left(\sum_{t=1}^{T} CF(t) \right) + d_1 \left(\sum_{t=1}^{T} t \, CF(t) \right) + d_2 \left(\sum_{t=1}^{T} t^2 \, CF(t) \right)$$

This provides the specification of a regression equation that can be estimated for a sample of bonds. Given the estimated coefficients, the discount function at any point in time can be determined by evaluating the estimated $DF(t)$ at that point, e.g., say $t = 2.5$ years then $DF(2.5) = d_0 + d_1(2.5) + d_2(2.5)^2$. An implied zero rate is obtained by inverting specific values of the discount function. In recent studies the polynomial function used is of the spline form, e.g., Fisher et al. (1995), that can be conceived as a piecemeal sequence of polynomial functions connected at appropriately specified knot points. However, despite the more sophisticated estimation techniques, the general procedure described is representative of the methodologies used to estimate the discount function.

    Another type of term structure estimation deals with the problem of fitting a model that best describes the evolution of the term structure over time. This estimation problem is significantly more complicated than the problem of fitting the discount function and has a number of different applications. Included in these applications are the pricing of fixed income securities with embedded options, e.g., callable bonds and mortgage backed securities, and the pricing of interest rate derivatives. An important feature of theoretical bond pricing models is the method of converting a stochastic model of the interest rate into a prediction about the evolution of the term structure. This can be illustrated by considering a *one factor model* of the term structure. In this case a stochastic model is assumed for the short term zero coupon interest rate. For simplicity, say the relevant rate is a one year rate, r_t. In addition to the observed one year rate that can be taken as given, $r_1 = z_1$, the fitted stochastic model for this interest rate is used to generate a sequence of future one year interest rates, $r_{1,2}, r_{2,3}, r_{3,4}, r_{4,5} \cdots$. These interest rates can be used to discount the contingent cash flows from securities with embedded options.

Chapter 6 devotes considerable attention to the valuation of fixed income securities with embedded options and the specification of various one factor models is discussed there. What remains to be discussed at this point is the *calibration* problem. In particular, under the UEH, a sequence of future interest rates can be interpreted as implied forward rates for one year securities. Assuming that the UEH is true, then the stochastic sequence of future interest rates can be used to recreate the current term structure, e.g., in a Monte Carlo framework the following relationships hold along any given path:[11]

$$(1 + z_2)^2 = (1 + z_1)(1 + f_{1,2}) = (1 + z_1)(1 + r_{1,2})$$

$$(1 + z_3)^3 = (1 + z_1)(1 + f_{1,2})(1 + f_{2,3}) = (1 + z_1)(1 + r_{1,2})(1 + r_{2,3})$$

$$(1 + z_4)^4 = (1 + z_1)(1 + f_{1,2})(1 + f_{2,3})(1 + f_{3,4}) = (1 + z_1)(1 + r_{1,2})(1 + r_{2,3})(1 + r_{3,4})$$

Because the stochastic model can be used to generate any number of equally likely future paths for short term interest rates, the equally weighted average of the implied zeros calculated using the above recursion is required to equal the observed term structure.

The calibration problem occurs because it is usually the case that the stochastic model is not capable of recreating the current term structure using the recursion procedure described above. As a consequence, the future sequence of stochastic rates, $r_{1,2}$, $r_{2,3}$, $r_{3,4}$, $r_{4,5} \ldots$, has to be "calibrated" by adding (or subtracting) some value sufficient to ensure that the current term structure is obtained. While this might seem somewhat suspicious, the need to calibrate is not surprising. The parameters of the stochastic model are estimated from past data and, as a consequence, are like an average of the stochastic behavior of the short rate over the sample period. Because the shape of the term structure changes over time, there is likely to be some deviation of the current term structure from the average of past values. The calibration problem arises because there is no theoretical direction given about how calibration is to be achieved. This raises questions about the validity of valuations based on arbitrary calibration methods.

To address the calibration problem a number of methods for estimating the term structure, e.g., Ho and Lee (1986), Black, Derman and Toy (1990) and Heath, Jarrow and Morton (1992), invert the process of model specification. The conventional process is to specify a stochastic model of interest rates, estimate the parameters of the model and then compute the implied zeros and the prices of the zero coupon bonds. The implied zeros are then compared with the implied zeros calculated from the observed Treasury yield curve and the parameters are calibrated to enable the model to fit actual prices. The calibrated procedures use the observed market data as a starting point and then determine the stochastic evolution of interest rates from that starting point. The various calibrated models that are available differ in the procedure by which this is done. Ho and Lee (1986), for example, model the evolution of the whole term structure using a binomial process, imposing arbitrage restrictions on admissible changes. Black, Derman and Toy (1990) model the evolution of spot rates while Heath, Jarrow and Morton (1992) model the evolution of forward rates.

In addition to estimating discount functions and stochastic models, term structure estimation also includes studies of the relationship between term structure shape and future economic activity, e.g., Harvey (1997), Plosser and Rouwenhorst (1994). This type of term structure estimation raises a number of econometric issues about the specification of the model generating the term structure, e.g., Is a VAR in levels appropriate? Is there cointegration? How are structural breaks to be incorporated? Leaving these issues aside, there is reasonably strong statistical evidence of a positive relationship between interest rate spreads and future growth rates in real GDP. In effect, the slope of the term structure is a leading indicator of economic growth, widening prior to expansions and contracting prior to downturns. This empirical result is consistent with mean reversion in the slope of the term structure.

4.4   BASICS OF CREDIT RISK AND DEFAULT RISK

The legal aspects of default

For analytical purposes, there are considerable advantages to abstracting from credit risk and embedded option features. Yet, the bulk of fixed income securities do not conform to this abstraction.[12] Even for bonds that would seem to conform to the abstraction of no credit risk, such as US Treasuries, there is still an element of credit risk that has to be addressed. For example, on rare occasions the US Congress has threatened to withhold legislation to increase the debt ceiling raising the possibility that the US Treasury would be unable to make scheduled interest or principal payments on outstanding debt issues, e.g., Nippani et al. (2001). Following Fabozzi (2002, ch. 7), credit risk can be decomposed into three parts: default risk; credit spread risk; and downgrade risk. For bonds, default risk relates to the possibility that the issuer will not fulfill the obligations set out in the bond indenture. This could be due to the failure to make a coupon payment or to return the principal value at maturity or to meet some other provision in the indenture, such as a covenant on net asset value. Such events have a number of possible implications.

Because the possibility of default varies across bond issuers, this will be reflected in the quoted prices and yields for different bond issues. The difference between yields for issues with different credit ratings is the *credit spread.* Due to a variety of factors, the credit spread changes over time. For example, in periods of contracting economic activity credit spreads will typically widen to reflect the pressure on firm cash flows needed to make debt payments. Credit spread risk relates to these changes in the difference between yields for issues with different credit ratings. To facilitate this assessment there are a number of services that provide ratings to the bond market. Related to credit spread risk is the concept of downgrade risk. While credit spread risk depends on general conditions such as aggregate economic activity, downgrade risk is more firm specific. For example, it is possible for, say, a telecom firm such as Worldcom to experience a credit downgrade from a rating agency at a time when the credit risk for telecom firms was narrowing relative to US Treasuries. Another example would be a firm that experienced an unfavorable result in litigation, e.g., Dow-Corning or Johns Mansville. Given this, it is expected that the factors causing a widening of credit spreads will also contribute to an increase in downgrades for individual firms.

Credit spread risk and downgrade risk are extensions of the issue of default risk. Credit spreads widen and narrow because of changes in the perception that default will occur. Downgrading of a firm's debt by a credit rating agency occurs because there is the perception that default is more imminent. Yet, while driven by economic factors, default is a legal event. As such, it is necessary to detail the relevant laws and legal remedies associated with default on a debt obligation.[13] A fixed income security is a debt instrument that is defined by a contract. For a corporate bond, this contract is the bond indenture. For publicly traded issues falling with the scope of the regulations of the Securities and Exchange Commission, such indentures must conform to the Trust Indenture Act (1939) that require appointment of a trustee to protect the interests of bondholders set out in the indenture. In addition, as publicly traded securities, the debt instruments must satisfy the relevant SEC rules regarding registration, resale of securities and the like. Debt instruments have a number of SEC Rules of specific relevance, such as Rule 415 on shelf registrations and Rule 144A on resale of privately placed securities.

Though there is considerable variation in the specifics of indentures, the American Bar Association (ABA) does provide examples of model contracts for specific bond indentures. For example, there are 15 articles, plus preamble, for the model debenture indenture and 16 articles, plus preamble, for the model mortgage bond indenture. Given that there is variation between specific indentures and the model indenture outlined by the ABA, the indenture contents do have a common set of essential characteristics. The preamble will typically make reference to the basis under which the indenture was issued, e.g., "the articles of incorporation permit the board of directors to authorize up to $xxx million of senior subordinated debentures." There will also be articles associated with the definition of terms, methods of notifying trustees, the specific wording on the security certificate, the denominations, the record dates and so on. While such articles are important from a legal standpoint, it is the articles relating to remedies and covenants that are of greatest interest to the assessment of default risk. Articles relating to mergers and consequences of changes in the status of assets are also important, as are preambles and articles that describe the property securing a secured debt issue.

The indenture sets out the conditions required to initiate a default proceeding. Conventionally, once a credit event sufficient to trigger a default has occurred, e.g., failure to make a scheduled coupon or principal payment, the trustee (or a holder of 25% or more of the outstanding debt) can demand payment in full of any outstanding obligations. Whether the trustee initiates such an action is not straight forward. Because the trustee has a fiduciary obligation to act in the best interest of the bondholders, the trustee may deem it more prudent to enter into negotiations with the issuer to attempt to get a resolution to the indenture violation. If the debtor is unable or unwilling to resolve the indenture violation, a US corporate issuer would likely respond by filing for bankruptcy under the relevant chapter of the Bankruptcy Reform Act (1978). Similarly, if the trustee wants to proceed with a default action, a bankruptcy filing can be made by a creditor as well as a debtor. The Bankruptcy Reform Act has 15 chapters dealing with different types of bankruptcy. For filings resulting from a corporate debt issuer violating an indenture, the relevant chapter governing the bankruptcy filing would be either Chapter 7, governing liquidation, or Chapter 11, governing reorganization.

The problems confronting a trustee having to decide the correct course in dealing with an issuer in default on an indenture provision are legally complex. Once the bankruptcy process is initiated for a corporation in default, a number of provisions of the bankruptcy code come into effect that create considerable uncertainty about the final disposition. In particular, a bankruptcy filing introduces the bankruptcy court into the decision making process. The law requires that there be an active role for judicial supervision and oversight. Decisions of the court are binding on the parties involved. Another provision of the bankruptcy code involves the imposition of a standstill agreement on all creditors. This is required to provide for an orderly process of liquidation or reorganization, preventing actions such as senior creditors seizing assets that are essential to the viability of the firm as a going concern or allowing the firm to make disbursements to certain creditors at the expense of others. One final provision of importance is the provision that the debtor retain control of firm operations during the period that the bankruptcy filing is being decided, unless a specific directive is ordered by the court such as the appointment of a receiver.

In theory, a bankruptcy proceeds under the *absolute priority rule.* This rule dictates that senior creditors are to be paid in full before junior creditors receive any payments. For a number of reasons, the absolute priority rule may not be followed. One of these reasons has to do with the judicially supervised negotiation process between the debtor and the creditors that commences with the bankruptcy filing. Under Chapter 7 filings, the negotiating process is usually not overly complicated and the division of assets conforms relatively closely to the absolute priority rule. However, under Chapter 11 filings, the negotiating process can be onerous. The process is complicated by two provisions: during the reorganization the court may permit the firm to undertake new financing that is given a senior claim to existing claims; and, the reorganization plan does not require unanimous consent, only a majority of all creditors holding two-thirds of the outstanding value in each debt classification. This legal structure makes a bankruptcy filing under Chapter 11 somewhat uncertain for debt holders.

Not surprisingly, there is considerable evidence that the distributions in Chapter 11 bankruptcies do not typically adhere to the absolute priority rule, e.g., Fabozzi et al. (1993), Weiss (1990). Due to all the legal complexities and other uncertainties, there are real incentives for the trustee and large individual creditors to avoid formal bankruptcy proceedings and to attempt a resolution outside the court process. In addition to monitoring bankruptcy filings, the major credit rating agencies also issue credit event releases that recognize various types of financial distress and the associated resolution. All this makes the securities of distressed firms, whether in bankruptcy or working toward a resolution outside the court process, a potentially fruitful area for identifying abnormal returns using the techniques of security analysis, e.g., John (1993).

Assessment of credit risk and default risk

Information on credit risk and default risk comes from two sources: ratings agencies and market prices. Because of the large number of traded fixed income securities, firms have emerged that specialize in providing credit ratings for a wide range of different debt issues. In the US, these firms are Standard and Poor's Corporation, Moody's Investors Services Inc. and Fitch Ratings (created by the merger of Fitch IBCA with Duff and Phelps Credit Rating Co.). It is often the case that firms pay the rating agencies to have their debt issues rated. In addition to ratings agency information, the larger investment banking firms and institutional investors will also have resources dedicated to doing credit analysis on specific firms and sectors that are of interest. There are also firms that specialize in ratings for specific industries such as Demotech, Inc. that assesses insurance companies and HMO's. As illustrated in table 4.6, there is a close

Table 4.6 Summary of corporate bond rating systems and symbols

Fitch	Moody's	S&P	Summary description
Investment grade – high credit worthiness			
AAA	Aaa	AAA	Gilt edge, prime, maximum safety
AA+	Aa1	AA+	
AA	Aa2	AA	High grade, high credit quality
AA−	Aa3	AA−	
A+	A1	A+	
A	A2	A	Upper-medium grade
A−	A3	A−	
BBB+	Baa1	BBB+	
BBB	Baa2	BBB	Lower-medium grade
BBB−	Baa3	BBB−	
Speculative – lower credit worthiness			
BB+	Ba1	BB+	
BB	Ba2	BB	Low-grade, speculative
BB−	Ba3	BB−	
B+	B1		
B	B2	B	Highly speculative
B−	B3		
Predominately speculative, substantial risk, or in default			
CCC+		CCC+	
CCC	Caa	CCC	Substantial risk, in poor standing
CC	Ca	CC	May be in default, very speculative
C	C	C	Extremely speculative
		C1	Income bonds – no interest being paid
DDD			
DD			Default
D		D	

Source: Rating agency websites

correspondence in the symbolic method of specifying ratings used by the different ratings agencies. However, this does not mean that the same methodologies are used by different ratings agencies to arrive at a credit rating for a specific firm.

Inspection of table 4.6 reveals three general categories of debt ratings: investment grade, rated BBB- (Baa3) and above; speculative, below investment grade, rated B (B-, B3) to BB- (Ba1); and, purely speculative, D to CCC+ (Caa). The ratings category that a debt issue falls into can have an important impact on the pricing of the issue in the market. In particular, various institutional borrowers, such as pension funds and insurance companies, are restricted from holding issues that are classified as being below investment grade. When a debt issue is downgraded to a rating below investment grade this can have a significant impact on the price of the issue. Similarly, certain types of bond funds, e.g., high yield funds, invest primarily in issues that are below investment grade. The implication is that lower rated issues typically have to offer substantially higher yields in order to attract the types of investors that purchase debt with below investment grade ratings.

Though there is a close correspondence between the credit rating issued by the rating services and, presumably, by the in-house credit analysts, the ratings do not translate precisely into pricing of debt issues. For example, it is possible for a bond with a lower credit rating to sell at a lower yield than a comparable bond with a higher credit rating. It is possible for this to happen because the relative credit ratings are not judged to be accurate by the market. However, it is more likely that this type of pricing occurs because the market price of an issue depends both on the credit rating and the potential *recovery rate*.[14] The recovery rate is the payout on the debt issue that takes place when default occurs. For example, the recovery rate for a corporate mortgage bond will depend on the value of the collateral securing the issue. If the collateral is sufficient to repay the principal value of the borrowing, a default by the issuer will not have severe consequences. Similarly, it is possible that, though default may be less likely, the recovery rate may also be lower in the event that default does occur, e.g., due to the asset structure of the company.

For a portfolio of bonds, it is possible to calculate the "default loss rate" as the product of the default rate and the recovery rate, e.g., Fabozzi (2002, p. 202). For example, if 10% of the issues in a portfolio defaulted and a weighted average of 50% of the value of the investment was recovered then the default loss rate was 5%. Ignoring costs associated with the disruption of cash flow associated with having to wait until the defaulted issue is paid out to bondholders, if the portfolio was initially purchased with a promised yield of more than 5% above Treasuries then the investor would, *ex post*, have done better than investing in Treasuries. As such, analysis of fixed income securities subject to credit risk requires both the default rate and the recovery rate to be assessed to determine an appropriate valuation. Table 4.7 provides evidence from Altman and Bana (2003) on both default rates and recovery rates for US high yield corporate bonds for 1978–2002. Accurate interpretation of table 4.7 requires understanding of how default rates are calculated.

The numerous studies of default rates use a variety of calculation methods. For example, Asquith et al. (1989) report that about one in three high yield bond issues default. This is a cumulative default rate that is calculated by using the total outstanding

Table 4.7 Default rates and losses,[a] 1978–2002

Year	Par value outstanding[a] ($ millions)	Par value of default ($ millions)	Default rate (%)	Weighted price after default	Weighted coupon (%)	Default loss (%)
2002	757,000	96,858	12.80	25.3	9.37	10.15[b]
2001	649,000	63,609	9.80	25.5	9.18	7.76
2000	597,200	30,295	5.07	26.4	8.54	3.95
1998	465,500	7,464	1.60	35.9	9.46	1.10
1996	271,000	3,336	1.23	51.9	8.92	0.65
1994	235,000	3,418	1.45	39.4	10.25	0.96
1992	163,000	5,545	3.40	50.1	12.32	1.91
1990	181,000	18,354	10.14	23.4	12.94	8.42
1988	148,187	3,944	2.66	43.6	11.91	1.66
1986	90,243	3,156	3.50	34.5	10.61	2.48
1984	40,939	344	0.84	48.6	12.23	0.48
1982	18,109	577	3.19	38.6	9.61	2.11
1980	14,935	244	1.50	21.1	8.43	1.25
1978	8,946	119	1.33	60.0	8.38	0.59
Arithmetic average[c] 1978–2001:			3.62	$43	11.14	2.19
Weighted average[c] 1978–2001:			5.49			3.16

[a] Excludes defaulted issues.
[b] Default 1 loss rate adjusted for fallen angels is 7.58%.
[c] Averages are based on the full annual sample while the table only reports detailed biannual values.
Source: Altman and Bana (2003)

amount of high yield debt issued in an initial year and dividing this value into the cumulative value of outstanding issues that defaulted for all issues for that year. In contrast, table 4.7 reports the default rate by dividing the par value of outstanding bonds that default in a given year by the total par value outstanding issues for that year. This provides a year-by-year estimate. For example, table 4.7 reports that the default rate on high yield bonds in 1996 was 1.23%. Until the wave of defaults in 2002, the highest level of default reported was for 1991 where a default rate of 10.27% is reported. Results in Altman and Bana (2003) are not confined to this method of estimating default rates, a wealth of other information is provided including defaults by original rating, years to default from original issue date, and defaults by industry.

Table 4.7 also provides information on recovery rates. This is calculated as the weighted average price after default, where the weights are the fraction of the par value of defaults in the year for that issue. Being all less than $30 per $100 par value, the recovery rates for 1999–2002 are at the bottom end of recovery rate values over the last two decades. The strong economic fundamentals of 1992–97 permitted recovery rates that were usually in excess of $50 per $100. Table 4.8 provides further useful information on recovery rates by decomposing the results by type of issue. It is significant that

Table 4.8 Weighted average recovery rates on defaulted debt by seniority per $100 face amount, 1978–2002

Default year	Senior secured		Senior unsecured		Senior subordinated		Subordinated		Discount and zero coupons		All seniorities	
	No.	$	No.	$	No.	$	No.	$	No.	$	No.	$
2002	37	52.81	254	21.82	21	32.79	0	0.00	28	26.47	340	25.32
2001	9	40.95	187	28.84	4	18.37	0	0.00	37	15.05	281	25.48
1998	6	70.38	21	39.57	6	17.54	0	0.00	1	17.00	34	37.27
1996	4	59.08	4	50.11	9	48.99	4	44.23	3	11.99	24	51.91
1994	5	48.66	8	51.14	5	19.81	3	37.04	1	5.00	22	39.44
1992	15	59.85	8	35.61	17	58.20	22	49.13	5	19.82	67	50.03
1990	12	32.18	31	29.02	38	25.0	24	18.83	11	15.63	116	24.66
1988	13	67.96	19	41.99	10	30.70	20	35.27			62	43.45
1986	8	48.32	11	37.72	7	35.20	30	33.39			56	36.60
1984	4	53.42	1	50.50	2	65.8	7	44.68			14	50.62
1982			16	39.31			4	32.91			20	38.03
1980			2	26.71			2	16.63			4	21.67
1978			1	60.00							1	60.00
Total/average	158	52.32	764	35.18	365	29.66	247	31.03	125	21.05	1,659	33.16
Median		55.75		41.99		31.91		31.00		17.50		39.44

Source: Altman and Bana (2003). Total/average values given are for the full sample while detailed information is only listed biannually. Total/average and median values are for all years from 1978–2002

senior secured debt does not provide full protection, with a low recovery rate of $26.90 in 1999 (not reported), below that of the recovery rate of senior unsecured debt in the same year. The implication is that the priority claim of security is less important than it would seem. Another interesting result is the absence of any defaults on subordinated debentures in 2001 and 2002. This is likely the result of less credit worthy companies being generally unable to issue this type of security.

The empirical evidence on credit risk and default risk

Even before Macaulay (1938), there were credit rating services and empirical studies of the relationship between crediting ratings and bond performance. Macaulay (1938, p. 58) captures the essence of the problem involved in making a credit rating:

> In grading bonds at any particular date, we are concerned with how good the bonds *were*, not with how good they *turned out to be*. It is, of course, true that, in a metaphysical sense, how good they turned out to be was how good they really were. But prices and yields can be *directly* affected only by *forecasts* of the future, never by the *facts* of the future. It is, therefore, to forecasts that we must restrict our concept of goodness. It is true that to grade bonds on any basis of how good they *seemed* to be, or even *should* have seemed to be, is to lean upon a flimsy reed. But there is clearly nothing else to do.
>
> Having come to this conclusion, we are faced with the question, should the grading be based on actual or on ideal forecasting, on how good the bonds seemed to be or on how good they *should* have seemed to be. At once we notice that any "should have seemed" grading is tarred with the same stick as grading based on what the future eventually revealed. It is almost always clear, *after the event*, that, though the future is essentially unknowable, a more shrewd and intelligent analysis of the facts that *were* available should have prevented much of the bad forecasting that actually occurred.

Macaulay (1938, pp. 59–60) provides the following assessment of the performance of credit ratings:

> the history of bond prices demonstrates conclusively that . . . bonds are usually graded very incorrectly by the market – and the statisticians. Collapse of the credit of a corporation is seldom seen far in advance; on the other hand, innumerable bonds that pay on time all coupons and the face of the bond are graded low throughout their existence. This is, of course, exactly what might be expected. As the future cannot be known, bonds must be graded on a probability basis and, unless they are of ultra-superior quality, the information available for grading them on such a basis is almost always quite inadequate.

Macaulay (1938) was largely concerned with developing indexes for interest rates. This is an exercise that has to deal directly with the problem of credit assessment in order to evaluate which securities to include in the indexes. As such, Macaulay was a leading authority in the assessment of credit risk.

Macaulay (1938, p. 58) dealt explicitly with the difficulty of developing a credit rating methodology:

this difficulty cannot be overcome by arbitrarily limiting the range of facts upon which forecasts "should have" been based. The essential element in any "should have" system of grading must clearly be that no pertinent and important consideration shall be neglected. To assume, for example, for purposes of yield comparisons, bonds can be more correctly graded by some simple mathematical formula whose variables are all derivable from either present or past financial reports of the debtor corporation than they are in fact graded in the open market is to exhibit an optimism that is difficult if not impossible to defend.

Interpretation of Macaulay's jaded views on credit evaluation needs to be tempered by the historical context. For example, Macaulay was faced with a more difficult problem of assessing credit risk than contemporary researchers, if only because US Treasury securities were not available as a benchmark. This was due to the use of US Treasury securities in the currency system, both before and after the creation of the Federal Reserve system, leading to yields that "were naturally much lower than if the bonds had been valued for their interest payments alone." Macaulay was also faced with the difficulty of obtaining accounting and other information about the firms being rated.

In general, modern credit rating firms do an impressive job of collecting and process-ing information in order to arrive at a credit rating for an individual firm. However, Macaulay's observation that "innumerable bonds that pay on time all coupons and the face of the bond are graded low throughout their existence" still applies today. Table 4.9 provides information from S&P on credit ratings drift over a one to ten year horizon. (Moody's does similar analysis.) The information is presented in the form of a transition matrix that gives the probabilities that a firm rated in one credit category will be in that category or another category a number of years in the future. For example, consider the five year transition matrix for an initially AAA rated firm. Only 60.6% of these firms were still AAA five years hence, while 0.11% had gone into default. In contrast, almost 20% of BBB rated firms and almost 40% of CCC rated had gone into default in five years. The importance of the NR (not rated) category in table creates some difficulty in interpretation.

Table **4.9** Selected transition matrices based on S&P rated issues

Average one-year transition rates

Initial rating	Ratings at end of first year (%)								
	AAA	AA	A	BBB	BB	B	CCC	D	N.R.
AAA	90.34	5.62	0.39	0.08	0.03	0.00	0.00	0.00	3.54
AA	0.64	88.78	6.72	0.47	0.06	0.09	0.02	0.01	3.21
A	0.07	2.16	87.94	4.97	0.47	0.19	0.01	0.04	4.16
BBB	0.03	0.24	4.56	84.26	4.19	0.76	0.15	0.22	5.59
BB	0.03	0.06	0.40	6.09	76.09	6.82	0.96	0.98	8.58
B	0.00	0.09	0.29	0.41	5.11	74.62	3.43	5.30	10.76
CCC	0.13	0.00	0.26	0.77	1.66	8.93	53.19	21.94	13.14

Table 4.9 (*Cont'd*)

Average two-year transition rates

Ratings at end of second year (%)

Initial rating	AAA	AA	A	BBB	BB	B	CCC	D	N.R.
AAA	81.51	10.14	1.05	0.18	0.06	0.03	0.00	0.00	7.04
AA	1.18	79.41	11.87	1.07	0.16	0.18	0.01	0.04	6.09
A	0.10	3.86	77.57	8.60	1.07	0.41	0.03	0.11	8.26
BBB	0.10	0.47	8.44	70.48	6.80	1.46	0.33	0.48	11.44
BB	0.03	0.11	0.87	10.79	56.21	10.11	1.61	2.95	17.32
B	0.00	0.14	0.54	0.92	8.8	53.85	3.83	11.01	20.84
CCC	0.14	0.00	0.57	1.72	2.15	11.61	32.09	28.37	23.35

Average five-year transition rates

Ratings at end of fifth year (%)

Initial rating	AAA	AA	A	BBB	BB	B	CCC	D	N.R.
AAA	60.60	17.32	3.41	0.93	0.14	0.11	0.00	0.11	17.39
AA	2.32	57.01	22.06	3.26	0.53	0.44	0.08	0.24	14.08
A	0.16	6.4	56.74	13.79	2.30	1.12	0.17	0.50	18.87
BBB	0.23	1.25	14.52	44.64	8.47	2.38	0.58	1.76	26.18
BB	0.05	0.30	2.35	15.16	24.23	9.37	1.45	9.14	37.94
B	0.00	0.15	0.87	2.53	10.41	19.42	2.05	19.98	44.59
CCC	0.18	0.00	0.35	2.65	3.36	6.54	7.77	39.22	39.93

Average ten-year transition rates

Ratings at end of tenth year (%)

Initial rating	AAA	AA	A	BBB	BB	B	CCC	D	N.R.
AAA	37.30	20.22	7.84	3.02	0.12	0.00	0.00	0.64	30.85
AA	2.88	33.41	28.09	6.49	0.84	0.24	0.11	0.95	27.00
A	0.37	6.29	37.47	15.23	3.34	1.16	0.11	1.75	34.29
BBB	0.35	1.77	15.71	26.17	6.48	1.57	0.20	4.30	43.45
BB	0.16	0.08	3.44	11.77	7.55	3.32	0.44	18.14	55.12
B	0.00	0.10	0.85	3.07	4.77	3.92	0.38	29.48	57.43
CCC	0.26	0.00	0.26	1.05	3.67	1.83	0.00	46.86	46.07

Source: Table 16 in Leo Brand and Reza Bahar, "Corporate defaults: will things get worse before they get better?" Special Report, Standard & Poor's Corporation

Table 4.10 Defaults by original rating (investment grades vs. non-investment grade, by year)

	Defaulted issues[a]	% originally rated investment grade	% originally rated non-investment grade
2002	321	39	61
2001	258	14	86
2000	142	16	84
1998	39	31	69
1996	24	13	88
1994	16	0	100
1992	59	25	75
1990	117	16	84
1988	64	42	58
1986	55	15	85
1984	14	21	79
1982	20	55	45
1980	4	25	75
1978	1	100	0
Total	1,511	23	77

[a] Where an original rating from either S&P or Moody's was available.
Source: Altman and Bana (2003). Total values given are for the full sample while detailed information is only listed biannually

Another approach to the assessment of default is provided in table 4.10 that reports on the percentage of defaults, by year, classified according to the original rating. The 41% of defaulting issues in 2002 that were originally rated as investment grade is almost disturbing. If included in table 4.9, this would also have an impact on the estimates of the credit ratings transition matrix.

Examining the evidence in table 4.11 reveals that, while the bulk of defaults occur within 5 years of the initial issue date, in years when default rates are high such as 2001–2, issues that have had a longer life also default. In periods of strong economic activity, e.g., 1996–8, few issues default that have been in the market for more than five years. In assessing credit ratings, it is important to recognize that the pricing implications of credit ratings relate to the credit spreads in yields.

Figure 4.1 captures the time series properties of investment quality bonds. Yet, the relationship between yields on such bonds needs to be carefully compared to yields on bonds that are considered to be below investment grade. The difficulty with making such a comparison is that the dispersion of yields from bond to bond is less systematic due to factors such as industry and firm characteristics. With this in mind, table 4.12 provides credit spreads for both investment and non-investment grade bonds for issuers that are banks. For a number of reasons, e.g., the regulatory structure, this group is

Table 4.11 Distribution of years to default from original issuance date (by year of default, 1990–2002)

Years to default	1990		1992		1993/4		1996	
	No. of issues	% of total	No. of issues	% of total	No. of issues	% of total	No. of issues	% of total
1	3	3	0	0	3	8	2	8
2	25	23	0	0	6	16	3	13
3	23	21	7	13	5	14	3	13
4	18	17	10	19	2	5	8	33
5	23	21	8	15	4	11	1	4
6	5	5	12	22	2	6	5	21
7	5	5	5	9	7	19	0	0
8	4	4	4	7	0	0	0	0
9	1	1	0	0	0	0	0	0
10	1	1	8	15	2	5	2	8
Total	108	100	54	100	37	100	24	100

Years to default	1998		2000		2001		2002	
	No. of issues	% of total	No. of issues	% of total	No. of issues	% of total	No. of issues	% of total
1	2	6	19	10	40	12	29	8
2	5	15	51	28	69	21	51	15
3	10	30	56	31	87	26	61	18
4	3	9	14	8	65	19	56	16
5	10	30	13	7	27	8	45	13
6	2	6	5	3	14	4	21	6
7	1	3	12	7	21	6	8	2
8	0	0	4	2	5	1	7	2
9	0	0	3	2	4	1	12	3
10	0	0	6	3	3	1	54	16
Total	33	100	183	100	335	100	344	100

Source: Altman and Bana (2003)

more homogeneous than, say, oil and gas drillers. Examination of table 4.12 dramatically illustrates an important characteristic of credit spreads: the sizable premium that appears when a bond is graded below investment grade BBB-. The empirical rationale for such a premium is not supported in the default by rating data or in the ratings drift statistics. Even though the observation date for table 4.12 is associated with relatively wide credit spreads, this result is robust across time.

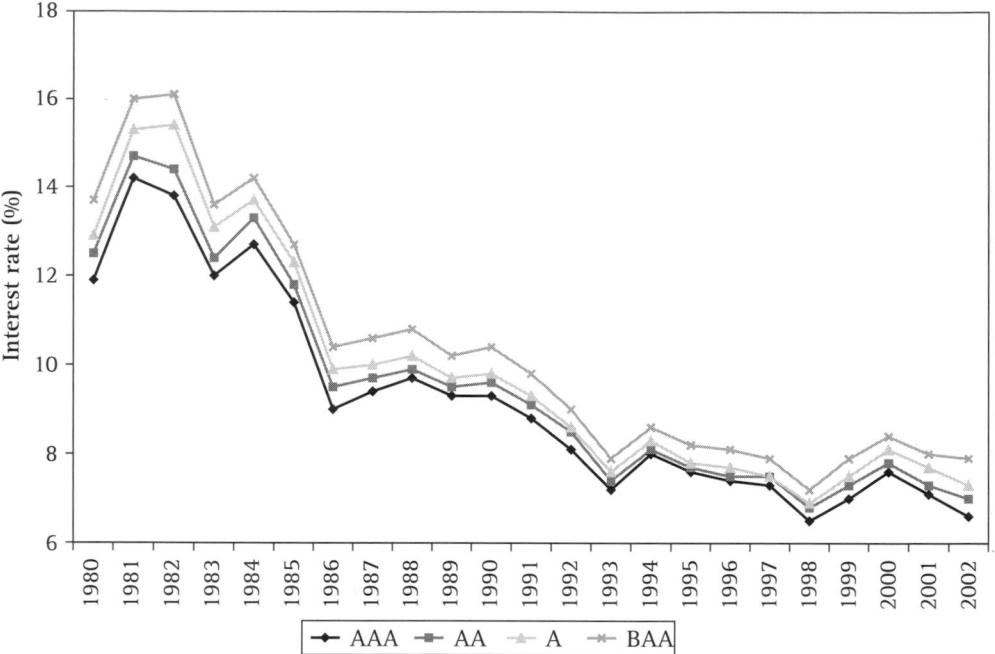

Figure 4.1 Interest spreads for investment grade bonds, 1980–2002

Table 4.12 Reuters corporate spreads for banks for February 10, 2003 (in basis points)

Ratings	1 year	2 year	3 year	5 year	7 year	10 year	30 year
Aaa/AAA	27	36	47	61	74	88	107
Aa1/AA+	33	49	53	61	84	99	118
Aa2/AA	35	54	56	75	87	101	121
Aa3/AA−	37	57	58	80	91	105	130
A1/A+	61	73	77	95	107	123	145
A2/A	64	76	79	97	108	125	148
A3/A−	68	79	82	101	115	128	150
Baa1/BBB+	81	98	104	124	153	180	202
Baa2/BBB	84	106	112	130	158	183	207
Baa3/BBB−	91	111	117	135	163	190	212
Ba1/BB+	605	615	625	635	655	675	695
Ba2/BB	615	625	635	645	665	685	705
Ba3/BB−	625	635	645	655	675	695	715
B1/B+	775	785	795	825	865	905	955
B2/B	785	795	805	835	875	915	965
B3/B−	795	805	815	845	885	925	975
Caa/CCC	1,195	1,205	1,215	1,240	1,270	1,330	1,280

Source: www.bondsonline.com (Bond Market Association website)

Questions ?

1 Your father is about to retire. His firm has given him the option of retiring with a lump sum of $50,000 or an annuity of $8,000 for 10 years. Which is worth more if the discount rate is: (a) 6%; (b) 18%?

2 You are in the market for a house. Your effective all-in market borrowing rate for a house mortgage from a bank is 10%. One of the houses you are considering purchasing has an assumable $200,000, 5 year mortgage at 8%, with a 20 year amortization. The asking price on the house is $400,000. What is the value of the concessionary financing for this house?

3 The following is a list of prices for (riskless) zero-coupon bonds of various maturities: 1 year, $97.10; 2 year, $92.50; 5 year, $74.70; 10 year, $50.80; 30 year, $13.10. Calculate: the yields to maturity of each bond; and, all possible implied forward rates.

4 Briefly explain the relationship between expectations of future interest rates and implied forward rates calculated from the current term structure of interest rates in the expectations, liquidity preference and market segmentation hypotheses.

5 A bond offers semi-annual coupon payments of $3 (i.e, it is a 6% coupon bond) and will repay its face value of $100 at the end of five years. You observe that other similar bonds have yields to maturity of 8%. How much is this bond worth? If the coupons are paid quarterly, how much is the bond worth?

6 Using the information in table 1.9, calculate the implied zero coupon rates for the US Treasury curve. Compare these rates to the observed interest rates for US Treasury strips. Using the information from table 4.5 plot the yield curve for government of Canada issues. Calculate the associated spot rate curve and plot the spot rate curve against the yield curve. Does the spot rate curve lie above or below the yield curve? Does your answer change if the yield curve is inverted?

7 Demonstrate that the duration formula for an annual coupon par bond is equal to:

$$\frac{1 + y}{y}\left[1 - \frac{1}{(1 + y)^T}\right].$$

NOTES

1 There are a number of excellent sources that cover in considerable detail the basics and beyond for fixed income analysis. Essential sources include Fabozzi (2000, 2002), Garbade (1996) and Sundaresan (2002). In addition to the generalist practitioner journals, such as the *Financial Analysts Journal* and the *Journal of Portfolio Management*, there are also some excellent journals dedicated to this topic such as the *Journal of Fixed Income*.

2 For more detail on the specific holdings in the Government Account Series see the *Treasury Bulletin*, table FD-3.

3 Due to complications associated with stripping callable bonds, since the introduction of the STRIPS program in 1985 the US Treasury has not issued bonds with call features. Prior to this date, the 30 year US Treasury bond issues had 25 years until the call date, i.e., the bonds were callable during the last five year period at the end of the term to maturity. As with corporate bonds, this feature was incorporated in order to facilitate refunding of the issue. As there was 25 years to the call date at primary issue, the cost of the call feature had a negligible impact on the new issue price Circa. 2003, there are about 15 callable Treasury issues outstanding.

4 Though the three types of closed-end bond funds differ in the tax treatment of the dividend income distribution, capital gains or losses are taxed the same as for other securities.

5 Unlike open-end funds, closed-end funds do not continuously offer their shares for sale. A fixed number of shares are sold at one time (in the initial public offering), after which the shares trade on a secondary market, such as the New York Stock Exchange (NYSE) or the American Stock Exchange (AMEX). The price of closed-end bond fund shares that trade on a secondary market after their initial public offering is determined by the market and may be greater or less than the shares' net asset value. Akhigbe and Madura (2001) examine the performance of seasoned offerings of closed-end funds.

6 For the specific dates examined, both these sources report that implied zero and strip rates are approximately equal at short maturities with implied zeros being slightly below strip rates at intermediate maturities and strip rates being well below the implied zero rate at long maturities. (See end of chapter exercises.)

7 If the settlement date is the same as the date the money market security is purchased, then $tsm = T - t$. However, as there is a usually a settlement lag, this is not usually the case. For longer term securities it is possible to ignore the settlement lag without having a significant impact on pricing. In addition, the impact of the settlement lag can be captured in the calculation of accrued interest, an element of the price that is being ignored for pedagogical reasons. However, the short term to maturity for money market securities and the absence of accrued interest makes the settlement lag an important element. The *tsm* notation is designed to recognize this impact.

8 There are a number of possible complications which can be introduced such as: the coupon payments (and compounding) occurring more than once a year; and, the dollar price change being required instead of % price change. Both these changes occurred in the 1994 exam.

9 References to Hicks (1939) are to the second edition of 1946. Changes between the first and second editions were largely aimed at correcting errors in the derivation of the consumer's choice problem and adding a brief discussion of the connection to Samuelson's dynamic treatment of the problems examined in Hicks (1939).

10 The "term structure of interest rates" terminology can also be used to refer to implied zero coupon rates derived from bonds with default risk, e.g., Bierwag et al. (1992) refer to the duration of bonds from different term structures where the term structures differ due to default risk. However, where further qualification is not given, the term structure of interest rates refers to default free securities.

11 In a binomial model these relationships would be somewhat more complicated as the evolution

of zero coupon interest rates is determined by taking the expected value of the interest rates at the two future nodes, discounted back at the interest rate for the previous node. This point is discussed in section 5.2.

12 The discussion in this section relates to bonds but the basic concepts apply to all fixed income securities. For example, there is default risk on a mortgage that will be reflected in, say, the requirement that mortgage insurance be purchased at the time the mortgage is issued. Loans at commercial banks will feature different rates of interest to reflect the different assessed credit ratings for borrowers.

13 Though default on federal, state and local government debt is possible, the legal implications are more complicated. Though only the case of corporate default is examined in detail, the basic principles of the issuer seeking protection under the bankruptcy laws and the purchaser seeking remedies under the terms of the debt contract still applies.

14 Other important factors that can influence the yield spread between two different debt issues are: the liquidity; differences in covenants and special provisions such as callability; and, the tax status of the coupon and principal payments.

Chapter
Summary

Chapter 5 *Convexity, Time Value and Immunization*

5.1   Fixed Income Portfolio Management
      Institutional considerations
      Classical immunization
      Portfolio management and international bond portfolios

5.2   Mathematics for Advanced Fixed Income Analysis*
      Taylor series solutions*
      Stochastic processes and Ito's lemma*
      Binomial models and other discrete processes*

5.3   The Time Value–Convexity Tradeoff*
      The contribution from convexity*
      The Taylor series representation of the time value–convexity tradeoff*
      A continuous time solution for the time value–convexity tradeoff*

5.4   Immunization with Non-parallel Yield Curve Shifts*
      Partial durations and convexities*
      Duration and convexity bounds*
      Some basic calculations and examples*

Questions
Notes

* Indicates sections and subsections that can be considered as advanced material

Convexity, Time Value and Immunization

 5.1   FIXED INCOME PORTFOLIO MANAGEMENT

Institutional considerations

The conventional starting point for an examination of fixed income portfolio management is the *classical immunization rules*. The development of immunization rules can be traced to Redington (1952) which provides theoretical conditions to address the general problem of ensuring that funds accumulating in a fixed income portfolio are sufficient to discharge a portfolio of future liabilities. Though Redington considered the case of a life insurance company, the rules apply to a wide range of situations. In most applications, the liabilities are well defined and the primary source of risk is the impact of future changes in interest rates on the return from a portfolio of fixed income securities. It is possible to generalize the asset portfolio to include other securities than just fixed income. More generally, immunization rules can be viewed as strategies for managing the balance sheet to control the impact of changes in interest rates.

A discussion of immunization strategies typically begins with the properties of fixed income securities, e.g., Bierwag (1987). To motivate the discussion, it is convenient to consider the potential interactions between the underlying business and the selection of securities required to address the immunization problem. There are numerous important applications of this problem, including *management of pension fund portfolios, life insurance funds* and *financial institution portfolios.* The structure of the portfolio management decision will differ depending on the specifics of the underlying business. For example, a property and casualty company may face the possibility of a large stochastic liability payout that can occur at the single date in the future due to, say, a large hurricane hitting the Florida coast. In contrast, a life insurance company will typically have a more predictable liability structure due to the connection with the more predictable payouts associated with the life table for the pool of policy holders.

Immunization is not the only possible portfolio management strategy that could be used to manage fixed income portfolios or, more generally, the balance sheets of financial institutions. Four of the most important strategies that can be used are: *dedication* or *cash flow matching*, where the cash flow from the fixed income assets is structured to match the requirements of a portfolio of predetermined liabilities; *immunization*, where the interest rate sensitivity of the cash flows from the fixed income assets and liabilities is matched (*contingent immunization* permits the fund manager to incorporate expectations into the immunization decision); *dollar duration matching*, which extends immunization to positive surplus situations; and, *horizon matching*, which combines dedication and immunization methods by dividing the assets and liabilities being managed into two parts, one part being managed with dedication and the other with immunization. The selection of a particular method of portfolio management will depend on the specifics of the situation. For example, if it is not possible to precisely specify the cash flow requirements associated with the liabilities, then it is not possible to use cash flow matching.

What is the appropriate strategy to use for, say, a life insurance company? In theory, the liability structure of a life company will depend on the age and health characteristics of the pool of policy holders. However, life companies offer a range of products including whole life, guaranteed insurance contracts (GIC's) and various of types of bundled and unbundled fixed income and life contingent securities.[1] These products may contain various types of embedded options such as floors, caps and collars. In addition, insurance companies operate in a competitive business environment for the products being sold requiring premiums and rates of return to be offered that are competitive with other types of financial intermediaries. Insurance companies are subject to a range of specific and general regulations, e.g., state insurance laws that impose actuarial restrictions on the composition and rate of return of the asset portfolio. Though it may be possible for insurance companies to employ some cash flow matching, immunization strategies provide greater potential for achieving competitive advantages from asset management.

In the US, insurance companies are subject to state regulation though there have been recent efforts to develop a federal presence. The National Association of Insurance Commissioners (NAIC) serves the role of bringing state regulators and regulations into collective agreement facilitating, for example, the reduction in the regulatory burden on insurance companies operating in multiple state jurisdictions and acting as a vehicle for the implementation of a collective accreditation program, e.g., Vaughan (2002). An important element of the NAIC initiatives is the introduction of a risk based capital system aimed to establish uniform minimum capitalization standards across states, e.g., Barth (2001). Introduced in 1993, the risk based capital (RBC) requirement met considerable resistance from the industry due to concerns about onerous capital requirements being imposed. The evolution of the implementation of RBC requirements reveals that these concerns were largely unfounded.

A number of useful points can be gleaned from the RBC implementation by insurance companies. For example, the asset portfolios of most insurance companies, both life and property/casualty contain a significant amount of non-fixed income securities, such as equities. By implication this would tend to reduce the applicability of a pure immunization model. Yet, despite some qualifications, Barth (2001, p. 240) is able to conclude:

> One of the most important outcomes of the RBC system is that the insurance industry itself now has a better understanding of financial risk. Insurers have long been recognized

experts on insurable risk, but the new emphasis on financial risk and capitalization have improved not only the safety but also the efficiency of the insurance industry. New private initiatives into risk measurement and modeling such as dynamic financial analysis and value-at-risk are becoming more prevalent throughout the industry.

Recognizing the duration and convexity can be interpreted as value-at-risk measures for interest rate changes, e.g., Jorion (2001), the relevance of immunization theory for the management of insurance companies is apparent.

Portfolio management for an insurance company is considerably more complicated than, say, for a private company pension fund where investment decisions can be more focused on the sole objective of maximizing the benefits accruing to fund beneficiaries, subject to the actuarial and legal requirements imposed on pension fund managers, e.g., FAS 87 governing the reporting of changes in pension surplus (deficit) in the firm's financial statements. Following Jorion (2001, ch. 17), value-at-risk modeling can be of some value in pension fund management, particularly for large funds that are involved in active trading. As such, classical immunization theory has value for the management of interest rate risk. However, much like insurance companies, the asset portfolios of most pension funds are invested in a range of interest sensitive and interest insensitive assets. As such, the connection may not be as clean as desired. Arguably, it is institutions such as commercial banks that provide the most important application for immunization strategies.

Many banking institutions fall within the scope of the risk based capital requirements that evolved from the 1988 Basle Accord and the subsequent revisions of 1996 and 1999. These accords institutionalize the use of risk management techniques such as value-at-risk for the assessment of capital requirements. This development lends considerable support to the importance of immunization methods when it is recognized that banking institutions in the US are subject to a range of regulations that restrict the balance sheet to largely interest sensitive securities. For example, there are restrictions on the ability of commercial banks to invest directly in equity securities. In addition, the large number of stochastic inflows and outflows make it impractical, if not impossible, for banking institutions to use cash flow matching.

Classical immunization

For pedagogical purposes, it is convenient to develop theoretical conditions for immunization under the assumptions of perfect markets. Particular assumptions can then be relaxed to allow the immunization conditions to be adapted to a specific situation. A key parameter governing the immunization problem is the date at which an obligation is to be discharged, i.e., the *planning* or *investment horizon*. The selection of the investment horizon is a problem for funds that have *multiple* planning periods making it difficult to administer using techniques that treat each individual liability separately by creating dedicated portfolios for each liability, i.e., using *cash flow matching*. The advantage of the immunization approach to portfolio management is that it is possible to treat all the different funds associated with the different possible planning periods and manage these funds as a single investment fund with a single investment horizon.

The initial statement and solution of the classical immunization problem is due to F.M. Redington (1952), a British actuary. Redington posed the following problem: What allocation of assets and liabilities would minimize a life insurance company's possibility of losses from unexpected changes in market rates of interest? If the initial difference between the market value of assets and liabilities is greater than or equal to zero, Redington proposed that if fund managers adhere to two rules there would be sufficient assets in the portfolio to discharge the liabilities. *Redington's rules*, known as the *classical immunization conditions*, are:

1 *Duration matching*: duration of cash inflows equals the duration of the outflows.
2 *Higher convexity of assets*: when there is more than one planning period for the fund to satisfy, the value of the cash inflows should be more "dispersed" around the duration than the value of the cash outflows.[2]

Together, (1) and (2) form the basis of the classical immunization approach to fixed income portfolio analysis.

Redington (1952, p. 290) derived these rules by specifying the "present value of the liability outgo" (V_L) and the "present value of the asset-proceeds" (V_A), both discounted at the same rate of interest. These two present values are then assumed to be equal with "any excess being 'free' funds to be separately invested." This means that Redington was not assuming a zero surplus fund, per se, but was modeling the immunization problem by creating a segmented problem with the surplus considered separately. Redington then evaluates the impact of a change in the interest rate using a Taylor series expansion (see section 5.2). Using the ε form of the expansion (see endnote 4), Redington states the expansion as:

$$V_A' - V_L' = (V_A - V_L) + \varepsilon \frac{d(V_A - V_L)}{dy} + \frac{\varepsilon^2}{2!} \frac{d^2(V_A - V_L)}{dy^2} + \dots$$

Redington then observes that the first term will be zero by assumption and: "In practice the first derivative is the most important for small changes of the rate of interest and I shall define a fund as immunized if the assets are invested so that $[d(V_A - V_L)/dy]$ is zero."

Redington deals with the convexity term by observing that if $[d^2(V_A - V_L)/dy^2] > 0$ then any change in interest "will result in a profit to the fund so long as the change is not so large that the higher terms in the expansion begin to take effect." Redington felt that higher convexity for assets relative to liabilities was "desirable" but used illustrations that showed "the point is not of great importance." Redington then states the theoretical conditions for "a satisfactory immunization policy" by specifying that the first derivative in the Taylor series be zero, i.e., equate the duration of assets and liabilities, and that the second derivative be positive, i.e., the convexity of assets be greater than the convexity of the liabilities. Given this result, the bulk of Redington (1952) is concerned with developing the implications of these immunization rules. For example, Redington

(p. 291) recognizes that the perpetuity represents a limit to the possible asset duration, i.e., the possibility of a duration gap is identified. There are so many insights contained in Redington (1952) that the contribution can still be considered required reading for those seeking to understand the application of immunization theory.

Introductory presentations of the classical immunization conditions assume there is one planning period and a liability with a single payout at a specific date in the future. In this case only the duration matching condition need be considered as the convexity condition is automatically satisfied. This leads to the result: when the initial market value of assets and liabilities is zero (there is no fund surplus or the surplus is treated separately) then immunization occurs when the Macaulay duration of assets equals the Macaulay duration of liabilities. The basic idea behind duration matching in this case requires assuming one planning period and that the liability is in the form of a single cash flow that has to be paid at T, the end of the investment horizon, and that there are only coupon bonds available for investment. If only one bond is purchased to fund the liability, duration matching requires that the liability be covered by buying a coupon bond with a longer term to maturity than the investment horizon. Term to maturity matching of the liability and the asset will fail.

Redington summaries the logic of the immunization rule for a life insurance company as:

> A sceptical reader may ask how it is possible to immunize existing business when, even if no new business is written, the funds will continue to grow for some years, and require the investment of that growth at unknown rates of interest. The verbal answer to this question is that, if the rate of interest falls, there will be a shortfall in the yield on the future investments which have to be made, but there will be an exactly balancing excess in the appreciation of existing investments which have been invested for longer terms than the liabilities they have to meet.

In other words, there are two risks from holding the bond: (1) coupon reinvestment risk; and, (2) risk of capital gain or loss on the bond when it is sold at the end of the investment horizon. Duration matching implies that the time required for investment accumulation associated with coupon reinvestment to offset any capital gain or loss from changing yields is exactly equal to the initial duration. Taking T to be the length of the investment horizon (the payout date on the single liability in the simple case), if $D_A > T$ then the capital gain or loss will dominate the coupon reinvestment return. If $D_A < T$ the coupon reinvestment return will exceed the capital gain or loss.

As Redington explicitly recognized, immunization requires that the portfolio be rebalanced as time goes on, e.g., after each coupon payment date, in order to ensure that the durations of assets and liabilities are equal. "The equations define the position at a moment of time. Their solutions change continuously." In the case of a life insurance company, these changes could be due to "changes in the constitution of the business" or, "for a fixed block of business," due to the diminishing term to maturity of the assets and liabilities with the passage of time. Redington recognizes that cash flow matching ("'absolute' matching") is a specific case of immunization where all the terms in the Taylor series are zero and changes in the rate of interest will have no impact "however violent." In addition, Redington recognizes: "The theory would be difficult to interpret in practice because of the existence of such assets as equity shares, properties, mortgages on an open basis, and so on. Either the income, or the term, or both, of many assets are indeterminate."

Classical immunization theory is, at heart, a hedging theory. As Redington observes: "It has to be remembered that apart from the minor second derivative profits the immunization is against profit as well as loss." Duration measures the $\%\Delta P_B$ when yields change instantaneously, it is not a measure of the return on a bond. For example, consider the case of a zero coupon bond. If the change in yields is zero the return is obtained as the price of the bond increases over time. Similarly, if yields do not change, then the price of par bonds will not change but the return will be obtained by the receipt of coupon income. Duration does not provide any guidance about return in these situations. However, it is possible to use immunization methods to design profitable strategies such as those aimed at "riding the yield curve." Similarly, contingent immunization theory can be used to model key problems in the fund management, such as surplus immunization, and in the management of financial institutions seeking duration gap management.

Portfolio management of international bond portfolios

Classical immunization proposes rules involving the duration and convexity of assets and liabilities. In this approach to fixed income portfolio management, duration is interpreted as the elasticity of the bond price with respect to $(1 + y)$. Even if the problem of currency translation is ignored, the extension of domestic duration to foreign bond prices still poses a problem:

$$-\frac{1+y}{P_{Bf}}\frac{dP_{Bf}}{d(1+y)} = -\frac{1+y}{1+y_f}\frac{1+y_f}{P_{Bf}}\frac{dP_{Bf}}{d(1+y_f)}\frac{d(1+y_f)}{d(1+y)}$$

$$= -\frac{1+y_f}{P_{Bf}}\frac{dP_{Bf}}{d(1+y_f)}\frac{1+y}{1+y_f}\frac{d(1+y_f)}{d(1+y)} = D_f^* \cdot \eta_{y_f,y}$$

where P_{Bf} is the price of the foreign bond denominated in foreign currency terms, y_f is the yield on the foreign bond, and D_f^* is the Macaulay duration (foreign duration) measured as the elasticity of the foreign bond price with respect to the foreign yield. This result shows that the elasticity of the foreign bond price with respect to a change in domestic interest rates is the product of two elasticities: the foreign duration, i.e., the elasticity of the foreign bond price with respect to $(1 + y_f)$; and, the elasticity of the foreign interest rate with respect to the domestic interest rate.

Given this, it follows that unless changes in foreign and domestic interest rates are highly correlated, then domestic duration will not be a useful measure of interest rate risk for a foreign bond. To get some idea of the size of the relationship between foreign and domestic interest rates, consider the correlation coefficients for changes in monthly 10 year government bond interest rates across major industrialized countries observed from 2/84 to 09/90 given in table 5.1.[3] (By construction, these bond interest rates are

Table 5.1 Correlation coefficients for monthly changes in 10-year government bond interest rates, February 1984–October 1990

	Canada	France	Italy	Japan	Netherlands	Switzerland	UK	W. Germany	US	US*
Canada	1	0.4400	0.1340	0.4865	0.3271	0.2243	0.3944	0.5657	0.8339	(0.70)
France	0.4400	1	0.2000	0.2868	0.5712	0.1364	0.3302	0.4727	0.4711	(0.65)
Italy	0.1340	0.2000	1	0.0923	0.1760	0.2251	−0.0522	0.1579	0.2155	(0.30)
Japan	0.4865	0.2868	0.0923	1	0.3503	0.3368	0.3456	0.5486	0.4517	(0.65)
Netherlands	0.3271	0.5712	0.1760	0.3503	1	0.2956	0.4881	0.6785	0.3894	(0.65)
Switzerland	0.2243	0.1364	0.2251	0.3358	0.2956	1	0.1889	0.2249	0.2780	(0.55)
UK	0.3944	0.3302	−0.0522	0.3456	0.4881	0.1889	1	0.5261	0.3081	(0.55)
W. Germany	0.5657	0.4727	0.1579	0.5486	0.6785	0.2249	0.5261	1	0.5123	
United States	0.8339	0.4711	0.2155	0.4517	0.3894	0.2780	0.3081	0.5123	1	

Sources: Government bond interest rates from Bloomberg Financial Markets, adapted from Dym (1992). Values in (US*) column are from Thomas and Willner (1997) for a monthly sample over 1977–95

calculated in terms of the currency of issue.) Though there is a high correlation of .8339 between the US/Canada, correlations are typically much lower with Italy and the UK, two members of the European Monetary System (EMS), even exhibiting negative correlations. (The EMS was a precursor of the European Monetary Union). As indicated by the bracketed correlation coefficients in table 5.1, empirical evidence from other sources for different sample periods indicates that there is some variation when different samples are used. On balance, these empirical results confirm that duration for foreign bonds (measured in terms of domestic interest rate changes) will tend to be inaccurate indicators of the price elasticity with respect to domestic interest rate changes.

Following Dym (1992) and Thomas and Willner (1997), it is possible to extend the duration measure to produce a risk measure for the change in a bond price, measured in terms of the issue currency. Recalling that the total derivative of $\ln[x]$, $d\{\ln[x]\} = (1/x)\, dx = dx/x$, manipulation of the duration formula gives:

$$d\{\ln[P_{Bf}]\} = \frac{dP_{Bf}}{P_{Bf}} = -D^* \cdot d\{\ln[1 + y_f]\}$$

This form directly illustrates the role played by duration in translating yield changes into bond price changes. A risk measure associated with domestic returns now follows from evaluating the standard deviation of dP/P:

$$RM = Risk = std[dP_{Bf}/P_{Bf}] = (D^*)\, std[d\{\ln[1 + y_f]\}]$$

where $std\,[\,\cdot\,]$ is the standard deviation operator. The resulting decomposition of the right hand side of the equation, together with the calculated risk measure, is provided in table 5.2. The large difference in the local yield volatility is apparent. Contrary to the

Table 5.2 Government bond interest rate risk measures, February 1984–October 1990[a]

Country	Macaulay duration	Yield volatility (×100)	Average yield (%)	RM (risk measure)	β (beta)
Canada	6.34	0.3867	10.55	0.0222	1.0838
France	6.48	0.3695	10.29	0.0217	0.6871
Italy	6.07	0.7696	12.19	0.0416	0.6052
Japan	7.33	0.3286	5.52	0.0228	0.8226
Netherlands	6.84	0.2366	7.16	0.0151	0.4767
Switzerland	7.35	0.1876	7.87	0.0128	0.2514
UK	6.22	0.4439	10.49	0.0250	0.7528
W. Germany	6.86	0.2503	7.01	0.0160	0.6018
US	6.92	0.3878	9.25	0.0246	1.1874

[a] β measures the change in the foreign government bond yield relative to changes in the Merrill Lynch Global Bond index measure of global interest rates.

prediction of the simple duration model, the riskiest bonds do not have the highest durations. Quite the opposite, the highest duration bond (Switzerland) has the lowest risk and the lowest duration bond (Italy) has the highest risk.

Ultimately, the domestic (US) currency return on a foreign bond requires incorporating exchange risk. In addition, it is useful to decompose a given bond interest volatility into the influence of local and global interest rate movements, where the global component is measured by a market size weighted average of long-term bond rates of industrialized countries as measured by the Merrill-Lynch global bond market index. In this case, a CAPM-type model for bond pricing can be introduced:

$$\Delta(1 + y_f) = \Delta y = \beta \, \Delta I + \Delta u$$

where I is the global interest rate and u is the random error term representing the country specific (local) component. Estimates for β are provided in table 5.2. Assuming independence of u and I gives:

$$var[\Delta(1 + y_f)] = \beta^2 \, var[\Delta(1 + I)] + var[\Delta(1 + u)]$$

where $var[\ \cdot \ ]$ is the variance operator. This result can be used to decompose the domestic currency denominated interest rate risk of a foreign bond into local and global components.

The results for bond returns denominated in the currency of issue confirm, to a certain extent, the importance of the composition of the global portfolio. This is reflected in the size of the global component in the individual country measures for interest rate risk. Given this, correlations among changes in the local factors (not reported) are typically small for the non-EMS currencies. Correlations between EMS currencies and the currencies that compose the bulk of the global market portfolio, i.e., Japan and the US, are typically negative. Given this information on the risk structure of the domestic currency denominated bond returns, it is now possible to extend the analysis to permit the return of each bond to be valued in US dollars. In this case the bond's US dollar value at time t, $V(t)$, will equal $P_{Bf}(t)/S(t)$, where $S(t)$ is measured in foreign (not US) direct terms. Taking logs and first differences gives:

$$\Delta \ln V = -D^* \cdot \Delta \ln [1 + y_f] - \Delta \ln e$$

where $e = dS/S$. Given this it is now possible to determine a domestic currency denominated risk measure that accounts for the risks of local and global interest rates and the exchange rate.

The procedure for developing the measure extends the method used for table 5.2. Consider first:

$$Std \ [\Delta \ln[V]] = \sqrt{(D^*)^2 \, var[\Delta \ln[1 + y_f]] + var[\Delta \ln[e]] + 2D^* \, cov[\Delta \ln[1 + y_f], \ \Delta \ln[e]]}$$

where $cov[\ \cdot \ ]$ is the covariance operator. Following Dym (1992, pp. 87–8), it is now possible to substitute the CAPM-type model of interest rates for $\Delta(1 + y_f)$ to provide

Table 5.3 Components of the risk of the domestic currency return for foreign government bonds divided by total foreign bond risk, February 1984–October 1990[a]

Country	Global interest rate	Local interest rate	Exchange rate	Global interest/ exchange rate covariance	Local interest/ exchange rate covariance
Canada	0.4226	0.2485	0.1834	0.0780	0.0672
France	0.0860	0.2255	0.6304	0.1005	−0.0425
Italy	0.0313	0.6013	0.3210	0.0501	−0.0039
Japan	0.1254	0.1233	0.5285	0.1533	0.0692
Netherlands	0.0469	0.0967	0.6951	0.0845	0.0766
Switzerland	0.0154	0.0908	0.7623	0.0516	0.0797
UK	0.0575	0.1914	0.4639	0.0518	0.2352
W. Germany	0.0746	0.0858	0.6561	0.1111	0.0722
US	0.7421	0.2579	–	–	–

[a] All values are expressed in terms of shares of $std[\Delta \ln[V]]$ where std is the standard deviation and V is the domestic (US) currency value of the foreign government bond. Values may not sum to one due to rounding error.

Source: Adapted from Dym (1992)

a decomposition of foreign bond risk into the relevant components associated with global interest rate risk, local interest rate risk and exchange rate risk. Recognizing that the local and global interest rate components have no covariance by construction, there will also be covariance terms for the exchange rate with the global and local interest rate components. Dividing these risk components by $std[\Delta \ln[V]]$ reexpresses the values in terms of percentage contribution to the total risk. These results are given in table 5.3.

Examination of table 5.3 reveals that, for a US investor, the addition that currency risk makes to total risk is similar to the results reported in table 1.14. More precisely, though there is significant variation in the exchange rate component across countries, the general result is that the bulk of the risk associated with unhedged holding of foreign government bonds is associated with the exchange rate. Excluding Canada and Italy, the impact of global and local interest rate changes is not much different from the covariance parts. In the Canadian case, the relatively stable US$/C$ exchange rate results in the contribution of currency risk to total risk for Canadian bonds being well below 20%. Another exception is Italy where more than 60% of the total risk was due to the local interest rate component. A number of countries exhibited high positive covariance terms, either with the global or local interest rate component. The variation in the local interest rate/exchange rate covariance shares could be partially due to the use of domestic interest rate policy to control the spot exchange rate.

5.2 MATHEMATICS FOR ADVANCED FIXED INCOME ANALYSIS*

*Taylor series solutions**

The Taylor series expansion is one of the most practical and widely used tools of real analysis, e.g., Rudin (1964). The technique is a special type of power series expansion that applies to **analytic functions.** The basic idea is a specific solution to the more general problem of approximation of functions, a topic that has occupied mathematicians for centuries. Functions appear in a wide range of situations. Real analysis is concerned with functions defined using real variables, i.e., defined over a subset of the real line ($\Re^1$) for functions of one variable and $\Re^1 \times \Re^1 \times \ldots$ for functions of n variables. The restriction that the function be "analytic" imposes further conditions on the function. For a function of one variable, these conditions are that the function be continuous and differentiable in the interval of convergence of the power series. In fixed income security analysis, the main function of interest is the value or price function. For default and option free bonds, the price function is convex in the yield to maturity, a property that easily satisfies the conditions required for a Taylor series to be used. With appropriate restrictions, Taylor series expansions can be used to extend the analysis to bonds with option features or the possibility of default.

The Taylor series technique can be illustrated by making a comparison between the discrete and continuous forms of discounting operators (where t^* is the fraction of the year remaining to maturity). Observe that for $t^* \leq 1$ with the continuous discounting operator $\ln[\exp\{-rt^*\}] = -rt^*$, the corresponding $\ln[(1 + rt^*)^{-1}]$ for the discrete compounding case does not provide a similar simple solution but can be evaluated by taking a **Taylor series expansion.** For a function of one variable, this expansion takes the general form:[4]

$$f[x] = f[a] + \frac{df[a]}{dx}(x - a) + \frac{1}{2!}\frac{d^2f[a]}{dx^2}(x - a)^2 + \frac{1}{3!}\frac{d^3f[a]}{dx^3}(x - a)^3 + \ldots$$

In other words, any function $f[x]$ that has continuous derivatives over some interval $[b, c]$ can be equivalently expressed as the converging infinite sum provided by the Taylor series. This expression expands the univariate function $f[x]$ about the fixed point a, where $b \leq a \leq c$. Each of the derivatives in the expansion are evaluated by setting $x = a$. For this expansion to be valid, the function $f[x]$ must have derivatives of all orders over $[b, c]$ (some of which can be zero).

Term by term inspection of the Taylor series reveals how the function $f[x]$ is approximated. The first term $f[a]$ is a point, the value of the function evaluated at the point $x = a$. The sum of the first term and the second term is the linear approximation to the function about the point a. Assuming that $f[x]$ is the price function for a default and option free bond, the linear approximation is illustrated in figure 5.1. Taking into account the third term in the Taylor series involves using a quadratic approximation. The implications of this are illustrated in figure 5.2. As illustrated, even though the assumed function is convex, it does not follow that a quadratic approximation will

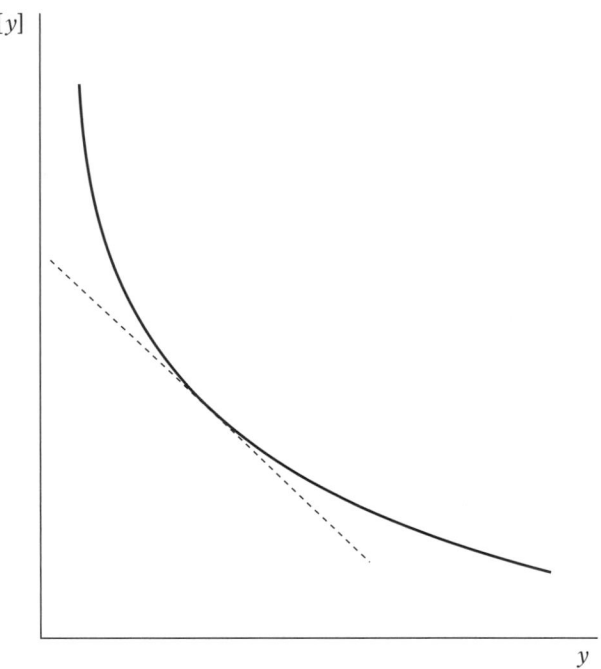

Figure 5.1 Linear approximation to a convex function

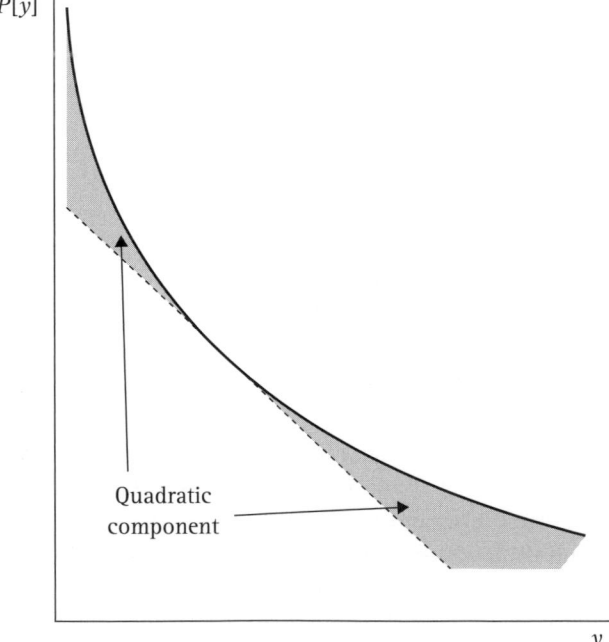

Figure 5.2 Quadratic approximation to a convex function

provide an exact fit to the function. In addition, because a Taylor series only possesses the property of uniform convergence, it does not follow that taking an additional term into account will necessarily produce a closer approximation. All that the Cauchy criterion for uniform convergence ensures is that if enough terms are taken into account then the approximation will be within ε of the true function, for all $\varepsilon > 0$.

A Taylor series is a specific form of the more general mathematical concept of a power series. Other types of power series can also be used to represent an admissible function as an expansion expressed as an infinite converging sum. Examples of such expansions occur frequently, particularly in mathematical statistics. Some of the more important are the Edgeworth expansion, Cornish-Fisher expansion and the Gram-Charlier expansion. The various types of power series are distinguished primarily in the method used for determining the coefficients for each of the terms in the expansion. The selection of one method of expansion over another depends on the specifics of the function being examined and the use required for the expansion. The Taylor series uses derivatives of the function $f[x]$ in order to determine the coefficients. An important special case of the Taylor series occurs where zero is used as the fixed point in the expansion. This form of the Taylor series is sometimes referred to as a Maclaurin series.

Applied to the function $f[r] = \ln[(1 + rt^*)^{-1}]$ evaluated around the origin $(a = 0)$ gives:

$$\ln\left[\frac{1}{1 + rt^*}\right] = -\ln[1 + rt^*] = -\left\{\ln[1 + (0)t^*] + \frac{t^*}{1 + (0)t^*}(r - 0)\right.$$
$$\left. - \frac{1}{2!}\frac{(t^*)}{(1 + (0)t^*)^2}(r - 0)^2 + \frac{1}{3!}\frac{(t^*)}{2(1 + (0)t^*)^3} - \cdots\right\}$$

$$= -\{0 + rt^* - r^2t^* + r^3t^* - \cdots\}$$

For small r, say r is .1, the terms involving squares, cubes and so on will be relatively small and the expansion reduces to $\ln[1/(1 + rt^*)]$ being approximately equal to $-rt^*$, which is the same as the exact value given when the log of the continuous discounting operator was evaluated. Using this approach, the difference between the continuous and discrete interest rates can be represented by the higher order terms which are being ignored in the Taylor series expansion. Application of the Taylor series to the geometric discounting operator produces: $\ln[(1 + r)^{-t^*}] = -t^* \ln[(1 + r)]$ which is also approximately $-rt^*$. However, unlike the linear form where the approximation to the log was taken for $(1 + rt^*)$, this approximation is $-t^*$ times $\ln[1 + r]$ which will, generally, produce a different error of approximation.

This discussion can also be used to clarify an approximation that is commonly used in financial calculation: $\ln[1 + x]$ is approximately equal to x when x is small. The question this operation raises is: how small can x be in order to ensure that substitution of x for $\ln[1 + x]$ does not produce sizeable errors of approximation? Examining the Taylor series for $\ln[1 + x]$ reveals that the square of x must be small relative to x. For example, if x is .1 then $x^2 = .01$ which, for many applications, is sufficiently small to permit the approximation. Similarly, if $x = .05$ then $x^2 = .0025$, and the approximation is again admissible in many situations. However, for $x = .5$, $x^2 = .25$, a value which is not small relative to x. In practice, the admissibility of the approximation will depend on the specific type of problem in which the approximation is used. It is always possible to improve the approximation by taking account of higher order terms in the expansion.

For present purposes, the application involves applying the Taylor series expansion to the bond price function. $P[y]$. This application goes back at least to Redington (1952). While it is possible to define the bond price function in terms of yield and time, i.e., $P[y, t]$, the conventional textbook explanation for the relationship between duration and convexity, e.g., Fabozzi (1993, ch. 4), is to treat the bond price as a univariate function of yield. Applying a Taylor series expansion to this function gives:

$$P_B[y] = P_B[y_0] + \frac{dP}{dy}(y - y_0) + \frac{1}{2}\frac{d^2P}{dy^2}(y - y_0)^2 + \ldots H.O.T.$$

$$\frac{P_B[y] - P_B[y_0]}{P_B[y_0]} \cong -DUR(y - y_0) + \frac{1}{2}CON(y - y_0)^2$$

where $DUR = D$ and CON are the modified duration and convexity of the bond. This result can be used to show that for two different fixed income portfolios, with equal initial yield and duration, that the higher convexity portfolio will have a more favorable percentage change in price, whether yields go up or down (see section 5.3 below).

As demonstrated by Christensen and Sorensen (1994) and others, this analysis is incomplete because the bond price function can be modeled as a function of two variables, yield and time. This expansion involves the application of a multivariate Taylor series:

$$P_B[y, t] = \sum_{t=1}^{T}\frac{C}{(1 + y)^t} + \frac{M}{(1 + y)^T}$$

$$= P_B[y_0, t_0] + \frac{\partial P}{\partial y}(y - y_0) + \frac{\partial P}{\partial t}(t - t_0)$$

$$+ \frac{1}{2}\left\{\frac{\partial^2 P}{\partial y^2}(y - y_0)^2 + \frac{\partial^2 P}{\partial t^2}(t - t_0)^2\right\} + \frac{\partial^2 P}{\partial y \partial t}(y - y_0)(t - t_0) + \ldots H.O.T.$$

Dividing through by $P_B[y_0, t_0]$ will produce the familiar expansion in terms of modified duration, convexity, theta and the cross product terms, e.g., Jordan and Chance (1995), Kang and Chen (2002). Though this expansion does clarify certain points, there are also some limitations in arriving at conclusions based on this form of the expansion (see section 5.3 below).

Stochastic processes and Ito's lemma*

BASIC BACKGROUND

As discussed in section 1.3, the theory of stochastic processes describes the behavior of random variables, the $X(t)$'s, over time, $t \in \mathfrak{F}$. A random variable is a function which maps from a prespecified domain, or sample space, to some portion of the real line, $\Re^1$. In certain financial applications, e.g., where X refers to a security price, X takes values only on the positive, half line. In this case as well as when the X values are allowed to assume any value along the real line, it is conventional to assume that there is a zero probability of X being equal to plus or minus infinity. When t is fixed at a given point, $X(t)$ has the conventional interpretation of a random variable, with associated (one-dimensional) probability density function. Specification of the stochastic process for X requires further specification of the joint density functions that relate X's at different points in time: the joint densities provide a probabilistic specification of how X evolves over time. This potentially complicated mapping can involve various combinations of discrete or continuous observations on X and t. While in financial applications X is usually continuous, time can be either. The terms *discrete stochastic process* and *continuous stochastic process* are used to refer to the time intervals at which $X(t)$ is observed. Applications of stochastic processes have contributed significantly in numerous fields, e.g., engineering, physics, biology and statistics.

A number of important notions from stochastic processes have received considerable attention in modern Finance. While martingales and random walks are possibly the most familiar,[5] most of the literature on option pricing is developed using diffusion processes. These concepts are all closely related. *Diffusions* are (strong) Markov processes, continuous in both X and t. In turn, diffusions are constructed from Weiner processes which are the continuous time representation of a discrete time random walk. Both types of processes obey the martingale property. The essential concept of a *Markov* process is most readily illustrated in discrete time. Using the conditional probability distribution $Pr[\cdot]$, the Markov property can be stated:

$$Pr[X(t + 1) = j \mid X(0) = a, \ X(1) = b, \ X(2) = c \ldots, \ X(t) = s]$$
$$= Pr[X(t + 1) = j \mid X(t) = s]$$

In effect, the Markov process is "memoryless," the past and future are statistically independent when the present is known.

While there are a number of subtle technical issues associated with the precise definition of Markov process, Markov families and diffusions (e.g., Rogers and Williams 1987), for current purposes it is sufficient to define a diffusion process as a Markov process in which both time and the state variable X are continuous. When expressed in the form of a *stochastic differential equation (SDE)*, diffusions can be used to concisely specify the joint density functions for the stochastic process. To adequately motivate stochastic differential equations, it is necessary to develop the basic concept of a Weiner process as the limit of a discrete "normal" random walk, defined by a stochastic difference equation. The discrete *random walk*, without drift, has the form:

$$X(t + 1) = X(t) + Z(t + 1) \quad \text{where } X(0) = 0, \text{ and } t \in \{1, 2, 3 \ldots\}$$

where $Z(1), \ Z(2), \ Z(3) \ldots$ form a stochastic process of independent random variables with the standard normal probability distribution: $Z(t) \sim N[0, 1]$. In other words, over the unit time interval $(\Delta t = 1)$ $Z(t)$ is a normal random variable with mean 0 and variance of one.

Types of diffusions

Consider what happens to a normal random walk as the time interval Δt shrinks. In this case, $Z(t + \Delta t)$ is no longer $N(0, 1]$, but rather $N[0, \Delta t]$ (e.g., Poitras 2002, pp. 545–6) where the random walk now has the form (see section 10.4):

$$X(t + \Delta t) = X(t) + Z(t + \Delta t) = X(t) + Z(t)\sqrt{\Delta t}$$

Reexpressing in difference form and using:

$$\lim_{\Delta t \to 0} \Delta t = dt$$

Gives the stochastic differential equation for the standard Weiner process:

$$dX(t) = Z(t)\sqrt{dt} \quad \Rightarrow \quad dX(t) = dW(t)$$

$W(t)$ is usually referred to as a ***standard Weiner process*** with a unit variance parameter. The terminology "Gaussian process" or "Brownian motion" is also used. As discussed in section 1.3, the ***ensemble*** of sample paths for $W(t)$ conform to the evolution of a random variable that is standard normal on the unit time interval.

Geometrically, the behavior of the standard Weiner process can be illustrated in two dimensions by taking $X(t)$ on the vertical axis and time on the horizontal axis. Starting from $X(0)$, which is a predetermined point, the Weiner process specifies an infinite number of possible paths originating from $X(0)$. The pattern of these paths conform to $N[0, \Delta t]$. To see this, select any time $t_1 > 0$, take a "slice" across the X paths and plot the distribution of the paths. The distribution of the paths will be a normal distribution, centered at $X(0)$, with variance t_1. Similarly, doing the same "slicing" operation for another time $t_2 > t_1$ and evaluating the density associated with the ensemble of X time paths will again produce a normal distribution, centered at $X(0)$, but with a larger dispersion. In this fashion, it is possible to make a connection with the distribution theory, familiar from traditional statistics, which is concerned with variables at a given point in time. The SDE technique is a method of describing the evolution over time of random variables that are functions of the class of normal random variables.

The Weiner process can be immediately generalized to allow for non-zero drift and variance that differs from Δt. When a trend or "drift" term μ and standard deviation σ ($\neq 1$) are admitted then the ***arithmetic Gaussian*** stochastic process (with constant coefficients μ and σ) is defined:

$$dX(t) = \mu dt + \sigma dW(t)$$

This constant coefficient process is also referred to as an arithmetic or absolute Brownian motion, e.g., Poitras (1998). The ensemble of time paths for this process are also normal but differ from the standard Weiner process by allowing for a different amount of variation around a constant trend. The standard Weiner process can be used to construct a wide range of SDE's, each of which is associated with a different specification for the joint density of the stochastic process. The construction of the Weiner process requires these densities to be functionally connected to the normal.

In general, the drift and standard deviation can be functions of both the state variable and time, such that $\alpha[x, t]$ is the drift and $\beta[x, t]$ is the volatility. Consider, a simple form of state dependence, where $\alpha[x, t] = \mu X$ and $\beta[x, t] = \sigma X$, with μ and σ being constants:

$$dX(t) = \mu X dt + \sigma X dW(t) \Rightarrow dX(t)/X = \mu dt + \sigma dW(t)$$

In this case, the instantaneous rate of change (dX/X) follows a Gaussian process. For this reason, the terms *geometric Gaussian process* or *geometric Brownian motion* are sometimes used to identify this process. It can be shown that for the geometric Gaussian process the paths of $X(t)$ correspond to a process that is lognormally distributed at each point in time. This is important for cases where $X(t)$ refers to prices which, like lognormal variables, cannot be negative (for $X(0) > 0$).[6]

The geometric Brownian motion has an important position in option pricing theory. Black and Scholes (1973) use this process to describe the behavior of the stock price in deriving their European option pricing formula. The process is often encountered in a variety of option pricing situations because geometric Brownian motion usually leads to a relatively simple closed form solution. While the empirical validity of this assumption can be questioned, the process is sufficiently close to real world processes that in many cases a reasonable approximation is provided.[7] However, in the case of fixed income securities and interest rates, geometric Brownian motion has definite limitations. For example, the price of fixed income securities such as Tbills or Tbonds will converge to the par value on the maturity date, which is inconsistent with unrestricted geometric Brownian motion. Even where the interest rate instead of the price is used as the stochastic variable, there is considerable evidence that the empirical process exhibits mean reversion, a property that is not consistent with geometric Brownian motion.

Despite the empirical limitations, it is still possible to use geometric Brownian motion as the process for stochastic modeling of interest rate behavior. For various reasons, it is useful to know the mean and variance of an assumed diffusion process. For example, a key step in the risk neutral valuation of the European option requires this result. For geometric Brownian motion:

$$E[X(t)] = X(0)e^{\alpha t} = X(0)\,e^{\left(\mu + \frac{\sigma^2}{2}\right)t} \qquad var[X(t)] = [X(0)]^2 e^{2\alpha t}[e^{\sigma^2 t} - 1]$$

These results are derived by directly evaluating the expectations. Applications of these results appear, for example, in the risk-neutral derivation of the Black-Scholes option pricing formula, e.g., Poitras (2002, ch. 8).

An important class of processes that is exploited in some pricing of options and stochastic modeling of interest rates are the variations of the *regular Ornstein-Uhlenbeck* (OU) process:[8]

$$dX(t) = \alpha X dt + \sigma dW(t)$$

Observe that an OU process has a positive probability of having negative values. In financial applications, the OU process is often presented as a *mean reverting* process:

$$dX(t) = \alpha[\mu - X]dt + \sigma dW(t)$$

where α can be interpreted as the speed of adjustment of $X(t)$ to the steady state mean μ. Different variations of the OU process have appeared. For example, Brennan and Schwartz (1979) and many others use the process:

$$dX(t) = \alpha[\mu - X]dt + \sigma X dW(t)$$

In this case, dX/X reduces to a mean-reverting OU.

Unlike the geometric and arithmetic Brownian motions, the $X(t)$ distribution associated with the OU process changes over time. At any time t, $X(t)$ is governed by a non-steady state distribution which is normal but with *conditional* means and variances that are time dependent, e.g., Cox and Miller (1965, pp. 225–7). For the *regular OU*:

$$E[X(t)] = X(0)e^{-\alpha t} \quad var[X(t)] = \frac{\sigma^2(1 - e^{-\alpha t})}{2\alpha}$$

Asymptotically, as $t \to \infty$ then the OU converges to a normal steady state distribution with mean zero and variance $\sigma^2/2\alpha$. This damping behavior of the OU is different from the geometric Brownian motion which increases indefinitely as $t \to \infty$. Similarly, the *mean-reverting OU* has conditional parameters:

$$E[X(t)] = \mu + (X(0) - \mu)e^{-\alpha t} \qquad var[X(t)] = \frac{\sigma^2}{2\alpha}\{1 - e^{-2\alpha t}\}$$

As $t \to \infty$ then the mean-reverting OU converges to a steady state normal distribution with mean μ and variance $\sigma^2/2\alpha$.

Cox, Ingersoll and Ross (1985) and others use a diffusion process, the square root process, in which volatility depends on the square root of X. In mean-reverting form, the SDE for this process is represented:

$$dX(t) = \alpha[\mu - X]dt + \sigma\sqrt{X}\,dW(t)$$

This process can be shown to be the continuous limit of a *noncentral* chi-squared distribution. In turn, the square root process is a special case of the more general *constant elasticity of variance* (CEV) process:

$$dX(t) = \alpha X dt + \sigma X^{\beta/2} dW(t)$$

where $\beta \in [0, 2)$. Unlike the other diffusions examined to this point, the CEV model describes a class of processes defined over the range of β. For $\beta = 1$, the CEV process is equivalent to a square root process. For $\beta = 2$, the process is lognormal.

The ***Brownian bridge*** process is a development on the Brownian motion process that incorporates a drift term which forces the process to a fixed endpoint. For a Brownian bridge process that starts at zero and ends at zero, the unit variance process takes the form:

$$dX(t) = -X(t)/(T - t)dt + dW(t)$$

The Brownian bridge process has been used in a number of papers, e.g., Ball and Torous (1983), Chiang and Okunev (1993), to model the bond price process. For this purpose, the Brownian bridge is attractive because the bond price converges to par value as the term to maturity endpoint is approached. Cheng (1991) explores problems that assuming a Brownian bridge has for arbitrage free pricing.

Unfortunately, the number of diffusion processes for which readily interpretable conditional probability densities can be derived is limited. While the density function for the general CEV process has been derived, the formula is complicated. In addition to the processes already described and immediate extensions, such as the Brownian bridge, the only other class of processes that have manageable density functions are Bessel processes which, in squared form, have the representation: $dX(t) = \alpha dt + 2\sqrt{X}dW(t)$. This form of the Bessel process is typically used because the associated densities are stable under convolutions, a useful property not shared by geometric Brownian motion. For example, Geman and Yor (1993) use this process to model the pricing of perpetuities and Asian options. In general, while not always the best empirical fit to the distribution for financial random variables, the analytical advantages of diffusion processes have played important roles in the application of stochastic processes to problems in finance and economics.[9]

With relatively little analytical complication, the general SDE model can be extended to include ***jump processes***. One of the properties of the diffusion is the continuity of its sample paths. This property can be generalized to permit certain types of jumps in the state variable to take place, usually modeled as a Poisson event process. In other words, the sample paths of the diffusion are continuous except at a countable number of discontinuity points, where the jumps are generated by a Poisson process. In this case, the SDE can be written:

$$dX(t) = \alpha[x, t]dt + \sigma[x, t]dW(t) + v[x, t]dQ(t)$$

where $v[x, t]$ obeys the same technical conditions imposed on α and σ, and $dQ(t)$ is a Poisson process assumed to be distributed independently of $W(t)$.[10] For this type of SDE, there is a generalized form of Ito's lemma, e.g., Malliaris and Brock (1982, p. 122). The usefulness of this result in applications is that it, theoretically, permits the valuation of jumps in the underlying process, e.g., Merton (1976), Cox and Ross (1976).

EMPIRICAL EVIDENCE ON STOCHASTIC PROCESSES FOR INTEREST RATES

Given all the possible diffusion processes that could be selected, it is natural to ask the question: what is the appropriate SDE to use for modelling an interest rate process?[11]

The answer to this question depends on the problem that the SDE is being used to analyse. In many applications, e.g., where the problem involves a one-factor model of the term structure, the objective is to select the SDE that has the best empirical fit to the short term interest rate that, in turn, may be used to determine the term structure of interest rates. Such applications arise in pricing interest rate contingent claims, including interest rate derivatives, bonds with embedded options and swaptions. The importance of determining the appropriate SDE (or non-linear discrete process) for the interest rate process has not escaped the proponents of modern Finance. Since the early 1990s, an impressive number of articles have been dedicated to this topic. Yet, Chapman and Pearson (2001, p. 91) conclude: "After all this research, we know a few important facts about the evolution of interest rates. Unfortunately, the list of things we do not know is as long as the list of things we do know."

The connection of this statement with the philosophical discussion in part I is difficult to ignore. However, it is still instructive to consider what "few important facts" have been identified. Chapman and Pearson (2001, p. 78) start with three "stylized facts" about short term interest rates:

> *Short rate fact #1*: The short-rate series is a "persistent" time series; that is, it spends long consecutive periods above or below the (sample estimate of the) unconditional, or long-run, mean.
> *Short rate fact #2*: In the 1979–82 period, the average level and volatility of the short rate was substantially higher than for other years in the 1971–2000 period.
> *Short rate fact #3*: The volatility of the short rate level appears to be both time varying and persistent.

Chapman and Pearson also observe that although the 5 year constant maturity Treasury yields (1962–2000) have "lower mean and volatility" than the short rate measured using the one-month Eurodollar yield, "the overall movements in levels and volatility are qualitatively similar." Hence, short term interest rate processes can be characterized by "persistence in level," structural breaks and "time-varying and persistent" volatility. "Strong contemporaneous correlations between rates of different maturities" is also observed leading Chapman and Pearson to conclude that "a limited number of common factors" determine "virtually all of the variability in weekly yield changes for bonds of maturities from six months to 18 years." Principal components analysis is used to "confirm" the results of Litterman and Scheinkman (1991) that there are three factors that determine the variation in yield changes. The first factor, which explains "88 percent of the variation," is the "level." The other two factors being "slope" and "curvature" explain a further 11 percent of the variation.

In addition to these "facts" Chapman and Pearson also present other "facts" such as: "the volatility of yields was decreasing for increasing terms to maturity." However, this empirical result does not hold over all sub-periods. There does appear to be high contemporaneous correlations between yield volatilities for all adjacent maturities "even for 1-month versus 10-year yields." In addition to these, "facts," Chapman and Pearson also present potentially illuminating results from working papers and forthcoming studies that are "very preliminary and, consequently, must be interpreted with caution." It seems this preliminary evidence indicates "patterns in term premiums do not permit distinguishing among competing models. It may be necessary to examine data on the dynamics of interest options to narrow the field of acceptable dynamic models" (p. 91). Perhaps the inability of techniques such as "two-factor regime switching models" to capture the *ex ante* behavior of interest rates and the term structure is due more to the failure of the assumptions of logical positivism?

In the end, Chapman and Pearson (2001) stands as an example of the extent to which logical positivism dominates the methodology of modern Finance. The discussion is predicated on the assumption that by examining more data with "better" statistical techniques the "true" model generating interest rates and the term structure can be identified. Some indication of the validity of this approach can be gained by considering the various models of the interest rate process that have been suggested in numerous studies over the last three decades. Almost a decade prior to Chapman and Pearson, Chan et al. (1992) provide a description and empirical evaluation of eight different diffusion specifications. In contrast to one of the "facts" provided by Chapman and Pearson, Chan et al. (1992, pp. 1224–5) find "no evidence of a structural shift in the interest rate process in October 1979 for the models which capture the conditional volatility of the interest rate process". In addition, Chan et al. stress the failures of available models to explain "the dependence of volatility on the level of the interest rate".

Despite the "progress" identified by Chapman and Pearson, Chan et al. (1992) still provides a useful taxonomy of the SDE models that are used to model the short term (riskless) interest rate. Eight such models are identified. These first of these specifications is the absolute Brownian motion used in Merton (1973) to model discount bond prices: $dr = \mu dt + \sigma dW$. This SDE suffers from a number of defects. One obvious limitation is the possibility of paths with negative interest rates. Another limitation is empirical, Chan et al. (p. 1210) find that the "the most important feature differentiating interest models" is the ability to capture the volatility of interest rates which is sensitive to the level of r. By modelling volatility as a constant, absolute Brownian motion does not recognize this empirical result. As such, this SDE is of interest primarily for the simplicity of the process in solving pricing problems.

A more plausible SDE is geometric Brownian motion: $dr = \mu r dt + \sigma r dW$. This process has been used in a number of studies including Rendleman and Bartter (1980). The empirical validity of this process has been questioned for allowing paths where the interest rate increases to levels that are not practical. The process does have desirable features such as sample paths that are only positive and, for option pricing purposes, the ability to access pricing results that have been derived for other cases, e.g., the Black-Scholes European option on a non-dividend paying stock. To value an option written on an interest rate, the Black (1976) version of the Black-Scholes formula is used where the implied forward rate is substituted for the forward price, the strike rate is used for the exercise price and the volatility is for the implied forward rate, e.g., Chance (1998, pp. 590–1).

Though there is considerable debate in economics about whether interest rate processes are unit root or mean reverting, e.g., Wu and Zhang (1996), at least since

Vasicek (1977) modern Finance has favored modelling interest rates as mean reverting processes. The Vasicek mean-reverting model of the short term interest rate has the OU form:

$$dr = \kappa(\mu - r)dt + \sigma dW$$

In this model, μ is the long run mean, κ is the speed of adjustment to the long run mean, and σ is the volatility of the short rate. Vasicek used this model to solve for discount bond prices and for a one factor model of the term structure (see end of chapter questions). Included among a large number of studies that have used the "Vasicek model," Jamshidian (1989) used this process to solve for options on zero coupon and coupon bearing bonds, e.g., Hull (2003, pp. 540–1). Gibson and Schwartz (1990) used this process to value the convenience yield for oil futures and forwards contracts.

While the Vasicek model accounts for the possibility of mean reversion in interest rates, this process suffers from the possibility that some sample paths may contain negative interest rates, though the presence of a mean reverting drift does mitigate this possibility. Another limitation is the assumption of constancy in the volatility. Both of these problems are at least partly addressed in the square root diffusion model employed by Cox, Ingersoll and Ross (1985), often referred to as the CIR model:

$$dr = \kappa(\mu - r)dt + \sigma \sqrt{r}\, dW$$

CIR used this process to solve for an equilibrium model of the term structure (see end of chapter questions). The empirical properties of the model have been investigated in numerous studies including Gibbons and Ramaswamy (1993), Pearson and Sun (1994) and Lamoureux and Witte (2002). While Pearson and Sun find the CIR model fits poorly, Lamoureux and Witte are able to extend the model to allow for additional "factors" that permit the CIR model to do "a very good job of fitting the time-series properties of short rates."

UNIVARIATE ITO'S LEMMA

Calculus is an important mathematical technique with numerous useful applications. As conventionally presented, calculus is applied to functions that are deterministic. In effect, the familiar rules associated with dy/dx, such as $y = x^2 \rightarrow dy/dx = 2x$, only apply when x is known. When x is a random variable the usual rules of calculus no longer apply. The importance of Ito's lemma is that it specifies the procedures for applying calculus to functions which contain random variables. More precisely, Ito's lemma provides a method for evaluating the total derivative of a function of a stochastic variable which follows a Markov diffusion process. As discussed above, the diffusion class includes a wide range of stochastic processes. Given this, the *univariate* form of Ito's lemma can be stated:[12]

Ito's lemma

Let $u[X, t]$ be a continuous random function mapping from $\Re^1 \times [0, T] \to \Re^1$ with continuous partial derivatives:

$$u_t = \frac{\partial u}{\partial t} \qquad u_x = \frac{\partial u}{\partial x} \qquad u_{xx} = \frac{\partial^2 u}{\partial x^2}$$

If $X(t)$ is a random process with a stochastic differential equation obeying a diffusion of the form:

$$dX(t) = a(t)dt + v(t)dW(t)$$

where $W(t)$ is a standard Wiener process and $a(t)$ and $v(t)$ are the drift and volatility of the diffusion, then the function $u(t) = u[X(t), t]$ also has a differential on $[0, T]$ given by:

$$du(t) = \{u_t + u_x a(t) + 1/2 u_{xx} v(t)^2\}dt + u_x v(t)dW(t)$$

This form of Ito's lemma generalizes in a natural fashion to the case where X is multidimensional, e.g., Malliaris and Brock (1982, pp. 85–6).[13]

While Ito's lemma has had numerous applications in financial economics, perhaps the most well known is the Black-Scholes application to call option valuation, where the non-dividend paying stock price $S(t)$ is assumed to follow a log-normal diffusion:

$$dS = \alpha S dt + \sigma S dW$$

In this case, $a(t) = \alpha S$ and $v(t) = \sigma S$ where α and σ are constants. The functional relationship between the call option price (C) and the stock takes the form: $C = C[S(t), t]$. Application of Ito's lemma gives:

$$dC = \{C_t + C_S \alpha S + 1/2 C_{SS} \sigma^2 S^2\}dt + \{C_S \sigma S\}dW$$

This solution plays a central role in the derivation of the Black-Scholes price of a European call. In particular, Black-Scholes are able to use the *riskless hedge portfolio* construction to provide an additional condition that permits elimination of the dW term. In this fashion, the call option pricing problem is transformed from an SDE problem which is not solvable in closed form with standard techniques, into a deterministic partial differential equation (PDE) problem that can be solved. However, complications associated with solving PDE's are such that closed form solutions are not always possible. This has at least two implications. First, there is an emphasis on problem specifications that can be solved in closed form, e.g., Black-Scholes, even though such solutions may not be fully realistic. And, secondly, there is the need to apply numerical methods to "solve" problems in which a precise specification of the problem is required.

Ito's lemma can also be used to transform one type of SDE into another. One useful example involves the function $G[S] = \ln[S]$ where the SDE for S is geometric Brownian motion. Application of Ito's lemma provides the SDE for $G[S]$, specified using the drift and volatility parameters for S. More precisely, $G_t = 0$, $G_S = 1/S$ and $G_{SS} = -(1/S)^2$. Using Ito's lemma it follows that:

$$dG = \{0 + \alpha - 1/2\sigma^2\}dt + \sigma dW = (\alpha - 1/2\sigma^2)dt + \sigma dW$$

The result that the log of a lognormally distributed random variable follows an arithmetic Brownian process is not surprising, but the specification of the drift is not obvious.

A straightforward extension of the univariate approach to the case of functions of two variables (and time) is provided by Fischer (1975) that examines the stochastic behavior of the real bond price $q = B/P$ where, using Fischer's notation, B is the nominal price of a riskless bond and P is the aggregate price level. In this case, the rate of change in the aggregate price level (dP/P) and the return on a zero-coupon continuously compounded nominal bond (dB/B) can be specified:

$$dP/P = \pi dt + \sigma dW \qquad dB/B = Rdt$$

Observing that when $q = u[B, P] = B/P$:

$$u_t = 0 \quad u_{BP} = -\{1/P\}^2 \quad u_{BB} = 0 \quad u_B = 1/P \quad u_P = -\{B/P^2\} \quad u_{PP} = 2\{B/P^3\}$$

It is now possible to apply the multivariate form of Ito's lemma to get:[14]

$$dq = \left\{\frac{1}{P}RB + \frac{-B}{P^2}\pi P + \frac{B}{P^3}P^2\sigma^2\right\}dt + \frac{-B}{P^2}\sigma PdW$$

Factoring out B/P gives the desired result:

$$dq/q = \{R - \pi + \sigma^2\}dt - \sigma dW$$

More developed applications of the multivariate form of Ito's lemma can be found in various sources, e.g., Gibson and Schwartz (1990), Schwartz (1982).

MULTIVARIATE ITO'S LEMMA

It is useful to proceed by example to illustrate the multivariate form of Ito's lemma. Briys and Solnik (1992) provide an interesting application to the case where the random process is multidimensional, involving two random variables (and time). This requires a more involved form of Ito's lemma. The Briys and Solnik example involves the domestic currency value of a foreign security, $V^* = VS$, where V is the random foreign currency value of the foreign security and S is the random spot exchange rate, producing V^* which is the random domestic currency value of the foreign security. In this case, processes are given for dV and dS with dV^* to be calculated using Ito's lemma.

To evaluate Ito's lemma for this case requires application of the associated multivariate total derivative. The resulting solution for the two random variable case, $y(t) = u[t, \{x(t)\}] = u[t, \{x_1(t), x_2(t)\}]$, takes the form:

$$dy = u_t dt + u_x dx + \frac{1}{2} tr\left[\Sigma u_{xx}\right] dt$$

where Σ is the variance–covariance matrix of the state variables and $tr[\cdot]$ is the trace operator. Because there are n state variables in the general form, u_x is a $n \times 1$ column vector containing the first partial derivatives, dx is a row vector containing the diffusion processes and u_{xx} is a symmetric $n \times n$ matrix of the second partial derivatives.

In the Briys and Solnik example, $dy = dV^*$ and V and S are assumed to follow the log-normal diffusions:

$$\frac{dV}{V} = \mu_V dt + \sigma_V dW_V \qquad \frac{dS}{S} = \mu_S dt + \sigma_S dW_S$$

The covariance between dW_S and dW_V per unit time is $cov(dW_S, dW_V) = \rho_{VS} dt$. It follows that $\sigma_{VS} = \rho_{VS}\sigma_V\sigma_S$. Recognizing that $y = u[x, t]$ in this case is $V^* = VS$, it follows that:

$$u_1 = \frac{\partial V^*}{\partial V} = S \qquad u_2 = \frac{\partial V^*}{\partial S} = V \qquad u_t = \frac{\partial V^*}{\partial t} = 0$$

$$u_{11} = \frac{\partial^2 V^*}{\partial V^2} = 0 = \frac{\partial^2 V^*}{\partial S^2} = u_{22} \qquad \frac{\partial^2 V^*}{\partial V \partial S} = 1 = \frac{\partial^2 V^*}{\partial S \partial V} = u_{1,2}$$

Because there are now two state variables, V and S, the variance–covariance matrix Σ is 2×2 with variances on the diagonal and covariances on the off-diagonal. Remembering from the univariate lognormal example that $v(t)^2 = \sigma^2 S^2$, evaluating $1/2\, tr[\cdot]$ for this case gives:

$$\frac{1}{2} tr\left\{\begin{bmatrix} \sigma_{11} & \sigma_{1,2} \\ \sigma_{2,1} & \sigma_{22} \end{bmatrix}\begin{bmatrix} u_{11} & u_{1,2} \\ u_{2,1} & u_{22} \end{bmatrix}\right\} = \frac{1}{2}\{\sigma_{11}u_{11} + \sigma_{1,2}u_{2,1} + \sigma_{2,1}u_{1,2} + \sigma_{22}u_{22}\}$$

$$= \sigma_{1,2} = \sigma_{VS} VS$$

Using the result that $1/2\, tr[\cdot] = \sigma_{VS} VS$. The solution to the total derivative is found to be:

$$dV^* = 0 + S(\mu_V V\, dt + \sigma_V V\, dW_V) + V(\mu_S S\, dt + \sigma_S S\, dW_S) + \sigma_{VS} VS\, dt$$

$$\frac{dV^*}{V^*} = (\mu_V + \mu_S + \sigma_{VS})dt + \sigma_V dW_V + \sigma_S dW_S$$

Given dV and dS, this is dV^*, the SDE for the domestic currency value of the foreign security.

Binomial models and other discrete processes*

Continuous time methods have a number of appealing properties in dealing with problems involving functions of random variables. For example, Ito's lemma provides a method for the intuition and analytical insight of deterministic calculus to be extended to functions of random variables. However, these appealing properties are obtained by making relatively strong restrictions on the structure of the valuation problem. In many cases, the complications associated with the continuous time approach are unnecessary to achieve a solution to the problem at hand. In other cases, the problem at hand is not fully solvable using continuous time methods. In these cases, solutions can be obtained using discrete time processes and the associated techniques of numerical methods. These techniques are particularly useful in valuing securities where the payout is *path dependent*, a property that is applicable to many of the important fixed income securities with embedded options, such as callable bonds and mortgage pass throughs. Path dependence occurs because the realized value of such securities depend on the specific stochastic path taken by, say, interest rates.

The simplest form of a discrete time process is the binomial process, sometimes called a two state process. As depicted in figure 5.3, given an initial starting point, the binomial process proceeds by specifying the probability of an up (down) move. Because there are only two possible states of the world, the probability of a down (up) move is determined by observing that the sum of the probabilities equals one. The binomial process is characterized by the number of periods or steps that are evaluated and by whether the process is *recombining* or *non-recombining.* A recombining process has the property that an up move followed by a down move will end up at the same outcome as a down move followed by an up move. For a two period recombining binomial process there will be three possible outcomes while for a two period non-recombining process there will be four possible outcomes. The computational advantages of a recombining process are considerable if the number of periods is large. In addition, there are absence of arbitrage restrictions that need to be considered in determining the probabilities of the binomial process.

In figure 5.3, the state variable used is the bond price. Specifying the appropriate state variable for modeling fixed income securities is not as obvious as for equity securities. Consider the case of bond valuation. It is possible to use the bond price as the state variable but, unlike equities, a bond has a fixed maturity date. As the maturity date is approached, the price will converge to the maturity value. This convergence property will affect the volatility along the binomial paths. This difficulty is avoided if the short term interest rate is used as the state variable. In a one factor model of the term structure, if enough periods are evaluated then the prices of zero coupon bonds can be determined from the short term interest rate paths. Following the discussion in section 4.3, this is typically done by assuming the unbiased expectations hypothesis and treating the future short term interest rates as implied forward rates. This procedure is complicated by the need to ensure that the interest rate paths do not admit arbitrage opportunities. This can happen, for example, if the future interest rates are not restricted from attaining negative values.

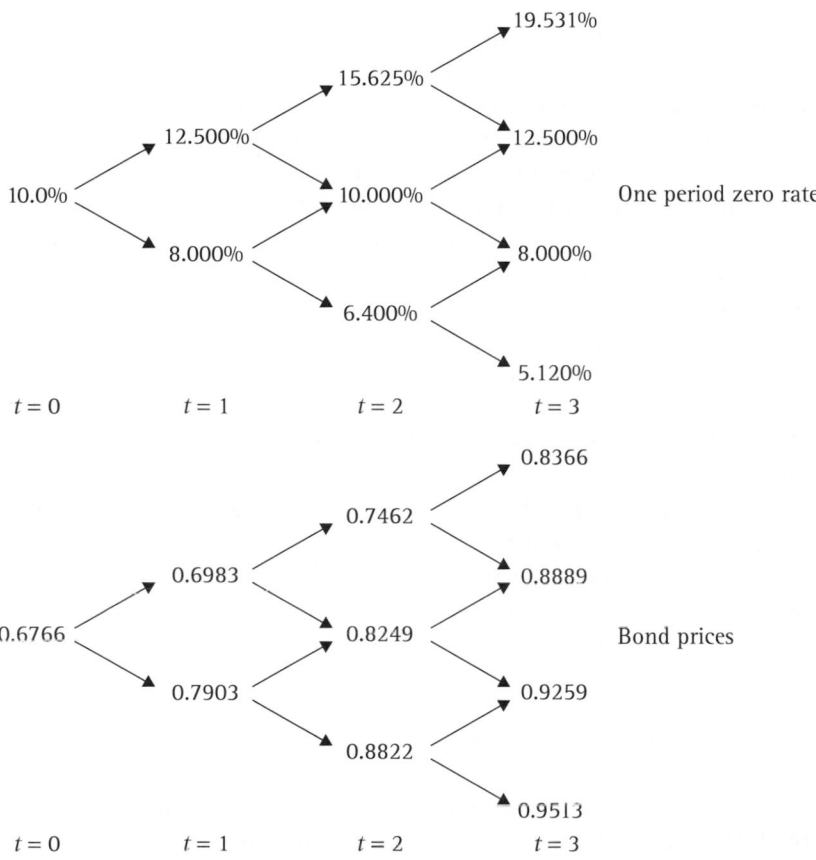

One period zero rates

Bond prices

Figure 5.3 Binomial process of the one-period zero and associated bond prices

Following Sundaresan (2002, pp. 599–604), the upper tree in figure 5.3 illustrates a 3 year evolution of a recombining binomial process for one year zero coupon interest rates. At $t = 0$, the one period interest rate is 10% and it is assumed that the probability of rates increasing or decreasing is 50%. If rates increase then the new rate will be 1.25 times the initial rate and if rates go down the factor is 0.8. As indicated in figure 5.3, this implies that an up move will produce a rate of 12.5% in one year and a down move will produce a rate of 8%. The probabilities and change factors are selected to produce a recombining tree. More complicated discrete processes, such as the self-calibrating processes, use more complicated methods of determining the size of the changes and, possibly, the probabilities. For example, if the process is restricted to be mean reverting the probabilities of up (down) moves will be reduced as the process moves farther above (below) the long run mean, i.e., the probabilities will also evolve over time (e.g., Sundaresan 2002, p. 607). Another example occurs in the Black, Derman and Toy model where the size of the changes are set using observed interest rate volatility and further subjected to an absence of arbitrage condition.

Even though figure 5.3 does not incorporate all the various possible complications, it does capture essential elements of the procedure for modelling the term structure using discrete time models. Given the binomial interest rate process, the lower tree in figure 5.3 provides the evolution of the price of a 4 year zero coupon bond. Determining bond prices involves starting from the last nodes of the interest rate tree and working backward to determine the various bond prices. Observing that the fifth node (not given) is the $t = 4$ maturity value of \$1, the four nodes at $t = 3$ are determined by evaluating $P(3, 4) = 1/(1 + r(3, 4))$. For example, .8366 = 1/(1.19531) and .9513 = 1/(1.0512). The $t = 2$ values can now be calculated by observing that the two connected $t = 3$ nodes are equally likely and that the expected value can be discounted back at the rate applicable at that node, i.e., $P(2, 4) = (.5P(3, 4)^u + .5P(3, 4)^d)/(1 + r(2, 3))$, where u and d represent up and down moves. This condition is required for *absence of arbitrage*. For example, .746162 = (.5(.8366) + .5(.8889))/(1.15625) gives the upper value on the bond price tree. This process is repeated to determine all the nodes on the zero coupon bond price tree.

Given the zero coupon bond price process, it is possible to calculate the zero coupon yield curve that, in turn, can be used to construct the price of coupon bonds and other types of fixed income securities. To see this let $P(0, T)$ represent the zero coupon bond price observed at $t = 0$ and maturing at $t = T$. For the binomial spot rate process it follows that $P(0, 4) = .6766 = 1/(1 + z_4)^4$ which can be solved to get $z_4 = .1026$. Using the same process that was used to construct the 4 year bond price of .6766, a three period tree can be constructed to get $P(0, 3) = .7475$ which can be solved to get $z_3 = .10187$ and again for a two period tree to get $P(0, 2) = .8249$ and $z_2 = .101$. Together with the initial starting value of $z_1 = .10$ the term structure from 1 to 4 years has been constructed. Following the discussion in section 4.3 observe that .6766 = 1/ $\{(1.1)((1.101)^2/(1.1))((1.10187)^3/(1.101)^2)((1.1026)^4/(1.10187)^3)\}$ = 1/$\{(1 + z_1)(1 + f_{1,2})(1 + f_{2,3})(1 + f_{3,4})\}$, i.e., the implied forward rates can be determined from the zero coupon interest rates. This absence of arbitrage condition is ensured by the method used to construct the binomial process. Sundaresan (2002, p. 604) demonstrates that the limit of the binomial process in figure 5.3 is lognormal, a process that does not have the most desirable properties for modelling the term structure.

The observation that the binomial process can be taken to the limit to derive the continuous time representation of the discrete process is significant. It recognizes the connection between the continuous and discrete approaches to modeling interest rate processes. The discrete and continuous models are complementary, not contradictory. Continuous time processes can lead to powerful analytical results but are difficult to apply in some situations. Binomial processes are useful in constructing solutions where continuous time methods are intractable. It is possible to extend the basic binomial model captured in figure 5.3 in a number of ways. In addition to the self-calibrating models, the binomial process can be used as the basis for Monte Carlo simulations (see section 6.3). In these models, a large number of binomial paths are generated using, say, a particular volatility assumption to generate the size of the steps. These various paths can be used to identify exercise decisions associated with embedded options. The specification of exercise decisions is explored further in chapter 6.

5.3   THE TIME VALUE–CONVEXITY TRADEOFF[#]

The contribution from convexity

The introduction of the convexity concept generated considerable initial enthusiasm among practitioners, e.g., Grantier (1988), Bierwag (1987, p. 306). The basis for this enthusiasm can be illustrated by examining the Taylor series expansion for the univariate bond price function $P_B[y]$:

$$\%\Delta P_B = \frac{P_B[y] - P_B[y_0]}{P_B[y_0]} \cong -DUR(y - y_0) + \frac{1}{2} CON(y - y_0)^2$$

Given this, consider a comparison of two bond portfolios (A and B), with values P_A and P_B. These portfolios are constructed to have equal duration ($D_A = DUR_A = DUR_A = D_B$), equal initial yield to maturity (y_0) and $CON_A > CON_B$. The initial durations and yields are set equal by appropriate selection of the bonds included in the two portfolios. The impact of an instantaneous interest rate change on these two portfolios would be approximately:

$$\%\Delta P_A - \%\Delta P_B \cong \frac{1}{2}(CON_A - CON_B)(y - y_0)^2$$

Observing that $CON > 0$ because the bond pricing function(s) are convex, it follows that whether yields go up or down, the portfolio with the higher convexity will have a better percentage change in price. This effect is further illustrated in figure 5.4.

To illustrate how the Taylor series expansion works to construct a function, consider table 5.4 which evaluates the impact of interest rate changes varying from 1 to 300 basis points on the price of a 20 year, 10% coupon par bond. Both increases and decreases in yield are considered. Because there is only one bond involved, it is straightforward to calculate the actual percentage price changes. Consistent with the convexity of the price function for a straight bond, the percentage change in price for a given change in yield is greater for a decrease in yield than for an increase in yield, e.g., −21.22% for a 300 bp increase versus +32.03 for a 300 bp decrease. Consistent with duration involving the derivative of the bond price function at a point, the price impact of small changes in yield are accurately estimated by duration. However, for changes as small as 10 bp there is some convexity impact. Consistent with convexity involving the second derivative, the impact of convexity on the (convex) default and option free bond price function is always positive.

Table 5.4 provides useful information about the properties of the Taylor series expansion of a convex function such as $P_B[y]$. In particular, for a given change in yield, the absolute value of the predicted change due to duration is the same for up moves as down moves. As a consequence, duration over-predicts the price impact of yield increases and under-predicts for yield decreases. Addition of the convexity term more than compensates for the yield increase case and does not sufficiently compensate for yield decrease. The result is that the first two terms of the Taylor series expansion do

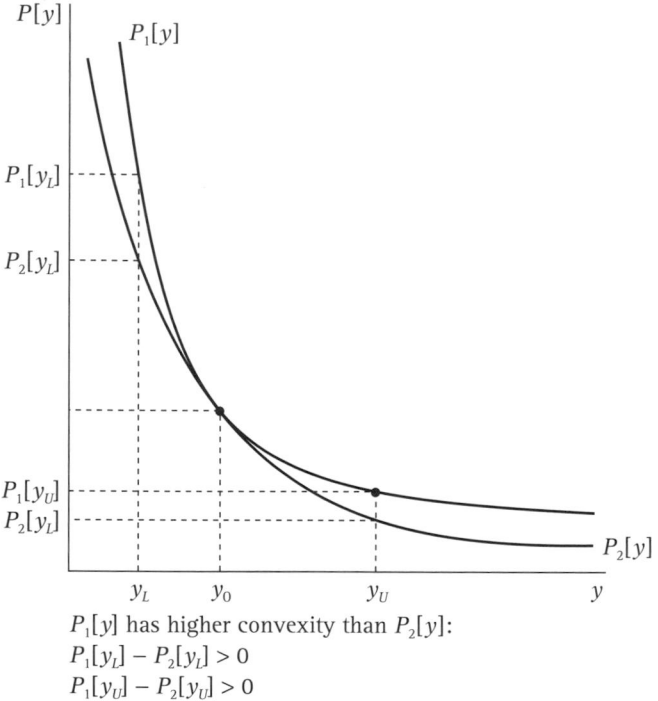

Figure 5.4 Higher convexity provides superior return

not completely explain all of the percentage change in price. Actual evaluation of the expansion follows from observing that $D = 8.5795$ and $CON = 117.478$. It follows that for, say, a 100 bp increase:

$$\%\Delta P_B = -D(.01) + \tfrac{1}{2}CON(.01)^2 = -8.58(.01) + \tfrac{1}{2}\,117.478(.01)^2$$

$$= -8.58\% + .5873\% = 7.99\%$$

This value compares to the actual price change of 8.023%.

To provide an illustration of the impact of convexity, consider the gains associated with the following self-financing portfolio:

1 Purchase one pure discount (zero coupon) bond with a 20 year maturity, with par value of $1 million.
2 Sell short 1.92 pure discount bonds with a 5 year maturity and par value of $1 million per unit. The full value of the short sale proceeds is immediately available.
3 Invest $1,127,490 in bonds with zero duration (cash has $D = 0$).

Without loss of generality, assume that the yield to maturity on all bonds is 5% initially. What is the initial investment in the portfolio? From an inspection of the balance sheet, it is apparent that no investment is required in the portfolio:

Table 5.4 Example of the % price change using modified duration and convexity for a 20-year 10% coupon bond selling at par to yield 10%

	Increase in required yield					
Required yield	10.01%	10.10%	10.50%	11.00%	12.00%	13.00%
Change in basis points	1	10	50	100	200	300
Estimated % change						
Duration	−0.09	−0.86	−4.29	−8.58	−17.16	−25.74
Convexity	0.00	0.01	0.14	0.57	2.27	5.10
Total	−0.09	−0.85	−4.15	−8.01	−14.89	−20.64
Actual % change	−0.09	−0.85	−4.15	−8.02	−15.05	−21.22

	Decrease in required yield					
Required yield	9.99%	9.90%	9.50%	9.00%	8.00%	7.00%
Change in basis points	−1	−10	−50	−100	−200	−300
Estimated % change						
Duration	0.09	0.86	4.29	8.58	17.16	25.74
Convexity	0.00	0.01	0.14	0.57	2.27	5.10
Total	0.09	0.87	4.43	9.15	19.43	30.84
Actual % change	0.09	0.86	4.44	9.20	19.79	32.03

Assets	Liabilities plus net worth
20 year bond $376,890 = 1 \text{ million}/(1.05)^{20}$	Short sale $1,504,370 = 1.92 \text{ million}/(1.05)^5$
Cash $1,127,480	Net worth = $0 (Self Financing)
Total: $1,504,370	

Computing the Macaulay duration of the assets and of the liability reveals that $D_A = (376,890/1,504,370)(20) + 0 = 5 = D_L$. Treating the liabilities as one portfolio and the assets as another, the position conforms to the requirement of equal duration and yield. Calculation of the convexity reveals that the convexity of the assets is $(21/6)$ times larger than the convexity of the liabilities. The portfolio is immunized according to the classical Redington conditions.

Consider what happens if the yield to maturity for all assets and liabilities immediately rises to 6%. In this case, the net value of the portfolio (value of assets less value of liabilities) changes to:

Assets		Liabilities plus net worth	
20 year bond	$311,800 = 1 million/(1.06)^{20}	Short sale	$1,434,740 = 1.92 million/(1.06)^5
Cash	$1,127,480	Net worth	4,540
Total:	$1,439,280		$1,439,280

Now consider what happens if the yield to maturity of all assets and liabilities immediately falls to 4%:

Assets		Liabilities plus net worth	
20 year bond	$456,390 = 1 million/(1.04)^{20}	Short sale	$1,573,100 = 1.92 million/(1.04)^5
Cash	$1,127,480	Net worth	10,770
Total:	$1,583,870		$1,583,870

This example illustrates that basic point: starting from a position of equal duration and yield for the assets and liabilities of the portfolio, whether yields increased or decreased the net worth of the portfolio increased.

Given this background, the initial enthusiasm for convexity is understandable. It appears as though there is a free lunch gain to be achieved from portfolios with higher convexity. In the context of portfolio immunization, this translates into a recommendation for using barbell asset positions to immunize single cash flow liabilities. The resolution of this apparent free lunch can be found in the time value–convexity tradeoff. This tradeoff can be illustrated by considering what happens to the portfolio in the example if yields remain unchanged. Consider the value of the portfolio in 1 year if yields are the same as on the initial portfolio creation date:

Assets		Liabilities plus net worth	
20 year bond	$395,734 = 1 million/(1.05)^{19}	Short sale	$1,579,590 = 1.92 million/(1.05)^4
Cash	$1,127,480	Net Worth	($55,276)
Total:	$1,524,214		$1,524,214

This illustrates the role of convexity. Setting the durations of the portfolios equal, higher convexity portfolios outperform low convexity portfolios whether interest rates go up or down. However, if rates do not change then higher convexity portfolios will underperform lower convexity portfolios. The large time value impact arises because this example does not adequately impose the condition that the initial yields of the two portfolios be equal (see end of chapter questions).

The Taylor series representation of the time value–convexity tradeoff*

The multivariate Taylor series expansion of the function $P_B[y, t]$ can be manipulated to produce the result:

$$\frac{P_B[y, t] - P_B[y_0, t_0]}{P_B[y_0, t_0]} = \frac{1}{P}\frac{\partial P}{\partial y}(y - y_0) + \frac{1}{P}\frac{\partial P}{\partial y}(t - t_0)$$

$$+ \frac{1}{2}\left\{\frac{1}{P}\frac{\partial^2 P}{\partial y^2}(y - y_0)^2 + \frac{1}{P}\frac{\partial^2 P}{\partial t^2}(t - t_0)^2\right\}$$

$$+ \frac{1}{P}\frac{\partial^2 P}{\partial y \partial t}(y - y_0)(t - t_0) + \ldots \; H.O.T.$$

$$\%\Delta P \cong -DUR(y - y_0) + \Theta(t - t_0)$$

$$+ \frac{1}{2}[CON \, (y - y_0)^2 + \Theta_2(t - t_0)^2] + CROSS(y - y_0)(t - t_0)$$

where $DUR = D$, θ is the theta of the bond, Θ_2 relates to the second derivative with respect to time and $CROSS$ relates to the cross product terms. In this presentation, the sign of θ requires interpretation. Much like an option, time counts backwards for a bond. Yet, as time increases, the time to maturity goes down and the value of the bond position increases, i.e., the time derivative is positive. Unlike options where the premium value falls as time increases, for θ to be taken as a positive value it is not necessary to define θ by multiplying by minus one.[15]

Evaluation of the relevant coefficients in the expansion is simplified considerably by using par bonds. This assumption permits the appropriate derivative to be used without having to deal with the valuation of the bond. For example, consider a semi-annual coupon par bond with $C = \$8$ ($C/2 = \$4$), $M = \$100$, $y = .08$ ($y/2 = .04$), $T = 5$ years:

$$P_B[y, t] = C\left[\frac{1}{\frac{y}{2}} - \frac{1}{\frac{y}{2}\left(1 + \frac{y}{2}\right)^{2T}}\right] + \frac{M}{\left(1 + \frac{y}{2}\right)^{2T}}$$

$$\frac{1}{P}\frac{\partial P}{\partial\left(1 + \frac{y}{2}\right)} = \frac{-811.09}{100} \; (in \; half \; years)$$

$$\rightarrow \; D = \frac{8.1109}{2} = 4.055 \; \rightarrow \; D^* = D(1.04) = 4.218$$

Evaluation of convexity follows appropriately:

$$\frac{1}{P}\frac{\partial^2 P}{\partial\left(1+\dfrac{y}{2}\right)^2} = \frac{8,075.43}{100} \; (in \; half \; years^2) \to CON = \frac{8,075.43}{4(100)} = 20.1886 \; (in \; years)$$

Division of the convexity value by four (instead of 2 as in the case of the calculation of duration for semi-annual coupon bonds) is because the derivative is expressed in units of half years squared.

Evaluation of theta is somewhat different. Duration and convexity deal with the change in price for an instantaneous change in yield. Theta deals with the change in value as time passes. Instead of the price impact, theta is concerned with the return earned from holding the bond over a given time period:

$$V[y, t] = P_B = \frac{C/2}{1 + y/2} + \frac{C/2}{(1 + y/2)^2} + \ldots + \frac{M + C/2}{(1 + y/2)^{2T}}$$

$$-\frac{\partial V}{\partial(T - t)} = \frac{\partial V}{\partial t} = \ln\left[1 + \frac{y}{2}\right](M + C/2) \quad (in \; half \; years)$$

This result applies to all bonds, independent of the term to maturity. Evaluating θ for the par bond example given previously $y/2 = .04$, $C/2 = \$4$ gives a half year value of $\theta = 0.04079$. In effect, the time value for a par bond is approximately equal to the coupon payment that is earned from holding the bond. For a non-par bond there will be an additional term associated with the capital gain (loss) due to the price change associated with the impact of time change on a discount (premium) bond, holding interest rates constant.

Adapting an exercise conducted in Chance and Jordan (1995), it is possible to compare the relative contributions for each component of the Taylor series to changes in price for various assumptions about changes in yield and time. Table 5.5 provides a benchmark table that can be used to compare with the results of table 5.4. Table 5.5 provides the values calculated above for D, CON and θ for the four par bond maturities being considered. The initial yield to maturity is 8% for all bonds. The percentage changes in price result from an instantaneous change in yield at all maturities; terms involving changes in time have no impact. The yield change considered is a 10 basis point increase. In table 5.4 it was demonstrated that, for such a small yield change, the D and CON terms in the Taylor series explain virtually all of the price change. Table 5.4 also illustrates that duration will over predict the fall in price due to the increase in yields and the positive impact of CON will offset this over prediction.

These results from table 5.4 are also indicated in table 5.5 where the prediction from D is more than the actual price change, i.e., values of $(D\Delta y/\%\Delta P) > 100\%$). For example, consider the 5 year bond, $D = 4.2177/1.04 = 4.05548$. The predicted $\%\Delta P = 4.05548(.001) = .00405548$. The actual $\%\Delta P$ is $= 99.5955 - 100/100 = -.004045$. Evaluating the absolute value of the predicted change divided by the actual change gives: $.00405548/.004045 = 1.00259 = 100.259\%$. Similarly, for the convexity adjustment: $\frac{1}{2}CON(\Delta y^2) = \frac{1}{2}(20.819)(.00001)$. Evaluating the convexity component divided by the actual price change gives: $-0.0000104095/.00405548 = -.2573\%$. The sum of

Table 5.5 Decomposition of the Taylor series expansion: default free par bonds from 1 year to 30 years to maturity*

Bond maturity (years)	1	5	15	30
Duration (D^*)	0.9808	4.2177	8.9919	11.7642
Convexity	1.3512	20.819	104.978	214.24
Theta (θ)	0.04079	0.04079	0.04079	0.04079
New price	99.9058	99.5955	99.1406	98.8795
$\%\Delta P$	-0.0009	-0.0041	-0.0086	-0.0112
$-(D\Delta y)/\%\Delta P$	100.0717	100.259	100.608	100.9486
$(\frac{1}{2}CON\Delta y^2)/\%\Delta P$	-0.0717	-0.2573	-0.6108	-0.956

*$\Delta y = 10$ basis points, $\Delta t = 0$

Table 5.6 Decomposition of the Taylor series expansion: default free par bonds from 1 year to 30 years to maturity*

Bond maturity (years)	1	5	15	30
Duration (D^*)	0.9808	4.2177	8.9919	11.7642
Convexity	1.3512	20.819	104.978	214.24
Theta (θ)	0.04079	0.04079	0.04079	0.04079
New price	99.9275	99.6174	99.1622	98.901
$\%\Delta V$	-0.0007	-0.0038	-0.0084	-0.011
$-(D\Delta y)/\%\Delta V$	130.0734	106.006	103.1982	102.9245
$(\theta\Delta t)/\%\Delta V$	-29.642	-5.646	-2.5651	-1.9554
$-(Cross\Delta y\Delta t)/\%\Delta V$	-0.3354	-0.040	-0.0093	-0.0019
$(\frac{1}{2}CON\Delta y^2)/\%\Delta V$	-0.0932	-0.2637	-0.625	-0.9747
$(\frac{1}{2}\Theta_2\Delta t^2)/\%\Delta V$	-0.0032	-0.0006	-0.0003	-0.0002

*$\Delta y = 10$ basis points, $\Delta t = 1$ day

the duration and the convexity terms in the Taylor series reproduces the actual price change almost exactly. Such calculations depend on the size of the assumed change in yield. Increasing the change to, say, 100 basis points will reduce the accuracy of the approximation.

Extending table 5.5 to incorporate a one-day change in time produces the results in table 5.6. Converting θ to an annual basis and evaluating the change in value for one day gives .08/365 = .000219. Observing the par value is $100 gives the difference in the "new prices" between tables 5.5 and 5.6. For example, for the five year par bond the actual price change in table 5.5 was $-.4045$. Taking into account the time value in table 5.6 gives an actual price change of $-.4045 + (.000219)(100) = -.3826$. This gives a new price of $100 - .3826 = 99.6174$. The various contributions follow appropriately: $(.00405548)/(.003826) = 106.006\%$. Recognizing the convention that theta has been defined as a positive value, the time value component can be calculated as .000216/.003826 =

Table 5.7 Decomposition of the Taylor series expansion: default free par bonds from 1 year to 30 years to maturity*

Bond maturity (years)	1	5	15	30
Duration (D^*)	0.9809	4.2177	8.9919	11.7642
Convexity	1.3512	20.819	104.978	214.24
Theta (θ)	0.04079	0.04079	0.04079	0.04079
Δy (%)	0.6500	0.4700	0.3875	0.3500
New price	100.084	98.7873	97.3825	96.8174
%ΔV	0.0008	−0.0121	−0.0262	−0.0318
$-(D\Delta y)/\%\Delta V$	−729.3730	157.1763	127.9986	124.3981
$(\theta\Delta t)/\%\Delta V$	767.1437	−53.1648	−24.6315	−20.2577
$-(Cross\Delta y\Delta t)/\%\Delta V$	56.4215	−2.0496	−0.3448	−0.0671
$(\frac{1}{2}CON\Delta y^2)/\%\Delta V$	3.3966	−1.8388	−3.0111	−4.1231
$(\frac{1}{2}\Theta_2\Delta t^2)/\%\Delta V$	2.473	−0.1714	−0.0794	−0.0653

*Δy = one standard deviation (historical), Δt = 30 days

5.646%. Table 5.6 illustrates the importance of the time value component relative to the convexity component. Even for a 30 year bond, the one day impact of interest income exceeds the contribution of convexity. For the type of scenario considered in table 5.6, the contributions from *CROSS* and Θ_2 are insignificant.

Though interesting, table 5.6 poses the difficulty that the values used for the time and yield change were arbitrary. For example, yield changes for short term bonds were assumed to be the same as for long term bonds when, in practice, short term yields are typically more variable than long term yields. In addition, bond trading horizons are often longer than one day. Table 5.7 extends the analysis to incorporate a longer period of time, 30 days, and yield changes that are one standard deviation in size for that time interval, i.e., are typical yield changes. One interesting feature of table 5.7 is the implication of the offsetting effects for time and yield on the results for the 1 year bond. The percentage change in the value of the position is so small, due to the offsetting impacts, that the individual duration and theta components are over seven times larger. Comparing the relative sizes of these two components reveals that for a 1 year bond the impact of a 30-day theta move exceeds the impact from a one-standard deviation duration move. In addition, the *CROSS* term is much larger than the convexity component, a result that extends to the 5 year bond. Even Θ_2 rivals convexity in size for the 1 year bond.

Another interesting result in table 5.7 is that, for a 30 year bond, the theta component of the change in value is about five times larger than the convexity value. For the 15 year bond theta is about eight times larger. Even when a two standard deviation change is considered (not reported), the theta term for the 30 year bond is still larger (9.55 to 7.75) than the convexity impact. This confirms results presented in Kang and Chen (2002) for Treasury bonds and other government bonds that demonstrated a greater role for theta than convexity in the changing value of bond positions. Table 5.7 also illustrates that for the longer term bonds, Θ_2 and *CROSS* are insignificant for both one or two standard deviation change scenarios. The upshot of the information contained in table 5.7 is that the shape of the yield curve imbeds a cost of convexity that appears as a time value. Setting duration and yield for two portfolios to be equal will have a time value cost that will be traded off against the convexity value. This point is discussed further below.

A continuous time solution of the time value–convexity tradeoff*

As demonstrated by Ingersoll (1987, pp. 348–9) and others, Ito's lemma can be derived by applying a Taylor series expansion to an appropriately specified function of a random variable. Given this, it is not surprising that the continuous time solution has a close resemblance to the multivariate Taylor series result. In a one-factor model, this approach starts with an assumption about the SDE driving the spot rate. In general, the SDE takes the form:

$$dr(t) = \mu_r[r,\ t]dt + \sigma_r[r,\ t]dW(t)$$

Following the discussion in section 4.3, this one factor interest rate model can be used to generate a set of current spot interest rates. It follows that $P_B = P[r,\ t]$ and application of Ito's lemma leads to:

$$\frac{dP[r,\ t]}{P[r,\ t]} = \mu_P[r,\ t]dt + \sigma_P[r,\ t]dW(t)$$

where:

$$\mu_P[r,\ t] = \frac{1}{2}\sigma_r^2\ CON - \mu_r[r,\ t]D + \theta \qquad \sigma_P[r,\ t] = \sigma_r[r,\ t]D$$

In words, Ito's lemma has been used to derive the SDE for the bond price from the SDE for the interest rate process.

The next step in the derivation of the continuous time solution to the tradeoff between time value and convexity involves a result that is often used in deriving option pricing models, e.g., Christensen and Sorensen (1994). For example, Garman and Kohlhagen (1983) use this result in deriving the pricing formula for a European currency option. The result can be stated:

$$\frac{\mu_p[r,\ t] - r(t)}{\sigma[r,\ t]} = \lambda[r,\ t]$$

where $\lambda[r,\ t]$ is the risk premium, measured per unit of standard deviation, that applies to all assets. Using absence of arbitrage arguments, it is possible to demonstrate that this λ is the same for all assets, e.g., Ingersoll (1987). Given the specification of λ, it is possible to substitute in the coefficients from the SDE for the bond price to produce a partial differential equation (PDE) that may be solvable.

Substituting the SDE coefficients into the definition for λ gives the PDE:

$$\frac{1}{2}\sigma_r^2 \frac{\partial^2 P}{dr^2} + [\mu_r - \lambda\sigma_r]\frac{\partial P}{\partial r} + \frac{\partial P}{\partial t} - rP = 0$$

$$\rightarrow \quad \frac{\sigma_r^2}{2} CON - [\mu_r - \lambda\sigma_r]D + \theta = r$$

This PDE specification is sufficient to define a tradeoff between convexity and time value. To do this, recognize that P can be specified to refer not only to individual bonds. More generally, P can also refer to portfolios of fixed income securities. With appropriate adjustments, it is possible for these portfolios to contain bonds with embedded options or that are subject to default risk, but this extension will not be considered here. Rather, consider the exercise of comparing two portfolios that are specified to have the same duration. It is possible for each of these portfolios to contain a single bond.

Examining the PDE it is apparent that the coefficients involving r will be the same for different P because the stochastic process for interest rates is the same for fixed income securities. Consider the relationship between the PDE's for two distinct portfolios. Because the PDE's for both portfolios are equal to r, it follows:

$$\frac{\sigma_r^2}{2} CON_1 - [\mu_r - \lambda\sigma_r]D_1 + \theta_1 = r = \frac{\sigma_r^2}{2} CON_2 - [\mu_r - \lambda\sigma_r]D_2 + \theta_2$$

For two portfolios with equal durations, $D_1 = D_2$, it follows that:

$$\frac{\sigma_r^2}{2}[CON_1 - CON_2] = \theta_2 - \theta_1$$

This is the continuous time version of the tradeoff between convexity and time value.

A number of different interpretations can be made of the tradeoff. One interpretation is straight forward: given two portfolios with equal durations, it does not follow that the portfolio with the higher convexity will be necessarily outperform the lower convexity portfolio. Higher convexity comes at the cost of lower time value. The higher convexity portfolio will outperform if the interest rate changes are sufficiently large. If interest rates do not change sufficiently then the lower time value will cause the higher convexity portfolio to underperform. The level, slope and shape of the yield curve at a given point in time reflect the prevailing tradeoff between time value and convexity. Yet, the different possible scenarios for the future term structure make it difficult to infer from a given yield curve shape precise predictions about future yield curve shape and, as a consequence, the relative performance of high and low convexity portfolios.

To see this, compare a barbell portfolio that combines a 1 year and 15 year bond with a portfolio that holds only a 5 year bond. If the yield curve is upward sloping, equating the durations of these two portfolios will involve holding a larger fraction of the portfolio value in the 1 year bond than in the 15 year bond. It follows that the barbell portfolio, which has a higher convexity, will have a lower time value than the portfolio with the 5 year bond. Hence, the shape of the yield curve at a given point in time represents the time value cost of convexity. By introducing fixed income derivative securities such as call options (for convexity adjustment) and futures (for duration adjustment), it may be possible to achieve both duration and convexity matching. Assuming that the one factor model of the term structure is valid, then such duration and convexity matching strategies will also be time value matching.

Another interpretation of the tradeoff can be made by observing that setting the durations of two portfolios equal will produce a given difference in convexity. Though it is possible to construct a large number of possible portfolios that will match the duration of a given portfolio, once a specific matching portfolio is selected the difference in convexities is given. As such, there will then be a tradeoff between the volatility of interest rates and the time value. In effect, the tradeoff involves not just convexity and time value but also interest rate volatility. At higher levels of interest rate volatility, the cost of convexity will be higher in terms of the time value that has to be paid. Following Phoa (1997), it is possible to invert this relationship to seek an explanation for the commonly observed hump-shaped yield curve where the yield on 30 year Treasuries is below the yield on, say, 20 year Treasuries. Because the 30 year Treasury has a higher convexity, the degree of hump in the yield curve could be due to the costs of convexity and used as a measure of the market's expectations of future interest rate volatility.

 ## 5.4 IMMUNIZATION WITH NON-PARALLEL YIELD CURVE SHIFTS*

*Partial durations and convexities**

Redington (1952) recognized that classical immunization theory may fail when shifts in the term structure are not parallel.[16] At least since Bierwag (1977), this failure has led to the development of alternative concepts of fixed income portfolio management such as the maxmin portfolio, e.g., Bierwag and Khang (1979), Prisman (1986), and the recognition of a connection between immunization strategy specification and the type of assumed shocks, e.g., Fong and Vasicek (1984), Chambers et al. (1988).[17] Risk measures associated with convexity, such as M^2, were developed to select the best duration matching portfolio from the set of potential portfolios. Being derived using a specific assumption about the stochastic process generating the term structure, these theoretically attractive models encountered difficulties in practice. In particular, "minimum M^2 portfolios *fail* to hedge as effectively as portfolios including a bond maturing on the horizon date" (Bierwag et al. 1993, p. 1165).[18] This empirical research led to the following result:

> using different data bodies, different term structure estimation procedures, different duration measures, and different time periods – the duration-matching portfolio containing a bond having a maturity matching the planning period length has a smaller portfolio-promised return deviation than portfolios not containing a maturity-matching bond. This empirical regularity is so pervasive that we may view it as an appropriate risk-minimizing duration-matching portfolio strategy. (Bierwag et al. 1993, p. 1148)

This empirical result is referred to as the "duration puzzle." Is this puzzle due to failings of the stochastic process assumption underlying the theoretically derived immunization measures or is there some deeper properties of the immunization process which are not being accurately modelled?

Instead of assuming a specific stochastic process and deriving the optimal immunization conditions, it is possible to leave the process unspecified and work directly with the properties of the expansion of the spot rate pricing function, i.e., employ directional derivatives. The use of directional derivatives to derive worst possible shocks and the associated upper bound on the loss of an "immunized" portfolio is found in Reitano (1991b, 1992), Bowden (1997) and Balbas and Ibanez (1998). This line of development has the attractive feature of allowing the introduction of partial durations and convexities associated with the relevant spot interest rates. In Reitano (1991b, 1992), the bounds are derived from Cauchy-Schwarz and quadratic form restrictions inherited from the normed vector space. A closely related problem is adequately solved by Bowden (1997) through the use of the Gateaux differential.

Reitano (1991a,b, 1992, 1996) provides a seminal, if not widely recognized, analysis of duration and bond portfolio immunization. Reitano evaluates a multivariate Taylor series for the asset and liability price functions specified using spot interest rates. Defining a norm applicable to a parallel yield curve shift, Reitano is able to identify bounds on the possible deviations from classical immunization conditions. In other words, even though classical immunization conditions are violated for non-parallel yield curve shifts, it is still possible to put theoretical bounds on the deviations from classical conditions. In addition, it is also possible to identify the specific types of shifts that represent the greatest loss or gain. Developing the Gateaux differential approach introduced by Bowden (1997), Balbas and Ibanez (1998) rediscover the possibility of defining such bounds, albeit in a more sophisticated mathematical framework. Balbas and Ibanez also introduce a novel innovation: a linear dispersion measure that, when minimized, permits identification of the "best" portfolio within the class of immunizing portfolios. More precisely, a strategy of matching duration and minimizing the dispersion measure identifies the portfolio that will minimize immunization risk and, as a consequence, provides an optimal upper bound for possible loss on the portfolio.

The multivariate Taylor series expansion can be applied to motivate the directional derivative approach to fixed income portfolio immunization. Recognizing that P_B is a function of the T spot interest rates contained in $z = \{z_1, z_2 \ldots z_T\}$, it is possible to apply a multivariate Taylor series expansion to this bond price formula, that leads to the concepts of partial duration and partial convexity:[19]

$$P(z) = P(z_0) + \sum_{t=1}^{T} \frac{\partial P(z_{t,0})}{\partial z_t}(z_t - z_{t,0}) + \frac{1}{2!}\sum_{i=1}^{T}\sum_{j=1}^{T}\frac{\partial^2 P(\cdot)}{\partial z_i \partial z_j}(z_i - z_{i,0})(z_j - z_{j,0}) + H.O.T.$$

$$\rightarrow \quad \frac{P(z) - P(z_0)}{P(z_0)} \cong -\sum_{t=1}^{T} D_t(z_t - z_{t,0}) + \frac{1}{2!}\sum_{i=1}^{T}\sum_{j=1}^{T} CON_{i,j}(z_i - z_{i,0})(z_j - z_{j,0}) \qquad (1)$$

where $z_0 = (z_{1,0}, z_{2,0}, \ldots, z_{T,0})'$ is the Tx1 vector of initial spot interest rates, D_t is partial duration associated with z_t, the spot interest rate for time t, and $CON_{i,j}$ is the partial convexity associated with the spot interest rates z_i and z_j for i,j defined over $(1, 2, \ldots T)$.[20] This formulation is useful for examining the impact of non-parallel yield curve shifts on fixed income portfolio strategies.

Observing that the partial durations can be identified with a $T \times 1$ vector $D_T = (D_1, D_2, \ldots D_T)'$ and the partial convexities with a $T \times T$ matrix C_T with elements $C_{i,j}$, the model proceeds by applying results from the theory of normed linear vector spaces to identify theoretical bounds on D_T and C_T. In the case of D_T, the Cauchy-Schwarz inequality is used.[21] For C_T the bounds are based on restrictions on the eigenvalues of C_T derived from the theory of quadratic forms. To access these results, it is necessary to specify a norm and the norm selected, often referred to as a *direction vector*, is intuitively appealing. More precisely, taken as a group, the $(z_t - z_{0,t})$ changes in the individual spot interest rates represent shifts in yield curve shape. These individual changes can be reexpressed as the product of a direction shift N and a magnitude Δi:

$$(z_t - z_{t,0}) = n_t \, \Delta i \quad \text{where:} \quad N = (n_1, n_2, \ldots, n_T)'$$

From this, the spot rate curve is shocked and the immunization bounds can be derived. This approach differs slightly from shocking the yield curve and deriving the associated change in the spot rate curve. Using the spot rate approach, it follows that $N_0 = (1, 1, \ldots, 1)'$ represents a parallel shift in the spot rate curve, with the size of the shift determined by Δi. Using this substitution (1) becomes:

$$\frac{P(z) - P(z_0)}{P(z_0)} \cong -\Delta i [N'D_T] + \Delta i^2 [N'C_T N]$$

Because the unit shift has been applied to spot rate rates, it is only for a parallel shift of a flat term structure that the partial duration and convexity measures, $N_0'D_T$ and $N_0'C_T N_0$. reduce to the classical definitions of duration and convexity, e.g., Reitano (1992, p. 38).

Duration and convexity bounds

Starting with the bond price function is instructive because it establishes a direct connection to the basic building blocks of the portfolio, the cash flows associated with individual assets and liabilities. Using the objective of fund surplus immunization, e.g., Messmore (1990), Reitano (1992) produces a slightly more complicated problem than calculating the partial durations and convexities for individual assets and liabilities in isolation. Surplus immunization involves recognizing the balance sheet relationship: $A = L + S$, where A is the assets held by the fund, L is the fund liabilities and S is the accumulated surplus. The objective of immunizing the portfolio surplus, $S = A - L$, against future changes in interest rates requires:

$$S(z) = \sum_{t=1}^{T} \frac{CF_t}{(1 + z_t)^t} \quad \rightarrow \quad \frac{S(z) - S(z_0)}{S(z_0)} = 0 \cong -\Delta i [N'D_T] + \Delta i^2 [N'C_T N] \tag{2}$$

where D_T and C_T are now defined for the fund surplus, $S(z)$, and the cash flows at time t, CF_t, are the sum of the asset (+) and liability (–) cash flows that occur at time t. Because CF_t will be negative when the liability cash outflow exceeds the asset cash inflow at time t, it is possible for either the duration of surplus or convexity of surplus to take negative values, depending on the selected portfolio composition and yield curve shape.

It is not difficult to identify the analytical importance of the directional derivative approach. For analytical reasons, it will be easier to work with unit shifts in the spot rate curves. This requires a connection between the key building blocks of the directional derivative approach, the partial durations and convexities, and the associated classical concepts, for both the unit yield curve and spot rate curve shifts. As noted previously, the concepts are only equivalent for parallel shifts of flat yield curves. If the yield curve is not flat to start, then a unit vector change in yields, $N_0 = (1, 1, \ldots 1)'$, is then spread differentially across the spot interest rates.[22] Heuristically, this can be seen by evaluating the total derivative of $S(z)$:[23]

$$dS(z) = \frac{\partial S}{\partial z_1} dz_1 + \frac{\partial S}{\partial z_2} dz_2 + \ldots + \frac{\partial S}{\partial z_T} dz_T \quad \rightarrow \quad \frac{dS(z)}{S} = \sum_{t=1}^{T} \frac{1}{S} \frac{\partial S}{\partial z_t} dz_t$$

If it is possible to set $dz_1 = dz_2 = \ldots = dz_T = dy$, then the unit yield curve shift result applies:

$$D^S = \frac{1}{S} \frac{dS}{dy} = \sum_{t=1}^{T} \frac{1}{S} \frac{\partial S}{\partial z_t} = \sum_{t=1}^{T} D_t = D_N{}^S$$

where D^S is the classical modified duration of surplus. Yet, the assumption of equal changes in spot rates and yields will only apply when starting from a flat yield curve. There is a dependence among the spot interest rates that cannot be arbitrarily ignored. Even when $N_0 = (1, 1, \ldots, 1)'$ it is not generally true that the sum of the partial durations calculated with a norm using a parallel change in spot rates will equal the classical duration. For example, unless the yield curve is flat, the classical duration for a coupon bond will not equal the duration calculated using the sum of the partial durations.[24] A similar comment applies to the convexity measures.

Using a unit change in spot rates to specify the norm can also lead to other theoretical confusions that can only be resolved by making reference to market reality. For example, Reitano selects an example with three relevant maturities, one maturity applicable to a 5 year zero coupon liability and two maturities applicable to a 6 month zero coupon asset and a 10 year coupon bond. Even though there will be partial durations and convexities associated with the regular coupon payments, only three maturity dates are incorporated into the analysis. Assuming *semi-annual* coupon payments, incorporating all the dates with cash flows would increase the number of elements in N_0 to $2T = 20$. Doing this would increase the parallel shift norming vector from $N_0'N_0 = 3$ to $N_0'N_0 = 20$. This would immediately increase the Cauchy-Schwarz bounds on $N'D_T$, even where the bounds are calculated directly from the extreme shift vector.[25] Following

Poitras (2003), consider the form of the extreme value solutions for the elements of N, e.g., for n_1^*, where the norming vector only identifies three yield curve points, i.e., $N_0 = (1, 1, 1)'$:

$$n_1^* = \sqrt{\frac{3}{1 + \left(\dfrac{D_2}{D_1}\right)^2 + \left(\dfrac{D_3}{D_1}\right)^2}}$$

Now consider the solution where the norming vector admits all the 20 cash flow points:

$$n_1^* = \sqrt{\frac{20}{1 + \left(\dfrac{D_2}{D_1}\right)^2 + \left(\dfrac{D_3}{D_1}\right)^2 + \ldots + \left(\dfrac{D_{20}}{D_1}\right)^2}}$$

Such N values would almost surely result in a substantial increase in the bounds with no substantive change in the underlying immunization situation.[26]

A mathematical resolution to this norming problem is achieved by making reference to market reality. Similar to the selection of an investment horizon, the initial specification of the optimization problem fixes the dimension of the term structure and then conducts calculations relative to this initial term structure. For example, this is the motivation for the "key rate durations" in Phoa and Shearer (1997). Once the dimension of T is set, it follows that for the semiannual payment frequency:

$$N_1 = \left(\frac{1}{\sqrt{2T}}, \frac{1}{\sqrt{2T}}, \ldots, \frac{1}{\sqrt{2T}}\right) \quad \rightarrow \quad N_1'N_1 = 1$$

where T is the longest maturity (in years) of the assets and liabilities contained in the portfolio. In this case, $N_1'N_1 = 1$ is independent of the number of cash flow payment dates.[27] This solution to the inherent problems with the use of $N_0 = (1, 1, \ldots, 1)'$ to specify the norm now requires interpretation of $N_1'D_T$ to involve multiplication by $2T^{1/2}$ to be equal to $N_0'D_T$. Even though this adjustment is inconsequential when the initial objective is to set the duration of surplus equal to zero, where comparisons with classical duration results are involved the adjustment by $2T^{1/2}$ is required. This difficulty can be readily resolved by factoring out $2T^{1/2}$ and redefining the magnitude of the shift as $(\Delta i/(2T)^{1/2})$. Scaling the magnitude of the shift in this fashion, as in Bowden (1997) and Balbas and Ibanez (1998), facilitates comparisons to be made across portfolios with different cash flow patterns, where norming with $N_1'N_1 = 1$ is an essential step.

Another related issue concerns the use of a key rate element vector when there is actually a larger number of cash flow payment dates. The advantage of this seemingly inconsistent reduction in the number of maturity points in the yield curve vector is that the calculated extreme bound vectors have the appearance of actual yield curve shifts. Where the yield curve or spot rate vectors are specified with all the actual number of cash flow payments, the optical appearance of the extreme shifts often seems unrealistic. More precisely, similar to the difficulties that led to the introduction of key rate durations, e.g., Ho (1992), Phoa and Shearer (1997), the yield curve shape associated with the extreme upper and lower bounds will have an unusual sawtooth pattern. The n_t will reflect the size of the cash flow in period t, small cash flow periods will have n_t close to zero and large cash flow periods will have relatively large n_t. Yet, as it turns out, exploring this apparent problem leads to insight into other quandaries in immunization analysis, such as the so-called "duration puzzle" (Bierwag et al. 1993). The essential step is to recognize that the duration matching (zero duration of surplus) portfolio is not unique. It is possible to pick the composition of the portfolio to reduce the sensitivity of the portfolio value against certain types of yield curve shifts. In terms of the directional derivative approach, it is possible to construct the portfolio to have the upper and lower extreme bounds that are "tighter" to the zero duration of surplus condition, e.g., Reitano (1996). However, achieving tightness does not necessarily undercut the possibility of extreme yield curves that possess the sawtooth pattern.

One final point of interest about the directional derivative concerns the associated convexity calculation. Consider the direct calculation of the partial convexity of surplus, $CON_{i,j}^S$, where $i \neq j$:

$$S(z) = \sum_{t=1}^{T} \frac{CF_t}{(1+z_t)^t} \;\;\rightarrow\;\; \frac{\partial S(z)}{\partial z_i} = \frac{iCF_i}{(1+z_i)^{i+1}} \;\;\rightarrow\;\; \frac{\partial^2 S(z)}{\partial z_i \partial z_j} = 0 \quad for \;\; i \neq j$$

where CF_t is the cash flow at time t for $t = (1, 2, \ldots T)$. From these, it follows that the quadratic form $N'C_T^S N$ reduces to:

$$N'C_T^S N = \sum_{t=1}^{T} n_t^2 \, CON_{t,t}^S = \sum_{t=1}^{T} n_t^2 \frac{1}{S(z_0)} \frac{\partial^2 S(z_0)}{\partial z_t^2}$$

In terms of the extreme bounds on convexity, this is a significant simplification. Because the TxT convexity matrix is diagonal, the extreme bounds are now given by the maximum and minimum diagonal ($CON_{i,i}$) elements. If the ith element is a maximal element, the associated N^{**} vector is a Tx1 with a one in the ith position and zeros elsewhere. Similar to the duration adjustment, there will be complications in directly comparing $N_1'C_T N_1$ with either the classical convexity or $N_0'C_T N_0$.

Some basic calculations and examples

To facilitate heuristic comparison with Reitano (1991a, 1991b, 1992, 1996), the fixed liability in the portfolio initially being examined is identical to that for the example of Reitano (1992): a \$100 million par value, zero coupon GIC maturing in year 5.[28] This liability is being hedged with the same two assets, 6 month commercial paper, with market value A_1, and a 12% coupon (semi-annual) 10 year bond, with market value A_2. Variation in the universe of assets and liabilities will eventually be introduced, though asset selection is restricted to combinations of short term, zero coupon money market instruments and longer term coupon bearing bonds. This is consistent with the absence in fixed income markets of competitively priced, zero coupon long term securities, i.e., long term fixed income markets have a preference for coupon bonds. The portfolio management objective is to choose the asset composition of the balance sheet such that the duration of surplus equal to zero is retained. Because variation in the market/par values of the balance sheet items will be permitted, a methodology is needed to determine the relevant values. Initially, the yield/spot interest rate curve from Fabozzi (1993) is selected. This *par bond* curve has semi-annual yields from 6 months to 10 years, i.e., $y = (.08, .083, .089, .092, .094, .097, .10, .104, .106, .108, .109, .112, .114, .116, .118, .119, .12, .122, 124, .125)'$. The 6 month and 1 year yields are for zero coupon securities, with the remaining yields applying to par coupon bonds. This yield curve produces the associated spot rate curve, $z = (.08, .083, .0893, .0925, .0946, .0979, .1013, .106, .1083, .1107, .1118, .1159, .1186, .1214, .1243, .1256, .1271, .1305, .1341, .1358)'$.[29]

The first point to illustrate involves the result that the sum of the partial durations will not typically equal the classical duration, which is the case here because the yield curve slopes up. Observe that the partial duration and classical duration formulas can be specified, using semi-annual cash flows, as:[30]

$$N_0 D_T = D_N^S = \frac{1}{S} \sum_{t=1}^{2T} \frac{\{t/2\} CF_t}{(1 + \{z_t/2\})^{t+1}} \qquad D^S = \frac{1}{S} \sum_{t=1}^{2T} \frac{\{t/2\} CF_t}{(1 + \{y/2\})^{t+1}}$$

where $N_0' D_T$ is the duration of portfolio surplus calculated using the partial durations and D^S is the classical duration of surplus measure. To use these formulas to calculate the durations of a coupon bond, with regular semi-annual coupon payments, set $C/2 = CF_t$ for $t = 1$ to $(2T - 1)$, and the coupon plus return of principal, $C/2 + M = CF_{2T}$. Observing that surplus is defined by the balance sheet identity $L + S = A$, set $L = 0$ and admit only one balance sheet asset, the coupon bond. This transforms the formulas into the appropriate form. Term by term comparison for the upward sloping yield curve case reveals that the sum of the partial durations for the coupon bond must be less than the classical duration, requiring that $N_0' D_T < D^S$. For example, for a $T = 10$ semi-annual coupon par bond with C = 12.5%, for the Fabozzi yield curve the (modified) classical duration is 5.62 and $N_0' D_T = 5.42$. This type of discrepancy can produce significant differences in the composition of immunizing portfolios, both for the initial portfolio as well as when yield curves change location and shape.[31]

Recognizing that the liability is a zero coupon security, the 5 year spot rate is used to determine the price, $P_L = \$58.3427$ million, and the partial duration, $D_L = 4.738$. The example immunization problem is to pick A_1 and A_2 such that the duration of surplus, D_N^S, equals zero. The balance sheet identity $S + L = A_1 + A_2$ provides an additional restriction. Allowing for the value of the surplus to be positive, the zero duration of surplus condition requires:

$$w_1 D_{A1} + w_2 D_{A2} - w_3 D_L = 0 \quad \rightarrow \quad D_L = x_1 D_{A1} + x_2 D_{A2}$$

where $w_1 = A_1/S$, $w_2 = A_2/S$, $w_3 = P_L/S$, $S = A_1 + A_2 - P_L$, $x_1 = A_1/P_L$ and $x_2 = A_2/P_L$. The relevant asset durations are $D_{A1} = 0.481$ and $D_{A2} = 5.462$. For the problem at hand, if S is undetermined, the system is over-identified with 2 equations and 3 unknowns. This provides for a theoretically infinite number of possible combinations of the two assets that would achieve the immunization condition. In practice, the surplus would also be given, inherited from the previous history of the fund's performance. With both the surplus and liability given, there are now two equations to satisfy with only two variables to choose. Unless more assets are available, which would often be the case in practice, it is not possible to arbitrarily fix one of the asset values, permitting the surplus immunization condition to determine the (positive) value of the other asset. Both asset values are determined once the market values of the surplus and liability are given. In addition, for purposes of calculating this example, because the long term asset is a discount bond it is necessary to have a methodology for determining the par value associated with the given market price.

More precisely, an additional complication arises when the coupon bond is not a par bond. This happens in the current example where the bond sells at a discount. Because the relevant yield curve is for **par bonds**, it is not appropriate to apply the 10 year yield to the price to calculate the coupon cash flows. Even though it is possible to calculate the price using the spot interest rates, this creates calculation difficulties when the value of the asset is being changed to, say, achieve an immunization objective. To get around this difficulty, it is expedient to unbundle the cash flows from the discount bond into a combination of a par bond and a zero coupon bond. This recognizes that, relative to a par bond, a discount bond has a larger portion of the cash flow occurring at maturity. For example, assume that the par value, M, of the 10 year discount bond is $48. The annual cash flow from the coupon will be $(.12)(48) = 5.76$ which is the same as the cash flow from a par bond with $M = 46.08$.[32] The difference between $48 - 46.08 = 1.92$ is the M for the relevant 10 year zero coupon bond. The price of the discount bond follows appropriately:

$$P_{A2} = \$46.08 + \frac{\$1.92}{(1 + \{.1358/2\})^{20}} = \$46.5963$$

This price can now be used to calculate the duration of the asset as the value weighted sum of the par bond duration and the zero coupon duration.

The initial balance sheet being investigated is "high surplus": $S (= 33.8387) + L (= 58.3427) = A_1 (= 45.5851) + A_2 (= 46.5963)$. It is readily verified that these values satisfy the immunization of surplus condition:

$$D_N^S = \frac{45.5851}{33.8387}(.4808) + \frac{46.5963}{33.8387}(5.4617) - \frac{58.3427}{33.8387}(4.7377) = 0$$

Now consider what happens when the $L + S$ side of the balance sheet is reconstructed to be "low surplus" by increasing the par value of the liability to $150 million, such that $L (= 87.5141) + S (= 4.6674)$. Even though the total of the $S + L$ side of the balance sheet is unchanged, the previous asset composition no longer immunizes the surplus:

$$D_N{}^S = \frac{45.5851}{4.6674}(.4808) + \frac{46.5963}{4.6674}(5.4617) - \frac{87.5141}{4.6674}(4.7377) = -29.61$$

The immunizing portfolio is now $A_1 = 17.8382$ and $A_2 = 74.3432$. The calculated par value for this bond price is 76.4928. This par value is needed for direct calculation of the coupon and principal cash flows in the partial durations.

Both the high and low surplus cases can be examined using the Fabozzi spots as the baseline spot rate curve. Table 5.8 reports the partial durations, the n_t and extreme duration bounds calculated from the Cauchy-Schwarz inequality. Comparison of the bounds between the low and high surplus cases depends crucially on the observation that the bounds relate to the percentage change in the surplus. Due to the smaller position in the 6 month asset, the larger bounds for the low surplus case still translate to a larger relative change when compared to the high surplus case. This result is calculated by multiplying the reported bound by the size of the surplus. As expected, the extreme shift vector, N^*, exhibits a sawtooth change, with about 80% of the worst shift concentrated on a fall in the 5 year yield and 17–20% on an increase in the 10 year rate.[33] This is an immediate implication of the limited exposure to cash flows in other time periods. However, even in this relatively simple portfolio management problem, the n_t provide useful information about the worst case shift. There is not much loss of content in heuristically "filling in" the sawtooth pattern, adjusting upward the small partial durations in the intervening periods. Consistent with basic intuition, the implication is that the worst type of shift has a sizeable fall in mid-term rates combined with smaller, but still significant rise in long term rates. As it turns out, filling in the sawtooth patterns in rates cannot be done arbitrarily but must satisfy basic absence of arbitrage conditions. When this is done, the extreme duration bounds are impacted.

Table 5.8 is constructed to be roughly comparable to the example in Reitano (1991, 1992, 1996). Of the range of possible extensions, increasing the number of assets to include the addition of a maturity matching bond is of topical interest. The impact of including such bonds is the source of the "duration puzzle" in Bierwag et al. (1993). Table 5.9 provides results for two cases with similar surplus levels but with somewhat different asset compositions. One case involves, a par bond with a maturity that matches that of the zero coupon liability ($T = 5$). This is referred to as the *maturity bond* portfolio. The other case does not include the maturity matching bond but, instead, uses 3 and 7 year par bonds. This is referred to as the *split maturity* portfolio. For both asset portfolios the 1/2 year and 10 year bonds of table 5.1 are included, with the position in the 10 year bond being the same in both asset portfolios. The 1/2 year bond position is permitted to vary, with the maturity matching portfolio holding a slightly higher market value of the 1/2 year asset. *A priori*, the split maturity portfolio would seem to have an advantage as four assets are being used to immunize instead of the three bonds in the maturity matching portfolio.

Given this, the results in table 5.9 are revealing. In particular, the asset portfolio with the maturity matching bond has much smaller extreme bounds even though more bonds are being selected in the split maturity portfolio. The partial durations reveal that, as expected, the presence of a maturity matching bond reduces the partial duration at $T = 5$ compared to the split maturity case. The partial durations at $T = 3$ and $T = 7$ are

Table 5.8 Partial durations, $\{n_t\}$ and extreme bounds for the high and low surplus examples[a]

| Date | High surplus | | Low surplus | |
	D	n^a	D	n^a
0.5	0.687	0.0775	2.292	0.0236
1.0	0.075	0.0085	0.870	0.0089
1.5	0.107	0.0121	1.238	0.0128
2.0	0.136	0.0153	1.569	0.0162
2.5	0.161	0.0182	1.863	0.0192
3.0	0.183	0.0206	2.111	0.0217
3.5	0.201	0.0226	2.318	0.0239
4.0	0.214	0.0241	2.472	0.0254
4.5	0.226	0.0255	2.611	0.0269
5.0	−7.933	−0.89545	−86.115	−0.88658
5.5	0.244	0.0275	2.815	0.0290
6.0	0.246	0.0277	2.837	0.0292
6.5	0.247	0.0279	2.854	0.0294
7.0	0.246	0.0278	2.845	0.0293
7.5	0.243	0.0275	2.810	0.0289
8.0	0.242	0.0273	2.792	0.0287
8.5	0.239	0.0269	2.758	0.0284
9.0	0.231	0.0260	2.664	0.0274
9.5	0.221	0.0249	2.551	0.0263
10.0	3.786	0.42733	43.742	0.45033
Extreme duration bounds:	Cauchy = |D| 8.860		Cauchy = |D| 97.131	
Surplus:	33.8387		4.66735	

[a] The high surplus portfolio is composed of ($45.581) 1/2 year and ($46.5963) 10 year bonds. The low surplus portfolio is composed of ($17.8382) 1/2 year and ($74.343) 10 year bonds. The liability for the high surplus portfolio is a 5 year zero coupon bond with $100 par value and market value of $58.3427. The liability for the low surplus portfolio is a 5 year zero coupon bond with $150 par value and market value of $87.514. The extreme Cauchy bounds are derived using $|N| = 1$.

proportionately higher in the split maturity case to account for the difference at $T = 5$. The small difference in the partial duration at $T = 10$ is due solely to the small difference in the size of the surplus. Examining the $n_t{}^*$ reveals that there is not a substantial difference in the sensitivity to changes in five year rates, as might be expected. Rather, the split maturity portfolio redistributes the interest rate sensitivity along the yield curve. In contrast, the maturity bond portfolio is more heavily exposed

Table 5.9 Partial durations, $\{n_i\}$ and extreme bounds for the maturity bond and split maturity examples[a]

Date	Maturity bond		Split maturity	
	D	n^a	D	n^a
0.5	0.476	0.0183	0.251	0.0063
1.0	0.454	0.0174	0.446	0.0112
1.5	0.646	0.0248	0.635	0.0159
2.0	0.818	0.0314	0.804	0.0201
2.5	0.971	0.0373	0.955	0.0239
3.0	1.101	0.0422	7.737	0.1939
3.5	1.208	0.0464	0.834	0.0209
4.0	1.288	0.0494	0.889	0.0223
4.5	1.361	0.0522	0.939	0.0235
5.0	−23.866	−0.91558	−36.998	−0.92716
5.5	0.636	0.0244	1.012	0.0254
6.0	0.641	0.0246	1.020	0.0256
6.5	0.645	0.0247	1.026	0.0257
7.0	0.643	0.0247	8.177	0.2049
7.5	0.635	0.0244	0.601	0.0151
8.0	0.631	0.0242	0.597	0.0150
8.5	0.623	0.0239	0.590	0.0148
9.0	0.602	0.0231	0.569	0.0143
9.5	0.577	0.0221	0.545	0.0137
10.0	9.884	0.37921	9.350	0.23430
Extreme duration bounds:	Cauchy = $\|D\|$ 26.07		Cauchy = $\|D\|$ 39.905	
Surplus:	10.32685		10.91804	

[a] The maturity bond portfolio is composed of ($5.13) 1/2 year, ($55.54) 5 year and ($37.172) 10 year bonds. The split maturity portfolio is composed of ($0.4105) 1/2 year, ($33.8435) 3 year, (27.0) 7 year and ($37.172) 10 year bonds. The liability is a 5 year zero coupon bond with $150 par value and market value of $87.5121. The extreme Cauchy bounds are derived using $\|N\| = 1$.

to changes in 10 year rates. This greater exposure along the yield curve by the split maturity portfolio results in wider extreme duration bounds because the norming restriction dampens the allowable movement in any individual interest rate. In other words, spreading interest rate exposure along the yield curve by picking assets across a greater number of maturities acts to increase the exposure to yield curve shifts of unit length.

? Questions

1*(a) The Vasicek (1977) mean-reverting SDE model of the short term rate can be used to solve for the price of a zero coupon bond that pays \$1 at time T as:

$$P(t, T) = A(t, T)e^{-B(t,T)r(t)}$$

where:

$$B(t, T) = \frac{1 - e^{\kappa(T-r)}}{\kappa}$$

$$A(t, T) = \exp\left[\frac{\{B(t, T) - (T - t)\}\{\kappa^2\mu - (\sigma^2/2)\}}{\kappa^2} - \frac{\sigma^2 B(t, T)^2}{4\kappa}\right]$$

Using these results, solve for an equation specifying the term structure of interest rates. (Hint: see Hull 2003, pp. 538–40.)

(b) The CIR (1985) mean-reverting square root model of the short term rate can be used to solve for the price of a zero coupon bond that pays \$1 at time T as:

$$P(t, T) = A(t, T)e^{-B(t,T)r(t)}$$

where:

$$B(t, T) = \frac{2(e^{\gamma(T-t)} - 1)}{2\gamma + (\kappa + \gamma + \lambda)(e^{\gamma(T-t)} - 1)}$$

$$A(t, T) = \left[\frac{2\gamma(e^{\gamma(T-t)} - 1)}{2\gamma + (\kappa + \gamma + \lambda)(e^{\gamma(T-t)} - 1)}\right]^{\frac{2\kappa\mu}{\sigma^2}}$$

$$\gamma = \sqrt{(\kappa + \lambda)^2 + 2\sigma^2}$$

and λ is a parameter that is related to the risk aversion properties of the representative investor. Following the approach used in (a), use this result to solve for the term structure.

2 What is the relationship between Macaulay duration and the term to maturity for: (a) a zero coupon bond; (b) a perpetuity; (c) discount bonds;

(d) par and premium bonds. Plot the relationship between these four cases in a single diagram. (Hint: see Bierwag et al. 1983, p. 17.)

3 In the example of section 5.3 it was assumed that the asset portfolio contained a combination of a twenty year zero and cash. Rework this example using a one year zero coupon bond and a twenty year zero. If a flat yield curve is assumed, what is your estimate of the change in the value of the liability and the asset if yields are unchanged and one year is allowed to pass. Rework your answer assuming the yield curve slopes up with the one year yield = 4%, the five year = 5% and the 20 year equal to 6%.

4* "Whether the bond market moves up or down, high-convexity portfolios will always outperform low-convexity portfolios of equal duration and yield." Explain the argument supporting this statement. What factors would tend to undermine this position?

5* Explain this statement: "the larger the convexity on a portfolio, the less the value of the portfolio rises over time if the interest rate remains unchanged." What are the implications of this result for the asset/liability managers seeking to control interest rate risk? Is it true that "the cost of a higher convexity is a lower yield"?

6* Tables 5.6 and 5.7 were calculated using an increase in yield and a reduction in time. Because value increases with time changes, due to the payment of interest income, and falls in value when yields increase, the contributions from yield and time changes act in opposite directions. Re-calculate the relevant values in these tables for a decrease in yield and a reduction in time.

7* "Classical immunization strategies, which explicitly assume parallel yield curve shifts, cannot in theory be expected to provide immunization when the yield curve shifts (are nonparallel) . . . However, these conditions readily generalize to conditions that insure immunization against any given yield curve shift assumption. Unfortunately, these conditions are not compatible in general. That is, immunization against a given type of shift will often create exposure to other types of shifts, causing immunization to fail as other shifts are realized."

Comment on the implications of this statement for asset and liability management. In your answer, be sure to identify what are "classical immunization strategies" and to explain how the generalized immunization conditions can be used to provide estimates of the degree of immunization risk.

NOTES

1 In Canada, a GIC (guaranteed investment certificate) can be issued by a financial institution such as a chartered bank. In the US such liabilities are referred to as certificates of deposit.

2 "Dispersion" is a description of the time profile of the cash flows. For example, a zero coupon bond has a cash flow without dispersion. The single cash flow is concentrated at a single maturity date. A coupon bond with the same maturity date has considerably more dispersion, as the coupon cash flows occur at dates prior to the maturity date. A fixed coupon annuity with the same maturity date has even more dispersion as the cash flows are concentrated evenly across all the payment dates. In theoretical examples, it is conventional to achieve greater dispersion by using a barbell portfolio of assets, where assets with only short and long maturities are used to immunize a liability with an intermediate term maturity.

3 Due to the absence of a 10 year instrument in Italy, Singapore and New Zealand, Dym (1992) uses the longest maturity active bond, without actually saying what was involved. As these three countries are involved in some of the atypical results, some caution must be taken because of possible yield curve distortions.

4 This expansion is sometimes presented by setting $a = x_0$ and considering a small region around x_0 by setting $x = x_0 + \varepsilon$. Using these substitutions, $x - a = \varepsilon$. Redington (1952) uses this form of the expansion.

5 Malliaris and Brock (1982) survey the range of applications in economics and finance.

6 To see this is not difficult. By construction, if y is lognormally distributed then for $\ln[y] = x$, x is normally distributed. A normally distributed variable is a real variable which can take values ranging over the real line from positive to negative infinity. Observing $\exp\{\ln[y]\} = y = \exp\{x\}$, if x takes the value of minus infinity, the lowest possible value for x on the real line, then y will take a value of zero. Hence, a lognormal variable is defined on the positive half-line, ranging from 0 to positive infinity.

7 The empirical literature on the distribution of security and derivative prices is voluminous. A useful introduction is included in Duffie (1989).

8 In the form given, the OU process is a form of arithmetic Gaussian process. Unlike the geometric case, this type of process admits the possibility of negative values for X. In certain cases, this difficulty can be rationalized away by arguing that only short term options are of interest. In other words, the probability of observing negative values increases with the length of the permissible time paths. If these paths are constrained to be short, then there will only be a negligible probability of observing negative values.

9 Analytically, the admissibility of a given diffusion for arbitrage free financial pricing depends on satisfaction of conditions required for Girsanov's theorem to hold. A discussion and application of this point to using Brownian bridge process to model bond prices is provided in Cheng (1991).

10 Extending analysis to this type of process can be motivated by observing that a diffusion process can be created from the countable combination of Poisson processes.

11 As discussed previously and elaborated in section 5.2, the interest rate is the most appropriate variable to model directly as a stochastic process. The bond price process can then be derived by applying Ito's lemma.

12 Various technical conditions associated with the lemma are suppressed, e.g., restrictions on f[·] and σ[·]. These details can be found in various sources, e.g., Arnold (1974). It should also be recognized that other approaches to differentiation and integration of stochastic functions is possible, e.g., Meyer (1976).

13 Ingersoll (1987, pp. 348–9) motivates Ito's lemma using a Taylor series expansion and ignoring terms which are of order Δt.

14 Because the nominal bond price does not have a Brownian component, no cross product terms of the form {dB dP} appear. This simplification is what makes Fischer's derivation uncomplicated.

15 A similar convention is used to define the theta for an option, e.g., Poitras (2002, ch. 9).

16 Classical immunization theory originates with Reddington (1952) where it was proposed that duration matching of assets and liabilities combined with a higher convexity of assets will minimize a life insurance company's possibility of loss from unexpected changes in market rates of interest.

17 Wu (2000) and Barber (1999) provide recent treatments of these alternative approaches to duration measures and the implications for immunization. Wu (2000) extends the use of CIR and Vasicek term structure models to derive duration measures and, as such, is a useful source for the relevant formulas.

18 Crack and Nawalkha (2000) and others continue to improve on the M^2 model by developing the properties of series solutions to capture changes in the level, slope and curvature of the yield curve.

19 The partial duration concept is closely related to the "key rate duration" of Ho (1992) and Phoa and Shearer (1997).

20 HOT refers to higher order terms which will be ignored. This assumption, which could be problematic for bonds with special features, such as call provisions, implies that the discussion centres on default free, straight bonds.

21 Reitano does not actually use the Cauchy-Schwarz inequality. Rather, the extreme yield curve shift is calculated and these values are used to calculate the bounds using $N*'D_T$. The result is tighter bounds than those provided by direct application of the Cauchy-Schwarz values. In Reitano's case, the upper and lower Cauchy-Schwarz bounds, calculated from the product of the inner products of N and D, are 303.6 and -303.6, respectively.

22 Conversely, unless the yield curve is flat, $N = (1, 1, \ldots, 1)$ for the spot rates will not translate into a parallel shift in the yield curve. In addition, even though the unit shift vector does retain the classical property that the classical duration of surplus, D^S, continues to equal zero after the shift, a property also exhibited by $D_N{}^S = 0$, the composition of the initial immunizing portfolios will differ when the initial yield curve is not flat.

23 The result is heuristic because the changes in z_t are infinitesimal and not discrete. Extending the result to discrete changes is straight forward.

24 For surplus immunization this implies that the composition of the classical and Reitano immunizing portfolios will be different, at least when there are coupon bearing securities and yield curves are not flat.

25 The case of the actual Cauchy-Schwarz bounds:

$$-\|N\| \|D\| \le N^T D \le \|N\| \|D\|$$

is obvious, as the length of N will grow with T. As T goes to infinity, as in the case of a perpetuity, the bounds will also go to plus/minus infinity and be, effectively, non-binding.

26 Heuristically, the dates where cash flows are small would have small partial durations which would explode the denominator value, resulting in near zero n_i for those time periods. This leaves the key cash flow points to take on similar values to the $N = (1, 1, 1)^T$ case, albeit scaled up due to the larger value in the numerator.

27 This norm specification is used in Bowden (1997). Luenberger (1969) is an accessible treatment of optimization theory in vector spaces.

28 It is conventional in immunization analysis to work with simplified balance sheets even though such cases are remote from important practical applications such as life companies and pension plans. Practical situations will impose additional limitations on portfolio composition, e.g., due to the need to hold near cash reserves sufficient to meet unanticipated payout requirements.

29 In tables 5.8 and 5.9, indexing of these vectors is assumed to be done in half-units, i.e., $t = (.5, 1, 1.5, \ldots, 9.5, 10)$. At other times, as in summation expressions, the indexing is done in integer units, i.e., $t = (1, 2, \ldots, 19, 20)$.

30 The problem of resolving the relevant yield to use for discounting cash flows in the classical case is suppressed. In practice, the durations of assets and liabilities would be calculated using the yields associated with the maturity of the security, which would result in cash flows occurring at the same time being discounted at

different rates. The stated classical formula assumes that there is only one yield.

31 To see this for the initial portfolio composition, observe that the duration of surplus is calculated as: $D_S = w_1 D_{A1} + w_2 D_{A2} - w_L D_L$. The stated result follows by observing that the difference between classical durations and durations calculated as the sum of partial durations will be largest for the long maturity securities.

32 This par value can be determined directly by taking the ratio of the coupon percentage and the yield and multiplying by original par value, e.g., $(.12/.125)(48) = 46.08$.

33 To see this, recall that the length of the shift vector is one. As a consequence, the sum of the squares will equal one and the square of each $n*$ is the percentage contribution of that particular rate to the extreme directional shift vector.

Chapter Summary

Chapter 6 *Bonds with Embedded Options*

6.1 Types of Bonds with Embedded Options
      Basics of bonds with embedded option features
      Callable bonds, sinking funds and convertible bonds
      Mortgage backed securities

6.2 Greeks for Bonds with Embedded Options*
      What are the Greeks?*
      Duration, convexity and the Greeks for callable bonds*
      Duration, convexity and the Greeks for other embedded option bonds*

6.3 Option Adjusted Spread Analysis*
      Static spread and cash flow assumptions*
      Generating the future spot rates and solving OAS*
      The OAS: examples and pitfalls*

6.4 Modeling and Analyzing Default Risk#
      Early approaches
      The continuous time framework*
      Recent developments in valuing defaultable bonds*

Questions
Notes

# Indicates some sub-sections contain advanced material
* Indicates complete section is advanced material

chapter 6 Bonds with Embedded Options

 6.1   TYPES OF BONDS WITH EMBEDDED OPTIONS

Basics of bonds with embedded option features

The basic discounted cash flow analysis used to value fixed income securities centers on bonds that are default and option free and that provide a fixed coupon and return of principal at maturity. Such securities are referred to as (default and option free) *bullet securities* or *straight bonds* (debt). The analytical advantages of working with straight bonds are apparent from the discussion in chapters 4 and 5. Though a sizeable fraction of the outstanding fixed income security issues can be more or less considered as straight debt, there is a larger fraction that does not qualify due to the presence of embedded options or default risk. Recognizing that default can be viewed as a type of option, the class of bonds with option features extends well beyond those issues with explicit features such as callability or convertibility. In a sense, even straight debt can be analyzed as having an option associated with the reinvestment of coupons. In addition to being useful in valuing non-straight debt, the techniques that are employed to value bonds with option features can also be used in the design of investment strategies for fixed income portfolios.

The price of a bond with an embedded option can be decomposed into two parts, the price of the straight bond without the option plus or minus the price of the embedded option. If the option is a *seller's option* then the option will make the bond less attractive to the purchaser and, as a result, the price of the option will be subtracted from the straight bond price. Examples of securities with seller's options include callable bonds and mortgage backed securities. It is also possible to view default as a type of seller's option. If the option is a *buyer's option* then the option will make the bond more attractive to the purchaser and the option price will be added to the straight bond price. Examples of securities with buyer's options include convertible bonds, putable bonds and extendible bonds. In most cases, it is not possible to directly unbundle the price of the straight bond and the price of the option, i.e., these values are not observed. All that is observed is the traded price of the bond with the embedded option attached.

If the value of the embedded option cannot be unbundled from the straight bond component of the observed bond price, this creates significant difficulties for the discounted cash flow valuation methods used to analyze the fixed income securities examined in chapters 4 and 5. Even if the option value can be unbundled, some method for determining the option value is still required in order to assess the impact of potential changes in, say, interest rate levels on the value of the option. This chapter is concerned with developing the different approaches to valuing bonds with embedded options. The valuation problem can be approached using either continuous time or discrete time methods. The objective is often to provide a method of adjusting the calculated yield to maturity to incorporate the embedded option feature. This is the objective of option adjusted spread analysis. Credit spread analysis seeks to explain the behavior of the difference between the yields on a default and option free bond and on a bond subject to credit risk.

The discounted cash flow valuation techniques used in chapters 4 and 5 did not incorporate the possibility of contingencies in the future cash flows arising from embedded options. Various analytical techniques are available to value fixed income securities with embedded options. Based on the impressive analytical advances associated with option pricing theory, e.g., Black-Scholes (1973), it would seem natural to apply continuous time methods to specify closed form solutions for the embedded options. For a number of reasons, this is not easily accomplished if only because interest rate derivatives pose complications that do not arise in valuing, say, options on common stock or currency. In addition, it is not straightforward to specify the riskless hedge portfolio for embedded options that is needed to specify the relevant PDE. Even when the PDE can be specified, specific features of the embedded option can make it difficult to derive a closed form solution and numerical methods are required in order to determine a security value.[1] In turn, application of numerical methods may produce "pricing errors that are too large for practical applications" (e.g., Buttler 1995). In some cases, all that can be practically adopted is portfolio management techniques such as the use of Greeks for general functional forms.

Recognizing that there may be potential complications and limitations, when closed form solutions derived from PDEs are not available to value bonds with embedded options, it is still possible to arrive at a solution by adopting other techniques of contingent claims analysis to value the embedded options. Where PDEs are available but closed forms cannot be determined, solutions can be obtained by application of numerical methods, e.g., Dunn and McConnell (1981) for GNMAs and Buttler (1995) for callable bonds. In addition, it is also possible to use discrete time methods such as binomial trees and Monte Carlo simulation. Whether such methods produce credible solutions depends, in part, on the user of the solutions. For example, a market maker required to determine a continuous bid/offer spread on a security has a higher need for precision than a bond portfolio manager trying to determine whether to buy bond A or bond B. Much of the theoretical analysis for bonds with embedded options takes the perspective of a market maker, where a high degree of pricing precision is required. For purposes of security analysis and investment strategy, the techniques are more useful as a guide to decision making than for determining "precise" values.

Callable bonds, sinking funds and convertible bonds

To the uninitiated, it is confusing to find that the "callability" option for a callable bond is quite different than the "call" option written on a stock or fixed income security. This is because callability is a seller's option while the call option is a buyer's option. Once it is recognized that the callability feature is a call option for the seller much of the confusion is removed. However, it is difficult to avoid the habit of taking the buyer's perspective. From this perspective, the conventional (buyer's) call option traded on, say, the Chicago Board Options Exchange is similar to the conversion feature embedded in convertible bonds, with the caveat that the currency used to exercise a convertible bond is usually the par value of the bond. In addition, there is considerable variation in the types of call provisions that are attached to bond issues. In some cases, such as the call provisions that were attached to US Treasury long bonds prior to 1986, the issuer's exercise decision was driven by considerations other than the level of interest rates, i.e., the US Treasury was more concerned with the impact of calls on the orderly marketing of issues than with saving on interest costs, per se (see box 6.1).

A pure "callable bond" combines a straight bond with the provision that the bond issuer can redeem/buy back/"call" the issue prior to the stated maturity date. In keeping with the terminology used in options markets, three general types of call provisions are possible: American, Bermudan and European. These references are only terminological and are not intended to represent anything about the geographical distribution for the use of a particular feature. An *American callable bond* can be redeemed at any time prior to maturity, subject to a possible initial *lockout period* where the bond is not callable; a *Bermudan (semi-American) callable bond* can only be redeemed on specific dates prior to maturity; a *European callable bond* can only be redeemed on one specific date. The date(s) on which the bond can be called is (are) the call date(s). An American callable bond that does not have any period for which the bond is not callable is *currently callable.* The price that the issuer pays to redeem the issue is the call price. For American and Bermudan callable bonds, the call price will typically vary across call dates. Call exercises for each type of bond are subject to a notice period, usually from 30 to 60 days.

A variety of different methods are used to set call prices. One common method is to set call prices starting at par plus coupon scaling down to par at some later date. Bonds called between coupon payment dates are adjusted for accrued interest. Wilson and Fabozzi (1996, p. 116) provide the example (box 6.2) of a callable 30 year issue of 10% sinking fund debentures made by Anheuser-Busch in mid-1988.

In addition to being currently callable, this issue is also subject to a sinking fund provision that may have different redemption prices. Given the wide possible variation in the terms of callable bond issues, Wilson and Fabozzi (1996, p. 112) correctly caution: "The importance of knowing the terms of bond issues, especially those relating to redemption, cannot be overstressed."

Rationality requires that, at primary issue, the bond issuer receives less for a bond that is callable than for a bond that is not callable. The issuer is willing to take less for the issue in order to obtain the benefits associated with the right to redeem the issue

Box 6.1 Graham and Dodd on bond call provisions

Graham, Dodd and Cottle (1962, pp. 753–4) provide a historical perspective on the use of call provisions. Beyond this statement, there is little discussion of call provisions.

The call provision of bonds
Nearly all corporate bonds issued for some decades past have a call provision which enables the company to pay them off before maturity at a stipulated price, which often declines as maturity approaches. (Most preferred stocks carry a comparable provision, but the call price rarely if ever changes with time.) Comparatively little attention was paid to the significance of these call features until the sharp drop in interest rates after 1933 – and the low rates continuing for more than twenty years thereafter – brought on an almost universal retirement of callable bond issues and their replacement by new ones carrying lower coupons. The effect of this provision was then seen to be the depriving of bondholders of most of the price benefit that should accompany a drop in interest rates, although they had no comparable option to safeguard them against a fall in the price of their bonds when interest rates advance. Otherwise stated, the call provision compels bondholders to accept a cut in their interest return when the general interest rate drops appreciably, but does not give them any increased income when the rate advances.

We have illustrated this point elsewhere by the following typical example: In 1928, American Gas & Electric Co. sold an issue of 100 year 5 percent debentures to the public at 101, yielding 4.95 percent. Four years later, in the depths of the depression, the debentures sold as low as 60, with a yield of 8.25 percent. This reflected the impact of unusually unfavorable economic and market conditions on a good-quality investment bond. Conversely, and under favorable circumstances, the interest rate applicable to bonds of this quality fell under 3 percent. This *should* have meant an advance in the price of this 5 percent issue to 160 or better. But at this point, in March, 1946, the call feature was availed of and the company redeemed the issue at only 106.

Since 1954 bondholders have experienced a third unfavorable experience of this sort – this time occasioned by a sharp rise in the basic interest rate. The low coupon bonds issued in the long period of low-interest rates sustained a severe decline. In the case of American Gas & Electric, its $3\frac{3}{8}$ percent debentures issued above par in 1952 sold as low as 80 in 1961. The purchasers of Consolidated Edison of New York $2\frac{3}{4}$'s at $102\frac{7}{8}$ in 1947 had the more disconcerting experience of seeing their price drop below 70 in 1959.

In our view the call feature in the typical bond contract is a thinly disguised instance of "heads I win, tails you lose." Its results may be summarized as follows: When interest rates go down the call feature forces the investor to lose the income he counted upon; when the interest rate goes up the investor loses in the principal value of his bond.

The SEC has taken the stand that a call provision is a necessary feature in public utility bond issues (under their jurisdiction) to safeguard the company against paying higher interest on its old bonds than the going rate in future years. This view is logical as far as it goes, but it completely ignores the contrary and equally legitimate interests of the bond investor. Perhaps the correct solution of this problem would be to make the interest payments on long-term bonds vary with changes in the basic rate; if the company wishes to retain a right to call the bonds – presumably for reasons of convenience – then a corresponding right should be given the holders to tender their bonds to the company at discount equal to the premium that the company would have to pay on call. A provision to vary the coupon with interest-rate conditions would bear some resemblance to that found in a number of foreign bonds which protect the holder against a fall in the gold or commodity value of the currency. However, our tentative suggestion would operate in both directions, to safeguard both parties to the bargain.

The triple "whipsawing" that institutional bondholders have submitted to since 1929 has led them to demand more protection as far as call features are concerned. Many, perhaps most, tax-free and industrial issues in recent years have been made noncallable for a substantial period after issuance. *Example*: In 1961 the State of California issued $100 million of bonds at various coupon rates and maturing serially from 1963 through 1987. This issue was made callable only between 1983 and 1987.

A more sophisticated arrangement permits an early call provided that interest rates have not fallen appreciably – which means that the bondholder would able to replace his called bonds at an equivalent coupon rate. Example: In 1962 Ohio Oil Co. sold at 100 a large issue of 4 percent debentures due 1987. For the first five years they were made nonredeemable "through a funding operation at an interest cost to the company of less than 4.36 percent." They could be redeemed in whole or in part out of "spare cash" at prices ranging from 104.6 in 1962 to 103.9 in 1966. Beginning in 1967 the company will be free to redeem bonds with any funds at prices gradually declining toward par in 1986. The analyst should be cognizant of the implications of the various types of provisions, and pay due heed to them in making his bond selections.

early. Typically, the desired benefit is the ability to take advantage of lower interest rates in the future. These lower rates would usually be due to a change in the general level of interest rates but could also be due to a narrowing of credit spreads for lower credit issuers or to an improvement in the credit status of the firm. In some cases, the call provision may be included to facilitate the implementation of a sinking fund provision. In other cases, such as the call provision on "old" Treasury long bonds, the benefits were associated with orderly refunding of the issue. In order to reduce the cost of the call feature, the issuer may introduce a range of additional features. For example, there may be a lockout period governing first possible call date. There may also be protection against redemptions done with refundings. In contrast, there may also be

Box 6.2 Redemption Schedule for Anheuser–Busch Companies, Inc., 10% Sinking Fund Debentures issued July 1, 1988 and due July 1, 2018

Redemption

The debentures will be redeemable at the option of the company at any time in whole or in part, upon not fewer than 30 nor more than 60 days' notice, at the following redemption prices (which are expressed in percentages of principal amount) in each case together with accrued interest to the date fixed for redemption:

If redeemed during the 12 months beginning July 1,

	%		%		%
1988	110.0	1995	106.5	2002	103.0
1989	109.5	1996	106.0	2003	102.5
1990	109.0	1997	105.5	2004	102.0
1991	108.5	1998	105.0	2005	101.5
1992	108.0	1999	104.5	2006	101.0
1993	107.5	2000	104.0	2007	100.5
1994	107.0	2001	103.5	2008 and thereafter	100.0

provided, however, that prior to July 1, 1998, the Company may not redeem any of the Debentures pursuant to such option, directly or indirectly, from or in anticipation of the proceeds of the issuance of any indebtedness for money borrowed having an interest cost of less than 10% per annum.

Source: **Prospectus dated June 23, 1988.**

features that increase the call probability, such as restrictive covenants designed to reduce default risk.

Refunding is the process of replacing a secondary bond issue by making a primary bond issue. Entities with a permanent stock of debt, such as the US Treasury, pay for maturing issues by refunding with (rolling over into) new issues. For corporate issuers, refunding takes on additional importance because most redemption of callable issues is accomplished with refunding. Protection against refunding is significant because it makes redemption more difficult. Ten year refunding protection is a common provision on long term corporate bond. However, call protection is stronger in protecting redemption from any source of funds, not just new bond issues. An important legal example occurred with the Archer-Daniels-Midland (ADM) issue of $125 million in 30 year, 16% sinking fund debentures in May 1981. This issue was currently callable but had 10 year refunding protection. In the following two years ADM made a series of lower cost bond issues, as well as issuing over $140 million in common equity. The redemption of the issue in August 1983 led to a lawsuit claiming that the refunding protection was violated. The courts sided with ADM.[2]

The decision for an issuing corporation about whether and when to redeem an outstanding bond issue is complicated. In turn, this complicates the problem of valuing a callable bond. Assuming that the redemption is paid for using a refunding, the process involves a corporation issuing a notice to call an issue, with payment usually 30 to 60 days later. This payment will be made using a new bond issue with a lower interest rate that may involve a lockout period. Because this process involves considerable fixed costs, it is not usually feasible or profitable for the corporation to undertake another redemption until rates fall significantly and a significant amount of time has gone by. Hence, in making a redemption decision a corporation has to identify the interest rate level at which it is optimal to exercise. In addition, there may be other factors that have to be taken into account than the interest rate level, e.g., there may be restrictive covenants in the debt issue that the corporation may want to extinguish by redeeming the issue.

In perfect capital markets with a zero notice period, the issuer will exercise the call on a nonconvertible callable bond as soon as possible following the market price of the bond reaching the call price (Ingersoll 1977; Brennan and Schwartz 1977). However, markets are not perfect and notice periods are not zero and, as a consequence, the call policies of issuers do not always follow the perfect capital markets result. In contrast to empirical studies of optimal exercise for callable convertible bonds, there are relatively few empirical studies on nonconvertible callable bonds. The most detailed study, King and Mauer (2000), examined over 1,600 US issues (1,126 utilities, 495 industrials and 21 transportation covering 530 different firms) over a 20 year period from 1975 to 1994. For these issues, King and Mauer find that 86% of issues were called long after the bond price first reaches the call price, with an average delay of 27 months; 56% of the delayed call issues traded at least 2% above the call price for 3 or more consecutive months and 25% traded above the call price for 12 or more consecutive months.

Prior to King and Mauer, Vu (1986) had presented an unusual empirical result based on a smaller sample of 102 issues: three-quarters of the nonconvertible callable bonds had a bond price *below* the call price immediately before the call announcement date. This result is unusual because calling a bond in this case would involve paying an exercise price that is higher than the observed price of the bond in the secondary market. This would indicate that the optimal call policy was influenced by factors other than interest cost minimization, e.g., the desire to eliminate the restrictive covenants contained in bond indentures. This result was not supported by King and Mauer where 81% of issues had a bond price above the call price immediately before the call announcement date. In addition, King and Mauer found that the call delay was shorter in periods of low interest rate volatility and steeper term structures. Firms that were larger and had a higher interest cost saving from calling the issue also tended to have short call delays. Market prices for the different issues appeared to reflect the call policies of the firms.

In addition to explicit call provisions, the bond indenture may also contain non-call exception features (e.g., Blanc and Gordon 1999). The four most common such provisions are: sinking funds; maintenance and replacement funds; release and substitution provisions; and, eminent domain provisions. The use of the terminology "sinking fund" can be traced back to the revolution in English government finance in the late seventeenth and early eighteenth century, e.g., Poitras (2000, ch. 11). The original idea was to create a fund that, over time, would be sufficient to pay off a specific government debt issue. The cash flow into the fund would be tied to a dedicated source of funding associated with the revenue from a specific tax. While "sinking funds" for government debt financing have long since disappeared, the notion is still important for corporate bond issues. The objective of the sinking fund provision is usually to raise the primary issue price by reducing the default risk. Though a number of variations are available, in general a sinking fund is an indenture provision that provides for the regular retirement of a portion of a debt issue. Sinking fund payments are made by the issuing corporation to the bond indenture trustees.

Sinking fund payments are usually made annually. On long term issues, the sinking fund payments may not begin until after the refunding protection expires, usually after ten years. While it is possible for a sinking fund provision to be satisfied by the issuing company depositing funds or property into a "fund" to be controlled by the trustees for the purpose of retiring the issue at maturity, it is more common for the issuer to redeem a specific amount of the debt issue at periodic intervals. In some *non-specific sinking funds*, a number of the outstanding bond issues may fall within the scope of the sinking fund. Such funds permit the sinking fund requirement to be "funneled" onto one issue, permitting the issuer to select the issue for redemption that provides the greatest cost savings. The funneling provision often appears on sinking funds for high yield issues.

How the sinking fund for a specific issue is handled varies from indenture to indenture. For example, redemption for sinking fund purposes may be at a different price than if the whole issue is called for refunding purposes. Par value is a common sinking fund redemption price. Issues that are called for sinking fund purposes are often selected by lot, affecting the expected maturity of a sinking fund issue for a bondholder. It is usually the case that, instead of calling a specific amount of the outstanding bonds, the issuing corporation is permitted to repurchase a sufficient amount of bonds in the open market and deliver those bonds to satisfy the sinking fund provision. This would be advantageous for the issuer when the issue was trading at a lower price than the sinking fund redemption price. Because the issuer would be purchasing a significant amount of bonds, this would be favorable for purchasers due to enhanced issue liquidity. However, if the issue is trading above the sinking fund redemption price, this would have the same type of negative impact as a call provision.

In addition to call provisions and non-call exceptions, the bond indenture may also contain a conversion provision. Pure "convertible" bonds can be defined as a combination of a straight bond and a (buyer's) option to convert the bond into the common stock of the issuing corporation. Occasionally, the conversion option permits the bond to be converted into other securities of the firm than the common stock. Other variations on the conversion option are usually given a different name. For example, an "exchangeable security" permits conversion of the bond into the common stock of another corporation. Such a feature is not typical. A more common "conversion" feature is the putable bond that permits the bond to be redeemed (converted to cash) at the option of the bondholder, e.g., Crabbe and Nikoulis (1997). The price of pure convertible bonds can be modeled as equal to the straight bond price plus the price of the buyer's conversion option. (Because exercise involves an increase in the number of common shares, the embedded conversion option is a form of warrant.) As such, pure convertible bonds are good candidates for applying the continuous time valuation methods developed for exchange traded call options, e.g., Black (1976). Unfortunately, convertible bond valuation is usually complicated by the market practice of issuing callable convertibles.

Though there may be a lockout period, over time most convertible bond indentures also have had a call provision. The presence of these two unobserved embedded options poses severe analytical problems. One option, exercisable by the bondholder, depends mostly on the common stock price and the other option, exercisable by the issuer, depends on a range of factors including the level of interest rates. Even under the simplifying assumptions that the conversion option depends solely on the common stock price/ conversion price relationship and that the callable feature depends solely on the level of interest rates, the valuation problem is quite intractable due to the presence of two random variables combined with the potential for both the issuer and bondholder to exercise an embedded option. In practice, there is empirical evidence that the prices of many convertible bonds are substantially underpriced, relative to the sum of the straight bond price plus the embedded conversion option, e.g., Greiner et al. (2002), Athanassokos and Carayannapoulos (2000). As this underpricing can occur for bonds trading significantly below par value (call price), the underpricing is at least partly due to factors other than the presence of the call feature.

Many of the empirical studies of convertible bonds are concerned with identifying the firm's optimal call strategy for callable convertibles, e.g., Ederington and Goh (2001). The objective is typically to explain the observed fall in the common stock price that usually occurs immediately following a conversion forcing call of a convertible bond. There has also been disagreement over whether the firm delays the call decision beyond the optimal call date. It is difficult to examine these studies without acquiring scepticism about the progress of "knowledge" in modern Finance. Much like the perfect markets result for a callable nonconvertible bond, the optimal call policy for a callable convertible bond with a zero notice period is to call the bond at the first date that conversion can be forced on the bondholder, e.g., Brennan and Schwartz (1977), Ingersoll (1977a). By forcing conversion, the value of the bondholders' conversion option, a liability of the firm, is minimized. In practice, Asquith (1995) and others demonstrated that convertible bonds are not called until the conversion premium is well above the minimum conversion value. Asquith, for example, estimates an average premium of the stock price over the conversion price on the call date of 26%.

Confronted with the empirical evidence about call delays and a falling stock price around the convertible call date, proponents of modern Finance, e.g., Harris and Raviv (1985), were able to exploit the strong theoretical preference for signaling models during the 1980s to provide a theoretical rationale for these two "stylized" facts. Calling a convertible issue was a "signal" from the firm that equity was overvalued. Firms that did not want to send this signal would not call the convertible resulting in a long delay of the convertible call decision. While there was initially "strong evidence" advanced in support of this hypothesis, the gradual demise of signaling theory during the 1990s has been accompanied by an accumulation of empirical evidence against the theoretical signaling explanation of convertible call policy. For example, Mazzeo and Moore (1992) and Ederington and Goh (2001) demonstrate that the drop in the stock price on the convertible call date is transitory, likely associated with the sudden increase in the floating supply of common stock. On average, the price decline is usually reversed within two to three weeks.

As for the delay in the convertible call decision, Butler (2002) argues that the perceived "delay" can be explained by properly modeling the call conversion decision with a non-zero notice period. Recognizing that typical notice periods are between 15–60 days, significant delay beyond the first possible conversion date is sensible because the call decision involves an exchange of the convertible bond, i.e., straight bond plus embedded warrant, for the common stock plus a put option. In effect, during a non-zero notice period the bondholder has the right to put the common stock back to the firm in exchange for the call price on the underlying debt issue. As such, observed call premiums are consistent with the firm seeking to minimize the value of the put by waiting until the put is sufficiently out of the money that it has zero or near zero value. The precise premium will depend on the conventional factors governing the put price, e.g., volatility of the stock, length of the notice period, spread between the call price and the price of the straight bond, the expected dilution of the common stock due to conversion.

The objective of the "delay" in convertible call conversion is to wait until the put value is sufficiently out of the money that the value is near zero. In addition to the basic problem of valuing the put, there are also other factors to consider that are associated with the costs of the put being in the money on the expiration date. The objective of a convertible call is to force the bondholder to convert the debt into common stock. A "busted call" occurs when the firm incorrectly judges the call decision and the put is in the money on the expiration date. This results in the bond issue being put back to the firm for cash. In such cases, the firm may have added expenses, if not difficulty, in obtaining on short notice the funds needed to refund the (unanticipated) bonds that are put back. The firm may also have to incur additional costs associated with further security issues to achieve the desired capital structure. The importance of the put option associated with convertible calls is recognized in the structure of recent convertible issues where zero coupons and short (1 year) put options have been added to the conventional callable convertible design (Dialynas et al. 2001, Springsteel 2002).

The convertible bond presents an attractive vehicle for the hedge funds, investment bankers and financial engineers seeking to profit from the modern renaissance in derivative securities (Poitras 2002, ch. 1). Pricing depends on the specific features of the bonds being examined and "structured" variations on convertible bonds, e.g., zero coupon-short put-callable-convertibles, can be complicated to value and market. A new terminology, Co-Co (contingent convertible), has been introduced to aid in the marketing effort. Such securities present excellent opportunities for the convertibles division of the large investment banks, such as Merrill Lynch, Goldman Sachs, Citigroup/Salomon and JP Morgan, to rationalize the big fees, usually 2% of proceeds, that are charged to firms seeking to "tailor" financing requirements to purchaser demands for specific security designs. (See box 6.3 for a description of a recent convertible deal.) For example, the leading US investment bank for convertibles issuance, Merrill Lynch, derived 9% of first half 2002 total investment banking income from convertibles issuance.

Box 6.3 The convertible bond

The following description of a convertible bond deal done by Silicon Integrated in 2002 illustrates the degree of complexity that such deals have attained:

"ING completed an $80m convertible bond issue for Silicon Integrated Systems Corp, Taiwan's second largest designer of computer chipsets, on Wednesday during London trading hours. Silicon Integrated has been waiting all this calendar year to sell an ADR issue through its chosen lead manager, Bear Stearns. A window of opportunity to raise new funds through a straight equity placement did not appear, and therefore the company opted to brave the inclement market conditions to sell bonds that it wants to ensure will convert into equity.

The $80m issue plus $20m greenshoe has a five year maturity and a put at the end of year two to yield 3.704%, equivalent to 100bp above US Treasuries. The conversion premium is just 8.2%. The zero coupon notes are 18 months to call and then subject to call at 125% of the accreted value. There are annual conversion premium downward re-fixes subject to an aggregate 80% floor. The bond also features a onetime special re-fix by which the issuer can effectively guarantee conversion by pushing the notes deep into the money. This allows the company to re-fix the conversion premium at 85% of the market share price.

ING declared itself pleased with the distribution and the structure. The bonds were sold with a theoretical value of 112.4%, based on a credit spread of Libor plus 350bp, a zero coupon, a stock borrow cost of 5% and a volatility assumption of 35%. The bond floor emerged at 94.4%, enough to encourage outright buyers to take up 50% of the placement and asset swappers to take a quarter of the book. Hedge funds took the remaining 25% of the notes. The lead said the book was made up of 40 accounts, half of which were European."

Source: "Silicon Integrated sells $80m CB despite stormy markets,"
Euroweek, July 12, 2002.

The observed mispricing of convertible bond prices has fostered the emergence of a large number of hedge funds aimed at "arbitraging" the mispricing that is commonly observed in convertible bond prices. For example, market observers estimate that hedge funds bought over 50% of new convertible issues during 2000–2002. Given that US convertibles issuance in 2001 was a record $105 billion, the market activities of hedge funds are considerable. As Evans (2002) observes: "Convertibles are a perfect product for sophisticated, liquidity-oriented hedge funds. They can trade the volatility, strip the products into their constituent debt and equity parts, buy and sell credit protection, asset swap the paper and exploit pricing arbitrages in the secondary market." Though convertible arbitrage strategies have been used for decades, e.g., Evans (1965), the general absence of pure arbitrage opportunities has meant that modern hedge fund strategies have had to extend into strategies that have a higher level of inherent risk. As discussed below, the Greeks provide an important risk management technique that is used by hedge funds to control the risk of convertible bond strategies, e.g., Krishnan and Mains (2002).

Convertible bonds are not the only equity-linked security available. A significant variation on equity-linked security design was the large scale Japanese warrant bond issues of the 1980s, e.g., Vaidya et al. (1995). At primary issue, a warrant bond is a combination of a straight bond and a detachable in the money warrant. A warrant bond issue explicitly recognizes that, from put-call parity, it is possible to unbundle the price of common stock into the sum of a straight bond and an in-the-money detachable warrant. More precisely, put-call parity for a non-dividend paying stock requires (e.g., Poitras 2002, ch. 7):

$$S(t) + PP[S, t; X, T, r, \sigma] = W[S, t; X, T, r, \sigma] + Xe^{-rt^*}$$

where W is the warrant price, t^* is the the number of years remaining until the expiration date of the put and warrant, r is the continuous time interest rate, σ is the volatility of the continuous rate of return on the stock, X is the exercise price and PP is the put price. (For simplicity a zero coupon continuously compounded debt issue has been assumed.) Observing that the put and warrant have the same expiration date and exercise price and are written on the same stock, it follows that when the warrant is deep in the money the put will be deep out of the money, i.e., the put price will be nearly zero.

Traditionally, convertible bonds were structured such that the embedded warrant was priced out of the money at primary issue. This makes the convertible similar to a path independent insured stock position (e.g., Poitras 2002, ch. 9), where the exercise price of the put is significantly above the current stock price. In addition, convertible bonds were long-dated with terms to maturity of 15 years and longer. Hence, at primary issue, a convertible bond was similar to a straight bond with an equity-linked "sweetener" that is only significant some considerable time in the future. (More recently, the structure of convertible bond issues has been more flexible and a variety of different structures are observed.) A warrant bond changes the traditional convertible bond structure in two important ways. First, by having the warrant deep in the money at primary issue, making the put price near zero, the warrant bond is closer to an equity issue than a debt issue. Second, by making the warrant detachable, a warrant bond issue enhances the marketability of the issue to a wider number of potential purchasers.

Unlike a traditional convertible bond that is similar to a straight bond issue, a warrant bond is a substitute for an equity issue. There are a number of advantages of using a warrant bond as a substitute for direct equity financing. Given that the warrant value could be anywhere from 15–35% of the initial value, the issuer gains by being able to raise debt with lower coupons. In turn, future warrant exercise would provide funds needed to repay the issue at maturity. Purchasers would have the advantage of being able to unbundle the components of an equity issue, selling off either the warrant or debt component if desired. For purchasers holding both parts, the bonds would provide a stable cash flow over the life of the bond and the return of principal would provide the funds needed to purchase the equity. Though this form of funding is still popular in east Asian markets, the collapse of the Japanese equity market following the large warrant bond issues of the 1980s has acted to stem the demand for such issues from international investors.

Mortgage backed securities[3]

One of the most remarkable features of the US capital markets is the process of funding mortgages. In Canada, for example, mortgages are funded primarily by financial institutions such as the chartered banks. When used to raise funds to finance a residential house purchase, the Canadian mortgage loan contract features an amortization period that is typically well in excess of the term of the loan. A conventional residential fixed rate mortgage would have a one to five year term with significant prepayment penalties. At the end of the term of the mortgage loan, the unpaid balance on the mortgage would be refinanced by creating a new fixed rate mortgage that reflects market interest rates prevailing at that time the mortgage is rewritten. At this time the borrower has the right to shift mortgage to another lender, using the funds raised to pay out the unpaid balance on the maturing mortgage without penalty. At the time the mortgage is rewritten the borrower has the ability to adjust the amortization period, select a different term and select other features such as a floating rate. In addition to the security of the property, these mortgage loans are also backed by the full faith and credit obligation of the borrower.

A borrower in the Canadian mortgage market can only dream of obtaining a 30 year fixed rate mortgage with minimal prepayment penalties and featuring a competitive rate of interest. The availability of this type of mortgage in the US can be attributed to the system of funding mortgages through the issuance of mortgage backed securities.[4] This institutional history of this system can be traced back to 1938 and the creation of the Federal National Mortgage Association (FNMA). This institution was created to purchase Federal Housing Administration (FHA) and Veterans Administration (VA) mortgages from lenders, providing a secure source of funds for that type of borrowing. The FNMA was restructured in 1968 into two separate entities: the Government National Mortgage Association (GNMA), an agency of the federal government situated within the Department of Housing and Urban Development; and the "new" FNMA that was rechartered by Congress as a private corporation responsible for making a secondary market in mortgages not insured by FHA or VA. Two years later, in 1970, the Federal Home Loan Mortgage Corporation (FHLMC) was established under a government charter, with ownership residing in the 12 Federal Home Loan Banks.

The key innovation in mortgage funding came with the introduction by GNMA of the mortgage pass-through security in 1970. The FHLMC started issuing pass-throughs in 1971 and, in 1981, the FNMA followed suit.[5] The basic idea behind a pass-through is to securitize the cash flows from a pool of mortgages. The mortgages are originated by financial institutions and then sold to the agency issuing the pass-through. These *mortgage originators* are primarily commercial banks, thrift institutions, mortgage brokers, insurance companies and pension funds. Cash flows from the mortgages are "passed through" to the purchasers of the security issue after the payment of a nominal servicing fee to the entity engaged in the relevant activities of collecting and processing the mortgage payments, initiating default proceedings where appropriate and the like. These activities can be handled by the originating institution or by some other *mortgage servicer.* Depending on the characteristics of the mortgage pool, there may be various types of *mortgage insurance* that are required. This insurance can include policies directly on individual mortgages, e.g., due to a high loan-to-value ratio, or credit risk policies written on the whole pool. Pools in specific regions may also be required to have specific peril insurance, e.g., tornado insurance in Florida.

Because the cash flows on a pass-through depend on the payments from the underlying pool of mortgages, a pass-through security is qualitatively different from a straight bond. The holder of a pass-through receives on a monthly basis the pro rata share of the scheduled interest and principal payments on the underlying mortgage pool. In addition, the holder also receives any unscheduled principal payments that result from prepayments and defaults. While the scheduled principal and interest payments are predictable, the unscheduled pre-payments are not, making the cash flows from a pass-through somewhat unpredictable. To increase the marketability of mortgage backed securities, starting in 1983 the FHLMC introduced the *collateralized mortgage obligation* (CMO) that rebundles the cash flow from a pass-through into tranches of different securities with different maturity dates.[6] One example of the advantages of a CMO is that financial institutions can purchase a security with a maturity date that better matches the maturity structure of deposits. Tax changes in the 1986 Tax Reform Act permitted CMOs to be issued as Real Estate Mortgage Investment Conduits (REMICs). Recognizing that almost all CMO issues are now in the form of REMICs, market convention is to use the terms REMIC and CMO interchangeably.

Taken together, pass-throughs and CMOs represent the class of mortgage backed securities (MBS). Though the bulk of MBS are issued by GNMA (Ginnie Mae), FNMA (Fannie Mae) and FHLMC (Freddie Mac), there is also some issuance of nonagency MBS, including MBS used to finance commercial mortgages, e.g., Fabozzi (2001, chs 27–8). Recognizing that it is difficult to obtain precise information on the size of the nonagency MBS market, the size of the market for agency MBS is given in table 6.1. Though the relationship between CMOs and pass-throughs varies over time, about 40% of pass-throughs are used to collateralize CMOs. For example, by mid-year 2002 there had been $241 billion in CMOs issued (Bond Market Association, 2002). Table 6.1 reveals that the market for MBS expanded rapidly during the 1980s. This was largely due to the ongoing collapse of the thrift institutions as a major source of long-term mortgage financing. The amount of MBS issued in any year is dependent on the demand for the underlying mortgages. Periods of declining interest rates, e.g., 2001–2, led to a large number of mortgage refinancings and higher levels of MBS issuance.

A mortgage pass-through is a key innovation from many perspectives. Even though there has been a secondary market for individual mortgages that goes back centuries, the introduction of MBS increases the marketability of secondary mortgages, significantly reduces the credit risk by introducing agency guarantees and alters the cash flow profile of the underlying security by aggregating the individual mortgage cash flows into a pool. The process of aggregating the cash flows from individual mortgages into the cash flow from a pool of mortgages is an essential element in valuing MBS. The basic cash flow characteristics of an individual mortgage are well known. A conventional fixed rate mortgage is self-amortizing, requiring a sequence of (usually) equal monthly payments made over the term of the mortgage. Each payment can be divided between interest and principal, with the size of principal paydown relative to interest increasing over the life of the mortgage until the full mortgage balance is paid off on the last scheduled payment date. Other types of mortgage structures, e.g., adjustable rate, two-step and balloon, are possible.

Table 6.1 Issuance of agency mortgage backed securities, 1980–2002[a] ($ billions)

Date	GNMA	FNMA	FHLMC	Total
1980	20.6	–	2.5	23.1
1981	14.3	0.7	3.5	18.5
1982	16.0	14.0	24.2	54.2
1983	50.7	13.3	21.4	85.4
1984	28.1	13.5	20.5	62.1
1985	46.0	23.6	41.5	111.1
1986	101.4	60.6	102.4	264.4
1987	94.9	63.2	75.0	233.1
1988	55.2	54.9	39.8	149.9
1989	57.1	69.8	73.5	200.4
1990	64.4	96.7	73.8	234.9
1991	62.6	112.9	92.5	268.0
1992	81.9	194.0	179.2	455.2
1993	138.0	221.4	208.7	568.1
1994	111.2	130.5	117.1	358.8
1995	72.9	110.4	85.9	269.2
1996	100.9	149.9	119.7	370.5
1997	104.3	149.4	114.3	368.0
1998	150.2	326.1	250.6	726.9
1999	151.5	300.7	233.0	685.2
2000	103.7	211.7	166.9	482.4
2001	174.6	528.4	389.6	1,092.6
2002[a]	174.0	723.3	547.1	1,444.4
2003	220.0	1,198.6	713.3	2,131.9

[a] As of September 30, 2002

Sources: GNMA, FNMA, FHLMC, Bond Market Association

A mortgage presents two types of risks that can impact the cash flow: prepayment risk and default risk. For a MBS, default risk is controlled by the use of mortgage insurance and agency guarantees. However, though principal is not at risk, a default will typically trigger an eventual prepayment of principal. As such, default risk on a MBS can be treated as a component of prepayment risk. The mortgages that form the pool for a MBS usually permit homeowners to prepay the outstanding mortgage balance in whole or in part at any time prior to maturity without penalty. The precise form of the prepayment provisions is governed by state and federal law and depend on the type of mortgage, e.g., adjustable rate mortgages are governed by federal law with fixed rate mortgages falling under state law. A small number of states do not permit prepayment penalties with some other states restricting the type of penalty. Another feature impacting prepayment risk is whether the mortgages in the pool are assumable. Mortgages in FNMA and FHLMC MBS pools are generally not assumable with GNMA pools being assumable.

Because the realized cash flows from a MBS depend on the mortgage prepayments, it is necessary to estimate prepayment flows in order to value these securities. Various methods and models are available, e.g., Deng et al. (2000). Though firms that are market makers in the MBS market have in-house prepayment models, the industry benchmark

Table 6.2 Mortgage pass-through cash flow, at 100% PSA

Month	Start balance	PSA mortal.	Mortgage payment	Principal	Interest	Prepayment	Service fee	Cash flow	End balance
1	100,000	0.000166	841	49	792	17	42	816	99,934
2	99,934	0.000333	841	50	791	33	42	832	99,851
3	99,851	0.000501	840	50	790	50	42	849	99,751
4	99,751	0.000669	840	50	790	67	42	865	99,634
5	99,634	0.000837	839	51	789	83	42	881	99,500
6	99,500	0.001005	839	51	788	100	41	897	99,349
7	99,349	0.001174	838	51	787	117	41	913	99,181
8	99,181	0.001343	837	52	785	133	41	929	98,996
18	96,584	0.003050	819	55	765	294	40	1,074	96,235
19	96,235	0.003223	817	55	762	310	40	1,087	95,870
20	95,870	0.003396	814	55	759	325	40	1,100	95,489
21	95,489	0.003569	812	56	756	341	40	1,113	95,093
31	90,860	0.005143	777	58	719	467	38	1,206	90,336
32	90,336	0.005143	773	58	715	464	38	1,200	89,814
33	89,814	0.005143	769	58	711	462	37	1,193	89,294
34	89,294	0.005143	765	58	707	459	37	1,187	88,777
99	60,354	0.005143	547	69	478	310	25	832	59,975
100	59,975	0.005143	544	70	475	308	25	827	59,597
209	27,372	0.005143	310	94	217	140	11	439	27,138
210	27,138	0.005143	309	94	215	139	11	436	26,905
211	26,905	0.005143	307	94	213	138	11	434	26,673
359	283	0.005143	143	141	2	1	0	144	141
360	141	0.005143	142	141	1	0	0	142	0

Where: Start balance is mortgage balance at the beginning of month; PSA mortal. is the mortality rate estimated for that month using 100% of PSA; Mortgage payment is the monthly mortgage payment = principal + interest; Prepayment is the estimated prepayment = (Start balance) (PSA mortal.); Service fee is the assumed contractually specified service fee; Cash flow is the payment made to holder of the pass through; and, End balance = Start balance – Principal – Prepayment.

Original mortgage balance: $100,000; mortgage rate: 9.5%; term of mortgage: 30 years (360 months); servicing fee: 0.5%; PSA = 100%.

was developed by the Public Securities Association (incorporated 1976, name changed to Bond Market Association in 1997). This benchmark is referred to as 100% PSA. With the demise of the PSA as the association name, the acronym now refers to Prepayment Speed Assumptions. Based on empirical experience with FHA mortgages, 100% PSA assumes a prepayment rate that increases each month for the first 30 months and then is level thereafter. Tables 6.2 and 6.3, adapted from Fabozzi (1989, pp. 246–8), illustrate the impact of assuming 100% PSA and 150% PSA on the cash flows of a pass-through. The prepayment amount for any month is determined by multiplying the prepayment mortality factor from the PSA by the outstanding mortgage principal amount. Increasing from 100% to 150% PSA involves multiplying the 100% PSA mortality factor by 1.5.

Table **6.3** Mortgage pass-through cash flow, at 150% PSA

Month	Start balance	PSA mortal.	Mortgage payment	Principal	Interest	Prepayment	Service fee	Cash flow	End balance
1	100,000	0.000250	841	49	792	25	42	824	99,926
2	99,926	0.000501	841	50	791	50	42	849	99,826
3	99,826	0.000753	840	50	790	75	42	874	99,701
4	99,701	0.001005	840	50	789	100	42	898	99,551
5	99,551	0.001258	839	51	788	125	41	923	99,375
6	99,375	0.001512	838	51	787	150	41	947	99,174
7	99,174	0.001767	836	51	785	175	41	970	98,947
8	98,947	0.002022	835	52	783	200	41	994	98,695
18	95,324	0.004615	809	54	755	440	40	1,209	94,830
19	94,830	0.004878	805	54	751	462	40	1,228	94,313
20	94,313	0.005143	801	54	747	485	39	1,247	93,774
21	93,774	0.005407	797	55	742	507	39	1,266	93,213
31	87,224	0.007828	746	55	691	682	36	1,392	86,487
32	86,487	0.007828	740	55	685	677	36	1,381	85,755
33	85,755	0.007828	734	55	679	671	36	1,369	85,028
34	85,028	0.007828	728	55	673	665	35	1,358	84,308
99	48,211	0.007828	437	55	382	377	20	794	47,779
100	47,779	0.007828	434	55	378	374	20	787	47,350
209	16,241	0.007828	184	56	129	127	7	304	16,059
210	16,059	0.007828	183	56	127	125	7	301	15,878
211	15,878	0.007828	181	56	126	124	7	299	15,699
359	112	0.007828	57	56	1	0	0	57	56
360	56	0.007828	56	56	0	0	0	56	0

Where: Start balance is mortgage balance at the beginning of month; PSA mortal. is the mortality rate estimated for that month using 150% of PSA; Mortgage payment is the monthly mortgage payment = principal + interest; Prepayment is the estimated prepayment = (Start balance) (PSA mortal.); Service fee is the assumed contractually specified service fee; Cash flow is the payment made to holder of the pass through; and, End balance = Start balance – Principal – Prepayment.

Original mortgage balance: $100,000; mortgage rate: 9.5%; term of mortgage: 30 years (360 months); servicing fee: 0.5%; PSA = 100%.

6.2 GREEKS FOR BONDS WITH EMBEDDED OPTIONS*

What are the Greeks?*

The "Greeks" refer to the names given to derivatives of option prices and other value functions, e.g., Poitras (2002, ch. 9). The most important of these names are *delta (Δ), gamma (Γ), theta (θ), rho (ρ)* and *vega*, hence the reference to Greeks, i.e., the various derivatives are referred to using Greek letters. In particular, the first derivative of the price of a call option (C) written on a stock, taken with respect to the stock price $(\partial C/\partial S)$, is the "delta" of that call option (Δ_c). Similarly, the delta of a put option on the common stock is the first derivative of the put price with respect to a change in the stock price (Δ_p). A partial derivative is taken because the call (put) option price is a function of other variables, such as time. In general, a "delta" refers to the first derivative of a price or value function taken with respect to the price of the underlying asset or commodity (the state variable price). The delta for an option written on a fixed income security would be the first derivative of the call option price with respect to the price of the fixed income security. For a bond with an embedded option, the delta of the option is typically the first derivative taken with respect to the price of a *riskless* bond.

Delta and the other Greeks were initially developed for use in the analysis of options, e.g., Cox and Rubinstein (1985). The Greeks are particularly useful in risk management. Delta, for example, measures the change in the value of a position with respect to a change in the state variable. The extension to more recent risk management techniques, such as value at risk, is straightforward, e.g., Jorion (2001). In almost all cases, the relevant risk is the change in a "price," e.g., the change in stock prices, the change in commodity prices, even the change in exchange rates. However, for assessing the risk of fixed income securities, the state variable "price" is an illusive concept. For this reason, risk management for fixed income securities has developed notions such as duration and convexity. In particular, duration measures the change in the value of a fixed income position with respect to a change in "interest rates." Though it is possible to conceive of reexpressing duration in terms of the change in, say, a riskless fixed maturity zero coupon bond, this would add more confusion to an already imprecise concept (as discussed in section 5.3). Instead, it is more practical to detail how the Greeks relate to the conventional notions of duration and convexity.

When referring to options on fixed income securities, whether the option is embedded or traded separately, the Greek concepts make sense. For example, the delta of an exchange traded bond option measures the change of the option price with respect to a change in the price of the underlying bond. When referring to a bond with an embedded option, including bonds subject to default risk, it is also possible to talk about the delta in terms of the change in the price of the embedded riskless straight bond. Letting P_{OB} be the price of the bond with the embedded option and P_B be the riskless straight bond price component of the embedded option price $(P_{OB} = P_B \pm \text{Embedded option price})$, it follows that:

$$\Delta_{OB} = \frac{dP_{OB}}{dP_B} = \frac{P_{OB}}{P_{OB}} \frac{P_B}{P_B} \frac{y}{y} \frac{dy}{dy} \frac{dP_{OB}}{dP_B} = \frac{P_{OB}}{P_B} \frac{D_{OB}}{D_B}$$

The delta of the embedded option bond equals the ratio of the price of the embedded option bond to the straight bond component multiplied by the ratio of the duration of the embedded option bond to the duration of the straight bond component. To interpret the delta of the embedded option bond consider the case where the embedded option has no value. In this case, $P_{OB} = P_B$ and the durations will also be equal. It follows that the delta will be one. Similarly, consider a currently callable bond where the callable bond price is above the call price. In this case, $P_{OB} < P_B$ and the duration of the embedded option bond will be significantly shorter than the duration of the straight bond because of the likelihood of an early call date. It follows that the delta of the embedded option bond will be much less than one, approaching zero as the probability of immediate call approaches one.

Given this, it is possible to provide another interpretation of the delta of an embedded option bond. Let $P_{OB} = P_B \pm P_O$, where P_O is the price of the embedded option. This specification follows because the embedded option price is subtracted from the straight bond price for a seller's (issuer's) option and added to the price for a buyer's option. It follows that:

$$\Delta_{OB} = \frac{dP_{OB}}{dP_B} = 1 \pm \frac{dP_O}{dP_B} = 1 \pm \Delta_O$$

In effect, when the embedded option is deep out of the money then the delta of the embedded option bond will be close to one and the price will change like a straight bond price. As the option goes into the money the delta of the embedded option bond will deviate from one. Recalling that the delta of the embedded option is a non-linear function of the state variable, this property is carried over to the change in the delta of the embedded option bond. One of the insights of option pricing theory is that it is possible to provide a functional form for the option delta.

Discussion of the other Greeks follows appropriately. In option pricing theory, the second derivative of a call option written on a stock, taken with respect to the stock price ($\partial^2 C / \partial S^2$) is the gamma of the call option on a stock. In general, gamma measures the changes in delta with respect to the change in the state variable. This Greek is important in risk management for portfolios where the objective is to attain a delta target, e.g., delta equal to zero. Because option deltas change as the state variable changes, it may be necessary to dynamically trade the position to achieve the delta target. Gamma gives information about the rebalancing frequency. Other derivatives follow appropriately: theta is the time derivative; "vega" is the volatility derivative; and rho is the riskless interest rate derivative.[7] In theory, each of these concepts can be extended to embedded option bonds (theta for straight bonds has already been examined in section 5.3). However, the precise method of doing this for vega or rho is not obvious. For example, vega could be assessed by assuming a specific stochastic process that, in turn, could be used to specify zero coupon bond prices (see end of chapter 5 questions) and embedded option prices. The method for doing this would, at best, be complicated.

The Greeks play a useful role in the analysis of portfolios that contain options. If a closed form option pricing formula is available, then the Greeks can be solved directly. While identifying a closed form is relatively straightforward for options on commodities and equities where there is a single price for the underlying state variable, e.g., stock prices or exchange rates, there are considerable problems for options written on fixed income securities (e.g., Hull 2003, pp. 530–1). To see this, consider the Black (1976) model for an option on a Eurodollar futures contract. This model requires the state variable to be lognormally distributed. This assumption is inappropriate for fixed income prices because par value is an upper bound on the price determined by the inability of interest rates to be negative. Following Stoll and Whalley (1993, pp. 369–73), this problem can be circumvented by choosing yields as the state variable. In this case, lognormality is consistent with the yield not being negative. By setting a short time to expiration and using observed implied volatilities, the possibility of Eurodollar futures prices going to zero as the yield increases without limit is effectively avoided.

Given this, the payoff for the call option on the expiration date can now be expressed as: $C_e(T) = \max[0, (100 - eu(T)) - X] = \max[0, (100 - X) - eu(T)]$ where C_e is the price of the Eurodollar call option, eu is the add-on interest rate on the Eurodollar deposit to be delivered, T is the expiration date and X is the exercise price. This is the first quirk associated with the Eurodollar interest rate option contract: the payoff on a call option has the same form as a payoff on a commodity put option, where the interest rate $eu[T]$ replaces $S[T]$ and the "exercise price" is expressed as $(100 - X)$ instead of X. Observing that $eu(t) = (100 - EU(t))$, where $EU(t)$ is the observed Eurodollar futures price, it is now possible to substitute directly into the Black (1976) formula for a European *put* option on a commodity futures contract to obtain the option pricing formula for a European *call* on a Eurodollar interest rate futures contract:[8]

$$C_e[EU, T; X, r, \sigma_e] = \exp^{-rt^*}[(100 - X)N[-d_2] - (100 - EU(t))N[-d_1]]$$

where:

$$d_1 = \frac{\ln\left[\dfrac{100 - EU(t)}{100 - X}\right] + .5\sigma_e^2 t^*}{\sigma_e\sqrt{t^*}} \qquad d_2 = d_1 - \sigma_e\sqrt{t^*}$$

In this formulation σ_e is the volatility of the Eurodollar add-on interest rate, t^* is the fraction of the year remaining to maturity, r is the "riskless" interest rate and $N[d]$ is the value of the cumulative normal distribution function evaluated at d (see table 6.4).

As an example of applying the formula consider the Eurodollar futures and options quotes in table 6.5. Assume that the "price" for the nearby March Eurodollar futures contract is $EU(t) = 98.69$ which translates to an annualized interest rate on the deliverable three month Eurodollar of $100 - 98.69 = 1.31\%$. The method of quoting Eurodollar futures options is somewhat different. For example, on February 4, 2002 the March delivery call with a $(X =) 98.75$ exercise price is .27 or 27 basis points. To calculate the price of this option observe that the $1 million par value 3 month Eurodollar deposit underlying the futures contract has a value of $25 per basis point. Hence, ignoring transactions costs a call for one Eurodollar futures with a 98.75 exercise price is selling for $(27)(\$25) = \$675$. Observing that the price quotes are for February 4 and the option will expire on March 17, the fraction of the year remaining to maturity is $t^* = (41/365) = .112$. To use the option pricing formula for this option now requires an estimate for the volatility σ_e and the riskless rate r. Given that the call option price is observed, it follows that the formula provides a joint estimate of implied volatility and the riskless rate.

Table 6.4 Cumulative normal distribution values

Values of $N(d)$ for selected values of d

d	$N(d)$	d	$N(d)$	d	$N(d)$
		−1.00	0.1587	1.00	0.8413
−2.95	0.0016	−0.95	0.1711	1.05	0.8531
−2.90	0.0019	−0.90	0.1841	1.10	0.8643
−2.85	0.0022	−0.85	0.1977	1.15	0.8749
−2.80	0.0026	−0.80	0.2119	1.20	0.8849
−2.75	0.0030	−0.75	0.2266	1.25	0.8944
−2.70	0.0035	−0.70	0.2420	1.30	0.9032
−2.65	0.0040	−0.65	0.2578	1.35	0.9115
−2.60	0.0047	−0.60	0.2743	1.40	0.9192
−2.55	0.0054	−0.55	0.2912	1.45	0.9265
−2.50	0.0062	−0.50	0.3085	1.50	0.9332
−2.45	0.0071	−0.45	0.3264	1.55	0.9394
−2.40	0.0082	−0.40	0.3446	1.60	0.9452
−2.35	0.0094	−0.35	0.3632	1.65	0.9505
−2.30	0.0107	−0.30	0.3821	1.70	0.9554
−2.25	0.0122	−0.25	0.4013	1.75	0.9599
−2.20	0.0139	−0.20	0.4207	1.80	0.9641
−2.15	0.0158	−0.15	0.4404	1.85	0.9678
−2.10	0.0179	−0.10	0.4602	1.90	0.9713
−2.05	0.0202	−0.05	0.4801	1.95	0.9744
−2.00	0.0228	0.00	0.5000	2.00	0.9773
−1.95	0.0256	0.05	0.5199	2.05	0.9798
−1.90	0.0287	0.10	0.5398	2.10	0.9821
−1.85	0.0322	0.15	0.5596	2.15	0.9842
−1.80	0.0359	0.20	0.5793	2.20	0.9861
−1.75	0.0401	0.25	0.5987	2.25	0.9878
−1.70	0.0446	0.30	0.6179	2.30	0.9893
−1.65	0.0495	0.35	0.6368	2.35	0.9906
−1.60	0.0548	0.40	0.6554	2.40	0.9918
−1.55	0.0606	0.45	0.6736	2.45	0.9929
−1.50	0.0668	0.50	0.6915	2.50	0.9938
−1.45	0.0735	0.55	0.7088	2.55	0.9946
−1.40	0.0808	0.60	0.7257	2.60	0.9953
−1.35	0.0885	0.65	0.7422	2.65	0.9960
−1.30	0.0968	0.70	0.7580	2.70	0.9965
−1.25	0.1057	0.75	0.7734	2.75	0.9970
−1.20	0.1151	0.80	0.7881	2.80	0.9974
−1.15	0.1251	0.85	0.8023	2.85	0.9978
−1.10	0.1357	0.90	0.8159	2.90	0.9981
−1.05	0.1469	0.95	0.8289	2.95	0.9984

Table 6.5 Eurodollar futures and options prices, January 14, 2004

Interest Rate Futures	Interest Rate Options

Interest Rate Futures

Treasury Bonds (CBT)-$100,000; pts 32nds of 100%

Mar	109–20	110–16	109–17	110–09	24	116–23	101–05	430,808
June	108–23	109–01	108–13	108–28	24	116–15	104–00	10,195

Est vol 114,656; vol Tue 134,747; open int 464,142, +4,406.

Treasury Notes (CBT)-$100,000; pts 32nds of 100%

Mar	112–01	12–235	111–30	112–20	22.0	116–10	106–29	928,020
June	–	–	111–04	22.0	111–15	107–13		290

Est vol 288,353; vol Tue 303,885; open int 941,864, –2.107.

10 Yr. Agency Notes (CBT)-$100,000; pts 32nds of 100%

Mar	–	–	–	na	–	–	–	0

Est vol 0; vol Tue 0; open int na, *.

5 Yr. Treasury Notes (CBT)-$100,000; pts 32nds of 100%

Mar	111–10	111–25	11–075	111–23	16.5	19–215	09–145	795,042

Est vol 125,149; vol Tue 148,419; open int 820,085, –7,560.

2 Yr. Treasury Notes (CBT)-$200,000; pts 32nds of 100%

Dec	07–202	107–21	107–18	107–21	6.7	07–287	106–06	10,470

Est vol 11,115; vol Tue 19,587; open int 160,113, +87.

30 Day Federal Funds (CBT)-$5,000,000; 100 – daily avg.

Dec	99.010	99.015	99.005	99.005	–	99.230	98.400	45,786
Ja04	99.00	99.00	99.00	99.00	–	99.24	98.66	51,238
Feb	98.99	99.00	98.99	98.99	0.01	99.22	98.70	77,544
Mar	98.99	98.99	98.98	98.98	0.01	99.16	98.74	51,695
Apr	98.97	98.97	98.96	98.97	0.01	99.17	89.96	63,198
May	98.88	98.89	98.88	98.88	0.01	99.79	98.40	27,107
June	98.87	98.87	98.86	98.87	0.02	98.96	98.38	15,844
July	98.75	98.77	98.75	98.77	0.04	98.89	98.20	14,668

Est vol 9,191; vol Tue 15,247; open int 349,596, +1,170.

10 Yr. Interest Rate Swaps (CBT)-$100,000; pts 32nds of 100%

Mar	109–19	110–07	109–19	110–07	21	111–00	107–20	36,929

Est vol 75; vol Tue 2,590; open int 36,930, +1,676.

10 Yr. Muni Note Index (CBT)-$1,000 × index

Mar	102–16	103–01	102–16	103–01	16	103–14	99–21	1,916

Est vol 498; vol Tue 170; open int 1,916, +4.
Index: Close na; Yield na.

	OPEN	HIGH	LOW	SETTLE	CHG	YIELD	CHG	OPEN INT

13 Week Treasury Bills (CME)-$1,000,000; pts of 100%

Jan	–	–	–	n.a.	–	–	–	0

Est vol n.a.; vol Tue 0; open int 0, unch.

1 Month Libor (CME)-$3,000,000; pts of 100%

Jan	98.88	98.88	98.88	98.88	–	1.12	–	18,951
Feb	98.87	98.87	98.87	98.87	0.01	1.13	–0.01	31,195

Est vol 1,601; vol Tue 3,205; open int 74,691, +1,179.

Eurodollar (CME)-$1,000,000; pts of 100%

Jan	98.83	98.83	98.82	98.82	–	1.18	–	103,770
Feb	98.81	98.81	98.79	98.81	0.01	1.19	–0.01	22,987
Mar	98.76	98.77	98.75	98.76	0.01	1.24	–0.01	810,547
Apr	98.72	98.72	98.72	98.72	0.03	1.28	–0.03	13,917
May	98.62	98.65	98.62	98.65	0.06	1.35	–0.06	9,886
June	98.51	98.57	98.51	98.56	0.07	1.44	–0.07	696,129
Sept	98.16	98.24	98.15	98.22	0.09	1.78	–0.09	576,374
Dec	97.71	97.83	97.69	97.81	0.13	2.19	–0.13	495,833
Mr05	97.27	97.41	97.28	97.40	0.12	2.60	–0.12	348,628
June	96.88	96.98	96.87	96.97	0.12	3.03	–0.12	278,748
Sept	96.52	96.61	96.49	96.60	0.13	3.40	–0.13	215,912
Dec	96.22	96.32	96.19	96.30	0.12	3.70	–0.12	176,090
Mr06	95.98	96.10	95.97	96.08	0.11	3.92	–0.11	141,182
June	95.77	95.86	95.76	95.85	0.10	4.15	–0.10	124,164
Sept	95.62	95.66	95.61	95.65	0.09	4.35	–0.09	102,376
Dec	95.37	95.46	95.37	95.45	0.09	4.55	–0.09	101,407
Mr07	95.23	95.29	95.21	95.29	0.08	4.71	–0.08	74,970
June	95.11	95.12	95.08	95.12	0.07	4.88	–0.07	65,690
Sept	94.90	94.96	94.90	94.97	0.07	5.03	–0.07	62,672
Dec	94.77	94.82	94.77	94.82	0.05	5.18	–0.05	53,056
Mr08	94.70	94.71	94.65	94.71	0.06	5.29	–0.06	46,171
June	94.59	94.61	94.54	94.61	0.06	5.39	–0.06	46,961
Sept	94.49	94.52	94.44	94.51	0.06	5.49	–0.06	29,345
Dec	94.40	94.42	94.40	94.41	0.08	5.59	–0.08	17,419

Est vol 236,941; vol Tue 435,250; open int 4,685,668, +1,398.

Interest Rate Options

T-Bonds (CBT)
$100,000; points and 64ths of 100%

Price	Jan	Feb	Mar	Jan	Feb	Mar
108	2–18	2–58	3–36	0–01	0–40	1–17
109	1–19	2–14	2–59	0–01	0–60	1–41
110	0–28	1–40	2–23	0–10	1–22	2–04
111	0–04	1–09	1–56	0–50	1–55	2–38
112	0–01	0–49	1–29	1–47	2–30	3–10
113	0–01	0–31	1–07	–	3–13	3–52

Est vol 38,507;
Tu vol 19,412 calls 25,929 puts
Op int Tues 395,173 calls 296,135 puts

T-Notes (CBT)
$100,000; points and 64ths of 100%

Price	Jan	Feb	Mar	Jan	Feb	Mar
111	1–41	2–07	2–37	0–01	0–31	0–61
112	0–43	1–23	1–60	0–03	0–52	1–20
113	0–05	0–57	1–26	0–29	1–17	1–50
114	0–01	0–32	0–62	1–25	1–56	2–22
115	0–01	0–16	0–42	2–24	2–40	–
116	0–01	0–07	0–26	–	–	3–50

Est vol 102,810 Tu 36 calls 71,317 puts
Op int Tues 767,793 calls 883,751 puts

5 Yr Treas Notes (CBT)
$100,000; points and 64ths of 100%

Price	Jan	Feb	Mar	Jan	Feb	Mar
11,050	1–14	1–35	1–52	0–01	0–21	0–39
11,100	0–47	1–11	1–32	0–01	0–29	0–50
11,150	0–18	0–54	1–12	0–04	0–40	0–62
11,200	0–04	0–38	0–59	0–22	0–56	1–13
11,250	0–01	0–26	0–46	–	–	–
11,300	0–01	0–16	0–35	–	–	–

Est vol 22,793 Tu 11,042 calls 28,596 puts
Op int Tues 123,621 calls 354,590 puts

Eurodollar (CME)
$ million; pts. of 100%

Price	Jan	Feb	Mar	Jan	Feb	Mar
9,825	5.15	–	5.22	0.00	0.05	0.07
9,850	2.70	–	2.80	0.05	0.10	0.15
9,875	0.45	0.60	0.70	0.30	0.45	0.55
9,900	0.00	–	0.10	–	–	2.45
9,925	–	–	0.02	–	–	4.87
9,950	–	–	0.00	–	–	7.35

Est vol 32,107;
Tu vol 22,091 calls 41,581 puts
Op int Tues 3,565,358 calls 3,786,058 puts

1 Yr. Mid-Curve Eurodlr (CME)
$1,000,000 contract units; pts. of 100%

Price	Jan	Feb	Mar	Jan	Feb	Mar
9,700	4.35	5.10	5.60	0.35	1.10	1.60
9,725	2.50	3.37	3.85	1.00	1.87	2.35
9,750	1.15	2.00	2.52	2.15	–	3.52
9,775	0.40	1.00	1.45	–	–	4.95
9,800	0.15	–	0.72	–	–	6.70
9,825	–	–	–	–	–	8.82

Est vol 5,952 Tu 17,956 calls 13,780 puts
Op int Tues 729,969 calls 570,966 puts

As a pedagogical exercise, set $r = 1\%$ and $\sigma_e = 1.866\%$. Using these values to calculate the call option price reveals:

$$d_1 = \frac{\ln[(100 - 98.69)/(100 - 98.75)] + .5(1.866)^2.112}{1.866\sqrt{.112}} = .3873 \quad \rightarrow \quad N[-d_1] = .35$$

$$d_2 = .3873 - 1.866\sqrt{.112} = -.2372 \quad \rightarrow \quad N[-d_2] = .585$$

$$C_e = \exp^{-.01(.112)}[(100 - 98.75)]N[-d_2] - (100 - 98.69)N[-d_1] = .2724$$

This is consistent with the observed call option price of 27 basis points. The use of yields as the state variable is well suited to Eurodollar futures options where the "futures price" $EU(t) = 100 - eu(t)$. Specification of the Black model for an option on a bond futures contract, where the futures and options quotes relate to bond prices, again raises the complications associated with assuming lognormality for a fixed income security price. In addition, there are complications associated with valuing changes in the term structure affecting the bond and bond option value.

In order to develop a more sensible bond option pricing model the discussion in section 5.2 about different stochastic processes for the interest rate now assumes relevance. For example, the Vasicek model can be used to solve for zero coupon bond prices that, in turn, can be used to solve the option pricing formula for a zero coupon bond. Because the underlying process is OU, this will result in a different specification for the volatility. Hull (2003, pp. 545–6) demonstrates that the Ho-Lee model leads to a zero coupon bond pricing formula that is "essentially the same as Black's model" with the proviso that the zero coupon bond prices are determined by the absence of arbitrage formula determined from the Ho-Lee model (see end of chapter 5 questions). Given the option pricing formulas for zero coupon bonds, coupon bearing bond options can be determined by treating each coupon payment as a zero coupon bond and summing across options for all payment periods. In any event, it is possible, in some fashion, to determine the Greeks for various fixed income options from the available valuation formulas or, where these are too complicated, using numerical procedures.

*Duration, convexity and the Greeks for callable bonds**

To derive the Greeks for a default free callable bond it is necessary to observe that the call feature is a seller's option. This leads to:

$$P_{CB} = P_B - C_B$$

where P_{CB} is the observed price of the callable bond, P_B is the unobserved price of the straight bond, and C_B is the unobserved price of the "callable option" feature.[9] The value of C_B is subtracted because a callable option is a seller's option. The delta of the callable option plays a key role in the interpretation of the duration for the callable bond price. To see this, consider the modified duration for the callable bond:

$$\frac{1}{P_{CB}}\frac{dP_{CB}}{dy} = \frac{1}{P_{CB}}\left[\frac{dP_B}{dy} - \frac{dC_B}{dy}\right] = \frac{P_B}{P_{CB}}\left[\frac{1}{P_B}\frac{dP_B}{dy} - \frac{1}{P_B}\frac{dC_B}{dy}\right]$$

It follows that the duration of a callable bond is related to the duration of the embedded straight bond and the embedded option delta.

To demonstrate that these two durations are connected by the delta of the callable option, consider the following manipulation:

$$\frac{1}{P_B}\frac{dC_B}{dy} = \frac{1}{P_B}\frac{dC_B}{dP_B}\frac{dP_B}{dy} = \Delta_C \Delta_B$$

where D_B is the modified duration of the embedded straight bond and $\Delta_C = (dC_B/dP_B)$ is the delta of the callable option. The introduction of the chain rule is applicable because the call price depends on the straight bond price which, in turn, is a function of the yield, i.e., the callable option is only an implicit function of the yield to maturity. The delta is evaluated with respect to the straight bond price because changes in the callable option price depend on changes in the straight bond price, with the callable bond price being a function of the straight bond and callable option prices.

Given this, the duration for the callable bond follows appropriately:

$$\frac{1}{P_{CB}}\frac{dP_{CB}}{dy} = D_{CB} = D_B(1 - \Delta_C)\frac{P_B}{P_{CB}}$$

This functional relationship between the modified durations of the callable and straight bonds is illustrated in figure 6.1. This figure is only indicative as the price function for the callable bond will be altered somewhat if different assumptions are made about variables such as the call price, call date and interest rate volatility. Following the discussion in section 5.3, the duration can be heuristically interpreted as the slope of the bond price function, $P[y]$. Recognizing that figure 6.1 is for a callable bond that is approaching the call date, at price levels well below (yield levels well in excess of) the call exercise price, the callable and straight bond price functions are identical ($P_{CB} = P_B$). In the formula for the modified duration, this implies that $\Delta_C = 0$ at that yield level. This follows because the callable option is deep out-of-the-money in this region implying a zero or near zero price for the embedded option.

Figure 6.1 indicates that as the price level rises (yields fall) to a level approaching the call exercise price, the callable and straight bond price functions start to diverge. This is an implication of the callable option getting closer to the money and, as a result, the delta of the option takes on a significant positive value. As the bond price rises above the call exercise price, the callable option goes into the money and the delta of the option increases above the at-the-money level of approximately one-half. As the option goes deep in the money, the delta goes to one and the duration of the callable bond goes to zero. This implies that the callable bond will have a price that is bounded above. This illustrates an important feature of callable bonds: the upward price increase of a callable bond due to falling yields is bounded above. This upper bound will be tighter for shorter call dates and higher levels of yield volatility.

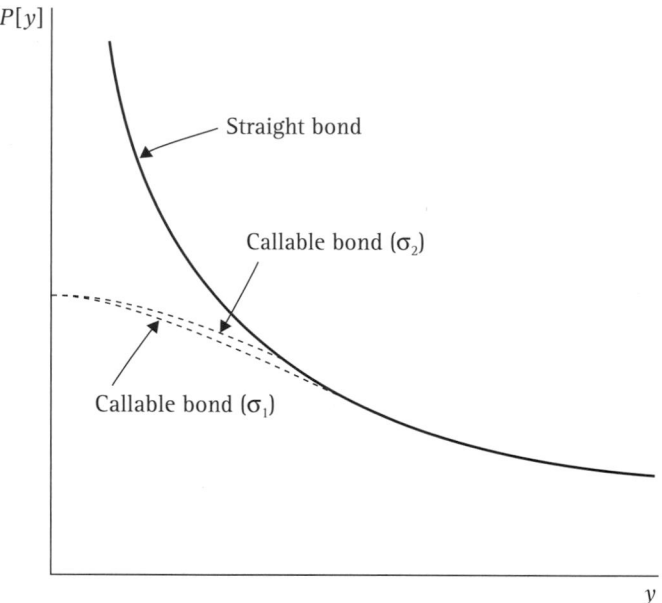

Figure 6.1 Price-yield relationship for a callable bond and a straight bond where $\sigma_2 > \sigma_1$

In much the same fashion that the duration of a callable bond is related to the delta of the embedded callable option, the convexity of the callable bond is related to the gamma of the embedded callable option. However, the relationship is analytically more complicated than for the duration–delta relationship. To see this consider the second derivative of the callable bond price:

$$\frac{dP_{CB}}{dy} = \frac{dP_B}{dy} - \frac{dC_B}{dP_B}\frac{dP_B}{dy}$$

$$\rightarrow \quad \frac{d^2P_{CB}}{dy^2} = \frac{d^2P_B}{dy^2} - \left[\frac{dP_B}{dy}\frac{d^2C_B}{dP_B^2}\frac{dP_B}{dy} + \frac{dC_B}{dP_B}\frac{d^2P_B}{dy^2}\right]$$

It follows that:

$$\frac{1}{P_{CB}}\frac{d^2P_{CB}}{dy^2} = CON_{CB} = \frac{P_B}{P_{CB}}\left[\frac{1}{P_B}\frac{d^2P_B}{dy^2} - \left(\frac{1}{P_B}\frac{dP_B}{dy}\frac{d^2C_B}{dP_B^2}\frac{dP_B}{dy} + \frac{1}{P_B}\frac{dC_B}{dP_B}\frac{d^2P_B}{dy^2}\right)\right]$$

Observing that:

$$\frac{1}{P_B}\frac{d^2P_B}{dy^2} = CON_B \qquad \frac{d^2C_B}{dP_B^2} = \Gamma_C$$

The formula for the convexity of a callable bond can be stated as:

$$CON_{CB} = \frac{P_B}{P_{CB}} [CON_B (1 - \Delta_C) - P_B \Gamma_C (D_B)^2]$$

This results reveals that, unlike a straight bond that has $CON_B > 0$, a callable bond can have convexity that is negative over some range of bond prices.

When will convexity be negative? This can be seen by again examining figure 6.1 (see also end of chapter questions). As with the result for callable bond duration, for bond prices well below (yields above), the callable option will be deep out of the money and both the delta and gamma will be zero or near zero. In this case, $CON_{CB} = CON_B$. The negative convexity emerges as the bond price increases (yield decreases) from a very low (high) level. Starting from, say 20% yield, the durations of both the callable and straight bond will increase as the yields fall (positive convexity). However as the yield approaches the range where the call provision becomes effective, the duration of the straight bond will continue to increase but the duration of the callable bond will start to fall. Recalling that duration involves the value of the first derivative multiplied by minus one, the property that the duration falls as yields fall is the meaning of negativity convexity. As the callability option goes farther and farther into the money, the impact of yield changes on the duration of the callable bond will dissipate, implying that convexity will start to increase from a negative value back to zero.

*Duration, convexity and the Greeks for other embedded option bonds**

Callable bonds provide a relatively clean solution to duration, convexity and the Greeks for bonds with embedded options. Some other types of embedded option bonds, e.g., bonds with put provisions, are also relatively clean. However, embedded option bonds such as MBS and bonds with default risk are more complicated. This happens because the mechanism for interest rate changes to impact bond prices requires some type of valuation model to be specified. For example, an MBS security requires the specification of a prepayment model. The relationship between prepayments and interest rates is decidedly more complicated than in the case of the callability provision. Because a conventional convertible bond is, by construction, a defaultable security, the case of convertible bonds is also complicated as it requires both the default risk and the conversion option to be modeled. While the conversion option can be modeled using option pricing techniques, the default risk component requires a valuation model for the market value of the firm. The process of modeling default risk is discussed in section 6.4.

To derive the Greeks for a default free putable bond it is necessary to observe that the put feature is a buyer's option. This leads to:

$$P_{PB} = P_B + PP_B$$

where P_{PB} is the observed price of the putable bond, P_B is the unobserved price of the straight bond, and PP_B is the unobserved price of the "putable option" feature.[10] The value of PP_B is added because a putable option is a buyer's option. As before, the delta of the putable option plays a key role in interpreting the duration of the putable bond price. To see this observe the modified duration for a putable bond:

$$\frac{1}{P_{PB}} \frac{dP_{PB}}{dy} = \frac{1}{P_{PB}} \left[\frac{dP_B}{dy} + \frac{dPP_B}{dy} \right] = \frac{P_B}{P_{PB}} \left[\frac{1}{P_B} \frac{dP_B}{dy} - \frac{1}{P_B} \frac{dPP_B}{dy} \right]$$

It follows that the duration of a putable bond is related to the duration of the embedded straight bond and the embedded option delta.

To demonstrate that these two durations are connected by the delta of the putable option, consider the following manipulation:

$$\frac{1}{P_B} \frac{dPP_B}{dy} = \frac{1}{P_B} \frac{dPP_B}{dP_B} \frac{dP_B}{dy} = \Delta_P D_B$$

where D_B is the modified duration of the embedded straight bond and $\Delta_P = (dPP_B/dP_B)$ is the delta of the putable option. The introduction of the chain rule is applicable because the put price depends on the straight bond price which, in turn, is a function of the yield, i.e., the putable option is only an implicit function of the yield to maturity. The delta is evaluated with respect to the straight bond price because changes in the putable option price depend on changes in the straight bond price, with the putable bond price being a function of the straight bond and putable option prices.

Given this, the duration for the putable bond follows appropriately:

$$\frac{1}{P_{PB}} \frac{dP_{PB}}{dy} = D_{PB} = D_B(1 + \Delta_P) \frac{P_B}{P_{PB}}$$

This functional relationship between the modified durations of the putable and straight bonds is illustrated in figure 6.2. As in figure 6.1 for the callable bond, this figure is only indicative as the price function for the putable bond will be altered somewhat if different assumptions are made about variables such as the put price, put date and interest rate volatility. Again following the discussion in section 5.3, the duration can be heuristically interpreted as the slope of the bond price function. For a putable bond that is approaching the put date, at putable bond price levels well above (yield levels well below) the put exercise price, the putable and straight bond price functions are identical ($P_{PB} = P_B$). In the formula for the modified duration, this implies that $\Delta_P = 0$ in this range of y. This follows because the putable option is deep out-of-the-money in this region implying a zero or near zero price for the embedded option.

Figure 6.2 indicates that as the price level falls (yields rise) to a level approaching the put exercise price, the putable and straight bond price functions start to diverge. This is an implication of the putable option getting closer to the money and, as a result, the delta of the put option starts to take on a significant *negative* value, i.e., as straight bond prices fall the value of a put option increases ($\Delta_P < 0$). As the bond price falls below the put exercise price, the putable option goes into the money and the delta of the option decreases below the at-the-money level of approximately minus one-half. As the option goes deep in the money, the delta goes to minus one and the duration of the putable bond goes to zero. This implies that the putable bond will have a price that is bounded below. This illustrates an important feature of putable bonds: the downward price decrease of a putable bond associated with rising yields is bounded below. With a

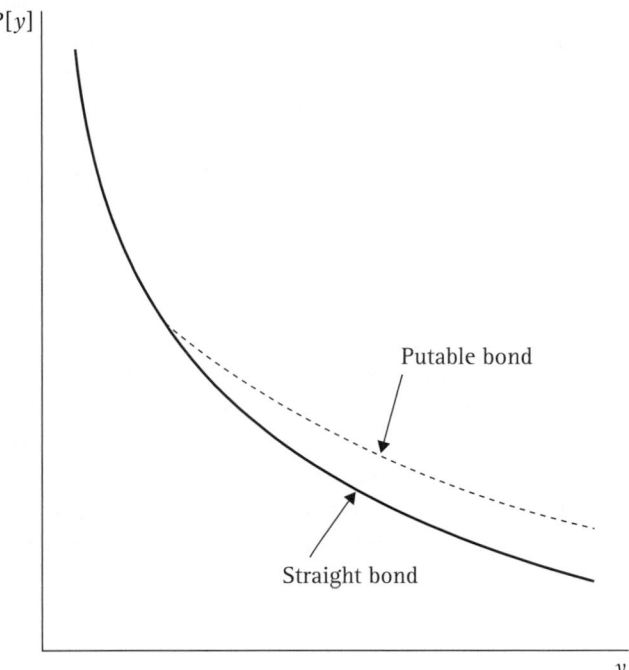

Figure 6.2 Price-yield function for a putable and a straight bond

zero notice period, this lower bound will be tighter for shorter put dates and higher levels of yield volatility.

As demonstrated by Chance (1990), Nawalka (1996) and Sarkar (1999), it is possible to extend the analysis to bonds subject to default risk and conversion features. Ignoring the topic of default risk for the moment, let the price of a convertible bond (P_{BW}, price of a bond with warrants) be equal to the straight bond price plus the value of the conversion feature that is set equal to W, the price of a warrant to purchase one share of stock, times N, the number of shares that can be obtained by fully converting the bond:

$$P_{BW} = P_B + NW \quad \rightarrow \quad D_{BW} = \frac{P_B}{P_{BW}} D_B - N \frac{1}{P_{BW}} \frac{dW}{dy}$$

This duration can be reexpressed as:

$$D_{BW} = D_B - \frac{NW}{P_{BW}} \left(D_B + \frac{1}{W} \frac{dW}{dy} \right)$$

When the rho of a warrant is, more or less, equal to the rho of an exchange traded call option, the Black-Scholes formula can be differentiated to show that $(dW/dr) > 0$, this implies that the duration of a convertible bond will be smaller than the duration of the straight bond component.

The formula for the duration of a convertible bond illustrates the need for a valuation model to make an adequate interpretation. For example, just because the rho of an exchange traded option calculated from the Black-Scholes formula is always positive, it does not necessarily follow that a warrant will have the same property in practice. The market value of a warrant depends on the market value of the underlying equity. Ignoring the potential dilution associated with warrant exercise, increases in interest rates can impact the value of the warrant by changing the market value of the assets and, hence, the value of the equity claim. Even though increases in interest rates will reduce the market value of the debt, it is theoretically possible for the equity claim to fall in value enough to cause $(dW/dr) < 0$, if the fall in the market value of assets is sufficiently greater than the reduction in the debt value. This could happen in various ways. One scenario is where a large fraction of the firm's debt is funded with short term rollover. If the leverage ratio for the firm is very high, an increase in interest rates could force the firm into default.

Sarkar (1999) illustrates the implications of using a valuation model to determine the duration of a convertible bond. Following Merton (1974), the model assumes that the market value of the firm (V) follows a lognormal diffusion (see section 6.4) with drift of μV and volatility σV. The convertible bond is assumed to be zero coupon and non-callable with par value of M. Firm value is the only source of randomness, i.e., the riskless interest rate is not modeled as being stochastic. The "conversion fraction" x is determined as $x = \#/(N + \#)$ where $\#$ is the number of shares outstanding prior to conversion. The only debt in the capital structure is this zero coupon convertible. Given this, the price of a zero coupon convertible bond can be derived as:

$$P_{BW} = VN[d_1] + xVN[d_2] + Me^{-rt*}(N[d_4] - N[d_3])$$

where:

$$d_1 = \frac{\ln\left[\dfrac{M}{V}\right] - (r + .5\sigma^2)t*}{\sigma\sqrt{t*}} \qquad d_2 = \frac{\ln\left[\dfrac{xV}{M}\right] + (r + .5\sigma^2)t*}{\sigma\sqrt{t*}}$$

$$d_3 = d_1 + \sigma\sqrt{t*} \qquad d_4 = -d_2 + \sigma\sqrt{t*}$$

Using this valuation formula, the duration for this special case of a convertible bond can be determined by evaluating the derivative with respect to the riskless interest rate r.

Given this, the duration can be derived as (Sarkar 1999, p. 180):

$$D_{BW} = t*\frac{Me^{-rt*}(N[d_4] - N[d_3])}{P_{BW}} = t*\frac{Me^{-rt*}(N[d_4] - N[d_3])}{VN[d_1] + xVN[d_2] + Me^{-rt*}(N[d_4] - N[d_3])}$$

Setting $x = 0$ will give the duration of a corporate zero coupon bond without the conversion provision. Chance (1990) provides a solution, without the conversion provision, that incorporates stochastic interest rates as well as randomness in firm value.

Observing that, with no default and no conversion, the expected value of the convertible bond price is $Me^{-rt^*}(N[d_4] - N[d_3]) > 0$, it follows that the duration for the convertible bond in this valuation model will be smaller than the duration for the straight bond component. Sankar (1999, pp. 182–3) provides a range of results from comparative static analysis for the convertible bond duration, e.g., convertible bond duration is decreasing in the volatility of firm value because this increases the probability of both default and conversion causing duration to fall. Inspection of the comparative static results reveals that the assumption of non-stochastic interest rates has substantive implications for the interpretation of convertible bond valuation and duration models (see section 6.4).

6.3 OPTION ADJUSTED SPREAD ANALYSIS*

*Static spread and cash flow assumptions**

Option adjusted spread (OAS) analysis is an extension of the static spread that incorporates randomness in the cash flows from the security. In turn, the *static spread* is an extension of traditional yield spread analysis that accounts for the timing of the cash flows of the two securities being compared, where accounting for the timing of the cash flows is affected by the term structure of interest rates. Fabozzi (1989, p. 340) illustrates traditional yield spread analysis by comparing two straight bonds, a Treasury and a corporate bond both with an 8.8% coupon and 25 years to maturity. The Treasury sells at $96.613 to yield 9.15% and the corporate sells for $87.08 to yield 10.24%. *Traditional yield spread* analysis would compare the value of these two bonds by observing the difference in the yields is 109 basis points. This yield spread would then be compared with the Treasury-corporate yield spread on other bonds of similar coupon and yield to maturity that are being assessed. After due consideration of the credit risk of the various bonds a decision would be made about the appropriate bond to purchase.

Traditional yield spread analysis has the attractive feature of simplicity. However, because promised yields to maturity are being compared, this approach fails to account for the shape of the term structure of interest rates. Consider valuing the corporate and Treasury bonds using implied zero interest rates. Because the implied zeros are derived from the Treasury yield curve, the price of the Treasury bond (P_B) would be evaluated as:

$$P_B = \sum_{t=1}^{2T} \frac{C/2}{\left(1 + \frac{z_t}{2}\right)^2} + \frac{M}{\left(1 + \frac{z_T}{2}\right)^{2T}} = \sum_{t=1}^{2T} \frac{C/2}{\left(1 + \frac{y}{2}\right)^2} + \frac{M}{\left(1 + \frac{y}{2}\right)^{2T}}$$

where coupons are paid semi-annually, T is the term to maturity in years and z_t and y are annualized. Comparing the yield to maturity calculation with the implied zero calculation it is apparent that if, say, the implied zero curve slopes up then the yield will "over discount" near term cash flows and "under discount" later cash flows.

In the same fashion that the yield to maturity "averages" over the yield curve by over and under discounting cash flows at specific points in time, traditional yield spread analysis will also be subject to "over and under discounting" specific cash flows. The static spread aims to address this problem by adding a fixed number of basis points to each of the implied zero interest rates to determine the price of the (semi-annual coupon) corporate bond (P_C):

$$P_C = \sum_{t=1}^{2T} \frac{C/2}{\left(1 + \frac{z_t}{2} + \frac{ss}{2}\right)^2} + \frac{M}{\left(1 + \frac{z_T}{2} + \frac{ss}{2}\right)^{2T}} = \sum_{t=1}^{2T} \frac{C/2}{\left(1 + \frac{y_C}{2}\right)^2} + \frac{M}{\left(1 + \frac{y_C}{2}\right)^{2T}}$$

where ss is the (annualized) static spread and y_C is the yield to maturity on the corporate bond. Using a spot rate curve that starts at 7% for the six month maturity and increases to 10.8% at 25 years, Fabozzi (1989, p. 345) demonstrates that evaluation of ss produces a value of 120 basis points, instead of the 109 basis point spread calculated using traditional yield curve analysis.

The static spread is a deterministic value that is used to construct the option adjusted spread (OAS) which is determined by doing a contingent claims valuation. Just like the static spread, the OAS gives a basis point value that captures the spread above Treasuries. However, due to the presence of randomness, there will not be one OAS but, rather, a range of OAS estimates that vary with the assumed volatility for the random variable(s). This is because the presence of an embedded option means that the future cash flows on the fixed income security are contingent on the future realization of some random variable. For example, the cash flows from a callable bond are contingent on the future realization of interest rates. If interest rates on the call date have fallen below the level at which it is cost effective to call the bond issue then there will be a cash flow at that point equal to the call price (plus accrued interest) and future cash flows from that point will be zero. However, if interest rates on the call date are not below the level at which it is cost effective to call the bond issue then there will continue to be a cash flow equal to the scheduled coupon payment.

In addition to the randomness in the future cash flows, the future behavior of interest rates also has to be modeled. Following the discussion in section 5.2, there are a number of different procedures that can be employed to generate future interest rates. The binomial process used in section 5.2 proceeded by generating paths for one period implied zeros. By working backwards through the binomial tree it was possible to determine the associated zero coupon bond prices for different maturities that could be used to solve for the implied forward rates. Monte Carlo methods provide an alternative procedure that is well adapted to solving for the OAS. In the Monte Carlo method, a large number of individual paths for the one period zeros are generated. Along each path, the one period zeros can be treated as implied forward rates that can be used to discount the random cash flows. The different values obtained can then be summed across each of the equally likely paths to obtain an estimate of the price of the contingent cash flows.

Generating the future spot rates and solving OAS*

Though it is possible to employ other methods, e.g., binomial trees as in Windas (1993), the Monte Carlo procedure for calculating the OAS is, perhaps, the easiest to illustrate. The sequence of steps involved in the Monte Carlo calculation of OAS is described by Fabozzi (1989, pp. 351–2):

1 Calculate the implied zero coupon interest rates from the observed Treasury yield curve. Use the implied zeros to calculate a full set of one period ahead implied forward rates ($f_{t,t+1}$). These values are used to calibrate the parameters used in the Monte Carlo process.
2 Identify the stochastic interest rate model that will be used in the Monte Carlo procedure to generate the one period Treasury spot rates. A range possible processes can be selected such as the self-calibrating one factor models of Black, Derman and Toy (1990) or Ho-Lee. The specification of the interest rate model will involve the selection of the volatility parameter.
3 Use the selected volatility and interest rate model to generate a sufficiently large number of interest rate paths. Each of the paths will be composed of a sequence of one period zeros that apply to future time periods. Treating the one period zeros as forward rates, construct the spot rates along each path.
4 Specify the decision rules used to determine the random cash flows. For example, a callable bond requires a rule for determining at what interest rate level the bond will be called.
5 Path by path, examine the relevant interest rate and determine when or whether the bond will be called along that path. Generate the contingent cash flow along that path.
6 Using the spot rates for each path, determine the present value of the cash flow along each path for a given level of the static spread.
7 For each static spread value, sum the present values across all the generated paths and divide by the number of paths. Repeat the process for a range of static spread values.
8 Compare the present values that were determined by averaging across the paths with the observed market price of the bond with the embedded option. When the observed bond price is equal to the value calculated from the Monte Carlo process, the associated value of the "averaged-across-paths" static spread is the option adjusted spread (OAS).
9 By repeating steps 3–8, recalculate the OAS for a different volatility assumption.

This 9 step process can be clarified by dissecting the simple example given in Fabozzi (1989, pp. 346–9).[11]

For simplicity, assume that the Monte Carlo simulation only requires ten interest rate paths to be generated. In practice, 1,000 or more paths would be used but this number is impractical for pedagogical purposes. Fabozzi is concerned with valuing an 8.8% semi-annual coupon, 10 year corporate bond that is currently callable with a call price of $103. The observed price of the corporate bond in the market is, say, $103.30. Observe that in step (2), the generated interest rate paths are for Treasury zeros. As there will be a credit spread between the Treasury curve and the corporate curve for bonds

Table 6.6 Monte Carlo simulation of ten binomial paths for 6 month one period Treasury zeros; initial zero rate of 7% with 10% binomial rate changes[a]

Semi-annual period	Short-term one period zero paths									
	1	2	3	4	5	6	7	8	9	10
1	7.0%	7.0%	7.0%	7.0%	7.0%	7.0%	7.0%	7.0%	7.0%	7.0%
2	7.7	7.7	7.7	6.3	6.3	6.3	7.7	6.3	7.7	7.7
3	8.5	6.9	6.9	6.9	5.7	5.7	8.5	5.7	8.5	8.5
4	7.6	6.2	6.2	7.6	5.1	6.2	9.3	6.2	9.3	9.3
5	6.9	6.9	5.6	8.4	4.6	6.9	8.4	6.9	8.4	8.4
6	7.5	7.5	5.1	9.2	4.1	6.2	7.5	7.5	7.5	7.5
7	8.3	8.3	4.5	10.1	4.5	5.6	6.8	8.3	6.8	6.8
8	9.1	9.1	5.0	11.2	5.0	5.0	6.1	9.1	6.1	6.1
9	10.0	10.0	5.5	12.3	5.5	4.5	5.5	8.2	6.7	6.7
10	9.0	9.0	6.1	13.5	6.1	4.1	5.0	7.4	6.1	7.4
11	9.9	8.1	6.7	12.2	6.7	4.5	4.5	8.1	5.4	6.7
12	8.9	8.9	7.3	10.9	7.3	4.0	4.0	8.9	4.9	6.0
13	8.1	9.8	8.1	9.8	8.1	4.4	3.6	9.8	4.4	5.4
14	8.9	8.9	7.2	8.9	7.2	4.0	3.2	10.8	4.0	4.9
15	9.7	8.0	6.5	8.0	6.5	4.4	2.9	9.7	4.4	5.3
16	8.8	7.2	7.2	8.8	7.2	3.9	3.2	10.7	4.8	4.8
17	7.9	6.5	7.9	9.6	7.9	3.5	3.5	9.6	5.3	4.3
18	7.1	7.1	8.7	10.6	8.7	3.2	3.9	10.6	5.8	4.8
19	7.8	7.8	7.8	11.7	9.6	2.9	4.3	11.7	6.4	5.2
20	8.6	7.0	8.6	10.5	8.6	3.2	4.7	12.8	7.0	4.7

[a] Each interest rate in a given path is the (annualized) 6 month zero coupon interest rate simulated for that path. Each value is calculated by randomly multiplying the interest rate for the previous period by either (1.1 = 1 + 0.1) or (0.9 = 1 − 0.1). Each path provides a different random result for the 6 month interest rate process.

with a given credit rating, this has to be taken into account in the valuation. Though it is possible to incorporate credit spreads into the binomial interest rate process, e.g., Finnerty (1999), the OAS will typically include both the credit risk and callable option values. The forward rate paths given in table 6.6 are determined in an elementary fashion by using a binomial process where up and down moves are equally likely and the size of the move is plus or minus 10% of the previous period yield. Given the initial starting value of 7%, path one proceeds with an up move to 7% (1.1) = 7.7% in period two followed by another up move to (7.7%) (1.1) = 8.47% (which is rounded to 8.5%) and a down move to 8.5% (.9) = 7.65% (rounded down to 7.6%).

The interest rate process used in table 6.6 suffers from a number of limitations. In particular, the process does not recombine, the step increments are relatively arbitrary and the process is not constructed to satisfy absence of arbitrage. In addition, the generating process does not capture the empirical property of mean reversion or allow the credit spread to change with interest rate level. As depicted in step (1), all this is assumed not to matter substantively if the generated paths are able to recreate the

Table 6.7 Calculated Treasury spot rates for the ten paths in table 6.6[a]

Semi-annual period	Paths 1	2	3	4	5	6	7	8	9	10
1	7.00%	7.00%	7.00%	7.00%	7.00%	7.00%	7.00%	7.00%	7.00%	7.00%
2	7.35	7.35	7.35	6.65	6.65	6.65	7.35	6.65	7.35	7.35
3	7.72	7.21	7.21	6.74	6.32	6.32	7.72	6.32	7.72	7.72
4	7.70	6.97	6.97	6.96	6.02	6.30	8.12	6.30	8.12	8.12
5	7.53	6.95	6.69	7.25	5.73	6.41	8.17	6.41	8.17	8.17
6	7.53	7.05	6.42	7.57	5.46	6.37	8.07	6.60	8.07	8.07
7	7.64	7.22	6.15	7.94	5.33	6.26	7.89	6.84	7.89	7.89
8	7.83	7.46	6.01	8.34	5.29	6.10	7.66	7.13	7.66	7.66
9	8.07	7.75	5.95	8.77	5.31	5.92	7.42	7.25	7.56	7.56
10	8.17	7.88	5.96	9.24	5.39	5.73	7.17	7.26	7.41	7.54
11	8.33	7.90	6.02	9.51	5.50	5.62	6.93	7.34	7.23	7.46
12	8.38	7.99	6.13	9.62	5.65	5.48	6.68	7.48	7.03	7.34
13	8.36	8.13	6.28	9.64	5.84	5.40	6.44	7.66	6.83	7.19
14	8.39	8.18	6.35	9.59	5.94	5.30	6.21	7.88	6.63	7.02
15	8.48	8.17	6.36	9.48	5.98	5.24	5.99	8.01	6.47	6.91
16	8.50	8.11	6.41	9.43	6.05	5.15	5.82	8.17	6.37	6.78
17	8.46	8.01	6.50	9.45	6.16	5.06	5.68	8.26	6.31	6.63
18	8.39	7.96	6.62	9.51	6.30	4.95	5.58	8.39	6.28	6.53
19	8.36	7.95	6.68	9.62	6.47	4.84	5.51	8.56	6.28	6.46
20	8.37	7.90	6.78	9.67	6.58	4.76	5.47	8.77	6.32	6.37

[a] Annualized semi-annual zero coupon interest rates calculated from the one period zeros in table 6.6 by assuming the local expectations hypothesis and observing that the hypothesis implies: $z_{t,t+1} = f_{t,t+1}$.

observed Treasury zero curve (even though such simple processes typically will not be able to accomplish such recreation). In the simple example in table 6.6, "calibration" to the observed Treasury zero curve could be accomplished by changing the up/down probabilities by deleting certain paths and adding others. For example, in table 6.6 only four of the ten paths start with a down move. This is followed by five up and five down moves and then another four down/six up. Unequal numbers of up moves relative to down moves result in a generating process with different up/down probabilities. This simplistic calibration procedure captures an element of arbitrage free processes that work by fitting the process by estimating the arbitrage free probabilities.

Under the (local) unbiased expectations hypothesis the one period ahead zero rates in table 6.6 can be treated as implied forward rates. This result permits the associated Treasury spot rate curve along each path to be calculated. Table 6.7 presents the calculated values for the Treasury spot rate curves. For example, along path one the period two value spot rate is determined as:

$$\left(1 + \frac{z_2}{2}\right)^2 = \left(1 + \frac{z_1}{2}\right)\left(1 + \frac{f_{1,2}}{2}\right) = \left(1 + \frac{.07}{2}\right)\left(1 + \frac{.077}{2}\right) = 1.03675 \quad \rightarrow \quad z_2 = 7.35\%$$

Averaging across the ten equally likely paths gives a two period spot rate (z_2) of 7.07%. Similar calculations give a three period spot rate (z_3) of 7.1% (see end of chapter questions). Given these spot rates, the OAS can be determined by adding a fixed static spread to the spot rates along each path to determine a value for the bond along that path, as in step (6). However, this requires the random cash flows along each path to be determined, as in steps (4) and (5).

An important limitation of Monte Carlo methods is the difficulty these methods have in valuing American style options. This happens because the decision rule about when to exercise along a given path is complicated to incorporate into the path-by-path simulation process. Though methods of getting around such difficulties have been available at least since Tilley (1993), the rule for exercising the callable bond proposed in the example of Fabozzi (1989, p. 346) is relatively naive:

> The refinancing opportunity for the corporation will be based not on the short-term forward rate but on a longer-term rate that reflects how much the issuer would have to pay to refund a bond issue. Let's make the simple assumption that the refinancing rate for the corporation is 100 basis points higher than the short-term forward rate . . . Suppose that the following rule is established for calling of the bond. If the refinancing rate is below 5.8% with at least three years remaining to maturity, then the bond will be called.

To arrive at table 6.8a, Fabozzi adds 100 basis points to the values in table 6.6. Each path is then examined to determine if a value below 5.8% is obtained. If so, then the bond is called. This procedure is used to generate the cash flows in table 6.8b. For example, there are no values in paths one and two that are below 5.8%. On path 3, a value of 5.5% is obtained in period 7. Given a call price of $103, plus the 4.4% semi-annual coupon, the payout in period 7 on path 3 is $107.40. As the bond is then retired, all future cash flows on that path are zero.

While useful as a general illustration of the Monte Carlo method, there are some apparent difficulties with this decision rule. For example, the refinancing rate selected is determined by adding 100 basis points to the one period Treasury spot rates. This assumes a constant credit spread at the short end of the yield curve. More importantly, the decision rule assumes that the firm will look at one period interest rates instead of the potential financing rate on any new debt that may be issued to refund the issue that is being called. Even if a refunding is not used, e.g., the issue is redeemed out of cash on hand, the operative refinancing decision would probably not be done by comparing the short-term rate with a target short-term rate. Other problems that arise include the use of a 300 basis point spread over the current coupon to determine redemption instead of comparing the call price with the market price of the bond. By comparing prices, this would permit different call prices to be used, consistent with the market practice of using call prices that decline over time. In addition, a 300 basis point buffer seems to be a relatively large value to use.

The final step in the OAS calculation involves the calculation of a fixed static spread along each path to determine a bond value, as in table 6.9. The bond values along each path are then averaged across all the paths and an average price determined associated with the assumed level of the static spread. This average value is then compared with

Tables 6.8a and 6.8b Refinancing rate paths and callable bond cash flow for each refinancing path[a]

6.8a

Semi-annual period	Refinancing rate paths									
	1	2	3	4	5	6	7	8	9	10
1	8.0%	8.0%	8.0%	8.0%	8.0%	8.0%	8.0%	8.0%	8.0%	8.0%
2	8.7	8.7	8.7	7.3	7.3	7.3	8.7	7.3	8.7	8.7
3	9.5	7.9	7.9	7.9	6.7	6.7	9.5	6.7	9.5	9.5
4	8.6	7.2	7.2	8.6	6.1	7.2	10.3	7.2	10.3	10.3
5	7.9	7.9	6.6	9.4	5.6	7.9	9.4	7.9	9.4	9.4
6	8.5	8.5	6.1	10.2	5.1	7.2	8.5	8.5	8.5	8.5
7	9.3	9.3	5.5	11.1	5.5	6.6	7.8	9.3	7.8	7.8
8	10.1	10.1	6.0	12.2	6.0	6.0	7.1	10.1	7.1	7.1
9	11.0	11.0	6.5	13.3	6.5	5.5	6.5	9.2	7.7	7.7
10	10.0	10.0	7.1	14.5	7.1	5.1	6.0	8.4	7.1	8.4
11	10.9	9.1	7.7	13.2	7.7	5.5	5.5	9.1	6.4	7.7
12	9.9	9.9	8.3	11.9	8.3	5.0	5.0	9.9	5.9	7.0
13	9.1	10.8	9.1	10.8	9.1	5.4	4.6	10.8	5.4	6.4
14	9.9	9.9	8.2	9.9	8.2	5.0	4.2	11.8	5.0	5.9
15	10.7	9.0	7.5	9.0	7.5	5.4	3.9	10.7	5.4	6.3
16	9.8	8.2	8.2	9.8	8.2	4.9	4.2	11.7	5.8	5.8
17	8.9	7.5	8.9	10.6	8.9	4.5	4.5	10.6	6.3	5.3
18	8.1	8.1	9.7	11.6	9.7	4.2	4.9	11.6	6.8	5.8
19	8.8	8.8	8.8	12.7	10.6	3.9	5.3	12.7	7.4	6.2
20	9.6	8.0	9.6	11.5	9.6	4.2	5.7	13.8	8.0	5.7

6.8b

Period	Cash flow paths									
	1	2	3	4	5	6	7	8	9	10
1	4.4	4.4	4.4	4.4	4.4	4.4	4.4	4.4	4.4	4.4
2	4.4	4.4	4.4	4.4	4.4	4.4	4.4	4.4	4.4	4.4
3	4.4	4.4	4.4	4.4	4.4	4.4	4.4	4.4	4.4	4.4
4	4.4	4.4	4.4	4.4	4.4	4.4	4.4	4.4	4.4	4.4
5	4.4	4.4	4.4	4.4	107.4	4.4	4.4	4.4	4.4	4.4
6	4.4	4.4	4.4	4.4	0.0	4.4	4.4	4.4	4.4	4.4
7	4.4	4.4	107.4	4.4	0.0	4.4	4.4	4.4	4.4	4.4
8	4.4	4.4	0.0	4.4	0.0	4.4	4.4	4.4	4.4	4.4
9	4.4	4.4	0.0	4.4	0.0	107.4	4.4	4.4	4.4	4.4
10	4.4	4.4	0.0	4.4	0.0	0.0	4.4	4.4	4.4	4.4
11	4.4	4.4	0.0	4.4	0.0	0.0	107.4	4.4	4.4	4.4
12	4.4	4.4	0.0	4.4	0.0	0.0	0.0	4.4	107.4	4.4
13	4.4	4.4	0.0	4.4	0.0	0.0	0.0	4.4	0.0	4.4
14	4.4	4.4	0.0	4.4	0.0	0.0	0.0	4.4	0.0	4.4
15	4.4	4.4	0.0	4.4	0.0	0.0	0.0	4.4	0.0	4.4
16	4.4	4.4	0.0	4.4	0.0	0.0	0.0	4.4	0.0	4.4
17	4.4	4.4	0.0	4.4	0.0	0.0	0.0	4.4	0.0	4.4
18	4.4	4.4	0.0	4.4	0.0	0.0	0.0	4.4	0.0	4.4
19	4.4	4.4	0.0	4.4	0.0	0.0	0.0	4.4	0.0	4.4
20	104.4	104.4	0.0	104.4	0.0	0.0	0.0	104.4	0.0	104.4

[a] Refinancing rate paths are determined by adding 100 basis points to the one period Treasury zero paths in table 6.6. Cash flow for each refinancing path is for an 8.8% semi-annual coupon 10 year corporate bond callable at 103. The call rule used is that if the refinancing rate falls to 5.8% or less and the bond has at least three years to maturity then the bond is called on the coupon payment date at 103 to produce a payment of 103 + 4.4 = 107.4.

Table 6.9 Present value of each path and average present value using various spreads

Trial OAS	Present value of path										Average PV
	1	2	3	4	5	6	7	8	9	10	
40 bp	100.6	103.5	107.5	93.73	108.5	111.5	107.9	100.4	107.7	112.4	105.4
50 bp	100.0	102.9	107.3	93.14	108.3	111.1	107.4	99.77	107.2	111.6	104.9
60 bp	99.35	102.2	107.0	92.55	108.0	110.7	106.9	99.13	106.7	110.8	104.3
70 bp	98.70	101.5	106.7	91.97	107.8	110.3	106.5	98.49	106.2	110.1	103.8
80 bp	98.06	100.8	106.4	91.40	107.5	109.9	106.0	97.86	105.7	109.3	103.3
90 bp	97.43	100.2	106.1	90.83	107.3	109.5	105.5	97.24	105.3	108.6	102.8
100 bp	96.80	99.58	105.9	90.26	107.1	109.1	105.1	96.62	104.8	107.9	102.3
110 bp	96.18	98.93	105.6	89.70	106.8	108.7	104.6	96.00	104.3	107.1	101.8
120 bp	95.56	98.29	105.3	89.14	106.6	108.3	104.2	95.39	103.8	106.4	101.3

the observed market price of the bond to identify the static spread value that was able to produce the market price. This averaged-across-paths static spread value is the option adjusted spread (OAS). Recalling that the market price was assumed to be $103.30, it follows that the OAS for this bond is 80 basis points. In effect, the OAS is the static spread that, when averaged across the interest rate paths, reproduces the observed market price. As such, the OAS will depend on the volatility assumption that was used to generate the one period spot interest rates. Because a different level of volatility will generate a different OAS, it is conventional to report a range of OAS for different volatility assumptions, which is indicated in step (9). Given this discussion, it is not surprising that considerable effort has been dedicated to identifying the pitfalls in the OAS technique.

The OAS: examples and pitfalls*

Table 6.10 presents a number of different examples of OAS calculations for bonds with different features. In assessing the information in table 6.10, it is important to remember that an OAS calculation is not like a yield to maturity calculation. Different OAS values can be calculated for the same bond, depending on the procedure employed to estimate the OAS. For example, as illustrated by Kupiec and Kah (1999), significantly different OAS estimates are calculated for the same security by MBS dealers on a regular basis, e.g., on a 7.5% MBS participation certificate the spread between the Lehman Bros and Bear Stearns OAS estimates was over 60 basis points with one estimate being almost double the other. Table 6.10 illustrates the impact of changing volatility on OAS values: as the predicted volatility of interest increases, the OAS will fall. This happens because the value of the option is subtracted from the straight bond price to determine the callable bond price or MBS price. Increasing predicted volatility raises the cost of the embedded option reducing the spread above Treasuries. Put differently, increasing predicted volatility will increase the probability the option will be exercised, lowering the "option adjusted spread" above Treasuries.

Table 6.10 Option adjusted spreads for various types of bonds with embedded options[a]

Callable Bonds (9/88)

Issuer	S&P rating	Maturity	Next call date	Next call price	Current price	Coupon (%)	Yield	Treasury yield spread	OAS at volatility of: 10%	15%	20%
ITT Fin.	A	07/01/92	07/01/89	100.00	101.58	10.800	10.27	168	57	30	-4
Marriot	A-	02/01/96	02/01/93	100.00	99.59	9.625	9.70	85	65	50	37
GMAC	AA-	07/15/07	now	104.00	84.19	8.000	9.86	82	71	54	41

Mortgage backed pass through (PT) vs. fixed coupon agency (6/88)

Security	Price	Term to maturity	Average life	Yield	Treasury spread	OAS at volatility of: 10%	15%	20%
FNMA 9% PT	95.3125	28.05	9.80	9.98	115	104	84	64
FNMA 9.35%	101.1875	7.7	7.70	9.13	38	38	38	38

GNMA 9 and collateralized mortgage obligations (5/88)

Class	Par amount	Price[a]	Coupon	Average life	Yield	Treasury spread	OAS at volatility of: 10%	15%	20%
GNMA 9	100	92.656	9.0	11	10.48	123	104	88	71
A	35.1	98.378	8.0	2	9.10	100	67	48	21
B	19.0	95.508	8.5	5	9.85	115	83	59	25
C	18.0	94.748	9.0	7	10.27	125	103	80	52
Z	27.9	80.999	9.0	17	10.87	150	102	79	52

[a] Callable bond values are based on closing prices and Treasury rates on September 20, 1988. The MBS values are based closing prices on June 29, 1988. All prices shown in decimal form. The GNMA 9 is assumed to have a remaining term to maturity of 28 years; the CMO is priced at 100% PSA. This table is adapted from Hayre and Lauterbach (1991).

For the simplifying case of an annual cash coupon bond, the OAS calculation can be expressed compactly as, e.g., Kupiec and Kah (1999), Babbel and Zenios (1992):

$$P_{OB} = \frac{1}{S} \sum_{s=1}^{S} \sum_{t=1}^{T} \frac{CF_t^s}{\prod_{i=1}^{t} (1 + z_{i-1,i}^s + OAS)}$$

where P_{OB} is the market price of the bond with the embedded option, S is the number of possible equally likely future states, T is the term to maturity, OAS is the option adjusted spread, CF_t^s is the cash flow at time t (= 1 to T) in state s (= 1 to S), and $z_{i-1,i}^s$ is the state s one period spot interest rate starting at $i - 1$ and ending at i for discounting cash flows occurring at $t = i$ with $z_{0,1}^s = z_1$ the one period zero rate observed on the pricing date $t = 0$. Under the local expectations hypothesis, the one period zeros will be equal to the one period ahead forward rates. The product operator in the numerator is used for analytical purposes, e.g., because the cash flows at time t in different states will not necessarily be the same; as with the static spread, the OAS is added to each of the one period zeros.[12]

The widespread use of OAS in assessing value for bonds with embedded options has led to a number of contributions aimed at identifying pitfalls in the implementation and interpretation of OAS, e.g., Babbel and Zenios (1992), Kopprasch (1994), Kupiec and Kah (1999). Some of these pitfalls have already been illustrated in detailing the Monte Carlo example of Fabozzi (1989). In particular, it was observed that the OAS calculation for a callable bond depended on the rule that was adopted to model the issuer's call decision. A similar observation applies to other types of bonds with embedded options, e.g., MBS where a prepayment model has to be specified. Kupiec and Kah (1999, p. 91) take an extreme position on this pitfall: "That there is an OAS in mortgage-backed securities at all is a consequence of misspecification of the prepayment function . . . In general it is not possible to modify the prepayment functional form or parameter values to fully compensate for the omission of factors that influence prepayment behavior." Another pitfall occurs with the use of one number, the OAS, to account for more than one option, e.g., default risk and the callability option for a callable corporate bond.

In addition to these concerns, another pitfall is that the OAS depends on the stochastic process selected to model the interest rate. Since the emergence of OAS, considerable effort has been dedicated to addressing this pitfall, such as the development of the self-calibrating processes proposed by Ho-Lee and Black, Derman and Toy. Unfortunately, though such processes do address certain fundamental problems, other problems such as the selection of a volatility assumption still remain. In addition to the size of volatility, the behavior of volatility over time needs to be addressed, e.g., is it appropriate to hold volatility constant over time? Security rankings based on OAS can change depending on assumptions made about the temporal behavior of volatility. This problem is exacerbated by another pitfall: the assumption of a constant OAS across time. As an option approaches its expiration date, the impact on the option value is non-linear. Yet the OAS calculation assumes that the OAS in the last period is the same size as in the first period.

The list of potential pitfalls in OAS modeling and interpretation goes on. Yet, despite the potential pitfalls, OAS is still a commonly used technique that permits practitioners to extend yield spread valuation techniques to bonds with embedded options. Practitioners have to make comparative valuations on a regular basis and OAS does have attractive features for this purpose. The ability to handle the impact of interest rate volatility and other potential sources of randomness on cash flow patterns requires some valuation methodology that can handle these contingencies and OAS is, in many cases, the best alternative available. Though there are pitfalls and limitations in OAS, such problems are not avoided by using other contingent claim valuation methodologies, e.g., Bookstaber (1991). For example, using much simpler valuation techniques, Longstaff (1992) values the embedded option in callable US Treasury securities and find estimates of negative prices for the embedded option. Such results raise more questions about the valuation methodology than the apparent conclusion that a basic property of option valuation (non-negative prices) has been violated.

In the end, OAS is a model dependent calculation. Alterations in the various modeling assumptions can, and likely will, impact the OAS that is estimated. Despite the analytical complexity, the problem of *ex post* estimates being used to make *ex ante* decisions cannot be avoided, e.g., in determining the appropriate level of predicted interest rate volatility to use. As illustrated in the Fabozzi (1989) example, much can be said about the value inherent in the process of arriving at the estimate, rather than the actual estimate that is obtained. The process requires various assumptions to be made about: the decision rules associated with exercising the option; the interest rate process used to generate the one period zeros; the presence of other options; the impact of other random variables; and, the impact of randomness on the future cash flows. Going through this process aids considerably in developing the intuition needed to arrive at a practical assessment of the relative value. The process is more relevant to the security analysis than the actual OAS number that is determined.

6.4 MODELING AND ANALYZING DEFAULT RISK[#]

Early approaches

In addition to developing the notion of duration, Macaulay (1938, pp. 60–2) also provides insight into the modeling of default risk. The discussion begins by observing the failures of a possible method of handling default probabilities:

> The simplest of all probability hypotheses is that the probability of each and every promised future payment is always the same, 9/10, for example. With this assumption, the *price* of the bond would, on any specified date, be 90 per cent of the price on the same date of a bond containing an identical set of promises but rated by the market as "absolutely secure." However, unless the bonds were perpetuities, the *yield* of the lower grade bond would fluctuate less than the yield of the "absolutely secure" bond.

Macaulay recognized that using bond price as a method of assessing credit risk is inadequate because taking the price of a lower grade bond as some percentage of the price of a higher grade bond reduces to assuming that the probabilities of all future payments are equal, a severe assumption that assumes the independence of the payment probabilities.

Macaulay proceeds to develop the implications of using the "much more appealing" approach of comparing yields to measure default risk. Explicitly recognizing that using yields can also lead to "strange conclusions." Macaulay (1938, p. 61) considers the problem of determining the default probabilities:

> The simplest assumption having any appreciable air of reality is that no payment will be met unless all preceding payments have first been met, but that, as soon as one payment has been met, the probability that the next payment will be met is the same as previously had been the probability that the preceding payment would be met. Under this compound assumption, if the probability that the first payment will be met is designated as p, the probability (as of the same date) that the second payment will be met will be p^2, and the probability that the nth payment will be met will be p^n.

Letting P_L be the price of a low grade bond, y the yield on an "absolutely secure" bond and, using Macaulay's notation, p the compounding payment probability, Macaulay proceeds to demonstrate that this leads to the result:

$$P_L = \sum_{t=1}^{T} \frac{p^t C}{(1 + y)^t} = \sum_{t=1}^{T} \frac{C}{\left(\dfrac{1 + y}{p}\right)^t}$$

Hence, in this case yield on the low grade bond (y_L) can be determined as $(1 + y_L) = (1 + y)/p$. This leads to the assessment of the default probability as $p = (1 + y)/(1 + y_L)$.[13]

While recognizing the importance of analyzing default risk in terms of yields and not prices, Macaulay is able to identify a number of problems with this compound probability approach. Being primarily concerned with preparing an indepth empirical analysis of interest rate and bond yield movements, Macaulay was concerned that the compound probability model did not accurately describe the empirical behavior of bond yields, i.e., the model predicts that yields for low grade bonds fluctuate less in percentage terms than high grade yields which is contrary to what Macaulay observed empirically. To see this let $y = 2\%$ and $p = .99$, it follows that $y_L = 3.03\%$. If the absolutely secure yield doubles to 4% then the low grade yield will increase to 5.05%. Macaulay observes that, even though it is possible to specify probabilities that would produce a larger percentage change in the low grade yield, "any such hypothesis would necessarily be a mere mathematical curiosity" (p. 62).

Macaulay demonstrates a subtle understanding of the empirical relationship between low grade and high grade bonds:

> startling as it may sound, we do not *know* that lower grade bonds actually do fluctuate in yield appreciably more than do higher grade bonds. Indeed, there are strong reasons for suspecting that the excessive fluctuations in the yields of so-called lower grade bonds is primarily an indication of fluctuation in the *grades* assigned by the market to such bonds

rather than an indication that violent fluctuations in yield normally accompany low, *but unchanging*, market grading.

Even though Macaulay was writing at a time when ratings agencies were considerably less sophisticated and information about bonds was substantially less, Macaulay (p. 65) makes a telling observation about bond grades: "The average and the whole distribution of grades undoubtedly drift in great secular swings, immense waves, and even up and down with the movements of the business cycle." Changes in the yield spreads between different bond grades reflect these swings, waves and cycles.

Macaulay identifies numerous factors that influence the yield on bonds: security, duration, taxation, marketability, embedded options such as convertibility and callability, legal restrictions (e.g., eligible for "trustee" investment), and currency of denomination. Macaulay also makes the following interesting observation:

> If the earnings of a corporation cover the interest charges on a bond thirty times, the market takes little or no notice of a change in conditions such that the charges are covered only twenty times. On the other hand, a change from one and a half times to once only will probably be considered extremely serious. The yield may rise violently. The lower the grade of a bond the more it tends to act like a common stock. It comes to be significantly affected not only by interest rate factors but also by potential earnings.

Yet, despite insightful comments, Macaulay (1938) is ultimately a study about the economics of the empirical behavior of bond yields and not about the methods to be used in picking individual bonds. It is a study about averages and tendencies.

In contrast, Graham, Dodd and Cottle (1962) (GDC) is directly concerned with picking individual bonds. Where Macaulay is concerned with average yields between bond grades, GDC is concerned with the determinants of specific bond yields. The focus is on the properties of the individual security and not the average. GDC (p. 310) structures the security analysis for corporate bonds around "Four Principles for the Selection of Issues of the Fixed-income Type":

> I. Safety is measured not by specific lien or other contractual rights but by the ability of the issuer to meet all its obligations.
> II. This ability should be measured under conditions of recession and depression rather than of prosperity.
> III. Deficient safety cannot be compensated for by an abnormally high coupon rate alone.
> IV. The selection of all senior securities for investment should be subject to rules of exclusion and to specific quantitative tests.

GDC make it explicit that analysis of a corporate bond needs to focus on the characteristics and strengths of the business issuing the debt and not on the property that is securing the issue. The basic intuition of this approach is illustrated in section 4.4 where empirical evidence was presented that the recovery rate on secured debt is significantly less than 100%.

Based on this general framework GDC make a number of recommendations about corporate bond selection. For example (p. 313): "The theoretically correct procedure for bond investment, therefore, is first to select a company meeting every test of strength and soundness, and then to purchase its highest-yielding obligation, which would usually mean its junior rather than its first-lien bonds." This recommendation is tempered with the observation that the junior issue must provide a sufficiently higher yield, which is usually the case. In general, selecting first-mortgage issues reflects a lack of confidence in the analysis of the business which begs the question: is it advisable to buy any bonds of a company that requires a first-lien to protect against adverse consequences associated with the business? GDC quotes Walter Bagehot with admiration: "If there is any difficulty or doubt the security should be declined." Unlike equity selection where the costs of rejecting a specific security can be considerable, bond selection is primarily a "*negative art*" where the avoidance of capital loss is of central concern.

Perhaps the most telling statement in GDC (p. 320) about bond selection is the following:

> In the traditional theory of bond investment a mathematical relationship is supposed to exist between the interest rate and the degree of risk incurred. The interest return is divided into two components, the first constituting "pure interest" – i.e., the rate obtainable with *no* risk of loss – and the second representing the premium obtained to compensate for the risk assumed. If, for example, the "pure interest rate" is assumed to be 3 percent, then a 4 percent investment is supposed to involve one chance in a hundred of losing the entire principal in one year.

GDC strongly question this view of bond interest rates. In contrast to the numerous theories that have been discussed in part II, GDC (p. 320) maintain there is no mathematically identifiable relationship between yield and risk:

> This view . . . seems to us to bear little relation to the realities of bond investment. Relative bond yields usually do reflect the rating of the market as to the relative degrees of risk involved in the investments, but these yields have not been computed by means of mathematical equations involving chance of loss on the one hand and required income on the other.

The actuarial computation of investment risks is "not a practicable undertaking." Despite the substantial amount of information about the history of bond performance, the nature of the "risks" contains enough "uncertainty" that mathematical formulations are impractical.

The continuous time framework*

The scepticism of Macaulay and, particularly, GDC, about the modeling of default risk stands in stark contrast to the approach of modern Finance to this subject. The techniques of contingent claims pricing have overtaken the subject. The initial connection between default risk and option pricing theory can be found in Merton (1974). Since this time, the continuous time approach to modeling default risk has been developed and extended in a number of ways, e.g., Jones et al. (1984), Ritchken (1987, ch. 14),

Kim et al. (1993) and Culp (2001). Though simplified, the Merton (1974) approach provides a foundation that requires description. The basic idea follows by extending the conventional embedded option relationship to the case where the default decision is viewed as an option for the firm to "put" the assets of the firm back to the bondholders. In other words: market value of a risky loan = market value of a default and option free loan – put value associated with default.

In this formulation the exercise price on the put option is the promised value of the outstanding fixed income securities. More precisely, assume that the firm has a relatively simple capital structure composed of common stock and continuously compounded zero coupon bonds maturing to a par value of M at time T. Assuming perfect capital markets the conventional market valuation equation for the firm applies: $V(t) = S(t) + B(t)$, where S is the market value of equity (number of shares times price per share), B is the market value of the debt and V is the market value of the firm. Observing that the zero coupon bonds permit the risk of default to be shifted to T, then at $t = T$ the holders of debt will receive: $\min[M, V(T)] = M - \max[0, M - V(T)] = B(T)$, where min (max) refers to the functions that select the minimum (maximum) of the values within the brackets. Observe that the value of a put option on the firm with an exercise price equal to M is $PM(T) = \max[0, M - V(T)]$. Discounting the value back to time t at the riskless rate r and taking (risk neutral) expectations gives: $B(t) = M \exp[-rt^*] - PM(t)$. Hence, the market value of the corporate debt equals the difference between the price of a riskless default free bond and a short position in the put option.

It is possible to approach this specification from another direction. More precisely, it is also possible to have: $\min[M, V(T)] = V(T) - \max[0, V(T) - M] = B(T)$. Again, discounting back at the riskless rate and taking expectations gives: $B(t) = V(t) - C_V(t)$ where C_V is the value of call option on the firm with exercise price equal to M. The interpretation of this relationship is that in issuing debt the common stockholders have, effectively, sold the firm to the bondholders in exchange for a call option that permits the stockholders to repurchase the firm at maturity in exchange for payment of the face value of the debt, i.e., $V(t) - B(t) = C_V(t) = S(t)$. In the absence of any coupon payments, all the default risk occurs at maturity of the debt and the option can be modeled as a European option. Assuming that the market value of the firm follows a geometric Brownian motion with volatility parameter σ_V, a Black Scholes equation for the call can be derived as:

$$C_V(t) = V(t)N[d_1] - e^{-rt^*}MN[d_2]$$

where:

$$d_1 = \frac{\ln\left[\dfrac{V(t)}{M}\right] + (r + .5\sigma_V^2)t^*}{\sigma_V t^*} \qquad d_2 = d_1 - \sigma_V t^*$$

It is difficult not to see this interpretation of the market value of the firm's equity as a remarkable insight.

Developing the alternative put option approach involves viewing the shareholders as having purchased the market value of the firm, plus a put option, offsetting the associated costs by borrowing funds with time T maturity value of M, i.e., $B(t) = V(t) - S(t) = M \exp[-rt^*] - PM(t)$ or $S(t) = V(t) + PM(t) - M \exp[-rt^*]$. Observing that this is a put on the market value of the firm, using the same assumptions as for the call the value of the put can be specified:

$$PM(t) = e^{-rt^*}MN[-d_2] - V(t)N[-d_1]$$

This can now be used for a value of $B(t)$ as:

$$B(t) = Me^{-rt^*} - PM(t) = Me^{-rt^*}\left[1 - N[-d_2] + \frac{V(t)N[d_1]}{Me^{-rt^*}}\right] \equiv Me^{-rt^*}K$$

This result is sufficient to derive the perfect markets, continuous time representation of the default risk spread.

To derive the default risk spread, let the risky interest rate be R and observe that the market value of corporate debt at t is $B(t) = M \exp[-Rt^*]$. It follows that:

$$Me^{-Rt^*} = Me^{-rt^*}K \quad \rightarrow \quad -Rt^* = -rt^* + \ln[K] \quad \rightarrow \quad R - r = \frac{\ln[K]}{t^*}$$

This provides a direct relationship between the credit (default risk) spread and K. Closer inspection of K reveals a number of important variables including the leverage ratio, the volatility of the market value of the firm and the term to maturity of the debt. While the presence of these variables is hardly surprising, what the Merton (1974) approach provides is a precise specification of how these particular variables interact. Following Culp (2001, p. 388), empirical implementation of this model is complicated by the difficulty of obtaining two important inputs, σ_V and the debt to equity ratio: "the volatility of equity tends to be a very noisy proxy for asset volatility and can be extremely sensitive to asset price changes . . . the capital structure of a firm is rarely as simple as equity plus zero-coupon debt with a single maturity date."[14]

Recent developments in valuing defaultable bonds*

Since Merton (1974), considerable effort has been given to the extension and application of contingent claims pricing models to the valuation of defaultable fixed income securities. Empirical evidence on the basic Merton model has demonstrated an inability to explain the large size of observed credit spreads, e.g., Kim et al. (1993). Explanations for the failure of the basic model focus on: the assumption that all default risk occurs at maturity; limitations of the assumed absolute priority rule; and, the assumption of constant riskless interest rates. Following Cathcart and El-Jahel (1998), relaxation of each of these assumptions has proceeded by extending the "structural" continuous time default model of Merton.[15] Extensions to the structural model have incorporated default prior to maturity by introducing first passage time to a boundary that may be either random or deterministic. Randomness in the short term riskless interest rate is incorporated into the structural model in a fashion that is all too familiar, for example, from the discussion in section 5.2. In addition, some contributions to the structural model also allow for exogenous violations of the absolute priority rule.

Longstaff and Schwartz (1995) is a useful example of the structural model extensions where the firm defaults on debt obligations when the value of assets falls below an exogenously determined threshold. Stochastic interest rates are modeled using a mean-reverting OU process. Deviations from the absolute priority rule are permitted by exogenously setting the payment to bondholders when default occurs. Cathcart and El-Jahel (1998) address some limitations in Longstaff and Schwartz by using a mean reverting square root process for the riskless short term interest rate and introducing a "signaling process" that determines default. As discussed in section 5.1, the square root process avoids the possibility of negative interest rates. The use of a signaling process avoids the need to use the value of assets to specify the occurrence of default. The signal is treated as a random variable following a diffusion. Default occurs when the signal variable hits a lower threshold. At this point, the debt is "reorganized" and the bondholder receives $(1 - \delta)$ in new default free discount bonds. The value of δ $(0 \leq \delta \leq 1)$ is exogenous with $\delta = 1$ representing a complete loss of bond value. The assumed process for the signal follows a geometric Brownian motion. No rationalization is given for the choice of this particular process and, though stylistically different, the conceptual gains compared to using the value of assets, as in Longstaff and Schwartz, does not appear substantive.

The linchpin of continuous time valuation models is the "fundamental partial differential equation" (PDE). For example, in section 5.3 a fundamental partial differential equation was derived for all interest rate dependent securities. Given the usefulness of closed form solutions, the trick is to structure the specifics of the valuation problem in such a way that the PDE can be solved in closed form. When there are two stochastic processes that have to be addressed, as in Cathcart and El-Jahel with the interest rate and signal processes, the PDE is more complicated. In order to reduce the complexity, it is analytically convenient to assume that the two random variables are not correlated. By making this assumption, Cathcart and El-Jahel can specify the PDE for the defaultable bond value (price) function $H[x, r, t^*]$ as:

$$rH = H_r\kappa(\mu - r) + H_x\alpha x + .5[H_{rr}r\sigma_r^2 + H_{xx}x^2\sigma_x^2] - H_t$$

where x is the random signal that follows a lognormal diffusion, r is the random riskless interest rate that follows a mean reverting square root process and $t^* = T - t$ (measured in years) is the time to maturity of the defaultable bond.

By making reference to the discussion of Ito's lemma in section 5.2, the definitions of the diffusions, and the associated parameters, are apparent from this specification of the PDE. The assumption that the short term riskless interest rate and the signal are not correlated allows the cross partial derivatives terms to be set to zero. Given this PDE, for the problem to be "well posed" appropriate initial and boundary conditions also have to be specified. Cathcart and El-Jahel provide five conditions: $H[x, r, 0] = 1$, if the bond reaches maturity then a par value of $1 is paid; $H[\infty, r, t^*] = P[r, t^*]$, as the signal goes to infinity, the price of the defaultable bond goes to the value of the riskless bond, $P[r, t^*] = P(t, T)$ (the notation used in chapter 5); $H[x = x_L, r, t^*] = (1 - \delta)P[r, t^*]$ when the signal reaches the lower threshold default value (x_L) then the "reorganization" of the debt will occur; and, two technical conditions associated with r, $0 < H[x, 0, t^*] < \infty$ and $H[x, \infty, t^*] = 0$. Because the riskless interest rate follows a square root process, closed form solutions for $P[r, t^*]$ are available (see end of chapter 5 questions).

With this mathematical setup, Cathcart and El-Jahel are able to solve for the price function for the defaultable bond as:

$$H[x, r, t^*] = P[r, t^*] - \delta P[r, t^*]\Lambda[x, t^*] = P[r, t^*](1 - \delta\Lambda[x, t^*])$$

where $\Lambda[x, t^*]$ is the inverse Laplace transform defined as:

$$\Lambda[x, t^*] = \frac{1}{2\pi i} \int_{c-100}^{c+100} \frac{e^{qt^*}}{q} \left(\frac{x}{x_L}\right)^{\lambda[q]} dq$$

with:

$$\lambda[q] = \frac{-\alpha + .5\sigma_x^2 - \sqrt{(\alpha - .5\sigma_x^2)^2 + 2\sigma_x^2 q}}{\sigma_x^2}$$

In this specification, q is the Laplace parameter and, heuristically, c is chosen so that the inverse Laplace transform integration makes sense. Leaving aside the obvious questions about how to actually do this calculation, observe that the credit spread in this model ($R - r$ in the Merton model) can be solved as: $-\ln[1 - \delta\Lambda[x, t^*]]/t^*$.

To the uninitiated, all this analytical structure might seem somewhat contrived. As discussed in sections 1.3 and 2.4, the propensity for practitioners of modern Finance to generate more heat than light is difficult to ignore. What relevance are the "structural models" of default risk to security analysts trying to determine the value of a defaultable bond? The simple answer lies in the functional form used to specify the default probability. The security analyst is interested in finding differences between the assessment of default (and the recovery rate) as reflected in the market price of a defaultable bond and the "true" *ex ante* assessment whether there will be a default and, if so, what the payout to bondholders will be. In the Cathcart and El-Jahel framework the probability of default is $\Lambda[x, t^*]$ and the recovery rate $(1 - \delta)$ is set exogenously. The function $\Lambda[x, t^*]$ can be associated with the probability of the first passage time from a given signal value x to the lower threshold x_L. As indicated, this function depends on the drift and volatility parameters of the assumed signal diffusion process. Though *ex post* estimates of the parameters could be obtained, and some rationalization given for x_L, the comments concerning the value of "process" made about the OAS procedure also seem to apply concerning models of default assessment.

Questions ?

1 (CFA Level II) The table below shows prices as a function of yields for four tranches of a collateralized mortgage obligation (CMO). Using the prices and yields in the Table, determine the effective duration of tranche T2. Assume that the relevant current interest rate is 6%. Identify the tranche with negative convexity. Justify your choice.

Table: price vs. yield for four CMO tranches

Yield	T-1	T-2	T-3	T-4
5.0	113	109	103.5	107
5.5	106	104	101.5	104
6.0	100	100	100	100
6.5	95	97	99.5	95
7.0	91	95	99.25	89

2 (CFA Level II) The table below shows the CMO option adjusted spreads declining as price volatility increases. Explain this pattern of option adjusted spreads.

Table: CMO option adjusted spreads for different pricing volatilities

Pricing Volatility	8%	12%	16%
Option Adjusted Spread (bp)	93	74	51

3 "For a callable bond, it is inappropriate to use modified duration (and convexity) because the expected cash flow changes as the yield changes . . . A change in interest rates will affect the price volatility of the noncallable bond component depending on the duration of the noncallable bond. It will also affect the price of the embedded call option."

Explain how the option adjusted duration measure is derived and how this measure can be used in the analysis of callable bonds and mortgage backed securities.

4 An important drawback of "traditional yield spread analysis" is the "failure to take into account future interest rate volatility that would affect the expected cash flow" of a fixed income security. What is option adjusted

spread analysis and how does this technique correct for this limitation of traditional yield spread analysis in the analysis of bonds with embedded option features. What are some important pitfalls of option adjusted spread analysis?

5(a) In the Fabozzi example of section 5.3, finish calculating the empirical spot rate curve, for the remaining 17 cash flow dates, by averaging the spot rates across the paths. Compare these values to the Treasury spot rate curve given in Fabozzi (1989, pp. 342–3). What adjustments could be made to the process to make these two curves approximately equal?

(b) Reconstruct the ten paths given in table 6.6 using an interest rate process that is mean-reverting. Repeat the exercise using the Black, Derman and Toy model and calibrate the model to the empirical spot rate curve in (a). (Hint: see Sundaresan 2002, pp. 605–8 and 612–16).

6(a) Using the Merton credit spread model of section 6.4, consider a firm with a market value of $V = 30$ and a zero coupon debt that matures in one year with a par value $M = 20$ and a term to maturity of $T = 1$. If the riskless interest rate $r = 10\%$ and the volatility of the market value $\sigma_V = .3$. Show that the market value of the bond is 17.96. Similarly, solve for the credit spread to show that $R - r = .7\%$ (70 basis points). (Hint: see Ritchken 1987, pp. 334–6.)

(b) Extend the Merton default risk model to the case where the firm issues both senior debt $B1$, with par value $M1$, and subordinated debt $B2$ with par value $M2$. In this case, $S(T) = \text{Max}[0, V(T) - (M1 + M2)]$, $B1(T) = \text{Min}[V(T), M1]$ and $B2(T) = \text{Max}[\text{Min}[V(T) - M1, M2], 0]$.

7(a) Given the duration for a putable bond derived in section 6.2, derive the formula for the convexity of a putable bond. What will happen to the value of convexity as interest rates change? Is it possible for a putable bond to have negative convexity?

(b) Given the duration of a convertible bond provided by Sarkar (1999) examined in section 6.2, derive a formula for the convexity of the convertible. What are the implications of introducing subordinated debt into the firm's capital structure? (Hint: see Sarkar, pp. 189–93.)

NOTES

1 What is a closed form? Though this terminology appears in numerous articles in modern Finance, a precise definition is difficult to identify. The basic intuition is that a closed form is an "exact formula." For example, numerical methods are used to solve option pricing problems when closed forms (exact formulas) are not available. Given this, when is a formula an exact formula? The Black-Scholes option pricing formula is clearly an exact formula as are the discounted cash flow formulas for pricing fixed income securities such as default free fixed

term annuities, perpetuities and option and default free bonds. However, as valuation formulas become more complicated terms may appear in formulas that, for example, are sums that are used to approximate an unknown function, e.g., Buttler and Waldvogel (1996, p. 62). For example, a truncated Taylor series could be used as an approximation to some unknown function. This sum is then truncated at some arbitrary point creating an "exact formula." Such formulas are little more than disguised numerical methods dressed up as formulas. In some sense, almost all numerical methods can be reduced to "exact formulas" describing the solution procedure. To avoid the associated semantic confusions, a closed form is defined here as an "exact formula" in the sense that a numerical method is not required to implement the formula. Heuristically, the formula can be solved by "plugging in" values. One important advantage of a closed form is that is can be differentiated to obtain closed form solutions for the Greeks.

2 The relevant legal citation is *Morgan Stanley Co.* vs. *Archer Daniels Midland Co.*, 570 F. Supp. 1529, 1532–33, (S.D.N.Y 1983). Blanc and Gordon (1999) examine the relevant legal issues of this case and other situations where firms seek to undertake surprise calls of issues that are either non-callable or have restrictive call provisions.

3 More detail on MBS can be found in Fabozzi (2001, chs 24–8).

4 Both before and after the introduction of the system for issuing mortgage backed securities, the supply of long term fixed rate mortgage funds in the US was facilitated by the savings and loan network of financial institutions. This network was given a variety of favorable institutional and legal preferences, e.g., Regulation Q restricting the payment of interest on demand deposits, that provided a supply of relatively low cost savings deposit funds that, in turn, were used to fund mortgages. The collapse of these preferences during the 1970s led, ultimately, to the end of this method of funding mortgages.

5 Technically, GNMA does not formally issue pass-throughs. Rather, GNMA adds a guarantee to privately-issued pass-throughs that are backed by FHA and VA mortgages. FNMA and FHLMC both issue and guarantee pass-throughs.

6 In addition to CMOs, pass-throughs are also used to collateralize stripped MBS. These securities unbundle the pass-through cash flow into interest only (IO) and principal only (PO) classes. The first stripped MBS were introduced in 1986. Some presentations, e.g., Carron (1992), treat stripped MBS as a type of CMO.

7 Even though "vega" is not a Greek letter, this is the name given to this "Greek."

8 For those unfamiliar with futures contracts on Eurodollars, Treasury bills and the like, the method of quoting futures prices is $EU(t) = 100 - eu(t)$, where $eu(t)$ is expressed in % terms. For example, $EU(t) = 96.45$ means that the add-on interest rate for the three month Eurodollar deposit to be delivered at maturity of the futures contract will be 3.55%. This method of quoting is consistent with the market practice of quoting money market securities in terms of yields while retaining the futures market convention that long (short) positions make money when "prices" rise (fall). The method of quoting futures contracts for longer term debt securities, e.g., Treasury notes and bonds, differs from the money market securities by using the "price" of a theoretical deliverable.

9 The reference to callable option is not meant to imply that the option is callable. Rather, the reference is a short form for the expression "the embedded option that permits the issuer to call the bond issue prior to the stated maturity date." This terminology is used in preference to referring to the embedded option as a call option which confuses the terminology with exchange traded and other call options that are buyer's options.

10 Unlike the callable bond, the reference to a putable option is meant to imply that the option is to put the bond back to the issuer, i.e., the option is a buyer's option. More precisely, the reference to putable is a short form for the expression "the embedded option that permits the bondholder to put the bond issue back to the issuer at a stated put price on the stated put date(s)."

11 Later editions of Fabozzi (1989) replaced the Monte Carlo example with a binomial solution to valuing the embedded option in a callable bond based on Kalotay et al. (1993). Recognizing the advantages of Monte Carlo methods for dealing with path dependent options and options subject to a number of random variables, Fabozzi (2000) retains the OAS method to value MBS.

12 As stated, the compact formula for the OAS differs slightly from the Monte Carlo calculation described in Fabozzi (1989). This is due to the OAS being added to the one period zero rate in the compact formula and to the z_t spot rate in the Fabozzi presentation. Even though the product of t (one plus the) one period ahead zeros will equal the product of (one plus the) z_t spot rate (raised to the t), it does not follow that adding the OAS to each of the one period zeros will give the same result as adding the OAS to the z_t spot rate. However, the difference will be typically small enough to ignore for all but the most precise calculations.

13 Based on the relationship between the yields of low grade and high grade bonds, Macaulay is able to conclude that, for the same term to maturity, the low grade bond will have a shorter duration than for a high grade bond.

14 Despite the potential complications, there are a number of commercial applications of credit risk measurement that have been inspired by the Merton credit risk model. The most well known of these applications is the KMV Corporation Credit Monitor® model. This model calculates the expected default frequency (EDF) for companies with publicly traded common stock, e.g., Culp (2001, pp. 388–9), Sundaresan (2002, pp. 645–6). The EDF calculation is used to predict future changes in a firm's credit rating. The EDF measure is an extension of the Merton approach that uses actual default probabilities to substitute for the cumulative normal distribution function value $(K - 1)$ which is the default probability in the Merton model.

15 In conjunction with the extension of the structural models, there has also been the development of "reduced form" models, e.g., Jarrow and Turnbull (1995). According to Cathcart and El-Jahel (1998, p. 66): "The reduced-form models are models in which default time is a stopping time of some given hazard function." A simpler description would be to describe these models as extensions of the self-calibrating binomial models where the objective is to estimate the martingale default probabilities. This definition would include, say, Finnerty (1999) in the reduced form category.

part 3

Equity Valuation and Investment Strategy

All I lost was two hundred and forty thousand dollars ... I would have lost more but that was all the money I had.

Groucho Marx joking about the losses he actually suffered during the stock market collapse of 1929 (Klein 2001, p. 231)

The basic ingredient in outstanding common stock management is the ability neither to accept blindly whatever may be the dominant opinion in the financial community at the moment nor to reject the prevailing view just to be contrary for the sake of being contrary. Rather, it is to have more knowledge and to apply better judgment, in thorough evaluation of specific situations and the moral courage to act "in opposition to the crowd" when your judgment tells you you are right.

Philip Fisher, Developing an Investment Philosophy (1980, p. 44)

I have little confidence even in the ability of analysts, let alone untrained investors, to select common stocks that will give better than average results. Consequently, I feel that the standard portfolio should be to duplicate, more or less, the DJIA.

Benjamin Graham, Memoirs of the Dean of Wall Street (1996)

Academics ... like to define investment "risk" differently, averring that it is the relative volatility of a stock or portfolio of stocks – that is, their volatility as compared to a large universe of stocks. Employing data bases and statistical skills, these academics compute with precision the "beta" of a stock – its relative volatility in the past – and then build arcane investment and capital-allocation theories around this calculation. In their hunger for a single statistic to measure risk, however, they forget a fundamental principle: It is better to be approximately right than precisely wrong.

Warren Buffett (1993), as quoted in Cunningham (2002, p. 82)

Chapter
Summary

Chapter 7 *Fundamental Analysis and Value Investing*

7.1 Characteristics of Equity Securities
The classification of securities
Preferred stock vs. corporate debt
Common stock and firm value

7.2 The Basics of Fundamental Analysis
Fundamental analysis and investment philosophy
Macroeconomics and common stock valuation
Philip Fisher on industry and company analysis

7.3 What is Value Investing?
Warren Buffett on value investing
Techniques of value investing
Value investing for special situations

7.4 Observations from the Classics
Graham, Dodd and Cottle (1962)
Philip Fisher and the growth stock
The Warren Buffett synthesis

Questions
Notes

chapter 7 — Fundamental Analysis and Value Investing

7.1 CHARACTERISTICS OF EQUITY SECURITIES

The classification of securities

Section 1.1 discussed basic characteristics of equity securities. Elements such as priority of claim, limited liability and the corporate charter were identified. The discussion in section 1.1 followed the conventional analytical classification of securities into bonds and stocks. The structure of this book also follows the convention by discussing fixed income securities in part II and equity securities in part III. This classification scheme conforms to the legal distinction between the equity holders as owners of the firm and the debt holders as creditors with a contractually defined claim against the firm, typically for interest and principal payments. The higher priority of claim suggests that debt securities possess a "higher degree of safety" while equity claims have a "lower degree of safety" that, presumably, is compensated by a greater potential for gain. While useful, this method of classifying corporate securities has limitations that, in some cases, can lead to confusions and misrepresentations. For example, Graham and Dodd (1934) recognized these problems and suggested an alternative classification scheme for securities that was more in keeping with the theme of investment versus speculation in security selection decisions.

The modern investment landscape has become considerably more complicated than in the days of Graham and Dodd (1934). The division of equity securities into common stocks and preferred stocks has been blurred by the presence of hybrid preferred issues such as mandatory convertible preferred shares, e.g., Battacharya (2001, p. 1138), that are closer to common stocks than the traditional non-convertible fixed coupon preferred stock. Yet, there is still considerable substance in *the "new classification scheme"* for securities recommended by Graham and Dodd (1934) and carried forward into Graham, Dodd and Cottle (1962, p. 101):

Class	Representative issue
I. Securities of the fixed-income and stable-value type.	A high grade bond or preferred stock
II. Senior securities of the fluctuating value type	
A. Well-protected issues with profit possibilities	A high-grade convertible issue
B. Inadequately protected issues	A lower-grade bond or preferred stock
III. Common-stock type	A common stock

Using more conventional terminology, these three classes can be described as: "I. Investment grade bonds and preferred stocks; II. Speculative grade bonds and preferred stocks, A. Convertibles, etc., B. Low-grade senior notes; III. Common stocks."

The basic idea behind the proposed classification scheme is to emphasize the investment characteristics of a security, as opposed to the "type" of security, i.e., bond vs. preferred vs. common. In particular, securities in class I "are bought in the reasonable expectation that the income therefrom will continue unchanged and that their market quotation will not deviate greatly from the purchase price" (GDC, p. 102). Securities in class I provide *safety of principal and a steady income.* Securities in class II are subject to significant possibilities about the safety of principal. The division of class II into A and B groups is to recognize the possibility of different factors contributing to price changes. In class A, the price change arises from the security combining a "straight investment" with a conversion right or some other privilege that carries the possibility of profit or loss. In class B, the possibility of profit or loss is inherent in the "straight security" and not in the attached provision. Securities in class B differ from common stock in two ways: the securities have an "effective priority" over some junior issue, which gives some degree of protection; the possibility for profit is limited in time and amount, in contrast to common stock where the possibility of gain is "theoretically or optimistically" unlimited.

As for the specific types of security in each class, "all *straight* bonds and preferred stocks of high quality selling at a normal price" belong in class I, together with "sound convertible issues" where the conversion option is well out of the money. Just because a bond is rated investment grade does not qualify the security as belonging in class I. If the bond sells at "any unduly low price" then the possibility of capital gain puts the bond in class II. Precisely where the dividing line between classes I, II and III is drawn is difficult to specify. The essence of the classification scheme is to shift the focus onto the price and cash flow characteristics of the security as opposed to more traditional features such as priority of claim. "Any issue which displays the main characteristics of a common stock belongs in Group III, whether it is entitled 'common stock,' 'preferred stock' or even 'bond'." This would apply, for example, to a convertible bond where the conversion right was deep in the money. Another example is a senior bond selling at a price so low that the junior bonds have no value. Such a bond "lacks the prime requisite of a senior security, viz., that it should be followed by a junior investment of substantial value."

Preferred stock vs. corporate debt

The origins of preferred shares can be traced to the triple contract used in medieval and Renaissance finance (Poitras 2000, ch. 2). Preferred share arrangements appear in the capital structure of early English joint stock companies and were an important financing feature of the US industrial trusts in the late nineteenth century. Initially, the basic notion of a preferred share related to the prior claim to dividend payments. Over time, other features have been added, such as the prior claim against assets in the event of a liquidation. In addition to *preference over common stock to dividend payments and assets in liquidation*, features that apply to all preferred issues, there are a range of other features that may or may not be part of the preferred structure. For example, most preferred shares are "cumulative," i.e., if preferred dividends are not paid then the unpaid amount "cumulates" and all cumulative unpaid preferred dividends have to be settled before any dividend payments can be made to common shareholders. Though preferred shares do not usually have the unrestricted voting rights associated with common stock, contingent voting rights provisions are often included that permit preferred stock to have voting rights when there are unpaid preferred dividends outstanding.[1]

As an equity claim, failure to make a dividend payment on preferred shares is not sufficient to initiate a bankruptcy proceeding (in contrast to the case of debt issues). The prospectus published at the time the preferred share is issued is the best source for finding information about the terms and conditions for a specific issue. The prospectus will specify the various protections afforded the preferred shareholder, such as the cumulative dividend provision and contingent voting rights. Other forms of protection may include restrictions on the ability to make additional issues of more senior securities. Another typical protective feature is a redemption or sinking fund provision that permits the corporation to retire outstanding preferred shares. Preferred share issues may also be convertible, though preferred shares with this provision appear less frequently than straight (non-convertible) preferred shares.[2] Convertible preferred stock is often issued to facilitate a merger or takeover. As illustrated in table 7.1, convertible preferred stock is more expensive to issue and there is considerable cross industry variation in convertible and straight preferred issues. As with debt issues, preferred shares are rated by the major ratings services, Moody's, S&P and Fitch, using the same ratings scheme as for bonds. The ratings agencies are another potential source of information about the terms of a specific preferred share issue.

Three basic types of *preferred share dividend payment provisions* are observed in modern financial markets: fixed-rate (fixed-dividend); adjustable rate; and auction/remarketed rate.[3] The fixed rate preferred is the traditional type of dividend payment provision. For this type of preferred, the dividend payment is based on a predetermined rate (percentage) of the par value. This may be expressed as a dollar value per share. For example, if the par value is $50 a 10% dividend preferred would have a $5.00 annual dividend payment. As with common stock dividends, the dividend payment is usually paid quarterly so the 10% dividend preferred ($50 par value) would make a regular payment of $1.25 each quarter. Even though preferred shares have redemption provisions and other features that can impact the yield calculation, e.g., conversion provisions, it is

Table 7.1 Cost of preferred stock of financial, utility and other companies, 1980–99

	Number of issues	Gross spread (%)	Other expenses (%)	Total cost (%)
Financial companies				
Straight preferred stock	1485	2.343	0.406	2.750
Convertible preferred stock	218	4.151	1.387	5.537
Utility companies				
Straight preferred stock	610	2.159	0.415	2.543
Convertible preferred stock	22	3.359	0.427	3.786
Other companies				
Straight preferred stock	265	2.970	0.643	3.613
Convertible preferred stock	442	5.123	2.734	7.857

Financial companies defined as those with SIC codes beginning with 6; Utility companies defined as those SIC codes beginning with 49; Gross spread (%) is the gross spread as a percentage of total proceeds, including management fee, selling concession, and reallowance fee.
Source: Adapted from Bajaj et al. (2002) and Securities Data Co.

conventional to quote the "dividend yield" (*Div/P*) for preferred stocks and use this as a method of assessing value much as in traditional yield spread analysis (see section 6.3). Given that this measure of the dividend yield is a current yield calculation (see section 4.1), this procedure is theoretically precise only if the preferred is a perpetuity.

Prior to 1982, all preferred shares traded in US stock markets were of the fixed-rate type. Following a practice that had started a few years earlier in the private placement market, starting in 1982 adjustable rate preferred stock issues began to appear to be followed, two years later, by auction rate preferred issues and, the following year, by remarketed preferreds. All of these types of preferred stock issues have a dividend payment that changes from period to period. Though a number of variations are possible, an adjustable rate preferred typically has a quarterly resetting of the dividend rate determined by some spread off the highest of three points on the Treasury yield curve, e.g., using the yields for 3 month, 10 year and 20 year maturities. This maximum rate may be subject to a floor rate below which the dividend payment rate will not fall, i.e., the adjustable rate preferred has a "collar." The spread off the Treasury yield can be positive or negative. A difficulty with this type of preferred stock design is that the method of adjusting the dividend payment rate is fixed. The spread does not change with market conditions or the risk of the issuer. As such there is some associated principal risk.

For reasons to be discussed below, purchasers of variable rate preferred stock are often corporate cash managers seeking a tax-exempt or tax-advantaged money market security (Wilson 2001, pp. 343–4). This type of investor is seeking a competitive interest rate without risk of principal. The auction rate preferred structure addresses the potential problem that the adjustable rate preferred poses for this type of investor. For this type of preferred stock, the dividend payment rate is set at regular intervals, usually every seven weeks, through auctions involving current holders of these preferred issues and other investors interested in purchasing the shares. In this fashion, the dividend payment rate reflects market conditions and changes in the risk of the issuer. The remarketed rate preferred stock issues are a variation on the auction rate preferred that uses a remarketing agent to reset the dividend payment rate. By avoiding the costs associated with the auction process, the remarketed issue can feature a shorter reset period, usually varying between one week and seven weeks. In this fashion, the auction rate and remarketed rate preferred issues avoid most of the principal risk associated with adjustable rate preferred stocks.

Since the first issues appeared, these variable dividend preferred issues have come to represent about half of new preferred issues, with the split between fixed and variable dividends varying from year to year. These changes in dividend structure were accompanied by a change in the composition of issuers. While the traditional issuer of preferred shares was a utility, i.e., electric, water, gas and telephone companies, more recently the financial companies such as banks, thrifts and insurance firms, have become significant sources of preferred share issues. These entities are important drivers of the variable rate preferred structures. For example, the first auction rate preferred stock issue, in 1984, was by American Express. From 1990 to 2003, it is estimated that $332 billion in new preferred stock was issued, much of this by financial companies (Tunick 2003). Combined with the approximately $60 billion of preferred issues outstanding in 1990, net of redemptions, the amount of the preferred stock outstanding is currently not larger than $350 billion. Even with these changes and considerable growth, the size of the outstanding preferred share market can be measured in the hundreds of billions of dollars, compared to the trillions in par value of outstanding issues in the debt market. Though the preferred share market is not important in terms of relative size, the preferred share does play an important role in security analysis.

The preferred share is a hybrid security, sharing some features of debt and some features of common stock. On the issue of whether to purchase a preferred stock or the debt of a company, Graham, Dodd and Cottle (1962, p. 382) observe:

> What yield advantage should the investor demand to compensate him for the contractual weakness of preferred stocks against bonds? We are inclined to think that an *individual* should not buy any preferred stock unless he is able to obtain *both* adequate safety and a differential of, say, 1 percent in the yield over that afforded by a bond of similar safety... What of preferred stocks of secondary or inferior grade which can be bought at tempting yields? Our attitude toward them is the same as that toward high-coupon bonds. It is unsound to accept inadequate security to obtain a higher income, *unless* the buyer obtains also an opportunity for a substantial increase in principal value and *unless also* he is prepared to take the speculative risk of loss involved in the transaction.

In addition to being an excellent illustration of the Graham and Dodd approach to speculation vs. investment in security analysis and selection, preferred shares are also an excellent illustration of the impact that tax treatment and regulations can have on a security. For example, the reason that GDC state individual investors will, typically, not be attracted to preferred stocks is due to the *different tax treatment compared to debt.*

For pedagogical purposes, it is difficult to systematically incorporate tax considerations when discussing the security analysis of each and every security. Taxes impact security purchasers and issuers in different ways, e.g., a high net worth individual subject to capital gains taxes will have different investment concerns than a tax-exempt charitable institution or pension trust. There are so many possible iterations that it is impractical to consider the different possible tax implications for, say, valuation of common stocks. In general, the tax rate of the marginal investor is usually too difficult to identify. Unlike common stocks where the tax motivations of purchasers and issuers are unclear, preferred shares provide a relatively clean security structure for examining the impact of tax considerations on the analysis of securities. (Another example is municipal bonds.) For the issuer, preferred shares have the disadvantage that dividends paid are not a deductible expense like the interest payments on corporate debt.[4] In the US, the Internal Revenue Code (IRC) section 243 provides a 70% deduction for dividend income received by corporate investors owing less than 20% of the paying corporation. This rises to 80% for ownership shares between 20% and 80% and is 100% for greater than 80% ownership.

The *valuation of preferred stock* depends on the tradeoff between: the increase in issuer opportunity cost due to the loss of the interest deductibility forgone by issuing preferred stock instead of debt; and the reduction in tax liabilities of corporate preferred share purchasers due to the partial income tax deductibility of dividends paid on preferred shares. The benefits to investors means that the coupons on preferred stock will be lower than on comparable debt issues. This makes preferred stocks an attractive source of financing relative to long term debt for firms with low expected marginal tax rates, e.g., Ely et al. (2002). In practice, the financing benefits of preferred stocks to issuers are reduced by the generally higher issue costs of preferred stocks relative to long term debt. These additional costs depend on a combination of factors related to the characteristics of the preferred being issued, e.g., convertible preferreds are more expensive to issue than fixed rate preferreds, the size of the issue, the credit risk rating and the type of issuer, e.g., financial company vs. public utility (Bajaj et al. 2002). Given this, the decision to issue preferred stock versus debt will depend on the tradeoff between the tax benefit to the marginal corporate investor and the incremental tax burden on the issuing corporation.

Despite some sweeping tax code changes associated with the Tax Reform Act (1986) and later reforms, little has changed for US individual investors in preferred stocks since GDC (1962, p. 382) wrote: "under present tax laws high-grade preferred stocks are not logical investments for individuals. They *are* logical investments for corporations, which can obtain a much higher net return from them than from corporate bonds of comparable quality." Despite some current proposals to reduce or eliminate the "double taxation" of dividends, US individuals receiving common stock or preferred stock dividends are subject to taxation on that income at their marginal tax rate. In the US, the coupon rates on preferred shares only make sense for corporate investors able to take advantage of the favorable dividend tax treatment. The US is unusual in applying the full marginal tax rate to dividend payments made to individuals. In Canada, for example, dividend income from both preferred and common stock is usually taxed at rates well below the marginal tax rate for individuals and not taxed when received by Canadian corporations.[5] Unfortunately, the theoretically attractive features of this reduction in "double taxation" of preferred dividends has, in practice, been characterized by numerous tax management schemes by corporations to reduce or eliminate corporate taxes paid.

In addition to tax consequences associated with dividend payments, the issuance of preferred shares can also be motivated by *regulatory considerations and other aspects of the tax code*, e.g., Callahan et al. (2001). In particular, the Tax Reform Act (1986) limited the deductibility of net operating loss carry forwards after a change in corporate ownership. Under the rules, straight preferred stock does not count toward the "change in ownership criteria" that measure ownership change in terms of holdings of common stock and convertibles. As firms with such loss carry forwards are usually subject to severe restrictions on the issue of debt, preferred shares are an attractive form of financing. A regulatory motivation for the issuance of preferred shares for financial institutions can be found in the capital adequacy requirements that have been introduced since the 1989 Basle accord. Because preferred stock is considered to be equity, this provides an added motivation for financial companies subject to the capital adequacy guidelines to issue preferred stock instead of debt. The ongoing trend for financial institutions to create equity/debt hybrids that are booked as equity has been an impetus to the proposed accounting standard FAS 149 that will require corporations to treat preferred share issues (and other equity/debt hybrids) as debt on the balance sheet.

Common stock and firm value

Common stock is, by far, the most important type of equity claim. As observed in section 1.1, common stock is the security that attracts the most attention in the popular media of financial newspapers, magazines and television shows. Yet, the valuation of individual common stocks has been relatively ignored in modern Finance. Where common stock valuation models are proposed, such as the Gordon constant growth model, the proposed formulas are usually elementary extensions of discounted cash flow techniques. Instead of focusing on individual stocks, modern Finance assumes that markets are efficient and concentrates on the properties of diversified portfolios. Though having become somewhat out-of-fashion in recent years, the efficient markets hypothesis implies that the search for abnormal returns in individual stock analysis is a futile exercise, incapable of generating abnormal returns. Faced with this view, practitioners involved in the security analysis industry have reacted with ridicule and indignation, implicitly or explicitly claiming that the generation of abnormal returns is an inherent property of the intellectual services that the industry sells to institutional and individual clients.

Common stock valuation is an intellectual quandary that defies a general solution. The security involved is a *residual claim* to whatever is left over after all the claims of other holders of a corporation's securities have been satisfied. (See section 1.1 for further discussion of common stock features.) Though the value of all other corporate securities are also dependent on the economic performance of the corporation, this dependency is amplified many times for common stock. Consider the value of the corporate debentures for two AAA rated US firms. If both of these securities are straight bonds with the same coupon and time to maturity and without any embedded options, the prices of these two debentures will be approximately the same. However, the valuation of the common stock for these two corporations likely would be much different. Absent the use of a par value for common stock, even a basic comparison of the common stock prices would require some restrictive convention like equality of the number of shares and the initial offering price.[6] Already the comparison is getting so abstract that the connection to the characteristics of the two corporations has been undermined. For example, different firms raising the same initial amount of equity would almost certainly be compelled to have different capital structures. It is difficult to construct even crude theoretical comparisons of common stock values across firms.

The *valuation of common stock* is intimately connected to the firm that issues the stock. GDC (1962, p. 443) observe: "The basic components in a common-stock valuation are fourfold, viz.: 1. The expected future earnings; 2. The expected future dividends; 3. The capitalization rates – or multiplers – of the dividends and earnings; 4. The asset value." This seems simple enough, but this observation is followed by:

> It should be pointed out that these four factors include, by implication, a number of elements which enter into both the quantitative and qualitative analysis of a common stock. Chief of these are the past and expected rates of profitability, stability and growth; the abilities of the management; and, the various underlying facts and hypotheses that will govern sales volume, costs, and profits after taxes.

Suddenly the common stock valuation problem does not seem so simple as looking at a few "basic components." Precisely how these "elements" fit together with the "four factors" is, at best, a heuristic exercise. The presence of "expected" dividends and "expected" earnings in the factors raises significant problems about *ex ante* versus *ex post* evaluations.

The common stock represents a residual claim to what is left over after the well defined claims of the corporation's other security holders have been settled. To make an analogy to economic theory, this residual claim has both *a "stock" and a "flow" component*. The "stock" component relates to the net asset value of the firm, a combination of the productive assets that were "purchased" with the initial equity issue plus the accumulation of retained earnings that were used to augment the asset base over time minus the economic depreciation of the assets over time. Though accounting makes an allowance in the form of depreciation each period to account for the payments made to maintain the assets, this allocation can be a fictional exercise conducted for the purposes of calculating the income tax liability that has to be settled. Even new assets can become obsolete or unproductive, though still eligible for depreciation write-downs. Similarly old assets that have long since been depreciated to zero (or to estimated salvage value) may continue to be productive. The accounting approach to depreciation has additional difficulties dealing with intangible assets that have not been "priced" by, say, the accurate creation of goodwill in a takeover. Even if priced in a takeover, the goodwill value may not be accurate. In terms of GDC factor 4, common stock valuation requires the *market value* of the stock of productive assets, both tangible and intangible, to be accurately valued.

The "flow" component of common stock valuation relates to GDC factors 1, 2 and 3: "expected future earnings," "expected future dividends" and "capitalization rates." These factors are associated with the ability of the "stock" of productive assets to generate the net cash flows over time. The factors are the primary components of the discounted cash flow valuation model: "The value of any stock, bond or business today is determined by the cash inflows and outflows – discounted at an appropriate interest rate – that can be expected to occur during the remaining life of the asset" (Cunningham 2000, p. 93). While there is general agreement from many perspectives about this basic approach to valuation, there is a confounding range of difficulties that arise in the implementation. These difficulties are apparent with even the simplest valuations. For example, consider the case of a resource company that owns the mineral rights to some property and is making a stock issue to fund exploratory drilling activities. Geological forecasting will give some notion about the types of minerals that could be found, e.g., it is not possible to find natural gas or oil in areas where drilling for precious metals is indicated. There may also be some information about drilling done at other sites in the same area. Given this, how is a value to be determined for this company?

Focusing on "expected future earnings," "expected future dividends" and "capitalization rates," it is apparent that the value of this resource company depends on the success of the exploratory drilling program. In most cases, the drilling will not produce an exploitable amount of ore and the value of the shares will fall to zero, or near zero, because the expected future earnings are zero.[7] If an exploitable amount of ore is found, then the property will have value to the large mining companies that specialize in the particular mineral, e.g., Inco Ltd. (N) for nickel or Barrick Gold Co. (ABX) for gold. In this case, the expected future earnings would be the sale price of the mineral rights. This requires a future market value for the property to be determined that will depend on factors such as the future market price of the mineral, the "quality" of the ore deposit, the costs of developing the property, and the date the property is sold. Having estimated these values, the "future earnings" have to be discounted back to the present using a "capitalization rate." It is conventional that the capitalization rate reflects the inherent risks in the project, the expected return on the market and the level of riskless interest rates. Even in this simple case, the difficulties of obtaining an estimate for the market value of the common stock of the mineral exploration company is evident.

One of the key failings of modern Finance is the inability to provide a plausible model of common stock valuation. Recalling the quote from Stickney in section 1.3, this inability stems from modern Finance being concerned with developing the average properties of common stocks. Central paradigms, such as the capital asset pricing model, are concerned with eliminating firm specific risk. Yet, the value of a common stock is intimately connected to the company that issued the stock. As such, the common stock valuation problem has to be concerned with the analysis of firm specific risk, not with the elimination of such risk. In general, firms are not homogeneous entities having properties that can be uncovered by examining the averages of different groupings or regressing returns on factors and the like. Though it may be possible to produce some crude relationships using averaging/grouping methods or regression techniques, type I (unjust acceptance) and type II (unjust rejection) errors are so hard to control that inaccurate inferences are difficult to avoid. Despite often being naive about the techniques of modern Finance, it difficult to ignore the widely held belief of practitioners that much of modern Finance is vacuous when it comes to common stock valuation.

7.2 THE BASICS OF FUNDAMENTAL ANALYSIS

Fundamental analysis and investment philosophy

Philosophy has dedicated considerable effort to developing the implications of how language is used.[8] From semantics to rhetoric, words have content that extend well beyond simple definitions. The use of the expression "fundamental analysis" in modern Finance provides a useful illustration of the basic point at hand. As used in modern Finance, fundamental analysis is interpreted in terms of a core theoretical proposition: the efficient markets hypothesis (EMH). As discussed in section 1.2, the EMH is usually presented as applying to specific information sets denoted as weak form, semi-strong form and strong form. Whereas the weak form relates to the information set used in "technical analysis," *the semi-strong form* relates to the information set applicable to "fundamental analysis." Under the EMH, if the market is semi-strong form efficient then it is not possible to earn abnormal returns by exploiting the information set used in "fundamental analysis," i.e., market prices fully and accurately reflect the relevant fundamental information. Based on this type of language, it would appear that if markets are semi-strong form efficient then there is little to be gained from doing fundamental analysis.

In modern Finance, fundamental analysis is defined relative to the core theory. The rejection of fundamental analysis is achieved by considering specific types of "publicly available" information such as announcements of earnings and dividends, disclosures of merger plans, changes in accounting practices and the like. Studies stretching back at least to Ball and Brown (1968) and Fama et al. (1969) have demonstrated that a wide range of publicly available information is "rapidly and accurately reflected in the price of the stock," e.g., Giammarino et al. (1996, p. 293).[9] By defining fundamental analysis in this fashion, language is being used in a confusing and misleading way. An important, complicated and diverse approach to the evaluation of securities is reduced to a statistical examination of how prices of specific securities, usually common stocks, react to changes in some type of publicly available information. The sophisticated methods and procedures involved in taking a body of fundamental information and translating that information into an evaluation of whether a stock is correctly valued does not correspond to whether, on average, changes in a particular type of information are rapidly translated into prices. Though there is some relationship, the connection between fundamental analysis and tests of semi-strong form efficiency is weak at best and misleading at worst.

In *Financial Statement Analysis and Security Valuation*, Penman (2001, p. 3) states: "Investors typically invest in a firm by buying equity shares or the firm's debt. Their primary concern is the amount to pay – the value of the shares or the debt. The analysis of information that focuses on valuation is called *valuation analysis, fundamental analysis*, or, when securities like stocks and bonds are involved, *security analysis*." Penman (2001) "develops the principles of fundamental analysis" and "shows how financial statement analysis is used in fundamental analysis." Penman focuses on *the accounting aspects of fundamental analysis*, covering the techniques involved in translating the information presented in accounting statements into estimates of the appropriate market value of specific securities. As such, Penman is providing a natural development of the traditional approach taken in accounting to the subject of financial statement analysis, e.g., Bernstein (1989). Casual inspection of Penman (2001) or Bernstein (1989) or any of a number of excellent texts in this area, e.g. Fridson and Alvarez (2002), reveals that the assessment and analytical manipulation of information in financial statements for purposes of valuing securities is considerably more complicated than determining if, say, an adverse or positive earnings announcement is rapidly reflected in common stock prices.

In contrast to those emphasizing the importance of financial statement analysis, there are other fundamental analysts that emphasize *the importance of economic analysis* in determining security values. A key aspect typically considered in the economic analysis are industry factors, such as the level of competition, barriers to entry and the regulatory environment. Also important are the macroeconomic factors such as the general level of the financial markets, interest rates and exchange rates. There are also qualitative economic factors about the firm not reflected in the financial statements, such as the depth and quality of management. Though the economic analysis will, almost always, be combined with various types of financial statement information to arrive at an assessment of the security value, the process by which this is done will vary across analysts. Evidence that, say, changes in money supply numbers announced by the Federal Reserve are "rapidly reflected" in prices has only ambiguous implications for fundamental analysis, other than to demonstrate that security prices react to the release of this type of information. Such evidence would seem to have more implications for theories of "noise trading" rather than for fundamental analysis.

Though there is a general methodological approach that characterizes fundamental analysis, it is not a homogeneous doctrine. The techniques of fundamental analysis are aimed at determining the value of a security or capital asset using a range of economic and accounting information. Selection of specific aspects for analysis and the interpretation depends on the "investment style" or "investment philosophy" or, in the spirit of the title for this book, the "investment strategy" of the analyst. Put differently, the fundamental analyst specifies a valuation model, such as the discounted cash flow model, and then assembles and evaluates the analyst-specific economic and accounting information needed to forecast the variables used in the model. Though it is a popular and widely recommended valuation model for fundamental analysts, the discounted cash flow model is neither a necessary nor sufficient condition for fundamental analysis. While modern Finance presents fundamental analysis as being, somehow, homogeneous, fundamental analysis is, at best, a loose-knit collection of somewhat different techniques. Perhaps more importantly, the application of the techniques is participant dependent.

To see this point, consider the question: is the P/E ratio for stock A "too high" to justify the purchase of the stock? The P/E ratio is a measure that is widely used in fundamental analysis. However, not all fundamental analysts give much consideration to the P/E ratio in deciding whether a stock is under-valued. Philip Fisher, for example, subordinates the P/E ratio to the characteristics of the business (see section 7.4). Other analysts use the P/E ratio as an initial filter to indicate what other types of fundamental information to examine before making a decision. For example, a "high" P/E ratio could be due to a potential source of earnings that is expected to materialize in the near future or to the price being driven primarily by the market value of assets. Even if the fundamental analyst determines that the P/E ratio indicates the stock is under-valued, different analysts may have different criteria for determining when to purchase a security, i.e., there will be variation across analysts in the different degrees of underpricing at which purchase decisions are triggered. In effect, in fundamental analysis there is not a simple functional relationship between the P/E ratio and the valuation of common stocks.

The observation that security analysis and investment strategy are intimately connected is not new. It has long been understood that the investment strategy selected makes specific demands about the type of information required and the way it is interpreted. In this vein, the observation that fundamental analysis is not a homogeneous subject applies directly to how industry and firm level information is used in security analysis. It also applies to the use of macroeconomic information. Graham, Dodd and Cottle (1962, pp. 26–7) explicitly attempt to deal with this point by introducing three general categories to describe distinct approaches to common stock valuation: the *anticipation approach*; the *relative value approach*; and, the *intrinsic value approach* also known as the absolute value approach.[10] Within each of these approaches to fundamental analysis there may be further differences in the security analysis style and usage of information. However, these differences in style and usage are small compared to the differences in investment strategy implied by each of the approaches.

According to GDC, *the anticipation approach* is the first and oldest approach to security analysis of common stocks. This approach takes the current market price to be an appropriate measure of the current value and attempts to identify stocks that will outperform by "anticipating" changes in current conditions. This usually involves detailed analysis of the business position and prospects of various companies. GDC observe:

> The anticipation approach is typified by the numerous published lists which suggest stocks which will "outperform" the market over some time span . . . The function of the security analyst . . . is to anticipate the new situation, to select the stocks that will benefit most therefrom, and to reject those that will fare badly . . . This approach, clearly, does not involve seeking an answer to the question: What is the stock worth?

The typical "anticipation" security analyst examines the price history of the stock and attempts to heuristically determine how the price changed in response to past *changes* in key variables such as earnings, new product innovations, production technology, management composition, capital structure, capital expenditures, mergers and acquisitions and so on. Based on breadth and depth of knowledge, the analyst attempts to predict or "anticipate" changes in key variables.

The anticipation approach has much in common with the "expectations investing" model specified by Rappaport and Mauboussin (2001) (see section 8.1). Though expectations investing explicitly incorporates the use of discounted cash flow modeling, this step is only used to determine the "price-implied expectations" associated with the market price. The specific value drivers – sales growth, incremental investment rate and operating profit margin – are predicted and compared to the level of those drivers consistent with the price implied expectations. This comparison provides the basis for a buy or sell recommendation based on an "anticipation" of the market revising expectations in line with the predictions of the analyst. The emphasis in both expectations investing and the anticipation approach is on *changes* in prices and not on the *level* of prices that is consistent with fundamentals. Though Rappaport and Mauboussin make reference to margin of safety, this inclusion in the methodology appears to be more of an after-thought. Consistent with other micro-fundamentalist approaches, both the anticipation approach and expectations investing place an emphasis on individual security valuation and the use of micro-fundamental information.

Keynes (1936, p. 155) provides a different perspective on the anticipation approach: "the professional investor is forced to concern himself with the anticipation of impending changes, in the news or in the atmosphere, of the kind by which experience shows the mass psychology of the market is most influenced." Keynes saw the negative macroeconomic implications of a market populated by professional investors driven by the anticipation approach. In a justly famous quote, Keynes (1936, pp. 155–6) observes:

> This battle of wits to anticipate the basis of conventional valuation a few months hence, rather than the prospective yield of an investment over the long term of years, does not even require the gulls amongst the public to feed the maws of the professional: – it can be played by professionals amongst themselves. Nor is it necessary that anyone should keep his simple faith in the conventional basis of valuation having any long-term validity. For it is, so to speak, a game of Snap, of Old Maid, of Musical Chairs – a pastime in which he is victor who says *Snap* neither too soon nor too late, who passes the Old Maid to his neighbour before the game is over, who secures a chair for himself when the music stops . . . we have reached the third degree where we devote our intelligence to anticipating what average opinion expects the average opinion to be.

Given this, Keynes recognized that the anticipation approach implies an investment strategy that is aimed at trading over horizons of three months and less: "it is not sensible to pay 25 for an investment of which you believe the prospective yield to justify a value of 30, if you also believe that the market will value it a 20 three months hence."

The relative value approach is similar to the anticipation approach in taking the current market price to be an appropriate measure of the current value and attempts to identify the "relative" attractiveness of various stocks. GDC observe that the relative value analyst:

> derives the capitalization rate for an individual issue in terms of the rate at which earnings or dividends for a cross section of the market – such as the Dow-Jones Industrial Average – are being capitalized or from the capitalization rate for a specific industry or other group which typifies the market for an individual share he is seeking to evaluate. His efforts, therefore, are devoted fundamentally to appraising the *relative* attractiveness of individual issues in terms of the then existing level of stock prices and not to determining the fundamental worth of a stock.

The relative value approach is, by default, the approach of necessity for a fund that is fully invested in equities. The precise method used to determine relative value will differ from analyst to analyst, though the GDC reference to "capitalization rates" is consistent with the market practice of comparing P/E ratios. The relative value approach could also contain elements of either the anticipation or intrinsic value approaches to rank prospects. Ultimately, however, the buy or sell decision would be based on a relative ranking. If anything, the implications of following the relative value approach is even closer to what Keynes observed as conventional market practice.

As illustrated by Hooke (1998, ch. 13), the relative value approach to security analysis is the most favored approach in the modern Wall Street approach to security analysis. Being at the core of day-to-day trading of common stocks, the financial community of investment bankers, securities firms, institutional fund managers and the like that compose Wall Street are, in aggregate, not unlike a fund that is fully invested in equities. Observing that professional security analysts seldom refer to intrinsic value, Hooke (1998, p. 232) provides the following description of the relative value approach used on Wall Street:

> Morgan Stanley analyst, Madhav Dhar, suggests there's no such thing as the "intrinsic value" of a stock. "You have to figure out where you are relative to everybody else," he says. "It's an investment decision overlaid by game theory." With many institutions sharing this view, practitioners increasingly turn to relative values to price companies. Instead of a fair price based on discounted cash flows, practitioners use "relative value" analysis where the positive and negative aspects of a stock are evaluated against those characteristics of similar stocks falling in the same industry category. Value parameters are then compared and contrasted, resulting in statements such as "Kroger is undervalued relative to Safeway, because Kroger's growth rate is higher, yet its P/E is lower." Other popular comparators include the Price/Book, Price/Sales, (Price + Debt)/EBITDA, and (Price + Debt)/EBIT ratios.

For many in the investment industry, DCF models involve too many variables to estimate, leading to interminable debates over this projection vs. that projection. In the marketing of stocks, it is easier to take the industry or sector multiple as given, and then to argue over the relative values of stocks in the sector using widely recognized valuation ratios such as P/E and P/BV. This is also consistent with the "Wall Street" practice of organizing research analysts along industry/sector lines.

The intrinsic value approach has been widely described, analyzed and recommended. Though Graham and Dodd (1934, p. 14) explicitly recognize that the intrinsic value approach has a much longer history, modern observers usually credit Graham and Dodd (1934) with originating the approach which is typically, though not always, referred to as "value investing." GDC (1962, p. 27) observe that the intrinsic value approach "attempts to value a stock independently of its current market price. If the value found is substantially above or below its current price, the analyst concludes that the issue should be bought or disposed of." The essence of this approach revolves around the definition of intrinsic value. Graham and Dodd (1934, p. 17) recognize the difficulties in providing a precise definition: "intrinsic value is an elusive concept. In general terms, it is understood to be that value which is justified by the facts, e.g., the assets, earnings, dividends, definite prospects, as distinct, let us say, from market quotations established by artificial manipulation or distorted by psychological excesses." For Keynes (1936), the intrinsic value was "the prospective yield of an investment over a long term of years."

Both Keynes (1936) and Graham and Dodd (1934) were profoundly influenced by the financial and economic collapse associated with the Great Depression. Both recognized the significance of the intrinsic value approach. Yet, both came to dissimilar conclusions about the prospects for this approach. Keynes (1936, p. 157) maintained that: "Investment based on genuine long-term expectation is so difficult to-day as to be scarcely practicable. He who attempts it must surely lead much more laborious days and run greater risks than he who tries to guess better than the crowd how the crowd will behave; and, given equal intelligence, he may make more disastrous mistakes." Keynes generally views the anticipation approach as the potentially most profitable. Graham and Dodd (1934, p. 22) cautiously take a different tack:

> The field of [security analysis] may be said to rest upon a twofold assumption: first, that the market price is frequently out of line with the true value; and, second, that there is an inherent tendency for these disparities to correct themselves . . . The second assumption is . . . true in theory, but its working out in practice is often unsatisfactory. Undervaluations caused by neglect or prejudice may persist for an inconveniently long time, and the same applies to inflated prices caused by overenthusiasm or artificial stimulants . . . The analyst must seek to guard himself against this danger as best he can.

Despite the qualifications, for Graham and Dodd the intrinsic value approach was the potentially most profitable.

Macroeconomics and common stock valuation

The bulk of security analysis falls within the realm of accounting and finance. As a consequence, the macro-fundamentals of common stock valuation are often overlooked. In addition, because the bulk of the analysis of macro-fundamentals is done by economists, the connection of the results with the needs of security analysts is often underdeveloped. It is even possible to develop *macro-fundamentalist* investment strategies that rely on the fundamental analysis of macroeconomic factors to identify investment opportunities. For example, a strategy of buying cyclical stocks, e.g., steels and autos, just before the upswing in the business cycle and switching to defensive stocks, e.g., consumer products and tobacco/alcohol, at the peak of the business cycle would be macro-fundamentalist. Security selection could be incorporated to identify stocks within a sector or industry that may outperform, but this is not necessary. Even if the analyst is not interested in using a macro-fundamentalist investment strategy, macro-variables such as GDP, interest rates and exchange rates can be important elements in the industry and company analysis associated with micro-fundamentalism.

The history of using macro-fundamentals to analyze securities predates Graham and Dodd. For example, prior to contributions of Lawrence Smith during the 1920s, it was hypothesized that stock returns would typically outperform bond returns during inflationary periods and vice versa during deflationary periods. The set of variables that a macro-fundamentalist could consider includes: inflation rates, the level and term structure of interest rates, exchange rates, unemployment rates, business cycles, national and international economic growth rates, money supply growth rates and changes in the supply and demand for credit. Whitman (1999, p. 73) reflects a widespread view among micro-fundamentalists: "One reason – but far from the only one – that value investors do not factor into their investment decisions any views about general economic outlooks, stock market outlooks, or about interest rate outlooks is that almost no one is any good at making such predictions." Though this view may be somewhat harsh, there is an apparently conflicting body of empirical and theoretical results about the relationships between macroeconomic variables and stock prices.

Much of the perceived difficulty that practitioners and "value investors" have in assessing studies on macro-fundamentals stems from a misunderstanding of the strongly positivist philosophical approach used in economics (see section 1.3). Much of the epistemological approach used in modern Finance is adopted directly from economics. These difficulties can be illustrated by perhaps the most widely debated macro-fundamental: *the relationship between stock prices and inflation.* The economic theorist is concerned with developing models that possess the property of money-neutrality or inflation-neutrality where real variables, e.g., price level deflated nominal variables such as stock prices and GDP, are not affected by changes in the value of the monetary unit. The assumptions of the model can then be selectively relaxed to theoretically determine if there is non-neutrality when a particular assumption is not imposed. The end product is a range of theoretical results where there may or may not be inflation neutrality, depending on the specific assumptions that are adopted. Such theorizing is uninteresting to the value investor wanting to know if stocks are an inflation hedge. Unfortunately, a similar confusion emerges in the empirical results.

Siegel (1998, pp. 158–9) presents an optimistic view of the evidence on the relationship between stock prices and inflation:

> Despite the overwhelming evidence that the returns on stocks compensate shareholders for increased inflation, investor acceptance of stocks as inflation hedges has undergone significant changes. In the 1950's, stocks were praised as hedges against rising commodity prices. For that reason, many investors stayed with stocks, despite witnessing the dividend yield on equities fall below the interest rate on bonds in 1958 for the first time ever. In the 1970's, however, stock prices were ravaged during the inflation triggered by OPEC oil price hikes and perpetuated by bad monetary policy. As a result, it became unfashionable to view equity as an effective hedge against inflation.

Siegel explains the poor performance of stocks in certain periods of high inflation with the claim that stocks are not adequate "short term" hedges against inflation but will provide long term protection. Following Smith (1925), Siegel believes that stocks will outperform bonds over periods of both rising and falling prices and, as a consequence, provide the best inflation protection among financial assets.

While it may be comforting to claim that there is "overwhelming evidence" for stocks being an inflation hedge, this was little comfort to those directly impacted by the poor performance of stocks during the high inflation of the 1970s.[11] To the uninitiated, it may seem somewhat odd that two important variables, such as stock returns and inflation, would be negatively related in the short term but positively related in the long term. What is the long term but a sequence of short terms?[12] Interpretation of the empirical relationship between common stock investment performance and inflation is complicated by the use of a number of different conventions to define the stock variable in empirical studies. For example, Rapach (2002) examines the long run response of real stock prices to a permanent inflation shock (where "real stock prices" are nominal stock prices divided by a price index such as the producer or consumer price index). In contrast, Anari and Kolari (2001) use nominal stock prices, while Sharpe (2002) uses real stock returns. The objectives of empirical work also vary, with studies such as Anari and Kolari (2001) and Rapach (2002) focusing just on the empirical fit between stock performance and inflation while others, such as Sharpe (2002), are concerned with explaining the causal mechanism, e.g., the impact of inflation on earnings growth.

Despite Siegel's claim for overwhelming evidence in favor of stocks being a long run inflation hedge, Anari and Kolari (2001, p. 588) observe that "few studies" report such evidence and these studies use very long sample periods, e.g., Boudoukh and Richardson (1993) use a sample period covering 1802–1990.[13] Results from sample periods of 100–200 years are of questionable usefulness for most practical security analysis applications. In contrast, there are a large number of studies that report a negative short term relationship between inflation and stock performance, e.g., Bodie (1974), Geske and Roll (1983). This negative relationship is usually considered anomalous because the impact of the "Fisher effect" is expected to be positive. To see this, consider the decomposition of the nominal stock return into the real return and inflation. (Following the convention used in section 1.1 and elsewhere, the $t = 0$ conditional expectation involved in the rate of return calculations is not explicitly stated but is understood.) Letting $RR(t)$ be the real return and $\pi(t)$ the aggregate price level at time t with $\dot{\pi}(t)$ as the inflation rate $(\Delta \pi / \pi)$ between $t - 1$ and t.:

$$\frac{P(0)}{\pi(0)} = \left[\frac{\dfrac{P(1)}{\pi(1)} + \dfrac{Div(1)}{\pi(1)}}{1 + RR(1)} \right]$$

$$\rightarrow \quad 1 + RR(1) = \frac{P(1) + Div(1)}{P(0)} \div \frac{\pi(1)}{\pi(0)} = \frac{(1 + R(1))}{(1 + \dot{\pi}(1))}$$

In this framework, if stocks are a perfect inflation hedge then real returns will be constant through time which requires nominal returns, R, to adjust upwards to offset changes in inflation. This requires stock returns and inflation rates to be positively related.[14]

The considerable evidence that stock returns and inflation are negatively related in the short run has produced numerous studies aimed at explaining the process by which inflation impacts the real return. For example, Sharpe (2002) presents empirical evidence that the negative relation between real stock returns and expected inflation is due to a combination of two effects. A rise in expected inflation is associated with lower expected earnings growth that, in turn, produces higher required real returns. Sharpe estimates that an increase of 1 percentage point in expected inflation raises real stock returns about 1 percentage point which implies a significant fall in nominal stock prices; hence, there is a negative short term relationship between stock returns and inflation. Yet, the impact of expected inflation on expected real stock returns is also observed in real long term Treasury bond yields, implying that expected inflation will have little effect on the real long run equity premium. This suggests that the impact of expected inflation on interest rates is another mechanism through which inflation can impact stock prices, e.g., by increasing borrowing costs and dampening sales on credit higher interest rates can have a significant effect on earnings.

Disentangling the impact of inflation on stock prices is sufficiently complicated that it is not surprising there is considerable disagreement on the mechanisms involved. Part of the disagreement is due to a failure to recognize that inflation can have a range of causes. Though monetarists are inclined to argue that "inflation is always a monetary phenomenon," it is possible for inflation to originate from real sector shocks, especially oil price shocks. Inflation originating from this source can produce the negative impact on earnings and subsequent reduction in stock prices, as observed by Sharpe (2002), Jones and Kaul (1996), Fama (1981) and others. However, inflation originating from largely monetary sources will likely operate through a different economic mechanism. For example, Henry (2002) presents empirical evidence that levels of inflation above 40% produce a different impact on stock prices than inflation levels below 40%. As high levels of inflation are almost always due largely to excessive monetary expansion, the source of the inflation will influence the type of impact on stock prices.

If the source of the inflation matters for the impact on stock prices, then there will likely be variation in the impact of inflation across firms. Developing the notion of *"money illusion"* contained in Modigliani and Cohn (1979), Ritter and Warr (2002) present evidence that inflation confuses investors in two important ways: the discount rate to use in valuing common stocks is miscalculated; and, the capital gains associated with the reduction in the real value of debt and other nominal contracts due to inflation is underestimated. The latter source of confusion will produce a variation in the impact of inflation across firms. Ritter and Warr make the fascinating argument that the bull market that started in 1982 and continued to early 2000 was due to the market under-valuation of common stocks associated with the "inflation illusion" of the 1970s. The reduction in inflationary expectations starting in the early 1980s dissipated the inflation illusion resulting in the emergence of corrected valuations. The resulting abnormal gains skewed the appearance of the equity risk premium and eventually resulted in overvalued common stocks as the bull market progressed to its logical conclusion in early 2000.

This discussion makes it apparent that inflation is a complicated and pervasive factor in common stock valuation. Analysis of the role of inflation on stock prices during this and other periods suggests that the degree of hedging protection provided by stocks is affected by the source(s) of the inflationary pressures. Following Ritter and Warr (2002), inflation can also induce "money illusion" resulting in valuation errors associated with incorrect estimation of capitalization rates and the real value of nominal contracts. In addition, inflation may have an impact on tax burdens, interest rates and investor risk perceptions. The impact on tax burdens can occur, for example, due to the impact of progressive tax rates resulting in a real higher tax as inflation-induced increases in nominal corporate earnings are taxed at higher marginal rates. Assuming "money illusion," higher nominal interest rates created by higher levels of inflationary expectations increase the attractiveness of bonds relative to stocks causing the composition of portfolios to be allocated more towards fixed income securities at the expense of stocks. Finally, inflation makes investing in common stocks a riskier, more uncertain proposition, necessitating a higher real risk premium to be paid to justify common stock purchases.

Even though Ritter and Warr (2002) makes fascinating reading, the lessons for security analysis are largely limited to the inflation adjusted presentation of the "residual income" model. It is difficult to draw lessons from the knowledge that a sustained period of high inflation resulted in "valuation errors" that produced abnormal returns in subsequent periods as inflationary expectations readjusted and valuation errors dissipated. Even if the story is correct, the *ex post* investment horizon was 1982–99 and the problems of when to buy, what to buy and when to sell are left unresolved. The analysis does not proceed much beyond the conventional "averaging methodologies" of modern Finance, e.g., making distinctions between "all firms" and "high debt firms." A similar comment applies to the general use of macro-fundamentals to formulate investment strategies. The investment horizons are typically long term, the buy and sell signals are difficult to determine and the mechanisms for identifying the appropriate securities to buy are unclear. The implied strategies usually focus on stock groups, e.g., industry groupings, and do not deal with individual stock values.

To the uninitiated, one of the most potentially attractive macro-fundamental investment strategies involves *the use of business cycle predictions* to either "time the market" or to trigger "industry rotation" portfolio reallocation. Siegel (1998, p. 169) describes the basic issues:

> The stock market . . . responds quite powerfully to changes in economic activity . . . Although there are many "false alarms" like 1987, when the market collapse was not followed by a recession, stocks almost always fall prior to a recession and rally rigorously at signs of an impending recovery. If you can predict the business cycle, you can beat the buy-and-hold strategy . . . But this is no easy task . . . to make money by predicting the business cycle, you must be able to identify peaks and troughs of economic activity *before* they actually occur, a skill few if any economists possess.

As numerous studies have demonstrated, aggregate stock market indexes are a leading, if somewhat noisy, indicator of business cycles. Putting aside the issues associated with how the business cycle is defined and identified, virtually all recessions and recoveries are preceded by corresponding stock market movements (see table 7.2).[15] Increases of 8% or greater in the aggregate stock index always occur prior to the trough of the cycle being reached, though decreases of 8% or greater often do not happen before the peak of the cycle is reached.

The gains to correct *business cycle timing* can be substantial, e.g., Siegel (1998, p. 176) estimates that a strategy of switching from 100% invested stocks to 100% in Tbills four months prior to a business cycle peak and switching back to 100% invested

Table 7.2 Post-World War II recessions, expansions and stock returns

Peak to trough

Business cycle	S&P peak	Business cycle peak	Months difference	S&P trough	Business cycle trough	Months Difference
Nov. 1948–Oct. 1949	May 1948	Nov 1948	6	May 1949	Oct. 1949	5
July 1953–May 1954	Dec. 1952	July 1953	7	Aug. 1953	May 1954	9
Aug. 1957–April 1958	July 1957	Aug. 1957	1	Dec. 1957	April 1958	4
April 1960–Feb. 1961	Dec. 1959	April 1960	4	Oct. 1960	Feb. 1961	4
Dec. 1969–Nov. 1970	Nov. 1968	Dec. 1969	13	June 1970	Nov. 1970	5
Nov. 1973–Mar. 1975	Dec. 1972	Nov. 1973	11	Sept. 1974	Mar. 1975	6
Jan. 1980–July 1980	Jan. 1980	Jan. 1980	0	Mar. 1980	July 1980	4
July 1981–Nov. 1982	Nov. 1980	July 1981	8	July 1982	Nov. 1982	4
July 1990–Mar. 1991	July 1990	July 1990	0	Oct. 1990	Mar. 1991	5
Mar. 2001–	Aug. 2000	Mar. 2001	7			

Source: National Bureau of Economic Research, (www.nber.org/cycles)

in stocks four months prior to the trough would have an excess return of 4.8% per year over the postwar period. Being able to predict peaks and troughs one month prior would have produced a 1.8% per year excess return. The bulk of these gains accrue to predicting troughs. Given the strong connection between the business cycle and corporate earnings, similar gains could be achieved from sector or individual stock selection strategies. Siegel (1998, pp. 179–80) provides a useful synopsis of these types of strategies:

> Stock values are based on corporate earnings, and the business cycle is a prime determinant of these earnings. The gains of being able to predict the turning points of the economic cycle are enormous. Yet doing so with any precision has eluded economists of all persuasions. And despite the growing body of economic statistics, predictions are not getting much better over time.
>
> The worst course an investor can take is to follow the prevailing sentiment about economic activity. This will lead to buying at high prices when times are good and everyone is optimistic, and selling at the low when the recession nears its trough and pessimism prevails.
>
> The lessons to investors are clear. Beating the stock market by analyzing real economic activity requires a degree of prescience that forecasters do not have. Turning points are rarely identified until several months after the peak or trough has been reached. By then, it is far too late to act in the market.

This wisdom is not unique to Siegel (1998); strikingly similar versions can be found in the writings of Warren Buffett, Philip Fisher, and Benjamin Graham, among others. In the absence of value enhancing insights into business cycles, security analysis has to depend heavily on micro-fundamentals.

Philip Fisher on industry and company analysis

In contrast to macro-fundamentalists that focus on aggregate economic variables, micro-fundamentalists examine the characteristics of industries and individual companies. Though some attention may be given to macroeconomic considerations, the focus is predominately at the firm and industry level. The specific process used by the micro-fundamentalist to evaluate industry and firm information and come to a valuation decision depends on the investment strategy of the analyst. This is a key point. For example, English (2001, pp. 34–7) is concerned with identifying whether firms are in competitive equilibrium. Applying notions from economic theory, English argues that when firms are in competitive equilibrium then there will be no incremental investment opportunities available with returns that exceed the cost of capital. In the jargon of the DCF model that English uses, there are no opportunities for "abnormal earnings." The expectations investing approach of Rappaport and Mauboussin focuses on "competitive strategy" factors as a method of identifying the important micro-fundamentals used to predict the inputs to a discounted free cash flow model. The potential number and variation of approaches to the industry and company analysis component of fundamental analysis is staggering.

Instead of attempting to provide a taxonomy of possible approaches to doing industry and company analysis, a more viable approach is to concentrate on the suggestions of an acknowledged master of the craft. Of the various possible names that come to mind, Philip Fisher stands out (see section 7.4). A recognized influence on Warren Buffett, Fisher (1958, 1975) provides a guide to the techniques that support a company and industry focused investment strategy. DCF models are not central to Fisher's analysis because his objective is to identify companies that are so outstanding that the stock price goes up, say, 500% in five to ten years. Unlike the somewhat mechanical approach of Graham and Dodd that puts heavy reliance on financial statement analysis and can produce portfolios containing a potentially large number of securities, Fisher was concerned with identifying a small number of outstanding companies. As a measure of recognition to Fisher's insights, examine the 1960 revised edition of Fisher (1958) *Common Stocks and Uncommon Profits* that lists the companies that were used as examples in the 1958 edition (see table 7.3). The companies identified in this list speak volumes.

Fisher has an easy how-to style of writing that makes tracing his suggestions a relatively easy task. However, as is common with how-to approaches, the suggestions sometimes lack precision and, on occasion, do not rise above being platitudes. Though Fisher (1958) is the acknowledged classic, Fisher (1975, 1980) provides a somewhat better road map to his suggestions about company and industry analysis. Fisher (1975) structures the discussion around "*four dimensions*": "superiority in production, marketing, research and financial skills," "the people factor," "investment characteristics of some businesses" and "the price of the investment." Fisher (1980) synthesizes the discussion of these four dimensions into a listing of the essential elements. Those looking for a security analysis panacea in this listing will likely be disappointed. A central theme running through Fisher's various writings is summarized in the following:

Table 7.3 Philip Fisher's eighteen common stocks used as examples in the 1958 edition of *Common Stocks and Uncommon Profits* 26 months later

	Price 9/20/57	Price 11/7/59	% Change
Long established institutional stocks			
Aluminum Corporation of America	$75\frac{1}{2}$	$99\frac{1}{4}$	31
American Cyanamid	41	60	46
Corning Glass	86	$144\frac{1}{4}$	68
Dow	53.05	$93\frac{1}{8}$	76
Du Pont	182	261	43
General American Transportation	$40\frac{3}{4}$	$56\frac{1}{2}$	38
International Business Machines	194.87	408	110
Rohm & Haas	350.80	688	96
Union Carbide & Carbon	$108\frac{1}{8}$	$138\frac{1}{2}$	28
Companies now attaining institutional status			
Food Machinery & Chemical	$25\frac{1}{4}$	51	102
Motorola	$45\frac{1}{2}$	122	168
Companies approaching institutional stock status			
Ampex	20	$107\frac{1}{2}$	437
Texas Instruments	$26\frac{1}{4}$	$169\frac{3}{4}$	547
Smaller companies			
Beryllium Corporation	16.16	$26\frac{1}{2}$	64
Gladding, McBean	$18\frac{3}{4}$	$21\frac{5}{8}$	15
Hewlett-Packard	16	$46\frac{1}{2}$	190
P.R. Mallory	35	$37\frac{1}{4}$	6
Huge potential profits at big risks			
Elox	10	$7\frac{5}{8}$	−24
Average of 18 stocks in this list			113
Dow Jones Industrial Average	466.75	650.92	40
Ratio of gains on the 18 stocks to the Dow Jones Industrial Average:			*2.82*

All stocks adjusted for stock splits and stock dividends; American Cyanamid and Elox eliminated from the Fisher & Co. portfolio during 1958; Hewlett-Packard was first offered in November 1957 at 16.

"All of my business life, I have believed that the success of my own business – or any business – depends on following the principles of two I's and an H. These principles are integrity, ingenuity, and hard work."

Fisher (1980) collects the main elements of the "*superiority in production, marketing, research and financial skills*" dimension and renames these elements as "functional factors" that an outstanding company will possess. The first of these factors concerns competitive position: "The firm must be one of the lowest-cost producers of its products or services relative to its competition, and must promise to remain so." Fisher provides a number of rationales as to why this factor is so important. In particular: "a comparatively low breakeven will enable this firm to survive depressed market conditions and to strengthen its market and pricing position when weaker competitors are driven out of the market"; and, "a higher than average profit margin enables the firm to generate more funds internally to sustain growth without as much dilution caused by equity sales or strain caused by overdependence on fixed-income financing." These suggestions are similar in tone to the competitive strategy value drivers – sales growth and profit margin – of Rappaport and Mauboussin but go well beyond in terms of depth and breadth.

Fisher put considerable stress on the ability of a firm to market and develop its products. This is emphasized in the next important functional factor: "A firm must have a strong enough customer orientation to recognize changes in customer needs and interests and then to react promptly to those changes in an appropriate manner. This capability should lead to generating a flow of new products that more than offset lines maturing or becoming obsolete." This is supplemented by another aspect of this factor: "Effective marketing requires not only understanding of what customers want, but also explaining to them (through advertising, selling or other means) in terms the customer will understand. Close control and constant monitoring of the cost/effectiveness of market efforts are required." Fisher uses as an example the failure of the US automobile industry to recognize the shift in public demand away from "big gas guzzlers" towards compacts that cost less, were cheaper to operate and easier to park. Fisher (1975, pp. 9–10) further observes: "in the business world customers simply do not beat a path to the door of the man with the better mousetrap. In the competitive world of commerce it is vital to make the potential customer aware of the advantage of a product or service."

Close examination of all the companies listed in table 7.3 reveals a strong emphasis on companies with successful R&D strategies. For Fisher, R&D was important for all types of companies not just those in technical areas. Fisher (1975) uses the example of banks, a type of service industry, where "low-cost electronic input devices and mini-computers are enabling them to offer accounting and bookkeeping services to customers, thus creating a new product line for these institutions." Recognition of the need to do R&D to develop products led Fisher to recommend: "Even nontechnical firms require a strong and well-directed research capability to produce newer and better products, and perform services in a more effective or efficient way"; and, "There are wide differences in the effectiveness of research. Two important elements of more productive research are market/profit consciousness, and the ability to pool necessary talent into an effective working team." For Fisher (1975, p. 11): "The best corporate research team in the world can become nothing but a liability if it develops only products that cannot readily be sold."

Writing at a time prior to the information systems revolution, Fisher was cognizant of the need to have excellent financial management systems in place. In particular, Fisher recognized that a firm with a strong financial team has a number of important advantages. The advantages Fisher identified include: "good cost information enabling management to direct its energies towards those products with the highest potential for profit contribution; a cost system that can pinpoint where production, marketing, and research costs are inefficient even in sub-parts of the operation; the ability to execute capital conservation through tight control of fixed and working capital investments." A strong financial team that has implemented advantageous financial systems can perform a critical finance function: "to provide an early warning system to identify influences that could threaten the profit plan sufficiently ahead of time to devise remedial plans to minimize adverse surprises." While factors such as the cost structure, marketing system and R&D could be evaluated off-site, Fisher was a strong proponent of on-site visits. Such visits would be necessary to assess the financial management functions identified by Fisher.

In addition to functional characteristics of the firm, Fisher was a strong proponent of the second dimension of corporate performance: "*people factors.*" For example, Fisher maintained that "to become more successful, a firm needs a leader with a determined entrepreneurial personality combining the drive, the original ideas, and the skills necessary to build the fortunes of the firm." In addition: "a growth-oriented chief executive must surround himself with an extremely competent team and delegate considerable authority to them to run the activities of the firm. Teamwork, as distinct from dysfunctional struggles for power, is critical." These elements are difficult to assess even with on-site visits. However, Fisher makes another suggestion useful to analysts without the capability to do on-site visits: "Attention must be paid to attracting competent managers at lower levels and to training them for larger responsibilities. Succession should largely be from the available talent pool. The need to recruit the chief executive from outside is a particularly dangerous sign." In effect, the analyst needs to examine the management structure in detail and determine the method of selection. Hiring a CEO from outside the firm is usually a very negative signal.

Though Fisher's simple how-to style is relatively easy to follow, the approach sometimes suffers from lack of precision. For example, Fisher makes the recommendation: "The entrepreneurial spirit must permeate the organization." Another such recommendation is: "Successful firms usually have some unique personality traits – some special ways of doing things that are particularly effective for their management team. This is a positive not a negative sign." Similarly, Fisher makes the vague recommendation: "Management must recognize and be attuned to the fact that the world in which they are operating is changing at an ever increasing rate. Every accepted way of doing things must be reexamined periodically, and new, better ways sought. Changes in managerial approaches involve necessary risks, which must be recognized, minimized and taken." Fortunately, Fisher rarely wrote in the abstract and usually illustrated recommendations with examples. On the topic of managerial adjustment to change, Fisher (1975) uses the example of Dow Chemical Company. A number of the key initiatives Fisher identified were dividing management into five separate groups organized along geographical lines and the expenditure of large sums for pollution control.

Not all of Fisher's recommendations on management were difficult to identify. For example, Fisher made observations about the general workforce: "There must be a genuine, realistic, conscious and continuous effort to have employees at every level, including the blue collar workers, believe that their company is really a good place to work. Employees must be treated with reasonable dignity and decency. The firm's work environment and benefits programs should be supportive of motivation. People must feel they can express grievances without fear and with reasonable expectation of appropriate attention and action." Fisher's example of this aspect of the people factor was the "people effectiveness program" at Texas Instruments, a key element in the success of that semiconductor manufacturer. Another example of these management issues was Motorola which pioneered the "management training institutes" model. Another Fisher "people factor" is the suggestion: "Management must be willing to submit to the disciplines required of sound growth. Growth requires some sacrifice of current profits to lay the foundation for worthwhile future improvement."

Fisher's (1975, p. 28) third dimension is concerned with: "the degree to which there does or does not exist *within the nature of the business itself* certain inherent characteristics that make possible above-average profitability for as long as can be seen in the future." As such, Fisher is concerned with **essential business characteristics.** There are many facets to this element. For example, Fisher observes: "Although managers rely heavily on return of assets in considering new investments, investors must recognize that historic assets stated at historic costs distort comparisons of firms' performance and can be highly misleading. Favorable profit to sales ratios, notwithstanding differences in turnover ratios, may be a better indicator of the safety of an investment, particularly in an inflationary environment." This suggestion puts flesh on the Rappaport and Mauboussin emphasis on "sales growth" and "operating profit margins" (see section 8.1). In this regard, Fisher extends the analysis well beyond the company level to consider industry dynamics: "High margins attract competition, and competition erodes profit opportunities. The best way to mute competition is to operate so efficiently that there is no incentive left for the potential entrant."

How is a firm to obtain and maintain industry leadership? Fisher identifies a number of answers to this question. Leading firms need to have a streamlined management structure because: "Efficiencies of scale are often counterbalanced by the inefficiencies of bureaucratic layers of middle management." Given Fisher's strong emphasis on product development and marketing, it is not surprising that, for Fisher: "Getting there first in a new product market is a long step towards becoming the leading firm in the industry. Some firms are better geared to be there first." As for maintaining leadership, Fisher (1975, p. 31) maintains: "when a company clearly becomes a leader in its field, not just in dollar volume but in profitability, it seldom gets displaced from this position as long as its management remains highly competent." **Leaders persist** and, if adequate attention is paid to the activities of the management that got the firm into the leadership position, then the investment gains associated with leadership will be sustainable.

However, product market assessment is not a static exercise: "Products are not islands. There is an indirect competition, for example, for consumers' dollars. As prices change, some products may lose attractiveness even in well-run, low cost companies." Fisher is suspicious of the potential profitability of companies that attempt to make inroads into established markets. "It is hard to introduce new, superior products in market arenas where established competitors already have a strong position. While the new entrant is building the production, marketing power, and reputation to be competitive, existing competitors can take strong defensive actions to regain the market threatened. Innovators have a better chance of success if they combine technology disciplines, e.g. electronics and a highly specialized area of chemistry, in a way that is novel relative to existing competitive competencies." Despite sometimes being considered the father of "growth investing," Fisher was not fixated on technology: "Technology is just one avenue to industry leadership. Developing a consumer franchise is another. Service excellence is still another. Whatever the case, a strong ability to defend established markets against new competitors is essential for a sound investment."

Fisher's fourth dimension goes beyond company and industry analysis to incorporate *the value of the stock* into the analysis. To make the connection between the company and the stock value, Fisher uses the P/E ratio. This dimension connects the industry and company analysis with investment strategy. It is one step to identify excellent companies, it is another step to connect this analysis with buy and sell decisions. Though this step is examined in considerable detail in section 8.3, a brief overview would recognize that Fisher is, probably, as close to Keynes as to GDC in interpreting common stock pricing. Fisher (1975, p. 42) recognizes that the common stock price for a given company is strongly dependent on the often "unrealistic appraisal" of the financial community: "*Every significant price move of any individual common stock in relation to stocks as a whole occurs because of a changed appraisal of that stock by the financial community.*" Stocks go in and out of favor. It may take months or years for an unrealistic expectation by the financial community to be corrected, typically followed by an over-correcting for the previous over (under) estimate.

For Fisher, the best protection against this potentially capricious valuation is to purchase stocks in companies with continuing upward movement in earnings. Even when such companies are out of favor with the financial community, sooner or later the earnings movement will be justified with prices that reflect the correct valuation. The best possible stock to buy is one that is out of favor and rates high on the first "three dimensions." Over time, this type of stock will benefit both from increases in the P/E and from earnings growth. For example, a stock with a P/E of 10 and earnings per share of $1 will increase 400% in value if the P/E rises to 20 while the earnings per share increases to $2. The next most attractive stock to buy is a stock that has "a price-earnings ratio reasonably in line with these fundamentals." This stock will not benefit from the upward revision of the P/E but will still benefit from the earnings growth. Even if the P/E is overvalued, the long term benefit of earnings growth associated with companies rating high on the first three dimensions is sufficient to warrant retaining such stocks (but not purchasing with "new funds") over stocks with P/E ratios that "seem cheap" but do not rank highly on the first three dimensions.

7.3   WHAT IS VALUE INVESTING?

Warren Buffett on value investing

McCloskey (1985, 1994) raises a philosophical quandary for Finance academics and practitioners, rhetorically known as the American question. To paraphrase McCloskey, the American question can be stated: "If you're so smart, why ain't you rich?" If the American question is a concern, a sensible, if inexact, approach to security analysis is to identify those individuals who have excelled in the investment profession and to examine the methods and strategies that those individuals have used to achieve success. Arguably, the individual who has excelled above all others is Warren Buffett, the "*oracle of Omaha*," reported by *Forbes* magazine to be the second richest person in the world.[16] Given Buffett's track record, it is not surprising that there are numerous books detailing his investment practices, e.g., Hagstrom (1995, 2000), Lowe (1994), Cunningham (2002). Examination of these sources reveals a number of confusions surrounding Buffett's approach to investing and the so-called "value investing" approach. While it is common for proponents of value investing, e.g., Greenwald et al. (2001), to claim that Buffett is a "value investor," others, including Buffett himself, disagree. In the end, it seems that such confusions originate because value investing is not a homogeneous concept.

Buffett describes the general security selection strategy used at Berkshire Hathaway as (Cunningham 2001, p. 92):

> Our equity investing strategy remains little changed from what it was when we said in the 1977 annual report: "We select our marketable securities in much the way we would evaluate a business for acquisition in its entirety. We want the business to be one (a) that we can understand; (b) with favorable long-term prospects; (c) operated by honest and competent people; and (d) available at a very attractive price." We have seen cause to make only one change to this creed: Because of both market conditions and our size, we now substitute "an attractive price" for "a very attractive price."

Of these basic principles, (d) corresponds closely with the description of "value investing" proposed by Greenwald (2001, p. 4): "the central process of value investing is disarmingly simple. A value investor estimates the fundamental value of a financial security and compares that value to the current price ... if the price is lower than value by a sufficient margin of safety, the investor buys the security." This approach is "the master recipe of Graham and Dodd investing." Using this approach, value investing follows the general guidelines set out by Graham and Dodd, adjusted for the "unique flavor" of the specific descendants.

Adherents of modern Finance, e.g., Fama and French (1998), have adopted the common terminology of market practitioners distinguishing "value investing" from "growth investing." For example, a search on Bloomberg (www.bloomberg.com) for the names of mutual funds that have "value" in the fund title reveals 1688 value funds.[17] With names like "American Century Small Cap Value Fund" (ACVIX) and "Armada Large Cap Value Fund" (ALVCX), it appears that most value funds are primarily concerned with equity investments. Similarly, a Bloomberg search for funds with "growth" in the fund title reveals 3121 funds, with name like "Advance Capital 1 Equity Growth Fund" (ADEGX) and "AIM Emerging Markets Growth Fund" (EMECX). As Buffett observes: "most analysts feel they must choose between two approaches customarily thought to be in opposition: 'value' and 'growth.' Indeed, many investment professionals see any mixing of the two terms as a form of intellectual cross dressing." Buffett explicitly objects to the conventional distinction between value and growth.

For Buffett, *the distinction between value and growth* is based on "fuzzy thinking." This follows because: "Growth is *always* a component in the calculation of value, constituting a variable whose importance can range from negligible to enormous and whose impact can be negative as well as positive." The semantics of "value investing" are also confusing to Buffett:

> the very term "value investing" is redundant. What is "investing" if it is not the act of seeking value at least sufficient to justify the amount paid? Consciously paying more for a stock than its calculated value – in the hope that it can soon be sold for a still higher price – should be labeled speculation (which is neither illegal, immoral nor – in our view – financially fattening).

All this might seem a little confusing. How is it that proponents of value investing identify Buffett as an example of the approach, while Buffett does not recognize the affiliation? How is it that value investing differs from growth investing when growth is an essential component of value? The answers to these types of questions can be traced to the lack of agreement about what value investing is.

Buffett has, over the years, consistently attacked various aspects of modern Finance.[18] His interpretation of value investing has a modern Finance flavor to it:

> Typically, [value investing] connotes the purchase of stocks having attributes such as a low ratio of price to book value, a low price-earnings ratio, or a high dividend yield. Unfortunately, such characteristics, even if they appear in combination, are far from determinative as to whether an investor is indeed buying something for what it is worth and is therefore truly operating on the principle of obtaining value in his investments. Correspondingly, opposite characteristics – high ratio of price to book value, a high price-earnings ratio, and a low dividend yield – are in no way inconsistent with a "value" purchase.

Modern Finance is keen to reduce "value investing" to the assessment of measures identified by Buffett, such as the price-to-book ratio, because this facilitates sorting large numbers of stocks into groups for the purpose of empirically testing. Buffett adopts this interpretation and, seemingly, identifies value investing with using specific accounting/market price measures to make investment decisions. While this interpretation might be appropriate for pedagogical purposes, there is a wide range of schemes and strategies that fall within the scope of value investing. To dismiss value investing on the basis of the interpretation given in modern Finance seems misguided.

Buffett makes a similar (mis)interpretation of the "growth" approach. Buffett seems to interpret the growth approach as equivalent with increasing in size (Cunningham 2001, p. 93):

> business growth, per se, tells us little about value. It's true that growth often has a positive impact on value, sometimes one of spectacular proportions. But such an effect is far from certain. For example, investors have regularly poured money into the domestic airline business to finance profitless (or worse) growth. For these investors, . . . the more the industry has grown, the worse the disaster for owners.

Excluding a number of special cases, e.g., Southwest Airlines (LUV), it is unlikely that many growth investors would select the airline industry as a candidate for investing opportunities. Buffett does identify an essential feature of the "growth approach":

"Growth benefits investors only when the business in point can invest at incremental returns that are enticing – in other words, when each dollar used to finance the growth creates over a dollar of long-term market value." Buffett is correct in observing: "In the case of a low return business requiring incremental funds, growth hurts the investor." However, it would be difficult to find many advocates of the growth approach looking for companies in low return businesses.

If Buffett is a value investor, then what type of approach does he recommend? Identifying the discounted cash flow model of Williams (1938) as a key starting point, Buffett states the general model:

> The investment shown by the discounted-flows-of-cash calculation to be the cheapest is the one that the investor should purchase – irrespective of whether the business grows or doesn't, displays volatility or smoothness in its earnings, or carries a high price or a low [price] in relation to its current earnings or book value. Moreover, though the value equation has usually shown equities to be cheaper than bonds, that result is not inevitable. When bonds are calculated to be the more attractive investment, they should be bought.

While Buffett's support for the J.B. Williams approach is comforting, it is not too revealing. A similar statement applies to the suggested strategy for picking a business: "the best business to own is one that over an extended period can employ large amounts of incremental capital at very high rates of return. The worst business to own is one that must, or *will*, do the opposite – that is, consistently employ ever greater amounts of capital at very low rates of return." As Buffett recognizes, the trick comes in putting all this together into practice.

A key practical difficulty with the discounted cash flow model is estimating the future cash flows. This is where Buffett's tenet about investing in businesses that the investor can understand comes into play. In Buffett's case, this means that the business is "relatively simple and stable in character." If businesses are complex and operating in business areas that are constantly changing, then it is difficult to make estimates of future cash flows. In addition, Buffett uses the following "equally important" prescription:

> we insist on a margin of safety in our purchase price. If we calculate the value of a common stock to be only slightly higher than its price, we're not interested in buying. We believe this margin-of-safety principle, so strongly emphasized by Ben Graham, to be the cornerstone of investment success.

These three elements, invest in companies that are capable of being understood, select the investment shown by the DCF model to be the "most attractive" and use the margin-of-safety principle, are the keys to the Buffett approach to value investing.

Techniques of value investing

There is so much confusion about the precise definition of value inventing that it is not surprising someone as well informed about investing as Warren Buffett has a slanted view of this approach. For example, consider two recent books on "value investing,"

Whitman (1999) and Greenwald et al. (2001). Whitman (p. 3) claims: "Value investing is different from other kinds of investing . . . The underlying approaches to and goals of value investing differ quite materially from those . . . that are part of fundamental analysis as described in the various editions of *Security Analysis* by Benjamin Graham, David Dodd, and Sidney Cottle, popularly known as Graham and Dodd." Greenwald et al. (pp. 3–4) take precisely the opposite view and refer to: "Value investing in the manner initially defined by Benjamin Graham and David Dodd . . . A value investor estimates the fundamental value of a financial security and compares the value to the current price . . . If the price is lower than value by a sufficient margin of safety, the value investor buys the security. We can think of this formula as the master recipe of Graham and Dodd value investing." Another definition of value investing is found in modern Finance, where value investing has been reduced to determining whether key ratios such as the dividend yield, the *P/E* ratio and the *P/BV* are low relative to other stocks.

As discussed previously, modern Finance identifies value investing with the examination of certain key ratios. Typically, value stocks have high dividend yield, low *P/E* and low price/book ratios compared to other stocks while stocks with low dividend yield, high *P/E* and high price/book ratios are considered to be "growth stocks." These criteria are often supplemented by the requirement that stocks with zero or negative criteria values are excluded from comparison. For example, Dimson et al. (2002, p. 139) observe: "To simplify computation of the value-growth premia, it is common to focus on companies whose dividends, earnings or book values are all positive before entering an index of value or growth stocks." To practitioners, the exclusion of stocks that have negative earnings or no dividend payout may seem odd in a comparison of growth vs. value stocks. However, as with most "knowledge" evaluations, it is better to examine the results that are produced than to condemn the methodology at the outset. Modern Finance is concerned with obtaining information about averages across stocks (see section 1.3), not with the evaluation of individual stocks.

Dimson et al. (2002, ch. 10) provide an overview of results for stock groups that are sorted annually according to the modern Finance value measures. To assess the performance of high dividend yield, over a 1926–2000 sample, Dimson et al. identify the 30% of US stocks that had the highest yield. The annualized return over the sample is compared with the 30% of lowest dividend yield stocks. Stocks paying no dividends are not included in the sample. The results of the averaging exercise indicate: "The annualized returns on the high [dividend] yield companies is 12.2 percent, compared with 10.4% for the low [dividend] yield stocks." This difference is too large to be explained by the difference in the tax rates for dividend income versus capital gains. These results about the *long term* relationship between dividend yields are consistent with those obtained from other studies, e.g., Litzenberger and Ramaswamy (1979), Hodrick (1992), Naranjo et al. (1998) and Wu and Wang (2000) to name only a few. Yet, these results are contradicted by Wolf (2000, p. 29) which uses a more sophisticated estimation procedure and a post-WWII sample to determine: "no convincing case for the predictability of stock returns from dividend yields can be made."

Disentangling the connection between stock returns and dividend yields is complicated by a number of issues. In particular, there is the substantive change in dividend

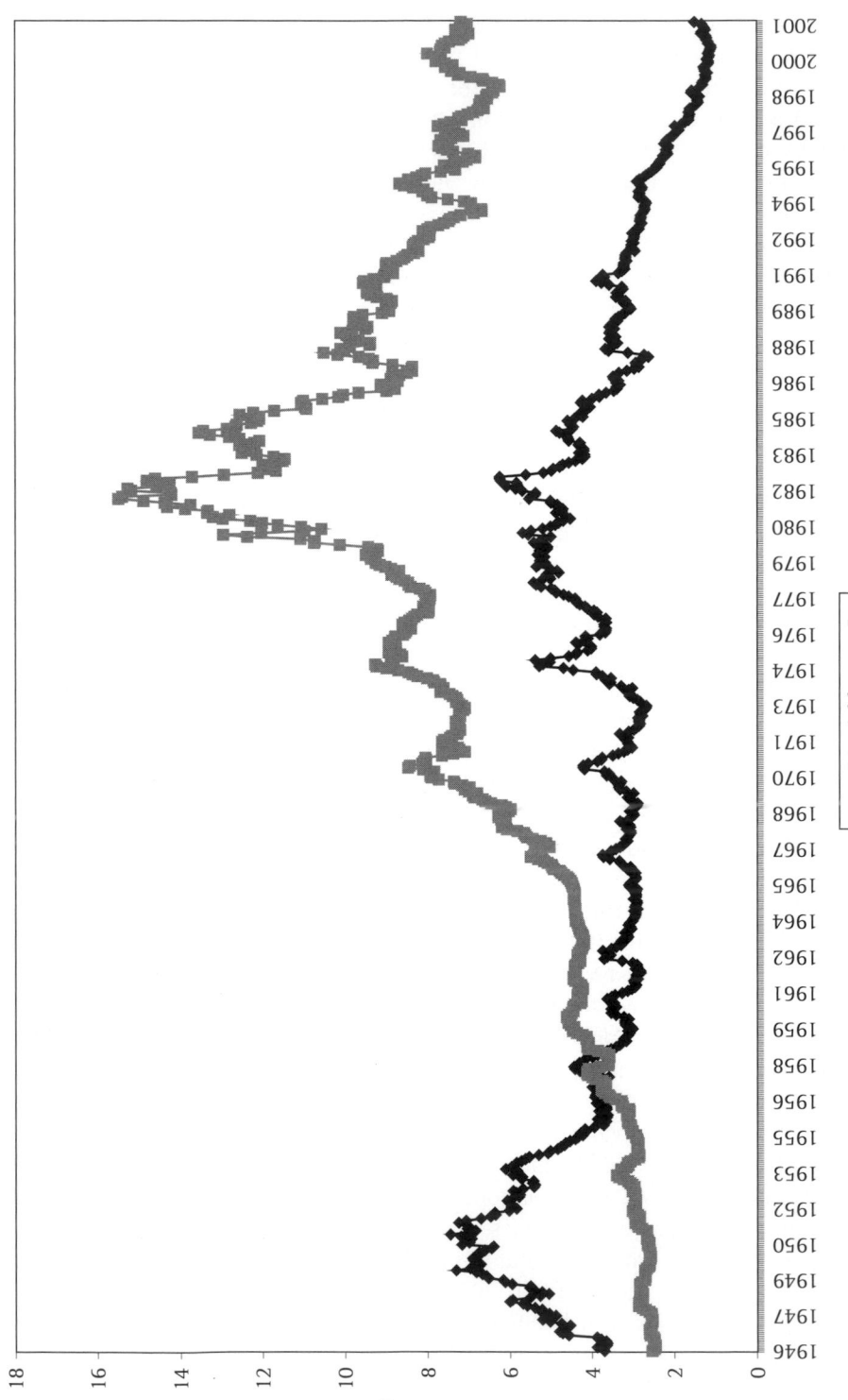

Figure 7.1 Dividend yields and AAA nominal bond yields

yields that has emerged in the post-World War II period (see figure 7.1). Starting around 1950, there has been a secular decline in dividend yields relative to nominal bond yields. In 1958, dividend yields fell below bond yields for the first time challenging conventional wisdom that this was a strong signal that stocks were overvalued. Since 1958, dividends yields have stayed below, usually substantially below, the nominal bond yield. In addition, at least since Lintner (1956), it has been recognized that firms tend to maintain a relatively stable level of dividends over time, increasing dividends to the "target payout ratio" only when an increase in earnings is judged to be permanent. This means that the "true" dividend is not directly observed, creating an unresolved statistical "errors in variables" problem. In addition, there are theoretical difficulties with the relationship, i.e., Miller and Modigliani (1961) demonstrated that, in perfect capital markets, the *dividend policy of the firm is irrelevant* to the firm's value. All this creates a complicated backdrop to the statistical evidence of a positive long-term relationship between dividend yield and stock returns.

The types of problems that arise with the "evidence" on dividend yields does not extend to another element of the modern Finance model of value investing: *the price-to-book ratio* (P/BV). The statistical evidence in favor of a positive relationship between price-to-book ratio and future stock returns is impressive. For example, Dimson et al. report results for the 1926–2000 sample of US stocks sorted annually by the price-to-book ratio or, in modern Finance terminology, the "book-to-market" ratio. Dimson et al. find: "The high book-to-market portfolio contains the 30 percent of stocks that rank highest on this criterion; the low book-to-market group contains the 30 percent of stocks that rank lowest . . . The annualized return from 1926–2000 is 13.7 percent for value [high book-to-market] stocks and 10.2 percent for growth [low book-to-market] stocks." Similar empirical results have been reported in numerous other studies. For example, Piotroski (2000) demonstrates the excess return performance of price-to-book portfolios can be improved by using other accounting information to include only financially healthy firms. For a sample of Japanese firms, Garza-Gomez (2001) demonstrate that higher levels of risk play only a weak role in the performance of price-to-book portfolios. In contrast to Piotroski, Griffin and Lemmon (2002) present evidence that the price-to-book effect could be associated with the presence of financially distressed firms.

Confronted with overwhelming statistical evidence, an undeniable obstacle for adherents of logical positivism, adherents of modern Finance have been driven to provide theoretical explanations for the price-to-book effect. Dimson et al. (2002, p. 141) summarize these developments:

> Why have value stocks outperformed growth stocks? There are three schools of thought. One is that investors become enthused about companies with good prospects, and bid their prices up to unrealistic levels . . . Another possibility is that since stock values are often for distressed companies, their higher returns are simply a reward for the greater risks they impose on investors . . . The third possibility . . . is that the outcome is simply a chance event: Siegel (1998) attributes the post-1963 value-growth premium to the 1973–83 oil price rise and its impact on large oil firms, an event that is not recurrent.

The first explanation is consistent with Fisher's observations about "stocks going in and out of favor." At any given time there are stocks that are overpriced and the bulk of these would appear as high price-to-book firms. While there may be some outstanding companies in the high price-to-book group, these companies would be less likely to appear than "overvalued" companies.

The investment strategy associated with "modern Finance value investing" differs significantly from the portfolios of "value investors" motivated by Graham and Dodd (see section 7.4). Assuming that the reported statistical results are correct, then what process is required to translate these results into superior portfolio performance? To generate the observed statistically significant excess returns associated with, say, low price-to-book ratios, the analyst begins with a large sample of stocks, e.g., the S&P 500 or all stocks traded on the NYSE. This sample of stocks is then segmented into, say, decile groupings ranked by P/BV (or P/E or dividend yield). The equally weighted portfolio of stocks defined by the decile with the lowest P/BV is then purchased on the start date, say, January 1. Following Piotroski (2000), a further refinement can be achieved by doing additional filtering of the stocks in the portfolio using other types of accounting information to ensure that only "financially strong," low P/BV firms are selected. The portfolio is then held for a fixed period, say, 1 year. The sample is then resorted and firms no longer in the lowest P/BV decile are sold and those now in the lowest decile are purchased. This process is repeated until the investment horizon is reached and the portfolio is liquidated.

A key step in this modern Finance value investing scenario occurs with the annual resorting process. According to Fisher (1975, p. 43) this resorting process would result in trading activities that are ill advised:

> In my opinion, there are important reasons . . . stocks [of outstanding companies] should be retained, even though their prices seem too high: If the fundamentals are genuinely strong, these companies will in time increase earnings not only enough to justify present prices but to justify considerably higher prices. Meanwhile, the number of truly attractive companies in regard to the first three dimensions is fairly small. Undervalued ones are not easy to find. The risk of making a mistake and switching into one that seems to meet all of the first three dimensions but actually does not is probably considerably greater for the average investor than the temporary risk of staying with a thoroughly sound but currently overvalued situation until genuine value catches up with current prices.

Armed only with heuristic arguments derived from years of market experience, Fisher (1975, p. 40) observes that many investors can be found:

> who over the years have prospered mightily from holding the right stocks for considerable periods of time. Their success may be due to understanding of basic investment rules. Or it may be due to just plain good luck. However, the common denominator in this success has been the refusal to sell certain unusual high-quality stocks simply because each has had such a sharp fast rise that its price-earnings ratio [or price-to-book ratio] looks high in relation to that to which the investment community has become accustomed.

While both the Graham and Dodd value investor and the modern Finance value investor or the Fisher value/growth investor may use the price-to-book ratio to do the security analysis used to identify investment opportunities, the implementation of the investment strategies differs dramatically.

Fisher sees "value" in companies, not in valuation ratios. It is not that Fisher ignores this information, rather, Fisher feels companies that are strong on the first three dimensions can still be successful investments even if valuation ratios indicate the stock is "overpriced." Fisher is a long term buy-and-hold investor in the common stock of a small number of companies. This is in contrast with both the modern Finance value investor and the Graham and Dodd value investor. Following Greenwald et al. (2001, p. 3) there are three key characteristic to being a *Graham and Dodd value investor*: the belief that market prices at any point in time are subject to "significant and capricious movements"; that there are "intrinsic values" for securities that are relatively stable, that can be identified through fundamental analysis and that the market price will ultimately come to reflect; and, an investment strategy of estimating the intrinsic value and purchasing the security when this estimated intrinsic value is below the market price by an appropriate *"margin of safety"* will produce superior returns in the long-run. This approach may involve holding a sizeable number of securities and selling the securities when market prices are at or above intrinsic value. This may or may not involve a long-term buy-and-hold.

Given the conventional distinction between "value" and "growth" strategies, can Fisher be considered a value investor? The essence of Fisher's approach is well defined because there is only the opinions of one person to examine. The emphasis on company characteristics and the overall approach is concerned with the identification of a small number of high growth companies. Hence, Fisher can be considered a growth stock investor. However, there are a large number of Graham and Dodd value investors that adhere to the key characteristics of the intrinsic value approach to investing but do have significantly different styles of implementing the approach. These styles vary across: methods of selecting stocks for valuation; techniques for estimating the intrinsic value; criteria for setting the margin of safety; restrictions on the portfolio specification and so on. Included in the list of possible areas of divergence within the value investing category are: the amount of diversification; how the value weights for each security are determined; whether fixed income securities will be included in the portfolio; and, criteria for deciding when to sell the security.

Fisher took an individualized approach to security selection. As such, even with a broad interpretation, it is not possible to classify Fisher as a Graham and Dodd value investor, if only because of Fisher's lack of adherence to the margin of safety principle. Fisher will not sell stocks that are "overvalued" using measures such as the P/E ratio. The objective for Fisher is to find excellent companies not to troll the market for stocks that undervalued using a DCF model. In a sense, Fisher does see excellent companies as "undervalued" even if the conventional valuations using, say, the P/E ratio would indicate otherwise. There is a margin of safety, but this is associated with the market's undervaluation of the true long-run strength of the company, not with an explicit DCF calculation. Whether Fisher is considered to be a value investor is more a question of semantics than of substance. In stressing the connection between company strength and conservation of investment value, *Philip Fisher demonstrates the qualities of a value investor.* In the end, it is difficult to escape Warren Buffett's observation that the emphasis on making a distinction between value and growth investing styles is misguided.

Value investing for special situations

A "*special situation*" is a catch-all expression aimed at capturing instances where conventional valuation techniques either do not apply or have to be adjusted significantly. In general, a special situation will depend on the valuation model and investment philosophy being used by the analyst. However, as it is conventional to use a DCF model for valuation, then special situations arise where the process of discounting expected cash flows either cannot be done, e.g., there are no cash flows to discount in the foreseeable future, or the expected cash flows are too difficult to determine in the usual fashion and some other valuation methodology is more appropriate, e.g., due to substantial material changes in the structure of the firm. From this perspective, the classic special situation is a firm in bankruptcy or about to enter bankruptcy due to severe financial distress. For a bankrupt firm facing liquidation, a DCF model is not too useful because the only expected net cash flows to discount are the distributions that will be made from the sale of assets. Firms in severe financial distress also pose difficulties for DCF models because the expected cash flows will be negative for the foreseeable future and there is the need to estimate the probability of bankruptcy and the type of bankruptcy filing, e.g., Chapter 7 vs. Chapter 11 (see section 4.4).

Depending on the type of DCF model employed, other potential kinds of special situations could include: privately held firms and firms about to go public; highly speculative stocks; firms that are going to be liquidated; certain types of mergers, acquisitions and recapitalizations; arbitrage operations; and, firms with significant amounts of intangible assets, product options or untraded warrants. It is even possible to include securities of firms in emerging markets or the natural resource sector. Special situations require either different valuation models than the conventional DCF model or using DCF models with unconventional adjustments. In particular, such alternative investment models include: *asset valuation* models; *breakup or liquidation* assessment techniques; *acquisition value* models; and, *cash-burn* models. Asset valuation models are applicable when asset values predominate in determining security prices, e.g., in situations where there is no observable cash flow or, as in the case of many natural resource companies, the observable cash flow is small relative to the asset base. Acquisition value models are applicable to valuation of takeover candidates, including leveraged buyout candidates. Breakup or liquidation assessment techniques are applicable to valuation of bankruptcies, equity carve-outs and the like. Finally, cash-burn models are applicable to technology startups, such as small biotechs and dot.coms.

In general, *asset valuation models* are not a competitor to DCF analysis, just an alternative approach that can be used to achieve the same endpoint. As illustrated in section 7.1, the residual claim represented by the common stock has both a "stock" and a "flow" component. In DCF analysis, it is the net cash flows generated by the stock of assets that determines the estimate of the firm's value. This approach is the most direct and appropriate avenue to estimating intrinsic value when it can be implemented. Alternatively, it is possible to estimate a market value of the assets and net the estimated market value of liabilities to determine an intrinsic market value for equity. Presumably, the market value of the assets of a firm would reflect the ability of those assets to generate the cash flows that are being valued in DCF analysis. However, there are numerous problems that can arise in determining an estimated market value for assets. For example, many types of assets are firm specific, non-traded or difficult to assess. Such assets pose a problem of estimating a market value. In addition, the cash flows generated by assets are often not the result of mechanistic activities but depend fundamentally on the effectiveness of "the people factor" to utilize those assets. Again, this poses problems for using asset values to estimate an intrinsic value for equity.

Because of the difficulties with arriving at intrinsic values, asset values are often largely ignored in "value investing." GDC (1962, p. 551) recognized this point:

> The basic fact is that – except in certain limited parts of the common-stock universe – asset values are virtually ignored in the stock market. Not only that; there is a sense in which tangible asset values are a negative factor in the company's exhibit. For, given any amount of earnings, the larger the net worth, the lower the profitability or percent earned on capital; hence the less favorable the showing. There is a temptation to accept this verdict of the market place and to confine our treatment of the asset factor to exceptional cases or the special areas in which the net worth can clearly be shown to exert an influence on average price.

The special areas identified by GDC as applicable for asset valuation or using asset valuation to supplement intrinsic value calculations based on DCF are: privately held corporations or partnerships; public utility companies; financial companies; natural resource companies; small initial public offerings; and companies where the price-to-book ratio lies outside the "roughly drawn" "normal range" of $\frac{2}{3}$ to 2. In contrast to "value investing" in modern Finance where the price-to-book ratio plays such an important role, GDC are not strong proponents of using book value to do valuations because of the numerous problems that can crop up with this measure.

The one situation where GDC (1962, pp. 561–6) were strong proponents of selecting common stocks using asset values was the *"net-current-asset value" rule*:

> We feel on more solid ground in discussing those cases in which the market price or computed value based on earnings and dividends is less than the *net current assets* applicable to common stock . . . From long experience with this type of situation we can say that it is always interesting and that the purchase of a diversified group of companies on the "bargain basis" is almost certain to result profitably within a reasonable period of time.

The relevant calculation involved here requires the deduction of all obligations and preferred stock from the working capital of the firm to determine the "net" current asset balance available to common stock. Though it is unusual in US stock markets to find companies with a market value of equity below net current asset value, there are some instances where such companies can be found in international markets. If such a company or group of companies is presently identified in US markets, there likely would be some significant offsetting factor, such as poor future earnings prospects requiring the cash and near-cash assets to be paid out in the near future to sustain firm operations. This type of situation is best examined using a "cash-burn" valuation model.

While not too useful in modern stock markets, this net current asset rule does have considerable historical interest, if only to illustrate how valuation practices are not immutable. GDC (1962, p. 562) provide a useful discussion:

> The historical development of the [net current asset] relationship has been interesting. Before the 1920's, common stocks selling under current-asset value were practically unknown. During the "new-era" market, when prime emphasis was placed on prospects to the exclusion of other factors, a few issues in depressed industries sold below their working capital. In the Great Depression of the early 1930's this phenomenon became widespread. Our computations show that about 40 percent of all industrial companies on the New York Stock Exchange were quoted at some time in 1932 at less than their net current assets. Many issues were actually sold for less than their net cash assets alone. Writing about this situation in 1932, we stated that the market prices as a whole seemed to indicate that American business was "worth more dead than alive." It seemed evident that the market had carried its pessimism much too far – to compensate, no doubt, for its reckless optimism of the 1920's.

By 1937, at the end of a run-up in stock prices, GDC estimate that there were few "net current asset" plays in the market but in the recession that preceded WWII, about 20% of all industrial stocks were selling below net current asset values. GDC suggest that from the early 1920s to the period leading up to the bull market of the 1960s, the fraction of shares in the stock market selling below net current asset value was a useful indicator of market strength or weakness. GDC also observe that it was not always the case that poor earnings prospects drove prices down to "too low" a level. In particular, during 1946–50, many stocks traded below net current asset values due to the accumulation of cash from high levels of earnings that were not correctly valued. Barring a brief period during the 1970s, since the early 1960s the net current asset rule has had little application as companies no longer trade at such low price levels relative to asset valuations.

The "net current asset" rule can be interpreted as a form of *liquidation assessment technique.* For GDC, net current assets provide a "minimum liquidating value," a conservative lower bound for computing the value of a company to be liquidated. Losses on working capital associated with converting these assets to cash are typically offset by the gains associated with the sale of assets from the property, plant and equipment account, as well as other miscellaneous assets. Hooke (1998, p. 385) describes the general process of doing a liquidation valuation:

> In performing a liquidation analysis, you examine the worth of each asset category in a quick sell-off, aggregate these liquidation values, and subtract from this sum the estimated cost of closing the business and paying off its liabilities . . . From this [value] must then be subtracted your time-adjusted rate of return requirement.
>
> Unless the business has substantial intangible assets such as well-respected brand-names, exclusive patents or quasi-monopoly operating rights, the first "back of the envelope" evaluation focuses on historical balance sheet financial data. For each balance sheet item, you determine an estimated range of "liquidated value" percentages, which are based on experiences for similar businesses. Later on, after further study, these percentages are adjusted to include the new information.

This general scheme needs to take account of additional factors such as: the uncertainty associated with the liquidation values; the "burn rate" on cash and near-cash assets to pay for earnings losses that the firm will sustain between the valuation date and the liquidation date; and whether there are any third parties that would be willing to acquire the firm's assets at a "going concern" price rather than at liquidation value.

Almost all liquidations are the result of financial distress or bankruptcy. As such, the equity claim is likely to be relatively small, if not zero. Firms that are in financial distress often pay for ongoing losses by borrowing against tangible assets and future cash flows. The experience of firms such as United Airlines or Bethlehem Steel are useful examples. The accumulation of debt on the balance sheet introduces a fixed cost component into the income statement that further erodes the profitability of the firm creating a downward spiral that is difficult to stop. The final result is the usually more than complete leveraging of the firm's assets leaving only secured debt holders with a claim against assets in liquidation. Hence, liquidation value calculations are usually aimed at determining the fraction of par value that debt holders will receive upon disposal of assets. The common stockholders have some say in the process by controlling the timing of the entry into bankruptcy and the type of bankruptcy filing that is made. Chapter 11 filings hold the possibility that the firm may be reorganized and reemerge from bankruptcy a "leaner and meaner" enterprise with common stockholders still in control. All these twists and turns makes a liquidation analysis a decidedly complicated exercise that extends well beyond simple calculation of disposal value of firm assets. However, disposal value does provide a useful lower bound within which further analysis can take place.

A basic assumption made in DCF analysis is that the firm being valued is a going concern. The cash flows are estimated based on an analyst specific analysis of the characteristics of the company and industry, possibly supplemented by some macro-economic considerations. An alternative method of arriving at a value estimate is to determine the "*acquisition value*" of the firm or, to use a Warren Buffett expression, the "private market value" of the firm. Unfortunately, one of the most difficult exercises in equity valuation is to determine the maximize value that one firm will pay to acquire or merge with another going concern.[19] The protracted infighting over the Compaq-HP merger in 2002 is just one recent example of these difficulties. Walter Hewlett, the son of a founding partner of Hewlett-Packard, was so seriously at odds with the HP management team led by Carla Fiorina over the valuation of Compaq that he initiated a proxy-fight to reject the merger and, when this was unsuccessful, filed suit in an attempt to prevent the merger on grounds that shareholders were misled by inaccurate financial statements concerning the merger. Though the suit was unsuccessful, it does serve as an extreme indicator of the difficulties in assessing the "private market value" for a firm such as Compaq. Ultimately, the determination of acquisition value will depend on a range of factors such as: whether the acquisition is a hostile takeover, friendly takeover or merger; what the synergies would be for the acquiring firm; what the alternative cost of acquiring the assets of the target firm would be; and whether the firm is a potential candidate for a leveraged buyout.

While the liquidation value of a firm is determined by calculating the disposal value of the assets, the acquisition value of a going concern is based on the "reproduction cost" of the assets. Unlike most liquidations where any "hidden assets" have long since been dissipated or sold off, going concerns often have a range of potentially valuable assets that are not recorded in the financial statements. For example, going concerns usually have well established customer relationships that will cost money for a new entrant to develop. Another example concerns R&D infrastructure that may be hard to replicate such as a drug company that has viable products that are in development but not yet generating cash flows. There may be licenses or franchises in place that permit the firm to carry on a business, such as a casino or a television station. Though it may be possible to obtain estimates for some of these hidden assets that were observed in related transactions, when the objective is to determine an estimated value for a going concern that is to be acquired there is a bundling of the hidden assets with tangible assets and management structure that makes the estimated value quite difficult to determine.

Following Hooke (1998, ch. 15) one method of determining an acquisition value is to assess the value of the company as a leveraged buyout (LBO) opportunity. Because an LBO does not place significant synergistic values on the target firm, *the LBO acquisition value* can be considered as a lower bound on the acquisition value. The relevance of the LBO estimate is supported by the approximately 150 investment firms that specialize in LBOs. According to Hooke, there are another 50 to 100 investment banks, venture capital firms and general investment funds that also do some occasional LBO business. The estimated equity value of the top five firms in the industry is approximately $10–$15 billion dollars. Though there is considerable variation in the types of LBO deals, the conventional LBO transaction operates under four principles: as far as possible use other people's money by leveraging the assets and cash flows of the target company; buy at relatively low multiples; search for targets in out-of-fashion industries; and, improve operating performance following acquisition. The actual valuations are done using "guideposts" of 80%/20% (4×) target debt to equity post-acquisition leverage and 1.4× interest coverage on cash flow.

The final special situation valuation method is the *cash-burn model.* This valuation methodology is applicable to firms that have no substantial performing assets and are using the capital raised in an equity issue to achieve a positive earnings situation. Examples where this valuation model could be applied include start-up biotechnology firms, junior mining and oil exploration companies and dot.coms. Because the operating structure of these type of companies is relatively simple, the period to period operating costs are usually quite predictable. After the initial costs of establishing the plant and equipment, the balance sheet will contain a sizeable amount of cash and near-cash assets that will be depleted as the project is in development. Because there is typically no revenues, the development/exploration costs represent a "cash burn" rate that permits a length of time before additional financing, usually another equity issue, is required. For example, a small biotechnology firm could be undertaking to clear the FDA Phase I–III trials in order to produce a drug that can be marketed to the public. The length of time to complete the trials is estimated and used to determine whether the cash-burn will exhaust the available cash and near-cash assets. Combined with an estimate of the revenues generated by the drug if trials are successfully completed, it is possible to determine an approximate value for the company.

7.4   OBSERVATIONS FROM THE CLASSICS

Graham, Dodd and Cottle (1962)

Knowledge can be transmitted in a variety of forms. Consistent with tenets of logical positivism, modern Finance proceeds by providing the logical development of a desired proposition, starting from initial assumptions and proceeding by logical progression until the proposition is established. Where appropriate, the proposition is then subjected to empirical verification. This pedagogical method can be contrasted with, say, the Socratic approach that develops notions using an interrogatory interplay. Various other methods of transmitting knowledge include: the parables of the New Testament; the sayings of Confucius or Sun Tzu; and, the fables of Aesop. Even Grimm's fairy tales or Mother Goose nursery rhymes convey knowledge in a fashion that is at odds with the "scientific" approach of logical positivism. Yet, it is difficult to claim that these different pedagogical methods do not have immense value. It is even possible to go in the other direction and claim that, in the human sciences, the false precision of logical positivism can shed more heat than light on matters. As Warren Buffett (Cunningham 2002, p. 82) observes about the modern Finance approach to measuring risk using beta: "In their hunger for a single statistic to measure risk . . . they forget a fundamental principle: It is better to be approximately right than precisely wrong."

Though justly recognized as a landmark text in security analysis, there is much in Graham, Dodd and Cottle (1962) (GDC) that can be found in other sources such as Ben Graham's, *The Intelligent Investor* (1949). Large parts of Graham and Dodd (1934) appear verbatim in GDC. Being a classic text from the era of "old Finance," GDC shares the institutional and descriptive pedagogical approach that characterizes old Finance (see section 2.4). Though there is a drift towards the approach of modern Finance, GDC is still clearly from a different tradition. The style used involves a heuristic discussion of a particular topic, typically illustrated with a number of practical examples using actual securities. Sometimes, usually where there is the potential for confusion in analyzing a particular situation, the discussion is followed by the statement of an investment principle. GDC is characterized by certain themes that permeate the analysis. These themes connect GDC with earlier versions of the text going back to Graham and Dodd (1934). However, GDC is more than an expanded discussion of earlier versions. Though the essence of the discussion is largely unchanged, there are some significant points of evolution and, on occasion, disagreement.

An important theme in GDC is *the distinction between speculation and investment.* This distinction is inherited directly from Graham and Dodd (1934) where the lessons of the stock market collapse of 1929–1933 and the "new era theory" of common stock investing were still fresh in the air. Though concern with the "new era" theory had been reduced to an historical discussion in GDC, the theme of investment versus speculation persisted: *"An investment operation is one which upon thorough analysis, promises safety of principal and satisfactory return. Operations not meeting these requirements are speculative"* (GDC, p. 49). This is an exact repetition of Graham and Dodd (1934, p. 54). GDC (e.g., pp. 51–2) explicitly recognize that security analysis has considerable limitations in *speculative* situations. Security analysis is "an adjunct rather than . . . a guide to speculation. It is only when chance plays a subordinate role that the analyst can properly speak in an authoritative voice and accept responsibility for the results of his judgments." By acknowledging limitations in the analysis of speculative securities, the range of common stocks and other securities to which the GDC techniques of security analysis apply is relatively narrow. More precisely, common stocks that have "too many uncertainties about its future to permit the analyst to estimate its earning power with any degree of confidence" are speculative in nature because: "a common stock purchase may not be regarded as a proper constituent of a true investment program unless it is possible to show by some rational calculation that it is worth at least as much as the price paid for it."

Another central theme in GDC (p. 105) can be summarized as: "All security analysis involves the analysis of financial statements." This viewpoint is qualified with the proviso: "the weight given to financial material may vary enormously, depending upon the kind of security studied and basic motivation of the prospective purchaser." However, GDC (p. 88) are clear on the relative importance of "quantitative" vs. "qualitative" factors in security analysis. *Quantitative factors* are associated with statistical information from the income statement, balance sheet and additional data on factors such as capacity utilization, unit prices, costs and so on. *Qualitative factors* include: the nature of the business; relative position of the company in the industry; physical, geographical, and operating characteristics; the character of management; the longer term outlook for the unit, industry and general business. The GDC approach to security analysis is fundamentally concerned with how quantitative and qualitative information is combined. On this point there is an apparent divergence of opinion across the various editions.

Comparing GDC with earlier versions, it is apparent that the weight to qualitative factors in security analysis varies considerably. Graham and Dodd (1934, p. 430) maintain: "*Quantitative data are useful only to the extent that they are supported by a qualitative survey of the enterprise.*" In contrast, GDC (p. 86) maintain that quantitative factors are always an essential element of the analysis:

> Broadly speaking, the important quantitative factors lend themselves to much more precise consideration in appraising a specific company than do the qualitative factors. The former are fewer in number, more easily obtainable, and better suited to the forming of definitive conclusions. Furthermore, the financial results themselves epitomize such qualitative elements as the ability of a reasonably long-entrenched management. This point of view does not minimize the importance of qualitative factors in appraising the performance of a company, but it does indicate that a detailed study of them – to be justified – should provide sufficient additional insight to assist significantly in appraising the company.

A further level of ambiguity on this issue is achieved when GDC (p. 50) provide an additional criterion for investment: "*An investment operation is one that can be justified on both qualitative and quantitative grounds.*" This change in emphasis away from qualitative factors towards quantitative factors associated with financial statements was probably due to the substantially increased reliability and availability of this source of information owing to historical developments such as the reform of securities laws that occurred around the time Graham and Dodd (1934) appeared.

Another important theme in GDC carried forward from previous editions, but subjected to change, was the concept of "intrinsic value." Whereas Graham and Dodd (1934, e.g., p. 17) emphasized the "*intrinsic value*" of a stock and provided heuristic methods for determining this "elusive concept" based on examination of a range of factors such as the record of dividends and the ability of earnings to sustain the dividend, GDC (p. 435) adopted the discounted cash flow (DCF) model as the theoretical mechanism for determining the intrinsic value:

> *The Valuation Process Briefly Described.* The standard method of valuation of individual enterprises consists of capitalizing the expected future earnings and/or dividends at an appropriate rate of return. The average earnings will be estimated for a period running ordinarily between five and ten years. In the case of an issue valued as a "growth stock" the projection may be of a terminal year – e.g., four to five years hence – rather than a long term average. The capitalization rate, or multiplier, applied to earnings and dividends, will vary with the quality of the enterprise and will thereby give recognition to the longer-term profit possibilities which cannot be established with precision. Asset values become a significant factor in the appraisal only at the extreme ranges, where either the tangible assets are very low in relation to earnings power value or the net current assets alone exceed the earning power value.

This approach leads GDC to identify the *four basic components of common stock value* identified in section 7.1: *expected future earnings, expected future dividends, capitalization rates and asset values.* The influence of J.B. Williams on GDC is difficult to ignore.

The GDC (pp. 438–441) approach to security analysis integrates the price estimates obtained from the DCF model with the "*margin of safety*" principle and the benefits of diversification: "In our opinion, margin of safety – in the form of an excess of estimated intrinsic value over current market price – is a prerequisite to investing in secondary [and primary] shares."[20] Because the margin of safety is not a guarantee that any given stock will not produce a loss, the diversification principle is also required: "A group of, say, twenty or more common stocks will usually average out the individual favorable and unfavorable developments. For this reason, the diversification or group approach is an integral part of the valuation concept itself." GDC (p. 448) later clarify this number to between twenty and thirty stocks drawn from a list of not more than 100 "primary" common stocks, i.e., large, prosperous and highly capitalized companies with a strong record of earnings. GDC suggest a further restriction on the amount invested in any one industry. The GDC recommendation that common stock portfolios contain "twenty or more" high grade common stocks that would be regularly adjusted is a distinct point of contrast with the recommendations of Philip Fisher.[21]

Though both the margin of safety and diversification concepts are carried forward from previous editions, there is a decided change in tone in GDC. For example, on the diversification principle, Graham and Dodd (1934, p. 320) state: "In our view, the purchase of a single common stock can no more constitute an investment than the issuance of a single policy on a life or a building can properly constitute insurance underwriting." However, GDC (p. 55) substantially qualify this view:

> There is a well-known argument *against* diversification based on Andrew Carnegie's maxim: "Put all your eggs in one basket and watch the basket." We believe this counsel has an application to security investment but only within its strictest interpretation. An investor may concentrate heavily on the shares of one corporation provided that he has a *personal connection* with it – as an executive or a member of a controlling group. Many large fortunes have been built up over the years by such concentration. But where the close personal connection with the company is lacking that policy rarely works out well. When the choice is in fact a very good one, there is a tendency to sell out at a comparatively early stage in the long-term advance. Any other kind of choice will, of course, appear to be a mistaken one during periods of declining prices.

GDC (pp. 447–9) also recommend a form of "*tactical asset allocation*" strategy (see section 10.2) where the composition of the investment portfolio would fluctuate between "an upper limit of 75 percent to be held in common stocks and a lower limit of 25 percent." The proportion held in common stocks at any point in time would be "geared to the analyst-investor's valuation of the DJIA, Standard & Poor's Composite Index, or some other measure of the market." In effect, GDC were advocates of index-tracking market timing strategies. In addition, GDC (p. 446) recommend "the sale of holdings that appear definitely overvalued or replacement of less by more attractive stocks." This implies a shorter holding period than the long-term buy-and-hold horizon of Philip Fisher.

    GDC were intimately aware of the dramatic progression: in securities markets; in the professional practice of security analysis; and in the emerging theories of modern Finance that occurred between 1934 and 1962. As observed above, the acceptance and adoption of valuation techniques for common stocks based on DCF modeling, started by Williams (1938), was explicitly recognized and rationalized. GDC (p. 416) acknowledge the changes that occurred in securities markets, particularly stock markets, during the 1950s, required "new points of view and standards of value":

> Our philosophy and its related standards of value were derived primarily from the actual experience of stock investors (and speculators) during many decades prior to the 1950's. They were consistent with stock-market conditions existing at the time our previous editions were published. We think they proved a useful guide to investors from 1934 through 1954. But, ... the latter half of the 1950's brought record high levels in stock prices and with them new points of view and standards of value. It is a difficult task to examine these new levels and standards as they exist at the beginning of the 1960's and to reach some conclusions as to their validity for investment purposes.

Consistent with the proposed use of DCF for common stock valuation, GDC (p. 434) criticize the observed practice of doing common stock valuations based on a "too abbreviated forecast of probable future earnings – covering generally only the next twelve months ... value cannot soundly be established on the basis of earnings shown over a short period of time."

On the historical evolution of common stocks, GDC (pp. 56–7) observe:

> During the past half-century the investment and speculative characteristics of common stocks as a whole have undergone a series of changes, some of which are as subtle as they are important. Before World War I the typical common stock was basically speculative, for reasons related chiefly to the company itself. The capitalization structure was often top-heavy, the working capital inadequate, the management deficient in various respects, the published information sketchy and unreliable. The junior issue's dividend history was nonexistent or erratic, its earnings subject to wide fluctuations, and its market action to crass manipulation. Virtually, all these defects have been greatly ameliorated or abolished, as far as today's representative common stocks are concerned.

GDC observe that the improvement in investment potential of common stocks led to "an upgrading in the public standing of common stocks generally," leading to the mis-perception that many "speculative" issues are actually of "investment" quality. This mis-perception had been complicated by the rapid pace of technological change that created the "growth stock" and led to more rapid erosion in the core business of certain "primary" stocks due to an inability to adapt to the pace of change. This *technological growth factor* "is not amenable to dependable prediction" and, as a consequence, stocks in the growth category are "fundamentally speculative." In contrast to Philip Fisher, GDC also maintain that the quality of the company alone is an insufficient indication of value without also considering the common stock price: "Strictly speaking, there can be no such thing as an 'investment issue' in the absolute sense, i.e., implying that it remains an investment regardless of price" (GDC p. 50).

Though GDC is generally a more sophisticated and developed treatment of security analysis than Graham and Dodd (1934), there are a number of points where GDC failed to recognize the value contained in the earlier edition and dropped material that still had considerable insight. The discussion of the "new era" theory is one of these cases. Graham and Dodd (1934, p. 307) provide the following description:

> During the post [WWI] war period, and particularly during the latter stage of the bull market culminating in 1929, the public acquired a completely different attitude towards the investment merits of common stocks. Two of the three elements [suitable and established dividend record and a satisfactory backing of tangible assets] lost nearly all of their significance and the third, the earnings record, took on an entirely novel complexion. The new theory or principle may be summed up in the sentence: "The value of a common stock depends entirely upon what it will earn in the future."
>
> From this dictum the following corollaries were drawn: 1. That the dividend rate should have slight bearing upon the value. 2. That since no relationship apparently existed between assets and earning power, the asset value was entirely devoid of importance. 3. That past earnings were significant only to the extent that they indicated what *changes* in the earnings were likely to take place in the future.
>
> This complete revolution in the philosophy of common-stock investment took place virtually without the realization by the stock-buying public and with only the most superficial recognition by financial observers.

It is difficult for a modern observer of equity markets to read these words and not be struck by the similarity of the "new era" theory to the common stock valuation philosophy which appeared during the technology/dot.com bubble that started around 1995 and continued to early 2000, e.g., the "Gorilla Finance" of Moore et al. (1999). Writing in the early 1960s when concerns with the stock market collapse of 1929–33 had largely faded from view, instead of a close examination of the "new era" theory all GDC (p. 57) could muster was a concern about "the shift of investment emphasis from values established by the past record to values to be achieved *solely* by future growth . . . we are skeptical of the ability of all but the most gifted analysts to chart with precision the growth rate of a given company for many years ahead."

Philip Fisher and the growth stock

As astute observers of "real-time" security markets, GDC were acutely aware of the growth stock phenomenon and of the implications that the views of growth stock proponents, such as Philip Fisher, had for the "Graham and Dodd" approach to security analysis. An acknowledged limitation of the GDC approach is the inability to deal with "speculative" securities – and technology driven growth stocks are viewed by GDC as "fundamentally speculative." Despite this, GDC (p. 57) give considerable attention to the emergence and assessment of growth stocks propelled by "the rapid stepping up of technological change":

> This has created opportunities for spectacular growth of profits for many companies, but it has also threatened the position of many others which have fallen behind in the technological race. To some degree these contrary occurrences can be projected well in advance by an unusually competent analyst who does some penetrating research of his own. But, broadly speaking, we think that modern technology has injected an important new factor in the affairs of many companies, which is not amenable to prediction and which for that reason must be recognized as fundamentally speculative.

While explicitly recognizing that "there have been investors capable of making [growth stock] selections with a high degree of accuracy and that they have benefitted hugely from their foresight and good judgment," GDC (p. 426) question "whether or not careful and intelligent investors as a class can follow this policy with fair success."

For GDC, growth stocks present three related questions that require addressing: "First, what is meant by a 'growth company'? Second, can the investor identify such companies with reasonable accuracy? Third, to what extent does the price paid for such stocks affect the success of the program?" GDC (pp. 425–33) give detailed attention to discussing these questions about growth stocks. The possibility of "growth industries" is admitted with "aluminum, electronics, drugs, office equipment, paper, and some branches of chemical manufacture" being explicitly identified. Not surprisingly, GDC are unable to shed much light on the subject. According to GDC, growth stocks are difficult to define, difficult to identify and difficult to tell if the price is too high. The prognosis for growth stocks is cloudy: "if the analysis of growth stocks is pursued with skill, intelligence, consistency and diligent study, it should yield satisfactory results." However, "it must represent the activity of a strong-minded and daring individuals rather than investment in accordance with accepted rules and standards." The incongruence between the "Graham and Dodd" and the "growth stock" approaches is apparent. It follows that, to get an accurate appreciation of security analysis and investment strategy for growth stocks, a leading "advocate" of the approach, such as Philip Fisher, needs to be examined.

Warren Buffett's approach to security selection has been described as 85% Benjamin Graham and 15% Philip Fisher. Given Buffett's substantial personal exposure to Graham, this is an extraordinary complement to Fisher. Closer examination of Buffett's approach to security analysis and investment strategy reveals that the 85%–15% split is, arguably, flattering to Graham. Given that there is considerable overlap in many of the basic notions advanced by Graham and Fisher, it is on points of emphasis and divergence that distinctions can be drawn. For example, Graham proposed methods of determining whether common stock prices were selling below intrinsic value, emphasizing the use of financial statements. In contrast, Fisher is concerned with the characteristics of the business, emphasizing the quality of management and the company's ability to generate sales and profits. Basic Buffett security selection dictums like searching for businesses with excellent management, focusing on a small number of core holdings (because there are only so many outstanding companies) and "buy a business not a stock" are more echoes of Philip Fisher than Ben Graham, though Graham did make passing reference to these concepts as well.

The legendary status achieved by Ben Graham is based at least partly on the phenomenal success of Warren Buffett. Though Graham's various investment firms, such as Graham-Newman, did achieve considerable success, the track record of Warren Buffett and Berkshire Hathaway has taken place in parallel with the emergence and ascendancy of modern Finance in academic circles. As Cunningham (2002, p. 10) observes:

> for more than forty years, Buffett has generated average annual returns of 20% or better, which double the market average. For more than twenty years before that, Ben Graham's Graham-Newman Corp. had done the same thing. As Buffett emphasizes, the stunning performances of Graham-Newman and Berkshire deserve respect: the sample sizes were significant; they were conducted over an extensive time period, and were not skewed by a few fortunate experiences; no data-mining was involved; and the performances were longitudinal, not selected by hindsight.

As discussed in chapter 10, the recent progression of modern Finance has attempted to incorporate quantitative elements of the "Graham" approach into the theoretical apparatus, e.g., Fama and French (1995, 1998). However, this is being done squarely within the positivist framework, without an indepth analysis of the prescriptions and dictums of the individuals whose track records stand as a disturbing contradiction to the underlying foundations of modern Finance.

Though it would seem sensible to have an intellectual history of the "old Finance" approach to security analysis and investment strategy, no such project has been produced. The excellent sources that are available, e.g., Bernstein (1992), tend to emphasize historical developments of theories and to take a viewpoint that is sympathetic to modern Finance. Even given the absence of general sources, it is still somewhat surprising that there has not been more interest sparked in Philip Fisher in academic circles. For example, Siegel (1998) has numerous references to Graham and Buffett but the only two Fishers that are discussed are Irving and Lawrence. The relative obscurity of Philip Fisher speaks to the process by which "knowledge" is generated in academic subjects. Fisher spent his working life outside of academia in the investment industry. His literary contributions are few (Fisher 1958, 1975, 1980) and generally targeted at the trade audience. He did not seek the limelight and usually had only a small, but selective, list of clients. For all but the beginning of his career as a fund manager, he did not need to promote himself to attract clients.

Fisher was not the originator of the "*growth stock*" approach. Though the growth stock phenomenon was widely recognized by the end of the 1950s, the basic concept has origins that predate World War II. For example, GDC (p. 426) examine a report by an investment trust, the National Investors Corporation (NIC), that explicitly identified growth stocks as "the most effective medium in the field of common stocks." This view was supported by "economic analysis and practical reasoning." For NIC, growth stocks were "companies whose earnings move forward from cycle to cycle, and are only temporarily interrupted by periodic business depressions." The modern disagreements over what constitutes a growth stock can be found in numerous contributions during the 1950s, e.g., Anderson (1955), Kennedy (1959). GDC (pp. 427) recommend the definition of Conklin (1958): "In the minds of the investing public, a 'growth stock' is a common stock which has recorded or gives promise of recording, a greater than average appreciation in market price over a span of several years." Bernstein (1956) even argues for a distinction between growth stocks and growth companies. Against this backdrop, a contribution by a successful practitioner of the growth stock approach was bound to have a substantial impact.

Fisher entered the investment industry somewhat later than Graham, though he did have substantive exposure to the "Great Bull Market of the 1920s" having entered the fledgeling Stanford Business School as a first year student in 1927–8. Though he started his own investment firm, Fisher & Company in 1931, this venture was a from-scratch startup in San Francisco by a young entrepreneur with little market experience. While the appearance of Graham and Dodd (1934) solidified Ben Graham's already considerable reputation in the New York financial community, by 1935 Fisher was just stabilizing his client list and achieving a small measure of success. It was not until the 1950s that Fisher rose to national prominence as an security analyst, a reputation that was solidified by Fisher (1958) a book that marks the beginning of systematic identification of the investment characteristics of "growth" stocks. Even though the investment philosophies of both Graham and Fisher were greatly influenced by events surrounding the Great Bull and Great Bear Markets of the late 1920s and early 1930s, there is a distinctly different flavor to their approaches to security analysis and investment strategy.

The popularity of Philip Fisher (1958) in the securities industry is due, at least partly, to the fashion in which the material is presented. Fisher was fond of providing point form summaries of his approach to investment analysis. In Fisher (1958), *fifteen key questions* are provided that need to be answered satisfactorily before a common stock is purchased. These questions, which are similar to those found in Fisher (1975) (see section 7.2) can be summarized as:

1 Do the company's products or services have sufficient market potential to make possible a significant *increase in sales* for at least several years?
2 Does the management have a desire and savvy to continue *developing products or processes* that will further increase total sales potential when the growth potential of current product lines have largely dissipated?
3 In relation to company size, how effective are the company's *research and development* efforts?
4 Does the company have an effective and efficient *sales organization*?
5 Does the company have a viable *profit margin*?
6 What is the company's strategy for maintaining or improving this profit margin?
7 Does the company have superior *labor and personnel* relations?
8 Does the company have superior relationships among the *executives*?
9 Does the company have strength and depth in its management structure?
10 Does the company have adequate cost analysis and *accounting controls*?
11 Are there other aspects of the business, specific to the industry, that will give the security analyst important clues to identifying if the company is outstanding in relation to its *competition*?
12 Does the company have an adequate short-range or a *long-range profit outlook*?
13 Is there potential common stock *dilution* in the foreseeable future, i.e., will the growth of the company require additional equity financing that will dilute the existing common stockholders' benefits from future anticipated growth?
14 Does the *management* willingly provide details about company activities when things are going well, but are reluctant to talk when troubles and disappointments occur?
15 Is the company management of unquestionable integrity and *honesty*?

By themselves, these questions are useful, if not overly revealing. The strength of Fisher (1958) is in the discussion and anecdotes that illustrate these various questions. In contrast to Graham and Dodd (1934), it is apparent that Fisher is "focused" on the characteristics of the company. The general approach can be summarized in the quote: "I don't want a lot of good investments; I want a few outstanding ones."

Though at the time still actively involved with his firm, Fisher (1980) was written when Fisher was well past the conventional age of retirement. The short monograph provides *eight key points in Philip Fisher's investment philosophy.* The key points are summaries, buttressed with practical, hands-on discussion of the various points using examples from his personal experiences. The accompanying discussion is short and largely autobiographical. From the perspective of fundamental analysis, these eight points are sufficiently insightful to warrant specific examination. The first point deals with the elements of the 15 points from Fisher (1958) and the first three dimensions of Fisher (1975):

- Buy into companies that have disciplined plans for achieving dramatic long-range growth in profits and that have inherent qualities making it difficult for newcomers to share in that growth. There are . . . many details, both favorable and unfavorable, that should also be considered in selecting one of these companies.

Fisher then refers to a summary of these ideas that is contained in the first three chapters of Fisher (1975). The essence of these ideas was discussed in section 7.2.

The overlap between the approaches of Graham and Fisher is illustrated in point 2 of Fisher's investment philosophy:

- Focus on buying these companies when they are out of favor; that is, when, either because of general market conditions or because the financial community at the moment has a misconception of its true worth, the stock is selling at prices well under what it will be when its true merit is better understood.

As stated, this recommendation is common sense and is not substantively different than the "Graham and Dodd" margin-of-safety approach. In Fisher (1975, p. 43), this recommendation is expanded to the case where the desired stock is fairly valued and over-valued:[22]

On the lowest end of the risk scale and most suitable for wise investment is the company that measures quite high in regard to the first three dimensions but currently is appraised by the financial community as less worthy, and therefore has a lower price-earnings ratio, than these fundamental facts warrant. Next least risky and usually quite suitable for intelligent investment is the company rating quite high in regard to the first three dimensions and having an image and therefore a price-earnings ratio reasonably in line with these fundamentals. This is because such a company will continue to grow if it truly has these attributes. Next least risky and, in my opinion, usually suitable for retention by conservative investors who own them but not for fresh purchase with new funds are companies that are equally strong in regard to the first three dimensions but, because these qualities have become almost legendary in the financial community, have an appraisal or price-earnings ratio higher than is warranted by even the strong fundamentals.

This explicit statement by Fisher contradicts the perception in modern Finance that "growth" investors bias purchases toward high *P/E* and, presumably, high *P/BV* stocks. Much like "value" investors, "growth" investors want to purchase the desired stocks as cheaply as possible. As illustrated, high P/E stocks are not desirable for "fresh purchase with new funds."

The desire to purchase targeted stocks as cheaply as possible is common sense and is found in virtually all analyses of securities trading and investment activities. The view is not unique to Fisher and GDC. Unlike GDC, Fisher does feel that if the company is good enough then buying the common stock is recommended when it is fairly valued in line with the fundamentals applicable to all companies. In advocating the use of intrinsic value and the margin of safety principle, GDC would seem to be in disagreement with this recommendation, per se, but this is could be due to a difference in semantics. Fisher is *using the P/E ratio to measure value*, i.e., the fourth dimension, while GDC is using DCF to measure intrinsic value. Presumably, Fisher is implying that the growth in earnings from companies that have the strongest fundamentals is not being fully captured by the *P/E*. Where Fisher is saying the *P/E* fairly reflects fundamentals, GDC could say that the intrinsic value is low enough to qualify for purchase using the margin of safety principle. However, the difficulties of estimating the future cash flows for the types of companies Fisher's first three dimensions identify may mean that GDC would not advocate a purchase.[23]

While there are possible interpretations that would have Fisher and GDC agreeing on criteria for purchasing common stocks, on the issue of when to sell there is unambiguous disagreement. GDC want to purchase common stocks that have the estimated intrinsic value less than the price by the margin of safety. These stocks are then held until an overvaluation is observed and then the stock is sold. In contrast, Fisher (1975, p. 43) is a long-term buy and hold investor in favor of retaining stocks "even though their prices seem too high. If the fundamentals are genuinely strong, these companies will in time increase earnings not only enough to justify present prices but to justify considerably higher prices." For Fisher there are only a small number of companies that genuinely qualify for selection using the first three dimensions. Selling such companies because the price reflects an "overvaluation" implies that there are similar companies available for purchase that are "undervalued." Yet this is unlikely due to the small number of such companies. Parking the money from the sale in cash and waiting for a pull back in price requires illusive market timing skills: "it is my observation that those who sell stocks to wait for a more suitable time to buy back these same shares seldom attain their objective."

What criteria does Fisher propose for when to sell a successful stock? Not surprisingly, the criteria are long run and relate to deterioration in the reasons why the stock was purchased in the first place:

- Hold the stock until either (a) there has been a fundamental change in its nature (such as a weakening of management through changed personnel), or (b) it has grown to a point where it no longer will be growing faster than the economy as a whole. Only in the most exceptional circumstances, if ever, sell because of forecasts as to what the economy or the stock market is going to do, because these changes are too difficult to predict. Never sell the most attractive stocks you own for short-term reasons. However, as companies grow, remember that many companies that are quite efficiently run when they are small fail to change management style to meet the different requirements of skill big companies need. When management fails to grow as companies grow, shares should be sold.

Fisher has a shorter horizon for determining whether an initial purchase was legitimate. In this regard, Fisher proposes a "*three year rule*" for any new purchase. If the company has not achieved the objectives set out when the stock was purchased, then it is time to consider selling. This leads to:

- Making some mistakes is as much an inherent cost of investing for major gains as making some bad loans is inevitable in even the best run and most profitable lending institution. The important thing is to recognize them as soon as possible, to understand their causes, and to learn how to keep from repeating the mistakes. Willingness to take small losses in some stocks and to let profits grow bigger and bigger in the more promising stocks is a sign of good investment management. Taking small profits in good investments and letting losses grow in bad ones is a sign of abominable investment judgment. A profit should never be taken just for the satisfaction of taking it.

Fisher basically wants to get in relatively early in the company growth cycle and hold onto the stock until the company has reached the point where future growth is problematic, always keeping a close eye on the first three dimensions. If the initial analysis is later found to be faulty, the position has to be unwound.

From Graham and Dodd (1934, ch. 29) onward, the "Graham and Dodd" approach has struggled with the importance of dividends: "From one point of view, the dividend rate is all-important; but from another and equally valid standpoint it must be considered an accidental and minor factor" (Graham and Dodd, p. 324). Similarly, GDC (p. 487) maintain: "The quality of common stock, which reflects itself in the multiplier applied to current or prospective earnings and dividends, is in most cases largely determined by the dividend record." Yet, GDC (p. 488) are willing to accept: "that a fundamental difference may exist between the appropriate payout policy for average and subaverage companies and that for the exceptional growth issue." Shareholders in growth companies will be better off if the company maintained a policy of complete retention of earnings. Recognizing the potential validity of the Miller and Modigliani (1961) argument on dividends (see section 2.4), GDC observe that "synthetic" dividend cash flows can be obtained by selling a fraction of the stock if desired. In addition, low or no dividend payout can have potential tax advantages for many stockholders due to the lower tax rate on capital gains vs. dividend income.

Fisher recognizes that outstanding companies will often have a real need funds to finance expansion. As a consequence, Fisher recommends:

- For those primarily seeking major appreciation of their capital, de-emphasize the importance of dividends. The most attractive opportunities are most likely to occur in the profitable, but low or no dividend payout groups. Unusual opportunities are much less likely to be found in situations where high percentage of profits is paid to stockholders.

This *low dividend payout aspect of the growth stock* profile is identified in modern Finance as being consistent with a desirable company characteristic advanced by "growth stock" advocates such as Fisher. However, this aspect is not even a necessary condition for Fisher (1975, p. 72): "As long as dividend policy is consistent, so that investors can plan ahead with some assurance, this whole matter of dividends is a far less important part of the investment picture than might be judged from the endless arguments frequently heard about the relative desirability of this dividend policy or that . . . dividend considerations should be given the least, not the most, weight by those desiring to select outstanding stocks." Retained earnings can just as easily be used to "enlarge the inefficient operation rather than to make it better." Allowances for increases in the capital stock can in some cases be achieved through depreciation rates.

Another fundamental point of difference between Fisher and GDC concerns portfolio composition. What is the optimal number of securities to own? On this point Fisher observes:

- There are a relatively small number of truly outstanding companies. Their shares frequently can't be bought at attractive prices. Therefore, when favorable prices exist, full advantage should be taken of the situation. Funds should be concentrated in the most desirable opportunities. For those involved in venture capital and quite small companies, say with annual sales of under $25,000,000, more diversification may be necessary. For larger companies, proper diversification requires investing in a variety of industries with different economic characteristics. For individuals (in possible contrast to institutions and certain types of funds), any holding of over twenty different stocks is a sign of financial incompetence. Ten or twelve is usually a better number. Sometimes the costs of the capital gains tax may justify taking several years to complete a move towards concentration. As an individual's holdings climb toward as many as twenty stocks, it nearly always is desirable to switch from the least attractive of these stocks to more of the attractive. It should be remembered that ERISA stands for Emasculated Results: Insufficient Sophisticated Action.

Whereas GDC recommended holding 20–30 stocks which are rebalanced on a regular basis, Fisher maintains that for individual investors this number is so large as to be "*a sign of financial incompetence.*" There is some need to diversify across industries and in cases where the holdings are in venture capital or small cap situations. The bulk of these holdings will be of the long term buy-and-hold variety.

To those indoctrinated into the modern Finance prescriptions about "efficient diversification," *the approach of holding a narrow stable of winners* will appear to be foolish and misguided. Yet, this approach is not unique to Fisher and can be found in other members of the old Finance school. For example, Loeb (1935; 1965, p. 11) observes: "Diversification is a necessity for the beginner. On the other hand, the really great fortuncs were made by concentration. The greater your experience, the greater your capability for running risks, and the greater your ability to chart your course yourself, the less you need to diversify." Given this, Fisher does maintain that some degree of diversification across industries (and possibly countries) is essential. Hyper-selective investment strategies, such as the Moore et al. (1999) gorilla game which preach investment only in selected technology stocks, are not advisable. Beyond this, the degree and extent of diversification depends on the predisposition of the investor. It is this slippery slope that is a major point of divergence between the views of GDC and those of Fisher.

The Warren Buffett synthesis

A brief overview of the Warren Buffett approach to security analysis and investment strategy was given in section 7.3. Buffett starts from the Graham and Dodd view that securities have an intrinsic value and that for a number of reasons, the prices of securities may not trade at intrinsic value creating trading opportunities. Following Williams (1938), Buffett advocates the use of the discounted cash flow model to estimate the intrinsic value. In order to overcome the difficulties of estimating the future cash flows, Buffett recommends examining only businesses that the analyst is capable of understanding: "You don't have to be an expert on every company or even many. You only have to be able to evaluate companies within your circle of competence. The size of the circle is not very important; knowing its boundaries, however, is vital" (Cunningham 2002, p. 100). Once the cash flows have been determined, the margin-of-safety principle is used to decide whether the security is a buying opportunity. Because there are only a few companies that will meet the appropriate criteria, a Buffett portfolio will have few securities and be relatively inactive in trading.

Examining the evolution of security analysis as reflected in the different editions of Graham and Dodd, it is apparent that the historical evolution of security markets has a profound impact on the prescriptions of security analysis. For example, whereas in the pre-World War II period it was possible at various times to identify significant numbers of companies with common stock prices trading below the net current asset value per share, such companies are relatively uncommon in current US stock markets. Where such situations are available, this is, more likely than not, a situation that is to be avoided because the large balance of net current assets is being soldiered to stave off an impending sequence of negative earnings. While the views of GDC and Fisher may have provided considerable insight into securities markets of earlier times, there is no assurance that markets have not evolved beyond the lessons contained in those texts. This speaks to the importance of the Warren Buffett synthesis. Buffett has obtained his track record more recently and, as such, his prescriptions are relevant to contemporary observers. To this end, table 7.4 provides evidence on the performance of Berkshire Hathaway vs. the S&P 500 and table 7.5 provides a listing of the companies in which Berkshire Hathaway currently has a substantial position.

Hagstrom (1995, 2000) has summarized the "*Buffett approach to investment*" into five principles. Though these principles do not do full justice to Buffett's value investing prescriptions, e.g., Cunningham (2001), the basic structure is sound.[24] These principles can be briefly summarized as:

1 Don't follow the day-to-day fluctuations in the stock market. The market is a forum for buying and selling, not for precisely setting value. Investors need to be able to ignore significant short-term reductions in the value of a common stock. Follow the market only when the objective is to sell a stock at prices well in excess of intrinsic value.
2 Don't try to predict the direction of the general economy. If the stock market cannot be predicted, then how is it possible to predict the economy?
3 Buy a business, not its stock. A stock purchase can be viewed as though the entire business is being purchased. Four important elements apply to valuing the business: business characteristics, management, financial numbers and value. Business characteristics include: the business needs to be simple and understandable to the investor and the business needs a consistent operating history and favorable long-term prospects. The management has to be honest, capable and candid with shareholders. Management with a high fraction of personal wealth invested in a company, e.g. Buffett and Munger at Berkshire Hathaway, have a greater incentive to manage effectively. Key financial numbers to examine are return on equity, as opposed to earnings per share, profit margin and the ability to add value with retained earnings (return on additions to equity greater than cost of capital).
4 Buffett requires the intrinsic value to be less than the market price by the margin of safety for a security to qualify as an eligible purchase.
5 Manage a portfolio of businesses – act like a business owner rather than a stock trader. The implication is that being widely diversified is inconsistent with being able to manage so many businesses.

In addition to these general principles, Buffett is credited with numerous interesting quotes such as: "It is just not necessary to do extraordinary things to get extraordinary

Table 7.4 Berkshire's Corporate Performance vs. the S&P 500

| Year | Annual % change | | |
	in per-share book value of Berkshire (1)	in S&P 500 with Dividends Included (2)	Relative results (1)–(2)
1965	23.8	10.0	13.8
1966	20.3	(11.7)	32.0
1967	11.0	30.9	(19.9)
1968	19.0	11.0	8.0
1969	16.2	(8.4)	24.6
1970	12.0	3.9	8.1
1971	16.4	14.6	1.8
1972	21.7	18.9	2.8
1973	4.7	(14.8)	19.5
1974	5.5	(26.4)	31.9
1975	21.9	37.2	(15.3)
1976	59.3	23.6	35.7
1977	31.9	(7.4)	39.3
1978	24.0	6.4	17.6
1979	35.7	18.2	17.5
1980	19.3	32.3	(13.0)
1981	31.4	(5.0)	36.4
1982	40.0	21.4	18.6
1983	32.3	22.4	9.9
1984	13.6	6.1	7.5
1985	48.2	31.6	16.6
1986	26.1	18.6	7.5
1987	19.5	5.1	14.4
1988	20.1	16.6	3.5
1989	44.4	31.7	12.7
1990	7.4	(3.1)	10.5
1991	39.6	30.5	9.1
1992	20.3	7.6	12.7
1993	14.3	10.1	4.2
1994	13.9	1.3	12.6
1995	43.1	37.6	5.5
1996	31.8	23.0	8.8
1997	34.1	33.4	0.7
1998	48.3	28.6	19.7
1999	0.5	21.0	(20.5)
2000	6.5	(9.1)	15.6
2001	(6.2)	(11.9)	5.7
2002	10.0	(22.1)	32.1
Average annual gain: 1965–2002	22.2	10.0	12.2
Overall gain: 1964–2002	214,433	3,663	

The table appears in the printed Annual Report on the facing page of the Chairman's Letter and is referred to in that letter. Data are for calendar years with these exceptions: 1965 and 1966, year ended 9/30; 1967, 15 months ended 12/31.

Starting in 1979, accounting rules required insurance companies to value the equity securities they hold at market rather than at the lower of cost or market, which was previously the requirement. In this table, Berkshire's results through 1978 have been restated to conform to the changed rules. In all other respects, the results are calculated using the numbers originally reported.

The S&P 500 numbers are **pre-tax** whereas the Berkshire numbers are **after-tax**. If a corporation such as Berkshire were simply to have owned the S&P 500 and accrued the appropriate taxes, its results would have lagged the S&P 500 in years when that index showed a positive return, but would have exceeded the S&P in years when the index showed a negative return. Over the years, the tax costs would have caused the aggregate lag to be substantial.

Table 7.5 Berkshire Hathaway Inc.: major operating companies

Company	Location	Website
Acme Building Brands	Fort Worth, TX	brick.com
Adalet[a]	Cleveland, OH	adalet.com
Ben Bridge Jeweler	Seattle, WA	benbridge.com
Benjamin Moore	Montvale, NJ	benjaminmoore.com
Berkshire Hathaway Credit Corporation	Omaha, NE	
Berkshire Hathaway Homestate Companies	Omaha, NE	bh-hc.com
Berkshire Hathaway Reinsurance Division	Stamford, CT	brkdirect.com
Borsheim's Jewelry	Omaha, NE	borsheims.com
The Buffalo News	Buffalo, NY	buffnews.com
CalEnergy[b]	Omaha, NE	calenergy.com
Campbell Hausfeld[a]	Harrison, OH	chpower.com
Carefree of Colorado[a]	Broomfield, CO	carefreeofcolorado.com
Central States Indemnity Co.	Omaha, NE	csi-omaha.com
CORT Business Services	Fairfax, VA	cortl.com
CTB International	Milford, IN	ctbinc.com
Dairy Queen	Edina, MN	dairyqueen.com
Douglas/Quikut[a]	Walnut Ridge, AR	quikut.com
Fechheimer Brothers	Cincinnati, OH	fechheimer.com
FlightSafety International	Flushing, NY	flightsafety.com
France[a]	Fairview, TN	franceformer.com
Fruit of the Loom	Bowling Green, KY	fruit.com
Garan	New York, NY	garanimals.com
GEICO	Washington, DC	geico.com
General Re Corporation	Stamford, CT	gcr.com
H.H. Brown Shoe Group	Greenwich, CT	hhbrown.com
Halex[a]	Cleveland, OH	halexco.com
Helzberg's Diamond Shops	North Kansas City, MO	helzberg.com
HomeServices of America[b]	Edina, MN	homeservices.com
Johns Manville	Denver, CO	jm.com
Jordan's Furniture	Avon, MA	jordansfurniture.com
Justin Brands	Fort Worth, TX	justinbrands.com
Kansas Bankers Surety Company	Topeka, KS	
Kern River Gas Transmission Company[b]	Salt Lake City, UT	kernrivergas.com
Kingston[a]	Smithville, TN	kingstonproducts.com
Kirby[a]	Cleveland, OH	kirby.com
Larson-Juhl	Norcross, GA	larsonjuhl.com
Meriam Instrument[a]	Cleveland, OH	meriam.com
MidAmerican Energy Company[b]	Des Moines, IA	midamerican.com
MiTek Inc.	Chesterfield, MO	mitekinc.com
National Indemnity Company	Omaha, NE	nationalindemnity.com
Nebraska Furniture Mart	Omaha, NE	nfm.com
NetJets	Woodbridge, NJ	netjets.com
Northern Natural Gas[b]	Omaha, NE	northernnaturalgas.com
Northern and Yorkshire Electric[b]	United Kingdom	northern-electric.co.uk

Table 7.5 (*cont'd*)

Company	Location	Website
Northland[a]	Watertown, NY	northlandmotor.com
The Pampered Chef	Addison, IL	pamperedchef.com
Precision Steel Warehouse	Franklin Park, IL	precisionsteel.com
See's Candies	South San Francisco, CA	sees.com
Shaw Industries	Dalton, GA	shawinc.com
Stahl[a]	Wooster, OH	stahl.cc
Star Furniture	Houston, TX	starfurniture.com
United Consumer Finance Company[a]	Cleveland, OH	ucfs.net
United States Liability Insurance Group	Wayne, PA	usli.com
Wayne Water Systems[a]	Harrison, OH	waynepumps.com
Wesco Financial Corp.	Pasadena, CA	
Western Enterprises[a]	Avon Lake, OH	westernenterprises.com
R.C. Willey Home Furnishings	Salt Lake City, UT	shoprcwilley.com
World Book[a]	Chicago, IL	worldbook.com
XTRA	Westport, CT	xtracorp.com

[a] A Scott Fetzer Company.
[b] A MidAmerican Energy Holdings Company.
Source: Berkshire Hathaway Annual Report 2002.

results" and "As far as I am concerned, the stock market . . . is there only as a reference to see if anybody is offering to do anything foolish."

Despite all the reverence given to Buffett as the proto-typical value investor, it is apparent that individual investors would have difficulty pursuing the types of strategies that have brought considerable success to Berkshire Hathaway (see end of chapter questions). For example, consider the "*Acquisition Criteria*" in table 7.6 that is published annually in the Berkshire Hathaway annual report. This buy-a-business approach is reiterated in Buffett's various writings. The following statement is contained in the Berkshire Hathaway (2003, p. 69) 2002 annual report:

> Our preference would be to reach our goal [of maximizing Berkshire's average annual rate of gain in intrinsic value on a per-share basis] by directly owning a diversified group of businesses that generate cash and consistently earn above-average returns on capital. Our second choice is to own parts of similar businesses, attained primarily through purchases of marketable common stocks by our insurance subsidiaries. The price and availability of businesses and the need for insurance capital determine any given year's capital allocation.

While it would be nice for individual investors to be able to search out companies and take a 100% interest, this is not practical for all but the select few investors (see table 7.5). The detailed emphasis on business characteristics, which usually requires on-site visits and access to senior management, also makes it difficult for individual investors.[25] In this regard and in the general approach to detailed fundamental analysis

Table 7.6 Berkshire Hathaway Inc.: acquisition criteria

We are eager to hear *from principals or their representatives* about businesses that meet all of the following criteria:

(1) Large purchases (at least $50 million of before-tax earnings),
(2) Demonstrated consistent earning power (future projections are of no interest to us, nor are "turnaround" situations),
(3) Businesses earning good returns on equity while employing little or no debt,
(4) Management in place (we can't supply it),
(5) Simple businesses (if there's lots of technology, we won't understand it),
(6) An offering price (we don't want to waste our time or that of the seller by talking, even preliminarily, about a transaction when price is unknown).

The larger the company, the greater will be our interest: We would like to make an acquisition in the $5–20 billion range. *We are not interested, however, in receiving suggestions about purchases we might make in the general stock market.*

We will not engage in unfriendly takeovers. We can promise complete confidentiality and a very fast answer – customarily within five minutes – as to whether we're interested. We prefer to buy for cash, but will consider issuing stock when we receive as much in intrinsic business value as we give.

Charlie and I frequently get approached about acquisitions that don't come close to meeting our tests: We've found that if you advertise an interest in buying collies, a lot of people will call hoping to sell you their cocker spaniels. A line from a country song expresses our feeling about new ventures, turnarounds, or auction-like sales: "When the phone don't ring, you'll know it's me."

---

of the business, Buffett has more in common with Philip Fisher than Graham and Dodd.

Being a practitioner rather than an academic, the folksy writing style that characterizes Buffett's published contributions often makes it difficult to untangle the analytical recommendations aimed at making 100% acquisitions from those associated with making fractional purchases of companies using common stock. However, this observation relates to the part of the Buffett synthesis that has a close connection to Philip Fisher, i.e., the economic analysis of the underlying business. Buffett's approach to fundamental analysis also has a component that is closely related to Ben Graham. Whereas Philip Fisher concentrated on business characteristics, for the Graham and Dodd approach: "all security analysis involves the analysis of financial statements." Unlike Fisher, who did not proceed much beyond the *P/E* ratio, profit margin and sales growth in the level of financial statement analysis, Buffett provides considerable insight into using financial accounting to identify investment opportunities (Cunningham 2002, p. 185): "In our own investing, we search for situations in which both [business analysis and financial statement analysis] give us the same answer."

Buffett's insights into the ***use of accounting numbers in business valuation*** are generally unrecognized. Yet, this aspect of the Buffett synthesis may be the most impressive and useful to individual investors. Buffett explicitly recognizes the importance and limitations of accounting numbers (Cunningham 2002, p. 213):

> Accounting numbers, of course, are the language of business and as such are of enormous help to anyone evaluating the worth of a business and tracking its progress. Charlie and I would be lost without these numbers; they invariably are the starting point for us in evaluating our own businesses and those of others. Managers and owners need to remember, however, that accounting is but an aid to business thinking, never a substitute for it.

Because the most important source of information for Buffett's views is the *Annual Reports* and *Letters to Shareholders* of Berkshire Hathaway, many of the comments are addressed to accounting aspects of that company. This means giving detailed attention to accounting for taxation, acquisitions and for different levels of ownership in the various companies that comprise the Berkshire Hathaway holding company.[26] However, there are also a number of general observations about accounting that appeal to a wider range of applications.

Buffett recognizes the failings of conventional interpretations of accounting numbers and related valuation measures (Cunningham 2002, p. 218): "Common yardsticks such as dividend yield, the ratio of price to earnings or to book value, and even growth rates have *nothing* to do with valuation except to the extent they provide clues as to the amount and timing of cash flows into and from the business." A common theme in Buffet's writings is that reference to "growth" and "value" strategies reflect an ignorance of the valuation process. Growth can destroy value if the cash required to increase assets exceeds the cash generation of those assets in the future. For Buffett:

> The primary test of managerial economic performance is the achievement of a high earnings rate on equity capital employed (without undue leverage, gimmickry, etc.) And not the achievement of consistent gains in earnings per share. In our view, businesses would be better understood by their shareholder owners, as well as the general public, if managements and financial analysts modified the primary emphasis they place on earnings per share, and upon yearly changes in that figure.

Earnings are too readily manipulated by unscrupulous management or misinterpreted by naive investors. The use of GAAP accounting does not ensure a meaningful earnings number, only that the earnings number is calculated according to "generally accepted accounting principles": "managers and investors alike must understand that accounting numbers are the beginning, not the end, of business valuation."

Buffett clearly states that the object is to maximize "economic earnings" and not "accounting earnings." This point is not original to Buffett. What Buffett brings to the table is the invaluable interpretations of an individual who has accumulated a remarkable record from understanding the difference. One example concerns "economic goodwill" versus "accounting goodwill": "You can live a full and rewarding life without ever thinking about Goodwill and its amortization. But students of investment and management should understand the nuances of the subject." On this subject, writing in 1983 Buffett makes a veiled reference to the incorrectness of the Graham and Dodd treatment of goodwill (Cunningham 2002, pp. 197–8):

My own thinking has changed drastically from 35 years ago when I was taught to favor tangible assets and to shun businesses whose value depended largely upon economic Goodwill. This bias caused me to make many important business mistakes of omission, although relatively few of commission.

Keynes identified my problem: "The difficulty lies not in the new ideas but in escaping from the old ones." My escape was long delayed, in part because most of what I had been taught by the same teacher had been (and continues to be) so extraordinarily valuable. Ultimately, business experience, direct and vicarious, produced my present strong preference for businesses that possess a large amount of enduring Goodwill and that utilize a minimum of tangible assets.

Unlike accounting goodwill, which is "excess of cost over equity in the net assets being acquired," economic goodwill is the capitalized value of the excess over market rates of return on net tangible assets. Both concepts are related to intangible assets, but in different ways.

Economic goodwill provides a connection to the "earnings power value" identified by proponents of "value investing" (Greenwald et al. 2001, ch. 5). To illustrate the concept of economic goodwill, Buffett examines the purchase of See's Candies in 1972, a basically debt free company that Berkshire Hathaway continues to own up to the present. The purchase price of this company was $25 million and the net tangible assets of the company was $8 million.[27] Observing that the after tax earnings of See's was approximately $2 million per year, it is apparent that the 25% return on assets represented more than just the market return earned on tangible assets. The excess return above what could be earned on the net tangible assets at prevailing market rates of return, capitalized at an appropriate discount rate, is the economic goodwill. See's had intangible assets associated with reputation, consumer loyalty and quality of product. In contrast, accounting goodwill would depend on a combination of factors, i.e., the premium over book value of the price paid for the firm, adjusted for fair value revaluation of inventories and tangible assets, plus amortization of goodwill and adjustments for deferred taxes. The resulting number may, or may not, capture the implicit value of the intangible assets.

Considerable discussion in value investing analysis is dedicated to the sources of "earnings power value" associated with "assets plus franchise." Businesses where the return on tangible assets is in excess of market rates of return are strong candidates for increased competition. This competition can arise in various forms, e.g., on the price side from competitors already in the market or from the entry of new firms. The end result is irresistible market pressures that force the return on assets to the market rate of return, or possibly below. What factors enable firms to resist these market pressures? Identifying *sustainable sources of competitive advantage* is the subject of numerous books and theories. A number of such sources of competitive advantage include: *licenses*, such as television or telecom broadcast rights; *production efficiencies* due to factors such as patents, specialized human capital or economies of scale; *access to cheaper sources of either capital, labor or other inputs*; and, *the franchise factor* associated with customer loyalty or acquired tastes.[28] It is not surprising that arguably the most important franchise factor business, Coca-Cola, is also a major holding of Berkshire-Hathaway.

Another key difference between accounting and economic values identified by Buffett involves the treatment of *depreciation*. This is directly related to the concept of "owner earnings" (Cunningham 2002, p. 211): "'owner's earnings'...represent (a) reported earnings plus (b) depreciation, depletion, amortization, and certain other non-cash charges...less (c) the average annual amount of capitalized expenditures for property plant and equipment, etc. that the business requires to fully maintain its long-term competitive position and its unit volume." Except in special cases, (c) will be difficult to estimate and, as a result, can only be a guess. However, for Buffett: "the owner earnings figure, not the [deceptively precise] GAAP figure [is] the relevant item for valuation purposes – both for investors in buying stock and for managers in buying entire businesses." Buffett cautions that the use of measures such as EBITDA to determine "cash flow" will likely lead to "faulty decisions." Economic depreciation is not the same as amortization and this is another essential feature required to take into account in arriving at an estimate of intrinsic value.

Questions ?

1 In section 7.4 the recommendations of Philip Fisher and Warren Buffett were surveyed. It was observed that some of these recommendations were not practical for individual investors. For example, a number of Philip Fisher's suggestions about analyzing a business would require on-site visits and access to senior management. Similarly, some of Warren Buffett's suggestions focus on the 100% acquisition of a business. Prepare a listing of three key recommendations of both Fisher and Buffett that would not be practical for individual investors to pursue.

2 Using the annual arithmetic return information in table 7.4, determine whether the performance of Berkshire Hathaway is statistically better than that of the S&P 500. (Hint: Use a t-test to determine whether the difference of the two means is different than zero, see Freund 1971.) Calculate the geometric means from table 7.4 and determine the test for statistical significance.

3(a) For the Fisher approach to company and industry analysis in section 7.3, evaluate the possibility of applying functional factors, people factors and business factors to the following sectors: oil and gas drillers; pulp and paper companies; automobile companies; and, biotechnology companies. For each of these company types, what elements of the three types of factors could not be identified? (Hint: what does being the lowest cost producer mean for an oil driller?)

(b) Assess the applicability of Fisher's four dimensions to three outstanding companies of the 1980–2000 period, e.g., Microsoft, Dell, Intel or Walmart.

NOTES

1 The NYSE requires contingent voting rights as a provision for listing "nonvoting" preferred shares. In the event of unpaid dividends, a range of voting provisions are possible. For example, some preferred shares are restricted to only electing two members to the board of directors while preferred shares of other companies have the same one vote per share rule as common stock.

2 In a large study of 3042 US preferred share issues from 1980 to 1999, Bajaj et al. (2002) found 682 convertible issues and 2360 non-convertible issues. As a measure of the completeness of this sample, between 1985 and 1999 there were 2,636 total preferred share issues raising $324.63 billion. In comparison, there were 7,017 seasoned equity offerings raising $606 billion.

3 Another form of dividend provision arises with participating preferred stock. This type of preferred stock is rare in modern financial markets, though the provision has appeared in isolated historical instances usually associated with mergers and acquisitions activity. Typically, a participating preferred has a prior claim to the initial round of dividends. After a certain amount of earnings has been paid as dividends to common stock, usually the same per share amount as the preferred dividend, then preferred and common stock share equally in any remaining dividend payments. While such an arrangement may seem disadvantageous to common shareholders, the absence of voting rights for preferred stock combined with a preferred redemption provision may provide sufficient offset in situations involving corporate takeovers.

4 There are exceptions to this rule. For example, IRC section 247 provides for a partial dividends paid deduction for "old money" preferred stocks issued by public utilities. In turn, the investors in these old money preferred shares are subject to a reduced dividend received tax credit under IRC section 244, e.g., Atwood (2002). Old money preferred stocks include public utility preferreds outstanding on October 1, 1942 and all subsequent preferred issues by that public utility used to replace these issues, including subsequent issues made through a tax-free reorganization.

5 Institutional information on Canadian securities markets, including topics such as relevant tax rates on securities, can be obtained from Canadian Securities Institute (1992).

6 The use of "par value" for common stocks was the convention until the practice was abandoned during the 1920s. While common stock still has a par value in an accounting sense, there is no connection to the original issue price. Common stock with a par value would be issued at, say, $100 per share and enough shares would be issued to achieve the equity funding target. In this fashion, if the stock traded at, say, $60 it could be readily assessed whether the stock had appreciated or depreciated relative to the initial offering price.

7 The value of the shares may not fall to zero because, in some cases, the shares themselves have value. For example, if controlling interest in the company's shares can be obtained cheaply, then it may be possible to use the shares to form a "shell company" for another venture. Shell companies are one method of avoiding the costs associated with making new equity issues.

8 Perhaps the most important twentieth-century philosopher emphasizing the importance of language was Ludwig Wittgenstein (1889–1951). For Wittgenstein, the aim of philosophy is to clear up muddle and confusion. The philosopher's proper concern is with what is conceivable. This depends on how concepts fit together using language. What is conceivable and what is not, what makes sense and what does not, depends on the grammatical rules of language. For example, in *Philosophical Investigations* Wittgenstein says: "Our investigation is a grammatical one. Such an investigation sheds light on our problem by clearing misunderstandings away. Misunderstandings concerning the use of words, caused, among other things, by certain analogies between the forms of expression in different regions of language."

9 The progression of the core theory of modern Finance has moved away from the largely indefensible position about the impact of fundamental information on security prices. At least since Fama and French (1995) it has become popular in modern Finance to incorporate additional (fundamental) "factors" to the traditional single-factor market model, with price-to-book and firm size being the most popular.

10 The GDC use of "anticipation approach" to describe one of the three approaches is somewhat unfortunate as all three approaches involve "anticipating" the future value of the stock by predicting specific variables. The key distinction between the three approaches is what variables are used to predict the future cash flows and how the estimation process is conducted. In this regard, the anticipation approach can also include the use, in whole or in part, of technical analysis, where variables that are used to "anticipate" future stock prices lie within the set of variables examined in technical analysis. There is also differences in the implied length of the holding period with the anticipation being the shortest and the intrinsic value approach being the longest.

11 Framing the discussion in terms of "common stocks being an inflation hedge" raises a semantical question about the usage of the word "hedge." In the analysis of derivative securities, a "hedged" position is protected against changes in a particular random variable, in this case inflation. This could mean the security value does not change when the random variable changes or that the position value will not decrease when the variable changes, depending on the usage. In either case, if there is a short-run negative impact on the value of the position then it is semantically incorrect to refer to there being a hedge in place. The case of stocks being a "hedge" against inflation uses the word "hedge" in the sense that the real return on the capital invested in common stocks does not change as (expected) inflation changes. As such, evidence of a negative short-term relationship between nominal stock returns and inflation violates the "hedge" condition.

12 The empirical question of what length of time constitutes a short-run and a long-run is addressed in Hakkio and Rush (1991).

13 Anari and Kolari (2001) also present evidence in favor of a positive long-run relationship between stock prices and inflation, i.e., that stock prices are a long-run inflation hedge. The sample in this study uses monthly observations from 1953 to 1999 for six countries. Using a sample of sixteen countries, Rapach (2002) presents evidence in favor of long-run neutrality that could also be interpreted as consistent with a positive long-run real stock price response to a permanent inflation shock. Rapach finds little evidence in favor of a negative long-run relationship.

14 Taking a log approximation produces the familiar result: $RR(t) \cong R(t) - \dot{\pi}(t)$. In other words, the real interest rate can be approximated by subtracting the inflation rate from the nominal interest rate. Numerous empirical studies have been conducted to examine the impact of inflation on nominal interest rates. These studies usually proceed by assuming a constant real rate and then fitting a distributed lag of inflation rates on nominal interest rates. In cases where the assumption that the real rate is constant is justified, this is usually done by having the real rate being determined by "real economic forces" that are determined outside the model. For example, the economy can be assumed to be on a steady state growth path.

15 The relevant website for information about business cycles is www.nber.org/cycles. The National Bureau of Economic Research is a private research organization that is responsible for dating business cycles. The history of the organization stretches back to 1920 and has produced, in addition to the analysis of economic conditions, seminal contributions by Wesley Mitchell, Arthur Burns and Frederick Macaulay.

16 There are alternatives to Buffett as the world's most successful investor, including Li Ka Shing, the Hong Kong billionaire, and Charles Munger, Vice Chairman of Berkshire Hathaway and Buffett's long time partner.

17 This number is inflated by the market practice of having more than one ticker symbol for the

same fund name. Technically, the funds usually differ in being separate entities managed by the same fund manager. For various reasons, mutual fund companies do not want individual funds to be larger than a given size. If the inflow to the fund results in a capital value larger than the upper bound, a new fund with the same or nearly the same name is created with a ticker symbol that differs from the original fund. It is possible for these funds to have different holdings, but any differences are typically quite small.

18 A representative example of these criticisms is the following (Cunningham 2001, p. 100): "To invest successfully, you need not understand beta, efficient markets, modern portfolio theory, option pricing, or emerging markets. You may, in fact, be better off knowing nothing of these. That, of course, is not the prevailing view at most business schools, whose finance curriculum tends to be dominated by such subjects. In our view, though, investment students need only two well-taught courses – How to Value a Business, and How to Think About Market Prices."

19 Based on aggregated empirical evidence given by Jensen and Ruback (1983), Jarrell et al. (1988) and others, it is safe to conclude the shareholders of target firms in successful acquisitions benefit substantially while acquiring firms experience either no significant or a small negative (> −5%) impact on stock returns. For example, for a sample of 663 successful tender offers, Jarrell et al. found bid premiums for the pre-announcement value of the target firm's stock price of 19% during the 1960s, 35% during the 1970s and 30% during the first half of the 1980s. The empirical evidence on corporate acquisitions has led to the use of crude rules of thumb regarding acquisitions such as: a 25–30% bid premium is required to obtain corporate control of a going concern in a friendly tender offer. Like most rules of thumb, such estimates of the bid premium will differ depending on the specifics of the acquisition involved.

20 GDC do not use the words "primary" and "secondary" in the fashion that is conventional in modern Finance where a primary issue is a "new" issue, such as an IPO for a common stock or a Treasury issue that has just been auctioned, and a "secondary" issue for a previously issued security, such as the common stocks traded on the NYSE or Treasury bonds traded in the OTC market. For GDC (p. 3) a "primary" stock issue is a "first line" or "standard" issue of "large and prominent companies, generally with a good record of earnings and of continued dividends." A "secondary" issue refers to the more marginal common stock issues that have not obtained "primary" quality. GDC estimate that about 80% of listed stocks and 90% or more of unlisted stocks belong in the secondary category.

21 The precise specification of the margin of safety is unclear. Recognizing that there is a target level of 20–30 stocks in a portfolio, presumably the margin of safety will change as the level of the market changes. When the market is "high" there will be a greater proportion of fairly valued and overvalued stocks and it will be necessary to have a lower margin of safety, say 10–15%, in order for there to be stocks that will qualify for selection as there will be "overvalued" stocks that were purchased previously that now require selling. Similarly when the market is "low" there will be a proportionately greater number of "undervalued" stocks to buy and less "overvalued" stocks in the portfolio to sell. This will require the margin of safety to be raised to, say, 25–30%, in order for the portfolio rebalancing exercise to make sense.

22 Fisher (1975) uses the term "conservative investor" in an unconventional sense. For Fisher, "a *conservative investment* is one most likely to conserve (i.e., maintain) purchasing power at a minimum of risk" and "conservative *investing* is understanding of what a conservative investment consists and then, in regard to specific investments, following a procedural course of action needed to properly determine whether specific investment vehicles are, in fact, conservative investments." In this context, Fisher sees the common stock of outstanding companies purchased as cheaply as possible as the best type of conservative investment.

23 The four dimensions are: (1) superiority in production, marketing , research and financial skill; (2) the people factor; (3) essential characteristics of the business; and, (4) the current value of the stock, measured in a relative *P/E* sense. This leaves Fisher with: *four dimensions*, used to structure the common stock selection strategy in Fisher (1975); *fifteen questions* used to assess business characteristics from Fisher (1980); and, *eight points* in the investment philosophy, given in Fisher (1980) but synthesized from Fisher (1958, 1975).

24 A more expanded version of the thirteen "owner related business principles" plus one added principle underlying Buffett's approach can be found in the Berkshire Hathaway annual report (2003, pp. 68–72).

25 For example, in the 2002 Berkshire Hathaway annual report (p. 4), Buffett recommends in reference to management: "to be a winner, work with winners." While this is good advice for Buffett who is able to secure a golf game, weekend retreat or cosy dinner with virtually any major figure in American corporate management, it is little comfort to a small individual investor seeking to make a purchase in, say, US Steel.

26 The reference to holding company is intended in a descriptive and not a legal sense. The description of Berkshire Hathaway in the 10-K filing refers to an insurance company that owns a range of non-insurance related businesses.

27 Any "economic value" calculation is subject to interpretation. The calculation of net tangible assets is no exception. A common convention is to use (cash + accounts receivable + inventory + property, plant and equipment) – (adjustments to reflect differences between the accounting value of the assets recorded on the balance sheet and the replacement cost of the assets).

28 Various descriptions of the value investing approach, in general, and the Buffett approach to value investing, in particular, stress the key role played by the franchise factor as the source of long run corporate advantage and "monopolistic" profit. However, while the franchise factor is of central importance in the many situations of sustainable competitive advantage, there are other sources that can also produce this result.

Chapter
Summary

Chapter 8 *Valuation Techniques for Equity Securities*

8.1 Discounted Cash Flow Modeling
     The history and variety of DCF models
     Damodaran on simplified DCF valuation
     Expectations investing

8.2 Interpreting Financial Statements
     Financial statement analysis
     Earnings, free cash flow and EVA
     Financial shenanigans

8.3 Forecasting the Inputs
     Identifying the value drivers
     From value drivers to valuations
     Alternatives to and hybrids of discounted cash flow models

Questions
Notes

chapter 8   Valuation Techniques for Equity Securities

8.1   DISCOUNTED CASH FLOW MODELING

The history and variety of DCF models

The connection between the academic and practitioner approaches to common stock valuation, if there is one, is the discounted cash flow model. The use of discounted cash flow (DCF) methods to value securities goes back centuries, e.g., Poitras (2000, ch. 4). Despite the ability to do such calculations for equity claims, the widespread recognition and acceptance of these methods by academics and some practitioners to value common stocks does not seem to predate John Burr Williams, *The Theory of Investment Value* (1938). For example, Graham and Dodd (1934) give no explicit discussion or recognition of discounted cash flow valuation for equities. The basic notion advanced in Williams (1938) was that the present value for a business or a security, such as a stock or bond, can be determined by discounting the future stream of expected cash inflows minus expected cash outflows at the appropriate rate of interest. This basic model was adapted and expanded in Gordon (1962) where the valuation of companies in regulated industries was a central concern. In recognition, the constant growth version of the discounted dividend form of the discounted cash flow model is often referred to as the "Gordon growth model," e.g., Damodaran (1994, p. 99).

To review the derivation of *the basic DCF model* for the security investor assume for the moment that the future is known with certainty and that perfect market assumptions apply. In the present context, this means there are no taxes and the term structure of discount rates is flat. Given this, consider the problem of determining the current price of a common stock. Assume that the stock to be valued is purchased at price $P(0)$ and held for one period and then sold. This current price can be modeled as the discounted value for the sum of the dividend to be received in the next period ($Div(1)$) and the price $P(1)$ received from selling the stock. Assuming the dividend is paid at the point the stock is sold:

$$P(0) = \frac{Div(1) + P(1)}{1 + k} \quad \rightarrow \quad k = \frac{P(1) - P(0)}{P(0)} + \frac{Div(1)}{P(0)}$$

This is the "*basic valuation equation*," sometimes inappropriately referred to as the "absence of arbitrage" condition. In effect, the (expected) return on the stock can be decomposed into two parts: the (expected) capital gain and the (expected) dividend yield. Dropping the assumption that future cash flows are known with certainty, leads to the result that $k = E[R_S]$, the expected return on the stock.

Accounting for randomness in the future cash flows by taking expectations conditional on information available at $t = 0$, the *discounted dividend model* is derived by making a progressive substitution for prices:

$$E[P(1)] = \frac{E[P(2)] + E[Div(2)]}{1 + k} \quad \rightarrow \quad P(0) = \frac{E[Div(1)]}{(1 + k)} + \frac{E[P(2) + Div(2)]}{(1 + k)^2}$$

$$P(0) = \sum_{t=1}^{T} \frac{E[Div(t)]}{(1 + k)^t} + \frac{E[P(T)]}{(1 + k)^T} \quad \rightarrow \quad P(0) = \sum_{t=1}^{\infty} \frac{E[Div(t)]}{(1 + k)^t}$$

The relevance of other perfect markets assumptions follows appropriately. For example, introducing taxes requires a distinction to be made between the stream of expected dividends and the expected capital gain, which will be taxed at different rates. Combining this with differences in the relative riskiness for these two types of cash flows leads to the possibility that different discount rates might be required for dividends and capital gains. In addition, relaxing the assumption of a flat term structure of discount rates requires different k's to be used to discount cash flows occurring at different points in time.

Despite impressions to the contrary, e.g., Cunningham (2000, p. 93), Williams (1938) did not originate the discounted cash flow model for security analysis. Rather, Williams popularized acceptance of the approach.[1] Prior to Williams, informed opinion was generally against the validity of the model. Macaulay (1938, pp. 130–2) captures the basic notions of using discounted cash flow analysis to value both stocks and bonds:

> Because the good that the common stock offers to its purchaser is an expectation of future money payments, the relation of its present-money price to its future-money payments is as unmistakably an interest phenomenon as is the relation of the present-money price of a bond to its future-money payments. In the fullness of time the stock will have a "realized" or "actual" yield just as will the bond. And, though the stock makes no "promise," as does the bond, and therefore has no "promised" or "hypothetical" yield, its price discounts *estimated* future payments as truly as does the price of a bond.

What disturbed Macaulay about this approach to common stock valuation was not the basic formulation but, rather, the difficulties of determining the future cash flows for stock:

> It is the absence of promises and the high degree of uncertainty as to what the stock will pay, with the resulting inadequate forecasting, that obscures the interest relation. The fundamental difference between an ultra high grade extremely long term bond and a low grade common stock is that the future-money returns of the bond can be forecast with more assurance than can those of the stock.

For Macaulay, the application of discounted cash flow techniques to assess the value of stocks, i.e., value as measured using model price vs. market price, depends fundamentally on the "*forecasting* of future payments."

Macaulay objected quite strongly to the practicality of using DCF methods to value stocks:

> The "assumption of payment," which must be made before the promised or "hypothetical" yield of a bond can be calculated . . . may, as we have seen, be a mere mathematical fiction for all except the highest grade of bonds. But, for common stocks it is not only a mathematical fiction but also an economic absurdity. Even if the chance that the promises contained in a bond will be kept is negligibly small that the promises are little more than mere words, they are at least *definite* words and, as such, can stand the strain of mathematical manipulation.

That Macaulay understood the mathematical and analytical basis of the DCF techniques that are credited to Williams and Gordon is evident. For example:

> If it be assumed that a share of common stock selling for $100 is to return $4 per annum *forever*, it may be thought of as having a promised or "hypothetical" yield of 4 per cent per annum. But, if the payments are to cease at the end of sixty years, the hypothetical yield must be less than $3\frac{1}{2}$ per cent per annum. If they are to cease at the end of 46 years, the yield must be less than 3 per cent per annum. If at the end of 35 years, the yield must be less than 2 per cent per annum. If they continue for just 25 years, the yield will be exactly zero per annum. With still shorter periods, the yields are negative.

Macaulay understood clearly that the return (yield) on a stock combined both the dividend yield and the capital gain resulting in the stock "yield" depending on two variables. "Sudden and great changes in the calculated 'yields' of a stock can occur not only because of changes in price but also because of changes in the dividend rate."

Though he clearly recognized the mechanics of the Gordon dividend growth model, Macaulay did not fully develop the mathematics for the formula. However, it is apparent that Macaulay (1938, p. 132) more than understood the nuances of the intuition. The discussion of the model is sufficiently interesting to warrant detailed examination:

> If such an assumption were made as that the dividend payments were to increase in geometric progression, the future that could be neglected would be still more distant. One of the strangest rationalizations of unending price rise that appeared in the months immediately preceding the stock market culmination of 1929 was evolved by a Wall Street economist. He presented to the directors of the investment trust with which he was associated statistical evidence that the wealth of the country increased in the long run about 3 per cent per annum. He then argued that corporations as a class should be expected to share in this growth at this rate and hence that their dividends should be expected, over the long run, to increase at least 3 per cent per annum; that is to say in such a series as $4.12, $4.24, $4.37, etc., or $4(1.03), $4(1.03)^2, $4(1.03)^3, etc. He then suggested that, with increasing financial stabilization in the country, these future dividends would eventually be discounted at a rate that would not exceed 3 per cent per annum. But, he

continued, if distant enough payments were assumed, discounting them at this rate would give very high prices for the stocks. The suggestion was even made that, as there seemed to be no necessary time limit to the 3 per cent rate of growth in wealth, there should logically be no "ceiling" whatever for stock prices. The phantasy was strangely reminiscent of the Petersburg Paradox in the mathematical theory of probability.

This discussion is remarkable, in providing evidence both that Macaulay understood the Gordon dividend growth model and that the basics of the model were known within the investment industry. In particular, Macaulay understood one of the conventional limitations of the model.

To see this, observe that the motivation for the Gordon growth model is to provide a simplification of the general form of the discounted dividend model, where determining the price involves evaluating the infinite sum of discounted dividends, a clearly impractical exercise. One immediate simplication is provided by the case where the dividend is assumed to be constant into perpetuity, i.e., $Div(t) = \bar{D}$ for all t.[2] In this case, the discounted dividend model reduces to the perpetuity pricing model discussed in section 4.1 and the resulting stock pricing model is: $P(0) = \bar{D}/k$. This pricing model is sometimes called *the preferred stock pricing model*. Because the dividend does not change, the preferred stock pricing model can be solved for the yield $k = \bar{D}/P(0)$ and this yield compared to the yield on other "fixed income" securities, much as in traditional yield spread analysis (see section 6.3). As Macaulay recognized, this model does not work for common stocks because both the dividend payment and the price are variable making the result of the yield calculation too "fuzzy" for practical applications.

The *Gordon dividend growth model* permits the dividend to change over time according to the assumption: $D(t + 1) = D(t)(1 + g)$, where g is the assumed constant growth rate in dividends. Dropping the expectation for ease of notation and substituting this result into the general form of the discounted dividend model produces the simplified DCF model:

$$P(0) = \sum_{t=1}^{\infty} \frac{Div(t)}{(1 + k)^t} = \sum_{t=1}^{\infty} \frac{D(0)(1 + g)^t}{(1 + k)^t}$$

$$= \frac{D(0)(1 + g)}{1 + k}\left[1 + \frac{1 + g}{1 + k} + \frac{(1 + g)^2}{(1 + k)^2} + \frac{(1 + g)^3}{(1 + k)^3} + \cdots\right]$$

$$= \frac{D(0)(1 + g)}{(1 + k)}\left[\frac{1}{1 - \dfrac{1 + g}{1 + k}}\right] = \frac{D(1)}{k - g}$$

By assuming that the dividend grows at a constant rate over time the Gordon growth model is able to provide a simple common stock valuation model: $P(0) = D(1)/(k - g)$. The example that Macaulay provides refers to the situation where $g \to k$ which gives "a very high price level for stocks."

In the context of the Gordon growth model with $g \to k$, Macaulay develops an interesting implication:

If the dividends were $4(1.03)$, $4(1.03)^2$, $4(1.03)^3$, etc. . . . and if these dividends were discounted at 3 per cent per annum, the price of a share of the stock that was to pay the dividends, should be just four times the *number of payments* that were to be made; in other words, four times the *number of years* that the succession of dividends was to continue.

Though this result is relatively obvious from inspection of the original sum, this result is not so obvious from inspection of the $D(1)/(k - g)$ formulation of the model. Over time, a number of developments of the basic Gordon growth model have appeared that introduce more complicated patterns for future dividend payments. For example, Malkiel (1963) has a two stage model where dividends grow at a constant rate for a finite number of years and then grow at a rate typical of other firms in the economy thereafter (see end of chapter questions). Molodovsky et al. (1965) has a three stage model where dividends initially grow at a constant rate, then decline over a second period to be followed by a constant steady state dividend payment thereafter. While theoretically appealing, such developments lack practical applications in all but the most specialized situations.

The Gordon growth model makes the precise statement that common stock pricing depends on three variables: the dividend to be received next period, $Div(1) = D(1)$; the expected return on the common stock, k; and the long term growth rate of dividends, g. In terms of expected returns the model maintains that: $E[R_S] = k = (D(1)/P(0)) + g$ and $(D(1)/P(0)) = (k - g)$. Returning to the "basic valuation equation," this implies that the expected capital gain is equal to the expected growth rate of dividends. While this might seem to be quite unrealistic, it does have a reasonable interpretation. If the P/E ratio does not change over time, the growth rate in earnings will equal the growth rate in dividends if the dividend payout ratio does not change over time. Under these assumptions, g will be translated into the capital gain. Yet, if these assumptions are adopted, then the model can be manipulated to produce other interesting results that can be used to interpret widely used valuation measures.

More precisely, assuming for the moment that the Gordon growth model is correct, it is possible to manipulate the model to provide precise statements for two important valuation measures, the price-earnings (P/E) ratio and the price-to-book value (P/BV) ratio. In turn, these values can be used to provide an interpretation for g. To convert the Gordon model to P/E form requires the *"clean surplus" equation* for earnings: $E(t) = Div(t) + RE(t) = Div(t) + (BV(t) - BV(t - 1))$, where $E(t)$ is earnings available to common stockholders, $RE(t)$ is the retained earnings and $BV(t)$ is the book value of equity, all observed at time t and expressed on a per share basis. In keeping with currently accepted accounting practice, e.g., Bernstein (1989, p. 747), the clean surplus equation requires that all items involving gain or loss in income are accounted for in the period in which these items occur. In effect, $E(t)$ is either paid out in dividends or is retained earnings and accounted for by changing the book value of equity. Though there are some accounting qualifications to this condition (see section 8.2), the clean surplus equation is sufficient for present purposes.

Letting b represent the dividend payout ratio $(Div(t)/E(t))$, i.e., $bE(t) = Div(t)$, substituting this result into the Gordon growth model produces the *simplified DCF P/E ratio*:

$$P(0) = \frac{bE(1)}{k - g} = \frac{bE(0)(1 + g)}{k - g} \quad \rightarrow \quad \frac{P(0)}{E(0)} = \frac{b(1 + g)}{k - g}$$

Taking the dividend payout ratio to be fixed over time produces: $D(t + 1) = bE(t + 1) = bE(t)(1 + g) \rightarrow E(t + 1) = E(t)(1 + g)$. In words, with a constant dividend payout ratio, the constant growth in dividends assumption translates into an assumption about the constant growth in earnings. To derive the price to book ratio involves observing that $(E(t)/BV(t - 1)) = ROE(t)$, where $ROE(t)$ is the return on equity at time t. (Though it is more conventional to use $BV(t)$ in defining $ROE(t)$, this definition will not be used here.) Making the appropriate substitution produces the *simplified DCF P/BV ratio*:

$$\frac{P(0)}{BV(0)} = \frac{b\dfrac{E(1)}{BV(0)}}{k - g} = \frac{bROE(1)}{k - g}$$

It follows that the price to book value ratio will depend on the dividend payout ratio, the ROE, the expected return on the stock and the growth rate in earnings.

A number of different variations on the DCF model can be derived.[3] English (2001, pp. 334–5) uses the clean surplus relationship, $BV(t) = BV(t - 1) + E(t) - D(t)$, to develop the following the *abnormal earnings form of the DCF model* (see end of chapter questions):

$$P(0) = \sum_{t=1}^{\infty} \frac{D(t)}{(1 + k)^t} = \sum_{t=1}^{\infty} \frac{E(t) - \Delta BV(t)}{(1 + k)^t}$$

$$= BV(0) + \sum_{t=1}^{\infty} \frac{(ROE(t) - k)BV(t - 1)}{(1 + k)^t} = BV(0) + \sum_{t=1}^{\infty} \frac{AE(t)}{(1 + k)^t}$$

where $AE(t) = (ROE(t) - k)BV(t - 1)$ is the "abnormal earnings attributable to equity in period t" and BV is expressed on a per share basis. Ritter and Warr (2002, p. 36) refer to this form the DCF model as the "*residual income model*" while Penman (2001, chap. 6) uses "*residual earnings model.*" Ritter and Warr make numerous adjustments to the model to account for the impact of inflation and the use of accounting accruals. Dechow et al. (1999) provides a detailed examination of this model while Penman and Sougiannis (1998) compare this DCF model with the free cash flow and dividend discount variants. This formula has intuitive appeal because it relates the current price to the initial value of capital raised, reflected in $BV(0)$ adjusted for the ability of the firm to earn more (or less) on invested capital (ROE) than the cost of maintaining the capital stock, as reflected in k. This formulation captures the idea that securities with superior investment potential create wealth ($ROE > k$) as opposed to destroying wealth ($ROE < k$).

Another useful manipulation of the basic Gordon growth model formulation provided by English (2001, pp. 353–4) follows from making a substitution for the dividend payout ratio, b, using the clean surplus relationship: $D(t) = bE(t) = (E(t) - (BV(t) - BV(t - 1)))$. Observing that constant growth in dividends with a constant dividend payout gives $BV(t) = (1 + g)BV(t - 1)$ (see end of chapter questions), it follows:

$$b = \frac{E(t) - gBV(t-1)}{E(t)} = 1 - \frac{g}{k}\left(\frac{kBV(t-1)}{E(t)}\right)$$

Recalling that the definition for $AE(t)$ requires, $kBV(t-1) = E(t) - AE(t)$, the expression for b can be manipulated to get:

$$b = \frac{1}{k}\left[k - g + g\left(\frac{AE(t)}{E(t)}\right)\right]$$

Substituting this result into the P/E ratio expression associated with the Gordon growth model produces the *abnormal earnings form of the P/E ratio*:

$$\frac{P(0)}{E(0)} = \frac{1+g}{k}\left\{1 + \left(\frac{AE(1)}{E(1)}\right)\left[\frac{g}{k-g}\right]\right\}$$

Compared to the simple Gordon growth model formulation of the P/E ratio, by making the connection between P/E and the ability to generate "abnormal earnings" this formulation is more revealing.

The relationship between the P/E ratio and growth of the firm is a subject that receives attention in almost every introductory investments textbook, e.g., Bodie et al. (1999). The conventional starting point is the *"present value of growth opportunities"* (*PVGO*) formulation of the P/E ratio. The simplifying, if somewhat confusing, assumption is made that there is benchmark "firm" that is able to generate a constant stream of earnings into perpetuity that are fully paid out to common shareholders, i.e., $b = 1$. The value of this firm would be $P(0)^* = E(1)/k$. The definition of the $PVGO$ reflected in the stock price for any given firm follows appropriately as: $P(0) = P(0)^* + PVGO$. Expressed as a P/E ratio, this formulation is: $(P(0)/E(1)) = (1/k)[1 + (PVGO/P(0)^*)]$. Hence, the P/E ratio will be higher for firms with higher growth opportunities. Within this framework, it can be shown that $g = ROE(1-b)$ and substituting into the Gordon growth model P/E ratio gives: $(P(0)/E(1)) = (b/\{k - (1-b)(ROE)\})$. In this case, firms with higher ROE, which reflects growth opportunities, will have a higher P/E ratio. If accurate, these types of formulas would provide precise information about the relationship between P/E and growth opportunities.

One application of the different formulas for the P/E ratio is to illustrate the behavior of the *"PEG" ratio*, or P/E to growth rate ratio. This ratio is sometimes used as a crude rule of thumb to determine under/over valuation for a common stock. For example, a PEG rule could be formulated as: if the PEG ratio is less than one then the stock is undervalued because the "cost of growth" as measured by the P/E is less than the actual growth. The AE form of the P/E can be used to show that this rule is difficult to apply in practice, even when simplifying assumptions are made, i.e.:

$$\frac{P(0)}{100gE(0)} = \frac{PEG}{100} = \frac{1}{100}\left[\frac{1+g}{kg} + \frac{1+g}{k}\frac{AE(1)}{E(1)}\frac{1}{k-g}\right]$$

Scaling by 100 follows from recognizing that the PEG rule assumes the growth rate is expressed as a percentage whole number. It follows that if $AE(1) = 0$ because, say, the firm is in "competitive equilibrium," then if $k = g = .1$ the PEG rule will be approximately correct. However, if $k = g = .05$, then the PEG will equal 4. Even without examining cases where $AE(1) \neq 0$, the PEG ratio rule can be seen to have significant limitations.

There is not complete agreement about what is to be considered a DCF model. To the capital budgeting purists, a DCF model discounts the net cash flows. In this case, the variable being discounted is cash flow and is to be interpreted in a cash accounting sense. Given that the only cash payments received by the buy-and-hold common stock investor are dividends, this leads to the discounted dividend model and its variants, such as the Gordon model. Others expand the DCF universe to include cash flows that involve accrual accounting numbers, as in the residual income models, or involve a combination of accrual and cash flow accounting, as in the *free cash flow to equity model* or the EVA models. These models seek to provide a more representative cash flow measure that captures a specific objective. Whether these techniques are successful at achieving that objective is unclear, with conflicting academic evidence on the issue. The free cash flow to equity model (*FCFE*) aims to measure the return to equity above the amount required to: maintain existing production levels; or, alternatively, to keep the firm on a particular growth path. The EVA models seek to discount the future "economic profit" generated by the firm.

To derive the *FCFE* DCF model, observe that the cash flow in this case is free cash flow (see section 8.2). Discounting of these cash flows leads to the general form of this DCF model:

$$P(0) = \sum_{t=1}^{\infty} \frac{FCFE^*(t)}{(1 + k)^t}$$

where $FCFE^*(t)$ is $FCFE(t)$ expressed on a per share basis. Recognizing that constant growth in dividends with a constant dividend payout does not ensure that *FCFE* will also grow at the same rate, it is possible to assume that *FCFE* grows at a constant rate g_f such that $FCFE(t) = FCFE(t - 1)(1 + g_f)$, this produces the simplified free cash flow valuation model: $P(0) = \{FCFE^*(0)(1 + g_f)\}/\{k - g_f\}$. Under appropriate assumptions, it is possible to assume $g = g_f$ though this may not be plausible in many situations (see end of chapter questions). Similar analysis can be applied to the EVA models.

Damodaran on simplified DCF valuation

It is not too difficult to inspect the simplified DCF models of stock valuation, such as the Gordon growth model, and dismiss these models based on superficial analysis of the model structure. For example, without simplifying assumptions such as "constant growth" the model is difficult to implement due to the larger number of terms that have to be estimated and calculated. Where the simplifying assumption of constant growth in dividends (earnings) is used, the empirical behavior of dividends (earnings) does not support the assumption that dividends (earnings) grow at a constant rate over time. In addition, the market practice of low or no dividend payout would seem to argue against straightforward application of DCF models where the cash flows are dividends. There are problems with obtaining estimates of k; there are problems with obtaining estimates of $D(1)$, and so it goes. However, consistent with Friedman's "positivist" approach, it does not follow that just because the assumptions of a model seem impractical or unrealistic, that the model is necessarily invalid. Before dismissing the model out of hand, it would be appropriate to examine the performance of the model in practice.

A search for the "best practices" approach to implementing the simplified DCF models leads to Damodaran (1994) where the implementation of the Gordon model and other types of DCF models reaches a relatively sophisticated stage of evolution.[4] Aswath Damodaran is a professor at the Stern School of Business at New York University (NYU) specializing in executive education and the author of a number of books along these lines. Given the just-around-the-corner proximity of the NYU business school campus to Wall Street, it is likely than many individuals in the New York financial community have been directly exposed to these ideas and have used, or attempted to use, the models in practical situations. Damodaran (1994) goes carefully over the appropriate procedures for estimating the discount rate, the cash flows and the growth rates. This background is then used to implement the dividend discount model and the free-cash-flow-to-equity discount model. Valuation results are provided for the common stocks of the firm types where the DCF model would be most likely to work.

Damodaran (1994, pp. 2–4) starts with six "*valuation myths*" that are useful to take into account in assessing the validity of the DCF technique. These myths are: "Since valuation models are quantitative, valuation is objective"; "A well-researched and well-done valuation is timeless"; "A good valuation provides a precise estimate of value"; "The more quantitative a model, the better the valuation"; "The market is generally wrong"; and, "The product of a valuation – the value – is what matters, the general process of valuation is not important." While it would be difficult to find many sources that adhere to or propose these "myths," dispelling the myths allows Damodaran to set a relatively low bar for the DCF modeling procedure. What follows is a sometimes insightful discussion and an honest attempt to implement the dividend discount model, both in Gordon model form and in two-stage and three stage form (see questions at the end of chapter). To do this specific companies are selected that are compatible with doing actual valuations with the dividend discount model.

The original Gordon model (Gordon 1962) was developed for valuation of companies in regulated industries. At that time, these types of companies included telephones and public utilities. The regulation of rates provided these companies with stable and relatively predictable cash flows. With this historical application in mind, a more modern *application of the Gordon dividend growth model* to Southwestern Bell illustrates the procedure followed by Damodaran (1994):

> Southwestern Bell has earnings per share of $4.33 in 1992 and paid out 63% of its earnings as dividends. Its earnings and dividends had grown at 6% a year between 1988 and 1992 and were expected to grow at the same rate in the long term. The beta for the stock was 0.95. The T-bond rate at the time of the analysis was 7%...

Cost of equity = 7% + 0.95 × 5.5% = 12.23%

Value of equity = $2.73 × 1.06/(0.1223 − 0.06) = $46.45

SW Bell was selling for $78.00 on the day of this analysis (May 1993).

Damodaran (1994, p. 103) then uses the $78.00 stock price to solve for g in the Gordon model as 8.43%. This is interpreted as the expected growth rate embedded in the current price which is 2.43% higher than the estimated historical growth rate.

There are many subtle features involved in this valuation. Consider the cost of equity that is estimated using a form of the capital asset pricing model (CAPM): $k_i = E[R_i] = r + \beta_i \{E[R_M] − r\}$. While it is conventional to use a short-term interest rate, such as the 3 month Treasury bill rate, for the riskless interest rate (r) in the estimating the CAPM, Damodaran uses the 30 year Treasury bond rate. This choice is made consciously with a rationale that "takes a strict view of matching the duration of the riskfree security with the duration of the asset being analyzed." Without stating how the duration of a common stock is calculated, Damodaran continues with the rationale: "At a practical level, in periods when the term structure follows historical patterns in the relationship between short rates and long rates and when the beta is close to one, all three variants will produce similar results" (p. 26). This is confusing because, if beta is close to one, then the riskless rate used will not matter in an arithmetic sense (as it will cancel out in the CAPM). However, in an estimation sense this will not be correct. It is not clear how "historical patterns" in yield curve slope will save the situation. All this is left unexplained in Damodaran (1994, ch. 3).

Another feature of Damodaran's analysis is the *estimation of the risk premium on the market*: $\{E[R_M] − r\}$ (see section 3.3). Damodaran estimates this value by using the difference of the annualized geometric means for a stock market index (10.08%) and the Treasury bond rate (4.58%) over a 1926–90 sample. This difference of 5.5% is used as the stock market risk premium to estimate the cost of equity from the CAPM that, in turn, is used as the discount rate (k) in the Gordon model. Damodaran recognizes that the difference of the geometric mean is smaller than the difference of the arithmetic means (12.13% − 4.90% = 7.23%). The rationale for this choice is stated as: "where cash flows over a long time horizon are discounted back to the present, the geometric mean provides a better estimate of the risk premium" (p. 22). Consistency would appear to require that geometric averages be used to estimate g but, despite recognition of this point (p. 68), it appears as though an arithmetic average is used. In addition, though there is no reference given to the specific stock market index used to calculate the geometric mean, comparison with evidence in Bodie et al. (1999) reveals that the index is the S&P Composite Index. Damodaran (1994, p. 103) explicitly recognizes that:

> the Gordon growth model is best suited for firms that are growing at a rate comparable to or lower than the nominal growth in the economy and that have well-established dividend-payout policies that they intend to continue into the future. The dividend payout of the firm has to be consistent with the assumption of stability, since stable firms generally pay substantial dividends. (The average payout for large stable firms in the United States is about 60%).

As illustrated in the use of SW Bell, large utilities qualify as examples of a "large stable firm." Another example used by Damodaran to illustrate a large stable firm that is not a utility is Exxon. In this case:

> Exxon has earnings per share of $3.82 in 1992 and paid out 74% of its earnings as dividends that year. The expected growth rate in earnings and dividends, in the long term, was expected to be 6%. The beta for Exxon was 0.75 and the T-Bond rate was 7% . . . Cost of equity = 7% + 0.75 × 5.5% = 11.13% . . . Value of equity per share = 2.83 × 1.06/(0.1113 − 0.06) = $58.47. Exxon was selling for $65.00 on the day of this analysis (May 1993).

Though the estimated value and the observed stock price are reasonably close, the analysis begs an obvious question about selection bias. Was Exxon selected more or less at random from the available group of "large stable non-utility" firms, or was Exxon selected because the Gordon growth model produced the most plausible price estimate from a group of such estimates?

The choice of Exxon as an example of a large stable firm suitable for application of the Gordon growth model seems misplaced because of the sensitivity of Exxon's earnings to developments in the oil sector. A more plausible type of firm would be a brewery such as Budweiser (BUD). Consider a valuation of Exxon, now Exxon-Mobil (XOM), in March 2003. The beta is relatively unchanged at 0.91 but the long Treasury bond rate has fallen to 5.375%. Solving for the cost of equity using the 5.5% long run risk premium on the market gives: 10.38% = 5.375% + 0.91(.055). Observing that the previous three years of dividends increase from .83 to .88 to .91 cents per share (2.68% dividend yield in the current year), gives a growth rate of $g = 4.4\%$. Dividend growth is used in favor of the more variable earnings growth. Using earnings over the three years, the dividend payout is less than 50%. Evaluating the Gordon growth model estimate of the price of the stock gives: (.91)(1.044)/(.1038 − .044) = 15.89. This does not compare favorably to the observed stock price of $34.37. Raising the growth rate to 5.4% (or lowering the market risk premium by 1/.91%) only raises the price estimate to $19.08. Solving for the growth rate that is consistent with the observed price gives $g = 7.7\%$.

How does Damodaran use the Gordon growth model to value a foreign stock? As another case of a "*stable large firm*," Damodaran (1994, p. 105) selects the second largest German bank, Dresdner Bank. It is estimated that Dresdner "maintained a growth rate of 5% in earnings and dividends between 1983 and 1992, and was expected to grow at this rate in the long term." The analysis continues that Dresdner:

> was also expected to have earnings per share of 34.05 DM in 1993 and to pay out 47.62% of its earnings as dividends. It had a beta of 0.87 in 1993, measured relative to the Frankfurt DAX. The ten-year bond rate in Germany at the end of July 1993 was 6.42% and the risk premium for stocks over bonds was assumed to be 3.5% . . . Cost of equity = 6.42% + (0.87 × 3.5%) = 9.45%
>
> Value of equity per share = 16.21 DM × 1.05/(0.0945 − 0.05) = 383.01 DM
>
> Dresdner Bank was trading at 408 DM per share in July 1993.

Similar to the Exxon and SW Bell estimates, Damodaran obtains a relatively close estimate of the observed stock price for Dresdner using the Gordon growth model. After examining the constant growth Gordon model, Damodaran (1994, ch. 6) goes on to consider two-stage and three-stage dividend growth models (see end of chapter questions), again obtaining reasonably accurate estimates of selected observed stock prices.

Damodaran's favorable, if relatively limited, application of the discounted dividend model to specific stocks is supported by Sorensen and Williamson (1985) which provides an *ex ante* application of the dividend discount model to 150 stocks in the S&P Composite Index. Valuation using a form of the dividend discount model was done in December 1980 and the stocks were held for two years with the result that stocks identified as "undervalued" significantly outperformed "overvalued" stocks. Further evidence in support of using the dividend discount model to identify undervalued stocks is provided by Haugen (1990) which examines the 1979–91 performance of a fund that used the dividend discount model to select undervalued stocks. Over the 1979–91 period, the quintile of stocks judged by the fund to be most undervalued using the dividend discount model outperformed the most overvalued by 1253% to 434%. Based on an examination of this evidence Damodaran (1994, p. 124) concludes: "The dividend discount model outperforms the market over five-year time periods, but there have been individual years when the model has significantly underperformed the market."

As with other adherents of modern Finance, Damodaran is not immune to the progress of received opinion. Confronted with a growing list of anomalies to the efficient markets hypothesis, modern Finance has shifted attention to assessing the differences between "value" and "growth" stocks. This distinction is defined by Dimson et al. (2002, p. 139):

> Since the earliest days of security analysis, experts stressed the potential benefits of buying at a price that is reasonable to fundamentals. The oldest yardstick is probably the price-to-dividend ratio, or its reciprocal, the dividend yield. But long ago, Graham and Dodd (1934) also urged investors to look for "a reasonable ratio of market price to average earnings," and further advised that "the book value deserves at least a fleeting glance by the public before it buys and sells shares." Stocks that trade at high dividend yield (a low price-to-dividend ratio), or a high earnings yield (a low price-to-earnings ratio), or a high ratio of book value of equity to the market value of equity, are often referred to as value stocks. Stocks that trade at a low dividend yield, low earnings yield, or low book-to-market are typically regarded as growth stocks.

Though a strong proponent of the discounted dividend model, this "*value vs. growth*" sentiment is echoed by Damodaran (1994, p. 125):

> The dividend-discount model weights expected earnings and dividends in near periods more than earnings and dividends in far periods, and it is biased towards finding low price/earnings-ratio stocks with high dividend yields to be undervalued and high price/earnings-ratio stocks with low- or no-dividend yields to be overvalued. Studies of market efficiency indicate that low P/E-ratio stocks have outperformed (in terms of excess returns) high P/E-ratio stocks over extended time periods. Similar conclusions have been drawn about high-dividend-yield stocks relative to low-dividend stocks. Thus the valuations of the model are consistent with the empirical irregularities observed in the market. It is unclear how much the model adds in value to investment strategies that use P/E ratios or dividend yields to screen stocks.

Decades after the DDM model was popularized by Gordon, proponents of modern Finance are still unable to make an accurate assessment of the validity of the model. Critics of the model correctly argue that the relevant variable to examine is cash that is returned to shareholders, which includes both dividends and net share repurchases (see end of chapter questions).

Expectations investing

The inadequacies of the simplified discounted cash flow (DCF) models, such as the Gordon model, stem from an attempt to over-generalize the common stock valuation problem. While the basic notion that the "true" stock price can be determined by appropriately discounting the expected net cash flows is fundamentally sound, the desire to develop general valuation formulas from this notion cuts the connection between the common stock and the specifics of the individual firm. Though there may be cases where the simplified DCF models provide a more than adequate estimate of the stock price, there are many other cases where the model gives misleading or incorrect results. Under the null hypothesis that a simplified DCF model such as the Gordon model is correct, it is possible to invert the model to solve for the growth rate that is consistent with the current stock price. This growth rate can then be compared with an estimate of the growth rate determined from, say, a fundamental analysis of the firm's operations to provide a framework for an investment decision. This type of exercise is a form of "expectations investing." As such, the natural progression from simplified DCF models to firm-by-firm fundamental analysis goes through the models such as the "expectations investing" model.

"*Expectations investing*" is a term coined by Rappaport and Mauboussin (2001) to characterize an investment strategy designed to "read market expectations and anticipate revisions to these expectations" as a "springboard for superior returns – long term returns above an appropriate benchmark." The basic intuition for expectations investing is derived from the idea that: "Stock prices express the collective expectations of investors, and changes in these expectations determine your investment success" (Rappaport and Mauboussin 2001, p. 2). This basic intuition is not new and can be found in prior contributions traceable to the beginnings of trading in joint stocks, e.g., the intuition is consistent with the intrinsic value approach of Graham and Dodd (1934). The approach is also consistent with the observation that a stock is worth what it will sell for in the market. This price reflects current "collective expectations." Assuming that there is some "true" value for the stock that depends on expectations consistent with economic fundamentals, then by comparing the market's collective estimate of this value with the true value then changes in expectations can be identified and an expectations investing decision can be made. What makes the "expectations investing" approach of interest is the method of estimating the "collective expectations" that are reflected in the current price and the process of determining the revision in expectations using "competitive strategy frameworks."

In order to estimate "*collective expectations*," the expectations investing approach uses the general discounted cash flow model to work backwards from the current price to arrive at an estimate of the expectations reflected in the current price. Though this can be done using, say, a simplified DCF model, Rappaport and Mauboussin (2001) claim "expectations investing" is "a sharp break from standard practice" because of the novel implementation of the DCF model. In addition, the method of estimating revisions in expectations, the "competitive strategy framework," focuses on firm specific "operating value drivers," i.e., sales growth, incremental investment rate and operating profit margins, and industry characteristics, such as barriers to entry and competition for market share, adjusted for the "value determinant," the cash tax rate. Given that this process can be implemented, it is claimed that expectations investing avoids the numerous limitations of traditional security analysis associated with using accounting numbers and the like to estimate economic values. This is in sharp contrast to English (2001, p. xii), for example, where: "the numbers produced by the GAAP financial accounting system, especially earnings measures, are the most useful single tool in equity analysis."

The beginnings of this connection between DCF valuation and the implied market expectation used in Rappaport and Mauboussin is available in Rappaport (1986). The basic principle of expectations investing follows from the mechanics of the general DCF model: the current price of the stock is the sum of the discounted expected value of future cash flows. Following Rappaport and Mauboussin (2001, p. 70):

> To accurately read the expectations wrapped in stock prices, you must think in the market's terms. The long-term discounted cash-flow model best captures the stock market's pricing mechanism. Yet investors justifiably think forecasting distant cash flows is extraordinarily hazardous. Credible long-term forecasts are difficult to make, and they only serve to reveal the forecasting investor's underlying biases. As Warren Buffett says, "Forecasts usually tell us more of a forecaster than of the future."

Given this, Rappaport and Mauboussin claim that the expectations investing procedure allows the user "to retain the discounted cash-flow model but frees you from the burden of cash-flow forecasts." The current stock price is used to "'read' what the market implies about a company's future performance."

While all this sounds exactly like what the doctor ordered, in practice the expectations investing process is a repackaged, if differently focused, type of fundamental analysis. There are a number of tip-offs in Rappaport and Mauboussin to the over-selling of the methodology, e.g., "be aware that reading expectations is as much an art as it is a science. The ability to read expectations improves with experience and industry know-ledge" (p. 71). To arrive at the cash flows to use in the DCF analysis, Rappaport and Mauboussin recommend the following process:

> You can consult a number of sources – Value Line Investment Survey, Standard & Poor's, Wall street reports (available directly or via services like Multex.com), and other research services – to establish a market consensus forecast for operating value drivers, that is, sales growth rate, operating profit margin, and incremental investment rate.

These "market consensus" estimates are then used to construct the cash flows using a pro forma procedure. But from the various possible measures available, what cash flows do Rappaport and Mauboussin suggest using in the DCF analysis?

As discussed in section 8.2, there are a number of possible candidates for the cash flows. Rappaport and Mauboussin (2001, p. 21) make the following recommendation:

> Exactly what do we mean by "cash flows," and how does it determine shareholder value? ...Let's take a quick road trip. The shareholder-value road map shows the following relationships: Sales growth and operating profit margin determine operating profit; Operating profit minus cash taxes yields net operating profit after taxes (NOPAT); NOPAT minus investments in working and fixed capital equals free cash flow. Think of free cash flow as the pool of cash available to pay the claims of debt-holders and shareholders; Free cash flows discounted at the cost of capital determine corporate value; Corporate value plus nonoperating assets minus the market value of debt equals shareholder value.

In the end for Rappaport and Mauboussin it is expected "*free cash flow*" that is the appropriate cash flow variable to discount in order to determine firm value. With some adjustments, estimated firm value is the basis for determining the estimate of the share price. Even though Rappaport and Mauboussin recommend working backward from the price, there is still the reliance on pro forma accounting numbers to generate the free cash flow inputs. The problems for accounting numbers raised by "economic value added" measures go unrecognized (see section 8.2).

The novelty of the general model of discounted cash flow valuation in Rappaport and Mauboussin (2001) is decidedly overstated. In recommending the use of free cash flow in the DCF analysis, Rappaport and Mauboussin do not differ substantively from, say, Damodaran (1994, ch. 7) where the dividend discount model is extended to discounted free-cash-flow-to-equity (FCFE): "The primary difference between the dividend-discount models ... and the FCFE models ... lies in the definition of *cash flows* – the dividend-discount model uses a strict definition of *cash flow* ... while the FCFE models uses an expansive definition of *cash-flow-to-equity* (the residual cash flow after meeting all financial obligations and investment)." Damodaran (1994, p. 143) is less enthusiastic about FCFE vs. dividends as the cash flow measure than Rappaport and Mauboussin, though still mildly positive: "When firms have dividends that are different from the FCFE, the values from these two [discounted cash flow] models will be different. In valuing firms for takeovers or in valuing firms in which there is a reasonable chance of changing corporate control, the value from the FCFE model provides a better estimate of value."

Similar to the DCF modeling approach advocated by corporate finance textbooks, Rappaport and Mauboussin use estimates of the firm's weighted average cost of capital for the discount rate. Recognizing that Rappaport and Mauboussin want to estimate firm value and then make appropriate adjustments to arrive at the value of equity, this is not particularly novel. What is somewhat different in the expectations investing, DCF modeling process is the approach to the problem of determining the number of future periods to use in obtaining the current market price:

> The final value determinant is the number of years of free cash flows required to justify the stock price. We call this horizon the *market-implied forecast period* (it's also called the "value growth duration" and "competitive advantage period"). Practically, the market-implied

forecast period measures how long the market expects a company to generate returns that exceed its cost of capital and consequently add no further value. The market implied forecast period for US stocks clusters between ten and fifteen years, but it can range from zero to as long as thirty years for companies with strong competitive positions.

It is the "*market-implied forecast period*" that Rappaport and Mauboussin adopted from Rappaport (1986). Rappaport and Mauboussin (2001, pp. 73–6) provide a practical application of the whole process to Gateway Computers where, for a valuation done in April 2000, the market-implied forecast period is estimated to be seven years.

The final Rappaport and Mauboussin (2001, p. 110) observation needed to confirm the lack of novelty in the expectations approach arises with the suggested process for the "buy decision":

> Stated simply, whenever you estimate that the expected value is greater than the stock price, you have potential opportunity to earn an excess return. However, the prospect of an excess return is by itself not enough to signal a genuine buying opportunity. You must still decide whether the excess return is sufficient to warrant purchase.
>
> Your decision depends on two factors. The first is the stock price's percentage discount to expected value, or its margin of safety. The greater is the discount to expected value, the higher the prospective excess return – and the more attractive a stock is for purchase. Inversely, the higher a stock's price premium to its expected value, the more compelling the selling opportunity.
>
> The second factor is how long it will take for the market to revise its expectations. The sooner the stock price converges toward the higher expected value, the greater the excess return. By the same logic, when expected value is below the current stock price, the faster the price converges toward expected value, and the greater the urgency to sell the stock.

In advocating the "*margin of safety*" principle, Rappaport and Mauboussin are adhering to a Graham and Dodd prescription. In considering "how long it will take for the market to revise its expectations," Rappaport and Mauboussin are doing little more than academic posturing. There is little in "expectations investing" that provides guidance on the speed of expectations convergence.

All things considered, does expectations investing represent a novel approach to equity analysis that is a "sharp break" from conventional approaches. Aside from the focus on "competitive strategy" analysis as a method for evaluating future firm performance, there does not seem to be much in expectations investing that is unconventional. Even the use of competitive strategy analysis is not overly novel when the drivers, such as sales growth and operating profit margins, are identified. The final nail in the expectations investing coffin concerns the valuation of Gateway Inc. (GTW), the firm that was used as the primary practical example to illustrate the relevant techniques. If there is "more art than science" in expectations investing then, perhaps, this would have been supported in an insightful evaluation of this firm. The valuation was initially done for April 2000 when GTW was selling for $52. The implied-market forecast of seven years was determined by using a "consensus" sales growth value of 20%, operating profit margin of 9%, cash tax rate of 35%, and incremental fixed-capital rate of 11% and an incremental working capital rate of –5%. Using these values, sales were projected to grow from $10.3 billion in 2000 to $30 billion in 2006.

Rappaport and Mauboussin (2001, pp. 103–10) revisit Gateway in early 2001, at a time that GTW is trading in the low twenties. To motivate the buy decision, Rappaport and Mauboussin apply expected value analysis to GTW, providing a sales growth rate range from 6% "low" to 28% "high," with a "*price implied expectations*" (PIE) growth of 20%. This leads to estimated low and high stock price values of $18.05 and $76. Simple expected value calculations are then recommended using, for example, 50% probability for PIE with 20% probability for the low growth rate and 30% probability for the high to recreate the $52 price observed in April 2000. The bearish "non-consensus" value of $26.06 is produced with probabilities of 80% low, 15% PIE and 5% high. Rappaport and Mauboussin do not address the actual change in GTW from April 2000 to early 2001, where the stock price was even lower than the "bearish non-consensus" value of $26.06. Even more disturbing, the next two years sales performance for GTW has witnessed a fall in sales from $9.6 billion (12/31/2000), to $6.08 billion (12/31/2001) to $4.17 billion (12/31/2002), a decline over the three years of –21.57% per year. Having done the expectations investing analysis on the verge of a major collapse in fundamentals for GTW, Rappaport and Mauboussin were unable to forecast the dramatic impending changes looming just ahead.

8.2 INTERPRETING FINANCIAL STATEMENTS

Financial statement analysis

One of the tenets of GDC (1962, p. 105) is: "All security analysis involves the analysis of financial statements." Warren Buffett's recommendation of the discounted cash flow (DCF) model raises a legitimate question about how "cash flows" are determined from the accounting and other information provided by the firm. Even Fisher's focus on the characteristics of the business requires interpreting information from the firm's financial statements in order to make assessments about the performance of the business. Penman (2001, p. 12) makes the observation: "Payoffs from operations have to be measured. Are they cash inflows minus cash outflows (net cash flows)? Are they revenues minus expenses (net income)? If so, how is revenue measured and how is expense measured? Specifying and measuring the payoffs is critical to valuation [fundamental] analysis. It is an accounting issue." The subject of financial statement analysis is concerned with the various methods for extracting information from the financial statements of the firm. This includes both the current and past statements, as well as forecasts of future statements, i.e., pro forma analysis.

Under US generally accepted accounting principles (*GAAP*), the accounting statements that are typically available for analysis are: the *balance sheet*, the *income statement*, the *cash flow statement*, and the *statement of stockholders' equity*. In addition to these statements, there is also the footnotes and other supplementary information that is provided along with the four basic statements. Best practices in the preparation of the annual report for the firm is to expand and detail the information that is contained in the financial statements. For example, the annual reports of the major Canadian banks contain a detailed discussion of the various sources of risk that face the firm, including value-at-risk estimates for the range of major market risks facing the firm arising from interest rates, exchange rates and commodity prices. Though a strict interpretation of financial statement analysis includes only "analysis of the financial statements," this "analysis" can be greatly aided by considering or incorporating the discussion that is included in the body of the annual report, 10-K or other document that is being used as the source of the financial statements. When such information is considered, the analyst cannot lose sight of the possible biases that can arise if the various pronouncements of the firm's management are taken at face value.

Following Penman (2001, ch. 2), analysis of financial statements requires discussion of both *form* and *content*. Form deals with the manner that the statements, and parts of the statements, fit together. Content deals with the various line items that are reported in the statements. Except for specific items of interest, detailed consideration of content falls within the realm of accounting theory and practice, a topic that lies outside the scope of this discussion. For US companies, content is largely determined by the GAAP formulated by the Financial Accounting Standards Board (FASB). For securities that are publicly traded in US securities markets (including many large cap Canadian stocks), SEC rules ensure adherence to GAAP.[5] There are numerous excellent sources on GAAP for financial accounting, e.g., Bernstein (1989). Accounting principles for securities traded outside the US are subject to accounting rules for those jurisdictions, with the International Accounting Standards Board (IASB) providing guidance in many non-US jurisdictions. While there are some jurisdictions that do impose "revealing" accounting standards, e.g., Canada and Singapore, it is unwise to expect the type of company information provided under US accounting standards to be available when foreign securities are being considered.

Though there are numerous constraints imposed by GAAP on financial accounting practices, *GAAP is not a strait-jacket.* There is some scope for working within GAAP to present accounts that are the most representative of the activities of the firm. This means that companies involved in different businesses or in more than one line of business will present accounts that do not have exactly the same content, e.g., because there is no information to report in certain content categories. There may also be some cosmetic differences in form. This is illustrated in table 8.1 that provides the "Sector Statement of Income" (income statement) for Ford Motor Company.[6] In addition to the consolidated form of the income statement, Ford also reports the sector income statement to recognize the two distinct parts of the business: automotive; and, financial services (about 80% Ford Credit and 17% Hertz). The typical form of the income statement is repeated for both of these parts, though the content items do differ. In addition to being the source of the important "net income" figure, i.e., the earnings generated by the firm for equity claimholders, the income statement contains numerous other items that can be used in the evaluation of company performance.

A model format for the income statement is given in Penman (2001, p. 33), based on the financial statement of Dell Computer (DELL):[7]

Table 8.1 Ford Motor Company and subsidiaries, sector statement of income, for the periods ended December 31, 2003 and 2002 ($ millions, except per share amounts)

	Full year	
	2003 (unaudited)	2002
Automotive		
Sales	138,442	134,273
Costs and expenses		
Cost of Sales	129,821	125,043
Selling, administrative and other expenses	10,152	9,758
Total costs and expenses	139,973	134,801
Operating income/(loss)	(1,531)	(528)
Interest income	870	834
Interest expense	1,370	1,368
Net interest income/(expense)	(500)	(534)
Equity in net income/(loss) of affiliated companies	74	(91)
Income/(loss) before income taxes		
Automotive	(1,957)	(1,153)
Financial Services		
Revenues	25,754	27,983
Costs and expenses		
Interest expense	6,320	7,468
Depreciation	8,779	10,162
Operating and other expenses	4,971	4,974
Provision for credit and insurance losses	2,357	3,275
Total costs and expenses	22,427	25,879
Income/(loss) before income taxes		
Financial Services	3,327	2,104
Total company		
Income/(loss) before income taxes	1,370	951
Provision for/(benefit from) income taxes	135	301
Income/(loss) before minority interests	1,235	650
Minority interests in net income/(loss) of subsidiaries	314	367
Income/(loss) from continuing operations	921	283
Income/(loss) from discontinued/held-for-sale operations	(8)	(62)
Loss on disposal of discontinued/held-for-sale operations	(154)	(199)
Cumulative effect of change in accounting principle	(264)	(1,002)
Net income/(loss)	495	(980)
Income/(loss) attributable to common and class B stock after preferred stock dividends	495	(995)

Table 8.1 (*Con'd*)

	Full year 2003 (unaudited)	2002
Average number of shares of common and class B stock outstanding	1,832	1,819
Amounts per share of common and class B stock		
Basic income/(loss)		
Income/(loss) from continuing operations	0.50	0.15
Income/(loss) from discontinued/held-for-sale operations	–	(0.04)
Loss on disposal of discontinued/held-for-sale operations	(0.09)	(0.11)
Cumulative effect of change in accounting principle	(0.14)	(0.55)
Net income/(loss)	0.27	(0.55)
Diluted income/(loss) Income/(loss) from continuing operations	0.50	0.15
Income/(loss) from discontinued/held-for-sale operations	–	(0.03)
Loss on disposal of discontinued/held-for-sale operations	(0.09)	(0.11)
Cumulative effect of change in accounting principle	(0.14)	(0.55)
Net income/(loss)	0.27	(0.54)
Cash dividends	0.40	0.40

> Net revenue – Cost of goods sold = Gross margin
> Gross margin – Operating expenses = Operating income before tax (EBIT)
> Operating income before tax – Interest expense = Income before taxes
> Income before taxes – Income taxes = Income after taxes (and before extraordinary items)
> Income before extraordinary items + Extraordinary items = Net income
> Net income – Preferred dividends = Net income available to common

In the Ford (F) income statement, "net revenue" is replaced by "sales" for the automotive component and "revenues" for financial services. Other variations are also possible. For example: Alcan Inc. (AL) uses a general category for "Revenues" and then provides subsections for "Sales and Operating Revenues" and "Other Income"; Transocean Inc. (RIG) reports a line item for "Operating Revenues"; and US Steel Group (X) reports a general category for "Revenues and other income" that includes "revenues," "income from investees," "net gains on disposal of assets" and "other income" (see table 8.2). Banks use a somewhat different format. For example, the income statement provided in the annual report for the Royal Bank of Canada (RY), which is prepared under Canadian GAAP, has two general categories, one for "interest income" and another for "other income." Each of these categories contains numerous subheadings that decompose income by source.

Table 8.2 United States Steel Corporation, statement of operations (unaudited: $ millions, except per share amounts)

	Year ended	
	December 31, 2003	December 31, 2002
Revenue and other Income		
Revenues	9,328	6,949
Income (loss) from investees	(11)	33
Net gains on disposal of assets	85	29
Other income	56	43
Total revenues and other income	9,458	7,054
Costs and expenses		
Cost of revenues (excludes items shown below)	8,469	6,158
Selling, general and administrative expenses	673	418
Depreciation, depletion and amortization	363	350
Restructuring charges	–	683
Total costs and expenses	10,188	6,926
Income (loss) from operations	(730)	128
Net interest and other financial costs	130	115
Income (loss) before income taxes, extraordinary loss and cumulative effect of change in accounting principles	(860)	13
Benefit for income taxes	(454)	(48)
Income (loss) before extraordinary loss and cumulative effect of change in accounting principle	(406)	61
Extraordinary loss, net of tax	(52)	–
Cumulative effect of change in accounting principle, net of tax	(5)	–
Net Income (loss)	(463)	61
Dividends on preferred stock	(16)	–
Net income (loss) applicable to common stock	(479)	61
Common stock data		
Per share basic and diluted:		
Income (loss) before extraordinary loss and cumulative effect of change in accounting principle	(4.09)	0.62
Extraordinary loss, net tax	(0.50)	
Cumulative effect of change in accounting principle, net of tax	(0.05)	–
Net income (loss)	(4.64)	0.062
Weighted average shares, in thousands		
Basic	103,179	97,426
Diluted	103,179	97,428
Dividends paid per share	0.20	0.20

The basic problem of financial statement analysis is to translate accounting numbers into a viable economic interpretation of the operations of the firm. As such, the cash flows in DCF analysis can be interpreted as the economic profits generated by the firm. In economics, profits are defined as revenues minus costs. Subject to adjustments for accruals, revenues can usually be taken directly from the income statement. However, the precise cost items to include in the calculation of economic profits is not obvious. The income statement provides various possible methods of determining costs. Inclusion of all cash and accrual costs items results in *the income statement accounting relationship*:

$$\text{Revenue} - \text{Costs} = \text{Net income.}$$

After deduction for preferred dividends, this is the "cash flow" or net income or "earnings" available to common shareholders. Under clean surplus accounting, these earnings are either paid out as dividends or retained by the firm and used to make additions to the assets of the firm. Yet, there are legitimate reasons to consider other ways of calculating economic profits than earnings available to common. For example, "depreciation costs" are a non-cash expense that is calculated according to accounting rules. The value used may or may not represent the economic depreciation of assets.

The various possible methods of calculating revenues minus costs is facilitated by the accounting procedures for reporting cost items. As such, the revenue item usually has considerably less components than the cost line. The components of cost almost always include four key items: cost of goods sold; selling general and administrative expenses; depreciation, depletion and amortization; and income taxes. If the firm has engaged in borrowing activities then there will be another item associated with the "interest expense" or "net interest expense," with both interest revenue and interest expense usually being reported in the latter case. For example, in table 8.1, Ford reports an interest expense item for both the automotive and financial services divisions, together with an interest revenue component for the automotive division. In table 8.2, US Steel reports only an item for "net interest and other financial costs." Information about the sources of interest revenue can be obtained from the balance sheet and the notes to the financial statements. For companies involved in financial intermediation, such as commercial and investment banks, the handling of interest costs and expenses will be decidedly more complicated.

Other important cost items may appear depending on the company's type of business. For example, oil and gas companies such as Suncor (SU) will include a line item for "exploration" and, possibly, "royalties." Technology companies, such as Genetech (DNA) or Intel (INTC), will include a line for "research and development." For companies that have been actively involved in mergers and acquisitions, e.g., Transocean, there will be an item for "goodwill amortization." There are also items that have a classification component. One such item is "gain (loss) from the sale of assets." US Steel classifies this item under revenue, while Transocean treats this as an expense. Both of these treatments involve accounting for this item in operating income before interest and taxes (EBIT). In certain situations, it is not straightforward to determine whether such items appear in EBIT or are subtracted afterward as "extraordinary gains and losses." This classification decision can have significant implications for analysis of profitability that uses measures such as EBIT and EBITDA.

In section 7.1, the common stock valuation problem was related to the "stock" and "flow" interaction encountered in the theoretical economic analysis of the firm. The "stock" of productive assets, both tangible and intangible, produces a "flow" of earnings. The income statement relates to the accounting for the flow component and the balance sheet relates to the "stock" component. Insofar as the *market value* of assets reflects the ability to generate cash flow, then the balance sheet can also be used as vehicle for valuation of the firm's securities. Because of the complicated interaction of tangible and intangible assets that is involved in the production of net income, it is usually not practical to sum the market value each asset to determine an aggregate market value of assets. Rather, it is more appropriate to assess the acquisition value of the firm's assets as a whole. Except for large sophisticated investors such as Warren Buffett, this is not typically an exercise that can be accomplished by individual investors. Rather, when an ability to estimate acquisition value is not available, then the balance sheet becomes an adjunct to analysis of the income statement, providing information about: the stock of assets used to generate net income; and, the capital structure used to finance those assets.

Theoretically, the balance sheet is the appropriate accounting statement to use for determining the value of common stock. This is apparent from the *basic balance sheet accounting identity*:

$$\text{Assets} - \text{Liabilities} = \text{Shareholders' equity.}$$

Netting out the value of preferred stock and dividing the remaining value of share-holders' equity (or, as in Ford's balance sheet, "stockholders' equity") by the number of shares outstanding gives a value for a share of common stock. Yet, for a whole range of reasons, this estimated value for common stock will differ significantly from the observed market price. In other words, the book value of equity does not typically provide an accurate estimate for the market value of the common stock. The book value of equity is an accounting number that reflects the initial capital invested in the business plus the accumulated retained earnings. Understanding how this accounting number can deviate from the economic or intrinsic value of equity is a key aspect of accurately doing a security analysis. The ratio of the *market capitalization of equity* (market cap) – the market price of common stock times the number of shares outstanding – to the book value of common stockholders' equity – *the price-to-book ratio (P/BV)* – is a key measure of this aspect of security analysis.

The composition of the balance sheet is considerably less complicated to understand than that of the income statement (see tables 8.3 and 8.4). However, simplicity and various problems associated with book values versus market values does not mean that the balance sheet is uninteresting. Depending on the specific valuation, there are numerous items on the balance sheet that are of interest. For example, GDC identified

Table 8.3 Ford Motor Company and subsidiaries, sector balance sheet ($ millions)

	December 31, 2003 (unaudited)	December 31, 2002
Assets		
Automotive		
Cash and cash equivalents	5,427	5,157
Marketable securities	10,749	17,464
Loaned securities	5,667	–
Total cash, marketable and loaned securities	21,843	22,621
Receivables, net	2,721	2,047
Inventories	9,181	6,977
Deferred income taxes	3,225	3,462
Other current assets	6,052	4,547
Current receivable from Financial Services	–	1,062
Total current assets	43,022	40,716
Equity in net assets of affiliated companies	1,930	2,470
Net property	41,993	36,352
Deferred income taxes	12,092	11,694
Goodwill	5,378	4,719
Other intangible assets	876	812
Assets of discontinued/held-for-sale operations	68	246
Other assets	15,282	10,781
Total Automotive assets	120,641	107,790
Financial Services		
Cash and cash equivalents	16,343	7,064
Investments in securities	1,123	807
Finance receivables, net	110,893	97,007
Net investment in operating leases	31,859	39,727
Retained interest in sold receivables	13,017	17,618
Goodwill	769	749
Other intangible assets	239	248
Assets of discontinued/held-for-sale operations	388	2,783
Other assets	17,292	16,626
Receivable from Automotive	3,356	4,803
Total Financial Services assets	195,279	187,432
Total assets	315,920	295,222
Liabilities and stockholders' equity		
Automotive		
Trade payables	15,289	14,579
Other payables	2,942	2,471
Accrued liabilities	32,171	27,615
Debt payable within one year	1,806	551
Current payable to Financial Services	124	–
Total current liabilities	52,332	45,216

Table 8.3 (*Cont'd*)

	December 31, 2003 (unaudited)	December 31, 2002
Senior debt	13,832	13,607
Subordinated debt	5,155	—
Total long-term debt	18,987	13,607
Other liabilities	45,104	46,887
Deferred income taxes	2,352	303
Liabilities of discontinued/held-for-sale operations	94	213
Payable to Financial Services	3,232	4,803
Total Automotive liabilities	122,101	111,029
Financial Services		
Payables	2,189	1,886
Debt	159,011	148,054
Deferred income taxes	11,061	11,629
Other liabilities and deferred income	9,211	9,441
Liabilities of discontinued/held-for-sale operations	37	861
Payable to Automotive	—	1,062
Total Financial Services liabilities	181,509	172,933
Company-obligated mandatorily redeemable preferred securities of subsidiary trusts holding solely junior subordinated debentures of the Company	—	5,670
Minority interests	659	—
Stockholders' equity		
Capital stock		
Common stock, par value $0.01 per share (1,837 million shares issued)	18	18
Class B stock, par value $0.01 per share (71 million shares issued)	1	1
Capital in excess of par value of stock	5,374	5,420
Accumulated other comprehensive income/(loss)	(414)	(6,531)
Treasury stock	(1,749)	(1,977)
Earnings retained for use in business	8,421	8,659
Total stockholders' equity	11,651	5,590
Total liabilities and stockholders' equity	315,920	295,222

Table 8.4 United States Steel Corporation, balance sheet data ($ millions)

	Dec. 31, 2003	Dec. 31, 2002
Cash and cash equivalents	316	243
Other current assets	2,869	2,197
Property, plant and equipment net	3,415	2,978
Pension asset	8	1,654
Other assets	1,223	905
Total assets	7,831	7,977
Current liabilities	2,137	1,372
Long-term debt	1,890	1,408
Employee benefits	2,375	2,601
Other long-term liabilities	336	569
Stockholders' equity	1,093	2,027
Total liabilities and stockholders' equity	7,831	7,977

the net current asset position per share as an important indicator of value. For both Ford and US Steel the employee pension and benefit plans are key items. For Ford, this item is bundled into "other liabilities" while for US Steel the item is reported as "employee benefits" and "prepaid pensions." Another important balance sheet item is the property, plant and equipment account. For Ford, this item is itemized as "net property." In both cases, the property, plant and equipment item (PPE) includes an allowance for accumulated depreciation. Because both Ford and US Steel are engaged in industries with large amounts tangible assets and relatively low intangible assets, evaluation of the market value of PPE is an important element in assessing the "acquisition value" of these companies.

As illustrated in figure 8.1, the income statement, cash flow statement and statement of changes in shareholders' equity conceptually capture different aspects of changes in the balance sheet. Yet another approach explaining balance sheet changes is the *clean surplus equation*:

$$E_t = D_t + RE_t = D_t + BV_t - BV_{t-1} \quad \rightarrow \quad E_t - D_t = \Delta A - \Delta L$$

Historically, accounting practice was content to provide only the income statement and the balance sheet. As discussed above, these statements alone have certain limitations for analytical purposes. To address some of these limitations, the cash flow statement and statement of changes in shareholders' equity are prepared. While the statement of changes in shareholders' equity has limited analytical uses, the cash flow statement can be invaluable. This statement is based on a rearrangement of balance sheet and income statement items into a form that is particularly well suited for identifying items of relevance in security analysis, such as free cash flow.

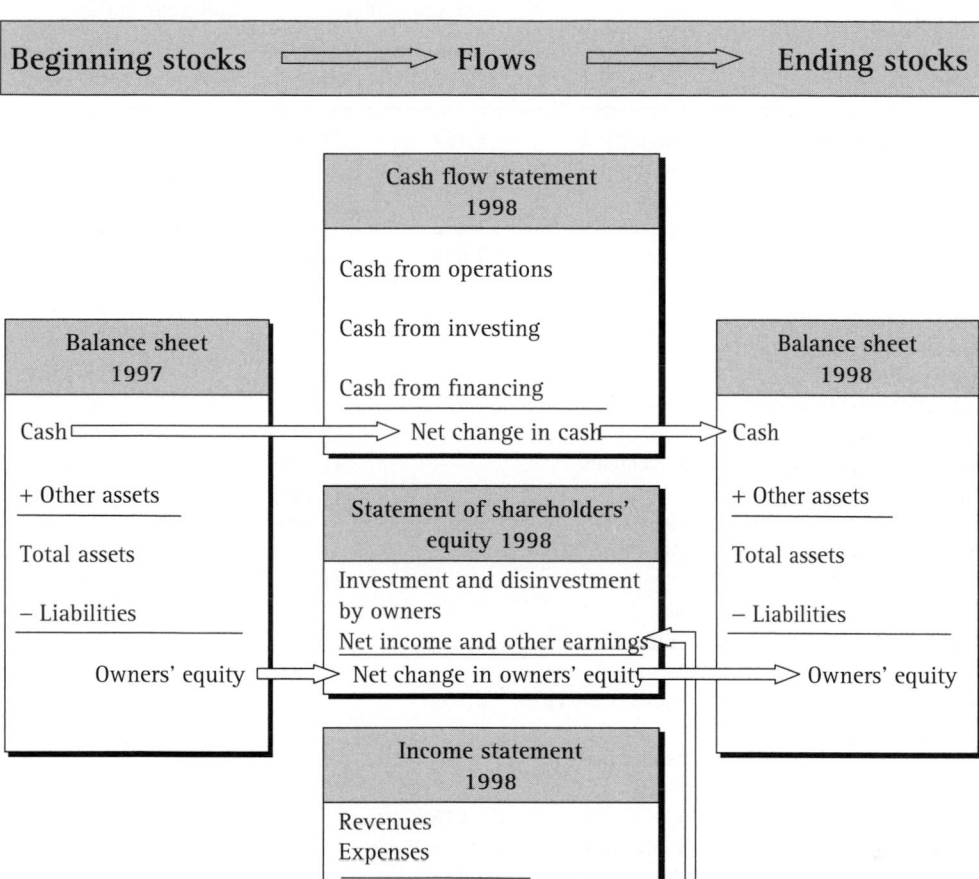

Figure 8.1 Relationship among the four financial statements
Source: Adapted from Penman (2001)

The *cash flow statement* is based on the following identity:

Change in cash = Cash from operations + Cash from investing activities
+ Cash from financing activities

Though it might seem that the change in cash is only an incidental item for most valuations, it is the process of arriving at the change that is important. By collecting items according to function, the activities of the firm reflected in the other accounting statements becomes more transparent. It is often stated that earnings are, in many ways, something of a fiction. The rationale for this observation is apparent in table 8.6 where,

Table 8.5 Ford Motor Company and subsidiaries, condensed sector statement of cash flows, for the periods ended December 31, 2003 and 2002 ($ millions)

	Full year 2003		Full year 2002	
	Automotive (Unaudited)	Financial Services	Automotive	Financial Services
Cash and cash equivalents at January 1	5,157	7,064	4,053	3,131
Cash flows from operating activities before securities trading	1,336	17,052	9,479	15,261
Net sales/(purchases) of trading securities	1,282	525	(6,206)	(23)
Net cash flows from operating activities	2,618	17,577	3,273	15,238
Cash flows from investing activities				
Capital expenditures	(7,370)	(379)	(6,774)	(502)
Acquisitions of receivables and lease investments	–	(62,980)	–	(81,690)
Collections of receivables and lease investments	–	42,727	–	45,767
Net acquisitions of daily rental vehicles	–	(1,505)	–	(1,846)
Purchases of securities	(8,925)	(1,149)	(3,446)	(609)
Sales and maturities of securities	8,673	709	3,445	479
Proceeds from sales of receivables and lease investments	–	21,145	–	41,289
Proceeds from sale of businesses	77	204	257	–
Repayment of debt from discontinued operations	–	1,421	–	–
Net investing activity with Financial Services	3,708	–	1,053	–
Cash paid for acquisitions	–	–	(289)	–
Cash recognized on initial consolidation of joint ventures	256	–	–	–
Other	716	55	–	407
Net cash (used in)/provided by investing activities	(2,865)	248	(5,754)	3,295
Cash flows from financing activities Cash dividends	(733)	–	(743)	
Net sales/(purchases) of Common Stock	9	–	287	
Proceeds from mandatorily redeemable convertible preferred securities	–	–	4,900	
Preferred Stock – Series B redemption	–		(177)	
Changes in short-term debt	(237)	1,542	(31)	(14,140)
Proceeds from issuance of other debt	1,144	21,942	318	15,524
Principal payments on other debt	(1,097)	(27,683)	(859)	(15,760)
Net financing activity with Automotive	–	(3,708)	–	(1,053)
Other	(15)	(4)	(23)	369
Net cash (used in)/provided by financing activities	(929)	(7,911)	3,672	(15,060)
Effect of exchange rate changes on cash	260	551	37	336
Net transactions with Automotive/Financial Services	1,186	(1,186)	(124)	124
Net increase/(decrease) in cash and cash equivalents	270	9,279	1,104	3,933
Cash and cash equivalents at December 31	5,427	16,343	5,157	7,064

in 2001, US Steel had a net income loss of $218 million compared to $21 million in 2000. Yet, cash provided by operating activities in 2001 was $669 million versus a loss of $627 million in 2000. Though similar capital expenditures were done in both years, the better earnings picture in 2000 was created by a $1.2 billion increase in debt whereas a debt repayment of $370 million was made in 2001. The cash flow statement reveals that the situation at Ford is the reverse. Table 8.5 reveals that the large loss in net income for Ford is due primarily to a deterioration of the core business, as reflected in the large drop in cash generated by operating activities. The impact of the weak operating situation on net income is mitigated by the allowance made for capital expenditures and acquisitions being at a lower level than in previous years as well as a lower level of payment in cash dividends.

The motivation for the *Statement of Stockholders' Equity* – to reconcile the items that produced the change in the book value of equity over the period – is well conceived. However the execution leaves much to be desired (and no examples of this statement are provided here). The basic accounting identity for this statement is, more or less, the same as the clean surplus equation: *Change in Shareholders' Equity = Earnings − Net cash paid to shareholders*. As Penman (2001, p. 35) observes: "Unfortunately, the statement is not presented as clearly as this reconciliation of beginning and ending equity prescribes. Indeed, . . . the accounting in this statement is rather poor." Yet, this does not mean this statement is always without value. For example, the impact of foreign currency translation losses and derivative accounting transactions on Ford Motor is revealed. Negative values for such items can, in some cases, be offset by positive values in later periods mitigating the impact on shareholders' equity. This type of revealing information is not always the case. For example, the statement of shareholders' equity reveals little about the operations of US Steel. There was some impact on equity associated with transactions between Marathon and US Steel (the two components of USX), but the nature of these transactions is not apparent from inspection of this statement.

Earnings, free cash flow and EVA

The central importance of DCF valuation models in modern security analysis begs an obvious question: *what is the appropriate "cash flow" to discount in the DCF model?* Given the potential limitations in the net income number identified in the discussion of the cash flow statement, this earnings number that receives so much attention in "sell side" security analysis would seem to be a relatively poor candidate, though this is not a clear cut issue. Buffett recommends using owner's earnings calculated as "reported income" (presumably net income) plus depreciation, depletion, amortization, and certain other non-cash charges minus the average annual amount of capitalized expenditures for property plant and equipment and other items that the business requires to fully maintain its long-term competitive position and its unit volume. This is similar enough to the calculation of free cash flow that it could be called "*economic free cash flow.*" In other places, Buffett recommends discounting the amount of cash that will be paid out of during the life of the firm. Both of these measures are difficult to implement

Table 8.6 United States Steel Corporation, cash flow statement (unaudited: $ millions)

	Year ended December 31	
Cash flow data ($ millions)	2003	2002
Cash provided from (used in) operating activities:		
Net income (loss)	(463)	61
Depreciation, depletion and amortization	363	350
Restructuring charges	594	—
Working capital changes	488	(69)
Other operating activities	(409)	(63)
Total	573	279
Cash used in investing activities:		
Capital expenditures	(311)	(258)
Acquisition of National Steel Corporation assets	(839)	—
Acquisition of U.S. Steel Kosice	(37)	(38)
Acquisition of U.S. Steel Balkan	(28)	—
Other investing activities	82	(13)
Total	(1,133)	(309)
Cash provided from financing activities and foreign exchange rate changes:		
Issuance of long-term debt	427	—
Preferred stock issued	242	—
Common stock issued	23	227
Other financing activities	(59)	(101)
Total	633	126
Total net cash flow	73	96
Cash at beginning of the year	243	147
Cash at end of the year	316	243

precisely. Both notions require estimating values that are effectively unknown. The desire for more precision in the numbers used in the DCF analysis dictates that only cash flow variants derived from manipulation of accounting numbers be considered as viable proxies, e.g., English (2001, chs 14–16).

The form of the financial statements is determined by GAAP. There is no such guidance available where analysis of the financial statements is involved. Construction of "earnings" numbers as inputs for use in DCF analysis and other techniques of security analysis is guided more by conceptual intuition than precise rules. An example of this is provided by the text for the Canadian Securities Course (Canadian Securities Institute 1992), a certification course required to work in the Canadian securities markets. This source defines earnings per common share (EPS) as: [*Net earnings* (*before extra-ordinary items*) *– Preferred dividends*]/*Number of common shares outstanding*, where "net earnings" means "net income." While the adjustment of net income for preferred dividend payments is consistent with Bernstein (1993, ch. 12), the deduction of extraordinary items is not. On this point, Bernstein (1993, p. 767) observes: "in determining the earning power of an enterprise, no item of income and expense should be excluded. Since every item of income or expense is part of the enterprise's operating experience, the question is only what year items should be assigned." It seems there is not even agreement in key sources on the calculation of the most basic earnings numbers used for analytical purposes.

While being clear on the calculation of earnings, Bernstein does recognize the adjustments that may be made for purposes of analysis:

> For purposes of analysis or comparison, analysts may, however, wish to focus on an adjusted level of earnings for a short period . . . This can be done by adding to, or removing from, reported earnings per share selected items of income or expense that were included therein. If this is to be done on a per share basis, every item must be adjusted for tax effect (by using the enterprise's effective tax rate unless the applicable tax rate is otherwise specified) and must be divided by the number of shares that are used in the basic computation of earnings per share.

Hence, even though the adjustment for extraordinary items in the Canadian Securities Course method of calculating EPS is acceptable on grounds of "analysis or comparison," there is no explicit recognition of the tax adjustment for the extraordinary items. Given the key role played by *EPS* in various aspects of security analysis, e.g., in the determination of the *P/E* ratio, it is not surprising that there are disparate opinions about the appropriate calculation of other less commonly used "cash flow" measures, such as free cash flow.

Higgins (1998, p. 19) observes: "So many conflicting definitions of cash flow exist today that the term has almost lost meaning." In the absence of "generally accepted cash flow calculation principles," there has been a proliferation of cash flow valuation models that purport to accurately capture the economics of equity valuation. In the management consulting industry, these models are also marketed as methodologies for "managing company value," "generating shareholder value" and accurately setting executive compensation. A partial list of these methodologies includes: Economic Value Added (EVA) from Stern Stewart & Company; the Economic Profit Model from McKinsey & Company; Economic Value Management from KPMG; and, Value Builder from Price-Waterhouse. The basic idea behind these methodologies is to make adjustments to GAAP numbers to produce measures of cash flow that can be used to better assess economic value. As Copeland et al. (1996) observe in describing the McKinsey & Company approach: "Cash is King." The number of adjustments to GAAP numbers can be considerable. For example, Weaver (2001) estimates that determining EVA from GAAP numbers can involve up to 164 adjustment items. The precise adjustments used will depend on subjective assessments of factors such as the nature of the industry and the availability of data.

To evaluate the different variations that arise in determining the "cash flow" variable to be used in DCF valuation it is helpful to examine the conceptual foundations of the technique. DCF valuation is a variation on the net present value (NPV) model used in capital budgeting. This model has a long history, with elements that can be traced to Frank Knight, Alfred Marshall and the Austrian capital theorists.[8] Though conventional microeconomic theory is largely static, the capital investment problem requires the introduction of expectations about future input and output prices, the length of the production period, the production plan, the accumulation of capital, the degree of competition in the industry and so on. In this theoretical approach: "the market value of the firm is a reflection of its expected future earnings . . . the object of the owner of the firm is to make this market value, called its *capitalized present value*, as large as possible" (Baumol 1970, p. 24). Earnings are defined: "The sum of the money value of his outputs during a period is the entrepreneur's total revenue for that period, and the sum of the money values of the inputs is the total cost incurred during period. The difference constitutes his total [profit] for that period" (Baumol 1970, p. 65). Profit, earnings and surplus are loosely used to capture the same concept.

Given this, the theoretical foundation for DCF analysis requires evaluating the discounted present value of the future stream of "economic profits," where profits are measured as the cash value of revenues minus the cash value of costs, including interest payments, adjusted for taxes. In capital budgeting, the terminology "net cash flow" or "cash earnings" is substituted for "economic profit." To determine *net cash flow* from GAAP numbers:[9]

$$\text{Net cash flow} = \text{Net income} \pm \text{Non-cash items}$$

From this conceptual starting point, the calculations become fuzzier. Ignoring the problems associated with GAAP recognizing revenues and costs when booked not when the cash is received, important non-cash expenses reported for almost all firms are: "depreciation, depletion and amortization" and "deferred taxes." In tables 8.1 and 8.2, Ford and US Steel also report other items that involve non-cash components, e.g., "Provision for credit and insurance losses."

Working backwards from net income to net cash flow involves disentangling "cash" from non-cash items. This can be a complicated exercise. In addition, there are cash items that may provide positive or negative cash flow to the company but are better considered differently when doing the "economic profit" calculation. The most important such item is cash adjustments to working capital that took place due to the firm's operations. All these considerations go into determining the "net cash flows from operating activities" reported in the Statement of Cash Flows (see tables 8.5, 8.6, 8.7). The analytical fuzziness of this cash flow calculation is captured in the treatment of "net interest expense" which is included in net income and not subtracted out in determining "net cash flows from operating activities," e.g., Penman (2001, p. 119). Whether an adjustment for net interest is required is not a clear cut issue.[10] If this adjustment is made, then the tax implications also need to be taken into account. In the end, this item only relates to the cash revenues (adjusted for some of the cash costs) part of "economic profit." Because "depreciation, depletion and amortization" has been

Table 8.7 Operating cash flows before securities trading, Ford Motor Company, 2000–2002 ($ millions)

	2002		2001		2000	
	Automotive	Financial Services	Automotive	Financial Services	Automotive	Financial Services
Net income/(loss) from continuing operations	(987)	1,271	(6,155)	806	3,664	1,792
Depreciation and special tools amortization	4,897	10,240	4,999	10,164	5,087	9,059
Impairment charges (depreciation and amortization)	–	–	3,828	–	1,100	–
Amortization of goodwill, intangibles	21	19	299	43	305	42
Net losses/(earnings) from equity investments in excess of dividends remitted	134	13	845	(5)	86	17
Provision for credit/insurance losses	–	3,276	–	3,661	–	1,957
Foreign currency adjustments	51	–	(201)	–	(58)	–
Loss on sale of business	519	–	–	–	–	–
Provision for deferred income taxes	(1,377)	595	(2,242)	538	706	1,449
Decrease/(increase) in accounts receivable other current assets	2,570	(2,499)	(1,201)	(813)	(523)	(1,049)
Decrease/(increase) in inventory	(650)	–	1,122	–	(1,369)	–
Increase/(decrease) in accounts payable and accrued and other liabilities	3,971	2,681	4,729	(969)	2,444	1,267
Other	338	(221)	(969)	(253)	567	(156)
Cash flows	9,487	15,375	7,456	13,172	12,009	14,378

Ford considers all highly liquid investments with a maturity of three months or less, including short-term time deposits and government, agency and corporate obligations, to be cash equivalents. Automotive sector cash equivalents at December 31, 2002 and 2001 were $4.4 billion and $3.3 billion, respectively: Financial Services sector cash equivalents at December 31, 2002 and 2001 were $5.3 billion and $2.2 billion, respectively.

added back, a further adjustment is required to account for the cash capital expenditures that were made to support the productive activities of the firm.

While the Statement of Cash Flows seems to be a promising source of accounting numbers for calculating the "economic profit" needed in the DCF calculation, it is apparent that numerous adjustments are required. These adjustments are not mechanical but, rather, require subjective assessments. This is especially the case for the capital expenditure adjustment. "Depreciation, depletion and amortization" was added back to net income because this item is a non-cash expense that, in most cases, does not reflect the underlying economic requirement for a cash expenditure item that reflects the assumptions about the length of the production period, the production plan, the accumulation of capital, the degree of competition in the industry and so on. More precisely, the forecasting of future economic profits embeds an assumption about a stream of capital expenditures required to sustain this projection. Firms facing an earnings squeeze may react by cutting back on capital expenditures and permitting a running down the capital stock. This could be what is happening with Ford in table 8.5. Hence, the cash outflow associated with capital expenditures (capex) derived from the cash flow statement may not provide a realistic picture of the capex required to keep a firm on the historical growth path. Adjusting for alternative growth scenarios is even more complicated.

Conceptually, the DCF calculation can be used to produce either a market value of the firm, by discounting cash flows going to the firm, or a market value of common equity, by discounting the cash flows going to common equity. The connection between these two approaches to DCF valuation follows from the ***market value balance sheet relationship***:

Market value of equity
= Market value of common stock + Market value of preferred stock
= Market value of assets − market value of liabilities

---

where the market value of assets is equal to the market value of the firm. In effect, the DCF calculation for the estimated market value of the firm adjusted for the market value of liabilities plus the market value of any preferred stock will theoretically be equal to the DCF calculation for the estimated market value of equity. This relationship is only theoretical because DCF valuations are only estimates. The implication is that the DCF value of items that are excluded from cash flows to equity and included in cash flows to the firm will be sufficient to reconcile the two approaches. Because these items are related to debt and preferred stock cash flows the market values and values estimated by DCF methods will likely be approximately equal. As a consequence, subtracting the market value of debt and preferred stock from a DCF estimation of the market value of the firm can be expected to give more-or-less the same value as doing DCF for common equity directly.

The cash flow variable that is most commonly calculated from GAAP numbers to be used in DCF analysis is *free cash flow* (FCF). The precise FCF calculation depends on whether the DCF valuation is for the firm or for common equity. Different presentations of the calculation of FCF are available, depending on the particular financial statement(s) used in the calculation and whether FCF for common equity (*FCFE*) or

FCF to the firm (*FCFF*) is required.[11] For example, Higgins (1998) gives the following calculation:

$$\text{FCFF} = \text{EBIT}(1 - \text{Tax rate}) + \text{Depreciation} - \text{Capital expenditures}$$
$$\pm \Delta \text{ Net working capital}$$

Following Higgins (1998, p. 323) the rationale for this FCF to the firm calculation is:

> The rationale for using free cash flows goes like this. EBIT is the income a company earns without regard to how the business is financed; so EBIT(1 − Tax rate) is income after tax excluding any effects of debt financing. Adding depreciation and any other significant noncash items yields the standard aftertax cash flows used in capital expenditure analysis. If management were prepared to run the company into the ground, it could distribute this cash to owners and creditors, and that would be the end of it. But in most companies, management retains some of this cash flow in the business to pay for new capital expenditures and possibly to increase net working capital. The cash available for distribution to owners and creditors is thus aftertax cash flow less capital expenditures and increases in net working capital. Reductions in net working capital are also possible, and they add to free cash flow.

This rationale captures the essential point that free cash flow is a "best efforts" attempt to use GAAP numbers to calculate a value for "economic profit."

The approach to calculating FCF given by Higgins differs somewhat from approaches that work backward from net income, e.g., Damodaran (1994, p. 127). Users of this approach are often motivated to obtain *FCFE*, because net income has already made provision for payments to debt holders. In this case, assuming no outstanding preferred share issues:

$$\text{FCFE} = \text{Net income} + \text{Depreciation} - \text{Capital expenditures} - \Delta \text{ Net working}$$
$$\text{capital} - \text{Debt principal repayments} + \text{Proceeds of new debt issues}$$

This formulation differs from the Higgins approach due, for example, to the inclusion of extraordinary items. Because FCF is an analytical concept, there is no "correct" method for calculating this value. The analyst is required to determine which calculation is most appropriate. If ease of calculation is a concern, comparison of this calculation with the cash flow statement reveals that *FCFF* and *FCFE* can be easily calculated as:

$$\text{FCFF} = \text{Cash flow from operations} - \text{Capital expenditures}$$
$$+ \text{Interest expense}(1 - \text{Tax rate})$$
$$\text{FCFE} = \text{Cash flow from operations} - \text{Capital expenditures} - \text{Preferred}$$
$$\text{dividends} - \text{Debt principal repayments} + \text{Proceeds of new debt issues}$$

For firms without any preferred stock and no changes in outstanding debt issues the *FCFE* calculation is simplified to the subtraction of two items from the cash flow statement: *FCFE = Cash flow from operations – Capital expenditures.*

Free cash flow is a practical attempt to use GAAP numbers to determine a value for economic profit. It is not difficult to see that FCF inherits many of the problems associated with reconciling GAAP numbers to be consistent with economic value. Unfortunately, the appropriate method for adjusting GAAP numbers is not obvious and is likely to vary from firm to firm, depending on particular circumstances. This situation has created an opportunity for the management consulting industry to sell customized adjustments on a fee-for-service basis. There is considerable attractiveness in this activity. On the one hand, there is the potential for measuring the "true value" of a company. Changes in that value can be used as a measure of management effectiveness and to provide a guide to management as to appropriate corporate policies to "enhance shareholder value." On the other hand, the conceptual difficulties of correctly manipulating GAAP accounting numbers can prevent corporations from accomplishing this task with in-house resources. Management consulting services can compete on service by "branding" the techniques and procedures used to produce "accurate economic value measures." As a consequence, there has emerged a significant number of such "branding exercises." "Economic Value Added" (EVA) is the registered trademark for the methodology developed by Stern Stewart & Company, e.g., Ehrbar (1998).

Despite the presence of proprietary techniques that are only known within Stern Stewart Company, *the basic elements of the EVA technique* do not differ substantively from, say, the "Economic Profit Model" developed by McKinsey & Company, e.g., Copeland et al. (1996).[12] Both techniques are usually applied to aid with corporate management decision making, so the corresponding FCF value is *FCFF*. Though there are a number of equivalent ways of calculating basic EVA, one revealing formulation is:

$$EVA = EBIT(1 - \text{Tax rate}) - \{(\text{Weighted average cost of capital})$$
$$(\text{Invested capital})\} = \text{Invested capital (return on invested capital} - \text{Weighted}$$
$$\text{average cost of capital}) = \text{Invested capital (ROIC} - \text{WACC})$$

where the return on invested capital (*ROIC*) is expressed after tax and depreciation.[13] The relevance of using of *EBIT*(1 – *Tax rate*) is captured by the introduction of a new terminology, either *NOPAT* or *NOPLAT* to refer to "net operating profit after tax" or "net operating profit less adjusted taxes."

The number in EVA that is somewhat complicated to determine is "invested capital." This number can be determined from either the side of the balance sheet, e.g., Copeland et al. (1996, p. 164):

> Invested capital represents the amount invested in the *operations* of the business. Invested capital is the sum of operating working capital; net property, plant and equipment; and net other assets (net of noncurrent, noninterest-bearing liabilities). Invested capital, plus any

Table 8.8 Example of different methods for calculating invested capital, Hershey Foods Corporation, 1990–92 ($ millions)

	1990	1991	1992
Operating current assets	661.8	702.3	760.9
Non-interest bearing current liabilities	(276.4)	(362.7)	(351.7)
Net working capital	385.4	339.7	409.2
Net property plant and equipment	952.1	1,145.7	1,296.0
Other operating assets, net of other liabilities	(18.9)	(50.9)	(55.8)
Operating invested capital	1,318.6)	1,434.4	1,649.4)
Excess marketable securities	0.0	42.1	0.0
Goodwill	417.6	421.7	399.8
Non-operating investments	0.0	0.0	179.1
Total investor funds	1,736.3	1,898.3	2,228.3
Equity	1,243.5	1,335.3	1,465.3
Deferred income taxes	154.5	172.0	203.5
Adjusted equity	1,398.0	1,507.3	1,668.8
All interest bearing debt	338.3	391.0	559.5
Total investor funds	1,736.3	1,898.3	2,228.3

Source: Adapted from Copeland et al. (1996)

nonoperating investments, measures the total amount invested by the company's investors, which we will call total investor funds. Total investor funds can also be calculated from the liability side of the balance sheet as the sum of all equity (plus quasi-equity items like deferred taxes) and interest-bearing debt.

Table 8.8 provides a basic example reconciling the two different approaches. This example does not provide an exhaustive list of the relevant right hand side balance sheet items that could be included. A partial listing of the items that could be used to calculate invested capital are:[14]

Invested capital = Bank indebtedness + Short-term debt + Dividends payable
+ Current portion of long term debt + Deferred taxes + Preferred shares
+ Share capital + Retained earnings + Other financial assets

Examination of tables 8.3 and 8.4 reveals a number of other items that have to be assessed (see end of chapter questions.)

The EVA approach is conceptually the same as the "Economic Profit Model" of McKinsey & Company. As described by Copeland et al. (1996, pp. 149–50), the economic profit model is an advance over DCF valuation using FCF:

> An advantage of the economic profit model over the [FCF] DCF model is that economic profit is a useful measure for understanding a company's performance in any single year, while free cash flow is not. For example, you would not track a company's progress by comparing actual and projected free cash flow, because free cash flow in any year is determined by highly discretionary investments in fixed assets and working capital. Management could easily delay investments simply to improve free cash flow in a given year at the expense of long term value creation.

According to proponents, EVA and the Economic Profit Model are conceptual advances over using FCF-based DCF:[15]

> Economic profit measures the value created in a company in a single period of time and is defined as follows:
>
> $$\text{Economic Profit} = \text{Invested Capital} \times (\text{ROIC} - \text{WACC})$$
>
> . . . The economic profit approach says that the value of a company equals the amount of capital invested, plus a premium or discount equal to present value of its projected economic profit:
>
> $$\text{Value} = \text{Invested Capital} + \text{Present value of projected Economic Profit.}$$
>
> The logic behind this is simple. If a company earned exactly its WACC every period, then the discounted value of its projected free cash flow should exactly equal its invested capital. In other words, the company is worth exactly what was originally invested. A company is worth more or less than its invested capital only to the extent that it earns more or less than its WACC. So the premium or discount relative to invested capital must equal the present value of the company's future economic profit.

Such claims beg an obvious question: are these approaches as superior to other DCF approach and other valuation techniques as the proponents claim?

EVA and the related techniques being marketed by the management consulting industry were initially proposed to measure corporate performance and assess the use of shareholder capital by management. Because this involves a valuation exercise, it is natural that the performance of EVA as a tool in security analysis was empirically examined. For example, Stern Stewart provide annual rankings of firm performance based on estimates of EVA and a related measure, market value added (MVA). Stern Stewart (www.sternstewart.com) describes the rankings and MVA as follows:

> Stern Stewart compiles annual performance rankings of large, publicly owned companies in most of the major countries of the world. The rankings are in terms of a measure that we call MVA, for Market Value Added. MVA is the difference between the market value of a company (both equity and debt) and the capital that lenders and shareholders have entrusted to it over the years in the form of loans, retained earnings and paid-in capital. As such, MVA is a measure of the difference between "cash in" (what investors have contributed)

Table 8.9 The top 30 firms in the Stern Stewart Performance 1000

MVA rank					MVA	EVA (average capital)	Capital (year-end operating capital)	Return on capital (R)	Cost of capital (WACC)
1999	1998	1994	TIC[a]	Company name	1999	1999	1999	1999	1999
1	1	10	MSFT	Microsoft	629,470	5,796	20,034	51.78	12.62
2	2	2	GE	General Electric	467,510	3,499	75,830	17.20	12.47
3	8	50	CSCO	Cisco Systems	348,442	182	23,653	13.72	12.78
4	5	3	WMT	Wal-Mart Stores	282,655	1,528	54,013	14.31	10.99
5	3	26	INTC	Intel	253,907	4,695	29,825	30.55	12.19
6	9	–	LU	Lucent Technologies	200,540	−1,828	65,594	9.81	13.96
7	23	425	AOL	American Online	187,558	−156	4,482	11.10	15.53
8	41	38	ORCL	Oracle	154.263	605	5,413	24.59	12.42
9	11	78	IBM	IBM	154,219	1,349	66,827	13.33	11.40
10	19	25	HD	Home Depot	148,358	884	16,145	16.60	10.49
11	10	6	XOM	Exxon Mobil	144,687	4,440	180,040	11.67	8.16
12	4	5	MRK	Merck	143,001	3,449	29,553	23.09	10.72
13	6	1	KO	Coca-Cola	134,149	1,562	18,120	21.80	12.31
14	47	307	SUNW	Sun Microsystems	133,953	595	5,954	23.85	13.03
15	14	430	DELL	Dell Computer	132,609	1,330	7,320	46.33	14.79
16	43	–	YHOO	Yahoo!	128,748	−862	8,847	−2.66	15.99
17	15	11	PG	Procter & Gamble	127,222	1,782	31,587	15.52	9.72
18	362	393	QCOM	QUALCOMM	126,323	78	3,521	15.80	13.05
19	30	133	AIG	American International Group	118,726	−119	48,774	10.44	10.70
20	12	10	BMY	Bristol-Myers Squibb	115,411	2,589	17,811	24.90	10.08
21	7	21	PFE	Pfizer	113,097	1,953	16,959	22.57	10.37
22	32	134	C	Citigroup	112,964	1,003	74,566	14.32	12.82
23	38	112	EMC	EMC	111,255	668	7,168	25.09	12.70
24	16	12	JNJ	Johnson & Johnson	107,564	1,555	29,570	16.24	10.39
25	28	8	T	AT&T	105,248	−6,379	176,869	4.39	9.22
26	18	349	WCOM	WorldCom	96,151	−4,736	94,105	5.55	10.78
27	34	36	HWP	Hewlett-Packard	92,842	−195	29,117	10.72	11.42
28	27	45	TWX	Time Warner	81,476	−1,354	48,588	6.35	9.80
29	26	37	VZ	Verizon Communications	74,563	1,854	57,673	11.12	7.74
30	52	128	TXN	Texas Instruments	71,813	−123	11,966	13.61	14.76

[a] = Ticker symbol.
Source: www.sternstewart.com

and "cash out" (what they could get by selling at today's prices). If MVA is positive, it means that the company has increased the value of the capital entrusted to it and thus created shareholder wealth. If MVA is negative, the company has destroyed wealth.

As illustrated in table 8.9, the MVA rankings for 2000 produce some odd results with Cisco, Lucent and Sun Micro all appearing in the top 15 of the 1000 firms being ranked.

Yook and McCabe (2001) even present evidence that MVA is negatively related with future stock returns. However, it does not follow that EVA and MVA will produce similar predictions about future returns. For example, the EVA for a number of firms in table 8.9 does seem to provide an indication of the impending poor performance.

Unfortunately, the promise of superior performance for EVA as a security analysis tool compared to traditional measures such as net income does not have much empirical support. For example, Clinton and Chen (1996) found that other traditional accounting measures, such as *P/E*, *EPS* and *ROA*, tracked stock returns more reliably than *EVA*. More recently, Cordeiro and Kent (2001) considered whether analysts that adopted EVA outperformed other analysts in forecasting future EPS and found "no significant relationship between EVA adoption and security analyst forecasts of future firm EPS performance." Biddle et al. (1997, 1998) find similar results. For example, Biddle et al. (1997) conclude: "earnings [are] more highly associated with returns and firm values than EVA, residual income, or cash flow from operations. Incremental tests suggest that EVA components add only marginally to information content beyond earnings . . . these results do not support claims that EVA dominates earnings in relative information content, and suggest rather that earnings generally outperform EVA."

Financial shenanigans

It is difficult to find a period since the enactment of the major securities legislation in 1933 and 1934 where the failures of the accounting profession have been so apparent than in the period surrounding the Enron collapse. Arthur Anderson, one of the contemporary big five accounting firms, was indicted and dismantled for practices that were seemingly devious and illegal. Collapses at firms, such as Worldcom, raised serious concerns about the ability of firms to manipulate the accounting numbers that were being presented in annual reports and regulatory filings. These are only two of a large number of similar situations that led Congress to introduce and pass legislation requiring substantive oversight of the accounting profession in the form of the Sarbanes-Oxley Act.[16] All this is clouded by the confusion over which activities were illegal frauds and which were legitimate, if somewhat unethical, "management" of accounting numbers. Even if accounting numbers are prepared according to Generally Accepted Accounting Practices (GAAP), there is still considerable leeway in massaging the accounting numbers to present a misleading description of the firm's financial performance.

Schilit (2002) is a now classic primer on the identification of financial shenanigans. The author, Howard Schilit is also the founder of the Center for Financial Analysis and Research (www.cfraonline.com), a provider of analysis about misleading information produced by the accounting practices of specific firms. The seven shenanigans identified in Schilit (2002, pp. 24–5) have achieved recognition in various other sources as a benchmark for discussing these issues, e.g., English (2001, p. 129). All that is provided here is an overview to give the flavor of the problems that can arise. The first shenanigan is:

Shenanigan no. 1: Recording revenue too soon or of questionable quality

- Recording revenue when future services remain to be provided
- Recording revenue before shipment or before the customer's unconditional acceptance
- Recording revenue even though the customer is not obligated to pay
- Selling to an affiliated party
- Giving the customer something of value as a quid pro quo
- Grossing up revenue

Each of the (•) items is a technique that can be used by a corporation to achieve the desired manipulation of the accounting numbers. Schilit usually provides an example or two of each technique. For example, in 1996 Sunbeam began using the technique of booking revenue to boost sales of gas grills, even though there was a significant probability of right-of-return in the sales. In such cases, FAS 48 requires recognition of such sales in revenue only when the cash is received. The SEC later determined that Sunbeam did overstate revenues on these sales.

The second shenanigan is related to the first, though the issues involved here have a greater element of unethical or fraudulent intent:

Shenanigan no. 2: Recording bogus revenue

- Recording sales that lack economic substance
- Recording cash received in lending transactions as revenue
- Recording investment income as revenue
- Recording as revenue supplier rebates tied to future required purchases
- Releasing revenue that was improperly held back before a merger

---

Surprisingly, it is not just "shady characters" that engage in such activities. Major companies such as Bausch & Lomb and Xerox have engaged in this type of activity. For example, Xerox improperly recognized revenue from lease operations that involved future deliveries of supplies and services. In addition to corporate giants, there are also smaller firms populated by shady characters that engage in such activities. An excellent source on such activities can be found in the writings of David Baines at the *Vancouver Sun* documenting, among other things, the phony revenue recognition schemes of various promoters that populated the Vancouver Stock Exchange and now operate on the OTC bulletin board and TSX Venture Exchange. Of course, bogus revenue schemes are not restricted to the small firms examined by Baines, as evidenced by the infamous ZZZZ Best bankruptcy of 1987 (Baliga 1995).

The third shenanigan is less insidious than the first two and, arguably, lies within the fair game area of managerial discretion. For example, consider an airline that is under earnings pressure and is anxious to avoid reporting poor earnings numbers. One option would be to sell or lease back an airplane that had a low book value due to substantial depreciation. Another example of a possible transaction that could be used to boost earnings is to sell a marketable security that was purchased at a price well below the price at which the security could be sold.[17] The listing of possible techniques for this type of shenanigan are:

Shenanigan no. 3: Boosting income with one-time gains

- Boosting profits by selling undervalued assets
- Including investment income or gains as part of revenue
- Reporting investment income or gains as a reduction in operating expenses
- Creating income by reclassification of balance sheet accounts

---

Schilit provides a number of examples where this boosting of income originated from the pooling of interests associated with a merger or acquisition.

The objective of accounting manipulations is to produce financial statements that are not accurate reflections of the position of the firm intended by GAAP. This usually involves a desire to inflate current earnings numbers, though there are some reasons to deflate current earnings in order to achieve better earnings in later periods. Shenanigans 1–3 relate to boosting earnings by inflating revenues. A similar result can be achieved by deflating expenses or by suppressing the recording of liabilities. This objective is covered in shenanigan 4:

Shenanigan no. 4: Shifting current expenses to a later or earlier period

- Capitalizing normal operating costs, particularly if recently changed from expensing
- Changing accounting policies and shifting current expenses to an earlier period
- Amortizing costs too slowly
- Failing to write down or write off impaired assets
- Reducing asset reserves

AOL provides an excellent recent example of this type of shenanigan where, according to the SEC, the costs of marketing to acquire customers were inappropriately capitalized. Other examples are: Snapple and JDS Uniphase where expenses were reclassified and booked against previous periods; Orion Pictures where costs of failed films were written off too slowly; and Lockheed where impaired assets, effectively new aircraft designs that were not feasible for production, were not written off quickly enough. Some financial institutions also engage in this type of activity by being too slow to make provisions for bad loans.

The fifth shenanigan has a number of dimensions. Perhaps the most topical aspect of this shenanigan is captured in the debate over the expensing of executive stock options:

Shenanigan no. 5: Failing to record or improperly reducing liabilities

- Failing to record expenses and related liabilities when future obligations remain
- Reducing liabilities by changing accounting assumptions
- Releasing questionable reserves into income
- Creating sham rebates
- Recording revenue when cash is received, even though future obligations remain

---

Warren Buffett (Cunningham 2002, p. 226) makes the following observation about the executive stock option aspect of this shenanigan:

> The most egregious case of let's-not-face-up-to-reality behavior of executives and accountants has occurred in the world of stock options ... even when options are structured properly, they are accounted for in ways that make no sense. The lack of logic is not accidental. For decades, much of the business world has waged war against accounting rulemakers, trying to keep the costs of stock options from being reflected in the profits of the corporations that issue them.

Buffett describes the accounting treatment for executive stock options as "outrageous." In addition to stock option abuses, this category also includes the "special purposes entities" that Enron used to disguise the true character of the company's financial statements.

The final two shenanigans are not concerned with inflating current profits but, rather, with deflating current profits in order to make profits in future periods more attractive. There are a number of possible reasons for such activities. Healthy companies may want to create a "reserve" for use in future periods. A weak company may want to "take a bath" and get all the bad news out of the way in order to "relieve future periods of these expenses." Companies involved in an acquisition may manipulate profits of the target firm in order to obtain a better purchase price or submerge bad news within the costs of the merger in order to disguise the true operating state of the acquiring firm. Given this, the two remaining shenanigans are related to deflating revenues, shenanigan six, and inflating expenses, shenanigan seven:

Shenanigan no. 6: Shifting current revenue to a later period

- Creating reserves and releasing them into income in a later period
- Improperly holding back revenue just before an acquisition closes

---

Shenanigan no. 7: Shifting future expenses to the current period as a special charge

- Improperly inflating an amount included in a special charge
- Improperly writing off in-process R&D costs from an acquisition
- Accelerating discretionary expenses into the current period

---

An example of shenanigan 6 is provided by W.R. Grace that used "a significant and unanticipated increase in revenue as a result of Medicare reimbursements" at a subsidiary in the early 1990s to create a reserve that was used to smooth income in later periods. As a consequence of the release of reserves in later periods, the subsidiary was able to report steady earnings growth between 27–31 percent instead of erratic earnings growth of −8% to 61% that would have been observed without the reserve. The activity led to an SEC enforcement action in 1998. Though not subject to any SEC actions, Microsoft is currently sitting on substantial reserves that could be used to manage future earnings. As for shenanigan 7, the recent goodwill writedowns that have taken place in the telecom sector is a potential area for this type of accounting manipulation.

At the time of writing, Schilit (2002) apparently did not have sufficient information or lead time to discuss the massive accounting frauds at *Enron and Worldcom.* These accounting frauds led to the two largest US corporate bankruptcies in history at the time of the bankruptcy filings. The accounting frauds at both firms involved more than one type of shenanigan. Two key manipulations involved in the accounting scandal that resulted in Worldcom filing for bankruptcy protection in July 2002 were: improper revenue recognition; and the capitalizing of operating expenses. Much of the revenue recognition related to the release of reserves into current revenue. The use of reserve accounts is common for telecom firms, e.g., to allow for customer accounts that are not paid. The release of these reserves into revenue when the potential losses are still likely to occur is designed to inflate revenue. This is a variant of shenanigan 3. The capitalizing of operating expenses involved the shift of operating expenses to the capital expenditure account. Not only did this give an incorrect impression of operating profits, it permitted the depreciation of those expenses over time. This is a variant of shenanigan 5.

Enron filed for bankruptcy protection in December 2001. The Enron bankruptcy was, from an accounting standpoint, more complicated and involved considerably more elements than the Worldcom case. At least five types of inter-related accounting irregularities can be identified. The primary vehicles in the accounting manipulations were the non-consolidated "special purpose entities" (SPEs) that Enron used to disguise losses and liabilities. These SPEs were privately held partnerships, usually "owned" by the Enron CFO or members of his family. FAS 94 requires that consolidation of accounts be used if there is an element of control between entities making the transactions. Though there was clearly an element of control in the Enron-SPE transactions, consolidation was not used. In addition, many of the SPE transactions involved the sale of stock in exchange for notes receivable. The SEC requires that such transactions be reflected in the balance sheet, which Enron did not do. Yet, another type of transaction involved derivative security transactions between Enron and the SPEs, allowing Enron to shift risk to the SPEs that was not reported due to absence of financial statement consolidation.

Examples of the types of transactions between Enron and the SPEs are described in Enron's 2000 financial statements where the company recognizes a transfer to the SPEs of assets valued at $1.2 billion, including $150 million in notes payable, 3.7 million restricted Enron shares and subscription rights to receive up to 18 million Enron common shares in March 2003, subject to certain conditions. Enron also transferred to the partnerships other assets valued at $309 million, including a $50 million note payable and "an investment in an entity that indirectly holds warrants convertible into common stock of an Enron equity method investee." In return for these considerations, Enron reports receiving "economic interests in the entities," $309 million in notes receivable against the SPE's and an additional $1.2 billion in SPE notes receivable as part of a "special distribution." The disclosure went on to mention a series of purchases by Enron of "share-settled options from the entities" on shares of Enron common stock. Through the selective use of hedge accounting rules, Enron was also able to disguise a range of derivative transactions done with the SPEs. In sum, the Enron transactions were sufficiently opaque that even the most well-informed accounting professionals could not make sense of the financial statements, a clear violation of the intent of GAAP which requires "information deemed necessary to an understanding of the effects of the transactions on the financial statements" be revealed.

Though an excellent and well organized source, Schilit (2002) is only one of a number of interesting studies of accounting manipulations.[18] The introduction of the securities laws of 1933–4 is a watershed in the history of accounting manipulations. Prior to this time, manipulations were the rule rather than the exception. Warren Buffett provides a delightful satire given to him by Ben Graham on various financial shenanigans of a fictitious company (Cunningham, pp. 185–91). Included in the accounting operations are an immediate writedown of assets to a large minus number in order to be able to claim a regular asset "appreciation," as opposed to depreciation, credit. Elimination of wage and salary expenses by making all such payments using stock options. This would also benefit the company with a large cash inflow as the options are exercised. The success of the accounting manipulations in inflating the market price of the stock by greatly inflating company earnings will be a windfall to employees receiving the stock options. And so the story goes, tongue-in-cheek but not without an almost depressing sense of reality.

8.3   FORECASTING THE INPUTS

Identifying the value drivers

Value is a concept with many possible interpretations. In general, the "value" is equal to the "true worth." This interpretation is too normative for practical purposes. Some method of determining true worth is needed. In one sense, the value of a security is equal to the price of the security observed in the market for that security. This interpretation of value is consistent with the spirit of a central proposition of modern Finance:

the efficient markets hypothesis. In security analysis, it is usually assumed that the market price does not necessarily capture the true worth of a security. At any point in time, the market price may be above or below the true value. In this sense, value is an economic concept. This economic value can be estimated using techniques such as discounted cash flow analysis but this requires estimates of the key inputs to the model, e.g., cash flows, capitalization rates, termination dates. A substantial portion of security analysis is concerned with interpreting the economic content of accounting numbers in order to determine the value of a security. A *value driver* is a factor that has a significant impact on the level and change of the value of a security. There are two key dimensions to value drivers: profitability and growth.

Reference to value drivers is a relatively new development in security analysis. The concept migrated into security analysis from the management consulting industry where value drivers were introduced as concepts to "measure, manage and maximize shareholder value." For example, Copeland et al. (1996, p. 107) observe:

> A value driver is simply any variable that affects the value of the company. To be useful, however, value drivers need to be organized so we can identify which have the greatest impact on value and assign responsibility for their performance to individuals who can help the organization meet its targets. Value drivers must be developed down to the level of detail that aligns the value driver with the decision variables directly under the control of line management.

If value drivers can be used to better manage a company to enhance shareholder value, then it is not difficult to extend this notion to using value drivers to measure the value of a company's common stock. Given the sizeable amount of management consulting done by the large accounting firms, it is not surprising that academic sources using the value driver terminology, e.g., Penman (2001), Liu et al. (2002), are primarily from the accounting stream, though there are also some studies using value drivers in a strategic management context.

Recognizing the connection between the use of value drivers and accounting, a useful starting point for the discussion of value drivers is the residual income model (see section 8.1). The numerator in the residual income model is: $(ROE(t) - k)BV(t-1)$ where ROE can be interpreted as the return on common equity. This can be mechanically transformed into a value driver format:

$$ROE = \frac{Net\ income}{Book\ value\ of\ equity}$$

$$= \left(\frac{Net\ income}{Sales}\right)\left(\frac{Sales}{Total\ assets}\right)\left(\frac{Total\ assets}{Book\ value\ of\ equity}\right)$$

Expressed in other words: Return on equity = (Profit margin) × (Asset Turnover) × (Financial Leverage). This approach to roughing out the value drivers is consistent with the management consulting approach where (Copeland et al. 1996, p. 107): "Generic value drivers such as sales growth, operating margins and capital turns, apply equally

Table 8.10 ROE and levers of performance for ten diverse companies, 1995

	Return on equity		Profit margin		Asset turnover		Financial leverage
Analog Devices, Inc.	18.2	=	12.7	×	0.94	×	1.53
Bank America Corporation	13.2	=	13.1	×	0.09	×	11.49
Duke Power	14.9	=	15.3	×	0.35	×	2.79
Exxon Corporation	16.0	=	5.3	×	1.33	×	2.26
Food Lion Inc.	15.7	=	2.1	×	3.10	×	2.40
Hewlett-Packard	20.6	=	7.7	×	1.29	×	2.06
Nike	20.4	=	8.4	×	1.51	×	2.60
Nordstrom Inc.	11.6	=	4.0	×	1.51	×	1.92
Southwest Airlines	12.8	=	6.4	×	0.88	×	2.28
Tiffany & Company	14.8	=	4.9	×	1.23	×	2.48

Source: Adapted from Higgins (1998)

well to all business units." Using this approach, there are three value drivers for the residual income model. The variation of these drivers across various sectors is illustrated in table 8.10. The next step in this approach is to decompose the profit margin, asset turnover and financial leverage to gain further insight into the value drivers, e.g., profit margin can be examined by considering elements of fixed and variable costs associated with the business.

The use of *ROE* to define the value drivers is only one possible approach. Even within the framework of the residual income DCF model, examination of the model variables, $(ROE(t) - k)BV(t - 1)$, reveals that k has not been taken directly into account. A more telling comment applies to the method of measuring the profit margin using net income divided by sales as a value driver. Presumably, the profit margin is concerned with the success of the operating component of the business. In this case, it is more conventional to measure profit margin using, say, *Gross profit margin = {Sales – Cost of goods sold}/ Sales* or *EBITDA profit margin = {Sales – Cost of goods sold – Selling, administrative and general expenses}/Sales*. In addition to having a range of accruals, net income may also include significant extraordinary items. Another complication associated with starting from *ROE* arises with the use of *Book value of equity* which does not directly account for the inherent increase in riskiness associated with leveraging. One method of addressing this concern is to use the *ROIC = {EBIT(1 – Tax rate)}/Invested capital* of the "economic profit model" as a starting point for specifying value drivers.

Taking a cue from the management consulting approach, the nuts-and-bolts problem of identifying value drivers for specific companies is not as easy to solve as the mechanical accounting formulas would suggest. Though the generic value drivers such as sales growth, operating margins and capital turnovers "apply equally well to all business units" these notions "lack specificity and cannot be used well at the grassroots level." This comment applies equally well to the use of value drivers in security analysis. Yet, when pressed for precisely how to identify value drivers, the management consulting approach is decidedly vague, e.g., Copeland et al. (1996, p. 111):

> Key value drivers are not static, they must be periodically reviewed . . . Identifying the key value drivers for a company can be difficult because it requires the company to think differently about its processes, and in many cases the company's reporting systems are not equipped to supply the necessary information. Identifying the key value drivers is also a creative process that requires trial and error. Mechanical approaches based on existing information and purely financial approaches rarely identify the key value drivers. Aligning the value drivers with decisions is the key . . . Nor can value drivers be considered in isolation from each other.

References are made to "decision trees" and "scenario analysis" as techniques for dealing with the difficulty of identifying value drivers, even though these techniques appear to involve substituting one form of mechanistic analysis for another. Similar difficulties arise when the value driver approach is applied to the valuation of the common stock of companies.

Ultimately, the format used to structure the identification of value drivers pales in comparison with the economics required to assess the underlying business. Consider the problem of identifying the value drivers for Coca-Cola, a company that Buffett describes as a "wonderful" organization. Penman (2001, p. 497) suggests that: "For Coca-Cola sales and margins are key drivers." These drivers are related to "brand creation and maintenance" and "product innovation." "Coca-Cola is a *brand management firm* where value is driven by exploiting a brand." The accounting information for Coca-Cola that is provided in Penman (2001, pp. 468, 497) covers the years 1990–7 and reflects a strong and steady increase in sales estimated to be 7.5% per year. This sales growth is used by Penman to provide an estimate of futures sales growth that, in turn, is used as a key input to a DCF valuation of the common stock of $56.20. Yet, table 8.11 reveals that sales from 1998–2002 did not conform with past patterns. Sales fell significantly in 2000 and 2001. Net Income fell from 2001 to 2002. Though dividends per share have been increased and the share buyback program has been stepped up, the *ROIC* fell.

Buffett is correct to characterize Coca-Cola (KO) as a "wonderful" company. In a macro-economic and stock market environment where many firms are suffering, both on an operating and common stock price basis, Coca-Cola is weathering the storm with some dignity. There are even glimmers of hope in table 8.11 that the corner may be in sight. However, this is only based on a casual inspection of accounting numbers. To make any plausible statement about future performance requires considerably more dissecting of factors such as the regional and product distribution of sales, developments in the marketing of the key brands (Coke, Fanta, Sprite, Minute Maid, etc.), roll-outs of new products, projected changes in the financial structure and so on. If there is a lesson to be learned from Philip Fisher it is that casual, or even intensive, analysis of accounting numbers is only of secondary importance relative to analyzing and understanding the business. The general accounting format for value drivers based, say, on a decomposition of *ROE* provides a motivation for which elements to examine. However, this is only a guide to where to channel energies in dissecting the business. It is at this point that the elements discussed in sections 7.3 and 7.4 have to be addressed.

Table 8.11 The Coca-Cola Company and subsidiaries, selected financial data ($ millions except per share data, ratios and growth rates)

	Compound growth rates		Year ended December 31,	
	5 years (%)	10 years	2002[a,b,c]	2001[c,d]
Summary of operations				
Net operating revenues	3.3	5.2	**19,564**	17,545
Cost of goods sold	3.4	3.5	**7,105**	6,044
Gross profit	3.3	6.3	**12,459**	11,501
Selling, general and administrative expenses	4.8	5.7	**7,001**	6,149
Other operating charges			—	—
Operating income	1.8	7.1	**5,458**	5,352
Interest income			**209**	325
Interest expense			**199**	289
Equity income (loss)			**384**	152
Other income (loss) – net			**(353)**	39
Gains on issuances of stock by equity investees			—	91
Income before income taxes and changes in accounting principles	(1.9)	7.2	**5,499**	5,670
Income taxes	(4.6)	5.8	**1,523**	1,691
Net income before changes in accounting principles	(0.8)	7.8	**3,976**	3,979
Net income	(5.9)	6.2	**3,050**	3,969
Average shares outstanding			**2,478**	2,487
Average shares outstanding assuming dilution			**2,483**	2,487
Per share data				
Income before changes in accounting principles – basic	(0.8)	8.3	**1.60**	1.60
Income before changes in accounting principles – diluted	(0.5)	8.5	**1.60**	1.60
Basic net income	(5.9)	6.9	**1.23**	1.60
Diluted net income	(5.6)	7.1	**1.23**	1.60
Cash dividends	7.4	11.1	**.80**	.72
Market price on December 31,	(8.0)	7.7	**43.84**	47.15
Total market value of common stock balance sheet and other data	(8.0)	7.1	**108,328**	117,226
Cash, cash equivalents and current marketable securities			**2,345**	1,934
Property, plant and equipment – net			**5,911**	4,453
Depreciation			**614**	502
Capital expenditures			**851**	769
Total assets			**24,501**	22,417
Long-term debt			**2,701**	1,219
Total debt			**5,356**	5,118
Share-owners' equity			**11,800**	11,366
Total capital			**17,156**	16,484

Table 8.11 (*Cont'd*)

	Year ended December 31,	
	2002[a,b,c]	2001[c,d]
Other key financial measures		
Total debt-to-total capital	31.2%	31.0%
Net debt-to-net capital	21.1%	22.6%
Return on common equity	34.3%	38.5%
Return on capital	24.5%	26.6%
Dividend payout ratio	65.1%	45.1%
Net cash provided by operations	4,742	4,110
Economic profit	2,375	2,466

[a] In 2002, Coca-Cola adopted SFAS No. 142, "Goodwill and Other Intangible Assets." Refer to Note 4 in the Consolidated Financial Statements.

[b] In 2002, Coca-Cola adopted the fair value method provisions of SFAS No. 123, "Accounting for Stock-Based Compensation," and it adopted SFAS No. 148, "Accounting for Stock-Based Compensation – Transition and Disclosure."

[c] In 2002, Coca-Cola adopted EITF Issue No. 01–9, "Accounting for Consideration Given by a Vendor to a Customer or a Reseller of the Vendor's Products." In 2001, it adopted EITF Issue No. 00–14, "Accounting for Certain Sales Incentives" and EITF Issue No. 00–22," Accounting for 'Points' and Certain Other Time-Based or Volume-Based Sales Incentive Offers, and Offers for Free Products or Services to be Delivered in the Future." All prior years were reclassified to conform to the current year presentation.

[d] In 2001, Coca-Cola adopted SFAS No. 133, "Accounting for Derivative Instruments and Hedging Activities."

[e] In 1998, Coca-Cola adopted SFAS No. 132, "Employers' Disclosures about Pensions and Other Postretirement Benefits."

Having conducted a detailed analysis of the business operations, the value drivers can be estimated to obtain the appropriate inputs to the DCF model. In certain cases where simple models such as the Gordon model are applicable, the DCF model can be inverted to provide, say, k and g parameters that would make sense of an observed price. In some cases, such as the valuation of resource companies with known reserves, the DCF model can be used to provide an estimate for the implied average future selling price for the commodity. However, in other cases, the DCF calculation is sufficiently complicated that the simple models do not apply. This is, arguably, the case with most of the firms in the airline industry following 9/11. As of the start of the US-led war in Iraq in March 2003, major carriers such as Delta (DAL), American Airlines (AMR) and United Airlines (UAL) are all bleeding staggering amounts of red ink. Problems in the industry are so severe that UAL entered Chapter 11 bankruptcy protection in early 2003 with considerable discussion about whether American will follow. Faced with competition from point-to-point low cost carriers such as Southwest Airlines (LUV), the large hub-based carriers are caught in a vice of intense competition on the most profitable routes, increased costs of security and a dramatic and potentially continuing fall in traffic generated by a combination of macro-economic, geopolitical and psychological factors.

What are the key value drivers for an airline such as Delta? Profit margins are negative and look to remain so for the near future. Prospects for improving asset turnover by, say, reducing routes and capacity to adjust to the decline in traffic are uncertain due to levels of competition, significant fixed cost elements and other factors. Increasing financial leverage raises interest costs that contribute to an erosion of the ability to compete on fares. Writing prior to the recent difficulties that have hit the airline industry, Penman (2001, p. 499) provides the following discussion of key drivers in the airline industry:

> The size of the fleet and gate allocation defines what the industry calls *available seat miles* (*ASM*). A *load factor* determines the *revenue miles seat* (*RMS*) and ticket prices determine the dollar yield per RMS. This yield, along with RMS, drives revenues so, for a given ASM, load factors and yields are the key drivers for airlines. The analyst cuts to these key factors but is also sensitive to any changes in available seat miles with new routes and gate allocations. Other drivers such as labor productivity, labor costs, commission rates to travel agents, and fuel costs per mile are also monitored.

It is possible to express the current situation for Delta common stock in terms of the factors identified by Penman, e.g., the need to increase debt to pay for current losses raises the breakeven load factor and further erodes the competitive position of the airline. However, the focus on numbers tends to mask essential conceptual questions such as: when or if this particular airline can return to profitability and what the restructured airline will look like if profitability can be achieved? The issues are discussed in more general detail in the *Cases for Fundamental Analysis*, available for download from the book website, and for airlines specifically in the case for Delta Airlines.

From value drivers to valuations

A quote from Hartley Withers (1911) about common stock valuation is worth repeating at this point: "The pedantic mind craves a precise formula ... But second thoughts put the formula into the waste-paper basket." The DCF model is a formula that suggests it is possible to arrive at a precise estimate for the value of a common stock. Reinventing Withers in the present, it is still true that *there is no precise formula* – though some techniques do perform better in particular situations. Acknowledging that there are cases where the cash flows and discount rate are more-or-less known with relative certainty, a DCF valuation will only be as precise as the inputs that are used. Because the relevant inputs are typically imprecise, the resulting estimated value obtained from a DCF model will also be imprecise. However, even though the formula does not yield a precise value, it does not follow that the waste-paper basket is the appropriate endpoint. The DCF model provides a process of constructing an estimated value that can provide insight into the future evolution of the value drivers that determine the common stock price. To what extent the estimated price determined from a DCF model can be used as the primary vehicle for conducting a security analysis will depend on a range of factors including the type of stock and the biases of the analyst.

Following GDC, Warren Buffett and other "value investors," the DCF price estimate puts a face on the "intrinsic value." Combining an intrinsic value with the "margin of safety" principle is an implicit recognition that the value estimates obtained from DCF models are inherently imprecise. Consistent with the underlying investment philosophy of value investors, at any given time a particular common stock may be overvalued or undervalued relative to the "true" intrinsic value that will eventually be reflected in the market price. DCF models are a theoretically sound if imprecise method of determining an estimate for the intrinsic value. Even if there is not enough confidence in the DCF estimate to make a trading decision, if the common stock price is significantly different than the DCF estimate, either above or below, then this is a flag to reexamine the assumptions and forecasts that were made for the value drivers and inputs to the DCF model. Hence, following Hooke (1998, ch. 12) and others, estimating a price using *a DCF model is a sound first step* in the security analysis process. It will not likely be sufficient to generate a trading decision and, even if it is, there will almost certainly be a number of iterations of the DCF price estimate before a trading decision is made.

Given that a DCF model is used to construct a first step value estimate, a number of key questions have to be addressed before the forecasts of the inputs are determined. One question concerns the specific type of DCF model to use. The various DCF alternatives to equity valuation differ according to the variable that is being discounted, i.e., dividends, accrual earnings or cash flow. In terms of the DCF models in conventional use, the associated alternatives can be classified as the dividend discount model, the residual income model and the free cash flow model.[19] Each of these models can be expressed in a simple format, e.g., the Gordon growth model version of the dividend discount model. Alternatively, each model can appear in a more flexible format that does not make, say, constant growth assumptions but calculates the price estimate by individually discounting a string of future cash flows. Though more conceptually appealing, because it is not feasible to discount cash flows out to infinity this approach requires some forecasting horizon to be specified and some method for estimating the terminal value. Following Penman and Sougiannis (1998), the different DCF models have different sensitivities to the selection of the forecast horizon.

A natural question arises about the practical differences between the simplified versions of these different models. In cases where dividend payouts are zero or not approximately based on a constant target dividend payout ratio, then there will be difficulties with applying the dividend discount model. In such cases, the residual income or free cash flow approaches will be superior. Which of these two simplified models works best depends on whether the inclusion or exclusion of accruals provides a better fit to the future stream of cash flows. Though there is some empirical accounting research on the relative ability of current cash flows and current earnings to predict future cash flows, this research is better suited to the more general DCF models that estimate a stream of future cash flows and a terminal value at the fixed horizon endpoint. There is little information about the relative performance of the different forms of the simplified DCF models. Though based on the same general DCF approach, this is no assurance that these simplified models will provide much the same results. Yet, these simplified models are well suited to providing a relatively quick check on the difference between the estimated intrinsic price and the observed stock price. Difficulty of application is one criticism that is often made of the DCF model by professional security analysis.

In order to provide some information on this point, consider a comparative valuation of Coca-Cola using three different simplified DCF models. To this end, recall the Gordon model from section 8.1: $P(0) = \{D(0)(1 + g)\}/\{k - g\}$. Deriving this model required a constant growth rate in dividends assumption. As discussed in section 8.1, to derive a similar version for the free cash flow to equity (*FCFE*) model, recall that the general form of this DCF model is specified:

$$P(0) = \sum_{t=1}^{\infty} \frac{FCFE^*(t)}{(1 + k)^t}$$

where $FCFE^*(t)$ is $FCFE(t)$ expressed on a per share basis. Recognizing that constant growth in dividends with a constant dividend payout does not ensure that *FCFE* will also grow at the same rate, it is possible to assume that *FCFE* grows at a constant rate g_f such that $FCFE(t) = FCFE(t - 1)(1 + g_f)$, this produces the simplified free cash flow valuation model: $P(0) = \{FCFE^*(0)(1 + g_f)\}/\{k - g_f\}$. Under appropriate assumptions, it is possible to assume $g = g_f$ though this may not be plausible in many situations (see end of chapter questions). Similarly, assuming that the book value of equity grows at a constant rate g_b such that $BV(t) = BV(t - 1)(1 + g_b)$, produces the simplified residual income model: $P(0) = BV(0)\{ROE(1) - g_b\}/\{k - g_b\}$. Again, under appropriate assumptions, it is possible to assume $g = g_b$ (see end of chapter questions). With constant dividend payout the "constant payout residual income model" becomes: $P(0) = BV(0)\{b\ ROE(1)\}/\{k - g\}$.

Coca-Cola (KO) is an excellent company to use for comparative purposes, if only because it has such helpful financial statements (see table 8.11). Other aspects that make it an attractive example are that, being a stock that is highly touted by Warren Buffett, it can be viewed as a classical example of a "value company." Such companies are likely to be excellent candidates for applying DCF techniques. Another attractive feature of Coca-Cola is that it is such a strong company that many problems that can arise in estimating the input values, e.g., where earnings have been negative for some time or dividends have been suspended, do not arise. Given this, consider *applying the Gordon model* where the five year growth for dividends is $g = 7.4\%$ with $D(0) = \$.80$ and $P(0) = \$40.73$ (27/03/03). With this information it is possible to solve for the implied expected return on equity as $k = \{.8(1.074)/\$40.73\} + .074 = 9.51\%$. Given that the beta for Coca-Cola is 0.624 and the long-term Treasury bond is yielding 5.375% using Damodaran's long-term market risk premium of $E[R_M] - r = 5.5\%$ the CAPM provides an estimate of the discount rate of 8.81%. This provides an estimated price of \$61.06.

In contrast to the price estimate provided by the Gordon model, the *simplified free cash flow* and *residual income* models for Coca-Cola are more difficult to evaluate. The constant payout residual income model can provide a bridge between the Gordon model and the residual income model. However, examination of the ten year (1992–2002) dividend payout ratio for Coca-Cola reduces confidence in the constant payout assumption. Though the dividend payout ratio was always below 45% and sometimes below 40% until 2000, the payout ratios in 2000 and 2002 were 77% and 65%. Nevertheless, taking $BV(0) = 11.8/2.478 = 4.762$ and assuming $b = .5$, it is possible to use the $\{k - g\}$ values from the dividend growth model to provide an estimate for the constant payout residual income model: $P(0) = 4.762\{.5(.35)\}/\{.0951 - .074\} = \$39.50$. The value for $ROE(1)$ is based on the 34.3% value observed in 2002 and similar values observed in a number of previous years. Using the CAPM discount rate estimate of 8.81% instead of the 9.51% rate from the Gordon model gives a price estimate of $59.10. The close correspondence of these values with the Gordon model price estimates reveals that .5 is close to the equilibrium dividend payout ratio that is consistent with the growth rate of 7.4% and discount rate of .0951 derived using the Gordon model.

In contrast to the steady 7.4% growth of per share for dividend payments, determining a growth rate for net income and book value of equity per share is more difficult. A five year horizon gives a growth rate for net income of −5.9% while the ten year rate is 6.2%. Return on equity is also quite variable with a high over the five year period of 61.6% in 1997 to a low of 23.1% in 2000. The growth rate for book value of equity is only somewhat more cooperative. For example, the three year compound growth rate for BV from 1999–2002 is 7.45%. (Using BV values from earlier periods result in an estimated growth rate for book value in excess of k, violating the stability condition). Evaluating the simplified residual income model with $k = .0951$ gives: $P(0) = BV(0) \{ROE(1) - g_b\}/\{k - g_b\} = 4.732\{.35 - .0745\}/\{.0951 - .0745) = \$63.69$, indicating the common stock is undervalued. The reliance of the residual income model on the book value of equity and net income is a substantive limitation on the effectiveness of this approach. BV and E are residual outcomes of a significant number of accounting calculations. Accrual values for items such as depreciation, company pension fund adjustments, methods of inventory valuation and so on can have a significant impact on this method of calculating a DCF price estimate.

In many presentations, reference to the DCF model implies the discounting of free cash flow. Net income and book value are accrual accounting numbers and, as such, are only proxies for "true" cash flows. Yet, free cash flow (FCF) is not without problems and limitations. One important limitation is that FCF requires a value for capital expenditures to be subtracted from "net cash provided by operating activities." While it is conventional to use the observed capital expenditure item(s) from the investing activities section of the cash flow statement, this is not conceptually correct. The logic of the DCF model requires the use of a capital expenditure expense that reflects the assumptions used to generate the future stream of free cash flows. English (2001, p. 295) provides a discussion of this point:

> My students often ask what level of capital expenditures (capex) to assume in a cash flow projection. Recommendations on this question vary. Some say capital expenditures sufficient to maintain existing operations are the appropriate choice. Or perhaps that level of capex should be adjusted for inflation. I believe that, once cash flow from operations is determined, a level of fixed investment, appropriate to the growth and production assumptions, is also determined . . . Analysts are often guided to capital expenditure assumptions by management. If management guidance on capex is used, then the analyst's operational scale assumptions are bounded. That is, the productive capacity implied in management's capital expenditure plans limits sales growth and operational scale assumptions. Unless that limitation is observed, the company's cash flow generating capacity could be seriously misstated.

Table 8.12 Financial highlights statement for RCCC

Financial highlights (For the years ended December 31: in thousands, except per share data)

	2001	2000	1999	1998	1997
Total revenues	$441,156	$356,097	$175,741	$113,518	$63,098
Operating income	$80,800	$49,286	$30,211	$7,999	$1,835
Net income (loss) applicable to common shares	($87,559)	($83,334)	($11,062)	($15,714)	($1,266)
Net income (loss) per share	($7.38)	($7.24)	($1.22)	($1.76)	($0.14)
EBITDA[a]	$193,377	$140,364	$71,488	$34,531	$14,293
Free cash flow[b]	$33,298	$(2,058)	$18,552	$(24,559)	$(26,700)
Weighted average shares outstanding	11,865	11,510	9,047	8,916	8,853

[a] Earnings before interest, taxes, depreciation and amortization.
[b] Free cash flow is defined as EBITDA less net interest expense and capital expenditures.

While the observation that management capital expenditure assumptions need to be recognized is sound advice, what if there is no direct guidance about capital expenditures provided by management? In this case English provides the almost vacuous response: "Essentially, any scale assumption the analyst feels comfortable with" is appropriate.

The use of the reported capital expenditure items as a baseline for evaluating the current level of *FCF* and the future capital expenditure stream is tempting but, depending on the specifics of the firm, can be potentially distorting. For example, consider a firm that is under considerable pressure on earnings due to a decline in sales. There is the temptation to reduce capital expenditures, sell productive assets and the like in order to improve the appearance of the accounting statements. Yet, this will have a substantive impact on the future ability of the firm to generate free cash flow. If exogenous change results in an improvement in the product market, the firm will be less able to take advantage of these changes. In this case, using reported capital expenditures will likely be inconsistent with the use of current "net cash from operations" to predict future "net cash." Another problem with free cash flow involves the handling of changes in the degree of financial leveraging. For example, *FCFE* is initially improved if the firm increases the level of debt. This will impact *FCFE* in latter periods as the interest expense of the additional debt is paid. Table 8.12 and figure 8.2 provide examples for a firm, Rural Cellular Corporation (RCCC), with positive free cash flow that is suffering a serious financial crisis (see end of chapter questions).

Coca-Cola does not report *FCF* as a separate line item in the 10-K financial statements. This value has to be calculated and, to this end, a number of conceptual problems arise. In particular, the calculation of capital expenditures is equated in the financial statements with purchases of property, plant and equipment. Yet, the line item "acquisitions and investments, principally trademarks and bottling companies" is sufficiently close to capital expenditures that it is appropriate to be included. Despite some opaqueness in the total debt number, debt repayments and debt issuance are directly identifiable

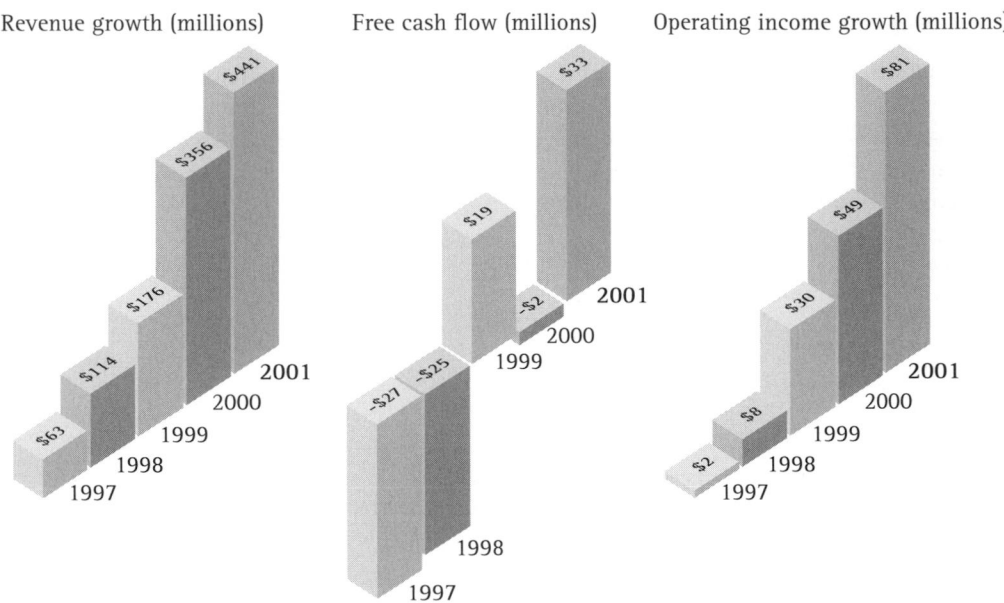

Figure 8.2 Financial highlights statement for RCCC

from the cash flow statement. Using this calculation process the following *FCFE* values are calculated:

Free cash flow to equity for Coca-Cola, 1996–2002 (millions US$)						
2002	2001	2000	1999	1998	1997	1996
$2591	$1770	$1870	$1894	$2551	$1244	$2370
(−544)	(−651)	(−397)	(−1876)	(−1428)	(−1100)	(−645)

The numbers in brackets below the free cash flow numbers is the "acquisitions and investments, principally trademarks and bottling companies" that is listed separately from the conventional capital expenditure number associated with purchases of property, plant and equipment.

Based on these FCF numbers setting $g_f = 0$ does appear to be a realistic assumption. The largest *FCFE* number occurs during 1998 and 2002 with 1996 being approximately the same as in 2002. Setting the fixed *FCFE** = $2,500/2,478 shares = $1.01/share and using the CAPM discount rate of 8.81% gives an estimated price of $11.51. If the "trademark and bottling companies" number is not included then the valuation produces *FCFE** = $3,100/2,478 = $1.25 with k = 8.81% for an estimated price of $14.20. Using the simple constant growth *FCFE* valuation model to estimate a projected growth rate for free cash flow to equity that is consistent with $P(0)$ = $40.73 produces g_f = 6.86%

for $k = 9.51\%$ and $g_f = 6.18\%$ for $k = 8.81\%$ with the "trademark" number included and $g_f = 6.25\%$ for $k = 9.51\%$ and $g_f = 5.57\%$ for $k = 8.81\%$ with the "trademark" number excluded. Why do the *FCFE* price estimates differ so much from the Gordon model and residual income model? In the case of the Gordon model, the growth rate in dividends is being achieved by a substantial increase in the payout ratio, a violation of an underlying assumption. The residual income model relies on the relationship between the book value of equity and net income. The book value is sensitive to retained earnings and not, directly, to how the assets purchased with those retained funds are used to generate cash flows in a given year.

Is Coca-Cola over-valued? The answer to this question depends on the confidence allotted to the three simple DCF models employed.[20] The sizeable difference in the price estimates lend support to the notion that estimates from these models are, at best, imprecise and subject to a number of vagaries. What the simple DCF models do provide is the first step in a structured approach to evaluating observed market prices. For example, the dividend discount model demonstrated that for a current dividend of $0.80 per share and $g = 7.4\%$ then a $k = 9.51\%$ is needed to make sense of the current price of $41. The CAPM estimated discount rate of 8.81% indicates the stock price is overvalued. But this could be due to the beta estimate or market risk premium used to determine the k from the CAPM. This raises the question: what expected return is appropriate for KO? Similarly, the residual income model raised the need to evaluate the erratic growth rate in earnings. Comparison of the residual income and free cash flow results indicate some concerns about whether retained earnings have been effectively employed in the purchase of cash flow generating assets. In addition, the difference between the accrual and cash flow estimates raises concern that the high value for $ROE = \{P/BV\}/\{P/E\} = \{E/BV\}$ may be masking price-to-book and price-to-earnings ratios that are "overvalued" at 8.5 and 23.

Lacking confidence in all three of the simple DCF valuation models, it would be possible to employ more detailed DCF models where cash flows for each individual time period up to the end of a forecasting horizon is specified.[21] In residual income model applications, the terminal period is often assumed to be where $ROE(T) = k$ and all future terms after the terminal period in the (infinite) sum can be set to zero. The economic rationale for this is that when $ROE(T) = k$ the firm has reached a "competitive equilibrium" where no further abnormal earnings are possible. If dividends or free cash flows are being discounted, the terminal period is often assumed to be where the relevant dividend or free cash flow is constant from that point forward, again being rationalized as an implication of the firm reaching a competitive equilibrium. The value of the cash flows beyond the terminal period is then determined using a perpetuity pricing model and that value discounted back to the present at the appropriate discount rate. Recognizing that "competitive equilibrium" may be an impractical endpoint because it cannot be attained in a foreseeable future, Penman and Sougiannis (1998, p. 347) suggest that, if the forecast horizon is truncated at a practical horizon of five to eight years, then accrual techniques, i.e., the residual income model, "yield lower valuation errors than those based on forecasting dividends or cash flows". The potential for accrual numbers to outperform cash flow numbers in forward-looking valuations is also supported by Barth et al. (2001).

Which DCF approach works better? Is it better to discount free cash flow, dividends, economic value added, residual income or some other cash flow measure? As the assessments of Coca-Cola and RCCC illustrate, the answer to this question is elusive. In general, the applicability of a certain model will depend on the specifics of the situation. The various DCF models are simplified characterizations of reality and are useful as an initial screen and a crude check on other aspects of the valuation exercise. As illustrated in the "cases for fundamental analysis" available on the book website, there is a need to do intensive study of a particular security in order to do an adequate valuation. Such study goes well beyond the confines of a simplified DCF calculation. In turn, the process of determining the inputs into the DCF calculation provides a structure within which the various sources of information about a particular security can be organized. Following GDC and others, DCF models generally work best with stable cash flow industries. As such, the performance of a specific DCF model will depend on the sources of cash flow instability. When possible, it is advisable to calculate an estimated security value from a number of DCF models and use the diversity or disagreement of the estimates as a guide to further investigations.

Alternatives to and hybrids of discounted cash flow models

In addition to the three DCF models, a number of hybrids have been proposed based on approaches such as EVA or *the economic profit model.* Penman (2001, p. 468) develops one such model, based on capitalizing the value of the cash flows from net operating assets. This model is used to estimate a price for Coca-Cola. Taking *VNOA* to be the estimated value of net operating assets, *ROIC* to be the return on invested capital, *IC* to be invested capital, *WACC* to be the weighted average cost of capital and g_s the growth rate of sales, Penman provides the following simple valuation formula:

$$VNOA(0) = IC(0) + \frac{(ROIC(0) - WACC(0))IC(0)}{WACC(0) - g_s(0)}$$

The connection with the economic profit model is apparent in the use of *WACC*, *ROIC* and *IC*. Based on the 2002 values in the Coca-Cola financial statements, $IC(0) = \$17,156$, $ROIC(0) = 24.5\%$ and $g_s = 3.3\%$ (5 year compound rate). Observing that $BV(0) = \$11,800$ with a value for debt of $5,356, completion of the valuation requires an estimate for the *WACC*. Taking the CAPM value of 8.81% and assuming a debt cost of 7% produces a *WACC* of 8.25%.

Arriving at price estimate based on this formula requires evaluating *VNOA*. This can be viewed as an estimate for the right hand side of the balance sheet. Deducting the (book) value of debt to obtain an estimate for the value of equity and dividing by the number of shares outstanding produces a common stock price estimate. Using the values given produces an estimate of $P(0) = \$27.51$. This value is sensitive to the assumption made about the growth rate in sales. If instead of the five year sales growth rate, the ten year sales growth rate of 6.3% is used then the common stock price estimate rises to $62.41. A growth rate of 5.1% produces a price estimate of $40.48. This method of valuation is a hybrid, mixing the economic profit model with simplifying assumptions needed to achieve a readily calculated pricing formula. Much like the residual income model, the methodology combines income statement and balance sheet items. The estimated values relate to capitalizing cash flows associated with net operating assets, hence the use of the sales growth rate. While the connection between a sales growth rate and the *WACC* may seem somewhat tenuous, g_s can be viewed as a proxy for other more conceptually appealing growth rates.

Despite widespread acknowledgment of the discounted cash flow methodology as the theoretically appropriate approach to specifying a common stock valuation model, *the "relative value" approach* (see section 7.3), also known as the "method of comparables" or "companion variable" approach, is often used in practice.[22] As English (2001, p. 289) observes:

> The discounted-cash-flow (DCF) technique is the most familiar and arguably the most rigorous of equity valuation techniques. Unfortunately, in the real world of equity analysis, it is among the most infrequently used – rightly so, in my view . . . The DCF model has a number of potentially serious limitations. It is poorly suited for comparative valuations, lacks the solid intuitive basis of accounting earnings, and is subject to whatever difficulties the capital asset pricing model itself may have.

Other sources, such as Hooke (1998, p. 241), agree with this view, adding the observation that DCF modeling depends on a range of assumptions and "practitioners . . . decided long ago not to argue interminably among themselves about the merits of one projection against another." Casual inspection of valuation practices used in "professional" equity analysis reveals a reliance on accounting-based, as opposed to cash flow-based, quantitative measures of common stock value. Important examples of these measures include the *P/E* and *P/BV* multiples. These measures are used despite the recognition of the limitations of GAAP in producing "economic," as opposed to accounting, measurements of firm performance.

Various arguments can be made against DCF modeling. English (2001, pp. 290–1) expands on one type of rationale, the need for professional security analysts to use "*combat finance*" techniques:[23]

> The stock valuation methods that working analysts actually use must be driven by the tremendous time demands of the analysts' world. Nevertheless, many finance writers and teachers begin and end the subject of equity valuation with the discounted-cash-flow technique. There is nothing wrong with DCF. It is certainly rigorous, complete, and familiar. And, at least for some companies they actually cover, most equity analysts already maintain detailed, multi-year financial models that could support DCF valuations . . . The fact is that DCF is a fine behind-the-lines method that works well, one company at a time out of the heat of battle. But the working analyst needs "combat finance" techniques that: work quickly; can accommodate a large number of stocks; and are framed in the market's valuation multiple language . . . Instead of discounted projected cash flows, working analysts and many professional investors rely instead on accounting-based valuation techniques, relative/multiple valuation.

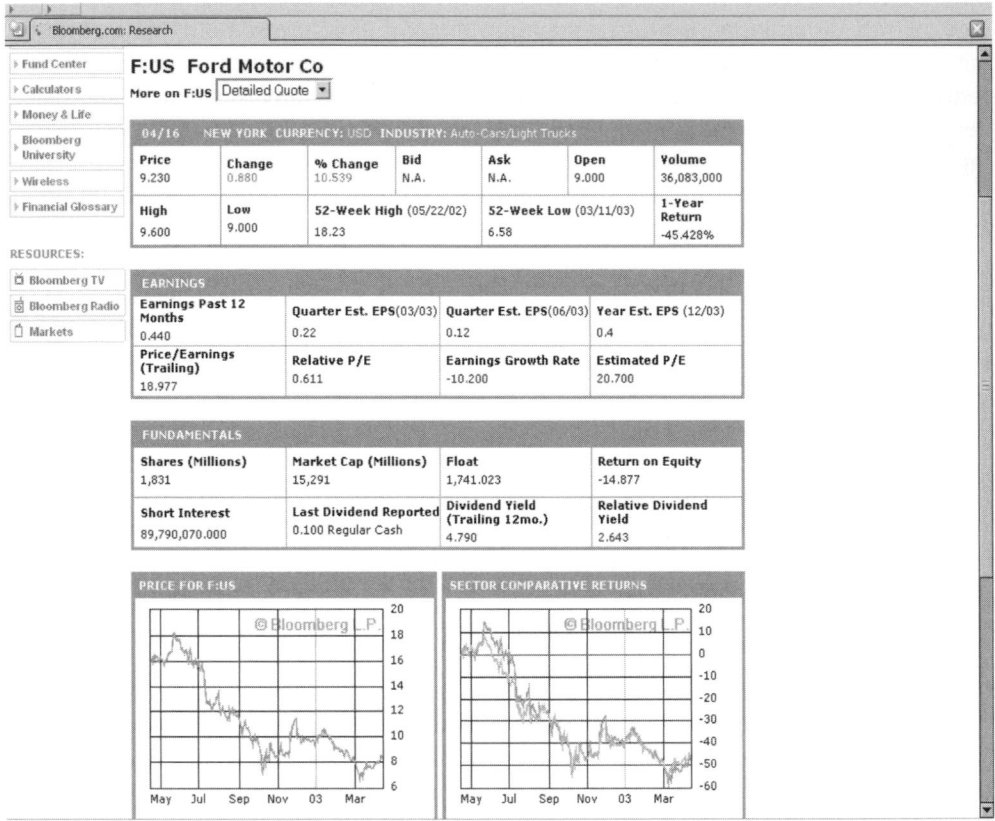

Figure 8.3 Internet site information for Ford Motor Company

Many of the important variables that are mostly commonly used in relative valuation analysis can be readily identified by examining the output on a www.bloomberg.com stock information screen (see figure 8.3). The dividend yield, the P/E ratio, realized and forecasted earnings, market capitalization and relative earnings forecast for the industry group compared to the S&P 500 are all prominent. In addition, the combat finance analyst may also have at hand the *P/BV*, *ROE* $(= E(t)/BV(t))$ or *ROBBV* (Return on Beginning Book Value, $E(t)/BV(t-1)$) and other comparables such as *P/Sales*.

There are a range of possible approaches to arriving at price estimates that can be associated with the method of comparables. For example, Philip Fisher did not advocate DCF modeling preferring to use comparative measures, especially *the P/E multiple*, to assess whether a stock was under or over valued relative to current stocks. Fisher would estimate a future level for the earnings per share and combine this with the *P/E* to determine an estimate for the future price. One example involved a stock that currently had *E* = $1 and *P/E* = 10 and was forecasted to have *E* = $2 and *P/E* = 20 in the future. The *P/E* is expected to increase because the current *P/E* is low compared to other similar companies or, possibly, to the level of the market. The earnings are forecasted to increase based on an analysis of the business. The numbers used in the example imply the common stock price will increase from $10 to $40. Though extremely simple, this example does capture the essence of one possible approach to relative valuation analysis. The *P/E* is used as a measure to compare relative value across firms. Forecasted earnings are then combined with a *P/E* forecast and used to provide a future price forecast.

An *illustration of the use of P/E multiples* for relative value analysis has to deal with the limitations of the *P/E* ratio as a valuation measure. In particular, the volatility in earnings over time, either from quarter to quarter or from year to year, makes it difficult to identify the appropriate *P/E* ratio to use. Are current earnings the appropriate value? Is some weighted average of past earnings or some forecast of future earnings a better approach? For example, using information from www.globeinvestor.com, consider a relative value comparison of General Motors (GM) and Ford (F). On September 4, 2003, GM had a *P/E* of 5.80 based on a price of $41.97 and *EPS* of $7.24 based on a trailing 12 months estimate of earnings. (Dividend payout has been held constant at $2 per share.) This value is up significantly from the $3.34 *EPS* that GM was earning in calendar year 2002 and the $4.58 for the trailing 12 month earnings estimate from the previous quarter. In contrast, Ford has a *P/E* of 20.30 based on a stock price of $11.94 and a trailing 12 month *EPS* of $0.58. This is up from the trailing 12 month *EPS* of $0.46 from the previous quarter and a loss of −$0.54 in calendar year 2002. (After suspending the dividend, Ford has resumed the dividend at a reduced payment of $0.40 per share.)

A comparison of the *P/E* multiples for GM and F is decidedly favorable to GM. Even if GM is unable to sustain the $7.24 *EPS* and falls back to the previous value of $4.58, a doubling of the *P/E* would still leave GM as an attractive purchase at (11.6)($4.58) = $53.12 which is considerably above the current price of $41.97. In contrast, even if F is able to double *EPS* to $1.16, at the same *P/E* value as used for GM this produces: (11.6)($1.16) = $13.46. Similarly, a doubling of the *EPS* for F still leaves the *P/E* at 10.15 if the stock price does not change. This type of analysis raises questions about the ability of F and GM to grow earnings. As of 3Q 2003, Ford is still in an earnings recovery mode, following a shakeup in senior management. If plans underway are successful, the prospects of a significant *EPS* increase are good. In comparison, GM did not experience the same problems as Ford and does not have a potential earnings upside that is comparable to Ford. Both companies have a pension overhang problem associated with previous contracts negotiated with the UAW. Yet, even with these mitigating factors, a relative value analysis based on *P/E* multiples is still decidedly favorable to GM.

Similar to the variation in DCF techniques there are a range of possible approaches to the relative value approach. The general approach of relative value analysis was discussed in section 7.3. Hooke (1998, p. 232) provides a description of the heuristic style involved:

Inevitably, a stock price is characterized as "20x earnings," "8x EBIT," or "3x book value." When the analyst is asked how he justifies this valuation, the response is invariably something like "comparable companies are trading at 20x earnings, 8x EBIT or 3x book value." If the subject company's multiples are higher than the comparables, the investor asks the obvious question, "Why is this firm's price higher than its peers?" The answer is typically a recitation of the firm's positive attributes, such as a better growth outlook, a better track record, or a better balance sheet.

There are a number of problems with such an approach. In particular, by comparing only companies within the same line of business, no evaluation is made about whether the group of comparables is appropriately valued. For example, General Motors (GM) may be comparably better value than Ford Motor (F) but the automobile sector as a whole may be overvalued relative to, say, non-alcoholic beverages. Another problem with the relative value approach is that company characteristics differ within the group of comparables. For example, though often classified into the same group of comparables, IBM (IBM), Dell (DELL) and Hewlett-Packard (HPQ) are substantively different companies operating in a range of over-lapping but not identical product markets.

English (2001, ch. 15) recommends an alternative approach to relative value analysis based on the ***use of regression techniques*** across comparable firms to identify the fitted relationship between, say, *P/BV* and *ROE*. To illustrate this approach, assume that Gateway has an *ROE* of 23.6% and a *P/BV* of 6.54. For all comparable firms in the computer industry a bivariate regression equation is fitted between the dependent variable *P/BV* and the independent variable *ROE*. The fitted equation is found to have an intercept of −1.2 and a slope coefficient of 35.4. Evaluating the predicted *P/BV* for Gateway gives: −1.2 + 35.4(.236) = 7.15 > 6.54.[24] This implies that Gateway is undervalued by 9%. English concludes: "Regardless of the reason for the deviation . . . it suggests further questions, causes the analyst to dig deeper, and provides a strong starting point for further inquiry." Just as the price estimate from the simple DCF model was used as a first step in the DCF valuation process, the fitted regression estimate is used as a first step in this version of the method of comparables. Though this approach may seem naive to those familiar with advanced econometric techniques, the approach is similar in spirit to the multi-factor models of modern Finance.

As observed, the method of comparables or relative value approach is the rule rather than the exception among professional security analysts. Though this observation sometimes comes as a surprise to the uninitiated, this point has long been recognized by academics, as reflected in a number of studies comparing the pricing performance of DCF models with techniques from the method of comparables. For example, S. Kaplan and Ruback (1995) examines the pricing performance of a cash flow DCF technique to value highly leveraged transactions and find that the DCF model performs as least as well as the method of comparables. Berkman et al. (2000) report similar results when cash flow DCF models are compared with *P/E* multiples to value IPO's, i.e., DCF methods and the method of comparables have similar accuracy. Liu et al. (2002) report that the use of valuation multiples, the most common approach to relative value analysis, provides superior results when compared to simplified residual income DCF models. Contrary to the general view that the performance of relative value analysis is sensitive to the industry being examined, Liu et al. find these results apply across industries.

Questions ?

1(a) Dividend discount models are based on the notion that firms have a target payout ratio for dividends that is stable over time. Funds that are not paid out are reinvested in the firm and the resulting growth in the firm's asset base sustains future growth in dividends. Yet, in practice, instead of paying out earnings as dividends or reinvesting in the firm, many firms return cash to shareholders by repurchasing shares. Explain how the dividend growth model has to be adjusted to account for share repurchases. Does your answer depend on whether the firm also makes extensive use of executive stock options?

(b) In section 8.1 it was observed that the Gordon growth model could be extended to two-stage and higher levels of dividend growth, where the different stages had a different growth rate for dividends. Demonstrate that where g_1 and g_2 are the dividend growth rates in the first (T period) and second ($T + 1$ to infinity) stages that the solution to the DCF valuation equation is:

$$P(0) = D(1)\left[\frac{1 - \left(\frac{1 + g_1}{1 + k}\right)^T}{k - g_1}\right] + \frac{D(1)(1 + g_1)^{T-1}(1 + g_2)}{(1 + k)^T(k - g_2)}$$

(Hint: observe that $D(T + 1) = D(0)(1 + g_1)^T(1 + g_2)$.)

2 Starting from the "clean surplus" equation (to substitute for the value of dividends in the general discounted dividend model) and using the results that:

$$E(t) = ROE(t)BV(t - 1) \qquad \frac{BV(t)}{1 + k} = BV(t) - \frac{kBV(t)}{1 + k}$$

Show that:

$$P(0) = BV(0) + \sum_{t=1}^{\infty}\frac{(ROE(t) - k)BV(t - 1)}{(1 + k)^t}$$

(Hint: see English 2001, pp. 334–5.) If it is assumed that $BV(t) = BV(t - 1)(1 + g_b)$, then show that the price to book ratio can be expressed as:

$$\frac{P(0)}{BV(0)} = 1 + \frac{ROE(1) - k}{k - g_b} = \frac{ROE(1) - g_b}{k - g_b}$$

(Due to the assumption of constant perpetual growth, this is the highest possible price-to-book ratio). What is the relationship between the constant growth assumption for book value and the constant growth assumption for dividends and earnings?

3 (a) Show that the expression for the earnings/dividend growth rate in the constant growth model, $g = ROE(t)(1 - b)$ can be derived from the value equation: $E(t + 1) = E(t) + (ROE(t + 1))RE(t)$, where RE is the retained earnings and b is the constant dividend payout ratio. Does this formulation depend on the "perpetual earnings model," i.e., that earnings can be maintained as a constant level in perpetuity if $b = 1$?
(b) Derive the relationship between the growth rates in $BV(t) = BV(t - 1)(1 + g_b)$ and $E(t) = E(t - 1)(1 + g)$. Under what conditions will $g = g_b$? (Hint: assume constant dividend payout and solve for the BV looking forward from a given $t = 0$ in terms of earnings. This will produce a geometric series solution in terms of $E(0)$. Because $t = 0$ is arbitrary, this solution will also hold for BV at $t = 1$ as a geometric series in terms of $E(1)$. Observing $E(t) = E(t - 1)(1 + g)$ and dividing $BV(1)$ by $BV(0)$ and solving gives the desired solution.)

4 For the three different formulas for the P/E given in section 8.1, let $b = \{0, .2, .4, .6, .8, 1\}$, $g = \{-.2, 0, .02, .04, .06, .08\}$ and $k = \{.06, .08, .10, .12\}$. Derive a tableau of values for the formulas by substitute these values into the formulas. What do you observe about the required relationships for AE, E and ROE? For what values of b, g and k do the formulas produce sensible values?

5 Explain the difference between: (a) accrual basis and cash basis accounting; (b) percentage-of-completion and completed contracts method of revenue recognition; (c) cash flow from operations and free cash flow; (d) primary earnings per share and fully diluted earnings per share.

6 Explain briefly how each of the following transactions would affect a company's balance sheet, income statement and cash flow statement: (a) purchase of a new building for $1 million using internal cash; (b) purchase of a new $1 million building, financed 60% with debt and 40% with cash; (c) receipt of a $100,000 payment from a customer on an account receivable; (d) repurchase of $10 million in company stock using internal cash.

7 XYZ Corporation earns a 12% profit margin on sale of its high-technology electronic calibrators. The manager of the calibrator division strongly opposes introduction of a new mass-market calibrator because its anticipated profit margin is only 6%, arguing that the new calibrator can only lower division returns. Is this a valid argument against the introduction of the new calibrator? Explain the various factors which have to be taken into account in making the decision.

8 Describe three ways in which a company could manipulate earnings and the book value of equity within the framework of GAAP (generally accepted accounting principles). (Hint: consider the seven shenanigans.)

9 There are certain accounting signals that can be used to identify deteriorating earnings capacity. Explain how the following could be used in this process: (a) increase in accounts receivable; (b) changes in accounting policies; (c) increases in intangible assets; (d) increase in non-recurring income; (e) manipulation of reserve accounts.

10 From the information in tables 8.3 and 8.4 calculate the "invested capital" for both Ford and US Steel using both the assets approach and the liabilities approach. What assumptions were made to achieve equality of the invested capital number for the two approaches? What conclusions can be drawn about the practical applicability of EVA given the difficulties associated with determining a number for invested capital?

11 The simplified free cash flow to equity DCF model uses the condition that, under appropriate assumptions, it is possible to assume $g = g_f$. Examining the definition for *FCFE* and net income given in the discussion of financial statement analysis in section 8.2, specify a set of conditions that are sufficient for this result to apply. (Hint: under what conditions will accrual accounting be equivalent to cash flow accounting?)

12 In table 8.12 and figure 8.2 the free cash flow situation for Rural Cellular is provided. Explain how a firm with a positive free cash flow can have such a large increase in the equity deficit? What role does preferred share financing have on the free cash flow situation?

NOTES

1 Williams (1938, p. 6) states: "investment value [is] the present worth of the future dividends in the case of a common stock, or the future coupon and principal in the case of a bond."

2 In what follows, do not confuse the use of $D(t)$ for D and D^* that appeared in part II in reference to either the Macaulay or adjusted durations. Except in the case where a bar appears over the D ($\bar{D}$) dividends are always referenced with a time date while the duration value is not.

3 The convention in accounting is to make a distinction between valuation methods that involve "cash flows" and "accruals." Using this distinction, discounted cash flow (DCF) techniques refer *only* to valuation methods that discount "cash flows" such as free cash flow or dividends. Valuation methods such as the residual income method (about to be introduced), which use accrual numbers, are not considered to be DCF techniques, e.g., Penman and Sougiannis (1998). While this distinction is useful in accounting studies, it is terminological overkill when the primary objective is discussing the valuation of securities. The operative cash flow in the residual income model, i.e., accounting earnings/net income, can be viewed either as a proxy for a cash flow or taken to be an accounting cash flow. In both cases, a cash flow is being discounted and the residual income model can be viewed as a DCF technique. This interpretation is used in what follows.

4 Damodaran (1994) is of interest because of the intensive examination of the discounted dividend approach to DCF valuation. As such, Damodaran differs from other sources in the depth of coverage. Useful textbook level

overviews of the different approaches to DCF analysis are available in a number of sources, e.g., Palepu et al. (2000) and Weston et al. (2001).

5 An American depository receipt (ADR) is a security that represents a claim to shares of a foreign security, almost always a common stock listed and traded on an exchange outside the US. Conceptually, an ADR can be viewed as an all equity financed closed end fund that holds a foreign security as the sole asset of the fund. While publicly traded on US exchanges, an ADR is only subject to SEC reporting requirements on the receipt. The company associated with the foreign security is only subject to reporting requirements imposed by the foreign market in which the security trades.

6 As with the use of Boeing in section 1.1, the selection of Ford is for pedagogical purposes. Ford was not selected as a model for how accounts are to be prepared or because it represents viable security selection opportunities. If anything, the method used by Ford is somewhat atypical and confusing. In some cases, the income statement is referred to using other terminology. For example, US Steel uses "Consolidated Statement of Operations."

7 In the following, ticker symbols appear after the company names to facilitate the retrieval of the company information from an appropriate information source such as www.bloomberg.com. In all cases, the information provided is obtained from the financial statements provided in the annual reports of the companies.

8 Baumol (1977, ch. 25) contains references to some of the early studies from the 1940s and 1950s where the capital budgeting theory currently taught in corporate finance was developed. Included in these studies are a number from engineering economics.

9 This definition corresponds with the "indirect method" of calculating cash from operations in the cash flow statement. More precisely, there are two methods of calculating the cash flow statement: the direct method and the indirect method, e.g., Penman (2001, p. 314). The indirect method calculates: *Net income + Accruals = Cash from operations*. Following Barth et al. (2001), the major components of accruals are: change in accounts receivable, change in accounts payable, change in inventory and depreciation/amortization. Barth et al. demonstrate that accruals have a statistically significantly ability to forecast future cash flows.

10 This adjustment can depend, for example, whether the DCF valuation is determining the market value of the firm or the market value of common equity. Adjustment for net interest expense is more appropriate if the market value of the firm is being calculated.

11 There is a procedural difference between these two numbers in determining a DCF value. If *FCFF* is used, then discounting is done at the weighted average cost of capital. If *FCFE* is used then discounting is done at the cost of equity.

12 Following Ehrbar (1998), the types of additional adjustments that are made involve: goodwill amortization; asset write-offs; full expensing of R&D; restructuring charges; and leasing arrangements.

13 Calculation of the weighted average cost of capital is discussed in introductory corporate finance texts, e.g., Giammarino (1996). The formula defines *ROIC* after taxes and depreciation as $ROIC = \{EBIT(1 - Tax\ rate)\}/Invested\ capital$.

14 The Canadian Securities Course (Canadian Securities Institute 1993, p. 97) does not include deferred taxes in the calculation of invested capital.

15 Though proponents of EVA and the economic profit model distinguish between these techniques and DCF models, there is no conceptual difference in the underlying methodology. The distinction is largely one of semantics. The intent is to distinguish between the types of cash flows being discounted, the EVA-type being closer to "economic profit" than the accounting determined FCF values.

16 Sutton (2002) provides a practical overview of the current crisis including a brief overview of the main points of the Sarbanes-Oxley Act. The text of this Act can be viewed from links at the SEC website.

17 Poitras et al. (2002b) discusses the different accounting standards that are used in various jurisdictions. In some locales, it is possible to revalue assets without doing an asset sale. In

practice, this transforms the earnings management decision into a classification problem.

18 The number of academic accounting studies on techniques of earnings management and earnings manipulation is difficult to estimate, certainly numbering in the hundreds. Dechow and Skinner (2000) examines the differences between views of various academics, practitioners and regulators about earnings management. Sutton (2002) discusses some of the issues associated with the reform of financial reporting.

19 Ruback (2002) suggests an alternative DCF model, the "capital cash flow model" that involves discounting free cash flow by the weighted average cost of capital. Because in this method the interest tax shields are included in the cash flows, the capital cash flow approach is easier to apply when debt is forecasted in levels instead of as a percent of total firm value.

20 Though the objective of doing a valuation for Coca-Cola was to illustrate the use of simple DCF models, the analysis indicates that KO is accurately valued with the balance pointing toward overvaluation. Mitigation comes from the reasonably robust improvement in variables such as free cash and earnings in 2002. In addition, this improvement has been accompanied by a fall in the common stock price level to values that are historically low for KO. However, with a *P/E* at 23, a *P/BV* of 8.5 and a deterioration in the dividend payout ratio there does not appear to be sufficient improvement in free cash flow to support significant upside price movement from the current price level. An expected increase in net operating revenue similar to what was experienced from 2001 to 2002 is indicated for the current common stock price to sustain the view that KO is still a legitimate "value investing" company. Whether such an increase in operating revenue is justified requires considerably more analysis than what has been provided. Such analysis would have to take into account the gains that could be obtained from purchasing, say, an investment grade corporate bond.

21 Modeling the future cash flows individually permits the introduction of *real option* values

into the valuation. In addition, variability and contingency in the future cash flows (or accruals) can be captured using Monte Carlo analysis (see section 6.3). However, while Monte Carlo methods are attractive when valuing fixed income securities with embedded options and real options are valuable for capital budgeting decisions, the problem of valuing a common stock is usually not sufficiently precise for these techniques to be as valuable in this type of application.

22 The method of comparables is not a technique that is unique to professional security analysts. Variations of this approach can be found in real estate appraisal, tax law, and probate law where valuations of untraded real assets and privately held businesses are required.

23 In section 7.3, GDC observed that relative valuation analysis (method of comparables) is sensible for a fund that is required to be always fully invested in common stocks. This observation can be used to provide another rationale for the widespread use of the method of comparables in professional security analysis. In effect, both the buy-side and sell-side institutions can be viewed as fully invested funds. In aggregate, the buy-side institutions hold the bulk of common stock and the sell-side institutions make a large fraction of firm revenue from supporting common stock trading activities. Unlike Warren Buffett who has the luxury of sitting on the sidelines for years if common stocks are estimated to be over-valued, the professional security analyst is, of necessity, required to support a position that is continuously invested in common stocks. Hence, even if a detailed DCF model determined that stocks, as a whole, were overvalued and that a shift into bonds and other assets, e.g., real estate, was indicated, such a conclusion could not be sustained by the nature of the job many professional security analysts are required to do.

24 This estimate is based on data from July 1999. Based on the performance of Gateway common stock since that time, it is apparent that the estimate of Gateway being undervalued was decidedly incorrect. As of March 2003, the stock is trading at historic lows and is on the bankruptcy watch list from Weiss ratings service.

Chapter
Summary

◤ **Chapter 9**   *Technical Analysis Demystified*

9.1   What is Technical Analysis?
       Different forms of technical analysis
       Conceptual foundations of technical analysis
       Modern Finance and technical analysis

9.2   The Technician's Toolkit
       The Dow theory
       Charting and moving average systems
       Contrarian and contrary opinion strategies

9.3   Behavioral Foundations?
       Heuristic-driven bias
       Frame dependence
       Inefficient markets

9.4   Relative Strength, Momentum and the Oscillator
       Relative strength
       Momentum and the "price rate of change"
       Oscillators

Questions
Notes

Technical Analysis Demystified

9.1 WHAT IS TECHNICAL ANALYSIS?[1]

Different forms of technical analysis

Much like "fundamental analysis" (see section 7.2), "technical analysis" suffers from an over-simplified interpretation given to this body of techniques. For many years, adherents of modern Finance maintained the empirical evidence against technical analysis was overwhelming. For example, Malkiel (1990, p. 133) claims:

> Technical rules have been tested exhaustively by using stock price data on both major exchanges, going back as far as the beginning of the 20th century. The results reveal conclusively that past movements in stock prices cannot be used to foretell future movements. The stock market has no memory. The central proposition of charting is absolutely false, and investors who follow its precepts will accomplish nothing but increasing substantially the brokerage charges they pay.

Yet, in a remarkable about-face, this "overwhelming" evidence has been contradicted and the prevailing academic view now seems to be: "Most recent studies investigating return predictability have concluded that security returns are predictable from information that investors can easily obtain" (Beller et al. 1998). It is not difficult to find similar views, e.g., Brock et al. (1992), Lo and MacKinlay (1999), Siegel (1998, ch.17). Despite this accumulating evidence some modern Finance stalwarts still maintain that *consistently* profitable trading rules have not yet been demonstrated and the results are probably due to "data snooping" and the like, e.g., Bessembinder and Chan (1998), Sullivan et al. (1999), Ready (2002).[2]

What can be concluded from the apparently conflicting empirical evidence that is now found in the body of academic studies on technical analysis? Does technical analysis provide effective methods for enhancing investment portfolio profitability through, say, improvements in market timing ability? This chapter does not attempt to answer these questions. Rather, it seeks only to provide an overview of the subject, describing various methods of technical analysis and identifying relevant studies that may give insights into the validity of specific techniques. Those seeking information about, say, the statistically significant evidence from momentum profits in Chan et al. (2002) are encouraged to examine the relevant sources directly. While there are many methods of technical analysis that fail to produce substantive improvements, it is difficult to deny that virtually all purchases of common stock and other securities involve at least a rudimentary form of technical analysis, i.e., an inspection of the historical price chart. Beyond this basic starting point, the application and extension of technical analysis tends to be a relatively subjective decision.

Much like fundamental analysis, technical analysis is an important, diverse and sometimes complicated approach to the evaluation of securities that has been overly simplified in tests of the "weak form" efficient markets hypothesis (see section 1.2). The methods and procedures involved in taking a body of "technical information" and translating that information into an evaluation of whether a stock is correctly valued does not correspond to conventional methods of testing whether, on average, changes in a particular type of technical information is rapidly translated into prices. The perception that technical analysis is an alternative and competitive approach to fundamental analysis is also inaccurate. *Much of technical analysis is concerned with speculative trading*, not with investment. Certain types of technical analysis may be used in conjunction with fundamental analysis, e.g., as a guide to market timing for determining when to purchase securities that have been identified using fundamental analysis. Some forms of technical analysis can be theoretically rationalized in terms of fundamentals. Even the precise dividing line between technical and fundamental analysis is unclear, with some "technical" trading rules exploiting information that would best be characterized as fundamental.

The boundaries of technical analysis can be defined with reference to the type of information that is being used in the specific trading rule or valuation model. More precisely, *technical analysis involves the use of "market generated data"* as inputs. This includes: current and past security prices; aggregations of these prices into market and sector indexes; total volume; up/down volume and ratios or differences for the number advancing issues to number of declining issues (e.g., the advance/decline line); implied volatilities for put and call options; relationships among bond yields, such as the "confidence index" published by *Barron's*; odd lot trading volume; and short sales positions in aggregate or by type of trader (specialist vs. odd lot). It is possible to extend the set of information to include other more circumspect types of "market generated" data, e.g.: mutual fund cash positions; credit and debit balances with brokerage firms; insider trading transactions (revealed through SEC filings such as Form 4); and, investment advisory opinions. Technical analysis involves the processing of these sources of information into valuation or market timing decisions about securities. In some cases the processing is cursory, in other cases the processing is quite sophisticated.

Technical analysts are often referred to as "chartists," e.g., Siegel (1998, p. 240), Lo et al. (2000, p. 1705). Though many types of technical analysis employ charts, this reference confuses the method of analysis with the type of information being analyzed and the type of signal that is expected. Though widely used by technical analysts, *charts are neither necessary nor sufficient for technical analysis.* Even when charts are being used, there is a range of possible techniques that can be employed. For the same set of data, different charting techniques may produce different trading signals. Some types of charting techniques may be aimed at specific sampling intervals, e.g., point-and-figure charts are often used to analyze intra-day price movements while moving average charts are applied to, say, time series of daily or weekly prices. Ultimately, charts are only visual aids. It is always possible to translate the information in a chart to mathematical or statistical expressions, though this may be difficult to accomplish in many cases, e.g., Treynor and Ferguson (1985). It is unfortunate that by stressing the connection of technical analysis with charting the theoretical foundation for the general approach is overlooked. Taken as a whole, technical analysis is much more than an atheoretical reading of the "tea leaves."

Technical analysis is a vast subject containing so many contributions that it is not possible in this chapter to provide more than a brief overview. Such an overview has to deal with selecting topics for examination. The subject has not been static. For example, classic texts, such as Edwards and Magee (1966), do not deal with numerous concepts such as oscillators and stochastics that have risen to popularity since the early 1970s and now form the grist of various online sites featuring technical indicators. In addition, significant contributions to the subject span both the commodity and securities markets. Initially, key contributions to technical analysis, such as the Dow theory, were concerned with stock markets. Over time, the emphasis on speculative trading of derivative securities in commodity markets resulted in many essential sources on technical analysis, e.g., Kaufman (1978), being concerned with commodity trading. In turn, the rapid development of day trading in stocks, enhanced execution ability, and the dramatic drop in transactions costs associated with online trading has created a resurgence of contributions concerned with stocks, e.g., Elder (1993), Blau (1995). Those interested in the current state of theory are advised to examine a number of the excellent websites featuring the "technical" approach, e.g., www.marketscreen.com, www.futuresource.com or clearstation.etrade.com.

Conceptual foundations of technical analysis

The current debate over the merits of technical analysis can be traced back to the beginnings of modern Finance in the late 1950s and early 1960s. Prior to this time, the potential benefits of technical analysis were generally acknowledged by many practitioners, though the subject was largely disparaged by adherents of "Old Finance" (see section 2.4), if only because of the emphasis on speculative trading strategies.[3] Technical analysis, in some form or other, has been practiced in securities markets at least since the sixteenth century (Poitras 2000). Nison (1996) finds evidence for the use of technical analysis in eighteenth-century Japan. Brock et al. (1992, p. 1731) observe: "In the United States, the use of trading rules to detect patterns in stock prices is probably as old as the stock market itself." Prior to the widespread availability of detailed and accurate financial statement information about publicly traded companies, market generated data were often the most important source of information about a security. The introduction of the NYSE stock ticker in 1867 marks the beginning of an important technological advance that brought "tape reading" into the lexicon of mainstream society. Prior to this time, the barriers to information transmission made the analysis of market generated data largely the preserve of those able to directly observe trading at the exchange.

Though a definitive intellectual history of technical analysis is yet to be written, the origin of modern technical analysis is usually traced to the late nineteenth century when Charles Dow originated the Dow-Jones Industrial Index.[4] Together with his successor at the *Wall Street Journal*, William Peter Hamilton, Dow was an active promoter of technical analysis based on market averages. These developments by Dow and Hamilton were not produced in isolation. As evidenced in Wyckoff (1910), other notions commonly used in modern chart reading, such as resistance and support levels, were in use around that time. Graham and Dodd (1934, p. 608) recognize that "technical study" had "increased immensely during the past ten years. Whereas security analysis suffered a distinct and continued loss of prestige beginning about 1927, chart reading apparently increased the number of its followers even during the long depression." These followers of chart reading were to be found in significant numbers in Wall Street. Graham and Dodd identify various references for these techniques including: Gartley (1934), which provides a development of moving average techniques examined in Gartley (1930); Schabacker (1930), which Kaufman (1978) describes as outstanding and a "must read"; and Rhea (1932) which is still an essential source for examining the Dow theory.

Graham and Dodd (1934) and later editions up to and including Graham, Dodd and Cottle (1962) took a dim view of "market analysis" which included technical analysis as a significant subset. A number of logical arguments were advanced against this approach. Though the connection was not recognized, the Graham and Dodd position against technical analysis was supported by statistical evidence that security price changes were serially uncorrelated which started to accumulate during the 1950s (see section 1.2).[5] These statistical studies were broadly interpreted as being strong evidence against technical analysis. Though some adherents of modern Finance have claimed that this interpretation of the evidence was incorrect (e.g., Lo et al. 2000, Jegadeesh and Titman 2001), at the time, enthusiasm for the evolving efficient markets paradigm of modern Finance outweighed the answers to the common sense question: if technical analysis is incapable of generating abnormal returns, why are so many technical analysts employed by the securities industry?[6] In the process of making a headlong rush to judgment, modern Finance was quick to dismiss conceptual arguments supporting the foundations of technical analysis.

While specific rationales for technical analysis have appeared more recently – such as behavioral finance motivations (Shefrin 2000) – Levy (1966) provided an assessment of the conceptual foundation for technical analysis prevailing at the time the efficient markets hypothesis was being formulated. A summary of this assessment can be stated as:

1 Market value is determined by the interaction of supply and demand.
2 Supply and demand are determined by numerous factors. These factors can be both rational and irrational. Included in these factors are those of importance to fundamental analysts, as well as moods, sentiment, guesses and blind faith. The market is a mechanism for weighing each of these factors on a continuing basis.

3 Though there are minor fluctuations in the market, *stock prices have a tendency to move in trends that persist for appreciable lengths of time.*
4 Changes in trend are the result of shifts in supply and demand. These shifts, no matter what factors determine the shift, can be detected sooner or later in analysis of market action.

The connection with behavioral finance appears in point 2. The connection with chartism is associated with point 4 where the detection of market action is achieved through the use of charts. The notion is that certain chart patterns will tend to recur and these patterns can be used to make forecasts of prices.[7]

Levy (1966) is not the only statement of the conceptual framework for technical analysis. Following Murphy (1999), the framework can be reduced to three propositions: *market movements discount all relevant information*; *prices move in trends*; and, *history repeats itself.* Though reference is made to "all relevant information" being incorporated into prices, hiding in the background is a view of security pricing that is decidedly contrary to the view of security pricing contained in the Graham and Dodd approach (see section 7.4). For example, Edwards and Magee (1966, p. 5) observe:

> It is futile to assign an intrinsic value to a stock certificate. One share of United States Steel, for example, was worth $261 in the early fall of 1929, but you could buy it for only $22 in June 1932. By March 1937, it was selling for $126 and just one year later for $38 . . . This sort of thing, this wide divergence between presumed value and actual value, is not the exception; it is the rule; it is going on all the time. The fact is that the real value of a share of United Steel common is determined at any given time solely, definitely and inexorably by supply and demand which are accurately reflected in the transactions consummated on the floor of the New York Stock Exchange.

Though not as sophisticated as the model of stock pricing proposed by Keynes (e.g., Poitras 2002a), technical analysts recognize that both rational and irrational factors can impact market prices. The resulting trading strategies are generally consistent with the "anticipation approach," as opposed to the "intrinsic value" approach, to security valuation (see section 7.3).

For Graham and Dodd (1934, p. 608), technical analysis is part of the more general subject of "market analysis" that seeks to predict the "short-term behavior of the stock market," as opposed to the "long-term market considerations" that are the basis of the intrinsic value approach. Two approaches to market analysis are identified. One approach uses "all sorts of economic factors," including general and specific business conditions, short-term interest rates, political considerations and so on. The other approach "finds the material for its predictions exclusively in the past action of the stock market," i.e., technical analysis. "The underlying theory of [this] approach may be summed up in the declaration that 'the market is its own best forecaster'." While it is always theoretically possible to reconstruct chart analysis in terms of mathematical or statistical equations, this will typically be difficult to do without the aid of computing power. Writing prior to the widespread introduction of mainframe computers, Graham and Dodd observe that technical analysts "generally studied [the behavior of the market] by means of charts on which are plotted the movements of individual stocks or of 'averages'." As a consequence, Graham and Dodd refer to technical analysis as "chart reading" and to technical analysts as "chartists." Though not fully descriptive, this terminology has carried forward into the modern lexicon.

The arguments advanced by Graham and Dodd (1934, p. 609) against technical analysis are:

1 Chart reading cannot possibly be a science.
2 It has not proved itself in the past to be a dependable method of making profits in the stock market, at least not one available to the general public.
3 Its theoretical basis rests on faulty logic and also upon mere assertion.
4 Its vogue is due to certain advantages it possesses over haphazard speculation, but these advantages tend to diminish as the number of chart students increases.

These arguments are carried verbatim into later editions. The intuition underlying each of these points is presented. All four points revolve around an observation that can be characterized as the "*feedback problem.*" This problem is illustrated in a discussion of the first point:

> If [technical analysis] were a science, its conclusions would be as a rule dependable. In that case, everybody could predict tomorrow's or next week's price changes, and hence every one could make money continuously by buying and selling at the right time. That is patently impossible. A moment's thought will show that there can be no such thing as a scientific prediction of economic events under human control. The very "dependability" of such a prediction will cause human actions which will invalidate it. Hence thoughtful [technical analysts] admit that continued success is dependent upon keeping the successful method known only to a few people.

There are two key observations being made here. One observation deals with the inherent unpredictability of events under human control. This is the essence of the epistemological problem confronting the human sciences (see section 1.3). The other point has to do with the need to keep successful technical analysis systems secret in order to prevent a "feedback problem" where trading on a successful system by large numbers of traders eliminates the profitability.[8] But if successful systems are secret, how can such systems be tested to assess *ex ante* profitability?

Graham and Dodd recognize that security analysis is not immune to the inherent unpredictability of events under human control. Yet, there are differences (GDC, p. 714):

> The past earnings of a company supply a useful indication of its future earnings – useful, but not *infallible.* Security analysis and [technical] analysis are alike, therefore, in the fact that they deal with past data that are not conclusive as to the future. However, we are inclined to the view that for the typical analyst the so-called "fundamental" information for investment-quality shares – sales, earnings, asset and capital data, etc. – lends itself to more meaningful interpretation than does [technical] information. Moreover . . . there is the added difference that the security analyst can protect himself by a *margin of safety* that is denied to the [technical] analyst.

This emphasis on the margin of safety is not the only difference. The longer time horizon of fundamental analysis looks beyond the near-term horizon that is reflected in the "consensus" forecast embedded in current stock prices generated by "the analysis and advice supplied in the financial district [that] rests upon the near-term business prospects of the company considered." In GDC, there is explicit recognition of the possibility that the feedback problem could also affect the intrinsic value approach. However, compared to the longer-term buy-and-hold intrinsic value approach, the reliance of technical analysis on near-term trading intensive techniques means that "the expense of trading weights the dice heavily" against this approach.

In addition to the logical objections presented by the feedback problem, Graham and Dodd observe that there is nothing in the structure of technical analysis that ensures adequate performance (GDC, pp. 714–15):

> You may learn a great deal about the technical position of individual stocks by studying charts of their past market performance, but the question is whether you learn enough to predict the future with sufficient accuracy to operate profitably over time in the stock market. In other words, does the information which you derive from the past market action of individual issues prove valuable *often enough* for you to invest profitably in common stocks?

Referring to the Levy (1966) four point conceptual foundation for technical analysis given above, all four points could be accepted without any assurance that sustainable and profitable strategies could be identified and pursued. While there may be certain situations where technical analysis provides "really convincing cases," such cases are not the norm: "such precise signals apparently occur at wide intervals, and all too often the chart configurations are such that chart readers 'find themselves adrift on a sea of ambiguities'."

The Graham and Dodd (1934, p. 615) objections to technical analysis extend to all forms of market analysis that seek to profit from making near-term predictions of common stocks:

> We are skeptical of the ability of the analyst to forecast with a fair degree of success the market behavior of individual issues over the near-term future – whether he bases his predictions upon the technical position of the market or upon the general outlook for business or upon the specific outlook for individual companies.

Despite arguing for the absence of a scientific approach to market analysis, Graham and Dodd were not able to shake the observation that such activities are widely used in the investment industry. This perception increased from edition to edition reaching the conclusion (GDC, p. 716):

> The more intelligent chart students recognize these theoretical weaknesses, we believe, and take the view that market forecasting is an *art* that requires talent, judgment, intuition, and other personal qualities. They admit that no rules of procedure can be laid down, the automatic following of which will ensure success. Hence the widespread tendency in Wall Street circles toward a composite or eclectic approach, in which a very thorough study of the market's performance is projected against the general economic background and the whole is subjected to the appraisal of experienced judgment.

While recognizing that the prevalence of market analysis in Wall Street circles implicitly supported the possibility of profitably pursuing such an approach, Graham and Dodd still left no room for the possibility of a systematic, quasi-scientific technical analysis.

Modern Finance and technical analysis

In recent years, modern Finance has revisited the possibility that there may be something in technical analysis beyond being a convenient punching bag for the efficient markets hypothesis. Consistent with the positivist philosophy that drives the subject, the process of "empirical verification" has guided this change of course. For example: "statistically significant evidence has been presented from momentum profits" (Chan et al. 2000); "a systematic and automatic approach to technical pattern recognition using nonparametric kernel regression . . . provide(s) incremental information and may have some practical value" (Lo et al. 2000); "trading strategies that buy past winners and sell past losers realize significant abnormal returns . . . relative strength profits cannot be attributed to lead-lag effects that result from delayed stock price reactions to common factors" (Jegadeesh and Titman 1993); "momentum profits have continued in the 1990's, suggesting that the . . . results were not the product of data snooping bias" (Jegadeesh and Titman 2001); "Hamilton's [Dow theory] timing strategies actually yield high Sharpe ratios and positive alphas for the period 1902 to 1929 . . . Neural net modeling to replicate Hamilton's calls provides interesting insight into the Dow Theory" (Brown et al. 1998).

The evidence in favor of various types of technical analysis has been accompanied by a range of other statistical studies that have questioned the empirical validity of the efficient markets hypothesis (see section 1.2). The scope of these studies includes evidence for: pricing anomalies, such as the January effect and the small firm effect (see section 1.2), e.g., Dimson et al. (2002); serial correlation in returns, e.g., Campbell et al. (1997), Lo and Mackinlay (1999); value stocks outperforming growth stocks, e.g., Fama and French (1998); and, various aspects of behavioral finance such as a bias to buying winners and selling losers, e.g., Shefrin (2000).[9] Confronted with "statistically significant evidence," a natural reaction for a positivist is to rethink the prevailing theory and construct new theories that explain the stylized empirical facts. This reaction has given particular impetus to the development of behavioral finance that seeks to explain deviations from market efficiency in terms of investor psychology. Strong prior beliefs will encourage those with attachments to the prevailing theory to question the statistical results in favor of the new theories, presenting claims such "data-snooping" or "data-mining." Others proceed cautiously down the new path, as evidenced in Jegadeesh and Titman (2001): "The evidence provides support for the behavioral models, but this support should be tempered with caution."

To those not well versed in the theories of modern Finance, discerning the distinction between technical analysis and modern Finance presents something of a quandary. Technical analysis is concerned with using market-generated data to predict future price behavior. Yet, core theories of modern Finance, such as the capital asset pricing model

(CAPM) and the Markowitz mean-variance optimization model (see sections 3.2 and 3.3), also use market generated data to form "optimal portfolios." Practical implementation of, say, the Markowitz mean-variance optimization model requires the analyst to examine the time series of returns for the securities of interest together with a proxy for the risk-free interest rate, e.g., Eun and Resnick (1988). "Optimal" portfolios are obtained by solving a quadratic optimization problem using *ex post* estimates of the means, variances and covariances of security returns. To the uninitiated, this is not substantively different than a technical analyst using the Dow theory, combined with a moving average system, to select a portfolio of speculative trading opportunities. Both approaches examine market generated data to identify security investment opportunities. However, the CAPM is decidedly unlike technical analysis in being derived from a coherent theory of equilibrium pricing.

Though there have been various attempts to extend the core theory of modern Finance to incorporate a range of other "factors," e.g., Jagannathan and Wang (2002), modern Finance has not proposed methods for determining which factors to include in "the model" that are not immune from the criticisms of data-snooping and ad hocery. In some cases, the factors that have been selected for inclusion have corresponded to measures that are widely used in the relative value analysis commonly practiced by "Wall Street" security analysts, e.g., Fama and French (1998). However, in the absence of a well-developed theoretical foundation for, say, the inclusion of "value factors" in asset pricing models, it is difficult to determine why this approach is immune from the criticisms that Graham and Dodd aimed at technical analysis. To see this, consider the following tongue-in-cheek adaptation of the four points raised against technical analysis:

1 Asset price modeling cannot possibly be a natural science.
2 It has not proved itself in the past to be a dependable method of making profits in the stock market, at least not one available to the general public.
3 Its theoretical basis rests on faulty logic due to invalid assumptions.
4 Its vogue is due to certain advantages it possesses over haphazard speculation, but these advantages tend to diminish as the number of asset pricing students increases.

Despite being tongue-in-cheek, there is a ring of truth in this variant of the four points raised by Graham and Dodd against technical analysis.

In particular, consider the question: Why cannot asset price modeling be considered a natural science? The answer to this question was discussed in detail in section 1.3 – the human sciences cannot operate under the same ground rules as the natural sciences. Just as with technical analysis, using asset price modeling to identify securities that will generate abnormal returns is also subject to the "feedback problem." Other aspects of the four points follow appropriately. By abandoning the belief in efficient markets and shifting the focus onto the identification of securities that generate abnormal returns, modern Finance is operating on a different battlefield. The various anomalies that have been identified may be *ex post* fictions that cannot be used to produce *ex ante* abnormal returns. Even the third point can be rationalized by referring to the severe limitations (faulty logic) that apply to the perfect capital market assumptions that are used to derive the asset pricing models of modern Finance.

The upshot is that the efficient markets hypothesis cannot be readily abandoned by practitioners of modern Finance. It is essential to the philosophical foundation upon which the edifice of modern Finance is constructed. It is the "Keynesian convention" (see section 9.3) that is used to deal with the uncertainty arising in security analysis and investment strategy, e.g., Poitras (2002a). By adopting this convention, modern Finance is able to avoid the logical contradiction of technical analysis: how can the market discount all relevant information and prices still follow trends? Why is the trend not considered to be part of "all relevant information"? Technical analysts avoid this logical contradiction by claiming specialized expertise in identifying the trends and refusing to reveal the forecasting system that is being used to identify the trend. Academic researchers cannot take refuge in this approach.

9.2   THE TECHNICIAN'S TOOLKIT

The Dow theory

The Dow theory has a long pedigree stretching back to Charles Dow and the creation of the Dow-Jones rail and industrial averages circa 1897 (see section 2.3).[10] The first key historical figure in the development of the theory is Charles Dow, founding editor of the *Wall Street Journal*. Dow originated the basic approach of using stock market averages to predict future movements in the market. The main source of information about Dow's views is fifteen *Journal* editorials written between 1899 and 1902. (Dow did not publish any books on the subject or make reference to the "Dow theory.") Reference to the "*Dow's theory*" can be traced to a collection of these editorials that was published by S. Nelson, a personal friend of Dow, under the title *The ABC of Stock Speculation*. Despite having started the ball rolling, Dow did not contribute much detail to the theory that has come to bear his name. Shortly after Dow's death in 1902, William P. Hamilton assumed the editorship of the *Journal* and developed the bulk of the theoretical structure for the Dow theory, mostly contained in *Journal* editorials published between 1903 and 1929.[11] Though Hamilton did write a book outlining the theory (Hamilton 1922), the essential primary source of his views on the theory are these editorials that discussed and forecasted major trends in US stock markets using the rudiments of the Dow theory. Brown et al. (1998) put the number of these editorials at 255.

One of the oddities of the Dow theory is the untimely deaths of the major historical figures responsible for developing the theory. Just as Dow died shortly after bringing the theory on line, Hamilton died in 1930 shortly after writing his last editorial on October 25, 1929 titled: "The Turn of the Tide." The demise of Hamilton marks a turning point in the evolution of the Dow theory from the preserve of *Journal* editors into the domain of the investment advisory industry. This stage begins with Robert Rhea, a key figure in detailing, refining and popularizing the theory as it had been developed by Hamilton, e.g., Rhea (1932). Though Rhea closely followed Hamilton in his explanations of the theory, Rhea had the instinct to develop the *"art" of the Dow theory*. This instinct permitted Rhea to call the bottom of the bear market almost exactly on July 8, 1932.

Rhea developed techniques for using the averages for trading secondary, as well as primary, market trends. In November 1932, Rhea launched "Dow Theory Comment," an investment advisory service that attracted considerable notoriety for being correctly bullish when the bears dominated market opinion. Rhea is also credited with correctly calling the bear market of 1937, a prognostication that added considerably to Rhea's already significant standing on Wall Street.

Throughout the 1930s, Rhea had been afflicted by tuberculosis, a disease that took his life in 1939. With the absence of its leading proponent in the investment advisory industry and without promotions on the editorial page of the *Journal*, it was not until after World War II that the Dow theory was rejuvenated by George Schaefer. This revival can be dated from 1948 when Schaefer started an investment advisory service, "Schaefer's Dow Theory Trader." Like Rhea, Schaefer had a keen instinct for the "art" of using the Dow theory to predict stock market trends. In June 1949, shortly after starting the advisory service, Schaefer correctly called, almost to the day, the beginning of the major bull market that was to continue until 1966. In his advisory service newsletter, Schaefer used a "new version" of the Dow theory to detail reasons for the start of a major bull market. Schaefer continued to be bullish throughout the seventeen year bull market, advising clients to accumulate stocks on the numerous dips and drawbacks associated with the secondary movements of the market. In a remarkable prognostication, Schaefer turned bearish in early 1966 and held that position until his death, by suicide, in 1974. In another quirk in the murky history of the Dow theory, the year of Schaefer's death marks the beginning of another primary bull market movement.[12]

As evidenced by continuing references to the Dow theory in the popular financial media, the theory continues to have a strong following of adherents in present day Wall Street, e.g., Du Bois (2000, 2001). The essence of the Dow theory is reflected in the words of Richard Russell, the modern version of the Dow theory investment advisor (see www.dowtheoryletters.com): "[The] Dow theory can't be summed up in one or two sentences. It's more of an art form than anything specific. It requires a lot of interpretation" (Du Bois 2001). This is consistent with the Graham and Dodd view that "intelligent technical analysts" adopt the view that the forecasting methodology employed has to be viewed as an art form and not a science. Given that an art form cannot be precisely defined, it is still possible to sketch the basic conceptual elements. The first element in the Dow theory is that there are *"three simultaneous movements in the market"* (Russell 1960, pp. 4–5):

> The first [is] the great primary trend or tide. In a bull market, for example, this is a broad upward movement, interrupted by frequent reactions. The primary trend may last from one year to a great many years. The next movements are the so-called secondary reactions, which reverse and correct the tidal moves. They usually last from three weeks to three months, and then to retrace one-third to two-thirds of the previous uncorrected primary moves. The final movements are the daily moves. These minor fluctuations admittedly can be manipulated by the news of the day. Although the least important, they are the ones to which the public pays the most attention. The single movement which every investor must be aware of at all times is the primary trend. Investors should always invest with this primary tide.

The Dow theory is a body of techniques that have been developed – partly based on empirical observation, partly based on intuition – to identify the primary trend in the stock market. As such, the Dow theory is concerned with timing the overall market and using the predictions to guide portfolio composition.

Since the inception, Dow theorists have made an analogy between the three movements in the market and movement of the ocean. The primary trend is like the tide while the secondary reactions resemble the waves with the daily movements being ripples. As Russell observes (Du Bois 2001): "It isn't the waves that make or break you in this business, it's the great ocean tide of the market." Sail with the tide, not against it. While the analogy to movements of the tide is helpful, it is also somewhat misleading. Unlike the gravitational pull of the moon that controls the tides and allows for accurate prediction, the primary trend in the stock market is considerably more difficult to determine. Dow theorists approach this problem by dividing the primary trend into phases. In the case of a primary bull market trend (Russell 1960, p. 5):

> Phase one is the rebound from the depressed conditions of the previous bear market. Here stocks return to known values. In the second and longest phase, shares advance in recognition of improving business and a rising economy. During the third phase they spurt skyward on the hopes and expectations of a continuing rosy future. This is the traditional period of great prosperity and unbounded optimism. It is here that the public enters the market wholeheartedly for the first time. The low-priced "cats-and-dogs" historically make great moves in this third phase, and market volume becomes excessive.

This distinction between the *three types of market movement – primary trend, secondary reaction and daily fluctuation* – and *three phases of a primary trend – recovery, recognition and exuberance* – can be a source of confusion.

Another potential source of confusion about the Dow theory arises with the method used for determining whether and when the primary trend indicates a bull market or a bear market. The basic notion, derived from Hamilton and Rhea, is the concept of *confirmation.* Russell (1960, pp. 5–6) describes the concept:

> Under Dow theory, it is a bullish sign when successive rallies penetrate previous high points, and ensuing declines terminate above preceding lows. It is a bearish indication when rallies fail to penetrate earlier highs, and ensuing declines carry below their former lows. It is crucial to remember that the movements of both Rail and Industrial Averages always must be considered together. The action of one Average must be confirmed by the other before reliable inferences can be considered. A penetration of one Average unconfirmed by the other is meaningless for prediction purposes and frequently can be deceptive.

The concept of confirmation relates to predictions of future market movements based on analysis of changes in the Dow-Jones Industrial Average (DJIA) having to be considered in conjunction with an analysis of changes in the Dow-Jones Transportation Average (DJTA) (see table 9.1). The confirmation of these two signals is usually expected to be accompanied by a high level of trading volume on the confirmation date (see figure 9.1 for an illustration). When asked to describe the Dow theory, it is this "confirmation of the industrial and transportation averages" statement of the theory

Table 9.1 Current components for Dow Jones Transportation average, Friday, April 25, 2003

Company	Exchange	Ticker sym.	Style	Primary group	Mkt. cap.	Wghtg.	US$ close
Airborne Inc.	New York SE	ABF	VAL	Air Freight	Sml. cap.	3.6311	19.89
Alexander & Baldwin Inc.	NASDAQ NMS	ALEX	VAL	Marine Transport	Sml. cap.	4.794	26.26
AMR Corp.	New York SE	AMR	VAL	Airlines	Sml. cap.	0.8033	4.4
Burlington Northern Santa Fe Corp.	New York SE	BNI	VAL	Railroads	Lrg. cap.	5.0916	27.89
CNF Inc.	New York SE	CNF	VAL	Trucking	Mid. cap.	5.3983	29.57
Continental Airlines Inc. Cl B	New York SE	CAL	GRO	Airlines	Sml. cap.	1.5335	8.4
CSX Corp.	New York SE	CSX	VAL	Railroads	Mid. cap.	5.6703	31.06
Delta Air Lines Inc.	New York SE	DAL	N/A	Airlines	Mid. cap.	2.1852	11.97
FedEx Corp.	New York SE	FDX	GRO	Air Freight	Lrg. cap.	10.7326	58.79
GATX Corp.	New York SE	GMT	VAL	Industrial Services	Sml. cap.	3.224	17.66
J.B. Hunt Transport Services Inc.	NASDAQ NMS	JBHT	N/A	Trucking	Sml. cap.	6.2599	34.29
Norfolk Southern Corp.	New York SE	NSC	VAL	Railroads	Mid. cap.	3.7607	20.6
Northwest Airlines Corp.	NASDAQ NMS	NWAC	GRO	Airlines	Sml. cap.	1.3071	7.16
Roadway Corp.	NASDAQ NMS	ROAD	N/A	Trucking	Sml. cap.	6.6561	36.46
Ryder System Inc.	New York SE	R	VAL	Transportation Services	Sml. cap.	4.3412	23.78
Southwest Airlines Co.	New York SE	LUV	GRO	Airlines	Lrg. cap.	2.7585	15.11
Union Pacific Corp.	New York SE	UNP	VAL	Railroads	Lrg. cap.	10.8367	59.36
United Parcel Service Inc. Cl B	New York SE	UPS	GRO	Air Freight	Lrg. cap.	11.0484	60.52
USFreightways Corp.	NASDAQ NMS	USFC	VAL	Trucking	Sml. cap.	5.1226	28.06
Yellow Corp.	NASDAQ NMS	YELL	VAL	Trucking	Sml. cap.	4.8451	26.54

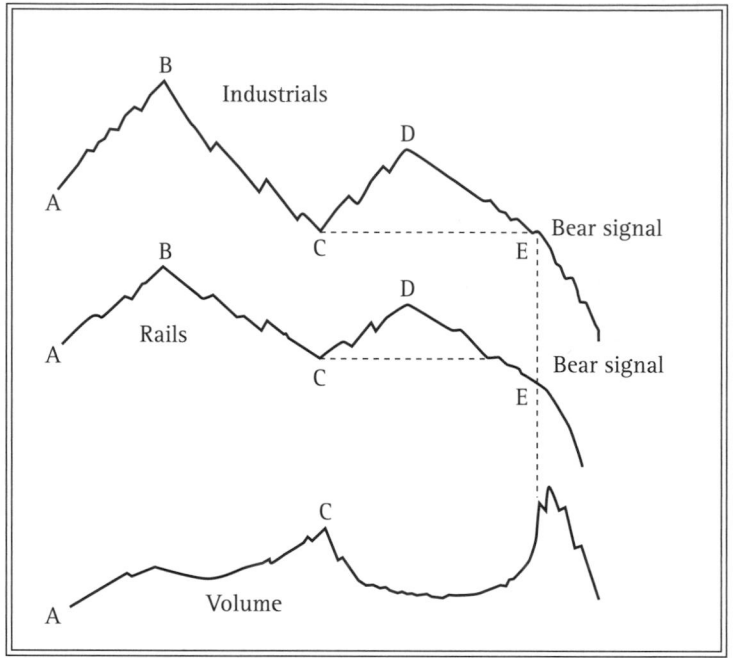

Figure 9.1 Example of a Dow theory confirmation signal
Source: Russell (1960)

that will typically be identified. Supplementary interpretation concepts such as penetration, reversal, break-out and so on follow appropriately.

As is evident from an inspection of figures 9.2 and 9.3, *identification of confirming signals* in the DJIA and DJTA is not an obvious exercise. For example, has a confirmation signal been achieved on March 11, 2003? Though it came close, the low in the DJTA that occurred in March 2003 was not quite confirmed by the DJIA which did not quite reach a new low on that date. The volume on that date was also not consistent with the "climax of volume" signal for a change in primary movement. Comparing Figures 9.2 and 9.3 with the stylized example in figure 9.1, it appears that the Dow theory has not produced a strong signal for the end of the primary bear market trend that began in May 1999. However, the market trading environment has changed significantly since Dow, Hamilton and Rhea developed the corpus of the theory.[13] For example, as illustrated in table 9.1, the DJTA is no longer an index composed entirely of railway companies. This change has been effective since 1970.

The implications of the significant change in the composition of the DJTA, when compared to the all-railway Dow (Railway) Transport index of Dow, Hamilton and Rhea, is difficult to formalize. The ability of leading Dow theorists to predict major primary market changes in 1974, 1982 and 1999 is strong evidence that the change in the DJTA did not substantively impact the predictive ability of the Dow theory. However, it is possible that the connection between the DJTA and DJIA may have been

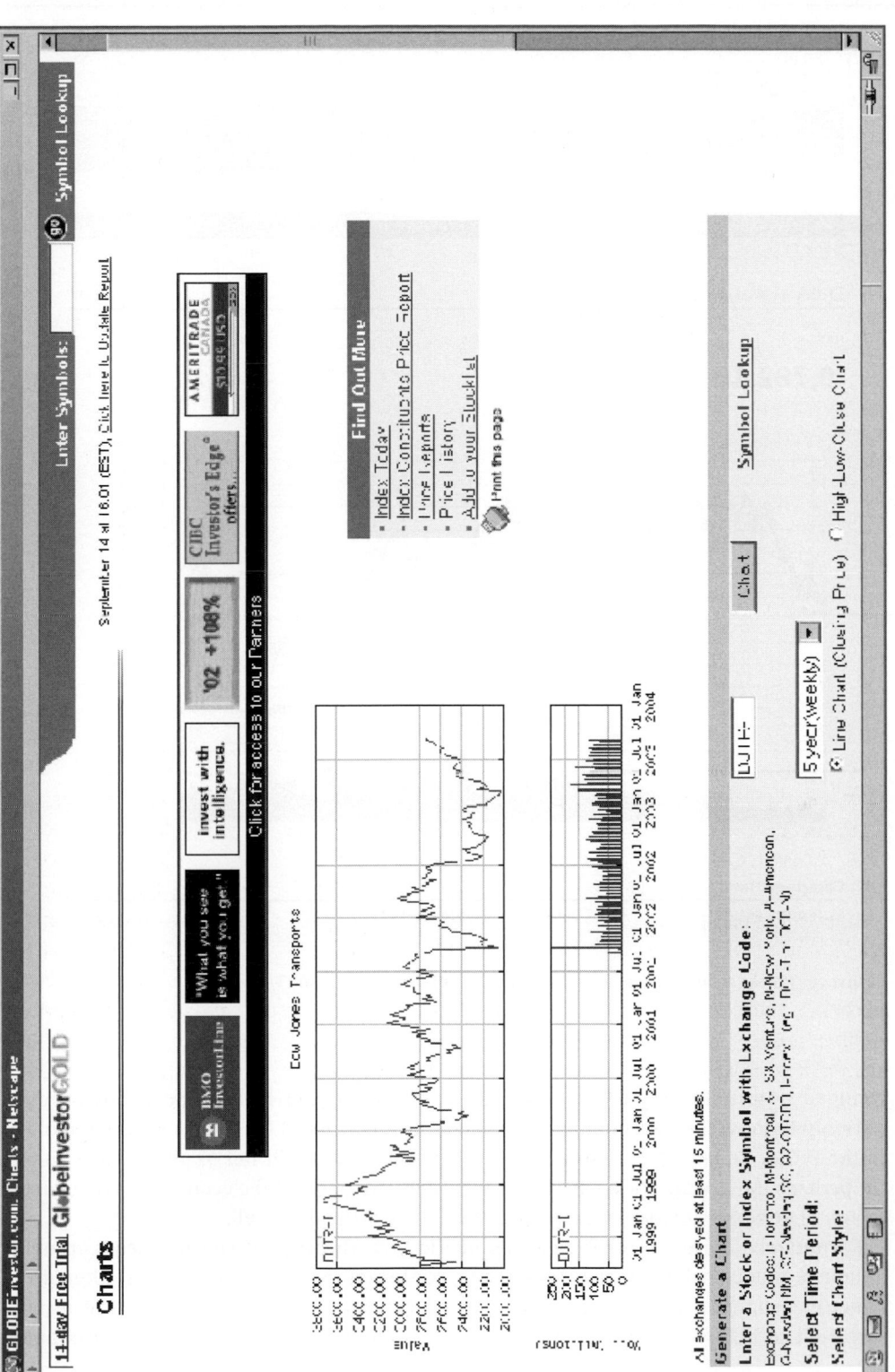

Figure 9.2 Dow Jones Transportation Index, 5 year, 09/98–09/03

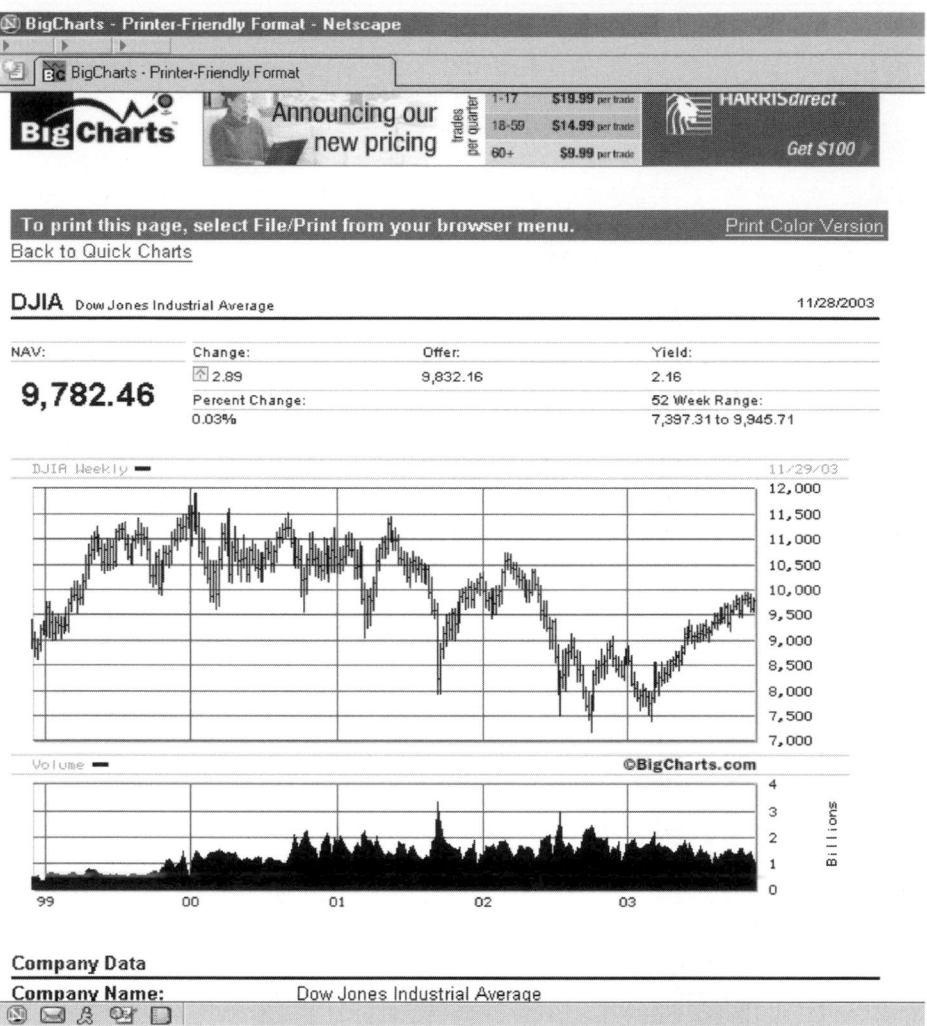

Figure 9.3 Five year DJIA chart, November 1998–November 2003

changed significantly by the impact that the events of 9/11 had on the airline industry – if only because the impact on airline valuations has reduced the share of this component in the DJTA. Perhaps this is an instance where the theory will fail to give a clear signal. Or, perhaps the structural changes in the securities markets and the economy have rendered theory ineffective for the foreseeable future. It is difficult to tell.

Fortunately, there are other elements of the Dow theory that can be used to provide guidance about whether the traditional confirmatory signal has been altered by structural changes. Those with only a casual exposure to the Dow theory are usually surprised to discover that there is considerable divergence among Dow theorists about the central role of the confirmation feature of the theory. *Old-style Dow theorists*, followers of Hamilton and Rhea, base the art of interpreting the averages primarily on further properties of the charts. As Rhea observes (Russell 1960, p. 7): "Beginners frequently make the mistake of basing conclusions wholly on the matter of penetration. Familiarity with the co-related factors of duration, extent, activity, divergence, and secondary implications of primary bull markets is needed to make the correct diagnosis." Yet, even old-style Dow theorists do not focus exclusively on the behavior of the averages, seeking also to identify elements that are expected to be present when there is a change in the primary movement. If these elements are not present, then confirmation of the averages alone is not sufficient.

For old-style Dow theorists a change in primary movement of the market from bull to bear can only occur during the third phase of the bull market. Rhea describes the characteristics of the third phase of a bull market:

> This is the time when brokers and soothsayers prosper, and when an excited public, lured by the bait of advancing prices, buys stocks without regard to values, basing their action on nothing more than hopes and expectations . . . this is the phase where worthless stocks are bought for no other reason than because they look cheap, and because gamblers hope they will double in price. This condition has always prevailed in the third phase of bull markets.

If these types of activities are not witnessed in the marketplace, then confirmation signals are likely to be false, second phase indications of a change in the primary market movement. Unfortunately, the three phases are not symmetric across bull and bear markets. While the characteristics of the three phases of a bull market are readily specified, guidance from the Dow theory about the three phases of a bear market is less precise. It is recognized that the extent and duration of a primary bear market will be shorter than for a primary bull market, with the drop in the averages being much more rapid in a bear market than the rise in the averages during a bull market.

Modern Dow theorists, such as Schaefer and Russell, put considerably less weight on the averages in determining the primary market movement. For example, Schaefer states: "A study of the Averages themselves can be highly rewarding. But in my opinion, a forecast based on past movements of the Averages cannot be conclusive. Predictions of events to come are more reliable if they can be reinforced by analysis of other technical and more conclusive factors." These other factors include: the 200-day moving average of the Dow; the short interest ratio; the advance-decline line; market sentiment; market phases; and the bond yield cycle. Russell takes this approach even further (Du Bois 2001): "[confirmation of the averages helps] to identify the primary trend. However, value, dividend yield and other factors also play an important role. Without understanding all of them you're lost." Unlike Hamilton and Rhea who promoted active trading on secondary phase reactions in bull and bear markets, Schaefer advised: "Once stocks are purchased, both the minor and secondary movements in the market should be completely disregarded." Second phase pullbacks in a bull market are buying (not rebalancing) opportunities, while second phase run-ups in bear markets are selling opportunities.

Starting from the contributions of Schaefer, the modern form of the Dow theory makes "value" the operative word. As Russell observes: "All other Dow theory considerations are secondary to the value thesis. Therefore, price action, support lines, resistance, confirmations, divergence — all are of much less importance than value considerations, although critics of the theory seem totally unaware of that fact." The transformation of the old-style Dow theorist to the modern Dow theorist can be gleaned from statements made by Russell in April 2001 about the previous bull market and the state of the ongoing bear market. The likelihood of non-confirmation at market peaks is explicitly acknowledged (Du Bois 2001):

> the long bull market that began in 1982 ended on May 12, 1999 when the DJIA and the Transports both hit peaks. The Industrials eventually topped out at 11,722.98 in January 2000, but the Transports failed by a wide margin to confirm that high. This bear market probably won't end until there's a final non-confirmation on the downside.

This statement recognizes the possibility that the global low point for the DJIA in the current primary bear market trend will not be confirmed by the DJTA. Rather, the bottom will come when the DJTA hits a global low and the DJIA hits a (local) low that is followed by an, unconfirmed, global low (or vice versa). This is something of a disconnect from the old-style Dow theory that, implicitly, assumed that the DJTA and DJIA confirmation would be associated with global values.

Another element distinguishing old-style and modern Dow theorists is the emphasis on using measures of value to supplement conventional analysis of the averages. This emphasis on value measures is evident in Russell's April 2001 analysis of the S&P 500 (Du Bois 2001):

> At its recent 1166, the S&P yielded about 1.2%. Were the yield to quadruple to 4.8% – and it's been higher than that in the past – the S&P would drop to about 300. Interestingly, the S&P now trades at over three times revenues, six times book value and 75 times dividends. These figures are well above peaks seen at previous bear-market tops, and illustrate just how overvalued the S&P 500 is.

However, there are still key elements of the old-style Dow theory left in the analysis:

> Bear markets usually last about 25%–33% as long as the preceding bull market. Assuming the recent bull market ran from a low in 1982 to a peak in 1999, we're talking 17–18 years. By this measure, I expect the decline to last four or five years, until 2005 or 2006. One possible difference this time is the speed at which the Nasdaq has plunged. If the Dow picks up momentum on the downside, the bottom could arrive sooner than 2003.

In considering the potential length of the current bear market, Russell still depends on the old-style notions of extent and duration.

And what advice was Russell dispensing in April 2001? After acknowledging that he had already shifted his personal portfolio into US Treasury bills, Russell observes:

Take this bear market seriously. It's never too late to do the right thing. In a primary bear market, the right thing is to play it safe. That means getting out of almost all common stocks and into US government paper. With cash in hand, you boost your buying power at the eventual bottom.

In retrospect, this advice was able to avoid the large drop in stock values but did not take advantage of the increase in bond prices associated with the downward shift in the Treasury yield curve that took place over the 2001–2 period. This said, the quality of the market prediction is solid. To provide context to the predictions that Russell was making consider the following:

resistance to believing we're in a bear market is mind-boggling. People still seem to be hanging on for the "long haul." This really is a tragedy. The losses in the average portfolio must be horrific. Foolish optimism and the speed of the Nasdaq decline literally have "locked in" millions of investors, the people who buy individual stocks and mutual funds... Way back at the turn of the 20th century, Charles Dow wrote that the most difficult concept to teach people is the inevitability of change. Sometimes the simplest ideas are the hardest to get across.

It is difficult to examine these notions and not be puzzled as to why so little attention has been given to the Dow theory in academic Finance.

This is not to say that the Dow theory has been completely ignored in modern Finance. As Brown et al. (1998, p. 1311) recognize, empirical testing of the Dow theory was the impetus for Cowles (1934) "a landmark in the development of empirical evidence about the informational efficiency of the [stock] market." However, unlike Cowles where it is found that "market timing based on the Dow theory results in returns that lag the market," Brown et al. arrive at the opposite conclusion:

we review Cowles evidence and find that it supports the contrary conclusion – the Dow theory, as applied by Hamilton over the period 1902 to 1929, yields positive risk-adjusted returns. The difference in the results is apparently due to the lack of adjustment for risk. Cowles compares the returns obtained from Hamilton's market timing strategy to a benchmark of fully invested stock portfolio. In fact, the Hamilton portfolio, as Cowles interprets it, is frequently out of the market. Adjustment for systematic risk appears to vindicate Hamilton as a market timer.

Yet, all this speaks to old questions surrounding the Dow theory and has only indirect implications about the prospects of using the Dow theory in contemporary securities markets.

Brown et al. beg a number of questions about whether the Dow theory is a viable method of market timing and about the feasibility of testing the Dow theory over a given sample. For example, there is the general question about whether it is possible to construct acceptable empirical tests of the Dow theory. Both Cowles and Brown et al. approach this problem by examining the prognostications of a specific, albeit important, early proponent of the Dow theory, W.P. Hamilton. However, at least since Bishop (1961) it has been recognized that the Dow theory has had to evolve through time, as market conditions and institutions change. As such, there is no "functional form" that is applicable to the Dow theory and can be estimated using, say, regression analysis. Rather, there are many Dow theorists, each with a distinct interpretation of what the theory says. While it is possible to estimate whether a basic feature of the Dow theory, such as the DJTA/DJIA confirmation signal, is capable of generating trading profits from market timing, the theory is more appropriately seen as a general qualitative guide to investment strategy as opposed to being a source of hard-and-fast trading signals.

Charting and moving average systems

The modern Dow theory is something of an oddity in the realm of technical analysis. While it is predicated on the basic notion of all technical analysis that prices move in trends, the objective is to predict long-term movements in stock market averages. In contrast, most technical analysis is concerned with shorter trading horizons, usually focusing on the performance of individual stocks or commodities. As such, the primary objective for much of this type of technical analysis is speculation whereas the Dow theory is more relevant as a supplement to investment strategy. Despite the rather chauvinistic attitude of fundamental purists and modern Finance believers, it is difficult to deny that some aspect of "charting" does not enter into every practical security analysis or investment strategy decision. Inspection of a three month, one year or three year price history is a typical first step in determining the value of a common stock. Similarly, the valuation process for, say, a corporate bond will examine the time series for credit spreads, yield curve shape and yield levels. Technical analysis attempts to bring more structure to this process. In the absence of a unified theoretical foundation, the resulting procedures are derived inductively. By construction, technical analysis will be subject to the problems of using *ex post* analysis for making *ex ante* decisions.

Even if an analyst has little belief in the efficacy of the various procedures used in technical analysis, it is difficult to deny that there are large numbers of traders that employ such techniques. At least in the short run, the activity of these traders can impact the price of specific securities.[14] As a consequence, even rigid nonbelievers in technical analysis can benefit from basic knowledge about certain elements of the approach. The starting point and, in many cases, the ending point for technical analysis is charts. As Edwards and Magee (1966, p. 7) observe:

> Charts are the working tools of the technical analyst. They have been developed in a multitude of forms and styles, to represent graphically almost anything and everything that takes place in the market or to plot an "index" derived therefrom. They may be monthly charts on which an entire month's trading record is condensed into a single entry, or weekly, daily, hourly, transaction, "point-and-figure", etc. They may be constructed on arithmetic, logarithmic or square-root scale, or projected as "oscillators." They may delineate moving averages, proportion of trading volume to price movement, average price

of "most active" issues, odd-lot transactions, the short interest, and an infinitude of other relations, ratios and indexes – all technical in the sense that they are derived, directly or indirectly, from what has actually been transacted on the exchange.

Though it is possible to use other "working tools" than charts to accomplish the same result, e.g., Lo et al. (2000), the bulk of technical analysis is presented in terms of chart interpretations. As a consequence, in order to explain and assess technical analysis it is necessary to examine charting techniques.

Outside the realm of technical analysis, the most commonly observed chart for common stocks is the *"close-only" chart*. This type of chart is simply a time series of closing prices or index values plotted using an arithmetic scale (see figures 9.2 and 9.3). The frequency of observation is typically daily, weekly or monthly depending on the length selected for the time period of interest. Observations for longer intervals, such as weekly or monthly, are usually for specific days, e.g., every Friday for weekly, though averages can also be used. Sometimes close-only charts are used because intra-day data is not available. In other cases, the close-only chart is selected because the technical analyst believes that the inclusion of high/low, open and other information on the chart tends to cloud the picture, i.e., the closing price is the appropriate summary of the key information. However, Schwager (1996, p. 21) reflects the typical view: "many important chart patterns depend on the availability of high/low data and one should think twice before ignoring this information."

While close-only charts can be used for various purposes, there are three other basic chart types that are more commonly used for doing basic technical analysis: bar charts (see figure 9.4); point-and-figure charts; and Japanese candlestick charts (see figure 9.5). *Point-and-figure charts* (not discussed here) are specialized charts more commonly used in futures markets, particularly by floor traders and day traders, than in stock markets.[15] These charts do not take account of time but, rather, view trading as a continuous process. For technical analysis of security prices, *the bar chart* is the most common type of chart. As indicated in figure 9.4, for a daily bar chart each day is represented by a vertical line defined by the high and low prices for the day with a small horizontal line indicating the close. Bar charts for longer intervals, such as a weekly or monthly bar chart, are analogous. For, say, a weekly bar chart the vertical line represents the high and low for the week with the small horizontal line representing the final closing price for the week. Because of the different appearance of charts for different sampling intervals, it is common for daily, weekly and monthly bar charts to be examined when doing a technical analysis for a given security.

Though the history of candlestick charts in Japan predates bar charts and point-and-figure charts, this method of charting was virtually unknown outside of East Asia prior to Nison (1991). Compared to bar charts, *candlestick charts* are more versatile and can generate more signals than bar charts. In effect, a candlestick chart contains all the information available in a bar chart and more. Because a candlestick chart has more information it is also somewhat more complicated and requires more preparation effort. While such charts are available at publicly accessible internet futures charting services such as www.futuresource.com (see figure 9.5), the format is currently only available at pay-for-service stock charting services, e.g., www.stockchart.com. The bar chart is still

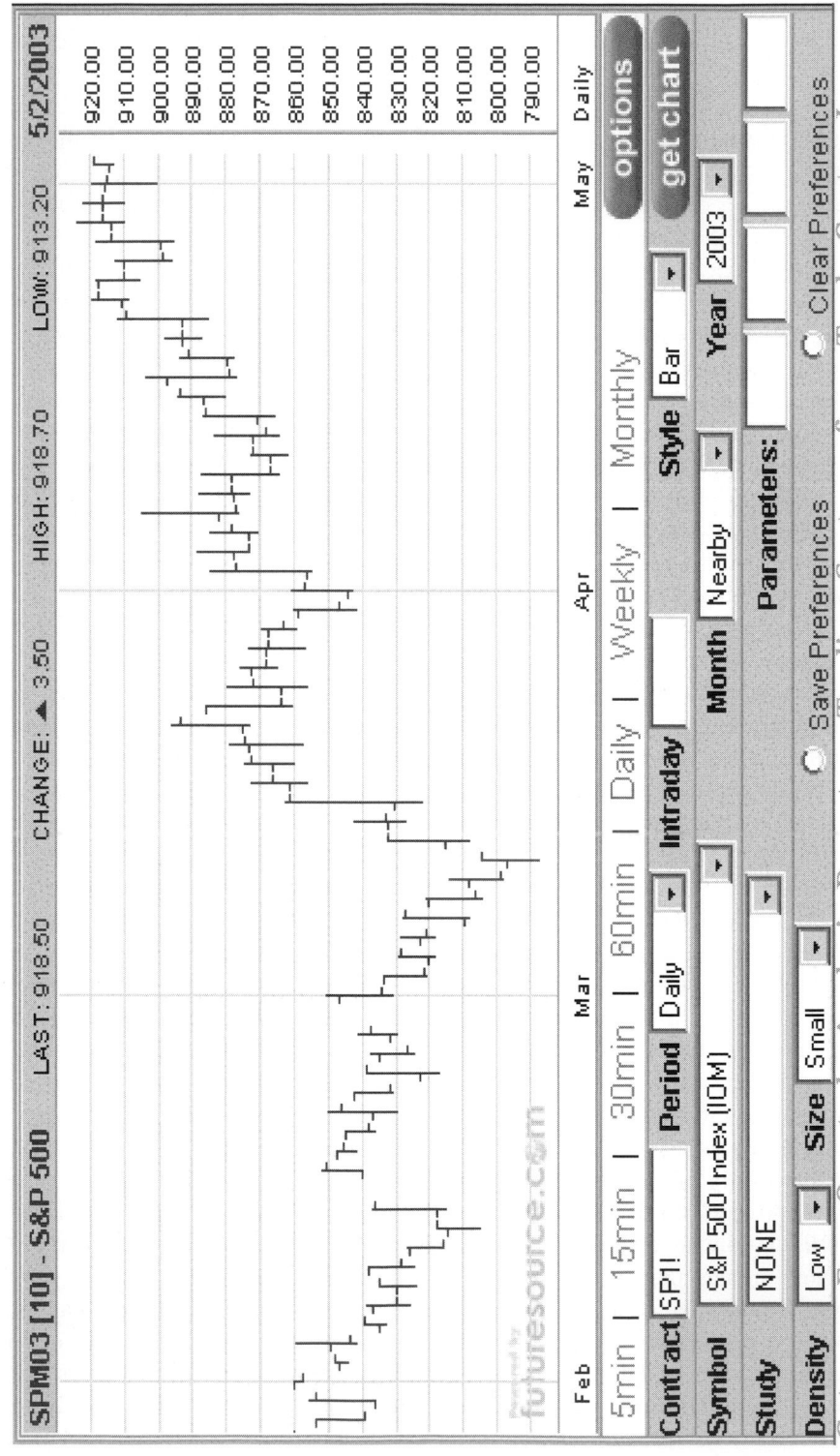

Figure 9.4 Bar chart, S&P 500 futures

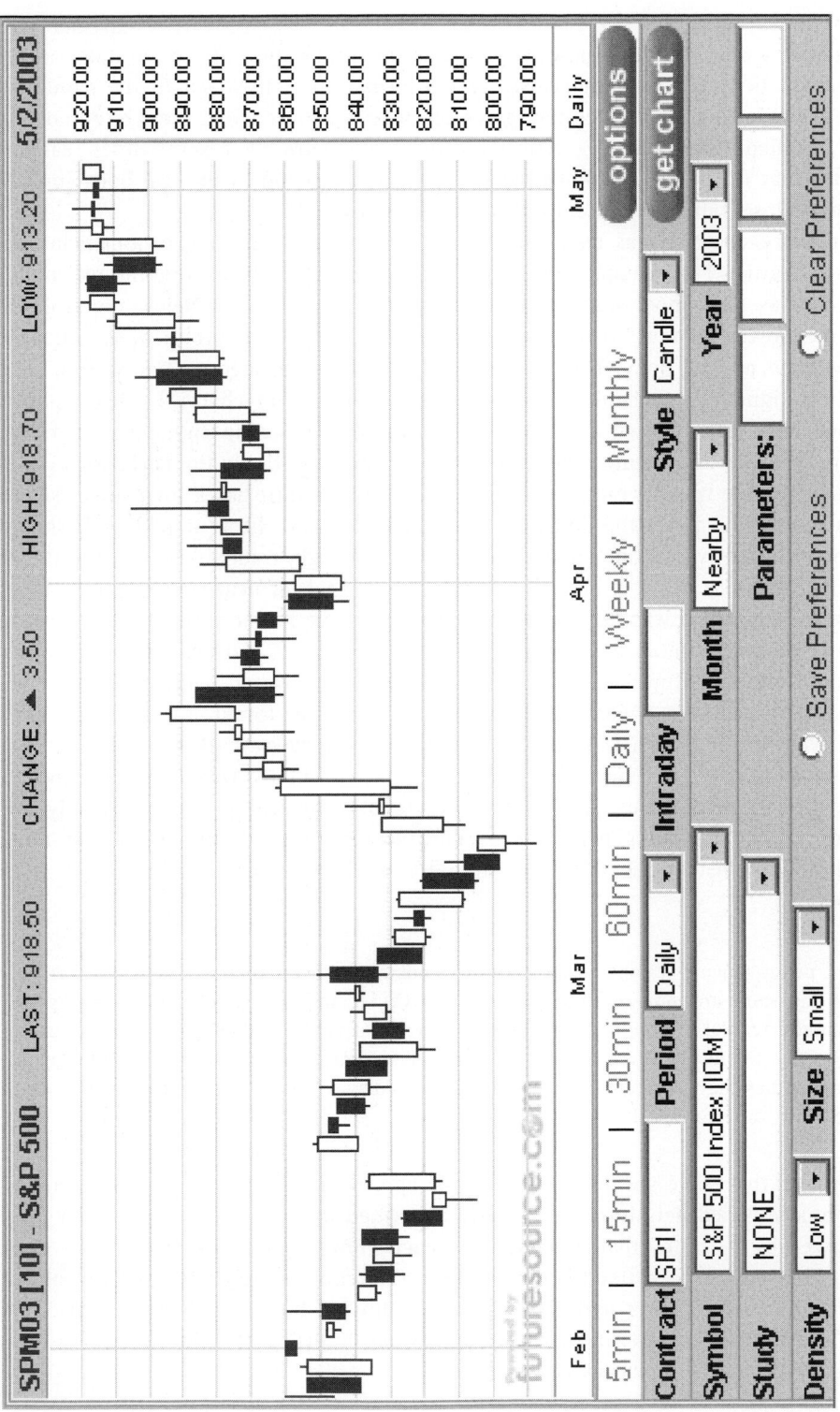

Figure 9.5 Candlestick chart, S&P 500 futures

the standard format for stock charts. Casual inspection of a bar chart reveals that while the high, low and close are indicated, there is no information about the open and the relationship between open and close. This information is included in the candlestick chart. The thin line on a given day gives the high and low while the white and black boxes – called "real bodies" – reflect the open and close. A black (white) real body indicates that the open was above (below) the close. The top of the real body indicates the open (close) with the bottom indicating the close (open).

Candlestick charting has many aesthetically pleasing features. The nomenclature is one such feature. For example, the part of the thin line that lies above the real body is referred to as the "upper shadow" with the part of the thin line below the real body being the "lower shadow." If the open and close are equal or approximately equal then there will be no real body. This is a "*doji*" – literally translated as "indecision." Dojis provide a signaling mechanism that is not available in bar charts. For example, the presence of a doji following a large white candle is a strong signal that a rally is stalling. Another key feature is *the hammer* which occurs where: the real body is at the upper end of the trading range (the color is not important); has a long lower shadow that is more than twice the height of the real body; and, little or no upper shadow. A hammer occurs when the market opened near the high, traded down during the day and rallied to close near the high. This is a bullish signal for near term trading. The one hammer in figure 9.5 was followed by a strong up move the next two trading sessions. There are numerous other features of candlestick charts, e.g., dark cloud cover, hanging man, morning star. However, discussion of these aspects would require more attention than is warranted here.[16] More detail on these issues can be found in Nison (1991, 1996) and at websites dedicated to technical analysis such as www.marketsource.com.

A key notion of technical analysis is that prices follow trends. Charts are used for identification of trends. As it turns out, trend identification is considerably more complicated than drawing a line on a chart. The process becomes subjective almost immediately. Consider the definition of a trend. Edwards and Magee (1966, p. 47) observe:

> Stock prices move in trends. Some of these trends are straight, some are curved; some are brief and some are long-continued; some are irregular and poorly defined and others are amazingly regular or "normal," produced in a series of action and reaction waves of great uniformity. Sooner or later these trends change direction; they may reverse (as from up to down) or they may be interrupted by some sort of sidewise movement and then after a time proceed in their former direction.

Recognizing that there are numerous possible approaches to specifying trends, consider the commonly used definition: an uptrend is defined by a sequence where each "high" is followed by a "high" that is higher and each "low" is followed by a "low" that is higher. Similarly, a downtrend is defined by a sequence where each "high" is followed by a "high" that is lower and each "low" is followed by a "low" that is lower. The "highs" and "lows" – often referred to as "relative highs" and "relative lows" – occur because price charts appear as jagged lines.

In drawing a trend line for a downtrend it is conventional to connect the sequence of lower relative highs. For an uptrend, the trend line will conventionally connect the sequence of relative lows. Where a trend line is drawn for both the relative lows and relative highs the resulting (hopefully) parallel lines form a *trend channel.* For a trend channel, the upper line is referred to as the "resistance line" and the lower line as the "support line" (Kaufman 1978, p. 139). The breaking of a trend line by a relative high or low is an indication that the trend *may* have ended. The practical difficulty that can arise with this exercise of defining a trend line is illustrated in figures 9.6 and 9.7 that provides a 1 year and 3 year bar chart for the S&P 500 (SPY). The trend line for the 1 year chart indicates that the downtrend has been broken in March 2003 while for the 3 year chart the relative high would have to be close to 100 for SPY (1000 on the S&P 500) before the trend line is broken (see end of chapter questions). Schwager (1996, p. 25) captures the type of conclusion that can be drawn from the breaking of a trend line: "It should be emphasized . . . that the disruption of the pattern of higher highs and higher lows (or lower highs and lower lows) should be viewed as a clue, not a conclusive indicator, of a possible long-term trend reversal."[17]

While technical analysis thrives on the presence of trends, in many situations there is no discernible trend. In these situations, prices move in a "horizontal corridor that contains price fluctuations for an extended period" (Schwager 1996, p. 57) referred to as a *trading range* also known as a rectangle (Edwards and Magee 1966, ch. 9).[18] An example of a trading range is provided in figure 9.8, where the 1 year price movement of Procter & Gamble is bounded above by $95 and below by about $80. Up-trends can stall out at the *resistance level* defined by the upper bound and downtrends can stall out at the *support level,* defined by the lower bound. A *breakout* occurs when prices penetrate either the resistance or support level. A breakout can be an important signal for securities with prices that have trading ranges. Once a breakout from a trading range has been established, the resistance level of the previous trading range becomes a support level for the next trading range. Determining whether a price chart represents a trading range or a trend is a key step in interpreting the chart. Most trading strategies used in technical analysis do not perform well in trading range markets. Those trading strategies that are designed to profit in trading range markets, such as oscillators (see section 9.4) will tend to perform poorly in trending markets. Similarly, techniques for analyzing charts in trending markets, e.g., head-and-shoulders, flags and gaps, have little meaning in trading range markets.

There are practical difficulties in identifying and interpreting the support and resistance levels for a trading range. One difficulty involves the appropriate length of time to use in *defining a trading range.* As with the drawing of trend lines, changing the sampling interval will change the interpretation of the chart. Schwager observes that for a trading range to be established the horizontal corridor has to last at least a couple of months. Trading ranges can last for years. In such cases, it is often possible for the long term trading range to be broken down into smaller trading ranges. In practice, breakouts from trading ranges are considered to be one of the most reliable technical indicators. Following Schwager (1996, p. 60), the *reliability of a breakout signal* depends on three

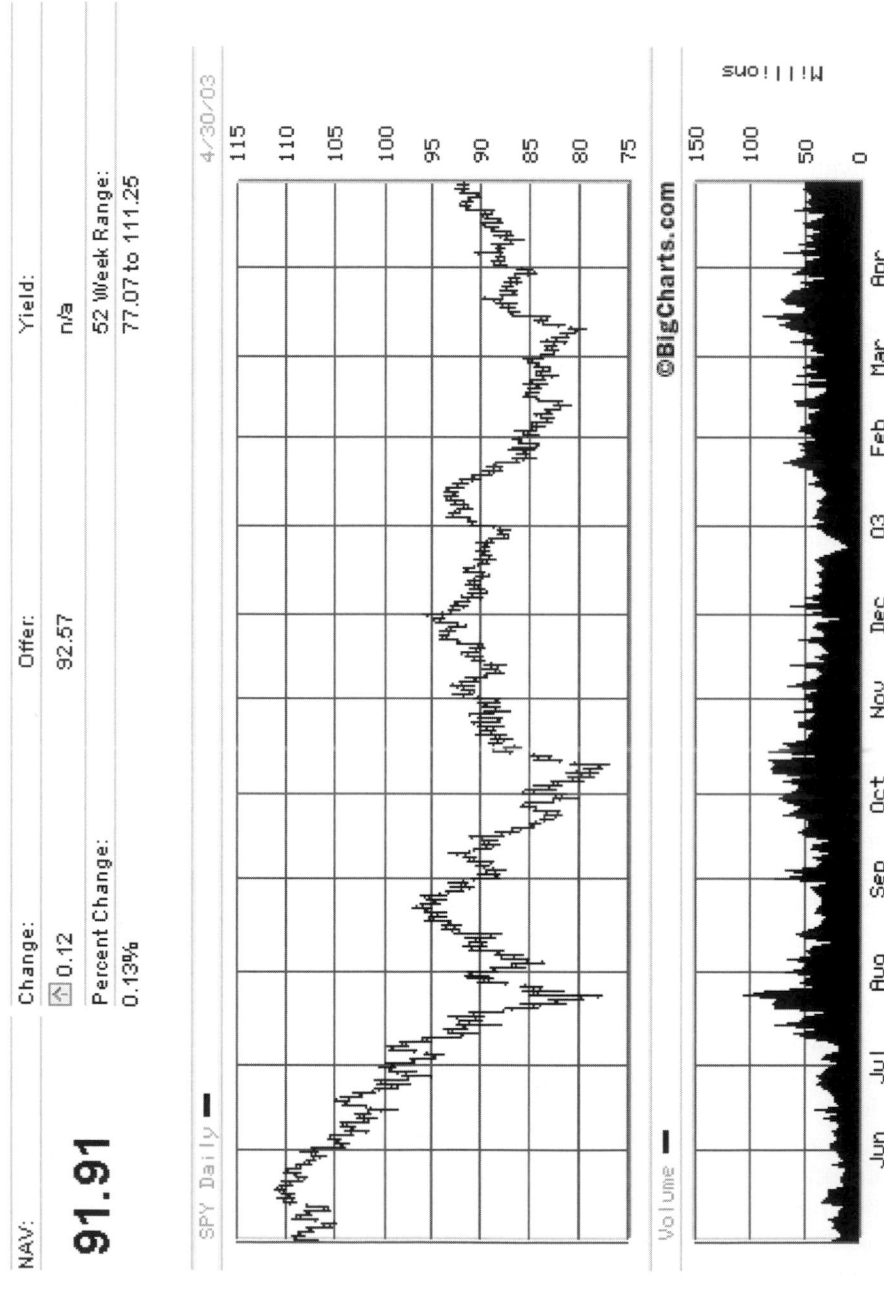

SPY SPDR Trust;1

4/30/2003 4:30 PM

NAV:	Change:	Offer:	Yield:
91.91	⬆ 0.12	92.57	n/a
	Percent Change: 0.13%		52 Week Range: 77.07 to 111.25

SPY Daily ▬

4/30/03

115
110
105
100
95
90
85
80
75

Volume ▬

©BigCharts.com

Millions

150
100
50
0

Jun   Jul   Aug   Sep   Oct   Nov   Dec   03   Feb   Mar   Apr

Figure 9.6 S&P 500 (SPY), 1 year sample, 05/02–05/03

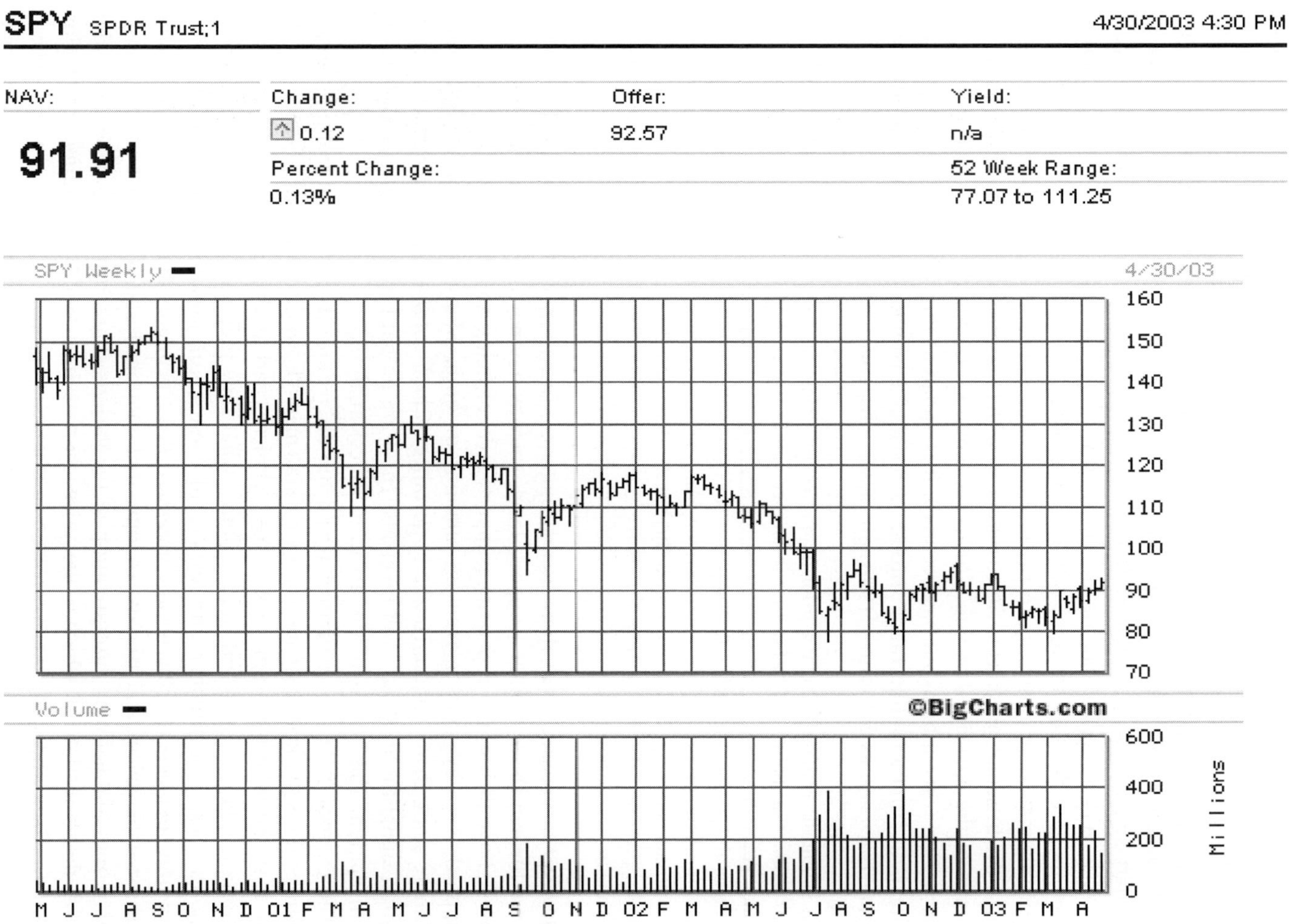

SPY SPDR Trust;1   4/30/2003 4:30 PM

NAV: Change: Offer: Yield:

91.91   ↑ 0.12   92.57   n/a

Percent Change: 52 Week Range:
0.13%   77.07 to 111.25

©BigCharts.com

Figure 9.7 S&P 500 (SPY), 3 year sample, 05/00–05/03

factors: the duration of the trading range, the longer the duration of the trading range the stronger the signal; the narrowness of the trading range, the narrower the range the more reliable the signal; and, the ability of the breakout to meet criteria for confirmation, simply penetrating the support or resistance level is usually not sufficient to produce a trading signal. The use of breakout signals to trigger trades has to be considered in the light of "the most important rule in chart analysis." Schwager (1996, p. 180) describes this *"failed signal" rule*: "A failed signal is among the most reliable of all chart signals. When a market fails to follow through in the direction of a chart signal, it very strongly suggests the possibility of a significant move in the opposite direction" (see the July move to $75 in figure 9.8).

All this may seem confusing to the uninitiated. A breakout is a strong trading signal unless the breakout provides a failed signal in which case it provides a strong signal of a move in the opposite direction. This is compounded by the difficulty that arises with interpreting when a breakout has occurred. It is apparent that when a chart pattern has a breakout from a trading range through a resistance (support) level this is a buy (sell) signal. However, as Schwager (1996, pp. 67–9) observes:

> It should be emphasized that a prior high does not imply that subsequent rallies will fail *at or below* that point, but rather that resistance can be anticipated in the *general vicinity* of that point. Similarly, a prior low does not imply that subsequent declines will hold *at or above* that point, but rather that support can be anticipated in the *general vicinity* of that point. Some practitioners of technical analysis treat prior highs and lows as points endowed with sacrosanct significance. If a prior high was 1078, then they consider 1078 to be major resistance, and if, for example, the market rallies to 1085, they consider resistance to be broken. This is nonsense.

Schwager recommends that there be a stronger confirmation signal than simply trading above (below) the resistance (support) level, such as having some minimum number of closes above (below) the resistance (support) level or being above (below) the resistance (support) level by some percentage amount or both. Many technical analysts that evaluate stock charts emphasize the importance of *high volume* as a prerequisite confirmation signal for breakouts and reversals. There are no hard-and-fast rules on breakout confirmation. This is part of the art in technical analysis.

The exercise reflected in figure 9.8 and the discussion of trends and trading ranges captures the significance of the following statement (Edwards and Magee 1966, p. 48): "the first and most important task of the technical chart analyst is to learn to know the important reversal formations and to judge what they may signify in terms of trading opportunities." The number and variety of these *chart formations* is unsettling: the head-and-shoulders and the necktie breakout; flags, pennants and wedges; scallops and saucers; gaps, spikes and islands; triangle tops (bottoms) and rounded bottoms (tops); and, V tops and bottoms. Interpretation of the various chart formations depends on the initial determination of whether the price chart is in a trend or trading range. For example, flags and pennants represent *continuation* signals in a major trend. These patterns are sideways price formations that are associated with a pause in a major trend. Triangles are a more complicated version of a continuation signal. Head-and-shoulders, double tops and bottoms and islands surrounded by gaps are indicators of reversals.

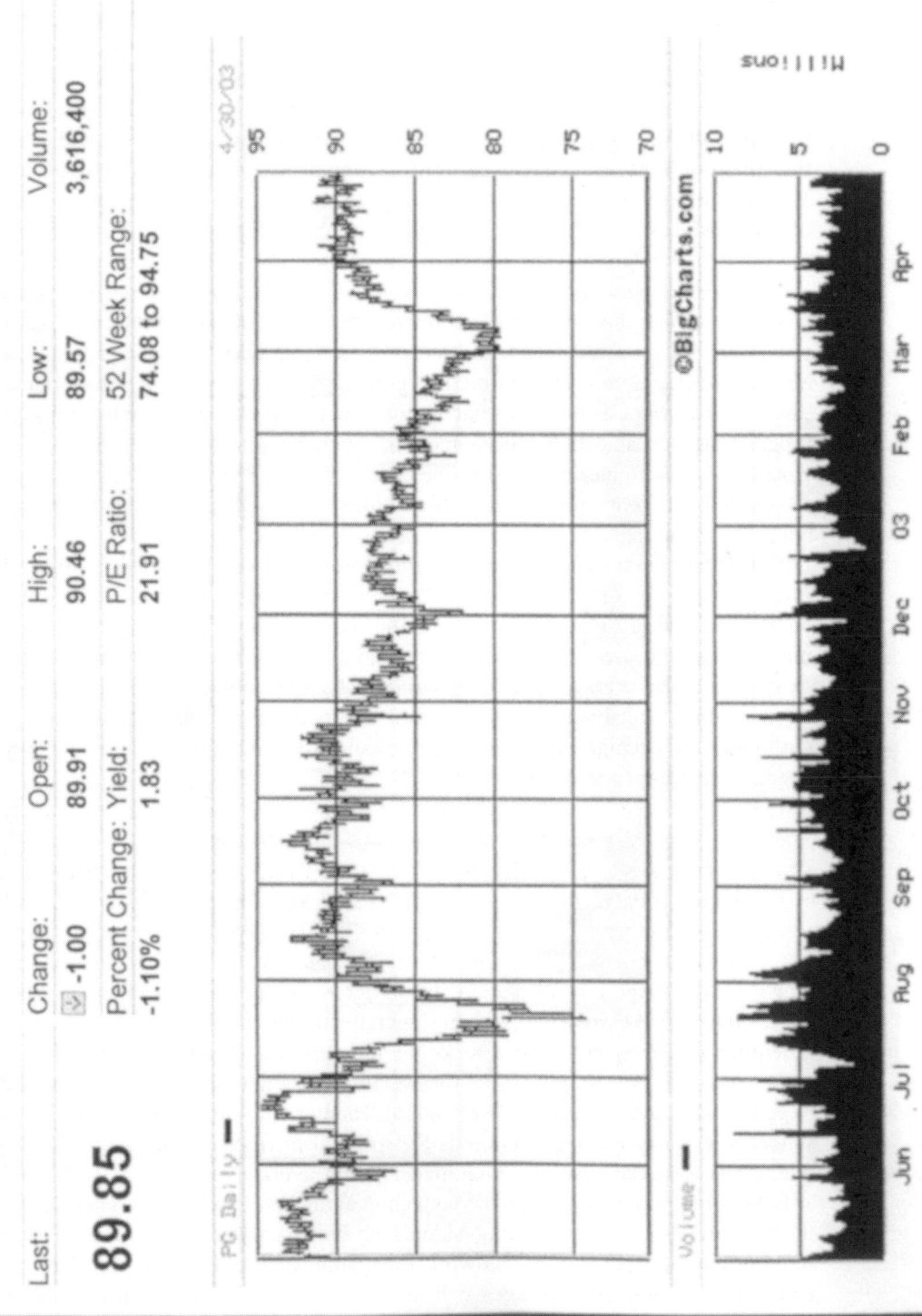

Figure 9.8 Trading range for Procter & Gamble

Combine this with the difficulties of determining whether the price chart reflects a trend or trading range and the conclusion of Schwager (1996, p. 147) is understandable: "chart analysis remains a highly individualistic approach, with success or failure critically dependent on the trader's skill and experience."

Breakouts, trading ranges, chart formations and the like are concepts that apply to the basic charts. Even the staunchest believer in technical analysis will acknowledge that the interpretation of chart patterns is complicated by the noisy character of prices. The drawing of lines on charts is a subjective process, at best. In order to remove some of the noisiness in prices, it is a natural development to consider further processing of the price data before plotting the information on a chart. Going back at least to Gartley (1930, 1934), technical analysts have explored the use of *moving average techniques* in order to smooth the time series of prices. Over time, more complicated processing of price data, such as oscillators and stochastics, have been introduced (see section 9.4). Moving averages have the attractive property that the unit of measurement is the same as for prices, something that is not always true of more complicated processing procedures. As a consequence, moving averages can be plotted onto the price charts and used to aid in assessing the chart patterns. Because moving averages smooth the price data, conventional chart formations such as flags and pennants will not be apparent in the moving average.

A moving average can take a variety of forms. The common element in the different forms is the use of a *fixed sampling window*. There is always a fixed number of observations used to calculate the moving average value for any given day. A T day moving average uses the current price and the most recent and the T-1 past prices to calculate the average at a given time t. As time moves forward, the most recent observation is added and the most distant observation is dropped, maintaining T observations in the average calculation. In particular the simple and weighted T day moving averages at time t are calculated as:

$$\text{Simple MA: } \bar{P}(t, T) = \frac{\sum_{i=0}^{T-1} P_{t-i}}{T} \qquad \text{Weighted MA: } \bar{P}(t, T)^W = \sum_{i=0}^{T-1} w_i P_{t-i}$$

where $\bar{P}(t, T)$ is the time t value of the simple moving average and $\bar{P}(t, T)^W$ is the time $t = 0$ value of the weighted moving average where the sum of the w_i (≥ 0) weights is required to be equal to one. The simple moving average weights each of the observations equally ($1/T$). Variations of the weighted moving average approach, such as the exponential moving average (see end of chapter questions), use different weighting schemes. A 1 day moving average is the original price chart. The simple T day moving average is a special case of a weighted moving average where $w_i = 1/T$.

Depending on the objectives of the technical analyst, moving averages can be used to identify trends, generate trading signals or both. Conventional wisdom recognizes a moving average as a trend following procedure. In trading range markets, which are often the case, moving averages will not typically be a useful tool. Because a moving average takes into account both current and lagged values of prices, the relationship between the observed price series and the moving average can be used to identify the trend. Due to the lagging nature of a moving average, in a rising market the moving average value for a given date will lie below the price for that date. Conversely, in a declining market the moving average will lie above the current price (see figures 9.9 and 9.10). Trend reversals, *crossovers*, occur when the sequence of current prices crosses the moving average. The transition from an uptrend to a downtrend occurs when the price series penetrates the moving average from above and vice versa for a downtrend to an uptrend. These crossovers are trading signals. In some cases, the moving average is compared with the original price series, in other cases a moving average of one length is compared with a moving average of another length, e.g., a 200 day moving average is compared with 10 day moving average as in figure 9.9.[19]

One difficulty of using a moving average to identify a trend or generate a trading signal is that, by construction, the moving average will lag the actual price series. The longer the moving average, the longer is this lag, e.g., a T day moving average will have a shorter lag than a $T + N$ day moving average. Examining the 200 day moving average in figure 9.9, it is apparent that the S&P peaked in mid-2000, the price series did not provide a confirmed crossover until almost a year later. The 50 day moving average gives much better results, though there is a hint of *whipsaws* where the price series crosses the moving average in one direction only to reverse course shortly thereafter and cross in the other direction. The 10 day moving average is replete with whipsaws and would only generate useful trend signals when the trading interval is short, e.g., day-to-day trading. While the 50 day moving appears to work well for the S&P 500 the failings of the moving average in a trading range market are apparent in figures 9.11 and 9.12 which provides results for 10 and 50 day moving averages for Procter & Gamble over a 1 year and 5 year sample period. Selecting the appropriate length for a moving average is a subject of considerable debate and study by technical analysts, e.g., Kaufman (1978, pp. 83–5). Further developments of moving average systems are discussed in section 9.4.

Finally, while the preceding discussion focused on price charts, the scope of technical analysis does include a much broader set of variables. Charting, moving averages, momentum, oscillators and the like apply to this broader set of variables in much the same fashion as with prices. For example, some technicians actively monitor a *breadth indicator* to get a sense of underlying market demand and the general near term or long term direction of the market. Technical indicators for market breadth involve calculations with advancing and declining issues, sometimes supplemented by volume. Included in these indicators are: the advance–decline line; advance–decline ratio; absolute breadth index; breadth thrust; McClellan oscillator; and the summation index (see www.marketscreen.com). Perhaps the mostly widely followed technical indicator of breadth is the advance–decline line – the cumulative, ongoing sum of the difference between the number of stocks closing higher minus the number of stocks closing lower each trading day (see figure 9.13). The weekly advance–decline line total is then plotted as in figure 9.13. An alternative method of calculation is to sum the advance–decline ratio – the ratio of advancing issues to declining issues.[20] The daily difference between the number of advancing and declining issues (not cumulated) is typically evaluated as a momentum indicator.

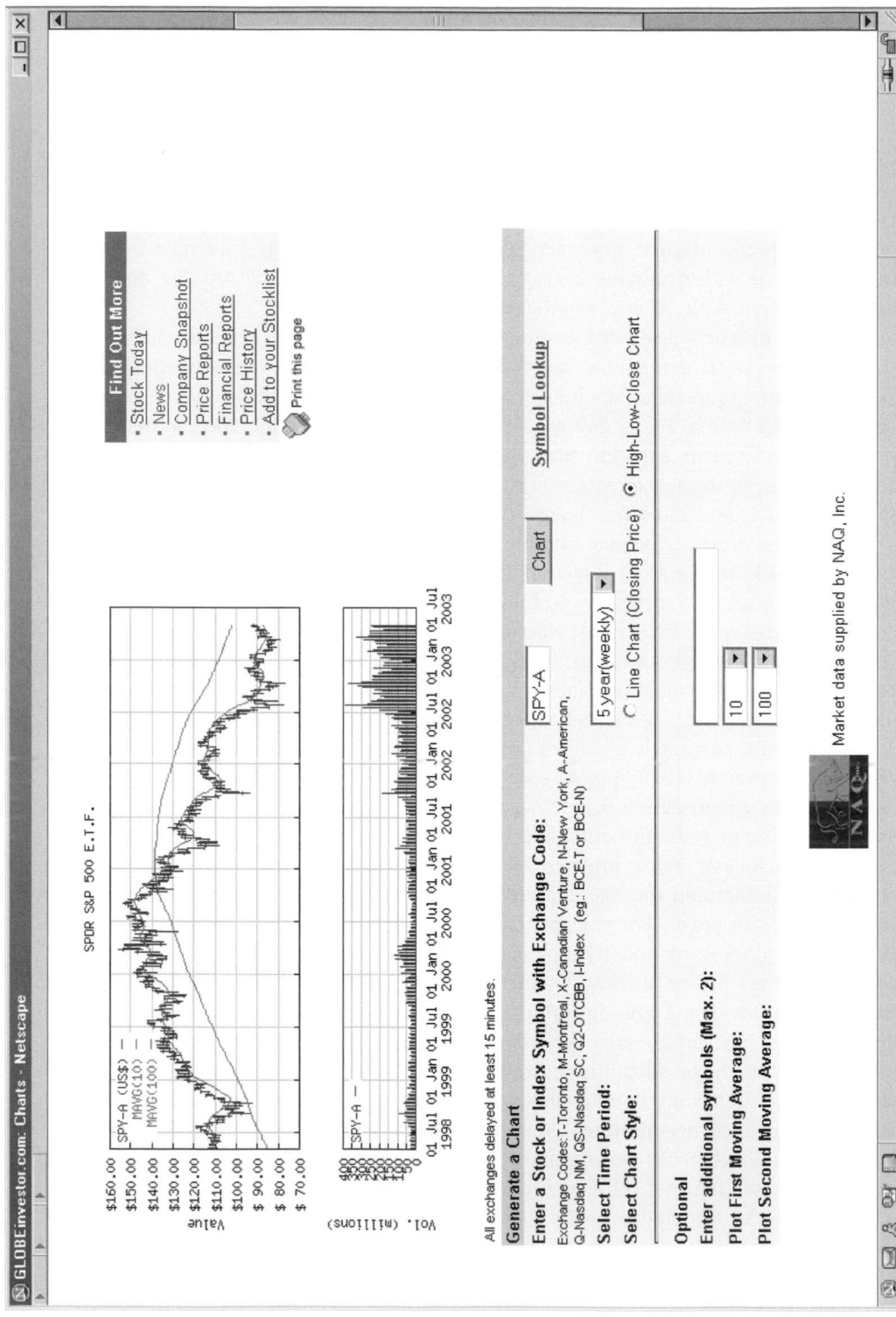

Figure 9.9 200 day vs. 10 day MA chart for SPY, July 1998–July 2003

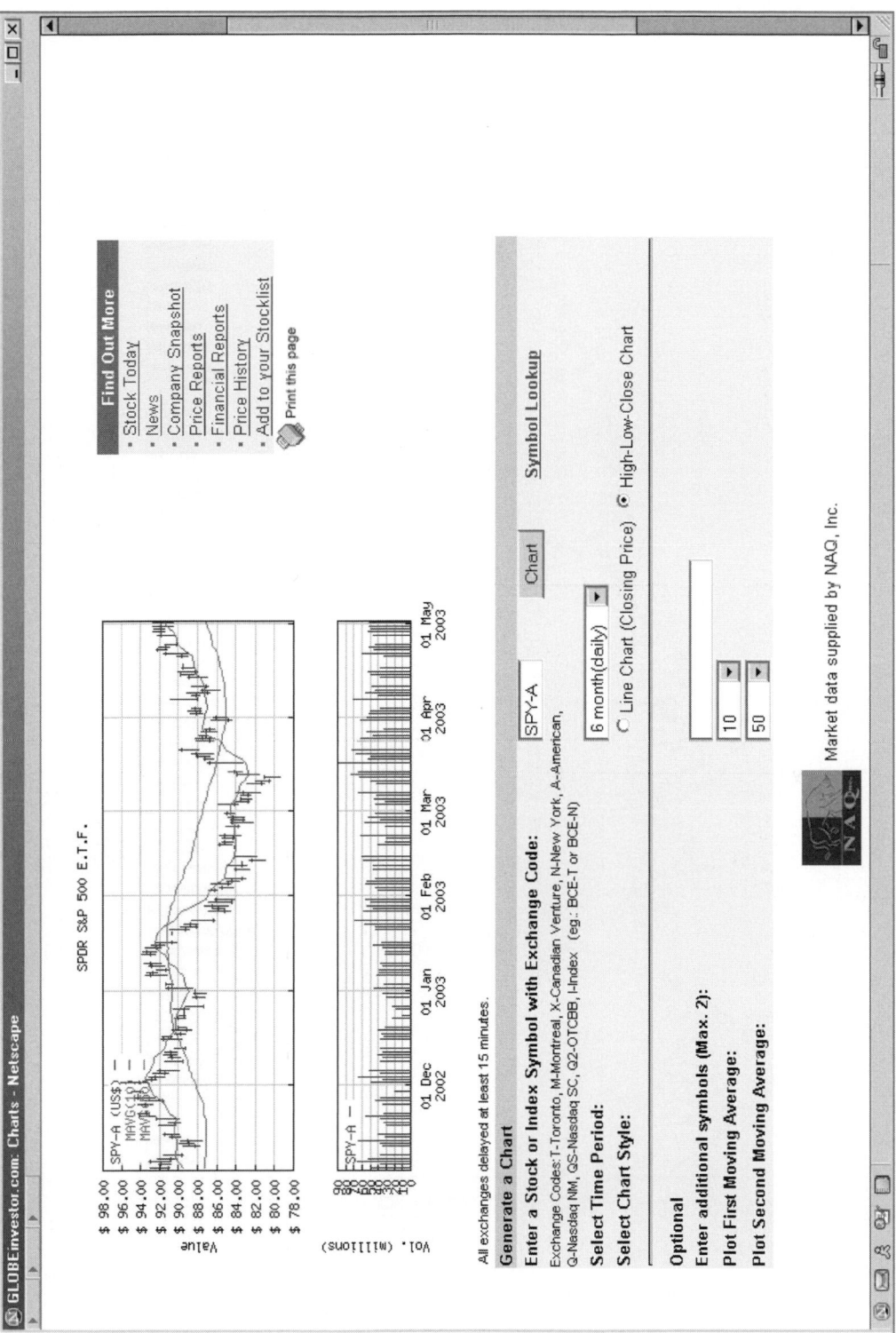

Figure 9.10 50 day MA chart for SPY, November 2002–May 2003

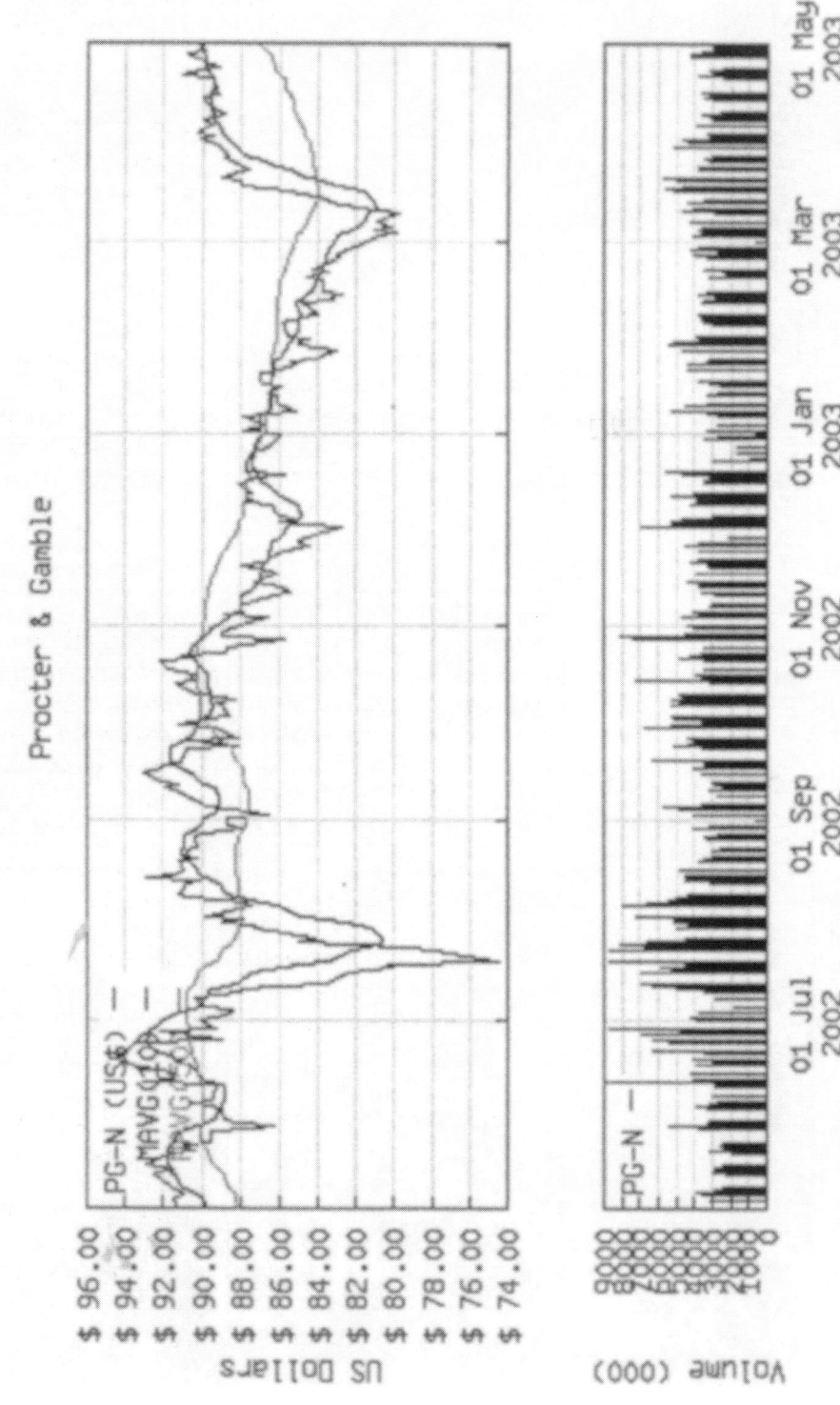

Figure 9.11 Procter & Gamble 50 day vs. 10 day MA, 1 year sample

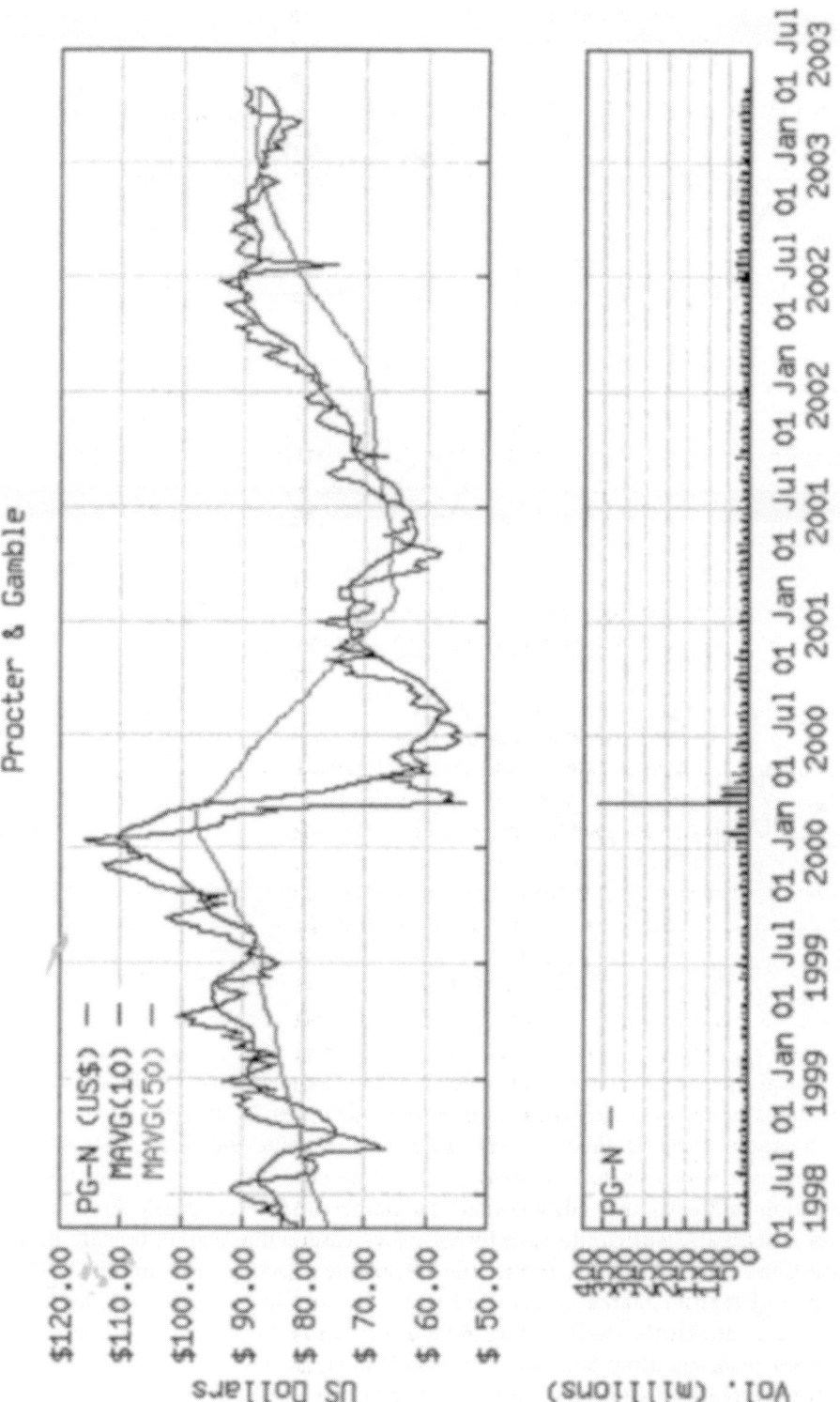

Figure 9.12 Procter & Gamble 50 day vs. 10 day MA, 5 year sample

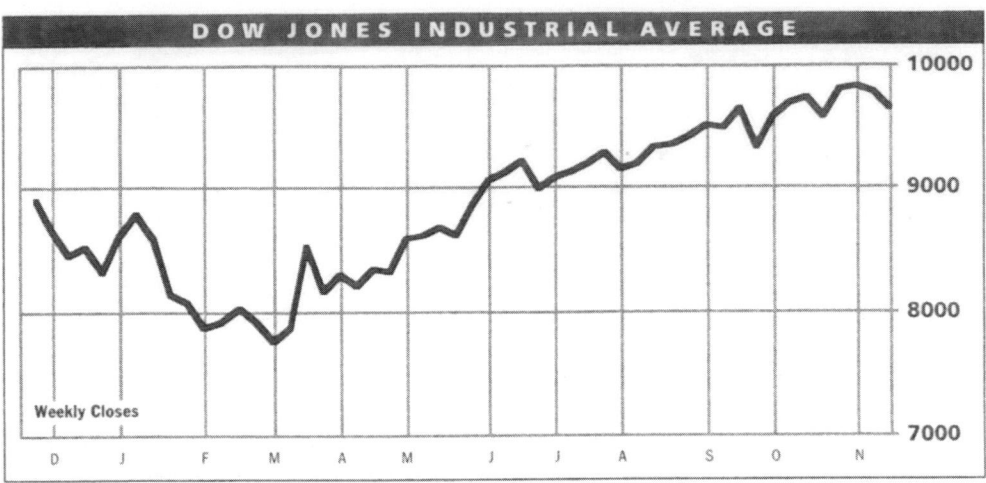

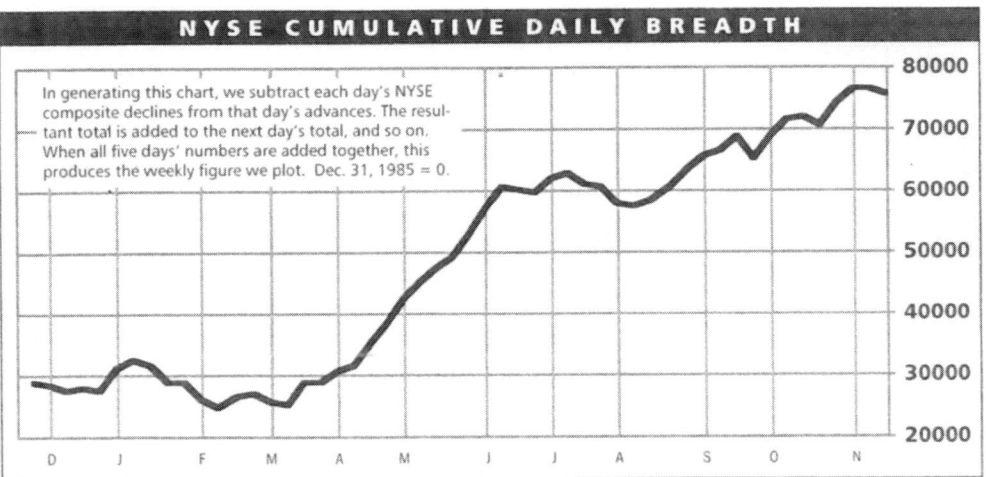

Figure 9.13 Advance–decline for DJIA, 11/02–11/03
Source: Barrons

The typical intuition used to assess a breadth indicator is based on the presumption that the direction of the major market averages tends to persist at trend reversal points. Market averages such as the 30 stock DJIA or the value weighted S&P 500 give disproportionate emphasis to a narrow group of stocks. This leads to the following interpretation of, say, the advance–decline ratio: at market peaks (troughs), the narrowly based DJIA will continue to increase (decrease) while market breadth declines (increases). In other words, a divergence in the advance–decline ratio and the DJIA is a signal of a change in market trend. Due to the day-to-day variation in the breadth indicator (and the DJIA), moving average methods can be used to smooth the series to give a better representation. Similarly, the market breadth indicator can be examined in isolation and used as a trend indicator. As with price charts, when the short term, say

10 day, moving average of the breadth measure cuts the long term, say 200 day, moving average from below (above) this is a signal for an upward (downward) movement in prices. In addition to changes in market trend, breadth indicators such as the McClellan oscillator can also be used to assess direction within trading range markets.

Contrarian and contrary opinion strategies

Like "value" and "growth" stocks, the "contrarian approach" to security analysis and investment strategy is another source of semantic confusion. The terminology "contrarian," "contrarian strategy" or "contrarian approach" can apply to a wide range of strategies involving different measures, applicable in a variety of different situations. The basic motivation of the contrarian strategy is to trade in the opposite direction of the trend in prices or market sentiment. Differences in definition arise from the theoretical rationale used to motivate the contrarian strategy. In modern Finance, the "contrarian" approach is often equated with "value investing." For example, Levis and Liodakis (2001) claim: "The profitability of contrarian investment strategies is now one of the most well known empirical facts in the finance literature" where "contrarian" refers "to various strategies based on buying/selling stocks that are low/high relative to three accounting measures of performance – earnings, cash flows, and book values – as well as strategies based on low/high EPS growth." This claim of "most well known empirical fact" is supported by references to a number of studies, including Fama and French (1998). Levis and Liodakis proceed to observe that: "the outperformance of such strategies has declined and even reversed in the most recent years."

The process of presenting "strong empirical evidence" that is later refuted is becoming a characteristic feature of modern Finance. This unsettling phenomenon is compounded by another confusing feature: the tendency to redefine words that have an established but different meaning in either old Finance or in practitioner usage. From the efficient markets hypothesis – where "technical analysis" and "fundamental analysis" are given interpretations that do not do justice to those approaches – to "contrarian" investment strategies – where the emphasis is placed on the use of accounting measures to select stocks – modern Finance has taken a seemingly chauvinistic attitude regarding previous approaches to the subject. Redefining words that already have established alternative meanings – such as "contrarian" investment strategy – shows either ignorance of other approaches to Finance or a disappointing lack of respect for these approaches.[21] It is not even clear that the use of "contrarian" is grammatically correct. The connection between the use of accounting measures and a contrarian outcome depends on an empirical assumption that, say, high (low) *P/E* or *P/BV* stocks are past winners (losers), e.g., Lakonishok et al. (1994). Only if the strategy involves buying losers and selling winners can the approach be interpreted as contrarian, and even then the meaning is substantively different than used in other contexts.

The attempt by adherents of modern Finance to redefine the contrarian approach is unfortunate because the long history of the contrarian approach contains many insights. The basis of this approach to security analysis and investment strategy is reflected, for example, by Keynes (1936, p. 155): "the professional investor is forced to concern himself with the anticipation of impending changes, in the news or in the atmosphere, of the kind by which experience shows that the mass psychology of the market is most influenced." In effect, prices in security markets are the outcome of "crowd psychology" or "mass psychology." As Neill (1954, p. 5) observes: "What it comes down to in the final analysis is that a 'crowd' thinks with its heart (that is, influenced by emotions) while an individual thinks with his brain." Keynes (1936, p. 154) provides more substance for this observation: "A conventional valuation which is established as the outcome of the mass psychology of a large number of ignorant individuals is liable to change violently as the result of a sudden fluctuation of opinion due to factors which do not really make much difference to the prospective yield; since there will be no strong roots of conviction to hold it steady." The contrarian attempts to be ahead of the crowd by identifying when mass psychology has driven prices too far in one direction.

Though the basis of the contrarian approach can be traced back to early writings on security markets, e.g., de la Vega (1688), the development of an organized approach aimed at trading securities did not occur until the 1950s. A well developed association of contrary opinion with technical analysis can be traced to Drew (1951) where the views of *Humphrey Neill* were recognized. Neill (1954, p. 15) appraises the state of the subject in the mid-1950s:

> The Theory of Contrary Opinion is not something that one reads about in books or histories. There is no literature on the subject. Nothing has been written directly on the use of contrary opinion that I am aware of, except an excellent chapter pertaining to "contrary *market* opinion" in [Drew 1951].

Neill had been developing and writing about contrary opinion since the 1920s, mostly in newspaper columns and an investment advisory newsletter, *Neill Letters of Contrary Opinion*. A driving concern for Neill's inquiries was the question: why is the public so often wrong? Neill sought the explanation for this question in the role of "human nature in finance," more specifically on the role of mass psychology and the actions of individuals in crowds.

For Neill the "*art of contrary thinking*" applies to a wide range of issues – political, social and economic: "The art of contrary thinking consists in training your mind to ruminate in directions opposite to general public opinions; but weigh your conclusions in light of current events and current manifestations of human behavior." Though Neill has insights into various realms of human activity, it is the implications of contrary thinking for technical analysis that has received the greatest recognition (Neill 1954, p. 16):

> One can interpret charts almost any way he wishes. He can read into their "formations" just about any probable result he hopes for. Which is to say, that if one is bullish at heart, his chart reading is likely to be interpreted optimistically; if bearishly inclined, charts accommodatingly will "say" that the market is going down. During one-way market trends (whether up or down) the trends are clearly enough defined on the charts; but when the market comes to an impasse and everybody is in a quandary as to the direction prices are likely to go, then the charts, too, are usually "silent."

It is in these periods of indecision in the charts that "each person would interpret 'technical action' in accordance with his deep-seated personal opinions." Wishful thinking takes over and the "inherent traits of hope, greed, pride-of-opinion, and similar human feelings" bias the analysis and contribute to making "successful speculation one of the most difficult arts to master."

For Neill (1954, pp. 44–6), the theory of contrary thinking is "intangible," it is a habitual approach to examining the world. The public, the crowd is *not* wrong all the time. "The public is perhaps right more of the time than not. In stock market parlance, the public is right *during* the trends but wrong at both ends!" In other words, the public is "wrong when it pays the most to be right." Neill recognizes that "when we adopt a contrary opinion, as a guide, we must recognize that we may be *too far* ahead of the crowd." This is because events are often slow to change. Weeks or months may pass before a trend changes and the contrary opinion proves to be correct. However, as "there is *no* known method of *timing* events or trends . . . it is wiser to be early than to be late – in most economic decisions." Neill makes the convincing point, based on years of heuristic inductive analysis, that consideration of contrary opinion improves forecasting ability: "Contrary thinking unquestionably helps one to avoid many common errors in forecasting – errors arising from miscalculating what the public will do." If anything, the art of contrary thinking will alert the individual to the bombardment of self-serving information and news that is dispensed from brokerage houses, government departments and agencies, and the popular financial media.

Making the theory of contrary thinking operational requires some method of measuring the sentiment of the "crowd." Since Neill, considerable effort has been dedicated to this task. In the absence of well-developed or acceptable measures, Neill (1954, p. 22) observes:

> you will have to peruse a pile of news and comments. However, our radios, and magazines unload such a flood of economic news and propaganda these days, it is not difficult to get a fairly accurate cross section of what people probably are thinking about and what the composite opinion is likely to be. Also – and this is important – of what some groups *want* us to accept and believe.

Neill identified official economic releases as another possible source for market sentiment, because of the weight such opinions have on the public. At Neill's time, the Council of Economic Advisors had an impact similar to what the Board of Governors would have at present. Neill also provides an important cue for later developments in the measurement of sentiment: "A consensus of businessmen – or brokers – is valuable in making an analysis of opinions 'to be opposite to' because of their influence on general sentiment." An example of how this notion has been made operational is provided by the Investor's Intelligence investment advisory service (www.investorsintelligence.com) that calculates a number of contrary opinion indicators based on surveys of market sentiment expressed: in investment advisory newsletters, e.g., Siegel 1998, p. 87; and by NYSE members (see figure 9.14).

In addition to surveys of investment advisory newsletters, opinions of floor traders and brokerage house recommendations, Siegel (1998, p. 89) makes reference to a

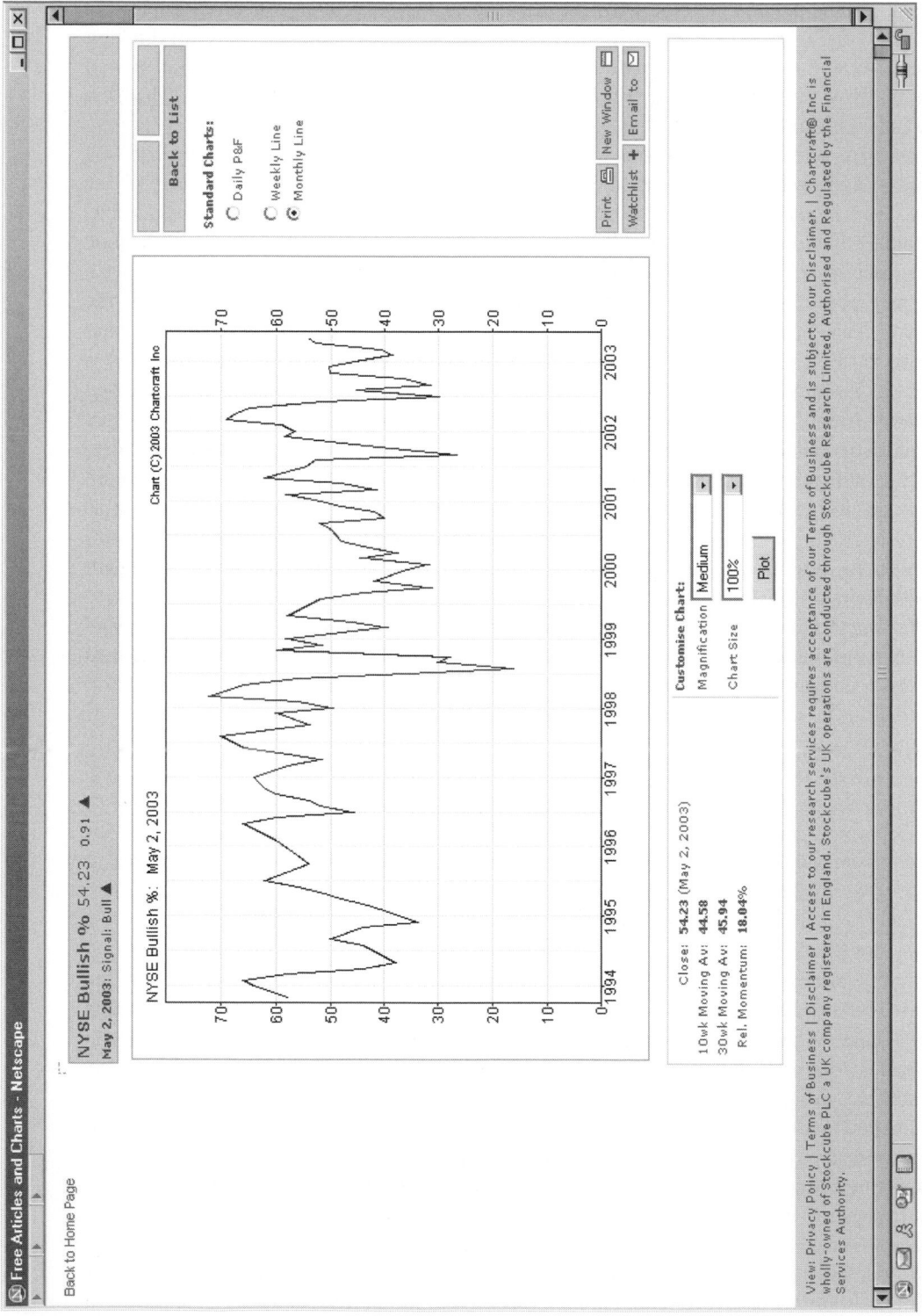

Figure 9.14 Investors' intelligence NYSE bullish

"sentiment indicator based on the recommended portfolio allocations of market analysts and portfolio managers. Whenever their recommended allocation to stocks falls below 50%, indicating a high level of pessimism about the market's prospects, subsequent returns have been high." Siegel claims that the Director of Quantitative and Equity Research at Merrill Lynch "calls this his single most powerful quantitative market-timing barometer." Like any mechanical investment strategy, there is the possibility that the feedback effect will undermine the effectiveness of such a contrarian strategy. However, *measures based on surveys and analysis of newsletters* have a number of features that would mitigate the feedback effect: the information is not widely disseminated and, in some cases, the measures are proprietary; being based on surveys and the like, the measures change slowly over time; and, the interpretation of the measure is subjective. It is arguable whether such contrarian measures are not more within the realm of fundamental analysis than technical analysis.

In considering the performance of contrary opinion and other contrarian indicators, *the forecasting horizon* is a key variable. Based on the limited evidence that is available, it appears that contrary opinion indicators have been effective for determining turning points in long term trends. However, the use of contrarian indicators for purposes of short term speculation – the main battlefield of technical analysis – is likely to be less effective, if only because contrarian indicators tend to have a long term focus. In order to be used for short term trading, the contrarian measures need to be based on information sets that change on a regular basis. This runs the risk of altering the conceptual foundation upon which the contrarian approach is based. Some indicators that have been suggested in the past that could be used for short term trading, such as the ratio of purchases to sales for odd-lot transactions (Kaish 1969) or mutual fund cash positions (Massey 1979), also seem to work best (if at all) for predicting long term turning points. In an odd twist, the "buying losers and selling winners" contrarian strategy suggested by modern Finance adherents seems to be the closest that a profitable "contrarian" strategy comes to a short term horizon.

9.3 BEHAVIORAL FOUNDATIONS?

Heuristic-driven bias

The "discovery" in modern Finance that technical analysis may provide a source of profitable trading rules has resulted in a rejuvenation of psychological explanations of market behavior, albeit with a modern twist. This empirically driven rejuvenation has been greatly aided by the experimentally based "*prospect theory*" of Kahneman and Tversky (1979) (see section 10.4). The view that psychological factors play an important and, at times, an overriding role in securities markets has been around for centuries. From de la Vega in the seventeenth century to Keynes in the twentieth century, the tension between bulls and bears has fascinated market observers. The importance of psychological factors to professional security analysts was recognized in GDC (p. 712):

In recent years the psychosomatic element in illness has been emphasized to such an extent that most doctors apparently have to be psychologists. In the security field a like situation has obtained almost from the beginning. Security analysts have felt the need to gauge the psychology or "technical position" of the stock market and to base their buying and selling recommendations on a combined consideration of underlying value *and* prospective market movement.

This suggested combination of technical analysis with "value" considerations has attracted considerable attention in modern Finance, e.g., Chan et al. (1996), Macedo (1995).

While the impact of psychological factors on stock markets and prices has a long history, recent developments have been gathered under the heading of "behavioral finance." Characterized as the "New Finance" by Haugen (see section 2.4), this "new subject" has been propelled by a desire to provide explanations for the empirical failings of modern Finance that have emerged in the form of "anomalies" (see section 1.2). Though decidedly more inductive, the philosophical and rhetorical approach of behavioral finance is consistent with the positivism of modern Finance.[22] As such, intellectual roots and historical progression of behavioral finance have been clouded by the perception that, somehow, the subject is a new evolution of the positivist approach. For example, Shefrin (2000, p. ix) claims: "Phil Cooley was among the first to apply the findings of psychologists and study the risk attitudes of portfolio managers, he published his work in the 1977 *Journal of Finance*. In fact, most of the major contributions to behavioral finance have appeared in academic journals." The connection between this statement and McCloskey's observation about the rhetorical aspects of journal articles and "conversations between academics" is difficult to avoid.

The claims of behavioral finance academics for being "first to apply" this or that notion to practical financial applications is, at best, overstated. Consider the "*heuristic-driven bias*" that Shefrin (2000, p. 4) identifies as one of three central themes in behavioral finance:[23]

Do financial practitioners commit errors because they rely on rules of thumb? Behavioral finance answers yes, and traditional finance answers no. Behavioral finance recognizes that practitioners use rules of thumb called heuristics to process data. One example of a rule of thumb is: "Past performance is the best predictor of future performance, so invest in a mutual fund having the best five-year record." Now, rules-of-thumb are like back-of-the-envelope calculations – they are generally imperfect. Therefore, practitioners hold biased beliefs that predispose them to commit errors. For this reason, I assign the label heuristic-driven bias to the first behavioral theme. In contrast, traditional finance assumes that when processing data, practitioners use statistical tools appropriately and correctly.

There are a number of oddities about the claims made in this statement. One oddity is that modern Finance is referred to as "traditional finance," as though Graham and Dodd and other contributors to Haugen's "Old Finance" (see section 2.4) were non-events. Intellectual progress is being measured relative to the inadequacies of modern Finance, as though Philip Fisher, J.M. Keynes, Ben Graham and a range of others that made essential insights into the analysis of securities markets had never contributed anything of substance. Conversations that took place outside the narrow confines of the academic circle of modern Finance are irrelevant, even though these conversations still have considerable relevance to behavioral finance.

To see the basis of this point, consider the following from J.M. Keynes (1936, ch. 12, pp. 149–50):

> The outstanding fact is the extreme precariousness of the basis of knowledge on which our estimates of prospective yield have to be made. Our knowledge of factors which will govern the yield of an investment some years hence is usually very slight and often negligible. If we speak frankly, we have to admit that our basis of knowledge for estimating the yield ten years hence of a railway, a copper mine, a textile factory, the goodwill of a patent medicine, an Atlantic liner, a building in the City of London amounts to little and sometimes to nothing; or even five years hence. In fact, those who seriously attempt to make any such estimate are often so much in the minority that their behavior does not govern the market.

For Keynes, the "uncertainty" that impacts financial decisions requires practitioners to employ "*convention.*" In the words of Keynes (1936, p. 152): "In practice, we have tacitly agreed, as a rule, to fall back on what is, in truth, a *convention*. The essence of this convention, though it does not, of course, work out quite so simply – lies in assuming that the existing state of affairs will continue indefinitely, except insofar as we have specific reasons to expect a change." Compare this with the heuristic given by Shefrin: "Past performance is the best predictor of future performance, so invest in a mutual fund having the best five-year record." Yet, Keynes goes well beyond the notion of heuristics to develop an insightful theory on the working of financial markets. This is not to say that the theories proposed by Keynes were correct. Rather, the pre-modern Finance contributions made by Keynes and others are not even acknowledged.

Keynes was far from being the only precursor of the ideas that behavioral finance is claiming to be the "first" to apply. Consider Neill (1954, pp. 55–7):

> Habit, of course, is one of the chief studies of psychology. Habits are of various types: fixed and changeable; likewise, physical, mental, and emotional. William Henry Mitchell tells us that "every division of the mind is habitualized ... Through habits we develop routines of action and thinking. This applies to business and financial thinking just as it does to the daily routine of eating and dressing ... Habits push our minds into ruts – and it takes a considerable amount of force and time to get out of the ruts. So, in contemplating crowd action (to which we may wish to be contrary) we have to consider not only the thought-habits of the crowd but our own thought-habits! This "rut-thinking" is regularly reflected in economics, politics, and in the stock market.

This connection between "habits" and financial decisions is not substantively different than the "heuristics" proposed by behavioral finance. Yet, Neill proposes a way of thinking that will permit the individual to avoid the "biased beliefs that predispose them to commit errors," as Shefrin describes the implications of decision-making using heuristics. In contrast, behavioral finance seeks to use heuristics to explain empirical observations that run contrary to received opinion in modern Finance. Neill provides sufficient references to indicate that these ideas about the implications of "habits" were relatively well developed by the 1950s. Because behavioral Finance shares the same positivist roots as modern Finance, there is a shared belief that "science" progresses linearly and ideas and insights from the past have been superseded by the progress of knowledge. As discussed in section 1.3, this incorrectly assumes that Finance is a natural science and not a human science.

All this is not meant to imply that behavioral finance is a watered down rehashing of unacknowledged ideas that were developed much earlier and in more insightful fashion – quite the contrary. Behavioral finance has extended and clarified notions that were, in some respects, relatively disorganized and underdeveloped. In particular, even though the implications and use of heuristics in financial decision making has long been recognized, behavioral finance provides a fresh and typically more developed perspective. Consider the evidence that buying losers and selling winners is profitable, e.g., De Bondt and Thaler (1985, 1987). Behavioral finance explains this outcome as a consequence of using stereotypes as a heuristic to make judgments, a practice that Kahneman and Tversky (1979) refer to as "*representativeness*" (Shefrin 2000, p. 14). The stereotyping of past winners and losers causes "overreaction" by analysts and stock traders. Shefrin identifies a range of other manifestations of heuristics such as availability bias, aversion to ambiguity, hindsight bias and overconfidence. "Because of their reliance on heuristics, practitioners hold biased beliefs that render them vulnerable to committing errors" (Shefrin 2000, p. 22). These errors can lead to the anomalies observed in a range of empirical studies that challenge the efficient markets hypothesis.

Frame dependence

Frame dependence is an obscure terminology that describes a range of interesting psychological responses to investment situations. Following Shefrin (2000, p. 4): "Behavioral finance postulates that in addition to objective considerations, practitioners' perceptions of risk and return are highly influenced by how decision problems are framed." *Loss aversion*, also known as the "disposition effect," is a useful example of frame dependence. Nofsinger (2002, p. 22) illustrates loss aversion with an investment situation where an individual wants to purchase a stock but has no cash and has to sell one of two stocks to raise the required capital:

> Stock A has earned a 20% return since you purchased it, whereas stock B has lost 20%. Which stock do you sell? Selling stock A validates your good decision to purchase it in the first place. You enjoy pride at locking in your profit. Selling stock B at a loss means realizing that your decision to purchase it was bad. You would feel the pain of regret. The disposition effect predicts that you will sell the winner, stock A. Selling stock A triggers a feeling of pride and avoids regret.

Loss aversion also leads to the "get-evenitis" disease, i.e., the extreme reluctance of individual investors to sell at a loss, which "has probably wrought more destruction on investment portfolios than anything else" (Gross 1982). The upshot of loss aversion is a tendency to sell winners too early and hold losers too long, e.g., Shefrin and Statman (1984). If present, the reduced returns associated with this tendency would be compounded by the adverse tax consequences; selling winners generates a taxable capital gain while selling a loser generates a capital loss that can be used to offset capital gains.

Behavioral finance aims to provide theoretical explanations to support empirical results contrary to the prescriptions of modern Finance. As such, frame dependence is a key theme in behavioral Finance because modern Finance assumes that individuals are frame independent. In addition to empirical anomalies such as the January effect and the small firm effect that appear to contradict the efficient markets hypothesis, there are a number of other empirical phenomena that provide puzzling examples of possibly irrational behavior. Perhaps the most significant example of such irrational behavior is the "*dividend puzzle*," e.g., Frankfurter (1999). This puzzle arises because investors consistently express a preference for dividends over capital gains, despite the unfavorable tax treatment of dividends. This preference is reflected empirically in the prices of stocks, as well as in investor surveys. The theoretical prescription that modern Finance advances to explain rational behavior toward dividends, the dividend irrelevance hypothesis of Modigliani and Miller (M and M), provides a popular illustration of frame independence. Underlying this hypothesis is the assumption that individuals will be guided by the desire to achieve the most favorable cash flow and will be indifferent between capital gains or dividends if the cash flows (end of period wealth) are not affected.

To derive the *dividend irrelevance hypothesis*, M and M proceed by assuming perfect markets. In the case of dividend payout, perfect markets is a conservative assumption because it ignores the negative tax implications of dividend payments. An all-equity financed firm is faced with two choices: paying dividends and financing further expansion by issuing additional stock; or forgoing dividend payments and using retained earnings to finance expansion. Using an arbitrage argument, M and M demonstrate that the dividend policy of the firm is irrelevant because, in the event the firm decides to forgo paying dividends, investors can create synthetic or "homemade" dividends by selling stock. The increase in the stock price in the no-dividends case will be just sufficient to compensate for the value of dividends that would have been paid in the dividend-payout case. The equity claim against assets is the same in both cases, though the number and price of shares will differ over time to reflect the new issue of shares in the dividend payout case and the increase in stock price for the retained earnings case due to the enhanced claim against assets. In the dividend payout case, the investor has cash in hand from dividends that is just equal to the cash in hand received from the sale of stock in the retained earnings case.

There are a range of effects that fall within the scope of frame dependence including: hedonic editing; self-control; cognitive dissonance; the snake bite; and money illusion. Both hedonic editing and the desire to achieve self-control can be used to motivate a psychological explanation for the dividend puzzle. *Hedonic editing* applies to the M and M dividend irrelevance case because (Shefrin 2000, p. 29): "hedonic editing offers some insight into investors' preferences for cash dividends. When stock prices go up, dividends can be savored separately from capital gains. When stock prices go down, dividends serve as a 'silver lining' to buffer a capital loss." Another reason given for the preference of dividends over capital gains is self-control (Shefrin 2000, p. 30):

> Older investors, especially retirees who finance their living expenditures from their portfolios, worry about spending their wealth too quickly, thereby outliving their assets. They fear a loss of self-control, where the urge for immediate gratification leads them to go on a spending binge. Therefore, they put rules into place to guard against the temptation to overspend. "Don't dip into capital" is akin to "don't kill the goose that lays the golden eggs." But if you don't dip into capital, how do you finance consumer expenditures – Social Security and pension checks alone? Not necessarily – this is where dividends come in. Dividends are labeled as income, not capital. And investors tend to frame dividends as income, not capital. Again, this is frame dependence.

Being a relatively new subject, the terminology for the various effects does differ. For example, Nofsinger (2002, p. 87) classifies this process of not dipping into capital under the general category of "mental accounting."

Following the approach used by Kahneman and Tversky (1979), behavioral finance typically proceeds by the use of stories, experiments and exercises. Though there are empirical studies that tend to support certain behavioral explanations, there are others that suggest the opposite. For example, Fama (1998) observes: "apparent overreaction to information is about as common as underreaction, and post-event continuation of pre-event abnormal returns is about as frequent as post-event reversal. Most important, consistent with the market efficiency prediction that apparent anomalies can be due to methodology, most long term return anomalies tend to disappear with reasonable changes in technique." To be sure, there are numerous empirical studies that are supportive of specific theoretical propositions advanced by behavioral finance. However, by proceeding along a positivist line, it is necessary for the results to be unambiguous and capable of rejecting appropriate alternative hypotheses. This goal has, to date, not been achieved. In the absence of convincing empirical evidence, the strength of the behavioral finance case relies heavily on stories and experiments – these are slender reeds to support the intellectually ambitious agenda of behavioral finance.

Inefficient markets

The last of the three central themes of behavioral finance identified by Shefrin (2000, p. 5) is market inefficiency: "heuristic-driven bias and framing effects cause market prices to deviate from fundamental values." The implication is that due to the pervasiveness of psychologically driven trading behavior, security markets will be inefficient. Behavioral finance seeks to provide explanations for why security markets can be inefficient. Yet, considerable confusion is created by the inductive character of this process. An empirical result is presented, such as a return anomaly, that is claimed to represent a market inefficiency, somehow defined. A behavioral explanation is then developed to account for the empirical result. Presumably, if the market is inefficient, the behavioral explanation would provide a method for identifying and understanding situations where abnormal returns can be obtained. Yet, beyond the original empirical result that identifies the anomaly, behavioral finance provides little guidance for "picking stocks to beat the market." It is difficult to shake the notion that behavioral finance does not proceed much beyond providing explanations for pricing inaccuracy, as opposed to pricing inefficiency.

The basic definition of market efficiency relates to security prices fully and rapidly reflecting the information contained in technical or fundamental or insider information sets (see section 1.2). If a market is inefficient with respect to a given information set then it is possible to use that information to generate an abnormal return. Yet, Shefrin (2000, p. 89) makes the following statement:

> it is harder to beat the market than most people think. That is an important reason why the moral . . . is *not* that investors can use behavioral finance to make a killing. I think most investors would be better off holding a well-diversified set of securities, mainly in index funds, than they would be trying to beat the market [using behavioral finance]. In other words, they would be better off acting as if Fama were right, that markets are efficient.

Hence, while behavioral finance can provide explanations for empirical "return anomalies" that indicate market inefficiencies, Shefrin does not put much credence in the potential for using such anomalies to actually generate an abnormal return. This view is not unique to Shefrin. For example, after detailing the contributions of behavioral finance, Nofsinger (2002, pp. 87–9) proposes the following guide to "beating the biases": understand the biases; know why you are investing; have quantitative investment criteria; diversify; and, control your investing environment. This guide does not suggest any potential for generating abnormal returns. Rather, the advice mostly concentrates on avoiding abnormal losses that can beset the novice investor.

Based on Shefrin (2000, p. 89), the absence of a connection between behavioral finance and market inefficiency is difficult to deny: "What about investing based on learning some behavioral finance? Well, understanding the relevance of representativeness means having a little knowledge, and you know what they say about a little knowledge. It is a dangerous thing." Is there any usable advice that security analysts or individual investors can find in behavioral finance to generate abnormal returns? Much like Nofsinger, Shefrin provides advice that is largely useful for novice investors:

> The moral of the [behavioral finance] story, for most investors, is not to be overconfident. Markets may fail to be efficient, but that doesn't mean it's easy to beat the market – either by oneself or by relying on the advice of some guru . . . If an investor picked just one brokerage firm in 1986 and stayed with it for the duration, the odds of beating the market were no better than even. Why? Because only half the brokerage firms recommended stocks that beat the market.

As for possible sources of market inefficiency or "strategies for beating the market," Shefrin falls back on the empirical evidence to find strategies to "beat the market," e.g., "momentum investing, large cap, and growth."

The discussion to this point is not designed to argue that behavioral finance makes little or no contribution to knowledge about financial activities. Rather, the primary objective of this section is to explore the potential for using behavioral finance to provide a theoretical rationale explaining how technical analysis can generate abnormal returns. Though there are explicit and implicit claims made by proponents of behavioral finance indicating that this would be the case, the process is largely inductive, working backward from empirical results to theoretical modeling. Behavioral finance is able to explain a wide range of alternative, possibly conflicting, hypotheses. Consider again the basic claim of behavioral finance: "heuristic-driven bias and framing effects cause market prices to deviate from fundamental values." This could be consistent with pursuing a range of approaches to security analysis and investment strategy, from value investing to technical analysis to two fund separation. The result that security prices, particularly common stock prices, differ from fundamental values is commonplace. Providing insight into the psychological biases that can generate investment errors does not translate into advice about how, say, to identify specific securities that are mispriced.

The theoretical proposition that "security prices differ from fundamentals" does not necessarily correspond to support for inefficiency. The test of inefficiency is the ability to generate abnormal returns using a given information set. This necessarily involves a joint hypothesis composed of the efficient market hypothesis (EMH) and the assumed return generating model. This complication permits believers in the EMH to claim that an empirical rejection of the EMH is actually a rejection of the return generating model. For example, if "abnormal" returns are observed, as in the case of the small firm effect, it is possible to claim that the returns were not properly "risk adjusted." If this is not possible, believers in the EMH can fall back on criticism of the statistical methodology, such as data mining, data snooping, survivor bias, bid-ask bounce and so on, e.g., Sullivan et al. (1999), Haugen (1999b, ch. 6). It is difficult to shake the assumption that individuals making financial decisions act rationally. This is an important source of attraction for behavioral finance. For positivists not wedded to the core beliefs of modern Finance, the subject provides a "rational" explanation for irrational investor behavior.

Accepting that the various empirical results demonstrating "returns anomalies" are correct, the number of possible theoretical explanations for such results is limited. A more or less complete list of possible explanations includes: institutional failure; information asymmetries; regulatory or institutional rigidities; psychological biases; and faulty interpretation of the statistical analysis. Of these explanations, psychological biases provide an attractive theoretical basis for return anomalies because the flexibility of this approach permits the explanation to be tailored to a specific anomaly. In addition, psychological explanations are adaptable to a range of historical and geographical situations that may not be possible with other types of explanations. This is particularly attractive when seeking a potential explanation for the profitability of technical analysis where the "chart patterns" are seen as independent of the institutional context. However, the flexibility of behavioral finance is also a limitation as approaches capable of explaining a wide range of empirical results are also difficult to reject. Given these caveats, *which of the psychological explanations is compatible with the potential profitability of technical analysis?*

Technical analysis is based on the notion that prices follow trends. As Edwards and Macgee (1966, p. 6) observe:

prices move in trends and trends tend to continue until something happens to change the supply-demand balance. Such changes are usually detectable in the action of the market itself. Certain patterns or formations, levels or areas, appear on the charts which have a meaning, can be interpreted in terms of probable future trend developments. They are not infallible, it must be noted, but the odds are definitely in their favor. Time after time, as experience has amply proved, they are far more prescient than the best informed and most shrewd of statisticians.

If there are identifiable and predictable trends in prices, then this is evidence of market inefficiency. Some of the reported "return anomalies" such as the January effect or the small firm effect as well as the profitability of buying winners and selling losers (or the reverse) could generate some types of identifiable trending in prices that are emphasized in technical analysis. However, as Edwards and Macgee claim, these return anomalies would be reflected in chart patterns: "[A technical analyst] could trade with profit in a stock knowing only its ticker symbol, completely ignorant of the company, the industry, what it manufactures or sells, or how it is capitalized. Needless to say, such practice is not recommended, but if your market technician is really experienced at his business he could, in theory, do exactly what he claims."

If there is identifiable and predictable trending in prices, then why don't rational individuals trade on the trends and generate sufficient price adjustment to eliminate the trends? In other words, if prices discount the future correctly, as technical analysts claim, then why are the trends not also discounted? Most adherents of technical analysis would answer this question by making reference to the struggle between bulls and bears – "heterogeneity" in preferences, tastes and expectations in the terminology of modern Finance. This struggle determines the supply and demand for securities in the market. Recall from section 9.1 the theoretical outline for technical analysis given by Levy (1966): "Supply and demand are determined by numerous factors. These factors can be both rational and irrational. Included in these factors are those of importance to fundamental analysts, as well as moods, sentiment, guesses and blind faith. The market is a mechanism for weighing each of these factors on a continuing basis." Unlike in modern Finance, investor rationality is not a requirement for technical analysis. As such, behavioral finance has the potential to provide rational explanations for the potentially irrational behavior that is required to sustain technical analysis.

Is there any aspect of technical analysis that receives unambiguous support from behavioral finance? Put differently, which theory or theories in behavioral finance provides the strongest support for technical analysis? There are a number of candidates. According to adherents of technical analysis, the trends, and turning points in the trends, that do appear in prices require skill and experience to discern. This suggests that the behavioral theories aimed at over-reaction and under-reaction are most applicable. Shefrin (2000, p. 85) summarizes the relevant empirical evidence:

> The winner-loser effect is puzzling in that if winners and losers are defined in terms of one-year past returns, rather than three-year past returns, an underreaction effect emerges, not an overreaction effect ... What we seem to have is overreaction at very short horizons, say less than one month ... momentum possibly due to underreaction for horizons between three and twelve months ... and overreaction for periods longer than one year ... This phenomenon is quite complex, and does not lend itself to easy explanations.

It seems that skill and experience are also required to interpret the empirical evidence emanating from the New Finance. Following from the practice of technical analysis, it is also likely that if a viable combination of empirical explanation and behavioral theory is eventually identified, the feedback effect would either prevent detailed documentation of techniques that are successful or create preconditions for the combination to become unsuccessful once recognized by the market.

9.4 RELATIVE STRENGTH, MOMENTUM AND THE OSCILLATOR

Relative strength

As discussed in section 1.3, modern Finance is firmly entrenched in the epistemology of logical positivism. Those instilled with this intellectual approach are compelled to develop theoretical models that are empirically tested on experimental data. (Hopefully such data is available.) Knowledge progresses linearly as more precise empirical observations are obtained and theoretical hypotheses are developed that have better predictive power. In the process of empirical testing and observation, insights are gained inductively that permit the development of theoretical models with a better fit to reality.[24] This intellectual process has produced enormous strides in the natural sciences, where an immutable physical reality is the object of analysis. The gains achieved by logical positivism have been more debatable in the human sciences where the exercise of free will by individuals undermines the assumption that the objective reality is immutable. Unlike modern Finance, the bulk of technical analysis proceeds by empirical observation. However, the "science of technical analysis" (Edwards and Magee 1966, p. 6) is still subject to the general criticism aimed at modern Finance, i.e., that objective reality in the human sciences is not immutable. The assumption that chart patterns repeat over time requires a degree of predictability for human behavior that is difficult to reconcile with the exercise of free will and the evolution of the social and historical context.

In any event, technical analysis is predicated on the assumption that "history repeats itself." The subject is "forward looking" in the sense that the reasons why history repeats are of relatively little interest compared to the identification of "repeatable patterns" that permit prediction of future price movements. Induction drives the method of analysis. Section 9.2 examined a range of these repeatable patterns: the various types of chart patterns and associated moving average techniques. These methods of technical analysis can be characterized as traditional, in the sense that the information of interest can be presented on a single price chart. Over time, technical analysis has evolved methods of analysis that are more sophisticated, in the sense that the information of interest is mapped from the price chart to another chart, or from two price charts onto another chart. Included in these more sophisticated methods are indicators of relative strength, momentum and oscillation. These indicators involve evaluating functions of the original price series. In keeping with the conventional approach of technical analysis, the charts of these more sophisticated indicators are usually used as the method of evaluation, though this is not necessary.

The indicators of relative strength, momentum and oscillation are closely related. In some presentations, relative strength and price momentum are used synonymously, e.g., Macedo (1995), though there are good reasons to make a distinction between the concepts. In an odd semantic twist, Wilder (1978) introduced a form of oscillator referred to as the "Relative Strength Index" that will be discussed below. In what follows, relative strength is interpreted in the traditional sense of Levy (1967, 1968) and others, e.g., Bohan (1981). To avoid potential semantic confusions, some sources refer to the traditional relative strength concept as *comparative relative strength*, e.g., www.marketscreen.com. Using the traditional definition, (comparative) relative strength is an extension of the basic notion in technical analysis that prices move in trends. The relative strength extension postulates that relative performance will also follow trends. Stocks or industries that are outperforming will continue to outperform until the trend is reversed. For stocks, this outperformance can be measured relative to the market average or to other stocks in the same industry or to some other stock or whatever. For industries, outperformance is measured relative to the market average or to other industries.

Relative strength is a widely used concept that can be measured in various ways. The simplest measure – plotting of the relevant price series on a close-only chart – is widely available from most online charting sites. For example, figure 9.15 compares the relative strength of GM, Ford and the S&P 500 using a one-year close-only chart. For many applications, this assessment of relative strength is sufficient. Analysts requiring more precise information can calculate indicators from the price series. A simple example of such a relative strength indicator would be the ratio of a stock's price to, say, the S&P 500. If this ratio increases over time, then the stock has relative strength compared to the index. However, the scale of this measure would not be directly comparable to the indicator value for another stock relative to the S&P. Consider figure 9.15, the indicator value around 1:30 EST on May 13, 2003 for Ford to the S&P is ($10.02/944.85) – .0106, for GM to the S&P is ($36.61/944.85) = .03875 and for Ford to GM is ($10.02/$36.61) = .2734. While it is possible to plot these individual series and use chart analysis techniques to identify trends, trading ranges, breakouts and so on, direct comparison of indicators across stocks is not feasible due to the absence of scale comparability. This can be corrected by scaling the indicator relative to some base period and multiplying by 100 to create an index number. The base year can be selected to correspond to, say, the last major reversal in the sector or the market.

Relative strength is somewhat different from most other technical indicators because it deals with the "co-movement" of prices. Even if successive price changes are serially uncorrelated, there may still be exploitable information in the co-movements. As Levy (1967) observes: "The intercorrelation or co-movement of stock prices could conceal existing dependencies in successive price changes." For example, unlike momentum that measures directional change, *relative strength can increase in both up markets and down markets*. Consider the relative strength of a stock measured using the ratio of the stock's price to the S&P 500. Both the price and the market average could be falling at the same time that the measure of relative strength is increasing. Typically, it is assumed that if, say, a given stock is outperforming the market, then this relative strength can also be expected to follow a trend. Using the tools of technical analysis,

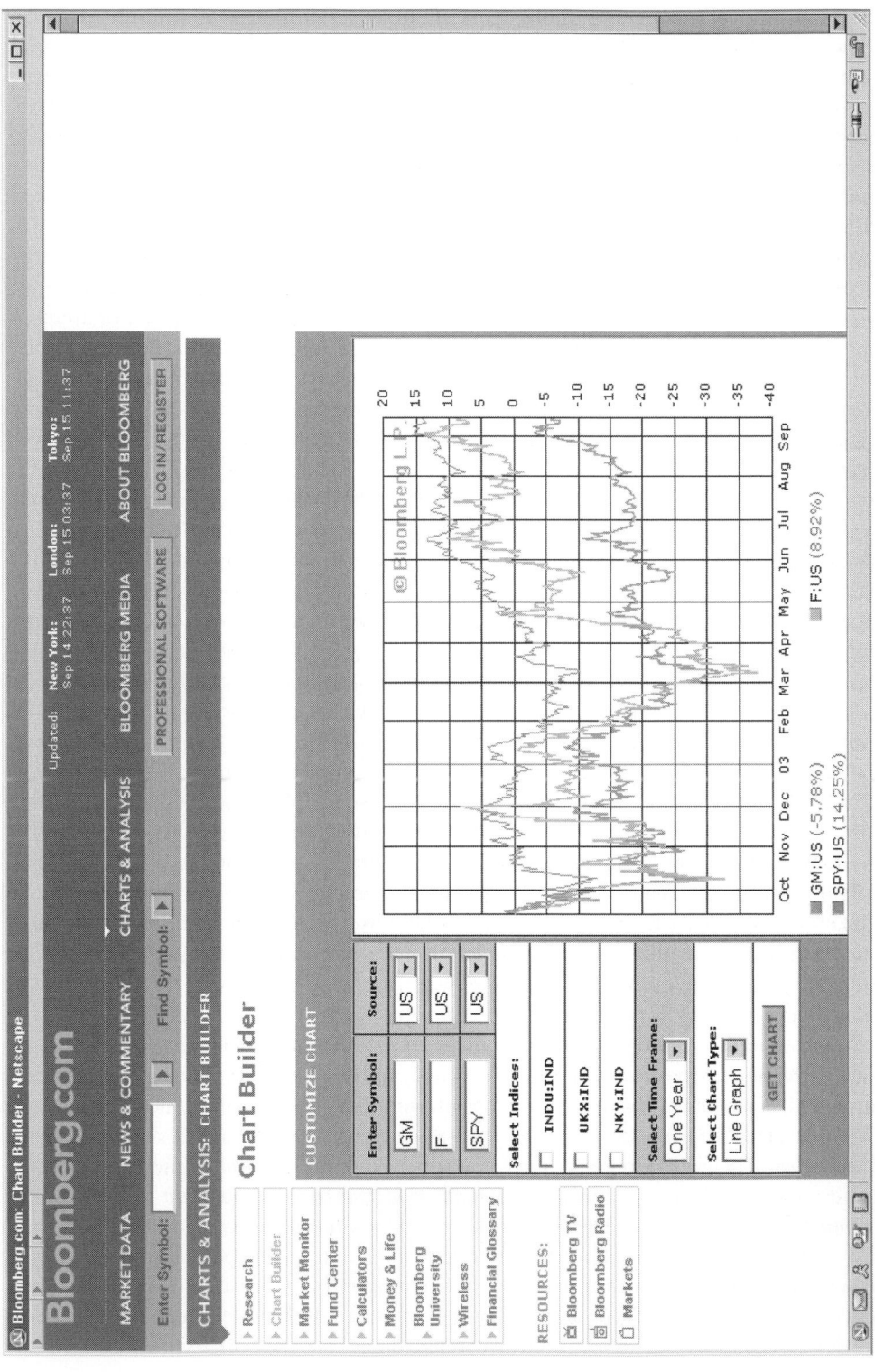

Figure 9.15 GM, Ford and S&P, September 2002–September 2003

these trends can be identified. As long as the relative strength trend is unbroken, stocks that are strong in bear markets can be expected to outperform when the primary trend changes to a bull market. This co-movement of stocks with market averages, between stocks, between industries and so on can be examined using a range of tools from technical analysis. Levy (1967), for example, suggests the uses of "divergence ranks" and "market ranks."

Despite holding considerable promise, there has been little interest in relative strength indicators in recent years. One possible reason for this is the emergence of the CAPM as an analytical tool. By construction, the market model representation of the CAPM provides two parameter estimates for a security: the alpha and the beta (see section 3.3). The information provided by these parameter estimates is a statistically sophisticated form of relative strength analysis. When expressed in excess return form, the beta measures the co-movement of the security return with the market return and the alpha measures the excess (deficit) return after adjusting the security return for equilibrium systematic risk compensation. In effect, the alpha of a security is a measure of relative strength, adjusted for systematic risk. As such, the use of alpha addresses concerns expressed in Levy (1967, pp. 609–10) and other early studies of relative strength indicators about "the riskiness of the various technical indicators." While useful, the temporal instability in the parameter estimates of the market model leaves room for improvement in the use of alpha as a relative strength indicator. Perhaps the use of charting techniques, moving averages and so on can be used to improve the usefulness of the market model?

Momentum and "price rate of change"

In section 9.2, it was observed that the development of technical analysis involved a gradual increase in the sophistication of techniques associated with the processing of price information. At least since Schabacker (1930) it has been recognized that, in order to deal with the noisiness of the raw price series, moving averages can be calculated. The values of a moving average are smoother than the price series and can be plotted directly on the price chart. The smoothing of the price information in this fashion alters basic chart patterns such as head and shoulders, flags and pennants that are the basic tools of chart analysis involving unprocessed prices. This leads to different trading rules for moving averages. Eventually, processing of price information had to achieve a level of sophistication where the resulting indicators could not be plotted directly on the price chart.[25] Another chart or series of charts has to be prepared in addition to the basic price chart. (This use of additional charts in technical analysis was already the case with volume information that cannot be plotted directly on the price chart.) Much like a moving average, the objective is to calculate some function of the underlying price series and use that to identify trends, determine trading signals or both. Because of the large number of potential functions that could be applied, the scope for these types of extensions to technical analysis are almost limitless.

Precisely when momentum entered the lexicon of technicians is unclear.[26] It is only since the 1970s that considerable attention from both practitioners and academics has focused on the concept. As with so many concepts in Finance, there is divergence both between practitioners and between academics and practitioners as to the definition of "momentum." For many practitioners, e.g., Schwager (1996), Blau (1995), Kaufman (1978), *momentum* is defined as the rate of change of prices over a period of time. More precisely, the k day momentum indicator, $M(t, k)$, is defined as $M(t, k) = P(t) - P(t - k)$, where P is the closing price. The k day *price rate of change*, $ROC(t, t - k)$, is defined as $ROC(t, k) = P(t)/P(t - k)$ (or in percentage change terms $ROC(t, k) = \{(P(t) - P(t - k))/P(t - k)\}100$). Other practitioners, e.g., www.marketscreen.com, use conflicting definitions by defining momentum as the ratio of prices k days apart and the price rate of change as the first difference or percentage change in prices. It is also possible to define momentum using other variables than closing prices. For example, a moving average of prices can be used for a momentum indicator calculated by taking the difference of the moving average values k days apart. It is also possible to take a moving average of the momentum value. However, if only because of the differing interpretation of the momentum chart patterns, it is more appropriate to refer to these more involved momentum measures using different terminology.

Whatever the definition, the basic intuition of momentum relates to the slope of the price chart. For purposes of illustration, consider a smooth non-linear function that starts at zero and increases monotonically to a maximum. (The cumulative normal distribution function is a practical example of such a function with the normal density function as the representation of the slope of that function.) Basic calculus provides the result that the slope of the function will initially increase and then start decreasing until the slope reaches zero when the function reaches a maximum. As such, the slope of the function signals a maximum prior to the maximum being reached; it follows that the momentum chart can theoretically provide a signal for a change from uptrend to downtrend. The momentum function will achieve a maximum prior to the price function, crossing zero when the price function maximum is achieved. A similar analysis applies for a minimum. This basic intuition of selling (buying) at the maximum (minimum) of the momentum function is complicated by the noisy fluctuations of market prices. Consider the simple case of the one-day momentum, $\{M(t, 1)\}$. It is usually the case that the one-day momentum chart is not a smooth function, crossing the zero line numerous times over the time period, making the momentum signal difficult to evaluate.

As illustrated in figure 9.16, the difficulty of interpreting the momentum function may possibly be improved by taking larger differencing intervals to define momentum. Though the momentum charts for $\{M(t, 3)\}$, $\{M(t, 9)\}$ and $\{M(t, 20)\}$ are still erratic, as the differencing interval is increased the function becomes less erratic. The *ex post* maximum and minimum values become easier to identify. The longer 20-day differencing interval does not have as many values in the extreme ranges. Recognizing that momentum can be interpreted as an oscillator, the maximum and minimum ranges can be used to define "overbought" and "oversold" levels that, in turn, can be used to specify trading signals (see below). Casual inspection of the $M(t, 20)$ chart reveals reasonably accurate trading signals at the minimum point around December and a maximum in February, though the up move that begins in mid-March is missed. The use of specific differencing intervals is much like the choice of a sample length for a moving average,

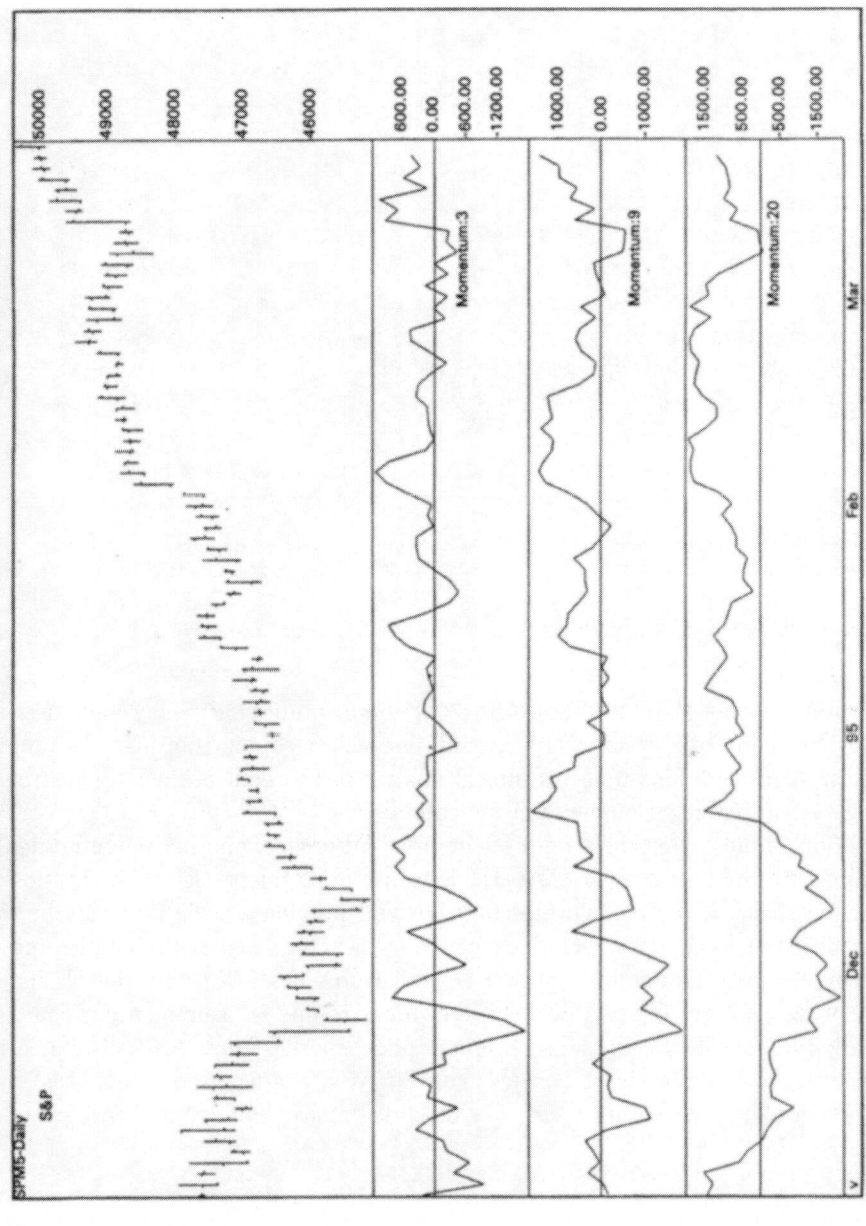

COMPARING DIFFERENT N-VALUES FOR THE MOMENTUM OSCILLATOR

This chart shows S&P futures with 3, 9 and 20 day momentum indicators, 1985.

Figure 9.16 Momentum: 3, 9, 20 day

Source: FutureSource; copyright © 1986–1995; all rights reserved

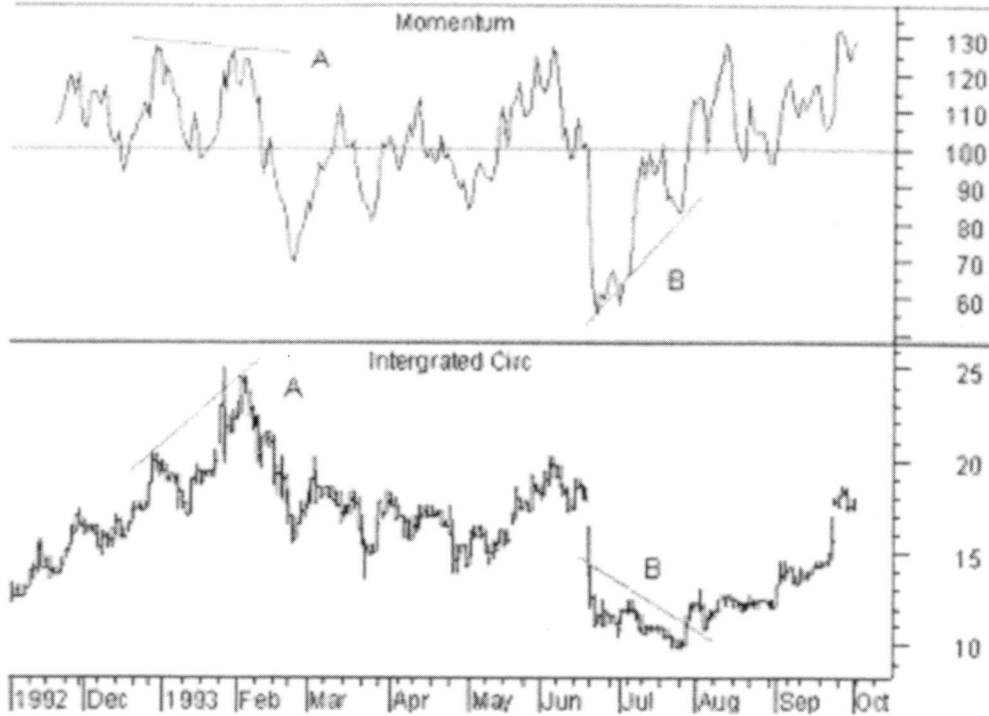

Figure 9.17 The 12-day momentum ratio $\{ROC(t, 12)\}$

100-day and 200-day ($M(t, 100)$ and $M(t, 200)$) momentum charts may have desirable properties. Selection of a specific differencing interval or comparison across a range of intervals are considerations that a technical analyst has to consider when constructing a trading system based on momentum indicators.

In addition to increasing the length of the price difference, another potential method for dealing with the noisiness in $\{M(t, 1)\}$ is to use price ratios. Using price ratios will not alter the shape of the momentum chart but will provide a scale that may be more interpretable. The price ratio technique can also be combined with lengthening the differencing interval. Examining figure 9.17 which provides $ROC(t, 12)$ reveals that, as in figure 9.16, a longer interval between the prices results in a momentum chart that is similar, but not identical, to the original price chart. Figure 9.17 also identifies *divergence* signals that can be associated with differing chart patterns, identified using trend lines, for the momentum chart and the price chart. Following Schwager (1996, p. 527):

> Bullish divergence occurs when a market makes a low, rallies, and then declines to a lower low, while [momentum] makes a low along with the market, rallies, and then fails to decline to a new low ... Bearish divergence occurs when a market makes a high, declines, and then rallies to a higher high, while [momentum] makes a high along with the market, declines, and then fails to rally to a new high.

These situations are indicated in figure 9.17 using trend lines. At point A, the higher highs on the price chart are not reflected by the "bearish divergence" of momentum. Similarly at B, the lower lows are not supported by the "bullish divergence" of momentum. The concept of divergence applies to oscillators, in general, not just momentum.

The difficulties of interpreting the erratic behavior of momentum for small K illustrated in figure 9.16 have generated a large number of techniques designed to enhance interpretation of the momentum chart in order to improve the signaling potential. Specification and interpretation of these often complicated transformations of momentum differs across technical analysts. Casual inspection of figure 9.16 reveals a number of relevant issues. As discussed above, the scale of the price difference is in terms of prices with the momentum value fluctuating about zero. Because price is the scale, it is not immediately clear when a momentum value is "too high" or "too low." A small price change of, say, $2 when the stock price is $50 will appear to be the same on the momentum chart as when the price is $10, when $2 is a large price change. While there is no theoretical maximum, the lowest possible value is $-P(t)$. The scaling of a momentum chart depends on the definition selected. One difference associated with defining k day momentum as the ratio of prices k days apart is that the indicator will fluctuate around 1.00 with zero as an absolute lower bound, as indicated in figure 9.17 that plots the momentum for $k = 12$ days. Using price ratios to define momentum does correct for the different impact of a $2 change on a $50 stock and a $10 stock, but the problem of defining when a momentum value is "too high" or "too low" still remains.

In conjunction with using bullish and bearish divergence signals, determining when a momentum chart generates a buy or sell signal typically can also be facilitated by specifying an upper or "overbought" boundary and lower or "oversold" boundary on the momentum function. As indicated in figure 9.17, the divergence assessments were evaluated in the maximum and minimum regions of the momentum chart. As with divergence, the concepts of overbought and oversold are general oscillator concepts and are not restricted to momentum indicators. Yet, even if these boundaries can be determined from, say, the past history of the stock price momentum, the erratic pattern of momentum indicated in figure 9.16 for $\{M(t, 3)\}$ indicates that it will be difficult to separate "false" signals from correct signals. While it may be possible to widen the differencing interval, as in figure 9.16, another natural approach is to use moving average techniques to smooth the momentum function. For this purpose, most technical analysts use exponential weighted moving averages (EMA), e.g., a 20-day EMA of $M(t,1)$ (see end of chapter questions). In some cases, e.g., Blau (1995), an EMA of different length is taken of the EMA resulting in, say, a 5-day EMA of the 20-day EMA of 1-day momentum. This process is called "*double smoothing.*"

In contrast to the wide diversity of definitions and interpretations associated with momentum that are used by practitioners, academic studies of momentum use a relatively simple approach to definition and interpretation. Consider the "momentum" strategy used by Jegadeesh and Titman (2001, p. 703) for a sample of all NYSE, Amex and Nasdaq stocks over a 1965–98 sample: "at the end of each month we rank the stocks in our sample period based on their past six-month returns . . . then group the stocks into 10 equally weighted portfolios based on these ranks. Each portfolio is then held for six months following the ranking month." While based on the notion of buying stocks using $M(t, 6\ month)$, the connection to the concept of momentum used by technical analysts is decidedly underdeveloped. This lack of correspondence is not surprising when it is recognized that Jegadeesh and Titman (1993, 2001) and other modern Finance adherents that have examined "momentum strategies," e.g., Chan et al. (2000), are not concerned with testing the profitability of technical analysis. Rather, the concern is with testing the hypothesis of "buying winners and selling losers" that is suggested by the behavioral finance challenge to the modern Finance orthodoxy.[27]

A number of academic studies have demonstrated the potential profitability of momentum strategies. The momentum differencing interval varies across studies, e.g., Jegadeesh and Titman use a six month interval while Chan et al. examine five differencing intervals varying between one week and six months. In contrast to the practice in technical analysis where an individual security is usually examined, the academic studies focus on classification of a universe of stocks into portfolios. Though these academic momentum studies have been subjected to the criticism of "data-snooping bias" by other studies, it is difficult to ignore the sharpness of the statistically significant results for the profitability of the simple momentum strategies. For example, for the full sample of stocks over three different sampling periods (1965–98, 1965–89, 1990–8), Jegadeesh and Titman (2001, p. 704) report monthly returns that decline monotonically from a high of (1.65, 1.63, 1.69) for the highest decile of equally weighted momentum portfolios down to the lowest decile portfolios (0.42, 0.46, 0.30). The strength of these results has led to the emergence of a "stylized fact" that investors "under-react" to short period returns. Whether this stylized fact will withstand closer scrutiny is, at present, unclear.

Oscillators

The reference to an "oscillator" is inherited from physics where the term was originally used to describe the graphical representation of alternating-current voltage flow. Recognizing that the fluctuations of the alternative voltage flow between a positive maximum and negative minimum display an oscillatory pattern, it follows that the name oscillator is associated with oscillation or frequent fluctuation. (The term now more generally refers to an electronic device used for the purpose of generating a signal.) In technical analysis, the term *oscillator* refers to a wide range of techniques that can be based on substantively different calculations and motivations. The unifying notion connecting the techniques is that the chart pattern calculated from the original price chart oscillates or fluctuates within a defined range. The defined range for an oscillator permits the specification of *overbought* and *oversold* levels for the oscillator that can be used to identify trading signals. Interpretation of overbought and oversold signals is aided by the concept of *divergence*. Because the oscillator is often constructed by taking the difference of two series, most oscillators are designed to be "counter-trend" systems. This leads to the following result (Schwager 1996, p. 556): "Oscillators perform well when a market is in a trading range – that is, a sideways trend. They work poorly, however, when a market is in a strong uptrend or downtrend."

The oscillator covers so many techniques that some technical analysis websites do not make any reference to the concept, e.g., www.marketscreen.com, opting instead to list specific types of oscillators directly. Other sites use a narrow definition of oscillator that excludes many types of techniques that would be considered oscillators using a wider definition. An example of a narrow definition is found at www.futuresource.com, which defines an oscillator as "the simple difference between two moving averages." Adopting the wider definition, momentum can be viewed as a type of oscillator. As illustrated in figures 9.16 and 9.17, the momentum chart oscillates above and below the zero slope line. $M(t, 1)$ is, arguably, the simplest form of oscillator. A number of more sophisticated oscillators, such as the Relative Strength Index and the Lane Stochastic, are developments on the momentum oscillator. Though some forms of oscillator, such as the Lane Stochastic, have been in use since the 1950s, the fascination with the oscillator is a relatively recent development in technical analysis, gaining popularity starting in the early 1970s. For example, the concept is given only passing recognition in Edwards and Magee (1966). Kaufman (1978, p. 91) restricts "the use of the term oscillator to a specific form of momentum, that which is normalized or expressed in terms of values ranging between +1 and −1 or +1 and 0." This definition would include the Relative Strength Index and the A/D oscillator.

In addition to oscillators based on momentum, a variety of alternative specifications are possible. In particular, another simple oscillator is the dual moving average (DMA) oscillator that is constructed by differencing two moving averages of different length: $DMA(t, j, k) = \bar{P}(t, j) - \bar{P}(t, k)$ where $j < k$ with the j period moving average being "fast" and the k period moving average being "slow." This oscillator is of interest because the moving average is a trend-following technique while an oscillator is a counter-trend technique. In effect, the *DMA oscillator* is designed to capture the momentum of the trend: "When the fast moving average is accelerating away from the slow one, prices are gaining momentum; when the fast moving average is decelerating toward the slow one, prices are losing momentum" (Schwager 1996, p. 524). The zero line is defined as the point where the two moving averages are equal. Unlike trend following systems that use the crossing of the zero line as a trade indicator, the DMA oscillator signals trades by specifying overbought and oversold regions on the DMA oscillator chart. It is also possible to examine divergence between the oscillator and the price chart. In the same fashion that using the zero line to signal trades will result in false signals and whipsaws in trading range markets, using the overbought and oversold regions will result in false signals in trending markets.

The DMA oscillator is a graphical representation of the dual moving average trading system that can be implemented directly on the price chart (see section 9.2). The analytical advantages that are gained by mapping particular price chart information into a different chart format are in this case, more or less, incidental. This suggests a natural extension of the DMA oscillator that does exploit the ability to map from the price chart to the oscillator chart: the Moving-Average Convergence-Divergence (*MACD*). Though in the form of an oscillator, the MACD is not usually referred to as an oscillator because the technique integrates both trend-following and counter-trend methods. Credited to Gerald Appel, the MACD constructs an *MACD line* by subtracting a 26 period EMA from a 12 period EMA.[28] This step is a special case of a DMA oscillator that uses specific sample periods for exponential moving averages. To generate trading signals the MACD technique proceeds to calculate the *signal line* which is a 9 period EMA of the MACD line. As illustrated in figure 9.18, it is conventional for MACD charts to also contain a histogram of the difference between the MACD line and the signal line. The histogram provides an oscillator-like chart that can be used to identify trades.

Because the signal line in the MACD involves taking a moving average of the price difference between two moving averages, the MACD can be classified as a "double-smoothed momentum indicator" (Blau 1995). The process for determining trades using the MACD line and the signal line is described in Schwager (1996, p. 538):

> The basic method for trading with MACD is to buy when the MACD line crosses above the signal line and to sell when the MACD line crosses below the signal line. However, entering and exiting trades based solely on MACD line-signal line crossovers results in frequent whipsaw losses. To make the best use of MACD, it is advisable to wait for crossovers that are preceded by divergence and confirmed by the subsequent price action of the market.

The MACD is the featured technical indicator at a number of high traffic websites dedicated to technical trading, including the e-trade site (see figure 9.19). Though usually classified as an oscillator, the MACD does differ from other oscillators in having better theoretical properties in trend following situations. For example, the website www.trade10.com provides the following observation about MACD: "the signals generated by the MACD are trend following, occurring after the market has made movement in a new direction. For this reason the MACD is used more as a conformational tool of the trend and can be used in trading decisions when combined with other indicators and platforms for decision and strategies." As with the momentum oscillator, the MACD also requires interpretation of the scale. To partially adjust for this shortcoming, figure 9.19 also reports information on the stochastic.

As discussed previously, a limitation of the momentum chart is difficulty in interpreting the scale. In other words, when is the value of the oscillator "high enough" to be overbought and "low enough" to be oversold? A number of popular oscillators, such as the *Relative Strength Index* (RSI) and the Lane Stochastic are designed to produce a momentum indicator that has a scale varying between 0 and 100%. This scaling permits the overbought and oversold regions to be specified in a transparent fashion. Conventionally, overbought is > 80% and oversold < 20%, though > 70% and < 30% are also popular boundaries. The methods required to produce such scaling are not obvious. For example, at time t the RSI developed by Wilder (1978), is calculated as:

$$RSI(t, k) = 100\left(\frac{RS(t, k)}{1 + RS(t, k)}\right)$$

where RS is the weighted average of daily price increases over the past k days divided by the weighted average of daily price decreases over the previous k days. Wilder used $k = 14$ days but this is not essential. Though the method of calculating the weighted averages requires detailed explanation, the intuition is clear: if there are a long string of

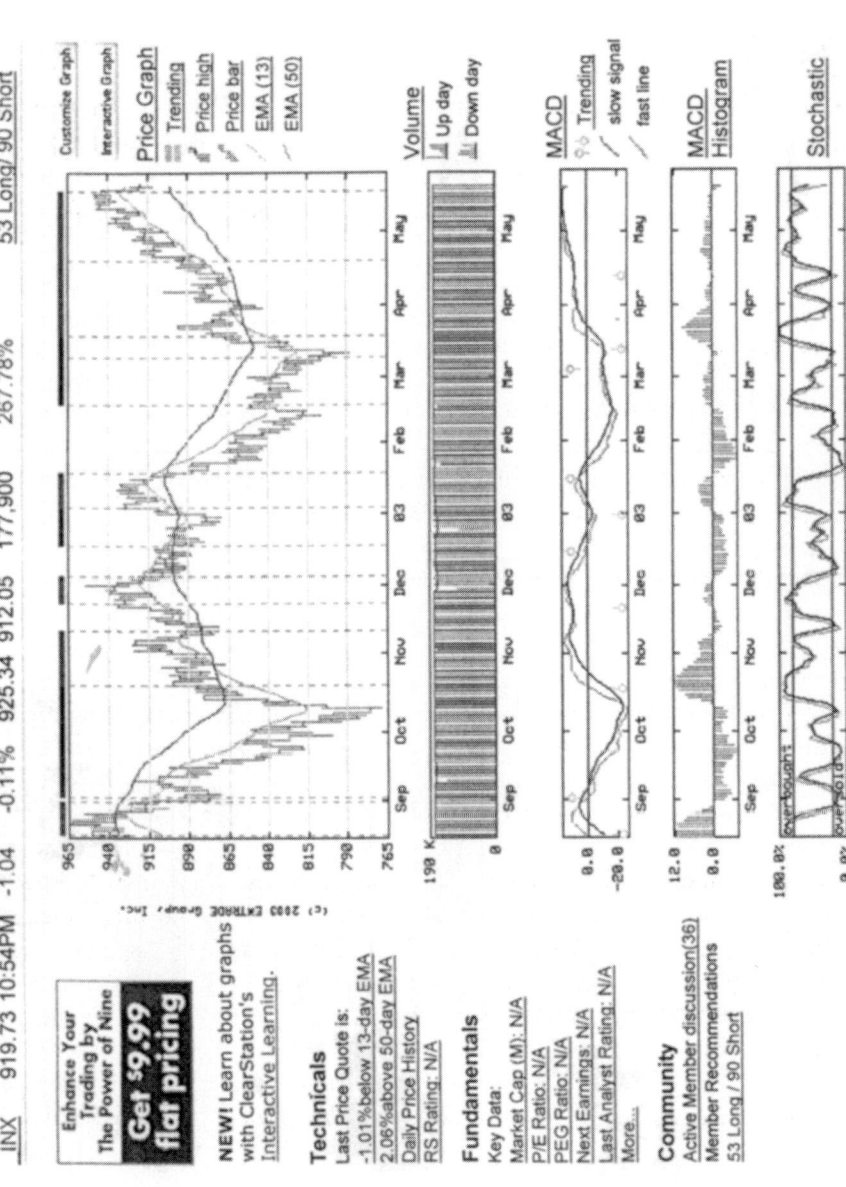

Figure 9.18 MACD diagram

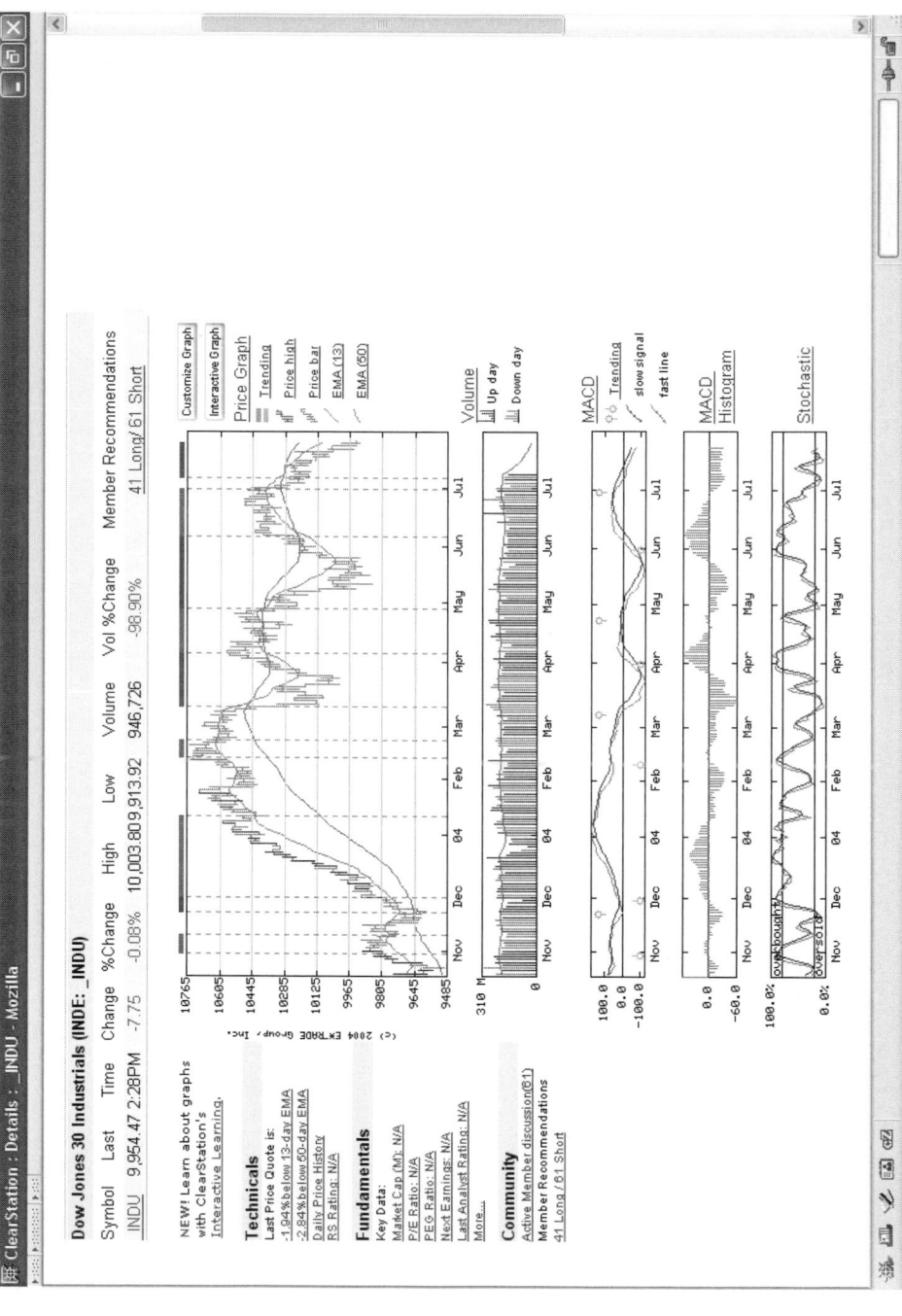

Figure 9.19 MACD and other technical indicators, DJIA, November 2003–July 2004

up moves then *RS* gets large and *RSI* goes to 100; if there are a long string of down moves then *RS* goes to zero and *RSI* goes to zero.

As noted previously, it is not possible in a single chapter to examine in any detail the wide array of possible methods that could be used in technical analysis. Even if the subject is narrowed to just include oscillators, the topic is still unmanageable. Despite having examined momentum oscillators, DMA oscillators, the MACD and the RSI, the number of undiscussed oscillators still includes: Williams %R, similar to the stochastic oscillators; volume oscillators; the Ultimate oscillator, that uses the weighted sum of three oscillators; detrended price oscillators; Lane's fast and slow stochastics, based on the location of closing and opening prices within the high-low range; the mass index, based on the high-low range; the McClellan oscillator, based on the number of advancing and declining issues; the True Strength Index (Blau 1995, p. 5); candlestick momentum; and the stochastic momentum index. Beyond the basic description of these oscillators, there is also a need to describe practical issues about the implementation. All this would take more space and time than is practical here. Those wanting more information are recommended to visit a number of the excellent technical analysis websites such as www.futuresource.com and www.marketscreen.com.

Questions /?

1 Following Shefrin (2000, pp. 55–6), do the following exercise:

Imagine that a coin is being tossed 100 times. Write down the sequence of heads and tails that is *imagined* to occur as the coin is flipped. Repeat this exercise by actually flipping a coin 100 times and writing down the sequence of heads and tails that correspond to the order observed as the coin is flipped.

Compare the length of runs in the two sequences. What is the longest "run" of heads and the longest "run" of tails in the imagined sequence and in the actual sequence? What is the relative frequency of runs of five, four, three, two and one? What theory in behavioral finance would explain these discrepancies?

2 Figure 9.6 in section 9.2 provides two trend lines for the S&P 500, one associated with a 1 year price chart and the other with a 3 year chart. Which trend line is most appropriate to use in making an assessment of the long-term trend in the S&P 500? (Hint: consider where the last reversal in the S&P 500 occurred.) Does your answer depend on the type of trading strategy that is being pursued?

3 In section 9.2, the specification of a trading range involved resistance and support levels. Provide a practical explanation for trading ranges in terms of stop-loss orders and market-if-reached orders. Does this suggest that resistance

and support levels for a trading range be defined in terms of a number of observations at the boundaries? (Hint: See Schwager 1996, pp. 73–7.) How would the activities of a stock exchange specialist affect the performance of a stock following a breakout?

4(a) An exponentially weighted moving average (*EMA*) has the form:

$$EMA(t) = \alpha P(t) + (1 - \alpha)EMA(t - 1)$$

where $0 < \alpha < 1$. Prove that the *EMA* can be expressed as a infinite weighted moving average with weights $w_i = \alpha(1 - \alpha)^i$. In other words:

$$EMA(t) = \alpha P(t) + \alpha(1 - \alpha)P(t - 1) + \alpha(1 - \alpha)^2 P(t - 2)$$
$$+ \alpha(1 - \alpha)^3 P(t - 3) + \ldots$$

(b) In various sources, e.g., Schwager (1996, p. 602), it is stated that the *EMA* "corresponds roughly to a simple moving average" with length T where: $\alpha = 2/(T + 1)$ or $T = (2 - \alpha)/\alpha$. Recognizing that simple moving averages weight each term in the moving average equally and that exponentially weighted moving averages have a declining weight scheme, specify conditions under which this mapping between a simple moving average and *EMA* make sense.

5 The following example of loss aversion is adapted from Kahneman and Tversky (1979). You currently own a stock that you purchased for $10,000 and has fallen to $2,500. If you hold onto the stock there is a 75% chance the company will go bankrupt and the stock price will fall to zero, and there is a 25% chance the stock will recover to its original value. Based on an intuitive inspection of this decision, should you sell the stock today and lock in a loss of −$7,500 or hold on? What is the expected value of the two transactions? Why does the decision to hold the stock reflect loss aversion?

6 In section 9.4, momentum was defined as $M(t, k) = P(t) - P(t - k)$. In section 9.2, the simple T day moving average $\bar{P}(t, T)$ was defined as:

$$\bar{P}(t, T) = \sum_{i=0}^{T-1} \frac{P(t - i)}{T}.$$ Setting $k = T$ what is the relationship between the

momentum and moving average indicators? (Hint: Consider the case of $k = 5$. In this case $M(t, 5) = P(t) - P(t - 5)$. Similarly, $\bar{P}(t, T) = \{P(t) + P(t - 1) + P(t - 2) + P(t - 3) + P(t - 4)\}/5$. But $\bar{P}(t, T) = \bar{P}(t - 1, T) + \{[P(t) - P(t - 5)]/5\}$ and it follows that $M(t, 5) = \{\bar{P}(t, T) - \bar{P}(t - 1, T)\}/5$. More precisely, show that in general for $k = T$:

$$M(t, k) = \{\bar{P}(t, T) - \bar{P}(t - 1, T)\}k$$

Given this result, what is the relationship between a momentum oscillator and a dual moving average oscillator?

7 Blau (1995, p. 13) makes the following statement: "Moving averages performed on prices introduce a lag. The longer the duration of the moving average, the greater is the lag. A 300-day moving average, for example, produces a tremendous amount of lag. *A single moving average performed on the momentum of price behaves in an altogether different manner. By contrast, the longer the duration of the moving average on momentum, the lower is the lag.* A 300-day moving average, for example, approximates a zero-lag situation. With emphasis, again: *A large moving average on momentum produces low lag price determination.*" Demonstrate the result that "the longer the duration of the moving average on momentum, the lower is the lag" and the result (Blau 1995, p. 14): "large moving averages of momentum . . . have, in the limit, the exact *shape* of price." (Hint: State the formula for an exponential moving average for price and substitute the formula of momentum for price.)

NOTES

1 The appearance of a chapter on technical analysis in a section on investment strategy may seem odd but, as discussed in chapter 10, market timing is an essential component of investment strategy. While applicable to both equity and fixed income security analysis, techniques of technical analysis are, arguably, more related to market timing strategies. If the speculative motivation for much of technical analysis is ignored, technical analysis is most appropriately discussed under "investment strategy."

2 The production of empirical results on technical analysis in modern Finance provides an interesting illustration of McCloskey's "conversations among academics." For example, a recent listing of eighteen studies, largely from the core journals of modern Finance, that provide either direct or indirect empirical support for technical analysis can be found in Lo et al. (2000, p. 1706). This list does not include the numerous studies outside the core journals of modern Finance, i.e., outside the conversation among strong adherents of modern Finance, that also provide support for technical analysis.

3 Wyckoff (1933, p. 105) quotes a newpaper reporter from the 1920s bemoaning "unwarranted market declines" caused "by purely mechanical interpretation of a meaningless set of lines" on "charts of professional stock traders."

4 There are a number of sources that do pay some attention to the history. For example, Kaufman (1978, chs 12–13) provides considerable background on the important, if unrecognized, individuals in the history of technical analysis such as: R.N. Elliot, developer of the "Elliot Wave Principle" based on Fibonnaci numbers, during the mid-1930s; the various systems developed by William Gann, starting in the mid-1930s and continuing until the 1950s; William Dunnigan, originator of "the thrust method," during the early 1950s; Eugene Nofri, originator of the "congestion-phase system;" Chester Keltner, originator of the "minor trend rule," during the late 1950s.

5 The statistical attack on technical analysis by academics can, arguably, be traced back to Cowles (1934) where the performance of the Hamilton version of the Dow theory is examined. As discussed in section 9.2, Cowles found

that returns from the Dow theory lagged the market which is inconsistent with the claim that the Dow theory can be used for market timing. Brown et al. (1998) reconsider Cowles' results and observe: "Cowles compares the returns obtained from Hamilton's market timing strategy to a benchmark of a fully invested stock portfolio. In fact, the Hamilton portfolio, as Cowles interprets it, is frequently out of the market. Adjustment for systematic risk appears to vindicate Hamilton as a market timer."

6 While there are a significant number of technical analysts on Wall Street, the preponderance of analysts are of the fundamental persuasion.

7 Kaufman (1978, p. 192) provides the following quote from R.N. Elliot, originator of the Elliot wave theory, that describes the epistemological approach of technical analysis: "Even though we may not understand the cause underlying a particular phenomenon, we can, by observation, predict the phenomenon's recurrence."

8 Practicing technical analysts are well-aware of the feedback problem. Consider the following statement from the Dow theorist, Richard Russell (Du Bois 2000): "I began publishing the Primary Trend Index (PTI) in 1971. It's a compilation of eight components that measure only market action. There's no subjective interpretation involved. I prefer not to name the components. If everybody followed the same ones in the same way, the PTI would lose its usefulness."

9 As discussed in section 9.3, the empirical evidence on the profitability of selling losers and buying winners is gathered from samples using returns that are generated over shorter time horizons, say one month, producing "under reaction" for periods up to one year. For returns generated over longer horizons, say a year or more, "over reaction" is reported where buying losers and selling winners becomes profitable.

10 A useful source on the history of the Dow theory is an article by Richard Russell that can be found on the website www.dowtheoryletters.com. The following discussion of Schaefer's approach to the Dow theory is based on Russell's discussion of Schaefer's advisory newsletters that is contained in that article. Edwards and Magee (1966, chs 3–5) has a useful overview of the main elements of the theory. This reference is to the fifth edition. There was not much change between this and the final seventh edition (1997) of this classic text.

11 Due to the presence of two brief tenures by others as *Wall Street Journal* editors following the death of Charles Dow, Hamilton was the fourth editor of the *Journal*. Hamilton held this position until his death in 1930.

12 Russell traces the bull market trend that ended in 1999 to a beginning in 1982 (Du Bois 2001). Much like Schaefer, the primary source of Russell's views on the Dow theory are an investment advisory newsletter – "Dow Theory Letters" – that Russell has produced continuously since 1958. Russell (1960) contains a collection of early newsletters. In addition to these sources, there a number of interviews and columns that have appeared in *Barron's*.

13 The possibility of a substantive change in the Dow theory was recognized by Richard Russell in an interview published in *Barron's* on June 12, 2000 (Du Bois 2000). Speaking of the first phase of the bear market that followed the change in primary market movement in May 1999, Russell observes: "In some ways, the current first phase is different from any other I've ever seen ... Because it has lasted longer, because many more individuals and institutions are involved ... and because a new phenomenon, the Internet, has emerged and is obviously changing the world. Then there's volatility. I've never seen anything like what we have now. Among the reasons for it are day-traders moving in and out of stocks." Structural changes such as the trading "circuit breakers" introduced following the market collapse of October 1987 may have altered the underlying dynamics sufficiently to prevent a strong signal for the end of a bear market to emerge.

14 The statement cannot be taken too literally. In general, it is not clear that technical analysts will move prices since technicians are not a homogeneous group. There are many different types of technical analysis and even analysts using the same approach may come up with conflicting buy and sell signals.

15 Observe that figures 9.4 and 9.5 are for futures prices, where the underlying commodity is a security index. This highlights the close connection between technical analysis in the commodity derivative markets and in the "cash market" for stocks and bonds. One service that does make extensive use of point and figure charts for stock analysis is Investor's Intelligence. Examples of point and figure charting for stocks can be viewed at the service website: www.investorsintelligence.com. Standard drawing of trend lines applies to point and figure charts in the same fashion as bar charts and candlestick charts. In addition, figures 9.4 and 9.5 are for futures prices. Because technical analysis is not limited to spot (cash) market trading, a number of important technical analysis sites are concerned with futures prices.

16 In addition to requiring considerable space for developing the requisite notions, there is also relatively little information available on the profitability of the various candlestick chart patterns. One study reported by Schwager (1996, pp. 296–305) provides results that "were not encouraging . . . The test . . . does not prove that candlestick charts have no value, but rather that a simplistic interpretation of candlestick patterns is not profitable." It seems that, like other forms of technical analysis, candlestick charts are sensitive to whether there is a trend or a trading range in the underlying price series.

17 Schwager (1996) is concerned with doing technical analysis for commodity futures contracts, not stocks. Following Edwards and Magee (1966, ch. 16), it is "true," in general, that techniques used in technical analysis of stocks and commodities are the same, as long as "proper allowance is made for intrinsic differences between commodity futures contracts and stocks and bonds." Included in these differences are: the limited life of individual futures contracts; the presence in futures markets of commercial traders involved in hedging which renders near-term support and resistance levels less effective for futures; the need to interpret volume differently and to account for open interest; and, the greater importance of certain news events such as droughts or flooding. Given these qualifications: "Under what might be called normal market conditions, those chart patterns which reflect trend changes in the most simple and logical fashion work just as well with commodities as with stocks." However, Edwards and Magee make an important qualification to this statement: "successful speculation in commodities requires far more specialized knowledge, demands more constant daily and hourly attention. The ordinary individual can hope to attain a fair degree of success in investing in securities by devoting only his spare moments to charts, but he might better shun commodity speculation unless he is prepared to make a career of it."

18 The distinction between a "trading range," a "rectangle" and a "consolidation" is not always clear. Following Edwards and Magee, a consolidation is a period of sideways movement in a trending market. Flags, pennants and wedges are consolidation formations, as are head-and-shoulders, scallops and saucers. Edwards and Magee (1966, p. 168) describe the rationale for consolidations: "An army that has pushed forward too rapidly, penetrated too far into enemy territory, suffered casualties and out-run its supplies, must halt eventually, perhaps retreat a bit to a more easily defended position and dig in, bring up replacements and establish a strong base from which later to launch a new attack. In the military parlance which we have all become more or less familiar these past few years, that process is known as *consolidating* one's gains." In other words, a consolidation is a "sidewise" chart pattern composed of minor fluctuations that continues until the market has "caught up to itself" and "is ready to go on again." In contrast to a consolidation, a "rectangle" "defines a contest between two groups of approximately equal strength . . . Nobody . . . can tell who is going to win until one line or the other is decisively broken." In effect, a rectangle more-or-less defines a trading range.

19 The use of two moving averages of different lengths to generate trading signals is a basic type of oscillator system, e.g., Schwager (1996, p. 524). Such systems are usually referred to as "dual moving average" or DMA systems. Oscillators are discussed in more detail in section 9.4.

20 The rise in the importance of breadth indicators is a relatively recent phenomenon. Edwards and Magee (1966), for example, do not examine breadth indicators. One example is the "breadth thrust" indicator developed by Martin Zweig, a frequent guest on *Wall Street Week* with L. Rukeyser.

21 Siegel (1998, ch. 5) is an exception. Siegel provides a brief discussion of Neill (1954) and overviews empirical evidence on a study of investor sentiment as captured in the indicator published by the investment advisory service Investor's Intelligence. This indicator is based on sentiment scoring of a large sample of market newsletters. Over a 35 year sample, the indicator was found to have "strong predictive power." However, Siegel (1998, p. 65) does contribute to the semantic confusion about "value investing" as a contrarian strategy: "Value investors are contrarians who believe that swings of optimism and pessimism about the market and individual stocks are frequently unjustified, so buying out of favor stocks is a winning strategy."

22 Approaching the impact of psychological factors on financial and economic events from a positivist perspective is not original to behavioral finance. For example, the interaction between psychology and economics is explored in Katona (1951), an early precursor of behavioral economics.

23 The three themes of behavioral finance proposed by Shefrin (2000) are not the only possible classification scheme for the subject. For example, Statman (1995) proposes four factors for behavioral finance: prospect theory; susceptibility to cognitive errors; aversion to regret; and imperfect self-control. Fisher and Statman (1999) provide an illustrative application of these four factors to the time diversification puzzle (see section 10.4).

24 In practice, the process of producing theoretical models is guided by "stylized facts" that have been identified in previous examinations of the data. This process of developing theoretical models from previously known empirical results and then testing those models as though there was no prior knowledge of the data has been explored by Leamer (1978). The progress of knowledge in economics and finance has been characterized by a variety of "specification searches" that are explored by Leamer.

25 Included in the more sophisticated group of technical indicators are techniques with appealing names such as Elliot waves, Bollinger bands, Moving Average Convergence–Divergence (MACD), Lane Stochastics, and Double-Smoothed Stochastics, e.g., Blau (1995).

26 Bierovic (1996, ch. 15 in Schwager 1996) observes that: "As early as the 1920's, technical analysts were creating oscillators to measure a market's momentum rather than limiting their efforts to determining the market's trend." However, no references are given. It is likely that Bierovic is referring to the introduction of "dual moving average" techniques. Recognizing that the more general term "oscillator" includes momentum as a special case, the logic of momentum analysis does have a long history.

27 McCloskey (1984, 1995) provided a general discussion of the rhetoric of economics and Finance, identifying how much of the persuasion used in modern Finance is targeted at "conversations between academics" that take place in selected academic journals. Jegadeesh and Titman (2001, p. 701) provides an interesting example of this discussion: "Because there are potentially large payoffs to any viable model that predicts stock returns (in terms of publications and/or money management revenues) many academics and practitioners have, no doubt, independently tested a wide variety of trading strategies." Putting aside the questionable empirical validity of the statement, the connection between "large payoffs" for academics and "publications" (presumably in the appropriate journals) is difficult to avoid.

28 Appel is a well-known technical analyst, publisher of the newsletter *Systems and Forecasts*, as well as a number of books on technical analysis, e.g., Appel and Zweig (1976), Appel (1974).

Chapter Summary

Chapter 10   *Investment Strategy*

10.1   Investment Strategy: Basic Concepts
Whose investment strategy?
The Dow Ten and dividend yield strategies
The hedge fund approach

10.2   Tactical and Strategic Asset Allocation
Strategic asset allocation and two fund separation
What is tactical asset allocation?
Cash management and dollar cost averaging

10.3   Investment Strategy for Value Investors
The Graham, Dodd and Cottle approach
The Warren Buffett approach
Practical investment strategy for individual value investors

10.4   Advanced Topics in Investment Strategy*
The interior decorator fallacy and other confusions*
The fallacy of large numbers and growth optimal portfolios*
Behavioral portfolio theory: Keynesian investment strategy?*

Questions
Notes

* Indicates section or sub-section contains advanced material

chapter 10 Investment Strategy

10.1 INVESTMENT STRATEGY: BASIC CONCEPTS

Whose investment strategy?

At numerous points in this book it has been observed that semantics, the meanings of words, are too often ignored in discussing topics in Finance. Important words – such as "fundamental analysis," "value investing," "growth stock" – can be interpreted in a number of ways. Even though specific words being used can have different meanings, the words are interpreted as having one precise meaning by the individual or text using the word.[1] A related semantic problem is encountered in other situations where more than one word is being used to identify the same general concept. This is the case with "investment strategy." Alternative references to this concept include "investment policy," "portfolio management" and "asset allocation strategy." Well specified distinctions between these words are not available. The terminology selected to describe the underlying concept is often associated with a particular approach to Finance. For example, "portfolio management" or "asset allocation strategy" is the terminology commonly used in modern Finance, e.g., Campbell and Viceira (2002), Bodie et al. (1999), while "investment policy" is more commonly used in old Finance, e.g., Graham, Dodd and Cottle (1962) (GDC, ch. 5).

Because the term *investment strategy* is not commonly attached to any particular approach, this is the terminology adopted in this book to describe the various approaches to selecting combinations of securities that form an investment portfolio. Investment strategy is an essential adjunct to security analysis, which is concerned with determining the value of individual securities. Because investment strategy is a dynamic decision, determination of portfolio value weights at a point in time, and varying of the value weights over time, falls within the scope of investment strategy. As a consequence, there are both short-term and long-term elements of the investment strategy decision. The "modern portfolio theory" that is at the core of modern Finance is concerned almost exclusively with investment strategy. The closely related notions of tactical asset allocation and strategic asset allocation are other examples of such "top down" investment strategies. In contrast, a "bottom up" investment strategy is where security analysis takes the central role, such as in the GDC approach. In bottom up approaches, the portfolio composition is determined through the incremental process of doing valuations on individual securities.

Whatever the terminology, the importance of the investment strategy decision is difficult to deny. For example, Lummer and Riepe (1994) observe: "Any security-specific selection decision is preceded, either implicitly or explicitly, by an asset allocation decision. Asset allocation is therefore the most fundamental of investment decisions." Brinson et al. (1991) estimate that for comparable portfolios, the strategic asset allocation decision – the long-term asset mix – is responsible for 91.5% of the variation in portfolio returns for a sample of 91 large US pension plans. The Brinson et al. result has generated considerable debate both within modern Finance, e.g., Statman (2001), and among practitioners, e.g., Jahnke (1997), Renkenthaler (1999), about various aspects of investment strategy. This involves assessing the relative importance of the long-term asset allocation mix versus portfolio rebalancing around that mix, subject to the cash management requirements of the investment portfolio.[2] Using a sample of UK pension plans, Blake et al. (1999) confirm and expand the results of Brinson et al., raising legitimate questions about the prevailing investment strategy practices of pension fund managers. There is a demonstrated need to extend these results to different institutional situations and wider asset mixes, e.g., including higher fractions of foreign assets.

While there is an ongoing, largely academic debate about the relative importance of the different aspects of investment strategy, Arnott (1998, p. 162) reflects the commonly held view of practitioners: "It is often said that asset allocation is the most important decision that an investment manager or fund sponsor faces. It is conventional wisdom, and is demonstrated in academic journals, that asset allocation has more influence on aggregate portfolio returns than any other single decision." Whether such statements are justified is difficult to determine in practice, if only because the effectiveness of a particular investment strategy decision cannot be accurately determined *ex ante*. Studies such as Blake et al. (1999) are limited by having to make assessments based on *ex post* performance. Conclusions such as security selection is a "zero expected-excess-return activity" (Blake et al. 1999, p. 459) have to be tempered by the specifics of the Blake et al. sample. In addition, the security selection strategies of, say, value investors also have implications in the realm of investment strategy, e.g., the process of buying undervalued securities and selling overvalued securities complements the tactical asset allocation decision. While specific pension plans may be ineffective at selecting securities, it is difficult to maintain that this is generally the case.

Analysis of investment strategy has progressed considerably from the early prognostications of the old Finance reflected in GDC. Though primarily concerned with security selection, GDC did give some attention to investment strategy. The essence of "investment strategy" as stated by GDC (p. 59) is: "the allocation of the available funds among the various types of securities, including variations in such proportions under changing conditions and decisions to hold cash for future commitments." This general statement still applies but the various aspects of investment strategy are now more explicitly identified and examined (see section 3.3). In particular, investment strategy is now considered to involve three related types of decisions (see section 10.2 for more precise definitions and detailed discussion): "*strategic asset allocation,*" where long-term portfolio composition objectives are determined; "*tactical asset allocation*," that involves portfolio rebalancing and investment timing decisions; and, *cash management*, which often involves the satisfaction of minimum cash balance requirements and other liquidity considerations.[3] Security analysis is considered to be an input to these three types of decisions.

Given this decomposition of investment strategy into three related decisions, modern Finance dedicates considerable attention to modeling the various aspects of the optimal investment strategy decision. Because there are a range of investors with different investment strategy objectives, there cannot be a unique optimal solution to the investment strategy decision problem applicable to all investors. However, by classifying investors into rough groupings, it is possible to identify significant differences in the decision problem that require solution. These differences impose constraints on the types of solutions that can be selected. For example: insurance companies are subject to restrictions on the quality of securities that can be purchased; or, due to capital and reserve requirements imposed by regulators, commercial banks have to hold a significant fraction of liquid or near liquid assets; or, due to the aggregate value of funds under management, large institutional investors have to purchase more than a small number of securities. Subject to such institutional constraints, the approach to investment strategy that is selected will depend on philosophical differences between fund managers, investors and the like about, say, the handling of uncertainty in security returns.

For purposes of analyzing the investment strategy decision, owners of securities can be roughly divided into two groups: individuals; and institutions. Institutions can be further subdivided according to *the degree of regulatory controls* on portfolio composition. Institutions subjected to wide ranging control include life insurance companies, depository institutions and certain types of trust funds. Fire and casualty insurance companies are subject to a lesser degree of regulatory control, with mutual funds, investment funds, commingled trusts and pension funds subject to the lowest level of regulatory control. This is not to imply that, say, a mutual fund is not subject to regulations on investment strategy. In addition to the legally binding fund prospectus that provides a general description of the investment strategy of the fund, the investment activities of the fund will be subjected to the range of legislation enforced by the SEC, state–blue-sky laws and so on. However, these controls are relatively light compared to the restrictions imposed on, say, depository institutions where there are restrictions on ownership of equity securities, fraction of assets invested in liquid securities needed to satisfy capital and reserve requirements and so on.

Turning to *investment strategy for individual investors*, there is also considerable diversity. At one extreme are the small individual investors dependent on the cash flows from an investment portfolio to pay day-to-day expenses. Such investors are driven by necessity to follow an investment strategy with characteristics that are not much different from that of, say, a life insurance company: conservative, primarily invested in high quality bonds that have little or no risk of capital loss.[4] Another type of individual investor with a specialized investment strategy would be the high net worth individual seeking to gain a tax advantage from trading in securities with favorable tax treatment, such as municipal bonds. Ignoring these special cases, GDC (p. 66) suggest decomposing individual investors into *defensive investors* and *enterprising investors*:

It would be most useful, we think, to classify [individual] security buyers into two groups – defensive investors and aggressive or enterprising investors. Defensive investors are those who should place their chief emphasis upon freedom from effort, annoyance and the necessity for making frequent investment decisions. The great majority of individual investors belong in the defensive category. Their specific training and experience with bonds and stocks are not adequate to warrant making independent decisions about the selection of securities ... The distinguishing feature of [enterprising investors] is their willingness and ability to devote time and care to the selection of sound and attractive investments. Their chief objective should be by training, intelligence and guidance to take advantage of the numerous opportunities in normal markets to buy securities for considerably less than they are worth.

For GDC, writing prior to the widespread availability of low management expense ratio index funds, the defensive investor with no cash management restrictions could hold a portfolio of equity investment (mutual) fund shares and US government bonds with the investment mix varying between (25% to 75%) equity and (75% to 25%) fixed income depending on the "subjective feeling" of the investor. The portfolios of the enterprising investor would follow the prescriptions of "intrinsic value" investing set out in chapters 7–9 of this book.

There has been considerable progress in the analysis of investment strategy since GDC. If modern Finance has made a single outstanding practical contribution beyond the realm of derivative security valuation, this contribution is asset allocation strategies. Starting from Markowitz and continuing to the present, the portfolio management problem, together with solutions derived using mean-variance optimization, has been a centerpiece for the teachings of modern Finance (see section 2.4 and chapter 3). More recently, this basic theory has been dressed up and repackaged in various forms under the guise of asset allocation strategies. Recognizing that there is a considerable diversity across investors leads to specific analysis of the long-term "strategic asset allocation" decision, e.g., Campbell and Viceira (2002). Because strategic asset allocation only deals with long-term solutions, considerations of market timing and portfolio rebalancing also need to be addressed. This falls within the scope of tactical asset allocation. Finally, the solutions to both strategic and tactical asset allocation depend on the types of asset classes that are being considered for inclusion in the portfolio, e.g., large capitalization (cap) stocks, small cap stocks, mortgage-backed securities, corporate bonds, and real estate. Allowing investment in international assets considerably complicates the asset allocation problem. These issues are examined in section 10.2.

The Dow Ten and dividend yield strategies

Investment strategies can take a wide variety of forms. In some cases, the investment strategy is intimately related to a strongly held investment philosophy. This could be the case with the "top down" investment strategies associated with modern Finance that systematically develop approaches to strategic and tactical asset allocation (see section 10.2). In this spirit, a top down investment strategy details an approach to security selection that either does not involve security analysis or incorporates security analysis at a later stage in the decision process. This investment strategy category can also be expanded to include mechanical methods of dealing with the common stock investment decision that do not directly involve security analysis but leave strategic asset decisions, such as the split between stocks and bonds, unresolved. One example of such a strategy is the *"Dogs of the Dow"* or "Dow Ten" (Dow 10) strategy that recommends buying the ten highest dividend yielding stocks from the Dow-Jones Industrial Average.[5] In this case, the investment strategy is driven by a security selection method that does not involve security analysis – other than calculation of the dividend yield. No consideration is given to the strategic asset mix, company earnings or whatever. The tactical allocation strategy is to change the portfolio whenever stocks enter and leave the Dow Ten list.

For purposes of assessing the Dow Ten strategy it is expedient to assume that the strategic asset allocation is 100% invested in equities, though this is not essential. Siegel (1998, p. 65) describes the history of the strategy:[6]

> The Dow 10 strategy, which calls for investors to buy the ten highest-yielding stocks in the Dow-Jones Industrial Average, has been regarded as one of the most successful investment strategies of all time. James Glassman of the *Washington Post* claimed that John Slatter, a Cleveland investment advisor and writer, invented the Dow 10 system in the 1980's. Harvey Knowles III and Damon Perry analyzed and praised the system in their book, the *Dividend Investor* written in 1992, as did Michael O'Higgins and John Downes in *Beating the Dow*.

In an odd twist, Siegel attempts to classify the Dow Ten theory as a form of value investing:

> The basic theory behind the Dow 10 strategy is grounded in "value investing." Value investors are contrarians who believe that the swings of optimism and pessimism about the market and individual stocks are frequently unjustified, so buying out-of-favor stocks is a winning strategy. Since firms reduce cash dividend payouts infrequently, stocks with a high dividend yield are often those that have fallen in price and are out of favor with investors. For this reason, the Dow 10 strategy is often called the "dogs of the Dow."

Ignoring the apparent semantic confusion over what constitutes value investing, Siegel is compelled to provide an explanation for the success of the Dow 10 that is reported. This explanation is found in the modern Finance interpretation of "value investing."

According to Siegel (1998, pp. 66–7) the Dow 10 strategy has had a stellar historical performance: "The Dow 10 strategy has outperformed both the overall Dow and the S&P 500 Index in every decade except the 1930's, besting the Dow 30 by an average of 3.26 percent per year and the S&P 500 Index by an even larger 3.7 percent per year since 1939." Siegel is unambiguous about the empirical track record of the Dow 10 strategy:

> You might think that these spectacular returns were achieved with higher risk, but that is not the case. The standard deviation of annual returns on the Dow 10 strategy was actually lower than the Dow 30 and only slightly more than the S&P 500 Stock Index. And the Dow 10 was spectacular during the 1973–74 bear market. During those two years when the Dow 30 was down by 26.5 percent and the S&P Index was down 37.3 percent, the Dow 10 strategy actually gained 2.9 percent!

Siegel also provides reasons for why the Dow 10 strategy "worked." This enthusiasm stands in stark contrast to the empirical results of Hirschey (2000) where the Dogs of the Dow strategy is referred to as a "myth." By finding evidence for a similar dividend-yield effect on the Toronto Stock Exchange ("Canadian dogs"), Visscher and Fillbeck (2003) provide evidence that the essence of the Dow 10 strategy is related to dividend payout by high market capitalization firms and not to specific characteristics of the Dow-Jones Industrial Index. Visscher and Fillbeck also report considerable market interest in "Euro dog" funds based on securities traded on the London, Frankfurt, Paris and Amsterdam exchanges.

The conflicting views over the past performance of the Dow 10 strategy would seem to be resolvable. The search for such a resolution motivated McQueen et al. (1997) but the goal was found to be illusive. Using a 50 year sample, results for the Dow 10 strategy were mixed. Though the crude return results of 3 percent plus per annum above the Dow described by Siegel are confirmed, when adjustment is made for transaction costs, tax implications and the increase in risk due to the loss of diversification inherent in comparing the Dow 10 with the 30 stock DJIA, the gain was less than 1 percent. Using a 1961–98 sample, Hirschey (2000) goes farther and finds that after adjustment for rebalancing costs and taxes there is no significant difference between the performance of the Dow 10 and the DJIA. Given the central role of empirical verification in logical positivism, the conflicting views over the performance of dividend-yield strategies, in general, and the Dow 10 strategy, in particular, is puzzling. Surely an empirical issue about the *ex post* performance of an investment strategy such as the Dow 10 is resolvable by an examination of past data?

The recognition that the Dow 10 strategy is a specific case of a ***dividend yield strategy*** is significant, if only because a connection is established to the empirical results in modern Finance concerning "value stocks." Along with a low price to book ratio and low *P/E* ratio, the dividend yield is one of the metrics that modern Finance uses to define a value stock. Visscher and Fillbeck (2003) provide the following summary of this research:

> The effectiveness of dividend yield strategies in enhancing portfolio returns has been debated for many years. Some studies have suggested that little or no relationship exists between dividend yield and share price returns (Black and Scholes 1974; Goetzmann and Jorion 1993, 1995). Many other studies, however, have identified a positive relationship between dividend yield and share price (Fama and French 1988; Hodrick 1992; Grant 1995). Benjamin Graham (see Rea 1977) reported an average compound growth rate between 1925 and 1975 of 19.5 percent for US stocks that had a dividend yield greater than two-thirds of the AAA bond yield, compared with a 7.5 percent return for the DJIA.

This largely empirical debate is accompanied by a related theoretical debate over the appropriate functional form for the relationship between dividend yields and stock returns. This debate revolved around the question of whether there was a U-shaped relationship where companies with high dividend yields and companies paying no dividends outperform companies with dividend yields lying between the extremes, e.g., Elton et al. (1983), Christie (1990).

Putting aside the semantic confusion arising from differing interpretations of value stocks and value investing, the empirical evidence assembled in modern Finance concerning value stocks, including those with high dividend yield, indicates the rudiments of a potentially profitable investment strategy.[7] Considerable attention in modern Finance has been given to the problem of designing practical investment strategies from core theories, such as those based on quadratic optimization techniques. For example, Grauer and Hakansson (1993, 1998) develop the *empirical probability assessment approach* where an appropriately specified quadratic optimization problem for portfolio returns is solved each rebalancing period using parameters that are re-estimated each period using a moving sample window. Similarly, the "value investing" approach of modern Finance (not to be confused with the value investing approach of old Finance) is based on a sorting approach. At each rebalancing point, the universe of common stocks is sorted and stocks that have a high weighted scoring based on the chosen value factors are selected. More precisely, the highest decile or quartile of stocks is chosen and held until the next rebalancing date. The scoring system is based on weights determined from empirical estimation of an appropriate multi-factor regression or factor analytic model

The hedge fund approach

The derivative securities industry, both in the US and globally, is immense. The industry continues to grow into new areas and offer a bewildering array of new products. Significant derivative security trading activity takes place in a variety of geographical locations around the globe and is subject to an ad hoc and sometimes competing collection of regulators and regulations. This situation is exacerbated by the competing venues in which derivatives are traded. Futures exchanges scattered around the globe compete for business while the OTC market continues to proliferate new derivative products. In addition to direct trading of derivative securities, the intellectual technology of derivatives trading has also permeated the cash markets, as evidenced by the introduction of trading techniques such as dynamic portfolio insurance (see section 3.4). In addition to dynamic trading in securities markets, a wide variety of possible distributional shapes for the portfolio return can be obtained by combining a securities position with a position in derivative securities. These positions are typically written with the security or some related security as the underlying commodity for delivery on the derivative security (e.g., Poitras 2002, ch. 6). Though of considerable interest, strategies combining securities positions with derivative positions are described in considerable detail elsewhere and will not be examined in any detail here.

Before the recent renaissance in derivative security trading, various forms of restrictions, legal and otherwise, were imposed on the use and availability of derivatives. Historical roots of these restrictions can be found in the speculative abuses associated with these products (Poitras 2000, ch. 9; Poitras 2002, ch. 1). The use of options has, at various times, been singled out for specific restrictions. In the absence of direct trading of derivative products, securities markets have often developed trading techniques that have essential features of a derivative security. *Short selling* is one such activity. While a short position in, say, a forward contract on the DJIA involves entering into a forward contract, a short sale would involve entering into a short sale agreement with the lender of the 30 component stocks. The sale and later repurchase of the DJIA stocks will generate cash flows that will likely involve further securities trading. The essential feature of the forward contract and the short sale is the creation of a position that will generate profit from a fall in the security price. However, as a consequence of the cash flow differences between a short sale and a short forward contract, it is often not practical to use the short sale to directly hedge an underlying securities position.

The short sale has a checkered history. For example, various edicts in seventeenth-century Holland banned the sale of a commodity for forward delivery not owned by the seller at the time the forward contract was created. This included company shares. As a legacy of this history, a range of restrictions, such as the "up tick" rule, still restrict short sellers in US markets. Individual investors often face restrictions on the ability to access the funds earned from the sale of securities. Where such access is available, it is possible to pursue hedge-fund-like investment strategies. By being short in one security (commodity) and long in another security (commodity), the profit functions for such strategies are similar in intuition to inter-commodity futures spread trades (Poitras 2002, ch. 3). However, there is an additional component of the profit function for a hedge fund related to the cash flows from the securities positions and the amount of capital invested in the fund. In combination with the capital size, the degree of leveraging determines the aggregate size of fund assets. By explicitly introducing over-valued securities into the universe of available opportunities, the hedge fund would seem to be a conceptual advance over traditional long-only funds.

Though the hedge fund concept appears to be a natural outlet for the GDC approach to value investing, there are practical reasons why GDC use the long-only approach. For example, there are the informational requirements associated with researching securities that are short selling opportunities. Such securities will almost certainly lie outside the universe of "100 or so primary stocks" that GDC use in selecting a long-only portfolio. Restricting short selling opportunities to the same securities as are considered for the long-only portfolio presents problems. Because most of these securities are selected due to the positive prospects, there will not be many short selling opportunities. In addition, secular market movements may cause bunching where most of the securities appear as short selling opportunities at much the same time. Another complication occurs with the types of strategies that fall within the hedge fund concept. The basic idea of leveraging fund capital using short sales can be extended to other commodities than securities, though there are liquidity and other factors that make securities an attractive trading vehicle for hedge fund purposes.

In a sense, the essence of a hedge fund is inherent in the process of financial intermediation, though it is not helpful to stretch this analogy too far. For example, viewed as a hedge fund a commercial bank is short demand and time deposits and long commercial loans. Price changes appear over time as changes in interest rates on liabilities and assets. However, unlike many actual hedge funds, commercial banks primarily aim to generate profits off the cash flows associated with the appropriately adjusted interest rate spread on the assets and liabilities, rather than on changes in prices. This analogy with a commercial bank does illustrate the range of possible strategies that could be pursued by hedge funds. Profitability could originate from a correct assessment of the long position, with the short position serving to leverage the fund's capital. As such, the class of hedge fund strategists would include a two fund separator that is borrowing at the risk free rate and purchasing additional units of the market portfolio. Bond traders that are speculating on changes in yield curve shape will typically short the expensive and buy the cheap parts of the yield curve. This is also a potential hedge fund strategy.

Caldwell (1995) traces *the beginnings of the modern hedge fund industry* to 1949 when Alfred Jones (1901–1989) set up a general partnership operating a fund with the requisite elements.[8] Prior to establishing this fund, Jones had led a full life. In addition to earning a Ph.D. in sociology from Columbia University in 1941, Jones was an associate editor for *Fortune* and a business writer for *Time* and other publications. Prior to being in the publishing industry, Jones had traveled the world, including a tour as vice consul at the US embassy in Berlin during the early days of Hitler's reign. Apparently, it was the research that Jones did for an article published by *Fortune* in March 1949 that provided the foundation for the establishment of his hedge fund. The research involved Jones interviewing many of the important players on Wall Street. The basic strategy guiding the fund was to combine short selling and leverage to create a relatively conservative investment portfolio aimed at capturing stock picking opportunities. At the time, this was a novel approach, given that both leverage and short sales were generally used to increase return variability, not reduce variability. Jones went beyond this to develop a measure of market exposure for his fund. The result was the first of the *market neutral* hedge funds.

Caldwell (1995, p. 7) describes the Jones approach to fund management:

> Jones regularly calculated the exposure of his capital to market risk . . . His method of quantifying market exposure is highly valued by traditional hedge fund managers for its intuitive relevance, yet it is largely ignored or misunderstood by academics and the financial media.

$$\text{Market exposure} = (\text{Long Exposure} - \text{Short Exposure})/\text{Capital}$$

> A typical asset allocation for Jones would look like this: Given $1,000 in capital, he would employ leverage to purchase shares valued at $1,100 and sell shares short valued at $400. His gross investment of $1,500 (150 percent of capital) would have a net market exposure of only $700 ($1,100 − $400), making this portfolio "70 percent net long." Although Jones valued stock picking over market timing, he increased or decreased the net market exposure of his portfolio based on his estimation of the strength of the market. Since the market generally rose, Jones was generally "net long."

As with other modern hedge funds, the Jones fund had an uncommonly high management fee. Though there was no high water marks or loss pay-backs, the 20% of realized profits to the general partner is in the realm of more recent arrangements. Also similar to recent hedge funds, Jones kept his entire investment capital in the fund, providing a strong managerial incentive for positive performance.

Jones introduced another innovation in 1954, reducing fund risk by bringing in other fund managers to run part of the portfolio, effectively starting the fund-of-funds approach to hedge fund management. Though there was oversight to ensure that duplication and cancellation was not happening, managers were given wide latitude to make investment decisions. Over the years, Jones would have as many as eight managers working the fund-of-funds portfolio. With this move, the Jones fund became an incubator for new hedge fund creation. Two of his early fund managers, Dick Ratcliffe and Carl Jones, eventually moved on to start their own hedge funds, Ratcliffe establishing Fairfield Partners in 1965 and C. Jones establishing City Associates in 1964. Certain elements of hedge fund structure were adapted by other funds. For example, the notion of hedge fund management fees, i.e., incentive-based partnership agreements, was adopted by, among others, Warren Buffett with Buffett Partners and Walter Schloss with WJS Partners. Though possessing some elements of hedge funds, these two funds did not regularly use short sales to create market neutral positions.

Caldwell (1995, p. 9) identifies another turning point in hedge fund history as the publication of an article by C. Loomis in *Fortune* magazine in April 1966. This article detailed the performance of the Jones fund, demonstrating that this fund was easily the best performing fund over the previous five years, even when account was taken of the 20% management fees. Loomis also provided a reasonably accurate description of how the Jones fund was run. Fuelled on the demand side by sudden investor demand for such investment vehicles and on the supply side by fund managers attracted by the high management fees, the result was a wave of new hedge funds being created (Caldwell 1995, p. 10):

> Although we don't know how many hedge funds were established in the three-year flurry following Loomis's article, estimates range from 140 to several hundred. Michael Steinhardt and George Soros were among those setting up funds at this time. The SEC found 215 investment partnerships in a survey for the year ending 1968 and concluded that 140 of these were hedge funds, with the majority formed that year.

The market contraction which started at the end of 1968 and continued until the end of 1974 demonstrated that there was considerably more to running a hedge fund than desire and marketing. Considering just the 28 largest US hedge funds at year end 1968, within two years there had been five funds shut down, with fund asset values down 70% due to losses and withdrawals.

Some hedge funds survived the tough years between 1968 and 1974 while others foundered. Why? There are no detailed empirical studies of hedge fund strategies during this period. Hedge funds are closely held and such information was and is difficult to obtain. Anecdotal evidence is strongly in favor of the hypothesis that most fund managers did not adequately establish sufficient short positions. Many so-called hedge funds were decidedly long, not market neutral. In effect, these "hedge funds" were more like traditional mutual funds, only with the high performance fees. Since the early 1970s, there has been a veritable explosion in the complexity, availability and variety of securities, including the introduction of a range of relatively complex derivative securities associated with financial commodities. This technological progress in the security design arena has been accompanied by the perception that there has been similar progress in the portfolio management and risk management systems that use these products. However, as evidenced by a string of high profile corporate collapses, "derivative debacles," and the like, this progress has also been accompanied by a systemic and partially uncontrollable increase in a range of manipulations that have exploited the leveraging potential of derivative security contracts.

It is not surprising that the renaissance in derivative securities has seen a remarkable resurgence of hedge funds. The *Report* of the President's Working Group on Financial Markets (1999) (PWGFM) investigating the collapse of Long Term Capital Management (LTCM) in 1998 makes the following observations about the growth in the hedge fund industry:[9]

> A 1968 survey by the Securities and Exchange Commission identified 140 hedge funds operating at that time. During the last two decades, however, the hedge fund industry has grown substantially. Although it is difficult to estimate precisely the size of the industry, a number of estimates indicate that as of mid-1998 there were between 2,500 and 3,500 hedge funds managing between $200 billion and $300 billion in capital with approximately $800 billion to $1 trillion in total assets. Collectively, hedge funds remain relatively small when compared to other sectors of the US financial markets. At the end of 1998, for instance, commercial banks had $4.1 trillion in total assets; mutual funds had assets of approximately $5 trillion; private pension funds had $4.3 trillion; state and local retirement funds had $2.3 trillion; and insurance companies had assets of $3.7 trillion.

Armed with the new risk management technologies, such as value-at-risk, a number of new style hedge funds actively use derivatives to leverage underlying capital. There is a substantial number of hedge fund strategies in place, only a small fraction of which are similar to the Jones model. Others, such as LTCM, are creatures of the renaissance in derivative securities.

The growth in the hedge fund industry has increased both the visibility and availability of information about hedge funds. For example, MARhedge is an important source of information, data and news about the hedge fund industry.[10] Data available through MARhedge has been thoroughly examined in Ackermann et al. (1999). In order to provide some degree of organization to the mis-mash of hedge fund strategies, MARhedge (www.MARhedge.com) classifies hedge funds into eight broad categories: *global macro funds* that take positions on changes in global economic conditions in equity, FX and debt markets using derivatives, including index derivatives, and leverage; *global funds* that are similar to macro funds but targeted at specific regions, often involving stock picking; *long-only (US opportunistic) funds* that are like traditional equity funds but with the hedge fund characteristics of leveraging and incentive fees for managers – listed strategies for these funds include the traditional value, growth and short-term trading approaches; *market-neutral funds* where the basic objective is to be long in one group of securities and short in another group, such that market risk is controlled or neutralized – this group would include the Jones funds as well as conversion arbitrages, derivative security arbitrages and, fixed income arbitrages, such as the long off-the-run

Treasuries and short on-the-run Treasuries strategy; *sectoral hedge funds* that have an industry focus including short-sale funds, which short sell over-valued securities, investing the balance in indexes or fixed income securities; *event-driven funds* that target special situations such as distressed securities of firms in reorganization or bankruptcy as well risk trading in takeovers that involve buying the target and selling the acquirer; *short sales funds* where the fund is positioned to benefit from market declines including funds that are index driven and those based on stock picking; and, the *fund of hedge funds* approach that may involve leveraging to acquire positions in the individual funds. Within each of these general groupings, a variety of different strategies could be pursued. Similarly, some funds may be involved in activities covering more than one fund category.

The large number of possible hedge fund strategies raises legitimate questions about how the term "hedge fund" is defined. As indicated, the term is generic, being used to describe a variety of different fund strategies that loosely share some similar characteristics. The PWGFM (p. 40) defines the term "to refer to a variety of pooled investment vehicles that are not registered under the federal securities laws as investment companies, broker-dealers, or public corporations." Both of these features, pooled investment vehicle and absence of registration, are important to identifying whether a given fund qualifies as a hedge fund. More precisely, in order to avoid the registration requirements specified under US federal securities laws for securities companies, hedge funds have to be privately structured and closely held. As such, the primary investors in hedge funds are high net worth individuals and institutional investors. Recently, certain fund operators have been successful in extending the market for hedge funds to smaller individual investors, e.g., minimum investment floor of $25,000. This has usually been accomplished by pursuing a fund-of-funds strategy and then registering that fund with the SEC.

Hedge funds are not the only securities that seek *specific exemptions from US securities laws*. For example, venture capital pools, asset securitization vehicles, family estate planning vehicles and investment clubs can receive such treatment. While it would seem sensible for a defining feature of hedge funds to be the types of strategies which the funds pursue there is so much variation in this area that it is difficult to isolate specific elements that apply to all hedge funds other than to say that the strategies usually involve a combination of long and short positions, including leveraging. Hedge funds are not conventional investment vehicles. Investor liquidity is often compromised with "lock-up periods of one year for initial investors and subsequent restrictions on withdrawals to quarterly intervals" (Ackermann et al. 1999, p. 834). The regulatory exemptions that hedge funds work under severely restricts the ability of hedge funds to advertise. Another untypical feature of hedge funds concerns their management (Ackermann et al. 1999):

> Hedge funds are . . . characterized by strong performance incentives. On average, hedge fund managers receive a 1 percent annual management fee and 14 percent of the annual profits. For most funds this bonus incentive fee is paid only if the returns surpass some hurdle rate or "high-water mark" – meaning there is no incentive fee until the fund has recovered from past losses. Although incentive fees and high-water marks could lead to

excess risk taking under some conditions, there are countervailing forces that may dampen risk. Hedge fund managers often invest a substantial amount of their own money in the fund. Furthermore, the managers of US hedge funds are general partners, so they may incur substantial liability if the fund goes bankrupt.

Perhaps the closest security comparable to a hedge fund are the shares in managed futures funds and commodity pools that have been traded for many years.

In contrast to mutual funds which have been and continue to be intensively studied, hedge funds have only started to receive attention relatively recently, though work on managed futures funds and commodity pools, which started somewhat earlier, is also applicable, e.g., Irwin and Brorsen (1985), Elton, Gruber and Rentzler (1987), Cornew (1988), Irwin et al. (1993), Edwards and Caglayan (2001). Some useful recent studies directly on hedge funds include Fung and Hseih (2000, 2002), Brown et al. (1999), Schneeweiss and Spurgin (1998), Ackermann et al. (1999), Liang (2000), Brown et al. (2001), Gregoriou (2002) and Goetzmann et al. (2003). A useful observation about studies of hedge fund performance is given by Caldwell (1995, p. 13):

> Considerable caution must be used when reviewing performance statistics for the hedge fund industry and its various segments. Even the best statistics are skewed by asset weighting (or lack thereof), voluntary selection and a strong survivorship bias. It's highly unlikely that hedge fund performance statistics accurately reflect the true, weighted average return to investors for any segment of this industry.

Though more recent studies have come some of the way to correcting these difficulties, e.g., Fung and Hseih (2002), there is still considerable uncertainly about how to measure and assess hedge fund performance. Gregoriou (2002) also reports: "The median (half-life) survival time of all hedge funds is exactly 5.50 years. It is found, however, that millions managed, redemption period, performance fee, leverage, monthly returns and minimum purchase have an impact on the mortality of hedge funds. It is also found that certain hedge fund classifications experience higher survival times than others."

What role can hedge funds play in the investment strategy of an individual investor? For a number of reasons, this practical question is difficult to answer. Because a large number of hedge funds operate under exemptions in US securities laws that restrict the allowable number of investors, such funds are not feasible investments for small investors due to the large initial investment (in the millions of dollars) that is required. Hedge funds that are publicly traded and feature an initial investment as small as, say, $25,000, are currently structured with the fund-of-funds approach. This creates difficulties for the small investor seeking to monitor the holdings of the various hedge funds contained in the mingled fund that is purchased. In addition, even for investors capable of making direct investment into individual hedge funds, due to the large number of hedge fund strategies it is difficult to make generalizations about hedge fund performance. However, intuition suggests that a form of MM1 (see section 2.4) will apply to hedge funds, significantly reducing the potential abnormal returns that would accrue to this type of investment.[11]

10.2 TACTICAL AND STRATEGIC ASSET ALLOCATION

Strategic asset allocation and two fund separation

Asset allocation involves determining the asset mix for a specific portfolio. As discussed in section 10.1, the asset allocation decision is a precursor to the security selection decision. Strategic asset allocation is a key first step that professional investment advisors take in the process of establishing new account parameters for unsophisticated investors. The new client is asked a range of questions regarding income level, risk tolerance, age, expected retirement age and the like. The types of questions asked are much the same across investment advisory firms. The end result is typically some target percentages for equity and fixed income holdings that will likely be slowly changed as the individual investor ages and the contribution levels to the portfolio change. This process is guided by the intuition that bonds are "safe" and equities are "risky." Investors approaching retirement with low levels of risk tolerance are directed to portfolios that are heavily weighted to fixed income while those investors that are younger and have a higher level of risk tolerance are funneled into portfolios heavily weighted to equities. Despite the practical importance of such asset allocation strategies, Elton and Gruber (2000, p. 27) observe: "almost no attention has been paid [by academics] to examining advice regarding the asset allocation decision."

Canner et al. (1997) initiated a discussion about the inconsistency between central propositions of modern Finance, such as the capital asset pricing model and the two fund separation theorem (see chapter 2), and the strategic asset allocation advice conventionally provided by professional investment advisors. In particular, the *two fund separation* theorem requires that the asset composition of the risky tangency portfolio – the market portfolio – is the same for all investors. Differences in risk tolerance across investors are handled by altering the value weights allocated to the riskless asset and the risky tangency portfolio. Hence, the ratio of stocks to bonds will not change across investors. This is inconsistent with the conventional strategic asset allocation advice of professional investment advisors. However, as Elton and Gruber (2000) illustrate, a range of qualifications are required to accommodate the various possible specifications of "modern portfolio theory" which includes the two fund separation theorem as a special case. Included in these qualifications are: the presence of a riskless asset; whether short sales are permitted; and the number and type of risky assets permitted in the risky portfolio.

The two fund separation result goes by a number of related names, such as the "portfolio separation theorem," "two mutual fund theorem" and the like, e.g., Ingersoll (1987, ch. 6), Elton and Gruber (1995).[12] The essence of the two fund separation result is that all investors will hold combinations of only two funds, the market portfolio and the riskless security. In the purest form, the investment strategy decision associated with two fund separation is solely a strategic asset allocation decision: how is the total amount of invested capital divided between the riskless asset and the market portfolio? Because two fund separation is predicated on the assumption of market efficiency, it is not feasible to engage in tactical asset allocation where the proportions invested in the two funds varies according to market timing decisions. The investment strategy decision is based on the risk attitudes of the investor. While the composition of the market portfolio is fixed externally, the proportion of the portfolio held in the riskless asset can be either positive (lending) or negative (borrowing). If the proportion is negative then the investor has borrowed at the riskless rate and has a leveraged position in the market portfolio.

The theoretical conditions required for two fund separation to apply are quite restrictive (see section 3.2). If all other assumptions of the model are maintained, the basic two fund separation result is not affected by whether short sales are allowed. Given the assumed homogeneity of investors, the tangency portfolio is the market portfolio because all assets have to be held in equilibrium. Short sales of the riskless asset are used to move the investor along the capital market line. Dropping the assumption that there is a riskless asset requires a zero beta portfolio to be determined as a substitute for the riskless asset. This will require a short sales assumption for the risky assets. Using the zero beta portfolio in place of the riskless asset, a version of the two fund separation theorem still holds with the additional implication that "all portfolios on the efficient frontier are a linear combination of any two other efficient portfolios" (Elton and Gruber 2000, p. 28). It follows that "any recommended portfolio must be a linear combination of any two other recommended portfolios." This provides an additional restriction on the properties of portfolios recommended by professional investment advisors.

Dropping both the riskless asset assumption and the short-sales-allowed assumption is sufficient to undermine the two fund separation theorem. Elton and Gruber (2000, pp. 28–9) provide a summary of the implications arising from dropping these assumptions:

> If short sales [and the riskless asset] are not allowed, the nature of the efficient frontier changes. The two-fund theorem no longer holds. Securities enter and leave the efficient frontier at different risk-return tradeoffs. The points where they enter or leave are called corner portfolios. Securities may be held in zero weight for a range of risk tolerance and some assets are never held. Generally, the maximum return portfolio on the efficient frontier will consist of one asset and the minimum risk portfolio will consist of multiple assets. Thus, if short sales are not allowed and advisors are rational, any allocation recommendation should not be a linear combination of any two others unless all three lie at or between adjacent corner portfolios.

It follows that the practical implications of modern portfolio theory depend on the assumptions made to generate the results of interest. Depending on the assumptions made and the empirical return data used to determine the associated portfolio allocations, a range of possible specifications have to be considered in determining whether specific professional investment advice is consistent with the prescriptions of modern portfolio theory.

The central impetus for Canner et al. (1997) was to develop tests of rationality consistent with modern portfolio theory that could be applied in assessing the validity of strategic asset allocation advice of professional investment advisors and financial planners. Though Canner et al. argue for the irrationality of a decrease in the ratio of bonds to stocks as investors' risk tolerance increases, Elton and Gruber (2000, p. 40) demonstrate: "whether or not short sales are allowed, the sign of the relationship between the bond stock ratio and risk hypothesized in Canner et al. cannot be used as a rationality test." In general, it seems that simple theoretical tests derived from modern portfolio theory are problematic and empirical properties of bond and stock returns have to be considered. Yet, once empirical properties are introduced this raises the problem of using *ex post* parameter estimates to determine the *ex ante* values required to make the strategic asset allocation decision. Ultimately, an underlying feature of this discussion is the implicit assumption that modern portfolio theory is the appropriate measure of rationality. Even if the epistemological approach of modern Finance is accepted, the various possible specifications of the model admit a range of sometimes conflicting strategic asset allocation prescriptions.

What is tactical asset allocation?

Tactical asset allocation is a catchall expression that is aimed at capturing gains to *market timing and portfolio rebalancing* decisions. Tactical asset allocation strategies can take a variety of forms. A common format is reflected in Ragsdale and Rao (1994, p. 209):

> In tactical asset allocation, the central question is: Which asset class will provide superior future returns? Because relative returns are more important than absolute returns in this particular setting, many tactical asset allocators have focused on expected return premiums or spreads. As a practical matter, the most important comparison is that between stocks and fixed income (either bonds or cash) and the forecast on which the most effort is expended is the expected return for stocks. The comparison between stocks and fixed income is crucial because these are the two largest pools of assets in institutional portfolios. Stock return forecasts are important because, historically, stocks have provided the highest and most volatile investment returns.

Though a number of methods can be used to determine tactical asset allocation decisions, the basic procedure involves starting from a *benchmark* asset mix derived from the strategic asset allocation decision and then employing tactical methods to systematically deviate from the benchmark mix. Precisely how much deviation from the benchmark is permitted depends on the specifics of the fund being managed. Using the studies in Lederman and Klein (1994) as a guide, it appears that tactical strategies based on mean-variance optimization techniques are an important component of the class of available strategies.

As portrayed in modern Finance, tactical asset allocation takes place prior to a security selection decision. As such, the composition of risky assets is usually associated with a stock fund, such as the S&P 500, and a bond fund. Following Fox (1999), this leaves two key elements in the tactical asset allocation decision: "the tilt" and *forecasting ability*. The *tilt* is concerned with the amount of deviation from the benchmark holdings of the risky assets. If the benchmark is, say, 60/40 stocks and bonds then a "full tilt size" could be 20% deviation, i.e., maximum values of 80/20 and 40/60. Fox uses this full tilt value in combination with a forecasting ability variable to simulate a range of tactical asset outcomes. Fox (1999, p. 46) describes some results of the simulation relationship: "In the long run, managers with forecasting ability of 60% or better will virtually never underperform the benchmark. For managers who have superior forecasting skill, increasing tilt size improves the entire range of possible return outcomes." As with other tactical asset allocation studies, performance is measured relative to the benchmark portfolio. In a study of the *tracking error* that arises in tactical asset allocation, Ammann and Zimmermann (2001, p. 32) demonstrate that the higher returns to forecasting ability are not at the expense of benchmark tracking accuracy: "imposing fairly large tactical asset allocation ranges produces surprisingly small tracking errors."

Another element in the tactical asset allocation exercise is the *rebalancing frequency*.[13] Fox (1999), for example, uses monthly rebalancing as do Ammann and Zimmermann (2001). Presumably, this fixed rebalancing interval is a restriction imposed by the requirements of the research design, rather than being reflective of actual fund manager practices. However, Fox (1999, p. 40) observes: "the relatively small size of the US [tactical asset allocation] universe. Other types of portfolio managers can be compared to fifty to eighty peers, each with a long investment history. [Tactical asset allocation] managers have many fewer counterparts and only a handful have long-enough observed histories for accurate assessment." It would appear that the relevance of the tactical and strategic asset allocation approach is due more to the connection to modern Finance than to the practical importance of the approach in the fund management industry. As such, there is little guidance from practicing fund managers as to the appropriate rebalancing interval. Perhaps a daily or weekly tilt would apply for some funds while a quarterly or annual tilt would apply for other funds? Perhaps an irregular rebalancing interval is most appropriate but, if so, the process for determining a rebalancing point needs to be adequately specified.

Though there are decided similarities with other approaches to investment strategy, the terminology "tactical asset allocation" is intimately tied to strategic asset allocation and, in turn, to the modern Finance approach to investment strategy. As for similarities with other approaches, tactical asset allocation strategies can be contrasted with, say, the Dow theory (see section 9.2) where: the tilt is usually a "bang-bang" solution, i.e., 100% stocks during bull markets shifting to 100% fixed income or cash during bear markets; the forecast is generated by interpreting the Dow theory signals; and the rebalancing period is determined by the movements of the market rather than by a fixed time interval such as monthly or quarterly frequency. Within the conventional tactical asset allocation framework, industry rotation and country rotation strategies are considered to be too close to the realm of security analysis. There are some practical reasons for this. For example, certain institutional investors, such as pension funds and life insurance companies, have restrictions on holdings of foreign assets. A similar comment applies to the allowable tilt, where there are also various restrictions on the tilt imposed on institutional investors.

As a consequence of being narrowly structured within the modern Finance approach, the connection between security analysis and tactical asset allocation is left largely unexplored by proponents. Yet, when security analysis is eventually added to the process, there are a number of potential feedbacks into the tactical asset allocation decision that have to be considered. For example, the tracking error associated with deviations from the benchmark portfolio could become substantial if the actual risky assets are small collections of individual securities (or even individual securities), as opposed to broadly diversified passive index portfolios. Another potential feedback concerns the rebalancing frequency. Using, say, a monthly rebalancing interval would require that securities be purchased and sold on specific days while security analysis typically requires that transactions be determined by value calculations. In effect, the tilt is determined by the number and variety of securities that satisfies the security analysis selection criteria at a given point in time. It is not obvious how to integrate security analysis, which involves decisions about a significant number of individual securities, into the tactical asset allocation framework, where stylized forecasts are made for a passive index.

Despite the connections between tactical asset allocation and modern Finance, there is a lack of agreement among modern Finance adherents about the efficacy of the practice. To purists, tactical asset allocation is another form of market timing strategy. Even when the potential for market timing is recognized, modern Finance purists usually observe that the range of optimal changes in portfolio weights is much less than typically recommended by tactical asset allocators. For example, Samuelson (1990) observes:

> If you do have timing ability, flaunt it! But in the absence Napoleonic pretensions to clairvoyance, your rational flauntings are more likely to involve switches of a few percent in your equity fraction around some optimal intermediate level rather than the swings from 100% in stocks to 10% in stocks that characterized many asset allocation systems.

The basic intuition behind the attack on tactical asset allocation is embedded in the terminology used by Samuelson (1990) to describe the practice: "across-time deviations from diversification." Market timing requires the investor to temporarily deviate from the allocations that provide optimal, long-term diversification. Hence, unless there are sufficient gains in expected returns, tactical asset allocation will produce a sub-optimal amount of diversification resulting in a lower measured performance using, say, the Sharpe ratio (see below). While this conclusion is strongest for iid returns and log utility, the basic result carries through to other situations.

Cash management and dollar cost averaging[14]

Despite being an integral part of investment strategy, little attention is given to the cash management element of the decision. For example, in the CAPM, which provides the theoretical basis for two fund separation, the cash management decision is modeled as a problem in riskless lending and borrowing. Yet, unless the investment horizon of the portfolio is exactly equal to the term to maturity of the default-free, zero coupon fixed income security used as the riskless asset, then there will be a reinvestment risk associated with rolling the security over at maturity.[15] In addition to confusions associated with specifying the riskless asset, there are also complications associated with the cash flow requirements of the portfolio over the investment horizon. The basic optimization model underlying the CAPM and two fund separation assumes that there is a fixed level of initial wealth that is invested at the beginning of the investment period. Depending on the specification of the optimization problem there may be rebalancing along the time path. In addition, in the consumption-investment form of the problem, allowance could be made for cash inflows or outflows along the time path, in the form of consumption that can take positive or negative values. In a practical context, this leads to consideration of trading strategies concerned with buying along the time path, such as dollar cost averaging, e.g., Leggio and Lien (2003).

Adherents of modern Finance have long recognized the *practical limitations of the riskless asset* concept, e.g., Roll (1978). This concept of "cash" as a riskless security that pays the riskless rate of interest differs from actual "cash" which is legal tender – Federal Reserve bank notes in the US – that do not pay interest. Even this type of cash is subject to the erosion of purchasing power associated with price level inflation. Ignoring inflation, it is possible to view cash as a "riskless" security but this requires the riskfree rate of interest to be set equal to zero. Perhaps an interest bearing chequeable bank account is a more appropriate security to use as cash? What about using a money market mutual fund? Both of these securities feature changing interest rates, violating the CAPM condition that the security is riskless unless the frequency of interest rate changes equals the portfolio rebalancing frequency. In models with a fixed rebalancing frequency of, say, 3 months, then it is possible to use a 3 month US Treasury bill as the riskless asset. In any event, the issue of defining cash is a significant complication in assessing the appropriate cash management strategy to pursue. However, because the resolution of this complication diverts attention from more germane issues, it will be assumed that, somehow, an appropriate cash asset has been identified.[16]

It is conventional in the modern Finance approach to investment strategy to unbundle the cash management decision from the investment management decision. There are a number of reasons given for this simplification. For example, the previous discussion illustrated the point that the cash management decision requires "cash" to be defined. Even when an acceptable definition for the cash asset(s) is given, the cash requirements for the portfolio decision are usually given exogenously. Over time, there may be cash inflows to the portfolio from net labor income or cash outflows due to drawdowns during retirement. However, such cash flows do not typically impact the optimal solution to the theoretical decision problem in a transparent fashion. Interpretation usually involves making sense of intertemporal marginal rates of substitution, correlations between labor income and investment returns, rates of time preference and the like. To avoid such complications, it is conventional to simplify the cash inflow/cash outflow component of the portfolio decision by assuming that a lump sum of initial wealth is invested at the beginning of the investment horizon and is held until the end of the horizon. This framework can be adjusted to permit the initial lump sum to be invested over a sequence of time periods, as in dollar-cost-averaging strategies.

Unbundling the cash management decision from the larger investment optimization problem permits a number of possible approaches to be pursued. Unfortunately, this unbundling does not necessarily lead to useful and practical recommendations. Following the theoretical approach used in economics, the optimal cash management solution will depend on the individual investor's supply and demand for cash. The supply of cash will depend on the initial capital and, possibly, other factors such as the cash flow requirements, investment returns and labor income over the time path. The demand for cash will have three basic elements: precautionary demand; transactions demand; and speculative demand. Unfortunately, using this approach opens a hornet's nest of conflicting opinions about: the specification of the different demand functions; the various definitions of money, from "high powered money" to "near-money" to "outside money"; the empirical properties of the possible demand function specifications and so on. Following Tobin (1958), the speculative demand for money can be modeled using much the same theoretical framework as that employed in the derivation of the Sharpe-Lintner CAPM. This approach reduces the solution of the cash management decision problem to that contained in the CAPM.

In the CAPM framework, optimal holding of the riskless asset (cash) depends on a combination of investor risk attitudes and the spread between the riskfree rate and the expected return on the risky portfolio. When appropriate, this optimal holding is adjusted at each of the potentially diverse number of rebalancings that occur over the investment horizon. In practice, this process reduces to deciding the optimal method of purchasing risky assets over the rebalancing period (investment horizon). Cash assets are held as a buffer to support such purchases. A number of possible methods are available. *Lump sum investing* involves purchasing the desired asset allocation at the beginning of the rebalancing period (investment horizon). The disadvantage of this approach is that the purchase decision may occur at a time when the risky assets are selling at "high" prices, somehow defined. In addition, the change in asset prices over time will cause the portfolio weights to deviate from the desired asset allocation. If no rebalancing is permitted along the path, or if the optimal lump sum allocation is 100% in risky assets, then the lump sum approach reduces to the *buy-and-hold* approach. In such cases, the tactical and strategic asset allocation decisions are identical.

At least since Merton (1973) it has been recognized that the buy-and-hold approach is generally sub-optimal (see end of chapter questions). A widely recommended alternative approach to buy-and-hold is *dollar cost averaging* (DCA) where the investor makes a fixed dollar investment at regular intervals during the rebalancing period. The underlying rationale for DCA is that the risk of buying at a market high associated with lump sum investing is avoided. In addition, for risky assets with volatile prices, the larger number of shares purchased at low prices will more than offset the smaller number of shares purchased at high prices, resulting in a net gain. An alternative to DCA is *value averaging* where, instead of investing a fixed dollar amount each period, the size of the investment is set to maintain a constant increase in the value of the portfolio each rebalancing period. For example, assume the objective is to increase the portfolio value $100 per month (the rebalancing window). If the portfolio increases 5% in the first month, then investment in the second month would be $95 (+ $105 = $200). If there is a 2% drop in the second month then the investment in the third month would be $104 (+ 196 = $300) and so on. Both value averaging and DCA are aimed at capturing the gains of "buy low, sell high."

In comparing these different approaches, it is useful to identify the various types of investment situations being compared. The conventional structure is associated with an inheritance. The investor acquires a sum of money at the beginning of the investment horizon and has to determine the strategy for achieving the highest level of expected utility at the end of the investment horizon, allowing for possible rebalancing within the horizon This basic structure would also apply to, say, a retired investor trying to determine the optimal method for withdrawing funds from an investment account to use for consumption expenses, e.g., Vora and McGinnis (2000). In this case the relevant question being determined can be described as: is it optimal for the retired investor to make one large withdrawal at the beginning and hold cash over the horizon or is it optimal to make regular withdrawals? To address these types of questions, Leggio and Lien (2003) set the rebalancing frequency at one month and the investment horizon at one year. Distributional information, such as average returns and standard deviation of returns, are then calculated over the sample of annual returns. This general approach tends to mask other possible aspects of the typical investment decision. For example, by working with the arithmetic average of returns, the growth in the value of the portfolio over time is not directly incorporated (see sections 1.1 and 10.4).

In addition to the structure of the underlying investment decision, to determine the optimal investment purchasing strategy some method of performance measurement is required. It has long been recognized that any claim about the optimality of this or that investment strategy also involves an implicit claim about *the method of performance measurement.* In turn, because optimality is usually situated within an expected utility framework, it follows that performance measurement be similarly situated. As such, it is conventional to take both the risk and return of the strategy into account, except in situations where the objective function imposes risk neutrality. The various limitations and failings of the CAPM have made the subject of performance measurement an active research area within modern Finance, e.g., Ferson and Schadt (1996). Included in the various issues that have arisen are: the method of measuring risk, e.g., beta vs. standard deviation; the structure of the investment problem, e.g., are cash inflows and outflows permitted; the method of measuring return, e.g., geometric return vs. arithmetic average vs. CAPM alpha; and, the types of portfolios being compared.

Perhaps the most widely used method of performance measurement in modern Finance is the *Sharpe ratio* (*SR*):

$$SR_p = \frac{E[R_p] - r}{\sigma_p}$$

where $E[R_p]$ and σ_p are the expected return and standard deviation of portfolio return (see section 3.1 for definitions) and r is the riskfree interest rate. Being the empirical representation of the capital market line, the Sharpe ratio is directly related to the CAPM. This measure is closely related to a number of other measures that are also based on the CAPM such as: Treynor's measure, which adjusts the *SR* by substituting the beta of the portfolio for σ_p; and, Jensen's alpha, which uses the alpha estimate from the market model expressed in excess return form. Because these measures are all based on the CAPM, it is possible to develop precise theoretical relationships between these measures (see end of chapter questions). Significantly, the reliance on the CAPM to measure performance raises some questions about these estimators.

In addition to portfolio performance measures associated directly with the CAPM, a number of other measures have been proposed. The primary insight of the CAPM measures is that both the risk and the return of the portfolio have to be considered in assessing performance, not just return alone. Though it is possible to consider higher moments of the distribution (see section 3.1), this is not conventional. The focus on risk and return leads to consideration of the various methods of estimating the relevant parameters. For example, the $E[R]$ could be estimated using the arithmetic or geometric averages.[17] Sortino et al. (1999) provide an illustration of a performance measure that does not employ standard estimators. More precisely, the *upside potential ratio* (UPR) is calculated by taking the ratio of the Sortino downside risk measure (δ) (Sortino and Price 1994) to an upside expected return measure (θ):

$$\delta^2 = \int_{-\infty}^{r} (r - x)^2 f[x]\, dx \qquad \theta = \int_{r}^{\infty} (x - r) f[x]\, dx$$

where r is the riskfree interest rate, x represents the random variable for security return and $f[x]$ is the return distribution.

As an illustration involving some of these performance measures, consider the Leggio and Lien (2003) empirical comparison of dollar cost averaging, value averaging and lump sum investing (see table 10.1). This study uses the monthly returns from the Ibbotson and Associates *Yearbook* from four different asset classes: large cap stocks, with returns calculated using the S&P composite index, small cap stocks, which is measured with the Ibbotson small cap index, with US corporate bonds and US government bonds measured using total return indexes for long-term maturities. The riskfree interest rate is US Treasury bills. The study uses the Sharpe ratio, *the Sortino ratio* ($\{E[R] - r\}/\delta$) and the upside potential ratio (θ/δ) to compare the strategies. In doing the calculations, the strategies are assumed to have an investment horizon of one year. It is assumed that a fixed amount of capital is received at the beginning of each period. Dollar cost averaging would then involve investing 1/12 of the capital in the risky asset each month while lump sum investing would invest all the capital in the risky asset at the beginning of the period. The $E[R]$ is then estimated as the arithmetic average of the annual returns over the sample, with other parameter estimates following appropriately. In calculating the results in table 10.1, a 1970–99 sample is used. Leggio and Lien also report results for other samples, such as 1950–1999 and 1926–1999, with some differences in results.

Table 10.1 is useful for comparing the trading strategies, as well as the properties of the performance measures. Leggio and Lien (2003, p. 219) describe the results:

> For the sample period of 1970–99 . . . the Sharpe ratio and Sortino ratio lead to identical rankings of investing strategies for all asset classes. For corporate bonds, the Upside Potential ratio also ranks the investing strategies consistently with the other ratios. However, for both large-cap stocks and government bonds, Upside Potential ratio ranks the preferred investing strategy as reported by the Sharpe ratio to be the least preferred strategy.

Table 10.1 Annualized excess returns and risk measures, 1970–99

Strategy	Mean	Standard deviation	Sharpe ratio	Sortino ratio	Upside potential ratio
A *Asset: large stocks*					
Lump Sum	7.76	16.18	0.48	4.95	2.93
Dollar Cost Average	3.60	8.88	0.41	4.46	3.46
Value Average	3.46	9.38	0.37	3.73	3.28
B *Asset: small stocks*					
Lump Sum	9.70	22.84	0.42	4.49	4.02
Dollar Cost Average	1.83	12.17	0.15	1.87	3.44
Value Average	6.96	13.35	0.52	4.93	3.93
C *Asset: corporate bonds*					
Lump Sum	3.01	11.91	0.25	3.79	5.69
Dollar Cost Average	2.79	6.85	0.41	6.24	6.19
Value Average	–0.13	5.22	–0.02	–0.34	4.60
D *Asset: government bonds*					
Lump Sum	2.90	12.33	0.24	3.91	4.87
Dollar Cost Average	3.00	6.71	0.45	7.07	4.78
Value Average	–0.40	5.96	–0.07	–1.15	5.20

Source: Leggio and Lien (2003)

As for the different trading strategies, the relative rankings reveal that, using the Sharpe and Sortino ratios, lump sum did best for large stocks, while value average did the best for small stocks – a case where DCA did significantly worse than the other two strategies. For corporate and government bonds, DCA had the best performance. Value averaging was disastrous for the two bond cases. Using the upside potential ratio to measure performance produced generally contrary results, e.g., value averaging had the best performance for government bonds. Such results raise substantive questions about the different possible methods used to measure portfolio performance. In addition, claims about the superior performance of DCA often made by practitioners are also brought into question.

Milevsky and Posner (2003) seek a theoretical resolution to the popularity of DCA among practitioners and individual investors. Working within a continuous time framework using Brownian bridges, Milevsky and Posner model DCA as a path dependent claim and develop a mathematical proposition that "proves": "the expected return from . . . the DCA strategy – conditional on knowing the final value of the security will uniformly exceed the return from the underlying security for all sufficiently large volatilities." In effect, DCA outperforms lump-sum investing. This leads to the conclusion that rational investors using DCA are working with target prices. In effect, adherents of DCA are working with conditional subjective expectations. In this framework, the more volatile is the underlying security price, "the greater is the benefit to dollar-cost averaging – conditional on knowing the final value." This result is in sharp contrast to what has been generally accepted wisdom about DCA, based on Constantinides (1979) and later theoretical studies where DCA is shown to be a dynamically inefficient trading strategy. Whether the Milevsky and Posner proposition clarifies or muddies the overall picture on DCA is, at present, unclear.

10.3   INVESTMENT STRATEGY FOR VALUE INVESTORS

The Graham, Dodd and Cottle approach

Writing just prior to the widespread acceptance of modern Finance in academic circles, GDC (p. 439) make the following revealing observation: "There is nothing to prevent the investor, whether an individual or an institution, from making actual investment purchases of a unit such as the Dow–Jones industrial group when the composite valuation indicates he is getting good value for his money. Such a policy may be unusual, but it is not illogical." Though there is an element of the old Finance intrinsic value approach in this statement, GDC capture the essence of the investment strategy inherent in the two fund separation theorem, albeit with the qualification that the Dow–Jones industrial average is only a crude proxy for the "market portfolio." What is revealing in the statement is how "unusual" an investment strategy that favored diversification over security selection was in the early 1960s. Though there were widely diversified investment funds available at the time, the concept of index funds was relatively undeveloped. The value of the "professionally managed investment fund," so strongly promoted by Irving Fisher and others three to four decades earlier (see section 2.3), was still the prevailing model.

Given the different possible approaches that fall within the "value investing" category (see section 7.4), the identification of a specific investment strategy for value investors is not possible. There is so much diversity that it is even possible for strategies similar to two fund separation to be included within the value-investing rubric. This point is reflected in GDC (p. 446):

> Those who practice [the intrinsic value approach] will use their conclusions as a basis for selecting issues to make up a common-stock portfolio, and for recommending the sale of holdings that appear definitely overvalued or the replacement of less by more attract-ive stocks ... Each security analyst, however, will develop his own approach to these problems in accordance with his investment philosophy, his interests and his individual capabilities. We have no desire to prescribe dogmatically any one course of procedure in this area.

As such, all that can be concluded about the GDC approach to value investing is that it involves "buy low, sell high" with intrinsic value, diversification and margin of safety being the guides for specific decisions. This approach does differ from, say, the value investing approach of Philip Fisher where a long-term investment horizon is used and outstanding stocks are retained because there are an insufficient number of opportunities for alternative investment and timing the market is too difficult. In other words, GDC visualize trading a portfolio of "primary stocks" while Philip Fisher has an aversion to trading.

Within this context, GDC do recognize that the intrinsic value approach imposes restrictions on the "model investment policy." The cumulative effect of determining whether the estimated intrinsic value of a security satisfies the margin of safety principle requires a dynamic security trading strategy. Restrictions on this trading strategy are imposed by the diversification principle, but this is insufficient guidance. This point is not lost on GDC: "Many of our readers would like as much guidance as we are able to give them in this highly important and intensely practical aspect of the work of the security analyst." Though GDC are largely concerned with security analysis, i.e., techniques for determining the value of individual securities, some attention is given to the problem of managing the aggregation of securities that are being bought and sold. However, as indicated, the motivation for this was largely driven by the desires of "many of our readers" as opposed to being included as an element of expertise or profound insight. What emerges is a suggested approach to investment strategy that has a certain incongruity with other elements of the GDC approach, but this is what is proposed so this is what is reported here.

GDC (p. 447) visualize a *three step investment strategy* process for an individual with sufficient funds to "make possible adequate diversification." This case is selected because it is the easiest to determine. Qualifications would be required for other cases. The *first step* in the process is to determine the proportion of the portfolio to be held in common stocks "at varying levels of the stock market." In more modern terminology, this is the "asset allocation" decision. The *second step* is to establish a process for selecting the common stocks to be included in the portfolio; this is one aspect of the "security analysis" decision. The *third step* relates to "rules for selling a security held or replacing one stock by another"; this is partly a security analysis decision and partly an asset allocation decision. To adherents of the Warren Buffett or Philip Fisher approach to "value investing," the first step in the GDC investment strategy process may seem to be at odds with the prescriptions of: not following day-to-day fluctuations in the stock market; and, not analyzing or worrying about the general economy. The description also seems to be at odds with decidedly negative statements about market timing made by GDC in chapter 53 that explicitly compares market analysis with security analysis.

Is it possible to take the view that step one does not involve predicting the direction of the stock market but, rather, is an artifact of steps two and three? To answer this question consider the GDC description of the first step:

> we shall assume that the typical individual investor would always have a fixed-value component in his portfolio. Accordingly, we would set an upper limit of 75 percent to be held in common stocks and a lower limit of 25 percent. This minimum proportion, which would be kept in common stocks irrespective of the level of the market or the outlook for equities, is in accord with the view . . . regarding the inclusion of common stocks in the ordinary investment portfolio.

This relatively innocuous statement is followed by:

> The proposed common stock proportions would be put into effect pursuant to a formula plan, which in turn would be geared to the analyst-investor's valuation of the DJIA, Standard & Poor's Composite Index, or some other measure of the market. Assume, for example, that the analyst accepts our unpopular valuation of the DJIA at between 540 and 570 at the beginning of 1962. The actual market level of 730 would then call for holding at or close to the minimum figure of 25 percent in common stocks. This percentage would not be increased until the level fell to the top of the *then* valuation range – not necessarily 570. It would be brought up to 50 percent of the portfolio within the new valuation range, and to the maximum of 75 percent at various levels below the range.

GDC qualify this with the statement: "Very few professionals or nonprofessionals in finance would at this time accept or follow the policy outlined above." The reasons for this are as expected: a formula-timing approach is not considered to be desirable; the assumption that the market has an estimable "central value" is "obsolete"; and, even if there is a central value, this value cannot be determined from "long-term past experience." Despite these qualifications, step one of the "model investment policy" still appears to have a tactical asset allocation component.

GDC recognize that step one can be separated from steps two and three. It is possible that application of the intrinsic value method plus "margin of safety" principle used in step two will provide an automatic adjustment of the portfolio proportion held in common stocks that has much the same effect as the "formula-timing" approach of step one. In particular, when the market is "overvalued" then there will be relatively few opportunities for investment in common stocks and vice versa when the market is "undervalued." Exogenous maximum and minimum bounds on the proportion invested in common stocks could be achieved by altering the margin of safety as the bounds are approached. Given this, step two involves picking 20–30 stocks from a "basic portfolio list" of not more than 100 "large, prosperous, soundly capitalized and well-known" common stocks. Stocks not on the basic list would only be considered if the estimated intrinsic value indicated the stock was "at least 25 percent" cheaper than the most "overvalued" stock on the primary list. Restrictions on the amount invested in any one industry would also be imposed.

The GDC (pp. 448–9) guidance on step three is somewhat vague. There is a reference to a formula-timing-motivated reduction in the fraction of the portfolio in common stocks: "The investor with a full 75 percent common-stock portfolio at a low market level would begin to sell off, on some graduated basis, after the market has again advanced to at least the upper limit of the (new) appraisal range." The reduction could occur by reducing all stocks proportionately "or by selling those issues which at the time of sale bear the least attractive relation to their then appraised [estimated intrinsic] value." This could be an implicit recognition by GDC of the inability that the intrinsic value plus margin of safety method has in providing a complete ranking for purposes of selling (and buying) stocks. In particular, the method does not rank stocks according to the size of the difference between the estimated intrinsic value and market price – this would put too much pressure on the precision of estimating intrinsic value. Rather, all that is provided by the method is a buy/no buy and sell/no sell decision.

Finally, GDC recommend that any replacement of one stock with another not be done unless there is a large advantage, "say, at least, one third."

In the end, the limited advice on asset-allocation-type investment strategy provided in GDC is largely incongruent with the rest of the text and does not rise substantially above the mundane. This is hardly surprising when it is recognized that GDC is dedicated to security analysis. The essential elements of the GDC approach – intrinsic value, margin-of-safety and diversification – do implicitly impose restrictions that generate a coherent tactical asset allocation strategy. In effect, GDC have a *security-analysis-driven investment strategy* (also referred to as a "bottom-up" strategy). However, this connection is not developed or even explicitly recognized by GDC. Presumably, investors adhering to the GDC approach would recognize the overvaluation (undervaluation) of almost all common stocks around market tops (bottoms) and would sell (buy) stocks and buy (sell) bonds resulting in a rapid tilt away from (toward) stocks during periods of declining (rising) stock prices. In technical terms, by rebalancing along the time path using intrinsic value as a selection criteria, GDC are implicitly pursuing a growth-optimal-like investment strategy (see section 10.4). If this outcome appears as wishful thinking, anecdotal evidence indicates otherwise.

The Warren Buffett approach

As observed in section 7.4, the Warren Buffett approach to value investing is not easily replicated by individual investors. Whereas Buffett, through Berkshire Hathaway, is able and willing to purchase whole companies, both publicly traded and privately held, individual investors are typically restricted to investing in companies by purchasing publicly traded corporate securities with investments in private companies not appearing on the menu of available choices. The advantage that Buffett has over the individual investor is apparent in the Berkshire-Hathaway annual reports where numerous purchases of whole companies are reported. For example, the 2002 Report (Buffett 2003) details direct purchases of Albecca and Fruit of the Loom as well as purchases through subsidiaries such as the purchase of pipelines by MEHC. In addition to positions in whole companies, Berkshire Hathaway has substantial positions in the insurance and re-insurance sector. These companies are also involved in the management of asset portfolios. Buffett makes no secret that the investment management activities of the insurance segment are incorporated into the investment decisions made by Berkshire Hathaway.

As discussed in section 7.3, Buffett is a strong adherent of the use of the GDC principles of intrinsic value and margin-of-safety. Application of these concepts in the US stock market during 1999–2002 leads Buffett to conclude that purchases of common stocks were not generally warranted during this period. More precisely, Berkshire Hathaway (2003, pp. 15–16) takes the following view of common stocks:

> Despite three years of falling prices which have significantly improved the attractiveness of common stocks, we still find *very* few that even mildly interest us. That dismal fact is testimony to the insanity of valuations reached during the Great Bubble. Unfortunately, the hangover may prove to be proportional to the binge.

Table 10.2 Common stock positions of Berkshire Hathaway, larger than $500 million, 12/31/02

Shares	Company	Cost ($ millions)	Market
151,610,700	American Express Company	$1,470	$5,359
200,000,000	The Coca-Cola Company	1,299	8,768
96,000,000	The Gillette Company	600	2,915
15,999,200	H&R Block, Inc.	255	643
6,708,760	M&T Bank	103	532
24,000,000	Moody's Corporation	499	991
1,727,765	The Washington Post Company	11	1,275
53,265,080	Wells Fargo & Company	306	2,497
	Others	4,621	5,383
	Total common stocks	$9,164	$28,363

The aversion to equities that Charlie and I exhibit today is far from congenital. We love owning common stocks – If they can be purchased at attractive prices. In my 61 years of investing, 50 or so years have offered that kind of opportunity. There will be years like that again. Unless, however, we see a very high probability of at least a 10% pre-tax return (which translates to 6%–7% after corporate tax), we will sit on the sidelines. With short-term money returning less than 1% after tax, sitting it out is no fun. But occasionally successful investing requires inactivity.

As indicated in table 10.2, this statement is not meant to imply that Berkshire Hathaway has no position in equities. Quite the contrary, the company has long standing common stock investments in a number of high profile companies, including Coca-Cola, Gillette and the Washington Post.[18] At the least, the view expressed about common stocks would have increased the tilt of Buffett's aggregate investment position towards fixed income securities. This tilt is further confirmed in the Report where a "sextuple" increase to $8.3 billion in Berkshire Hathaway junk bond holdings during 2002 is reported.

The actual experience of Berkshire Hathaway relates directly, if anecdotally, to the implementation of the GDC security-analysis-driven investment strategy, with the qualification that the value investing approach of Warren Buffett is not precisely the same as GDC. For example, Buffett has a stronger bias to buy-and-hold than GDC. The replacement of overvalued securities with undervalued securities is a more important part of the security analysis process for GDC than for Buffett. Berkshire Hathaway has some practical reasons for this buy-and-hold bias. Large positions in common stocks are difficult to unwind and repurchase. If there is a positive long-term view on the security of a company then the gains to trading, particularly in trading range markets, will likely be illusory. In addition, though the security selection methodology is similar, Buffett has adapted the GDC approach to include the Philip Fisher great-companies model. This synthesis reinforces the buy-and-hold bias of Buffett's investment strategy. There are only so many great companies in the world, and the securities, particularly the common stock, of such companies are scarce. In this regard, Buffett goes well beyond Fisher in extending the universe of securities to include purchases of whole companies.

It is one of the intellectual oddities of modern Finance that, despite rafts of studies on arcane and incidental issues, so little attention has been given to anecdotal study of the security market activities and writings of Warren Buffett. The bulk of information and discussion about Buffett is to be found in the trade press. While there are some academic efforts along this line, e.g., Statman and Scheid (2002), it is difficult for proponents of modern Finance to reconcile the inconsistency with efficient markets that Warren Buffett presents. In addition, there is also the general epistemological unwillingness to consider anecdotal evidence. Perhaps Buffett has just been lucky? In any game there will be winners. In big games, there will be big winners. As Stickney (1997) observes (see section 1.3): "academic research focuses on the average relation between selected accounting information and stock prices across a large number of firms." The intellectual oddity arises because a potentially important source of insights into securities markets is being ignored. It appears that the observations of Frank Knight (1925) still apply: "One who aspires to explain or understand human behavior must be, not finally but first of all, an epistemologist." In this context, the logical positivism of modern Finance is not structured to generate knowledge from the type of anecdotal evidence provided by Warren Buffett, despite the potential practical significance of such knowledge.

Some evidence on the performance of Berkshire-Hathaway has already been provided in section 7.4. Table 7.4 documents the remarkable performance of the company. Table 7.5 lists the major operating companies owned by Berkshire Hathaway with Table 7.6 listing the acquisition criteria. All of this information was obtained from the 2002 Annual Report (Buffett 2003). These Berkshire Hathaway annual reports are an essential source on the views of Warren Buffett. As such, it is surprising that the most recent annual Report is not required reading in introductory investment classes, if not in more advanced classes. Yet, courses with such a requirement are the exception rather than the rule in the academic curriculum. Those perusing the 2002 Report will find the thirteen "Owner Related Business Principles" that Buffett includes to provide a precise description of the managerial approach at Berkshire Hathaway. These principles were originally developed in 1983 and were initially circulated to shareholders in 1996. In addition to such gems, the annual reports can also be examined to address a range of important questions such as: how does Berkshire Hathaway make money? and, what are the current views of Buffett and Charles Munger on securities markets?

From the Report it is possible to partially unravel the complex current financial composition of Berkshire Hathaway, and determine sources of profit. As illustrated in tables 10.3 and 10.4, the insurance business plays a key role in the overall revenue and earnings of Berkshire-Hathaway. The insurance business is particularly attractive for an operator such as Buffett because of the ability to gain competitive advantage from superior performance of the investment portfolio. This is another aspect of the Buffett approach that is not accessible to individual value investors. This element goes back to the creation of Berkshire Hathaway in 1967. The life and times of Warren Buffett and Berkshire Hathaway have been examined in detail elsewhere (e.g., Hagstrom 1995, 2000; Lowenstein 1995), so only a brief excerpt will be given here. The company was formed from a merger of Berkshire Cotton Manufacturing, a textile company, and Hathaway Manufacturing. Also included in the merger were two insurance companies.

Table 10.3 Berkshire Hathaway Inc. and subsidiaries, selected financial data ($ millions except per share data)

	2002	2001	2000	1999	1998
Revenues					
Insurance premiums earned	19,182	17,905	19,343	14,306	5,481
Sales and service revenues	17,347	14,902	7,361	5,918	4,675
Interest, dividend and other investment income	3,061	2,815	2,725	2,314	1,049
Revenues of finance and financial products businesses	2,126	1,658	1,505	987	394
Realized investment gains[a]	637	1,363	3,955	1,365	2,415
Total revenues	42,353	38,643	34,889	24,890	14,014
Earnings					
Net earnings[a,c,d]	4,286	795	3,328	1,557	2,830
Net earnings per share[d]	2,795	521	2,185	1,025	2,262
Year-end data[b]					
Total assets	169,544	162,752	135,792	131,416	122,237
Notes payable and other borrowings of non-finance businesses	4,807	3,485	2,663	2,465	2,385
Notes payable and other borrowings of finance businesses	4,481	9,019	2,116	1,998	1,503
Shareholders' equity	64,037	57,950	61,724	57,761	57,403
Class A equivalent common shares outstanding, in thousands	1,535	1,528	1,526	1,521	1,519
Shareholders' equity per outstanding Class A equivalent common share	41,727	37,920	40,442	37,987	37,801

	2002	2001	2000	1999	1998
Net earnings as reported	4,286	795	3,328	1,557	2,830
Goodwill amortization, after tax	–	636	548	476	111
Net earnings as adjusted	4,286	1,431	3,876	2,033	2,941
Earnings per class A equivalent common share:					
As reported	2,795	521	2,185	1,025	2,262
Goodwill amortization	–	416	360	313	88
Earnings per share as adjusted	2,795	937	2,545	1,338	2,350

[a] The amount of realized investment gains and losses for any given period has no predictive value, and variations in amount from period to period have no practical analytical value, particularly in view of the unrealized appreciation now existing in Berkshire's consolidated investment portfolio. After-tax realized investment gains were $383 million in 2002, $842 million in 2001, $2,392 million in 2000, $886 million in 1999, and $1,553 million in 1998.

[b] Year-end data for 1998 includes General Re Corporation acquired by Berkshire on December 21, 1998.

[c] Net earnings for the year ending December 31, 2001 includes pre-tax underwriting losses of $2.4 billion in connection with the September 11th terrorist attack. Such loss reduced net earnings by approximately $1.5 billion and earnings per share by $982.

[d] Effective January 1, 2002, Berkshire adopted Statement of Financial Accounting Standards ("SFAS") No. 142 "Goodwill and Other Intangible Assets." SFAS No. 142 changed the accounting for goodwill from a model that required amortization of goodwill, supplemented by impairment tests, to an accounting model that is based solely upon impairment tests.

A reconciliation of Berkshire's Consolidated Statements of Earnings for each of the five years ending December 31, 2002 from amounts reported to amounts exclusive of goodwill amortization is shown below. Goodwill amortization for the years ending December 31, 2001 and 2000 includes $78 million and $65 million, respectively, related to Berkshire's equity method investment in MidAmerican Energy Holdings Company.

Table 10.4 Berkshire Hathaway, sources of profit ($ millions)

	Revenues		
	2002	2001	2000
Operating businesses			
Insurance group:			
Premiums earned:			
GEICO	6,670	6,060	5,610
General Re	8,500	8,353	8,696
Berkshire Hathaway Reinsurance Group	3,300	2,991	4,712
Berkshire Hathaway Primary Group	712	501	325
Investment income	3,067	2,844	2,796
Total insurance group	22,249	20,749	22,139
Apparel	1,619	726	678
Building products	3,702	3,269	178
Finance and financial products	2,126	1,658	1,505
Flight services	2,837	2,563	2,279
Retail	2,103	1,998	1,864
Scott Fetzer Companies	899	914	963
Shaw Industries	4,334	4,012	–
Other businesses	1,983	1,488	1,436
	41,852	37,377	31,042
Reconciliation of segments to consolidated amount			
Realized investment gains	637	1,363	3,955
Other revenues	29	35	54
Eliminations	(56)	(65)	(26)
Purchase-accounting adjustments	(109)	(67)	(136)
	42,353	38,643	34,889

	Operating Profit before taxes		
	2002	2001	2000
Operating businesses			
Insurance group operating profit:			
Underwriting profit (loss):			
GEICO	416	221	(224)
General Re	(1,393)	(3,671)	(1,254)
Berkshire Hathaway Reinsurance Group	534	(647)	(162)
Berkshire Hathaway Primary Group	32	30	25
Net investment income	3,050	2,824	2,773
Total insurance group operating profit (loss)	2,639	(1,243)	1,158
Apparel	229	(33)	6
Building products	516	461	34
Finance and financial products	1,016	519	530
Flight services	225	186	213
Retail	166	175	175
Scott Fetzer Companies	129	129	122
Shaw Industries	424	292	–
Other businesses	691	377	320
	6,035	863	2,558
Reconciliation of segments to consolidated amount			
Realized investment gains	603	1,320	3,955
Interest expense[a]	(86)	(92)	(92)
Corporate and other	2	8	22
Goodwill amortization and other purchase-accounting adjustments	(119)	(630)	(856)
	6,435	1,469	5,587

[a] Amounts of interest expense represent interest on borrowings under investment agreements and other debt exclusive of that of finance and financial products businesses and interest allocated to certain other businesses.

An initial key to the future success of Berkshire Hathaway can be found in the substantial profit generated by Buffett after assuming management of the insurance company asset portfolios.

During the 1970s, the insurance aspect of the business was expanded considerably with the purchase of three additional insurance companies and the creation of five more. The textile segment was closed and a holding company was created. Management of the aggregate Berkshire Hathaway asset portfolio led naturally to the acquisition of non-insurance related businesses. The role of these businesses in the company has gradually risen from about 1/3 to 40% of revenue in the early 1990s to almost 50% currently (see table 10.4). Included in the asset purchases of Berkshire Hathaway have been a number of large common stock purchases in Coca-Cola, Gillette, American Express and other high profile companies. Table 10.2 reveals the success of these particular purchases. Given the size of these positions, even when common stock purchases are considered, the Buffett approach is not directly accessible for the typical individual investor. A position of, say, 200,000,000 shares in Coca-Cola differs substantively from a 500 share position, if only in terms of access to senior management. The upshot is that the typical individual value investor would have considerable difficulty in formulating a complete investment strategy from the experience of Warren Buffett.

Practical investment strategy for individual value investors

What are appropriate investment strategy concerns for an individual investor with a relatively small capital base seeking to pursue the value investing approach? The potential for smaller investors to pursue such an approach has been greatly enhanced in recent years with the explosion in investment information both on-line and in a range of financial media. If used with sufficient skepticism, these information sources permit the individual investor to obtain a depth and breadth of information about publicly traded companies that was available only to professional investors even a couple of decades previously. Legislative changes in the US have permitted IRAs, 401 (k) and other tax advantaged retirement savings plans (RRSPs in Canada) that now provide a pool of investment funds representing a significant fraction of the individual investor's net worth. Many of these plans provide sufficient flexibility for the individual investor to, say, pursue strategic and tactical asset allocation strategies that are consistent with personal investment philosophy. The accumulated evidence about the below benchmark performance of the average actively managed mutual fund provides considerable incentive for the individual investor to formulate and implement individual investment strategies based on the value investing approaches suggested by the likes of GDC and Philip Fisher, and popularized by Warren Buffett.

For reasons discussed previously, it is difficult for individual value investors to directly pursue the Warren Buffett investment strategy. Similarly, the guidance of GDC appears to be aimed at the practicing professional security analysts and portfolio managers that are involved in trading securities on a regular basis. Consideration also has to be given to historical changes in securities markets that have taken place since

GDC considered investment strategy. Yet, despite the historical evolution, there are certain constants that gives the GDC approach to value investing a timeless quality. One constant is the emphasis on distinguishing between *speculation and investment.* The individual investor has to determine the amount and degree of speculation that will be undertaken. The value investing approach is aimed at capturing superior investment returns. In this process, there is an element of speculation involved in predicting future security price performance. However, speculative activities such as the short-term trading of securities to earn profit are not directly employed. GDC do discuss "market analysis," a category that would include technical analysis and the Dow theorists. However, the discussion is superficial. As such, value investors have to ignore the returns accruing to predominately speculative situations when making investment decisions.

Sorting out the distinction between speculation and investment involves the identification of an individual *investment philosophy.* By taking the value investor route, the individual implicitly accepts elements that are contained in the investment philosophy of leading value investors, such as GDC. Even though there is some variation in certain aspects of philosophy across different value investors, where speculative securities are concerned there is general agreement. Such securities fail to conform to the criteria required to undertake an accurate assessment of intrinsic value. Given this, there is scope for honest disagreement over which particular securities are speculative. However, such disagreements revolve around factors concerned with the valuation methodology rather than with the criteria required to identify speculative situations. For example, some value investors may be attracted to the debentures of a bankrupt corporation such as Worldcom, based on an assessment that the potential payout of, say, 35 cents on the dollar is sufficiently in excess of the current price of 21 cents on the dollar. Other value investors may feel that, given their knowledge about bankruptcy law, Worldcom and the telecom industry, it is not possible to make an accurate enough assessment of the asset values and other factors to make a decision that is not overly speculative in nature.

Issues of investment philosophy are at the core of many investor decisions. Value investing requires the future cash flows of a security to be estimated. In turn, this requires the individual investor to acquire sufficient information to make reasoned decisions about the estimated cash flows. This imposes substantial demands regarding information collection, processing and analysis. Given that there are thousands of potential securities domestically and ten of thousands if international securities are included, this poses a quandary for individual investors. In the face of potential information overload, what are the appropriate methods to use in arriving at an investment decision for a given security? Faced with this quandary, value investors have used a variety of different methods. For example, Warren Buffett recommends only investing in securities of businesses that the investor can understand. This approach considerably narrows the field of potential securities. GDC divide investors into *defensive investors* and *enterprising investors* (see section 10.1) where "[t]he great majority of individual investors belong in the defensive category." In general, such investors are well served by the two-fund separation theorem.

The individual enterprising investor requires guidance well beyond that of the individual defensive investor. For example, while the defensive investor will automatically achieve a high level of diversification associated with having a position in a broadly-based stock index such as the S&P 500, the enterprising value investor needs to consider the treatment of diversification. As discussed above, though the *benefits of diversification* are explicitly recognized by value investors, this is expressed only in terms of, say, not concentrating invested capital in a small number of companies in one industry. Close reading of the editions of Graham and Dodd (1934) up to GDC reveals that modern issues of investment strategy – strategic and tactical allocation – are largely irrelevant. In the value investing approach, the asset allocation decision is determined by available security investment opportunities. The decision process starts with security analysis and works backward to tactical and strategic asset allocation considerations. Following Philip Fisher, the enterprising investor may well be confident in holding only a small number of securities, subject to the restriction that there be diversification across industries: "any holding of over twenty different stocks is a sign of financial incompetence." In contrast, GDC visualize picking the best 20–30 stocks from a pool of 100.

Casual consideration of the diversification issue leads to a natural question for value investors to consider: what is the desired frequency of trading for the portfolio? A sound and widely recommended rule-of-thumb is, if possible, *avoid transactions costs and management fees*. Defensive investors can partially achieve this outcome by using low management fee, high liquidity index funds. However, even defensive investors have to decide on a long run allocation between stocks, bonds and cash and whether there will be rebalancing of the portfolio at regular intervals. This rebalancing decision will depend on whether the investor wants to make a market call. As discussed in chapter 10, there are good reasons to engage in such prognostications, even if the call is weakly supported. Various factors come into play, such as: whether the market is in a trading range or a trend; and, whether it is in a secular bull or secular bear phase. Forecasting ability does not have to be that acute in order to undertake a shift to bonds and other fixed income securities in a stock market downdraft. As the Dow theorists suggest, look for the signs of speculative excess and do not be too worried about getting out early.

It seems that a defensive investor pursuing an active rebalancing strategy may engage in more securities trading – albeit in index funds and bonds – than an enterprising investor following a Philip Fisher, buy-and-hold approach. In pursuing this approach, the defensive investor is motivated by the observation that, while stocks may outperform bonds in the long run, bonds can outperform stocks over investment horizons of significant length. General results about asset classes, such as the equity premium that is of concern in modern Finance, can belie actual results for individual investors trading specific securities over a given investment horizon. Properly executed, a strategy of rebalancing between index funds and fixed income securities would provide attractive returns. This strategy also has a grounding in the principles of modern Finance. If security analysis is judged to be a zero or negative expected value activity (due, for example, to the perception that markets are efficient) then two-fund separation is a rational investment strategy. Recognizing that two fund separation involves an optimal allocation between the risky market portfolio and the riskless asset, rebalancing along the path to maintain the optimal weights is indicated.

While there is attractive potential returns in the rebalancing strategy of the defensive investor, such returns are dwarfed by the possible gains for the enterprising investor. It is not surprising that, in practice, such gains are almost always accompanied by an enhanced element of speculation. In the technical analysis context (see chapter 10), speculation is typically associated with active trading strategies. In contrast, the enterprising value investor following, say, the *Philip Fisher approach* (see section 7.4) would have the buy-and-hold strategy of a long-term investor. Only a limited amount of rebalancing is admitted. The speculative element comes primarily from narrowing the number of securities in the portfolio. "There are a relatively small number of truly outstanding companies." The difficulty with this approach centers on the *ex ante* identification of the truly outstanding companies. As indicated in chapter 9, it is not necessary or practical to have knowledge of the full set of securities. With the thousands of common stocks and bonds traded on securities markets, it is only necessary to develop a comfortable knowledge about a smaller universe of securities. This raises natural questions about the construction of this smaller universe from the larger, unmanageable universe with tens of thousands of stocks in hundreds of industries and countries.

In selecting this universe, a sensible first step is to follow Warren Buffett's dictum (see sections 7.4 and 10.3): *concentrate on the securities of companies that are understandable.* This dictum is implied in the essence of value investing because purchasing securities in companies that are not understood is speculative. Other dictates of Warren Buffett about the characteristics of these understandable companies follow appropriately: look for companies that have a consistent operating history and favorable long-term prospects. Included in the consistent operating history will, in most cases, be a strong and sustained profit margin. Company management needs to be closely scrutinized and desired rules of conduct verified. Though Buffett tends to favor companies with a franchise that is needed by consumers and has strong brands, such as Coca-Cola or Gillette, companies that compete primarily on a price/net cost basis, such as oil and gas producers, can also be acceptable as long as these companies satisfy the criteria for a value investment. One such criterion is that management has been able to use past retained earnings to generate a more than compensating change in market value.

Each value investor needs to specify the particular criteria that is to be applied in identifying feasible companies for investment. Though there will be considerable overlap in these criteria across value investors, there will be significant variation in the application across investors. Given this, the amount of time and energy an individual investor can devote to gaining and maintaining information about a group of stocks will determine the size of the universe. Individual investors with relatively little time can pursue *hybrid strategies* that mix defensive and enterprising styles. While maintaining a sizeable position in the passive market index, the hybrid investor will also have a small stable of securities in individual companies. The objective of the hybrid investor is to incrementally outperform the market index return. The dedicated individual enterprising investor is assisted by the securities market information that can be rapidly found on the internet, cable television and in modern print sources such as the *Wall Street Journal*. Even with effortless information access, it is unlikely that there is enough time for an individual to exceed the 100 stock universe identified in

GDC. Probably, the total number of stocks that could carefully be followed would be much less.

The question of the number of securities and companies to follow is closely related to the number of industries that these companies fall within. From this point, it is difficult to provide general guidance. Some value investors may favor the *"buy-low–sell-high" approach* of GDC and take the *ex ante* view that such opportunities arise because of across industry differences in valuation. By rotating the portfolio across industries, these differences in valuation can be obtained. Such a value investor would, almost certainly, cover a larger number of industries than an enterprising investor seeking to follow, say, the Philip Fisher approach. In this case, there would only be a cursory examination of cross-industry valuations. Because considerable effort is expended in finding only a small number of securities, a paring process takes place that quickly reduces the list of potential candidates. If an attractive opportunity appears in an unfamiliar industry or area to the investor, time and effort is expended in acquiring the understanding. Additions and, if necessary, subtractions from the portfolio take place at glacial speed. As a consequence, the time and effort given to each trading decision is considerable. Fisher would be disappointed to find that any investor following his approach has as many as twenty securities in the portfolio.

10.4   ADVANCED TOPICS IN INVESTMENT STRATEGY

*The interior decorator fallacy and other confusions**

The investment strategy decision for institutional investors is often constrained by regulatory considerations. In addition, institutions usually have substantial internal resources: to determine the long-term portfolio allocation between stocks, bonds and cash within allowable limits; to make short-term, market timing adjustments to the long-term portfolio composition; and, to make security selection decisions designed to enhance overall portfolio returns. Some institutions may tolerate only slight deviations from long-term portfolio composition targets, preferring to enhance returns through reliance on security selection within defined asset groupings. Other institutions may permit significant deviation from long-term targets in order to enhance returns through market timing and security selection strategies. These decisions are guided by the constraints facing the specific institution. For example, mutual funds will be driven by the requirements set out in the fund prospectus and the need to obtain competitive returns relative to competing funds in the same grouping. Due to the diversity of institutions and institutional investment objectives, combined with the considerable internal expertise available within most institutions, it is difficult to briefly make helpful generalizations about the investment strategy decisions of institutions. As a consequence, in what follows discussion focuses on the investment strategy for individual investors.

Relative to the variation in investment strategies across institutions, the investment strategy decision for individual investors is more homogeneous. Due to the perceived lack of sophistication, the investment strategy decision for many individual investors is guided by recommendations provided through the advisory services of brokerage firms and investment banks, either directly or through mutual funds offered by these firms. These advisory services are an important linchpin of revenue generation for many securities firms. Fees are obtained for providing services required to design and implement "customized" portfolios for specific investors. These bundled and unbundled services include brokerage, in-house mutual funds, accounting management, investment research and the like. Since the inception of securities markets, financial sector firms have demonstrated considerable ingenuity and adaptability in generating revenue from the investment advisory process. In recent years, challenges have been presented by the deregulation of brokerage fees, the emergence of discount brokers, the rise of online trading and the enhanced accessibility of index funds with low management fees. In the face of these challenges, the advisory services of securities firms have thrived based, it seems, largely on the perception of the typical individual investor that, somehow, the investment strategy decision is "too complicated" and specialized advice is required.

Is the individual investment strategy decision sufficiently complicated to warrant the compensation that financial planners, investment advisors and securities firms are paid to facilitate this decision? In many cases, there are reasons to expect that the compensation is excessive. As discussed in section 3.2, the two fund separation theorem suggests that, for the typical investor, a strategy of holding the market portfolio and the riskless asset is optimal. While this solution is idealized, the basic intuition suggests that holding low management fee, passively managed stock market index fund(s) combined with long-term government bonds and a sufficient level of cash is an appropriate strategy for a wide range of investors. The long-term weights of bond, index fund and cash can be determined by the individual investor after due reflection, without the need to pay sizeable fees for advisory services. This view is supported, for example, by numerous empirical studies that have found the *ex post* performance of the "average" actively managed mutual fund underperforms the appropriate index benchmark fund after expenses, e.g., Daniel et al. (1997). As Campbell and Viceira (2002, p. 3) observe: "Financial planners have traditionally resisted [this] simple investment advice . . . This resistance may to some extent be self-serving."

Despite the apparent overcharging for services exhibited by various investment advisory services, "almost no attention [in academic studies] has been paid to examining advice regarding the asset allocation decision" (Elton and Gruber 2000, p. 27). As evidenced by Bernstein (1992), Canner et al. (1997), Campbell and Viceira (2002) and others, this lack of attention is surprising given that the asset allocation advice dispensed by investment advisory services is seemingly in conflict with the tenets of the investment strategy proposed in modern Finance: "as Peter Bernstein points out in his 1992 book *Capital Ideas*, many financial planners and advisors justify their fees by emphasizing the need for each investor to build a portfolio reflecting his or her unique personal situation" (Campbell and Viceiria 2002, p. 3).[19] For example, younger investors and aggressive investors are encouraged to hold "riskier" portfolios than older investors and conservative investors, usually by investing a larger fraction of the portfolio in stocks versus bonds plus cash (see table 10.5). This need to tailor investment portfolios to the specific characteristics of individual investors is referred to as the *interior deco-*

Table 10.5 Asset allocations recommended by selected financial advisors

Advisor and investor type	% of portfolio Cash	Bonds	Stocks	Ratio of bonds to stocks
A Fidelity				
Conservative	50	30	20	1.50
Moderate	20	40	40	1.00
Aggressive	5	30	65	0.46
B Merrill Lynch				
Conservative	20	35	45	0.78
Moderate	5	40	55	0.73
Aggressive	5	20	75	0.27
C Jane Bryant Quinn				
Conservative	50	30	20	1.50
Moderate	10	40	50	0.80
Aggressive	0	0	100	0.00
D The New York Times				
Conservative	20	40	40	1.00
Moderate	10	30	60	0.50
Aggressive	0	20	80	0.25

Source: Canner et al. (1997)

rator fallacy by Bernstein and others.[20] This terminology makes a connection to the strong role that personal preferences and tastes play in interior decoration. The fallacy arises because much of the advice is either unnecessary or inconsistent with the portfolio theory of modern Finance.

The interior decorator fallacy begs the question: can sound reasons be provided for recommending distinct investment strategies for different investors? Theoretically, there appears to be considerable support for the need to tailor investment portfolios. Included in the possible reasons that have been proposed for differences between individual investors are: tax status, usually associated with income, capital gains and estate taxes; the length of the investment horizon, where young persons typically have long horizons and retired persons have short horizons; the cash payout requirements; the randomness of labor income and stock market returns, including the correlation between these two variables; different investor attitudes towards risk, often characterized as "aggressive" or "conservative"; short sales constraints, that are more costly for non-institutional investors; the level of current wealth; and, illiquidity of assets in the aggregate investor portfolio, such as real estate or privately held businesses. The diversity and number of possible factors makes it difficult to develop a general framework for individualized asset allocation.[21] Instead, considerable effort has been dedicated to studying specific aspects of the problem. The resulting diversity of possible solutions gives the appearance of a complicated decision problem when, for most investors, a rational investment strategy is not difficult to determine.

While security analysis is viewed as a zero expected return activity and is largely ignored in modern Finance, the subject of investment strategy – albeit in the guise of "portfolio management" – has a long history with numerous substantive contributions. The bulk of these largely theoretical contributions involve, in some fashion, the risk aversion properties of expected utility functions (see section 3.3).[22] In particular, the relative risk aversion property of the expected utility function determines the fraction of wealth held in risky assets as the level of investor wealth increases. Relative risk aversion plays a key role in many of the solutions to the portfolio management problem proposed in modern Finance. An early example is the solution to the *time diversification puzzle* provided by Samuelson (1963) and re-examined in Samuelson (1994), Bodie (1995), Kritzman and Rich (1998), Fisher and Statman (1999) and Kritzman (1994, 2000). This puzzle arises from the conventional recommendation that investors with longer investment horizons allocate a higher fraction of the portfolio to riskier assets, i.e., common stocks. Time diversification requires that, somehow, the riskiness of stocks is "diversified" as the investment horizon increases. The logic of this view is described by Siegel (1998, p. 26): "Although it might appear to be riskier to hold stocks than bonds, precisely the opposite is true [for long investment horizons]; the safest long-term investment for the preservation of purchasing power has clearly been stocks, not bonds."

Does the length of the investment horizon matter to the portfolio allocation decision? Is the optimal portfolio for short-term and long-term investors the same? Samuelson (1963) states a set of *three sufficient theoretical conditions* for expected utility maximizing investors to hold a constant fraction of a portfolio in risky assets as the investment horizon increases, e.g., Kritzman (2000, p. 48):

1. Investors have constant relative risk aversion, which means that they maintain the same percentage exposure to risky assets regardless of changes in wealth.
2. Investment returns are independently and identically distributed, which means that they follow a random walk.
3. Future wealth depends only on investment results and not on human capital or consumption habits.

Being based on logical deduction, these three conditions can be used to assess the rationale for making different asset allocation recommendations based on the length of the investment horizon. The first point is sensible if investors are expected utility maximizers; constant relative risk aversion requires that the investor keep the fraction of the portfolio invested in risky assets constant as wealth increases.[23] Recognizing that investor wealth changes over the life cycle, this condition is needed to ensure that time diversification does not apply as wealth levels change over time. However, the use of expected utility theory in this context may be undermined by, say, the *Friedman-Savage puzzle* where the expected utility function does not display a uniform attitude towards risk across wealth levels, e.g., Shefrin and Statman (2000).[24]

Condition two is more complicated to interpret, if only because the statistical implications of a random walk are subject to misunderstanding. It is helpful to reference a result concerning the standard deviation for a sum of standard normal random variables. More precisely, the discrete time random walk can be specified as:

$$X(t) = X(t - 1) + Z(t) \quad \text{where } X(0) = 0, \text{ and } t \in \{1, 2, 3 \dots \}$$

where $Z(1)$, $Z(2)$, $Z(3) \dots$ form a stochastic process of *independent* random variables with the standard normal probability distribution: $Z(t) \sim N[0, 1]$ (see section 1.3).[25] This requires the $Z(t)$ to be identically, independently distributed (iid) random variables. Over any time interval 0 to T, the variance of $\Delta X(t)$ can be evaluated by determining the variance:

$$var\left\{\sum_{t=1}^{T} Z(t)\right\} = E\left[\sum_{t=1}^{T} Z(t)\right]^2 = \sum_{t=1}^{T} \sigma_Z^2 = T\sigma_Z^2 = T$$

Hence, when $\Delta t = T$, the Z is $N[0, T]$. Now, consider what happens when the time interval Δt shrinks. Because $Z(t)$ is $N[0, \Delta t]$ over any arbitrary time interval, the random walk now has the form:

$$X(t + \Delta t) = X(t) + Z(t + \Delta t)\sqrt{\Delta t}$$

In Samuelson's condition two, the variable $X(t)$ is the investment return. It follows that if investment returns are iid then the variance will increase proportionally with time while the standard deviation will increase with the square root of time.

What is the relevance of this result for time diversification? In general, time diversification requires that the expected utility of terminal wealth increases as the length of the investment horizon increases. If returns follow a random walk, then the riskiness of the investment – as measured by the standard deviation of returns – will increase with the square root of time. Whether this increases or decreases expected utility will depend on the connection between the increase in risk and the weight attached to risk in the expected utility function. For example, where the expected utility functions is risk loving, then time diversification holds by construction when returns are iid. For functions displaying risk aversion, then time diversification will depend on the desired holding of risky assets as the wealth level increases. When returns are not iid, the picture is much cloudier and results can depend on the specific process selected. For example, as discussed below, Siegel (1998) relies on the assumption of mean reversion to motivate time diversification.[26]

Given that returns are iid, the application of condition two now requires the evaluation of a risky investment as time increases *for an investor with a constant relative risk aversion utility function*. Though it is possible to demonstrate this result in general terms, it is expedient to illustrate this point using an example. Consider the expected log utility function, $E[\ln[W]]$, that displays the constant relative risk aversion property (see end of chapter 1 questions). Condition two states that if the return generating process is iid then an investor making decisions using expected log utility will be indifferent between a certain outcome and a wealth process that grows according to the iid return process. For illustrative purposes, let the iid process be binomial. Following

Kritzman and Rich (1998), construct a certainty equivalent comparison between a certain outcome, say $100, and a one-step ahead binomial process for wealth. Choosing the probability of the up and down moves to be 50%, let the outcome in the up state be $133.33, a one-third gain, and the down state to be $75, a one-quarter loss. It is possible to show that $E[\ln W(1)] = .5[\ln[133.33] + \ln[75]] = 4.6052 = \ln[100]$. Hence, the appropriate return generating (recombining) binomial process has a one-third gains on the upside and a one-quarter loss on the downside, with equal probabilities of up and down moves (see end of chapter questions).

Given initial wealth, $W(0)$, of $100, it follows that $W(1) = .5[133.33 + 75] = 104.17$, implying an expected return of 4.17%. In this example, time diversification requires that the expected utility will increase as the risky expected wealth process evolves through time. In other words, comparing the expected utility of terminal wealth for a one period investor and a T period investor ($T > 1$), the expected utility will be equal across the horizon. To see this, consider the recombining binomial process taken one more period ahead where $E[\ln W(2)] = .25\ln[177.28] + .25\ln[56.25] + .5\ln[100] = E[\ln W(1)] = .5[\ln[133.33] + \ln[75]] = 4.6052 = \ln[100]$. The expected utility of terminal wealth is unchanged as the investment horizon gets longer. Time diversification does not apply as there is no incentive to change the investment in the risky asset based on the length of the investment horizon. Kritzman (2000, p. 53) observes: "this result is not restricted to investors with log-wealth utility functions. It applies to all investors who have constant relative risk aversion as long as returns follow a random walk. If [time diversification was] true, we would observe an increase in expected utility as the number of periods of the investment increases."

One of the strongest academic proponents of time diversifications is Siegel (1998). The rationale provided in favor of "stocks for the long-run" focuses on the empirical properties of the "standard measures of risk" (Siegel 1998, pp. 31–2):

> stocks are riskier than fixed-income investments over short-term holding periods. But once the holding period increases to between 15 and 20 years, the *standard deviation* of average annual returns, which is the measure of the dispersion of returns used in portfolio theory, become *lower* than the standard deviation of average bond or bill returns. Over 30-year periods, equity risk falls to only two-thirds that of bonds or bills. As the holding period increases, the standard deviation of stocks falls nearly twice as fast as that of fixed-income assets.

Siegel explicitly denies the validity of the random walk hypothesis: "data show that the random walk hypothesis cannot be maintained and that the risk of stocks declines far faster when the holding period increases more than predicted. This is a manifestation of the *mean reversion* of equity returns." For Siegel, time diversification is predicated on an empirical foundation. Condition two in Samuelson (1963) is denied and an alternative empirical model for stock prices, based on **mean reversion** (see section 5.2), is proposed. Kritzman (2000, pp. 57–8) claims that when the stock price process is mean reverting, then constant relative risk aversion still does not exhibit time diversification. However, Barberis (2000, p. 227) argues that mean-reversion will lower the variance of cumulative returns over long horizons: "This makes stocks appear less risky to long-horizon investors and leads them to allocate more to equities than would investors with shorter-horizons" (see end of chapter questions).[27] In any event, time diversification with mean-reversion could still follow if condition one is dropped and replaced by an increasing relative risk aversion utility function, such as the quadratic.

Some care has to be taken in interpreting the Siegel arguments in favor of time diversification. For example, similar to a host of other academics that approach Finance from an economist's perspective, Siegel uses "real" returns to measure performance. As this involves dividing one random variable, the nominal return, by another random variable, the inflation rate (see section 7.3), the statistical properties and the practical intuition of this variable are unclear.[28] During investment time periods where the inflation rate is low, the differences between real and nominal returns will be small. However, for long time horizons, there will likely be periods where real and nominal returns diverge significantly due to the level and volatility of inflation rates. For a number of reasons, it is more meaningful to assume that investors are concerned with actual returns, not "real" returns. The process by which an individual investor makes adjustments for changes in price levels varies considerably. For example, some investors, such as retired investors with income streams that are fixed in nominal terms, will experience an erosion in real income as prices rise. In contrast, other investors with, say, labor income streams that increase with inflation will have an offset to potential "real" investment income losses.

Another issue arising from the Siegel mean-reversion-based argument concerns the process of implementing a time diversification agenda as a portfolio management strategy. The basic Samuelson (1963) result, which appears to be carried forward by Siegel, is predicated on a *buy-and-hold investment strategy*. This involves purchasing stocks at the beginning of the holding period and selling at the end. Alternatively, it is possible to pursue a rebalancing strategy where the portfolio is adjusted at regular or irregular intervals according to some set of criteria. There are also hybrid strategies where the buy-and-hold strategy involves the purchase of investments that have a predetermined rebalancing mechanism. For example, if the stocks in the buy-and-hold portfolio are a broadly diversified value-weighted market index fund, such as the S&P 500, this implicitly involves passive rebalancing to reflect changes in index value weights as relative stock prices change. Yet, if mean reversion is the basis for the claim of time diversification, this implies that some process of active rebalancing is being used to exploit the time series properties of security returns. The precise connection between the rebalancing and the empirical assumption of mean-reversion is unclear.

As modern portfolio theory evolved, the significance of portfolio rebalancing was explicitly recognized. However, the analytical apparatus required to incorporate *optimal rebalancing* is considerably more involved than the buy-and-hold approach where the optimization problem is modeled using only a decision date and a terminal date. Techniques such as stochastic dynamic programming are required to theoretically solve the optimization problem when more than one decision date is permitted. For example, in continuous time this leads to the derivation of a partial differential equation (PDE) that can be solved for the optimal weights.[29] Depending on the specification of the problem, the PDE may or may not admit closed form solutions. Simplifying conditions required to obtain a solution were provided in early contributions by Samuelson (1969) and Merton (1969). These studies demonstrated that combining the assumptions of iid security returns with the constant relative risk aversion power utility function is sufficient to generalize the one decision date result. In other words, using the simplifying conditions permits the portfolio time path to have the same asset allocation across possible investment horizons.

As the study of the optimal portfolio management progressed, theoretical features were introduced into the problem that altered the basic structure of the solutions. Consistent with concerns arising from microeconomic theory, the portfolio optimization problem was formulated as a *consumption-investment problem.* This involves an explicit concern with consumption along the time path. Following Merton (1973), this transforms the focus of the problem to measuring asset return risk using the covariance with the marginal utility of the investor. As Campbell (1996, p. 299) observes: "In an intertemporal setting, this need not be the same as covariance with the market return, because innovations in marginal utility can be driven by changing expectations of future returns, which determine the marginal productivity of wealth, as well as by increments to wealth itself." The upshot is that concern shifted from a theoretical framework in which asset allocations were readily identifiable to a framework where investor marginal utilities and hedging demands take center stage, e.g., Ingersoll (1987, ch. 13). While the elegance and rigor of the solutions was considerably enhanced by these changes, the practical applicability of the optimal solutions was correspondingly reduced.

The final condition given by Samuelson (1963) anticipates these sorts of theoretical complications by explicitly ruling out the potential impact of human capital and consumption effects on the portfolio allocation decision. Yet, much of the theoretical development of modern portfolio theory since Samuelson (1963) has taken place in a theoretical framework that incorporates such effects. Merton (1969) and Samuelson (1969) were able to deal with one aspect of this issue by demonstrating that "retirement is irrelevant for portfolio decisions if investment opportunities are constant and human capital is tradable." However, Merton (1971) "shows that time-varying investment opportunities result in portfolio rules with an intertemporal hedging component whose magnitude depends on the investment horizon of the investor" (Viceira 2001, p. 433). Merton (1973a) expands this notion in the context of an intertemporal capital asset pricing model to demonstrate that investors with long investment horizons will allocate more to equities if the utility function is more risk averse than log utility. This result provided further impetus to the theoretical shift from utility functions defined using terminal wealth, to consumption-portfolio problems using utility functions that included the time path of consumption as well as terminal wealth. As evidenced by recent studies such as Campbell and Viceria (2002), Constantinides (2002), Viceira (2001), and Lettau and Ludvigson (2001) this theoretical framework is still the convention, though there are some exceptions that work only with terminal wealth, e.g., Barberis (2000).

The fascination with dynamic asset pricing and optimal consumption-portfolio rules that was initiated by Fama (1970a), Hakansson (1970) and Merton (1971, 1973a) has continued to the present producing a bewildering array of theoretical contributions. However, while inherently interesting to economists with a theoretical orientation, the concern with the consumption-savings-portfolio decision masks essential elements that are of interest in practical Finance. To see this, consider the rhetoric of the following description provided by Viceria (2001, p. 435):

[this] paper builds a stationary model in which it is possible to explore life-cycle effects on portfolio choice and savings while preserving the analytical advantage of infinite-horizon models. Retirement is defined as a permanent zero-labor income episode ... by comparing the optimal allocations of investors with different retirement horizons, it is possible to understand portfolio allocations over the life cycle because, if discount rates and the expected growth rate of labor income are constant over the life cycle, the investor's retirement horizon is relevant for her portfolio decisions only in that it determines her remaining human capital.

In this time separable power utility of consumption framework, Viceria (2001, p. 433) concludes: "With idiosyncratic labor income risk, the optimal allocation to stocks is unambiguously larger for employed investors than for retired investors, consistent with the typical recommendations of investment advisors." Though this result seems to favor time diversification, this conclusion is elusive: "Increasing idiosyncratic labor income risk raises investor's willingness to save and reduces their stock portfolio allocation towards the level of retired investors." Ultimately, as is common in economic theorizing, conditions for a contrary conclusion are also provided: "Positive correlation between labor income and stock returns has a further negative effect and can actually reduce stockholdings below the level of retired investors."

In defense of Viceria (2001), this "on-the-one-hand-and-on-the-other-hand" theorizing establishes a number of key issues that can possibly be subjected to empirical analysis. Is the correlation between labor income and stock returns positively and significantly correlated? Is labor income tradable? To what extent is it possible to borrow against future labor income? To what extent is labor income idiosyncratic? Unfortunately, empirical analysis of these types of questions raises a range of additional problems. For example, consider the Siegel rationale for time diversification that arises from mean reversion in stock returns. This empirical model restricts the future expected returns from wandering too far from the long run mean, thereby lowering the variance of cumulative returns over long horizons compared to the random walk model.[30] In an intertemporal portfolio management framework that permits optimal rebalancing, mean reversion allows investors to "predict" expected returns from realized returns and to adjust portfolios appropriately.[31] Theoretically, this will result in investors holding "substantially more equities at longer horizons, but only when they are more risk-averse than log utility investors" (Barberis 2000, p. 227). However, such results require accurate empirical estimates for the process generating stock returns.

A key difficulty with using an empirical assumption, such as mean reversion of stock returns, to justify time diversification is that implementation requires parameter estimates. While this may not present much difficulty in a theoretical setting, when it comes to making actual trades based on these estimates, the resulting parameter uncertainty poses real problems. Barberis (2000, p. 227) finds: "in both the static buy-and-hold and the dynamic rebalancing problem, incorporating parameter uncertainty changes the optimal allocation significantly ... In some situations, we find that uncertainty about parameters can be large enough to reverse the direction of the results. Instead of allocating more to stocks at long horizons, investors may actually allocate *less* once they incorporate parameter uncertainty properly." Barberis (2000) derives these results using a utility model with constant relative risk-aversion power utility defined over terminal wealth. The upshot is that the issue of time diversification is too complicated to provide a definitive solution with practical validity. By implication, it is not possible to resolve other theoretical issues that arise from the interior decorator fallacy. Consistent with the interior decorator approach, it may be safe to say that the allocation between stocks, bonds and cash will vary across individuals. However, a theoretical resolution of precisely what those individual allocations are is currently unavailable.

The fallacy of large numbers and growth optimal portfolios*

Though widely accepted in modern Finance, the mean-variance optimization model is not the only model of portfolio choice that has been explored and proposed. One important alternative is the portfolio that is "growth optimal," i.e., the portfolio that provides the highest expected (log) return over the investment horizon. Casual reflection about the properties of this portfolio raises questions about the riskiness of the return. The highest expected return will likely come with downside as well as upside. Investors that are risk averse will not find such a portfolio to be as attractive as some other "optimal" portfolio with less upside and downside. It follows that analysis of the growth optimal portfolio will have to account for the investor's expected utility function. At this point in the analysis confusion arises because, if the investment horizon is long enough, then the strong law of large numbers (see section 1.3) suggests that the growth optimal portfolio will outperform, with probability one, all other portfolios. In other words, in the limit, the actual cumulative return on the portfolio will converge to the expected value. Hence, for long term buy-and-hold investors, it would seem to be irrational for investors with any sensible expected utility function to select any other portfolio than the growth optimal portfolio.

As it turns out, the use of the law of large numbers to justify selection of the growth optimal portfolio has led to description of this argument as the *fallacy of large numbers*. Following Samuelson (1963), this fallacy is often motivated by referring to an individual accepting a sequence of bets involving an iid random variable with positive expected value when an individual bet is unacceptable. A possible example would be a coin flipping game where the individual loses $9 for heads but gains $10 for tails. One trial of such a game may be unacceptable while a sufficiently long sequence of trials for such a game is acceptable. For Samuelson, this represents a misunderstanding of the law of large numbers, which applies to averages, because both the variance and expected return from the game apply to a sum that will increase with the number of trials. It is possible, though highly unlikely, for there to be a long string of heads consuming most of the sequence, resulting in a loss that cannot be sustained. A connection to the St Petersburg paradox is suggested as the solution for that game involved determining a cost of play that depends on the number of trials. Though the number of trials also enters the fallacy of large numbers the connection is weak because of the additional connections to the growth optimal portfolio decision problem.[32]

The fallacy of large numbers assumes an important place in modern Finance because of the implications for expected utility theory, e.g., Ross (1999), Peköz (2002).

Considerable debate has surrounded the implications of accepting a sequence of good bets when a single bet would be rejected. For example, Pratt and Zeckhauser (1987) define "proper risk aversion" as a property of expected utility functions where, if a single bet is rejected, then combinations of such single bets will also be rejected. Various studies have developed conditions on expected utility functions where a single good bet would be rejected but a sequence of such bets would be accepted, e.g., Nielson (1985). The basic intuition of these studies is provided by Peköz (2002, p. 2): "if the utility function decreases faster than exponentially in the negative direction, the small risk of loss can be magnified to overwhelm the benefits of a gain even for an arbitrary sequences of good bets." Attention has focused on properties of the independent random variables forming the sequence such as bounded or unbounded sample paths; and, identical or nonidentical distributions. The connection of these studies to mathematical statistics is illustrated by Peköz (2002) where the implications of permitting optional stopping – quitting the game early – are examined.

The debate surrounding the growth optimal portfolio is related to the fallacy of large numbers and, indirectly, to the time diversification puzzle because of a connection to the solution for the expected utility maximization problem with log utility. To see this consider the basic maximization problem for an investor with log utility defined for terminal wealth:

$$\max E[\ln[W(T)]] \quad \rightarrow \quad \max E\left[\ln\left[\frac{W(T)}{W(0)}\right]\right] = \max E[\ln[1 + R(0, T)]]$$

The division of $W(T)$ by $W(0)$ and resulting conversion of the problem into maximizing the expected return $E[R(0, T)]$ follows because the expected utility function is unique up to a linear transformation. (The maximization is a choice problem involving the portfolio value weights for the securities that determine $W(T)$.) Assuming a discrete time and state model, the expectation taken over N possible states can be written as:

$$\max E[\ln[1 + R(0, T)]] = \max \sum_{\xi=1}^{N} Pr_\xi \ln[1 + R(0, T)_\xi] = \max \sum_{\xi=1}^{N} \ln[1 + R(0, T)_\xi]^{Pr_\xi}$$

From this point, it can observed that the sum of the logs is equal to the log of the products. In addition, ergodicity (see section 1.3) can be invoked to convert states to equally likely time periods to get:

$$\max \sum_{\xi=1}^{N} \ln[1 + R_\xi(0, T)]^\xi = \max \ln\left[\prod_{\xi=1}^{N} [1 + R_\xi(0, T)]^\xi\right] = \max \ln\left[\prod_{t=1}^{T} (1 + R(0, t))\right]$$

It follows that maximizing the expected log utility of terminal wealth corresponds to a strategy that maximizes the geometric mean return, e.g., Ingersoll (1987, pp. 255–8).

The debate surrounding the growth optimal portfolio is theoretically connected to the underlying portfolio strategy that is being pursued and to the specification of the expected utility function. The argument connecting the maximization of the expected log utility of terminal wealth with the growth optimal solution is structured in a portfolio choice problem that involves no additions or withdrawals from invested wealth until the investment horizon is reached. The consumption-investment problem along the time path is suppressed. Given this, though the growth optimal portfolio will have the highest *expected return* in the long run, it does not follow that this portfolio will have the highest *expected utility* for all investors. Ross (1999, p. 323) captures the point:

> At the root of a contentious literature on economic behavior in the face of repeated random choices is the observation that maximizing the geometric growth rate of a portfolio will, with probability one, asymptotically outperform any other choice. This result has led some to suggest that any other choice would be irrational. Samuelson (1971), however, argued that convergence in probability is too weak to support such a strong behavioral conclusion. Indeed, since maximizing the geometric growth rate is equivalent to maximizing the expected log of wealth, the position of its advocates is tantamount to judging all other utility functions as irrational choices.

Ultimately, the debate over the growth optimal portfolio is not theoretically resolvable because the issues involved are too complex. As the solutions become more sophisticated the connection with the underlying portfolio management problem is lost and replaced with concerns about, say, the properties of convergent sequences and whether there is an option to quit the game early.

Behavioral portfolio theory: Keynesian investment strategy?

Behavioral finance has gradually emerged as a potential alternative to the approach of modern Finance (see sections 1.2, 2.4 and 9.3). This raises the possibility that an alternative investment strategy can be developed that incorporates the essential elements of behavioral finance while still retaining methodological features that are familiar to adherents of modern Finance. Given the central role the von Neumann-Morgenstern expected utility approach plays in the development of the central propositions of modern Finance, it is not surprising that the starting point for a *behavioral portfolio theory* begins with an alternative method for modeling decision making under uncertainty.[33] Such an alternative approach to portfolio theory is likely to produce theoretical results that are at odds with the mean-variance optimization model that is used to generate the CAPM and two fund separation results. Such an extension is provided in Shefrin and Statman (2000) where the *prospect theory* of Kahneman and Tversky (1979) is combined with Security-Potential/Aspiration theory of Lopes (1987) to produce a "behavioral portfolio theory" (BPT).

Prospect theory was proposed by Kahneman and Tversky to address failings identified in expected utility theory, such as those proposed by Allais (1953). The theory was extended to a version referred to as *cumulative prospect theory* in Tversky and Kahneman (1992). Following Levy and Levy (2002, pp. 1334–5), cumulative prospect theory is characterized by four propositions:

The main features of prospect theory are: (a) Investors make decisions based on *change* of wealth rather than *total* wealth, in contrast to what is advocated by expected utility theory ... (b) Investors maximize the expectation of value function $V(x)$ where x stands for the *change* in wealth (rather than total wealth). $V(x)$ is S-shaped $V'(x) > 0$ for all $x \neq 0$, $V''(x) > 0$ for $x < 0$ and $V''(x) < 0$ for $x > 0$. The parameters of the value function may change with wealth ... but the S-shaped property is general to all initial wealth levels. (c) Investors subjectively distort probabilities. They make decisions based on the subjective cumulative distribution F^* which is given by $F^* = T(F)$ where F denotes the objective cumulative distribution and T is some subjective transformation such that $T' > 0$, $T(0) = 0$ and $T(1) = 1$ (this is the main modification of cumulative prospect theory in comparison to prospect theory). (d) The "framing" of alternative outcomes may strongly affect subjects' choices.

Though prospect theory is supported in a series of experimental studies conducted by Kahneman and Tversky, Levy and Levy (2002) question the validity of the design used for these experiments. In particular, the choices given to subjects involved only negative or positive outcomes when mixed outcomes provide a better description of actual investment situations. When mixed outcomes are admitted, Levy and Levy provide evidence against the S-shaped value function that is a core proposition of prospect theory.

Despite the potential limitations, prospect theory has assumed an important position in the emerging subject of behavioral finance, in general, and BPT, in particular. As Shefrin and Statman (2000, p. 128) observe: "Mean-variance investors choose portfolios by considering mean and vaiance. In contrast, BPT investors choose portfolios by considering expected wealth, desire for security and potential, aspiration levels, and probabilities of achieving aspiration levels." While the two fund separation theorem of modern Finance implies that rational investors will hold combinations of the riskless asset and the market portfolio, a key feature of optimal BPT portfolios is the resemblance to combinations of bonds and lottery tickets. Facing the same investment opportunities, Shefrin and Statman demonstrate that the BPT efficient frontier does not coincide with the mean-variance efficient frontier. Recognizing that the BPT portfolios being identified contain security combinations that are not transparently comparable to commonly observed "real world securities," Shefrin and Statman (2000, p. 149) observe:

> Treasury bills are right for investors with very low aspiration levels, while equity participation notes are right for investors with higher aspiration levels. Investors with even higher aspiration levels choose stocks and those with yet higher aspiration levels choose out-of-the-money call options and lottery tickets. Stocks, call options, and lottery tickets feature many states with zero payoffs, but they also feature states with payoffs that meet high, even exceedingly high, aspiration levels.

The flexibility of BPT permits this approach to provide an adequate solution to the interior decorator fallacy. Yet, following Fisher and Statman (1999), this is a general result in behavioral finance, resulting from inherent modification of conventional risk concepts used in modern Finance.

The Shefrin and Statman (2000) BPT results are obtained by exploiting alternative approaches to von Neumann-Morgenstern expected utility theory. In particular, BPT has decided similarities to the **safety-first portfolio theory** initially proposed by Roy (1952). Together with the approaches of maximizing the geometric mean and stochastic dominance, safety first provides a consistent method of making decisions in the face of random outcomes.[34] In comparison with using the expected utility approach, safety-first has a number of desirable and not so desirable properties. For example, safety-first avoids the Friedman-Savage puzzle where individuals buy both insurance and lottery tickets. This phenomenon presents complications for expected utility theory where concave utility functions defined over terminal wealth are employed. Such concavity requires a uniform attitude toward risk that leads to the Friedman-Savage puzzle. No such theoretical problem arises if safety-first is used. Similarly, the relatively straight-forward decision problem associated with safety first avoids the complicated calculations that can arise when solving expected utility optimization problems.

The basic idea of safety-first is appealing. Instead of doing an expected utility calculation, individuals are assumed to use a less complicated decision-making model that aims to avoid unacceptable outcomes. To see this, let s denote the lower bound on terminal wealth, then the optimization problem for the safety-first investor is:

$$\min_{\{w_i\}} Prob \; \{W(T) < s\} \quad \rightarrow \quad \min_{\{w_i\}} Prob \; \left\{\frac{W(T)}{W(0)} < \frac{s}{W(0)}\right\}$$

By dividing through by initial wealth it is possible to reexpress this specification in terms of returns. Where s is identified as a minimum subsistence level, then the problem is said to involve minimizing the probability of ruin. Assuming returns (or terminal wealth) are normally distributed then it follows that the optimal solution will be that portfolio which is the most standard deviations above the subsistence level. To see this consider three portfolios $\{A, B, C\}$ with expected returns = $\{7\%, 12\%, 16\%\}$ and standard deviations = $\{4\%, 5\%, 10\%\}$. Given $\{s/W(0)\} = R_s = 4\%$, then the number of standard deviations above 5% for $\{A, B, C\} = \{.75\sigma, 1.6\sigma, 1.5\sigma\}$. It follows that portfolio B is optimal for the safety first investor because it is the portfolio that has the greatest separation, measured in terms of standard deviation, from the subsistence return level.

Under the critical assumption of normally distributed returns, it is possible to convert this safety-first optimization problem to a more familiar form:

$$\min_{\{w_i\}} Prob \; \left\{\frac{W(T)}{W(0)} < \frac{s}{W(0)}\right\} \quad \rightarrow \quad \min_{\{w_i\}} \frac{R_S - R_p}{\sigma_p} = \max_{\{w_i\}} \frac{R_p - R_S}{\sigma_p}$$

If R_S is set equal to the riskless rate r then it is apparent that the safety-first optimization problem is the same as maximizing the Sharpe ratio, the basic approach underlying the CAPM and two fund separation results. Geometrically, the safety-first investor can define preference lines in mean-standard deviation space that identify sets of portfolios for which the investor will be indifferent (see end of chapter questions). The efficient frontier for the safety-first investor will be that line with maximum slope. Introducing the investment opportunity set defines the available portfolios that can be obtained.

It follows that the optimal safety-first portfolio is identified by the portfolio preference line that is just tangent to the investment opportunity set. When $R_S = r$ this is qualitatively the same solution as in the mean-variance optimization model, with the qualification that all assets are risky in the safety-first decision problem.

From this basic framework, a number of extensions have been pursued. For example, the safety-first optimization problem assumes that all assets are risky. Hence, though the mean-variance and safety-first portfolios are equal when $R_S = r$, the absence of a riskless asset means that two-fund separation does not apply in a safety first framework. Extending the model to include riskless lending and borrowing raises undesirable possibilities such as infinite borrowing as well as complete investment in the riskless asset (see end of chapter questions). Another complication arises when the assumption of normally distributed returns is dropped. In this case, Elton and Gruber (1984, pp. 224–5) argue that Chebyshev's inequality can be used to demonstrate that the results can be generalized to distributions with finite first and second moments. However, Shefrin and Statman (2000, p. 138) demonstrate that this result is incorrect. Telser (1955), Arzac (1974) and Arzac and Bawa (1977) reformulate the safety-first decision problem as:

$$\max_{\{w_i\}} R_p \quad subject\ to: \quad Prob\ \{R_p < R_S\} \le \alpha$$

where α is the probability of ruin. In Telser (1955), α is fixed while in Arzac and Bawa (1977) the value is allowed to vary. This approach presents a number difficulties, such as the possible absence of a feasible solution.

In section 10.3, it was argued that Keynes (1936, esp. ch. 12) is a sophisticated precursor of a number of views that have been popularized in behavioral finance. This begs the question: to what extent can BPT be used as a surrogate for a *Keynesian investment strategy*? Keynes (1936) gives a central role to uncertainty and the use of conventions to make decisions in the face of uncertainty. Yet, the type of uncertainty visualized by Keynes differs from the random variables that motivate BPT. Consistent with the approach used in modern Finance, uncertainty in BPT appears as measurable risk. Variables such as the return on the portfolio have a well defined probability distribution, complete with expected values and standard deviations. For Keynes (1936, p. 148): "It would be foolish, in forming our expectations, to attach great weight to matters which are very uncertain." Keynes is more concerned about the "state of confidence" that is determined by the interaction of the confidence that various traders have in the expectations that are the basis of investment decisions. It is the instability in the state of confidence that is a significant source macroeconomic disturbance.

Keynes (1936, ch. 12) proposes two general types of investment strategies. On the one hand, there is the approach to: "Investment based on genuine long-term expectation." Though Keynes does not provide much fleshing out of this approach, it is reasonable to connect this approach with value investing. Yet, Keynes (1936, p. 157) felt this approach "is so difficult to-day as to be scarcely practicable" and "evidence from experience" indicates this approach is not likely to be "most profitable." Those seeking to follow this approach are advised not to use borrowed money, i.e., do not purchase stocks on margin or otherwise leverage invested capital. Keynes argued that the "most profitable" investment strategy would be one that Graham and Dodd referred to as the *anticipation approach,* where the objective is to trade based on estimates of the "waves of optimistic and pessimistic sentiment" and "anticipating what average opinion expects average opinion to be." This approach has a short-term trading horizon of three months and less. Implicitly, Keynes appears to be assuming that this approach will involve trading on margin. However, the role that leveraging plays in the profitability of this approach is not precisely specified.

The anticipation approach encompasses a range of investment strategies, including the bulk of the trading intensive approaches found in technical analysis. Though Keynes did not spell out precisely how "average opinion about average opinion" is to be estimated, it is clear that he did not intellectually favor these types of investment strategies. However, based apparently on anecdotal evidence, Keynes did believe that such strategies were likely to be the most profitable. Keynes was intellectually disposed to a general value investing approach, even though such an approach could present real challenges to the investor. Though it is comforting to feel that the substantial progress in securities markets that has taken place since Keynes (1936) has turned the tables on the value investor making these investors the dominant market players, there is still considerable evidence that "waves of optimistic and pessimistic sentiment" still drive security price determination. For example, it is difficult to avoid this conclusion based on an examination of technology stock pricing during the 1998–2000 period The upshot is that there is no identifiable Keynesian investment strategy. Both value investors and technical analysts could, arguably, find some support in Keynes (1936).

? Questions

1 In section 10.2, it was observed that the buy-and-hold approach to investment is sub-optimal if rebalancing is permitted along the time path. This result arises because changes in asset prices along the time path cause deviations from the optimal weights determined at the beginning of the investment horizon. What is the assumed investment situation that is associated with this result? For example: what is the initial capital? what is the rebalancing frequency? what are the cash flows along the path? (Hint: see Constantinides 1979.) Rebalancing to maintain the optimal weights will result in higher expected utility at the terminal date for the investor. In a discrete time model, what theoretical conditions are required for this result to apply? What further conditions are required for the result to extend to cases where the length of the rebalancing interval is arbitrary or diverse? (Hint: see Levy and Samuelson 1992.)

2 In section 10.2, three measures of performance evaluation directly related to the CAPM were introduced: the Sharpe ratio (SR); Treynor's measure (TM); and, Jensen's alpha (J). Letting the subscript p denote the portfolio of interest and M the market portfolio, derive the following results:

$$TM_p = \frac{E[R_p] - r}{\beta_p} = \frac{\alpha_p}{\beta_p} + TM_M = \frac{J_p}{\beta_p} + TM_M$$

$$SR_p = \frac{E[R_p] - r}{\sigma_p} = \frac{\alpha_p}{\sigma_p} + \rho SR_M = \frac{J_p}{\sigma_p} + \rho SR_M$$

where ρ is the correlation between the return on the market and the return on the portfolio of interest. (Hint: see Bodie, Kane and Marcus 1999.)

3 In section 10.4, an example involving the expected log utility function and a binomial process was used to illustrate the Samuelson (1963) conditions. The binomial process set the probability of up and down moves to be equal at 50% with the upside gain equal to 1/3 and the downside loss equal to 1/4. What is the mean and variance of the associated wealth process and return process? How is this process iid? Referring to the discussion of the random walk in the previous paragraph, re-express this binomial process as a discrete random walk: $X(t) = X(t - 1) + Z(t)$. (Hint: In order for $Z(t)$ to be a mean zero process, this will be a random walk for the expected return process.) What are the mean and variance of the sum of the $\{Z(t)\}$?

4 In section 10.4, it was observed Kritzman (2000) argues that mean-reversion in stock returns is insufficient to produce time diversification if the investor has a constant relative risk aversion utility function. Barberis (2000) claims the opposite. Using the binomial techniques developed in section 5.1 for mean-reverting interest rate processes, evaluate directly whether the expected utility will increase over an increasing time horizon for a mean-reverting stock return process. Assume that the investor has: a log utility function; and, a power utility function. Compare the results for these two cases. Do your results confirm the conclusions of Ingersoll (1987, p. 257) that the log utility function is completely "myopic" while the power utility function is only myopic if security returns are statistically independent?

5 In section 10.4, the safety-first decision model led to the specification of lines in expected return-standard deviation space that defined portfolios of equal preference. Explain how these lines are defined (Hint: see Elton and Gruber 1984, pp. 222–4). This solution depends on there being only risky assets in the choice problem. If riskless borrowing and lending is permitted, demonstrate that this raises the possibility of infinite lending and borrowing or complete investment in the riskless asset (Hint: see Elton and Gruber 1984, pp. 238–9). Finally, explain the limitations of using Chebyshev's inequality (see section 1.3) to generalize the safety-first approach to distributions other than the normal (Hint: see Shefrin and Statman 2000, p. 139).

NOTES

1 Whitman (1999, ch. 11) also discusses the "sloppy" terminology used in the financial community. Some important words that are identified as having imprecise meanings are: investor, speculator, value, price, company, risk, margin of safety, capital, earnings and cash flow.

2 Kritzman and Page (2002) is a recent example of studies that dispute the relative importance of asset allocation versus security selection: "Contrary to the widely held view, it turns out that choosing stocks within the equity component of a portfolio is substantially more important than choosing a portfolio's exposure among stocks, bonds and cash." Recognizing that there are methodological difficulties in making a comparison between gains to asset allocation and security selection, Kritzman and Page find the gains from security selection relative to asset allocation vary across countries, ranging from just over two times to almost four times.

3 Another example of potentially confusing semantics in this area occurs with the use of "strategic asset allocation" to refer to the normal, long-term asset mix and "tactical asset allocation" to refer to the market timing decision. The definition used here follows Ragsdale and Rao (1994).

4 In the jargon of the trade, such investors are referred to as "widows and orphans." This terminology makes reference to an earlier time where social support systems, such as Social Security, were not available and bequests and inheritances were an often essential source of financial support. Because the husband was, typically, the primary breadwinner, upon the death of her husband, a widow would often be dependent on the income from a bequest or inheritance to pay for day-to-day expenses. As such, the potential for disruption of cash flow associated with, say, a downturn in equity values and dividend payouts, would be an important consideration in the investment strategy decision.

5 In addition to Siegel, the "Dogs of the Dow" strategy is touted by L. Kudlow on the regularly scheduled CNBC show *Kudlow and Kramer.*

6 Visscher and Fillbeck (2003, p. 100) provide much the same history, dating the *Washington Post* story to 1988 and observing that Slatter worked for Prescott, Ball and Turben of Cleveland, Ohio.

7 A number of investment strategies that incorporate dividend yield have been proposed in modern Finance. For example, the PEGY models (see section 8.1) aim to incorporate P/E ratios, growth rates and dividend yields to estimate the modern Finance version of the "intrinsic value" for a stock.

8 The fund was converted to a limited partnership in 1952.

9 The collapse of LTCM has been exhaustively examined in a number of sources, e.g., Dunbar (2000). Many of the regulatory aspects of the collapse are examined in PWGFM (1999). Poitras (2002, pp. 64–7) provides a brief overview.

10 Links to a number of hedge fund sources can be found at www.sfu.ca/~poitras/links.htm. The President's Working Group on Financial Markets (PWGFM) that examined the hedge fund industry in the wake of the collapse of LTCM has led to a process of discussion and examination of the hedge fund industry. The most recent round in the process that was initiated by the PWGFM *Report* (1999) is a SEC sponsored Roundtable on Hedge Funds held in May 2003. The submissions to this Roundtable (accessible through the SEC website www.sec.gov) are a useful source for information on the current state of hedge fund regulation.

11 A number of links to hedge fund websites can be found in the Security Analysis section on the author's links page at www.sfu.ca/~poitras/links.htm. Included in the links are the MARhedge site, Hedgeworld at Deutschebank, Van Hedge Fund Advisors and Magnum Funds.

12 The "two fund separation" terminology can be found in various sources. For example, Levy and Samuelson (1992, p. 1530) observe: "The Sharpe-Lintner CAPM can be derived by assuming either a quadratic utility function or

normally distributed returns. In a multiperiod framework, the quadratic utility assumption also leads to the two-fund Separation Theorem, and hence implies the CAPM."

13 Among others, Levy and Samuelson (1992) provide four sets of sufficient conditions for multiperiod generalization of the single-period Sharpe-Lintner CAPM where investors are permitted to have diverse holding periods and rebalancing frequencies. In the multiperiod context, if portfolio rebalancing is not permitted then the CAPM and two fund separation do not hold, even in the restrictive case of quadratic utility.

14 Portfolio performance measurement is an important aspect of modern Finance. Yet, as demonstrated in Campbell et al. (1997) and Cochrane (2001), adequate treatment of this topic takes the discussion decidedly in the direction of sophisticated financial econometrics. Unfortunately, this requires the development of techniques and notions that are outside the general framework of this book. As a consequence, this topic is only given a cursory treatment which is incongruent with the relevance of this topic to investment strategy, in general, and modern Finance, in particular. Included in the useful recent studies on this topic are Brown et al. (1992), Elton et al. (1996) and Carpenter and Lynch (1999) which consider the problem of *survivorship bias* in studies of fund (or common stock) performance. This bias can arise in empirical studies of mutual fund performance because poorly performing funds disappear and are typically deleted from the sample because the price history does not cover the full sample (and other reasons). The result is that the samples used for fund performance studies may be biased toward over-representation of the better performing funds. Other recent studies of portfolio performance measurement include Pastor and Stambaugh (2002), Carhart (1997) and Ferson and Schadt (1996).

15 This assumes that nominal returns are the variable of interest. If, as is common in modern Finance, the real return is the variable of interest, even a default-free, zero coupon fixed income security with maturity date equal to the investment horizon will be risky. Even though the nominal return will be certain, there is still purchasing power risk associated with inflation. This complication can be handled by using an inflation-indexed default-free fixed income security as the riskless asset.

16 An alternative approach to defining cash is provided by the corporate financial statements where there is a "cash and cash equivalents" item. There is also the "cash flow statement."

17 Strictly speaking, the return in the Sharpe ratio requires that the holding period for the return equals the investment horizon.

18 The need to reveal the size and change in equity positions at Berkshire Hathaway is another feature that distinguishes Warren Buffett from the small individual investor. As reflected in numerous sources, Buffett has consistently and persistently complained about having to reveal his equity positions. Among other negative aspects, this creates difficulties for unwinding the positions due to "front-running" when Berkshire-Hathaway is adding or adjusting common stock positions. However, compared to other investors that also have to report equity positions, Buffett does have the benefit of two classes (A and B) of Berkshire Hathaway common stock (BRK.A and BRK.B) that simplifies the process of making substantial changes in portfolio composition. Finally, relative to the dividend yield strategies of section 10.1, Berkshire-Hathaway does not engage in stock splits or cash dividend payouts. As such, Berkshire Hathaway is a useful example of a company that does not pay dividends but would qualify as an excellent investment for a wide range of investors able to make the sizable investment required to purchase an individual share.

19 Not all studies support the view that the advice of financial planners is inconsistent with, say, modern portfolio theory. For example, in an empirical study using a sample of TIAA-CREF participants, Bodie and Crane (1997) conclude: "Individual asset allocations are consistent with the advice of expert practitioners and with the prescriptions of economic theory." Included in the type of advice dispensed by expert practitioners is the following (Bodie and

Crane 1997, p. 14): "The fraction of assets invested in equities should decline as an investor's age advances. A popular rule-of-thumb regarding the age-equity relationship is that the percentage of one's portfolio to invest in equities should be 100 minus one's age. So, a person thirty years old should invest 70 percent in equities, and a person 70 years old should invest 30 percent in equities."

20 Bernstein (1992, p. 63) credits Richard Brealey with the introduction of this terminology.

21 This lack of a generalized framework is not for lack of trying. The extent of the efforts is reflected in Viceira (2001, p. 435): "This paper extends the previous literature in three directions. First, it incorporates retirement into a dynamic model of optimal consumption and portfolio choice with uninsurable labor income risk. Second, it explores the ability of stocks to hedge consumption from unexpected falls in labor income when labor income is correlated, but not possibly perfectly correlated, with stock returns. Third, it derives an approximate analytical solution of the model . . . This is particularly useful to understand the effects of an uncompensated increase in labor income risk on savings and portfolio decisions."

22 This is not meant to imply that the "portfolio management" aspect of modern Finance lacks empirical contributions. Quite the contrary, consistent with the methodology of logical positivism, there are numerous empirical explorations of portfolio management theories. However, despite decades of empirical analysis, the difficulties of estimating expected returns, *ex post*, from non-experimental data, for use in practical *ex ante* applications of the theory is still elusive, e.g., Elton (1999). As such, the contributions of the portfolio management theory of modern Finance lie primarily in the theoretical sphere.

23 Included in the class of constant relative risk aversion (CRRA) utility functions are the log-wealth, square root wealth and power utility functions. Despite sharing the CRRA property, these functions do not typically generate the same solutions. For example, the log-wealth utility function often produces an intertemporal solution that is the same as the single-period

solution, a result that is only achieved by power utility in special cases.

24 The Friedman-Savage puzzle is concerned with the shape of the expected utility function. In particular, assuming risk aversion requires that the function $EU[W]$ be everywhere concave (downwards). Similarly, the expected utility function for a risk-lover is everywhere convex. The puzzle posed in Friedman and Savage (1948) concerns the shape of the expected utility function for an individual that both gambles (risk lover) and buys insurance (risk averter). Because a large number of individuals do engage in both sorts of activities, Friedman and Savage argue that the expected utility function is concave at low incomes, convex at middle incomes and concave again at high incomes. The puzzle revolves around the assumption, say in the mean-variance optimization framework, that individuals are risk-averse, which implies an everywhere concave expected utility function.

25 In words, the notation $Z(t) \sim N[0, 1]$ means that the continuous (or possibly discrete) random variable $Z(t)$ is distributed normally with mean equal to zero and variance equal to one.

26 Another variant of a time diversification strategy would be to invest in higher beta stocks for long investment horizons and lower beta stocks for short investment horizons. For individual investors able to select the investment horizon, then time diversification suggests a preference for high beta stocks with long investment horizons. When Fama and French (1992) examined such strategies, no statistically significant difference was found between the performance of the high and low beta portfolios.

27 The connection between mean reversion and time diversification is not original to Siegel (1998) and Barberis (2000). As indicated in section 5.2, the result follows from the solutions for the expected return and variance of a mean-reverting process. Lee (1990) is an earlier study that demonstrates mean reversion will lead to time diversification because the non-iid character of the time paths means that the variances of risky assets will converge to values that are smaller than in the iid case.

28 Inflation also has a range of theoretical implications. For example, a fixed income security with no default risk and a term to maturity equal to the investment or rebalancing horizon has the properties of a riskless asset if the model uses nominal returns. However, if real returns or used, then the fixed income security will not be riskless. Though it is possible to argue for the use of inflation-indexed Treasuries as a candidate for the riskless asset when real returns are used, there are a number of practical difficulties that arise in this case.

29 An illustration of the optimization problem, solution procedure and optimal weights that can be derived in continuous time is provided in Ingersoll (1987, pp. 271–6). Discrete-time solutions are given in Ingersoll (1987, ch. 11). These optimal consumption-portfolio models are usually expressed in terms of an additively separable intertemporal utility function defined over consumption between the decision date $t = 0$ and the terminal date $t = T$ with the terminal value of wealth also entering the utility function, i.e., $U[C(0), C(1), \ldots, C(T), W(T)]$. In addition to consumption and terminal wealth a separate bequest motive function, defined over terminal wealth, is typically also included.

30 Following Campbell and Viceira (2002, p. 89): "Any evidence that risk does not scale with horizon . . . is indirect evidence for the predictability of asset returns." Hence, Siegel's claim that mean-reversion in stock returns results in a lower level for the variance of cumulative returns compared to the random walk model implies that there is some empirical model that can be used to predict future returns.

31 In addition to the intertemporal optimal rebalancing case, mean reversion has empirical implications for time diversification in the buy-and-hold approach. The extent of mean reversion depends on the parameter values such as the size of the adjustment coefficient (see section 5.2). If the adjustment coefficient is relatively small, it is possible for a mean-reverting process to wander quite far from the long run mean. Hence, to exploit the potential reduction in the variance of cumulative returns provided by mean-reversion, a buy-and-hold investor would have to determine if the time path of realized returns had permitted the level of stock prices to rise to a level that was so high the potential gains in variance reduction would not likely be obtained within the investor's investment horizon. Hence, while mean-reversion may be theoretically consistent with time diversification, this result may not be applicable to specific points in time for buy-and-hold investors. The pressure this puts on obtaining accurate empirical estimates is evident.

32 The resolution of the St Petersburg paradox is given in Feller (1957) where it is demonstrated that the paradox is a result of attempting to determine a fixed entry fee for a game that has a theoretically infinite number of trials (see section 1.3). The game will have a finite entry value if the number of possible trials is also finite.

33 In this case, the semantic use of "uncertainty" is consistent with the conventional usage in modern Finance where uncertainty is associated with random variables. In turn, these variables have well defined distributions resulting in a measurable form of uncertainty. This usage is not consistent with the use of "uncertainty" by, say, Frank Knight and Keynes (see section 1.2).

34 The stochastic dominance approach will not be examined in detail here, if only because the pairwise comparisons involved in employing stochastic dominance make this approach generally infeasible for portfolio management applications. Elton and Gruber (1984, pp. 229–36) provides a introductory overview of this approach.

References

Ackerman, C., R. McNally and D. Ravenscraft (1999), "The performance of hedge funds: risk, return and incentive," *Journal of Finance* 54: 833–74.

Adams, C.F. and H. Adams (1871), *Chapters of Erie and Other Essays*, Boston: James Osgood.

Akhigbe, A. and J. Madura (2001), "Motivation and performance of seasoned offerings by closed-end funds," *Financial Review* 36: 101–23.

Alexander, G., W. Sharpe and J. Bailey (1993), *Fundamentals of Investments*, 2nd edn, Englewood Cliffs, NJ: Prentice-Hall.

Allais, M. (1953), "Le Comportement de l'homme rational devant le risque, Critique des postulates de l'ecole Americaine," *Econometrica* 21: 503–46.

Alter, G. and J. Riley (1986), "How to bet on lives: a guide to life contingency contracts in early Modern Europe," in P. Uselding (ed.), *Research in Economic History* 10: 1–53.

Altman, E. and G. Bana (2003), "Defaults and returns on high yield bonds: the year 2002 in review," NYU Working Paper (http://pages.stern.nyu.edu/~ealtman/Q3-2003.pdf).

Altman, E. and V. Kishore (1998), "Defaults and returns on high yield bonds," in F. Fabozzi (ed.), *The Handbook of Corporate Debt Instruments*, New Hope, PA: Frank Fabozzi Associates.

Ammann, M. and H. Zimmermann (2001), "Tracking error and tactical asset allocation," *Financial Analysts Journal* (March/April): 32–43.

Anari, A. and J. Kolari (2001), "Stock prices and inflation," *Journal of Financial Research* 24: 587–602.

Anderson, R. (1955), "Unrealized potentials in growth stocks," *Harvard Business Review* (March/April), 5–67.

Appel, G. (1974), *Winning Market Systems: 83 Ways to Beat the Market*, Great Neck, NY: Signalalert.

Appel, G. and M. Zweig (1976), *New Directions in Technical Analysis*, Great Neck, NY: Signalalert.

Arnold, L. (1974), *Stochastic Differential Equations*, New York: Wiley.

Arnott, R. (1998), "Active asset allocation," chapter 7 in Bernstein and Damodaran (eds).

Arzac, E. (1974), "Utility analysis of chance-constrained portfolio selection," *Journal of Financial and Quantitative Analysis* 8: 993–1007.

Arzac, E. and V. Bawa (1977), "Portfolio choice and equilibrium in capital markets with safety-first investors," *Journal of Financial Economics* 4: 277–88.

Asquith, P. (1995), "Convertible bonds are not called late," *Journal of Finance* 50: 1275–89.

Asquith, P., D. Williams and E. Wolff (1989), "Original issue high yield bonds: aging analysis of defaults, exchanges and calls," *Journal of Finance* (Sept.): 923–52.

Athanassokos, G. and P. Carayannapoulos (2000), "Bargains in the corporate convertible bond market," *Canadian Journal of Administrative Sciences* 17: 153–65.

Babbel, D. and S. Zenios (1992), "Pitfalls in the analysis of option-adjusted spreads," *Financial Analysts Journal* (July/Aug.): 65–9.

Bajaj, M., S. Mazumdar and A. Sarin (2002), "The costs of issuing preferred stock," *Journal of Financial Research* 25: 577–93.

Bailey, E. (2002), "Aviation policy: past and present," *Southern Economic Journal* 69: 12–20.

Balbas, A. and A. Ibanez (1998), "When can you Immunize a Bond Portfolio?", *Journal of Banking and Finance* 22: 1571–95.

Baliga, W. (1995), "U.S. district court makes summary judgment ruling," *Journal of Accountancy* 179: 20.

Ball, C. and W. Torous (1983), "Bond price dynamics and options," *Journal of Financial and Quantitative Analysis* 17: 517–31.

Ball, R. and P. Brown (1968), "An empirical evaluation of accounting income numbers," *Journal of Accounting Research* 6: 159–78.

Barber, T. (1999), "Bond immunization and affine term structures," *Financial Review* 34: 137–40.

Barberis, N. (2000), "Investing for the long run when returns are predictable," *Journal of Finance* 55: 255–64.

Barney, J. (1997), *Gaining the Sustaining Competitive Advantage*, Reading, MA: Addison-Wesley.

Barth, M. (2001), "Risk-based capital," *Journal of Insurance Regulation* 20: 233–43.

Barth, M., D. Cram and K. Nelson (2001), "Accruals and the prediction of future cash flows," *Accounting Review* 76: 27–58.

Basu, S. (1977), "Investment performance of common stocks in relation to their price-earnings ratios: a test of the efficient markets hypothesis," *Journal of Finance* 32: 663–82.

Basu, S. (1983), "The relationship between earnings yield, market value and the return for NYSE common stocks: further evidence," *Journal of Financial Economics* 12: 129–56.

Battacharya, M. (2001), "Convertible securities and their valuation," chapter 51 in Fabozzi.

Baumol, W. (1970), *Economic Dynamics*, 3rd edn, London: Macmillan.

Baumol, W. (1977), *Economic Theory and Operations Analysis*, 4th edn, Englewood Cliffs, NJ: Prentice-Hall.

Beller, K., J. Kling and M. Levinson (1998), "Are industry stock returns predictable?," *Financial Analysis Journal* 54 (Sept.–Oct.): 42–58.

Berkman, H., M. Bradbury and J. Ferguson (2000), "The accuracy of price-earnings and discounted cash flow methods of IPO equity valuation," *Journal of International Financial Management & Accounting* 11: 71–83.

Berkshire Hathaway (2003), *Annual Report 2002*, obtained from www.berkshirehathaway.com.

Benninga, S. and M. Blume (1985), "On the optimality of portfolio insurance," *Journal of Finance* (Dec.): 1341–52.

Bernoulli, N. (1709; 1975), *De Usu Artis Conjectandi in Jure*, Basel; reprinted in *Die Werke von Jakob Bernoulli*, (vol. 3), Basel: Birkhauser.

Bernstein, L. (1989; 1993), *Financial Statement Analysis*, 4th edn (5th edn 1993), Homewood, IL: Irwin.

Bernstein, P. (1992), *Capital Ideas: The Improbable Origins of Modern Wall Street*, New York: Free Press.

Bernstein, P. (1997), "How long can you run: and where are you running?", *Journal of Post-Keynesian Economics* 20: 183–9.

Bernstein, P. (1998), "Stock market risk in a post-Keynesian world," *Journal of Post-Keynesian Economics* 21: 15–24.

Bernstein, P. and A. Damodaran (eds) (1998), *Investment Management*, New York: John Wiley.

Bernstein, P.I. (1956), "Growth companies vs. growth stocks," *Harvard Business Review* (Sept./Oct.): 87–98.

Bessembinder, H. and K. Chan (1998), "Market efficiency and the returns to technical analysis," *Financial Management* 27: 5–17.

Bhaskar, R. (1978), *A Realist Theory of Science*, 2nd edn, Brighton, UK: Harvester.

Biddle, G., R. Bowen and J. Wallace (1997), "Does EVA beat earnings? Evidence on association of stock returns and firm values," *Journal of Accounting and Economics* 24: 201–336.

Biddle, G., R. Bowen and J. Wallace (1998), "Economic value added: some empirical EVAdence," *Managerial Finance* 24: 60–71.

Bierman, H. (1991), *The Great Myths of 1929 and the Lessons to be Learned*, Westport, CN: Greenwood Press.

Bierman, H. (1998), *The Causes of the 1929 Stock Market Crash*, Westport, CN: Greenwood Press.

Bierwag, G. (1977), "Duration and the term structure of interest rates," *Journal of Financial and Quantitative Analysis* 12: 725–42.

Bierwag, G. (1987), *Duration Analysis, Managing Interest Rate Risk*, Cambridge, MA: Ballinger.

Bierwag, G. and C. Khang (1979), "An immunization strategy is a maxmin strategy," *Journal of Finance* 37: 379–89.

Bierwag, G., I. Fooladi and G. Roberts (1993), "Designing an immunized portfolio: is M-squared the key?", *Journal of Banking and Finance* 17: 1147–70.

Bierwag, G., G. Kaufman and A. Toevs (1983), "Duration: its development and use in bond portfolio management," *Financial Analysts Journal* (July/Aug.): 15–35.

Bishop, G. (1961), "Evolution of the Dow theory," *Financial Analysts Journal* 17 (Sept./Oct.): 25–36.

Black, F. (1976), "The pricing of commodity contracts," *Journal of Financial Economics* 3: 167–79.

Black, F. and M. Scholes (1973), "The pricing of options and corporate liabilities," *Journal of Political Economy* 81: 637–59.

Black, F., E. Derman and W. Toy (1990), "A one-factor model of interest rates and its application to treasury bond options," *Financial Analysis Journal* (February): 33–9.

Blanc, R. and R. Gordon (1999), "Reforming the unbargained contract: avoiding bondholder claims for surprise calls," *Business Lawyer* 55: 317–49.

Blake, D., B. Lehmann and A. Timmermann (1999), "Asset allocation dynamics and pension fund performance," *Journal of Business* 72: 429–61.

Blau, W. (1995), *Momentum, Direction and Divergence*, New York: John Wiley.

Blaug, M. (1978), *Economic Theory in Retrospect*, 3rd edn, Cambridge, UK: Cambridge University Press.

Blaug, M. (1992), *The Methodology of Economics: Or, How Economists Explain*, Cambridge, UK: Cambridge University Press.

Blume, M. and I. Friend (1975), "The asset structure of individual portfolios and some implications for utility functions," *Journal of Finance* 10: 585–603.

Bodie, Z. (1974), "Common stocks as a hedge against inflation," *Journal of Finance* 31: 459–70.

Bodie, Z. (1995), "On the risk of stocks in the long run," *Financial Analysts Journal* (May/June): 18–22.

Bodie, Z. and D. Crane (1997), "Personal investing: advice, theory and evidence," *Financial Analysts Journal* (Nov./Dec.): 13–23.

Bodie, Z., A. Kane and A. Marcus (1999), *Investments*, Boston: Irwin, 4th edn.

Bohan, J. (1981), "Relative strength: further positive evidence," *Journal of Portfolio Management* 7: 39–46.

Bond Market Association (2002), "An investors guide to collateralized mortgage obligations."

Bond, D. (2003), "The big downside: this year's FAA forecast sees slower growth. Unfortunately, that's the good news," *Aviation Week and Space Technology*, Mar. 24.

Bookstaber, R. (1991), "The valuation and exposure management of bonds with embedded options," chapter 38 in Fabozzi.

Bookstaber, R. and R. Clarke (1983), *Option Strategies for Institutional Investment Management*, London: Addison Wesley.

Borenstein, S. and N. Rose (1994), "Competition and price dispersion in the US airline industry," *Journal of Political Economy* 103: 653–83.

Boudoukh, J. and M. Richardson (1993), "Stock returns and inflation: a long-horizon perspective," *American Economic Review* 83: 1346–55.

Bowden, R. (1997), "Generalizing interest rate duration with directional derivatives: direction X and applications," *Management Science* 43: 198–205.

Box, G. and G. Jenkins (1970), *Time Series Analysis, Forecasting and Control*, San Francisco: Holden Day.

Brealey, R. (1991), "Harry M. Markowitz's contributions to financial economics: bibliography of Markowitz's Publications, 1952–1990," *Scandinavian Journal of Economics* 93: 7–21.

Brealey, R. and S. Myers (1991), *Principles of Corporate Finance*, 4th edn, New York: McGraw-Hill.

Brennan, M. and E. Schwartz (1976), "The pricing of equity-linked life insurance policies with an asset value guarantee," *Journal of Financial Economics* 4: 195–213.

Brennan, M. and E. Schwartz (1977), "Savings bonds, retractable bonds and callable bonds," *Journal of Financial Economics* 5: 67–88.

Brennan, M. and E. Schwartz (1979), "A Continuous time approach to the pricing of bonds," *Journal of Banking and Finance* 3: 133–55.

Brennan, M. and E. Schwartz (1987), "Time invariant portfolio insurance strategies," UCLA Working Paper (September).

Brieman, L. (1960), "Investment policies for expanding businesses optimal in a long run sense," *Naval Research Logistics Quarterly* 7: 647–51.

Brinson, G., B. Singer and G. Beebower (1991), "Determinants of portfolio performance II: an update," *Financial Analysts Journal* (May/June): 40–8.

Briys, E. and B. Solnick (1992), "Optimal currency hedge ratios and interest rate risk," *Journal of International Money and Finance* 11: 431–46.

Brock, W., J. Lakonishok and B. LeBaron (1992), "Simple technical trading rules and stochastic properties of stock returns," *Journal of Finance* 47: 1731–64.

Brockett, P. and Y. Kahane (1992), "Risk, return, skewness and preference," *Management Science* 38: 851–66.

Brown, S., W. Goetzmann, R. Ibbotson and S. Ross (1992), "Survivorship bias in performance studies," *Review of Financial Studies* 5: 553–80.

Brown, S., W. Goetzmann and A. Kumar (1998), "The Dow theory: William Peter Hamilton's track record reconsidered," *Journal of Finance* 53: 1311–33.

Brown, S., W. Goetzmann and R. Ibbotson (1999), "Offshore hedge funds: survival and performance, 1989–1995," *Journal of Business* 72: 91–117.

Brown, S., W. Goetzmann and J. Park (2001), "Careers and survival: competition and risk in the hedge fund and CTA industry," *Journal of Finance* 56: 1869–86.

Bruecker, J. (2003), "International airfares in the age of alliances," *Review of Economics and Statistics* 85: 105–18.

Buckley, H. (1924), "Sir Thomas Gresham and the foreign exchanges," *Economic Journal* 34: 589–601.

Busse, M. (2002), "Firm financial condition and airline price wars," *Rand Journal of Economics* 33: 298–318.

Butler, A. (2002), "Revisiting optimal call policy for convertibles," *Financial Analysts Journal* (Jan./Feb.): 50–5.

Buttler, H. (1995), "Evaluation of callable bonds: finite difference methods, stability and accuracy," *Economic Journal* 105: 374–84.

Buttler, H. and J. Waldvogel (1996), "Pricing callable bonds by means of Green's function," *Mathematical Finance* 6: 53–89.

Caldwell, T. (1995), "Introduction: the model for superior performance," chapter 1 in Lederman and Klein (eds.).

Callahan, C., W. Shaw and W. Terando (2001), "Tax and regulatory motivations for issuing non-voting, non-convertible preferred stock," *Journal of Accounting Research* 39: 463–81.

Campbell, J. (1996), "Understanding risk and return," *Journal of Political Economy* 104: 298–345.

Campbell, J. and L. Viceira (2002), *Strategic Asset Allocation: Portfolio Choice for Long-Term Investors*, New York: Oxford University Press.

Campbell, J., A. Lo and A. MacKinley (1997), *The Econometrics of Financial Markets*, Princeton, NJ: Princeton University Press.

Canadian Securities Institute (1992), *The Canadian Securities Course*, Toronto: Canadian Securities Institute.

Canner, N., G. Mankiw and D. Weil (1997), "An asset allocation puzzle," *American Economic Review* 87: 181–91.

Carhart, M. (1997), "On persistence in mutual fund performance," *Journal of Finance* 52: 57–82.

Carpenter, J. and A. Lynch (1999), "Survivorship bias and attrition effects in measures of performance persistence," *Journal of Financial Economics* 54: 337–74.

Carron, A. (1992), "Understanding CMOs, REMICs and other mortgage derivatives," *Institutional Investor* (June): 65–82.

Cathcart, L. and L. El-Jahel (1998), "Valuation of defaultable bonds," *Journal of Fixed Income* (June): 65–78.

Chambers, D., W. Carleton and R. McEnally (1988), "Immunization default-free bond portfolios with a duration vector," *Journal of Financial and Quantitative Analysis* 23: 89–104.

Chan, K., A. Hameed and W. Tong (2000), "Profitability of momentum strategies in the international equity markets," *Journal of Financial and Quantitative Analysis* 35: 153–72.

Chan, K., N. Jegadeesh and J. Lakonishok (1996), "Momentum strategies," *Journal of Finance* 51: 1681–1713.

Chan, K.C., G. Karolyi, F. Longstaff and A. Sanders (1992), "An empirical comparison of alternative models of the short-term interest rate," *Journal of Finance* 47: 1209–27.

Chance, D. (1990), "Default risk and the duration of zero-coupon bonds," *Journal of Finance* 45: 265–74.

Chance, D. (1998), *An Introduction to Derivatives*, 4th edn, New York: Dryden Press.

Chance, D. and J. Jordan (1996), "Duration, convexity and time as components of bond returns," *Journal of Fixed Income* (Sept.): 88–96.

Chapman, D. and N. Pearson (2001), "Recent advances in estimating term structure models," *Financial Analysts Journal* (July/Aug.): 77–93.

Chen, G., M. Firth and J.-B. Kim (2002), "The use of accounting information for the valuation of dual-class shares listed on China's stock markets," *Accounting and Business Research* 32: 123–31.

Cheng, S. (1991), "On the feasibility of arbitrage-based option pricing when stochastic bond price processes are involved," *Journal of Economic Theory*, 53: 185–98.

Chiang, R. and J. Okunev (1993), "An alternative formulation on the pricing of foreign currency options," *Journal of Futures Markets* 903–7.

Christensen, P. and B. Sorensen (1994), "Duration, convexity and time value," *Journal of Portfolio Management* (winter): 51–60.

Christie, W. (1990), "Dividend yield and expected returns: the zero-dividend puzzle," *Journal of Financial Economics* 28: 95–126.

Cipolla, C. (ed.) (1974), *The Fontana Economic History of Europe*, vol. 2, Glasgow: Collins.

Clews, H. (1908), *Fifty Years on Wall Street*, New York: Irving Press; reprinted by New York: Arno Press (1973).

Clinton, D. and S. Chen (1996), "Do new performance measures measure up?", *Management Accounting* 80: 38–43.

Cochrane, J. (2001), *Asset Pricing*, Princeton, NJ: Princeton University Press.

Cohen, J. (1953), "The element of lottery in British government bonds, 1694–1919," *Economica* (Aug.): 237–46.

Conklin, H. (1958), "Growth stocks: a critical view," *Analysts Journal* (Feb.).

Conrad, J. and G. Kaul (1993), "Long-term market overreaction or biases in computed returns?", *Journal of Finance* (March): 39–63.

Constantinides, G. (1979), "A note on the suboptimality of dollar-cost averaging as an investment policy," *Journal of Financial and Quantitative Analysis* 14: 443–50.

Constantinides, G. (2002), "Rational asset prices," *Journal of Finance* 57: 1566–82.

Coolidge, J.L. (1990), *The Mathematics of Great Amateurs*, 2nd edn, Oxford: Clarendon.

Cootner, P. (ed.) (1965), *The Random Character of Stock Market Prices*, Cambridge, MA: MIT Press.

Cope, S. (1978), "The stock exchange revisited: a new look at the market in securities in London in the eighteenth century," *Economica* 45: 1–21.

Copeland, T., T. Koller and J. Murrin (1996), *Valuation: Measuring and Managing the Value of Companies*, 2nd edn, New York: Wiley.

Cordeiro, J. and D. Kent (2001), "Do EVA adopters outperform their peers? Evidence from security analyst earnings forecasts," *American Business Review* 19: 57–63.

Cornew, R. (1988), "Commodity pool operators and their pools: expenses and profitability," *Journal of Futures Markets* 8: 617–37.

Cowles, A. (1934), "Can stock market forecasters forecast?", *Econometrica* 1: 309–24.

Cox, D. and H. Miller (1965), *The Theory of Stochastic Processes*, London: Chapman and Hall.

Cox, J. and S. Ross (1976), "The valuation of options for alternative stochastic processes," *Journal of Financial Economics* 3: 145–66.

Cox., J. and M. Rubinstein (1985), *Option Markets*, Englewood Cliffs, NJ: Prentice-Hall.

Cox, J., J. Ingersoll and S. Ross (1985), "A theory of the term structure of interest rates," *Econometrica* (March): 385–407.

Crabbe, L. and P. Nikoulis (1997), "The putable bond market: structure, historical experience and strategies," *Journal of Fixed Income* (Dec.): 47–60.

Crack, T. and S. Nawalkha (2000), "Interest rate sensitivities of bond risk measures," *Financial Analysts Journal* (Jan./Feb.): 34–43.

Culp, C. (2001), *The Risk Management Process*, New York: Wiley.

Cunningham, L. (ed.) (2002), *The Essays of Warren Buffett: Lessons for Investors and Managers*, revised edn, New York: John Wiley.

Damodaran, V. (1994), *Damodaran on Valuation: Security Analysis for Investment and Corporate Finance*, New York: John Wiley.

Daniel, K., M. Grinblatt, S. Titman and R. Wermers (1997), "Measuring mutual fund performance with characteristic based benchmark," *Journal of Finance* 52: 1035–58.

Daston, L. (1987), "The domestication of risk: mathematical probability and insurance 1650–1830," in L. Kruger, L. Daston and M. Heidelberger (eds), *The Probabilistic Revolution*, vol. 1, London: MIT Press, ch. 10.

Daston, L. (1988), *Classical Probability in the Enlightenment*, Princeton, NJ: Princeton University Press.

Davidson, P. (1991), "Is probability theory relevant for uncertainty?: a post-Keynesian perspective," *Journal of Economic Perspectives* 3: 29–43.

Dechow, P. and D. Skinner (2000), "Earnings management: reconciling the views of accounting academics, practitioners, and regulators," *Accounting Horizons* 14: 235–50.

Dechow, P., A. Hutton and R. Sloan (1999), "An empirical assessment of the residual income valuation model," *Journal of Accounting and Economics* 26: 1–34.

De Bondt, W. and R. Thaler (1985), "Does the stock market overreact?", *Journal of Finance* 40: 793–805.

De Bondt, W. and R. Thaler (1987), "Further evidence on stock market overreaction and stock market seasonality," *Journal of Finance* 42: 557–81.

de Marchi, N. and P. Harrison (1994), "Trading 'in the wind' and with guile: the troublesome matter of the short selling of shares in seventeenth-century Holland," in N. de Marchi and M. Morgan (eds), *Higgling: Transactors and their Markets in the History of Economics*, Annual Supplement to *History of Political Economy* 26.

Deng, Y., J. Quigley and R. van Order (2000), "Mortgage terminations, heterogeneity and the exercise of mortgage options," *Econometrica* 68: 275–307.

Dewing, A. (1953), *The Financial Policy of Corporations*, New York: Ronald Press.

Dhrymes, P. (1974), *Econometrics, Statistical Foundations and Applications*, New York: Springer-Verlag.

Dhrymes, P. (1981), *Distributed Lags: Problems of Estimation and Formulation*, 2nd edn, New York: North Holland.

Dialynas, C., S. Durn and J. Ritchie (2001), "Convertible securities and their investment characteristics," chapter 50 in Fabozzi.

Dickson, P. (1967), *The Financial Revolution in England*, New York: St Martin's Press.

Dimson, E., P. Marsh and M. Staunton (2002), *Triumph of the Optimists: 101 Years of Global Investment Returns*, Princeton, NJ: Princeton University Press.

Donkers, B., B. Melenberg and A. van Soest (2001), "Estimating risk attitudes using lotteries: a large sample approach," *Journal of Risk and Uncertainty* (March) 22: 165–95.

Dresner, M., R. Windle and Y. Yao (2002), "Airport barriers to entry in the US," *Journal of Transport Economics and Policy* 36: 389–405.

Drew, G. (1951), *New Methods for Profit in the Stock Market*, Boston: Metcalf Press.

Du Bois, P. (2000), "The oracle of Dow," *Barron's*, June 12: 39–40.

Du Bois, P. (2001), "Dow 2500, anyone? An interview with Richard Russell," *Barron's*, Apr. 16: 28–30.

Duffie, D. (1988), *Securities Markets, Stochastic Models*, New York: Academic Press.

Duffie, D. (1989), *Futures Markets*, Englewood Cliffs, NJ: Prentice-Hall.

Duffie, D. (2001), *Dynamic Asset Pricing Theory*, 3rd edn, Princeton, NJ: Princeton University Press.

Dunbar, N. (2000), *Inventing Money: The Story of Long-term Capital Management and the Legends Behind It*, New York: Wiley.

Dunn, K. and J. McConnell (1981), "Valuation of GNMA mortgage-backed securities," *Journal of Finance* 36: 599–616.

Durand, D. (1957), "Growth stocks and the Petersburg paradox," *Journal of Finance* 12: 348–63.

Durand, D. (1959), "The cost of capital, corporation finance and the theory of investment: comment," *American Economic Review* 49: 639–55.

Durand, D. (1960), "Portfolio selection: efficient diversification of investments, review," *American Economic Review* 50: 234–6.

Dym, S. (1992), "Global and local components of foreign bond risk," *Financial Analysts Journal*, (Mar./Apr.): 83–91.

Eaker, M. et al. (1991), "Investment in foreign equities: diversification, hedging and risk," *Journal of Multinational Financial Management* 1: 1–21.

Eames, F. (1894), *The New York Stock Exchange*, New York: Greenwood Press; reprint (1968).

Ederington, L. and J. Goh (2001), "Is a convertible bond call really bad news?", *Journal of Business* 74: 459–76.

Edwards, F. and M. Caglayan (2001), "Hedge fund and commodity fund investment in bull and bear markets," *Journal of Portfolio Management* 27: 97–108.

Elton, E., M. Gruber, and J. Rentzler (1987), "Professionally managed, publicly traded commodity funds," *Journal of Business* 60: 175–200.

Edwards, R. and J. Magee (1958), *Technical Analysis of Stock Trends*, 4th edn, Springfield, MA: John Magee.

Edwards, R. and J. Magee (1966), *Technical Analysis of Stock Trends*, 5th edn, Springfield, MA: John Magee.

Ehrbar, A. (1998), *EVA: The Real Key to Creating Wealth*, New York: Wiley.

Eiteman, W. and F. Smith (1953), *Common Stock Value and Yields*, Ann Arbor, MI: University of Michigan Press.

Elder, A. (1993), *Trading for a Living*, New York: John Wiley.

Elton, E. (1999), "Expected return, realized return and asset pricing tests," *Journal of Finance* 54: 1199–1220.

Elton, E. and M. Gruber (1974), "An algorithm for maximizing the geometric mean," *Management Science* (Dec.): 483–8.

Elton, E. and M. Gruber (1984), *Modern Portfolio Theory and Investment Analysis*, 2nd edn, New York: Wiley.

Elton, E. and M. Gruber (1995), *Modern Portfolio Theory and Investment Analysis*, 5th edn, New York: Wiley.

Elton, E. and M. Gruber (2000), "The rationality of asset allocation recommendations," *Journal of Financial and Quantitative Analysis* 36: 27–41.

Elton, E., M. Gruber and J. Rentzler (1983), "A simple examination of the empirical relationship between dividend yields and deviations from the CAPM," *Journal of Banking and Finance* 7: 135–46.

Elton, E., M. Gruber and C. Blake (1996), "Survivorship bias and mutual fund performance," *Review of Financial Studies* 9: 1097–1120.

Ely, D., A. Houston and C. Houston (2002), "Taxes and the choice of issuing preferred stock vs. debt," *Journal of the American Taxation Association* 24: 29–46.

English, J. (2001), *Applied Equity Analysis*, New York: McGraw-Hill.

Eun, C. and B. Resnick (1988), "Exchange rate uncertainty, forward contracts and international portfolio selection," *Journal of Finance* 43: 197–215.

Eun, C. and B. Resnick (1995), "International diversification of investment portfolios: US and Japanese perspectives," *Management Science* 40: 140–61.

Evans, M. (1965), *Arbitrage in Domestic Securities in the United States*, W. Nyack, NY: Parker.

Evans, N. (2002), "Is the game over for hedge funds?", *Euromoney* (Jan.): 10–12.

Fabozzi, F. (1989), *Bond Markets, Analysis and Strategies*, 2nd edn, Englewood Cliffs, NJ: Prentice-Hall.

Fabozzi, F. (1991), *Handbook of Fixed Income Securities*, 3rd edn, New York: McGraw-Hill.

Fabozzi, F. (2000), *Bond Markets, Analysis and Strategies*, 4th edn, Englewood Cliffs, NJ: Prentice-Hall.

Fabozzi, F. (2001), *Handbook of Fixed Income Securities*, 6th edn, New York: McGraw-Hill.

Fabozzi, F. (2002), *Fixed Income Securities*, New York: Wiley.

Fabozzi, F., J. Howe, T. Makabe, and T. Sudo (1993), "Recent evidence on the distribution patterns in Chapter 11 reorganizations," *Journal of Fixed Income* (spring): 6–23.

Fama, E. (1998), "Market efficiency, long-term returns, and behavioral finance," *Journal of Financial Economics* 49: 283–306.

Fama, E. (1965), "The behavior of stock market prices," *Journal of Business* 38: 34–105.

Fama, E. (1970), "Efficient capital markets: a review of theory and empirical work," *Journal of Finance* 25 (March): 383–417.

Fama, E. (1970a), "Multiperiod consumption-investment decisions," *American Economic Review* 60: 163–74.

Fama, E. (1976), *Foundations of Finance*, New York: Basic Books.

Fama, E. (1981), "Stock returns, real activity, inflation and money," *American Economic Review* 71: 545–65.

Fama, E. and M. Blume (1966), "Filter rules and stock market trading profits," *Journal of Business* 39: 226–41.

Fama, E. and J. MacBeth (1973), "Risk, return and equilibrium: empirical tests," *Journal of Political Economy* 81: 607–36.

Fama, E. and K. French (1992), "The cross-section of expected stock returns," *Journal of Finance* 47: 427–66.

Fama, E. and K. French (1995), "Size and book-to-market factors in earnings and returns," *Journal of Finance* 50: 131–84.

Fama, E. and K. French (1998), "Value vs. growth: the international evidence," *Journal of Finance* 53: 1975–99.

Fama, E., L. Fisher, M. Jensen and R. Roll (1969), "The adjustment of stock prices to new information," *International Economic Review* 10: 1–21.

Feller, W. (1957), *An Introduction to Probability Theory and Its Applications*, vol. 1, 2nd edn, New York: Wiley.

Feller, W. (1966), *An Introduction to Probability Theory and Its Applications*, vol. 2, New York: Wiley.

Ferson, W. and R. Schadt (1996), "Measuring fund strategy and performance in changing economic conditions," *Journal of Finance* 51: 425–62.

Finnerty, J. (1999), "Adjusting the binomial model for default risk," *Journal of Portfolio Management* (winter): 93–103.

Fischer, S. (1975), "The demand for index bonds," *Journal of Political Economy* 83: 509–34.

Fishburn, P. (1982), *The Foundations of Expected Utility*, Dordrecht: Reidel.

Fisher, I. (1896), *Appreciation and Interest*, New York: Macmillan.

Fisher, I. (1906), *The Nature of Capital and Income*, New York: A.M. Kelley reprint (1965).

Fisher, I. (1907), *The Rate of Interest: Its Nature, Determination and Relation to Economic Phenomena*, New York: Macmillan.

Fisher, I. (1912), *How to Invest when Prices are Rising*, Scranton, PA: Lynn Sumner.

Fisher, I. (1930), *The Stock Market Crash: And After*, New York: Macmillan.

Fisher, I. (1930a), *The Theory of Interest: As Determined by Impatience to Spend Income and Opportunity to Invest in It*, New York: Macmillan.

Fisher, K. and M. Statman (1997), "The mean-variance optimization puzzle: security portfolios and food portfolios," *Financial Analysts Journal* (July/Aug.): 41–50.

Fisher, K. and M. Statman (1999), "A behavioral framework for time diversification," *Financial Analysts Journal* (May/June): 88–97.

Fisher, L. and J. Lorie (1964), "Rates of return on investment in common stocks," *Journal of Business* 37: 1–21.

Fisher, P. (1958), *Common Stocks and Uncommon Profits* (revised edn, 1960), New York: Harper and Row.

Fisher, P. (1975), *Conservative Investors Sleep Well*, New York: Harper and Row.

Fisher, P. (1980), *Developing an Investment Philosophy*, Charlottesville, VA: Financial Analysts Research Foundation.

Fong, C. and O. Vasicek (1984), "A risk minimizing strategy for portfolio immunization," *Journal of Finance* 39: 1541–6.

Foster (1986), *Financial Statement Analysis*, 2nd edn, Englewood Cliffs, NJ: Prentice-Hall.

Fox, S. (1999), "Assessing TAA manager performance," *Journal of Portfolio Management* (fall): 40–9.

Francis, J. (1983), *Management of Investments*, New York: McGraw-Hill.

Frankfurter, G. (1999), "What is the puzzle in the 'dividend puzzle'?", *Journal of Portfolio Management* (summer): 76–85.

Freund, J. (1971), *Mathematical Statistics*, 2nd edn, Englewood Cliffs, NJ: Prentice-Hall.

Fridson, M., (ed.) (1996), *Extraordinary Popular Delusions and the Madness of Crowds; and, Confusion de Confusiones* (reprints of classic texts), New York: Wiley.

Fridson, M. and F. Alvarez (2002), *Financial Statement Analysis*, New York: John Wiley.

Friedman, M. (1953), "The methodology of positive economics," in M. Friedman, *Essays in Positive Economics*, Chicago: University of Chicago Press.

Friedman, M. and L. Savage (1948), "The utility analysis of choices involving risk," *Journal of Political Economy* 56: 279–304.

Fung, W. and D. Hsieh (2000), "Performance characteristics of hedge funds and commodity funds: natural vs. spurious biases," *Journal of Financial and Quantitative Analysis* 35: 291–307.

Fung, W. and D. Hsieh (2002), "Benchmarks of hedge fund performance: information content and measurement biases," *Financial Analysts Journal* 58: 22–34.

Gadamer, H.-G. (1960), *Truth and Method*, New York: Seabury Press (1975) translation of the 2nd German edn of (1965).

Garbade, K. (1996), *Fixed Income Analytics*, Cambridge, MA: MIT Press.

Garman, M. and S. Kohlhagen (1983), "Foreign currency option values," *Journal of International Money and Finance* 2: 231–37.

Gartley, H. (1930), *Profits in the Stock Market*, Pomeroy, WA: Lambert-Gann.

Gartley, H. (1934), *Charting the Stock Market*, New York: Harper & Brothers.

Garza-Gomez, X. (2001), "The information content of the book-to-market ratio," *Financial Analysts Journal* 57: 78–95.

Gatto, M., R. Geske, R. Litzenberger and H. Sosin (1980), "Mutual fund insurance," *Journal of Financial Economics* 7: 283–317.

Geisst, C. (1997), *Wall Street: A History*, New York: Oxford University Press.

Geman, H. and M. Yor (1993), "Bessel processes, Asian options and perpetuities," *Mathematical Finance* (Oct.): 349–75.

Geske, R. and R. Roll (1983), "The fiscal and monetary linkages between stock returns and inflation," *Journal of Finance* 38: 1–33.

Giammarino, R., E. Maynes, R. Brealey, S. Myers and A. Marcus (1996), *Fundamentals of Corporate Finance*, (first Canadian edn), New York: McGraw-Hill.

Gibbons, M. and K. Ramaswamy (1993), "The term structure of interest rates: empirical evidence," *Review of Financial Studies* 6: 619–58.

Gibson, R. and E. Schwartz (1990), "Stochastic convenience yield and the pricing of oil contingent claims," *Journal of Finance* 45: 959–76.

Gittell, J. (2003), *The Southwest Airlines Way*, New York: McGraw-Hill.

Goetzmann, W., J. Ingersoll and S. Ross (2003), "High water marks and hedge fund management contracts," *Journal of Finance* 58: 1685–1718.

Gordon, J.S. (1999), *The Great Game: The Emergence of Wall Street as a World Power 1653–2000*, New York: Scribner.

Gordon, M. (1962), *The Investment Financing and Valuation of the Corporation*, Homewood, IL: Irwin.

Grabbe, O. (1991), *International Financial Markets*, New York: Elsevier.

Graham, B. (1949; 1973), *The Intelligent Investor: A Book of Practical Counsel*, 4th edn, New York: Harper and Row.

Graham, B. and D. Dodd (1934), *Security Analysis*, New York: McGraw-Hill.

Graham, B., D. Dodd and S. Cottle (1962), *Security Analysis*, New York: McGraw-Hill.

Graham, B., D. Dodd and C. Tatham (1951), *Security Analysis*, New York: McGraw-Hill.

Grauer, R. and N. Hakanson (1987), "Gains from international diversification: 1968–85 returns on portfolios of stocks and bonds," *Journal of Finance* 42: 721–42.

Grauer, R. and N. Hakanson (1993), "On the use of mean-variance and quadratic approximations in implementing dynamic investment strategies," *Management Science* 39: 856–71.

Grauer, R. and N. Hakanson (1998), "On naive approaches to timing the market: the empirical probability assessment approach with an inflation adaptor," in W. Ziemba and J. Mulvey (eds), *Worldwide Asset and Liability Modeling*, Cambridge, UK: Cambridge University Press.

Gray, M. (2002), "New technique defines the limits of upgrading heavy oils, bitumens," *Oil and Gas Journal* (Jan. 7): 50–4.

Greenwald, B., J. Kahn, P. Sonkin and M. van Biema (2001), *Value Investing, From Graham to Buffett and Beyond*, New York: Wiley.

Greenwood, M. (1940), "A statistical mare's nest," *Journal of the Royal Historical Society* 103: 246–8.

Gregoriou, G. (2002), "Hedge fund survival lifetimes," *Journal of Asset Management* 3: 237–52.

Greiner, D., A. Kalay and H. Kiyoshi (2002), "The market for callable-convertible bonds: evidence from Japan," *Pacific Basin Finance Journal* 10: 1–27.

Griffin, J. and M. Lemmon (2002), "Book-to-market equity, distress risk, and stock returns," *Journal of Finance* 57: 2317–36.

Gross, L. (1982), *The Art of Selling Intangibles*, New York: New York Institute of Finance.

Grubel, H. (1968), "Internationally diversified portfolios: welfare gains and capital flows," *American Economic Review* 58: 1299–1314.

Hagstrom, R. (1995), *The Warren Buffett Way: Investment Strategies of the World's Greatest Investor*, New York: John Wiley.

Hagstrom, R. (2000), *The Warren Buffett Portfolio*, New York: John Wiley.

Hahm, J. (1998), "Consumption adjustment to real interest rates: intertemporal substitution revisited," *Journal of Economic Dynamics and Control* (February) 22: 293–320.

Haines, L. (2001), "Alberta's heavy oils," *Oil & Gas Investor* 21 (October): 30–41.

Hakansson, N. (1970), "Optimal investment and consumption strategies under risk for a class of utility functions," *Econometrica* 38: 587–607.

Hakansson, N. (1971), "Capital growth and the mean-variance approach to portfolio selection," *Journal of Financial and Quantitative Analysis* 6: 517–57.

Hakkio, C. and M. Rush (1991), "Cointegration: how short is the long run?," *Journal of International Money and Finance* 10: 571–81.

Hald, A. (1990), *A History of Probability and Statistics and Their Applications before 1750*, New York: Wiley.

Haley, C. and L. Schall (1979), *The Theory of Financial Decisions*, New York: McGraw-Hill.

Halley, E. (1693), "An estimate of the degrees of mortality of mankind, drawn from the curious tables of births and funerals of the city of Breslaw; with an attempt to ascertain the price of annuities upon lives," *Philosophical Transactions*: 596–656.

Hamilton, E. (1947), "Origin and growth of the national debt in western Europe," *American Economic Review* (May): 118–30.

Hamilton, W. (1922), *The Stock Market Barometer*, New York: Barrons'.

Hammond, J. and B. Hammond (1919), *The Skilled Labourer, 1760–1832*, New York: A.M. Kelley (1967 reprint).

Harris, M. and A. Raviv (1985), "A sequential signaling model of convertible debt call policy," *Journal of Finance* 45: 1263–81.

Harris, R. (1994), "The Bubble Act: its passage and its effects on business organization," *Journal of Economic History* 54 (Sept.): 610–27.

Harvey, C. (1997), "The relation between the term structure of interest rates and Canadian economic growth," *Canadian Journal of Economics* 30: 169–93.

Hassett, M., S. Sears and G. Trennepohl (1985), "Asset preference, skewness and the measurement of expected utility," *Journal of Economics and Business* 37: 35–47.

Haugen, R. (1990), *Modern Investment Theory*, Englewood Cliffs, NJ: Prentice-Hall.

Haugen, R. (1999a), *The New Finance, The Case Against Efficient Markets*, 2nd edn, Upper Saddle River, NJ: Prentice-Hall.

Haugen, R. (1999b), *The Inefficient Stock Market: What Pays Off and Why*, Upper Saddle River, NJ: Prentice-Hall.

Hayek, F. (1955), *The Counter-Revolution of Science*, London: Collier-Macmillan.

Hayre, L. and K. Lauterbach (1991), "Option-adjusted spread analysis," chapter 37 in Fabozzi.

Heaney, J. and G. Poitras (1992), "Distributions for diffusions subject to constant reflecting barriers: a decomposition result," SFU Working Paper.

Heath, D., R. Jarrow and A. Morton (1992), "Bond pricing and the term structure of interest rates: a new methodology," *Econometrica* 60: 77–105.

Hecksher, E. (1955), *Mercantilism*, 2 vols., 2nd edn, edited by E. Soderlund from the trans. by M. Shapiro (1935), London: Allen and Unwin.

Heizl, M. (2003), "Canadian craze: investment trusts – investors flock to vehicles seeking their high yields but might not know risks," *Wall Street Journal* (Jan. 20): 2003.

Henderson, J. and R. Quandt (1980), *Microeconomic Theory*, 3rd edn, New York: McGraw-Hill.

Hendry, D. (1995), *Dynamic Econometrics*, New York: Oxford University Press.

Henry, P. (2002), "Is disinflation good for the stock market?," *Journal of Finance* 57: 1617–48.

Heywood, G. (1985), "Edmond Halley: astronomer and actuary," *Journal of the Institute of Actuaries*: 279–301.

Hicks, J. (1939), *Value and Capital: An Inquiry into some Fundamental Principles of Economic Theory* (2nd edn, 1946), Oxford, UK: Clarendon Press.

Higgins, R. (1998), *Analysis for Financial Management*, 5th edn, Homewood, IL: Irwin.

Hirschey, M. (2000), "The 'dogs of the Dow' myth," *Financial Review* 35: 1–16.

Ho, T. and S. Lee (1986), "Term structure movements and pricing of interest rate contingent claims," *Journal of Finance* 41: 1011–29.

Hobsbawm, E. (1965), *Labouring Men: Studies in the History of Labour*, New York: Basic Books.

Hodrick, R. (1992), "Dividend yields and expected stock returns: alternative procedures for inferences and measurement," *Review of Financial Studies* 5: 357–86.

Hooke, J. (1998), *Security Analysis on Wall Street*, New York: John Wiley.

Houtzager, D. (1950), *Life Annuities and Sinking Funds in the Netherlands before 1672*, Schiedam: Hav-Bank.

Hull, J. (2003), *Options, Futures and Other Derivatives*, 5th edn, Saddle River, NJ: Prentice-Hall.

Ibbotson, R. and R. Sinquefield (1976), "Stocks, bonds, bills and inflation: year-by-year historical returns (1926–74)," *Journal of Business* 49: 11–43.

Ingersoll, J. (1977), "A contingent claims valuation of convertible securities," *Journal of Financial Economics* 4: 289–321.

Ingersoll, J. (1977a), "An examination of corporate call policies on convertible securities," *Journal of Finance* 32: 463–78.

Ingersoll, J. (1987), *Theory of Financial Decision Making*, Savage, MD: Rowman and Littlefield.

Irwin, S. and W. Brorsen (1985), "Public futures funds," *Journal of Futures Markets*, 5: 149–72.

Irwin, S., T. Krukemyer and C. Zulauf (1993), "Investment performance of public commodity pools: 1979–1990," *Journal of Futures Markets*, 13: 799–820.

Jahnke, W. (1997), "The asset allocation hoax," *Journal of Financial Planning* 10 (Feb.): 109–13.

Jamshidian, F. (1989), "An exact bond option formula," *Journal of Finance* 44: 205–9.

Jangannathan, R. and Z. Wang (2002), "Empirical evaluation of asset-pricing models: a comparison of the SDF and beta methods," *Journal of Finance* 58: 2337–67.

Jarrell, G., J. Brickley and J. Netter (1988), "The market for corporate control: the empirical evidence since 1980," *Journal of Economic Perspectives* 2: 49–68.

Jarrow, R. and S. Turnbull (1995), "Pricing options on financial securities subject to default risk," *Journal of Finance* 50: 53–86.

Jegadeesh, N. and S. Titman (1993), "Returns to buying winners and selling losers: implications for stock market efficiency," *Journal of Finance* 48: 65–91.

Jegadeesh, N. and S. Titman (2001), "Profitability of momentum strategies: an evaluation of alternative explanations," *Journal of Finance* 56: 699–702.

Jensen, M. and R. Ruback (1983), "The market for corporate control," *Journal of Financial Economics* 11: 5–50.

Jianakoplos, N. and A. Bernasek (1998), "Are women more risk averse?", *Economic Inquiry* (October) 36: 620–30.

John, K. (1993), "Managing financial distress and valuing distressed securities: a survey and a research agenda," *Financial Management* 22: 60–78.

Jones, C. and G. Kaul (1996), "Oil and stock markets," *Journal of Finance* 51: 463–91.

Jones, E., S. Mason and E. Rosenfeld (1984), "Contingent claims analysis of corporate capital structures," *Journal of Finance* 39: 611–25.

Jorion, P. (1985), "International portfolio diversification with estimation risk," *Journal of Business* 58: 259–78.

Jorion, P. (2001), *Value at Risk*, 2nd edn, New York: McGraw-Hill.

Kahneman, D. and A. Tversky (1979), "Prospect theory: an analysis of decision making under risk," *Econometrica* 47: 263–91.

Kaish, S. (1969), "Odd-lot profit and loss performance," *Financial Analysts Journal* (Mar./Apr.): 83–9.

Kalotay, A., G. Williams and F. Fabozzi (1993), "A model for valuing bonds and embedded options," *Financial Analysts Journal* (May/June): 35–46.

Kang, J. and A. Chen (2002), "Evidence on theta and convexity in Treasury returns," *Journal of Fixed Income* 12: 41–50.

Kaplan, S. and R. Ruback (1995), "The valuation of cash flow forecasts: an empirical analysis," *Journal of Finance* 50: 1059–94.

Karlin, S. and H. Taylor (1975), *A First Course in Stochastic Processes*, New York: Academic Press.

Katona, G. (1951), *Psychological Analysis of Economic Behavior*, New York: McGraw-Hill.

Kaufman, P. (1978), *Commodity Trading Systems and Methods*, New York: John Wiley.

Keithahn, C. (1979), *The Brewing Industry*, Washington, DC: Federal Trade Commission.

Kellenbenz, H. (1957), "Introduction" to de la Vega, *Confusion de Confusiones*, reprinted in Fridson (1996).

Kendall, M. (1953), "The analysis of economic time series, part I: prices," *Journal of the Royal Statistical Society*, Series A, 15: 11–34.

Kendall, M. and A. Stuart (1963), *The Advanced Theory of Statistics*, vol. 1, 2nd edn, London: Griffin.

Kennedy, R. (1959), "Growth stocks and the chemical products industry," *Analysts Journal* (Feb.).

Keynes, J. (1936), *The General Theory of Employment, Interest and Money*, New York: Harcourt (Harbinger edn 1964).

Kim, I., K. Ramaswamy and S. Sundaresan (1993), "Valuation of corporate fixed-income securities," *Financial Management* 22: 60–78.

Kindleberger, C. (1989), *Manias, Panics and Crashes*, New York: Basic Books.

King, T. and D. Mauer (2000), "Corporate call policy for nonconvertible bonds," *Journal of Business* 73: 403–44.

Klamer, A., R. Solow and D. McCloskey (eds) (1988), *The Consequences of Economic Rhetoric*, New York: Cambridge University Press.

Klein, M. (2001), *Rainbow's End: The Crash of 1929*, New York: Oxford University Press.

Kocherlakota, N. (1996), "The equity premium: it's still a puzzle," *Journal of Economic Literature* 34: 42–71.

Kopprasch, R. (1994), "Option-adjusted spread analysis: going down the wrong path?", *Financial Analysts Journal* (May/June): 48–53.

Krishnan, H. and N. Mains (2002), "Hedging and diversification among convertible bond arbitrage strategies: an option-based approach," *Derivatives Use, Trading and Regulation* 8: 67–75.

Kritzman, M. (1994), "What practitioners need to know . . . about time diversification," *Financial Analysts Journal* (Jan./Feb.): 14–18.

Kritzman, M. (2000), *Puzzles of Finance*, New York: John Wiley.

Kritzman, M. and S. Page (2002), "Asset allocation versus security selection: evidence from global markets," *Journal of Asset Management* 3: 202–13.

Kritzman, M. and D. Rich (1998), "Beware of dogma: the truth about time diversification," *Journal of Portfolio Management* (summer): 66–77.

Kroll, Y., H. Levy and H. Markowitz (1984), "Mean-variance versus Direct Utility Maximization," *Journal of Finance* 39: 47–61.

Kupiec, P. and A. Kah (1999), "On the origin and interpretation of OAS," *Journal of Fixed Income* (Dec.): 82–92.

Lakonishok, J., A. Shleifer and R. Vishny (1994), "Contrarian investment, extrapolation and risk," *Journal of Finance* 49: 1541–78.

Lamoureux, C. and H.D. Witte (2002), "Empirical analysis of the yield curve: the information in the data viewed through the window of Cox, Ingersoll and Ross," *Journal of Finance* 57: 1479–1520.

Latane, H. (1959), "Criteria for choice among risky ventures," *Journal of Political Economy* (April): 144–55.

Lawson, T. (1997), *Economics and Reality*, London: Routledge.

Leamer, E. (1978), *Specification Searches*, New York: John Wiley.

Lederman, J. and R. Klein (1994), *Global Asset Allocation*, New York: John Wiley.

Lederman, J. and R. Klein (eds) (1995), *Hedge Funds*, New York: McGraw-Hill.

Lee, W. (1990), "Diversification and time: do investment horizons matter?", *Journal of Portfolio Management* (spring): 21–26.

Lefèvre, E. (1923), *Reminiscences of a Stock Operator*, New York: Wiley (reprint 1994).

Leggio, K. and D. Lien (2003), "An empirical examination of the effectiveness of dollar-cost averaging using downside risk performance measures," *Journal of Economics and Finance* 27: 211–23.

Leitch, G. and E. Tanner (1991), "Economic forecast evaluation: profits versus the conventional error measures," *American Economic Review* 81: 580–90.

Leland, H. (1980), "Who should buy portfolio insurance?," *Journal of Finance* 35: 581–96.

Lettau, M. and S. Ludvigson (2001), "Resurrecting the (C)CAPM: a cross-sectional test when risk premia are time varying," *Journal of Political Economy* 109: 1238–87.

Levis, M. and M. Liodakis (2001), "Contrarian strategies and investor expectations: the U.K. evidence," *Financial Analysts Journal* (Sept./Oct.): 43–57.

Levy, M. and H. Levy (2002), "Prospect theory: much ado about nothing?", *Management Science* 48: 1334–49.

Levy, H. and P. Samuelson (1992), "The capital asset pricing model with diverse holding periods," *Management Science* 38: 1529–42.

Levy, R. (1966), "Conceptual foundations for technical analysis," *Financial Analysts Journal* (July/Aug.): 83–9.

Levy, R. (1967), "Relative strength as a criterion for investment selection," *Journal of Finance* 23: 595–610.

Levy, R. (1968), *The Relative Strength Concept of Common Stock Price Forecasting*, Larchmont, NY: Investor's Intelligence.

Lewin, C. (1970), "An early book on compound interest: Richard Witt's *Arithmeticall Questions*," *Journal of the Institute of Actuaries*: 121–32.

Liang, B. (2000), "Hedge funds: the living and the dead," *Journal of Financial and Quantitative Analysis* 35: 309–26.

Lintner, J. (1965), "Security prices, risk, and maximal gains from diversification," *Journal of Finance* (Dec.): 587–615.

Lintner, J. (1956), "Distribution of incomes of corporations among dividends, retained earnings and taxes," *American Economic Review* 46: 93–113.

Linton, O., E. Mammen, J. Niels and C. Tanggaard (2001), "Yield curve estimation by kernel smoothing methods," *Journal of Econometrics* 105: 185–201.

Litterman, R. and J. Scheinkman (1991), "Common factors affecting bond returns," *Journal of Fixed Income* 3: 54–61.

Litzenberger, R. and K. Ramaswamy (1979), "The effect of personal taxes and dividends on capital asset prices: theory and empirical evidence," *Journal of Financial Economics* 7: 163–95.

Liu, J., D. Nissim and J. Thomas (2002), "Equity valuation using multiples," *Journal of Accounting Research* 40: 135–72.

Livingston, M. (1996), *Money and Capital Markets*, 3rd edn, Cambridge, MA: Blackwell.

Lo, A. and A. MacKinlay (1988), "Stock prices do not follow random walks," *Review of Financial Studies* 1: 41–66.

Lo, A. and A. MacKinlay (1999), *A Non-Random Walk Down Wall Street*, Princeton, NJ: Princeton University Press.

Lo, A., H. Mamaysky and J. Wang (2000), "Foundations for technical analysis: computational algorithms, statistical inference and empirical implementation," *Journal of Finance* 55: 1705–70.

Loeb, G. (1935), *The Battle for Investment Survival*, New York: Simon & Schuster (11th edn, 1965, with the 4th printing by Simon & Schuster in 1993).

Loistl, O. (1976), "The erroneous approximation of expected utility by means of a Taylor's series expansion: analytic and computational results," *American Economic Review* 66: 904–10.

Longstaff, F. (1992), "Are negative option prices possible? The callable U.S. Treasury-bond puzzle," *Journal of Business* 65: 571–93.

Longstaff, F. and E. Schwartz (1995), "A simple approach to valuing risky fixed and floating rate debt," *Journal of Finance* 50: 789–819.

Lopes, L. (1987), "Between hope and fear: the psychology of risk," *Advances in Experimental Social Psychology* 20: 255–95.

Lowe, J. (1994), *Benjamin Graham on Value Investing: Lessons from the Dean of Wall Street.*

Lowenstein, R. (1995), *Buffett*, New York: Random House.

Luenberger, D. (1969), *Optimization by Vector Space Methods*, New York: Wiley.

Luenberger, D. (1998), *Investment Science*, New York: Oxford University Press.

Luhnow, D. (2003), "Why Corona is big here, and Miller is so scarce in Mexico: beer makers south of the border dominate market using methods that would be illegal in the U.S." *Wall Street Journal* Jan. 17, 2003: B1.

Lummer, S. and M. Riepe (1994), "Taming your optimizer: a guide through the pitfalls of mean-variance optimization," ch. 1 in Lederman and Klein.

Macaulay, F. (1938), *The Movement of Interest Rates, Bonds, Yields and Stock Prices in the United States Since 1865*, New York: National Bureau of Economic Research.

Macedo, R. (1995), "Value, relative strength, and volatility in global equity country selection," *Financial Analysts Journal* (Mar./Apr.): 70–78.

Malkiel, B. (1990; 1995), *A Random Walk Down Wall Street*, 5th and 6th edns, New York: Norton.

Malkiel, B. (1995a), "Returns from investing in mutual funds, 1971–1991," *Journal of Finance* 50: 549–72.

Malkiel, B. (1963), "Equity yields, growth and the structure of share prices," *American Economic Review* 53: 1004–31.

Malliaris, A. and Brock, W. (1982), *Stochastic Methods in Economics and Finance*, Amsterdam: North Holland.

Markowitz, H. (1952), "Portfolio selection," *Journal of Finance* 7: 77–91.

Markowitz, H. (1959), *Portfolio Selection: Efficient Diversification of Investments*, New York: John Wiley.

Markowitz, H. (1999), "The early history of portfolio theory," *Financial Analysts Journal* (July/August): 5–16.

S. Mason, R. Merton, A. Perold and P. Tufano (1995), *Cases in Financial Engineering*, Prentice-Hall.

Massey, P. (1979), "The mutual fund liquidity ratio: a trap for the unwary," *Journal of Portfolio Management* 5: 18–21.

Mazzeo, M. and W. Moore (1992), "Liquidity costs and stock price response to convertible security calls," *Journal of Business* 65: 353–69.

McCulloch, J.H. (1971), "Measuring the term structure of interest rates," *Journal of Business* 44: 19–31.

McCloskey, D. (1985), *The Rhetoric of Economics*, Madison: University of Wisconsin Press.

McCloskey, D. (1994), *Knowledge and Persuasion in Economics*, Cambridge: Cambridge University Press.

McGahan, A. (1991), "The emergence of the national brewing oligopoly: competition in the American market, 1933–58," *Business History Review* 65: 229–84.

McKenna, E. and D. Zannoni (1993), "Philosophical foundations of post-Keynesian economics," *Journal of Post-Keynesian Economics* 15: 395–407.

McQueen, G., K. Shields and S. Thorley (1997), "Does the 'Dow 10 Investment Strategy' beat the Dow statistically and economically?", *Financial Analysts Journal* (July/Aug.): 66–72.

Medbery, J. (1870), *Men and Mysteries of Wall Street*, New York: Greenwood Press reprint (1968).

Mehra, R. and E. Prescott (1986), "The equity premium: a puzzle," *Journal of Monetary Economics* 15: 145–61.

Merton, R. (1969), "Lifetime portfolio selection: the continuous time case," *Review of Economics and Statistics* 51: 247–57.

Merton, R. (1971), "Optimal consumption and portfolio rules in a continuous time model," *Journal of Economic Theory* 3: 373–413.

Merton, R. (1973), "The theory of rational option pricing," *Bell Journal of Economics and Management Science*, 4: 141–83.

Merton, R. (1973a), "An intertemporal capital asset pricing model," *Econometrica* 41: 867–87.

Merton, R. (1974), "On the pricing of corporate debt: the risk structure of interest rates," *Journal of Finance* 29: 449–70.

Merton, R. (1976), "Option pricing when the underlying stock returns are discontinuous," *Journal of Financial Economics*, 125–44.

Messmore, T. (1990), "The duration of surplus," *Journal of Portfolio Management* (winter): 19–22.

Meyer, P. (1976), *Un Cours sur les Integrales Stochastiques*, Lecture Notes in Mathematics, no. 511, New York: Springer-Verlag.

Milevsky, M. and S. Posner (2003), "A continuous-time reexamination of dollar-cost averaging," *International Journal of Theoretical & Applied Finance* 6: 173–95.

Miller, M. and F. Modigliani (1961), "Dividend policy, growth and the valuation of shares," *Journal of Business* 34: 411–33.

Modigliani, F. and R. Cohn (1979), "Inflation, rational valuation and the market," *Financial Analysts Journal* 35: 24–44.

Modigliani, F. and M. Miller (1958), "The cost of capital, corporation finance and the theory of investment," *American Economic Review* 48 (June): 261–97.

Molodovsky, N., C. May and S. Chottinger (1965), "Common stock valuation," *Financial Analysts Journal* (Mar./Apr.): 104–23.

Moore, G., P. Johnson and T. Kippola (1999), *The Gorilla Game: Picking Winners in High Technology* (revised edn), New York: Harper.

Morgan, V. and W. Thomas (1962), *The Stock Exchange*, New York: St Martin's.

Mortimer, T. (1761), *Everyman His Own Broker; or a Guide to Exchange Alley*, 2nd edn, London: S. Hooper; 18th edition published (1801).

Mossin, J. (1966), "Equilibrium in a capital asset market," *Econometrica* 34: 261–76.

Mossin, J. (1973), *Theory of Financial Markets*, Englewood Cliffs, NJ: Prentice-Hall.

Murphy, J. (1999), *Technical Analysis of the Financial Markets*, Saddle River, NJ: Prentice-Hall.

Naranjo, A., M. Nilmalendran and M. Ryngaert (1998), "Stock returns, dividend yields and taxes," *Journal of Finance* 53: 2029–57.

Nawalka, S. (1996), "A contingent claims analysis of the interest rate risk characteristics of corporate liabilities," *Journal of Banking and Finance* 20: 227–45.

Neill, H. (1954), *The Art of Contrary Thinking*, Caldwell, ID: Caxton Printers.

Nielson (1985), "Attractive compounds of unattractive investments and gambles," *Scandanavian Journal of Economics* 87: 463–73.

Nippani, S., P. Liu and C. Schulman (2001), "Are Treasury securities free of default?", *Journal of Financial and Quantitative Analysis* 36: 251–65.

Nison, S. (1991), *Japanese Candlestick Charting Techniques: A Contemporary Guide to the Ancient Investment Techniques of the Far East*, New York: New York Institute of Finance.

Nison, S. (1996), "An introduction to Japanese candlestick charts," chapter 13 in Schwager.

Nofsinger, J. (2002), *The Psychology of Investing*, Upper Saddle River, NJ: Prentice-Hall.

Nofsinger, J. and R. Sias (1999), "Herding and feedback trading by institutional and individual investors," *Journal of Finance*, 54: 2263–95.

Noonan, J. (1957), *The Scholastic Analysis of Usury*, Cambridge, MA: Harvard University Press.

Ofek, E. and M. Richardson (2003), "Dotcom mania: the rise and fall of internet stock prices," *Journal of Finance* 58: 1113–37.

Ogborn, M. (1962), *Equitable Assurances*, London: Allen and Unwin.

Oppenheimer, H. (1981), *Common Stock Selection: An Analysis of Benjamin Graham's Intelligent Investor Approach*, Ann Arbor, MI: UMI Research Press.

Ormiston, M. and J. Quiggin (1994), "Two-parameter decision models and rank-dependent expected utility," *Journal of Risk and Uncertainty* 8: 273–82.

Palepu, K., P. Healy and V. Bernard (2000), *Business Analysis and Valuation*, Cincinnati: Southwestern.

Parente, G. and J. Weintraub (1987), "Eurodollar perpetual floating-rate note market: description and analysis," Salomon Bros. Bond Market Research.

Parker, G. (1974), "The emergence of modern finance in Europe 1500–1730," in C. Cipolla (ed.), ch. 7.

Partch, M. (1987), "The creation of a class of limited voting common stock and shareholder wealth," *Journal of Financial Economics* 18 (June): 313–39.

Pastor, L. and R. Stambaugh (2002), "Investing in equity mutual funds," *Journal of Financial Economics* 63: 351–80.

Pearson, E.S. (ed.) (1978), *The History of Statistics in the 17th and 18th Centuries, Lectures by Karl Pearson*, London: Charles Griffen.

Pearson, N. and T. Sun (1994), "Explaining the conditional density in estimating the term structure: an application of the Cox, Ingersoll and Ross Model," *Journal of Finance* 49: 1279–1304.

Peköz, E. (2002), "Samuelson's fallacy of large numbers and optional stopping," *Journal of Risk and Insurance* 69: 1–7.

Penman, S. (2001), *Financial Statement Analysis and Security Valuation*, New York: McGraw-Hill.

Penman, S. and T. Sougiannis (1998), "A comparison of dividend, cash flow and earnings approaches to equity valuation," *Contemporary Accounting Research* 15: 343–83.

Phoa, W. (1997), "Can you derive volatility forecasts from the yield curve convexity bias?," *Journal of Fixed Income* (June): 43–54.

Phoa, W. and M. Sheaver (1997), "A note on arbitrary yield curve reshaping sensitivities using key rate durations," *Journal of Fixed Income* (December): 67–71.

Piotrosky, J. (2000), "Value investing: the use of historical financial statement information to separate winners from losers," *Journal of Accounting Research* 38: 1–41.

Plosser, C. and K.G. Rouwenhorst (1994), "International term structure and real economic growth," *Journal of Monetary Economics* 33: 133–55.

Poitras, G. (1998), "Spread options, exchange options and arithmetic Brownian motion," *Journal of Futures Markets* 18: 487–517.

Poitras, G. (2000), *The Early History of Financial Economics, 1478–1776*, Aldershot, UK: E. Elgar.

Poitras, G. (2002), *Risk Management, Speculation and Derivative Securities*, New York: Academic Press.

Poitras, G. (2002a), "The philosophy of investment: a post-Keynesian perspective," *Journal of Post-Keynesian Economics* 25: 105–21.

Poitras, G. (2004), "Immunization bounds for non-parallel yield curve shifts," *Journal of Financial Research* (forthcoming).

Poitras, G. and J. Heaney (1999), "Skewness preference, mean-variance and the optimal demand for put options," *Managerial and Decision Economics* 20: 327–42.

Poitras, G., T. Wilkins and Y. Kwan (2002b), "Earnings management and the timing of asset sales," *Journal of Business, Finance and Accounting* 29: 903–34.

Porter, M. (1980), *Competitive Strategy*, New York: Free Press.

Porter, M. (1985), *Competitive Advantage*, New York: Free Press.

Pratt, J. and R. Zeckhauser (1987), "Proper risk aversion," *Econometrica* 55: 143–54.

Presidential Working Group on Financial Markets (1999), *Report*: "Hedge funds, leverage and the lessons of long-term capital management," Washington, DC: US Government Printing Office.

Prisman, E. (1986), "Immunization as a maxmin strategy: a new look," *Journal of Banking and Finance* 10: 491–509.

Ragsdale, E. and G. Rao (1994), "Tactical asset allocation at Kidder, Peabody," chapter 12 in Lederman and Klein (1994).

Rapach, D. (2001), "Macro shocks and real stock prices," *Journal of Economics and Business* 53: 5–26.

Rapach, D. (2002), "The long-run relationship between inflation and real stock prices," *Journal of Macroeconomics* 24: 331–51.

Rappaport, A. (1986), *Creating Shareholder Value: The New Standard for Business Performance*, New York: Free Press.

Rappaport, A. and M. Maboussin (2001), *Expectations Investing: Reading Stock Prices for Better Returns*, Boston: Harvard Business School Press.

Ready, M. (2002), "Profits from technical trading rules," *Financial Management* 31: 43–62.

Redington, F. (1952), "Review of the principles of life office valuations," *Journal of the Institute of Actuaries* 78: 286–340.

Reitano, R. (1991a), "Multivariate duration analysis," *Transactions of the Society of Actuaries* 43: 335–91.

Reitano, R. (1991b), "Multivariate immunization theory," *Transactions of the Society of Actuaries* 43: 392–438.

Reitano, R. (1992), "Non-parallel yield curve shifts and immunization," *Journal of Portfolio Management* (spring): 36–43.

Reitano, R. (1996), "Non-parallel yield curve shifts and stochastic immunization," *Journal of Portfolio Management* (winter): 71–8.

Rendleman, R. and B. Bartter (1980), "The pricing of options on debt securities," *Journal of Financial and Quantitative Analysis* 15: 11–24.

Renkenthaler, J. (1999), "Strategic asset allocation: make love, not war," *Journal of Financial Planning* 12 (Sept.): 32–4.

Rhea, R. (1932), *The Dow Theory*, New York: Barrons.

Ritchken, P. (1987), *Options: Theory, Strategy and Applications*, London: Scott, Foresman.

Ritter, J. and R. Warr (2002), "The decline of inflation and the bull market of 1982–1999," *Journal of Financial and Quantitative Analysis* 37: 29–61.

Rogers, L. and D. Williams (1987), *Diffusions, Markov Processes and Martingales: Ito Calculus*, vol. 2, New York: Wiley.

Roll, R. (1973), "Evidence on the 'growth-optimum' model," *Journal of Finance* 28: 551–66.

Roll, R. (1978), "Ambiguity when performance is measured by the security market line," *Journal of Finance* 33: 1051–69.

Ronan, C. (1978), "Edmond Halley," in *Dictionary of Scientific Biography*, C. Gillespie (ed.), vol. 6, New York: Scribner, pp. 67–72.

Ross, S. (1999), "Adding risks: Samuelson's fallacy of large numbers revisited," *Journal of Financial and Quantitative Analysis* 34: 323–39.

Roy, A. (1952), "Safety first and the holding of assets," *Econometrica* 20: 431–49.

Ruback, R. (2002), "Capital cash flows: a simple approach to valuing risky cash flows," *Financial Management* 31: 85–104.

Rubinstein, M. (1985), "Alternative paths to portfolio insurance," *Financial Analysts Journal* (July/Aug.): 42–51.

Rubinstein, M. (2002), "Markowitz's 'portfolio selection': a fifty-year retrospective," *Journal of Finance* 57: 1041–6.

Rubinstein, M. (2003), "Great moments in financial economics," *Journal of Investment Management* 2: 16–31.

Rubinstein, R. and H. Leland (1981), "Replicating options with positions in stock and cash," *Financial Analysts Journal* (July/Aug.): 63–72.

Russell, R. (1960), *The Dow Theory Today*, New York: R. Russell Associates.

Samuelson, P. (1945), "The effect of interest rate increases on the banking system," *American Economic Review* (March): 16–27.

Samuelson, P. (1963), "Risk and uncertainty: a fallacy of large numbers," *Scientia* (April/May): 1–6.

Samuelson, P. (1965), "The rational theory of warrant pricing," *Industrial Management Review* 6: 13–31.

Samuelson, P. (1969), "Lifetime portfolio selection by stochastic dynamic programming," *Review of Economics and Statistics* 51: 239–46.

Samuelson, P. (1971), "The 'fallacy' of maximizing the geometric mean in a long sequence of investing or gambling," *Proceedings of the National Academy of Sciences* 68: 2493–6.

Samuelson, P. (1990), "Asset allocation could be dangerous to your health," *Journal of Portfolio Management* 17 (spring): 5–8.

Samuelson, P. (1994), "The long-term case for equities," *Journal of Portfolio Management* 21: 15–24.

Santoni, G. (1987), "The great bull markets of 1924–29 and 1982–87: speculative bubbles or economic fundamentals?", Federal Reserve Bank of St. Louis *Economic Review* (November): 16–29.

Sarkar, S. (1999), "Duration and convexity of zero-coupon convertible bonds," *Journal of Economics and Business* 51: 175–92.

Sass, T. and D. Saurman (1993), "Mandated exclusive territories and economic efficiency," *Journal of Law and Economics* 36: 153–77.

Savage, L. (1954), *The Foundations of Statistics*, New York: Wiley.

Schabacker, R. (1930), *Stock Market Theory and Practice*, New York: B.C. Forbes.

Scherer, F. (1996), *Industry Structure, Strategy and Public Policy*, New York: Harper Collins.

Scherer, F. and D. Ross, *Industrial Market Structure and Economic Performance*, Boston: Houghton Mifflin.

Schilit, H. (2002), *Financial Shenanigans*, 2nd edn, New York: McGraw-Hill.

Schneeweis, T. and R. Spurgin (1998), "Multifactor analysis of hedge funds, managed futures, and mutual fund return and risk characteristics," *Journal of Alternative Investments* 1: 1–24.

Schwager, J. (1996), *Technical Analysis*, New York: John Wiley.

Schwartz, E. (1982), "The pricing of commodity-linked bonds," *Journal of Finance* 37: 525–39.

Schwed, F. (1940), *Where Are the Customers' Yachts?: Or a Good Hard Look at Wall Street*: New York: John Wiley (1995 reprint).

Sears, R. and G. Trennepohl (1983), "Diversification and skewness in option portfolios," *Journal of Financial Research* 6: 199–212.

Sharpe, S. (2002), "Reexamining stock valuation and inflation: the implications of analysts' earnings forecasts," *Review of Economics and Statistics* 84: 632–48.

Sharpe, W. (1963), "A simplified model of portfolio analysis," *Management Science* 9: 277–93.

Sharpe, W. (1964), "Capital asset prices: a theory of market equilibrium under conditions of risk," *Journal of Finance* (Sept.): 425–42.

Shefrin, H. (2000), *Beyond Greed and Fear, Understanding Behavioral Finance and the Psychology of Investing*, Boston: Harvard Business School Press.

Shefrin, H. and M. Statman (1984), "The disposition to sell winners too early and ride losers too long: theory and evidence," *Journal of Finance* 40: 777–90.

Shefrin, H. and M. Statman (2000), "Behavioral portfolio theory," *Journal of Financial and Quantitative Analysis* 35: 127–51.

Siegel, J. (1998), *Stocks for the Long Run: The Definitive Guide to Financial Market Returns and Long-Term Investment Strategies*, 2nd edn, New York: McGraw-Hill.

Simaan, V. (1993), "Portfolio selection and asset pricing: three parameter framework," *Management Science* 39: 568–77.

Smith, E. (1925), *Common Stocks as Long-Term Investments*, New York: Macmillan.

Smith, E. (1927), "Market value of industrial equities," *Review of Economics and Statistics* 9: 37–40.

Smith, E. (1931), "Tests applied to an index of the price level for industrial stocks," *Journal of The American Statistical Association* (supplement March): 127–35.

Sorensen, E. and D. Williamson (1985), "Some evidence on the value of the dividend discount model," *Financial Analysts Journal* 41: 60–9.

Sortino, F. and L. Price (1994), "Performance measurement in a downside risk framework," *Journal of Investing* 3: 59–64.

Sortino, F., R. van der Meer and A. Plantinga (1999), "The Dutch triangle: a framework to measure upside potential relative to downside risk," *Journal of Portfolio Management* 26: 50–8.

Springsteel, I. (2002), "The covert boomerang," *Investment Dealers Digest*, Mar. 11: 1.

Stansbury, C. (1960), *The Dow Theory Explained*, New York: R. Russell Associates.

Statman, M. (1995), "Behavioral framework for dollar-cost-averaging," *Journal of Portfolio Management* 22: 70–8.

Statman, M. (2001), "How important is asset allocation?", *Journal of Asset Management* 2: 128–35.

Stattman, D. (1980), "Book values and expected stock returns," unpublished MBA Honors paper, University of Chicago.

Statman, M. and J. Scheid (2002), "Buffett in foresight and hindsight," *Financial Analysts Journal* (July/Aug.): 11–18.

Stickney, C. (1997), "The academic's approach to securities research: is it relevant to the analyst?," *Journal of Financial Statement Analysis* (summer): 52–60.

Stigum, M. (1990), *The Money Market*, 2nd edn, Homewood, IL: Dow Jones-Irwin.

Stoll, H. and R. Whalley (1993), *Futures and Options*, Cincinnati: SouthWestern.

Sullivan, R., A. Timmermann and H. White (1999), "Data-snooping, technical trading rule performance, and the bootstrap," *Journal of Finance* 54: 1647–1691.

Sundaresan, S. (2002), *Fixed Income Markets and Their Derivatives*, 2nd edn, Cincinnati, OH: South-Western.

Sutton, M. (2002), "Financial reporting at a crossroads," *Accounting Horizons* 16: 319–28.

Telser, L. (1955), "Safety first and hedging," *Review of Economic Studies* 23: 1–16.

Thomas, L. and R. Willner (1997), "Measuring the duration of an internationally diversified bond portfolio," *Journal of Portfolio Management* (fall): 93–9.

Thomis, M. (1970), *The Luddites: Machine-breaking in Regency England*, Hamden, CN: Archon Books.

Tilley, J. (1993), "Valuing American options in a path simulation model," *Transactions of the Society of Actuaries* 45: 83–104.

Tobin, J. (1958), "Liquidity preference as behavior towards risk," *Review of Economic Studies* 25: 62–85.

Tosini, P. (1988), "Stock index futures and stock market activity in October 1987," *Financial Analysts Journal* (Jan./Feb.): 28–37.

Tracy, J. (1985), *A Financial Revolution in the Hapsburg Netherlands*, Los Angeles: University of California Press.

Treynor, J. and R. Ferguson (1985), "In defense of technical analysis," *Journal of Finance* 40: 757–76.

Tversky, A. and D. Kahneman (1992), "Advances in prospect theory: cumulative representation of uncertainty," *Journal of Risk and Uncertainty* 5: 297–323.

US Department of Transportation (1996), *The Low Cost Airline Service Revolution*, Washington, DC: Government Printing Office.

Vaidya, S., G. Poitras and A. Talib (1995), "International accounting implications of bond-cum-warrant issues," *International Journal of Accounting* 30: 25–36.

van Horne, J. (2001), *Financial Market Rates and Flows*, 6th edn, Upper Saddle River, NJ: Prentice-Hall.

Vasicek, O. (1977), "An equilibrium characterization of the term structure," *Journal of Financial Economics* 5: 177–88.

Vaughan, E. (1982), *Fundamentals of Risk and Insurance*, New York: Wiley.

Vaughan, T. (2002), "The NAIC's 2002 agenda: toward a more efficient system of insurance regulation," *Journal of Insurance Regulation* 20: 251–70.

Vega, J. de la (1688), *Confusion de Confusiones* reprinted in Fridson, M. (ed.) (1996).

Velde, F. and D. Weir (1992), "The financial market and government debt policy in France, 1746–1793," *Journal of Economic History* 52: 1–39.

Viceira, L. (2001), "Optimal portfolio choice for long-horizon investors with nontradable labor income," *Journal of Finance* 56: 433–70.

Victor, R. (1998), "Contrived competition: airline regulation and deregulation," *Business History Review* 64: 61–108.

Visscher, S. and G. Fillbeck (2003), "Dividend-yield strategies in the Canadian stock market," *Financial Analysts Journal* (Jan./Feb.): 99–106.

von Neumann, J. and O. Morgenstern (1947), *Theory of Games and Economic Behavior*, Princeton: Princeton University Press.

Vora, P. and J. McGinnis (2000), "The asset allocation decision in retirement: lessons from dollar-cost averaging," *Financial Services Review* 9: 47–63.

Vu, J. (1986), "An empirical investigation of non-convertible bonds," *Journal of Financial Economics* 16: 235–65.

Weatherford, L. and P. Belobaba (2002), "Revenue impacts of fare input and demand forecast accuracy in airline yield management," *Journal of the Operational Research Society* 53: 811–21.

Weaver, S. (2001), "Measuring economic value added: a survey of the practices of EVA proponents," *Journal of Applied Finance* (fall/winter): 3–9.

Weintraub, R. (1991), *Stabilizing Dynamics: Constructing Economic Knowledge*, Cambridge: Cambridge University Press.

Weir, D. (1989), "Tontines, public finance and revolution in France and England, 1688–1789," *Journal of Economic History* 49 (Mar.): 95–124.

Weiss, L. (1990), "Bankruptcy resolution: direct costs and violation of priority claims," *Journal of Financial Economics* 27: 285–314.

Wendt, L. (1982), *The Wall Street Journal: The Story of the Dow Jones and the Nation's Business Newspaper*, Chicago: Rand McNally.

Weston, J., J. Siu and B. Johnson (2001), *Takeovers, Restructuring and Corporate Governance*, Upper Saddle River, NJ: Prentice-Hall.

Whitman, M. (1999), *Value Investing*, New York: John Wiley.

Wilder, J. (1978), *New Concepts in Technical Trading Systems*, Winston-Salem, NC: Hunter Publishing.

Williams, J.B. (1938), *The Theory of Investment Value*, Cambridge, MA: Harvard University Press.

Wilson, C. (1941), *Anglo-Dutch Commerce and Finance in the Eighteenth Century*; reprinted by Cambridge University Press: London (1966).

Wilson, R. and F. Fabozzi (1996), *Corporate Bonds, Structures and Analysis*, New Hope, PA: Frank Fabozzi Associates.

Windas, T. (1993), *An Introduction to Option-Adjusted Spread Analysis*, New York: Bloomberg.

Withers, H. (1911), *Stocks and Shares*, London: Smith, Elder and Co.

Witt, R. (1613), *Arithmeticall Questions*, London: Richard Redmer.

Wolf, M. (2000), "Stock returns and dividend yields revisited: a new way to look at an old problem," *Journal of Business and Economic Statistics* 18: 18–30.

Wu, C. and X. Wang (2000), "The predictive ability of dividends and earnings yields for long-term stock returns," *Financial Review* 35: 97–124.

Wu, X. (2000), "A new stochastic duration based on the Vasicek and CIR term structure theories," *Journal of Business, Finance and Accounting* 27: 911–32.

Wu, Y. and H. Zhang (1996), "Mean reversion in interest rates: new evidence from a panel of OECD countries," *Journal of Money, Credit and Banking* 28: 604–21.

Wyckoff, R. (1910), *Studies in Tape Reading*, Burlington, VT: Fraser Publishing.

Wyckoff, R. (1930), *Wall Street Ventures and Adventures Through Forty Years*, New York: Harper and Row, reprinted by Greenwood Press: New York (1968).

Wyckoff, R. (1933), *Stock Market Technique, Number One*, New York: Wyckoff Associates.

Yook, K. and McCabe (2001), "MVA and the cross-section of expected stock returns," *Journal of Portfolio Management* 27: 75–87.

Young, W. and T. Roberts (1969), "Geometric mean approximations of individual securities and portfolio performance," *Journal of Financial and Quantitative Analysis* 4: 179–99.

Index

absolute Brownian motion 267
absolute Gaussian stochastic process 262, 270
absolute priority rules 232
absolute risk aversion 162–3
accounting, professional 112, 113, 437–8
accounting numbers 412–13
Ackermann, C. 569–70
acquisition models 390, 393–4
acquisitions and mergers 393, 462
actuarial science 184, 185
Adams, C.F. 94
Adams, H. 94
adjustable rate preferred stock 358, 359, 360
advance–decline line 519, 524
after-hours trading markets 68 n. 6
agency marketing 17
aggressive stocks 155
aleatory contracts 71
alpha 155, 541
American Airlines 470
American Bar Association 231
American callable bonds 304
American depository receipts 486 n. 5
American Eugenics Society 133 n. 21
American Express 360
American Gas & Electric Co. 305
American Institute of Certified Public
    Accountants 112
American Stock Exchange 17
Ammann, M. 574
Amsterdam 76, 79, 87, 88, 92
Anari, A. 372
Anheuser–Busch 304, 307

annual percentage rate (APR) 199
annual reports 97, 438
anticipation approach 367–8, 370, 493, 608
AOL 462
Appel, Gerald 547
Archer–Daniels–Midland (ADM) 307–8
arithmetic average return 27–9
arithmetic Brownian motion 262, 270
ARMA models 40
Arnott, R. 559
Arthur Anderson 460
asset pricing models 38, 41
asset valuation models 390–1
asymptotic distribution theory 39
auction rate preferred stock 358, 359–60
auditing 113
authority, human sciences 57, 58
axiomatic approach to decision making 157,
    159
Ayer, A.J. 52

Babson, Roger 100
Bacon, Francis 52
Bagehot, Walter 344
Baines, David 461
balance sheet 437, 442, 443–7
Balbas, A. 286, 289
balloon maturity 190
banking institutions 249
bankruptcy 10–11, 231–2, 390, 464
Bankruptcy Reform Act (1978) 16, 231
Barberis, N. 598–9, 601–2
bar charts 509, 510, 512

Barth, M. 248–9
Basle Accord 249, 362
Basu, S. 44
Baumol, W. 452
Bausch & Lomb 461
Bayes, Thomas 31
behavioral finance 496
　behavioral portfolio theory (BPT) 604–8
　efficient markets hypothesis 45
　frame dependence 532–4
　heuristic-driven bias 529–32
　inefficient markets 534–8
Beller, K. 489
Bergstresser, Charles 97
Berkman, H. 482
Berkshire Hathaway 382, 408–15, 584–9
　see also Buffett, Warren
Bermuda callable bonds 304
Bernoulli, Nicholas 72, 76, 85–6
Bernstein, Peter 127, 128, 402, 451, 594, 595
Bessel processes 265
best efforts marketing 17
beta 155, 149–50
Bethlehem Steel 393
Biddle, G. 460
Bierman, H. 110
Bierwag, G. 214, 216–17, 244 n. 10, 285
binomial models 272–4, 332, 334
Black, Fischer 167, 263
Black model 320–4
Black–Scholes formula 130, 168–9
　default risk 345
　dynamic portfolio insurance 172, 175,
　　177
　Greeks 329–30
　Ito's lemma 269
　stochastic processes for interest rates 267
Blake, D. 559
Blue-Sky Law Reporter 16
blue-sky laws 16
Blume, M. 43, 164
Bodie, Z. 223, 611–12 n. 19
Boeing Corporation 7–10
bond market securities 19, 20–3, 24–5
bonds
　credit risk and default risk 230–1
　duration 211–13, 214–15, 218–20
　with embedded options 302–48
　Fisher, Irving 104

human sciences, truth and method in 56–7
indentures 10
national markets, relative size of 7
risk and return tradeoff 30, 46–7
Smith, Edgar Lawrence 103–4
time value–convexity tradeoff 279–82
types and features 190–6
valuation 209–10
Withers, H. 115
see also Part II; specific bond types
Bookstaber, R. 174
book-to-market effect 44, 387
　see also price-to-book value (*P/BV*) ratio
bootstrap technique 202, 220–2
bought deals 17
Bowden, R. 286, 289
Box, G. 40
breadth indicators 519–25
breadth thrust indicator 556 n. 20
breakeven interest rate 202–3
breakouts 513–16, 518
Brennan, M. 168
Breslau 79–80
Brinson, G. 559
British East India Company 90
Briys, E. 270, 271
Brock, W. 491
Brockett, P. 164
brokers 18
Brown, S. 496, 507–8, 554 n. 5
Brownian bridge process 265
Buffett, Warren 354, 395, 407–15
　Coca-Cola 414, 468, 473
　financial shenanigans 463, 465
　financial statement analysis 437, 449
　Fisher's influence on 376, 401
　on forecasts 434
　hedge funds 567
　value investing 381–4, 389, 582, 584–9,
　　590, 592
business cycles 374–5
Buttonwood Agreement 92–3
buy-and-hold approach 577, 585, 599
buyer's options 302

Caldwell, T. 566, 567, 570
calendar and seasonality effects 44
calibration problem 229
callability, classifying securities by 69 n. 9

callable bonds 190, 224 n. 3, 304–8, 319–20, 324–7
  option adjusted spread analysis 332, 333, 336–8, 339, 340
call date 304
call feature 190, 310–11
call price 304
Campbell, J. 35, 594, 600, 613 n. 30
Canada
  accounting standards 438
  annual percentage rate 199
  common stock 13
  discount rate 205
  extendible bonds 191
  government bonds 17, 253, 254, 256
  guaranteed insurance contracts 298 n. 1
  mortgages 314
  risk and return tradeoff 30, 69 n. 11
  taxation 361
  yield to maturity 198
Canadian Securities Course 450–1
candlestick charts 509–12
Canner, N. 571, 572–3
capital allocation lines 143–6
capital asset pricing model (CAPM) 150–4
  cash management 575–6, 577, 578–9
  discounted cash flow modeling 430
  efficient markets hypothesis 44
  equity valuation 476, 477
  market model 154–5
  mean-variance portfolio analysis 140, 146
  modern Finance 127, 129, 130–1
  and technical analysis, differences between 496–7, 541
  two fund separation 149–50
capital cash flow model 487 n. 19
capital market line 144–5, 148, 149, 150
caps 191
Carnap, Rudolf 52
Carnegie, Andrew 95, 398
cash-burn models 390, 391, 394
cash flow matching 247–8, 251
cash flows
  expectations investing 434–5
  financial statement analysis 449–50, 451, 452–6
  net 452
  option adjusted spread analysis 331–2

see also discounted cash flow; free cash flow; free cash flow to equity
cash flow statement 437, 446–9, 452–4
cash management 560, 575–81
Cathcart, L. 347–8, 352 n. 15
Cauchy–Schwarz inequality 287, 288, 293
caution coefficient 120
census contracts 72–3
central limit theorem 61, 62, 65
certificates of deposit 20
Chan, K. 267, 496, 546
Chapman, D. 266–7
Chapter 11 filings 393
charting systems, technical analysis 508–25
Chebyshev's inequality 39, 61–2
Chicago Board Options Exchange 167
Chicago Stock Exchange 68 n. 6
China 13
Clarke, R. 174
classical economic theory 31
classified common stock 13
clean surplus equation 425, 446, 449
Clews, Henry 91, 92, 94, 96–7
closed end funds 18, 68 n. 5, 192–6
closed-form solutions 303
close-only chart 509
Coca-Cola 414, 468, 469–70, 473–4, 475–8
collars 191, 359
collateralized mortgage obligations (CMOs) 315, 339
"combat finance" techniques 479–80
Commercial and Financial Chronicle 92, 98
commercial paper 19–20, 206
Commodity Exchange Act (1936) 5
common stock 11–15
  Buffett, Warren 584–5
  classes of 13
  epistemology of modern Finance 50
  and firm value 362–4
  Fisher, Philip 405
  Graham, Dodd and Cottle 405–6
  historical evolution 399
  quotes 13–15
  risk and return tradeoff 46–7
  valuation 363–4, 367–75, 381, 398, 443
  see also Part III
company analysis 376–81
Compaq 11, 393
competitive advantage 414

Comte, Auguste 52
confirmation 500–2, 504–5, 506
Conklin, H. 402
Conrad, J. 69 n. 15
Consolidated Edison 305
consolidations 555 n. 18
consols 207
constant elasticity of variance (CEV) 264, 265
Constantinides, G. 48–9, 581
constant relative risk aversion 596
consumer choice theory 159–60
consumption–investment problem 600
contingent claims analysis 77, 130–1, 344, 346
contingent immunization 248
contrarian strategies 525–6, 529
contrary opinion strategies 526–9
conventions 106, 107, 114, 531
conversion feature 69 n. 9, 191, 358, 359
convertible bonds 69 n. 9, 191, 304, 309–13, 327, 329–31
convexity 275–8
  bounds 287–90
  classical immunization 250, 251, 252
  Greeks 319, 324–31
  immunization with non-parallel yield curve shifts 285–90
  partial 285–7
  time value–convexity tradeoff 278–85
Cooley, Phil 530
Cootner, P. 40, 42
Cope, S. 89
Copeland, T. 456–7, 458, 466–7, 468
Cordeiro, J. 460
corporate bonds 10, 20, 23, 233–42
  see also Part II
corporate charter 13
corporate debt 358–62
  see also bonds
corporate securities 7–16, 17, 189–90
corporate tax 11, 361
corporation law 13
Corporation Law Guide 13
cost items, financial statements 442–3
Cottle, Sidney see Graham and Dodd/Graham, Dodd and Cottle (GDC)
covariance stationarity 63, 64
Cowles, A. 507, 508, 553–4 n. 5
Cox, J. 268

Crane, D. 611–12 n. 19
credit quality, classifying securities by 69 n. 9
credit risk 230, 232–42, 346
credit spread 230
credit spread risk 230–1
critical realism 54
crossovers, moving average systems 519
Culp, C. 346
cumulative prospect theory 604–5
cumulative voting rights 12–13
Cunningham, L. 364, 401
curb trading 93
currently callable bonds 304
current yield 204

Damadoran, Aswath 429–33, 435
Davidson, P. 58–9, 158–9
daylight-savings-time effect 44
day-of-the-week effects 44
debentures 11
debt securities 7–11
dedication (cash flow matching) 247–8, 251
default, legal aspects 230–2
default loss rate 234–5
default risk 230–1
  assessment 232–7
  empirical evidence 237–42
  Greeks 327, 329
  modeling and analyzing 341–8
  mortgage backed securities 316
  perpetuities 208
defensive investors 560–1, 590–2
defensive stocks 155
de la Vega, Joseph 87–9
delta 318–20, 324–6, 327, 328
Delta Airlines 470, 471
de Marchi, N. 87, 133 n. 16
de Moivre, Abraham 81–5
Demotech, Inc. 233
Denmark 75
depreciation 415
derivative securities 5, 165–77, 564, 568
  see also specific derivatives
Dewing, A. 124
de Witt, Jan 76–9, 84
Dhar, Madhav 369
Dhrymes, P. 59
Dice, Charles Amos 101
diffusions 261–5

Dimson, E. 23, 44–5, 47–8, 385, 386
direct bootstrap approach 221–2
direction vector 287
discount bonds 210, 292
discounted cash flow (DCF)
  alternatives and hybrids 478–82
  common stock valuation 364
  equity valuation 471–8
  expectations investing 433–7
  financial statement analysis 451–2, 454, 458
  Fisher, Irving 101
  fixed income valuation 186
  fundamental analysis 366, 369
  Graham, Dodd and Cottle 397, 398
  history and variety of models 421–8
  simplified valuation 428–33
  value drivers 470
  value investing 384, 390–1, 393
discounted dividend valuation 422, 424, 429, 432–3
discount function 227–8
discount rate 204–6
discrete processes 272–4
discrete rebalancing, dynamic portfolio insurance 175, 176
dispersion 298 n. 2
disposition effect 532–3
divergence 544–5, 546
diversifiable risk 140
diversification *see* portfolio diversification
dividend discount model 472, 477
  see also Gordon dividend growth model
dividend irrelevance hypothesis 533–4
dividend puzzle 533–4
dividends
  common stock 13
  discounted cash flow modeling 421–2, 423–7, 429, 431–2
  growth stocks 406
  modern Finance, emergence 129
  preferred stock 11, 358–60, 361
  value investing 385–7
dividend yield strategies 563–4
Dodd, David 92
  see also Graham and Dodd/Graham, Dodd and Cottle
Dodson, James 82, 83
Dogs of the Dow strategy 561

dojis 512
dollar cost averaging (DCA) 66, 575–81
dollar duration 213
dollar duration matching 248
double smoothing 545
double tops and bottoms, charting systems 516
Dow, Charles 97–8, 492, 498, 502, 507
Dow Jones & Co. 97–8
Dow Jones Index 98
Dow Jones Industrial Average (DJIA)
  advance-decline line 524
  current stocks 100
  Dow Ten strategy 562–3
  Dow theory 500–5, 506
  history 98, 99, 169
Dow Jones Industrial Index 492
Dow Jones Transportation Average (DJTA) 500–5, 506
downgrade risk 230–1
Dow Ten strategy 561
Dow theory 492, 498–508, 574
Dow Transportation Index 98
Dresdner Bank 431
Drew, Daniel 94, 95, 526
dual-class shares 13
dual moving average (DMA) oscillator 547–8, 555 n. 19
Duer, William 93
Dunnigan, William 553 n. 4
Durand, D. 127
duration
  bounds 287–90
  concept 210–14
  gap 216
  Greeks 319–20, 324–31
  historical background 214–18
  immunization with non-parallel yield curve shifts 285–90, 291–5
  international bond portfolio management 254–5
  matching 250, 251, 252
  partial 285–7, 291, 293–5
  puzzle 286, 290, 293
  time value-convexity tradeoff 275, 280, 282, 285
  uses and calculation of 218–20
  see also Macaulay duration; modified duration
Dutch East India Company 86–7, 88

Eaker, M. 146
earnings 449–51, 452
  per share (EPS) 450–1
economic analysis 366
economic profit model 456, 458, 478–9
Economic Value Added (EVA) 428, 435, 449,
  451, 456–60
Edwards, R. 493, 537
  charting systems 508–9, 512, 516, 555
    n. 17, 555 n. 18
effective interest rate 199–201
efficient markets hypothesis (EMH)
  anomalies 42–6
  basic insights 34–9
  common stock and firm value 362
  efficient frontier 141–2, 143–4, 148
  ergodicity hypothesis 59
  fundamental analysis 365
  and Keynes 106, 107
  modern Finance 130
  questions 66–7
  risk and return tradeoff 46–50
  technical analysis 490, 492, 496, 498,
    536
  testing 39–42
  value drivers 466
Eiteman, W. 47
El-Jahel, L. 347–8, 352 n. 15
Elliot, R.N. 553 n. 4, 554 n. 7
Elton, E. 42, 50, 52, 154, 564, 607
  asset allocation 571, 572, 573, 594
empirical probability assessment approach
  564
empiricism 53
encashability feature 190
England *see* United Kingdom/England
English, J. 376, 482
  discounted cash flow modeling 426, 434,
    474–5, 479
Enron 460, 463, 464–5
enterprising investors 560–1, 590–1, 592
epistemology of modern Finance 50–4
equity risk premium 49
equity securities 7–11
  classification 356–7
  common stock and firm value 362–4
  discounted cash flow modeling 421–37
  forecasting the inputs 465–82
  interpreting financial statements 437–65

preferred stock vs. corporate debt 358–62
  valuation 471–82
  see also Part III
ergodic hypothesis 58–65, 67–8, 159
Erie Railroad Company 94–5, 97
ethical issues 109, 110
Eurodollars 20, 205, 320–4
European callable bonds 304
Evans, N. 312
exchange rate 29–30
exchange risk 255–6
executive stock options 463
expectations investing 367–8, 433–7
expected return
  efficient markets hypothesis 37, 39
  estimators 26–30
  mean-variance portfolio analysis 137, 139,
    140, 146–7
expected utility (EU) 157–61
  behavioral portfolio theory 605–6
  growth optimal portfolios 604
  mean-variance portfolio analysis 144–6
  and moment preference 164–5
  risk aversion properties 596
  time diversification puzzle 597–8
exponential weighted moving averages (EMA)
  545
extendible feature 191
Exxon-Mobil 431

Fabozzi, F. 331, 332, 341
  bonds with embedded options 304
  corporate management, responsibilities
    181
  implied zeros 202
  Monte Carlo procedure 333, 336, 340, 352
    n. 11, 352 n. 12
  traditional yield spread analysis 197
failed signal rule 516
fair game model 36–7, 39
Falcidian fourth 71
fallacy of large numbers 602–3
Fama, E.
  behavioral finance 534
  capital asset pricing model 152
  efficient markets hypothesis 35, 39, 42, 43,
    45
  modern Finance 130, 134 n. 28
federal funds 20

Federal Home Loan Mortgage Corporation (FHLMC) 314, 315, 316
Federal Housing Administration (FHA) 314
Federal National Mortgage Association (FNMA) 314, 315, 316
feedback problem 494, 495, 497
Feller, W. 36, 37, 61-2
Fellowship of Merchant Adventurers 86
Fillbeck, G. 563
filter rule trading strategy 43
Financial Accounting Standards Board 438
financial engineering 165-77
financial management systems 378-9
financial statement analysis 365-6, 437-49
    earnings, free cash flow and EVA 449-60
    financial shenanigans 460-5
Fiorina, Carla 393
Fischer, S. 270
Fisher, Irving
    efficient markets hypothesis 34
    fixed income valuation 192
    history of security analysis 91, 98-105, 110
    modern Finance 127
    portfolio diversification theory 120-1
    professionally managed investment funds 581
    risk and return tradeoff 47
Fisher, K. 556 n. 23
Fisher, L. 47
Fisher, Philip
    and Buffett 412, 585
    equity valuation 480
    financial statement analysis 437
    growth stock 400-7
    industry and company analysis 376-81
    portfolio diversification 397
    price/earnings ratio 366
    stock management 353
    value drivers 468
    value investing 387, 388-9, 581-2, 591, 592, 593
Fisher effect 372
Fisk, James 94, 95
Fitch Ratings 233-4
fixed rate preferred stock 358-9
flags, charting systems 516
Flanders 74
floating rate notes 191

floating rate perpetuities 207, 208
floors 191
Ford Motor Company
    equity valuation 480, 481, 482
    financial statement analysis 438-40, 442, 444-6, 448-9, 452-4
    technical analysis 539, 540
forecasting ability, tactical asset allocation 573-4
foreign securities 20, 25, 29-30, 177, 190, 431
fore-meanings 56-7
fourth market for securities trading 68 n. 6
Fox, S. 573-4
frame dependence 532-4
France 72-3, 74, 75, 76, 121-2
    government bonds 253, 254, 256
franchise factor 414
Francis, J. 68 n. 1
free cash flow (FCF) 454-6, 472, 474-5, 476
free cash flow to equity (FCFE) 428, 435, 455-6, 473, 475, 476-7
free cash flow to the firm (FCFF) 455
French, K. 45
Friedman, Milton 52-3, 54
Friedman-Savage puzzle 596, 606
Friend, I. 164
fundamental analysis 66-7
    Fisher, Irving 121
    Fisher, Philip 376-81
    and investment philosophy 365-70
    Keynes 107-8, 109
    macroeconomics and common stock valuation 370-5
    Mortimer 90
    and technical analysis 490, 495
futures contracts 5, 168, 169, 170, 351 n. 8
    Eurodollar 205, 320-4

Gadamer, H.-G. 51, 54-8
Galton, Francis 31
gambling 89
gamma 318, 320, 326
Gann, William 553 n. 4
Gateaux differential 286
Gateway Computers 436-7, 482
Gaussian distribution 63
General Electric 46

generally accepted accounting principles
(GAAP)
financial shenanigans 460, 462, 465
financial statement analysis 437–40, 451,
452, 454–5, 456
latitude within 10
General Motors 481, 482, 539, 540
Geneva 121–2
geometric average return 27, 28–9
geometric Brownian motion 263, 267, 270,
347
Germany 76, 253, 254, 256
Girsanov's theorem 298 n. 9
goodwill, economic vs. accounting 413–15
Gordon, J.S. 92, 112
Gordon, M. 421
Gordon dividend growth model 421, 423–7,
429–33, 473–4, 477
Gould, Jay 94, 95, 97
Government Account Series 186
government bonds 17, 20, 25, 254–6
Government National Mortgage Association
(GNMA) 314, 315, 316, 339
government securities 7, 18–19, 73–4, 186–90
Graham, Benjamin 91–2, 119, 131
and de la Vega, similarities between 89
price/earnings ratio 44
stock selection 353
value investing 384
Graham and Dodd/Graham, Dodd and Cottle
(GDC) 395–400
anticipation approach 607–8
and Buffett 412, 413–14, 585
callable bonds 305–6
classification of securities 356–7
common stock valuation 363, 367, 369–70
corporate bond selection 181
default risk 343–4
discounted cash flow modeling 421
dividends 406
expectations investing 433
financial shenanigans 465
financial statement analysis 437, 443–6
fixed income analysis 185, 214
fundamental analysis 134 n. 25
growth stocks 400–1, 402, 404–5
history of security analysis 91–2, 97, 112,
110–19, 123–4
investment strategy 559, 560–1, 565, 581–4

and Macaulay 215
preferred stock vs. corporate debt 360, 361
price-to-book value 46
securities, defining 5, 7
security analysis, defining 115–17
technical analysis 492, 493–7, 499, 529–30
value investing 382, 385, 388–9, 391–2,
589–91
Grauer, R. 147, 564
Greeks 318–31
Greenwald, B. 382, 385, 414
Gregoriou, G. 570
Gross, Bill 91, 532
growth optimal portfolios 602, 603–4
growth stocks 382–4, 385, 387, 389, 400–7
Gruber, M. 42, 50, 52, 154, 564, 607
asset allocation 571, 572, 573, 594

Hagstrom, R. 408
Hahm, J. 164
Hakanon, N. 147, 564
Hald, A. 133 n. 12
Halley, Edmond 79–81, 82, 83
Hamilton, Alexander 93
Hamilton, E. 73
Hamilton, William Peter 492, 498, 500, 502,
505–8
hammers 512
Harleysville Mutual Insurance Company 168
Harrison, P. 87, 133 n. 16
Haugen, R. 123–6, 134 n. 27, 432
Hayek, F. 51
head-and-shoulders, charting systems 516
Heckscher, E. 86, 132 n. 9
hedge funds 312–13, 564–70
hedonic editing 533–4
Heidegger, Martin 56
Helmholtz, Hermann 55
Hershey Foods 457
heuristic-driven bias 529–32
Hewlett, Walter 393
Hewlett-Packard 11, 393
Hicks, J. 215–16
Higgins, R. 451, 455
high yield bonds 20, 24
Hirschey, M. 563
history of security analysis
early European writers 86–91
emergence of modern Finance 119–31

Fisher, stock valuation and the 1929 crash
 98–105
Graham, Dodd and Cottle 110–19
Keynes, uncertainty and the stock market
 105–10
life annuity valuation 71–86
reminiscences of US stock operators 91–8
Holland *see* Netherlands/Holland
Hooke, J. 369, 392, 394, 479, 481–2
horizon matching 248
Houghton, John 6
Houtzager, D. 76
Hudde, Jan 77, 78
Hull, J. 173
human sciences
 duration, historical background 214
 fixed income valuation 186
 technical analysis 497
 truth and method in 54–8, 116, 123
Huygens, Christian 77
hyperbolic absolute risk aversion (HARA)
 162–3

Ibanez, A. 286, 289
Ibbotson, R. 23, 47
IBM 46
immunization
 classical rules 247, 249–52
 contingent 248
 fixed income portfolio analysis 247–8
 with non-parallel yield curve shifts
 285–95
 Redington 217–18, 247, 250–2
implied forward interest rates 202–3
implied zero coupon interest rate
 (spot interest rate) 201–2, 220–2
income statement 437, 438–43, 446–7
incorporation 13
indexes, stock market 97–8
inductive method 55–6
industry analysis 376–81
inefficient markets 534–8
inflation 371–4, 599
inflation-indexed Treasury securities 189
Ingersoll, J. 158, 162, 225, 268
initial public offering 16, 192
Institute of Accountants and Bookkeepers
 112
insurance companies 248–9, 251

interest rates
 binomial models 272–4
 and duration 211, 213, 215–18, 219
 fixed income valuation problems 206–10
 immunization 247, 249
 and inflation 417 n. 14
 international bond portfolio management
 252–4
 option adjusted spread analysis 332,
 333–4
 stochastic processes 265–8
 term structure 199, 220–30
 time value–convexity tradeoff 284, 285
 types 196–206
interior decorator fallacy 594–6, 602, 605
internal rate of return 196
Internal Revenue Code (IRC) 361, 416 n. 4
International Accounting Standards Board
 438
international bonds 20, 25, 196, 252–6
intrinsic value approach 367, 369–70, 472,
 495
 Graham, Dodd and Cottle 116–17, 397,
 581–2, 583
invested capital 456–7
investment banks 16–17
Investment Company Act (1940) 16, 68 n. 5
Investment Company Institute 192, 193, 196
investment horizon 249–50
Investor's Intelligence 527, 528
investment strategy
 behavioral portfolio theory 604–8
 cash management and dollar cost averaging
 575–81
 Dow Ten and dividend yield strategies
 561–4
 fallacy of large numbers and growth
 optimal portfolios 602–4
 hedge fund approach 564–71
 interior decorator fallacy and other
 confusions 593–602
 strategic asset allocation and two fund
 separation 571–3
 tactical asset allocation 573–5
 for value investors 581–93
 whose? 558–61
 see also portfolio management
islands, charting analysis 516
isoelastic utility function 163

Italy 73, 76
  government bonds 253, 254, 255, 256, 298
    n. 3
Ito's lemma 265, 268–71, 283, 347

January effect 44–5
Japan 253, 254, 255, 256, 313
JDS Uniphase 462
Jegadeesh, N. 496, 545–6, 556 n. 27
Jenkins, G. 40
Jensen's alpha 578
Jevons, Stanley 31
Jews 88
joint stock companies 86–9
Jones, Alfred 566–7
Jones, Carl 567
Jones, Edward 97
Jorion, P. 146–7
jump processes 265

Kah, A. 340
Kahane, Y. 164
Kahneman, D. 529, 604, 605
Kaplan, S. 482
Karlin, S. 59, 69 n. 20
Kaufman, P. 547
Kaul, G. 69 n. 15
Keltner, Chester 553 n. 4
Kendall, M. 35
Kent, D. 460
Keynes, J.M.
  anticipation approach 368
  behavioral finance 531
  behavioral portfolio theory 607–8
  contrarian strategies 525–6
  efficient markets hypothesis 34
  and Hicks 215
  history of security analysis 91, 98, 105–10,
    114, 131
  intrinsic value approach 370
  and Macaulay 214
  relative value approach 369
  risk and uncertainty 31, 33–4
  stock market valuation and macroeconomic
    activity 49
Kindleberger, C. 125
King, T. 308
KMV Corporation Credit Monitor® model 352
    n. 14

Knight, Frank 31–3, 34, 586
Kolari, J. 372
Kritzman, M. 598, 610 n. 2
Kupiec, P. 340

Lagrangian problem 159–60
Lane Stochastic oscillator 547, 548
large numbers, law of 39, 60–1, 64, 65
  fallacy of large numbers 602–4
Lee, W. 612 n. 27
Lefèvre, Edwin 91, 92
Leggio, K. 578, 579
Lehman Brothers 69 n. 9
Leitch, G. 41, 42
leveraged buyout (LBO) 394
Levis, M. 525
Levy, H. 604–5, 610–11 n. 12, 611 n. 13
Levy, M. 604–5
Levy, R. 492–3, 495, 537, 539–41
Lewin, C. 207
Lien, D. 578, 579
life annuity valuation 71–86
life contingent contracts 71–5, 121–2
life insurance companies 248, 251
limited liability 11
Liodakis, M. 525
liquidation 11, 68 n. 3
  assessment techniques 390, 392–4
  see also bankruptcy
liquidity premia hypothesis 222–3, 225–7
Little, Jacob 93–4
Liu, J. 482
Lo, A. 35, 496
Lockheed 462
Loeb, G. 407
logical positivism 52, 53–4, 123, 267, 395,
    586
log utility function 163
London 92
London Times 92
Longstaff, F. 347
Long Term Capital Management (LTCM)
    568
Loomis, C. 567
Lorie, J. 47
loss aversion 532–3
Lowe, J. 119
Lummer, S. 559
lump sum investing 577, 580

Macaulay, F. 237–8, 341–3, 344, 422–5
Macaulay duration 84, 181, 211–13, 251, 277
  history 214–15, 216
MacKinlay, A. 35
Maclaurin series 259
macroeconomics 370–5
Magee, J. 493, 537
  charting systems 508–9, 512, 516, 555
    n. 17, 555 n. 18
Malkiel, B. 425, 489
management fees 591
managers, company analysis 379, 380
Marathon 449
margin of safety principle 407, 436, 494–5
  Graham, Dodd and Cottle 397, 494–5, 583
MARhedge 568–9
market capitalization of equity 443
market-implied forecast period 435–7
marketing, company analysis 378
market model 129, 154–7
market portfolio 146, 149, 150, 153
market segmentation hypothesis 223, 226–7
market value added 458–60
market value balance sheet relationship 454
Markowitz, H. 23, 34, 141, 150–1
  modern Finance 127–8, 129, 130–1
  portfolio diversification theory 98, 119–20,
    121, 127
Markov processes 261
martingale difference sequences 38–9, 40
martingale limit theory 38
martingale processes 36–9, 40, 261
maturity, classifying securities by 19
maturity bond portfolio 293–5
Mauboussin, M. 367–8, 376, 380, 433, 434–7
Mauer, D. 308
maxmin portfolio 285
Mazarin, Cardinal 75
McClellan oscillator 525
McCloskey, D. 23, 530
McCulloch, J.H. 227
McKenna, E. 106, 134 n. 23
McKinsey & Company 456, 458
mean reversion 268, 324, 598–9, 601
mean-square ergodicity theorem 64
mean-variance expected utility functions 163
mean-variance portfolio analysis
  analytical preliminaries 136–40
  capital allocation lines 143–4

capital asset pricing model 152
capital market line and capital equilibrium
  144–6
  criticism 146–8
  optimization model 140–2, 150–1, 152, 159
  riskfree assets 143–4
mergers 393, 462
Merrill Lynch 16, 311
Merton, Robert 167, 345–7, 600
Microsoft 464
Milevsky, M. 580–1
Miller, M. 127, 128–9, 406, 533
minimum variance portfolio 138–9
Mitchell, William Henry 531
modern Finance
  Buffett 383
  common stock valuation 364
  contrarian strategies 525, 529
  derivative security renaissance 166
  efficient markets hypothesis 45–6, 47–50
  epistemology 50–4
  evolution 45, 119–31
  Graham, Dodd and Cottle 118
  redefinitions of words 525
  technical analysis 492, 496–8
  value investing 383, 385, 386, 388
modern portfolio theory 23
modified duration 211–13, 216, 277, 324–5,
  327–8
Modigliani, F. 127, 128–9, 406, 533
Molodovsky, N. 425
moment preference 164
moments of linear combinations of random
  variables 136–7
momentum 538–9, 541–6, 547
"money illusion" 373–4
money market securities 19–20, 204–6
Monte Carlo simulations 274, 332–6, 340,
  352 n. 12, 487 n. 21
Moody's Investor Services Inc. 10, 233
Morgenstern, O. 157, 159
mortgage backed securities 20, 24, 187,
  314–18, 327
  option adjusted spread analysis 338, 339,
    340
mortgage insurance 314–15
mortgage originators 314
mortgage servicers 314
Mortimer, Thomas 87, 89–91

Motorola 380
Moving-Average Convergence-Divergence
    547–8, 549–50
moving average systems, technical analysis
    518–25, 541, 542, 545
multi-country bonds 196
municipal bonds 20, 24
Murphy, J. 493

NASDAQ 17
National Association of Insurance
    Commissioners 248
National Bureau of Economic Research 417
    n. 15
National Investors Corporation 402
national municipal funds 192
natural sciences
    fixed income valuation 184, 185, 186
    and human sciences 54–8, 116, 123
    technical analysis 497
negative exponential utility function 163
neglected firm effect 44
Neill, Humphrey 526–7, 531–2
Nelson, S. 498
neo-classical approach 134 n. 23
net current asset rule 391–2
Netherlands/Holland
    Amsterdam 76, 79, 87, 88, 92
    government bonds 253, 254, 256
    life annuities 75, 76, 77–8, 79
    portfolio diversification 122
    public debt, emergence 74–5
    short selling 565
    stock market history 87, 88
net present value (NPV) model 451–2
new era theory 111, 399–400
New Finance 45, 123–4, 125–6
New York 92
New York Stock Exchange (NYSE) 13, 14–15,
    17, 171, 491–2
    history 93, 96, 97, 132 n. 5
New York Times 92
New Zealand 298 n. 3
Nofri, Eugene 553 n. 4
Nofsinger, J. 532, 534, 535
nondiversifiable risk 140
non-recombining processes 272
Noonan, J. 73
Noyes, Alexander 91

Ogborn, M. 83
Ohio Oil Company 306
Old Finance 45, 46, 123, 124–5, 127–30
old money preferred stock 416 n. 4
one factor models of term structure 228–9
open-end funds 17, 192
Oppenheimer, H. 119
option adjusted spread (OAS) analysis 303
    examples and pitfalls 338–41
    generating future spot rates and solving
        OAS 333–8
    static spread and cash flow assumptions
        331–2
option contracts 5, 6, 168, 172
option pricing theory 261, 263, 320, 344
option replication strategies 168
order placement strategies 168
Orion Pictures 462
Ormiston, M. 164
Ornstein–Uhlenbeck (OU) process 263–4, 268
oscillators 513, 538–9, 546–51, 555 n. 19
over-the-counter (OTC) market 17–18

Page, S. 610 n. 2
par bond bootstrap approach 221–2
par bonds 210, 291–3
partial differential equations (PDEs) 269,
    283–4, 303, 347–8
participating preferred stock 416 n. 3
par value 363, 416 n. 6
pass-throughs 314–15, 317–18, 339
Pearson, Karl 80, 82, 83–4, 132 n. 9
Pearson, N. 266–7
Peköz, E. 603
Penman, S. 365–6, 426, 468, 471, 477, 478
    financial statement analysis 437, 438–40,
        449
pennants, charting systems 516
pension funds 249
performance measurement 578–9
perpetuities 207–9, 213, 216, 251
Philadelphia 92
philosophy of fixed income analysis 184–6
philosophy of investment
    epistemology of modern Finance 50–4
    ergodic hypothesis 58–65
    fundamental analysis 365–70
    truth and method in the human sciences
        54–8

point-and-figure charts 509
Poitras, G. 167, 177
portfolio diversification 98
  Fisher, Philip 406–7
  Graham, Dodd and Cottle 397–8, 407, 582
  history 119–22, 123
  market model 156–7
  mean-variance portfolio analysis 139
  value investing 582, 591
portfolio insurance 168–77
portfolio management
  duration 219–20
  fixed income 247–56
  see also investment strategy
portfolio theory 166
positivism 58, 62
  epistemology of modern Finance 51, 52–4,
    69 n. 18, 126–7, 130
  logical 52, 53–4, 123, 267, 395, 586
Posner, S. 580–1
power series 259
  see also Taylor series expansion
power utility function 163
Pratt, J. 603
Prebon Yamane 18
preemptive rights 13
preferred habitat hypothesis 223, 226–7
preferred stock 11, 12, 358–62, 424
prejudices 57
premium bonds 209–10
prepayment flows 316–17
prepayment risk 316
Prepayment Speed Assumptions 317–18
present value of growth opportunities 427
Price, Richard 82
price-earnings (*P/E*) ratio
  abnormal earnings form 427
  discounted cash flow modeling 425–6,
    427
  efficient markets hypothesis 44
  Fisher, Irving 102–3
  fundamental analysis 366–7
  industry and company analysis 381
  multiples 480–2
price-earnings to growth ratio 427–8
price-to-book value (*P/BV*) ratio 46, 387–8,
  425, 426, 443
  see also book-to-market effect
primary government securities dealers 18–19

primary issues 16
principal risk 219
priority of claim 10, 11, 232
Procter & Gamble 513, 517, 519, 522–3
production efficiencies 414
profitability 466, 467
program trading 171
prospect theory 529, 604–5
prospectuses 358
proxy fights 11
proxy voting 11
Prudential Insurance Company 168
public debt 74–5
Public Securities Association 317–18
Public Utility Holding Company Act (1935)
  16
public utility preferred stock 416 n. 4
pure risks 185
putable bonds 190, 327–9
put feature 190

quadratic utility function 163
quantitative vs. qualitative factors in security
  analysis 396–7
Quiggin, J. 164

Ragsdale, E. 573
random walk models 35, 40–1, 261, 262,
  596–7, 598
Rao, G. 573
Rapach, D. 372, 417 n. 13
Rappaport, A. 367–8, 376, 380, 433, 434–7
Ratcliffe, Dick 567
ratings agencies 232–3, 358
rational economic model 48–9
Real Estate Mortgage Investment Conduits
  315
rebalancing frequency 574, 575, 578, 591–2
recombining processes 272
reconstituted securities 189
recovery rates 234, 235–7
rectangles 513, 555 n. 18
Redington, F. 217–18, 247, 250–2, 260, 285,
  298 n. 4
refunding 307–8
regression techniques 482
Regulation Q 351 n. 4
reinvestment risk 219
Reitano, R. 286, 287–8, 290, 299 n. 21

relative risk aversion 162–3
relative strength 538–41, 548–51
relative value approach 367, 368–9, 479,
    481–2
Remington Rand Company 133 n. 21
remarketed rate preferred stock 358, 359,
    360
rentes 72–3, 74
repurchase agreements 20
rescontre system 87
research and development 378
residual income model 426, 466–7
    equity valuation 472, 473, 474, 477
resistance level 513, 516
resistance line 513
restricted shares 13
returns
    efficient markets hypothesis 35, 37–8,
        39–41
    expected *see* expected return
    and risk tradeoff 23–30, 46–50
Rhea, Robert 498–9, 500, 502, 505, 506
rho 318, 320, 329–30
Riepe, M. 559
risk aversion 162–4, 225–6, 596
risk based capital requirement 248
riskfree assets 143–4, 148–9
risk premia hypothesis 222–3, 225–7
risks
    common stock valuation 364
    cost of 161–2
    Greeks 319
    pure vs. speculative 185
    and return tradeoff 23–30, 46–50
    in trading rules 41–2
    and uncertainty 31–4
    see also specific risks
risk tolerance function 162
Ritter, J. 373–4, 426
"robber barons" 95
Rockefeller, J.D. 95
Ross, S. 268, 604
Rothschild, Meyer 96
Roy, A. 23
Royal Bank of Canada 440
Ruback, R. 482
Rubinstein, M. 127, 129
runs tests 42–3
Rural Cellular Corporation 475, 476

Russell, Richard 449–500, 505–7, 554 n. 8,
    554 n. 12, 554 n. 13

safety-first portfolio theory 606–7
safety margin *see* margin of safety principle
Saint Petersburg paradox 602
Salomon Smith Barney 18
Samuelson, P. 35, 58–9, 216–17, 602, 604,
    610–11 n. 12
    tactical asset allocation 575, 611 n. 13
    time diversification puzzle 596, 597, 599,
        600
Santoni, G. 110
Sarbanes–Oxley Act (2002) 16, 460
Sarkar, S. 330–1
Savage, L. 159
Savings bonds 186, 189
Schaefer, George 499, 505, 506
Schilit, Howard 460, 461, 462, 464, 465
Schloss, Walter 567
Scholes, M. 263
    see also Black–Scholes formula
Schwager, J. 544
    charting systems 509, 513–16, 518, 555
        n. 16
    oscillators 546, 547, 548
Schwartz, E. 168, 347
seasoned primary issues 16
secondary issues 16, 17
securities
    classification 356–7
    defining 4–7
    types and markets 186–96
Securities Act (1933 and amendments) 4–6,
    16, 97, 165
Securities and Exchange Act (1934) 16
Securities and Exchange Commission (SEC)
    16, 231, 306, 438
    financial shenanigans 461, 462, 464
securities universe, institutions and
    regulations 7–23
security analysis 115–17
security market line 150, 151
See's Candies 414
self-control 534
self-regulation of stock market 94, 97, 112
seller's options 302
semi-American callable bonds 304
Sharpe, W. 127, 129, 372–3

Sharpe ratio 578–80
Shefrin, H.
  behavioral finance 530, 531, 532, 533–4,
    535, 537
  behavioral portfolio theory 605, 607
shell companies 416 n. 7
Sherman Anti-Trust Act (1890) 16, 96
short selling 147–8, 564–5
short squeeze 94
Siegel, J.
  business cycles 374–5
  contrarian and contrary opinion strategies
    527–9, 556 n. 21
  Dow Ten strategy 562–3
  history of security analysis 98, 99–101
  risk and return tradeoff 23, 47, 48
  stock prices and inflation 371, 372
  time diversification puzzle 596, 597, 598,
    599, 601
signaling process 347
signaling theory 310–11
signal line 548
Silicon Integrated 312
Singapore 298 n. 3, 438
single country international bonds 196
single index model (market model) 129,
  154–7
sinking funds 190, 304, 306, 307–8, 309
  Anheuser–Busch 304, 307
  preferred stock 358
Sinquefield, R. 23, 47
small firm effect 44
Smith, Edgar Lawrence 47, 91, 102, 103–4
Smith, F. 47
Snapple 462
social matrix 106, 107
Solnik, B. 270, 271
Sorensen, E. 432
Sortino, F. 579
Sortino ratio 579–80
Southwest Airlines 470
Southwestern Bell 429–30, 431
speculation 6
  and investment, distinction between 395–6,
    590
speculative risks 185
split maturity portfolio 293–5
spot interest rate (implied zero coupon
    interest rates) 201–2

square root diffusion model 268
square root process 264, 347, 348
Standard and Poor's 500 169
Standard and Poor's Corporation 102, 233,
    238–9
standard deviation of returns 27, 137–8, 139,
    140
Standard Oil 96
standby underwriting 17
state municipal funds 193
static spread 331–2, 333, 336–8
stationarity of stochastic processes 63
Statman, M. 45, 556 n. 23, 605, 607
statutory voting procedure 12
Stern Stewart & Company 456, 458–9
Stevin, Simon 75
Stickney, C. 50, 586
stochastic differential equations (SDEs)
    diffusions 261, 262–3, 264, 265
    interest rates 265–6, 267
    Ito's lemma 270, 271
    time value–convexity tradeoff 283–4
stochastic processes
    background 260–1
    continuous 261
    definition 59
    diffusions, types of 262–5
    discrete 261
    ergodicity hypothesis 59–60, 62–5
    interest rates 265–8
    Ito's lemma 268–71
    option adjusted spread analysis 340
    stationarity 63
stock exchanges 17
stockholders' equity, statement of 437, 446–7,
    449
stock market collapses 99–101, 103, 110–11,
    169
stock markets 17, 18, 86–115
stocks 11
    duration 213–14
    Fisher, Irving 104–5
    and fixed income valuation 186
    human sciences, truth and method in 56–7
    risk and return tradeoff 25, 26, 30, 46–7
    Smith, Edgar Lawrence 102–4
    value investing 385–8
    Withers, H. 115
    see also Part II; specific stocks

stop-out price 68 n. 8
St Petersburg paradox 602
straight bonds 209, 302
strategic asset allocation 559–60, 561, 571–3, 574
strict stationarity 63, 64
stripped mortgage backed securities 351 n. 6
STRIPS 187–9, 201–2
submartingale processes 37–8
Sunbeam 461
Sundaresan, S. 201–2
support level 513, 516
support line 513
survivorship bias 611 n. 14
Switzerland 253, 254, 255, 256
syndicates 16–17
systematic risk 140, 155–6

tactical asset allocation 398, 560, 561, 573–5
takeovers 393, 463
tangency portfolio 145–6, 148, 149, 150, 152, 153
Tanner, E. 41, 42
taxable bond funds 192
taxation 11, 360–2, 373–4
tax-exempt (municipal) bonds 20, 24
Tax Reform Act (1986) 315, 361, 362
Taylor, H. 59, 69 n. 20
Taylor series expansion 257–60
    classical immunization 250
    expected utility 159, 164–5
    partial duration and partial convexity 286–7
    time value–convexity tradeoff 275–6, 279–83
technical analysis 66
    charting and moving average systems 508–25
    conceptual foundations 491–6
    contrarian and contrary opinion strategies 525–9
    Dow theory 498–508
    forms of 489–91
    frame dependence 532–4
    heuristic-driven bias 529–32
    inefficient markets 534–8
    and modern Finance 496–8
    momentum and "price rate of change" 541–6

    oscillators 546–51
    profitability of 43
    relative strength 538–41
technological growth factor 399
term structure of interest rates 199, 220–30
Texas Instruments 380
theta 279, 280–2, 318, 320
third market for securities trading 68 n. 6
tilt, tactical asset allocation 573–4
time diversification puzzle 596–602, 603
time value–convexity tradeoff 283–5, 279–83
Titman, S. 496, 545–6, 556 n. 27
Tobin, J. 129
Tonti, Lorenzo 75
tontines 75
tracking error, tactical asset allocation 574, 575
Tracy, J. 72–3, 132 n. 3
trading range 513–18, 525
trading rules 41–2, 43
tradition 58
transactions costs 591
Treasury-online program 189
Treasury securities 18, 19, 20–2, 143, 189
    discount rate 205, 206
    risk and return tradeoff 25, 26
trends 512–13, 514–15, 516–19, 536–7
Treynor's measure 578
triangles, charting systems 516
Trust Indenture Act (1939) 231
trusts 95–6
turn-of-the-year effect 44–5
Tversky, A. 529, 604, 605
two fund separation 148–50, 153, 571–3, 590–1, 594

Ulpian 71–2
unbiased expectations hypothesis (UEH) 222–5, 226, 229, 272
uncertainty
    behavioral portfolio theory 604
    cost of risk and risk aversion properties 161–4
    expected utility theory 157–61, 164–5
    fixed income analysis 184, 185, 186
    Keynes on 105–10
    and risk 31–4
underwriting 16–17
United Airlines 393, 470

United Kingdom/England
  efficient markets hypothesis 45
  government bonds 17, 253, 254, 256
  history of portfolio insurance 168
  life annuities 76, 79
  Mortimer 89–91
  public debt, emergence 75
  sinking funds 309
  tontines 75
United States Steel Corporation 450
  balance sheet 446
  cash flow statement 449, 452
  income statement 440, 441, 442
unit investment trusts 68 n. 5
unseasoned primary issues 16
unsystematic risk 155–7
upside potential ratio (UPR) 579–80
usufructs 132 n. 2

value-at-risk modeling 249
value averaging 577, 580
value drivers 465–71
value investing
  Buffett, Warren 381–4, 584–9
  contrarian approach 525
  Dow Ten strategy 562
  Graham, Dodd and Cottle 581–4
  practical investment strategy 589–93
  for special situations 390–4
  techniques 384–9
Vanderbilt, "Commodore" Cornelius 94–5
van Horne, J. 223
van Schooten, Frans 77
van Strum, K. 104
variance of portfolio returns 137–8, 139
Vasicek mean reversion model 268, 324
Vaughan, E. 185
vega 318–19, 320
Velde, F. 122
Veterans Administration 314
Viceira, S. 594, 600–1, 612 n. 21, 613 n. 30
Visscher, S. 563

von Neumann, J. 157, 159
voting rights 358
Vu, J. 308

Wall Street 93–4
Wall Street Journal 92, 97, 98
Warr, R. 373–4, 426
warrant bonds 191, 313, 329–30
weak stationarity 63, 64
weekend effect 44
Weiner processes 261, 262–3
Weir, D. 122
whipsaws 519
Whitman, M. 371, 385
widows and orphans 610 n. 4
Wilder, J. 539, 548–51
Williams, John Burr 91, 120, 127, 397, 407
  discounted cash flow modeling 384, 398,
    421, 422
Williamson, D. 432
Wilson, R. 181, 304
Withers, Hartley 91, 92, 112–15, 131, 471
Witt, R. 207
Wittgenstein, Ludwig 416 n. 8
Wolf, M. 385
workforce, company analysis 379–80
Worldcom 460, 464, 590
Wyckoff, Richard 98, 492, 553 n. 3

Xerox 461

years' purchase, life annuities 76
yield curve 20, 197–9, 222, 227, 285–95
yield spread analysis 331–2
yield to maturity 196–9, 201, 210, 222

Zannoni, D. 106, 134 n. 23
Zeckhauser, R. 603
zero coupon bonds 197, 209, 211, 218, 292
Zimmermann, H. 574
Zweig, Martin 556 n. 20
ZZZZ Best 461